Critical Research Into Bhagavad-Gita

Prof. Ratnakar Narale

Pustak Bharati
Toronto, Canada

Author :

Dr. Ratnakar Narale, Ph.D (IIT), Ph.D. (Kalidas Sanskrit Univ.)

Prof. Hindi. Ryerson University, Toronto.

www.ratnakar-narale.com

Title :

Critical Research Into Bhagavad-Gita

This is a critical research work. **This book is a** lifetime study **for one who has dedication and patience to learn and** contemplate **on every word of the divine Gita. This is the right resource** for a critical study **for those who wish to go beyond. If one wants to learn or teach** Gita through Sanskrit and Sanskrit through Gita**, there is no substitute. From an elementary level to most scholarly level, to know the "Gita** in Krishna's Own Sanskrit Words,**" this book is the** sole authority**. Regardless of how many books on Gita you may have read, studied or written, while going through this** treasure of information**, you will discover** many **Surprises**, Interesting facts and Important points**, which you would not have known without going through this book. This books removes** misconceptions and wrong notions **one has collected without properly knowing what the Sanskrit words of Krishna truly mean.** Seeing is believing.

Published by :

Pustak Bharati (Books-India)

www.pustak-bharat-canada.com

Published for :

Kavikulaguru Kalidas Sanskrit University, Nagpur

Available at :

www.amazon.com

ISBN 978-1-989416-79-2

ISBN : 978-1-989416-79-2

The Story of the Divine Dialogue

दिव्यौ शंखौ प्रदध्मतुः।

Scene of Lord Krishna's dialogue with Arjuna according to the verses of the Gītā

for story explanation, see the next page

Scene of Lord Krishna's dialogue with Arjuna, according to the verses of the Gītā
श्रीमद्भगवद्गीतायाः प्रसङ्गः ।

1. During the dialogue (संवादमिदम् अद्भुतम् Gita 18.76), horses of the chariot were standing, they were NOT running. Gītā was not spoken in a running chariot (स्थापयित्वा रथोत्तमम् Gita 1.24).
2. Krishna and Arjuna were sitting in the chariot (रथोपस्थ उपाविषत् Gita 1.47). Even though the pose looks very nice for a sketch, they were NEITHER standing or sitting on the ground nor standing on the chariot. During the dialogue, Arjuna was sitting in the middle part of the chariot. Krishna was sitting at the front, talking to Arjuna. At the behest of Krishna (तस्मात् उत्तिष्ठ Gita 11.33), finally at the end of the last chapter, Arjuna said, "I will stand up" (करिष्ये वचनं तव Gita 18.73)
3. Arjuna was sitting sadly in the middle part of the chariot. He was NOT sitting at the back or in the front chambers of the chariot (रथोपस्थे उपाविषत् Gita 1.47, upastha = middle part) . It means Arjuna had a big chariot (महति स्यन्दने स्थितौ Gita 1.14 and रथोत्तमम् Gita 1.24), and it had three chambers. It had white horses (श्वेतैर्हयैर्युक्ते Gita 1.14).
4. Arjuna removed and kept his bow and quivers of arrows in the chariot itself. They were NOT thrown on the ground (विसृज्य सशरं चापं Gita 1.47).
5. During the dialogue, Arjuna's face was dejected (शोकसंविग्नमानसः Gita 1,47). He was NOT excited like a mad warrior, standing at the front of the chariot eager to fight (न योत्स्ये Gita 2.9). Lord Krishna had a pleasant face (प्रहसन्निव Gita 2.10), sitting on the chariot.
6. During the dialogue, both armies were standing quitely in the background, oblivious and non-functional. No one was engaged in fighting, arrows were not flying, slaughtered men were not lying in the pool of blood...etc. Gita is NOT a book on war. It is book of righteous (धर्मक्षेत्रे Gita 1.1) spiritual guidance (धर्म्यं संवादमावयोः Gita 18.70), for all times.
7. It was a day time.
8. Arjuna's chariot had a flag bearing Hanumana's image (कपिध्वजः Gita 1.20)
9. Lord Krishna's divine (दिव्यौ Gita 1.14) conch shell (पाञ्चजन्यम् हृषीकेषः Gita 1.15) and Arjuna's divine conch shell (देवदत्तं धनञ्जयः Gita 1.15) are part of the scene. Lord Krishna was nor bearing the *Sudarshana-chakra.* During the Gita, Krishna was only an unarmed charioteer.
10. The Pandavas were on the 'right' side (धर्म्यं Gita 18.70).

INDEX

anukramaṇikā अनुक्रमणिका

सत्यमेव जयते

डा. मुरली मनोहर जोशी
DR. MURLI MANOHAR JOSHI

मानव संसाधन विकास मंत्री
भारत
नई दिल्ली - ११० ००१
MINISTER OF
HUMAN RESOURCE DEVELOPMENT
INDIA
NEW DELHI-110 001

FOREWORD

Swami Madhusudan Saraswati has written nine beautiful verses entitled *'Gitadhyanam'*. The very first verse is illuminating and highlights the profundity of Gita. The sermon of Gita was delivered by Narayana Himself to his dear disciple Arjuna and this sermon has been made part of Mahabharat by the great Vedvyasa. Gita showers the nectar of philosophy of non-duality (Advaita) in 18 chapters and delivers those who meditate on it from the cycle of birth and death.

Parthaya pratibodhitam Bhagwata Narayanena Swayam
Vyasena grathitam puranmunina Madhye Mahabharatam
Advaitamritavarshinim Bhagawatim ashtadashadhyanim
Amb twamanusandhami Bhagwatgite Bhawadveshinim.

The essence of Indian philosophical thought is contained in the Brahmasutras, Upanishad and Bhagwadgita. However, Bhagwadgita is the single repository of Bhrahmavidya, Yogshastra and the Upanishads. Aldous Huxley says, *"The Gita is one of the clearest and most comprehensive summaries of the Perennial Philosophy ever to have been made. Hence its enduring value, not only for Indians, but for all mankind.....".*

Innumerable commentaries have been written on Bhagwadgita. The great masters like Adi Shankara, Anandgiri, Shridhara, Ramanuja and Madhwacharya etc. have explained Bhagwadgita in their own way. Many great men of our times Lokmanya Tilak and Gandhiji have been inspired by this great text. Millions all over the world read Bhagwadgita as a matter of discipline.

Gita teaches us to have faith in the Lord and oneself and engage in action without being obsessed of the result. In the course of life we are always in the midst of action. It is important to understand that the binding quality of action lies in the motive or the desire that prompts it. Gita shows us the path of detachment from desires along with devotion to our work. Action alone is our right but we have no control on the fruits of action because success and failure do not depend on individual but on many other factors. To accept happiness and sorrow, success and failure and continue to do ones duty with the evenness on mind is called Yoga. This is illustrated in a beautiful parable of Sri Ramakrishna *"Be in the world as a maid servant in a rich man's house. For all intents and purposes she claims her master's children and property as her own. But at the core of her heart she knows that they do not belong to her. As the maid servant can with ease relinquish her assumed ownership of the master's property, be prepared for separation from earthly possession".*

Gita teaches us to learn equanimity of mind to rid of selfishness and achieve devotion and excellence in our actions. Swami Vivekananda said, *"A Yogi seated in Himalayan cave allows his mind to wander on unwanted things. A Cobbler in a corner at the crossing of several busy streets of the city, is absorbed in mending a shoe, as an act of service. Of these two the latter is a better Yogi than the former".*

The rich nations and the people with all the resources at their command to fulfill their desire are ever striving for more and more but in the process have lost peace and happiness. In a situation like this all the world has to be aware that peace and happiness is not achieved by pursuing and satisfying desires. Peace is enjoyed by those in whom desires are merged even as rivers flow into the ocean which is full and unmoving. .

> *"Apuryamanam acalapratistham samudramapah pravisanti yadvat tadvat kama yam pravisanti sarve sa santim apnoti na kama-kami"*

In the context of modern problems I am deeply concerned about the quality of the human beings. The winds of change are devastating and in our present day situation people have hardly any time to think. It is a mad rush of materialism. Bhagwad Gita shows us the way out of the predicament and to be on the path of spirituality. One has to endear oneself to the Divine to be merged in Him.

Gita Darshan in 3 volumes is a profound study of Gita. In addition to normal explanation of each verse the author has explained each word and has analyzed each and every word grammatically. Thus the work is unique for those who wish to understand the nuances of Gita. The volumes are also useful for cross-reference.

I am deeply impressed by the scholarship of Dr. Ratnakar Narale, which shows his command on Sanskrit, English, Hindi, Marathi etc. Gita Darshan is in Hindi. The Foreword in English is to comply with the request of Dr. Narale.

In Bhagwatgita chapter 18 verses 68 & 69 Krishna says *"Those who teach this supreme mystery of the Gita to all who love me perform the greatest act of love; they will come to me without a doubt. No one can render me more devoted service; no one on earth can be more dear to me".*

I feel that the grace of Lord Krishna is already on Dr. Narale.

(Dr. Murli Manohar Joshi)

New Delhi.

List of Abbreviations

1◦ The 1st Class of verbs भ्वादि – √भू (to be, become)

भवामि (आमि) भवावः (आवः) भवामः (आमः) *bhavāmi bhavāvaḥ bhavāmaḥ*

2◦ The 2nd Class of verbs अदादि – √अद्(to eat)

अद्मि (मि) अद्वः (वः) अद्मः (मः) *admi advaḥ admaḥ*

3◦ The 3rd Class of verbs जुहोत्यादि – √हु (to offer)

जुहोमि (ओमि) जुहुवः (वः) जुहुमः (मः) *juhomi juhuvaḥ juhumaḥ*

4◦ The 4th Class of verbs दिवादि – √दिव् (to shine)

दीव्यामि (आमि) दीव्यावः (आवः) दीव्यामः (आमः) *dīvyāmi dīvyāvaḥ dīvyāmaḥ*

5◦ The 5th Class of verbs स्वादि – √सु (to sprinkle, bathe)

सुनोमि (आमि) सुनुवः (वः) सुनुमः (मः) *sunomi sunuvaḥ sunumaḥ*

6◦ The 6th Class of verbs तुदादि – √तुद् (to strike)

तुदामि (आमि) तुदावः (आवः) तुदामः (आमः) *tudāmi tudāvaḥ tudāmaḥ*

7◦ The 7th Class of verbs रुधादि – √रुध् (to stop)

रुणध्मि (मि) रुन्ध्वः (वः) रुन्ध्मः (मः) *ruṇadhmi rundhvaḥ rundhmaḥ*

8◦ The 8th Class of verbs तनादि – √तन् (to spread)

तनोमि (ओमि) तन्वः–तनुवः (वः) तन्मः–तनुमः (मः) *tanomi tanuvaḥ tanumaḥ*

9◦ The 9th Class of verbs क्रयादि – √क्रय् (to buy)

क्रीणामि (आमि) क्रीणीवः (आवः) क्रीणीमः (आमः) *krīṇāmi krīṇīvaḥ krīṇīmaḥ*

10◦ The 10th Class of verbs चुरादि – √चुर् (to steal)

चोरयामि (यामि) चोरयावः (यावः) चोरयामः (यामः) *ćorayāmi ćorayāvaḥ ćorayāmaḥ*

11◦ The 11th Class of verbs कण्ड्वादि – √कण्डु (to itch)

कण्डूयामि (यामि) कण्डूयावः (यावः) कण्डूयामः (यामः) *kaṇḍūyāmi kaṇḍūyāvaḥ kaṇḍūyāmaḥ*

1nom◦	Nominative Case	प्रथमा–विभक्तिः,	कर्ता–कारकम्
2acc◦	Accusative Case	द्वितीया–विभक्तिः,	कर्म–कारकम्
3inst◦	Instrumental Case	तृतीया–विभक्तिः,	करण–कारकम्
4dat◦	Dative Case	चतुर्थी–विभक्तिः,	सम्प्रदान–कारकम्
5abl◦	Ablative Case	पञ्चमी–विभक्तिः,	अपादान–कारकम्
6pos◦	Possessive Case or Genetive Case	षष्ठी–विभक्तिः,	सम्बन्धः
7loc◦	Locative Case	सप्तमी–विभक्तिः,	अधिकरण–कारकम्
8voc◦	Vocative Case	सम्बोधनम्	

1st-per∘ First Person, the speaker उत्तम-पुरुषः

2nd-per∘ Second Person, to whom the speaker is talking मध्यम-पुरुषः

3rd-per∘ Third Person, about whom the speaker is talking प्रथम-पुरुषः

act∘ Active, Active Voice कर्तरि-प्रयोगः

adj∘ Adjective विशेषणम्

adv∘ Adverb क्रियाविशेषणम्

ātmane∘ *ātmanepadī,* when the fruit of action accrues to the doer आत्मनेपदी

caus∘ Causative प्रयोजकम्

des∘ Desiderative Mood इच्छार्थकम्, सन्नन्तप्रक्रिया

dual∘ Dual Number द्विवचनम्

f∘ Feminine Gender स्त्रीलिङ्गम्

Definite, Periphrastic Future, First Future or Future अनतने लुट्

Future Tense, Second Future, Indefinite Future अपूर्ण-भविष्यति लृट्

imperative∘ Imperative Mood विध्यादौ लोट्

ind∘ Indeclinable अव्ययम्

inf∘ Infinitive तुमुन्, तुमन्त-अव्ययम्

Indeclinable Past Participle, Gerund पूर्वकालिक-धातुसाधित- अव्ययम्

Past Participle with an indeclinable prefix other than अ; (ल्यप्, ल्यबन्त-अव्ययम्)

m∘ Masculine Gender पुल्लिङ्गम्

n∘ Neuter Gender नपुंसकलिङ्गम्

num∘ Numerical संख्याविशेषणम्

potential∘ Potential Mood विध्यर्थी, वाख्यातम्, विधिलिङ्म्

parasmai∘ *Parasmaipadī,* fruit of the action accrues to someone other than the subject परस्मैपदी

pass∘ Passive, Passive Voice कर्मणि-प्रयोगः

past∘ Past Tense भूतकालः

past-imp∘ Imperfect Tense, Imperfect Past Tense अनद्यतने भूते लङ्

pastind∘ Past Indefinite tense, Aorist or Third Preterite भूते लुङ

past-perf∘ Perfect, Perfect Tense परोक्षे लिट्

pl∘ Plural बहुवचनम

ppp∘ Past Passive Participle भूतभूतसाधितम्

pres∘ Present tense वर्तमाने लट्

pron∘ Pronoun सर्वनामन्, सर्वनाम, सार्वनामिक-

prop∘ Proper noun, given name

s-avyayi◦	Adverbial Compound	अव्ययीभाव–समास:
s-bahuvrī◦	Attributive or Relative Compound	बहुव्रीहि–समास:
s-dvandva◦	Dual or Aggregative Compound	द्वंद्व–समास:
s-dvigu◦	Numeral or Collective Compound	द्विगु–समास:
s-karmadha◦	Appositional Compound	कार्मधारय–समास:
s-n.bahuvrī◦	Negative *Attributive* Compound	नञ्–बहुव्रीहि–समास:
s-n.tatpu◦	Negative Determinitive Compound	नञ्–तत्पुरुष–समास:
s-sbahuvrī◦	Instrumental Attributive Compound	सहबहुव्रीहि–समास:
s-tatpu◦	Determinitive, Dependent Compound	तत्पुरुष–समास:
śatṛ◦	Present Participle of *parasmaipada* (शतृ) formed with suffix अत	
śānać◦	Present Participle of *ātmanepada* (शानच्) formed with affix आन, मान	
sing◦	Singular Number	एकवचनम्
◦	*ubhayapadī*, where the action applies both to the subject and the object उभयपदि	
v◦	Verb	क्रियापदम् ।
vi◦	Intransitive Verb	अकर्मक–क्रिया ।
vt◦	Transitive Verb	सकर्मक–क्रिया
Elsewhere◦	In other translations, commentaries or books on the Gītā.	

The term on left side comes from the one on right.→ The term on right side comes from the one on left.

↑ Please see above, Referred above. (↑) See above in this paragraph itself.

↓ Please see below, Referred later.

NOTE :

The ̖ : and ′ accent-marks used with the Roman Saṁskṛt characters such as ḥ:, ḍ , ḳ , m̃, m̖ , n̖ , s̖, t̖ , ć and ćh in this book are employed only **for the purpose of the ease of their corelation with the *devanāgarī* Saṁskṛt counterparts**. The discreet readers may simply ignore them if they do not need this improvisation. However, some readers may find it to be a very useful innovation over the common systems of transliteration.

THE GREAT FAMILY-TREE FROM THE MAHABHARATA *

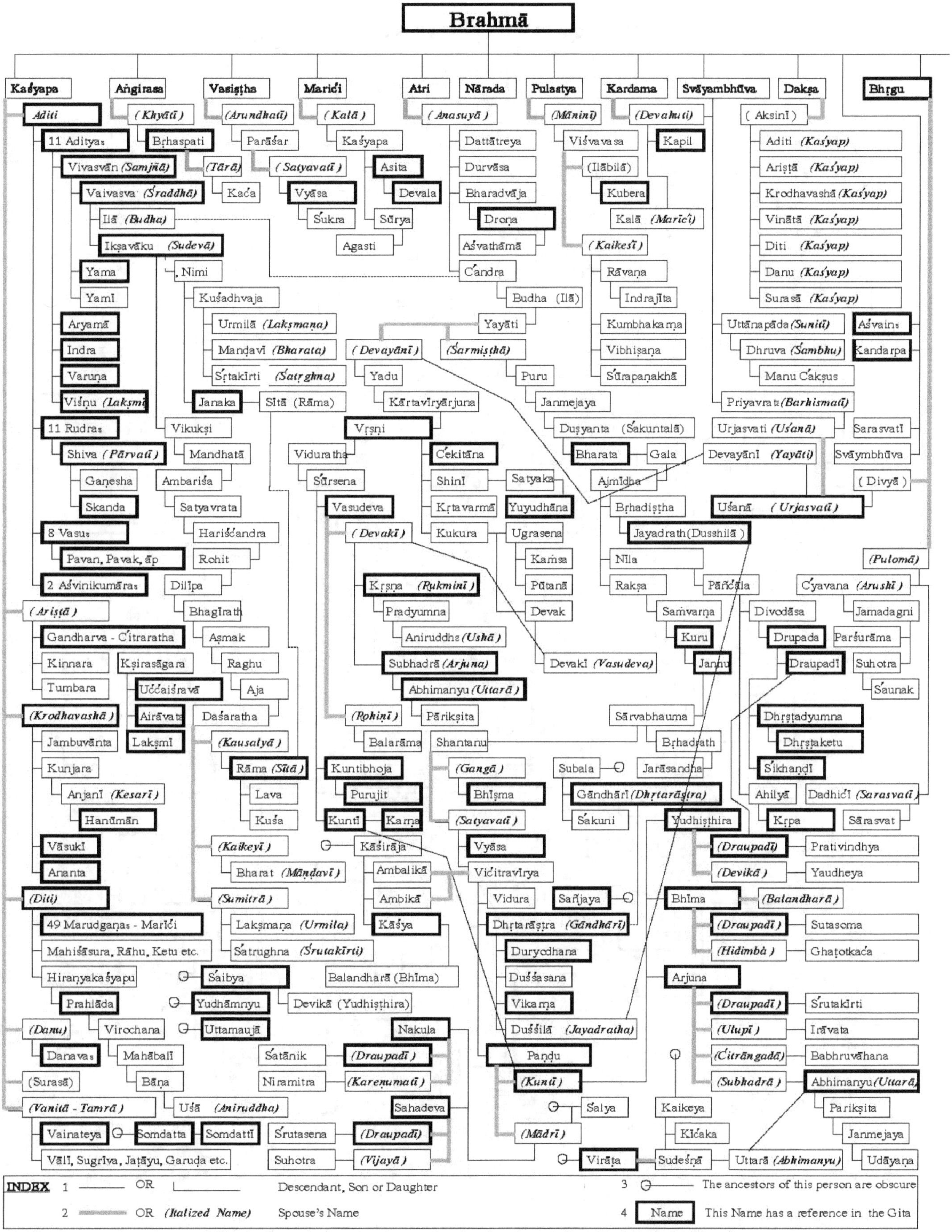

* This family-tree is shown here in a greatly reduced version to indicate its relation to the Gita only.

महाभारतीय विशाल वंशवृक्ष

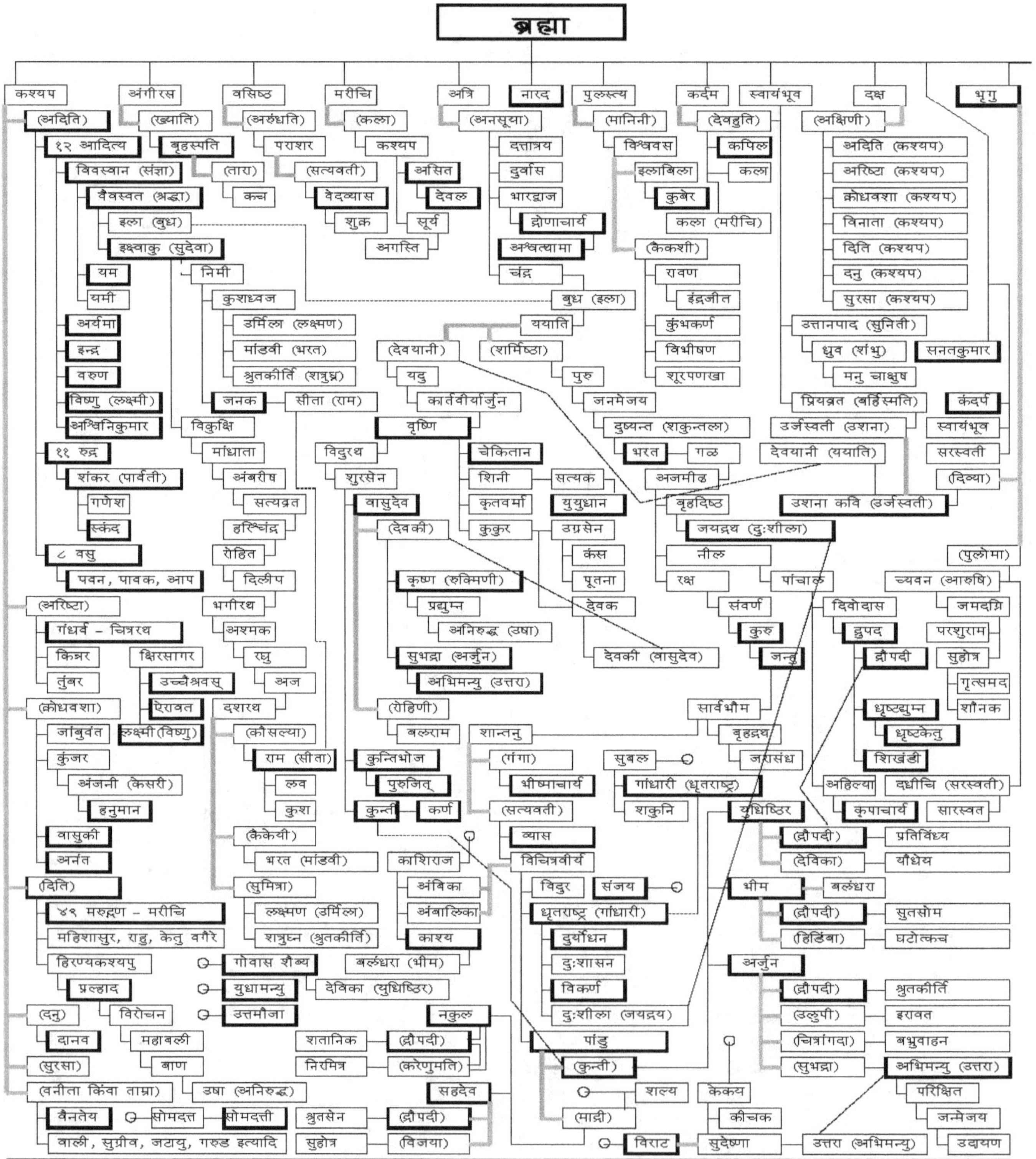

खुलासा १ ——— अथवा └—— वंशज, पुत्र अथवा पुत्री
२ ▬▬▬ अथवा पत्नी अथवा पति का नाम
३ O——— अपरिचित पूर्वज की व्यक्ति
४ [नाम] इस नाम का संदर्भ भगवद्गीता में है.

* यह महाभारतीय विशाल वंशवृक्ष यहां केवल श्रीगीता की मर्यादा में सीमित अतिसंक्षिप्त रूप से दिखाया गया है ।

THE BASIC GRAMMAR OF THE GITA

The 25 Rules of Conjunction required to understand the Gītā

सन्धिनियमाः

(1) Conjunction between similar letters :

When a short vowel (a, i, u, ṛ अ, इ, उ, ऋ) or a long vowel (ā, ī, ū, ṝ आ, ई, ऊ, ॠ) is followed by a similar short or long vowel, the two similar vowels combine together to produce one long vowel (ā, ī, ū, ṝ आ, ई, ऊ, ॠ). This conjunction is also called **long conjunction** (दीर्घसन्धिः). e.g.

1/1 अ + अ = आ) एव अभिरक्षन्तु → एवाभिरक्षन्तु a + a = ā eva abhirakṣantu → evābhirakṣantu (1.11)

1/2 अ + आ = आ) एव आश्रयेत् → एवाश्रयेत् a + ā = ā eva āśrayet → evāśrayet (1.36)

1/3 आ + अ = आ) उक्त्वा अर्जुनः → उक्त्वार्जुनः ā + a = ā uktvā arjunaḥ → uktvārjunaḥ (1.47)

1/4 आ + आ = आ) परया आविष्टः → परयाविष्टः ā + ā = ā parayā āviṣṭaḥ → parayāviṣṭaḥ (1.27)

1/5 इ + इ = ई) भ्रमति इव → भ्रमतीव i + i = ī bhramati iva → bhramatīva (1.30)

1/6 इ + ई = ई) उत्क्रामति ईश्वरः → उत्क्रामतीश्वरः i + ī = ī utkramati īśvaraḥ → utkramatīśvaraḥ (15.8)

1/7 ई + इ = ई) त्यागी इति → त्यागीति ī + i = ī tyāgī iti → tyāgīti (18.11)

1/8 उ + उ = ऊ) तेषु उपजायते → तेषूपजायते u + u = ū teṣu upajāyate → teṣūpajāyate (2.62)

when any consonant (k, t, n क्, त्, न्) is followed by a similar consonant (ka, ta, na क, त, न), the two similar consonants conjunct to form a compound consonant (kka, tta, nna क्क, त्त, न्न)

1/9 क + क = क्क पृथक् केशिनिषूदन → पृथक्केशि॰ k + k = kk pṛthak keśiniṣūdana → pṛthakkeśi॰ (18.1)

1/10 त् + त = त्त हस्तात् त्वक् → हस्तात्त्वक् t + t = tt hastāt tvak → hastāttvak (1.30)

त् + त्र = त्त्र एतत् त्रयम् → एतत्त्रयम् t + tr = ttr etat trayam → etattrayam (16.21)

1/11 न् + न = न्न तान् निबोध → तान्निबोध n + n = nn tān nibodha → tānnibodha (1.7)

(2) Conjunction between dissimilar vowels :

When the vowel a or ā (अ, आ) is followed by a dissimilar short vowel i, u or ṛ (इ, उ, ऋ) or a dissimilar long vowel sauch as ī, ū or ṝ (ई, ऊ, ॠ) then the two dissimilar vowels form letters e, o or r (ए, ओ, र्), respectively. e.g.

2/1 अ + इ = ए न इमे → नेमे a + i = e na ime → neme (2.12)

2/2 अ + उ = ओ विनद्य उच्चैः → विनद्योच्चैः a + u = o vinadya uććaiḥ → vinadyoććaiḥ (1.12)

अ + ऊ = ओ च + ऊर्ध्वम् → चोर्ध्वम् a + ū = o ća ūrdhvam → ćordhvam (15.1)

2/3 आ + इ = ए दृष्ट्वा इमम् → दृष्ट्वेमम् ā + i = e dṛṣṭvā imam → dṛṣṭvemam (1.28)

2/4 आ + उ = ओ त्यक्त्वा उत्तिष्ठ → त्यक्त्वोत्तिष्ठ ā + u = o tyaktvā uttiṣṭha → tyaktvottiṣṭha (2.3)

(3) ***Vriddhi*** Conjunction :

📖 When the vowel a or ā (अ, आ) is followed by a dipthong e, ai, o or au (ए, ऐ, ओ, औ) then this vowel a or ā (अ, आ) undergoes *vriddhi* to form a compound letters ai or au (ऐ, औ) respectively.

3/1 अ + ए = ऐ च एव → चैव a + e = ai ća eva → ćaiva (1.1)

3/2 अ + ओ = औ च ओषधिः → चौषधिः a + o = au ća oṣadhīḥ → ćauṣadhīḥ (15.13)

3/1 आ + ए = ऐ तथा एव → तथैव ā + e = ai tathā eva → tathaiva (1.8)

(4) ***Yaṇa*** Conjunction :

📖 When a short vowel i, u or ṛ (इ, उ, ऋ) or a long vowel ī, ū or ṝ (ई, ऊ, ॠ) is followed by any dissimilar vowel, this vowel i, ī, u, ū, ṛ, ṝ (इ, ई, उ, ऊ, ऋ, ॠ) becomes y, y, v, v, r, r (य्, य्, व्, व्, र्, र्) respectively. This group of letters y, y, v, v, r, r (य्, य्, व्, व्, र्, र्) is called as ***yaṇa*** by Pāṇini (इको यणचि । -aṣṭādhyāyī 6:1.76). e.g.

4/1 इ + अ = य् + अ = य शक्नोमि अवस्थातुम् → शक्नोम्यवस्थातुम्

i + a = ya śaknomi avasthātuṁ → śaknomyavasthātum (1.30)

4/2 इ + आ = य् + आ = या क्लेदयन्ति आपः → क्लेदयन्त्यापः

i + ā = yā kledayanti āpaḥ → kledayantyāpaḥ (2.23)

4/3 इ + उ = य् + उ = यु अभिभवति उत → अभिभवत्युत

i + u = yu abhibhavati uta → abhibhavatyuta (1.40)

4/4 इ + ए = य् + ए = ये यद्यपि एते → यद्यप्येते i + e = ye yadyapi ete → yadyapyete (1.38)

4/5 ई + अ = य् + अ = यइन्द्रियाणी अन्ये → इन्द्रियाण्यन्ये ī + a = y indriyāṇi anye → indriyāṇyanye (4.26)

4/6 उ + अ = व् + अ = व तु अनयो → त्वनयो u + a = va tu anayoḥ → tvanayoḥ (2.16)

4/7 उ + आ = व् + आ = वा तु आत्मरतिः → त्वात्मरतिः u + ā = vā tu ātmaratiḥ → tvātmaratiḥ (3.17)

4/8 उ + इ = व् + इ = वि तु इदम् → त्विदम् u + i = vi tu idam → tvidam (1.10)

4/9 उ + ए = व् + ए = वे तु एव → त्वेव u + e = ve tu eva → tveva (2.12)

(5) ***Ayādi*** Conjugation :

📖 When the compound vowel e or ai (ए, ऐ) coming at the end of a word is followed by any vowel other than the short vowel a (अ), then this vowel e or ai (ए, ऐ) is replaced by letters ay and āy (अय्, आय्) respectively. The y (य्) in the letters ay and āy (अय्, आय्) may optionally be deleted.

5/1 (आ) श्रीकृष्णार्जुनसंवादे आत्मसंयमयोगः → श्रीकृष्णार्जुनसंवाद आत्मसंयमयोगः

(ā) śrīkṛṣṇārjunasaṁvāde ātmasaṁyamayogaḥ → śrīkṛṣṇārjunasaṁvāda ātmasaṁyamayogaḥ (6.47)

5/2 (इ) ते इमे → त इमे (i) te ime → ta ime (1.33)

5/3 (उ) रथोपस्थे उपाविशत् → रथोपस्थ उपाविशत् (u) rathopasthe upāviśat → rathopastha upāviśat (1.47)

5/4 (ए) सर्वे एव → सर्व एव (e) sarve eva → sarva eva (1.6)

📖 When the compound vowel o or au (ओ, औ) coming at the end of a word is followed by any vowel other than the short vowel a (अ), then this vowel o or au (ओ, औ) is replaced by letters av and āv (अव्, आव्) respectively. The va (va`) in the letters av and āv (अव्, आव्) may optionally be deleted.

NOTE : The resulting letters in the group 5 *sandhi* are ay, āy, av, āv, etc. (अय्, आय्, अव्, आव् आदि), therefore, this sandhi is called ***ayādi*** (अय् आदि, अयादि) by Pāṇini (एचोऽयवायाव: ।-aṣṭādhyāyī 6:1.77).

5/5 (अ) पूजार्हौ अरिसूदन → पूजार्हावरिसूदन (a) pūjārhau arisūdana → pūjārhāvarisūdana (2.4)

5/6 (इ) द्वौ इमौ → द्वाविमौ (i) dvau imau → dvāvimau (15.16)

5/7 (उ) नि:श्रेयसकरौ उभौ → नि:श्रेयसकरावुभौ (u) niḥśreyasakarau ubhau → niḥ-śreyasakarāvubhau (5.2)

(6) ***Pūrvarūpa*** **Conjugation :**

📖 When the compound vowel e or o (ए, ओ) at the end of a word is followed by short vowel a (अ), then this short vowel a (अ) is replaced with an *avagraha* ' (ऽ). This group of compound vowel e or o (ए, ओ) is called as ***eḍh*** (एड) by Pāṇini (एड: पदान्तादति ।-aṣṭādhyāyī 6:1.107). e.g.

6/1 (ए) मे अच्युत → मेऽच्युत (e) me aćyuta → me'ćyuta (1.21)

(7) ***Prgṛhya*** **exception in the case of dual number words :**

📖 When a word of dual number (whether noun, pronoun or verb) that ends in vowel ī, ū or e (ई, ऊ, ए) is followed by any vowel, there is no sandhi (blending) between the two opposite vowels. Such vowel as ī, ū or e (ई, ऊ, ए) that does not congugate, or the word that ends in such non-blending vowel, is termed as ***pragṛhya*** by Pāṇini (ईदूदेद्द्विवचनं प्रगृह्यम् । aṣṭādhyāyī 1:1.11). e.g.

7/1 (उ) अनादी उभौ → अनादी उभौ (u) anādī ubhau → anādī ubhau (13.20)

(8) Third-Consonant and Vowel Conjugation :

📖 When any consonant from any of the five classes (k, ć, ṭ, t, p, क्, च्, ट्, त्, प्), except any nasal consonant, is followed by any vowel, this consonant from a class is replaced by the third consonant from the same class and this third consonant then conjugates with vowel that follows it. e.g.

Consonant k (क्)

8/1 (उ) क् + उ = ग् + उ = गु सम्यक् उभयो: → सम्यगुभयो:

(u) k + u = g + u = gu samyak ubhayoḥ → samyagubhayoḥ (5.4)

Consonant t (त्)

8/2 (अ) त् + अ = द् + अ = द तत् अस्माकम् → तदस्माकाम्

(a) t + a = d + a = da tat asmākam → tadasmākam (1.10)

8/3 (आ) त् + आ = द् + आ = दा स्यात् आत्मतृप्तः → स्यादात्मतृप्तः

(ā) t + ā = d + ā = dā syāt ātmatṛptaḥ → syādātmatṛptaḥ (3.17)

8/4 (इ) त् + इ = द् + इ = दि बलात् इव → बलादिव (i) t + i = d + i = di balāt iva → balādiva (3.36)

8/5 (ई) त् + ई = द् + ई = दी यत् ईदृशम् → यदीदृशम् (ī) t + ī = d + ī = dī yat īdṛśam → yadīdṛśam (6.42)

8/6 (उ) त् + उ = द् + उ = दु रणात् उपरतम् → रणादुपरतम्

(u) t + u = d + u = du raṇāt uparatam → raṇāduparatam (2.35)

8/7 (ऊ) त् + ऊ = द् + ऊ = दू श्रीमत् ऊर्जितम् → श्रीमदूर्जितम्

(ū) t + ū = d + ū = dū śrīmat ūrjitam → śrīmadūrjitam (10.41)

8/8 (ऋ) त् + ऋ = द् + ऋ = दृ एतत् ऋतम् → एतदृतम् (ṛ) t + ṛ = d + ṛ = dṛ etat ṛtam → etadṛtam (10.14)

8/9 (ए) त् + ए = द् + ए = दे यावत् एतान् → यावदेतान् (e) t + e = d + e = de yāvat etān → yāvadetān (1.22)

8/10 (ॐ) त् + ॐ = द् + ॐ (ओम्) = दोम् तस्मात् ॐ (ओम्) → तस्मादोम्

(om) t + om = d + om = dom tasmāt om → tasmādom (17.24)

When a nasal consonant n or m (न्, म्) is followed by a vowel, they form a full letter as given below. But, if a short vowel precedes the nasal consonant n (न्), it conjugates according to the sandhi rules 13/1-5.

Consonant n (न्)

8/11 (अ) योद्धुकामान् अवस्थितान् → योद्धुकामानवस्थितान्

(a) yoddhukāmān avasthitān → yoddhukāmānavasthitān (1.22)

8/12 (आ) एतान् आततायिनः → एतानाततायिनः (ā) etān ātatāyinaḥ → etānātatāyinaḥ (1.36)

8/13 (इ) कुरून् इति → कुरूनिति (i) kurun iti → kuruniti (1.25)

8/14 (ई) श्रीभगवान् उवाच → श्रीभगवनुवाच (ī) śrībhagavān uvāća → śrībhagavānuvāća (2.2)

8/15 (उ) यान् एव → यानेव (u) yān eva → yāneva (2.6)

Consonant m (म्)

8/16 (अ) किम् अकुर्वत् → किमकुर्वत् (a) kim akurvata → kimakurvata (1.1)

8/17 (आ) पाण्डुपुत्राणाम् आचार्य → पाण्डुपुत्राणामाचार्य (ā) pāṇḍuputrāṇām āćārya → ◦putrāṇāmāćārya (1.3)

8/18 (इ) वाक्यम् इदम् → वाक्यमिदम् (i) vākyam idam → vākyamidam (1.21)

8/19 (ई) भूतानाम् ईश्वरः → भूतानामीश्वरः (ī) bhūtānām īśvaraḥ → bhūtānāmīśvaraḥ (4.6)

8/20 (उ) आचार्यम् उपसङ्गम्य → आचायमुपसङ्गम्य (u) āćāryam upasaṅgamya → āćāryamupasaṅgamya (1.2)

8/21 (ऋ) असपत्नम् ऋद्धम् → असपत्नमृद्धम् (ṛ) asapatnam ṛddham → asapatnamṛddham (2.8)

8/22 (ए) भीष्मम् एव → भीष्ममेव (e) bhīṣmam eva → bhīṣmameva (1.2)

8/23 (ऐ) योगम् ऐश्वरम् → योगमैश्वरम् (ai) yogam aiśvaram → yogamaiśvaram (9.5)

8/24 (ओ) पवित्रम् ओङ्कार:→ पवित्रमोङ्कार: (o) pavitram oṅkāraḥ → pavitramoṅkāraḥ (9.17)

8/25 (औ) अहम् औषधम् → अहमौषधम् (au) aham auṣadham → ahamauṣadham (9.16)

(9) Third-Consonant and Consonant Conjugation :

📖 When a consonant, other than any nasal consonant, comes after a hard consonant from any of the five classes (k, ć, ṭ, t, p, क्, च्, ट्, त, प्), then this hard consonant from a class is replaced by the third consonant from the same class or optionally by the last (nasal) consonant from that class. e.g.

Consonant k (k')

9/1 (ब) पृथक् बाला: → पृथग्बाला: (b) pṛthak bālāḥ → pṛthagbālāḥ (5.4)

9/2 (म) ईदृक् मम → ईदृङ्मम (m) idṛk mama → idṛṅmama (11.49)

9/3 (व) सम्यक् व्यवसित: → सम्यग्व्यवसित: (v) samyak vyavasitaḥ → samyagvyavasitaḥ (9.30)

Consonant t (त्) : Consonant t (त्) follows the *sandhi* rules 9 and 11

9/4 त् + ग् = द् + ग् = द्ग यत् गत्वा → यद्गत्वा t + g = d + g = dg yat gatvā → yadgatvā (15.6)

9/5 त् + द् = द् + द् = द्द् विद्यात् दु:खसंयोगवियोगम् → विद्याद्दु:खसंयोगवियोगम्

t + d = d + d = dd vidyāt duḥkhasaṁyogaviyogam → vidyādduḥkhasaṁyogaviyogam (6.23)

9/6 त् + ध् = द् + ध् = द्ध बुद्धियोगात् धनञ्जय → बुद्धियोगाद्धनञ्जय

t + dh = d + dh = ddh buddhiyogat dhanañjaya → buddhiyogaddhanañjaya (2.49)

9/7 त् + ब् = द् + ब् = द्ब स्मृतिभ्रंशात् बुद्धिनाश: → स्मृतिभ्रंशाद्बुद्धिनाश:

t + b = d + b = db smṛtibhraṁśāt buddhināśaḥ → smṛtibhraṁśādbuddhināśaḥ (2.63)

9/8 त् + भ् = द् + भ् = द्भ क्रोधात् भवति → क्रोधाद्भवति

t + bh = d + bh = dbh krodhāt bhavati → krodhādbhavati (2.63)

9/9 त् + य् = द् + य् = द्य् अपनुद्यात् यत् → अपनुद्याद्यत् t + y = d + y = dy (apanudyāt yat → ◦nudyādyat)(2.8)

9/10 त् + र् = द् + र् = द्र् यत् राज्यसुखलोभेन → यद्राज्यसुखलोभेन

t + r = d + r = dr yat rājyasukhalobhena → yadrājyasukhalobhena (1.45)

9/11 त् + व् = द् + व् = द्व एतत् विद्म: → एतद्विद्म: t + v = d + v = dv etat vidmaḥ → etadvidmaḥ (2.6)

9/12 त् + ह् = द् + ह् = द्ध धर्म्यात् हि → धर्म्याद्धि t + h = d + h = ddh dharmyāt hi → dharmyādhi (2.31)

(10) First-Consonant Conjugation :

📖 When a consonant from any of the five classes (k, ć, ṭ, t, p, क्, च्, ट्, त, प्), except a nasal consonant, is followed by any dissimilar hard consonant (k, kh, ć, ćh, ṭ, ṭh, t, th, p, ph, ś, ṣ s क्, ख्, च्, छ्, ट्, ठ्, त, थ्, प्, फ्, श्, ष्, स्), that consonant from any class is replaced by the first (hard) consonant from the same class. However, if the consonant t (त्) is followed by ć or ćh (च्, छ्) then the congugation follows the *sandhi* rule number 11↓

Consonant k (क्) :

10/1 (च्) त्वक् च → त्वक्च (ć) tvak ća → tvakća (1.30)

10/2 (प्) पृथक् पृथक् → पृथक्पृथक् (p) pṛthak pṛthak → pṛthakpṛthak (1.18)

10/3 (श्) प्राक् शरीरविमोक्षणात् → प्राक्शरीरविमोक्षणात् (ś) prāk śarīravimokṣaṇa → prākśarīravimokṣaṇa (5.23)

10/4 (स्) ऋक् साम → ऋक्साम (s) ṛk sāma → ṛksāma (9.17)

Consonant t (त्) : Consonant t follows the *sandhi* rules 10 and 11

10/5 (क्) पुरुजित् कुन्तिभोजः → पुरुजित्कुन्तिभोजः (k) purujit kuntibhojaḥ → purujitkuntibhojaḥ (1.5)

(क्ष्) अन्यत् क्षत्रियस्य → अन्यत्क्षत्रियस्य (kṣ) anyat kṣatriyasya → anyatkṣatriyasya (2.31)

10/6 (प्) आश्चर्यवत् पश्यति → आश्चर्यवत्पश्यति (p) āśćaryavat paśyati → āśćaryavatpaśyati (2.29)

10/7 (स्) अपश्यत् स्थितान् → अपश्यत्स्थितान् (s) apaśyat sthitān → apaśyatsthitān (1.26)

(11) Same order Consonant-Consonant Conjugation :

When any consonant from t (त्) class (t, th, d, dh, n त्, थ्, द्, ध्, न्), is followed by any consonant from ć (च्) class (ć, ćh, j, jh, ñ च्, छ्, ज्, झ्, ञ्), then that consonant from t (त्) class is replaced by the consonant of same order from the ć (च्) class. However, if the consonant n (न्) is followed by ć (च्) then the congugation follows the *sandhi* rule number 13/6↓

Consonants t (त्) and n (न्)-

11/1 (च) त् + च् = च् + च् = च्च् आश्चर्यवत् च → आश्चर्यवच्च

(ć) t + ć = ć + ć = ćć āśćaryavat ća → āśćaryavaćća (2.29)

11/2 (ज) त् + ज् = ज् + ज् = ज्ज् स्यात् जनार्दन → स्याज्जनार्दन

(j) t + j = j + j = jj syāt janārdana → syājjanārdana (1.36)

(ज्ञ) त् + ज्ञ् = ज् + ज्ञ् = ज्ज्ञ् यत् ज्ञात्वा → यज्ज्ञात्वा

(jñ) t + jñ = j + jñ = jjñ yat jñātvā → yajjñātvā (4.16)

11/3 (न) न् + ज् = ञ् + ज् = ञ्ज् सपृशन् जिघ्रन् → सपृशञ्जिघ्रन्

(n) n + j = ñ + j = ñj spṛśan jighran → spṛśañjighran (5.8)

When any consonant from t (त्) class (t, th, d, dh, n त्, थ्, द्, ध्, न्), is followed consonant ś (श्), then that consonant from t (त्) class (t, th, d, dh, n त्, थ्, द्, ध्, न्), is replaced by the consonant of same order from the ć (च्) class (ć, ćh, j, jh, ñ च्, छ्, ज्, झ्, ञ्). And the following consonant ś (श्) is optionally replaced by consonant ćh (छ) e.g.

11/4 (त) यत् शोकम् → यच्छोकम् yat śokam → yaććhokam (2.8)

युद्धात् श्रेयः → युद्धाच्छ्रेयः yuddhāt śreyaḥ → yuddhāććhreyaḥ (2.31)

11/5 (न) पश्यन् शृण्वन् → पश्यञ्छृण्वन्, पश्यन्शृण्वन्, पश्यञ्श्रुण्वन्, पश्यञ्शृण्वन्

paśyan śṛṇvan → paśyañćhṛṇvan, paśyanśṛṇvan, or paśyañśruṇvan, paśyañśṛṇvan (5.8)
महानुभावान् श्रेयः → महानुभावाञ्श्रेयः mahānubhāvān śreyaḥ → mahānubhāvāñśreyaḥ (2.5)

📖 But, When the consonant t (त्) or d (द्) is followed by consonant l (ल्) then that consonant t (त्) or d (द्) is always replaced by consonant l (ल्). e.g.

11/6 (त) आब्रह्मभुवनात् लोकाः → आब्रह्मभुवनाल्लोकाः (t) ābrahmabhuvanāt lokāḥ → ◦bhuvanāllokāḥ (8.16)

(12) *Anunāsic* (nasal) Conjugation :

📖 When any consonant, other than a nasal consonant, from any of the five classes (k, ć, ṭ, t, p क्, च्, ट्, त् प्), is followed by a nasal consonant, then this consonant from that class is optionally replaced by the nasal (last) consonant from the same class. e.g.

Consonant *t* (त्)

12/1 त् + न = न् + न = न्न तस्मात् न → तस्मान्न t + n = n + n = nn tasmāt na → tasmānna (1.37)

12/2 त् + म = न् + म = न्म तत् मे → तन्मे t + m = n + m = nm tat me → tanme (1.46)

Consonant d (द्)

12/3 द् + म = न् + म = न्म सुहृद् मित्र → सुहृन्मित्र d + m = n + m = nm suhṛd mitra→ suhṛnmitra (6.9)

(13) Conjugation of the word ending in n (न्)

📖 When a word ending in n (न्) is preceeded by any short vowel and is followed by any vowel, the ending n (न्) is doubled and becomes nn (न्न). e.g.

13/1 (अ) अनिच्छन् अपि → अनिच्छन्नपि (a) aniććhn api → aniććhnnapi (3.36)

13/2 (आ) पश्यन् आत्मनि → पश्यन्नात्मनि (ā) paśyan ātmani → paśyannātmani (6.20)

13/3 (इ) विषीदन् इदम् → विषीदन्निदम् (i) viṣīdan idam → viṣīdannidam (1.27)

13/4 (उ) गृह्णन् उन्मिषन् → गृह्णन्नुन्मिषन् (u) gṛhṇan unmiṣan → gṛhṇannunmiṣan (5.9)

13/5 (ए) युञ्जन् एवम् → युञ्जन्नेवम् (e) yuñjan evam → yuñjannevam (6.15)

📖 When a word ending in n (न्) is followed by ć, ćh, ṭ, ḍ, t or th (च्, छ्, ट्, ड्, त्, थ्), then the ending n (न्) is replaced by an *anusvāra* (ं the nasal dot) and a *visarga* (:). This visarga then may change to ś, ṣ or s (श्, ष्, स्) according to the *sandhi* rules 17 and 18↓. e.g.

13/6 (च्) प्रज्ञावादान् च → प्रज्ञावादांश्च (ć) prajñāvādān ća → prajñāvādāṁśća (2.11)

13/7 (त्) सखीन् तथा → सखींस्तथा (t) sakhin tathā → sakhiṁstathā (1.26)

📖 When a word ending in consonant n (न्) is followed by a word starting with l (ल्), then a *ćandra-anusvāra* (ँ the special nasal dot) comes on the letter that is before n (न्), and that n (न्) is replaced with letter l (ल्) e.g.

13/8 श्रद्धावान् लभते → श्रद्धावाँल्लभते śraddhāvān labhate → śraddhāvām̐llabhate (1.26)

📖 When a word ending in consonant n (न्) is followed by any consonant other than ć, ćh, ṭ, ḍ, t, th, n, l or ś (च्, छ्, ट्, ड्, त्, थ्, न्, ल्, श्), then the n (न्) and the following consonant conjugate to fom a compound nasal consonant.

13/9 न् + क = न्क धार्तराष्ट्रान् कपिध्वजः → धार्तराष्ट्रान्कपिध्वजः

n + k = nk dhārtarāṣṭrān kapidhvajaḥ → dhārtarāṣṭrānkapidhvajaḥ (1.20)

13/10 न् + ग = न्ग् अश्नन् गच्छन् → अश्नन्गच्छन् n + g = ng aśnan gaććhan → aśnangaććhan (5.8)

13/11 न् + द = न्द् शङ्खान् दध्मुः → शङ्खान्दध्मुः n + d = nd śaṅkhān dadhmuḥ → śaṅkhāndadhmuḥ (1.18)

13/12 न् + ध = न्ध् धर्मकामार्थान् धृत्या → धर्मकामार्थान्धृत्या

n + dh = ndh arthān dhṛtyā → arthāndhṛtyā (18.34)

13/13 न् + प न्प् स्थितान् पार्थः → स्थितान्पार्थः n + p = np sthitān pārthaḥ → sthitānpārthaḥ (1.26)

13/14 न् + ब न्ब् तान् ब्रवीमि → तान्ब्रवीमि n + b = nb tān bravīmi → tānbravīmi (1.7)

13/15 न् + भ = न्भ् भवान् भीष्मः → भवान्भीष्मः n + bh = nbh bhavān bhīṣmaḥ → bhavānbhīṣmaḥ (1.8)

13/16 न् + म = न्म् आचार्यान् मातुलान् → आचार्यान्मातुलान्

n + m = nm āćāryān mātulān → āćāryānmātulān (1.26)

13/17 न् + य न्य् अस्मिन् यथा → अस्मिन्यथा n + y = ny asmin yathā → asminyathā (2.13)

13/18 न् + र = न्र् अस्मिन् रणसमुद्यमे → अस्मिन्रणसमुद्यमे n + r = nr asmin raṇa◦ → asminraṇa◦ (1.22)

13/19 न् + व = न्व् बहून् वदिष्यन्ति → बहून्वदिष्यन्ति n + v = nv bahūn vadiṣyanti → bahūnvadiṣyanti (2.36)

13/20 न् + स न्स् एतान् समवेतान् → एतान्समवेतान् n + s = ns etān samavetān → etānsamavetān (1.25)

न् = श ञ्श पश्यन् शृण्वन् → पश्यञ्शृण्वन् n + ś = ñś paśyan śṛṇvan → paśyañśṛṇvan (5.8)

13/21 न् + ह = न्ह सञ्जनयन् हर्षम् → सञ्जनयन्हर्षम्

n + h = nh sañjanayan harṣam → sañjanayanharṣam (1.12)

(14) m (ma`) becomes a nesal dot (ं *anusvāra*)

📖 When a word ending in letter m (म्) is followed by a word strating with any consonant, then that letter m (म्) becomes a nasal dot (ं) that is placed over the character that is before m (म्). e.g.

14/1 पाण्डवानीकम् व्यूढम् → पाण्डवानीकं व्यूढम् pāṇḍavānīkam vyūḍham → pāṇḍavānīkaṁ vyūḍham (1.2)

📖 However, when the word ending in letter m (म्) is at the end of the sentence, then that letter m (म्) remains unchanged.

14/2 पश्यैतां पाण्डुपुत्राणामाचार्य महतीं चमूम् । (1.3) अपर्याप्तं तदस्माकं बलं भीमाभिरक्षितम् ।। (1.10)

paśyaitāṁ pāṇḍuputrāṇāmāćārya mahtiṁ ćamūm (1.3)

paryaptaṁ tvidameteṣaṁ balaṁ bhīmābhirakṣitam (1.10)

(15) *Visarga* (:) becomes letter o (ओ)

📖 When vowel 'a' (अ) comes before and after the *visarga* (:), then that *visarga* (:) becomes letter u (उ). This letter u (उ) then joins with the vowel a (अ) that came before the *visarga* (:) and becomes letter o (ओ) according to the *sandhi* rule 2/2↑. And the letter a (अ) that came after the *visarga* (:) becomes an *avagraha* ' (ऽ), e.g.

15/1 तुमुलः अभवत् → तुमुलोऽभवत् tumulaḥ abhavat → tumulo'bhavat (1.13)

📖 When vowel a (अ) comes before the *visarga* (:) and any soft consonant comes after *isarga* (:), then that *visarga* (:) becomes letter u (उ). This letter u (उ) then joins with the vowel a (अ) that came before the *visarga* (:) and becomes letter o (ओ) according to the *sandhi* rule 2/2↑

15/2 (ग) हृषीकेशः गुडाकेशेन → हृषीकेशो गुडाकेशेन (g) hṛṣīkeśaḥ guḍākeśena → hṛṣīkeśo guḍākeśena (1.24)

15/3 (ज) नः जयेयुः → नो जयेयुः (j) naḥ jayeyuḥ → no jayeyuḥ (2.6)

(ज्ञ) बहवः ज्ञानतपसा → बहवो ज्ञानतपसा (jñ) bahavaḥ jñānatapasā → bahavo jñānatapasā (4.10)

15/4 (द) सौभद्रः द्रौपदेयाः → सौभद्रो द्रौपदेयाः (d) saubhadraḥ draupadeyāḥ → saubhadro draupadeyāḥ (1.6)

15/5 (ध) घोषः धार्तराष्ट्राणाम् → घोषो धार्तराष्ट्राणाम्

(gh) ghoṣaḥ dhārtarāṣṭrāṇam → ghoṣo dhārtarāṣṭrāṇam (1.19)

15/6 (न) सङ्करः नरकाय → सङ्करो नरकाय (n) saṅkaraḥ narakāya → saṅkaro narakāya (1.42)

15/7 (ब) बुद्धिनाशः बुद्धिनाशात् → बुद्धिनाशो बुद्धिनाशात्

(b) buddhināśaḥ buddhināśāt → buddhināśo buddhināśāt (2.63)

15/8 (भ) वासः भवति → वासो भवति (bh) vasaḥ bhavati → vaso bhavati (1.44)

15/9 (म) ध्रुवः मृत्युः → ध्रुवो मृत्युः (m) dhruvaḥ mṛtyuḥ → dhruvo mṛtyuḥ (2.27)

15/10 (य) कुन्तीपुत्रः युधिष्ठिरः → कुन्तीपुत्रो युधिष्ठिरः

(y) kuntīputraḥ yudhiṣṭhiraḥ → kuntīputro yudhiṣṭhiraḥ (1.16)

15/11 (र) नः राज्येन → नो राज्येन (r) naḥ rājyena → no rājyena (1.32)

15/12 (ल) प्रवृद्धः लोकान् → प्रवृद्धो लोकान् (l) pravṛddhaḥ lokān → pravṛddho lokān (11.32)

15/13 (व) युयुधानः विराटः → युयुधानो विराटः (v) yuyudhānaḥ virāṭaḥ → yuyudhāno virāṭaḥ (1.4)

15/14 (ह) उक्तः हृषीकेशः → उक्तो हृषीकेशः (h) uktaḥ hṛṣīkeśaḥ → ukto hṛṣīkeśaḥ (1.24)

(16) *Visarga* (:) becomes letter r (र्) -

📖 When any vowel other than a or ā (अ, आ) comes before a *visarga* (:) and any vowel comes after the *visarga* (:), then that *visarga* (:) becomes r (र्) and this r (र्) conjugates with the vowel following that *visarga* (:). e.g.

16/1 (इ) मुनिः उच्यते → मुनिरुच्यते (i) munih ućyate → munirućyate (2.56)

16/2 (ई) निराशीः अपरिग्रहः → निराशीरपरिग्रहः (ī) nirāśīḥ aparigrahaḥ → nirāśīraparigrahaḥ (6.10)

16/3 (उ) धनुः उद्यम्य → धनुरुद्यम्य (u) dhanuḥ udyamya → dhanurudyamya (1.20)

16/4 (ऐ) दोषैः एतैः → दोषैरेतैः (ai) doṣaiḥ etaiḥ → doṣairetaiḥ (1.43)

16/5 (ओ) सेनयोः उभयोः → सेनयोरुभयोः (o) senayoḥ ubhayoḥ → senayorubhayoḥ (1.21)

📖 If a vowel other that a or ā (अ, आ) comes before a *visarga* (:) and any soft consonant comes after the *visarga* (:), then that *visarga* (:) becomes r (र्) and this r (र्) is placed as a sofr r (र्‍) over the letter following that *visarga* (:)

16/5 (इ) प्रपश्यद्भिः जनार्दन → प्रपश्यद्भिर्जनार्दन

(i) prapaśyadbhiḥ janārdana → prapaśyadbhir janārdana (1.39)

16/6 (ई) स्थितधीः मुनिः → स्थितधीर्मुनिः (ī) sthitadhīḥ muniḥ → sthitadhīrmuniḥ (2.56)

16/7 (उ) मृत्युः ध्रुवम् → मृत्युर्ध्रुवम् (u) mṛtyuḥ dhruvam → mṛtyurdhruvam (2.27)

16/8 (ऊ) भूः मा → भूर्मा (ū) bhūḥ mā → bhūrmā (2.47)

16/9 (ए) दुर्बुद्धेः युद्धे → दुर्बुद्धेर्युद्धे (e) durbuddheḥ yuddhe → durbuddheryuddhe (1.23)

16/10 (ऐ) श्वेतैः हयैः → श्वेतैर्हयैः (ai) śvetaiḥ hayaiḥ → śvetairhayaiḥ (1.14)

16/11 (ओ) उभयोः मध्ये → उभयोर्मध्ये (o) ubhayoḥ madhye → ubhayormadhye (1.21)

(17) *Visarga* (:) becomes letter ś (श्)

📖 When ć or ćh (च्, छ्) comes after a *visarga* (:), then that *visarga* (:) changes to ś (श्). But, if ṭ or ṭh comes, then that *visarga* (:) becomes ṣ (ष्). e.g.

17/1 (च) पाण्डवाः च → पाण्डवाश्च (ć) pāṇḍavāḥ ća → pāṇḍavāśća (1.1)

17/2 (छ) उभयविभ्रष्टः छिन्नाभ्रम् → उभयविभ्रष्टश्छिन्नाभ्रम्

(ćh) vibhraṣṭaḥ ćhinnābhram → vibhraṣṭaśćhinnābhram (6.38)

(18) *Visarga* (:) becomes letter s (स्)

📖 When letter t or th (त्, थ्) comes after a *visarga* (:) then that *visarga* (:) changes to s (स्). e.g.

18/1 (त) दुर्योधनः तदा → दुर्योधस्तदा (t) duryodhanaḥ tadā → duryodhanastadā (1.2)

(त्र) लिङ्गैः त्रीन् → लिङ्गैस्त्रीन् (tr) liṅgaiḥ trīn → liṅgaistrīn (14.21)

(त्य) कर्मफलत्यागः त्यागात् → कर्मफलत्यागस्त्यागात् (ty) tyāgaḥ tyāgāt → tyāgastyāgāt (12.12)

(त्व) कुतः त्वा → कुतस्त्वा (tv) kutaḥ tvā → kutastvā (2.2)

(19) *Visarga* (:) after vowel a (अ) is deleted

📖 When vowel a (अ) comes before a *visarga* (:) and any vowel other than a (अ) comes after the *visarga* (:) then that *visarga* (:) is deleted.

19/1 (आ) निर्योगक्षेम: आत्मवान् → निर्योगक्षेम आत्मवान् (ā) yogakṣemaḥ ātmavān → ◦kṣema ātmavān (2.45)

19/2 (इ) अन्तवन्त: इमे → अन्तवन्त इमे (i) antavantaḥ ime → antavanta ime (2.18)

19/3 (ई) अव्यय: ईश्वर: → अव्यय ईश्वर: (ī) avyayaḥ īśvaraḥ → avyaya īśvaraḥ (15.17)

19/4 (उ) धृतराष्ट्र: उवाच → धृतराष्ट्र उवाच (u) dhṛtarāṣṭraḥ uvāća → dhṛtarāṣṭra uvāća (1.1)

19/5 (ऊ) अत: ऊर्ध्वम् → अत ऊर्ध्वम् (ū) ataḥ ūrdhvam → ata ūrdhvam (12.8)

19/6 (ऋ) ओङ्कार: ऋक् → ओङ्कार ऋक् (ṛ) oṅkāraḥ ṛksāma → oṅkāra ṛksāma (9.17)

19/7 (ए) य: एनम् → य एनम् (e) yaḥ enam → ya enam (2.19)

(20) *Visarga* (:) after vowel ā (आ) is deleted

📖 When vowel ā (आ) comes before a *visarga* (:) and any vowel comes after the *visarga* (:) then that *visarga* (:) is deleted. e.g.

20/1 (अ) देवा: अपि → देवा अपि (a) devāḥ api → devā api (11.52)

20/2 (आ) अपहृतज्ञाना: आसुरम् → अपहृतज्ञाना आसुरम् (ā) apahṛtajñānāḥ āsuram → ◦jñānā āsuram (7.15)

20/3 (इ) मणिगणा: इव → मणिगणा इव (i) maṇigaṇāḥ iva → maṇigaṇā iva (7.7)

20/4 (उ) षण्मासा: उत्तरायणम् → षण्मासा उत्तरायणम् (u) ṣaṇmāsāḥ uttarāyaṇam → ṣaṇmāsā uttarāyaṇam (8.24)

20/5 (ए) कामोपभोगपरमा: एतावत् → कामोपभोगपरमा एतावत्

(e) kāmopabhogaparamāḥ etāvat → kāmopabhogaparamā etāvat (16.11)

📖 When vowel ā (आ) comes before a *visarga* (:) and any soft consonant comes after the *visarga* (:) then that *visarga* (:) is deleted.

20/6 (ग) गुणा: गुणेषु → गुणा गुणेषु (g) guṇāḥ guṇeṣu → guṇā guṇeṣu (3.28)

20/7 (ज) स्वर्गपरा: जन्मकर्मफलप्रदाम् → स्वर्गपरा जन्मकर्मफलप्रदाम्

(j) svargaparāḥ janmakarmaphalapradām → svargaparā janmakarmaphalapradām (2.43)

20/8 (द) देवा: दास्यन्ते → देवा दास्यन्ते (d) devāḥ dāsyante → devā dāsyante (3.12)

20/9 (ध) पुरुषा: धर्मस्य → पुरुषा धर्मस्य (dh) paruṣāḥ dharmasya → paruṣā dharmasya (9.3)

20/10 (न) देहा: नित्यस्य → देहा नित्यस्य (n) dehāḥ nityasya → dehā nityasya (2.18)

20/11 (ब) व्यवसायात्मिका: बुद्धि → व्यवसायात्मिका बुद्धि

(b) vyavasāyātmikāḥ buddhiḥ → vyavasāyātmikā buddhiḥ (2.41)

20/12 (भ) महेश्वासा: भीमार्जुनसमा: → महेश्वासा भीमार्जुनसमा:

(bh) maheṣvāsāḥ bhīmārjunasamāḥ → maheṣvāsā bhīmārjunasamāḥ (1.4)

20/13 (म) शूरा: महेश्वासा: → शूरा महेश्वासा: (m) śūrāḥ maheṣvāsāḥ → śūrā maheṣvāsāḥ (1.4)

20/14 (य) समवेता: युयुत्सव: → समवेता युयुत्सव: (y) samavetāḥ yuyutsavaḥ → samavetā yuyutsavaḥ (1.1)

20/15 (र) धार्तराष्ट्राः रणे → धार्तराष्ट्रा रणे (r) dhārtarāṣṭrāḥ raṇe → dhārtarāṣṭrā raṇe (1.46)

20/16 (ल) कामकामाः लभन्ते → कामकामा लभन्ते (l) kāmakāmāḥ labhante → kāma-kāmā labhante (9.21)

20/17 (व) अर्हाः वयम् → अर्हा वयम् (v) arhāḥ vayam → arhā vayam (1.37)

20/18 (ह) बहुशाखाः हि → बहुशाखा हि (h) bahuśākhāḥ hi → bahu-śākhā hi (2.41)

📖 However, when vowel ā (आ) comes before a *visarga* (:) and any hard consonant comes after the *visarga* (:) then that *visarga* (:) is not deleted. e.g.

मामकाः पाण्डवाः → मामकाः पाण्डवाः māmakāḥ pāṇḍavāḥ → māmakāḥ pāṇḍavāḥ (1.1)

(21) *Visarga* (:) after eṣaḥ and saḥ (एषः, सः) is deleted

📖 When any consonant or any vowel other than letter a (अ), comes before a *visarga* (:) then that *visarga* (:) is deleted.

21/1 (एषः) एषः वः → एष वः eṣaḥ eṣaḥ vaḥ → eṣa vaḥ (3.10)

21/2 (सः) सः शब्द → स शब्द saḥ saḥ shabdaḥ → sa shabdaḥ (1.13)

(22) *Visarga* (:) remains unchanged

📖 When any vowel comes before a *visarga* (:) and a hard consonant such as k, kh, p, ph, ś, ṣ or s (क्, ख्, प्, फ्, श्, ष्, स्) comes after the *visarga* (:) then that *visarga* (:) is remains unchanged. e.g.

22/1 (क्) चेकितानः काशिराजः → चेकितानः काशिराजः (k) ćekitānaḥ kāśirājaḥ→ ćekitānaḥ kāśirājaḥ (1.5)

(क्ष्) सुखिनः क्षत्रियाः → सुखिनः क्षत्रियाः (ks) sukhinaḥ kṣatriyāḥ → sukhinaḥ kṣatriyāḥ (2.32)

22/2 (ख्) वायुः खम् → वायुः खम् (kh) vāyuḥ kham → vāyuḥ kham (7.4)

22/3 (प्) मामकाः पाण्डवाः → मामकाः पाण्डवाः (p) māmakāḥ pāṇḍavāḥ → māmakāḥ pāṇḍavāḥ (1.1)

22/4 (फ्) कृपणाः फलहेतवः → कृपणाः फलहेतवः (ph) kṛpaṇāḥ phalahetavaḥ → kṛpaṇāḥ phala◦ (2.49)

22/5 (श्) बहवः शूराः → बहवः शूराः (ś) bahvaḥ śūrā → bahvaḥ śūrā (1.9)

22/6 (ष्) शुक्लः षण्मासाः → शुक्लः षण्मासाः (ṣ) śuklaḥ ṣaṇmāsā → śuklaḥ ṣaṇmāsā (8.24)

22/7 (स्) नानाशस्त्रप्रहरणाः सर्वे → नानाशस्त्रप्रहरणाः सर्वे

(s) nānāśastrapraharaṇāḥ sarve → nānāśastrapraharaṇāḥ sarve (1.9)

📖 When a *visarga* (:) comes at the end of a sentence, then that *visarga* (:) remains unchanged. e.g.

22/8 धर्मक्षेत्रे कुरुक्षेत्रे समवेताः युयुत्सवः । (1.1) युयुधानो विराटश्च द्रुपदश्च महारथः ।। (1.4)

dharmakṣetre kurukṣetre samavetā yuyutsavaḥ (1.1) yuyudhāno virāṭaśća drupadaśća mahārathaḥ (1.4)

(23) Conjugation within and between sentences

📖 As said above, conjunction in the internal structure of words is necessary. Conjunction between the root and its prefix is also required. Conjugation is also necessary in the समास (two words being compounded). Though it is not necessary, conjunction between the congruent words of a sentense makes it a good prose; but not doing so in the poetry is a fault.

(*saṁhitaikapade nityā nityā dhātūpasargayoḥ, nityā samāse vākye tu sā vivakṣāmapekṣte.* संहितैकपदे नित्या नित्या धातूपसर्गयो: । नित्या समासे वाक्ये तु सा विवक्षामपेक्षते ।। -सिद्धान्तकौमुदि:) e.g.

23/1 दृष्ट्वा तु पाण्डवानीकं व्यूढं दुर्योधनस्तदा आचार्यमुपसङ्गम्य राजा वचनमब्रवीत् ।

dṛṣṭvā tu pāṇḍavānīkaṁ vyūḍhaṁ duryodhanastadā ācāryamupasaṅgamya rājā vacanamabravīt।। (1.2)

(24) Change of n (न्) to ṇ (ण्) at the end of a word

📖 When letter n (न्) at the end of a word is preceeded by letter ṛ, ṝ, r or ṣ (ऋ, ॠ, र्, ष्); and between this n (न्) and the letter ṛ, ṝ, r or ṣ (ऋ, ॠ, र्, ष्) even if any vowel or *anusvāra* (nasal dot) or a consonant from class k (क) or a consonant from class p (प) or letter y, r, v or h (य्, र्, व् ह्) comes, in all these cases the n (न्) changes to ṇ (ण्).

24/1	(एन) गुडाकेशेन (1.24) द्रुपदपुत्रेण (1.3)	(ena) guḍākeśena (1.24) drupadapautreṇa (1.3)
24/2	(न:) सम्बन्धिन: (1.34) शरीरिण: (2.18)	(naḥ) sambandhinaḥ (1.34) śarīriṇaḥ (2.18)
24/3	(नम्) वचनम् (1.2) अश्रुपूर्णाकुलेक्षणम् (2.1)	(nam) vacanam (1.2) aśrupūrṇākulekṣaṇam (2.1)
24/3	(ना) आत्मना (2.55) कर्मणा (3.20)	(nā) ātmanā (2.55) karmaṇā (3.20)
24/3	(ना:) अनुद्विग्नमना: (2.56) नानाशस्त्रप्रहरणा: (1.9)	(nāḥ) anudvignamanāḥ (2.56) śastrapraharaṇāḥ (1.9)
24/3	(नाम्) कुलीनाम् (1.42) पाण्डुपुत्राणाम् (1.3)	(nām) kulaghnānām (1.42) pāṇḍuputrāṇām (1.3)
24/3	(नि) हृदयानि (1.19) गात्राणि (1.29)	(ni) hṛdayāni (1.19) gātrāṇi (1.29)
24/3	(नी) ज्ञानी (7.16) अव्यभिचारिणी (13.10)	(nī) jñānī (7.6) avyabhicāriṇī (13.10)
24/3	(ने) स्यन्दने (1.14) रणे (1.46)	(ne) syandane (1.14) raṇe (1.46)

(25) Change of s (स्) to ṣ (ष्) at the end of a word

📖 When letter any vowel other than a or ā (अ, आ) or any consonant from the class k (क्) or letter r (र्) comes after a word ending in the case suffixes such as saḥ, sā, sāma, si, su, syati, syate, syanti, syāmi, sye, sva, etc. (स:, सा, साम्, सि, सु, स्यति, स्यते, स्यन्ति, स्यामि, स्ये, स्व), then in all these cases the s (स) in these suffixes changes to ṣ (ष्). e.g.

25/1	(स:) स: (1.13) एष: (3.10)	(saḥ) saḥ (1.13) eṣaḥ (3.10)
25/1	(सा) सा (2.69) एषा (2.39)	(sā) sā (2.69) eṣā (2.39)
25/1	(साम्) अपहृतचेतसाम् (2.44) एतेषाम् (1.10)	(sām) apahṛtacetasām (2.44) eteṣam (1.10)
25/1	(सि) वासांसि (2.22) करोषि (9.27)	(si) vāsānsi (2.22) karoṣi (9.27)
25/1	(सु) दुष्टासु (1.41) अयनेषु (1.11)	(su) duṣṭāsu (1.41) ayaneṣu (1.11)

25/1 (स्यति) स्थास्यति (2.53) परिशुष्यति (1.29) (syati) sthāsyati (2.53) pariśuṣyati (1.29)

25/1 (स्यन्ति) नमस्यन्ति (11.36) कथयिष्यन्ति (2.34) (syanti) namasyanti (11.36) kathayiṣyanti (2.34)

25/1 (स्यते) मंस्यन्ते (2.35) विशिष्यते (7.17) (syate) mansyante (2.35) viśiṣyate (7.17)

25/1 (स्यामि) प्रतियोत्स्यामि (2.4) कथयिष्यामि (10.19) (syāmi) pratiyotsyāmi (2.4) kathayiṣyāmi (10.19)

25/1 (स्ये) योत्स्ये (2.9) हनिष्ये (16.14) (sye) yotsye (2.9) haniṣye (16.14)

25/1 (स्व) तितिक्षस्व (2.14) कुरुष्व (9.27) (sva) titikṣasva (2.14) kuruṣva (9.27)

NOTE : Once any *sandhi* rule is applied between two words, those two words do not congugate again with any of the other *sandhi* rules. e.g.

vikrāntaḥ uttamaujāḥ → vikrānta uttamaujāḥ (1.6)

In this case, vikrāntaḥ and uttamaujāḥ are congugated into vikrānta uttamaujāḥ using *sandhi* rule 19/1. Now, vikrānta uttamaujāḥ can not be conjugated as vikrāntottamaujāḥ using *sandhi* rule 2/2.

EXCEPTION TO THIS RULE : THE PARASAVARNA SANDHI
परसवर्णसंधिः ।

Once a *sandhi* is made according to Rule no. 14/1, the *anuswara* (nasal dot) may be changed to the corresponding nasal consonant and this new nasal consonant will form a ***parasavarṇa sandhi*** with the next consonant. e.g.

(ञ्) उक्तम् च → उक्तं च → उक्तञ्च । (ñ) uktam ća → uktaṁ ća → uktañća

सर्वेषाम् च महीक्षिताम् → सर्वेषां च महीक्षिताम् → सर्वेषाञ्च महीक्षिताम् →

sarveṣām ća mahīkṣitām → sarveṣāṁ ća mahīkṣitām → sarveṣāñća mahīkṣitām → (1.25)

(ङ्) पापम् कर्तुम् → पापं कर्तुम् → पापङ्कर्तुम् । (ṅ) pāpam kartūm → pāpaṁ kartum → pāpaṅkartum (1.45)

पदम् गच्छन्त्यनामयम् → पदं गच्छन्त्यनामयम् → पदङ्गच्छन्त्यनामयम् ।

padam gaćchantyanāmayam → padaṁ gaćchantyanāmayam → padaṅgaćchantyanāmayam

(न) कृतम् दोषं → कृतं दोषं → कृतन्दोषं (n) kṛtam doṣam → kṛtaṁ doṣam → kṛtandoṣam (1.39)

NOTE :

For All Aspects of the GRAMMAR OF THE GITA, see our "Sanskrit Grammar and Reference Book" at amazon

ॐ

atha śrīmadbhagavadgītā prārabhyate
अथ श्रीमद्भगवद्गीता प्रारभ्यते ।

CHAPTER 1

prathamo'dhyāyaḥ:[1]
प्रथमोऽध्यायः ।

YOGA OF THE MELANCHOLY[2]
(THE YOGA THAT OVERWHELMED AND HUMBLED ARJUNA)

viṣādayogopaniṣhat
विषादयोगोपनिषत् ।

Dhritarashtra Said to Sanjaya

Vyāsa's divine saṁskṛt words :

Dhṛtarāṣṭra said (Dhṛtarāṣṭra uvāća धृतराष्ट्र उवाच ।)

1.1 धर्मक्षेत्रे कुरुक्षेत्रे समवेता युयुत्सवः ।
मामकाः पाण्डवाश्चैव किमकुर्वत सञ्जय ।।

dharmakṣetre kurukṣetre samavetā yuyutsavaḥ:,
māmakāḥ: pāṇḍavāśćaiva kimakurvata sañjaya. (1.1)

---

[1] NOTE : The additional innovative accent marks attached with the characters such as Ć ć d̦ ḥ: k̦ m̦ n̦ ș ț etc. are devised only for associating these English characters closely with their Saṁskṛt counterparts च् च् द् : म् न् त् स् respectively, and to differentiate them from the common English characters C, c, d, h, k, m, n, s and t that appear elsewhere in the English text. e.g. (i) 'vaćanam̦ is a collective noun;' as against (ii) 'vacanam is a collective noun.' These accents are purposefully innovated **as a visual help** for the discreet readers. The readers who do not need them, or refuse to adopt or accept them, may simply ignore them.

[2] Elsewhere◦ *arjunaviṣādayoga* → Arjuna's Vishad Yooga, Yoga of Arjuna's Despondency, Arjuna Yoga, Arjuna's Melancholy ...etc.

📖 Each chapter in the Gītā is an Upaniṣhat. This Upaniṣhad in the Gītā is the ***yoga* of 'melancholy.'** The Melancholy, that affected Arjuna. The **'melancholy,'** that overwhelmed and humbled Arjuna, should affect you and me to make us benevolent to hear an advise from elders. It is **not** given by Lord Krishna as the yoga of **only** 'od Arjuna' or 'Arjuna's melancholy.' Remember : Lord Krishna gave the 'Yoga of Melancholy' to Vivasvān much before he gave it to Arjuna.

PLEASE NOTE THAT, in all verses of in this book :

(§1) = Analysis of the verse, with the 25 Sandhi Rules explained above,

(§2) = Grammatical analysis of each Sanskrit word with the rules given earlier,

(§3) = Plain grammatical English meaning of each Sanskrit word of the shloka based on the grammar given in Step §2. These exact English words are used in step §5 below,

(§4) = Sanskrit words re-arranged in the order of English syntax,

(§5) = English meaning of the shloka, exactly as translated in step (§3) above.

(§1) Dissection of the verse, with the 25 Sandhi Rules explained above :

अथ श्रीमत् भगवत् गीता प्रारभ्यते । प्रथमः अध्यायः । अर्जुन-विषाद-योगः । धृतराष्ट्रः उवाच । धर्मक्षेत्रे कुरुक्षेत्रे समवेताः युयुत्सवः । मामकाः पाण्डवाः च एव किम् अकुर्वत सञ्जय ।

atha śrīmaṭ (rule 9/sub-rule 8) bhagavaṭ (r∘ 9/4)[3] gītā prārabhyate. prathamaḥ: (r∘ 15/1) adhyāyaḥ:. arjunaviṣādayogaḥ:. dhṛtarāṣṭraḥ: (r∘ 19/4) uvāća.

dharmakṣetre kurukṣetre samavetāḥ: (r∘ 20/14) yuyutsavaḥ: (r∘ 22/8) māmakāḥ: (r∘ 22/3) pāṇḍavāḥ: (r∘ 17/1) ća (r∘ 3/1) eva kiṃ (r∘ 8/16) akurvata sañjaya (1.1)

(§2) **Grammatical Analysis of Each Sanskrit Word with the Rules given earlier :**

atha (see verse 1.20[4]↓); *śrīmadbhagavadgītā* (f∘ 1nom∘ sing∘ ←tatpu∘ *śrīmaṭ-bhagavaṭ-gītā*, श्रीमतः भगवतः गीता ←adj∘ *śrīmaṭ* 6.41 ↓ + adj∘ *bhagavaṭ* 10.14 ↓ + f∘ *gītā* ←ppp∘ adj∘ *gīta* 13.5 ↓); *prārabhyate* (3rd-per∘ sing∘ pres∘ वर्तमान्-लट् ātmane∘ ←1∘प्र-आ-√रभ् (to brgin)). *prathamaḥ:* (m∘ 1nom∘ sing∘ ←num∘ adj∘ *prathama* ←1∘√प्रथ् (to grow) 1.18↓); 📖*adhyāyaḥ:* (chapter) (1nom∘ sing∘ ←m∘ *adhyāya* ←1∘अधि√इ (to enter, come, go).[5] *arjunaviṣādayogaḥ:* (m∘ 1nom∘ sing∘ ←tatpu∘ *arjuna-viṣāda-*

---

[3] PLEASE NOTE : In each Section (§1), the r∘ (for example : r∘ 9/4) refers to rule∘ number, i.e. one of the 25 the Sandhi Rules mentioned in the Euphonic Conjunctions used in Gītā सन्धिमीमांसा section in the chapter on "THE BASIC GRAMMAR OF THE GITA," earlier in this book. For detailed grammar, see my "*Sanskrit Grammar and Reference Book.*"

[4] PLEASE NOTE : In each Section (§2), the 1∘ in the expressions such as ←1∘अधि√इ refers to one of the Eleven classes of the of Verbs mentioned in the List of Abbreviations. Here (in 1∘अधि√इ), the 1∘ indicates that the root verb √इ belongs to Class 1, the भ्वादि गणः of the verbs.

[5] PLEASE NOTE : In each Section (§2), the numer in the expressions such as (1.20) refers to the Gita Chapter Number and The verse number in that Chapter. Therefore, 1.20 = Verse 20 in Chapter 1, and so on. This is done to avoid the repetition of the same explanation over and over in the subsequent chapters.

yoga, अर्जुनम् अभिभूतस्य विषादस्य योगः ←m◦ prop◦ *arjuna* 1.4 ↓ + m◦ 🕮*viṣāda* (melancholy) 1.27 ↓ + m◦ *yoga* 2.39 ↓). 🕮*dhṛtarāṣṭraḥ:* (m◦ 1nom◦ sing◦ ←bahuvrī◦ adj◦ or prop◦ *dhṛtarāṣṭra*, धृतम् राष्ट्रम् राजपालयति यः ←ppp◦ adj◦ *dhṛta* ←1◦√धृ (to bear) + n◦ rāṣṭra ←1◦√राज् (to rule); 🕮*uvāća* (said) (1.25 ↓).

dharmakṣetre (n◦ 7loc◦ sing◦ ←tatpu◦ *dharma-kṣetra*, धर्मयुक्तकर्माणाम् क्षेत्रम् । धार्मिकम् क्षेत्रम् । धर्मयुक्तकर्मभ्यः प्रसिद्धं क्षेत्रम् ←m◦ 🕮**dharma**[6] (what ought to be done) ←1◦√धृ (to bear) + n◦ 🕮**kṣetra** (land) ←6◦√क्षि (to stay); *kurukṣetre* (n◦ 7loc◦ sing◦ ←tatpu◦ *kuru-kṣetra*, कुरुणां क्षेत्रम् । कुरुणा वा कुरुभिः वा धर्मयुक्तकुरुभिः प्रस्थापितम् क्षेत्रम् ←m◦ adj◦ **kuru**, कुरोः गोत्रापत्यम् + n◦ *kṣetra* ↑);[7] 🕮*samavetāḥ:* (m◦ 1nom◦ plu◦ ←ppp◦ adj◦ **samaveta** (assembled) ←2◦सम्-अव√इ (to enter) ←ind◦ **saṃ** ←4◦√सो (to complete) + ind◦ *ava* ←1◦√इ (to come); 🕮*yuyutsavaḥ:* (m◦ 1nom◦ plu◦ ←desi◦ adj◦ **yuyutsu** ←f◦ **yudh** ←4◦√युध् (to fight) + सन्); 🕮*māmakāḥ:* (m◦ 1nom◦ plu◦ ←adj◦ **māmaka** (my) ←pron◦ *asmad* 1.7↓); *pāṇḍavāḥ:* (1nom◦ plu◦ ←m◦ -taddhita◦ ***pāṇḍva***, पाण्डोः अपत्यम् ←prop◦ ***pāṇḍu*** ←10◦√पण्ड् (to be learned) ; ***ća*** (and) (ind◦ aggregative ←5◦√चि (to gather) ; ***eva*** (ind◦ ←1◦√इ (to come); ***kiṃ*** (what?) (ind◦ adv◦ or n◦ 2acc◦ sing◦ ←pron◦ *kiṃ*, -what?); *akurvata* (did) (3rd-per◦ plu◦ -past-imper◦ लङ् भूत◦ ātmane◦ ←8◦√कृ (to do); *sañjaya* (m◦ 8voc◦ sing◦ ←prop◦ ***sañjaya*** ←1◦सम्√जि (to win) (1.1)

---

[6] PLEASE NOTE : In each Section (§2), the underline suggests that this word appears for the first time in the Gītā in this verse and that it also appears at more places ahead after this verse. Its grammatical analysis is given only in this shloka. And after this point, wherever it appears again, it is referred to this shloka for its grammatical analysis. This method is used in all sholkas, to avoid unnecessary repetitions of the explanations.

[7] कुरुक्षेत्रम् : निमिषं निमिषार्धं वा यत्र तिष्ठन्ति योगिनः । तत्र तत्र कुरुक्षेत्रं प्रयागो नैमिषं वनम् ।। (uttaragītā 3.9)

HOW TO READ THE ANALYSIS GIVEN IN STEP (§2)

for example :

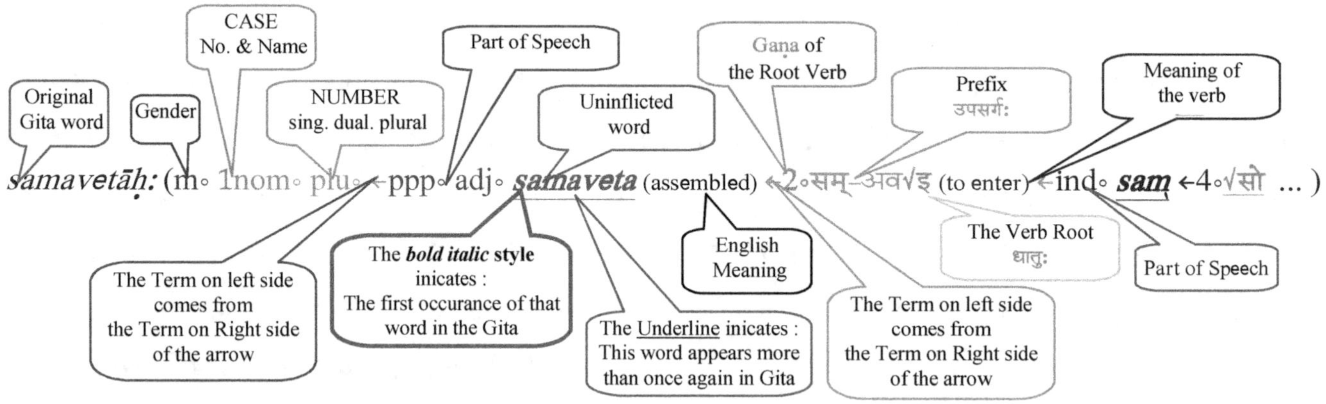

(§3) Plain Grammatical Meaning of each one of the Sanskrit words of the shloka (exact same English words to be used in step 5 below) :

atha (Now, as follows); *śrīmadbhagavadgītā* (subj◦ the Celestial Gītā); *prārabhyate* (vi◦ it begins). *prathamaḥ:* (adj◦-subj◦ the first); *adhyāyaḥ:* (subj◦ the chapter). *arjunaviṣādayogaḥ:* (The Yoga of the Melancholy that overwhelmed Arjuna). *dhṛtarāṣṭraḥ:* (subj◦ Dhṛatarāṣṭra); *uvāća* (vt◦ he said). *dharmakṣetre kurukṣetre* (on the sacred land of Kurukṣetra, on the place established by the Kurus for righteous works);[8] *samavetāḥ:* (adj1◦-subj1-2◦ assembled) *yuyutsavaḥ:* (adj2◦-subj1-2◦ those who are eager for battle); *māmakāḥ:* (subj1◦ mine); *pāṇḍavāḥ:* (subj2◦ sons of Pāṇḍu; Pāṇḍu's sons); *ća* (and); *eva* (and, also); *kiṃ* (what?); *akurvata* (did they do); *sañjaya* (O Sañjaya!). (1.1)

(§4) Sanskrit words re-arranged in the order of English Syntax :

atha prārabhyate śrīmadbhagavadgītā. prathamaḥ: adhyāyaḥ:. arjunaviṣādayogaḥ:. dhṛtarāṣṭraḥ: uvāća. sañjaya! kiṃ māmakāḥ: ća pāṇḍavāḥ: -yuyutsavaḥ: eva samavetāḥ: dharmakṣetre kurukṣetre- akurvata? (1.1)

(§5) English Meaning of the shloka, exactly "as translated" in step (§3) above[9]

---

[8] A note for the readers who know Hindī language: For *the essential history and background* of the Gītā, answers to your questions, clarification of your doubts and definitions of the key words, please read my 'संगीत-कृष्ण-रामायण' ISBN 978-1-897416-43-3).

[9] **The true meaning of an original verse, as it is, lies ONLY within Kṛṣṇa's and Vyāsa's Sanskṛt words, and nowhere else.** It can only be obtained by understanding the original Saṁskṛt words and then deducting your own heartfelt meaning. There is no better way. No translation or commentary is a substitute. For your help, alternate *Saṁskṛt* words are provided for most of the KEY WORDS. They are your second best guide.

(additional connecting or filler words, if any, are enclosed in brackets) :

Now begins the Celestial Gītā. The first chapter. The Yoga of the Melancholy (The Yoga that overwhelmed Arjuna).

Dhṛatarāṣṭra said :

O Sañjaya! What did mine[10] and Pāṇḍu's sons --eager for battle[11] and assembled[12] on the sacred land[13] of Kurukṣetra-- do? (verse 1.1)

Sanjaya said (sañjaya uvāća सञ्जय उवाच ।)

1.2 दृष्ट्वा तु पाण्डवानीकं व्यूढं दुर्योधनस्तदा ।
आचार्यमुपसङ्गम्य राजा वचनमब्रवीत् ।।

dṛṣṭvā tu pāṇḍavānīkaṁ vyūḍhaṁ duryodhanastadā,
āćāryamupasaṅgamya rājā vaćanamabravīt. (1.2)

(§1) सञ्जयः उवाच । दृष्ट्वा तु पाण्डवानीकम् व्यूढम् दुर्योधनः तदा । आचार्यम् उपसङ्गम्य राजा वचनम् अब्रवीत् । *sañjayaḥ:* (r◦ 19/4) *uvāća. dṛṣṭvā tu pāṇḍavānīkam* (r◦ 14/1) *vyūḍham* (r◦ 14/1) *duryodhanaḥ:* (r◦ 18/1) *tadā* (r◦ 23/1) *āćāryam* (r◦ 8/20) *upasaṅgamya rājā vaćanam* (r◦ 8/16) *abravīt* (1.2)

(§2) *sañjayaḥ:* (m◦ 1nom◦ sing◦ ←prop◦ *sañjaya* 1.1); *uvāća* (1.25). 📖**dṛṣṭvā** (ipp◦ ind◦ ←1◦√दृश् (to see); **tu** (ind◦ ←6◦√तुद् (to strike); *pāṇḍavānīkam* (n◦ or m◦ 2acc◦ sing◦ ←tatpu◦ *pāṇḍavānīka,* पाण्डवानाम् अनीकम् or अनीकः ←m◦ *pāṇḍava* 1.1 + n◦ or m◦ 📖**anīka** (army) ←4◦√अन् (to move); *vyūḍham* (n◦ m◦ 2acc◦ sing◦

PLEASE treat English meaning of *Saṁskṛt* text as an approximation only. Do not depend solely on translation and defeat the purpose of this book. Please use it only as a guide, if and when you need help. Giving the English translation is not within the objectives of this book, however, it is provided just to complete the step-by-step flow and proper termination of the process of explanation. Notwithstanding, to render an honest translation in step 5, care is taken to use the same English words given as meaning in step 3 above. It holds good for the entire book.

[10] Elsewhwre◦ *māmakāḥ* → my sons

📖 मामक adj◦ = my, mine, belonging to me, belonging to my side ...etc.)

[11] Elsewhere◦ *yuyutsavaḥ* → desiring (gerund)

📖 युयुत्सु is not a gerund or verb. It is a desederative adj◦ → he who is desirous or eager for the battle.

[12] Elsewhere◦ *Samavetāḥ* → they are assembled, when they assembled ...etc. (verb).

📖 समवेता: is not a verb. It is a ppp◦ adj◦ → assembled people, as an adjective. समवेता: युयुत्सव: मामका: किम् अकुर्वत?

[13] Elsewhere◦ धर्मक्षेत्रम् = धर्मस्य क्षेत्रम् । कुरुक्षेत्रम् = कुरो: क्षेत्रम् ।

←ppp◦ adj◦ ***vyūḍha*** (arrayed) ←1◦**√वह्** (to carry); *duryodhanaḥ:* (m◦ 1nom◦ sing◦ ←prop◦ *duryodhana* ←adj◦ *duryodha* ←ind◦ ***dur*** ←5◦**√दु** (be bad) + f◦ *yudh* 1.1); ***tadā*** (then) (ind◦ ←pron◦ ***tad***, -that ←8◦**√तन्** (to spread); *ā́cāryam* (m◦ 2acc◦ sing◦ ←taddhita◦ ***ā́cāraya,*** (guru) आचारयति यः ←m◦ ***ā́cāra*** ←1◦आ**√चर्** (to move); 📖*upasaṅgamya* (past-participle lyp◦ ind◦ ←1◦उप-सम्**√गम्** (to go); 📖***rājā*** (1nom◦ sing◦ ←m◦ ***rājan*** (king) ←1◦√राज् (to rule); 📖***vaćanam*** (2acc◦ sing◦ ←n◦ *vaćana* (expression) ←2◦**√वच्** (to speek); ***abravīt*** (said) (3rd-per◦ sing◦ -past-imper◦ लङ् भूत◦ parasmai◦ ←2◦**√ब्रू** (to speak) (1.2)

(§3) *sañjayaḥ:* (subj◦ Sañjaya); *uvāća* (said). *dṛṣṭvā* (having seen, seeing, beholding); *tu* (an emphatic expletive particle; and then); *pāṇḍavānīkam* (obj1◦ the army of the Pāṇḍavas) *vyūḍham* (adj◦-obj1◦ strategically arranged, arrayed in phalanx); *duryodhanaḥ:* (subj◦ Duryodhana); *tadā* (at that time); *ā́cāryam* (obj2◦ ā́cārya, Droṇā́cārya); *upasaṅgamya* (having approached); *rājā* (adj◦-subj◦ King); *vaćanam* (obj3◦ the expression); *abravīt* (said). (1.2)

(§4) tadā dṛṣṭvā pāṇḍavānīkam vyūḍham tu upasaṅgamya ā́cāryam rājā duryodhanaḥ: abravīt vaćanam

(§5) At that time, beholing the army[14] of the Pāṇḍavas, arrayed in phalanx, and then having approached[15] Droṇā́cārya, King Duryodhana said (this) expression.[16] (1.2)

1.3 पश्यैतां पाण्डुपुत्राणामाचार्य महतीं चमूम् ।
व्यूढां दृपदपुत्रेण तव शिष्येण धीमता ।।

paśyaitāṁ pāṇḍuputrāṇāmā́cārya mahtīṁ ćamūm,
vyūḍhāṁ drupadaputreṇa tava śiṣyeṇa dhīmatā. (1.3)

(§1) पश्य एताम् पाण्डुपुत्राणाम् आचार्य महतीम् चमूम् । व्यूढाम् दृपदपुत्रेण तव शिष्येण धीमता । *paśya* (r◦ 3/1) *etām* (r◦ 14/1) *pāṇḍuputrāṇām* (r◦ 24/6, 8/17) *ā́cārya mahtīm* (r◦ 14/1) *ćamūm* (r◦ 14/2) *vyūḍhām* (r◦ 14/1) *drupadaputreṇa* (r◦ 24/1) *tava śiṣyeṇa* (r◦ 24/1) *dhīmatā* (1.3)

---

[14] Elsewhere◦ *anīkam* → soldiers

📖 It should be (collective) singular, e.g. army

[15] Elsewhere◦ *upasaṅgamya* → went, approached ...etc. (past tense)

📖 उपसङ्गम्य is not a tense. It is a उप-सम्√गम् lyp◦ ipp◦ gerund participle → having gone, having approached.

[16] Elsewhere◦ *vaćanam* → words, these words (plural)

📖 वचनम् should be translated singular, may be as a colloective singular noun, such as : word, expression, utterance, statement, wording. The same is true for the word *vākyam* वाक्यम् in 1.21 and 2.1; and *vaćaḥ* वचः in 2.10

(§2) ***paśya*** (2nd-per◦ sing◦ imperative◦ निवेदनार्थ-लोट् parasmai◦ ←1◦√दृश् (to see); ***etām*** (f◦ 2acc◦ sing◦ ←pron◦ ***etad***, (to this) ←1◦√इ (to come); *pāṇḍuputrāṇām* (6pos plu◦ ←m◦ tatpu◦ *pāṇḍu-putra*, पाण्डोः पुत्रः ←prop◦ *pāṇḍu* 1.1 + m◦ ***putra*** (son) ←1◦पुत्√त्रै (to protect); *āćārya* (8voc◦ sing◦ ←m◦ *āćārya* 1.2); *mahtīm* (f◦ 2acc◦ sing◦ ←adj◦ ***mahat*** (great) ←1◦√मह् (to respect); *ćamūm* (2acc◦ sing◦ ←f◦ *ćamū* (army) ←1◦√चम् (to eat); *vyūḍhām* (f◦ 2acc◦ sing◦ ←ppp◦ adj◦ *vyūḍha* 1.2); *drupadaputreṇa* (m◦ 3inst◦ sing◦ ←tatpu◦ *drupada-putra*, द्रुपदस्य पुत्रः ←prop◦ ***drupada*** ←1◦√द्रु (to flow) + m◦ *putra* ↑); ***tava*** (6pos sing◦ ←personal pron◦ ***yuṣmad***, (you) ←1◦√युष् (to serve); *śiṣyeṇa* (3inst◦ sing◦ ←m◦ ***śiṣya*** (disciple) ←2◦√शास् (to rule); *dhīmatā* (m◦ 3inst◦ sing◦ ←adj◦ ***dhīmat*** (talented) ←f◦ ***dhī*** (talent) ←1◦√ध्यै (to meditate) + taddhita◦ suffix *matup*, ***mat*** मत्) (1.3)

(§3) *paśya* (behold); *etām* (adj1◦-obj◦ this); *pāṇḍuputrāṇām* (of the sons of Pāṇḍu; of the Pāṇḍavas); *āćārya* (O Āćārya!; O Āćārya Droṇa); *mahtim* (adj2◦-obj◦ great); *ćamūm* (obj◦ army); *vyūḍhām* (adj3◦-obj◦ the one that is arrayed in phalanx); *drupadaputreṇa* (subj◦ by the son of king Drupada; by Dhṛṣṭadyumna, the son of Drupada); *tava* (your); *śiṣyeṇa* (adj1◦-subj◦ by the disciple); *dhīmatā* (adj2◦-subj◦ by the talented)

(§4) paśya! āćārya! etām mahtim ćamūm pāṇḍuputrāṇām, vyūḍhām tava dhīmatā śiṣyeṇa drupadaputreṇa

(§5) O Āćārya Droṇa! behold this great army of the Pāṇḍavas, arrayed in phalanx by your talented disciple Dhṛṣṭadyumna, the son of Drupada. (1.3)

1.4 अत्र शूरा महेष्वासा भीमार्जुनसमा युधि ।
युयुधानो विराटश्च द्रुपदश्च महारथः ।।

atra śūrā maheṣvāsā bhīmārjunasamā yudhi,
yuyudhāno virāṭaśća drupadaśća mahārathaḥ:; (1.4)

(§1) अत्र शूराः महेष्वासाः भीमार्जुनसमाः युधि । युयुधानः विराटः च द्रुपदः च महारथः । ***atra śūrāḥ:*** (r◦ 20/13) ***maheṣvāsāḥ:*** (r◦ 20/12) ***bhīmārjunasamāḥ:*** (r◦ 20/14) ***yudhi yuyudhānaḥ:*** (r◦ 15/13) ***virāṭaḥ:*** (r◦ 17/1) ***ća drupadaḥ:*** (r◦ 17/1) ***ća mahārathaḥ:*** (r◦ 22/8);

(§2) *atra* (place or time indicating ind◦ ←pron◦ *idam* 1.10 or *tad* 1.3); ***śūrāḥ:*** (m◦ 1nom◦ plu◦ ←adj◦ ***śūra*** (brave) ←10◦√शूर् (to be brave); *maheṣvāsāḥ:* (m◦ 1nom◦ plu◦ ←adj◦ *maheṣvāsa* इष्वासेषु महान् ←adj◦ *mahā* (great) 1.15↓ + bahuvrī◦ *iṣvāsa* (archer) ←इषुम् अस्यति यः । इषुः अस्यते येन । ←m◦ ***iṣu*** (arrow) ←1◦√ईष् (to fly) + m◦ ***āsa*** (bow) ←2◦√आस् (to sit); *bhīmārjunasamāḥ:* (m◦ 1nom◦ plu◦ ←bahuvrī◦ adj◦ *bhīmārjuna-sama*, भीमस्य वा अर्जुनस्य वा समः यः । ←m◦ prop◦ ***bhīma*** ←3◦√भी (to fear) + m◦ prop◦ ***arjuna***

←1∘√अर्ज् (to earn) + adj∘ **sama** (such as) ←1∘√सम् (to be equanimous, equal); *yudhi* (7loc∘ sing∘ ←f∘ *yudh* 1.1); *yuyudhānaḥ:* (m∘ 1nom∘ sing∘ ←prop∘ *yuyudhāna* ←4∘,3∘युध्√धा (to put); **virāṭaḥ:** (m∘ 1nom∘ sing∘ ←prop∘ *virāṭa* ←ind∘ prefix **vi** वि -indicating excess or uniqueness ←2∘√वा (to move) + m∘ *rāṭ* ←1∘√राज् (to rule); *ća* (and); *drupadaḥ:* (m∘ 1nom∘ sing∘ ←prop∘ *drupada* 1.3); *ća* (and); **mahārathaḥ:** (m∘ 1nom∘ sing∘ ←bahuvrī∘ **mahāratha** महान् रथी यः ←adj∘ *mahā* (great) 1.3 + m∘ **ratha** or adj∘ **rathin** (charioteer) ←1∘√रम् (to rejoice); (1.4)

(§3) *atra* (here); *śūrāḥ:* (adj1∘-subj1-13∘ brave men); *maheṣvāsāḥ:* (adj2∘-subj1-13∘ great archers); *bhīmārjunasamāḥ:* (such as Bhima and Arjuna) *yudhi* (on the battle field, in the war); *yuyudhānaḥ:* (subj1∘ Yuyudhāna); *virāṭaḥ:* (subj2∘ Virāṭa, king Virāṭa); *ća* (and); *drupadaḥ:* (subj3∘ Drupada, king Drupada); *ća* (and); *mahārathaḥ:* (adj∘-subj3∘ the great charioteer, the great commander); (1.4)

(§4) atra yudhi maheṣvāsāḥ: śūrāḥ: ća bhīmārjunasamāḥ: yuyudhānaḥ: virāṭaḥ: ća mahārathaḥ: drupadaḥ:;

(§5) Here, on the battlefield, (there are) great archers[17] and brave men, such as Bhima and Arjuna,[18] (and) Yuyudhāna, Virāṭa and the great charioteer[19] Drupada;[20] (1.4)

---

[17] Elsewhere∘ *maheṣvāsāḥ:* → mighty bowed, big bowed...etc.

The adj∘ महा in the *bahuvrīhi samāsa* महेष्वासा: does not glorify or clasify the bows (tatpurusha samāsa), but it rather qualifies the bowmen or the archers, because a great bow is not as important as a great archer.

[18] Elsewhere∘ *bhīmārjunasamāḥ:* → equal to Bhīma and Arjuna, equals of Bhima and Arjuna, equal of Bhima and Arjuna.

If we say each of them is equal to Bhīma and Arjuna, it would mean that each of these men is equal in power to Bhīma + Arjuna added together i.e. double than Bhīma or Arjuna, which means Bhima and Arjuna were the weakest among them. Therefore, it should be SUCH AS Bhima AND Arjuna. Not, he is equal to Bhima + Arjuna. No warrior was equal to Bhima or to Arjuna, let alone Bhima + Arjuna.

[19] Elsewhere∘ *mahārathaḥ* → great fighters, great chariot fighters, chariot warriors, great warriors, great charioteers; one who has a great chariot, the master of a great chariot, ...etc.

महारथ: is a singular adj∘ a great charioteer. It should be attached to one nearest singular person i.e. Drupada. Similarly, in the next verse the adjectives वीर्यवान् and नरपुङ्गव: qualify kāśya and śaibya only. NOTE : महारथ: is not just a great charioteer, but a great charioteer who is the commander (महारथी) of a great army composed of all four wings of the combat (चतुरांगिणी सेना).

[20] NOTE : In this book, the semicolon (;) at the end of a verse indicates that the present verse continues into the following verse or verses.

1.5 धृष्टकेतुश्चेकितानः काशिराजश्च वीर्यवान् ।
पुरुजित्कुन्तिभोजश्च शैब्यश्च नरपुङ्गवः ।।

dhṛṣṭaketuśćekitānaḥ kāśirājaśća vīryavān,
purujitkuntibhojaśća śaibyaśća narapuṅgavaḥ:; (1.5)

(§1) धृष्टकेतुः चेकितानः काशिराजः च वीर्यवान् । पुरुजित् कुन्तिभोजः च शैब्यः च नरपुङ्गवः । *dhṛṣṭaketuḥ:* (r◦ 17/1) *ćekitānaḥ:* (r◦ 22/1) *kāśirājaḥ:* (r◦ 17/1) *ća vīryavān* (r◦ 23/1) *purujit* (r◦ 10/5) *kuntibhojaḥ:* (r◦ 17/1) *ća śaibyaḥ:* (r◦ 17/1) *ća narapuṅgavaḥ:* (r◦ 22/8)

(§2) *dhṛṣṭaketuḥ:* (m◦ 1nom◦ sing◦ ←prop◦ *dhṛṣṭaketu* ←1◦धृष√चाय् (to discern)or 1◦√चित् (to percceive); *ćekitānaḥ:* (m◦ 1nom◦ sing◦ ←prop◦ *ćekitāna* ←चि1◦√कित् (to examine); *kāśirājaḥ:* (m◦ 1nom◦ sing◦ ←bahuvrī◦ *kāśi-rāja*, काश्याः राजा यः ←f◦ prop◦ ***kāśi*** + m◦ *rājan* 1.2); *ća* (and); ***vīryavān*** (m◦ 1nom◦ sing◦ ←taddhita◦ adj◦ *vīryavat* (mighty) ←n◦ ***vīrya*** (might) ←10◦√वीर् (to be brave) + taddhita◦ affix *vatup*, ***vat*** वत् – indicating an inclusion of one thing into another thing); *purujit* (m◦ 1nom◦ sing◦ ←prop◦ *purujit* ←5◦√पृ (to be pleased); *kuntibhojaḥ:* (m◦ 1nom◦ sing◦ ←prop◦ *kuntibhoja* ←1◦√कम् (to desire); *ća* (and); *śaibyaḥ:* (m◦ 1nom◦ sing◦ ←taddhita◦ *śaibya*, शिब्याः राजा ←f◦ prop◦ *śibi* + m◦ *rājan* 1.2); *ća* (and); *narapuṅgavaḥ:* (m◦ 1nom◦ sing◦ ←bahuvrī◦ *nara-puṅgava*, नरेषु पुङ्गवः इव यः ←m◦ ***nara*** (man) ←9◦√नॄ (to take away) + m◦ *puṅgava* (bull) ←1◦√पू (to cleanse) (1.5)

(§3) ***dhṛṣṭaketuḥ:*** (subj4◦ **Dhṛṣṭaketu**); ***ćekitānaḥ:*** (subj5◦ **Ćekitāna**); ***kāśirājaḥ:*** (subj6◦ **Kāśirāja, the king of Kāśi**); ***ća*** **(and)**; ***vīryavān*** (adj◦-subj6◦ **mighty, powerful**); ***purujit*** (subj7◦ **Purujit**); ***kuntibhojaḥ:*** (subj8◦ **Kuntibhoja**); ***ća*** **(and)**; ***śaibyaḥ:*** (subj9◦ **Śaibya, King of Śibi**); ***ća*** **(and)**; ***narapuṅgavaḥ:*** (adj◦-subj9◦ **the one who is powerful like a bull among men**) (1.5)

(§4) ća dhṛṣṭaketuḥ: ćekitānaḥ: vīryavān kāśirājaḥ: purujit ća kuntibhojaḥ: ća śaibyaḥ: narapuṅgavaḥ:;

(§5) and Dhṛṣṭaketu; Ćekitāna; mighty Kāśirāja, the king of Kāśi; Purujit and Kuntibhoja and King of Śibi, the one who is powerful like a bull among men; (1.5)

1.6 युधामन्युश्च विक्रान्त उत्तमौजाश्च वीर्यवान् ।
सौभद्रो द्रौपदेयाश्च सर्व एव महारथाः ।।

yudhāmanyuśća vikrānta uttamaujāśća vīryavān,
saubhadro draupadeyāśća sarva eva mahārathāḥ:. (1.6)

(§1) युधामन्युः च विक्रान्तः उत्तमौजा च वीर्यवान् । सौभद्रः द्रौपदेयाः च सर्वे एव महारथाः । *yudhāmanyuḥ:* (r◦ 17/1) *ća vikrāntaḥ:* (r◦ 19/4) *uttamaujāḥ:* (r◦ 17/1) *ća vīryavān* (r◦ 23/1) *saubhadraḥ:* (r◦ 15/4) *draupadeyāḥ:*

(r◦ 17/1) *ća sarve* (r◦ 5/4) *eva mahārathāḥ:* (r◦ 22/8)

(§2) *yudhāmanyuḥ:* (m◦ 1nom◦ sing◦ ←prop◦ *yudhāmanyu* ←4◦युध्√मन् (to think) ; *ća* (and); *vikrāntaḥ:* (m◦ 1nom◦ sing◦ ←ppp◦ adj◦ *vikrānta* (valorous) ←1◦वि√क्रम् (to step) ; *uttamaujāḥ:* (1nom◦ sing◦ ←m◦ prop◦ *uttamaujas* ←5◦√उ (ask); *ća* (and); *vīryavān* (1.5); ***saubhadraḥ:*** (m◦ 1nom◦ sing◦ ←taddhita◦ m◦ *saubhadra*, सुभद्रायाः अपत्यम् ←f◦ prop◦ *subhadrā* ←1◦सु√भन्द् (to be fortunate); ***draupadeyāḥ:*** (m◦ 1nom◦ plu◦ ←taddhita◦ m◦ *draupadeya*, द्रौपद्याः अपत्यम् ←f◦ prop◦ *draupadī* ←1◦√द्रु (to flow); *ća* (and); ***sarve*** (m◦ 1nom◦ plu◦ ←pron◦ *sarva* (all) ←1◦√सृ (to go); *eva* (1.1); ***mahārathāḥ:*** (m◦ 1nom◦ plu◦ ←adj◦ *mahāratha* 1.4) (1.6)

(§3) ***yudhāmanyuḥ:*** (subj10◦ Yudhāmanyu); ***ća*** (and); ***vikrāntaḥ:*** (adj◦-subj10◦ valorous); ***uttamaujāḥ:*** (subj11◦ Uttamaujas); ***ća*** (and); ***vīryavān*** (adj◦-subj11◦ powerful); ***saubhadraḥ:*** (subj12◦ Saubhadra; Abhimanyu, son of Subhadra); ***draupadeyāḥ:*** (subj13◦ five sons of Draupadī); ***ća*** (and); ***sarve*** (adj1◦-subj1-13◦ all of them); ***eva*** (indeed); ***mahārathāḥ:*** (adj2◦-subj1-13◦ great charioteers) (1.6)

(§4) ća vikrāntaḥ: yudhāmanyuḥ: vīryavān ća uttamaujāḥ: saubhadraḥ: ća draupadeyāḥ: sarve eva mahārathāḥ:

(§5) and, valorous Yudhāmanyu; powerful Uttamaujas and Abhimanyu, the son of Subhadrā and the sons of Draupadī, all of them[21] indeed great charioteers. (1.6)

1.7 अस्माकं तु विशिष्टा ये तान्निबोध द्विजोत्तम ।
नायका मम सैन्यस्य संज्ञार्थं तान्ब्रवीमि ते ।।

asmākaṁ tu viśiṣṭā ye tānnibodh dvijottama,
nāyakā mama sainyasya sañjñārthaṁ tānbravīmi te. (1.7)

(§1) अस्माकम् तु विशिष्टाः ये तान् निबोध द्विजोत्तम । नायका मम सैन्यस्य संज्ञार्थम् तान् ब्रवीमि ते । *asmākam* (r◦ 14/1) *tu viśiṣṭā* (r◦ 20/14) *ye tān* (r◦ 1/11) *nibodha dvijottama nāyakāḥ:* (r◦ 20/13) *mama sainyasya sañjñārtham* (r◦ 14/1) *tān* (r◦ 13/14) *bravīmi te*

(§2) ***asmākam*** (6pos plu◦ ←personal pron◦ ***asmad***, (I, we) ←2◦√अस् (to be); *tu* (1.2); *viśiṣṭāḥ:* (m◦ 1nom◦

---

[21] *sarve eva mahārathāḥ:* may only qualify subj◦ 13 (द्रौपदेयाः), however, better still, along with अत्र शूराः, महेश्वासाः, भीमार्जुनसमाः, the adjecties सर्वे and महारथाः must qualify all subjects 1-13 (युयुधानः, विराटः, द्रुपदः, धृष्टकेतुः, चेकितानः, काशिराजः, पुरुजित्, कुन्तिभोजः, शैब्यः, युधामन्युः, उत्तमौजा, सौभद्रः, द्रौपदेयाः), and thereby perform the function of tying the shlokas 1.4 to 1.6 together. Otherwise, these three verses remain unconnected, independent.

plu◦ ←ppp◦ adj◦ *viśiṣṭa* (distinguished) ←7◦वि√शिष् (to leave remainder); ***ye*** (m◦ 1nom◦ plu◦ ←pron◦ adj◦ ***yad***, (which) ←1◦√यज् (to offer); ***tān*** (m◦ 2acc◦ plu◦ ←pron◦ tad 1.2); 📖***nibodha*** (please take note!) (2nd-per◦ sing◦ imperative◦ लोट् parasmai◦ ←1◦नि√बुध् (to comprehend); *dvijottama* (m◦ 8voc◦ sing◦ ←bahuvrī◦ adj◦ *dvijottama*, द्विजेषु उत्तमः यः ←bahuvrī◦ adj◦ ***dvija***, द्वौ जन्मसंस्कारौ जायेते यस्य ←adj◦ ***dvi*** (twice) ←1◦√द्वृ (to hinder) + m◦ ***ja*** (born) ←4◦√जन् (to be born, give birth) + adj◦ ***uttama*** (noblest) ←ind◦ *ud* ←4◦√उ (ask) + superlative affix *tama* तम); 📖*nāyakāḥ:* (1nom◦ plu◦ ←m◦ *nāyaka* (learer) ←1◦√नी (to carry); ***mama*** (ind◦ or 6pos◦ sing◦ ←pron◦ *asmad* ↑); 📖*sainyasya* (6pos sing◦ ←n◦ or m◦ *sainya* (army) ←5◦√सि (to bind); 📖*sañjñārtham* (m◦ 2acc◦ sing◦ ←tatpu◦ *sañjñārtha*, संज्ञायाः अर्थः ←f◦ ***sañjñā*** (information) ←9◦सम्√ज्ञा (to know) + m◦ 📖***artha*** (for) ←10◦√अर्थ् (to want); *tān* (↑); 📖*bravīmi* (1st-per◦ sing◦ pres◦ वर्तमान्-लट् parasmai◦ ←2◦√ब्रू (to speak); ***te*** (2acc◦ sing◦ ←pron◦ *yuṣmad* 1.2) (1.7)

(§3) *asmākam* (among us); *tu* (and now); *viśiṣṭāḥ:* (adj1◦-subj◦ those who are distinguished); *ye* (adj2◦-subj◦ those who are); *tān* (obj◦ to them); *nibodha* (please know, take note of); *dvijottama* (O Noblest of the twice-born!); *nāyakāḥ:* (subj◦ the leaders); *mama* (my); *sainyasya* (of army); *sañjñārtham* (for information); *tān* (obj◦ them, to them); *bravīmi* (I tell; I name); *te* (obj◦ to you) (1.7)

(§4) tu dvijottama nibodha ye asmākam viśiṣṭāḥ: nāyakāḥ: mama sainyasya bravīmi tān te sañjñārtham

(§5) And now, O Noblest of the twice-born![22] please take note of those who are distinguished among us, the leaders of my army.[23] I name them[24] to you for (your) information. (1.7)

---

[22] Elsewhere◦ *dvijottama*→ best of the Brāhmaṇas, Best among the Brāhmaṇas, Best Among the Brahmins ...etc.

📖 The word *dvija* द्विज is not dependent upon one's actual birth, second birth, but on *saṅskara karma* (civilization) only, so also the words *vipra* and *brāhmaṇa*.

जन्मनि जायते शूद्रः संस्कारात् द्विज उच्यते । वेदाभ्यासाद्भवेद्विप्रो ब्रह्मज्ञानात्तु ब्राह्मणः ।।

By birth **everyone** is *śūdra*, by becoming civilized one is *dvija* (that is his second birth into civilized stage), by study of scriptures one becomes *vipra* and by knowing Supreme self (brahma), one becomes *brāhmaṇa*.

[23] Elsewhere◦ *asmākaṁ tu viśiṣṭā ye* ***tānnibodh*** *dvijottama, nāyakā* ***mama*** *sainyasya* → let me tell you about the captains who are especially qualified to lead my military force, let me introduce you the highly qualified commanders of our army,

📖 The words अस्माकम्, तान्निबोध, मम and तान्ब्रवीमि need to be translated carefully with respect to their associated grammar. अस्माकम् and मम in Possessive 6th case singular, तान् in Accusative 2nd case, निबोध in Imperative लोट् mood, and ब्रवीमि in a Present tense (simple or continuous).

[24] Elsewhere◦ *bravīmi* → I will name them, I shall name them, I shall mention, let me introduce, let me tell

1.8 भवान्भीष्मश्च कर्णश्च कृपश्च समितिञ्जयः ।
अश्वत्थामा विकर्णश्च सौमदत्तिस्तथैव च ।।

bhavānbhīṣmaśća karṇaśća kṛpaśća samitiñjayaḥ:,
aśvatthāmā vikarṇaśća saumadattistathaiva ća; (1.8)

(§1) भवान् भीष्मः च कर्णः च कृपः च समितिञ्जयः । अश्वत्थामा विकर्णः च सौमदत्तिः तथा एव च । *bhavān* (r◦ 13/15) *bhīṣmaḥ:* (r◦ 17/1) *ća karṇaḥ:* (r◦ 17/1) *ća kṛpaḥ:* (r◦ 17/1) *ća samitiñjayaḥ:* (r◦ 22/8) *aśvatthāmā vikarṇaḥ:* (r◦ 17/1) *ća saumadattiḥ:* (r◦ 18/1) *tathā* (r◦ 3/3) *eva ća*

(§2) ***bhavān*** (m◦ 1nom◦ sing◦ ←honorific pron◦ adj◦ ***bhavat*** (you) ←2◦√भा (to shine); 📖***bhīṣmaḥ:*** (m◦ 1nom◦ sing◦ ←prop◦ ***bhīṣma*** ←3◦√भी (to fear); *ća* (and); 📖*karṇaḥ:* (m◦ 1nom◦ sing◦ ←prop◦ ***karṇa*** ←10◦√कर्ण् (to pierce); *ća* (and); *kṛpaḥ:* (m◦ 1nom◦ sing◦ ←prop◦ *kṛpa* ←1◦√कृप् (to imagine); *ća* (and); 📖*samitiñjayaḥ:* (m◦ 1nom◦ sing◦ ←bahuvrī◦ *samitiñjaya,* समितिं जयति यः ←m◦ *samiti* (battle) ←1◦सम्√इ (to enter, come, go) + m◦ ***jaya*** (victory) ←1◦√जि (to win); *aśvatthāmā* (m◦ 1nom◦ sing◦ ←bahuvrī◦ prop◦ *aśvatthāman,* अश्वस्य इव स्थाम धैर्यं यस्य ←m◦ ***aśva*** (horse) ←5◦√अश् (to pervade) + adj◦ *sthāman* (steadiness) ←1◦√स्था (to stay); *vikarṇaḥ:* (m◦ 1nom◦ sing◦ ←prop◦ *vikarṇa* ←10◦वि√कर्ण् (to pierce); *ća* (and); *saumadattiḥ:* (m◦ 1nom◦ sing◦ ←taddhita◦ *saumadatti,* सोमदत्तस्य अपत्यम् ←1◦√सु (to deliver); ***tathā*** (as well) (ind◦ ←pron◦ tad 1.2); *eva* (1.1); *ća* (and) (1.8)

(§3) ***bhavān*** **(subj1◦ Your honour, Droṇāćārya);** ***bhīṣmaḥ:*** **(subj2◦ Bhīṣma, Bhīṣmāćārya);** ***ća*** **(and);** ***karṇaḥ:*** **(subj3◦ Karṇa);** ***ća*** **(and);** ***kṛpaḥ:*** **(subj4◦ Kṛpa, Kṛpāćārya);** ***ća*** **(and);** ***samitiñjayaḥ:*** **(adj◦-subj4◦ ever victorious, ever victorious in the battles);** ***aśvatthāmā*** **(subj5◦ Aśvatthāman);** ***vikarṇaḥ:*** **(subj6◦ Vikarṇa);** ***ća*** **(and);** ***saumadattiḥ:*** **(subj7◦ Somadatta's son Bhūriśravas);** ***tathā*** **(as well as);** ***eva*** **(also);** ***ća*** **(and)** (1.8)

(§4) bhavān ća bhīṣma ća karṇaḥ: ća samitiñjayaḥ: kṛpaḥ: ća aśvatthāmā ća vikarṇaḥ: tathā saumadattiḥ: eva

(§5) Your honour and Bhīṣmāćārya and Karṇa and ever victorious[25] Kṛpāćārya and Aśvatthāman and Vikarṇa as well as Somadatta's son Bhūriśravas also; (1.8)

...etc.

📖 ब्रवीमि is not a future tense or a potential mood, it is a present tense.

[25] Elsewhere◦ *samitiñjayaḥ* → who are always victorious in battle.

📖 समितिञ्जयः is singular adj◦ and should qualify only one nearest noun, subj4◦ i.e. Kṛpa.

1.9 अन्ये च बहवः शूरा मदर्थे त्यक्तजीविताः ।
नानाशस्त्रप्रहरणाः सर्वे युद्धविशारदाः ॥

anye ća bahvaḥ: śūrā madarthe tyaktajīvitāḥ:,
nānāśastrapraharaṇāḥ: sarve yuddhaviśāradāḥ:. (1.9)

(§1) अन्ये च बहवः शूराः मदर्थे त्यक्तजीविताः । नानाशस्त्रप्रहरणाः सर्वे युद्धविशारदाः । *anye ća bahvaḥ:* (r∘ 22/5) *śūrāḥ:* (r∘ 20/13) *madarthe tyaktajīvitāḥ:* (r∘ 22/8) *nānāśastrapraharaṇāḥ:* (r∘ 24/5, 22/7) *sarve yuddhaviśāradāḥ:* (r∘ 22/8)

(§2) ***anye*** (m∘ 1nom∘ plu∘ ←adj∘ 📖***anya*** (other) ←4∘√अन् (to move); *ća* (and); 📖***bahvaḥ:*** (m∘ 1nom∘ plu∘ ←num∘ adj∘ ***bahu*** (many) ←1∘√**बंह** (to make firm); *śūrāḥ:* (intrepid fighters) (1.4); 📖*madarthe* (= mama-**arthe**, m∘ 7loc∘ sing∘ ←tatpu∘ ***madartha*** (for my sake) मम अर्थः ←5abl∘ sing∘ pron∘ ***mat*** ←pron∘ *asmad* 1.7 + m∘ *artha* 1.7); 📖*tyakta-jīvitāḥ:* (m∘ 1nom∘ plu∘ ←bahuvrī∘ adj∘ *tyakta-jīvita* त्यक्तम् जीवितम् यस्य । समर्पितम् जीवनम् येन सः ←ppp∘ adj∘ ***tyakta*** (abandoned) ←1∘√**त्यज्** (to renounce) + n∘ *jīvita* (life) ←1∘√**जीव्** (to live); 📖***nānā*** (various) (num∘ adj∘ or ind∘ ←ind∘ *na* 1.30); *śastrapraharaṇāḥ:* (m∘ 1nom∘ plu∘ ←bahuvrī∘ *śastra-praharaṇa*, one who is armed with weapons शस्त्राणि प्रहरणानि यस्य सः ←n∘ 📖***śastra*** = (weapon) ←1∘√**शस्** (to leap) + n∘ 📖*praharaṇa* = (arm, weapon) ←1∘प्र√**हृ** (to take); *sarve* (1.6); *yuddhaviśāradāḥ:* (m∘ 1nom∘ plu∘ ←tatpu∘ *yuddha-viśārada*, युद्धे विशारदः ←n∘ 📖***yuddha*** (warfare) ←4∘√युध् (to fight) + adj∘ 📖*viśārada* (skillful) ←1∘वि-शाल√**दा** (to give) (1.9)

(§3) ***anye*** **(adj1∘-subj∘ other);** ***ća*** **(and);** ***bahvaḥ:*** **(adj2∘-subj∘ many);** ***śūrāḥ:*** **(subj∘ intrepid fighters);** ***madarthe*** **(for my sake);** ***tyakta-jīvitāḥ:*** **(bahuvrī∘ adj3∘-subj∘ those who have abandoned their lives)** ***nānā*** **(various);** ***śastrapraharaṇāḥ:*** **(bahuvrī∘ adj4∘-subj∘ those with arms and weapons);** ***sarve*** **(adj5∘-subj∘ all);** ***yuddhaviśāradāḥ:*** **(adj6∘-subj∘ skillful in warfare)** (1.9)

(§4) ća bahvaḥ: anye śūrāḥ: nānā śastrapraharaṇāḥ: tyakta-jīvitāḥ: madarthe sarve yuddhaviśāradāḥ:

(§5) And, many other intrepid fighters, with various arms with various weapons,[26] those who have abandoned their lives[27] for my sake, all skillful in warfare (are here). (1.9)

---

[26] Elsewhere∘ *nānāśastrapraharaṇāḥ:* → weilding various weapons for attack, all of them are well equipped with..., who possess various kinds of weapons and missiles, they are equipped with..., attacking with various weapons ...etc.

📖 प्रहरण is not a verb, gerund or ppp∘ It is a n∘ noun. प्रहरण प्र√हृ + ल्युट् = arm, weapon, आयुधम् ।

[27] Elsewhere∘ *tyaktajīvitāḥ* → are prepared to lay down their lives, are ready to die, are determined to give up their lives, prepared to risk life, renouncing their lives ...etc.

1.10 अपर्याप्तं तदस्माकं बलं भीष्माभिरक्षितम् ।
पर्याप्तं त्विदमेतेषां बलं भीमाभिरक्षितम् ।।

aparyāptaṁ tadasmākaṁ balaṁ bhīṣmābhirakṣitam,
paryāptaṁ tvidameteṣaṁ balaṁ bhīmābhirakṣitam. (1.10)

(§1) अपर्याप्तम् तदस्माकम् बलम् भीष्माभिरक्षितम् । पर्याप्तम् तु इदम् एतेषाम् बलम् भीमाभिरक्षितम् । *aparyāptam* (r◦ 14/1) *tat* (r◦ 8/2) *asmākam* (r◦ 14/1) *balam* (r◦ 14/1) *bhīṣmābhirakṣitam* (r◦ 14/2) *paryāptam* (r◦ 14/1) *tu* (r◦ 4/8) *idam* (r◦ 8/22) *eteṣām* (r◦ 25/3, 14/1) *balam* (r◦ 14/1) *bhīmābhirakṣitam* (r◦ 14/2)

(§2) 📖*aparyāptam* (n◦ 1nom◦ sing◦ ←n.tatpu◦ *a-paryāpta* (limitless) नास्ति पर्याप्तम् इति ←negative affix *a* (अ) ←1◦√अव् (to protect) + ppp◦ adj◦ ***paryāpta*** (just enough) ←5◦परि√आप् (to attain, get); ***tat*** (n◦ 1nom◦ sing◦ ←pron◦ *tad* (that) 1.2); *asmākam* (1.7); 📖***balam*** (1nom◦ sing◦ ←n◦ ***bala*** (army) ←10◦√बल् (to support); *bhīṣmābhirakṣitam* (n◦ 1nom◦ sing◦ ←adj◦ tatpu◦ *bhīṣmābhirakṣita,* भीष्मेन अभिरक्षित ←m◦ *bhīṣma* 1.8 + ppp◦ adj◦ 📖***abhirakṣita*** (protected) ←1◦अभि√रक्ष् (to protect); 📖*paryāptam* (n◦ 1nom◦ sing◦ ←adj◦ *paryāpta* (limited) ↑); *tu* (1.2); ***idam*** (n◦ 1nom◦ sing◦ ←pron◦ ***idam*** (it, this) ←1◦√इन्द् (to be lofty); *eteṣām* (m◦ 6pos◦ plu◦ ←pron◦ *etad* (this) 1.3); *balam* (↑); *bhīmābhirakṣitam* (n◦ 1nom◦ sing◦ ←adj◦ tatpu◦ *bhīmābhirakṣita,* भीमेन अभिरक्षित ←m◦ 📖*bhīma* 1.4 + adj◦ *abhirakṣita* ↑) (1.10)

(§3) ***aparyāptam*** **(adj1◦-subj1◦ limitless, boundless, endless; extensive, infinite, vast);** ***tat*** **(adj2◦-subj1◦ that, the one that is further from here);** ***asmākam*** **(adj3◦-subj1◦ our);** ***balam*** **(subj1◦ army);** ***bhīṣmābhirakṣitam*** **(adj4◦-subj1◦ the one that is protected by Bhīṣma);** ***paryāptam*** **(adj1◦-subj2◦ limited, measurable);** ***tu*** **(but);** ***idam*** **(adj2◦-subj2◦ this, the one that is closer to us);** ***eteṣām*** **(adj3◦-subj2◦ of these people);** ***balam*** **(subj2◦ army);** ***bhīmābhirakṣitam*** **(adj4◦-subj2◦ the one that is protected by Bhīma)** (1.10)

(§4) tat asmākam balam bhīṣmābhirakṣitam aparyāptam tu idam balam eteṣām bhīmābhirakṣitam paryāptam

(§5) That our army, protected by Bhīṣma, (is) limitless; but this army of these people,[28] protected

---

📖 Being prepared or determined to die is not a त्यक्तजीवित । There is a difference between त्यक्त and सज्ज, विचारित or निर्णित । *tyaktajīvita* is a ppp◦ adj◦ → he who has layed down his life.

[28] While standing near and talking to Droṇa about the two facing armies, Duryodhana calls his own army THAT (तत्) and the army of the Pāṇḍavas as THIS (इदम्) army of THESE people (एतेषाम्). Similarly in 1.3 also, he refers to the Pāṇḍavas' army as THIS army (एताम्). It shown that even though Droṇa was fighting for

by Bhīma,[29] (is) limited.[30] (1.10)

1.11 अयनेषु च सर्वेषु यथाभागमवस्थिताः ।
भीष्ममेवाभिरक्षन्तु भवन्तः सर्व एव हि ।।

ayaneṣu ća sarveṣu yathābhāgamavasthitāḥ:,
bhīṣmamevābhirakṣantu bhavantaḥ: sarva eva hi. (1.11)

(§1) अयनेषु च सर्वेषु यथाभागमवस्थिताः । भीष्मम् एव अभिरक्षन्तु भवन्तः सर्वे एव हि । *ayaneṣu* (r◦ 25/5) *ća sarveṣu* (r◦ 25/5) *yathābhāgam* (r◦ 8/16) *avasthitāḥ:* (r◦ 22/8) *bhīṣmam* (r◦ 8/22) *eva* (r◦ 1/1) *abhirakṣantu bhavantaḥ:* (r◦ 22/7) *sarve* (r◦ 5/4) *eva hi*

(§2) 📖*ayaneṣu* (7loc◦ plu◦ ←n◦ ***ayana*** (enerance point) ←1◦√अय् (to go); *ca* (1.1); ***sarveṣu*** (n◦ 7loc◦ plu◦ ←pron◦ *sarva* 1.6); 📖*yathābhāgam* (adv◦ ←ind◦ *yathā* (as) ←pron◦ *yad* 1.7 + *bhāga* (appointment) ←1◦√भज् (to divide); यथा + भागम् = यथाभागम्; samas.avyayi◦); 📖***avasthitāḥ:*** (m◦ 1nom◦ plu◦ ←ppp◦ adj◦ ***avasthita*** (firmly stood) ←1◦अव√स्था (to stay); ***bhīṣmam*** (m◦ 2acc◦ sing◦ ←prop◦ *bhīṣma* 1.8); *eva* (1.1); 📖*abhirakṣantu* (3rd◦ plu◦ imperative◦ आज्ञार्थ–लोट् parasmai◦ ←1◦ अभि√रक्ष् (to protect); *bhavantaḥ:* (honorific pron◦ m◦ 1nom◦ plu◦ ←adj◦ *bhavat* 1.8); *sarve* (1.6); *eva* (1.1); ***hi*** (ind◦ ←3◦√हा (to go) (1.11)

(§3) *ayaneṣu* (in the gates, at the entrance points); *ća* (and); *sarveṣu* (in all); *yathābhāgam* (as appointed); *avasthitāḥ:* (adj1◦-subj◦ firmly stood); *bhīṣmam* (obj◦ Bhīṣma); *eva* (only); *abhirakṣantu* (please protect from all sides); *bhavantaḥ:* (subj◦ you); *sarve-eva* (adj2◦-subj◦ all); *hi* (by all means)

(§4) ća avasthitaḥ: yathābhāgam sarveṣu ayaneṣu bhavantaḥ: sarve eva hi abhirakṣantu bhīṣmam eva

(§5) And, firmly stood[31] as appointed, in all the entrance points, you all protect Bhīṣma only, by

---

the Kauravas, he had stationed himself on the side of the Pāṇḍavas' army, away from the Kauravas'.

[29] Elsewhere◦ *bhīṣmābhirakṣitam* and *bhīṣmābhirakṣitam* → is protected by Bhīṣma and is or are protected by Bhīma.

📖 बलं भीमाभिरक्षितम् and भीष्माभिरक्षितम् are not लट् present tense. They are ppp◦ adj◦ of the two armies. They mean → the army that is protected by Bhīṣma and the army that is protected by Bhīma.

[30] Elsewhere◦ (i). *aparyāptaṁ tadasmākaṁ balam* → That army of ours...is insufficient and incapable of fighting, Our army...is insufficient ...etc. (ii) *paryāptaṁ tvidameteṣāṁ balam* → That army of theirs...is sufficient and capable of fighting, their army...is sufficient ...etc.

[31] Elsewhere◦ *yathābhāgamavasthitaḥ:* → staying at strategic points (क्त्वा), keeping to your respective stations (क्त्वा), stand at your strategic points (लोट्), as differently situated (क्रिवि◦) ...etc.

📖 यथाभागम् अवस्थित is not a क्त्वा gerund, adverb or an imperative verb. It is a ppp◦ adj◦ tatpu◦ → stood, stood

all means. (1.11)

1.12 तस्य सञ्जनयन्हर्षं कुरुवृद्धः पितामहः ।
सिंहनादं विनद्योच्चैः शङ्खं दध्मौ प्रतापवान् ॥

tasya sañjanayanharṣaṁ kuruvṛddhaḥ: pitāmahaḥ:,
siṁhanādaṁ vinadyoććaiḥ: śaṅkhaṁ dadhmau pratāpavān. (1.12)

(§1) तस्य सञ्जनयन् हर्षम् कुरुवृद्धः पितामहः । सिंहनादम् विनद्य उच्चैः शङ्खम् दध्मौ प्रतापवान् । *tasya sañjanayan* (r∘ 13/21) *harṣam* (r∘ 14/1) *kuruvṛddhaḥ:* (r∘ 22/3) *pitāmahaḥ:* (r∘ 22/8) *siṁhanādam* (r∘ 14/1) *vinadya* (r∘ 2/2) *uććaiḥ:* (r∘ 22/5) *śaṅkham* (r∘ 14/1) *dadhmau pratāpavān* (1.12)

(§2) ***tasya*** (m∘ 6pos∘ sing∘ ←pron∘ *tad* 1.2); 📖*sañjanayan* (m∘ 1nom∘ sing∘ ←śatṛ∘ caus∘ *sañjanayat* (increasing) ←1∘सम्√जन् (to beget); 📖*harṣam* (2acc∘ sing∘ ←m∘ ***harṣa*** (joy) ←1∘**√हृष्** (to be joyful); *kuru-vṛddhaḥ:* (m∘ 1nom∘ sing∘ ←bahuvrī∘ adj∘ *kuruvṛddha*, कुरुषु वृद्धतमः यः ←m∘ *kuru* 1.1 + ppp∘ adj∘ *vṛddha* (old) ←1∘**√वृध्** (to grow); ***pitāmahaḥ:*** (m∘ 1nom∘ sing∘ ←taddhita∘ ***pitā-maha*** (grandsire) पितुः पिता or bahuvrī∘ पितृषु महान् यः ←m∘ ***pitṛ*** ←2∘**√पा** (to protect) + adj∘ *mahat* 1.3); 📖*siṁhanādam* (m∘ 2acc∘ sing∘ ←tatpu∘ *siṁha-nāda*, सिंहस्य इव नादः ←m∘ *siṁha* (lion) ←7∘**√हिंस्** (to be violent) + m∘ *nāda* (roar) ←1∘**√नद्** (to make sound); *vinadya* (deriv∘ greund ←1∘वि√नद् (to make sound); 📖*uććaiḥ:* (adv∘ ←3inst∘ plu∘ ←adj∘ ućća (loud) ←5∘उद√चि (to gather); 📖***śaṅkham*** (2acc∘ sing∘ ←m∘ ***śaṅkha*** (conch shell) ←4∘**√शम्** (to be calm); ***dadhmau*** (3rd-per∘ sing∘ past-perf∘ लिट् भूत∘ parasmai∘ ←1∘**√ध्मा** (to blow); 📖*pratāpavān* (m∘ 1nom∘ sing∘ ←adj∘ *pratāpavat* (valiant) ←m∘ *pratāpa* ←4∘प्र**√तप्** (to do penance, heat up) + suffix *vat* 1.5) (1.12)

(§3) ***tasya*** **(his);** ***sañjanayan*** **(adj1∘-subj∘ while causing to increase, while bringing forth);** ***harṣam*** **(obj1∘ joy);** ***kuru-vṛddhaḥ:*** **(adj2∘-subj∘ the oldest among the Kurus);** ***pitāmahaḥ:*** **(subj∘ grandsire; grandsire Bhīṣma);** ***siṁha-nādam*** **(obj2∘ a sound like a lion);** ***vinadya*** **(having made a roar, roaring);** ***uććaiḥ:*** **(loudly); śaṅkham (obj3∘ conch shell);** ***dadhmau*** **(he blew);** ***pratāpavān*** **(adj3∘-subj∘ the valiant)** (1.12)

(§4) sañjanayan tasya harṣam pratāpavān pitāmahaḥ: kuru-vṛddhaḥ: uććaiḥ: vinadya siṁha-nādam dadhmau śaṅkham

(§5) While increasing Duryodhana's joy,[32] the valiant grandsire Bhīṣma, the oldest among the

---

firmly, firmly stood etc.

[32] Elsewhere∘ *tasya sañjanayanharṣaṁ* → giving Duryodhana joy (क्त्वा), cheering Duryodhana (क्त्वा), to the great joy of Duryodhana (accusative or dative), in order to cheer him (dative) ...etc.

Kurus, roaring loudly like a lion, blew (his) conch shell. (1.12)

1.13 ततः शङ्खाश्च भेर्यश्च पणवानकगोमुखाः ।
सहसैवाभ्यहन्यन्त स शब्दस्तुमुलोऽभवत् ।।

tahaḥ: śankhāśća bheryaśća paṇavānakagomukhāḥ:,
sahasaivābhyahanyanta sa shabdastumulo'bhavaṭ. (1.13)

(§1) ततः शङ्खाः च भेर्यः च पणवानकगोमुखाः । सहसा एव अभ्यहन्यन्त सः शब्दः तुमुलः अभवत् । *tataḥ:* (r∘ 22/5) *śankhāḥ:* (r∘ 17/1) *ća bheryaḥ:* (r∘ 17/1) *ća paṇavānakagomukhāḥ:* (r∘ 22/8) *sahasā* (r∘ 3/3) *eva* (r∘ 1/1) *abhyahanyanta saḥ:* (r∘ 21/2) *shabdaḥ:* (r∘ 18/1) *tumulaḥ:* (r∘ 15/1) *abhavaṭ*

(§2) ***tataḥ:*** (time indicating ind∘ *tataṣ* (thereuopn) ←pron∘ *taḍ* 1.2); *śankhāḥ:* (1nom∘ plu∘ ←m∘ *śankha* 1.12); *ća* (and); *bheryaḥ:* (1nom∘ plu∘ ←f∘ *bherī* (kettle-drum) ←3∘√भी (to fear); *ća* (and) ; *paṇavānaka-gomukhāḥ:* (m∘ 1nom∘ plu∘ ←dvandva∘ पणवाः च आनकाः च गोमुखाः च ←m∘ *paṇava* (trumpet) ←2∘पण√वा (to move) + m∘ *ānaka* ←4∘√अन् (to move) + m∘ or n∘ *gomukha* (cow horn) ←1∘√गम् (to go) + 1∘√खन् (to dig); 📖*sahasā* (immediately) (adv∘ ind∘ ←4∘सह√सो (to complete); *eva* (1.1); *abhyahanyanta* (pass∘ -past-imper∘ लङ् भूत∘ 3rd-per∘ plu∘ ←2∘अभि–आ√हन् (to hurt); ***saḥ:*** (m∘ 1nom∘ sing∘ ←pron∘ *taḍ* 1.2); 📖***shabdaḥ:*** (1nom∘ sing∘ ←m∘ ***śabda*** (noise) ←10∘√शब्द् (to sound); 📖***tumulaḥ:*** (m∘ 1nom∘ sing∘ ←adj∘ *tumula* (tumultuous) ←2∘√तु (to thrive); *abhavaṭ* (became) (3rd-per∘ sing∘ -past-imper∘ लङ् भूत∘ parasmai∘ ←1∘ √भू (to be, become) (1.13)

(§3) ***tataḥ:*** **(after this, thereupon);** ***śankhāḥ:*** **(subj1∘ conch shells);** ***ća*** **(and);** ***bheryaḥ:*** **(subj2∘ kettle-drums);** ***ća*** **(and);** ***paṇavānaka-gomukhāḥ:*** **(subj3∘ cymbals, trumpets and cow horns);** ***sahasā*** **(adv∘ just immediately, suddenly, all together);** ***abhyahanyanta*** **(vi∘ blared forth, sounded);** ***saḥ:*** **(adj1∘-subj4∘ that);** ***shabdaḥ:*** **(subj4∘ sound, noise);** ***tumulaḥ:*** **(adj2∘-subj4∘ tumultuous);** ***abhavaṭ*** **(vi∘ became)** (1.13)

(§4) sahasā tataḥ: śankhāḥ: ća bheryaḥ: ća paṇavānaka-gomukhāḥ: abhyahanyanta saḥ: shabdaḥ: abhavaṭ tumulaḥ:

(§5) Just immediately thereupon, conch shells and kettle-drums and cymbals, trumpets and cow-

---

📖 सञ्जनयन् to the great? सञ्जनयत् is a present active participle → increasing, while increasing. It should be : Increasing or while increasing his (तस्य, Duryodhana's - 6th case, not 4th or 2nd case) joy (हर्षम् m∘ 2nd case - object); NOTE : सञ्जनयत् is not the adjective of the object हर्षम्, but it is one of the three adjectives of the subject पितामहः । e.g. सञ्जनयन् कुरुवृद्धः प्रतापवान् पितामहः ।

PLEASE REMEMBER : If you understand which ones are the subjects and which ones are the objects and which ones are their corresponding adjectives in each *shloka*, you just can not go wrong. You will not make such mistakes.

horns blared forth. That noise became[33] tumultuous. (1.13)

1.14 ततः श्वेतैर्हयैर्युक्ते महति स्यन्दने स्थितौ ।
माधवः पाण्डवश्चैव दिव्यौ शङ्खौ प्रदध्मतुः ।।

tataḥ: śvetairhayairyukte mahati syandane sthitau,
mādhavaḥ: pāṇḍavaścaiva divyau śaṅkhau pradadhmatuḥ:. (1.14)

(§1) ततः श्वेतैः हयैः युक्ते महति स्यन्दने स्थितौ । माधवः पाण्डवः च एव दिव्यौ शङ्खौ प्रदध्मतुः । *tataḥ:* (r◦ 22/5) *śvetaiḥ:* (r◦ 16/11) *hayaiḥ:* (r◦ 16/11) *yukte mahati syandane sthitau mādhavaḥ:* (r◦ 22/3) *pāṇḍavaḥ:* (r◦ 17/1) *ća* (r◦ 3/1) *eva divyau śaṅkhau pradadhmatuḥ:* (r◦ 22/8)

(§2) *tataḥ:* (1.13) *śvetaiḥ:* (m◦ 3inst◦ plu◦ ←adj◦ *śveta* (white) ←1◦√श्वित् (to brighten); 📖*hayaiḥ:* (3inst◦ plu◦ ←m◦ *haya* (horse) ←5◦√हि (to impel); *yukte* (m◦ 7loc◦ sing◦ ←ppp◦ adj◦ 📖***yukta*** (equipped with) ←7◦√युज् (to unite); 📖*mahati* (m◦ 7loc◦ sing◦ ←adj◦ *mahaṭ* (magnificent) 1.3); 📖*syandane* (7loc◦ sing◦ ←m◦ *syandana* (chariot) ←1◦√स्यन्द् (to carry); 📖*sthitau* (m◦ 1nom◦ dual◦ ←ppp◦ adj◦ ***sthita*** (seated) ←1◦√स्था (to stay); *mādhavaḥ:* (m◦ 1nom◦ sing◦ ←bahuvrī◦ ***mādhava,*** मायाः धवः यः ←f◦ *mā* (lakshmī) ←3◦√मा (to measure) + m◦ *dhava* (husband) ←5◦√धु (to shake); ***pāṇḍavaḥ:*** (m◦ 1nom◦ sing◦ ←taddhita◦ *pāṇḍava,* पाण्डोः अपत्यम् 1.3); *ća* (and); *eva* (1.1); *divyau* (m◦ 2acc◦ dual◦ ←pot◦ adj◦ ***divya*** (celestial) taddhita◦ दिवः भावः । देवस्य भावः । ←4◦√दिव् (to shine); *śaṅkhau* (2acc◦ dual◦ ←m◦ n◦ 📖*śaṅkha* 1.12); *pradadhmatuḥ:* (3rd-per◦ dual◦ past-perf◦ लिट् भूत◦ parasmai◦ ←1◦प्र√ध्मा (to blow)

(§3) ***tataḥ:*** (after this, threupon); ***śvetaiḥ:*** (with spotless); ***hayaiḥ:*** (with horses); ***yukte*** (in equipped); ***mahati*** (in the magnificent); ***syandane*** (in the chariot); ***sthitau*** (adj◦-subj1-2◦ seated both); ***mādhavaḥ:*** (subj1◦ Mādhava, Śrī Kṛṣṇa); ***pāṇḍavaḥ:*** (subj2◦ Pāṇḍava, Arjuna); ***ća-eva*** (and); ***divyau*** (adj◦-obj◦ divine, celestial); ***śaṅkhau*** (obj◦ two conch shells); ***pra-dadhmatuḥ:*** (they both blew loudly) (1.14)

(§4) tataḥ: sthitau mahati syandane yukte śvetaiḥ: hayaiḥ: mādhavaḥ: ća pāṇḍavaḥ: eva pradadhmatuḥ: divyau śaṅkhau

(§5) After this, seated in the magnificent chariot equipped with spotless horses, Śrī Kṛṣṇa and Arjuna both blew (their) celestial conch shells loudly. (1.14)

1.15 पाञ्चजन्यं हृषीकेशो देवदत्तं धनञ्जयः ।
पौण्ड्रं दध्मौ महाशङ्खं भीमकर्मा वृकोदरः ।।

---

[33] Elsewhere◦ *abhavat* → was.

📖 √भू = to become; अभवत् = became.

pāñćajanyaṁ hṛṣīkeśo devadattaṁ dhanañjayaḥ:,
pauṇḍraṁ dadhmau mahāśaṅkhaṁ bhīmakarmā vṛkodaraḥ:; (1.15)

(§1) पाञ्चजन्यम् हृषीकेशः देवदत्तम् धनञ्जयः । पौण्ड्रम् दध्मौ महाशङ्खम् भीमकर्मा वृकोदरः । *pāñćajanyam̩* (r◦ 14/1) *hṛṣīkeśaḥ:* (r◦ 15/4) *devadattam̩* (r◦ 14/1) *dhanañjayaḥ:* (r◦ 22/8) *pauṇḍram̩* (r◦ 14/1) *dahdmau mahāśaṅkham̩* (r◦ 14/1) *bhīmakarmā vṛkodaraḥ:* (r◦ 22/8)

(§2) *pāñćajanyam̩* (m◦ 2acc◦ sing◦ ←prop◦ *pāñćajanya*, name of the celestial conch shell); ***hṛṣīkeśaḥ:*** (m◦ 1nom◦ sing◦ ←bahuvrī◦ ***hṛṣīkeśa***, हृषीकाणाम् ईशः यः ←n◦ *hṛṣīka* (sense organ) ←1◦√हृष् (to be joyful) + adj◦ ***īśa*** (lord) ←2◦**√ईश्** (to prosper); *devadattam̩* (m◦ 2acc◦ sing◦ ←prop◦ *devadatta*, name of a conch shell); ***dhanañjayaḥ:*** (m◦ 1nom◦ sing◦ ←bahuvrī◦ ***dhanañjaya***, धनं जयति यः ←n◦ ***dhana*** (wealth) ←1◦**√धन्** (to scurry) + m◦ *jaya* (win) 1.8); *pauṇḍram̩* (m◦ 2acc◦ sing◦ ←prop◦ *pauṇḍra*, name of a conch shell); *dahdmau* (1.12); ***mahā*** (the expression of word mahat̩ महत् to be used in a samāsa is *mahā* महा ←adj◦ *mahat̩* 1.3); *śaṅkham̩* (1.12); *bhīmakarmā* (m◦ 1nom◦ sing◦ ←bahuvrī◦ *bhīma-karman̩*, भीमं कर्म यस्य ←adj◦ *bhīma* (scary) 1.4 + n◦ ***karman̩*** (deed) ←8◦√कृ (to do); *vṛkodaraḥ:* (m◦ 1nom◦ sing◦ ←bahuvrī◦ adj◦ *vṛkodara*, वृकस्य इव उदरं यस्य ←m◦ *vṛka* (jackal) ←1◦**√वृक्** (to hold) + n◦ ***udara*** (stomach) ←1◦उद्**√ऋ** (to attain, get) (1.15)

(§3) ***pāñćajanyam̩*** **(obj1◦ the Pāñćajanya);** ***hṛṣīkeśaḥ:*** **(subj1◦ Hṛṣīkeśa, Śrī Kṛṣṇa);** ***devadattam̩*** **(obj2◦ the Devadatta);** ***dhanañjayaḥ:*** **(subj2◦ Dhanañjaya; Arjuna);** ***pauṇḍram̩*** **(obj3◦ Pauṇḍra);** ***dahdmau*** **(he blew);** ***mahā*** **(adj◦-obj3◦ the great);** ***śaṅkham̩*** **(obj3◦ conch shell);** ***bhīmakarmā*** **(adj1◦-subj3◦ Bhīmakarman̩; the performer of scary deeds);** ***vṛkodaraḥ:*** **(adj2◦-subj3◦ Vṛkodara, Bhīma)** (1.15)

(§4) hṛṣīkeśaḥ: pāñćajanyam̩ dhanañjayaḥ: devadattam̩ vṛkodaraḥ: bhīmakarmā dahdmau pauṇḍram̩ mahā śaṅkham̩

(§5) Śrī Kṛṣṇa (blew) the Pāñćajanya; Arjuna (blew) the Devadatta; Bhīma, the performer of scary deeds, blew Pauṇḍra, the great conch shell; (1.15)

1.16 अनन्तविजयं राजा कुन्तीपुत्रो युधिष्ठिरः ।
नकुलः सहदेवश्च सुघोषमणिपुष्पकौ ।।

anantavijayaṁ rājā kuntīputro yudhiṣṭhiraḥ:,
nakulaḥ: sahadevaśća sughoṣamaṇipuṣpakau; (1.16)

(§1) अनन्तविजयम् राजा कुन्तीपुत्रः युधिष्ठिरः । नकुलः सहदेवः च सुघोषमणिपुष्पकौ । *anantavijayam̩* (r◦ 14/1) *rājā kuntīputraḥ:* (r◦ 15/10) *yudhiṣṭhiraḥ:* (r◦ 22/8) *nakulaḥ:* (r◦ 22/7) *sahadevaḥ:* (r◦ 17/1) *ća sughoṣamaṇipuṣpakau*

(§2) *anantavijayaṃ* (m∘ 2acc∘ sing∘ ←prop∘ *anantavijaya,* name of a conch shell); *rājā* (1.2); *kuntīputraḥ:* (m∘ 1nom∘ sing∘ ←bahuvrī *kuntīputra,* कुन्त्या: पुत्र: ←f∘ prop∘ **kuntī** ←1∘√कम् (to desire) + m∘ *putra* 1.3); *yudhiṣṭhiraḥ:* (m∘ 1nom∘ sing∘ ←aluk-tat∘ samāsa, *yudhiṣṭhira,* युधि स्थिर: ←f∘ *yudh* 1.1 + adj∘ **sthira** (unwavering) ←1∘√स्था (to stay); *nakulaḥ:* (m∘ 1nom∘ sing∘ ←prop∘ *nakula* ←1∘न√कुल (to related); *sahadevaḥ:* (m∘ 1nom∘ sing∘ ←prop∘ *sahadeva* ←4∘सह√दिव् (to shine); *ća* (1.1); *sughoṣa-maṇipuṣpakau* (m∘ 2acc∘ dual∘ dvandva सुघोषम् च मणिपुष्पकम् च ←prop∘ *sughoṣa* + prop∘ *maṇipuṣpaka,* names of the two conch shells) (1.16)

(§3) *anantavijayaṃ* (obj4∘ the Anantavijaya); *rājā* (adj1∘-subj4∘ king); *kuntīputraḥ:* (adj2∘-subj4∘ the son of Kuntī); *yudhiṣṭhiraḥ:* (subj4∘ Yudhiṣṭhira); *nakulaḥ:* (subj5∘ Nakula); *sahadevaḥ:* (subj6∘ Sahadeva); *ća* (and); *sughoṣa-maṇipuṣpakau* (obj5∘ the Sughoṣa and obj6∘ the Maṇipuṣpaka) (1.16)

(§4) rājā yudhiṣṭhiraḥ: kuntīputraḥ: anantavijayaṃ nakulaḥ: ća sahadevaḥ: sughoṣa-maṇipuṣpakau

(§5) King Yudhiṣṭhira, the son of Kuntī (blew) the Anantavijaya; Nakula and Sahadeva (blew) the Sughoṣa and the Maṇipuṣpaka; (1.16)

1.17 काश्यश्च परमेष्वास: शिखण्डी च महारथ: ।
धृष्टद्युम्नो विराटश्च सात्यकिश्चापराजित: ॥

kāśyaśća parameṣvāsaḥ: śikhaṇḍī ća mahārathaḥ:,
dhṛṣṭadyumno virāṭaśća sātyakiśćāparājitaḥ:; (1.17)

(§1) काश्य: च परमेष्वास: शिखण्डी च महारथ: । धृष्टद्युम्न: विराट: च सात्यकि: च अपराजित: । *kāśyaḥ:* (r∘ 17/1) *ća parameṣvāsaḥ:* (r∘ 22/5) *śikhaṇḍī ća mahārathaḥ:* (r∘ 22/8) *dhṛṣṭadyumnaḥ:* (r∘ 15/13) *virāṭaḥ:* (r∘ 17/1) *ća sātyakiḥ:* (r∘ 17/1) *ća* (r∘ 1/1) *aparājitaḥ:* (r∘ 22/8)

(§2) *kāśyaḥ:* (m∘ 1nom∘ sing∘ ←taddhita *kāśya* काश्या: राजा ←f∘ prop∘ *kāśi* 1.5); *ća* (and); ▯*parameṣvāsaḥ:* (m∘ 1nom∘ sing∘ ←bahuvrī *parameṣvāsa,* परम: इष्वास: य: ←adj∘ **parama** (great) ←5∘√पॄ (to be pleased) + m∘ *iṣu* 1.4 + m∘ *āsa* 1.4); *śikhaṇḍī* (m∘ 1nom∘ sing∘ ←adj∘ *śikhaṇḍin* ←m∘ *śikhaṇḍ* ←1∘शिखा√अम् (to afflict); *ća* (and); *mahārathaḥ:* (1.4); *dhṛṣṭadyumnaḥ:* (m∘ 1nom∘ sing∘ ←bahuvrī prop∘ *dhṛṣṭadyumna,* धृष्टम् द्युम्नम् यस्य ←ppp∘ adj∘ *dhṛṣṭa* (courageous) ←5∘√धृष् (to be proud) + n∘ *dyumna* (prowess) ←1∘द्यु√म्ना (to remember); *virāṭaḥ:* (1.4); *ća* (and); *sātyakiḥ:* (m∘ 1nom∘ sing∘ ←taddhita *sātyaki,* सत्यकस्य अपत्यम् पुमान् ←prop∘ *satyaka* ←2∘√अस् (to be) + m∘ *putra* 1.3); *ća* (and); ▯*aparājitaḥ:* (m∘ 1nom∘ sing∘ n.tatpu *a-parājita,* न पराजित: ←ppp∘ adj∘ *parājita* (defeated) ←1∘परा√जि (to win) (1.17)

(§3) *kāśyaḥ:* (subj7∘ Kāśya, king of Kāśi); *ća* (and); *parameṣvāsaḥ:* (adj∘-subj7∘ the great archer);

śikhaṇḍī (subj8◦ Śikhaṇḍīn); ***ća*** (and); ***mahārathaḥ:*** (adj◦-subj8◦ the great charioteer); ***dhṛṣṭadyumnaḥ:*** (subj9◦ Dhṛṣṭadyumna); ***virāṭaḥ:*** (subj10◦ Virāṭa, king Virāṭa, king Virāṭa of Pāñćāla); ***ća*** (and); ***sātyakiḥ:*** (subj11◦ Sātyaki, son of Satyaka); ***ća*** (and); ***aparājitaḥ:*** (adj◦-subj11◦ ever victorious) (1.17)

(§4) ća kāśyaḥ: parameṣvāsaḥ: śikhaṇḍī mahārathaḥ: ća dhṛṣṭadyumnaḥ: ća virāṭaḥ: ća aparājitaḥ: sātyakiḥ:

(§5) And, king of Kāśi, the great archer;[34] Śikhaṇḍīn, the great charioteer; and Draupadī's brother Dhṛṣṭadyumna; and king Virāṭa of Pāñćāla; and ever victorious son of Satyaka; (1.17)

1.18 द्रुपदो द्रौपदेयाश्च सर्वशः पृथिवीपते ।
सौभद्रश्च महाबाहुः शङ्खान्दध्मुः पृथक्पृथक् ।।

drupado draupadeyāśća sarvaśaḥ: pṛthivīpate,
saubhadraśća mahābāhuḥ: śankhāndadhmuḥ: pṛthakpṛthak. (1.18)

(§1) द्रुपदः द्रौपदेयाः च सर्वशः पृथिवीपते । सौभद्रः च महाबाहुः शङ्खान् दध्मुः पृथक् पृथक् । *drupadaḥ:* (r◦ 15/4) *draupadeyāḥ:* (r◦ 17/1) *ća sarvaśaḥ:* (r◦ 22/3) *pṛthivīpate saubhadraḥ:* (r◦ 17/1) *ća mahābāhuḥ:* (r◦ 22/5) *śankhān* (r◦ 13/11) *dadhmuḥ:* (r◦ 22/3) *pṛthak* (r◦ 10/2) *pṛthak*

(§2) *drupadaḥ:* (m◦ 1nom◦ sing◦ ←prop◦ *drupada* 1.3); *draupadeyāḥ:* (1.6); *ća* (and); ***sarvaśaḥ:*** (adv◦ ←ind◦ *sarvaśaṣ* (from all sides) ←pron◦ *sarva* 1.6 + adverb forming affix *śas); pṛthivīpate* (m◦ 8voc◦ sing◦ ←bahuvrī◦ *pṛthivīpati* (king) पृथिव्याः पतिः इव यः ←f◦ ***pṛthivī*** (earth) ←1◦√प्रथ् (to grow) + m◦ ***pati*** (lord) ←2◦√पा (to protect); *saubhadraḥ:* (1.6); *ća* (1.1); *mahābāhuḥ:* (m◦ 1nom◦ sing◦ ←bahuvrī◦ ***mahābāhu***, महान्तौ बाहू यस्य ←adj◦ *mahā* (mighty) 1.3 + m◦ ***bāhu*** (arm) ←1◦√बाध् (to opress); *śankhān* (2acc◦ plu◦ ←m◦ *śankha* 1.12); *dadhmuḥ:* (3rd-per◦ plu◦ past-perf◦ लिट् भूत◦ parasmai◦ ←1◦√ध्मा (to blow); 📖*pṛthak-pṛthak* (adv◦ ind◦ ***pṛthak*** (distinct) ←1◦√प्रथ् (to grow) (1.18)

(§3) ***drupadaḥ:*** (subj12◦ Drupada; king Drupada); ***draupadeyāḥ:*** (subj13◦ five sons of Draupadī); ***ća*** (and); ***sarvaśaḥ:*** (adv◦ from all sides); 📖***pṛthivīpate*** (O Pṛthivīpati! O King Dhṛtarāṣṭra!); ***saubhadraḥ:*** (subj14◦ son of Subhadrā; Abhimanyu); ***ća*** (and); ***mahābāhuḥ:*** (adj◦-subj14◦ mighty armed); ***śankhān*** (obj◦ conch shells); ***dadhmuḥ:*** (they blew); ***pṛthak-pṛthak*** (each differently, distinctly) (1.18)

(§4) ća pṛthivīpate! drupadaḥ: draupadeyāḥ: ća mahābāhuḥ: saubhadraḥ: dadhmuḥ: śankhān pṛthak-

---

[34] Elsewhere◦ *parameṣvāsaḥ:* → mighty bowed.

📖 परमेष्वासः = महेष्वासः see the footnote in 1.4

pṛthak sarvaśaḥ:

(§5) And, O King Dhṛtarāṣtra! King Drupada; sons of Draupadī; mighty armed son of Subhadrā blew conch shells each distinctly,[35] from all sides.[36] (1.18)

1.19 स घोषो धार्तराष्ट्राणां हृदयानि व्यदारयत् ।
नभश्च पृथिवीं चैव तुमुलो व्यनुनादयन् ।।

sa ghoṣo dhārtarāṣṭrāṇāṁ hṛdayāni vyadārayat,
nabhaśca pṛthivīṁ caiva tumulo vyanunādayan. (1.19)

(§1) सः घोषः धार्तराष्ट्राणाम् हृदयानि व्यदारयत् । नभः च पृथिवीम् च एव तुमुलः व्यनुनादयन् । *saḥ:* (r◦ 21/2) *ghoṣaḥ:* (r◦ 15/5) *dhārtarāṣṭrāṇam* (r◦ 24/6, 14/1) *hṛdayāni vyadārayat* (r◦ 23/1) *nabhaḥ:* (r◦ 17/1) *ca pṛthivīm* (r◦ 14/1) *ca* (r◦ 3/1) *eva tumulaḥ:* (r◦ 15/13) *vyanunādayan*

(§2) *saḥ:* (1.13); *ghoṣaḥ:* (1nom◦ sing◦ ←m◦ *ghoṣa* (sound) ←1◦√घुष् (to rub); *dhārtarāṣṭrāṇām* (m◦ 6pos◦ plu◦ ←taddhita◦ ***dhārtarāṣtra***, धृतराष्ट्रस्य पुत्रः ←prop◦ *dhṛtarāṣtra* 1.1 + m◦ *putra* 1.3); *hṛdayāni* (2acc◦ plu◦ ←n◦ ***hṛdaya*** (heart) ←1◦√हृ (to take); *vyadārayat* (3rd-per◦ sing◦ -past-imper◦ लङ् भूत◦ parasmai◦ caus◦ ←9◦वि√दॄ (to rip); *nabhaḥ:* (2acc◦ sing◦ ←m◦ ***nabhas*** (sky) ←4◦√नह् (to bind), or m◦ *nabhasa* (sky) ←1◦√नभ् (not to be); *ca* (and); *pṛthivīm* (2acc◦ sing◦ ←f◦ *pṛthivī* (earth) 1.18); *ca* (and); *eva* (1.1); *tumulaḥ:* (1.13); *vyanunādayan* (1nom◦ sing◦ caus◦ ←śatṛ◦ adj◦ *vyanunādayat* ←1◦वि–अनु√नद् (to make sound, play) (1.19)

(§3) ***saḥ:*** **(adj1◦-subj◦ that);** ***ghoṣaḥ:*** **(subj◦ sound, uproar);** ***dhārtarāṣṭrāṇām*** **(of the Kauravas; of the sons of Dhṛtarāṣtra);** ***hṛdayāni*** **(obj1◦ hearts);** ***vyadārayat*** **(it caused to shake; caused to burst asunder)** ***nabhaḥ:*** **(obj2◦ the sky);** ***ca*** **(and); pṛthivīm (obj3◦ the earth);** ***ca eva*** **(and);** ***tumulaḥ:*** **(adj2◦-subj◦ tumultuous);** ***vyanunādayan*** **(adj3◦-subj◦ causing to reverberate, resonate, resound)** (1.19)

(§4) saḥ: tumulaḥ: ghoṣaḥ: vyanunādayan pṛthivīm ca-eva nabhaḥ: vyadārayat hṛdayāni

---

[35] Elsewhere◦ *pṛthak-pṛthak* → respective, स्व स्व, each his own, several, ...etc. (adj◦ qualifying noun शङ्खान्)

पृथक् is not an adjective, so it can not qualify a noun. It is an ind◦ adv◦ It must qualify the verb दध्मुः (e.g. separately, singly, severally; differently, distinctly ...etc.), not the noun शङ्खान् (e.g. own, respective, several). Therefore, not सर्वशः पृथक्पृथक् शङ्खान् but सर्वशः पृथक्पृथक् दध्मुः ।

[36] Elsewhere◦ *sarvaśaḥ:* → all (adj◦)

सर्वशः is not an adjective. It is an ind◦ adv◦ It must qualify the verb दध्मुः, not the subjects ...द्रुपदः, द्रौपेयाः, सौभद्रः ...etc.

dhārtarāṣṭrāṇām

(§5) That tumultuous sound, causing to reverberate the earth and the sky, caused to burst asunder[37] hearts of the Kauravas. (1.19)

1.20 अथ व्यवस्थितान्दृष्ट्वा धार्तराष्ट्रान्कपिध्वजः ।
प्रवृत्ते शस्त्रसम्पाते धनुरुद्यम्य पाण्डवः ।।

atha vyavasthitāndṛṣṭvā dhārtarāṣṭrānkapidhvajaḥ:,
pravṛtte śastrasampāte dhanurudyamya pāṇḍavaḥ:; (1.20)

(§1) अथ व्यवस्थितान् दृष्ट्वा धार्तराष्ट्रान् कपिध्वजः । प्रवृत्ते शस्त्रसम्पाते धनुः उद्यम्य पाण्डवः । *atha vyavasthitān* (r∘ 13/11) *dṛṣṭvā dhārtarāṣṭrān* (r∘ 13/9) *kapidhvajaḥ:* (r∘ 22/8) *pravṛtte śastrasampāte dhanuḥ:* (r∘ 16/3) *udyamya pāṇḍavaḥ:* (r∘ 22/8)

(§2) ***atha*** (after this) (time indicating ind∘ ←10∘√अर्थ् (to want); *vyavasthitān* (m∘ 2acc∘ plu∘ ←ppp∘ adj∘ ***vyavasthita*** (prepared to act) ←1∘वि–अव√स्था (to stay); *dṛṣṭvā* (1.2); ***dhārtarāṣṭrān*** (2acc∘ plu∘ ←m∘ *dhārtarāṣṭra* 1.19); *kapidhvajaḥ:* (m∘ 1nom∘ sing∘ ←bahuvrī∘ *kapidhvaja,* कपिः ध्वजे यस्य ←m∘ *kapi* (Hanumāna) ←1∘√कम्प् (to tremble) + m∘ *dhvaja* (flag) ←1∘√ध्वज् (to go); *pravṛtte* (m∘ 7loc∘ sing∘ ←ppp∘ adj∘ ***pravṛtta*** (commencement) ←4∘प्र√वृत् (to choose); *śastrasampāte* (m∘ 7loc∘ sing∘ ←tatpu∘ *śastra-sampāta* (clash of weapons) शस्त्राणाम् सम्पातः ←n∘ *śastra* (weapon) *1.9* + m∘ *sampāta* (clash) ←1∘सम्√पत् (to fall); *dhanuḥ:* (2acc∘ sing∘ ←n∘ ***dhanuṣ*** (bow) ←1∘√धन् (to scurry); *udyamya* (lyp∘ past-participle ←1∘उद्√यम् (to restrain); *pāṇḍavaḥ:* (1.14) (1.20)

(§3) ***atha*** **(after this, thereupon);** ***vyavasthitān*** **(adj∘-obj1∘ those who are reunited, repositioned, poised, prepared to act);** ***dṛṣṭvā*** **(having seen, seeing);** ***dhārtarāṣṭrān*** **(obj1∘ the sons of Dhṛtarāṣṭra; the Kauravas);** ***kapidhvajaḥ:*** **(adj∘-subj∘ the bearer of the standard with the image of Hanūmāna);** ***pravṛtte*** **(at the commencement of);** ***śastrasampāte*** **(at the clash of weapons);** ***dhanuḥ:*** **(obj2∘ the bow; the Gāṇḍīva bow);** ***udyamya*** **(having raised);** ***pāṇḍavaḥ:*** **(subj∘ Pāṇḍava; Arjuna) (1.20)**

(§4) atha dṛṣṭvā dhārtarāṣṭrān vyavasthitān pāṇḍavaḥ: kapidhvajaḥ: udyamya dhanuḥ: pravṛtte

---

[37] Elsewhere∘ *vyadārayat* → became uproarious (v.i∘) ..etc.

vyadaryat is not an v.i∘ It is a v.t∘ causative verb. The non-causative verb would be वि–अददरत्, व्यददरत्; but it is a causative व्यदारयत् → caused to shatter. It is not, the sound itself became (अभवत्) uproarious (an intransitive action), but it should be, the sound caused the hearts to shatter (a transitive causative action). The hearts are the object; sound is the subject, the causative performer of the verb shake; on the hearts, the object; through fear, the causative agent.

śastrasampāte

(§5) After this, having seen[38] the Kauravas prepared to act, Arjuna, the bearer of the standard with the image of Hanūmāna, having raised the Gāṇḍīva bow,[39] at the commencement of the clash of weapons;[40] (1.20)

1.21 हृषीकेशं तदा वाक्यमिदमाह महीपते ।
सेनयोरुभयोर्मध्ये रथं स्थापय मेऽच्युत ।।

hṛṣīkeśaṁ tadā vākyamidamāha mahīpate,
senayorubhayormadhye rathaṁ sthāpaya me'cyuta. (1.21)

(§1) हृषीकेशम् तदा वाक्यम् इदम् आह महीपते । सेनयो: उभयो: मध्ये रथम् स्थापय मे अच्युत । *hṛṣīkeśam* (r∘ 14/1) *tadā vākyam* (r∘ 8/18) *idam* (r∘ 8/17) *āha mahīpate senayoḥ:* (r∘ 16/5) *ubhayoḥ:* (r∘ 16/12) *madhye ratham* (r∘ 14/1) *sthāpaya me* (r∘ 6/1) *acyuta*

(§2) ***hṛṣīkeśam*** (2acc∘ sing∘ ←m∘ *hṛṣīkeśa* 1.15); *tadā* (1.2); 📖***vākyam*** (2acc∘ sing∘ ←collective noun n∘ ***vākya*** (utterance) ←1∘√वच् (to speek); *idam* (1.10); 📖***āha*** (3rd-per∘ sing∘ pres∘ वर्तमान्-लट् parasmai∘ ←5∘√अह् (to speak) or optional form ←2∘√ब्रू (to speak); 📖*mahīpate* (m∘ 8voc∘ sing∘ ←bahuvrī∘ *mahīpati* (king) मह्या: पति: इव य: ←f∘ ***mahī*** ←1∘√मह् (to respect) + m∘ *pati* 1.18); ***senayoḥ:*** (6pos∘ dual∘ ←f∘ ***senā*** (army) ←5∘√सि (to bind); ***ubhayoḥ:*** (f∘ 6pos∘ dual∘ ←pronominal adj∘ *ubhaya* (opposing two) ←6∘√उभ् (to join two); 📖***madhye*** (7loc∘ sing∘ ←adj∘ m∘ ***madhya*** (middle) ←1∘√मह् (to respect); 📖*ratham* (2acc∘ sing∘ ←m∘ *ratha* (chariot) 1.4); *sthāpaya* (place!) (2nd-per∘ sing∘ imperative∘ प्रार्थनार्थक-लोट् parasmai∘ caus∘ ←1∘√स्था (to stay); ***me*** (6pos sing∘ ←pron∘ *asmad* 1.7); ***acyuta*** (m∘ 8voc∘ sing∘ ←n.bahuvrī∘ *acyuta,* न च्युत: य: ←negative affix अ 1.10 + ppp∘ adj∘ *cyuta* ←1∘√च्यु (to drop) (1.21)

(§3) ***hṛṣīkeśam*** **(obj1∘ to Hṛṣīkeśa; to Śrī Kṛṣṇa);** ***tadā*** **(at that time, then);** ***vākyam*** **(obj2∘ utterance);** ***idam*** **(adj∘-obj2∘ this);** ***āha*** **(subj∘ he said);** ***mahīpate*** **(O Mahīpati! O King! O Dhṛtarāṣṭra!);** ***senayoḥ:*** **(in the middle of two armies);** ***ubhayoḥ:*** **(in the middle of both, the opposing);** ***madhye*** **(in the middle**

---

[38] Elsewhere∘ *atha...dṛṣṭvā* → when he saw, then the son of Pāndu (Arjuna) saw, then Arjuna looked at ...etc.
📖 'saw or looked' is a perfect action अपश्यत्, दृष्टवान् । But दृष्ट्वा is an ind∘ क्त्वा∘ participle.

[39] Elsewhere∘ *dhanurudyamya* → took up his bow.
📖 'took up' is a perfect verb, but उद्यम्य is an ind∘ lyp∘ participle.

[40] Elsewhere∘ *pravṛtte śastrasampāte* → when the missiles were about to be discharged, prepared to shoot his arrows, realized that missiles were about to be discharged,

of); ***ratham*** (obj3◦ the chariot); ***sthāpaya*** (please position, place!); ***me*** (adj◦ 4dat◦ for me; 6pos◦ my); ***aćyuta*** (O Aaćyuta! O Śrī Kṛṣṇa!) (1.21)

(§4) mahīpate tadā āha hṛṣīkeśam idam vākyam me aćyuta sthāpaya ratham madhye ubhayoḥ: senayoḥ:

(§5) O King! at that time, (Arjuna) said to Śrī Kṛṣṇa this[41] utterance, "O My Aaćyuta![42] please place the chariot in the middle of the opposing two armies;" (1.21)

Arjuna said (arjuna uvāća अर्जुन उवाच ।)

1.22 यावदेतान्निरीक्षेऽहं योद्धुकामानवस्थितान् ।
कैर्मया सह योद्धव्यमस्मिन्रणसमुद्यमे ।।

yāvadetānnirīkṣe'haṁ yoddhukāmānavasthitān,
kairmayā saha yoddhavyamasminraṇasamudyame. (1.22)

(§1) यावत् एतान् निरीक्षे अहम् योद्धुकामान् अवस्थितान् । कैः मया सह योद्धव्यम् अस्मिन् रणसमुद्यमे । arjuna (r◦ 19/4) uvāća. *yāvat* (r◦ 8/9) *etān* (r◦ 1/11) *nirīkṣe* (r◦ 6/1) *aham* (r◦ 14/1) *yoddhukāmān* (r◦ 8/11) *avasthitān* (r◦ 23/1) *kaiḥ:* (r◦ 16/11) *mayā saha yoddhavyam* (r◦ 8/16) *asmin* (r◦ 13/18) *raṇasamudyame*

(§2) *arjunaḥ:* (m◦ 1nom◦ sing◦ ←prop◦ *arjuna* 1.4); *uvāća* (1.25). ***yāvat*** (meanwhile) (limit indicating ind◦ ←pron◦ *yad* 1.7); ***etān*** (m◦ 2acc◦ plu◦ ←pron◦ *etad* (this) 1.3); 🕮*nirīkṣe* (1st-per◦ sing◦ pres◦ वर्तमान्-लट् ātmane◦ ←1◦निर्√ईक्ष् (to see); ***aham*** (1nom◦ sing◦ ←pron◦ *asmad* 1.7); 🕮*yoddhukāmān* (m◦ 2acc◦ plu◦ adj◦ ←bahuvrī◦ *yoddhu-kāma,* योद्धुम् अस्ति कामः यस्य, कामना यस्य ←f◦ *yudh* (fight) 1.1 + m◦ ***kāma*** (desire) ←1◦√कम् (to desire); 🕮***avasthitān*** (m◦ 2acc◦ plu◦ ←ppp◦ adj◦ *avasthita* 1.11); ***kaiḥ:*** (m◦ 3inst◦ plu◦ ←pron◦ *kim* 1.1); ***mayā*** (m◦ 3inst◦ sing◦ ←pron◦ *asmad* 1.7); ***saha*** (with) (aggregative adj◦ or ind◦ ←1◦√सह् (to endure); *yoddhavyam* (n◦ 1nom◦ sing◦ ←potential◦ विधि◦ adj◦ -*yoddhavya* ←4◦√युध् (to fight) ; ***asmin*** (m◦ 7loc◦ sing◦

---

[41] Elsewhere◦ *idaṁ vākyam* → these words (plu◦), the following words (plu◦) ...etc.

🕮 इदम् = singular n◦ this (इदम् this, इमे, इमानि these), वचनम् = singular - saying, speech, oration, talk, utterence, expression (see footnote in 1.2).

[42] Elsewhere◦ *me'ćyuta!* मेऽच्युत! → O Aćtuta! my chariot.

🕮 The pronominal adjective मे being just previous to the noun अच्युत! and Śrī Kṛṣṇa being very dear to Arjuna, the expression *me'ćyuta!* should naturally and appropriately mean → मे अच्युत! O My Aćyuta! Like Rāmānuja's त्वमेव विद्या द्रविण त्वमेव, त्वमेव सर्वम्, मम (मे) देव देव!

←pron◦ *idam* (this) 1.10); 📖*raṇasamudyame* (m◦ 7loc◦ sing◦ ←tatpu◦ *raṇa-samudyama* (battle) रणस्य समुद्यमः ←n◦ ***raṇa*** (battle field) ←1◦√रण् (to rattle, battle) + derivative noun m◦ *samudyama* (assemble) ←1◦सम्-उद्√यम् (to restrain) (1.22)

(§3) *yāvat* (Meanwhile; until); *etān* (obj◦ these people); *nirīkṣe aham* (subj1◦ I observe); *yoddhukāmān* (adj1◦-obj◦ who are desirous of fighting); *avasthitān* (adj2◦-obj◦ those who are arrayed in formations); *kaiḥ:* (subj2◦ by whom); *mayā saha* (with me); *yoddhavyam* (adj3◦-obj◦ ought to be fought, fighting should be done); *asmin* (in this); *raṇasamudyame* (in this battle, on this battlefield) (1.22)

(§4) yāvat nirīkṣe aham etān yoddhukāmān avasthitān kaiḥ: (yuddham) yoddhavyam mayā saha asmin raṇasamudyame

(§5) Meanwhile I observe these people, who are desirous of fighting (and) are arrayed in formations, by whom fighting should be done with me[43] in this battle. (1.22)

1.23 योत्समानानवेक्षेऽहं य एतेऽत्र समागताः ।
धार्तराष्ट्रस्य दुर्बुद्धेर्युद्धे प्रियचिकीर्षवः ।।

yotsamānānavekṣe'haṁ ya ete'tra samāgatāḥ:,
dhārtarāṣṭrasya durbuddheryuddhe priyacikīrṣavaḥ:. (1.23)

(§1) योत्समानान् अवेक्षे अहम् ये एते अत्र समागताः । धार्तराष्ट्रस्य दुर्बुद्धेः युद्धे प्रियचिकीर्षवः । *yotsamānān* (r◦ 8/11) *avekṣe* (r◦ 6/1) *aham* (r◦ 14/1) *ye* (r◦ 5/4) *ete* (r◦ 6/1) *atra samāgatāḥ:* (r◦ 22/8) *dhārtarāṣṭrasya durbuddheḥ:* (r◦ 16/10) *yuddhe priyacikīrṣavaḥ:* (r◦ 22/8)

(§2) *yotsamānān* (m◦ 2acc◦ plu◦ ←śānac◦ -desi◦ adj◦ *yotsamān* ←3rd-per◦ sing◦ pres◦ वर्तमान्-लट् ātmane◦ *yotsate* ←4◦√युध् (to fight); 📖*avekṣe* (sing◦ 1st-per◦ pres◦ वर्तमान्-लट् ātmane◦ ←1◦अव√ईक्ष् (to see); *aham* (1.22); *ye* (1.7); ***ete*** (m◦ 1nom◦ plu◦ ←pron◦ *etad* (this) 1.3); *atra* (here) (1.4); 📖*samāgatāḥ:* (m◦ 1nom◦ plu◦ ←ppp◦ adj◦ *samāgata* (assembled) ←1◦सम्-आ√गम् (to go); 📖*dhārtarāṣṭrasya* (m◦ 6pos◦ sing◦ ←bahuvrī◦ *dhārtarāṣṭra* 1.19); 📖*durbuddheḥ:* (m◦ 6pos◦ sing◦ ←bahuvrī◦ *durbuddhi* दुर् वा दुष्टा वा बुद्धिः

---

[43] Elsewhere◦ *kaiḥ: mayā saha yoddhavyam* → with whom (obj◦) I (subject) should fight (active◦), with whom I shall have to fight (future◦), with whom I have to contend (active◦) with whom I should fight at the commencement of the battle, with whom I must contend, with whom I must strive, with whom I must fight, let me know with whom I have to fight, those who are going to engage in battle with me ...etc.

📖 प्रयोगे कर्मवाच्यस्य तृतीया स्यात्तु कर्तरि – (कैः) । by whom (subj◦) fighting should to be done (adjective of the subject) with me (object).

यस्य सः ←derogatory ind◦ *dur̥* (evil) 1.2 + f◦ ***buddhi*** (mind) ←1◦√बुध् (to comprehend); ***yuddhe*** (7loc◦ sing◦ ←n◦ *yuddha* (battle) 1.9); 📖*priyaćikīrṣavaḥ:* (m◦ 1nom◦ plu◦ ←tatpu◦ *priya-ćikīrṣu* ←adj◦ ***priya*** (good, well) ←9◦√प्री (to please) + desi◦ adj◦ 📖*ćikīrṣu* (wisher) ←8◦√कृ (to do) (1.23)

(§3) *yotsamānān̥* (obj◦ the people who wish to fight) *avekṣe aham̥* (subj1◦ I observe; I am observing, viewing); *ye* (adj1◦-subj2◦ who); *ete* (adj2◦-subj2◦ these, these people); *atra* (here); *samāgatāḥ:* (adj3◦-subj2◦ those who are assembled); *dhārtarāṣṭrasya* (of Dhṛtarāṣtra's son; of Duryodhana); *durbuddheḥ:* (of the one who is evil minded); *yuddhe* (in the battle); *priyaćikīrṣavaḥ:* (adj4◦-subj2◦ with the desire of wishing well) (1.23)

(§4) avekṣe aham̥ yotsamānān̥ ete ye samāgatāḥ: atra priyaćikīrṣavaḥ: durbuddheḥ: dhārtarāṣṭrasya yuddhe.

(§5) I am observing the people who wish to fight.[44] These people[45] (are) assembled here with the desire of wishing well of evil-minded Duryodhana in the battle. (1.23)

Sanjaya said (sañjaya uvāća सञ्जय उवाच ।)

1.24 एवमुक्तो हृषीकेशो गुडाकेशेन भारत ।
सेनयोरुभयोर्मध्ये स्थापयित्वा रथोत्तमम् ।।

evamukto hṛṣīkeśo guḍākeśena bhārata,
senayorubhayormadhye sthāpayitvā rathottamam̥; (1.24)

(§1) एवम् उक्तः हृषीकेशः गुडाकेशेन भारत । सेनयोः उभयोः मध्ये स्थापयित्वा रथोत्तमम् । *sañjayaḥ:* (r◦ 19/4) *uvāća. evam̥* (r◦ 8/20) *uktaḥ:* (r◦ 15/14) *hṛṣīkeśaḥ:* (r◦ 15/2) *guḍākeśena bhārata senayoḥ:* (r◦ 16/5) *ubhayoḥ:*

---

[44] Elsewhere◦ *yotsyamānān* → with the object of fighting, those who will be fighting ...

[45] Elsewhere◦ *ye ete* → I desire to discern those that throng here to fight, let me see those who have come to fight, I desire to have a glance at those who are assembled here to fight, I wish to look at those who are assembled here, I see those who are gathered here ready ...etc. (like the object)

📖 If we say I desire to see (discern, glance, look) those who are gathered (throng, have come, assembled), then in that case, those and who become pronominal adjectives of the objective in Accusative case, यान् and एतान्. But, ये and एते both are Nominative case subj◦, and therefore, can not be connected to the verb of the subject अवेक्षे अहम् । *ye* (ये) and *ete* (एते) are adjectives of the subject in Nominative case समागताः (independent of अवेक्षे अहम्). It is, 'these people (who) are assembled here' ये एते अत्र समागताः (subj◦), 'to them' *yotsyamāmān* (obj◦), 'I am observing' (तान् योत्स्यमानान् अवेक्षे अहम् ।) NOTE : The thing to remember is that योत्स्यमानान् relates to obj◦ and समागताः relates to subj◦ as its adjective ये – एते ।

(r∘ 16/12) *madhye sthāpayitvā rathottamam̦* (r∘ 14/2)

(§2) *sañjayah̤:* (1.2); *uvāća* (1.25). 📖***evam̦*** (in this manner) (mode indicating ind∘ ←1∘√इ (to enter, come, go); 📖***uktah̤:*** (m∘ 1nom∘ sing∘ ←ppp∘ adj∘ ***ukta*** (addressed) ←2∘√वच् (to speek); *hr̤s̤īkeśah̤:* (m∘ 1nom∘ sing∘ ←m∘ *hr̤s̤īkeśa* 1.15); *gud̤ākeśena* (m∘ 3inst∘ sing∘ ←bahuvrī∘ ***gud̤ākeśa,*** गुडाकाया: ईश: य: ←f∘ *gud̤ākā* (sleep) ←1∘गुड–आ√कै (to sound) + adj∘ *īśa* (lord) 1.15); ***bhārata*** (m∘ 8voc∘ sing∘ ←taddhita∘ *bhārata,* भरतस्य गोत्रापत्यम् ; in 1.24 = dhr̤tarās̤t̤ra); *senayoh̤:* (1.21); *ubhayoh̤:* (1.21); *madhye* (1.21); *sthāpayitvā* (ipp∘ ind∘ caus∘ ←1∘√स्था (to stay); 📖*rathottamam̦* (m∘ 2acc∘ sing∘ ←bahuvrī∘ *rathottama,* रथेषु उत्तम: य: ←m∘ *ratha* (chariot) 1.4 + superlative adj∘ *uttama* (grand) 1.7) (1.24)

(§3) *evam̦* (in this manner); *uktah̤:* (adj∘-obj1∘ the one who was addressed) *hr̤s̤īkeśah̤:* (obj∘ Hr̤s̤īkeśa; Śrī Kr̤s̤n̤a); *gud̤ākeśena* (subj∘ by Gud̤ākeśa, by Arjuna); *bhārata* (O Bharata! O Dhr̤tarās̤t̤ra!); *senayoh̤:* (in the midst of the two armies;); *ubhayoh̤:* (in the midst of both, opposing); *madhye* (in the midst of); *sthāpayitvā* (having caused to be placed) *rathottamam̦* (obj2∘ the grand chariot) (1.24)

(§4) bhārata! hr̤s̤īkeśah̤:, uktah̤: gud̤ākeśena evam̦, sthāpayitvā rathottamam̦ madhye ubhayoh̤: senayoh̤:;

(§5) O Dhr̤tarās̤t̤ra! Śrī Kr̤s̤n̤a, the one who was addressed[46] by Arjuna in this manner, having caused the grand chariot to be placed[47] in the midst of the two opposing armies; (1.24)

1.25 भीष्मद्रोणप्रमुखत: सर्वेषां च महीक्षिताम् ।
उवाच पार्थ पश्यैतान्समवेतान्कुरूनिति ।।

bhīs̤madron̤apramukhatah̤: sarves̤ām̐ ća mahīks̤itām̦,
uvāća pārtha pasyaitānsamavetānkurūniti. (1.25)

(§1) भीष्मद्रोणप्रमुखत: सर्वेषाम् च महीक्षिताम् । उवाच पार्थ पश्य एतान् समवेतान् कुरून् इति । *Bhīs̤madron̤apramukhatah̤:* (r∘ 22/7) *sarves̤ām̦* (r∘ 25/3, 14/1) *ća mahīks̤itām̦* (r∘ 14/2) *uvāća pārtha paśya* (r∘ 3/1) *etān̦* (r∘ 13/20) *samavetān̦* (r∘ 13/9) *kurūn̦* (r∘ 8/13) *iti*

---

[46] Elsewhere∘ *evam ukth̤:* उक्त: → having been addressed (gerund∘), was addressed (present tense∘) ...etc.

📖 उक्त: is not a gerund or a verb. It is a Nominative case ppp∘ adjective, and thus it qualifies the Nominative case noun हृषीकेष: । Thus addressed, Hr̤s̤īkes̤a, (i.e. Hr̤s̤īkes̤a, who was addressed thus, ...)

[47] Elsewhere∘ *sthāpayitvā* → drew up, placed, stationed ...etc. (perfect tense)

📖 स्थापयित्वा is not a past tense. It is a क्त्वा∘ Past Participle, indicating a subordinate action having done, before the following main action began → having caused to be placed, drawn, stationed ..etc.

(§2) 📖*Bhīṣma-droṇa-pramukhataḥ:* (adv∘ भीष्मस्य च द्रोणस्य च प्रमुखत: ←m∘ prop∘ *bhīṣma* 1.8 + m∘ prop∘ ***droṇa*** ←1∘√द्रु (to flow) + adj∘ ***pramukha*** (presense) ←1∘प्र√खन् (to dig); ***sarveṣām*** (m∘ 6pos∘ plu∘ ←pron∘ *sarva* 1.6); *ća* (and); *mahīkṣitām* (6pos plu∘ ←m∘ *mahīkṣit* (king) मही क्षियते येन ←f∘ *mahī* 1.21 + affix *kṣit*, क्षीयते येन); ***uvāća*** (3rd-per∘ sing∘ past-perf∘ लिट् भूत∘ parasmai∘ ←2∘√वच् (to speek); ***pārtha*** (m∘ 8voc∘ sing∘ ←taddhita∘ ***pārtha***, पृथाया: पुत्र: ←f∘ prop∘ *pṛthā* ←1∘√प्रथ् (to grow) + m∘ *putra* 1.3); *paśya* (1.3); *etān* (1.22); 📖*samavetān* (m∘ 2acc∘ plu∘ ←ppp∘ adj∘ *samaveta* (assembled) 1.1); *kurūn* (m∘ 2acc∘ plu∘ ←bahuvrī∘ *kuru* 1.1); ***iti*** (that) (mode indicating ind∘ or ind∘ used for closing a quotation ←1∘√इ (to enter, come, go) (1.25)

(§3) ***Bhīṣma-droṇa-pramukhataḥ:*** **(in front of or in the presense of Bhīṣma and Droṇa)** ***sarveṣām*** **(of all);** ***ća*** **(and);** ***mahīkṣitām*** **(of the kings);** ***uvāća*** **(he said);** ***pārtha*** **(O Pārtha!; O Arjuna!);** ***paśya*** **(please see!);** ***etān*** **(adj1∘-obj∘ these);** ***samavetān*** **(adj2∘-obj∘ those who are assembled);** ***kurūn*** **(obj∘ Kurus);** ***iti*** **(that, so, thus)** (1.25)

(§4) uvāća bhīṣma-droṇa-pramukhataḥ: ća sarveṣām mahīkṣitām iti pārtha! paśya! etān kurūn samavetān

(§5) (Śrī Kṛṣṇa) said, in the presense of[48] Bhīṣma and Droṇa and of all the kings, that O Arjuna! please see these Kurus[49] who are assembled (here)! (1.25)

1.26 तत्रापश्यत्स्थितान्पार्थ: पितॄनथ पितामहान् ।
आचार्यान्मातुलान्भ्रातॄन्पुत्रान्पौत्रान्सखींस्तथा ।।
श्वशुरान्सुहृदश्चैव सेनयोरुभयोरपि ।

tatrāpaśyatsthitānpārthaḥ: pitṝnatha pitāmahān,

---

[48] Elsewhere∘ *pramukhataḥ* → facing (gerund).

📖 ∘प्रमुखत: is not a gerund, adj∘ or an ipp∘, it is an adverb qualifying the verb उवाच ।

[49] Elsewhere∘ *kurūn* कुरून् → behold all the Karuavas, see the Kauravas, look at these assembled Kauravas ...etc.

📖 Only the Kauravas were not the Kurus. Pāṇḍavas also belonged to the Kuru dynasty. When Kṛṣṇa said see these Kurus, he clearly ment **'behold these Kauravas and Pāṇḍavas.'** And, therefore, to follow Kṛṣṇa's instruction dutifully, the obedient devotee Arjuna looked at both the armies (सेनयोरुभयोरुपि). It is not possible that Kṛṣṇa asked Arjuna to look at the Kauravas, and he looked at the Pāṇḍavas. In the Gītā, Vyāsa has used the word 'Kuru कुरु' for Kaurava-Pāṇḍavas in 1.1 कुरुक्षेत्र; for Bhīṣma कुरुवृद्ध (1.12); for Arjuna कुरुनन्दन (2.42, 6.43, 14.13), कुरुप्रवीर (11.48), कुरुश्रेष्ठ (10.19), कुरुसत्तम (4.31). Remember that in the Gītā, in order to address only the Kauravas, Vyāsa has used words धार्तराष्ट्र (1.19-20, 1.36-37, 1.46, 2.6) and धृरातष्ट्रस्य पुत्रा: (11.26).

ā́ćāryānmātulānbhrātṛ́nputrānpautrānsakhīṁstathā;

ś́vaś́urānsuhṛdaś́ćaiva senayorubhayorapi. (1.26)

(§1) तत्र अपश्यत् स्थितान् पार्थः पितॄन् अथ पितामहान् । आचार्यान् मातुलान् भ्रातॄन् पुत्रान् पौत्रान् सखीन् तथा । श्वशुरान् सुहृदः च एव सेनयोः उभयोः अपि । *tatra* (r◦ 1/1) *apaś́yat* (r◦ 10/7) *sthitān* (r◦ 13/13) *pārthaḥ:* (r◦ 22/3) *pitṛ́n* (r◦ 8/11) *atha pitāmahān* (r◦ 23/1) *ā́ćāryān* (r◦ 13/16) *mātulān* (r◦ 13/15) *bhrātṛ́n* (r◦ 13/13) *putrān* (r◦ 13/13) *pautrān* (r◦ 13/20) *sakhin* (r◦ 13/7) *tathā ś́vaś́urān* (r◦ 13/20) *suhṛdaḥ:* (r◦ 17/1) *ća* (r◦ 3/1) *eva senayoḥ:* (r◦ 16/5) *ubhayoḥ:* (r◦ 16/5) *api*

(§2) ***tatra*** (there) (ind◦ ←pron◦ *tat* 1.10); 📖***apaś́yat*** (3rd-per◦ sing◦ -past-imper◦ लङ् भूत◦ parasmai◦ ←1◦√दृश् (to see); 📖*sthitān* (m◦ 2acc◦ plu◦ ←ppp◦ adj◦ *sthita* (stood) 1.14); ***pārthaḥ:*** (1nom◦ sing◦ ←m◦ *pārtha* 1.25); ***pitṛ́n*** (2acc◦ plu◦ ←m◦ *pitṛ* 1.12); *atha* (1.20); *pitāmahān* (2acc◦ plu◦ ←m◦ *pitāmaha* 1.12); *ā́ćāryān* (2acc◦ plu◦ ←m◦ *ā́ćārya* 1.2); *mātulān* (2acc◦ plu◦ ←m◦ -taddhita◦ ***mātula*** (uncle) मातुः भ्राता, ←f◦ ***mātṛ*** ←10◦**√मान्** (to worship); *bhrātṛ́n* (2acc◦ plu◦ ←m◦ *bhrātṛ* ←1◦**√भ्राज्** (to shine); *putrān* (2acc◦ plu◦ ←m◦ *putra* 1.3); *pautrān* (2acc◦ plu◦ ←m◦ taddhita◦, ***pautra*** (grandson) पुत्रस्य पुत्रः ←m◦ *putra* 1.3); *sakhin* (2acc◦ plu◦ ←m◦ ***sakhi*** (friend) ←2◦√ख्या (to declare); *tathā* (1.8); *ś́vaś́urān* (2acc◦ plu◦ ←m◦ ***ś́vaś́ura*** (father-in-law) ←9◦शु√अश् (to eat); *suhṛdaḥ:* (2acc◦ plu◦ ←m◦ ***suhṛd*** (companion) ←1◦सु√हृ (to take); *ća* (and); *eva* (1.1); *senayoḥ:* (1.21); *ubhayoḥ:* (1.21); ***api*** (aggregative ind◦ ←2◦√पा (to protect) (1.26)

(§3) ***tatra*** **(there);** ***apaś́yat*** **(saw, he saw);** ***sthitān*** **(adj◦-**obj1-10◦ **those who were standing);** ***pārthaḥ:*** (subj◦ **Pārtha);** ***pitṛ́n*** (obj1◦ **fathers; fatherly people);** ***atha*** **(and);** ***pitāmahān*** (obj2◦ **grandfathers; elderly people);** ***ā́ćāryān*** (obj3◦ **Gurus; tutors, venerable people);** ***mātulān*** (obj4◦ **maternal uncles);** ***bhrātṛ́n*** (obj5◦ **brothers);** ***putrān*** (obj6◦ **sons; young people);** ***pautrān*** (obj7◦ **grandsons, very young people);** ***sakhin*** (obj8◦ **friends);** ***tathā*** **(as well);** ***ś́vaś́urān*** (obj9◦ **father-in-laws);** ***suhṛdaḥ:*** (obj10◦ **companions);** ***ća*** **(and);** ***eva*** **(also);** ***senayoḥ:*** **(in both armies);** ***ubhayoḥ:*** **(in both; in opposing);** ***api*** **(even, also)** (1.26)

(§4) tatra pārthaḥ: apaś́yat pitṛ́n pitāmahān ća ā́ćāryān mātulān bhrātṛ́n putrān pautrān sakhin eva ś́vaś́urān tathā suhṛdaḥ: sthitān api senayoḥ: ubhayoḥ:

(§5) There Arjuna saw[50] fatherly, elderly and venerable people, uncles, brothers, young people, very young people, friends, also father-in-laws, as well as companions, standing even in both opposing armies. (1.26)

---

[50] Elsewhere◦ *apaś́yat* → Arjuna could see, he could see ...etc.

📖 अपश्यत् is 1st preterite past tense, he saw.

1.27 तान्समीक्ष्य स कौन्तेयः सर्वान्बन्धूनवस्थितान् ।
कृपया परयाविष्टो विषीदन्निदमब्रवीत् ।।

tānsamīkṣya sa kaunteyaḥ: sarvānbandhūnavasthitān,
kṛpayā parayāviṣṭo viṣīdannidamabravīt. (1.27)

(§1) तान् समीक्ष्य सः कौन्तेयः सर्वान् बन्धून् अवस्थितान् । कृपया परया आविष्टः विषीदन् इदम् अब्रवीत् । *tān* (r◦ 13/20) *samīkṣya saḥ:* (r◦ 21/2) *kaunteyaḥ:* (r◦ 22/7) *sarvān* (r◦ 13/14) *bandhūn* (r◦ 8/11) *avasthitān* (r◦ 23/1) *kṛpayā parayā* (r◦ 1/4) *āviṣṭaḥ:* (r◦ 15/13) *viṣīdan* (r◦ 13/3) *idam* (r◦ 8/16) *abravīt*

(§2) *tān* (1.7); 📖*samīkṣya* (lyp◦ past-participle gerund ind◦ ←f◦ *samīkṣā* (observation) ←1◦सम्√ईक्ष् (to see); *saḥ:* (1.13); *kaunteyaḥ:* (m◦ 1nom◦ sing◦ ←taddhita◦ **kaunteya**, कुन्त्याः पुत्रः ←f◦ prop◦ *kuntī* 1.16 + m◦ *putra* 1.3); **sarvān** (m◦ 2acc◦ plu◦ ←pron◦ *sarva* 1.6); *bandhūn* (2acc◦ plu◦ ←m◦ **bandhu** (brother) ←m◦ **bandha** (tie) ←9◦√**बन्ध्** (to tie); *avasthitān* (1.22); **kṛpayā** (3inst◦ sing◦ ←f◦ *kṛpā* (pity) ←1◦√कृप् (to imagine); **parayā** (3inst◦ sing◦ ←f◦ **parā** (deep) ←5◦√पृ (to be pleased); 📖*āviṣṭaḥ:* (1nom◦ sing◦ ←ppp◦ adj◦ **āviṣṭa** (possessed) ←3◦आ√**विष्** (to detach); *viṣīdan* (adv◦ or 1nom◦ sing◦ ←śatṛ◦ adj◦ *viṣīdat* (desponding) ←m◦ 📖**viṣāda** (melancholy) ←6◦वि√**सद्** (to sit); *idam* (1.10); *abravīt* (1.2) (1.27)

(§3) ***tān*** **(adj1◦-obj◦ them, to those);** ***samīkṣya*** **(having observed); saḥ: (adj1◦-subj◦ he, that); kaunteyaḥ: (subj◦ Kaunteya; Arjuna);** ***sarvān*** **(adj2◦-obj◦ all);** ***bandhūn*** **(obj◦ brothers); avasthitān (adj3◦-obj◦ arrayed in battle formation);** ***kṛpayā*** **(with pity);** ***parayā*** **(with deep);** ***āviṣṭaḥ:*** **(adj2◦-subj◦ overwhelmed, posessed);** ***viṣīdan*** **(adj3◦-subj◦ despairing);** ***idam*** **(this);** ***abravīt*** **(he said) (1.27)**

(§4) samīkṣya sarvān tān bandhūn avasthitān saḥ: kaunteyaḥ: āviṣṭaḥ: parayā kṛpayā viṣīdan abravīt idam -

(§5) Having observed all those[51] brothers arrayed in battle formation, that Arjuna, possessed with deep pity[52] (and) desponding,[53] said this : (1.27)

Arjuna said (arjuna uvāća अर्जुन उवाच ।)

---

[51] Elsewhere◦ *tān sarvān bandhūn samīkṣya* → seeing all these kinsmen, when Arjuna saw all these different grades of friends and relatives, he saw all these kinsmen, when Arjuna saw all these linsmen ...etc.

[52] Elsewhere◦ *āviṣṭaḥ:* → he became overwhelmed, he was overcome ...etc. (past tense◦)

📖 आविष्टः is not an Indefinite Past लङ् tense. It is a ppp◦ adjective of the subject.

[53] Elsewhere◦ *viṣīdan* → in grief (adv◦), in sadness (adv◦), out of grief (adv◦), in dejection (adv◦), sorrowfully (adv◦), ...etc.

📖 विषीदत् is not an adverb qualifying the verb अब्रवीत् । It is an ipp◦ adjective of the subject Arjuna. विषीदन् अर्जुनः इदम् अब्रवीत् ।

1.28 दृष्ट्वेमं स्वजनं कृष्ण युयुत्सुं समुपस्थितम् ।

dṛṣṭvemaṁ svajanaṁ kṛṣṇa yuyutsuṁ samupasthitam̦; (1.28)

(§1) दृष्ट्वा इमम् स्वजनम् कृष्ण युयुत्सुम् समुपस्थितम् । *arjunaḥ:* (r∘ 19/4) *uvāća. dṛṣṭvā* (r∘ 2/3) *imam̦* (r∘ 14/1) *svajanam̦* (r∘ 14/1) *kṛṣṇa yuyutsum̦* (r∘ 14/1) *samupasthitam̦* (r∘ 14/2)

(§2) *arjunaḥ:* (m∘ 1nom∘ sing∘ ←prop∘ *arjuna* 1.4); *uvāća* (1.25). *dṛṣṭvā* (1.2); ***imam̦*** (m∘ 2acc∘ sing∘ ←pron∘ *idam̦* 1.10); 🕮***svajanam̦*** (m∘ 2acc∘ sing∘ ←s-karm∘ *sva-jana* (kinsmen) स्वेषाम् जना: or aggregative noun स्वेषाम् जनानाम् समहार: । स्वस्य जन: । ←pron∘ ***sva*** (own) ←1∘√स्वन् (to sound) + m∘ ***jana*** (people) ←4∘√जन् (to be born, give birth); ***kṛṣṇa*** (m∘ 8voc∘ sing∘ ←prop∘ ***kṛṣṇa*** ←adj∘ ***kṛṣṇa*** ←6∘√कृष् (to cultivate); *yuyutsum̦* (m∘ 2acc∘ sing∘ ←des∘ adj∘ *yuyutsu* 1.1); 🕮***samupasthitam̦*** (m∘ 2acc∘ sing∘ ←ppp∘ adj∘ *samupasthita* (present) ←1∘सम्–उप्√स्था (to stay)

(1.28)

(§3) ***dṛṣṭvā*** **(having seen, seing);** ***imam̦*** **(adj1∘-obj∘ this);** ***svajanam̦*** **(obj∘ the mass of kinsmen);** ***kṛṣṇa*** **(O Kṛṣṇa!);** ***yuyutsum̦*** **(adj2∘-obj∘ anxious to fight)** ***samupasthitam̦*** **(adj3∘-obj∘ the one that has come; the one that is present)** (1.28)

(§4) kṛṣṇa dṛṣṭvā imam̦ samupasthitam̦ svajanam̦ yuyutsum̦;

(§5) O Kṛṣṇa! seeing this mass of kinsmen that is present (here, and) anxious to fight;[54] (1.28)

1.29 सीदन्ति मम गात्राणि मुखं च परिशुष्यति ।
वेपथुश्च शरीरे मे रोमहर्षश्च जायते ।।

sīdanti mama gātrāṇi mukhaṁ ća pariśuṣyati,
vepathuśća śarīre me romaharṣaśća jāyate; (1.29)

(§1) सीदन्ति मम गात्राणि मुखम् च परिशुष्यति । वेपथु: च शरीरे मे रोमहर्ष: च जायते । *sīdanti mama gātrāṇi* (r∘ 24/7) *mukham̦* (r∘ 14/1) *ća pariśuṣyati* (r∘ 25/6) *vepathuḥ:* (r∘ 17/1) *ća śarīre me romaharṣaḥ:* (r∘ 17/1) *ća jāyate*

(§2) 🕮*sīdanti* (3rd-per∘ plu∘ pres∘ वर्तमान्–लट् parasmai∘ ←6∘√सद् (to sit); *mama* (1.7); 🕮*gātrāṇi* (1nom∘ plu∘ ←n∘ *gātra* (limb) ←1∘√गम् (to go); 🕮*mukham̦* (1nom∘ sing∘ ←n∘ ***mukha*** (mouth) ←1∘√खन् (to dig); *ća* (and); *pariśuṣyati* (3rd-per∘ sing∘ pres∘ वर्तमान्–लट् parasmai∘ ←4∘परि√शुष् (to dry); 🕮*vepathuḥ:* (1nom∘ sing∘

---

[54] Elsewhere∘ *yuyutsum̦* → in a fighting spirit (adv∘), prompted by war (instrumental∘)...etc.

🕮 युयुत्सुम् is a Desiderative Accusative adjective → desirous, anxious, eager, wishing to fight.

←m◦ *vepathu* (shiver) ←1◦√वेप् (to quiver); *ća* (and); ***śarīre*** (7loc◦ sing◦ ←n◦ 📖***śarīra*** (body) ←9◦√शॄ (to smash); *me* (1.21); 📖*romaharṣaḥ:* (m◦ 1nom◦ sing◦ ←tatpu◦ ***romaharṣa*** (horripillation) रोमनि हर्षः ←n◦ ***roman*** (hair) ←2◦√रु (to cry) + m◦ *harṣa* 1.12); *ća* (and); ***jāyate*** (3rd-per◦ sing◦ pres◦ वर्तमान्-लट् ātmane◦ ←4◦√जन् (to be born, give birth) (1.29)

(§3) ***sīdanti*** **(they are failing);** ***mama*** **(my);** ***gātrāṇi*** **(subj1◦ limbs);** ***mukham*** **(subj2◦ mouth);** ***ća*** **(and);** ***pariśuṣyati*** **(it is drying up);** ***vepathuḥ:*** **(subj3◦ a shiver);** ***ća*** **(and);** ***śarīre*** **(in the body);** ***me*** **(my);** ***romaharṣaḥ:*** **(subj4◦ horripillation);** ***ća*** **(and);** ***jāyate*** **(it is occuring)** (1.29)

(§4) mama gātrāṇi sīdanti ća mukham pariśuṣyati ća vepathuḥ: me śarīre ća romaharṣaḥ: jāyate

(§5) My limbs are failing; and mouth is drying up;[55] and (there is) a shiver in my body; and horripillation is occuring;[56] (1.29)

1.30 गाण्डीवं स्रंसते हस्तात्त्वक्चैव परिदह्यते ।
न च शक्नोम्यवस्थातुं भ्रमतीव च मे मनः ।।

gāṇḍīvaṁ sraṁsate hastāttvakćaiva paridahyate,
na ća śaknomyavasthātuṁ bhramatīva ća me manaḥ:. (1.30)

(§1) गाण्डीवम् स्रंसते हस्तात् त्वक् च एव परिदह्यते । न च शक्नोमि अवस्थातुम् भ्रमति इव च मे मनः । *gāṇḍīvam* (r◦ 14/1) *sraṁsate hastāt* (r◦ 1/10) *tvak* (r◦ 10/1) *ća* (r◦ 3/1) *eva paridahyate na ća śaknomi* (r◦ 4/1) *avasthātum* (r◦ 14/1) *bhramati* (r◦ 1/5) *iva ća me manaḥ:* (r◦ 22/8)

(§2) *gāṇḍīvam* (1nom◦ sing◦ ←n◦ prop◦ *gāṇḍīva* bow); 📖*sraṁsate* (3rd-per◦ sing◦ pres◦ वर्तमान्-लट् ātmane◦ ←1◦√स्रंस् (to fall); *hastāt* (5abl◦ sing◦ ←m◦ 📖***hasta*** (hand) ←1◦√हस् (to laugh); *tvak* (1nom◦ sing◦ *tvak* or *tvag* ←f◦ *tvać* (skin) ←6◦√त्वच् (to cover); *ća* (and); *eva* (1.1); 📖*paridahyate* (3rd-per◦ pres◦ वर्तमान्-लट् ātmane◦ ←1◦परि√दह् (to burn); ***na*** (negative ind◦ ←4◦√नह् (to bind); *ća* (and); *śaknomi* (1st-per◦ sing◦ pres◦

---

[55] Elsewhere◦ *pariśuṣyati* → is parched, has dried, is parched up, is dried up ...etc. (perfect◦ or ppp◦)
📖 परिशुष्यति is not a perfect tense or ppp◦. It is a present, simple or continuous वर्तमान्-लट् tense.

[56] Elsewhere◦ (1) *vepathuśća śarīre me* → my body is trembling, my body quivers, my whole body quivers, my body trembles, my body shakes, a tremor comes on my body ...etc. and (2) *romaharṣaśća jāyate* → hair stands on end, my hairs stand, my hair is standing ...etc.
📖 In वेपथुश्च शरीरे मे रोमहर्षश्च जायते, body (शरीरं) and hair (रोम) are not the two subjects performing the verb जायते । The nouns वेपथुः (shiver) and रोमहर्षः (horripillation) are the subjects, performing the two separate verbs अस्ति and जायते. NOTE : शरीरे (in the body) is Locative 7th case.

वर्तमान्-लट् parasmai◦ ←4◦√शक् (to be able); *avasthātum* (inf◦ ind◦ ←1◦अव√स्था (to stay); *bhramati* (*bhramati* or *bhramyati* ←3rd-per◦ sing◦ pres◦ वर्तमान्-लट् parasmai◦ ←4◦√भ्रम् (to be deluded); ***iva*** (as if) (mode indicating ind◦ ←1◦√इ (to enter, come, go); *ća* (and); *me* (1.21); ***manaḥ:*** (1nom◦ sing◦ ←n◦ ***manas*** (mind) ←4◦√मन् (to think) (1.30)

(§3) ***gāṇḍīvam*** (subj1◦ Gāṇḍīva bow); ***sraṁsate*** (it is slipping); ***hastāt*** (from hand); ***tvak*** (sub2◦ the skin); ***ća*** (and); ***eva*** (also); ***paridahyate*** (is burning); ***na*** (not); ***ća*** (and); ***śaknomi*** (subj3◦ I am able); ***avasthātum*** (for standing, to stand); ***bhramati*** (it is whirling, reeling, confusing); ***iva*** (as if); ***ća*** (and); ***me*** (my); ***manaḥ:*** (subj4◦ mind) (1.30)

(§4) gāṇḍīvam sraṁsate hastāt ća tvak eva paridahyate ća na śaknomi avasthātum ća me manaḥ: bhramati iva

(§5) Gāṇḍīva bow is slipping from hand; and the skin is also burning; and I am not able to stand; and my mind is as if whirling; (1.30)

1.31 निमित्तानि च पश्यामि विपरीतानि केशव ।
न च श्रेयोऽनुपश्यामि हत्वा स्वजनमाहवे ।।

nimittāni ća paśyāmi viparītāni keśava,
na ća śreyo'nupaśyāmi hatvā svajanamāhave. (1.31)

(§1) निमित्तानि च पश्यामि विपरीतानि केशव । न च श्रेयः अनुपश्यामि हत्वा स्वजनम् आहवे । *nimittāni ća paśyāmi viparītāni keśava na ća śreyaḥ:* (r◦ 15/1) *anupaśyāmi hatvā svajanam* (r◦ 8/17) *āhave*

(§2) *nimittāni* (2acc◦ plu◦ ←n◦ ***nimitta*** (omen) ←4◦नि√मिद् (to be soft); *ća* (and); ***paśyāmi*** (1st-per◦ sing◦ pres◦ वर्तमान्-लट् parasmai◦ ←1◦√दृश् (to see); *viparītāni* (n◦ 2acc◦ plu◦ ←ppp◦ adj◦ ***viparīta*** (adverse) ←1◦वि-परि√इ (to enter, come, go); ***keśava*** (m◦ 8voc◦ sing◦ ←bahuvrī◦ prop◦ ***keśava*** कः ईशः वा ←m◦ *kaḥ:* (is he) 8.2 + m◦ *īśa* (a god) 1.15 + ind◦ *vā* (or what?) 1.32); *na* (1.30); *ća* (and); ***śreyaḥ:*** (n◦ 2acc◦ sing◦ ←comparative adj◦ ***śreyas*** (better) ←2◦√ई (to go); *anupaśyāmi* (1st-per◦ sing◦ pres◦ वर्तमान्-लट् parasmai◦ ←1◦अनु√दृश् ↑); ***hatvā*** (ipp◦ ind◦ ←2◦√हन् (to hurt); *svajanam* (1.28); *āhave* (7loc◦ sing◦ ←m◦ *āhava* (battle) ←1◦आ√ह्वे (to call) (1.31)

(§3) ***nimittāni*** (obj1◦ omens, signs); ***ća*** (and); ***paśyāmi*** (I see); ***viparītāni*** (adj◦-obj1◦ adverse, bad); ***keśava*** (O Keśava! O Śrī Kṛṣṇa!); ***na*** (not, do not); ***ća*** (and, moreover); ***śreyaḥ:*** (obj2◦ a better, a better gain); ***anupaśyāmi*** (I anticipate); ***hatvā*** (having slayed); ***svajanam*** (obj3◦ the kinsmen); ***āhave*** (in the battle) (1.31)

(§4) ća keśava paśyāmi viparītāni nimittāni ća na anupaśyāmi śreyaḥ: hatvā svajanam āhave

(§5) And, O Śrī Kṛṣṇa! I see adverse omens; moreover, I do not anticipate a better[57] gain having slayed[58] the kinsmen in the battle. (1.31)

1.32 न काङ्क्षे विजयं कृष्ण न च राज्यं सुखानि च ।
किं नो राज्येन गोविन्द किं भोगैर्जीवितेन वा ।।

na kāṅkṣe vijayaṁ kṛṣṇa na ća rājyaṁ sukhāni ća
kiṁ no rājyena govinda kiṁ bhogairjīvitena vā. (1.32)

(§1) न काङ्क्षे विजयम् कृष्ण न च राज्यम् सुखानि च । किम् नः राज्येन गोविन्द किम् भोगैः जीवितेन वा । *na kāṅkṣe vijayam* (r◦ 14/1) *kṛṣṇa na ća rājyam* (r◦ 14/1) *sukhāni ća kim* (r◦ 14/1) *naḥ:* (r◦ 15/11) *rājyena govinda kim* (r◦ 14/1) *bhogaiḥ:* (r◦ 16/11) *jīvitena vā*

(§2) *na* (1.30); *kāṅkṣe* (1st-per◦ sing◦ pres◦ वर्तमान्-लट् ātmane◦ ←1◦√काङ्क्ष् (to desire); *vijayam* (2acc◦ sing◦ ←m◦ ***vijaya*** (victory) ←1◦वि√जि (to win); *kṛṣṇa* (1.28); *na* (1.30); *ća* (and); ***rājyam*** (2acc◦ sing◦ ←n◦ ***rājya*** (kingdom) ←1◦√राज् (to rule); ***sukhāni*** (2acc◦ sing◦ ←n◦ or adj◦ ***sukha*** (pleasure) ←10◦√सुख् (to please); *ća* (and); *kim* (1.1); ***naḥ:*** (4dat◦ plu◦ ←pron◦ *asmad* 1.7); *rājyena* (3inst◦ sing◦ ←n◦ *rājya* ↑); *govinda* (m◦ 8voc◦ sing◦ ←bahuvrī◦ ***govinda,*** गाम् विन्दति यः ←f◦ ***go*** (cow) ←5◦√गै (to sing) + adj◦ *vindati* (secures) 4.38↓); ***kim*** (ind◦ ←pron◦ *kim* (what?) 1.1); *bhogaiḥ:* (3inst◦ plu◦ ←m◦ *bhoga* (pleasure) ←7◦√भुज् (to enjoy, experience); *jīvitena* (n◦ 3inst◦ sing◦ ←ppp◦ adj◦ *jīvita* (alive) ←1◦√जीव् (to live, stay alive); ***vā*** (ind◦ ←2◦√वा (to move) (1.32)

(§3) ***na*** **(neither);** ***kāṅkṣe*** **(I do wish);** ***vijayam*** **(obj1◦ a victory);** ***kṛṣṇa*** **(O Śrī Kṛṣṇa!);** ***na*** **(not);** ***ća*** **(and);** ***rājyam*** **(obj2◦ a kingdom);** ***sukhāni*** **(obj3◦ the pleasures);** ***ća*** **(and);** ***kim*** **(what?);** ***naḥ:*** **(for us, to us);** ***rājyena*** **(with kingdom);** ***govinda*** **(O Govinda! O Śrī Kṛṣṇa!);** ***kim*** **(what is?);** ***bhogaiḥ:*** **(with pleasures);** ***jīvitena*** **(with being alive);** ***vā*** **(or)** (1.32)

(§4) ća kṛṣṇa na kāṅkṣe vijayam na rājyam ća sukhāni govinda kim rājyena vā kim jīvitena bhogaiḥ: naḥ:

---

[57] Elsewhere◦ *śreyaḥ:* → good.

श्रेयस् is a comparative expression (comparison between two attributes) - better.

[58] Elsewhere◦ *hatvā* → from killing, from the slaughter, from slaying, by slaying, out of the killing, in killing, in destroying ...etc.

हत्वा is not an Ablative or Locative or any other case of gerund 'killing, slaying or destroying'. It is a क्त्वा ind◦ participle = having killed, slayed etc.

(§5) And, O Śrī Kṛṣṇa! neither do I wish[59] a victory not a kingdom and the pleasures; O Śrī Kṛṣṇa! what is kingdom or what is being alive with pleasures, for us? (1.32)

1.33 येषामर्थे काङ्क्षितं नो राज्यं भोगाः सुखानि च ।
त इमेऽवस्थिता युद्धे प्राणांस्त्यक्त्वा धनानि च ।।

yeṣāmarthe kāṅkṣitaṁ no rājyaṁ bhogāḥ: sukhāni ća,
ta ime'vasthitā yuddhe prāṇānstyaktvā dhanāni ća. (1.33)

(§1) येषाम् अर्थे काङ्क्षितम् नः राज्यम् भोगाः सुखानि च । ते इमे अवस्थिताः युद्धे प्राणान् त्यक्त्वा धनानि च । *yeṣām* (r◦ 25/3, 8/16) *arthe kāṅkṣitam* (r◦ 14/1) *naḥ:* (r◦ 15/11) *rājyam* (r◦ 14/1) *bhogāḥ:* (r◦ 22/7) *sukhāni ća te* (r◦ 5/2) *ime* (r◦ 6/1) *avasthitaḥ:* (r◦ 20/14) *yuddhe prāṇān* (r◦ 13/7) tyaktvā dhanāni ća

(§2) ***yeṣām*** (m◦ n◦ 6pos◦ plu◦ ←pron◦ *yad* 1.7); *arthe* (1.9); 📖*kāṅkṣitam* (1nom◦ sing◦ ←desi◦ ppp◦ adj◦ *kāṅkṣita* (desired) ←1◦√काङ्क्ष् (to desire); ***naḥ:*** (6pos plu◦ ←pron◦ *asmad* (we) 1.7); *rājyam* (2acc◦ 1.32); ***bhogāḥ:*** (1nom◦ plu◦ ←m◦ *bhoga* 1.32); *sukhāni* (2acc◦ 1.32); *ća* (and); ***te*** (m◦ 1nom◦ plu◦ ←pron◦ *tad* (that) 1.2); ***ime*** (m◦ 1nom◦ plu◦ ←pron◦ *idam* (this) 1.10); *avasthitāḥ:* (1.11); *yuddhe* (1.23); ***prāṇān*** (2acc◦ plu◦ ←m◦ ***prāṇa*** (life) ←4◦प्र√अन् (to move); 📖***tyaktvā*** (ipp◦ ind◦ ←1◦√त्यज् (to renounce); *dhanāni* (2acc◦ plu◦ ←n◦ *dhana* (wealth) 1.15); *ća* (and) (1.33)

(§3) ***yeṣām*** **(of whose);** ***arthe*** **(in sake, for sake);** ***kāṅkṣitam*** **(adj◦-obj1-3◦ the one that is desired - collective);** ***naḥ:*** **(of us);** ***rājyam*** **(obj1◦ the kingdom);** ***bhogāḥ:*** **(obj2◦ enjoyments);** ***sukhāni*** **(obj3◦ pleasures);** ***ća*** **(and);** ***te*** **(adj1◦-subj◦ they, those);** ***ime*** **(subj◦ these, they);** ***avasthitāḥ:*** **(adj2◦-subj◦ arrayed);** ***yuddhe*** **(in battle);** ***prāṇān*** **(obj4◦ lives);** ***tyaktvā*** **(having abandoned, sacrificed);** ***dhanāni*** **(obj5◦ riches);** ***ća*** **(and)** (1.33)

(§4) te, yeṣām arthe rājyam bhogāḥ: ća sukhāni kāṅkṣitam naḥ: ime avasthitaḥ: yuddhe tyaktvā prāṇān ća dhanāni

(§5) They, of whose sake the -kingdom, enjoyments and pleasures- is desired of us,[60] they,

---

[59] Elsewhere◦ *na kāṅkṣe* → nor can I desire ...etc.

📖 'Nor can I' would mean, I wish to desire the victory, kingdom and pleasures... but I am not able to .... Like न शक्नोमि अवस्थातुम् I wish to stand, but I can not stand.

[60] Elsewhere◦ *kāṅkṣitam naḥ:* → we desire, we may have desire, we seek, we covet ...etc.

📖 काङ्क्षितम् is not a verb of Active voice. Therefore, in the passive construction in Sanskrit (even though in English it differs), ppp◦ काङ्क्षितम्, the adj◦ of the obj◦1-3 is in Nominative case → desired of us, desired by us (passive).

arrayed[61] in battle, having abandoned (their) lives and riches; (1.33)

1.34 आचार्याः पितरः पुत्रास्तथैव च पितामहाः ।
मातुलाः श्वशुराः पौत्राः श्यालाः सम्बन्धिनस्तथा ।।

ā́ćāryāḥ: pitaraḥ: putrāstathaiva ća pitāmahāḥ:,
mātulāḥ: śvaśurāḥ: pautrāḥ: śyālāḥ: sambandhinstathā; (1.34)

(§1) आचार्याः पितरः पुत्राः तथा एव च पितामहाः । मातुलाः श्वशुराः पौत्राः श्यालाः सम्बन्धिनः तथा । *ā́ćāryāḥ:* (r∘ 22/3) *pitaraḥ:* (r∘ 22/3) *pautrāḥ:* (r∘ 18/1) *tathā* (r∘ 3/3) *eva ća pitāmahāḥ:* (r∘ 22/8) *mātulāḥ:* (r∘ 22/5) *śvaśurāḥ:* (r∘ 22/3) *pautrāḥ:* (r∘ 22/5) *śyālāḥ:* (r∘ 22/7) *sambandhinaḥ:* (r∘ 18/1) *tathā*

(§2) 🕮*ā́ćāryāḥ:* (1nom∘ plu∘ ←m∘ *ā́ćārya* (tutor) 1.2); ***pitaraḥ:*** (1nom∘ plu∘ ←m∘ *pitṛ* (fatherly person) 1.12); ***putrāḥ:*** (1nom∘ plu∘ ←m∘ *putra* (son) 1.3); *tathā* (1.8); *eva* (1.1); *ća* (and); 🕮*pitāmahāḥ:* (1nom∘ plu∘ ←m∘ *pitāmaha* (elderly person) 1.12); *mātulāḥ:* (1nom∘ plu∘ ←m∘ *mātula* (uncle) 1.26); *śvaśurāḥ:* (1nom∘ plu∘ ←m∘ *śvaśura* (father-in-law) 1.26); *pautrāḥ:* (1nom∘ plu∘ ←m∘ *pautra* (young person) 1.26); *śyālāḥ:* (1nom∘ plu∘ ←m∘ *śyala* (brother-in-law) ←1∘√श्यै (to go, be conjested); 🕮*sambandhinaḥ:* (1nom∘ plu∘ ←m∘ *sambandhin* (kinsman) ←9∘सम्√बन्ध् (to tie); *tathā* (1.8) (1.34)

(§3) *ā́ćāryāḥ:* (subj1∘ tutors, gurus); *pitaraḥ:* (subj2∘ fatherly people); *putrāḥ:* (subj3∘ sons, youthful people); *tathā eva* (also); *ća* (and); *pitāmahāḥ:* (subj4∘ grandfathers, elderly people); *mātulāḥ:* (subj5∘ maternal uncles); *śvaśurāḥ:* (subj6∘ fathers in law); *pautrāḥ:* (subj7∘ grandsons, young people); *śyālāḥ:* (subj8∘ brothers in law); *sambandhinaḥ:* (subj9∘ kinsmen); *tathā* (as well as) (1.34)

(§4) ā́ćāryāḥ: pitaraḥ: putrāḥ: tathā ća eva pitāmahāḥ: mātulāḥ: śvaśurāḥ: śyālāḥ: sambandhinaḥ: tathā pautrāḥ:

(§5) Tutors, fatherly people, youthful people and also elderly people, uncles, father-in-laws, brothers-in-law, kinsmen as well as young people; (1.34)

1.35 एतान्न हन्तुमिच्छामि घ्नतोऽपि मधुसूदन ।
अपि त्रैलोक्यराज्यस्य हेतोः किं नु महीकृते ।।

etānna hantumićchāmi ghnato'pi madhusūdana,
api trailokyarājyasya hetoḥ: kiṁ nu mahīkṛte. (1.35)

---

[61] Elsewhere∘ *avasthitāḥ:* → they stand, they are now arrayed, they are standing, are here standing ...etc.
🕮 अवस्थित is not a present tense or any other verb. It is a ppp∘ adjective of pronoun ते (*te*)

(§1) एतान् न हन्तुम् इच्छामि घ्नतः अपि मधुसूदन । अपि त्रैलोक्यराज्यस्य हेतोः किम् नु महीकृते । *etān* (r◦ 1/11) *na hantum* (r◦ 8/18) *iććhāmi ghnataḥ:* (r◦ 15/1) *api madhusūdana* (r◦ 23/1) *api trailokyarājyasya hetoḥ:* (r◦ 22/1) *kiṃ* (r◦ 14/1) *nu mahīkṛte*

(§2) *etān* (1.25); *na* (1.30); **hantum** (inf◦ ind◦ ←2◦√हन् (to hurt); ***iććhāmi*** (1st-per◦ sing◦ pres◦ वर्तमान्-लट् parasmai◦ ←6◦√इषु (to desire); *ghnataḥ:* (m◦ 2acc◦ plu◦ ←śatṛ◦ pres◦ participle◦ adj◦ *ghnaṭ* (being killed) ←adj◦ ***ghna*** √हन् + क (killer) ←2◦√हन् (to hurt); *api* (1.26); **madhusūdana** (m◦ 8voc◦ sing◦ ←bahuvrī◦ ***madhu-sūdana,*** मधुनामानं दैत्यं सूदितः येन ←1◦मधु√सूद् (to thrash); *api* (1.26); *trailokyarājyasya* (n◦ 6pos◦ sing◦ ←tatpu◦ *trai-lokya-rājya,* त्रैलोक्यस्य राज्यम् ←dvigu◦ n◦ *trailokya* (the three worlds) ←1◦तृ√लोक् (to see, seek) + n◦ *rājya* 1.32); *hetoḥ:* (6pos sing◦ ←m◦ ***hetu*** (purpose) ←5◦√हि (to impel); *kiṃ* (1.1); **nu** (ind◦ ←6◦√नुद् (to push); *mahīkṛte* (7loc◦ sing◦ ←m◦ *mahī-kṛta* ←f◦ *mahī* (earth) 1.21 + ppp◦ adj◦ **kṛta** (for the sake of) ←8◦√कृ (to do) (1.35)

(§3) ***etān*** **(adj◦-obj◦ these, to these people);** ***na*** **(not);** ***hantuṃ*** **(for killing, to kill);** ***iććhāmi*** **(I do wish);** ***ghnataḥ:*** **(obj◦ being killed);** ***api*** **(also);** ***madhusūdana*** **(O Madhusūdana! O Śrī Kṛṣṇa!);** ***api*** **(even);** ***trailokyarājyasya hetoḥ:*** **(for the reason of the sovereignty of the three worlds);** ***kiṃ*** **(what? how?);** ***nu*** **(then, now);** ***mahīkṛte*** **(for the sake of the earth)** (1.35)

(§4) madhusūdana ghnataḥ: api na iććhāmi hantuṃ etān api trailokyarājyasya hetoḥ: kiṃ nu mahīkṛte

(§5) O Śrī Kṛṣṇa! being killed[62] (by them), to them also I do not wish kill, even for the purpose of the sovereignty of the three worlds; how then[63] (would I) for the sake of the earth? (1.35)

1.36 निहत्य धार्तराष्ट्रान्नः का प्रीतिः स्याज्जनार्दन ।
पापमेवाश्रयेदस्मान्हत्वैतानाततायिनः ॥

nihatya dhārtarāṣṭrānnaḥ: kā prītiḥ: syājjanārdana,
pāpamevāśrayedasmānhatvaitānātatāyinaḥ:. (1.36)

---

[62] Elsewhere◦ *ghnataḥ:* → they were to kill me (conditional◦), they might kill me (potential), I were to be killed by them (potential◦), though they kill me (conditional), even if they should kill me (potential◦) ... etc.

घ्नतः is not a verb. It is not a ppp◦ It is not singular. It is a plural (of घ्नत्) . It is a Present Tense Active Participle adjective of object 'me.' It is in Accusative case → to me, being killed by them. NOTE : Its purpose is to confirm that Arjuna was very sure that if he does not fight or if he turns his back, the Kauravas will surely kill the Pāṇḍavas; as they had tried many times before (see the Background of the Gita).

[63] Elsewhere◦ *kiṃ nu* → much less.

(§1) निहत्य धार्तराष्ट्रान् नः का प्रीतिः स्यात् जनार्दन । पापम् एव आश्रयेत् अस्मान् हत्वा एतान् आततायिनः । *nihatya dhārtarāṣṭrān* (r◦ 1/11) *naḥ:* (r◦ 22/1) *kā* *prītiḥ:* (r◦ 22/7) *syāt* (r◦ 11/2) *janārdana pāpam* (r◦ 8/22) *eva* (r◦ 1/2) *āśrayet* (r◦ 8/2) *asmān* (r◦ 13/21) *hatvā* (r◦ 3/3) *etān* (r◦ 8/12) *ātatāyinaḥ:* (r◦ 22/8)

(§2) *nihatya* (past-participle lyp◦ ind◦ ←2◦नि√हन् (to hurt); *dhārtarāṣṭrān* (1.20); *naḥ:* (1.32 or 1.33); ***kā*** (f◦ 1nom◦ sing◦ ←pron◦ *kim* (what?) 1.1); *prītiḥ:* (1nom◦ sing◦ ←f◦ ***prīti*** (joy) ←9◦√प्री (to please); ***syāt*** (3rd-per◦ sing◦ potential◦ विधि◦ parasmai◦ ←2◦√अस् (to be); ***janārdana*** (m◦ 8voc◦ sing◦ ←bahuvrī◦ *janārdana*, दुष्टजनानाम् अर्दनः यः सः ←m◦ *jana* (people, bad people) 1.28 + n◦ *ardana* (killing) ←10√अर्द् (to afflict); ***pāpam*** (1nom◦ sing◦ ←n◦ *pāpa* (sin) ←1◦√पा (to drink); *eva* (1.1); *āśrayet* (3rd-per◦ sing◦ potential◦ विधि◦ -ubhay◦ ←1◦आ√श्रि (to attain); *asmān* (2acc◦ plu◦ ←pron◦ *asmad* 1.7); *hatvā* (1.31); *etān* (1.22); *ātatāyinaḥ:* (2acc◦ plu◦ ←m◦ *ātatāyin* (offender) ←1◦√अय् (to go) (1.36)

(§3) ***nihatya*** **(having killed);** ***dhārtarāṣṭrān*** **(obj1◦ the sons of Dhṛtarāṣṭra, the Kauravas);** ***naḥ:*** **(for us, to us);** ***kā*** **(what?);** ***prītiḥ:*** **(sub1◦ joy);** ***syāt*** **(would be);** ***janārdana*** **(O Janārdana! O Śrī Kṛṣṇa!);** ***pāpam*** **(subj2◦ sin);** ***eva*** **(only);** ***āśrayet*** **(it may cling, stick);** ***asmān*** **(obj2◦ to us);** ***hatvā*** **(having killed);** ***etān*** **(adj◦-obj3◦ these);** ***ātatāyinaḥ:*** **(obj3◦ felons, offenders, desperados)** (1.36)

(§4) janārdana kā syāt prītiḥ: naḥ: nihatya dhārtarāṣṭrān eva pāpam āśrayet asmān hatvā etān ātatāyinaḥ:

(§5) O Śrī Kṛṣṇa! what would be joy for us having killed[64] the Kauravas? Only sin may cling us, having killed[65] these offenders. (1.36)

1.37 तस्मान्नार्हा वयं हन्तुं धार्तराष्ट्रान्स्वबान्धवान् ।
स्वजनं हि कथं हत्वा सुखिनः स्याम माधव ।।

tasmānnārhā vayaṁ hantuṁ dhārtarāṣṭrānsvabāndhavān,
svajanaṁ hi kathaṁ hatvā sukhinaḥ: syāma mādhava. (1.37)

(§1) तस्मात् न अर्हाः वयम् हन्तुम् धार्तराष्ट्रान् स्वबान्धवान् । स्वजनम् हि कथम् हत्वा सुखिनः स्याम माधव । *tasmāt* (r◦ 12/1) *na* (r◦ 1/1) *arhāḥ:* (r◦ 20/17) *vayam* (r◦ 14/1) *hantum* (r◦ 14/1) *dhārtarāṣṭrān* (r◦ 13/20)

---

[64] Elsewhere◦ *nihatya* → by slaying, by doing away, from killing, we had then better, ...etc.

निहत्य is not an Instrumental case. It is a lyp◦ participle.

[65] Elsewhere◦ *hatvā* → if we kill (conditional◦), even if they should kill (cond◦), by killing (inst◦), ...etc.

हत्वा is not लृङ् conditional (विधि) mood. It is a क्त्वा participle gerund (having done). See the footnote in 1.37

svabāndhavān (r◦ 23/1) *svajanam* (r◦ 14/1) *hi katham* (r◦ 14/1) *hatvā sukhinaḥ:* (r◦ 22/7) syāma mādhava

(§2) ***tasmāt*** (ind◦ or m◦ 5abl◦ sing◦ (therefore) ←pron◦ *tad* 1.2); *na* (1.30); *arhāḥ:* (m◦ 1nom◦ plu◦ ←adj◦ 📖*arha* (suitable) ←1◦√अर्ह् (to deserve); ***vayam*** (1nom◦ plu◦ ←pron◦ *asmad* 1.7); *hantum* (1.35); *dhārtarāṣṭrān* (1.20); *svabāndhavān* (m◦ 2acc◦ plu◦ ←taddhita◦ *sva-bāndhava*, स्वस्य बान्धवः ←adj◦ *sva* (own) 1.28 + *taddhita*◦ *bāndhava* (brother) ← m◦ *bandhu* 1.27); *svajanam* (2 acc◦ our people 1.28); *hi* (1.11); 📖***katham*** (ind◦ (how?) ←pron◦ *kim* 1.1); *hatvā* (1.31); 📖**sukhinaḥ:** (m◦ 1nom◦ plu◦ ←adj◦ *sukhin* (happy) ←10◦√सुख् (to please); ***syāma*** (1st-per◦ plu◦ potential◦ विधि◦ parasmai◦ ←2◦√अस् (to be); *mādhava* (8voc◦ sing◦ ←m◦ *mādhava* 1.14) (1.37)

(§3) ***tasmāt*** **(therefore);** ***na*** **(not);** ***arhāḥ:*** **(adj◦-subj1◦ suitable, justified, proper, qualified);** ***vayam*** **(subj1◦ we, we are);** ***hantum*** **(for killing, to kill);** ***dhārtarāṣṭrān*** **(obj1◦ the sons of Dhṛtarāṣṭra, the Kauravas;);** ***svabāndhavān*** **(adj◦-obj1. our brothers);** ***svajanam*** **(obj2◦ our own people);** ***hi*** **(because);** ***katham*** **(how? why?);** ***hatvā*** **(having killed);** ***sukhinaḥ:*** **(adj◦-subj2◦ happy);** ***syāma*** **(subj2◦ we would be);** ***mādhava*** **(O Mādhava!; O Kṛṣṇa!)** (1.37)

(§4) tasmāt vayam na arhāḥ: hantum svabāndhavān dhārtarāṣṭrān hi mādhava katham syāma sukhinaḥ: hatvā svajanam

(§5) Therefore,[66] we are[67] not suitable to kill our brothers, the Kauravas; because,[68] O Kṛṣṇa! how would we be[69] happy having killed[70] our own people? (1.37)

---

[66] See the footnote for *hi* (हि) in verse 2.15

[67] Elsewhere◦ *arhaḥ vayam* → it is not proper for us to kill, we should not kill, it is not right that we slay, we are not justified in killing ...etc.

📖 अर्ह is an adjective, not a verb or gerund. 'it is not proper, it is not right ...etc.' are verbs. 'should not kill, we slay ...etc.' are also verbs, they are not adjectives; 'killing' is a gerund. वयं is Nominative case, 'for us' is Dative or Possessive case.

[68] See footnote in 2.15, हि and तस्मात्

[69] Elsewhere◦ *katham syāma* → how can.

[70] Elsewhere◦ *hatvā* → by killing (inst◦), in killing (locative◦), if we kill (cond◦) ...etc.

📖 हत्वा is not Instruental case, Locative case or a conditional clause. it is a Past Participle Gerund, and thus, it should mean a subordinate action having done, *hatvā* → having killed, the main clause being सुखिनः स्याम । See footnote in 1.36

1.38 यद्यप्येते न पश्यन्ति लोभोपहतचेतसः ।
कुलक्षयकृतं दोषं मित्रद्रोहे च पातकम् ।।

yadyapyete na paśyanti lobhopahatacetasaḥ:,
kulakṣayakṛtaṁ doṣaṁ mitradrohe ca pātakam̧. (1.38)

(§1) यद्यपि एते न पश्यन्ति लोभोपहतचेतसः । कुलक्षयकृतम् दोषम् मित्रद्रोहे च पातकम् । *yadyapi* (r◦ 4/4) *ete na paśyanti lobhopahatacetasaḥ:* (r◦ 22/8) *kulakṣayakṛtam̧* (r◦ 14/1) *doṣam̧* (r◦ 14/1) *mitradrohe ca pātakam̧* (r◦ 14/2)

(§2) ***yadi̧*** (ind◦ (if) ←pron◦ *yad* 1.7); *api* (1.26); *ete* (1.23); *na* (1.30); ***paśyanti*** (3rd-per◦ plu◦ pres◦ वर्तमान्-लट् parasmai◦ ←1◦√दृश् (to see); *lobhopahatacetasaḥ:* (m◦ 1nom◦ plu◦ ←bahuvrī◦ *lobhopahata-ćetaṣ* लोभेन उपहतं चेत: यस्य स: ←m◦ ***lobha*** (greed) ←4◦√लुभ् c(to covet) + ppp◦ adj◦ ***upahata*** (overpowered) ←2◦उप√हन् (to hurt) + n◦ ***ćetaṣ*** (heart) ←1◦√चित् (to percceive); ***kulakṣayakṛtam̧*** (m◦ 2acc◦ sing◦ ←ppp◦ adj◦ *kula-kṣaya-kṛta* ←n◦ ***kula*** (family) ←1◦√कुल् (to related) + m◦ ***kṣaya*** (destruction) ←6◦√क्षि (to stay) + ppp◦ adj◦ *kṛta* 1.35); ***doṣam̧*** (2acc◦ sing◦ ←m◦ ***doṣa*** (the evil) ←4◦√दुष् (to spoil); *mitradrohe* (m◦ 7loc◦ sing◦ ←tatpu◦ *mitra-droha,* मित्रेण मित्रस्य वा द्रोहः ←m◦ ***mitra*** (friend) ←4◦√मिद् (to be soft) + m◦ ***droha*** (trechery) ←4◦√द्रुह् (to be hostile); *ća* (and); *pātakam̧* (2acc◦ sing◦ ←n◦ *pātaka* (sin) ←1◦√पत् (to fall) (1.38)

(§3) ***yadi̧ api*** **(even though);** ***ete*** **(subj◦ these; these people);** ***na*** **(do not);** ***paśyanti*** **(see, perceive, understand);** ***lobhopahatacetasaḥ:*** **(adj◦-subj◦ those whose hearts are overpowered with greed);** ***kulakṣayakṛtam̧*** **(adj◦-obj◦ the one that is caused by the destruction of the family);** ***doṣam̧*** **(obj1◦ the evil);** ***mitradrohe*** **(in the treachery to a friend or friends);** ***ća*** **(and);** ***pātakam̧*** **(obj2◦ the sin)** (1.38)

(§4) yadi̧ api ete lobhopahatacetasaḥ: na paśyanti doṣam̧ kulakṣayakṛtam̧ ća pātakam̧ mitradrohe

(§5) Even though these people, whose hearts are overpowered with greed, do not see the evil that is caused by the destruction of the family[71] and the sin (that is) in the treachery to friends; (1.38)

1.39 कथं न ज्ञेयमस्माभिः पापादस्मान्निवर्तितुम् ।
कुलक्षयकृतं दोषं प्रपश्यद्भिर्जनार्दन ।।

---

[71] Elsewhere◦ *kulakṣayakṛtam̧ doṣam* → in killing ones's family, if we kill our, by killing our..., in destroying the family, in the extension of a fimily ...etc.

kulakṣayakṛtam̧ is not Instrumental case, conditional mood or a gerund. It is a tatpu◦ ppp◦ adj◦ of the object *doṣa*. Therefore, कुलक्षयकृत → the doṣa that is caused by the destruction of the family or families. Same is true for verse 1.39 also.

kathaṁ na jñeyamasmābhiḥ: pāpādasmānnivartitum,
kulakṣayakṛtaṁ doṣaṁ prapaśyadbhirjanārdana. (1.39)

(§1) कथम् न ज्ञेयम् अस्माभिः पापात् अमात् निवर्तितुम् । कुलक्षयकृतम् दोषम् प्रपश्यद्भिः जनार्दन । *katham* (r◦ 14/1) *na jñeyam* (r◦ 8/16) *asmābhiḥ:* (r◦ 22/3) *pāpāt* (r◦ 8/2) *asmāt* (r◦ 12/1) *nivartitum* (r◦ 14/2) *kulakṣayakṛtam* (r◦ 14/1) *doṣam* (r◦ 14/1) *prapaśyadbhiḥ:* (r◦ 16/6) *janārdana*

(§2) *katham* (1.37); *na* (1.30); 📖***jñeyam*** (m◦ 1nom◦ sing◦ ←pot◦ adj◦ ***jñeya*** (should be known) ←9◦√ज्ञा (to know); *asmābhiḥ:* (3inst◦ plu◦ ←pron◦ *asmad* 1.7); *pāpāt* (5abl◦ sing◦ ←n◦ *pāpa* (sin) 1.36); *asmāt* (5abl◦ sing◦ ←pron◦ *idam* 1.10); 📖*nivartitum* (inf◦ ind◦ ←4◦नि√वृत् (to choose); *kulakṣayakṛtam* (m◦ 2acc◦ 1.38); *doṣam* (1.38); *prapaśyadbhiḥ:* (m◦ 3inst◦ plu◦ ←śatṛ◦ adj◦ *prapaśyat* (knower) ←1◦प्र√दृश् (to see); *janārdana* (1.36) (1.39)

(§3) ***katham*** **(how?);** ***na*** **(not);** ***jñeyam*** **(adj◦-obj1◦ it should be understood, known);** ***asmābhiḥ:*** **(subj◦ by us);** ***pāpāt*** **(from the sin);** ***asmāt*** **(from this);** ***nivartitum*** **(for turning away, to refrain, to desist from);** ***kulakṣayakṛtam*** **(adj◦-obj2◦ the one that is caused by the destruction of the family);** ***doṣam*** **(obj2◦ the evil, the sin);** ***prapaśyadbhiḥ:*** **(adj◦-subj◦ by the discerning ones; by the knowers of)** ***janārdana*** (O Janārdana!; O Kṛṣṇa!) (1.39)

(§4) janārdana! katham na jñeyam asmābhiḥ:, prapaśyadbhiḥ: kulakṣayakṛtam doṣam, nivartitum asmāt pāpāt

(§5) O Kṛṣṇa! how should it not be known by us,[72] the knowers of[73] the sin that is caused by the

---

[72] Elsewhere◦ *katham na jñeyam asmābhiḥ:*→ why should we not have wisdom, why should we engage, why should not we learn, why should we not learn, why should we not know enough, how can we remain unaware, why should we not turn away, why then should we not desist, should not we learn ...etc. (active voice constructions)

📖 कथं न ज्ञेयम् अस्माभिः is a not an active voice. It is a passive Sanskrit construction, therefore, the use of the Instrumental case for the subject. अस्माभिः (by us) and its adjective दोषं-प्रपश्यद्भिः (by those who can see the evil) प्रयोगे कर्मवाच्यस्य तृतीया स्यात्तु कर्तरि । *asmābhiḥ* = 'by us' not 'we.' Thus, Instrumental case for the subj◦ and Nominative case for the object ज्ञेयम् (ought to be known).

[73] Elsewhere◦ *prapaśyadbhiḥ:* → we who see, those who can see, we who clearly see, ...etc. (present tense)

📖 प्रपश्यत् is not a present tense लट् । It is not a verb or a tense. It is a Present Participle, i.e. it is instrumental case adj◦ gerund derived from the root √दृश्। It should mean discerning, knowing, seeing; while discerning, while knowing, while seeing; knower, seer, etc. to qualify the subj◦ *asmābhiḥ:* अस्माभिः । Therefore, it is अस्माभिः:प्रपश्यद्भिः ।

destruction of the family, to refrain from this sin? (1.39)

1.40 कुलक्षये प्रणश्यन्ति कुलधर्माः सनातनाः ।
धर्मे नष्टे कुलं कृत्स्नमधर्मोऽभिभवत्युत ।।

kulakṣaye praṇaśyanti kuladharmāḥ: sanātanāḥ:,
dharme naṣṭe kulaṁ kṛtsnamadharmo'bhibhavatyuta. (1.40)

(§1) कुलक्षये प्रणश्यन्ति कुलधर्माः सनातनाः । धर्मे नष्टे कुलम् कृत्स्नम् अधर्मः अभिभवति उत । *kulakṣaye praṇaśyanti kuladharmāḥ:* (r∘ 22/7) *sanātanāḥ:* (r∘ 22/8) *dharme naṣṭe kulam* (r∘ 14/1) *kṛtsnam* (r∘ 8/16) *adharmaḥ:* (r∘ 15/1) *abhibhavati* (r∘ 4/3) *uta*

(§2) *kulakṣaye* (m∘ 7loc∘ sing∘ ←tatpu∘ *kula-kṣaya*, कुलस्य क्षयः or कुलानाम् क्षयः ←n∘ *kula* (family) 1.38 + m∘ *kṣaya* (destruction) 1.38); *praṇaśyanti* (3rd-per∘ plu∘ pres∘ वर्तमान्-लट् parasmai∘ ←4∘प्र√नश् (to ruin); ***kuladharmāḥ:*** (m∘ 1nom∘ plu∘ ←tatpu∘ *kula-dharma*, कुलस्य धर्मः or कुलानां धर्मः ←n∘ *kula* 1.38 + m∘ *dharma* (righteousness) 1.1); *sanātanāḥ:* (m∘ 1nom∘ plu∘ ←adj∘ ***sanātana*** ←time indicating ind∘ ***sadā*** (ever) ←1∘√सद् (to sit); *dharme* (7loc∘ sing∘ ←m∘ *dharma* 1.1); *naṣṭe* (7loc∘ sing∘ ←ppp∘ adj∘ ***naṣṭa*** (downfall) ←4∘√नश् (to ruin); *kulam* (2acc∘ sing∘ ←n∘ *kula* 1.38); ***kṛtsnam*** (adv∘ or n∘ 2acc∘ sing∘ ←adj∘ ***kṛtsna*** (the entire) ←7∘√कृत् (to surround); *adharmaḥ:* (m∘ 1nom∘ sing∘ ←n.tatpu∘ ***a-dharma*** (unrighteousness) ←1∘अ√धृ (to bear); *abhibhavati* (3rd-per∘ sing∘ pres∘ वर्तमान्-लट् parasmai∘ ←1∘अभि√भू (to be, become); ***uta*** (ind∘ ←5∘√उ (ask) (1.40)

(§3) ***kulakṣaye*** (in the ruin of the family or families); ***praṇaśyanti*** (perish, they perish); ***kuladharmāḥ:*** (subj1∘ the duties of the family or families; the customs of righteousness for families); ***sanātanāḥ:*** (adj∘-subj1∘ the ancient, the eternal); ***dharme*** (in the righteousness); ***naṣṭe*** (in the loss of, in the downfall of); ***kulam*** (obj∘ the family); ***kṛtsnam*** (adj∘-obj∘ the whole, the entire); ***adharmaḥ:*** (subj2∘ unrighteousness); ***abhibhavati*** (it dominates, it overpowers); ***uta*** (and, also) (1.40)

(§4) kulakṣaye sanātanāḥ: kuladharmāḥ: praṇaśyanti; uta naṣṭe dharme adharmaḥ: abhibhavati kṛtsnam kulam

(§5) In the destruction of the families, the eternal customs of the-righteousness-for-the-families perish;[74] and in the downfall of the righteousness, unrighteousness overpowers the entire

---

[74] Elsewhere∘ *kulakṣaye praṇaṣyanti kuladharmāḥ:* → with the destruction of families, the eternal family tradition is destroyed; the destruction of the family is bound to result in..., when the family decays...etc.

family.[75] (1.40)

1.41 अधर्माभिभवात्कृष्ण प्रदुष्यन्ति कुलस्त्रियः ।
स्त्रीषु दुष्टासु वार्ष्णेय जायते वर्णसङ्करः ।।

adharmābhibhavātkṛṣṇa praduṣyanti kulastriyaḥ:,
strīṣu duṣṭāsu vārṣṇeya jāyate varṇasaṅkaraḥ:. (1.41)

(§1) अधर्माभिभवात् कृष्ण प्रदुष्यन्ति कुलस्त्रियः । स्त्रीषु दुष्टासु वार्ष्णेय जायते वर्णसङ्करः । *adharmābhibhavāt* (r◦ 10/5) *kṛṣṇa praduṣyanti kulastriyaḥ:* (r◦ 22/8) *strīṣu* (r◦ 25/5) *duṣṭāsu vārṣṇeya jāyate varṇasaṅkaraḥ:* (r◦ 22/8)

(§2) *adharmābhibhavāt* (m◦ 5abl◦ sing◦ ←tatpu◦ *adharmābhibhava*, अधर्मस्य अभिभवः । दुराचारस्य प्राधान्यम् ←m◦ *adharma* (unrighteoussness) 1.40 + m◦ 📖*abhibhava* (dominance) ←1◦अभि√भू (to be, become); *kṛṣṇa* (1.28); 📖*praduṣyanti* (3rd-per◦ plu◦ pres◦ वर्तमान्-लट् parasmai◦ ←4◦प्र√दुष् (to spoil); *kulastriyaḥ:* (f◦ 1nom◦ plu◦ ←tatpu◦ *kula-strī,* कुलस्य स्त्री or कुलीना स्त्री ←n◦ *kula* 1.38 + f◦ ***strī*** (lady) ←1◦**√स्त्यै** (to gather); *strīṣu* (7loc◦ plu◦ ←f◦ *strī* ↑); *duṣṭāsu* (f◦ 7loc◦ plu◦ ←ppp◦ adj◦ *duṣṭa* (corrupted) ←4◦√दुष् (to spoil); ***vārṣṇeya*** (m◦ 8voc◦ sing◦ ←taddhita◦ *vārṣṇeya,* वृष्णि गोत्रापत्यम् ←prop◦ ***vṛṣṇi*** ←1◦**√वृष्** (to shower); *jāyate* (1.29); *varṇasaṅkaraḥ:* (m◦ 1nom◦ sing◦ ←tatpu◦ ***varṇa-saṅkara,*** वर्णानाम् सङ्करः ←m◦ ***varṇa*** (class) ←10◦**√वर्ण्** + m◦ ***saṅkara*** (admixture) ←8◦सम्√कृ (to do) (1.41)

(§3) *adharmābhibhavāt* (from the dominance of unrighteousness); *kṛṣṇa* (O Śrī Kṛṣṇa!); *praduṣyanti* (they become polluted; they become corrupt); *kulastriyaḥ:* (ladies of the family or families, ladies of good linage); *strīṣu* (among the ladies); *duṣṭāsu* (among the spoiled, corrupted); *vārṣṇeya* (O Vārṣṇeya! O Śrī Kṛṣṇa!); *jāyate* (it takes birth, it occurs); *varṇasaṅkaraḥ:* (subj◦ the admixture of the four classes) (1.41)

(§4) kṛṣṇa adharmābhibhavāt kulastriyaḥ: praduṣyanti vārṣṇeya duṣṭāsu strīṣu varṇasaṅkaraḥ: jāyate

(§5) O Śrī Kṛṣṇa! from the dominance of unrighteousness the ladies of good linage become

---

[75] Elsewhere◦ *kulaṁ adharmaḥ abhibhavati* → family yields to lawlessness, family becomes involved in irreligion, entire family is overcome by adharma, whole family is seized with unrighteousness ...etc.
📖 कुलं is not the subject in Nominative case. It is the object in Accusative case. Here, the subject in Nominative case is अधर्मः, the performer of the verb अभि√भू, on the accusative object कुलम् । It is activee voice construction. अधर्मः कृत्स्नं कुलं अभिभवति ।

corrupt. O Śrī Kṛṣṇa! among the corrupted ladies, admixture of the four classes[76] takes birth. (1.41)

1.42 सङ्करो नरकायैव कुलघ्नानां कुलस्य च ।
पतन्ति पितरो ह्येषां लुप्तपिण्डोदकक्रियाः ॥

saṅkaro narakāyaiva kulaghnānāṁ kulasya ća,
patanti pitaro hyeṣāṁ luptapiṇḍodakakriyāḥ:. (1.42)

(§1) सङ्करः नरकाय एव कुलघ्नानाम् कुलस्य च । पतन्ति पितरः हि एषाम् लुप्तपिण्डोदकक्रियाः । *saṅkaraḥ:* (r◦ 15/6) *narakāya* (r◦ 3/1) *eva kulaghnānāṃ* (r◦ 14/1) *kulasya ća patanti pitaraḥ:* (r◦ 15/14) *hi* (r◦ 4/4) *eṣāṃ* (r◦ 25/3, 14/1) *luptapiṇḍodakakriyāḥ:* (r◦ 22/8)

(§2) *saṅkaraḥ:* (1nom◦ sing◦ ←m◦ *saṅkara* (admixture) 1.41); *narakāya* (4dat◦ sing◦ ←m◦ or n◦ **naraka** (downfall) ←9◦√नॄ (to take away); *eva* (1.1); ***kulaghnānāṃ*** (m◦ 6pos◦ plu◦ ←tatpu◦ *kula-ghna*, कुलस्य घ्नः । कुलानां घ्नः ←n◦ *kula* (family) 1.38 + adj◦ *ghna* (destroyer) 1.35); *kulasya* (6pos sing◦ ←n◦ *kula* 1.38); *ća* (and); ***patanti*** (3rd-per◦ plu◦ pres◦ वर्तमान्–लट् parasmai◦ ←1◦√पत् (to fall)); *pitaraḥ:* (1.34); *hi* (1.11); *eṣāṃ* (m◦ 6pos◦ plu◦ ←pron◦ *idaṃ* 1.10); *luptapiṇḍodakakriyāḥ:* (m◦ 1nom◦ plu◦ ←tatpu◦ *lupta-piṇḍodaka-kriyā*, लुप्ते पिण्डस्य च उदकस्य च क्रिये यस्य । लुप्ताः पिण्डोदकादयः क्रियाः यस्य ←adj◦ *lupta* (deprived) ←6◦√लुप् (to vanish) + n◦ or m◦ *piṇḍa* (an offering) ←10◦√पिण्ड् (to unite) + n◦ **udaka** (water) ←7◦√उन्द् (to wet) + f◦ ***kriyā*** (rite) ←8◦√कृ (to do) (1.42)

(§3) ***saṅkaraḥ:*** (subj◦ the admixture of classes) ***narakāya*** (for the downfall; for going to hell); ***eva*** (only); ***kulaghnānāṃ*** (of the destroyers of the family or families); ***kulasya*** (of the family); ***ća*** (and); ***patanti*** (they fall, they get defiled); ***pitaraḥ:*** (subj◦ the forefathers); ***hi*** (because); ***eṣāṃ*** (of these people); ***luptapiṇḍodakakriyāḥ:*** (adj◦-subj◦ those who are deprived of the rites of the deceased) (1.42)

(§4) saṅkaraḥ: narakāya eva kulaghnānāṃ ća kulasya; hi pitaraḥ: eṣāṃ luptapiṇḍodakakriyāḥ: patanti

---

[76] Elsewhere◦ *varṇasaṅkaraḥ:* → unwanted progeny, unwanted children, intermixing of castes, confusion of castes, caste confusion, intermingling of castes, ...etc.

वर्णः (√वृ to describe) is not a caste. It is one of the four discriptions, categories, groups, classes or classifications, depending on the description of one's own गुण–स्वभावः and कर्म । The caste is जातिः (√ज to be born). The classes are four, and natural. The castes are man-made and unlimited in number. They are made to suite man's self serving interest. It is utter दुर्भाग्यं that even the Hindu writers are deluded, confused, misled or unaware of the distinction between वर्णः and जातिः class and caste.

(§5) The admixture of the classes[77] (is) certainly (the reason) for the downfall of the destroyers of the family and of the family[78] (also); because the forefathers of these people, who are deprived of the rites of the deceased,[79] get defiled. (1.42)

1.43 दोषैरेतैः कुलघ्नानां वर्णसङ्करकारकैः ।
उत्साद्यन्ते जातिधर्माः कुलधर्माश्च शाश्वताः ।।

doṣairetaiḥ: kulaghnānāṁ varṇasaṅkarakārakaiḥ:,
utsādyante jātidharmāḥ: kuladharmāśća śāśvatāḥ:. (1.43)

(§1) दोषैः एतैः कुलघ्नानाम् वर्णसङ्करकारकैः । उत्साद्यन्ते जातिधर्माः कुलधर्माः च शाश्वताः । *doṣaiḥ:* (r◦ 16/4) *etaiḥ:* (r◦ 22/1) *kulaghnānāṃ* (r◦ 14/1) *varṇasaṅkarakārakaiḥ:* (r◦ 22/8) *utsādyante jātidharmāḥ:* (r◦ 22/1) *kuladharmāḥ:* (r◦ 17/1) *ća śāśvatāḥ:* (r◦ 22/8)

(§2) *doṣaiḥ:* (3inst◦ plu◦ ←m◦ *doṣa* (sin) 1.38); *etaiḥ:* (m◦ 3inst◦ plu◦ ←pron◦ *etaḍ* 1.3); *kulaghnānāṃ* (1.42); *varṇasaṅkarakārakaiḥ:* (m◦ 3inst◦ plu◦ ←bahuvrī◦ *varṇa-saṅkara-kāraka*, वर्णस्य सङ्करस्य कारकः यः ←m◦ *varṇasaṅkara* (admixture of the classes) 1.41 + adj◦ *kāraka* (doer) ←8◦√कृ (to do); 📖*utsādyante* (3rd-per◦ plu◦ pres◦ वर्तमान्-लट् ātmane◦ caus◦ ←6◦उद्√सद् (to sit); *jātidharmāḥ:* (m◦ 1nom◦ plu◦ ←tatpu◦ *jāti-dharma*, जात्याः धर्मः । जातीनां धर्मः ←f◦ *jāti* (custom of castes) ←4◦√जन् (to be born, give birth) + m◦ *dharma* (righteous duty) 1.1); *kuladharmāḥ:* (1.40); *ća* (and); 📖*śāśvatāḥ:* (m◦ 1nom◦ plu◦ ←adj◦ **śāśvata** (eternal) ←1◦√शश् (to leap) (1.43)

(§3) ***doṣaiḥ:*** (subj◦ by the sins); ***etaiḥ:*** (adj1◦-subj◦ by these); ***kulaghnānāṃ*** (of the destroyers of family

---

[77] Elsewhere◦ *saṅkaraḥ:* → unwanted population, admixture of castes, intermingling of castes, caste admixture, confusion ...etc.

📖 सङ्करः ←सम्√कृ mixing together, intermixing, doing one. The word is not caste-*saṁkaraḥ*, जातिसङ्करः, the word is वर्णसङ्करः । For clear distinction between वर्णः and जातिः (class and caste), please see the footnote in verse 1.41 above.

[78] Elsewhere◦ *luptapiṇḍodakakriyāḥ:* → the performances for... are stopped, because the last rites of... are lost ...etc., treating this word as a f◦ *karmadhāraya tatpu◦ samāsa* with f◦ क्रिया as the control word and लुप्त as its adj◦

📖 लुप्तपिण्डोदकक्रिया is the m◦ plu◦ *bahuvrīhi* adj◦ of the m◦ plu◦ noun पितरः → They (the *pitaraḥ*), who are deprived of the last rites (क्रियाः) of *udaka* and *piṇḍa*...

[79] Elsewhere◦ कुलघ्नानां कुलस्य च → the family of these destroyers of families also ...etc.

or families); ***varṇasaṅkarakārakaiḥ:*** (adj2∘-subj∘ by the doers of the admixture of the classes);[80] ***utsādyante*** (they are caused to be obliterated, uprooted); ***jātidharmāḥ:*** (obj1∘ the customs of the castes); ***kuladharmāḥ:*** (obj2∘ the righteous duties of the families); ***ća*** (and); ***śāśvatāḥ:*** (adj∘-obj1-2∘ the eternal); (1.43)

(§4) doṣaiḥ: etaiḥ: kulaghnānām, śāśvatāḥ: jātidharmāḥ: ća kuladharmāḥ: utsādyante, varṇasaṅkarakārakaiḥ:

(§5) By these sins of the destroyers of families, the eternal[81] customs of the castes and the righteous duties of the families are caused to be uprooted,[82] through[83] the admixture of classes. (1.43)

1.44 उत्सन्नकुलधर्माणां मनुष्याणां जनार्दन ।
नरकेऽनियतं वासो भवतीत्यनुशुश्रुम ।।

utsannakuladharmāṇām manuṣyāṇam janārdana,
narake'niyatam vaso bhavatityunuśuśruma. (1.44)

(§1) उत्सन्नकुलधर्माणाम् मनुष्याणाम् जनार्दन । नरके अनियतम् वासः भवति इति अनुशुश्रुम । ***utsannakuladharmāṇām*** (r∘ 24/6, 14/1) ***manuṣyāṇām*** (r∘ 24/6, 14/1) ***janārdana narake*** (r∘ 6/1) ***aniyatam*** (r∘ 14/1) ***vāsaḥ:*** (r∘

---

[80] Elsewhere∘ *varṇasaṅkarakārakaiḥ:* → from these...that leads to a mixture of castes, together with the emergrgence of mixed castes, by creating intermixture of caste, by casste-confusing misdeeds, which cause intermingling of castes, by...bringing about caste pollution, by...and thus give rise to unwanted children, because of the caste-confusion created by the bad deeds, from these sins...that lead to a mixture of castes, through thase evils bringing about an intermixture of castes...etc.

📖 See footnote in 1.41 on *varṇasaṅkaraḥ:*

[81] Arjuna confirms his baffled state of mind (भ्रमतीव च मे मनः 1.30) by saying that (*śāśvata*) eternal customs are destroyed (*utsādyante*). He is so confused (भ्रमितः, भ्रष्टः) that he even forgot that if the जातिधर्माः can be destroyed, how can he call them शाश्वताः । A *śāśvata* can not be destroyed. And, therefore, the जातिधर्मः is not शाश्वतः, it is a नश्वरः (impermanent) thing. His so called 'words of wisdom' had no meaning, which Śrī Kṛṣṇa has pointed out in the next chapter (प्रज्ञावादांश्च भाषसे 2.11).

[82] Elsewhere∘ *utsādyante* → would inevitably lead to the destruction.

[83] *utsādyante* (they cause to obliterate) is a causative verb, therefore, to impart a causative meaning in the translation of this verb, *utsādyante* उत्साद्यन्ते is translated as 'through' rather than 'by' because even if both words are appropriate for an Instrumental case, the word 'by' imparts a double meaning. Thus, by sins दोषैः through admixture of classes ...

15/8) *bhavati* (r◦ 1/5) *iti* (r◦ 4/1) *anuśuśruma*

(§2) *utsannakuladharmāṇām* (m◦ 6pos◦ plu◦ ←bahuvrī◦ *utsanna-kula-dharma*, उत्सन्नः कुलस्य धर्मः यस्य । उत्सन्नाः कुलस्य धर्माः यस्य ←ppp◦ adj◦ *utsanna* (uprooted) ←6◦उद्√सद् (to sit) + n◦ *kula* (family) 1.38 + m◦ *dharma* (righteous tradition) 1.1); ***manuṣyāṇām*** (m◦ 6pos◦ plu◦ ←taddhita◦ ***manuṣya***, मनोः अपत्यम् ←m◦ prop◦ ***manu*** ←4◦√मन् (to think); *janārdana* (1.36); ***narake*** (7loc◦ sing◦ ←m◦ *naraka* (hell) 1.42); *aniyatam* (adv◦ ←n.tatpu◦ *a-niyata* ←adj◦ ***niyata*** (perpetual) ←1◦नि√यम् (to restrain); *vāsaḥ:* (1nom◦ sing◦ ←m◦ *vāsa* (stay) ←1◦√वस् (to stay); ***bhavati*** (3rd-per◦ sing◦ pres◦ वर्तमान्-लट् parasmai◦ ←1◦√भू (to be, become); *iti* (1.25); *anuśuśruma* (1st-per◦ plu◦ past-perf◦ लिट् भूत◦ parasmai◦ ←1◦अनु√श्रु (to hear) (1.44)

(§3) ***utsannakuladharmāṇām*** **(of those whose righteous traditions of the family are uprooted or obliterated);** ***manuṣyāṇām*** **(of the people);** ***janārdana*** **(O Janārdana!, O Kṛṣṇa!);** ***narake*** **(in hell);** ***aniyatam*** **(adv◦indefinite);**[84] ***vāsaḥ:*** **(subj◦ the stay);** ***bhavati*** **(occurs, becomes);** ***iti*** **(this, so);** ***anuśuśruma*** **(we have heard)** (1.44)

(§4) janārdana vāsaḥ: utsannakuladharmāṇām manuṣyāṇām bhavati aniyatam narake iti anuśuśruma

(§5) O Kṛṣṇa! the stay of those people, whose righteous traditions of the family are obliterated, becomes perpetual[85] in hell, so we have heard. (1.44)

1.45 अहो वत महत्पापं कर्तुं व्यवसिता वयम् ।
यद्राज्यसुखलोभेन हन्तुं स्वजनमुद्यताः ।।

aho vata mahatpāpaṁ kartuṁ vyavasitā vayam,
yadrājyasukhalobhena hantuṁ svajanamudyatāḥ:. (1.45)

(§1) अहो वत महत्पापम् कर्तुम् व्यवसिताः वयम् । यत् राज्यसुखलोभेन हन्तुम् स्वजनम् उद्यताः । *aho bata mahatpāpam* (r◦ 14/1) *kartum* (r◦ 14/1) *vyavasitāḥ:* (r◦ 20/17) *vayam* (r◦ 14/2) *yat* (r◦ 9/10) *rājyasukhalobhena hantum* (r◦ 14/1) *svajanam* (r◦ 8/20) *udyatāḥ:* (r◦ 22/8)

(§2) *aho* (exclamatory ind◦ ←3◦√हा (to go); *vata* (exclamatory ind◦); *mahatpāpam* (n◦ 2acc◦ *mahat* (great) + *pāpa* (sin) महत् + पापम् ←adj◦ *mahat* 1.3 + n◦ *pāpam* 1.36); ***kartum*** (inf◦ ind◦ ←8◦√कृ (to do); *vyavasitāḥ:*

---

[84] Elsewhere◦ *a-niyatam* → infinite period, is inevitable (adj◦)...etc.

[85] Elsewhere◦ अनियतम् वासः भवति → are doomed to live perpetually, are bound to live perpetually in hell, dwell in hell..., dwell always in hell, must live in hell, dwell indefinitely in hell, living becomes inevitable ...etc.
वासः is a noun; भवति is a verb of the Present tense; अनियतम् is an adverb. Therefore, वासः (noun) अनियतम् (adv◦) भवति (verb) = The stay becomes perpatual.

(m◦ 1nom◦ plu◦ ←ppp◦ adj◦ ***vyavasita*** (resolved) ←4◦वि–अव√सो (to complete); *vayam* (1.37); ***yat*** (n◦ 2acc◦ sing◦ ←pron◦ *yad* (that) 1.7); *rājyasukhalobhena* (m◦ 3inst◦ sing◦ ←tatpu◦ *rājya-sukha-lobha,* राज्यस्य सुखस्य लोभ: ←n◦ *rājya* 1.32 + n◦ *sukha* (pleasure) 1.32 + m◦ *lobha* (greed) (1.38); *hantum* (1.35); *svajanam* (own people) (1.28); *udyatāḥ:* (m◦ 1nom◦ plu◦ ←ppp◦ adj◦ **udyata** (prepared to) ←1◦उद्√यम् (to restrain) (1.45)

(§3) ***aho*** **(alas!);** ***vata*** **(how sad!);** ***mahatpāpam*** **(obj◦ a great sin);** ***kartum*** **(to do, for doing, to commit);** ***vyavasitāḥ:*** **(adj1◦-subj◦ the ones who are resolved);** ***vayam*** **(subj◦ we);** ***yat*** **(adj◦-obj1◦ that);** ***rājyasukhalobhena*** **(through the greed for the pleasures of the kingdom; through the greed for the pleasures and the kingdom);** ***hantum*** **(for killing, to kill);** ***svajanam*** **(obj2◦ our own people);** ***udyatāḥ:*** **(adj2◦-subj◦ those who are prepared, inclined)** (1.45)

(§4) aho! vata! vayam vyavasitāḥ: kartum mahatpāpam yat udyatāḥ: hantum svajanam rājyasukhalobhena

(§5) Alas! How sad! We, resolved[86] to commit a great sin, are prepared to kill our own people, through the greed for the pleasures of the kingdom. (1.45)

1.46 यदि मामप्रतीकारमशस्त्रं शस्त्रपाणयः । धार्तराष्ट्रा रणे हन्युस्तन्मे क्षेमतरं भवेत् ।।

yadi māmapratīkāramaśastraṁ śastrapāṇayaḥ:,
dhārtarāṣṭrā raṇe hanyustanme kṣemataraṁ bhavet. (1.46)

(§1) यदि माम् अप्रतीकारम् अशस्त्रम् शस्त्रपाणयः । धार्तराष्ट्राः रणे हन्युः तत् मे क्षेमतरम् भवेत् । *yadi mām* (r◦ 8/16) *apratīkāram* (r◦ 8/16) *aśastram* (r◦ 14/1) *śastrapāṇayaḥ:* (r◦ 22/8) *dhārtarāṣṭrāḥ:* (r◦ 20/15) *raṇe* (r◦ 24/9) *hanyuḥ:* (r◦ 18/1) *tat* (r◦ 12/2) *me kṣemataram* (r◦ 14/1) *bhavet*

(§2) *yadi* (even if) (1.38); ***mām*** (2acc◦ sing◦ ←pron◦ *asmad* 1.7); *apratīkāram* (2acc◦ sing◦ n.bahuvrī◦ ←m◦ *pratīkāra* (unresisting) ←8◦प्रति√कृ (to do); *aśastram* (2acc◦ sing◦ ←adj◦ n.tatpu◦ *a-śastra* (unarmed) ←1◦अ√शस् (to leap); *śastrapāṇayaḥ:* (m◦ 1nom◦ plu◦ ←bahuvrī◦ adj◦ *śastra-pāṇi,* शस्त्राणि पाण्योः यस्य ←n◦ *śastra* (arm) 1.9 + m◦ ***pāṇi*** (hand) ←1◦√पण् (to deal); ***dhārtarāṣṭrāḥ:*** (1nom◦ plu◦ ←m◦ *dhārtarāṣṭra* (Kaurav) 1.19); ***raṇe*** (7loc◦ sing◦ ←n◦ *raṇa* (battlefield) 1.22); *hanyuḥ:* (3rd-per◦ plu◦ potential◦ विधि◦ parasmai◦

---

[86] Elsewhere◦ *vyavasitāḥ:* → we have resolved (perfect), we are preparing, are perpetrating, are making ...etc. (present tense)

व्यवसित is not Present tense or any other tense or a gerund. It is a ppp◦ adjective of the subject वयम् (we). The same is true for adjective उद्यता: in this śloka.

←2◦√हन् (to hurt); *tat* (pron◦ *tad* 1nom◦ 1.2); *me* (1.21); *kṣemataram* (n◦ 1nom◦ sing◦ ←comparative adj◦ *kṣema-tara* ←adj◦ ***kṣema*** (benefit) ←6◦√क्षि (to stay) + taddhitaa affix ***tara*** (more) (तर); indicating a comparison between two things ←1◦√तॄ (to swim across); ***bhavet*** (3rd-per◦ sing◦ potential◦ विधि◦ parasmai◦ ←1◦√भू (to be, become) (1.46)

(§3) ***yadi*** **(if, even if);** ***mām*** **(adj1◦-obj◦ me, to me; Obj◦ Arjuna);** ***apratīkāram*** **(*****bahuvrī◦*** **adj2◦-obj◦ to one who is not resisting, unresisting);** ***aśastram*** **(*****bahuvrī◦*** **adj3◦-obj◦ the unarmed);** ***śastrapāṇayaḥ:*** **(adj◦-subj◦ those who are holding weapons in their hands; the armed);** ***dhārtarāṣṭrāḥ:*** **(subj◦ the sons of Dhṛtarāṣṭra; the Kauravas);** ***raṇe*** **(on the battlefield);** ***hanyuḥ:*** **(should they kill; they may kill);** ***tat*** **(subj◦2 that, that thing);** ***me*** **(for me);** ***kṣemataram*** **(adj◦-subj2◦ more beneficial, better);** ***bhavet*** **(would become, would be)** (1.46)

(§4) yadi śastrapāṇayaḥ: dhārtarāṣṭrāḥ: hanyuḥ: mām raṇe apratīkāram aśastram tat bhavet kṣemataram me

(§5) Even if the armed Kauravas should kill, the unarmed (and) unresisting me on the battlefield , that would be better for me. (1.46)

Sanjaya said (sañjaya uvāća सञ्जय उवाच ।)

1.47 एवमुक्त्वार्जुनः सङ्ख्ये रथोपस्थ उपाविशत् ।
विसृज्य सशरं चापं शोकसंविग्नमानसः ।।

evamuktvārjunaḥ: saṅkhye rathopastha upāviśat,
visṛjya saśaraṁ ćāpaṁ śokasaṁvignamānasaḥ:. (1.47)

(§1) एवम् उक्त्वा अर्जुनः सङ्ख्ये रथोपस्थे उपाविशत् । विसृज्य सशरम् चापम् शोकसंविग्नमानसः । *sañjayaḥ:* (r◦ 19/4) *uvāća. evam* (r◦ 8/20) *uktvā* (r◦ 1/3) *arjunaḥ:* (r◦ 22/7) *saṅkhye rathopasthe* (r◦ 5/3) *upāviśat* (r◦ 23/1) *visṛjya saśaram* (r◦ 14/1) *ćāpam* (r◦ 14/1) *śokasaṁvignamānasaḥ:* (r◦ 22/8)

(§2) *sañjayaḥ:* (1.2); *uvāća* (1.25). *evam* (1.24); 📖*uktvā* (ipp◦ ind◦ ←2◦√वच् (to speek); *arjunaḥ:* (1.28); 📖***saṅkhye*** (7loc◦ sing◦ ←n◦ *saṅkhya* (battlefield) ←2◦सम्√ख्या (to declare); 📖*rathopasthe* (m◦ 7loc◦ sing◦ ←tatpu◦ *rathopastha,* रथस्य उपस्थः ←m◦ *ratha* (chariot) 1.4 + m◦ *upastha* (middle part) ←1◦उप√स्था (to stay); *upāviśat* (3rd-per◦ sing◦ -past-imper◦ लङ् भूत◦ parasmai◦ ←6◦उप–आ√विश् (to enter); 📖*visṛjya* (adv◦ -past-participle lyp◦ ind◦ ←6◦वि√सृज् (to produce); *saśaram* (n◦ 2acc◦ sing◦ ←bahuvrī◦ *sa-śara* (with arrows) शरैः सह ←m◦ 📖*śara* (arrow) ←9◦√श्री (to prepare) + adj◦ *saha* (with) 1.22); *ćāpam* (2acc◦ sing◦ ←m◦ 📖*ćāpa* (bow) ←1◦√चप् (to encourage); *śokasaṁvignamānasaḥ:* (m◦ 1nom◦ sing◦ ←bahuvrī◦ *śoka-saṁvigna-mānasa,* शोकेन संविग्नं मानसं यस्य सः ←m◦ 📖***śoka*** (grief) ←1◦√शुच् (to lament) + ppp◦ adj◦ 📖*saṁvigna* (overcome) ←6◦सम्√विज्

(to tremble) + n∘ mānasa (mind) ←1∘√मन् (to think) (1.47)

(§3) ***evam*** (in this manner; like this); ***uktvā*** (having spoken); ***arjunaḥ:*** (subj∘ Arjuna); ***sankhye*** (on the battlefield); ***rathopasthe*** (in the middle part of the chariot)[87] ***upāviśat*** (he sat); ***visṛjya*** (having kept aside, casting aside); ***saśaram*** (with arrows); ***ćāpam*** (the bow); ***śokasaṁvignamānasaḥ:*** (bahuvri∘ adj∘-subj∘ he whose mind was overcome with grief, Arjuna); (1.47)

(§4) arjunaḥ: śokasaṁvignamānasaḥ: uktvā evam sankhye upāviśat rathopasthe visṛjya ćāpam saśaram

(§5) Arjuna, whose mind was overcome with grief,[88] having spoken in this manner on the battlefield,[89] sat in the middle part of the chariot,[90] having kept aside the bow with arrows. (1.47

---

[87] Elsewhere∘ *rathopasthe* → on the seat, on the chariot, on the back seat, on the front seat ...etc.

1. Upa-stha = middle or inner part of anything (**Sir Monier Monier-William,** *A Sanskrrit English Dictionary*)

2. उपस्थः = the middle part in general (V. S. Apte, *The Student's Sanskrit English Dictionary*)

3. उपस्थः = (उप+स्था+क) मध्य भाग (**वा. शि. आप्टे,** 'संस्कृत-हिन्दी कोश')

4. उपस्थ (पुं∘) (उप√स्था+क) = मध्यभाग (**व्याकरणवेदान्ताचार्य पण्डित तारिणीश झा,** 'संस्कृत-शब्दार्थ-कौस्तुभ')

NOTE : The word रथोपस्थे has also been used in the Mahābhārata, Karṇa Parva, Verse 51.1, with the above meaning. Therefore, रथोपस्थे → middle part of the chariot. It also indicates that, the great chariot (महास्यन्दनः 1.14) of Pārtha had three compartments, sections, parts.

[88] Please note that : शोकसंविग्नमानसः = Not his mind overwhelmed with grief, but he whose mind overwhelmed with grief = Arjuna, *bahuvrīhi samasa.*

[89] Elsewhere∘ एवम् उक्त्वा अर्जुनः सङ्ख्ये विसृज्य सशरम् चापम् → casting away, throwing down - his bow and arrows on the battlefield, cast aside his bow and arrows in the midst of the battle ...etc.

Note that at this point the battle has not yet started. No weapon clashed. Everbody is quiet and dismayed. They are woundring why Arjuna asked Krishna to place their chariot in the middle of the two opposing armies, why he is giving 'advice' to Krishna and then why he removed and kept his bow and arrow down and moved to the inner part of the chariot. This Arjuna's dialogue with Krishna on the battlrground refers to the words, "एवम् उक्त्वा अर्जुनः सङ्ख्ये" (Arjuna, having thus spoken on the battlefield). Here, सङ्ख्ये is battlefield, not the battle which Arjuna has so far refused to start.

[90] Elsewhere∘ (उक्त्वा अर्जुनः सङ्ख्ये) रथोपस्थे उपाविशत् → sat down on the chariot in that battle, sat down on the chariot in the midst of the battle, sat down on the seat of the chariot, ...etc.

रथोपस्थे see previous footnote. The phrase should be एवम् उक्त्वा अर्जुनः सङ्ख्ये or अर्जुनः सङ्ख्ये उक्त्वा (having spoken on the battlefield), not सङ्ख्ये रथोपस्थे उपाविशत् (sat on chariot in that battle, in the midst of the battle),

इति श्रीमद्भगवद्गीतासूपनिषत्सु ब्रह्मविद्यायां योगशास्त्रे श्रीकृष्णार्जुनसंवादेऽर्जुनविषादयोगो नाम प्रथमोऽध्यायः ।

iti śrīmadbhagavadgītāsūpaniṣatsu brahmavidyāyāṁ yogaśāstre,
śrīkṛṣṇārjunasaṁvāde'rjunaviṣādayogo nāma prathamo'dhyāyaḥ:..

(§1) *iti śrīmadbhagavadgītāsu* (r◦ 1/8) *upaniṣatsu brahmavidyāyām* (r◦ 14/1) *yogaśāstre śrīkṛṣṇārjuna-saṁvāde* (r◦ 6/1) *arjunaviṣādayogaḥ:* (r◦ 15/6) *nāma prathamaḥ:* (r◦ 15/1) *adhyāyaḥ:* (r◦ 22/8)

(§2) *iti* (1.25); *śrīmadbhagavadgītāsu* (f◦ 7loc◦ plu◦ tatpu◦ *śrīmad-bhagavad-gītā* ←adj◦ *śrīmat* (lofty) 6.41↓ + adj◦ *bhagavat* (divine) 10.14↓ + f◦ *gītā* ←5◦√गै (to sing); *upaniṣatsu* (7loc◦ plu◦ ←f◦ *upaniṣad* ←6◦उप-नि√सद् (to sit); *brahmavidyāyām* (f◦ 7loc◦ sing◦ ←tatpu◦ *brahma-vidyā,* ब्रह्मणः विद्या ←n◦ *brahman* 2.72↓ + *vidyā* (knowledge) 5.18↓); *yogaśāstre* (n◦ 7loc◦ sing◦ ←tatpu◦ *yoga-śāstra,* योगानाम् शास्त्रम् । योगस्य शास्त्रम् । ←m◦ *yoga* 2.39↓ + n◦ *śāstra* (science) 15.20↓); *śrīkṛṣṇārjunasaṁvāde* (m◦ 7loc◦ sing◦ ←tatpu◦ *śrī-kṛṣṇārjuna-saṁvāda,* श्रीकृष्णस्य च अर्जुनस्य च संवादः ←adj◦ *śrī* 10.34↓ + m◦ prop◦ *kṛṣṇa* 1.28 + m◦ prop◦ *arjuna* 1.4 + m◦ *saṁvāda* (dialogue) 18.70↓); *arjunaviṣādayogaḥ:* (m◦ 1nom◦ sing◦ ←tatpu◦ *arjuna-viṣāda-yoga,* अर्जुनस्य विषादस्य योगः ←prop◦ *arjuna* 1.4 + m◦ 📖*viṣāda* (melancholy) 1.27 + m◦ *yoga* (discipline) 2.39↓); *nāma* (1nom◦ sing◦ ←n◦ *nāman* (name) ←1◦√म्ना (to remember); *prathamaḥ:* (m◦ 1nom◦ sing◦ ←num◦ adj◦ *prathama* (first) ←1◦√प्रथ् (to grow) ; *adhyāyaḥ:* (1nom◦ sing◦ ←m◦ *adhyāya* (chapter) ←1◦अधि√इ (to enter, come, go)

(§3) ***iti*** **(thus);** ***śrīmadbhagavadgītāsu upaniṣatsu*** **(among the upaniṣads of Śrīmad-Bhagavadgītā);** ***brahmavidyāyām*** **(of the eternal wisdoms);** ***yogaśāstre*** **(in the science of Yoga);** ***śrīkṛṣṇārjunasaṁvāde*** **(in the dialogue between Śrī Kṛṣṇa and Arjuna);** ***arjunaviṣādayogaḥ:*** **(adj1◦-subj◦ Arjuna-viṣāda-yoga);** ***nāma*** **(called)** ***prathamaḥ:*** **(adj2◦-subj◦ first);** ***adhyāyaḥ:*** **(subj◦ discourse)**

(§4) śrīmadbhagavadgītāsu upaniṣatsu yogaśāstre brahmavidyāyām iti prathamaḥ: adhyāyaḥ: nāma arjunaviṣādayogaḥ: śrīkṛṣṇārjunasaṁvāde

(§5) Among the upaniṣads of the Śrīmad-Bhagavadgītā, in the science of Yoga of self realization, thus (is) the first discourse called *Arjuna-viṣāda-yoga,* in the dialogue between Śrī Kṛṣṇa and Arjuna.

---

because untill now and at this point in time there was no battle no rattle.

GITA CHAPTER TWO

THE CRUX OF THE KARMAYOGA

श्रीमद्भगवद्गीताया द्वितीयोऽध्यायः कर्मयोगस्य मूलम् ।

dvitīyo'dhyāyaḥ:

द्वितीयोऽध्यायः ।

YOGA OF KNOWLEDGE

OF RENUNCIATION OF THE AUTHORSHIP OF KARMA[91]

sāṅkhya-yogopaniṣhat

साङ्ख्ययोगोपनिषत् ।

Sanjaya said (sañjaya uvāća सञ्जय उवाच ।)

2.1 तं तथा कृपयाविष्टमश्रुपूर्णाकुलेक्षणम् ।

विषीदन्तमिदं वाक्यमुवाच मधुसूदनः ।।

taṁ tathā kṛpayāviṣṭamaśrupūrṇākulekṣaṇam,

viṣīdantamidaṁ vākyamuvāća madhusūdanaḥ:. (verse 2.1)

PLEASE NOTE THAT, in all verses of in this book :

(§1) = Analysis of the verse, with the 25 Sandhi Rules explained above,

(§2) = Grammatical analysis of each Sanskrit word with the rules given earlier,

(§3) = Plain grammatical English meaning of each Sanskrit word of the shloka based on the grammar given in Step §2. These exact English words are used in step §5 below,

(§4) = Sanskrit words re-arranged in the order of English syntax,

(§5) = English meaning of the shloka, exactly as translated in step (§3) above.

(§1) तम् तथा कृपयाविष्टम् अश्रुपूर्णाकुलेक्षणम् । विषीदन् तम् इदम् वाक्यम् उवाच मधुसूदनः । *dvitīyaḥ:* (r◦ 15/1) *adhyāyaḥ:* (r◦ 22/8). *sāṅkhyayogaḥ:* (r◦ 22/8). *sañjayaḥ:* (r◦ 19/4) *uvāća. taṃ* (r◦ 14/1) *tathā kṛpayā* (r◦ 1/4) *āviṣṭaṃ* (r◦ 8/16) *aśrupūrṇākulekṣaṇaṃ* (r◦ 14/2, 24/3) *viṣīdantaṃ* (r◦ 8/18) *idaṃ* (r◦ 14/1) *vākyaṃ* (r◦ 8/20) *uvāća madhusūdanaḥ:* (r◦ 22/8)

(§2) *dvitīyaḥ:* (m◦ 1nom◦ sing◦ ←sequence indicating num◦ adj◦ *dvitīya* (second) ←adj◦ *dvi* ←1◦√द्व (to hinder);

[91] Elsewhere◦ *Saṅkhyayoga* = Yoga of knowledge. Yoga of Renunciation.

adhyāyaḥ: (1nom∘ sing∘ ←m∘ *adhyāya* (chapter) ←1∘अधि√इ (to enter, come, go). *sāṅkhyayogaḥ:* (m∘ 1nom∘ sing∘ ←tatpu∘ *sāṅkhya-yoga*, सांख्ययोगः । सांख्यस्य योगः । सांख्यतत्त्वस्य योगः । सांख्यसंन्यासिभ्यः योगः । सांख्यज्ञानिभ्यः योगः । सांख्ययोगिभ्यः योगः । संन्यासस्य ज्ञानस्य योगः । संन्यासयोगः । ज्ञानयोगः (see the answer to Question 9, in the previous section) ←m∘ *sāṅkhya* 2.39 + m∘ *yoga* 2.39). *sañjayaḥ:* (1.2); *uvāća* (1.25).

tam (m∘ 2acc∘ sing∘ ←pron∘ *tad* 1.2); *tathā* (in that manner) (1.8); 📖*kṛpayā* (with compassion) (1.27); 📖*āviṣṭam* (m∘ 2acc∘ sing∘ ←adj∘ *āviṣṭa* (possessed) 1.27); *aśrupūrṇākulekṣaṇam* (m∘ 2acc∘ sing∘ ←bahuvrī∘ *aśrupūrṇākulekṣaṇa*, अश्रुभिः पूर्णे आकुले च ईक्षणे यस्य सः । अश्रुभिः पूर्णे अश्रुभिः च आकुले ईक्षणे यस्य सः ←n∘ *aśru* (tear) ←9∘√अश् (to eat)+ adj∘ *pūrṇa* (filled) ←6∘√पूर् (to fill) + adj∘ 📖*ākula* (agitated) ←1∘आ√कुल् (to related) + n∘ 📖*īkṣaṇa* (eye) ←2∘√ई (to go); 📖**viṣīdantam** (m∘ 2acc∘ sing∘ ←śatṛ∘ adj∘ *viṣīdat* (desponding) ←6∘वि√सद् (to sit); *idam* (1.10); *vākyam* (word) (2acc∘ 1.21); *uvāća* (1.25); *madhusūdanaḥ:* (1nom∘ sing∘ ←m∘ bahuvrī∘ *madhusūdana* 1.35) (2.1)

(§3) ***dvitīyaḥ:*** (adj∘-subj∘ the second); ***adhyāyaḥ:*** (subj∘ the discourse, the chapter). ***sāṅkhyayogaḥ:*** (Sāṅkhya-yoga, yoga of knowledge of renunciation). ***sañjayaḥ:*** (subj∘ Sañjaya); ***uvāća*** (he said). ***tam*** (obj1∘ him; to that; to that Arjuna); ***tathā*** (thus, in that manner); ***kṛpayā*** (with compassion; with pity); ***āviṣṭam*** (adj1∘-obj1∘ possessed with; engulfed with); ***aśrupūrṇākulekṣaṇam*** (adj2∘-obj1∘ to him whose eyes were filled and agitated with tears; he whose eyes were filled with tears and were agitated); ***viṣīdantam*** (adj3∘-obj1∘ to him who was desponding, despairing); ***idam*** (adj∘-obj2∘ this); ***vākyam*** (obj2∘ word; speech); ***uvāća*** (he said); ***madhusūdanaḥ:*** (subj∘ Madhusūdana; Śrī Kṛṣṇa) (2.1)

(§4) dvitīyaḥ: adhyāyaḥ:. sāṅkhyayogaḥ:. sañjayaḥ: uvāća. tathā āviṣṭam kṛpayā aśrupūrṇākulekṣaṇam viṣīdantam tam madhusūdanaḥ: uvāća idam vākyam

(§5) The Second Discourse. Sāṅkhya-yoga (Yoga of Knowledge of Renunciation of the Authorship of *karma*).

Sañjaya said : In that manner possessed with compassion (and) whose eyes were filled and agitated with tears,[92] to that desponding Arjuna Śrī Kṛṣṇa said this word.[93] (2.1)

2.2 कुतस्त्वा कश्मलमिदं विषमे समुपस्थितम् ।
अनार्यजुष्टमस्वर्ग्यमकीर्तिकरमर्जुन ।।

---

[92] *aśrupūrṇākulekṣaṇam* अश्रुभिः पूर्णे अश्रुभिः च आकुले ईक्षणे यस्य → he whose eyes were filled and agitated with tears; अश्रुभिः पूर्णे आकुले च ईक्षणे यस्य → he whose eyes were filled with tears and were agitated.

[93] See footnote in verse 1.2

kutastvā kaśmalamidaṁ viṣame samupasthitam,

anāryajuṣṭamasvargyamakīrtikaramarjuna. (2.2)

(§1) कुतः त्वा कश्मलम् इदम् विषमे समुपस्थितम् । अनार्यजुष्टम् अस्वर्ग्यम् अकीर्तिकरम् अर्जुन । *śrībhagavān* (r◦ 8/14) *uvāća. kutaḥ:* (r◦ 18/1) *tvā kaśmalam* (r◦ 8/18) *idam* (r◦ 14/1) *viṣame samupasthitam* (r◦ 14/2) *anāryajuṣṭam* (r◦ 8/16) *asvargyam* (r◦ 8/16) *akīrtikaram* (r◦ 8/16) *arjuna*

(§2) *śrī-bhagavān* (m◦ 1nom◦ sing◦ ←adj◦ *śrī* (10.34); + m◦ 1nom◦ sing◦ ←adj◦ *bhagavat* 10.14); *uvāća* (1.25). 📖***kutaḥ:*** (time or place indicating interrogatory ind◦ *kutaṣ* (from where) ←pron◦ *kim* 1.1); ***tvā*** (= *tvām* (to you) त्वाम्; 2acc◦ sing◦ ←pron◦ *yuṣmad* 1.3); 📖*kaśmalam* (1nom◦ sing◦ ←n◦ *kaśmala* (cowardice) ←1◦√कश् (to sound); *idam* (this) (1.10); 📖*viṣame* (n◦ or m◦ 7loc◦ sing◦ वि-समे, वि-समये, समस्य विरुद्धे, सामान्यस्य विरुद्धे ←adj◦ *viṣama* (wrong juncture) ←1◦वि√सम् (to be equanimous, equal); *samupasthitam* (came) (n◦ 1nom◦ 1.28); *anāryajuṣṭam* (n◦ 1nom◦ sing◦ ←tatpu◦ adj◦ *anārya-juṣṭa,* अनार्यः जुष्टः यिस्मिन् । अनार्यः जुषते येन । आर्य न जुष्टः यस्मिन् । आर्यः न जुषते येन –इति ←adj◦ *anārya* (not noble) ←1◦अन्√ऋ (to attain) + ppp◦ adj◦ 📖*juṣṭa* (pleased) ←6◦√जुष् (to inspire); 📖*asvargyam* (n◦ 1nom◦ sing◦ ←n.tatpu◦ -pot◦ adj◦ *a-svargya* (unheavenly) न स्वर्ग्यम् ←m◦ ***svarga*** (heaven) ←1◦सु√ऋज् (to attain); 📖*akīrtikaram* (n◦ 1nom◦ sing◦ ←n.tatpu◦ *a-kīrti-kara,* न कीर्तिः करोति इति ←n.tatpu◦ ***akīrti*** (infamy) ←f◦ ***kīrti*** (fame) ←10◦√कॄत् (to announce) + affix ***kara*** or adj◦ ***kāra*** or adj◦ *kāraka* (causer) ←8◦√कृ (to do); ***arjuna*** (m◦ 8voc◦ sing◦ ←prop◦ *arjuna* 1.4) (2.2)

(§3) ***śrī-bhagavān*** (subj◦ **Lord; Lord Śrī Kṛṣṇa);** ***uvāća*** **(said).** ***kutaḥ:*** **(from where? whence?);** ***tvā*** **(= त्वाम्** obj◦ **to you; have you, did you);** ***kaśmalam*** (subj◦ **the timidity, the the cowardice, pusillanimity);** ***idam*** **(adj1◦-**subj◦ **this);** ***viṣame*** **(in the wrong time and place, at the wrong moment, at the wrong juncture);** ***samupasthitam*** **(adj2◦-**subj◦ **the one that has come);** ***anāryajuṣṭam*** **(adj3◦-**subj◦ **that by which noble people are not pleased);** ***asvargyam*** **(adj4◦-**subj◦ **the one that is not heavenly; that which is not divine);** ***akīrtikaram*** **(adj5◦-**subj◦ **the one that causes infamy, which does not give credit);** ***arjuna*** **(O Arjuna!)** (2.2)

(§4) arjuna idam kaśmalam anāryajuṣṭam asvargyam akīrtikaram samupasthitam tvā viṣame kutaḥ:

(§5) O Arjuna! this cowardice - that by which the noble men are not pleased,[94] that is not

---

[94] Elsewhere◦ *anāryajuṣṭam* → practiced by anārya, unknown to men of noble mind, entertained by unenlightened, cherished by the unworthy ...etc.

📖 अनार्यजुष्टः, अनार्यः जुष्टः यस्मिन्, आर्यः अजुष्टः यस्मिन्, अनार्यः जुषते येन, आर्यः न जुषते येन ← √जुष् (आत्म◦) to be pleased, to be in favour; जुष्ट ppp◦ one who is pleased. अनार्यजुष्टः by which *anārya* is pleased, by which *ārya* (a noble man) is not pleased.

heavenly, that causes infamy has come[95] to you at the wrong juncture,[96] from where? (2.2)

2.3 क्लैब्यं मा स्म गमः पार्थ नैतत्त्वय्युपपद्यते ।
क्षुद्रं हृदयदौर्बल्यं त्यक्त्वोत्तिष्ठ परन्तप ।।

klaibyaṁ mā sma gamaḥ: pārtha naitattvayyupapadyate,
kṣudraṁ hṛdayadaurbalyaṁ tyaktvottiṣṭha parantapa. (2.3)

(§1) क्लैब्यम् मा स्म गमः पार्थ न एतत् त्वयि उपपद्यते । क्षुद्रम् हृदयदौर्बल्यम् त्यक्त्वा उत्तिष्ठ परन्तप । *klaibyam* (r◦ 14/1) *mā sma gamaḥ:* (r◦ 22/3) *pārtha na* (r◦ 3/1) *etat* (r◦ 1/10) *tvayi* (r◦ 4/3) *upapadyate kṣudram* (r◦ 14/1) *hṛdayadaurbalyam* (r◦ 14/1) *tyaktvā* (r◦ 2/4) *uttiṣṭha parantapa*

(§2) 📖*klaibyam* (2acc◦ sing◦ ←n◦ *klaibya* (cowardice) ←1◦√क्लीब् (to be weak); ***mā*** (opposition indicating ind◦ (don't) ←3◦√मा (to measure); *sma* (stress or certainty indicating ind◦ ←1◦√स्मि (to smile); *gamaḥ:* (2nd-per◦ sing◦ -pastind◦ लुङ् भूत parasmai◦ indicating an advice ←1◦√गम् (to go); *pārtha* (1.25); *na* (1.30); ***etat*** (n◦ 1nom◦ sing◦ ←pron◦ *etad* (this) 1.3); *tvayi* (7loc◦ sing◦ ←pron◦ *yuṣmad* 1.3); ***upapadyate*** (3rd-per◦ sing◦ pres◦ वर्तमान्-लट् ātmane◦ ←4◦उप√पद् (to go); 📖*kṣudram* (n◦ 2acc◦ sing◦ ←adj◦ *kṣudra* (lowly) ←7◦√क्षुद् (to trample); *hṛdayadaurbalyam* (n◦ 2acc◦ ←tatpu◦ *hṛdaya-daurbalya*, हृदयस्य दौर्बल्यम् ←n◦ *hṛdaya* (heart) 1.19 + n◦ 📖*daurbalya* (weakness) ←5◦√दु (be bad); *tyaktvā* (1.33); 📖***uttiṣṭha*** (2nd-per◦ sing◦ imperative◦ लोट् parasmai◦ ←1◦उद्√स्था (to stay); ***parantapa*** (m◦ 8voc◦ sing◦ ←bahuvrī◦ *parantapa*, परान् तापयति यः ←adj◦ ***para*** (other) ←3◦√पॄ (to fill) + m◦ *tapa* ←1◦√तप् (to do penance, heat up) (2.3)

(§3) *klaibyam* (obj1◦ cowardice, impotence); *mā sma* (don't); *gamaḥ:* (you yield to -, you should go for); *pārtha* (O Son of Pṛthā! O Pārtha! O Arjuna!); *na* (not, does not); *etat* (adj◦-obj◦ it, this); *tvayi* (on you); *upapadyate* (it becomes fit, it befits; it looks befitting); *kṣudram* (adj◦-obj2◦ the lowly, base, vile, ignoble); *hṛdayadaurbalyam* (obj2◦ weakheartedness); *tyaktvā* (having cast aside, having shaken off); *uttiṣṭha* (you please arise! you please stand up!); *parantapa* (O Parantapa! O Arjuna!) (2.3)

(§4) pārtha mā sma gamaḥ: klaibyam etat na upapadyate tvayi parantapa uttiṣṭha tyaktvā kṣudram hṛdayadaurbalyam

---

[95] Elsewhere◦ *samupasthitam* → these have come upon you, you have got these, this has come to thee, has come on you, has come upon you, ...etc.

📖 समुपस्थित is not a present or past tense. it is not a verb. It is not plural. It is singular. It is a ppp◦ adj◦ for the noun कश्मलम् । It is the Subject in Nominative case.

[96] Elsewhere◦ *viṣame* → at this crisis, in this hour of crisis, during the crisis of war, in such a critical situation, in danger ...etc.

(§5) O Arjuna! don't you yield to cowardice. It does not look befitting on you. O Arjuna! please stand up, having shaken off the lowly weak heartedness. (2.3)

Arjuna said (arjuna uvāća अर्जुन उवाच ।)

2.4 कथं भीष्ममहं सङ्ख्ये द्रोणं च मधुसूदन ।
इषुभिः प्रतियोत्स्यामि पूजार्हावरिसूदन ।।

kathaṁ bhīṣmamahaṁ saṅkhye droṇaṁ ća madhusūdana,
iṣubhiḥ: pratiyotsyāmi pūjārhāvarisūdana. (2.4)

(§1) कथम् भीष्मम् अहम् सङ्ख्ये द्रोणम् च मधुसूदन । इषुभिः प्रतियोत्स्यामि पूजार्हौ अरिसूदन । *arjunaḥ:* (r∘ 19/4) *uvāća. katham* (r∘ 14/1) *bhīṣmam* (r∘ 8/16) *aham* (r∘ 14/1) *saṅkhye droṇam* (r∘ 14/1, 24/3) *ća madhusūdana* (r∘ 23/1) *iṣubhiḥ:* (r∘ 22/3) *pratiyotsyāmi pūjārhau* (r∘ 5/5) *arisūdana*

(§2) *arjunaḥ:* (1.28); *uvāća* (1.25). *katham* (1.37); *bhīṣmam* (1.11); *aham* (1.22); *saṅkhye* (1.47); ***droṇam*** (m∘ 2acc∘ sing∘ ←prop∘ *droṇa* 1.25); *ća* (1.1); *madhusūdana* (1.35); *iṣubhiḥ:* (3inst∘ plu∘ ←m∘ *iṣu* (arrow) 1.4); *pratiyotsyāmi* (1st-per∘ sing∘ fut2∘ लृट् भविष्य∘ parasmai∘ ←4∘प्रति√युध् (to fight); 📖*pūjārhau* (m∘ 2acc∘ -dual ←tatpu∘ *pūjārha*, पूजायाः अर्हः ←f∘ ***pūjā*** (worship) ←10∘√पूज् (to worship) + adj∘ *arha* (worthy) ←1∘√अर्ह् (to deserve); *arisūdana* (m∘ 8voc∘ sing∘ ←bahuvrī∘ *ari-sūdana*, अरिणाम् सूदनः यः ←m∘ ***ari*** (enemy) ←1∘√ऋ (to attain) + adj∘ *sūdana* (destroyer) ←1∘√सूद् (to thrash) (2.4)

(§3) ***katham*** **(how?);** ***bhīṣmam*** **(obj1∘ Bhīṣma);** ***aham*** **(subj∘ I);** ***saṅkhye*** **(on the battlefield);** ***droṇam*** **(obj2∘ to Droṇa);** ***ća*** **(and);** ***madhusūdana*** **(O Madhusūdana! O Śrī Kṛṣṇa!);** ***iṣubhiḥ:*** **(with arrows);** ***pratiyotsyāmi*** **(I shall fight against);** ***pūjārhau*** **(adj∘-obj1,2∘ the two venerable-);** ***arisūdana*** **(O Arisūdana! O Śrī Kṛṣṇa!)** (2.4)

(§4) arisūdana katham aham pratiyotsyāmi pūjārhau bhīṣmam ća droṇam iṣubhiḥ: saṅkhye arisūdana

(§5) O Śrī Kṛṣṇa! how shall I fight against the two venerable,[97] Bhīṣma and Droṇa, with arrows on the battlefield? O Arisūdana! (2.4)

2.5 गुरूनहत्वा हि महानुभावाञ्श्रेयो भोक्तुं भैक्ष्यमपीह लोके ।

---

[97] Elsewhere∘ *pūjārhau* → they are worthy to be worshipped, are worthy of worship, they both are venerable, who are worthy of respect, who are only worthy of, ...etc.

📖 पूजार्हौ is not a present tense Nominative (1st) case dual verb (स्तः). It is not a verb. It is Accusative (2nd) case, dual, m∘ adjective of dual noun gurū (गुरू) → the two venerable, the two venerable ones.

हत्वार्थकामांस्तु गुरूनिहैव भुञ्जीय भोगान्रुधिरप्रदिग्धान् ॥

gurūnahatvā hi mahānubhāvāñśreyo bhoktuṁ bhaikṣyamapīha loke,
hatvārthakāmānstu gurūnihaiva bhuñjīya bhogānrudhirapradigdhāṇ.
(2.5)

(§1) गुरून् अहत्वा हि महानुभावान् श्रेयः भोक्तुम् भैक्ष्यम् अपि इह लोके । हत्वा अर्थकामान् तु गुरून् इह एव भुञ्जीय भोगान् रुधिरप्रदिग्धान् । *gurūn* (r◦ 8/11) *ahatvā hi mahānubhāvān* (r◦ 11/5) *śreyaḥ:* (r◦ 15/8) *bhoktum* (r◦ 14/1) *bhaikṣyam* (r◦ 8/16) *api* (r◦ 1/5) *iha loke hatvā* (r◦ 1/3) *arthakāmān* (r◦ 13/7) *tu gurūn* (r◦ 8/13) *iha* (r◦ 3/1) *eva bhuñjīya bhogān* (r◦ 13/18) *rudhirapradigdhān*

(§2) ***gurūn*** (2acc◦ plu◦ ←m◦ or adj◦ ***guru*** (guru) **←10◦√गृ** (to to know properly); *a-hatvā* (-ve◦ ipp◦ ←ind◦ *hatvā* 1.31); *hi* (because) (ind◦ ←5◦√हि (to impel) or 3◦√हा (to go); *mahānubhāvān* (m◦ 2acc◦ plu◦ ←bahuvrī◦ *mahānubhāva* (noble) महान् अनुभवः यस्य ←adj◦ *mahā* 1.3 + m◦ *anubhava* (experience) ←1◦अनु√भू (to be, become); ***śreyaḥ:*** (1nom◦ sing◦ ←n◦ *śreyaṣ* (better) 1.31); *bhoktum* (inf◦ ind◦ ←7◦√भुज् (to enjoy, experience); *bhaikṣyam* (1nom◦ sing◦ ←n◦ *bhaikṣya* (alms) ←1◦√भिक्ष् (to ask for, beg); *api* (1.26); ***iha*** (time or place indicating ind◦ ←pron◦ *idam* 1.10); ***loke*** (7loc◦ sing◦ ←aggregative m◦ ***loka*** (world) ←1◦√लोक् (to see, seek); *hatvā* (1.31); *arthakāmān* (m◦ 2acc◦ plu◦ ←bahuvrī◦ *artha-kāma*, अर्थम् कामयति यः ←m◦ *artha* (wealth) 1.7 + m◦ or n◦ *kāma* (slave) 1.22); *tu* (1.2); *gurūn* (↑); *iha* (↑); *eva* (1.1); *bhuñjīya* (1st-per◦ sing◦ -pot◦ ātmane◦ ←7◦√भुज् (to enjoy, experience); ***bhogān*** (2acc◦ plu◦ ←m◦ *bhoga* (pleasure) 1.32); *rudhirapradigdhān* (m◦ 2acc◦ plu◦ ←tatpu◦ *rudhira-pradigdha* (tainted with blood) रुधिरेण प्रदिग्धः ←n◦ *rudhira* (blood) ←7◦√रुध् (to stop) + ppp◦ adj◦ *pradigdha* (tainted) ←2◦प्र√दिह् (to smear) (2.5)

(§3) ***gurūn*** (obj1◦ the gurus); ***ahatvā*** (having not killed, not killing); ***hi*** (because); ***mahānubhāvān*** (adj1◦-obj1◦ the noble); ***śreyaḥ:*** (adj◦-subj◦ better, better is); ***bhoktum*** (for suffering; to suffer); ***bhaikṣyam*** (subj◦ alms, the life on alms); ***api*** (also); ***iha*** (here); ***loke*** (in this world); ***hatvā*** (having killed); ***arthakāmān*** (adj2◦-obj1◦ they who covet wealth; the ones who are the slaves of wealth); ***tu*** (indeed); ***gurūn*** (obj1◦ the gurus); ***iha*** (here, in this world); ***eva*** (only); ***bhuñjīya*** (I may experience); ***bhogān*** (obj2◦ the pleasures); ***rudhirapradigdhān*** (adj◦-obj2◦ tainted with blood) (2.5)

(§4) ahatvā mahānubhāvān gurūn iha loke, śreyaḥ: bhoktum bhaikṣyam api, hi iha hatvā gurūn arthakāmān tu bhuñjīya eva bhogān rudhirapradigdhān

(§5) Having not killed the noble gurus here in this world, better is to suffer the life on alms also.

Because,[98] in this world, having killed the *gurus*, (even) the ones who are the slaves of wealth,[99] indeed I may experience[100] only the pleasures tainted with blood. (2.5)

2.6 न चैतद्विद्मः कतरन्नो गरीयो यद्वा जयेम यदि वा नो जयेयुः ।
यानेव हत्वा न जिजीविषामस्तेऽवस्थिताः प्रमुखे धार्तराष्ट्राः ।।

na ćaitadvidmaḥ: kataranno garīyo yadvā jayema yadi vā no jayeyuḥ:,
yāneva hatvā na jijīviṣāmaste‘vasthitāḥ: pramukhe dhārtarāṣṭrāḥ:. (2.6)

(§1) न च एतत् विद्मः कतरत् नः गरीयः यद्वा जयेम यदि वा नः जयेयुः । यान् एव हत्वा न जिजीविषामः ते अवस्थिताः प्रमुखे धार्तराष्ट्राः । *na ća* (r◦ 3/1) *etat* (r◦ 9/11) *vidmaḥ:* (r◦ 22/1) *katarat* (r◦ 12/1) *naḥ:* (r◦ 15/2) *garīyaḥ:* (r◦ 15/10) *yat* (r◦ 9/11) *vā jayema yadi vā naḥ:* (r◦ 15/3) *jayeyuḥ:* (r◦ 22/8) *yān* (r◦ 8/15) *eva hatvā na*

---

[98] See the footnote in verse 2.15

[99] Elsewhere◦ *arthakāmān* → my enjoyment, with desire for worldly gain, for the sake of worldly gains, we shall be enjoying pleasures of wealth, pleasures in the form of wealth and sense-enjoyments, for the pleasures derived from the acquisition of wealth and fulfillment of desires, I should enjoy the pleasures of wealth, ...etc. (noun purpose or adjective attached to 1st person subj◦ Arjuna or his folk).

📖 अर्थकामान् is the plural adjective qualifying plural obj◦ (acc◦ 2nd case) the gurus गरून्, same as *mahānubhāvān* महानुभावान् । It does not qualify subj◦ Arjuna, which is neither the obj◦ nor a plural noun. It should mean → they (the gurus) who covet wealth; those who are the slaves of wealth. महानुभावान् अर्थकामान् गुरून् अहत्वा – रुधिरप्रदिग्धान् भोगान् भुञ्जीय ।

By saying so, Arjuna refers back to Droṇa's recent declaration to Yudhiṣṭhira (M. Bh◦ Bhi◦ 43:56). Just few moments earlier, when Yudhiṣṭhira asked Droṇa as to, why he was fighting on Kauravas' side when he clearly knows that it is the unrighteous behaviour of the Kauravas that has brought the war on the Pāṇḍavas? Guru Droṇa had replied : O Dharmaraja! I know that at the end the victory will be yours, for you are on the righteous side (सत्यमेव जयते). I have stationed myself on Pandavas' side and, still I am fighting on Kauravas' side because :

अर्थस्य पुरुषो दासो, दासस्त्वर्थो न कस्यचित् ।
इति सत्यं महाराज! बद्धोऽस्म्यर्थेन कौरवैः ।।

O King! Yudhiṣṭhira! Man is salve of wealth, wealth is slave of none. Bound by wealth, therefore, I am a monetary slave of the Kauravas.

[100] Elsewhere◦ *bhuñjīya* → I shall be enjoying, my enjoyments, we enjoy, we shall be enjoying, the pleasures would be, all my enjoyments will be, my enjoyment will be, my pleasures will be, we shall after all enjoy ...etc.

📖 भुञ्जीय is not a future tense or a gerund. It is 1st person, singular, potential mood of the verb √भुज् (to experience) : I may experience.

jijīviṣāmaḥ: (r∘ 18/1) *te* (r∘ 6/1) *avasthitāḥ:* (r∘ 22/3) *pramukhe dhārtarāṣṭrāḥ:* (r∘ 22/8)

(§2) *na* (1.30); *ća* (1.1); ***etaṭ*** (this) (n∘ 2acc∘ sing∘ ←pron∘ *etaṭ* 2.3); 📖*vidmaḥ:* (1st-per∘ plu∘ pres∘ वर्तमान्-लट् parasmai∘ ←2∘√**विद्** (to know); *kataraṭ* (n∘ 1nom∘ sing∘ ←adj∘ *kataraṭ* or *ktaraṣ* ←pron∘ adj∘ *katara* (which one of two) ←pron∘ *kiṃ* (what) 1.1); *naḥ:* (4dat∘ 1.33); *garīyaḥ:* (n∘ 1nom∘ sing∘ ←adj∘ 📖***garīyaṣ*** (better) ←9∘√**गॄ** (to praise); *yaṭ* (1.45); *vā* (1.32); *jayema* (1st-per∘ plu∘ potential∘ विधि∘ parasmai∘ ←1∘√जि (to win); *yadi* (if) (1.38); *vā* (or) (1.32); *naḥ:* (2acc∘ plu∘ ←pron∘ *asmaḍ* 1.7); *jayeyuḥ:* (3rd-per∘ plu∘ des∘ potential∘ विधि∘ parasmai∘ ←1∘√जि (to win); *yāṇ* (m∘ 2acc∘ plu∘ ←pron∘ *yaḍ* 1.7); *eva* (1.1); *hatvā* (1.31); *na* (1.30); *jijīviṣāmaḥ:* (m∘ *ji* ←1∘√जि (to win) + *viṣāmaḥ:* 1st-per∘ plu∘ des∘ pres∘ वर्तमान्-लट् parasmai∘ ←3∘√विष् (to detach); *te* (1.33); *avasthitāḥ:* (1.11); 📖*pramukhe* (adv∘ or n∘ 7loc∘ sing∘ ←adj∘ *pramukha* (in front) 1.25); *dhārtarāṣṭrāḥ:* (1.46) (2.6)

(§3) ***na*** **(do not);** ***ća*** **(and);** ***etaṭ*** **(obj∘1 this);** ***vidmaḥ:*** **(we know);** ***kataraṭ*** **(subj1∘ which one of the two?);** ***naḥ:*** **(for us);** ***garīyaḥ:*** **(adj∘-subj1∘ is better)** ***yad-vā*** **(whether);** ***jayema*** **(we should conquer);** ***vā*** **(or);** ***naḥ:*** **(obj∘2 to us);** ***jayeyuḥ:*** **(they should conquer);** ***yāṇ*** **(adj1∘-obj3∘ to whom);** ***eva*** **(even);** ***hatvā*** **(having killed);** ***na*** **(do not);** ***jijīviṣāmaḥ:*** **(we wish to live);** ***te*** **(adj1∘-subj2∘ they);** ***avasthitāḥ:*** **(adj2∘-subj2∘ those who are arrayed in battle formation);** ***pramukhe*** **(adv∘ facing, in front);** ***dhārtarāṣṭrāḥ:*** **(subj2∘ the sons of Dhṛtarāṣṭra; the Kauravas)** (2.6)

(§4) ća etaṭ na vidmaḥ: kataraṭ garīyaḥ: naḥ: yad-vā jayema vā jayeyuḥ: naḥ: te dhārtarāṣṭrāḥ: avasthitāḥ: yāṇ hatvā na eva jijīviṣāmaḥ: (*santi*) pramukhe.

(§5) And this (also) we do not know (that) - which one of the two (is) better[101] for us. Whether we should conquer[102] (them) or should they conquer[103] us. They, the Kauravas, who are arrayed in battle formation,[104] to whom having killed[105] we do not even wish to live,[106] (are) in front. (2.6)

---

[101] Elsewhere∘ *garīyaḥ:* → which will be better, which would be better.

[102] Elsewhere∘ *jayema* → We should slay, we shall win, we shall conquer, we conquer, conquering them ...etc.

📖 जयेम is not a future tense, present tense or gerund. It is a potential mood from verb 1∘√जि

[103] Elsewhere∘ *jayeyuḥ:* → they shall conquer us, they will conquer us, being conquered by them, they conquer us, they should slay us, ...etc.

📖 जयेयु: is not a future tense, present tense or gerund. It is a potential mood from verb 1∘√जि

[104] Elsewhere∘ *avasthitāḥ:* → are standing, they are now standing, they stand ...etc. (like a present tense)

📖 अवस्थित is not a tense. It is a ppp∘ adj∘ of the subj∘ धार्तराष्ट्र। Therefore, धार्तराष्ट्रा: अवस्थिता: = the Kauravas, who are arrayed.

NOTE : In Sanskṛt, the verb *asti* (अस्ति) is not always actually written but it is understood; especially so, in the

2.7 कार्पण्यदोषोपहतस्वभावः पृच्छामि त्वां धर्मसम्मूढचेताः ।
यच्छ्रेयः स्यान्निश्चितं ब्रूहि तन्मे शिष्यस्तेऽहं शाधि मां त्वां प्रपन्नम् ।।

kārpaṇyadoṣopahatasvabhāvaḥ: pṛćchāmi tvāṁ dharmasammūḍhaćetāḥ:, yaććhreyaḥ: syānniśćitaṁ brūhi tanme śiṣyaste'haṁ śādhi māṁ tvāṁ prapannam; (2.7)

(§1) कार्पण्यदोषोपहतस्वभावः पृच्छामि त्वाम् धर्मसम्मूढचेताः । यच्छ्रेयः स्यात् निश्चितम् ब्रूहि तत् मे शिष्यः ते अहम् शाधि माम् त्वाम् प्रपन्नम् । *kārpaṇyadoṣopahatasvabhāvaḥ:* (r◦ 22/3) *pṛćchāmi tvāṃ* (r◦ 14/1) *dharmasammūḍhaćetāḥ:* (r◦ 22/8) *yaṭ* (r◦ 11/4) *śreyaḥ:* (r◦ 22/7) *syāṭ* (r◦ 12/1) *niśćitaṃ* (r◦ 14/1) *bruhi taṭ* (r◦ 12/2) *me śiṣyaḥ:* (r◦ 18/1) *te* (r◦ 6/1) *ahaṃ* (r◦ 14/1) *śādhi māṃ* (r◦ 14/1) *tvāṃ* (r◦ 14/1) *prapannaṃ* (r◦ 14/2) (2.7)

(§2) *kārpaṇyadoṣopahatasvabhāvaḥ:* (m◦ 1nom◦ sing◦ ←bahuvrī◦ *kārpaṇya-doṣopahata-svabhāva,* कार्पण्यस्य दोषेन उपहतः स्वभावः यस्य सः ←n◦ 📖*kārpaṇya* (pity) ←1◦√कृप् (to imagine) + m◦ *doṣa* (feebleness) 1.38 + adj◦ 📖*upahata* (impaired) 1.38 + m◦ s-karm◦ 📖***svabhāva*** ←pron◦ adj◦ *sva* (own) 1.28 + m◦ ***bhāva*** (nature) ←1◦√भू (to be, become); *pṛćchāmi* (1st-per◦ sing◦ pres◦ वर्तमान्-लट् parasmai◦ ←6◦√प्रच्छ् (to ask); ***tvāṃ*** (2acc◦ sing◦ ←pron◦ *yuṣmaḍ* 1.3); *dharmasammūḍhaćetāḥ:* (m◦ 1nom◦ sing◦ ←bahuvrī◦ *dharma-sammūḍha-ćetaṣ,* धर्मे सम्मूढम् चेतः यस्य ←m◦ *dharma* (righteousness) 1.1 + ppp◦ adj◦ 📖***sammūḍha*** (confused) ←4◦सम्√मुह् (to be deluded) + n◦ *ćetaṣ* (mind) 1.38); *yaṭ* (1.45); *śreyaḥ:* (better) (2.5); *syāṭ* (may be) (1.36); ***niśćitaṃ*** (certainly) (n◦ 1nom◦ = adj◦ ***niśćita*** (certail) ←5◦निस्√चि (to gather); ***bruhi*** (2nd-per◦ sing◦ imperative◦ लोट् ←2◦√ब्रू (to speak); ***taṭ*** (that) (n◦ 2acc◦ sing◦ ←pron◦ *taḍ* 1.10); ***me*** (me) (4dat◦ sing◦ ←pron◦ *asmaḍ* 1.7); *śiṣyaḥ:* (m◦ 1nom◦ sing◦

---

use of ppp◦ adjectives in active voice. For example, रामः गतः means Rāma (is or is the one who has) gone; where Rāma is a noun and gone is the adjective, not a verb; the verb 'is' is silent and understood. पाण्डवाः शूराः means the Paṇḍavas (are) brave. ते अवस्थिताः युद्धे means they (are) the ones present in the battle. Here अवस्थिताः is not a verb, it is adj◦ of subj◦ ते । The verb 'are (सन्ति),' is understood. NOTE : for a very clear understanding on the distinction between a past tense verb and a past participle adj◦ (ppp◦), or any other topic, please refer my handy book, '*Learn Sanskrit through English Medium.*'

[105] Elsewhere◦ *hatvā* → If we killed them, if we slew, by killing ...etc.

📖 हत्वा is not a conditional (लृङ्) mood; and it is also not Instrumental case.

[106] Elsewhere◦ *na jijīviṣāmaḥ:* → we should not desire to live, we would not like to live any longer, would result in our disinclination to continue, we should not care to live, we would not want to live ...etc.

📖 जिजीविषाम is not a potential mood. It is a desiderative present tense = we do not wish to live.

←m◦ *śiṣya* (disciple) 1.3); ***te*** (your) (m◦ 6pos◦ sing◦ ←pron◦ *yuṣmad* 1.3); *aham* (I) (1.22); *śādhi* (2nd-per◦ sing◦ imperative◦ लोट् parasmai◦ ←2◦√शास् (to govern); *mām* (me) (1.46); *tvām* (to you) (2.7); 📖*prapannam* (m◦ 2acc◦ sing◦ ←ppp◦ adj◦ ***prapanna*** (suppliant) शरणागत ←4◦प्र√**पद्** (to go) (2.7)

(§3) ***kārpaṇyadoṣopahatasvabhāvaḥ:*** (adj1◦-subj◦ he whose nature is impaired by the feebleness of pity); ***pṛcchāmi*** (I ask, I am asking); ***tvām*** (obj1◦ you); ***dharmasammūḍhacetāḥ:*** (adj2◦-subj◦ he whose mind is confused in the matter of righteousness i.e. what is right and what is not); ***yat*** (subj2◦ which, what); ***śreyaḥ:*** (adj◦-subj2◦ better); ***syāt*** (it may be, it should be); ***niścitam*** (certainly, decisively, specifically, for sure); ***bruhi*** (you please tell); ***tat*** (obj2◦ that); ***me*** (dat◦ to me); ***śiṣyaḥ:*** (adj3◦-subj◦ disciple, pupil); ***te*** (your); ***aham*** (subj◦ I; I am); ***śādhi*** (you please instruct); ***mām*** (obj3◦ me); ***tvām*** (obj1◦ to you); ***prapannam*** (adj4◦-subj◦ the one who is suppliant, fallen at feet) (2.7)

(§4) kārpaṇyadoṣopahatasvabhāvaḥ: dharmasammūḍhacetāḥ: pṛcchāmi tvām tat bruhi me niścitam yat syāt śreyaḥ: aham te śiṣyaḥ: prapannam tvām śādhi mām

(§5) Nature impaired by the feebleness of pity, mind confused in the matter of what is right and what is not,[107] I am asking you to please tell me decisively what may be better. I am your disciple, suppliant to you.[108] Please instruct me; (2.7)

HERE CONCLUDES THE "VISHAD YOGA." THE YOGA THAT OVERWHELMED AND HUMBLED ARJUNA.

2.8 न हि प्रपश्यामि ममापनुद्याद्यच्छोकमुच्छोषणमिन्द्रियाणाम् ।
अवाप्य भूमावसपत्नमृद्धं राज्यं सुराणामपि चाधिपत्यम् ।।

na hi prapaśyāmi mamāpanudyādyacchokamucchoṣaṇamindriyāṇām,
avāpya bhūmāvasapatnamṛddham rājyam surāṇāmapi cādhipatyam. (2.8)

---

[107] Elsewhere◦ *dharmasammūḍhacetāḥ:* → my mind is confused, I have lost all composure, with my mind bewildered, my understanding is confused ...etc.

📖 धर्मसम्मुढचेतस् is not a *tatpuruṣa samāsa.* It is not a verb of perfect or any other tense. It is not in Instrumental case. It is Nominative masculine adjective of the subject I (i.e. Arjunaḥ). The word declines like m◦ चन्द्रमस् (चन्द्रमा:, चन्द्रमसौ, चन्द्रमस: । पु◦ ◦चेता:, ◦चेतसौ, ◦चेतस:). Therefore, it is NOT 'my mind', but it is 'I' (Arjun).

[108] Elsewhere◦ *prapannam* → I have surrendered myself, I have taken refuge, I surreeunder to you, I surrender at your feet, I am seeking ...etc.

📖 प्रपन्न is not a verb, it is an adj◦ qualifying the subject I, therefore → I, the one who is fallen at feet.

(§1) न हि प्रपश्यामि मम अपनुद्यात् यत् शोकम् उच्छोषण् इन्द्रियाणाम् । अवाप्य भूमौ असपत्नम् ऋद्धम् राज्यम् सुराणाम् अपि च अधिपत्यम् । *na hi prapaśyāmi mama* (r◦ 1/1) *apanudyāt* (r◦ 9/9) *yat* (r◦ 11/4) *śokam* (r◦ 8/20) *ućchoṣaṇam* (r◦ 8/18, 24/3) *indriyāṇām* (r◦ 24/6, 14/2) *avāpya bhūmau* (r◦ 5/5) *asapatnam* (r◦ 8/21) *ṛddham* (r◦ 14/1) *rājyam* (r◦ 14/1) *surāṇām* (r◦ 24/6, 8/16) *api ća* (r◦ 1/1) *adhipatyam* (r◦ 14/2)

(§2) *na* (1.30); *hi* (because) (1.11); *prapaśyāmi* (1st-per◦ sing◦ pres◦ वर्तमान्-लट् parasmai◦ ←1◦प्र√दृश् (to see) 1.31); *mama* (1.7); *apanudyāt* (3rd-per◦ sing◦ -benedictive◦ आशि◦ parasmai◦ ←6◦अप√नुद् (to push); *yat* (1.45); 📖***śokam*** (2acc◦ sing◦ ←m◦ *śoka* (grief) 1.47); 📖*ućchoṣaṇam* (2acc◦ sing◦ ←n◦ *ućchoṣaṇa* (drying) ←4◦उद्√शुष् (to dry); ***indriyāṇām*** (6pos plu◦ ←n◦ ***indriya*** (organ) ←1◦√इन्द् (to be lofty); *avāpya* (past-participle lyp◦ ind◦ ←5◦अव√आप् (to attain, get); *bhūmau* (7loc◦ sing◦ ←f◦ ***bhūmi*** (earth) ←1◦√भू (to be, become); 📖*a-sapatnam* (2acc◦ sing◦ n.tatpu◦ ←n◦ ***sapatna*** (obstruction) ←1◦√पत् (to fall); 📖*ṛddham* (n◦ 2acc◦ sing◦ ←adj◦ *ṛddha* (affluent) ←3◦√ऋध् (to be pleaseed, grow); *rājyam* (kingdom) (obj◦ 1.32); *surāṇām* (6pos plu◦ ←m◦ ***sura*** (god) ←2◦सु√रा (to bestow); *api* (1.26); *ća* (1.1); 📖*adhipatyam* (n◦ 2acc◦ sing◦ ←taddhita◦ *adhipatya* (sovereignty) ←m◦ ***adhipa*** (king) ←2◦अधि√पा (to protect) (2.8)

(§3) *na* (not); *hi* (because); *prapaśyāmi* (I see, clearly see, think); *mama* (my); *apanudyāt* (it may remove, take away); *yat* (which, that); *śokam* (obj1◦ the grief, sorrow, pain); *ućchoṣaṇam* (obj2◦ the withering, the drying); *indriyāṇām* (of organs; or senses); *avāpya* (having gained, having obtained); *bhūmau* (on the earth, in the world); *asapatnam* (adj1◦-obj3◦ unrivalled, without enemies; unobstructed); *ṛddham* (adj2◦-obj3◦ extended, affluent); *rājyam* (obj3◦ kingdom); *surāṇām* (of the gods); *api* (also); *ća* (and); *adhipatyam* (obj4◦ the sovereignty, supremacy, authority) (2.8)

Correct Sanskrit Syntax is : न हि प्रपश्यामि यत् अवाप्य भूमौ असपत्नम् ऋद्धम् राज्यम् च सुराणाम् अधिपत्यम् च अपि अपनुद्यात् मम इन्द्रियाणाम् शोकम् च उच्छोषण् च ।

(§4) hi na prapaśyāmi yat avāpya asapatnam ṛddham rājyam bhūmau adhipatyam surāṇām api apanudyāt śokam ća ućchoṣaṇam mama indriyāṇām

(§5) Because,[109] I do not think that having gained unobstructed affluent kingdom on the earth (or)[110] the sovereignty of the gods, may also take away the grief and the drying[111] of my organs.

---

[109] See the footnote in verse 2.15

[110] Elsewhere◦ → with, and, also ...etc.

[111] Elsewhere◦ *ućchoṣaṇam* → which dries up, which burns up, which is drying up, parches, which is blasting, that is utterly drying up, which withers my senses, ...etc.

📖 उच्छोषणम् is neither a verb nor it is an adjective of the m◦ noun शोकः or n◦ noun इन्द्रियाणि । It is a n◦ noun,

(2.8)

Sanjaya said (sañjaya uvāća सञ्जय उवाच ।)

2.9 एवमुक्त्वा हृषीकेशं गुडाकेशः परन्तप ।
न योत्स्य इति गोविन्दमुक्त्वा तूष्णीं बभूव ह ।।

evamuktvā hṛṣīkeśaṁ guḍākeśaḥ: parantapa,
na yotsya iti govindamuktvā tūṣṇīṁ babhūva ha. (2.9)

(§1) एवम् उक्त्वा हृषीकेशम् गुडाकेशः परन्तप । न योत्स्ये इति गोविन्दम् उक्त्वा तूष्णीम् बभूव ह । *sañjayaḥ:* (r∘ 19/4) *uvāća. evam̦* (r∘ 8/20) *uktvā hṛṣīkeśam̦* (r∘ 14/1) *guḍākeśaḥ:* (r∘ 22/3) *parantapa na yotse* (r∘ 5/2) *iti govindam̦* (r∘ 8/20) *uktvā tūṣṇīm̦* (r∘ 14/1) *babhūva ha*

(§2) *sañjayaḥ:* (1.2); *uvāća* (1.25). *evam̦* (1.24); *uktvā* (1.47); *hṛṣīkeśam̦* (1.20); *guḍākeśaḥ:* (1nom∘ sing∘ ←m∘ *guḍākeśa* 1.24); *parantapa* (in 2.3 = Arjuna; in 2.9 = Dhṛtarāṣṭra); *na* (1.30); ***yotse*** (1st-per∘ sing∘ fut2∘ लृट् भविष्य∘ ātmane∘ ←4∘√युध् (to fight); *iti* (1.25); *govindam̦* (2acc∘ sing∘ ←m∘ *govinda* 1.32); *uktvā* (1.47); *tūṣṇīm̦* (silently) (adv∘ ind∘ ←4∘√तुष् (to be content); *babhūva* (3rd-per∘ sing∘ past-perf∘ लिट् भूत∘ parasmai∘ ←1∘√भू (to be, become); *ha* (stress or certainty indicating ind∘ ←3∘√हा (to go) (2.9)

(§3) ***sañjayaḥ:*** **(Sañjaya);** ***uvāća*** **(said).** ***evam̦*** **(in this manner);** ***uktvā*** **(having said);** ***hṛṣīkeśam̦*** **(**obj∘ **to Hṛṣīkeśa; to Śrī Kṛṣṇa);** ***guḍākeśaḥ:*** **(**subj∘ **the Guḍākeśa; Arjuna);** ***parantapa*** **(O Parantapa! O Dhṛtarāṣṭra!);** ***na*** **(not);** ***yotse*** **(I shall fight);** ***iti*** **(that, thus);** ***govindam̦*** **(**obj∘ **to Govinda; to Śrī Kṛṣṇa);** ***uktvā*** **(having said; saying);** ***tūṣṇīm̦*** **(silently, quietly, without speaking)** ***babhūva ha*** **(he stayed)** (2.9)

(§4) guḍākeśaḥ: uktvā hṛṣīkeśam̦ evam̦ parantapa uktvā govindam̦ iti na yotse babhūva ha tūṣṇīm̦

(§5) Arjuna, having spoken to Śrī Kṛṣṇa in this manner, O Dhṛtarāṣṭra![112] (and then) saying to

---

that has सम्बन्धः (genetive or possessive 6th case relationship) with n∘ इन्द्रियाणि । Thus, it should mean → n∘ noun उच्छोषणम् 'the drying' of the *indriya*s, इन्द्रियाणाम् उच्छोषणम् । NOTE : Correct Sanskrit Syntax is : न हि प्रपश्यामि यत् अवाप्य भूमौ असपत्नम् ऋद्धम् राज्यम् च सुराणाम् अधिपत्यम् च अपि अपनुद्यात् मम इन्द्रियाणाम् शोकम् च उच्छोषण् च ।

[112] परन्तप → arjuna, scorcher of enenies; Arjuna, the harasser of foes; Gudakesa (Arjuna), the scorcher of foes; Arjuna, the destroyer of the enemies; Gudakesha, the tormenter of; Gudakesa, the terror to the foes; ...etc

In the Mahābhārata, while speaking to Dhṛtarāṣṭra, (सञ्जय उवाच) as customary, Sañjaya has always used some glorified expression to address his Master. Similarly in Gītā 2.9 also, Sañjaya has addressed Dhṛtarāṣṭra with an expression of *parantapa!* परन्तप!, and there is nothing odd about it.

However, some patronizing critics ideologically translate this परन्तप! (vocative) word as an adjective of

Śrī Kṛṣṇa[113] that "I shall not fight," he stayed silently.[114] (2.9)

2.10 तमुवाच हृषीकेशः प्रहसन्निव भारत ।
सेनयोरुभयोर्मध्ये विषीदन्तमिदं वचः ।।

tamuvāća hṛṣīkeśaḥ: prahasanniva bhārata,
senayorubhayormadhye viṣīdantamidaṁ vaćaḥ:; (2.10)

(§1) तम् उवाच हृषीकेशः प्रहसन् इव भारत । सेनयोः उभयोः मध्ये विषीदन्तम् इदम् वचः । *tam* (r◦ 8/20) *uvāća hṛṣīkeśaḥ:* (r◦ 22/3) *prahasanniva* (r◦ 13/3) *iva bhārata senayoḥ:* (r◦ 16/5) *ubhayoḥ:* (r◦ 16/12) *madhye viṣīdantaṃ* (r◦ 8/18) *idaṃ* (r◦ 14/1) *vaćaḥ:* (r◦ 22/8)

(§2) *taṃ* (2.1); *uvāća* (1.25); *hṛṣīkeśaḥ:* (1.15); 📖*prahasan* (1nom◦ sing◦ śatṛ◦ adj◦ *prahasaṭ* (smiling) ←1◦प्र√हस् (to laugh)); *iva* (1.30); *bhārata* (1.24); *senayoḥ:* (1.21); *ubhayoḥ:* (1.21); *madhye* (1.21); *viṣidantaṃ* (2.1); *idaṃ* (1.10); ***vaćaḥ:*** (2acc◦ sing◦ ←n◦ *vacaṣ* (word) ←2◦√वच् (to speek)

(§3) ***taṃ*** **(obj1◦ to him, to Arjuna);** ***uvāća*** **(said);** ***hṛṣīkeśaḥ:*** **(subj◦ Hṛṣīkeśaḥ:; Śri Kṛṣṇa);** ***prahasan*** **(adj◦-subj◦ while smiling, smiling);** ***iva*** **(like, as if, as it were, so to speak);** ***bhārata*** **(O Bhātara! O King**

Arjuna. They argue, "as Dhṛtarāṣṭra was blind, he could not command his enemies. He was elder but could not become king. He was installed on the throne only as a result of Pāṇḍu's death. He was a weak king." Having intelligently argued so, they translate the vocative परन्तप as गुडाकेशः परन्तप अर्जुनः, but this conjecture can not be supported by Sanskrit gammar. Knowing this difficulty, some other critics have substituted the original word परन्तप with परन्तपः so that (with गुडाकेशः परन्तपः अर्जुनः) they could glorify Arjuna, who had become fainthearted at that time. But, even in this case, if you change परन्तप to परन्तपः, then the reference (to सञ्जय उवाच), to whom Sañjaya is talking, gets lost.

Thus, what Vyāsa has chosen in his poetry should be left alone, whether we favour the Kauravas or not. When Vyāsa has given epithet of महीपति in Sajnaya's mouth to address Dhṛtarāṣṭra, in Gītā 1.21 and elswhere in the Mahābhārata he has addressed the blind King as भरतशार्दूल, भरतश्रेष्ठ, भरतर्षभ, भरतसत्तम, कुरुशार्दूल, कुरुश्रेष्ठ, then what is the problem if Sañjaya addressed his master as परन्तप in the Gītā 2.9?

The construction and the context of this line of this verse, with a four-way dialogue between Arjuna and Krisṇa and between Dhṛtarāṣṭra and Sañjaya, is same as in the verses 1.24 (एवमुक्तो ...) and (तमुवाच ...) ; except that the vocative भारत! is replaced with परन्तप!

[113] Elsewhere◦ *govindam* → Govind! (vocative)

[114] Elsewhere◦ →*tūṣṇīṃ* → became silent, became calm, became quiet ...etc.

📖 तूष्णीम् is not a noun, verb or adjective. It is an ind◦ adverb, it must qualify a verb or an adj◦ or of another adverb = silently, calmly, quietly.

Dhṛtarāṣṭra!); ***senayoḥ:*** (of the two armies); ***ubhayoḥ:*** (of the both, of the two opposing); ***madhye*** (in the middle); ***viṣidantam̦*** (adj∘-obj1∘ to him who was lamenting, despairing); ***idam̦*** (this); ***vaćaḥ:*** (obj2∘ word, a group of words, a speech) (2.10)

(§4) bhārata iva prahasan hṛṣīkeśaḥ: uvāća tam̦ viṣidantam̦ madhye ubhayoḥ: senayoḥ: idam̦ vaćaḥ:

(§5) O King Dhṛtarāṣṭra! as if smiling, Śri Kṛṣṇa said to him, who was lamenting[115] in the middle of the two opposing armies, this word;[116] (2.10)

The Lord said (śrībhagavānuvāća श्रीभगवानुवाच ।)

2.11 अशोच्यानन्वशोचस्त्वं प्रज्ञावादांश्च भाषसे ।
गतासूनगतासूंश्च नानुशोचन्ति पण्डिताः ।।

aśoćyānanvaśoćastvaṁ prajñāvādāṁśća bhāṣase,
gatāsūnagatāsūṁśća nānuśoćanti paṇḍitāḥ:. (2.11)

(§1) अशोच्यान् अन्वशोचः त्वम् प्रज्ञावादान् च भाषसे । गतासून् अगतासून् च न अनुशोचन्ति पण्डिताः । *śrībhagavān̦* (r∘ 8/14) *uvāća. aśoćyān̦* (r∘ 8/11) *anvaśoćaḥ:* (r∘ 18/1) *tvam̦* (r∘ 14/1) *prajñāvādān̦* (r∘ 13/6) *ća bhāṣase gatāsūn̦* (r∘ 8/11) *agatāsūn̦* (r∘ 13/6) *ća na* (r∘ 1/1) *anuśoćanti paṇḍitāḥ:* (r∘ 22/8)

(§2) *śrībhagavān̦* (2.2); *uvāća* (1.25). *aśoćyān̦* (m∘ 2acc∘ plu∘ ←pot∘ adj∘ *aśoćya* (not worthy of grief) ←1∘अ√शुच् (to lament); *anvaśoćaḥ:* (अनु + अशोच्यः = अन्वशोच्यः 2nd-per∘ sing∘ -past-imper∘ लङ् भूत∘ parasmai∘ ←1∘अनु√शुच् (to lament); ***tvam̦*** (1nom∘ sing∘ ←pron∘ *yuṣmad̦* 1.3); *prajñāvādān̦* (m∘ 2acc∘ plu∘ ←tatpu∘ *prajñā-vāda* (word of wisdom) प्रज्ञावाद = प्रज्ञायाः वादः ←f∘ ***prajñā*** (wisdom) ←9∘प्र√ज्ञा (to know) + m∘ ***vāda*** (word) ←2∘√वच् (to speek); *ća* (1.1); *bhāṣase* (2nd-per∘ sing∘ pres∘ वर्तमान्-लट् ātmane∘ ←1∘√भाष् (to speak); *gatāsūn̦* (m∘ 2acc∘ plu∘ ←bahuvrī∘ ***gatāsu*** (dead) गतः असुः यस्य ←ppp∘ adj∘ ***gata*** (gone) ←1∘√गम् (to go) + m∘ *asu* (life) ←2∘√अस् (to be); *a-gatāsūn̦* (m∘ 2acc∘ plu∘ n.tatpu∘ ←adj∘ *gatāsu* ↑); *ća* (1.1); *na* (1.30); *anuśoćanti* (3rd-per∘ plu∘ pres∘ वर्तमान्-लट् parasmai∘ ←1∘अनु√शुच् (to lament); ***paṇḍitāḥ:*** (m∘ 1nom∘ plu∘ ←taddhita∘ ***paṇḍita*** (hte learned) पण्डा सञ्जाता यस्य ←f∘ *paṇḍā* (learning) ←10∘√पण्ड् (to collect, be learned) (2.11)

---

[115] Elsewhere∘ →*viṣidantam̦* → grief-striken, depressed, dejected one ...etc.

विषीदत् is not a past passive participle. Notice that in विषीदत् the ending त् is half (हलन्त). It is a present active participle, not a ppp∘ विषीदत । It is an adjective gerund. It means → he who was desponding or while desponding, lamenting, grieving, despairing.

[116] Elsewhere∘ →*idam vćaḥ:* → these words.

(§3) ***śrībhagavān*** (subj∘ Lord); ***uvāća*** (said). ***aśoćyān*** (obj1∘ to those who ought not to be grieved for); ***anvaśoćah:*** (you have grieved); ***tvam*** (subj1∘ you); ***prajñāvādān*** (obj2∘ the words of wisdom); ***ća*** (and); ***bhāṣase*** (you speak, you are speaking); ***gatāsūn*** (obj3∘ those whose life has gone; those who are dead); ***a-gatāsūn*** (obj4∘ those whose life has not gone away; those who are alive); ***ća*** (and, as well as); ***na*** (do not); ***anuśoćanti*** (they grieve for); ***paṇḍitāḥ:*** (subj2∘ the wise, the learned ones) (2.11)

(§4) tvam anvaśoćah: aśoćyān ća bhāṣase prajñāvādān paṇḍitāḥ: na anuśoćanti gatāsūn ća agatāsūn

(§5) You have grieved[117] (for) those who ought not to be grieved for and you are speaking[118] the words of wisdom. The learned ones do not grieve for those whose life has gone as well as for those who are alive. (2.11)

2.12 न त्वेवाहं जातु नासं न त्वं नेमे जनाधिपाः ।
न चैव न भविष्यामः सर्वे वयमतः परम् ।।[119]

na tvevāhaṁ jātu nāsaṁ na tvaṁ neme janādhipāḥ:,
na ćaiva na bhaviṣyāmaḥ: sarve vayamataḥ: param. (2.12)

(§1) न तु एव अहम् जातु न आसम् न त्वम् न इमे जनाधिपाः । न च एव न भविष्यामः सर्वे वयम् अतः परम् । *na tu* (r∘ 4/9) *eva* (r∘ 1/1) *aham* (r∘ 14/1) *jātu na* (r∘ 1/2) *āsam* (r∘ 14/1) *na tvam* (r∘ 14/1) *na* (r∘ 2/1) *ime janādhipāḥ:* (r∘ 22/8) *na ća* (r∘ 3/1) *eva na bhaviṣyāmaḥ:* (r∘ 22/7) *sarve vayam* (r∘ 8/16) *ataḥ:* (r∘ 22/3) *param* (r∘ 14/2)

(§2) *na* (1.30); *tu* (1.2); *eva* (1.1); *aham* (1.22); ***jātu*** (ever) (time indicating ind∘ ←4∘√जन् (to be born, give birth); *na* (1.30); *āsam* (1st-per∘ sing∘ -past-imper∘ लङ् भूत∘ parasmai∘ ←2∘√अस् (to be); *na* (1.30); *tvam* (2.11); *na* (1.30); *ime* (these) (1.33); *janādhipāḥ:* (m∘ 1nom∘ plu∘ ←tatpu∘ *janādhipa* (king) जनानाम् अधिपः ←m∘ *jana* (people) 1.28 + m∘ *adhipa* (lord) 2.8); *na* (1.30); *ća* (1.1); *eva* (1.1); *na* (1.30); *bhaviṣyāmaḥ:* (1st-per∘ plu∘ fut2∘ लृट् भविष्य∘ parasmai∘ ←1∘√भू (to be, become); *sarve* (1.6); *vayam* (we) (1.37); ***ataḥ:*** (= abstract ind∘ *ataś* ←pron∘ *idam* 1.10); ***param*** (ind∘ ←5∘√पृ (to be pleased) (2.12)

---

[117] Elsewhere∘ →*anvaśoćaḥ:* → thou grievest, you are lamenting, you are mourning, you grieve ...etc. (present tense लट् ।)

अन्वशोचः is लङ् past tense. It should mean → you have lamented, grieved, mourned ...etc.

[118] Elsewhere∘ →*bhāṣase* → while speaking, talking ...etc. (like a gerund)

[119] संयोगश्च वियोगश्च वर्तते न च ते न मे ।
न त्वं नाहं जगन्नेदं सर्वमात्मैव केवलम् ।। (avadhūtagītā 15)

(§3) ***na*** (not, not that); ***tu*** (verily); ***eva*** (also); ***aham̦*** (subj1∘ I); ***jātu*** (at anytime, ever); ***na*** (not there); ***āsam̦*** (I was); ***na*** (not that); ***tvam̦*** (subj2∘ you); ***na*** (not); ***ime*** (adj∘-subj3∘ these); ***janādhipāḥ:*** (subj3∘ kings); ***na*** (not, were not there); ***ća*** (and); ***eva*** (also); ***na*** (not that); ***bhaviṣyāmaḥ:*** (we shall be, we shall exist); ***sarve*** (adj∘-subj4∘ all); ***vayam̦*** (subj4∘ we); ***ataḥ: param̦*** (from here onwards, in the future) (2.12)

(§4) na tu aham̦ āsam̦ na jātu; eva na tvam̦ ća ime janādhipāḥ: eva na; na vayam̦ sarve na bhaviṣyāmaḥ: ataḥ: param̦

(§5) Not that verily I was not there at anytime; also not that you and these kings also were not there; (and) not that we all shall not exist, from here onwards. (2.12)

IN POSITIVE TERMS (by removing the double negative expressions) : I was there at all times; also that you and these kings also were there; (and) that we all shall exist, from here onwards.

2.13 देहिनोऽस्मिन्यथा देहे कौमारं यौवनं जरा ।
तथा देहान्तरप्राप्तिर्धीरस्तत्र न मुह्यति ।।[120]

dehino'sminyathā dehe kaumāraṁ yauvanaṁ jarā,
tathā dehāntaraprāptirdhīrastatra na muhyati. (2.13)

(§1) देहिनः अस्मिन् यथा देहे कौमारम् यौवनम् जरा । तथा देहान्तरप्राप्तिः धीरः तत्र न मुह्यति । *dehinaḥ:* (r∘ 15/1) *asmin̦* (r∘ 13/17) *yathā dehe kaumāram̦* (r∘ 14/1) *yauvanam̦* (r∘ 14/1) *jarā tathā dehāntaraprāptiḥ:* (r∘ 16/6) *dhīraḥ:* (r∘ 18/1) *tatra na muhyati*

(§2) 📖***dehinaḥ:*** (6pos sing∘ ←m∘ ***dehin̦*** (embodied one) ←2∘√दिह् (to smear); *asmin̦* (1.22); *yathā* (just as) (1.11); 📖***dehe*** (7loc∘ sing∘ ←m∘ *deha* (body) ←2∘√दिह् (to smear); 📖*kaumāram̦* (n∘ 1nom∘ sing∘ ←adj∘ *kaumāra* (childhood) ←10∘√कुमार् (to play as a child); 📖*yauvanam̦* (1nom∘ sing∘ ←n∘ *yauvana* (youth) ←2∘√यु (to join); 📖*jarā* (1nom∘ sing∘ ←f∘ ***jarā*** (old age) ←4∘√जॄ (to grow old); *tathā* (similarly) (1.11); *dehāntaraprāptiḥ:* (f∘ 1nom∘ sing∘ ←tatpu∘ *dehāntara-prāpti,* देहान्तरस्य प्राप्तिः । नवदेहस्य प्राप्तिः ←m∘ *deha* ↑ + n∘ ***antara*** (another) ←4∘√अन् (to move) + f∘ *prāpti* (attainment) ←5∘प्र√आप् (to attain, get); 📖***dhīraḥ:*** (1nom∘ sing∘ ←m∘ ***dhīra*** (self-possesses person) ←2∘धी√रा (to bestow); *tatra* (in that matter) (1.26); *na* (1.30); ***muhyati*** (3rd-per∘ sing∘ pres∘ वर्तमान्–लट् parasmai∘ ←4∘√मुह् (to be deluded) (2.13)

(§3) ***dehinaḥ:*** (of the embodied one); ***asmin̦*** (in this); ***yathā*** (as, just as); ***dehe*** (in the body); ***kaumāram̦*** (subj1∘ the childhood); ***yauvanam̦*** (subj2∘ the youth); ***jarā*** (subj3∘ the old age); ***tathā*** (adv∘ similarly, as

---

[120] अशरीरंशरीरेष्वनवस्थेष्ववस्थितम् । महान्तं विभुमात्मानं मत्वा धीरो न शोचति । (kaṭhopaniṣad 1:2.21)

well as); ***dehāntaraprāptiḥ:*** (subj4◦ the attainment of another body; the acquisition of a new body); ***dhīraḥ:*** (subj5◦ the self-possessed, steadfast person); ***tatra*** (there, in that matter); ***na*** (not); ***muhyati*** (he does get deluded) (2.13)

(§4) yathā asmin dehe kaumāram yauvanam jarā tathā dehāntaraprāptiḥ: (santi) dehinaḥ:, tatra dhīraḥ: na muhyati

(§5) Just as in this body the childhood, the youth, the old age as well as the attainment[121] of another body are the experiences of the ātmā;[122] in that matter the self-possessed person[123] does not get deluded. (2.13)

2.14 मात्रास्पर्शास्तु कौन्तेय शीतोष्णसुखदु:खदा: ।
आगमापायिनोऽनित्यास्तांस्तितिक्षस्व भारत ।।

mātrāsparśāstu kaunteya śītoṣṇasukhaduḥ:khadāḥ:,
āgamāpāyino'nityāstānstitikṣasva bhārata. (2.14)

(§1) मात्रास्पर्शा: तु कौन्तेय शीतोष्णसुखदु:खदा: । आगमापायिन: अनित्या: तान् तितिक्षस्व भारत । *mātrāsparśāḥ:* (r◦ 18/1) *tu kaunteya śītoṣṇasukhaduḥ:khadāḥ:* (r◦ 22/8) *āgamāpāyinaḥ:* (r◦ 15/1) *anityāḥ:* (r◦ 18/1) *tān* (r◦ 13/7) *titikṣasva bhārata*

(§2) 📖*mātrāsparśāḥ:* (m◦ 1nom◦ plu◦ ←tatpu◦ *mātrā-sparśa*, मात्राया: स्पर्श: ←f◦ *mātrā* (sense object) ←3◦√मा (to measure) + m◦ ***sparśa*** (contact) ←10◦√स्पर्श् (to touch); *tu* (1.2); ***kaunteya*** (8voc◦ sing◦ ←m◦ *kaunteya* 1.27); *śītoṣṇasukhaduḥ:khadāḥ:* (m◦ 1nom◦ plu◦ ←bahuvrī◦ *śītoṣṇa-sukha-duḥ:kha-da*, शीतं च उष्णं च सुखं च दु:खं च ददाति य: ←adj◦ *śīta* (pleasing) ←1◦√श्यै (to go, be conjested) + adj◦ *uṣṇa* (painful) ←1◦√उष् (to burn) + n◦ *sukha* (pleasure) 1.32 + n◦ ***duḥ:kha*** (pain) ←10◦√दु:ख् (to pain) + adj◦ *da* ←1◦√दा (to give); 📖*āgamāpāyinaḥ:* (m◦ 1nom◦

---

[121] Elsewhere◦ देहान्तरप्राप्ति: → so does it attain, it attains, so it takes, ...etc.

📖 देहान्तरप्राप्ति: is not a verb, प्राप्नोति is a verb. देहान्तरप्राप्ति: (◦attainment) is a feminine Nominative noun SUBJECT, not the object. देही is NOT a subject. And कौमारम्, यौवनम्, जरा, देहान्तरप्राप्ति: are NOT the Accusative objects in this verse.

[122] *dehinaḥ* → As said above, please note that the देही is NOT a subject (कर्ताकारक) and कौमारम्, यौवनम्, जरा, देहान्तरप्राप्ति: are NOT the objects (कर्मकारक) in this verse. Please look at the grammar.

[123] Elsewhere◦ *dhīraḥ:* → the wise, the wise one, the intelligent, the sober person, the wise man ...etc.

📖 The adj◦ धीर: does not come from the word धी or बुद्धि (intellect, intelligence), with root 1◦√बुध् (to know, to understand). It comes from adj◦ धीर (courageous, enduring), with roots 1◦√ध्यै (to contemplate) and 2◦√रा (to bestow). Thus it should mean → courageous, brave, intrepid, valiant, chivalorous. Same holds good for 2.15↓

plu∘ ←dvandva∘ आगमः च अपायी च ←m∘ ***āgama*** (coming) ←1∘आ√गम् (to go) + m∘ *apāyin* (departing) ←2∘अप्√इण् (to go); *anityāḥ:* (m∘ 1nom∘ plu∘ ←adj∘ n.tatpu∘ *a-nitya* (impermanent) ←adj∘ *nitya* 2.18↓); *tān* (1.7); *titikṣasva* (2nd-per∘ sing∘ -desi∘ imperative∘ लोट् ātmane∘ ←f∘ तितिक्षा[124] (endurance) ← 1∘√तिज् (to endure); *bhārata* (1.24) (2.14)

(§3) *mātrāsparśāḥ:* (subj∘ the contacts of the senses; the experiences derived from the sense objects; the sensory perceptions); *kaunteya* (O Kaunteya! O Arjuna!); *śītoṣṇasukhaduḥ:khadāḥ:* (adj1∘-subj∘ the ones that give pleasure and pain); *āgamāpāyinaḥ:* (adj2∘-subj∘ the one which begin and end; the ones that come and go); *anityāḥ:* (adj3∘-subj∘ the ones which are temporary, impermanent); *tān* (obj∘ to them); *titikṣasva* (you please bear, endure); *bhārata* (O Bhārata! O Arjuna!) (2.14)

(§4) kaunteya śītoṣṇasukhaduḥ:khadāḥ: mātrāsparśāḥ: āgamāpāyinaḥ: anityāḥ:; bhārata titikṣasva tān

(§5) O Arjuna! the experiences derived from the sense objects (are) the ones that give pleasure and pain,[125] ones that come and go, ones which are impermanent. O Arjuna! you please endure them. (2.14)

2.15 यं हि न व्यथयन्त्येते पुरुषं पुरुषर्षभ ।
समदुःखसुखं धीरं सोऽमृतत्वाय कल्पते ।।[126]

yaṁ hi na vyathayantyete puruṣaṁ puruṣrṣabha,
samaduḥ:khasukhaṁ dhīraṁ so'mṛtatvāya kalpate. (2.15)

(§1) यम् हि न व्यथयन्ति एते पुरुषम् पुरुषर्षभ । समदुःखसुखम् धीरम् सः अमृतत्वाय कल्पते । *yam* (r∘ 14/1) *hi na vyathayanti* (r∘ 4/4) *ete puruṣam* (r∘ 14/1) *puruṣrṣabha samaduḥ:khasukham* (r∘ 14/1) *dhīram* (r∘ 14/1) *saḥ:* (r∘ 15/1) *amṛtatvāya kalpate*

---

[124] सहनं सर्वदुःखानामप्रतीकारपूर्वकम् । चिन्ताविलापरहितं सा तितिक्षा निगद्यते ।

Tolerance for all sorrows without resistance, worry and crying about them, is *titikṣā.* (vivekchuḍāmani24)

[125] Elsewhere∘ दाः in *śītoṣṇa-sukha-duḥ:kha-dāḥ:* → produces, give rise to, give, results in ...etc. (like present tense)

Suffix द when attached to a substantive, it does not produce a verb of present tense; it produces an adjective. Therefore, ∘दुःखद does not mean 'it gives' pain, but it means → the giver, the one that gives (द = giver). The same holds good for the इन् suffix, in the taddhita word आगमापायिन् ।

[126] समदुःखसुखः पूर्ण आषानैराश्ययोः समः ।

समजीवितमृत्युः सन्नेवमेव लयं व्रज ।। (aṣṭāvakragītā 5.4)

(§2) **yam** (m∘ 2acc∘ sing∘ ←pron∘ *yad* 1.7); *hi* (1.11); *na* (1.30); *vyathayanti* (3rd-per∘ plu∘ pres∘ वर्तमान्-लट् parasmai∘ caus∘ ←1∘√व्यथ् (to be pained)); *ete* (1.23); 📖*puruṣam* (2acc∘ sing∘ ←m∘ 📖*puruṣa* (person) ←6∘√पुर् (to fill)); 📖*puruṣrṣabha* (m∘ 8voc∘ sing∘ ←bahuvrī∘ *puruṣrṣabha*, पुरुषाणां वृषभ: इव य: ←m∘ *puruṣa* ↑ + m∘ *vṛṣabha* (bull) ←1∘√वृष् (to rain)); *samaduḥ:khasukham* (m∘ 2acc∘ sing∘ ←bahuvrī∘ **sama-duḥ:kha-sukha**, दु:खं च सुखं च समं यस्य स: ←adj∘ or ind∘ *sama* (equanimous) 1.4 + n∘ *duḥ:kha* (pain) 2.14 + n∘ *sukha* (pleasure) 1.32); *dhīram* (2acc∘ sing∘ ←m∘ *dhīra* (delf-controlled) 2.13); *saḥ:* (1.13); 📖*amṛtatvāya* (4dat∘ sing∘ ←n∘ *amṛtatva* ←n.tatpu∘ adj∘ or n∘ **amṛta** (immortality) ←6∘√मृ (to die); **kalpate** (3rd-per∘ sing∘ pres∘ वर्तमान्-लट् ātmane∘ ←1∘√कॢप् (to be fit, deserve) (2.15)

(§3) *yam* (adj1∘-obj∘ whom, to whom); *hi* (because); *na* (do not); *vyathayanti* (they cause distress; they cause to waver); *ete* (adj∘-subj1∘ these); *puruṣam* (obj∘ to a man, to a person); *puruṣrṣabha* (O Puruṣrṣabha! O Arjuna!); *samaduḥ:khasukham* (adj2∘-obj∘ to him who is equanimous to pain and pleasures); *dhīram* (adj3∘-obj∘ to the person who is self-controlled);[127] *saḥ:* (subj2∘ he, that person); *amṛtatvāya* (for immortality, for eternal life); *kalpate* (he is fit) (2.15)

(§4) hi puruṣrṣabha samaduḥ:khasukham dhīram puruṣam yam ete na vyathayanti, saḥ: kalpate amṛtatvāya

(§5) Because,[128] O Arjuna! to him who is equanimous to pain and pleasures, to the person who is

---

[127] Elsewhere∘ *dhīram* → wise person.
📖 see footnote in 2.14 धीर:

[128] Elsewhere∘ *hi* हि → indeed, certainly, truly ...etc. Same footnote is the footnote for *tasmāt* (तस्मात्)
📖 The translators who do not fully appreciate the foundation of Hindu ethos, do flatly treat the word हि as a filler word with meaningless expression such as indeed, certainly, truly, verily ...etc. However, otherwise, हि is a very important key word in the Gītā, as She is, in any other Hindu scripture. In the Gītā, it invirably means '**because.**' This word (along with *tasmāt* तस्मात्) actually separates the Hindu Scriptures from all other religious and dogmatic texts where reasoning has no place and no importance.
हि (because) always has तस्मात् (therefore) associated or understood with it. The Gītā, like any other typical Hindu scripture, is based on questioning, reasoning, understanding, seeing and then believing. In (2.14) the Lord says 'O Arjuna! you endure the pain and pleasures ...' not as I say, but (2.15) 'because (हि) the self-controlled person is equanimous to pain and pleasures... therefore (तस्मात्) you endure them .'
NOTE : Everywhere in Gītā, while giving any advice, the reasoning is given with expressions हि and (or) तस्मात् । By flatly translating हि and तस्मात् as 'indeed,' you take away this beautiful and unique quality of the Gītā and turn it into a dogmatic and ritualistic blind faith, which it is not.

self-controlled,[129] to the person whom these (*mātrāsparśāḥ:*) do not cause distress,[130] he is fit for eternal life. (2.15)

2.16 नासतो विद्यते भावो नाभावो विद्यते सतः ।
उभयोरपि दृष्टोऽन्तस्त्वनयोस्तत्त्वदर्शिभिः ।।

nāsato vidyate bhāvo nābhāvo vidyate sataḥ:,
ubhayorapi dṛṣṭo'ntastvanayostattvadarśibhiḥ:. (2.16)

(§1) न असतः विद्यते भावः न अभावः विद्यते सतः । उभयोः अपि दृष्टः अन्तः तु अनयोः तत्त्वदर्शिभिः । *na* (r◦ 1/1) *asataḥ:* (r◦ 15/13) *vidyate bhāvaḥ:* (r◦ 15/6) *na* (r◦ 1/1) *abhāvaḥ:* (r◦ 15/13) *vidyate sataḥ:* (r◦ 22/8) *ubhayoḥ:* (r◦ 16/5) *api dṛṣṭaḥ:* (r◦ 15/1) *antaḥ:* (r◦ 18/1) *tu* (r◦ 4/6) *anayoḥ:* (r◦ 18/1) *tattvadarśibhiḥ:* (r◦ 22/8)

(§2) *na* (1.30); 📖*asataḥ:* (n◦ 6pos◦ sing◦ ←śatṛ◦ adj◦ with affix *aṭ* (अत्); **asaṭ** (non-existence)←2◦अ√अस् (to be); 📖***vidyate*** (3rd-per◦ sing◦ pres◦ वर्तमान्-लट् ātmane◦ ←4◦√विद् (to exist); 📖***bhāvaḥ:*** (m◦ 1nom◦ sing◦ ←m◦ *bhāva* (existence) 2.7); *na* (1.30); 📖***abhāvaḥ:*** (m◦ 1nom◦ sing◦ ←n.tatpu◦ *abhāva* (non-existence) ←1◦अ√भू (to be, become); *vidyate* (↑); 📖*sataḥ:* (n◦ 6pos◦ sing◦ ←śatṛ◦ adj◦ **saṭ** (existence) ←2◦√अस् (to be); *ubhayoḥ:* (of both) (1.21); *api* (1.26); 📖*dṛṣṭaḥ:* (m◦ 1nom◦ sing◦ ←ppp◦ adj◦ **dṛṣṭa** (perceived) ←1◦√दृश् (to see); ***antaḥ:*** (1nom◦ sing◦ ←m◦ or adj◦ **anta** (inference) ←1◦√अम् (to afflict); *tu* (1.2); *anayoḥ:* (of these two) (6pos◦ 2nd-per◦ ←m◦ pron◦ *idaṃ* (this) 1.10); 📖*tattvadarśibhiḥ:* (m◦ 3inst◦ plu◦ ←adj◦ **tattva-darśiṇ** (seer of truth) ←n◦ **tattva** (truth) ←8◦√तन् (to spread) + adj◦ *darśiṇ* (seer) ←1◦√दृश् (to see) (2.16)

(§3) ***na*** **(does not);** ***asataḥ:*** **(of non-existence);** ***vidyate*** **(it becomes; it exists, it occurs);** ***bhāvaḥ:*** (subj◦ **existence, being);** ***na*** **(does not);** ***abhāvaḥ:*** (subj2◦ **non-existence, non-being);** ***vidyate*** **(↑);** ***sataḥ:*** **(of existence);** ***ubhayoḥ:*** **(of both);** ***api*** **(verily);** ***dṛṣṭaḥ:*** **(the one that is seen, known, perceived);** ***antaḥ:*** (obj◦ **the conclusion, inference);** ***tu*** **(indeed);** ***anayoḥ:*** **(of these two);** ***tattvadarśibhiḥ:*** (subj◦3 **by the seers, by the visionaries of truth, reality, facts)** (2.16)

(§4) tu bhāvaḥ: asataḥ: na vidyate abhāvaḥ: sataḥ: na vidyate antaḥ: anayoḥ: ubhayoḥ: api dṛṣṭaḥ:

---

[129] Elsewhere◦ *dhīram* → the wise person, who is wise, wise man, ...etc.

[130] Elsewhere◦ *yam na vyathayanti* → the person who is not disturbed by, the man who is not troubled by, he who is not afflicted with ...etc.

📖 व्यथयन्ति is a third person, plural, causative, active voice. It is an action applied to the obj◦ 'to him.' It is not a singular adj◦ of the subject 'he, a person'. It is *parasmaipadī* usage, not a (Sanskrit) passive voice with Instrumental case for subject.

tattvadarśibhiḥ:

(§5) Indeed, existence of non-existence[131] does not occur[132] (and) non-existence of existence[133] does not occur. The inference of both of these is verily perceived by the seers of truth. (2.16)

In other words: Existence of non-existence never existed, does not exist and will never exist; and non-existence of existence never existed, does not exist and will never exist.

2.17 अविनाशि तु तद्विद्धि येन सर्वमिदं ततम् ।
विनाशमव्ययस्यास्य न कश्चित्कर्तुमर्हति ।।

avināśī tu tadviddhi yena sarvamidaṁ tatam,
vināśamavyayasyāsya na kaścitkartumarhati. (2.17)

(§1) अविनाशि तु तत् विद्धि येन सर्वम् इदम् ततम् । विनाशम् अव्ययस्य अस्य न कश्चित् कर्तुम् अर्हति । *avināśi tu tat* (r◦ 9/11) *viddhi yena sarvam* (r◦ 8/18) *idam* (r◦ 14/1) *tatam* (r◦ 14/2) *vināśam* (r◦ 8/16) *avyayasya* (r◦ 1/1) *asya na kaścit* (r◦ 10/5) *kartum* (r◦ 8/16) *arhati*

(§2) 🕮*avināśi* (n◦ 2acc◦ sing◦ ←n.bahuvrī◦ *avināśin* (imperishable) विनाश: नास्ति यस्य ←4◦अ–वि√नश् (to ruin); *tu* (1.2); *tat* (2.7); 🕮**viddhi** (2nd-per◦ sing◦ imperative◦ उपदेशार्थ लोट् parasmai◦ ←2◦√विद् (to know); ***yena*** (by which) (n◦ 3inst◦ sing◦ ←pron◦ *yad* 1.7); ***sarvam*** (1nom◦ sing◦ ←pron◦ *sarva* (all) 1.6); *idam* (this) (1.10); ***tatam*** (1nom◦ sing◦ ←ppp◦ adj◦ *tata* (spread) ←8◦√तन् (to spread); 🕮*vināśam* (2acc◦ sing◦ ←m◦ ***vināśa*** (destruction) ←4◦वि√नश् (to ruin); ***avyayasya*** (n◦ 6pos◦ sing◦ ←adj◦ n.bahuvrī◦ ***avyaya*** (indestructible) नास्ति व्यय: यस्य ←1◦अ–वि√इ (to enter, come, go); ***asya*** (n◦ 6pos◦ sing◦ ←pron◦ *idam* 1.10); *na* (1.30); 🕮***kaścit*** (anyone) (adj◦ m◦ pron◦ sing◦ ←pron◦ *kim* + indeclinable affix ***cit*** -one, any one, any person, any thing ←1◦√चित् (to percceive); *kartum* (1.45); *arhati* (one is able) (3rd-per◦ sing◦ pres◦ वर्तमान्–लट् parasmai◦ ←1◦√अर्ह् (to deserve) (

---

[131] Elsewhere◦ *asataḥ:* → of untruth, of non-truth, of false, of the unreal, ...etc.

[132] Elsewhere◦ नासतो विद्यते भाव: → there is no coming to be of the non-existent, of the non-existent there is no coming to be, ...etc.

🕮 If one says, 'of the non-existent,' then it means that there is such a **thing** as 'non-existence,' and thus it means non-existence has existence, which in itself is contradictory. Therefore, नासतो विद्यते भाव: = non-existence never existed, does not exist and will never exist. There is no such thing as non-existence. It is a false concept. It is often said that "at first there was nothing, and after destruction it will be back to nothing" which is not true. It is like saying 'beyond infinity or before zero. No such things, नासतो विद्यते भाव: everything was, is and will always be there, in some form or other.

[133] Elsewhere◦ *asataḥ:* → of truth, of the real, of brahma, of reality...etc.

2.17)

(§3) ***avināśi*** (adj∘-obj1∘ imperishable, indestructible); ***tu*** (to be); ***tat*** (obj1∘ that); ***viddhi*** (you understand, know); ***yena*** (subj1∘ by which); ***sarvam*** (adj1∘-obj2∘ all, everything); ***idam*** (obj2∘ this); ***tatam*** (adj∘3-obj1∘ spread, evolved) ***vināśam*** (obj3∘ destruction) ***avyayasya*** (of the indestructible); ***asya*** (of this); ***na kaścit*** (adj∘-subj2∘ no one); ***kartum*** (for doing; to do); ***arhati*** (Subj2∘ he is able) (2.17)

(§4) viddhi tat tu avināśi yena idam sarvam tatam; na kaścit arhati kartum vināśam asya avyayasya

(§5) Know[134] THAT to be imperishable, by which this everything (is) spread.[135] No one is able to do destruction[136] of THIS indestructible. (2.17)

2.18 अन्तवन्त इमे देहा नित्यस्योक्ताः शरीरिणः ।
अनाशिनोऽप्रमेयस्य तस्माद्युद्ध्यस्व भारत ।।

antavanta ime dehā nityasyoktāḥ: śarīriṇaḥ:,
anāśino'prameyasya tasmādyuddhyasva bhārata. (2.18)

(§1) अन्तवन्तः इमे देहाः नित्यस्य उक्ताः शरीरिणः । अनाशिनः अप्रमेयस्य तस्मात् युद्ध्यस्व भारत । ***antavantaḥ:*** (r∘ 19/2) ***ime dehāḥ:*** (r∘ 20/10) ***nityasya*** (r∘ 2/2) ***uktāḥ:*** (r∘ 22/5) ***śarīriṇaḥ:*** (r∘ 24/2, 22/8) ***anāśinaḥ:*** (r∘ 15/1) ***aprameyasya tasmāt*** (r∘ 9/9) ***yuddhyasva bhārata***

(§2) 📖*antavantaḥ:* (m∘ 1nom∘ plu∘ ←adj∘ **antavat** (impermanent) ←m∘ anta 2.16 + affix *vat* 1.5); *ime* (these)

---

[134] Elsewhere∘ विद्धि → should be recognized as ...etc.

📖 विद्धि is not a potential mood. It is not a third person verb. It is second person imperative mood.

[135] Elsewhere∘ येन सर्वम् इदं ततम् → That which pervades entire body, by which the body and things like it are pervaded, which pervades this universe, by which all this universe is pervaded, by which all this is pervaded, by which this entire body is pervaded ...etc.

📖 ततम् is not a verb. It is a ppp∘ adj∘ by which (येन) this everything is spread or from this everything is evolved (ततम्). Thus, सर्वम् ततम् → not only the 'body,' but everything, because THAT is everything. Also, That does not 'pervade,' it, but everything 'IS' that. When everything 'IS' THA,, how can it pervade Itself. If It did, then it will be separate from That, and That will not be It, and then तत्सर्वम्, सर्वं खल्विदं ब्रह्म, प्रज्ञानं ब्रह्म, तत्त्वमसि, अहं ब्रह्मास्मि, अयमात्मा ब्रह्म... will not hold good. Just as, the ring is not pervaded by gold, but the gold IS the ring, or the ring evolves from the gold or gold is spread or transformed in the shape of a ring.

[136] Elsewhere∘ *vināśam* → to destroy.

📖 विनाशम् is not a verb. It is a m∘ noun → destruction (obj∘).

(1.33); 🕮*dehāḥ:* (1nom∘ plu∘ ←m∘ *deha* (body) 2.13); *nityasya* (m∘ 6pos∘ sing∘ ←adj∘ ***nitya*** (eternal) ←1∘√नी (to carry); *uktāḥ:* (m∘ 1nom∘ plu∘ ←ppp∘ adj∘ *ukta* ←2∘√वच् (to speek) or 2∘√ब्रू (to speek); *śarīriṇaḥ:* (m∘ 6pos∘ sing∘ ←adj∘ or m∘ *śarīriṇ* (possessor of the body) ←9∘√शॄ (to smash); 🕮*anāśinaḥ:* (m∘ 6pos∘ sing∘ ←adj∘ or m∘ n.bahuvrī∘ *a-nāśiṇ* (indestructible) नास्ति नाशः यस्य ←4∘अ√नश् (to destroy); *aprameyasya* (m∘ 6pos∘ sing∘ n.bahuvrī∘ ←adj∘ or n∘ ***prameya*** (unfathomable) ←3∘प्र√मा (to measure); *tasmāt* (1.37); ***yuddhyasva*** (2nd-per∘ sing∘ imperative∘ उपदेशार्थ लोट् ātmane∘ ←4∘√युध् (to fight); *bhārata* (1.24) (2.18)

(§3) *antavantaḥ:* (adj1∘-obj∘ having an end; impermanent); *ime* (adj2∘-obj∘ these); *dehāḥ:* (obj∘ the bodies); *nityasya* (of the eternal one; possessed by the eternal one); *uktāḥ:* (adj∘3-obj∘ are called; are said to be); *śarīriṇaḥ:* (of the possessor-of-the-bodies, body bearer); *anāśinaḥ:* (of the indestructible one); *aprameyasya* (of the unfathomable; of the immeasurable); *tasmāt* (therefore); *yuddhyasva* (you join in the war); *bhārata* (O Bhārata! O Arjuna!) (2.18)

(§4) ime dehāḥ: anāśinaḥ: aprameyasya nityasya śarīriṇaḥ: uktāḥ: antavantaḥ: tasmāt bhārata! yuddhyasva.

(§5) These bodies possessed by the indestructible, unfathomable (and) eternal possessor-of-the-bodies, are said to be impermanent, therefore,[137] O Arjuna! you join in the war. (2.18)

2.19 य एनं वेत्ति हन्तारं यश्चैनं मन्यते हतम् ।
उभौ तौ न विजानीतो नायं हन्ति न हन्यते ।।[138]

ya enaṁ vetti hantāraṁ yaśćainaṁ manyate hatam,
ubhau tau na vijānito nāyaṁ hanti na hanyate. (2.19)

(§1) य एनम् वेत्ति हन्तारम् यः च एनम् मन्यते हतम् । उभौ तौ न विजानीतः न अयम् हन्ति न हन्यते । ***yaḥ:*** (r∘ 19/7) ***enaṃ*** (r∘ 14/1) ***vetti hantāraṃ*** (r∘ 14/1) ***yaḥ:*** (r∘ 17/1) ***ća*** (r∘ 3/1) ***enaṃ*** (r∘ 14/1) ***manyate hataṃ*** (r∘ 14/2) ***ubhau tau na vijānitaḥ:*** (r∘ 15/6) ***na*** (r∘ 1/1) ***ayaṃ*** (r∘ 14/1) hanti na hanyate

(§2) ***yaḥ:*** (he who) (m∘ 1nom∘ sing∘ ←pron∘ *yad* 1.7); ***enaṃ*** (m∘ 2acc∘ sing∘ ←pron∘ *etad* (this) 1.3); 🕮***vetti***

---

[137] This is the key word. They are only "said to be" impermanent (by the laymen), because they are perpetually transforming, as part of THAT eternal. The laymen are the subject of this verse.

[138] हन्ता चेन्मन्यते हन्तुं हतःश्चेन्मन्यते हतम् ।
उभौ तौ न विजानितो नायं हन्ति न हन्यते ।। (kaṭhopaniṣad 1.2.19)
आत्मानं सततं विद्धि सर्वत्रैकं निरन्तरम् ।
अहं ध्याता परं ध्येयमखण्डं खण्ड्यते कथम् ।। (avadhūtagītā 12)

(3rd-per∘ sing∘ pres∘ वर्तमान्-लट् parasmai∘ ←2∘√विद् (to know); 📖*hantāram* (2acc∘ sing∘ ←adj∘ or m∘ *hantṛ* (slayer) ←2∘√हन् (to hurt); *yaḥ:* (↑); *ća* (1.1); *enam* (↑); 📖**manyate** (3rd-per∘ sing∘ pres∘ वर्तमान्-लट् ātmane∘ ←4∘√मन् (to think); 📖*hatam* (m∘ 2acc∘ sing∘ ←ppp∘ adj∘ **hata** (slain) ←2∘√हन् (to hurt); **ubhau** (m∘ 2acc∘ dual∘ ←pron∘ **ubha** (both) ←6∘√उभ् (to join two); **tau** (m∘ 2acc∘ dual∘ ←pron∘ *tad* 1.2); *na* (1.30); 📖*vijānitaḥ:* (3rd-per∘ dual∘ pres∘ वर्तमान्-लट् parasmai∘ ←9∘वि√ज्ञा (to know); *na* (1.30); **ayam** (m∘ 1nom∘ sing∘ ←pron∘ *idam* 1.10); **hanti** (3rd-per∘ sing∘ pres∘ वर्तमान्-लट् parasmai∘ ←2∘√हन् (to hurt); *na* (1.30); **hanyate** (3rd-per∘ sing∘ pres∘ वर्तमान्-लट् ātmane∘ ←2∘√हन् (to hurt) (2.19)

(§3) ***yaḥ:*** (subj1∘ he who); ***enam*** (obj1∘ to this); ***vetti*** (he thinks; he imagines); ***hantāram*** (adj1∘-obj1∘ slayer); ***yaḥ:*** (subj2∘ he who); ***ća*** (and); ***enam*** (obj1∘ to this); ***manyate*** (he thinks); ***hatam*** (adj2∘-obj1∘ slain); ***ubhau*** (adj1∘-subj1,2∘ both); ***tau*** (adj2∘-subj1,2∘ they both); ***na*** (do not); ***vijānitaḥ:*** (they both know); ***na*** (neither); ***ayam*** (adj∘-subj3∘ this, he); ***hanti*** (he slays); ***na*** (not); ***hanyate*** (he is slain) (2.19)

(§4) yaḥ: vetti enam hantāram ća yaḥ: manyate enam hatam tau ubhau na vijānitaḥ: na ayam hanti na hanyate

(§5) He who thinks this (ātmā to be a) slayer and he who thinks this (to be) slain; they both do not know,[139] neither he (ātmā) slays not he is slain. (2.19)

2.20 न जायते म्रियते वा कदाचिन्नायं भूत्वा भविता वा न भूयः ।
अजो नित्यः शाश्वतोऽयं पुराणो न हन्यते हन्यमाने शरीरे ।।[140]

na jāyate mriyate vā kadāćinnāyam bhūtvā bhavitā vā na bhūyaḥ:,
ajo nityaḥ: śāśvato'yam purāṇo na hanyate hanyamāne śarīre. (2.20)

(§1) न जायते म्रियते वा कदाचित् न अयम् भूत्वा भविता वा न भूयः । अजः नित्यः शाश्वतः अयम् पुराणः न हन्यते हन्यमाने शरीरे । na jāyate mriyate vā kadāćit (r∘ 12/1) *na* (r∘ 1/1) *ayam* (r∘ 14/1) *bhūtvā bhavitā vā na bhūyaḥ:* (r∘ 22/8) *ajaḥ:* (r∘ 15/6) *nityaḥ:* (r∘ 22/5) *śāśvataḥ:* (r∘ 15/1) *ayam* (r∘ 14/1) *purāṇaḥ:* (r∘

---

[139] उभौ तौ न विजानितो → both are ignorant (adj∘), both of them are ignorant, are equally ignorant, both of them are wrong, both of them fail to perceive ...etc.

📖 विजानितौ is a verb not an adj∘, but 'ignorant' is an adj∘. It is not a verb.

[140] न जायते म्रियते वा विपश्चिन्नायं कुतश्चिन्नायं बभूव कश्चित् ।
अजो नित्यः शाश्वतोऽयं पुराणो न हन्यते हन्यमाने शरीरे ।। (kaṭhopaniṣad 1.2.18)
न जायते म्रियते न स वर्धते न क्षीयते नो विकरोति नित्यः ।
विलीयमानोऽपि वपुष्यमुष्मिन्न लीयते कुम्भ इवाम्बरं स्वयम् ।। (vivekachuḍāmaṇi 134)

15/6) *na hanyate hanyamāne śarīre*

(§2) *na* (1.30); *jāyate* (1.29); *mriyate* (3rd-per∘ sing∘ pres∘ वर्तमान्-लट् ātmane∘ ←6∘√मृ (to die); *vā* (1.32); *kadācit* (ever) (time indicating ind∘ ←pron∘ *kim* 1.1 + affix *da* (द) + affix *cit* 2.17); *na* (1.30); *ayam* (2.19); ***bhūtvā*** (ipp∘ ind∘ ←1∘√भू (to be, become); ***bhavitā*** (3rd-per∘ sing∘ fut1∘ लुट् parasmai∘ ←1∘√भू (to be, become); *vā* (1.32); *na* (1.30); 📖***bhūyah:*** (= ind∘ *bhūyas* (again) ←1∘√भू (to be, become); ***ajah:*** (m∘ 1nom∘ sing∘ ←n.tatpu∘ adj∘ ***aja*** (birthless) न जायते इति ←m∘ *ja* 1.7); ***nityah:*** (m∘ 1nom∘ sing∘ ←adj∘ or ind∘ *nitya* (perpetual) 2.18); *śāśvatah:* (m∘ 1nom∘ sing∘ ←adj∘ *śāśvata* (eternal) 1.43); *ayam* (2.19); 📖***purāṇah:*** (m∘ 1nom∘ sing∘ ←adj∘ ***purāṇa*** (primeval) ←1∘पुरा√नी (to carry); na (1.30); *hanyate* (2.19); *hanyamāne* (7loc∘ sing∘ ←śānac∘ adj∘ *hanyamāna* ←2∘√हन् (to hurt); *śarīre* (1.29) (2.20)

(§3) ***na*** **(neither);** ***jāyate*** **(he takes birth)** ***mriyate*** **(he dies);** ***vā*** **(or; not);** ***kadācit*** **(ever, at any time);** ***na*** **(not);** ***ayam*** **(subj1∘ this, this ātmā);** ***bhūtvā*** **(having been);** ***bhavitā*** **(he will be);** ***vā*** **(either);** ***na*** **(not);** ***bhūyah:*** **(again);** ***ajah:*** **(adj∘-subj∘ birthless)** ***nityah:*** **(adj2∘-subj∘ perpetual);** ***śāśvatah:*** **(adj3∘-subj∘ eternal);** ***ayam*** **(subj∘ this; this ātmā);** ***purāṇah:*** **(adj4∘-subj∘ primeval, primordial); na (not);** ***hanyate*** **(he is slain);** ***hanyamāne*** **(in being slain);** ***śarīre*** **(in the body)** (2.20)

(§4) na jāyate vā mriyate kadācit na ayam bhūtvā bhūyah: na bhavitā ayam ajah: nityah: śāśvatah: purāṇah: hanyate na śarīre hanyamāne vā

(§5) Neither he takes birth[141] not he dies ever; not this *ātmā* having been,[142] again will not be. This birthless,[143] perpetual eternal, primeval (ātmā) is not slain in the body being slain either. (2.20)

2.21 वेदाविनाशिनं नित्यं य एनमजमव्ययम् ।

---

[141] Elsewhere∘ *na jāyate* → it is never born, He is not born, it is not born, neither born, ...etc. (ppp∘)

📖 जायते is not a ppp∘ It is a simple Present tense of Active voice (लट्, कर्तरिप्रयोग:).

न जायते = he-she-it does not take birth.

[142] Elsewhere∘ भूत्वा → being born.

[143] Elsewhere∘ *ajah:* → unborn.

📖 Adjective 'unborn' is attached to one that is yet to be born, not yet born or not born (e.g. an unborn child). Adjective अज is attached to the one that is born, but not from a womb or not by a normal birth process. Originally this word was coined to describe Brahmā, who was born, not to Mahālakṣmi's womb, but to Mahāviṣṇu, the *puruṣa*, through his navel. So, Brahmā ब्रह्मा (the personified or manifest Brahma ब्रह्म), born from Viṣṇu, is अज: ।

कथं स पुरुषः पार्थ कं घातयति हन्ति कम् ।

vedāvināśinaṁ nityaṁ ya enamajamavyayam,
kathaṁ sa puruṣaḥ: pārtha kaṁ ghātayati hanti kam. (2.21)

(§1) वेद अविनाशिनम् नित्यम् य एनम् अजम् अव्ययम्। कथम् सः पुरुषः पार्थ कम् घातयति हन्ति कम् । *veda* (r◦ 1/1) *avināśinam* (r◦ 14/1) *nityam* (r◦ 14/1) *yaḥ:* (r◦ 19/7) *enam* (r◦ 8/16) *ajam* (r◦ 8/16) *avyayam* (r◦ 14/2) *katham* (r◦ 14/1) *saḥ:* (r◦ 21/2) *puruṣaḥ:* (r◦ 22/3) *pārtha kam* (r◦ 14/1) *ghātayati hanti kam* (r◦ 14/2)

(§2) 📖***veda*** (3rd-per◦ sing◦ pres◦ वर्तमान्-लट् parasmai◦ ←2◦√विद् (to know); 📖*avināśinam* (m◦ 2acc◦ sing◦ ←adj◦ *avināśin* (indestructible) ←4◦अ-वि-√नश् (to destroy); ***nityam*** (m◦ 2acc◦ sing◦ ←adv◦ or adj◦ *nitya* (perpetual) 2.18); *yaḥ:* (2.19); *enam* (m◦ 2.19); ***ajam*** (m◦ 2acc◦ sing◦ ←adj◦ *aja* (birthless) 2.20); 📖***avyayam*** (m◦ 2acc◦ sing◦ ←adj◦ *avyaya* (imperishable) 2.17); *katham* (1.37); *saḥ:* (1.13); ***puruṣaḥ:*** (1nom◦ sing◦ ←m◦ *puruṣa* (person) 2.15); *pārtha* (1.25); ***kam*** (whom) (m◦ 2acc◦ sing◦ ←pron◦ *kim* 1.1); *ghātayati* (3rd-per◦ sing◦ pres◦ वर्तमान्-लट् parasmai◦ caus◦ ←2◦√हन् (to hurt); *hanti* (2.19); *kam* (↑) (2.21)

(§3) ***veda*** **(he knows);** ***avināśinam*** **(adj1◦-obj1◦ indestructible);** ***nityam*** **(adj2◦-obj1◦ perpetual);** ***yaḥ:*** **(adj1◦-subj◦ he who);** ***enam*** **(obj1◦ this; this ātmā);** ***ajam*** **(adj3◦-obj1◦ birthless);** ***avyayam*** **(adj4◦-obj1◦ imperishable);** ***katham*** **(how does?);** ***saḥ:*** **(adj2◦-subj◦ he, that person);** ***puruṣaḥ:*** **(subj◦ person);** ***pārtha*** **(O Pārtha! O Arjuna!);** ***kam*** **(obj2◦ anyone?);** ***ghātayati*** **(he causes to slay);** ***hanti*** **(he slays, does he slay);** ***kam*** **(obj3◦ whom?)** (2.21)

(§4) yaḥ: veda enam avināśinam nityam ajam avyayam pārtha katham saḥ: puruṣaḥ: ghātayati kam kam hanti?

(§5) He who knows this[144] indestructible, perpetual, birthless (and) imperishable *ātmā*, O Arjuna! how does he causes to slay anyone (and) whom does he slay? (2.21)

2.22 वासांसि जीर्णानि यथा विहाय नवानि गृह्णाति नरोऽपराणि ।

---

[144] Elsewhere◦ *veda enam* → he who knows that it is, who knows this self to be, he who knows that the Soul is, he who knows this One as ..., who knows This to be ..., who recognizes the Atman as, knows Him as, ...etc.
📖 *enam* एनम् is not Nominative. The soul is not the subject of this clause. *enam* is in Accusative. It is the object. Thus, it should NOT be 'he who knows that this soul (subj◦) is indestructible (adj◦-subj◦) ...,' instead it should be, 'he who knows this indestructible, eternal, undecaying, birthless (adj◦-obj◦) ... *ātmā* (obj◦).'
The difference is this : (i) The first case indicates that *ātmā* has only these four qualities. (ii) Whereas, in the second case : he who knows the true nature of *ātmā,* (in addition to being) the possessor these four qualities, as well as the qualities mentioned in 2.24, 2.25 etc. and much more), he ...

तथा शरीराणि विहाय जीर्णान्यन्यानि संयाति नवानि देही ।।

vāsāṁsi jīrṇāni yathā vihāya navāni gṛhṇāti naro'parāṇi,
tathā śarīrāṇi vihāya jīrṇānyanyāni saṁyāti navāni dehī. (2.22)

(§1) वासांसि जीर्णानि यथा विहाय नवानि गृह्णाति नरः अपराणि । तथा शरीराणि विहाय जीर्णानि अन्यानि संयाति नवानि देही । *vāsāṁsi jīrṇāni yathā vihāya navāni gṛhṇāti naraḥ:* (r◦ 15/1) *aparāṇi* (r◦ 24/7) *tathā śarīrāṇi* (r◦ 24/7) *vihāya jīrṇāni* (r◦ 4/1) *anyāni saṁyāti navāni dehī*

(§2) *vāsāṁsi* (2acc◦ plu◦ ←n◦ *vāsaṣ* (cloth) ←1◦√वस् (to stay); ***jīrṇāni*** (n◦ 2acc◦ plu◦ ←ppp◦ adj◦ 📖*jīrṇa* (discardable) ←4◦√जॄ (to grow old); *yathā* (1.11); 📖***vihāya*** (past-participle lyp◦ ind◦ ←3◦वि√हा (to go); 📖***navāni*** (n◦ 2acc◦ plu◦ ←adj◦ *nava* (new) ←2◦√नु (to commend); *gṛhṇāti* (3rd-per◦ sing◦ pres◦ वर्तमान्–लट् parasmai◦ ←9◦√ग्रह (to take); ***naraḥ:*** (1nom◦ sing◦ ←m◦ *nara* (person) 1.5); *aparāṇi* (n◦ 2acc◦ plu◦ ←pron◦ adj◦ ***a-para*** (other) ←adj◦ or n◦ *para* 2.3); *tathā* (1.8); *śarīrāṇi* (2acc◦ plu◦ ←n◦ *śarīra* 1.29); *vihāya* (↑); *jīrṇāni* (↑); *anyāni* (n◦ 2acc◦ plu◦ ←adj◦ *anya* 1.9); ***saṁyāti*** (3rd-per◦ sing◦ pres◦ वर्तमान्–लट् parasmai◦ ←2◦सम्√या (to go); *navāni* (↑); 📖***dehī*** (1nom◦ sing◦ ←m◦ *dehiṇ* (ātmā) 2.13) (2.22)

(§3) ***vāsāṁsi*** **(obj1◦ the clothes);** ***jīrṇāni*** **(adj◦-obj1◦ the discardable ones);** ***yathā*** **(as, just as);** ***vihāya*** **(having cast off);** ***navāni*** **(adj1◦-obj2◦ new, aanaother);** ***gṛhṇāti*** **(he wares, he takes);** ***naraḥ:*** **(subj1◦ a man, a person);** ***aparāṇi*** **(adj2◦-obj2◦ other);** ***tathā*** **(so);** ***śarīrāṇi*** **(obj3◦ bodies);** ***vihāya*** **(having cast off);** ***jīrṇāni*** **(adj◦-obj3◦ the discardable, unwanted);** ***anyāni*** **(obj4◦ other);** ***saṁyāti*** **(he does get);** ***navāni*** **(adj◦-obj4◦ new);** ***dehī*** **(subj2◦ the embodied; the ātmā)** (2.22)

(§4) yathā naraḥ: gṛhṇāti aparāṇi navāni vāsāṁsi vihāya jīrṇāni tathā dehī saṁyāti anyāni navāni śarīrāṇi vihāya jīrṇāni

(§5) Just as a person takes other new clothes, having cast off[145] the discardable[146] ones; so does the ātmā get new bodies, having cast off the discardable ones. (2.22)

2.23 नैनं छिन्दन्ति शस्त्राणि नैनं दहति पावकः ।
न चैनं क्लेदयन्त्यापो न शोषयति मारुतः ।।

nainaṁ ćhindanti śastrāṇi nainaṁ dahati pāvakaḥ:,
na ćainaṁ kledayantyāpo na śoṣayati mārutaḥ:. (2.23)

---

[145] Elsewhere◦ *vihāya* → casts off, gives up, discards, ...etc.

📖 विहाय is not a present लट् tense. It is a past participle gerund → having cast off.

[146] Elsewhere◦ *jirnaāni* → used, wor out.

(§1) न एनम् छिन्दन्ति शस्त्राणि न एनम् दहति पावकः । न च एनम् क्लेदयन्ति आपः न शोषयति मारुतः । *na* (r◦ 3/1) *enam̦* (r◦ 14/1) *ćhindanti śastrāṇi* (r◦ 24/7) *na* (r◦ 3/1) *enam̦* (r◦ 14/1) *dahati pāvakaḥ:* (r◦ 22/8) *na ća* (r◦ 3/1) *enam̦* (r◦ 14/1) *kledayanti* (r◦ 4/2) *āpaḥ:* (r◦ 15/6) *na śoṣayati mārutaḥ:* (r◦ 22/8)

(§2) *na* (1.30); *enam̦* (2acc◦ 2.19); *ćhindanti* (3rd-per◦ plu◦ pres◦ वर्तमान्-लट् parasmai◦ ←7◦√छिद् (to cut); 📖*śastrāṇi* (1nom◦ plu◦ ←n◦ *śastra* (weapon) 1.9); *na* (1.30); *enam̦* (2.19); *dahati* (3rd-per◦ sing◦ pres◦ वर्तमान्-लट् parasmai◦ ←1◦√दह् (to burn); 📖***pāvakaḥ:*** (1nom◦ sing◦ ←m◦ *pāvaka* (fire) ←1◦√पू (to cleanse); *na* (1.30); *ća* (1.1); *enam̦* (2.19); *kledayanti* (3rd-per◦ plu◦ pres◦ वर्तमान्-लट् parasmai◦ caus◦ ←4◦√क्लिद् (to wet); 📖***āpaḥ:*** (1nom◦ -collective noun sing◦ ←n◦ *āpa* (water) ←10◦√आप् (to attain, get); *na* (1.30); *śoṣayati* (3rd-per◦ sing◦ pres◦ वर्तमान्-लट् parasmai◦ caus◦ ←4◦√शुष् (to dry); 📖*mārutaḥ:* (1nom◦ sing◦ ←m◦ *māruta* (wind) ←6◦√मृ (to die) (2.23)

(§3) *na* (do not); *enam̦* (adj◦-obj◦ this); *ćhindanti* (they cleave, cut); *śastrāṇi* (subj1◦ weapons); *na* (does not); *enam̦* (adj◦-obj◦ this, it); *dahati* (it burns); *pāvakaḥ:* (subj2◦ fire); *na* (does not); *ća* (and); *enam̦* (adj◦-obj◦ this, it); *kledayanti* (they make it wet); *āpaḥ:* (subj3◦ the waters; water); *na* (does not); *śoṣayati* (it dries it up); *mārutaḥ:* (subj4◦ wind) (2.23)

(§4) śastrāṇi na ćhindanti enam̦ pāvakaḥ: na dahati enam̦ āpaḥ: na enam̦ kledayanti ća mārutaḥ: na śoṣayati

(§5) Weapons do not cleave[147] this (ātmā), fire does not burn it, water does not make it wet, and wind does not dry it up. (2.23)

2.24 अच्छेद्योऽयमदाह्योऽयमक्लेद्योऽशोष्य एव च ।
नित्यः सर्वगतः स्थाणुरचलोऽयं सनातनः ।।[148]

aććhedyo'yamadāhyo'yamakledyo'śoṣya eva ća,
nityaḥ: sarvagataḥ: sthāṇuraćalo'yaṁ sanātanaḥ:; (2.24)

(§1) अच्छेद्यः अयम् अदाह्यः अयम् अक्लेद्यः अशोष्यः एव च । नित्यः सर्वगतः स्थाणुः अचलः अयम् सनातनः । *aććhedyaḥ:* (r◦ 15/1) *ayam̦* (r◦ 8/16) *adāhyaḥ:* (r◦ 15/1) *ayam̦* (r◦ 8/16) *akledyaḥ:* (r◦ 15/1) *aśoṣyaḥ:* (r◦ 19/7) *eva ća nityaḥ:* (r◦ 22/7) *sarvagataḥ:* (r◦ 22/7) *sthāṇuḥ:* (r◦ 16/3) *aćalaḥ:* (r◦ 15/1) *ayam̦* (r◦ 14/1)

---

[147] Elsewhere◦ *ćhindanti* → cannot cut, can never be cut by, can not be cleaved, ...etc.
📖 छिन्दन्ति is a simple active habitual present tense. Same is the problem with दहति, क्लेदयन्ति and शोषयति ।

[148] अखण्डोऽहमनन्तोऽहं परिपूर्णोऽहमद्वयम् ।
सच्चिदानन्दरूपोऽहं ज्योतिषां ज्योतिरस्म्यहम् ।। (ramagītā 8.17)

sanātanaḥ: (r∘ 22/8)

(§2) *aććhedyaḥ:* (m∘ 1nom∘ sing∘ ←adj∘ n.tatpu∘ -pot∘ adj∘ *a-ććhedya* (uncleavable) ←7∘अ√छिद् (to cut); *ayam̧* (this) (2.19); *adāhyaḥ:* (m∘ 1nom∘ sing∘ ←n.tatpu∘ -pot∘ adj∘ *a-dāhya* (incombustible) ←1∘अ√दह् (to burn); *ayam̧* (2.19); *akledyaḥ:* (m∘ 1nom∘ sing∘ ←n.tatpu∘ -pot∘ adj∘ *a-kledya* (non-wettable) ←4∘अ√क्लिद् (to be wet); *aśoṣyaḥ:* (m∘ 1nom∘ sing∘ ←n.tatpu∘ -pot∘ adj∘ *a-śoṣya* (non-dryable) ←4∘अ√शुष् (to dry); *eva* (1.1); *ća* (1.1); 🕮*nityaḥ:* (2.20); 🕮*sarvagataḥ:* (m∘ 1nom∘ sing∘ ←tatpu∘ ***sarva-gata*** (omnipresent) सर्वस्मिन् गतः ←pron∘ *sarva* 1.6 + adj∘ *gata* 2.11); 🕮*sthāṇuḥ:* (m∘ 1nom∘ sing∘ ←adj∘ *sthāṇu* (steady) ←1∘√स्था (to stay); 🕮*aćalaḥ:* (m∘ 1nom∘ sing∘ ←n.bahuvrī∘ adj∘ ***a-ćala*** (permanent) ←1∘अ√चल् (to walk, move); *ayam̧* (2.19); 🕮***sanātanaḥ:*** (m∘ 1nom∘ sing∘ ←adj∘ *sanātana* (eternal) 1.40) (2.24)

(§3) *aććhedyaḥ:* (adj1∘-subj∘ uncleavable; which can not be cut); *ayam̧* (subj∘ this); *adāhyaḥ:* (adj2∘-subj∘ incombustible; which can not be burnt); *ayam̧* (this); *akledyaḥ:* (adj3∘-subj∘ which can not be wetted, soddened); *aśoṣyaḥ:* (adj4∘-subj∘ which can not be dried up); *eva* (also); *ća* (and); *nityaḥ:* (adj5∘-subj∘ perpetual); *sarvagataḥ:* (adj6∘-subj∘ all-encompassing); *sthāṇuḥ:* (adj7∘-subj∘ steady); *aćalaḥ:* (adj8∘-subj∘ permanent); *ayam̧* (subj∘ this); *sanātanaḥ:* (adj9∘-subj∘ eternal) (2.24)

(§4) ayam̧ nityaḥ: sarvagataḥ: sthāṇuḥ: aćalaḥ: ayam̧ sanātanaḥ: aććhedyaḥ: adāhyaḥ: akledyaḥ: ća ayam̧ aśoṣyaḥ: eva;

(§5) This[149] perpetual, all-encompassing, steady, permanent (and) this eternal (ātmā) which can not be cut, which can not be burnt, which can not be soddened and this (ātmā) which can not be dried up also; (2.24)

2.25 अव्यक्तोऽयमचिन्त्योऽयमविकार्योऽयमुच्यते ।
तस्मादेवं विदित्वैनं नानुशोचितुमर्हसि ।।

avyakto'yamaćintyo'yamavikāryo'yamućyate,
tasmādevaṁ viditvainaṁ nānuśoćitumarhasi. (2.25)

(§1) अव्यक्तः अयम् अचिन्त्यः अयम् अविकार्यः अयम् उच्यते । तस्मात् एवम् विदित्वा एनम् न अनुशोचितुम् अर्हसि । *avyaktaḥ:* (r∘ 15/1) *ayam̧* (r∘ 8/16) *aćintyaḥ:* (r∘ 15/1) *ayam̧* (r∘ 8/16) *avikāryaḥ:* (r∘ 15/1) *ayam̧* (r∘ 8/20) *ućyate tasmāţ* (r∘ 8/9) *evam̧* (r∘ 14/1) *viditvā* (r∘ 3/3) *enam̧* (r∘ 14/1) *na* (r∘ 1/1) *anuśoćitum̧* (r∘ 8/16) *arhasi*

(§2) 🕮***avyaktaḥ:*** (m∘ 1nom∘ sing∘ ←ppp∘ adj∘ n.tatpu∘ ***avyakta*** (unmanifest) ←7∘अ–वि√अञ्ज् (to make); *ayam̧*

---

[149] Elsewhere∘ *ayam̧* → He, this individual soul, It, ...etc.

(this) (2.19); *acintyaḥ:* (m◦ 1nom◦ sing◦ ←n.tatpu◦ -pot◦ adj◦ ***acintya*** (incomprehensible) ←10◦अ√चिन्त् (to think); *ayaṃ* (2.19); *avikāryaḥ:* (m◦ 1nom◦ sing◦ ←n.tatpu◦ adj◦ *avikārya* (immutable) ←8◦अ-वि√कृ (to do); *ayaṃ* (2.19); ***ucyate*** (pass◦ pres◦ वर्तमान्-लट् 3rd-per◦ sing◦ ātmane◦ ←2◦√वच् (to speek); *tasmāt* (therefore) (1.37); *evaṃ* (in this manner) (1.24); ***viditvā*** (ipp◦ ind◦ ←2◦√विद् (to know); *enaṃ* (2.19); *na* (1.30); *anuśocitum* (inf◦ ind◦ ←1◦अनु√शुच् (to lament); ***arhasi*** (2nd-per◦ sing◦ pres◦ वर्तमान्-लट् parasmai◦ ←1◦√अर्ह् (to deserve, be fit) (2.25)

(§3) *avyaktaḥ:* (adj1◦-subj◦ unpersonified; unmanifest); *ayaṃ* (subj◦ this); *acintyaḥ:* (adj2◦-subj◦ incomprehensible); *ayaṃ* (subj◦ this); *avikāryaḥ:* (adj3◦-subj◦ immutable); *ayaṃ* (subj◦ this); *ucyate* (he is said to be); *tasmāt* (therefore); *evaṃ* (in this manner; in this way); *viditvā* (having understood; having known); *enaṃ* (obj◦ this); *na* (not); *anuśocitum* (for lamenting, to lament, to grieve); *arhasi* (you should, you ought to; you are worthy of) (2.25)

(§4) ayaṃ avyaktaḥ: ayaṃ acintyaḥ: ayaṃ ucyate avikāryaḥ: tasmāt viditvā enaṃ evaṃ arhasi na anuśocitum

(§5) This unmanifest, this incomprehensible, is said to be immutable, therefore,[150] having understood this (ātmā) in this manner, you ought not to grieve. (2.25)

2.26 अथ चैनं नित्यजातं नित्यं वा मन्यसे मृतम् ।
तथापि त्वं महाबाहो नैवं शोचितुमर्हसि ।।[151]

atha cainaṁ nityajātaṁ nityaṁ vā manyase mṛtam,
tathāpi tvaṁ mahābāho naivaṁ śocitumarhasi. (2.26)

(§1) अथ च एनम् नित्यजातम् नित्यम् वा मन्यसे मृतम् । तथापि त्वम् महाबाहो न एवम् शोचितुम् अर्हसि । *atha ca* (r◦ 3/1) *enaṃ* (r◦ 14/1) *nityajātaṃ* (r◦ 14/1) *nityaṃ* (r◦ 14/1) *vā manyase mṛtaṃ* (r◦ 14/2) *tathāpi tvaṃ* (r◦ 14/1) *mahābāho na* (r◦ 3/1) *evaṃ* (r◦ 14/1) *śocituṃ* (r◦ 8/16) *arhasi*

(§2) *atha* (ind◦ 1.20); *ca* (1.1); *enaṃ* (2.19); *nitya* (2.18); *jātaṃ* (m◦ 2acc◦ sing◦ ←ppp◦ adj◦ ***jāta*** (born) ←4◦√जन् (to be born, give birth); *nityaṃ* (2.21); *vā* (1.32); ***manyase*** (2nd-per◦ sing◦ pres◦ वर्तमान्-लट् ātmane◦ ←4◦√मन् (to think) 2.19); *mṛtaṃ* (m◦ 2acc◦ sing◦ ←ppp◦ adj◦ ***mṛta*** (dead) ←6◦√मृ (to die); *tathā* (1.8); *api* (1.26); *tvaṃ* (2.11); ***mahābāho*** (m◦ 8voc◦ sing◦ ←bahuvrī◦ *mahābahu* 1.18); *na* (1.30); *evaṃ* (adv◦ 1.24);

---

[150] See the footnote in verse 2.15

[151] हन्ता चेन्मन्यते हन्तुं हतश्चेन्मन्यते हतम् ।
उभौ तौ न विजानीतो नायं हन्ति न हन्यते ।। (kaṭhopaniṣad 1.2.19)

śócitum (inf◦ ind◦ ←1◦√शुच् (to lament) 2.25); *arhasi* (2.25) (2.26)

(§3) *atha* (further, after this); *ća* (and); *enaṃ* (obj◦ this); *nitya-jātaṃ* (adj1◦-obj◦ that which is born again and again); *nityaṃ* (ever); *vā* (or); *manyase* (you think); *mṛtaṃ* (adj2◦-obj◦ that which is dead); *tathā api* (even then); *tvaṃ* (subj◦ you); *mahābāho* (O Mahābahu!, O Arjuna!); *na* (not); *evaṃ* (in this manner, like this); *śócitum* (for grieving, to grieve); *arhasi* (you should; you are worthy) (2.26)

(§4) ća atha manyase enaṃ nitya jātaṃ vā mṛtaṃ nityaṃ tathā api mahābāho tvaṃ arhasi na śócitum evaṃ

(§5) And after this, (if) you think this (to be) that which is born again and again or that which is ever dead;[152] even then, O Arjuna! you should not grieve like this. (2.26)

2.27 जातस्य हि ध्रुवो मृत्युर्ध्रुवं जन्म मृतस्य च ।
तस्मादपरिहार्येऽर्थे न त्वं शोचितुमर्हसि ॥

jātasya hi dhruvo mṛtyurdhruvaṃ janma mṛtasya ća,
tasmādaparihārye'rthe na tvaṃ śócitumarhasi. (2.27)

(§1) जातस्य हि ध्रुवः मृत्युः ध्रुवम् जन्म मृतस्य च । तस्मात् अपरिहार्ये अर्थे न त्वम् शोचितुम् अर्हसि । *jātasya hi dhruvaḥ:* (r◦ 15/9) *mṛtyuḥ:* (r◦ 16/8) *dhruvaṃ* (r◦ 14/1) *janma mṛtasya ća tasmāt* (r◦ 8/2) *aparihārye* (r◦ 6/1) *arthe na tvaṃ* (r◦ 14/1) *śócitum* (r◦ 8/16) *arhasi*

(§2) *jātasya* (m◦ 6pos◦ sing◦ ←adj◦ *jāta* (born) 2.26); *hi* (1.11); 📖*dhruvaḥ:* (m◦ 1nom◦ sing◦ ←adj◦ **dhruva** (certain) ←1◦√धृ (to bear); **mṛtyuḥ:** (1nom◦ sing◦ ←m◦ **mṛtyu** (death) ←6◦√मृ (to die); **dhruvaṃ** (n◦ 1nom◦ sing◦ ←adj◦ *dhruva* ↑); 📖**janma** (1nom◦ sing◦ ←n◦ **janman** (birth) ←4◦√जन् (to be born, give birth); *mṛtasya* (m◦ 6pos◦ sing◦ ←ppp◦ adj◦ *mṛta* (dead) 2.26); *ća* (1.1); *tasmāt* (therefore) (1.37); 📖*a-parihārye* (m◦ 7loc◦ sing◦ n.tatpu◦ ←pot◦ adj◦ *parihārya* (avoidable) ←1◦परि√ह (to take); *arthe* (matter) (1.9); *na* (1.30); *tvaṃ* (2.11); *śócitum* (2.26); *arhasi* (2.25) (2.27)

(§3) *jātasya* (of the born); *hi* (because); *dhruvaḥ:* (adj◦-subj1◦ certain, definite, inevitable); *mṛtyuḥ:* (subj1◦ the death); *dhruvaṃ* (adj◦-subj2◦ inevitable); *janma* (subj2◦ the birth); *mṛtasya* (of the dead); *ća* (and); *tasmāt* (therefore); *aparihārye* (in the unavoidable); *arthe* (in consequence; in matter); *na* (not); *tvaṃ* (subj3◦ you); *śócitum* (for grieving, to grieve); *arhasi* (you ought to; you are worthy) (2.27)

---

[152] Elsewhere◦ *mṛtam* → dies, ever dying, subject to death, ...etc.
📖 मृतम् is not a verb of present tense. It is a past passive participle adj◦ = dead; that which has already died.

(§4) hi mṛtyuḥ: jātasya dhruvaḥ: ća janma mṛtasya dhruvam tasmāt aparihārye arthe tvam na arhasi śoćitum

(§5) Because[153] the death of the born (is) certain and the birth of the dead[154] (is) inevitable,[155] therefore,[156] in the unavoidable matter, you ought not to grieve.[157]

(2.27)

2.28 अव्यक्तादीनि भूतानि व्यक्तमध्यानि भारत ।
अव्यक्तनिधनान्येव तत्र का परिदेवना ।।

avyaktādīni bhūtāni vyaktamadhyāni bhārata,
avyaktanidhanānyeva tatra kā paridevanā. (2.28)

(§1) अव्यक्तादीनि भूतानि व्यक्तमध्यानि भारत । अव्यक्तनिधनानि एव तत्र का परिदेवना । *avyaktādīni bhūtāni vyaktamadhyāni bhārata* (r∘ 23/1) *avyaktanidhanāni* (r∘ 4/4) *eva tatra kā paridevanā*

(§2) *avyaktādīni* (n∘ 1nom∘ plu∘ ←bahuvrī∘ adj∘ *avyaktādi,* अव्यक्तम् आदिम् यस्य तत् ←adj∘ *avyakta* (unmanifest) 2.25 + adj∘ ***ādi*** (begining) ←1∘आ√दा (to give); ***bhūtāni*** (1nom∘ plu∘ ←n∘ ***bhūta*** (being) ←1∘√भू (to be, become); *vyaktamadhyāni* (n∘ 1nom∘ plu∘ ←bahuvrī∘ adj∘ *vyakta-madhya,* व्यक्तम् मध्यम् यस्य तत् ←ppp∘ adj∘ *vyakta* (manifest) ←7∘वि√अञ्ज् (to make)+ adj∘ *madhya* (interim) 1.21); *bhārata* (1.24); *avyaktanidhanāni* (n∘ 1nom∘ plu∘ ←bahuvrī∘ *avyakta-nidhana,* अव्यक्तम् निधनम् यस्य तत् ←adj∘ *avyakta* 2.25 + n∘ ***nidhana*** (death) ←3∘नि√धा (to put); *eva* (1.1); *tatra* (1.26); *kā* (1.36); 📖*paridevanā* (1nom∘ sing∘ ←f∘ *paridevanā* (whimper) ←4∘परि√दिव् (to shine) (2.28)

(§3) ***avyaktādīni*** **(adj1∘-subj1∘ whose begining is the Unmanifest, Unpersonified, Invisible);** ***bhūtāni***

---

[153] See the footnote in verse 2.15

[154] Elsewhere∘ *mṛtasya* → to one who dies
📖 see footnote in 2.26

[155] सर्वं कृतं विनाशान्तं जातस्य मरणं ध्रुवम् ।
आशाश्वतं हि लोकेऽस्मिनसदा स्थावरजङ्गमम् ।। (anugītā 28.20)

[156] See the footnote in verse 2.15

[157] यथा जातानि जातानि चान्यान्यन्यानि कालतः । वृक्षात्पर्णानि शीर्यन्ते शरीराणि तथा नृणाम् ।
जायन्ते च म्रियन्ते च शरीराणि शरीरिणाम् । पादपानां च पर्णानि का तत्र परिदेवना ।।

Human bodies fade and fall away in time, like the withered leaves of tree. The bodies of all beings are equally doomed to be born and die in their time, as the leaves of tree, why then lament at the loss of what is surely to be lost (Yogavāsiṣṭha 3.6.32.49-50).

(subj1◦ the beings); ***vyaktamadhyāni*** (adj2◦-subj1◦ whose interim state is manifest, personified, visible); ***bhārata*** (O Bharata! O Arjuna!); ***avyaktanidhanāni*** (adj3◦-subj1◦ after the death who are unmanifest, impersonified, invisible); ***eva*** (also, and again); ***tatra*** (there, in that matter); ***kā*** (what, what is?); ***paridevanā*** (subj2◦ the whimper, the grieving; the cry) (2.28)

(§4) bhārata bhūtāni avyaktādīni vyaktamadhyāni eva avyaktanidhanāni, tatra kā paridevanā?

(§5) O Arjuna! the beings[158] (are) whose begining is the Unmanifest; whose interim state is manifest and after the death who are again unmanifest, in that matter what is the whimper? (2.28)

2.29 आश्चर्यवत्पश्यति कश्चिदेनमाश्चर्यवद्वदति तथैव चान्यः ।
आश्चर्यवच्चैनमन्यः शृणोति श्रुत्वाप्येनं वेद न चैव कश्चित् ।।

āśćaryavatpaśyati kaśćidenamāśćaryavadvadati tathaiva ćānyaḥ:,
āśćaryavaććainamanyaḥ: śṛṇoti śrutvāpyenaṁ veda na ćaiva kaśćiṭ.

(2.29)

(§1) आश्चर्यवत् पश्यति कश्चित् एनम् आश्चर्यवत् वदति तथा एव च अन्यः । आश्चर्यवत् च एनम् अन्यः शृणोति श्रुत्वा अपि एनम् वेद न च एव कश्चित् । *āśćaryavaṭ* (r◦ 10/6) *paśyati kaśćiṭ* (r◦ 8/9) *enaṃ* (r◦ 8/17) *āśćaryavaṭ* (r◦ 9/11) *vadati tathā* (r◦ 3/3) *eva ća* (r◦ 1/1) *anyaḥ:* (r◦ 22/8) *āśćaryavaṭ* (r◦ 11/1) *ća* (r◦ 3/1) *enaṃ* (r◦ 8/16) *anyaḥ:* (r◦ 22/5) *śṛṇoti śrutvā* (r◦ 1/3) *api* (r◦ 4/4) *enaṃ* (r◦ 14/1) *veda na ća* (r◦ 3/1) *eva kaśćiṭ*

(§2) 📖***āśćaryavaṭ*** (adv◦ ←adj◦ or n◦ 📖***āśćarya*** (wonder) ←1◦आ√चर् (to move) + ind◦ affix ***vaṭ*** वत् indicating an equality or a simile ←√वा (to move); 📖***paśyati*** (3rd-per◦ sing◦ pres◦ वर्तमान्-लट् parasmai◦ ←1◦√दृश् (to see)1.31); *kaśćiṭ* (2.17); *enaṃ* (2.19); 📖*āśćaryavaṭ* (↑); *vadati* (3rd-per◦ sing◦ pres◦ वर्तमान्-लट् parasmai◦ ←1◦√वच् (to speek); *tathā* (1.8); *eva* (1.1); *ća* (1.1); ***anyaḥ:*** (m◦ 1nom◦ sing◦ ←adj◦ *anya* (someone else) 1.9); *āśćaryavaṭ* (↑); *ća* (1.1); *enaṃ* (2.19); *anyaḥ:* (↑); *śṛṇoti* (3rd-per◦ sing◦ pres◦ वर्तमान्-लट् parasmai◦ ←1◦√श्रु (to hear); ***śrutvā*** (ipp◦ ind◦ ←1◦√श्रु (to hear); *api* (1.26); *enaṃ* (2.19); *veda* (2.21); *na* (1.30); *ća* (1.1); *eva* (1.1); *kaśćiṭ* (2.17) (2.29)

(§3) ***āśćaryavaṭ*** (like a wonder; as if a surprise); ***paśyati*** (one sees, one perceives); ***kaśćiṭ*** (subj1◦ someone); ***enaṃ*** (adj◦-obj◦ this); ***āśćaryavaṭ*** (like a wonder; as if a surprise); ***vadati*** (he speaks of); ***tathā eva ća*** (and similarly); ***anyaḥ:*** (subj2◦ someone else); ***āśćaryavaṭ*** (like a wonder; as if a surprise);

---

[158] Elsewhere◦ *bhūtāni* → all that are created, all created beings ...etc.

📖 Verb भू in भूत does not mean to "create" or created.

ća (and); *enaṃ* (adj∘-obj∘ this); *anyaḥ:* (subj3∘ somebother person); *śṛṇoti* (one hears about); *śrutvā* (having heard about); *api* (even); *enaṃ* (adj∘-obj∘ this); *veda* (one knows; they know); *na* (no); *ća eva* (and); *kaśćit* (subj4∘ someone, one) (2.29)

(§4) kaśćit paśyati enaṃ āśćaryavat tathā eva ća anyaḥ: vadati āśćaryavat ća anyaḥ: śṛṇoti enaṃ āśćaryavat eva ća api śrutvā enaṃ na kaśćit veda

(§5) Someone perceives this like a wonder; and similarly someone else speaks of (this) like a wonder; and some other person hears about this like a wonder; and even having heard about this, no one[159] (really) knows (this). (2.29)

2.30 देही नित्यमवध्योऽयं देहे सर्वस्य भारत ।
तस्मात्सर्वाणि भूतानि न त्वं शोचितुमर्हसि ।।[160]

dehī nityamavadhyo'yaṃ dehe sarvasya bhārata,
tasmātsarvāṇi bhūtāni na tvaṃ śoćitumarhasi. (2.30)

(§1) देही नित्यम् अवध्य: अयम् देहे सर्वस्य भारत । तस्मात् सर्वाणि भूतानि न त्वम् शोचितुम् अर्हसि । *dehī nityam* (r∘ 8/16) *avadhyaḥ:* (r∘ 15/1) *ayam* (r∘ 14/1) *dehe sarvasya bhārata tasmāt* (r∘ 10/7) *sarvāṇi* (r∘ 24/7) *bhūtāni na tvam* (r∘ 14/1) *śoćitum* (r∘ 8/16) *arhasi*

(§2) *dehī* (2.22); *nityaṃ* (2.21); ▯*avadhyaḥ:* (m∘ 1nom∘ sing∘ ←pot∘ adj∘ n.tatpu∘ *avadhya* (inviolable) ←1∘अ<u>वध्</u> (to kill); *ayaṃ* (2.19); *dehe* (2.13); **sarvasya** (m∘ 6pos∘ sing∘ ←pron∘ *sarva* 1.6); *bhārata* (1.24); *tasmāt* (1.37); **sarvāṇi** (n∘ 2acc∘ plu∘ ←pron∘ *sarva* 1.6); *bhūtāni* (2acc∘ ←n∘ pron∘ *bhūta* (being) 2.28); *na* (1.30); *tvam* (2.11); *śoćitum* (2.26); *arhasi* (2.25) (2.30)

(§3) *dehī* (subj1∘ the body bearer, the ātmā); *nityaṃ* (adv∘ eternally); *avadhyaḥ:* (adj1∘-subj1∘ uncleavable, inviolable); *ayaṃ* (adj2∘-subj1∘ this); *dehe* (in the body); *sarvasya* (of everyone); *bhārata* (O Bharata! O Arjuna!); *tasmāt* (therefore); *sarvāṇi* (adj∘-obj∘ to all, for all); *bhūtāni* (obj∘ beings); *na* (not); *tvam* (subj2∘ you); *śoćitum* (for grieving, to grieve); *arhasi* (you should, you ought to) (2.30)

(§4) ayaṃ avadhyaḥ: dehī nityaṃ dehe sarvasya tasmāt bhārata tvam arhasi na śoćitum sarvāṇi

---

[159] Elsewhere∘ न एव कश्चित् → others, yet another, none are, some other, some other again, someone else, yet others, ...etc.

[160] यस्मिन्सर्वाणि भूतान्यात्मैवाभूद्विजानतः ।
तत्र को मोहः कः शोक एकत्वमनुपश्यतः ।।

When one sees the oneness of all beings with the ātmā, then for that wise parson where is attachment and what is sorrow for? (īśāvāsyopanishad 7)

(§5) This ātmā (is) eternally[161] inviolable in the body of everyone, therefore,[162] O Arjuna! you ought not grieve for all beings.[163] (2.30)

2.31 स्वधर्ममपि चावेक्ष्य न विकम्पितुमर्हसि ।
धर्म्याद्धि युद्धाच्छ्रेयोऽन्यत्क्षत्रियस्य न विद्यते ।।

svadharmamapi ćāvekṣya na vikampitumarhasi,
dharmyāddhi yuddhāććhreyo'nyatkṣatriyasya na vidyate. (2.31)

(§1) स्वधर्मम् अपि च अवेक्ष्य न विकम्पितुम् अर्हसि । धर्म्यात् हि युद्धात् श्रेयः अन्यत् क्षत्रियस्य न विद्यते । *svadharmam* (r◦ 8/16) *api ća* (r◦ 1/1) *avekṣya na vikampitum* (r◦ 8/16) *arhasi dharmyāt* (r◦ 9/12) *hi yuddhāt* (r◦ 11/4) *śreyaḥ:* (r◦ 15/1) *anyat* (r◦ 10/5) *kṣatriyasya na vidyate*

(§2) ***svadharmam*** (m◦ 2acc◦ sing◦ ←karmadhāray◦ ***sva-dharma***, स्वस्य धर्मः ←pron◦ adj◦ *sva* (own) 1.28 + m◦ *dharma* (natural inclination) 1.1); *api* (1.26); *ća* (1.1); *avekṣya* (lyp◦ past-participle ind◦ ←1◦अव√ईक्ष् (to see); *na* (1.30); *vikampitum* (inf◦ ind◦ ←1◦वि√कम्प् (to tremble); *arhasi* (2.25); *dharmyāt* (n◦ 5abl◦ sing◦ ←pot◦ adj◦ ***dharmya*** (righteous) ←m◦ *dharma* 1.1); *hi* (1.11); *yuddhāt* (5abl◦ sing◦ ←n◦ *yuddha* (battle) 1.9); *śreyaḥ:* (1.31); ***anyat*** (1nom◦ sing◦ ←n◦ *anyat* ←adj◦ *anya* (else) 1.9); *kṣatriyasya* (m◦ 6pos◦ sing◦ ←taddhita◦ ***kṣatriya***, क्षत्रे भावः । क्षत्रत्राणात्ततः क्षत्रिय उच्यते । ←m◦ *kṣatra* ←√क्षण् (to injure, cause wound) + *bhāva* 2.7); *na* (1.30); *vidyate* (2.16)
(2.31)

(§3) ***svadharmam*** (obj◦ your own guṇa; your own natural inclination; your own varṇa, your own class, your inherant properties, your inborn attributes); ***api*** (also); ***ća*** (and); ***avekṣya*** (having seen; beholding, considering); ***na*** (not); ***vikampitum*** (for wavering; to hesitate); ***arhasi*** (you should; you are obliged); ***dharmyāt*** (righteous than-); ***hi*** (because) ***yuddhāt*** (than battle); ***śreyaḥ:*** (better, more); ***anyat*** (subj◦

---

[161] Elsewhere◦ देही नित्यम् अवध्यः अयम् देहे → The self in everyone's body is indestructible (adj◦), the dweller in the body of every one is eternal (adj◦), the indweller is eternal and imperishable, ...etc.
(i) नित्यम् is an adv◦ with Accusative form. It is not an adj◦ of Nominative m◦ देही । Nominative m◦ अवध्यः is adj◦ of m◦ देही । Therefore, नित्यम् is adv◦ of adj◦ अवध्यः । नित्यम् is not a m◦ nominative adjective, it can not be an adjective of m◦ nominative noun देही । (ii) अवध्यः does not imply imperishable (intransitive). The verb √वध् = to slay (transitive).

[162] See the footnote in verse 2.15

[163] Elsewhere◦ *sarvāṇi bhūtāni* → for any creature, for any living being, for the beings, ...etc.

anything else); ***kṣatriyasya*** (of a warrior; for a Kṣatriya); ***na*** (does not); ***vidyate*** (it exists) (2.31)

(§4) ća avekṣya svadharmam̦ api arhasi na vikampitum̦ hi kṣatriyasya anyaț na vidyate śreyaḥ: dharmyāț yuddhāț

(§5) And, beholding your own natural inclination also, you should not hesitate, because[164] for a *Kṣatriya*[165] nothing else exists than a righteous battle.[166] (2.31)

2.32 यदृच्छया चोपपन्नं स्वर्गद्वारमपावृतम् ।
सुखिनः क्षत्रियाः पार्थ लभन्ते युद्धमीदृशम् ।।

yadṛćchayā ćopapannaṁ svargadvāramapāvṛtam̦,
sukhinaḥ: kṣatriyāḥ: pārtha labhante yuddhamīdṛśam̦. (2.32)

(§1) यदृच्छया च उपपन्नम् स्वर्गद्वारम् अपावृतम् । सुखिनः क्षत्रियाः पार्थ लभन्ते युद्धम् इदृशम् । *yadṛćchayā ća* (r∘ 2/2) *upapannam̦* (r∘ 14/1) *svargadvāram̦* (r∘ 8/16) *apāvṛtam̦* (r∘ 14/2) *sukhinaḥ:* (r∘ 22/1) *kṣatriyāḥ:* (r∘ 22/3) *pārtha labhante yuddham̦* (r∘ 8/18) *īdṛśam̦* (r∘ 14/2)

(§2) *yadṛćchayā* (adv∘ or 3inst∘ sing∘ ←f∘ ***yadṛććhā*** (own accord) ←6∘यद्√ऋच्छ् (to go); *ća* (1.1); *upapannam̦* (n∘ 1nom∘ sing∘ ←ppp∘ adj∘ *upapanna* (stumbled) ←4∘उप√पद् (to go); *svargadvāram̦* (n∘ 1nom∘ sing∘ ←tatpu∘ *svarga-dvāra*, स्वर्गस्य द्वारम् ←m∘ *svarga* (heaven) 2.2 + n∘ ***dvāra*** (gate) ←1∘√द्वृ (to hinder); *apāvṛtam̦* (n∘ -1mon∘ sing∘ ←ppp∘ adj∘ *apāvṛta* (opened) ←4∘अप–आ√वृत् (to choose); *sukhinaḥ:* (1.37); *kṣatriyāḥ:* (1nom∘ plu∘ ←m∘ *kṣatriya* 2.31); *pārtha* (1.25); ***labhante*** (3rd-per∘ plu∘ pres∘ वर्तमान्–लट् ātmane∘ ←1∘√लभ् (to obtain); *yuddham̦* (2acc∘ sing∘ ←n∘ *yuddha* (war) 1.9); *īdṛśam̦* (n∘ 2acc∘ sing∘ ←adj∘ *idṛśa* (like this), ***idam̦*** ←1∘इदम्√दृश् (to see)

(2.32)

---

[164] See the footnote in verse 2.15

[165] Elsewhere∘ (i) *svadharmam* → own caste duty, own religious principles, ...etc.
(ii) *kṣatriyasya* → member of warrior caste, ...etc.

स्वधर्म is not a caste. Caste is जातिः। *jāti* (caste) denotes which parents one is born to. Whereas स्वधर्मः refers to your own गुणः *(guṇaḥ:)*. धर्मः also means गुणः । and स्वधर्मः is स्वगुणः or स्वगुणाः collectively. People who have not understood Hindu philosophy and culture properly, do misunderstand the distinction between गुणः, जातिः, वर्णः, धर्मः, caste and class. Srī Kṛṣṇa talks about four classes or divisions based on one's natural inclination (गुणः), not about the castes. In Gītā, *dharma* (धर्मः) is not a religion. It is righteous duty (कर्तव्यम्) virtue, or *guṇaḥ:* (गुणः ।)

[166] Elsewhere∘ *dharmyāt yuddhāt* → than fighting on religious principles.

(§3) *yadṛcchayā* (subj∘ by its own accord; by itself); *ća* (and); *upapannaṃ* (adj1∘-obj1∘ stumbled upon, discovered, found); *svargadvāraṃ* (obj1∘ the gate to heaven); *apāvṛtaṃ* (adj2∘-obj1∘ opened); *sukhinaḥ* (adj∘-subj2∘ fortunate, lucky; happy); *kṣatriyāḥ* (subj2∘ Kṣatriyas); *pārtha* (O pārtha! O Arjuna!); *labhante* (they get); *yuddhaṃ* (obj2∘ a war); *īdṛśam* (adj∘-obj2∘ like this) (2.32)

(§4) pārtha svargadvāraṃ upapannaṃ apāvṛtaṃ yadṛcchayā ća yuddhaṃ īdṛśam sukhinaḥ kṣatriyāḥ labhante

(§5) O Arjuna! (to be) stumbled upon[167] the gate to heaven opened[168] by itself, and, a war like this, (only) fortunate *kṣatriyas*[169] get.[170] (2.32)

2.33 अथ चेत्त्वमिमं धर्म्यं सङ्ग्रामं न करिष्यसि ।

---

[167] Elsewhere∘ *yadṛcchayā upapannaṃ* (in यदृच्छया अपावृतं स्वर्गद्वारम् उपपन्नम्) → battle that comes unsought, battle which has come of its own, fighting opportunity comes unsought, war comes of its own accord, fighting opportunity comes unsought opening the doors..., such a war comes of its own accord, such a war that comes unsought, battle which has come of its own accord and is an open gateway, a battle which presents itself unsought, a war which has come of its own accord ...etc.

 (i) उपपन्नम् (nominative∘) is not a verb. It is not an adjective of obj∘ युद्धम् (accusative∘). It is adj∘ of the subj∘ स्वर्गद्वारम् (nominative∘). ईदृशम् (accusative∘) is the adjective of noun युद्धम् (accusative) । If you attach उपपन्नम् to युद्धम्, then ईदृशम् has no connection. (ii) उपपन्नम् is not a present tense verb (comes, presents). उपपन्नम् is a past passive participle adj∘ = found, obtained, attained, got.

[168] Elsewhere∘ स्वर्गद्वारम् अपावृतम् → is an open gateway to heaven, is a gate way to heaven, which would serve as a gateway to heaven, opening for them the doors of the heavenly planets, ...etc.

 अपावृतम् (nominative) is not a present or any other tense. It is a ppp∘ adj∘ of (nominative) स्वर्गद्वारम् = opened, the one that has opened.

[169] Elsewhere∘ *sukhinaḥ kṣatriyāḥ* → happy are the kṣatriyas to whom, happy are the kṣatriyas who, fortunate indeed are the kshatriyas, happy are those kṣatriyas whom, Fortunate are the warriors, ...etc.

 In order to translate this verse with these expressions, you need insertion of additional conjunctions such as : whom, to whom, who, for whom etc. सुखिन: is not a verb, is adjective of the noun क्षत्रिया: and लभन्ते is the verb.

[170] Elsewhere∘ *kṣatriyāḥ labhante* → kṣatriyas who are called to fight, kṣatriyas who get such a battle, for whom such a war comes, to whom such war comes, Fortunate are the warriors who encounter, ...etc.

 (i) *labhante* is not an adjective of *Kṣatriyas*. It is a verb. (ii) The verb लभन्ते (plural) is not performed by the war (singular). The doers (subject) of this verb are the Kṣatriyas (plural) . (iii) Therefore, it should be *sukninaḥ kṣatriyāḥ labhante* = the fortunate Kṣatriyas get (the oppurtinity).

ततः स्वधर्मं कीर्तिं च हित्वा पापमवाप्स्यसि ।।

atha ćettvamimaṁ dharmyaṁ saṅgrāmaṁ na kariṣyasi,
tataḥ: svadharmaṁ kīrtiṁ ća hitvā pāpamavāpsyasi. (2.33)

(§1) अथ चेत् त्वम् इमम् धर्म्यम् सङ्ग्रामम् न करिष्यसि । ततः स्वधर्मम् कीर्तिम् च हित्वा पापम् अवाप्स्यसि । *atha ćet* (r∘ 1/10) *tvaṃ* (r∘ 8/18) *imaṃ* (r∘ 14/1) *dharmyaṃ* (r∘ 14/1) *saṅgrāmaṃ* (r∘ 14/1) *na kariṣyasi tataḥ:* (r∘ 22/7) *svadharmaṃ* (r∘ 14/1) *kīrtiṃ* (r∘ 14/1) *ća hitvā pāpaṃ* (r∘ 8/16) *avāpsyasi*

(§2) *atha* (1.20); 🕮***ćeṭ*** (if) (ind∘ ←1∘√चित् (to percceive); *tvaṃ* (2.11); *imaṃ* (1.28); 🕮***dharmyaṃ*** (m∘ 2acc∘ sing∘ ←adj∘ *dharmya* (righteous) 2.31); 🕮*saṅgrāmaṃ* (2acc∘ sing∘ ←m∘ *saṅgrāma* (battale) ←10∘√सङ्ग्राम् (to fight); *na* (1.30); ***kariṣyasi*** (2nd-per∘ sing∘ fut2∘ लृट् भविष्य∘ parasmai∘ ←8∘√कृ (to do); *tataḥ:* (1.13); *svadharmaṃ* (2.31); 🕮*kīrtiṃ* (2acc∘ sing∘ ←f∘ *kīrti* (honour) 2.2); *ća* (1.1); *hitvā* (ipp∘ ind∘ ←3∘√हा (to go); 🕮***pāpaṃ*** (2acc∘ sing∘ ←n∘ *pāpa* (sin) 1.36); 🕮***avāpsyasi*** (2nd-per∘ sing∘ fut2∘ लृट् भविष्य∘ parasmai∘ ←5∘अव√आप् (to attain, get) (2.33)

(§3) ***atha*** **(now after this; and now);** ***ćeṭ*** **(if);** ***tvaṃ*** **(subj∘ you);** ***imaṃ*** **(adj1∘-obj1∘ this, such);** ***dharmyaṃ*** **(adj2∘-obj1∘ bound by righteousness);** ***saṅgrāmaṃ*** **(obj1∘ battle);** ***na*** **(not);** ***kariṣyasi*** **(you will do);** ***tataḥ:*** **(then);** ***svadharmaṃ*** **(obj2∘ your own righteous duty);** ***kīrtiṃ*** **(obj3∘ honour);** ***ća*** **(and);** ***hitvā*** **(having forfeited);** ***pāpaṃ*** **(obj4∘ sin),** ***avāpsyasi*** **(you will incur)** (2.33)

(§4) atha ćeṭ tvaṃ kariṣyasi na imaṃ dharmyaṃ saṅgrāmaṃ tataḥ: hitvā svadharmaṃ ća kīrtiṃ avāpsyasi pāpaṃ

(§5) And now if[171] you will not[172] do such battle bound by righteousness,[173] then having forfeited your own righteous duty and honour, you will incur sin.[174] (2.33)

2.34 अकीर्तिं चापि भूतानि कथयिष्यन्ति तेऽव्ययाम् ।
सम्भावितस्य चाकीर्तिर्मरणादतिरिच्यते ।।

akīrtiṁ ćāpi bhūtāni kathayiṣyanti te'vyayāṃ,
sambhāvitasya ćākīrtirmaraṇādatirićyate. (2.34)

---

[171] Elsewhere∘ अथ चेत → if however, if, but if, on the other hand if, ...etc.

[172] Elsewhere∘ *na kariṣyasi*→ do not perform, doest not, do not fight, don't participate ...etc.

🕮 करिष्यसि is not present tense. It is a future tense.

[173] Elsewhere∘ *dharmyaṃ* → as a religious duty.

[174] Elsewhere∘ *pāpaṃ* → sins (pl∘).

(§1) अकीर्तिम् च अपि भूतानि कथयिष्यन्ति ते अव्ययाम् । सम्भावितस्य च अकीर्तिः मरणात् अतिरिच्यते । *akīrtim* (r◦ 14/1) *ća* (r◦ 1/1) *api bhūtāni kathayiṣyanti* (r◦ 25/7) *te* (r◦ 6/1) *avyayām* (r◦ 14/2) *sambhāvitasya ća* (r◦ 1/1) *akīrtiḥ:* (r◦ 16/6) *maraṇāt* (r◦ 8/2) *atirićyate*

(§2) 📖*akīrtim* (2acc◦ sing◦ ←f◦ *akīrti* 2.2); *ća* (1.1); *api* (1.26); *bhūtāni* (2.28); *kathayiṣyanti* (3rd-per◦ plu◦ fut2◦ लृट् भविष्य◦ parasmai◦ ←10◦√कथ् (to tell); *te* (m◦ 6pos◦ sing◦ ←pron◦ *yuṣmad* 1.3); 📖*avyayām* (2acc◦ sing◦ ←n.tatpu◦ f◦ adj◦ *avyayā* ←1◦वि√इ (to enter, come, go); 📖*sambhāvitasya* (6pos sing◦ ←ppp◦ adj◦ *sambhāvita* (gentle) ←1◦सम्√भू (to be, become); *ća* (1.1); *akīrtiḥ:* (1nom◦ sing◦ ←f◦ *akīrti* 2.2); 📖*maraṇāt* (5abl◦ sing◦ ←n◦ ***maraṇa*** (death) ←6◦√मृ (to die); 📖*atirićyate* (3rd-per◦ sing◦ pres◦ वर्तमान्-लट् ātmane◦ ←7◦अति√रिच् (to leave) (2.34)

(§3) ***akīrtim*** (obj◦ infamy, dishonour); ***ća*** (and); ***api*** (also); ***bhūtāni*** (subj1◦ beings, people); ***kathayiṣyanti*** (they will talk, they will gossip); ***te*** (your); ***avyayām*** (adj◦-obj◦ undying); ***sambhāvitasya*** (of a respectable person, for an honourable person); ***ća*** (and); ***akīrtiḥ:*** (subj2◦ the infamy; dishonour); ***maraṇāt*** (than death); ***atirićyate*** (it excels; it feels worse) (2.34)

(§4) ća api bhūtāni kathayiṣyanti te avyayām akīrtim ća sambhāvitasya akīrtiḥ: atirićyate maraṇāt

(§5) And also, people will gossip your undying[175] dishonour. And, for an honourable person, the infamy excels death. (2.34)

2.35 भयाद्रणादुपरतं मंस्यन्ते त्वां महारथाः ।
येषां च त्वं बहुमतो भूत्वा यास्यसि लाघवम् ।।

bhayādraṇāduparataṁ maṁsyante tvāṁ mahārathāḥ:,
yeṣaṁ ća tvaṁ bahumato bhūtvā yāsyasi lāghavam. (2.35)

(§1) भयात् रणात् उपरतम् मंस्यन्ते त्वाम् महारथाः । येषाम् च त्वम् बहुमतः भूत्वा यास्यसि लाघवम् । *bhayāt* (r◦ 9/10) *raṇāt* (r◦ 8/6) *uparatam* (r◦ 14/1) maṁsyante tvām (r◦ 14/1) *mahārathāḥ:* (r◦ 22/8) *yeṣām* (r◦ 25/3, 14/1) *ća tvam* (r◦ 14/1) *bahumataḥ:* (r◦ 15/8) *bhūtvā yāsyasi lāghavam* (r◦ 14/2)

(§2) 📖***bhayāt*** (5abl◦ sing◦ ←n◦ ***bhaya*** (fear) ←3◦√भी (to fear); *raṇāt* (5abl◦ sing◦ ←n◦ or m◦ *raṇa* 1.22); 📖*uparatam* (2acc◦ sing◦ ←ppp◦ adj◦ *uparata* (ran away) ←1◦उप√रम् (to rejoice); 📖*maṁsyante* (3rd-per◦ plu◦

---

[175] Elsewhere◦ *avyayām akīrtiṁ kathayiṣyanti* → always speak of your infamy, ever recount thy ill-fame, ever speak of your infamy, ever recount your infamy, infamy for ever, infamy endlessly, ...etc.

📖 अव्ययाम् is not an adverb, and thus, it can not qualify the verb कथयिष्यन्ति । अव्ययाम् is feminine accusative adjective of the f◦ noun अकीर्ति (अव्ययाम् अकीर्तिम् Accusative 2nd case).

fut2◦ लृट् भविष्य◦ ātmane◦ ←4◦√मन् (to think); *tvām* (2.7); *mahārathāḥ:* (1.6); *yeṣām* (1.33); *ća* (1.1); *tvam* (2.11); 📖*bahumataḥ:* (1nom◦ sing◦ ←dvigu◦ *bahu-mata* (well respected) ←adj◦ *bahu* 1.9 + ppp◦ adj◦ ***mata*** ←4◦√मन् (to think); *bhūtvā* (2.20); ***yāsyasi*** (2nd-per◦ sing◦ fut2◦ लृट् भविष्य◦ parasmai◦ ←2◦√या (to go); 📖*lāghavam* (2acc◦ sing◦ ←n◦ *lāghava* (contempt) ←1◦√लाघृ (to be short, be competent) (2.35)

(§3) *bhayāt* (from fear, out of fear); *raṇāt* (from the battlefield); *uparatam* (adj◦-obj1◦ the one who ran away, a deserter); *mam̐syante* (they will think); *tvām* (obj1◦ you); *mahārathāḥ:* (subj1◦ the charioteers, the great warriors); *yeṣām* (of whom; among whom); *ća* (and); *tvam* (subj2◦ you); *bahumataḥ:* (adj◦-subj2◦ one who is looked upon with great respect); *bhūtvā* (having been); *yāsyasi* (you will come; you will become); *lāghavam* (obj2◦ a disgrace, contempt; a subject for contempt) (2.35)

(§4) mahārathāḥ: yeṣām tvam bhūtvā bahumataḥ: mam̐syante tvām uparatam raṇāt bhayāt ća yāsyasi lāghavam

(§5) The great warriors, among whom you having been looked upon with great respect, they will think you (as) one who has ran away[176] from the battlefield out of fear; and you will become[177] a matter for disgrace. (2.35)

2.36 अवाच्यवादांश्च बहून्वदिष्यन्ति तवाहिताः ।
निन्दन्तस्तव सामर्थ्यं ततो दुःखतरं नु किम् ।।

avāćyavādām̐śća bahūnvadiṣyanti tavāhitāḥ:,
nindantastava sāmarthyaṁ tato duḥ:khataraṁ nu kim. (2.36)

(§1) अवाच्यवादान् च बहून् वदिष्यन्ति तव अहिताः । निन्दन्तः तव सामर्थ्यम् ततः दुःखतरम् नु किम् । *avāćyavādān* (r◦ 13/6) *ća bahūn* (r◦ 13/19) *vadiṣyanti* (r◦ 25/7) *tava* (r◦ 1/1) *ahitāḥ:* (r◦ 22/8) *nindantaḥ:* (r◦ 18/1) *tava sāmarthyam* (r◦ 14/1) *tataḥ:* (r◦ 15/4) *duḥ:khataram* (r◦ 14/1) *nu kim* (r◦ 14/2)

(§2) 📖*avāćyavādān* (m◦ 2acc◦ plu◦ ←n.tatpu◦ *avāćya-vāda*, अवाच्यः वादः ←adj◦ *avāćya* (unspeakable)

---

[176] Elsewhere◦ *uparatam* → you have withdrawn, you have left, thou hast abstained, thou hast withdrawn ...etc.
📖 उपरतं is not a verb. It is a ppp◦ adjective of pronoun त्वाम् ।

[177] Elsewhere◦ *yāsyasi* → you will be thought of lightly by those, they will make light of thee, they will consider you..., you will be lightly held by them, will look down on you, ...etc.
📖 The verb यास्यसि is for Second person Subject, i.e. an action performed by you (Arjuna), NOT by Third person : they, by them, by those ...etc. It is an active voice. It is not a Sanskrit passive voice.

←2◦अव√वच् (to speek) + m◦ *vāda* 2.11); *ća* (1.1); *bahūn̦* (m◦ 2acc◦ plu◦ ←adj◦ *bahu* 1.9); *vadis̩yanti* (3rd-per◦ plu◦ fut2◦ लृट् भविष्य◦ parasmai◦ ←1◦√वद् (to speak); *tava* (1.3); ***ahitāh̦:*** (m◦ 1nom◦ plu◦ ←n.tatpu◦ *ahita* (enemy) ←5◦अ√हि (to impel); *nindantah̦:* (m◦ 1nom◦ plu◦ ←śatr̥◦ अपूर्णकालिक adj◦ *nindat̩* (rediculing) ←1◦√निन्द् (to criticize); *tava* (1.3); *sāmarthyam̦* (2acc◦ sing◦ ←taddhi◦ n◦ *sāmarthya* (prowess) ←adj◦ ***samartha*** ←10◦सम्√अर्थ् (to want); *tatah̦:* (1.13); *duh̦:khataram̦* (1nom◦ sing◦ ←n◦ *duh̦:kha* 2.14 + comparative affix *tara* 1.46); *nu* (1.35); ***kim̦*** (n◦ 2acc◦ ←pron◦ *kim̦* 1.1) (2.36)

(§3) ***avāćyavādān̦*** **(obj1◦ unspeakable words);** ***ća*** **(and);** ***bahūn̦*** **(adj◦-obj1◦ many);** ***vadis̩yanti*** **(they will say);** ***tava*** **(your);** ***ahitāh̦:*** **(subj1◦ enemies);** ***nindantah̦:*** **(adj◦-subj1◦ while rediculing);** ***tava*** **(your);** ***sāmarthyam̦*** **(obj2◦ prowess; power);** ***tatah̦:*** **(then, then after that);** ***duh̦:khataram̦*** **(subj2◦ greater pain);** ***nu*** **(truly);** ***kim̦*** **(adj◦-subj◦2 what; what could be?)** (2.36)

(§4) ća tava ahitāh̦: vadis̩yanti bahūn̦ avāćyavādān̦ nindantah̦: tava sāmarthyam̦ tatah̦: kim̦ nu duh̦:khataram̦?

(§5) And, your enemies will say many unspeakable words, while rediculing[178] your prowess; then after that what could truly be a greater pain? (2.36)

2.37 हतो वा प्राप्स्यसि स्वर्गं जित्वा वा भोक्ष्यसे महीम् ।
तस्मादुत्तिष्ठ कौन्तेय युद्धाय कृतनिश्चयः ।।
hato vā prāpsyasi svargam̐ jitvā vā bhoks̩yase mahīm̦,
tasmāduttis̩t̩ha kaunteya yuddhāya kr̥taniśćayah̦:. (2.37)

(§1) हतः वा प्राप्स्यसि स्वर्गम् जित्वा वा भोक्ष्यसे महीम् । तस्मात् उत्तिष्ठ कौन्तेय युद्धाय कृतनिश्चयः । ***hatah̦:*** (r◦ 15/13) ***vā prāpsyasi svargam̦*** (r◦ 14/1) ***jitvā vā bhoks̩yase mahīm̦*** (r◦ 14/2) ***tasmāt̩*** (r◦ 8/6) ***uttis̩t̩ha kaunteya yuddhāya kr̥taniśćayah̦:*** (r◦ 22/8)

(§2) ***hatah̦:*** (m◦ 1nom◦ sing◦ ←adj◦ *hata* (slain) 2.19); *vā* (1.32); ***prāpsyasi*** (2nd-per◦ sing◦ fut2◦ लृट् भविष्य◦ parasmai◦ ←5◦प्र√आप् (to attain, get); *svargam̦* (2acc◦ sing◦ ←m◦ *svarga* 2.2); ***jitvā*** (ipp◦ ind◦ ←1◦√जि (to win); *vā* (1.32); *bhoks̩yase* (2nd-per◦ sing◦ fut2◦ लृट् भविष्य◦ ātmane◦ ←7◦√भुज् (to enjoy, experience); *mahīm̦* (2acc◦ sing◦ ←f◦ *mahī* 1.21); *tasmāt̩* (1.37); *uttis̩t̩ha* (2.3); *kaunteya* (2.14); ***yuddhāya*** (4dat◦ sing◦ ←n◦ *yuddha* 1.9); *kr̥taniśćayah̦:* (m◦ 1nom◦ sing◦ ←bahuvrī◦ *kr̥ta-niśćaya*, कृतः निश्चयः येन ←adj◦ *kr̥ta* 1.35

---

[178] Elsewhere◦ *nindantah̦:* → will scorn, will slander, will ridicule, ...etc.

निन्दन्तः is not a Future tense. It is a Present participle adjective of the subject अहिताः → ridiculing, while ridiculing.

+ m◦ **niśćaya** (resolve) ←5◦निर्√चि (to gather) (2.37)

(§3) ***hataḥ:*** (adj1◦-subj◦ slain, killed); ***vā*** (either); ***prāpsyasi*** (you will attain); ***svargaṃ*** (obj1◦ the heaven); ***jitvā*** (having won); ***vā*** (or); ***bhokṣyase*** (you will enjoy); ***mahīṃ*** (obj2◦ the earth); ***tasmāṭ*** (therefore); ***uttiṣṭha*** (please stand up; please arise); ***kaunteya*** (O Kaunteya! O Arjuna!); ***yuddhāya*** (for battle); ***kṛta-niśćayaḥ:*** (adj2◦-subj◦ one who has done a resolve; one who is resolved; one who has made up his mind; one who is determined, resolved) (2.37)

(§4) vā hataḥ: prāpsyasi svargaṃ vā jitvā bhokṣyase mahīṃ tasmāṭ kaunteya uttiṣṭha kṛta-niśćayaḥ: yuddhāya

(§5) Either, slain[179] you will attain the heaven, or, having won,[180] you will enjoy the earth; therefore,[181] O Arjuna! please arise, resolved for battle.[182] (2.37)

2.38 सुखदुःखे समे कृत्वा लाभालाभौ जयाजयौ ।
तततो युद्धाय युज्यस्व नैवं पापमवाप्स्यसि ।।

sukhaduḥ:khe same kṛtvā lābhālābhau jayājayau,
tato yuddhāya yujyasva naivaṁ pāpamavāpsyasi. (2.38)

(§1) सुखदुःखे समे कृत्वा लाभालाभौ जयाजयौ । ततः युद्धाय युज्यस्व न एवम् पापम् अवाप्स्यसि । *sukhaduḥ:khe same kṛtvā lābhālābhau jayājayau tataḥ:* (r◦ 15/10) *yuddhāya yujyasva na* (r◦ 3/1) *evaṃ* (r◦ 14/1) *pāpaṃ* (r◦ 8/16) *avāpsyasi*

(§2) *sukha-duḥ:khe* (n◦ 2acc◦ dual◦ ←dvandva◦ सुखं च दुखं च ←n◦ *sukha* 1.32 + n◦ *duḥ:kha* 2.14); 📖*same* (n◦ 2acc◦ dual◦ ←adj◦ *sama* 1.4); ***kṛtvā*** (ipp◦ ind◦ ←8◦√कृ (to do); *lābhālābhau* (m◦ 2acc◦ dual◦ ←dvandva◦ लाभः च अलाभः च ←m◦ 📖***lābha*** (gain) ←1◦√लभ् (to obtain)+ n.tatpu◦ 📖*a-lābha* (loss) ←m◦ *lābha* ↑); *jayājayau* (m◦ 2acc◦ dual◦ ←dvandva◦ जयः च अजयः च ←m◦ *jaya* (victory) 1.8 + n.tatpu◦ *a-jaya* (defeat) ←m◦ *jaya* 1.8); *tataḥ:* (1.13); *yuddhāya* (2.37); ***yujyasva*** (2nd-per◦ sing◦ imperative◦ उपदेशार्थ लोट्

---

[179] Elsewhere◦ *hataḥ:* → being killed, you will be killed, by dying ...etc.

📖 हत: is not a gerund or future tense. It is a ppp◦ adj◦ of Arjuna. It should mean → killed, he who is killed, slain.

[180] Elsewhere◦ *jitvā* → you will conquer, by conquering, by winning ...etc.

[181] See the footnote in verse 2.15

[182] Elsewhere◦ *yuddhāya* → you fight! (Imperative mood)

📖 युद्धाय is not imperative mood. उत्तिष्ठ is imperative mood.

ātmane◦ ←7◦√युज् (to unite); *na* (1.30); *evam̹* (1.24); *pāpam̹* (1.36); *avāpsyasi* (2.33) (2.38)

(§3) ***sukha-duḥ:khe*** (obj1◦ pleasure and pain); ***same*** (adj◦-obj1-3◦ both same; both alike, indifferent); ***kṛtvā*** (having made; having considered); ***lābhālābhau*** (obj2◦gain and loss); ***jayājayau*** (obj3◦ victory and defeat); ***tataḥ:*** (after that, with this mind-set); ***yuddhāya*** (for battle; for the sake of battle); ***yujyasva*** (you engage); ***na*** (not); ***evam̹*** (this way); ***pāpam̹*** (obj4◦ sin); ***avāpsyasi*** (you will incur) (2.38)

(§4) kṛtvā sukha-duḥ:khe lābhālābhau jayājayau same tataḥ: yujyasva yuddhāya evam̹ na avāpsyasi pāpam̹

(§5) Having considered pleasure and pain, gain and loss (and) victory and defeat both same,[183] with this mind-set, you engage for the battle. This way you will not incur sin. (2.38)

2.39 एषा तेऽभिहिता साङ्ख्ये बुद्धिर्योगे त्विमां शृणु ।
बुद्ध्या युक्तो यया पार्थ कर्मबन्धं प्रहास्यसि ।।[184]

eṣā te'bhihitā sāṅkhye buddhiryoge tvimāṁ śṛṇu,
buddhyā yukto yayā pārtha karmabandhaṁ prahāsyasi. (2.39)

(§1) एषा ते अभिहिता साङ्ख्ये बुद्धिः योगे तु इमाम् शृणु । बुद्ध्या युक्तः यया पार्थ कर्मबन्धम् प्रहास्यसि । *eṣā* (r◦ 25/2) *te* (r◦ 6/1) *abhihitā sāṅkhye buddhiḥ:* (r◦ 16/6) *yoge tu* (r◦ 4/8) *imām̹* (r◦ 14/1) *śṛṇu buddhyā yuktaḥ:* (r◦ 15/10) *yayā pārtha karmabandham̹* (r◦ 14/1) *prahāsyasi*

(§2) ***eṣā*** (f◦ 1nom◦ sing◦ ←pron◦ *etad* 1.3); *te* (1.7); 📖*abhihitā* (f◦ 1nom◦ sing◦ ←ppp◦ adj◦ *abhihita* (told) ←3◦अभि√धा (to put); ***sāṅkhye*** (m◦ 7loc◦ sing◦ ←adj◦ ***sāṅkhy*** (Sankhya Philosophy) ←2◦सम्√ख्या (to declare); ***buddhiḥ:*** (1nom◦ sing◦ ←f◦ *buddhi* (thinking) 1.23); *yoge* (7loc◦ sing◦ ←m◦ 📖***yoga*** (buddhi-yoga) ←7◦√युज् (to unite); *tu* (1.2); ***imām̹*** (f◦ 2acc◦ sing◦ ←pron◦ *idam̹* 1.10); ***śṛṇu*** (2nd-per◦ sing◦ imperative◦ उपदेशार्थ लोट् parasmai◦ ←1◦√श्रु (to hear); ***buddhyā*** (3inst◦ sing◦ ←f◦ *buddhi* 1.23); 📖***yuktaḥ:*** (1nom◦ sing◦ ←adj◦ *yukta* 1.14); ***yayā***

---

[183] Elsewhere◦ सुखदुःखे समे कृत्वा → making oneself same in pleasure and pain, having balanced mind in pleasure and pain, without condidering happiness or distress, staying even in pain and pleasure, being equal in pain and pleasure, ...etc.

📖 Here in this *dvandva samāsa,* सुखदुःखे is (accusative case) सुखं च दुःखं च, not (locative case) सुखे च दुःखे च । In pain and pleasure (locative) = सुखदुःखयोः not सुखदुःखे । Here, the object (in accusative case) is सुखदुःखे not "oneself."

[184] बुद्धिर्योगे : → Please note that, it is not बुद्धियोगे । It is बुद्धिर्योगे । ीत सि न्श्त ा समस. It is just a sandhi between बुद्धिः + योगे । । एषा ते साङ्ख्ये बुद्धिः अभिहिता = एषा बुद्धिः ते साङ्ख्ये अभिहिता, योगे तु इमाम् शृणु । योगे = बुद्धियोगे ।

(f∘ 3inst∘ sing∘ ←pron∘ *yad* 1.7); *pārtha* (1.25); *karmabandham* (m∘ 2acc∘ sing∘ ←tatpu∘ *karma-bandha*, कर्मण: बन्धम् ←n∘ *karman* 1.15 + m∘ *bandha* (bondage) 1.27); ***prahāsyasi*** (2nd-per∘ sing∘ fut2∘ लृट् भविष्य∘ jau∘ parasmai∘ ←3∘प्र√हा (to go) (2.39)

(§3) *eṣā* (adj1∘-subj1∘ this); *te* (obj1∘ to you); *abhihitā* (adj2∘-subj1∘ spoken); *sāṅkhye* (in the way of *Sāṅkhya* discipline); *buddhiḥ:* (subj1∘ thinking); *yoge* (in the way of the *yoga*, in the way of *buddhi-yoga, in the way of the yoga of equanimity*); *tu* (now); *imām* (obj2∘ it); *śṛṇu* (please hear); *buddhyā* (with thinking, vision, knowledge; with equanimous thinking, with *buddhi-yoga*); *yuktaḥ:* (adj∘-subj2∘ equipped); *yayā* (with which); *pārtha* (O Pārtha! O Arjuna!); *karmabandham* (obj3∘ the bondage, fetter or attachment to *karma*); *prahāsyasi* (subj2∘ you will abandon, you will cast away)[185]

(2.39)

(§4) pārtha eṣā buddhiḥ: te abhihitā sāṅkhye tu śṛṇu imām yoge yuktaḥ: yayā buddhyā prahāsyasi karmabandham

(§5) O Arjuna! this thinking, spoken to you, (was) in the way of *Saṅkhya* discipline, now please hear it in the way of the *buddhi-yoga.*[186] Equipped with which (mind), you will abandon the

---

[185] Elsewhere∘ *prahāsyasi* → you can be released, you may be freed, you will free yourself ...etc.

प्रहास्यसि is a future tense of the *parasmaipadī* transitive verb 3∘√हा (to abandon, to renounce something). Therefore, प्रहास्यसि → you will renounce, you will cast away. You is the subject, not the object. The object in Accusative case is कर्मबन्धम् (not ablative कर्मबन्धनात्). The same is true for the words जहाति in 2.50 and प्रजहाति in 2.55↓

[186] Elsewhere∘ (i) सांख्ये → through analytical study, ideal of self-knowledge, wisdom of self-knowledge, mental attitude towards the self, Yoga doctrine of practice, standpoint of self-realization, path of knowledge, ...etc.

(ii) बुद्धियोगे → in respect of the way of action, working without fruitive results, practice of self-knowledge, yoga of intelligence ...etc.

The terms *Sāṅkhya* and *Yoga* are used in the Gītā (in this chapter) in a bit different sense than the systems known as Sākhya philosophy of Kapila and Yoga and Meditation system of Patañjalī. Here, *Sāṅkhya* refers to the knowledge (ज्ञानम्) of renunciation (संन्यास:) of desire for the authorship (कर्तृत्वम्) of *karma* i.e. the *yoga* of selfless *karma.* (1) Therefore, *Sāṅkhya* is also known as *Jñāna-yoga* or *Sanyasa-yoga.* (2) *Buddhi or Buddhiyoga* refers to the discipline (योग:) of equanimity of mind (बुद्धि:). However, (3) The *Yoga* or *Karma-yoga* or *Niṣkāma-karma-yoga* refers to the discipline (योग:) of **renunciation (त्याग:)** of the desire or MOTIVE (हेतु:, कामना, काम) behind the fruit (फलम्) of action (कर्म). Where *niṣ-kāma* refers to not-having-a-motive (निस्-कामना, निस्-काम); i.e. not pre-meditated towards fruit, but doing purely as a duty, **ACCEPTING** whatever the fruit may be. See answer to the Question 9 in previous section.

attachment[187] to *(sakāma)karma.*[188] (2.39)

2.40 नेहाभिक्रमनाशोऽस्ति प्रत्यवायो न विद्यते ।
स्वल्पमप्यस्य धर्मस्य त्रायते महतो भयात् ॥

nehābhikramanāśo'sti pratyavāyo na vidyate,
svalpamapyasya dharmasya trāyate mahato bhayāt. (2.40)

(§1) न इह अभिक्रमनाशः अस्ति प्रत्यवायः न विद्यते । स्वल्पम् अपि अस्य धर्मस्य त्रायते महतः भयात् । *na* (r◦ 2/1) *iha* (r◦ 1/1) *abhikramanāśaḥ:* (r◦ 15/1) *asti pratyavāyaḥ:* (r◦ 15/6) *na vidyate svalpam* (r◦ 8/16) *api* (r◦ 4/1) *asya dharmasya trāyate mahataḥ:* (r◦ 15/8) *bhayāt*

(§2) *na* (1.30); *iha* (2.5); *abhikramanāśaḥ:* (m◦ 1nom◦ sing◦ ←tatpu◦ *abhikrama-nāśa*, अभिक्रमस्य नाशः ←m◦ *abhikrama* (undertaking) ←1◦अभि√क्रम् (step) + m◦ ***nāśa*** ←4◦√नश् (to ruin); ***asti*** (3rd-per◦ sing◦ pres◦ वर्तमान्–लट् parasmai◦ ←2◦√अस् (to be); *pratyavāyaḥ:* (1nom◦ sing◦ ←m◦ *pratyavāya* (adverse reaction) ←1◦प्रति–अव√अय् (to go); *na* (1.30); *vidyate* (2.16); 📖*svalpam* (1nom◦ sing◦ ←n◦ adj◦ *svalpa* (short) ←1◦सु√अल् (to prevent, make short); *api* (1.26); *asya* (2.17); ***dharmasya*** (6pos sing◦ ←m◦ *dharma* 1.1); ***trāyate*** (3rd-per◦ sing◦ pres◦ वर्तमान्–लट् ātmane◦ ←1◦√त्रै (to protect); ***mahataḥ:*** (n◦ 5abl◦ sing◦ ←adj◦ *mahat* 1.3); 📖*bhayāt* (2.35) (2.40)

(§3) ***na*** **(not);** ***iha*** **(here, in this, in this** ***buddhiyoga*****);** ***abhikramanāśaḥ:*** (subj1◦ **fruitlessness or waste of the work that has been undertaken; fruitlessness for the effort that has been put in the work-);** ***asti*** **(is);** ***pratyavāyaḥ:*** (subj2◦ **contrary effect);** ***na*** **(does not);** ***vidyate*** **(it exists; it happens);** ***svalpam*** (subj3◦ **a little, small practice);** ***api*** **(even);** ***asya*** **(of this);** ***dharmasya*** **(of the righteous way);** ***trāyate*** **(it protects);** ***mahataḥ:*** **(from great);** ***bhayāt*** **(from danger, hazard, peril)** (2.40)

(§4) iha abhikramanāśaḥ: asti na pratyavāyaḥ: na vidyate api svalpam asya dharmasya trāyate mahataḥ: bhayāt

(§5) In this (*buddhi-yoga*), fruitlessness for 'the effort that has been put in the work'[189] is not (there). Contrary effect[190] does not exist. Even a little[191] (practice) of this righteous way protects

---

[187] तृष्णामात्रात्मको बन्धस्तन्नाशो मोक्ष उच्यते । (aṣṭāvakragītā 10.4)

[188] Elsewhere◦ karma → action. See : the footnote attached with verse 2.49, *karma*

[189] Fruitlessness or waste of efforts does not occur, because one is not motivated by the desire of the fruit in the first place. The effort can not be be fruitless when the fruit is not expected and the result of the work (loss or gain) is accepted with equanimity or indifference (बुद्धियोगः).

[190] Elsewhere◦ *pratyavāyaḥ:* → chance of incuring sin, transgression, ...etc.

(us) from great peril.[192] (2.40)

2.41 व्यवसायात्मिका बुद्धिरेकेह कुरुनन्दन ।
बहुशाखा ह्यनन्ताश्च बुद्धयोऽव्यवसायिनाम् ।।

vyavasāyātmikā buddhirekeha kurunandana,
bahuśākhā hyanantāśća buddhayo'vyavasāyinām. (2.41)

(§1) व्यवसायात्मिका बुद्धिः एका इह कुरुनन्दन । बहुशाखाः हि अनन्ताः च बुद्धयः अव्यवसायिनाम् । *vyavasāyātmikā* (r◦ 20/11) *buddhiḥ:* (r◦ 16/1) *ekā* (r◦ 2/3) *iha kurunandana bahuśākhāḥ:* (r◦ 20/18) *hi* (r◦ 4/1) *anantāḥ:* (r◦ 17/1) *ća buddhayaḥ:* (r◦ 15/1) *avyavasāyinām* (r◦ 14/2)

(§2) 🕮***vyavasāyātmikā*** (f◦ 1nom◦ sing◦ ←adj◦ taddhita◦ *vyavasāyātmikā*, व्यवसायः आत्मा यया सा (resolute) ←m◦ ***vyavasāya*** ←4◦वि–अव√सो (to complete) + m◦ ***ātman*** ←1◦√अत् (to wandet constantly); *buddhiḥ:* (2.39); *ekā* (f◦ 1nom◦ sing◦ ←adj◦ ***eka*** ←1◦√इ (to enter, come, go); *iha* (2.5); ***kurunandana*** (m◦ 8voc◦ sing◦ ←bahuvrī◦ *kuru-nandana*, कुरुणां नन्दनः ←m◦ *kuru* 1.1 + adj◦ *nandna* (son) ←1◦√नन्द् (to rejoice); *bahuśākhāḥ:* (1nom◦ plu◦ ←f◦ bahuvrī◦ adj◦ *bahu-śākhā*, बहवः शाखाः यस्याः सा (diversified) ←adj◦ *bahu* 1.9 + f◦ ***śākhā*** (branch) ←1◦√शाखृ (to branch); *hi* (1.11); 🕮*anantāḥ:* (f◦ 1nom◦ plu◦ ←adj◦ ***ananta*** (unending) ←1◦√अम् (to afflict); *ća* (1.1); *buddhayaḥ:* (1nom◦ plu◦ ←f◦ *buddhi* 1.23); 🕮*avyavasāyinām* (m◦ 6pos◦ plu◦ ←adj◦ n.tatpu◦ *a-vyavasāyin* (non-rosolute) ←m◦ *vyavasāya* ↑) (2.41)

(§3) ***vyavasāyātmikā*** **(adj1◦-subj1◦ the demeanour of firm determination; of the resolute nature; the resolute);** ***buddhiḥ:*** **(subj◦ the insight, the mind);** ***ekā*** **(adj2◦-subj1◦ one pointed; focused);** ***iha*** **(here, in this discipline);** ***kurunandana*** **(O Kurunandana! O Arjuna!);** ***bahuśākhāḥ:*** **(adj1◦-subj2◦ multi-pointed;**

---

[191] Elsewhere◦ *svalpam* → a little of this dharma, a little of this devotion, a little of this righteousness, even a modicum of this religion, even a small measuer of this Dharma, even the least bit of this religion, even a little of this righteousness, even a little of this discipline, even a little of this knowledge, ...etc.

🕮 स्वल्पम् (सुष्ठु अल्पम्, प्रादि–समासः) is a nominative (1st case) adjective and it must be used as an adjective of a subject, and not as a noun (a little). स्वल्पम् is neuter gender Nominative case, and therefore, it qualifies a neuter gender nominative noun आचरणम्, which is not actually given, but is implied. स्वल्पम् आचरणम् is the subject performing the verb त्रायते । Here, धर्मस्य is not the subject in Nominative case in this verse. धर्मस्य has only an external (genitive 6th case) relationship with the subject स्वल्पम् आचरणम् (small practice), अस्य धर्मस्य स्वल्पम् आचरणम्, a little practice of this *dharma.* स्वल्पम् आचरणं अपि अस्य धर्मस्य त्रायते महतः भयात्

[192] Fear of loss or gain exists only when one works with a desire for gain only. With equanimous mind (बुद्धियोगः), one is indifferent to loss or gain, and it protects one from the great fear of loss automatically.

non-pointed; non-focused); ***hi*** (whereas); ***anantāḥ:*** (adj2◦-subj2◦ endless, imprecise, indefinite, non-specific, uncertain); ***ća*** (and); ***buddhayaḥ:*** (subj2◦ the thoughts, the minds); ***avyavasāyinām*** (of the non-resolute ones) (2.41)

(§4) kurunandana iha vyavasāyātmikā buddhiḥ: ekā hi buddhayaḥ: avyavasāyinām bahuśākhāḥ: ća anantāḥ:

(§5) O Arjuna! in this discipline, the resolute mind[193] (is) one pointed;[194] whereas the minds of the non-resolute ones (are) non-focused and imprecise. (2.41)

2.42 यामिमां पुष्पितां वाचं प्रवदन्त्यविपश्चितः ।
वेदवादरताः पार्थ नान्यदस्तीति वादिनः ।।

yāmimāṁ puṣpitāṁ vāćaṁ pravadantyavipaśćitaḥ:,
vedavādaratāḥ: pārtha nānyadastīti vādinaḥ:; (2.42)

(§1) याम् इमाम् पुष्पिताम् वाचम् प्रवदन्ति अविपश्चितः । वेदवादरताः पार्थ न अन्यत् अस्ति इति वादिनः । *yām* (r◦ 8/18) *imām* (r◦ 14/1) *puṣpitām* (r◦ 14/1) *vāćam* (r◦ 14/1) *pravadanti* (r◦ 4/1) *avipaśćitaḥ:* (r◦ 22/8) *vedavādaratāḥ:* (r◦ 22/3) *pārtha na* (r◦ 1/1) *anyat* (r◦ 8/2) *asti* (r◦ 1/5) *iti vādinaḥ:* (r◦ 22/8)

(§2) ***yām*** (f◦ 2acc◦ sing◦ ←pron◦ *yad* 1.7); *imām* (2.39); 📖*puṣpitām* (f◦ 2acc◦ sing◦ ←ppp◦ adj◦ *puṣpita* (flowery) ←4◦√पुष्प् (to blossom); *vāćam* (2acc◦ sing◦ ←f◦ ***vāć*** ←2◦√वच् (to speek); ***pravadanti*** (3rd-per◦ plu◦ pres◦ वर्तमान्-लट् parasmai◦ ←1◦प्र√वद् (to speak); 📖*avipaśćitaḥ:* (n.tatpu◦ m◦ 1nom◦ sing◦ ←adj◦ *vipaśćita* or 1nom◦ plu◦ ←adj◦ ***vipaśćit*** (descerning) ←10◦वि–प्र√चित् (to percceive); *vedavādaratāḥ:* (m◦ 1nom◦ plu◦ ←tatpu◦ *veda-vāda-rata*, वेदस्य वादे रतः ←m◦ ***veda*** ←2◦√विद् (to know)+ m◦ *vāda* (discussion) 2.11 + ppp◦ adj◦ ***rata*** (engaged) ←1◦√रम् (to rejoice); *pārtha* (1.25); *na* (1.30); *anyat* (2.31); *asti* (2.40); *iti* (1.25); 📖*vādinaḥ:* (1nom◦ plu◦ ←m◦ ***vādin*** (speaker) ←1◦√वद् (to speak) (2.42)

---

[193] Elsewhere◦ *vyavasāyātmikā* → Those who are on this path are resolute, to the firm-in-mind, those who are resolute ... to them, ...etc.

📖 व्यवसायात्मिका (f◦ singular) is not an adjective of 'those people' (m◦ plural). It is f◦ adj◦ of the f◦ subject बुद्धिः । Therefore, व्यवसायात्मिका बुद्धिः = the resolute mind, the persistent thinking.

[194] Elsewhere◦ *ekā* → those who are resolute... their aim is one.

📖 Similar to व्यवसायात्मिका, एका is also f◦ singular and thus it can not qualify m◦ plural pronoun 'their.' In this clause, it talks about the 'mind' (एका बुद्धिः the one pointed thinking) of the people, not about people themselves. Then, the second clause of this verse talks about the minds of the people who have ...

(3) ***yām imām*** (adj1◦-obj◦ this); ***puṣpitām*** (adj2◦-obj◦ flowery, embellished); ***vāćam*** (obj◦ speech)' ***pravadanti*** (they say); ***a-vipaśćitaḥ:*** (subj◦ the undescerning ones); ***vedavādaratāḥ:*** (adj1◦-subj◦ those who rejoice in the words of the Veda); ***pārtha*** (O Pārtha! O Arjuna!); ***na anyat*** (nothing else); ***asti*** (is; there is); ***iti*** (that); ***vādinaḥ:*** (adj2◦-subj◦ those who say, ones who say) (2.42)

(§4) pārtha vedavādaratāḥ: avipaśćitaḥ: vādinaḥ: na anyat asti iti pravadanti yām imām puṣpitām vāćam

(§5) O Arjuna! those who rejoice in the words of the Veda, those undescerning ones who say[195] that "there is nothing else," they say this embellished speech;[196] (2.42)

2.43 कामात्मनः स्वर्गपरा जन्मकर्मफलप्रदाम् ।
क्रियाविशेषबहुलां भोगैश्वर्यगतिं प्रति ।।

kāmātmanaḥ: svargaparā janmakarmaphalapradām,
kriyāviśeṣabahulāṁ bhogaiśvaryagatiṁ prati; (2.43)

(§1) कामात्मनः स्वर्गपरा जन्मकर्मफलप्रदाम् । क्रियाविशेषबहुलाम् भोगैश्वर्यगतिम् प्रति । ***kāmātmanaḥ:*** (r◦ 22/7) ***svargaparāḥ:*** (r◦ 20/7) ***janmakarmaphalapradām*** (r◦ 14/2) ***kriyāviśeṣabahulām*** (r◦ 14/1) ***bhogaiśvaryagatim*** (r◦ 14/1) ***prati***

(§2) *kāmātmanaḥ:* (m◦ 1nom◦ plu◦ ←bahuvrī◦ *kāmātman*, कामः आत्मा यस्य (covetous) ←m◦ *kāma* 1.22 + m◦ *ātman* 2.41); *svargaparāḥ:* (m◦ 1nom◦ plu◦ ←bahuvrī◦ *svarga-para,* स्वर्गः परमः यस्य (heaven seeker) ←m◦ *svarga* 2.2 + adj◦ *para* 2.3); *janmakarmaphalapradām* (f◦ 2acc◦ sing◦ ←bahuvrī◦ *janma-karma-phala-prada,* जन्मनः च कर्मणः च फलं प्रददाति या ←n◦ *janman* 2.27 + n◦ *karman* 1.15 + n◦ ***phala*** (fruit, reward)

---

[195] Elsewhere◦ *vādinaḥ:* → they say, the unwise say, they declare that, declaring ...etc

वादिनः is not a verb. वादिन् is an adjective (वादी, वादिनौ, वादिनः) of the subject. वादिन् = he who says, वादिनः = those who say, those people who say.

[196] Elsewhere◦ *imām puṣpitāṁ vāćam* → the flowery words of the Vedas.

f◦ singular adjective पुष्पितां does not qualify the m◦ plural noun Vedas. It qualifies the utterance (f◦ वाचम्) of the अविपश्चितः । In अविपश्चितः प्रवदन्ति, what the unwise people say, that saying (f◦ वाचम्) is qualified by adj◦ पुष्पिताम् । In the next clause also, reference is made to those people (अविपश्चितः वादिनः) who debate the vedas (वेदवादरतः), not 'the Vedas say.' The अविपश्चितः people are the subject performing the verb प्रवदन्ति पुष्पितां वाचम्, not the Vedas. The flowery words are of the अविपश्चितः people, not of the Vedas. The flowery words of the people are given in the next verse which is in continuation with this verse. Therefore, प्रवदन्ति from 2.42 is the verb for the verse 2.43

←1∘√फल् (to bare fruit) + 3rd-per∘ sing∘ v∘ *pradadāti* ←1∘प्र√दा (to give); *kriyāviśeṣabahulāṃ* (f∘ 2acc∘ sing∘ ←bahuvrī∘ *kriyā-viśeṣa-bahulā*, क्रियाया: विशेषा: बहुला: रीतय: यस्यां सा ←f∘ *kriyā* 1.42 + adj∘ ***viśeṣa*** (special) ←7∘वि√शिष् (to leave remainder) + adj∘ ***bahula*** (multitude) ←1∘√बंह् (to make firm); *bhogaiśvaryagatiṃ* (f∘ 2acc∘ sing∘ ←tatpu∘ collective *bhogaiśvarya-gati*, भोगस्य च ऐश्वर्यस्य च गती ←m∘ *bhoga* (enjoyment) 1.32 + n∘ ***aiśvarya*** (opulence) ←2∘√ईश् (to prosper) + f∘ ***gati*** (state) ←1∘√गम् (to go); ***prati*** (ind∘ ←1∘√प्रथ् (to grow) (2.43)

(§3) *kāmātmanaḥ:* (subj∘ desire-ridden selves); *svargaparāḥ:* (adj∘-subj∘ those people for whom heaven is the highest aim); *janmakarmaphalapradāṃ* (adj∘-obj1∘ the one that results in birth as a reult of *karma*); *kriyāviśeṣabahulāṃ* (obj1∘ the special rite of which there are of many varieties); *bhogaiśvaryagatiṃ* (obj2∘ to the attainment of enjoyment and affluence); *prati* (towards, for) (2.43)

(§4) kāmātmanaḥ: svargaparāḥ: kriyāviśeṣabahulāṃ bhogaiśvaryagatiṃ janmakarmaphalapradāṃ

(§5) Those desire-ridden selves, to whom heaven is the highest aim, (suggest) the special rite, of which there are many varieties[197] for the attainment of enjoyment and affluence (and), that results in birth as a result of *karma;*[198] (2.43)

2.44 भोगैश्वर्यप्रसक्तानां तयाऽपहृतचेतसाम् ।
व्यवसायात्मिका बुद्धि: समाधौ न विधीयते ।।

bhogaiśvaryaprasaktānāṃ tayāpahṛtaćetasāṃ ,
vyavasāyātmikā buddhiḥ: samādhau na vidhīyate. (2.44)

(§1) भोगैश्वर्यप्रसक्तानाम् तया अपहृतचेतसाम् । व्यवसायात्मिका बुद्धि: समाधौ न विधीयते । *bhogaiśvaryaprasaktānāṃ* (r∘ 14/1) *tayā* (r∘ 1/3) *apahṛtaćetasāṃ* (r∘ 14/2) *vyavasāyātmikā buddhiḥ:* (r∘ 22/7) *samādhau na vidhīyate*

(§2) *bhogaiśvaryaprasaktānāṃ* (m∘ 6pos∘ plu∘ ←tatpu∘ *bhogaiśvarya-prasakta*, भोगे च ऐश्वर्ये च प्रसक्त: ←m∘ *bhoga* 1.32 + n∘ *aiśvarya* 2.43 + ppp∘ adj∘ ***prasakta*** (fond of) ←1∘प्र√सञ्ज् (to attach); ***tayā*** (f∘ 3inst∘

---

[197] Elsewhere∘ *kriyāviśeṣabahulāṃ* → actions replete with specific rites, various fruitive activities, various specialized rites, words are laden with specific rites, full of various special rites ...etc.

क्रियाविशेषबहुला is (f∘ singular accusative noun) a special rite (क्रिया) of which there are many varieties.

[198] Elsewhere∘ *janmakarmaphalapradāṃ* → they utter words which lead to birth, these flowery words that result in rebirth, they offer birth as the fruit ...etc.

∘प्रदाम् is f∘ singular adjective of f∘ singular noun क्रियाम् । Not the 'words,' but the "क्रिया" is विशेषबहुला and जन्मकर्मफलप्रदा ।

sing◦ ←pron◦ *taḍ* 1.2); 📖*apahṛtaćetasāṃ* (m◦ 6pos◦ plu◦ ←tatpu◦ *apahṛta-ćetaṣ*, अपहृतम् चेतः यस्य सः ←ppp◦ adj◦ ***apahṛta*** (stolen) ←1◦अप√हृ (to take) + n◦ *ćetaṣ* 1.38); *vyavasāyātmikā* (2.41); *buddhiḥ:* (2.39); ***samādhau*** (7loc◦ sing◦ ←f◦ ***samādhi*** (concentration) ←3◦सम्√धा (to put); *na* (1.30); *vidhīyate* (3rd-per◦ sing◦ pres◦ वर्तमान्-लट् ātmane◦ ←3◦वि√धा (to put) (2.44)

(§3) ***bhogaiśvaryaprasaktānāṃ*** (of those who are devoted to enjoyment and affluence); ***tayā*** (f◦ adj◦-subj1◦ by that, by that flowery speech); ***apahṛtaćetasāṃ*** (of those whose thinking is stolen away); ***vyavasāyātmikā*** (adj◦-obj◦ firm); ***buddhiḥ:*** (obj◦ the mind); ***samādhau*** (in concentration; in own self); ***na*** (does not); ***vidhīyate*** (it fixes, it establishes; it gets established) (2.44)

(§4) tayā buddhiḥ: bhogaiśvaryaprasaktānāṃ apahṛtaćetasāṃ na vidhīyate vyavasāyātmikā samādhau

(§5) By that flowery speech,[199] the mind of those who are devoted to enjoyment and affluence (and) whose thinking is stolen away, does not get established firm in own self. (2.44)

2.45 त्रैगुण्यविषया वेदा निस्त्रैगुण्यो भवार्जुन ।
निर्द्वन्द्वो नित्यसत्त्वस्थो निर्योगक्षेम आत्मवान् ।।

traiguṇyaviṣayā vedā nistraiguṇyo bhavārjuna,
nirdvandvo nityasattvastho niryogakṣema ātmavāṇ. (2.45)

(§1) त्रैगुण्यविषयाः वेदाः निस्त्रैगुण्यः भव अर्जुन । निर्द्वन्द्वः नित्यसत्त्वस्थः निर्योगक्षेमः आत्मवान् । *traiguṇyaviṣayāḥ:* (r◦ 20/17) *vedāḥ:* (r◦ 20/10) *nistraiguṇyaḥ:* (r◦ 15/8) *bhava* (r◦ 1/1) *arjuna nirdvandvaḥ:* (r◦ 15/6) *nityasattvasthaḥ:* (r◦ 15/6) *niryogakṣemaḥ:* (r◦ 19/1) *ātmavāṇ*

(§2) *traiguṇyaviṣayāḥ:* (m◦ 1nom◦ plu◦ ←bahuvrī◦ *traiguṇya-viṣaya*, त्रैगुण्यं विषयः यस्य ←taddhita◦ n◦ 📖*traiguṇya* ←num◦ adj◦ ***tri*** (three) ←1◦√तॄ (to swim across) + m◦ ***guṇa*** (attribute) ←10◦√गुण् (to multiply, possess a property) + m◦ 📖***viṣaya*** (subject) ←5◦वि√सि (to bind); ***vedāḥ:*** (1nom◦ plu◦ ←m◦ *veda* 2.42); 📖*nistraiguṇyaḥ:* (indifferent to the effect of the three gunas = *guṇātītaḥ* 14.25 m◦ 1nom◦ sing◦ ←ind◦ with opposition indicating negative prefix ***niṣ*** (निस्); or ***nir*** (निर्) ←9◦√नॄ (to take away) + n◦ taddhita◦ *traiguṇya* ↑); ***bhava*** (2nd-per◦

---

[199] Elsewhere◦ *tayā* → by these words of the Veda; by such things, the mind of these ...etc.

📖 तया is f◦ singular pronominal adjective in the Instrumental case and does not relate to the *vāda* of Veda (m◦), these things (plu◦) or mind the *buddhi* (f◦ nominative 1st◦ case). In this context, the *kriyā-vishesha-bahulām* is the only f◦ sing◦ obj◦ that has just been referred in 2.43. Therefore, तया is the pronoun for the subject क्रिया, which is not actually given in 2.44, but is understood. See the footnotes given in 2.42 and 2.43. Please note that verses 2.43 and 2.44 are one continuous verse, connected by a semi-colon. (;)

sing∘ imperative∘ उपदेशार्थ लोट् parasmai∘ ←1∘√भू (to be, become); *arjuna* (2.2); 📖**nirdvandvaḥ:** (m∘ 1nom∘ sing∘ ←n.tatpu∘ *nir-dvandva* ←ind∘ *nir̥* ↑ + n∘ **dvandva** (duality) ←1∘√द्वृ (to hinder); 📖*nityasattvasthaḥ:* (m∘ 1nom∘ sing∘ ←s-tat∘ *nitya-sattvastha,* नित्यं सत्त्वे स्थित: ←adj∘ *nitya* 2.18 + n∘ **sattva,** सत: भाव: ←adj∘ or n∘ *sat̥* 2.16 + adj∘ **stha** (situated, steady) ←1∘√स्था (to stay); *niryogakṣemaḥ:* (1nom∘ sing∘ ←m∘ *nir-yoga-kṣema,* निर् योग: च क्षेम: च ←ind∘ *nir̥* ↑ + m∘ *yoga* 2.39 + adj∘ m∘ or n∘ *kṣema* 1.46); *ātmavān̥* (1nom∘ sing∘ ←adj∘ **ātmavat̥** (self-possessed) ←m∘ ātman̥ 2.41 + affix **vat̥** वत् 1.5)

(2.45)

(§3) *traiguṇyaviṣayāḥ:* (adj∘-subj∘ the derivatives of the three *guṇas* are the subject matter of); *vedāḥ:* (subj1∘ the Vedas); *nistraiguṇyaḥ:* (adj1∘-subj2∘ one who has controlled the balance of three guṇas, one who is unaffected by the three *guṇas*); *bhava* (you please be); *arjuna* (O Arjuna!); *nirdvandvaḥ:* (adj2∘-subj2∘ indifferent to the dualities); *nityasattvasthaḥ:* (adj3∘-subj2∘ ever established in the *sattva guṇa*); *niryogakṣemaḥ:* (adj4∘-subj2∘ free from the worry about acquisition; free from attachment and possession); *ātmavān̥* (adj5∘-subj2∘ self possessed, one who has controlled himself, self-controlled) (2.45)

(§4) traiguṇyaviṣayāḥ: vedāḥ: arjuna bhava nistraiguṇyaḥ: nirdvandvaḥ: nityasattvasthaḥ: niryogakṣemaḥ: ātmavān̥

(§5) The derivatives of the three *guṇas* are the subject matter of the *Vedas*. O Arjuna! you please be the one who has controlled the balance of the three *guṇas*,[200] indifferent to the dualities,[201]

---

[200] Elsewhere∘ निस्त्रैगुण्य: → free from from the triad of the gunas, free from the three gunas, without the three gunas, beyond the tri-giNa, ...etc.

📖 It is *nistraiguṇya* is not *nirguṇa.* Only the *brahma* (ब्रह्म) is निर्गुणम्, nothing else can be *nirguṇa* (निर्गुणं नेतरद्भवेत् ।) The Gītā says, 'there is no being on the earth or even in heaven or among Gods, who is free from the three guṇas (18.40).' Also, निस्त्रैगुण्य: is not above or transcendental to the three guṇas, because Gītā (3.27, 3.33) says everyone is helplessly caused to act by the guṇas. Guṇas are the doer (कर्ता). what one can do only is control the balance of the three guṇas in you to make your sat̥ guṇa more dominant to make you act in a righteous manner. Therefore, the *taddhit* word *nistraiguṇya* is *guṇātīta* (गुणातीत), the one who has controlled the balance of the three *guṇas,* one who has supressed his *rajas̥* and *tamas̥ guṇa.*

[201] Elsewhere∘ निर्द्वन्द्व: → free from all dualities, beyond the pairs of opposites, free from the pairs of opposites, free from the pairs of duality, ...etc. Previous footnote (निस्त्रैगुण्य) holds good for inaV√nV also. There is no such thing as free from or beyond dualities, just as there is no such thing as "One-sided-coin". All one can do is become indifferent to the dualities.

ever established in the *sattva guṇa*, free from the worry about acquisition, (and) be self possessed. (2.45)

2.46 यावानर्थ उदपाने सर्वतः सम्प्लुतोदके ।
तावान्सर्वेषु वेदेषु ब्राह्मणस्य विजानतः ।।[202]

yāvānartha udapāne sarvataḥ: samplutodake,
tāvānsarveṣu vedeṣu brāhmaṇasya vijānataḥ:. (2.46)

(§1) यावान् अर्थः उदपाने सर्वतः सम्प्लुतोदके । तावान् सर्वेषु वेदेषु ब्राह्मणस्य विजानतः । *yāvān* (r∘ 8/11) *arthaḥ:* (r∘ 19/4) *udapāne sarvataḥ:* (r∘ 22/7) *samplutodake tāvān* (r∘ 13/20) *sarveṣu* (r∘ 25/5) *vedeṣu* (r∘ 25/5) *brāhmaṇasya vijānataḥ:* (r∘ 22/8)

(§2) ***yāvān*** (1nom∘ sing∘ ←adj∘ *yāvat* (as much) 1.22); *arthaḥ:* (1nom∘ sing∘ ←m∘ *artha* (meaning) 1.7); *udapāne* (7loc∘ sing∘ ←m∘ *udapān* (water tank) ←1∘उद्√पा (to drink); ***sarvataḥ:*** (= ind∘ *sarvatas* ←pron∘ *sarva* 1.6); *samplutodake* (n∘ 7loc∘ sing∘ ←tatpu∘ *samplutodaka*, सम्प्लुतं उदकम् (flooded) ←ppp∘ adj∘ *sampluta* ←1∘सम्√प्लु (to float) + n∘ *udaka* (water) 1.42); *tāvān* (1nom∘ sing∘ ←adj∘ *tāvat* (that much) ←pron∘ *tad* 1.2); *sarveṣu* (1.11); ***vedeṣu*** (7loc∘ plu∘ ←m∘ *veda* 2.42); *brāhmaṇasya* (6pos sing∘ ←adj∘ ***brāhmaṇa*** (brahma-knower) ब्रह्मज्ञानी ←1∘√बृंह् (to grow); *vijānataḥ:* (m∘ 6pos∘ sing∘ ←śatṛ∘ adj∘ *vijānat* (knowledgeable) ←9∘वि√ज्ञा (to know) (2.46)

(§3) *yāvān* (as much); *arthaḥ:* (subj∘ meaning; use; object); *udapāne* (in the water near a well); *sarvataḥ:* (at the time when the earth is flooded with water all over); *tāvān* (so much); *sarveṣu* (in all); *vedeṣu* (in the Veda, the scriptures); *brāhmaṇasya* (of the *brahma*); *vijānataḥ:* (for a knower) (2.46)

(§4) yāvān arthaḥ: udapāne sarvataḥ: samplutodake tāvān sarveṣu vedeṣu vijānataḥ: brāhmaṇasya

(§5) As much meaning (is there) in a water tank near a well[203] at the time when the earth is flooded with water all over, so much (meaning is there) in all the scriptures, for a knower of the *brahma*. (2.46)

2.47 कर्मण्येवाधिकारस्ते मा फलेषु कदाचन ।

---

[202] यथाऽमृतेन तृप्तस्य पयसा किं प्रयोजनम् ।
एवं तत्परं ज्ञात्वा वेदे नास्ति प्रतोजनम् ।। (uttaragītā 1.17)

[203] *udapān* (उद, water; पान drinking) is the small water pool that is built next to a well, and kept filled with water from that well, as a handy source of available water for animals and people.

मा कर्मफलहेतुर्भूर्मा ते सङ्गोऽस्त्वकर्मणि ॥

karmaṇyevādhikāraste mā phaleṣu kadāćana,
mā karmaphalaheturbhūrmā te saṅgo'stvakarmaṇi. (2.47)

(§1) कर्मणि एव अधिकारः ते मा फलेषु कदाचन । मा कर्मफलहेतुः भूः मा ते सङ्गः अस्तु अकर्मणि । *karmaṇi* (r◦ 24/7, 4/4) *eva* (r◦ 1/1) *adhikāraḥ:* (r◦ 18/1) *te mā phaleṣu* (r◦ 25/5) *kadāćana mā karmaphalahetuḥ:* (r◦ 16/8) *bhūḥ:* (r◦ 16/9) *mā te saṅgaḥ:* (r◦ 15/1) *astu* (r◦ 4/6) *akarmaṇi* (r◦ 24/7)

(§2) ***karmaṇi*** (7loc◦ sing◦ ←n◦ *karmaṇ* 1.15); *eva* (1.1); 📖*adhikāraḥ:* (1nom◦ sing◦ ←m◦ *adhikāra* (right, authority) ←8◦अधि√कृ (to do); *te* (2.7); *mā* (2.3); *phaleṣu* (7loc◦ plu◦ ←n◦ *phala* 2.43); ***kadāćana*** (time indicating ind◦ (ever) ←pron◦ *kiṃ* 1.1 + limit indicating ind◦ *ćana,* -not more ←1◦√चन् (to sound); *mā* (2.3); *karmaphalahetuḥ:* (m◦ 1nom◦ sing◦ ←bahuvrī◦ *karma-phala-hetu,* कर्मणः फले हेतुः यस्य ←n◦ *karmaṇ* 1.15 + n◦ *phala* 2.43 + m◦ *hetu* 1.35); *bhūḥ:* (2nd-per◦ sing◦ mood.sub◦ ←1◦√भू (to be, become); *mā* (2.3); *te* (6pos◦ 2.7); 📖***saṅgaḥ:*** (1nom◦ sing◦ ←m◦ ***saṅga*** (attachment) ←1◦√सञ्ज् (to attach); ***astu*** (3rd-per◦ sing◦ imperative◦ उपदेशार्थ लोट् parasmai◦ ←2◦√अस् (to be); ***akarmaṇi*** (7loc◦ sing◦ ←n◦ n.tatpu◦ ***akarmaṇ*** (non-performance of duty) ←8◦अ√कृ (to do) (2.47)

(§3) *karmaṇi* (in *karma*; in the prescribed *karma,* in the righteous work); *eva* (only); *adhikāraḥ:* (subj1◦ duty, authority); *te* (your); *mā* (not); *phaleṣu* (in the fruit; in the fruit of *karma*); *kadāćana* (ever); *bhūḥ:* (subj2◦ be, you be); *mā* (do not); *karmaphalahetuḥ:* (adj◦-subj2◦ the one who has motive in the fruit of the *karma*); *mā* (do not); *te* (your); *saṅgaḥ:* (subj3◦ attachment); *astu* (let there be); *akarmaṇi* (in not performing the prescribed *karma*) (2.47)

(§4) te adhikāraḥ: karmaṇi eva, mā kadāćana phaleṣu, mā bhūḥ: karmaphalahetuḥ:, mā astu te saṅgaḥ: akarmaṇi.

(§5) Your duty (is) in the 'prescribed *karma*'[204] only; not ever in the fruit of *karma.*[205] You do not be the one who has 'motive' in the fruit of the *karma.*[206] Do not let your attachment be in 'not

---

[204] Elsewhere◦ *karmaṇi* → in karma, in action, ...etc.
📖 any kind of action : good, bad and evil?

[205] Elsewhere◦ मा फलेषु कदाचन → never claim its result (imperative लोट्), but you are not entitled to the fruit of action, but lay not claim to its fruits (imperative◦), ...etc.

[206] Elsewhere◦ मा भूः कर्मफलहेतुः → let not results of action be your motive, let not the result of action be thy motive, let not the fruits of action be thy motive, let not the fruits of action be your motive, never allow the results to become the motive, be you not the producer of the fruits, ...etc.

performing' the prescribed *karma*.[207] (2.47)

2.48 योगस्थः कुरु कर्माणि सङ्गं त्यक्त्वा धनञ्जय ।
सिद्ध्यसिद्ध्योः समो भूत्वा समत्वं योग उच्यते ।।

yogasthaḥ: kuru karmāṇi saṅgaṁ tyaktvā dhanañjaya,
siddhyasiddhyoḥ: samo bhūtvā samatvaṁ yoga ućyate. (2.48)

(§1) योगस्थः कुरु कर्माणि सङ्गम् त्यक्त्वा धनञ्जय । सिद्ध्यसिद्ध्योः समः भूत्वा समत्वम् योगः उच्यते । *yogasthaḥ:* (r◦ 22/1) *kuru karmāṇi* (r◦ 24/7) *saṅgaṃ* (r◦ 14/1) *tyaktvā dhanañjaya siddhyasiddhyaoḥ:* (r◦ 22/7) *samaḥ:* (r◦ 15/8) *bhūtvā samatvaṃ* (r◦ 14/1) *yogaḥ:* (r◦ 19/4) *ućyate*

(§2) *yogasthaḥ:* (1nom◦ sing◦ ←ppp◦ adj◦ *yogastha*, कर्मयोगे स्थितः ←m◦ *yoga* 2.39 + adj◦ *sthita* 1.14 or *stha* 2.45); ***kuru*** (2nd-per◦ sing◦ imperative◦ उपदेशार्थ-लोट् parasmai◦ ←8◦√कृ (to do); ***karmāṇi*** (2acc◦ plu◦ ←n◦ *karmaṇ* 1.15); ***saṅgaṃ*** (2acc◦ sing◦ ←m◦ *saṅga* 2.47); *tyaktvā* (1.33); ***dhanañjaya*** (8voc◦ sing◦ ←m◦ *dhanañjaya* 1.15); ***siddhyasiddhyoḥ:*** (f◦ 7loc◦ dual◦ ←dvandva◦ सिद्धौ च असिद्धौ च ←f◦ 🕮***siddhi*** (accomplishment, success) ←4◦√सिध् (to be successful)+ f◦ n.tatpu◦ ***a-siddhi*** (non-accomplishment) ←4◦अ√सिध् (to be successful); ***samaḥ:*** (1nom◦ sing◦ ←adj◦ *sama* 1.4); *bhūtvā* (2.20); 🕮*samatvaṃ* (1nom◦ sing◦ ←n◦ *samatva* (equanimity) ←adj◦ *sama* 1.4); ***yogaḥ:*** (1nom◦ sing◦ ←m◦ *yoga* 2.39); *ućyate* (2.25) (2.48)

(§3) ***yogasthaḥ:*** (adj1◦-subj1◦ being established in yoga, disciplined); ***kuru*** (please do, perform); ***karmāṇi*** (obj1◦ righteous works, prescribed work, duties); ***saṅgaṃ*** (obj2◦ motive, attachment, attachment to the desire for the fruit of the ***karma***); ***tyaktvā*** (giving up; renouncing, leaving aside); ***dhanañjaya*** (O Dhanañjaya! O Arjuna!); ***siddhyasiddhyoḥ:*** (in success and non-success); ***samaḥ:*** (adj◦2-subj1◦ indifferent to); ***bhūtvā*** (having become); ***samatvaṃ*** (subj2◦ the discipline of equanimity; the discipline of indifference); ***yogaḥ:*** (subj3◦ yoga; ***buddhi-yoga, sama-buddhi-yoga***); ***ućyate*** (this is called) (2.48)

🕮 here the subject of verb भू: (be) is 2nd person 'you.' It is not 3rd person 'result or fruits' of action. you = you, the one who has motive in the fruit of action.

[207] Elsewhere◦ मा ते सङ्गः अस्तु अकर्मणि → never be attached to inaction, nor should you be attached to inaction, never be attached to not doing your duty, nor be attached to inaction, neither shall you lean towards inaction, nor be thou to inaction attached, ...etc.

🕮 the verb अस्तु belongs to 3rd person subject सङ्गः, not 2nd person 'you.' Pronoun ते (your) is Possesive 6th case, not not Nominative 1st case (you, be). in ते सङ्गः the सङ्गः (attachment) is Nominative subject, it is not a verb (be attached).

(§4) dhanañjaya kuru karmāṇi yogasthaḥ: *tyaktvā* saṅgam bhūtvā samaḥ: siddhyasiddhyoḥ: samatvam ućyate yogaḥ:

(§5) O Arjuna! perform (your) duties[208] being established in yoga, renouncing attachment to the desire for the fruit of the *karma* (and) having become indifferent[209] to success and non-success. This 'discipline of indifference' is called *buddhi-yoga.*[210] (2.48)

2.49 दूरेण ह्यवरं कर्म बुद्धियोगाद्धनञ्जय ।
बुद्धौ शरणमन्विच्छ कृपणाः फलहेतवः ।।

dūreṇa hyavaraṁ karma buddhiyogāddhanañjaya,
buddhau śaraṇamanvićcha kṛpaṇāḥ: phalahetavaḥ:. (2.49)

(§1) दूरेण हि अवरम् कर्म बुद्धियोगात् धनञ्जय । बुद्धौ शरणम् अन्विच्छ कृपणाः फलहेतवः । *dūreṇa* (r∘ 24/1) *hi* (r∘ 4/1) *avaram* (r∘ 14/1) *karma buddhiyogāt* (r∘ 9/6) *dhanañjaya buddhau śaraṇam* (r∘ 8/16, 24/3) *anvićcha kṛpaṇāḥ:* (r∘ 24/5, 22/4) *phalahetavaḥ:* (r∘ 22/8)

(§2) *dūreṇa* (adv∘ ←adj∘ ***dūra*** (far) ←5∘√दु (be bad); *hi* (1.11) *avaram* (n∘ 1nom∘ sing∘ ←adj∘ *avara* (inferior) ←2∘अव√रा (to bestow); ***karma*** (1nom∘ sing∘ ←n∘ *karman* 1.15); *buddhiyogat* (m∘ 5abl∘ sing∘ ←tatpu∘ ***buddhi-yoga***, समबुद्ध्याः योगः । तटस्थमनसः योगः ←f∘ *buddhi* 1.23 + m∘ *yoga* 2.39); *dhanañjaya* (2.48); *buddhau* (7loc∘ sing∘ ←f∘ *buddhi* 1.23); ***śaraṇam*** (2acc∘ sing∘ ←n∘ *śaraṇa* (refuge) ←9∘√शॄ (to smash); *anvićcha* (2nd-per∘ sing∘ imperative∘ उपदेशार्थ-लोट् parasmai∘ ←6∘अनु√इषु (to desire); *kṛpaṇāḥ:* (m∘ 1nom∘ plu∘ ←adj∘ *kṛpaṇa* (wretched) ←1∘√कृप् (to imagine); *phalahetavaḥ:* (m∘ 1nom∘ plu∘ ←bahuvrī∘ *phala-hetu,* फले हेतुः यस्य ←n∘ *phala* 2.43 + m∘ *hetu* (objective) 1.35) (2.49)

(§3) ***dūreṇa*** **(greatly; in a high degree);** ***hi*** **(because);** ***avaram*** **(adj∘-subj1∘ inferior);** ***karma*** **(subj1∘ the** ***karma*****);** ***buddhiyogat*** **(than the** ***samabuddhi-yoga*****; than the** ***yoga*** **or discipline of equanimity of mind);** ***dhanañjaya*** **(O Dhanañjaya! O Arjuna!);** ***buddhau*** **(in** ***samabuddhi-yoga*****; in equanimity of mind);** ***śaraṇam*** **(obj∘ refuge, shelter, support);** ***anvićcha*** **(you please seek, desire);** ***kṛpaṇāḥ:*** **(adj∘-subj2∘**

---

[208] Elsewhere∘ कुरु कर्माणि → perform actions, perform action, undertake actions, ...etc.

[209] Elsewhere∘ समः भूत्वा → have no concern about (imperative∘), be balanced (imperative), with evenness (instrumental∘), unconcerned as to (instrumental∘), treating success and failure (gerund), ...etc.

भूत्वा is gerund participle = having become (√भू = to become + क्त्वा), adj∘ of the subject 'you.'

[210] *buddhiyoga* → see the footnotes in 2.39 and 3.3 and the Answer to Question 9 in Vol. I

any kind of action : good, bad and evil?

wretched); ***phalahetavaḥ:*** (subj2◦ those who keep alterior motive in the fruit; who are driven by the desire of gain) (2.49)

(§4) karma dūreṇa avaraṃ buddhiyogaṭ dhanañjaya anviccha śaraṇaṃ buddhau hi phalahetavaḥ: kṛpaṇāḥ:

(§5) The *sakāma-karma*[211] (is) greatly inferior than (done with) the discipline of equanimity of mind *(buddhi-yoga).*[212] O Arjuna! (therefore,) you please seek refuge in *buddhi-yoga*, because[213] those who keep alterior motive in the fruit (are) wretched. (2.49)

2.50 बुद्धियुक्तो जहातीह उभे सुकृतदुष्कृते ।
तस्माद्योगाय युज्यस्व योगः कर्मसु कौशलम् ।।

buddhiyukto jahātīha ubhe sukṛtaduṣkṛte,
tasmādyogāya yujyasva yogaḥ: karmasu kauśalaṃ. (2.50)

(§1) बुद्धियुक्तः जहाति इह उभे सुकृतदुष्कृते । तस्मात् योगाय युज्यस्व योगः कर्मसु कौशलम् । *buddhiyuktaḥ:* (r◦ 15/3) *jahāti* (r◦ 1/5) *iha* (r◦ 2/2) *ubhe sukṛtaduṣkṛte tasmāṭ* (r◦ 9/9) *yogāya yujyasva yogaḥ:* (r◦ 22/1) *karmasu kauśalaṃ* (r◦ 14/2)

(§2) *buddhiyuktaḥ:* (m◦ 1nom◦ sing◦ ←bahuvrī◦ ***buddhi-yukta***, बुद्ध्या युक्तः यः ←f◦ *buddhi* 1.23 + adj◦ *yukta* (equipped) 1.14); *jahāti* (3rd-per◦ sing◦ pres◦ वर्तमान्-लट् parasmai◦ ←3◦√**हा** (to go); *iha* (2.5); *ubhe* (n◦ 2acc◦ dual◦ ←pron◦ *ubha* (both) 2.19); *sukṛta-duṣkṛte* (n◦ 2acc◦ -dvan◦, सुकृतं च दुष्कृतं च ←n◦ 📖***sukṛta*** (merit) ←adj◦ *sukṛṭ* ←8◦सु√कृ (to do) + n◦ 📖*duṣkṛta* ←adj◦ ***duṣkṛta*** (demerit) ←ind◦ *duṣ* or *dus* + affix ***kṛṭ*** ←8◦√कृ

---

[211] Elsewhere◦ *karma* → action.

📖 At this place *karma* does not refer to every action or all actions. *karma* कर्म could be *sakāma* or *niṣkāma.* A *sakāma-karma* सकामकर्म is work done with-a-motive (स-काम) in the fruit of action; *niṣkāma-karma* निष्कामकर्म is work done without-a-motive (निस्-काम) in the fruit. Therefore, here *karma* does not refer to all actions. It refers to a *sakāma karma* that is performed with a desire for the fruit. It does not refer to a *niṣkāma karma*, that is performed with equanimity of mind. Also, A *karma* could also be सुकर्म or कुकर्म । Karma could be नित्यकर्म or अनित्यकर्म.

[212] Elsewhere◦ *buddhiyogaḥ* → discipline of intelligence, yoga of wisdom, yoga of descrimination, yoga of mental determination, yoga of intuitive determination, mind undisturbed by thoughts of results, devotion in wisdom, action guided by wisdom, ...etc.

📖 see the footnotes in 2.39 and 3.3 and the Answer to Question 9 in Vol. I

[213] See the footnote in verse 2.15

(to do); *tasmāt* (1.37); *yogāya* (4dat∘ sing∘ ←m∘ *yoga* 2.39); *yujyasva* (2.38); *yogaḥ:* (2.48); ***karmasu*** (7loc∘ plu∘ ←n∘ *karman* 1.15); 📖*kauśalam* (1nom∘ sing∘ ←n∘ *kauśala* or *kauśalya* (skill) ←1∘√कृ (to make sound) (2.50)

(§3) ***buddhiyuktaḥ:*** (subj1∘ the person equipped with the mind of equanimity; a person equipped with the buddhi-yoga); ***jahāti*** (he renounces, he casts away); ***iha*** (here; in this life itself); ***ubhe*** (adj∘-obj1∘ both); ***sukṛta-duṣkṛte*** (obj1∘ merit and demerit); ***tasmāt*** (therefore); ***yogāya*** (to the yoga; to the buddhi-yoga, to the yoga of equanimity); ***yujyasva*** (you please attach yourself, please make yoga your way of life); ***yogaḥ:*** (subj2∘ yoga); ***karmasu*** (in performing the karmas); ***kauśalam*** (subj3∘ the skill) (2.50)

(§4) buddhiyuktaḥ: jahāti ubhe sukṛta-duṣkṛte iha tasmāt yujyasva yogāya yogaḥ: kauśalam karmasu

(§5) The person equipped with the mind of equanimity[214] renounces (the passion for)[215] both merit and demerit (of *karma*) in this life itself. Therefore,[216] you please make *yoga* of equanimity your way of life. The skill in performing the *karmas* (equanimously)[217] is yoga. (2.50)

2.51 कर्मजं बुद्धियुक्ता हि फलं त्यक्त्वा मनीषिणः ।

---

[214] Elsewhere∘ *buddhiyuktaḥ:* → united to pure reason, born of wisdom, united with knowledge, yolked his intelligence, engaged in devotional services, he who is endowed with wisdom, endowed with intelligence, ...etc.

📖 बुद्धियुक्तः is not a *sandhi* between two words बुद्धिः and युक्ताः (बुद्धिर्युक्ताः) । The word बुद्धि in this *tatpuruṣa samāsic* word बुद्धियुक्तः does not literally mean intelligence or intelligent person, but it logically means समबुद्धिः or more precisely the बुद्धियोगः, समबुद्धियोगः (बुद्धियोगयुक्तः). The same is true for the word बुद्धौ in 2.49

सङ्कल्पनं मनोविद्धि सङ्कल्पात्तन्न भिद्यते ।
यथा द्रवत्वात्सलिलं तथा स्पन्दो यथा निलात् ।।

Know the volition to be same as mind, which is nothing different from the thinking, just as fluidity is same as water and the air is same as wind (Yogavāsiṣṭha 3.6.3.11).

[215] जहाति सुकृतदुष्कृते → In Gita sense it is जहाति वासनां सुकृतदुष्कृतयोः । One can not renounce or remove his *pāpa* (demerit) or *puṇya* (merit) or the fruit thereof. If one is able to renounce his sins, one will be free to do sinful acts, keep on renouncing them and get away clean easily. It doesn't work that way, for a good reason.

[216] See the footnote in verse 2.15

[217] Elsewhere∘ योगः कर्मसु कौशलम् → Yoga is the skill in working, Yoga is skill in actions, Yoga is skill in work, Yoga is skill in works, Yoga is skillfulness in work, yoga is the art of all work, yoga is none other than skill in the field of activity, work done to perfection is verily yoga, yoga is truly a helthy approach to action, ...etc.

जन्मबन्धविनिर्मुक्ताः पदं गच्छन्त्यनामयम् ।।

karmajaṁ buddhiyuktā hi phalaṁ tyaktvā manīṣiṇaḥ:,

janmabandhavinirmuktāḥ: padaṁ gac̓c̓hantyanāmayam. (2.51)

(§1) कर्मजम् बुद्धियुक्ताः हि फलम् त्यक्त्वा मनीषिणः । जन्मबन्धविनिर्मुक्ताः पदम् गच्छन्ति अनामयम् । *karmajam* (r◦ 14/1) *buddhiyuktā* (r◦ 20/18) *hi phalam* (r◦ 14/1) *tyaktvā manīṣiṇaḥ:* (r◦ 22/8) *janmabandhavinirmuktāḥ:* (r◦ 22/3) *padam* (r◦ 14/1) *gac̓c̓hanti* (r◦ 4/1) *anāmayam* (r◦ 14/2)

(§2) *karmajam* (n◦ 2acc◦ sing◦ ←bahuvrī◦ adj◦ ***karma-ja***, कर्मात् जायते यत् ←n◦ *karman* 1.15 + m◦ *ja* (born) 1.7); *buddhiyuktāḥ:* (m◦ 1nom◦ plu◦ ←m◦ *buddhi-yukta* 2.50); *hi* (1.11); ***phalam*** (2acc◦ sing◦ ←n◦ *phala* 2.43); *tyaktvā* (1.33); 📖*manīṣiṇaḥ:* (1nom◦ plu◦ ←adj◦ or m◦ ***manīṣin*** (wise) ←4◦√मन् (to think); *janmabandhavinirmuktāḥ:* (m◦ 1nom◦ plu◦ ←tatpu◦ adj◦ *janma-bandha-vinirmukta* ←जन्मनः बन्धात् विमुक्तः ←n◦ *janman* 2.27 + m◦ *bandha* (bondage) 1.27 + ppp◦ adj◦ *vinirmukta* (freed) ←6◦वि–निर्√मुच् (to liberate); ***padam*** (2acc◦ sing◦ ←n◦ ***pada*** (state, place) ←4◦√पद् (to go); ***gac̓c̓hanti*** (3rd-per◦ plu◦ pres◦ वर्तमान्–लट् parasmai◦ ←1◦√गम् (to go); 📖***anāmayam*** (n◦ 2acc◦ sing◦ ←adj◦ n.bahuvrī◦ *anāmaya*, नास्ति आमयं यस्मिन् तत् (blissful) ←m◦ ***āmaya*** (distemper) ←2◦आम√या (to go) (2.51)

(§3) ***karmajam*** (adj◦-obj1◦ the one that is born out of karma); ***buddhiyuktāḥ:*** (adj1◦-subj◦ endowed with the buddhi-yoga of equanimity); ***hi*** (because) ***phalam*** (obj1◦ the fruit, the desire for the fruit); ***tyaktvā*** (having renounced); ***manīṣiṇaḥ:*** (subj◦ the wise people); ***janmabandhavinirmuktāḥ:*** (adj2◦-subj◦ those who are freed from the cycle of rebirth, from the bondage of birth and death); ***padam*** (obj2◦ a state); ***gac̓c̓hanti*** (they attain); ***anāmayam*** (adj◦-obj2◦ blissful) (2.51)

(§4) manīṣiṇaḥ: buddhiyuktāḥ: janmabandhavinirmuktāḥ: hi tyaktvā phalam karmajam gac̓c̓hanti anāmayam padam

(§5) The wise people,[218] endowed with the *buddhi-yoga* of equanimity[219] (are) freed from the cycle of rebirth,[220] because,[221] having renounced[222] the desire[223] for fruit that is born out of

---

[218] Elsewhere◦ मनीषिणः → attaining self-realization, people, humans, ...etc.

📖 मनीषिणः is not a gerund. It is noun or an adj◦ of a noun. Self realization is आत्मज्ञानम्, आत्मबोधः ।

[219] Elsewhere◦ *buddhiyuktāḥ:* → intelligent ones, equipped with knowledge, united to Pure Reason, being engaged in devotional service, devoted to wisdom, endowed with wisdom, disciplined in intuitive discrimination, one who has his intelligence with the Divine, men of wisdom, yoked in intelligence, ...etc.

📖 see the footnotes in 2.50

[220] Elsewhere◦ *janmabandhavinirmuktāḥ:* → they become free from .., having become free from ... renounce

karma, they attain a blissful state. (2.51)

2.52 यदा ते मोहकलिलं बुद्धिर्व्यतितरिष्यति ।
तदा गन्तासि निर्वेदं श्रोतव्यस्य श्रुतस्य च ।।

yadā te mohakalilaṁ buddhirvyatitariṣyati,
tadā gantāsi nirvedaṁ śrotavyasya śrutasya ća; (2.52)

(§1) यदा ते मोहकलिलम् बुद्धिः व्यतितरिष्यति । तदा गन्तासि निर्वेदम् श्रोतव्यस्य श्रुतस्य च । *yadā te mohakalilam* (r◦ 14/1) *buddhiḥ:* (r◦ 16/6) *vyatitariṣyati* (r◦ 25/6) *tadā gantāsi nirvedam* (r◦ 14/1) *śrotavyasya śrutasya ća*

(§2) *yadā* (time indicating ind◦ ←pron◦ *yad* 1.7); *te* (2.34); 📖*mohakalilam* (n◦ 2acc◦ sing◦ ←tatpu◦ *moha-kalila,* मोहरुपं कलिलम् ←m◦ 📖*moha* (delusion) ←4◦√मुह् (to be deluded) + n◦ 📖*kalila* (mire) ←1◦√कल् (to hold); *buddhiḥ:* (2.39); 📖*vyatitariṣyati* (3rd-per◦ sing◦ fut2◦ लृट् भविष्य◦ parasmai◦ ←1◦वि–अति√तृ (to swim across); *tadā* (1.2); *gantāsi* (2nd-per◦ sing◦ fut1◦ लुट् parasmai◦ ←1◦√गम् (to go); 📖*nirvedam* (2acc◦ sing◦ ←m◦ *nirveda* (indifference) ←7◦निर√विद् (to think); *śrotavyasya* (6pos sing◦ ←pot◦ adj◦ *śrotavya* (to be heard) ←1◦√श्रु (to hear); *śrutasya* (6pos sing◦ ←ppp◦ adj◦ *śruta* (heard) ←1◦√श्रु (to hear); *ća* (1.1) (2.52)

(§3) ***yadā*** **(when);** ***te*** **(your);** ***mohakalilam*** **(**obj1◦ **the muddiness of the delusion);** ***buddhiḥ:*** **(**subj◦ **mind, thinking);** ***vyatitariṣyati*** **(it will cross over);** ***tadā*** **(then, at that time);** ***gantāsi*** **(you will attain);** ***nirvedam*** **(**obj2◦ **an indifference);** ***śrotavyasya*** **(what is to be heard);** ***śrutasya*** **(what is heard);** ***ća*** **(and)** (2.52)

(§4) yadā te buddhiḥ: vyatitariṣyati mohakalilam tadā gantāsi nirvedam śrutasya ća śrotavyasya

(§5) When your mind[224] will cross over the mire of the delusion,[225] at that time you will attain an

---

the fruit of, ...etc.

📖 विनिर्मुक्तः is not a gerund or a verb of present tense. It is a ppp◦ adj◦ → freed from.

[221] See the footnote in verse 2.15 हि ।

[222] Elsewhere◦ *tyaktvā* → they free themselves, who have abandoned, who have cast off ...etc.

📖 त्यक्त्वा is not a a present tense verb, or imperative or a ppp◦ adj◦ It is a past participle gerund → having renounced.

[223] Elsewhere◦ फलं त्यक्त्वा = कर्मफलं त्यक्त्वा → please see the footnote in verse 12.12 (in this volume) for the proper meaning of फलत्यागः ।

[224] Elsewhere◦ बुद्धिः → intelligence, intellect, ...etc.

indifference[226] (to) what is heard and what is to be heard.[227] (2.52)

2.53 श्रुतिविप्रतिपन्ना ते यदा स्थास्यति निश्चला ।
समाधावचला बुद्धिस्तदा योगमवाप्स्यसि ।।

śrutivipratipannā te yadā sthāsyati niśćalā,
samādhāvaćalā buddhistadā yogamavāpsyasi. (2.53)

(§1) श्रुतिविप्रतिपन्ना ते यदा स्थास्यति निश्चला । समाधावचला बुद्धिः तदा योगम् अवाप्स्यसि । *śrutivipratipannā te yadā sthāsyati niśćalā samādhau* (r◦ 5/5) *aćalā buddhiḥ:* (r◦ 18/1) *tadā yogam̧* (r◦ 8/16) *avāpsyasi*

(§2) *śrutivipratipannā* (f◦ 1nom◦ sing◦ ←tatpu◦ 📖*śruti-vipratipannā*, श्रुतिभिः विप्रतिपन्ना ←f◦ ***śruti*** m◦ ***śruta*** (heard) ←1◦√श्रु (to hear) + ppp◦ adj◦ *vipratipanna* (bewildered) ←4◦वि–प्रति√पद् (to go); *te* (2.34); *yadā* (2.52); *sthāsyati* (3rd-per◦ sing◦ fut2◦ लृट् भविष्य◦ parasmai◦ -v-i◦ ←1◦√स्था (to stay); 📖*niśćalā* (f◦ 1nom◦ sing◦ ←adj◦ *niśćala* (firm) ←1◦निर्√चल् (to move, walk); *samādhau* (2.44); 📖*aćalā* (f◦ 1nom◦ sing◦ ←adj◦ *aćala* (unwavering) 2.24); *buddhiḥ:* (2.39); *tadā* (1.2); ***yogam̧*** (2acc◦ sing◦ ←m◦ *yoga* 2.39); 📖*avāpsyasi* (2.33) (2.53)

(§3) ***śrutivipratipannā* (adj1◦-subj◦ distracted, perplexed, bewildered by whatever you have heard); *te* (adj2◦-sub◦ your); *yadā* (when); *sthāsyati* (will stay, it will stay); *niśćalā* (adj3◦-subj◦ unwavering; firm); *samādhau* (in concentration, in a focused state); *aćalā* (adj4◦-subj◦ tranquil; stable); *buddhiḥ:* (subj◦ mind); *tadā* (then, at that time); *yogam̧* (obj◦ yoga); *avāpsyasi* (you will attain)** (2.53)

(§4) yadā te buddhiḥ: śrutivipratipannā sthāsyati niśćalā aćalā samādhau tadā avāpsyasi yogam̧

(§5) When your mind, bewildered by whatever you have heard,[228] will stay[229] unwavering (and)

📖 Intelligence is बुद्धिचातुर्यम्, चातुर्यम्, विज्ञता, कुशलता, कौशल्यम्, वैचक्षण्यम्, विदग्धता, वैदग्ध्यम् ...etc.

[225] Elsewhere◦ *mohakalilam̧* → forest, mist, thicket, turbidity, faint, mire, pile, heap, ...etc.

[226] Elsewhere◦ *nirvedam̧* → you will become become indefferent, ...etc.

📖 निर्वेद is a m◦ noun (not an adj◦ or adv◦) → indifference, indifference in worldly objects, a feeling that gives rise to quietude = वैराग्यम् । Remember : inavae|dma` is an Accusative 2nd case object, not a Nominative 1st case subject.

[227] Elsewhere◦ श्रोतव्य → what is yet to be heard, whatever you are going to hear, ...etc.

[228] Elsewhere◦ श्रुतिविप्रतिपन्ना → disurbed by the flowery language of the Vedas, disregarding Vedic doctrine, perplexing things you may hear, ...etc.

[229] Elsewhere◦ *sthāsyati* → becomes, has become, it remains, stays, ...etc. (present tense)

📖 स्थास्यति is a लृट् future tense.

tranquil in concentration, then you will attain[230] yoga. (2.53)

Arjuna said (arjuna uvāća अर्जुन उवाच ।)

2.54 स्थितप्रज्ञस्य का भाषा समाधिस्थस्य केशव ।
स्थितधीः किं प्रभाषेत किमासीत व्रजेत किम् ।।

shtitaprajñasya kā bhāṣā samādhisthasya kes̒ava,
sthitadhīḥ: kiṁ prabhāṣeta kimāsīta vrajeta kiṃ. (2.54)

(§1) स्थितप्रज्ञस्य का भाषा समाधिस्थस्य केशव । स्थितधीः किम् प्रभाषेत किम् आसीत व्रजेत किम् । *arjunaḥ:* (r◦ 19/4) *uvāća. shtitaprajñasya kā bhāṣā samādhisthasya kes̒ava sthitadhīḥ:* (r◦ 22/1) *kiṃ* (r◦ 14/1) *prabhāṣeta kiṃ* (r◦ 8/17) *āsīta vrajeta kiṃ* (r◦ 14/2)

(§2) *arjunaḥ:* (1.28); *uvāća* (1.25). 📖*shtitaprajñasya* (m◦ 6pos◦ sing◦ ←bahuvrī◦ ***shtitaprajña***, स्थिता प्रज्ञा यस्य ←adj◦ *sthita* 1.14 + f◦ *prajñā* (thinking, mind) 2.11); *kā* (1.36); 📖*bhāṣā* (1nom◦ sing◦ ←f◦ *bhāṣā* (definition) ←1◦√भाष् (to speak); *samādhisthasya* (m◦ 6pos◦ sing◦ ←tatpu◦ adj◦ *samādhistha*, समाधौ स्थितः, bahuvrī◦ समाधौ स्थीयते यः (concentrated) ←f◦ *samādhi* 2.44 + adj◦ *sthita* 1.14 or *sthīyate* 3rd-per◦ sing◦ pres◦ वर्तमान्–लट् ātmane◦ ←1◦√स्था (to stay); *kes̒ava* (1.31); ***sthitadhīḥ:*** (m◦ 1nom◦ sing◦ ←bahuvrī◦ *sthitadhī*, स्थिता धीः यस्य ←adj◦ *sthita* (steady) 1.14 + f◦ *dhī* (thinking, mind) ←1◦√ध्यै (to meditate); *kiṃ* (1.1); *prabhāṣeta* (3rd-per◦ sing◦ potential◦ विधि◦ ātmane◦ ←1◦प्र√भाष् (to speak); *kiṃ* (1.1); ***āsīta*** (3rd-per◦ sing◦ potential◦ विधि◦ ātmane◦ ←2◦√आस् (to sit); *vrajeta* (3rd-per◦ sing◦ potential◦ विधि◦ ātmane◦ ←1◦√व्रज् (to go); *kiṃ* (1.1) (2.54)

(§3) *shtitaprajñasya* (of Shtitaprajña; of a person of sound thinking; of a stable minded person); *kā* (what, what is?); *bhāṣā* (subj1◦ the definition, meaning; description); *samādhisthasya* (of a person established in concentration); *kes̒ava* (O Kes̒ava! O S̒rī Kṛṣṇa!); *sthitadhīḥ:* (subj2◦ a person of sound mind); *kiṃ* (how?); *prabhāṣeta* (he may speak); *kiṃ* (how?); *āsīta* (he may sit); *vrajeta* (he may walk); *kiṃ* (how?) (2.54)

(§4) kes̒ava kā bhāṣā shtitaprajñasya kiṃ sthitadhīḥ: samādhisthasya kiṃ prabhāṣeta āsīta kiṃ vrajeta

(§5) O S̒rī Kṛṣṇa! what is the definition of *Shtitaprajña*? How a person of sound mind,[231] established in concentration, may speak?[232] How he may sit? How he may walk? (2.54)

---

[230] Elsewhere◦ *avāpsyasi* → you will have attained, you attain, you have attained, ...etc.

[231] Elsewhere◦ स्थितप्रज्ञः → man of steady wisdom, one whose consciousness is merged in transcendence, man of steadfast wisdom, man who has this firmly founded wisdom, deeply meditative man, ...etc.

[232] Elsewhere◦ प्रभाषेत → how does he talk, how does he speak, how does one, ...etc. (habitual present tense)

The Lord said - (śrībhagavānuvāća श्रीभगवानुवाच ।)

2.55 प्रजहाति यदा कामान्सर्वान्पार्थ मनोगतान् ।
आत्मन्येवात्मना तुष्टः स्थितप्रज्ञस्तदोच्यते ।।

prajahāti yadā kāmānsarvānpārtha manogatān,
ātmanyevātmanā tuṣṭaḥ: sthitaprajñastadoćyate. (2.55)

(§1) प्रजहाति यदा कामान् सर्वान् पार्थ मनोगतान् । आत्मनि एव आत्मना तुष्टः स्थितप्रज्ञः तदा उच्यते । *śrībhagavān* (r◦ 8/14) *uvāća. prajahāti yadā kāmān* (r◦ 13/20) *sarvān* (r◦ 13/13) *pārtha manogatān* (r◦ 23/1) *ātmani* (r◦ 4/4) *eva* (r◦ 1/2) *ātmanā tuṣṭaḥ:* (r◦ 22/7) *shtitaprajñaḥ:* (r◦ 18/1) *tadā* (r◦ 2/4) *ućyate*

(§2) *śrībhagavān* (2.2); *uvāća* (1.25). 📖*prajahāti* (3rd-per◦ sing◦ pres◦ वर्तमान्-लट् parasmai◦ ←3◦प्र√हा (to go) 2.50); *yadā* (2.52); ***kāmān*** (2acc◦ plu◦ ←m◦ *kāma* 1.22); *sarvān* (1.27); *pārtha* (1.25); 📖*manogatān* (m◦ 2acc◦ plu◦ ←tatpu◦ *manogata*, मनसि आगत (arose in mind) ←n◦ *manas* 1.30 + adj◦ *āgata* 4.10); ***ātmani*** (7loc◦ sing◦ ←m◦ *ātman* 2.41); *eva* (1.1); ***ātmanā*** (3inst◦ sing◦ ←m◦ *ātman* 2.41); *tuṣṭaḥ:* (m◦ 1nom◦ sing◦ ←ppp◦ adj◦ ***tuṣṭa*** (satisfied) ←4◦√तुष् (to be content); *shtitaprajñaḥ:* (1nom◦ sing◦ ←m◦ *shtitaprajña* 2.54); *tadā* (1.2); *ućyate* (2.25) (2.55)

(§3) ***prajahāti*** **(one renounces);** ***yadā*** **(when);** ***kāmān*** **(obj◦ the desires);** ***sarvān*** **(adj1◦-obj◦ all);** ***pārtha*** **(O Pārtha! O Arjuna!);** ***manogatān*** **(adj2◦-obj◦ arose in mind);** ***ātmani*** **(in self; in himself);** ***eva*** **(only);** ***ātmanā*** **(by self; by himself);** 📖***tuṣṭaḥ:*** **(adj◦-subj◦ satisfied, contented);** ***shtitaprajñaḥ:*** **(subj◦ shtitaprajña; a person of sound mind);** ***tadā*** **(then; at that time);** ***ućyate*** **(he is called; he is said to be)** (2.55)

(§4) pārtha yadā prajahāti sarvān kāmān manogatān tuṣṭaḥ: ātmani eva ātmanā tadā ućyate shtitaprajñaḥ:

(§5) O Arjuna! when one renounces all the desires arose in mind,[233] contented in himself by himself only, then he is called *'shtitaprajña.'* (2.55)

2.56 दुःखेष्वनुद्विग्नमनाः सुखेषु विगतस्पृहः ।

📖 प्रभाषेत is not a present tense. प्रभाषते is present tense. There is same problem with the other two potential verbs आसीत and व्रजेत in this verse.

[233] Elsewhere◦ *manogatān* → emerging in mind, originating in mind, desires of mind, desires of the mind, emerging from mind, ...etc.

📖 आगत is a ppp◦ → arose, emerged, come to, borne.

वीतरागभयक्रोधः स्थितधीर्मुनिरुच्यते ।।

duḥ:kheṣvanudvignamanāḥ: sukheṣu vigataspṛhaḥ:,

vītarāgabhayakrodhaḥ: sthitadhīrmunirućyate. (2.56)

(§1) दुःखेषु अनुद्विग्नमनाः सुखेषु विगतस्पृहः । वीतरागभयक्रोधः स्थितधीः मुनिः उच्यते । *duḥ:kheṣu* (r◦ 25/5, 4/6) *anudvignamanāḥ:* (r◦ 22/7) *sukheṣu* (r◦ 25/5) *vigataspṛhaḥ:* (r◦ 22/8) *vītarāgabhayakrodhaḥ:* (r◦ 22/7) *sthitadhīḥ:* (r◦ 16/7) *muniḥ:* (r◦ 16/1) *ućyate*

(§2) *duḥ:kheṣu* (7loc◦ plu◦ ←n◦ *duḥ:kha* 2.14); *anudvignamanāḥ:* (m◦ 1nom◦ sing◦ ←bahuvrī◦ *anudvigna-manaṣ*, नास्ति उद्विग्नं मनः यस्य (unagitated) ←ppp◦ adj◦ 📖*udvigna* ←m◦ 📖**udvega** (agitated) ←6◦उद्√विज् (to tremble) + n◦ *manaṣ* 1.30); *sukheṣu* (7loc◦ plu◦ ←n◦ *sukha* 1.32); ***vigataspṛhaḥ:*** (m◦ 1nom◦ sing◦ ←bahuvrī◦ *vigata-spṛha*, विगता स्पृहा यस्य ←adj◦ ***vigata*** (departed) ←1◦वि√गम् (to go) + f◦ 📖***spṛhā*** (want, desire) ←10◦√स्पृह् (to want); *vītarāgabhayakrodhaḥ:* (m◦ 1nom◦ sing◦ ←bahuvrī◦ ***vīta-rāga-bhaya-krodha***, वीताः रागः च भयः च क्रोधः च यस्य ←ppp◦ adj◦ 📖*vīta* (departed) ←1◦वि√इ (to enter, come, go) + m◦ 📖***rāga*** (attachment) ←4◦√रञ्ज् (to be colourful) + n◦ *bhaya* (fear) 2.35 + m◦ 📖***krodha*** (anger) ←4◦√क्रुध् (to angry); 📖*sthitadhīḥ:* (2.54); ***muniḥ:*** (1nom◦ sing◦ ←m◦ ***muni*** ←1◦√मन् (to think); *ućyate* (2.25) (2.56)

(§3) ***duḥ:kheṣu*** (in the miseries); ***anudvignamanāḥ:*** (adj1◦-subj◦ he whose mind is not agitated); ***sukheṣu*** (in pleasures); ***vigataspṛhaḥ:*** (adj2◦-subj◦ he whose desire has gone away); ***vītarāgabhayakrodhaḥ:*** (adj3◦-subj◦ he whose attachment, fear and anger are departed); ***sthitadhīḥ:*** (adj4◦-subj◦ person of sound mind); ***muniḥ:*** (subj◦ a Muni, an ascetic); ***ućyate*** (he is called) (2.56)

(§4) anudvignamanāḥ: duḥ:kheṣu sukheṣu vigataspṛhaḥ: vītarāgabhayakrodhaḥ: sthitadhīḥ: ućyate muniḥ:

(§5) He whose mind is not agitated in the miseries, he whose desire in pleasures has gone away (and) he whose attachment, fear and anger are departed, (that) person of sound mind[234] is called a

---

[234] Elsewhere◦ स्थितधीर्मुनिरुच्यते → is called a sage of steady mind, of steady wisdom, of setteld wisdom, that sage is said to be of ...etc.

📖 स्थितधीर्मुनिः is not a *sāmāsic* word. If it was tatpu◦ samās, the word would be स्थितधीमुनिः । But, स्थितधीर्मुनिः is just a *visarga-sandhiḥ:* between two nominative m◦ words *sthitadhīḥ:* and *muniḥ:* (स्थितधीः and मुनिः). Here, there is no possessive, genetive or accusative relationship between the words स्थितधीः and मुनिः । स्थितधीः is not an adjective of मुनिः । If at all, the word मुनिः is the adjective or a title of m◦ स्थितधीः । As अनुद्विग्नमनाः, विगतस्पृहः and वीतरागः are the other three adjectives of the स्थितधीः । **Such a three way qualified स्थितधीः is called a मुनिः** । Therefore, such a स्थितधिः is called a *muni* = मुनिः उच्यते । ईदृशः स्थितधीः मुनिः उच्यते ।

'Muni.' (2.56)

2.57 यः सर्वत्रानभिस्नेहस्तत्तत्प्राप्य शुभाशुभम् ।
नाभिनन्दति न द्वेष्टि तस्य प्रज्ञा प्रतिष्ठिता ।।

yaḥ: sarvatrānabhisnehastattatprāpya śubhāśubham,
nābhinandati na dveṣṭi tasya prajñā pratiṣṭhitā. (2.57)

(§1) यः सर्वत्र अनभिस्नेहः तत् तत् प्राप्य शुभाशुभम् । न अभिनन्दति न द्वेष्टि तस्य प्रज्ञा प्रतिष्ठिता । *yaḥ:* (r◦ 22/7) *sarvatra* (r◦ 1/1) *anabhisnehaḥ:* (r◦ 18/1) *tat* (r◦ 1/10) *tat* (r◦ 10/6) *prāpya śubhāśubham* (r◦ 14/2) *na* (r◦ 1/1) *abhinandati na dveṣṭi tasya prajñā pratiṣṭhitā*

(§2) *yaḥ:* (2.19); ***sarvatra*** (place or time indicating ind◦ (fully) ←pron◦ *sarva* 1.6); *anabhisnehaḥ:* (1nom◦ sing◦ ←bahuvrī◦ adj◦ *anabhisneha* (unattached) ←4◦अन्–अभि√**स्निह्** (to love); *tat* (2.7); *tat* (↑); ***prāpya*** (lyp◦ past-participle ind◦ ←10◦प्र√आप् (to attain, get); *śubhāśubham* (n◦ 2acc◦ sing◦ ←dvandva◦ शुभं वा अशुभं वा । शुभं च अशुभं च (good or bad) ←adj◦ ***śubha*** ←1◦√**शुभ्** (to look good) + n.tatpu◦ adj◦ ***aśubha*** ←1◦अ√शुभ् (to look good); *na* (1.30); *abhinandati* (3rd-per◦ sing◦ pres◦ वर्तमान्–लट् parasmai◦ ←1◦अभि√नन्द् (to rejoice); *na* (1.30); ***dveṣṭi*** (3rd-per◦ sing◦ pres◦ वर्तमान्–लट् parasmai◦ ←2◦√**द्विष्** (to loath); *tasya* (1.12); *prajñā* (2.11); ***pratiṣṭhitā*** (f◦ 1nom◦ sing◦ ←ppp◦ adj◦ ***pratiṣṭhita*** (steady) ←1◦प्रति√स्था (to stay) (2.57)

(§3) *yaḥ:* (subj1◦ he who); *sarvatra* (from all sides, in everything, in every way; totally); *anabhisnehaḥ:* (adj◦-subj1◦ he who is free from attachment); *tat tat* (that and that; whatever); *prāpya* (having obtained); *śubhāśubham* (obj◦ auspicious and-or inauspicious); *na* (neither); *abhinandati* (he rejoices); *na* (nor, not); *dveṣṭi* (he hates; he dislikes); *tasya* (his, of that person); *prajñā* (subj2◦ the intellect, buddhi, mind, the judgement); *pratiṣṭhitā* (adj◦-subj2◦ established; steadfast) (2.57)

(§4) yaḥ: *anabhisnehaḥ:* sarvatra prāpya tat tat śubhāśubham na abhinandati na dveṣṭi prajñā tasya pratiṣṭhitā

(§5) He who is free from attachment in every way[235] (and) having obtained whatever auspicious or inauspicious, neither he rejoices nor he hates (it), the mind of that person (is) steadfast (in *sama-buddhi-yoga*); (2.57)

Defination (भाषा) of a स्थितधिः is given in the earlier verse (2,55 स्थितप्रज्ञः) and in the next verse 2.57 प्रतिष्ठितप्रज्ञः). This verse (2.56) tells which स्थितधीः is called a मुनिः । It means a स्थितधीः or स्थितप्रज्ञः or प्रतिष्टितप्रज्ञः (like Arjuna) may not be a मुनिः, but a *muni* (like Vyāsa) is a स्थितधीः, स्थितप्रज्ञः as well as प्रतिष्ठितप्रज्ञः ।

[235] Elsewhere◦ *sarvatra* → anywhere, on any side, whatever, ...etc.

2.58 यदा संहरते चायं कूर्मोऽङ्गानीव सर्वशः ।
इन्द्रियाणीन्द्रियार्थेभ्यस्तस्य प्रज्ञा प्रतिष्ठिता ।।

yadā saṁharate ćāyaṁ kūrmo'ṅgānīva sarvaśaḥ:,
indriyāṇīndriyārthebhyastasya prajñā pratiṣṭhitā; (2.58)

(§1) यदा संहरते च अयम् कूर्मः अङ्गानि इव सर्वशः । इन्द्रियाणि इन्द्रियार्थेभ्यः तस्य प्रज्ञा प्रतिष्ठिता । *yadā saṁharate ća* (r◦ 1/1) *ayaṃ* (r◦ 14/1) *kūrmaḥ:* (r◦ 15/1) *aṅgāni* (r◦ 1/5) *iva sarvaśaḥ:* (r◦ 22/8) *indriyāṇi* (r◦ 24/7, 1/5) *indriyārthebhyaḥ:* (r◦ 18/1) *tasya prajñā pratiṣṭhitā*

(§2) *yadā* (2.52); *saṁharate* (3rd-per◦ sing◦ pres◦ वर्तमान्–लट् ātmane◦ ←1◦सम्√हृ (to take); *ća* (1.1); *ayaṃ* (2.19); *kūrmaḥ:* (1nom◦ sing◦ ←m◦ *kūrma* (turtle) ←1◦√कु (to make sound); *aṅgāni* (2acc◦ plu◦ ←n◦ ***aṅga*** ←1◦√अङ्ग् (to count); *iva* (1.30); *sarvaśaḥ:* (1.18); ***indriyāṇi*** (2acc◦ plu◦ ←n◦ *indriya* (organ, limb) 2.8); ***indriyārthebhyaḥ:*** (m◦ 5abl◦ plu◦ ←tatpu◦ ***indriyārtha***, इन्द्रियस्य इन्द्रियाणां वा अर्थः ←n◦ *indriya* 2.8 + m◦ *artha* 1.7); *tasya* (1.12); *prajñā* (2.11); *pratiṣṭhitā* (2.57) (2.58)

(§3) *yadā* (when); *saṁharate* (he withdraws); *ća* (and); *ayaṃ* (adj◦-subj1◦ this); *kūrmaḥ:* (subj1◦ the turtle, tortoise); *aṅgāni* (obj1◦ limbs); *iva* (as, like); *sarvaśaḥ:* (from all sides, altogether); *indriyāṇi* (obj2◦ the sense organs; the senses); *indriyārthebhyaḥ:* (from their sense objects); *tasya* (his, of that person); *prajñā* (subj2◦ mind, the judgement); *pratiṣṭhitā* (adj◦-subj2◦ established; steadfast)

(§4) ća yadā saṁharate sarvaśaḥ: indriyāṇi indriyārthebhyaḥ: iva ayaṃ kūrmaḥ: aṅgāni prajñā tasya pratiṣṭhitā

(§5) And, when he withdraws[236] altogether[237] the sense organs from their sense objects, as this tortoise (withdraws its) limbs, his mind (is) steadfast (*in buddhi-yoga*). (2.58)

2.59 विषया विनिवर्तन्ते निराहारस्य देहिनः ।
रसवर्जं रसोऽप्यस्य परं दृष्ट्वा निवर्तते ।।

viṣayā vinivartante nirāhārasya dehinaḥ:,
rasavarjaṁ raso'pyasya paraṁ dṛṣṭvā nivartate. (2.59)

---

[236] Elsewhere◦ *saṁharate* → is able to withdraw, he can withdraw ...etc.

संहरते is an *ātmanepadī* लट् present tense verb → he withdraws.

[237] Elsewhere◦ *sarvaśaḥ:* → all organs, all limbs ...etc.

सर्वशः is not adjective. It is not the adjective of n◦ अङ्गानि । *sarvaśaḥ:* is an adverb. It is qualifying the verb संहरते→ he withdraws limbs from all sides, altogether.

(§1) विषयाः विनिवर्तन्ते निराहारस्य देहिनः । रसवर्जम् रसः अपि अस्य परम् दृष्ट्वा निवर्तते । *viṣayāḥ:* (r◦ 20/17) *vinivartante nirāhārasya dehinaḥ:* (r◦ 22/8) *rasavarjam* (r◦ 14/1) *rasaḥ:* (r◦ 15/1) *api* (r◦ 4/1) *asya param* (r◦ 14/1) *dṛṣṭvā nivartate*

(§2) *viṣayāḥ:* (1nom◦ plu◦ ←m◦ *viṣaya* (sense object) 2.45); 📖*vinivartante* (3rd-per◦ plu◦ pres◦ वर्तमान्–लट् ātmane◦ ←1◦वि–नि√वृत् (to be); 📖*nirāhārasya* (6pos sing◦ ←tatpu◦ *nirāhāra* (abstinent) ←ind◦ *nir* 2.45 + m◦ ***āhāra*** ←1◦आ√हृ (to take); *dehinaḥ:* (2.13); *rasavarjam* (adv◦ रसः वर्जम्, रसः वर्जितः कृतः ←m◦ ***rasa*** (apetite) ←10◦√रस् (to taste) + m◦ *varja* ←2◦√वृज् (to shun); ***rasaḥ:*** (1nom◦ sing◦ ←m◦ *rasa* ↑); *api* (1.26); *asya* (2.17); *param* (2acc◦ sing◦ ←adj◦ ***para*** (Supreme) ←√पृ 2.12); *dṛṣṭvā* (1.2); 📖*nivartate* (3rd-per◦ sing◦ pres◦ वर्तमान्–लट् ātmane◦ ←1◦नि√वृत् (to be) 1.39) (2.59)

(§3) ***viṣayāḥ:*** (subj1◦ **the sense objects**); ***vinivartante*** **(they turn away);** ***nirāhārasya*** **(of the abstemious, abstinent, austere person);** ***dehinaḥ:*** **(of the embodied; of the person);** ***rasavarjam*** **(except the appetite; other than the thirst, craving, lust, passion, desire);** ***rasaḥ:*** (subj2◦ **the apetite);** ***api*** **(also);** ***asya*** **(his);** ***param*** (obj◦ **the Supreme);** ***dṛṣṭvā*** **(having seen, having realised);** ***nivartate*** **(it goes away)** (2.59)

(§4) viṣayāḥ: rasavarjam nirāhārasya dehinaḥ: vinivartante asya rasaḥ: api nivartate dṛṣṭvā param

(§5) The sense objects, except the appetite,[238] of the austere person[239] turn away. His apetite also goes away, having realized the Supreme. (2.59)

2.60 यततो ह्यपि कौन्तेय पुरुषस्य विपश्चितः । इन्द्रियाणि प्रमाथीनि हरन्ति प्रसभं मनः ।।

yatato hyapi kaunteya puruṣasya vipaśćitaḥ:,
indriyāṇi pramāthīni haranti prasabhaṁ manaḥ:; (2.60)

(§1) यततः अपि कौन्तेय पुरुषस्य विपश्चितः । इन्द्रियाणि प्रमाथीनि हरन्ति प्रसभम् मनः । *yatataḥ:* (r◦ 15/14) *hi* (r◦ 4/1) *api kaunteya puruṣasya vipaśćitaḥ:* (r◦ 22/8) *indriyāṇi* (r◦ 24/7) *pramāthīni haranti prasabham* (r◦ 14/1) *manaḥ:* (r◦ 22/8)

---

[238] Elsewhere◦ *rasavarjam* → giving up the taste, abstaining from the taste, ceasing engageent ...etc.

📖 रस = the sweetness, craving, lust, longing, thirst, apetite; वर्ज = except, other than. रसवर्ज is not a gerund or a verb. It is an adverb that qualifies the verb निवर्तते । रसवर्ज = other than the passion for it.

[239] Elsewhere◦ *nirāhārasya* → by negative restrictions, may be restricted from ...etc.

📖 निर्–आहार → noun◦ non-indulgence; the non-indulging person.

(§2) 📖*yatatah:* (m◦ 6pos◦ sing◦ ←śatṛ◦ adj◦ ***yatat*** ←1◦√यत् (to strive); *hi* (1.11); *api* (1.26); *kaunteya* (2.14); *puruṣasya* (6pos sing◦ ←m◦ *puruṣa* 2.15); *vipaścitaḥ:* (m◦ 6pos◦ sing◦ ←adj◦ *vipaścit* (2.42); ***indriyāṇi*** (1nom◦ plu◦ ←n◦ *indriya* 2.8); 📖*pramāthīni* (n◦ 1nom◦ plu◦ ←adj◦ ***pramāthin*** (stimulating) ←1◦प्र√मथ् (to churn); *haranti* (3rd-per◦ plu◦ pres◦ वर्तमान्-लट् parasmai◦ ←1◦√हृ (to take); 📖***prasabham*** (adv◦ ind◦ ←s.prādi bah◦ *prasabha* (forcibly) ←2◦प्र-सह√भा (to shine); *manaḥ:* (2acc◦ 1.30) (2.60)

(§3) ***yatataḥ:*** (of the striving person); ***hi*** (because); ***api*** (also, even); ***kaunteya*** (O Kaunteya! O Arjuna!); ***puruṣasya*** (of a man, of a person); ***vipaścitaḥ:*** (of wise); ***indriyāṇi*** (subj◦ the sense organs, the senses); ***pramāthīni*** (adj◦-subj◦ the arousing, stimulating, exciting); ***haranti*** (they overpower); ***prasabham*** (adv◦ forcibly; against the wishes); ***manaḥ:*** (obj◦ the mind) (2.60)

(§4) hi kaunteya pramāthīni indriyāṇi prasabham haranti manaḥ: api yatataḥ: vipaścitaḥ: puruṣasya

(§5) Because,[240] O Arjuna! the arousing[241] sense organs forcibly overpower the mind even of the striving wise person;[242] (2.60)

2.61 तानि सर्वाणि संयम्य युक्त आसीत मत्परः ।
वशे हि यस्येन्द्रियाणि तस्य प्रज्ञा प्रतिष्ठिता ।।

tāni sarvāṇi saṁyamya yukta āsīta matparaḥ:,
vaśe hi yasyendriyāṇi tasya prajñā pratiṣṭhitā. (2.61)

(§1) तानि सर्वाणि संयम्य युक्तः आसीत मत्परः । वशे हि यस्य इन्द्रियाणि तस्य प्रज्ञा प्रतिष्ठिता । ***tāni sarvāṇi*** (r◦ 24/7) ***saṁyamya yuktaḥ:*** (r◦ 19/1) ***āsīta matparaḥ:*** (r◦ 22/8) ***vaśe hi yasya*** (r◦ 2/1) ***indriyāṇi*** (r◦ 24/7) ***tasya prajñā pratiṣṭhitā***

(§2) ***tāni*** (n◦ 2acc◦ plu◦ ←pron◦ *tad* 1.2); *sarvāṇi* (2acc◦ 2.30); 📖*saṁyamya* (lyp◦ past-participle ind◦ ←1◦सम्√यम् (to restrain); 📖*yuktaḥ:* (2.39); *āsīta* (pot◦ 2.54); 📖*matparaḥ:* (m◦ 1nom◦ sing◦ ←bahuvrī◦ *mat-para,* मयि परायणः यः (devoted to me) ←pron◦ *mat* 1.9 + adj◦ *para* 2.3); *vaśe* (7loc◦ sing◦ ←m◦ or n◦ 📖*vaśa* ←2◦√वश् (to control); *hi* (1.11); *yasya* (m◦ or n◦ 6pos◦ sing◦ ←pron◦ *yad* 1.7); *indriyāṇi* (1nom◦ 2.60); *tasya* (1.12); *prajñā* (2.11); *pratiṣṭhitā* (2.57) (2.61)

(§3) ***tāni*** (adj1◦-obj◦ to them; to those arousing organs); ***sarvāṇi*** (adj2◦-obj◦ all); ***saṁyamya*** (having restrained); ***yuktaḥ:*** (subj1◦ the disciplined, the disciplined person, the ***yogī***); ***āsīta*** (should stay);

---

[240] See the footnote in verse 2.15

[241] Elsewhere◦ *indriyāṇi pramāthīni* → The senses are so strong, dangerous senses, ...etc.

[242] Elsewhere◦ *yatataḥ:* → striving for perfection, striving after perfection, of the one who strives, ...etc.

matparaḥ: (adj∘-subj1∘ he for whom I am the ultimate goal; he who is devoted to me); ***vaśe*** (in control); ***hi*** (because) ***yasya*** (he whose); ***indriyāṇi*** (subj2∘ sense organs, senses); ***tasya*** (his, of that person); ***prajñā*** (subj3∘ mind, the judgement); ***pratiṣṭhitā*** (adj∘-subj3∘ established; steadfast) (2.61)

(§4) saṁyamya sarvāṇi tāni yuktaḥ: āsīta matparaḥ: hi yasya indriyāṇi vaśe prajñā tasya pratiṣṭhitā

(§5) Having restrained all those arousing organs, the disciplined person should stay[243] devoted to Me. Because,[244] he whose sense organs (are) under control, his mind (is) steadfast (in *buddhi-yoga*). (2.61)

2.62 ध्यायतो विषयान्पुंसः सङ्गस्तेषूपजायते ।
सङ्गात्सञ्जायते कामः कामात्क्रोधोऽभिजायते ॥

dhyāyato viṣayānpuṁsaḥ: saṅgasteṣūpajāyate,
saṅgātsañjāyate kāmaḥ: kāmātkrodho'bhijāyate. (2.62)

(§1) ध्यायतः विषयान् पुंसः सङ्गः तेषु उपजायते । सङ्गात् सञ्जायते कामः कामात् क्रोधः अभिजायते । *dhyāyataḥ:* (r∘ 15/13) *viṣayān* (r∘ 13/13) *puṁsaḥ:* (r∘ 22/7) *saṅgaḥ:* (r∘ 18/1) *teṣu* (r∘ 25/5, 1/8) *upajāyate saṅgāt* (r∘ 10/7) *sañjāyate kāmaḥ:* (r∘ 22/1) *kāmāt* (r∘ 10/5) *krodhaḥ:* (r∘ 15/1) *abhijāyate*

(§2) *dhyāyataḥ:* (6pos sing∘ ←śatṛ∘ adj∘ ***dhyāyat*** ←1∘√ध्यै (to meditate); ***viṣayān*** (2acc∘ plu∘ ←m∘ *viṣaya* 2.45); 📖*puṁsaḥ:* (6pos sing∘ ←m∘ ***puṁs*** (person) ←1∘√पू (to cleanse); *saṅgaḥ:* (2.47); ***teṣu*** (m∘ 7loc∘ plu∘ ←pron∘ *tad* 1.2); 📖***upajāyate*** (3rd-per∘ sing∘ pres∘ वर्तमान्-लट् ātmane∘ ←4∘उप√जन् (to beget); *saṅgāt* (5abl∘ sing∘ ←m∘ *saṅga* 2.47); ***sañjāyate*** (3rd-per∘ sing∘ pres∘ वर्तमान्-लट् ātmane∘ ←4∘सम्√जन् (to beget); ***kāmaḥ:*** (1nom∘ sing∘ ←m∘ *kāma* 1.22); *kāmāt* (5abl∘ sing∘ ←m∘ *kāma* 1.22); ***krodhaḥ:*** (1nom∘ sing∘ ←m∘ *krodha* 2.56); ***abhijāyate*** (3rd-per∘ sing∘ pres∘ वर्तमान्-लट् ātmane∘ ←4∘अभि√जन् (to beget) (2.62)

(§3) ***dhyāyataḥ:*** (adj∘ while contemplating; while thinking of); ***viṣayān*** (obj∘ the sense objects); ***puṁsaḥ:*** (of a person); ***saṅgaḥ:*** (subj1∘ the attachment); ***teṣu*** (in those, in those sense objects); ***upajāyate*** (originates, develpos); ***saṅgāt*** (from the attachment); ***sañjāyate*** (arises, takes birth); ***kāmaḥ:*** (subj2∘ desire); ***kāmāt*** (from desire); ***krodhaḥ:*** (subj3∘ anger); ***abhijāyate*** (grows) (2.62)

(§4) dhyāyataḥ: viṣayān saṅgaḥ: puṁsaḥ: teṣu upajāyate saṅgāt sañjāyate kāmaḥ: kāmāt abhijāyate krodhaḥ:

---

[243] Elsewhere∘ *āsīta* → sits.

📖 आसीत is not a present tense. It is potential mood.

[244] See the footnote in verse 2.15

(§5) While thinking of[245] the sense objects, the attachment of a person[246] in those sense objects develpos; from the attachment arises desire; from desire grows anger; (2.62)

2.63 क्रोधाद्भवति सम्मोहः सम्मोहात्स्मृतिविभ्रमः ।
स्मृतिभ्रंशाद्बुद्धिनाशो बुद्धिनाशात्प्रणश्यति ॥

krodhādbhavati sammohaḥ: sammohātsmṛtivibhramaḥ:,
smṛtibhraṁśādbuddhināśo buddhināśātpraṇaśyati. (2.63)

(§1) क्रोधात् भवति सम्मोहः सम्मोहात् स्मृतिविभ्रमः । स्मृतिभ्रंशात् बुद्धिनाशः बुद्धिनाशात् प्रणश्यति । *krodhāt* (r◦ 9/8) *bhavati sammohaḥ:* (r◦ 22/7) *sammohāt* (r◦ 10/7) *smṛtivibhramaḥ:* (r◦ 22/8) *smṛtibhraṁśāt* (r◦ 9/7) *buddhināśaḥ:* (r◦ 15/7) *buddhināśāt* (r◦ 10/6) *praṇaśyati*

(§2) *krodhāt* (5abl◦ sing◦ ←m◦ *krodha* 2.56); *bhavati* (1.44); 🕮*sammohaḥ:* (1nom◦ sing◦ ←m◦ ***sammoha*** (delusion) ←4◦सम्√मुह् (to be deluded); *sammohāt* (5abl◦ sing◦ ←m◦ *sammoha* ↑); *smṛtivibhramaḥ:* (m◦ 1nom◦ sing◦ ←tatpu◦ *smṛti-vibhrama*, स्मृतेः विभ्रमः ←f◦ ***smṛti*** (thinking) ←1◦√स्मृ (to remember) + m◦ 🕮*vibhrama* (confusion) ←1◦वि√भ्रम् (to be deluded); *smṛtibhraṁśāt* (m◦ 5abl◦ sing◦ ←tatpu◦ *smṛti-bhraṁśa*, स्मृतेः भ्रंशः ←f◦ *smṛti* ↑ + m◦ *bhraṁśa* (confusion) ←4◦√भ्रंश् (to fall) or 1◦√भ्रंस् (to fall); *buddhināśaḥ:* (m◦ 1nom◦ sing◦ ←tatpu◦ ***buddhi-nāśa***, बुद्धेः नाशः ←f◦ *buddhi* 1.23 + m◦ *nāśa* 2.40); *buddhināśāt* (5abl◦ sing◦ ←m◦ *buddhināśa* ↑); ***praṇaśyati*** (3rd-per◦ sing◦ pres◦ वर्तमान्-लट् parasmai◦ ←4◦प्र√नश् (to ruin) प्रादि-समासः 1.40) (2.63)

(§3) ***krodhāt*** (from anger); ***bhavati*** (becomes, arises); ***sammohaḥ:*** (subj1◦ delusion); ***sammohāt*** (from delusion); ***smṛtivibhramaḥ:*** (subj2◦ the confusion of the mind); ***smṛtibhraṁśāt*** (from confusion of mind); ***buddhināśaḥ:*** (subj3◦ the loss of judgement, righteous thinking, discrimination, preception, comprehension, understanding); ***buddhināśāt*** (from the loss of comprehension); ***praṇaśyati*** (one gets destroyed totally) (2.63)

---

[245] Elsewhere◦ *dhyāyataḥ:* → a person who dwells, when a man dwells, by musing, when a man thinks, ...etc.
🕮 ध्यायत् is not a verb. It is not in Instrumental or Nominative case. It is a gerund. It is an adjective. It is in the Possessive 6th case because it qualifies the noun पुंसः which is in the Possessive case.

[246] Elsewhere◦ *puṁsaḥ: saṅgaḥ: (teṣu) upajāyate* → a person develops attachment, man develops attachment, man conceiveth an attachment ...etc.
🕮 In पुंसः सङ्गः ... तेषु उपजायते, 'the man' (पुंसः) is not the subject or doer of verb उपजायते । Also, attachment (सङ्गः) Nominative case is not the object in the Accusative 2nd case. सङ्गः is the subject, that is performing the verb उपजायते । Ttherfore, it is in the Nominative 1st case. पुंसः has only an external (Ginitive 6th case) relationship with सङ्गः in this clause.

(§4) krodhāt bhavati sammohaḥ: sammohāt smṛtivibhramaḥ: smṛtibhraṁśāt buddhināśaḥ: buddhināśāt praṇaśyati

(§5) From anger arises delusion, from delusion the confusion of the mind,[247] from confusion of mind the loss of righteous thinking, (and) from the loss of righteous thinking one gets destroyed totally. (2.63)

2.64 रागद्वेषवियुक्तैस्तु विषयानिन्द्रियैश्चरन् । आत्मवश्यैर्विधेयात्मा प्रसादमधिगच्छति ।।

rāgadveṣaviyuktaistu viṣayānindriyaiśćaran,
ātmavaśyairvidheyātmā prasādamadhigaććhati. (2.64)

(§1) रागद्वेषवियुक्तैः तु विषयान् इन्द्रियैः चरन् । आत्मवश्यैः विधेयात्मा प्रसादम् अधिगच्छति । *rāgadveṣaviyuktaiḥ:* (r◦ 18/1) *tu viṣayān* (r◦ 8/13) *indriyaiḥ:* (r◦ 17/1) *ćaran* (r◦ 23/1) *ātmavaśyaiḥ:* (r◦ 16/11) *vidheyātmā prasādam* (r◦ 8/16) *adhigaććhati*

(§2) *rāgadveṣaviyuktaiḥ:* (3inst◦ plu◦ ←tatpu◦ *rāga-dveṣa-viyukta,* रागेण च द्वेषेण च वियुक्तः ←m◦ *rāga* 2.56 + m◦ **dveṣa** (loath) ←2◦√द्विष् (to loath) 2.57 + adj◦ 📖**viyukta** (freed) ←4◦वि√युज् (to unite); *tu* (1.2); *viṣayān* (2.62); **indriyaiḥ:** (3rd-per◦ plu◦ ←n◦ *indriya* 2.8); 📖*ćaran* (1nom◦ sing◦ ←śatṛ◦ adj◦ **ćarat** ←1◦√चर् (to move); 📖*ātmavaśyaiḥ:* (m◦ 3inst◦ plu◦ ←adj◦ *ātma-vaśya,* आत्मनः वशः ←m◦ *ātman* 2.41 + m◦ *vaśa* 2.61); 📖*vidheyātmā* (m◦ 1nom◦ sing◦ ←bahuvrī◦ *vidheyātman,* विधेयः आत्मा यस्य ←adj◦ *vidheya* ←3◦वि√धा (to put) + m◦ *ātman* 2.41); 📖*prasādam* (2acc◦ sing◦ ←m◦ **prasāda** (tranquility) ←1◦प्र√सद् (to sit); 📖**adhigaććhati** (3rd-per◦ sing◦ pres◦ वर्तमान्-लट् parasmai◦ ←1◦अधि√गम् (to go) (2.64)

(§3) *rāgadveṣaviyuktaiḥ:* (adj1◦-inst◦ with ... freed from attachment and repugnance); *tu* (even); *viṣayān* (obj1◦ the objects of the senses); *indriyaiḥ:* (inst◦ with the sense organs); *ćaran* (adj◦-subj◦ while experiencing, performing functions) *ātmavaśyaiḥ:* (adj2◦-inst◦ with ... brought under control); *vidheyātmā* (subj◦ the self restrained person); *prasādam* (obj2◦ peace, tranquility); *adhigaććhati* (he attains) (2.64)

(§4) vidheyātmā tu ćaran viṣayān indriyaiḥ: rāgadveṣaviyuktaiḥ: ātmavaśyaiḥ: adhigaććhati prasādam

---

[247] Elsewhere◦ *smṛtivibhramaḥ:* → loss of memory, failure of memory, impairs memory, ...etc.

📖 verb 1◦√भ्रम् is to wander; वि√भ्रम् is to be deluded, confused; विभ्रमः is delusion, confusion, misapprehension, error, mistake, a misunderstanding, straying, deviation, wandering away ... स्मृतिविभ्रमः → delusion of mind.

(§5) The self restrained person, even while experiencing the objects of the senses,[248] with the sense organs freed from attachment and repugnance[249] (as well as) brought under control, attains tranquility. (2.64)

2.65 प्रसादे सर्वदुःखानां हानिरस्योपजायते ।
प्रसन्नचेतसो ह्याशु बुद्धिः पर्यवतिष्ठते ।।

prasāde sarvaduḥ:khānām hānirasyopajāyate,
prasannaćetaso hyāśu buddhiḥ: paryavatiṣṭhate. (2.65)

(§1) प्रसादे सर्वदुःखानाम् हानिः अस्य उपजायते । प्रसन्नचेतसः हि आशु बुद्धिः पर्यवतिष्ठते । *prasāde sarvaduḥ:khānām* (r◦ 14/1) *hāniḥ:* (r◦ 16/1) *asya* (r◦ 2/2) *upajāyate prasannaćetasaḥ:* (r◦ 15/14) *hi* (r◦ 4/2) *āśu buddhiḥ:* (r◦ 22/3) *paryavatiṣṭhate*

(§2) *prasāde* (7loc◦ sing◦ ←m◦ *prasāda* 2.64); *sarva* (1.6); *duḥ:khānām* (6pos plu◦ ←n◦ *duḥ:kha* 2.14); 📖*hāniḥ:* (1nom◦ sing◦ ←f◦ *hāni* (destruction) ←3◦√हा (to go)); *asya* (2.17); *upajāyate* (2.62); *prasannaćetasaḥ:* (6pos sing◦ ←bahuvrī◦ *prasanna-ćetaṣ*, पसन्नं चेतः यस्य ←adj◦ 📖***prasanna*** (at peace) ←प्र√सद् (to sit) + n◦ *ćetaṣ* (mind) 1.38); *hi* (1.11); 📖*āśu* (adv◦ (quickly) ←9◦√अश् (to eat); *buddhiḥ:* (2.39); 📖*paryavatiṣṭhate* (3rd-per◦ sing◦ pres◦ वर्तमान्–लट् ātmane◦ ←1◦परि–अव√स्था (to stay) (2.65)

(§3) ***prasāde*** (in tranquility, in peace); ***sarva-duḥ:khānām*** (of all miseries, woes, griefs); ***hāniḥ:*** (subj◦ non-existence; loss; destruction); ***asya*** (of his); ***upajāyate*** (it occurs); ***prasannaćetasaḥ:*** (of him whose mind is tranquil; of him whose heart is at peace); ***hi*** (because) ***āśu*** (rapidly, soon); ***buddhiḥ:*** (subj◦ the mind, thinking); ***paryavatiṣṭhate*** (it becomes stable, stabilizes) (2.65)

(§4) prasāde upajāyate hāniḥ: sarva-duḥ:khānām asya hi buddhiḥ: prasannaćetasaḥ: paryavatiṣṭhate

(§5) In tranquility occurs destruction of all his woes. Because,[250] the thinking of him, whose mind

---

[248] Elsewhere◦ विषयान् चरन् → moving among sense sense objects, moves about amidst sense-objects, approaches objects, even as he engages, ...etc.

[249] Elsewhere◦ *rāgadveṣaviyuktaiḥ:* → by one who has become free from ..., the self controlled person without attachment and aversion, a person free from attachment and aversion, self-controlled, one who has eliminated, one who is free, a self-disciplined man with his, ...etc.

📖 रागद्वेषवियुक्तैः (Instrumental 3rd case, plural) is an adjective of इन्द्रियैः (Instrumental 3rd case, plural); it can not qualify विधेयात्मा (nominative, singular). Same is also true for आत्मवश्यैः in this *śloka.* Please note the inst◦, adj1◦-inst◦ and adj2◦-inst◦ remarks. (रागद्वेषवियुक्तैः आत्मवश्यैः इन्द्रियैः विषयान् चरन् विधेयात्मा प्रसादम् अधिगच्छति ।)

[250] See the footnote in verse 2,15

is tranquil, becomes stable[251] rapidly. (2.65)

2.66 नास्ति बुद्धिरयुक्तस्य न चायुक्तस्य भावना ।
न चाभावयतः शान्तिरशान्तस्य कुतः सुखम् ।।

nāsti buddhirayuktasya na ćāyuktasya bhāvanā,
na ćābhāvayataḥ: śāntiraśāntasya kutaḥ: sukham. (2.66)

(§1) नास्ति बुद्धिः अयुक्तस्य न च अयुक्तस्य भावना । न च अभावयतः शान्तिः अशान्तस्य कुतः सुखम् । *na* (r∘ 1/1) *asti buddhiḥ:* (r∘ 16/1) *ayuktasya na ća* (r∘ 1/1) *ayuktasya bhāvanā na ća* (r∘ 1/1) *abhāvayataḥ:* (r∘ 22/5) *śāntiḥ:* (r∘ 16/1) *aśāntasya kutaḥ:* (r∘ 22/7) *sukham* (r∘ 14/2)

(§2) *na* (1.30); *asti* (2.40); *buddhiḥ:* (2.39); 📖***ayuktasya*** (6pos sing∘ ←adj∘ n.tatpu∘ ***ayukta*** (not-disciplined) ←4∘अ√युज् (to unite), see युक्तः 2.39); *na* (1.30); *ća* (1.1); *ayuktasya* (↑); *bhāvanā* (1nom∘ sing∘ ←f∘ 📖*bhāvanā* (faith, feeling) ←1∘√भू (to be, become); *na* (1.30); *ća* (1.1); 📖*abhāvayataḥ:* (m∘ 6pos∘ sing∘ n.tatpu∘ ←śatṛ∘ adj∘ ***abhāvayat*** (faithless) ←1∘√भू (to be, become); 📖***śāntiḥ:*** (1nom∘ sing∘ ←f∘ ***śānti*** (peace) ←4∘√शम् (to be calm); 📖*aśāntasya* (m∘ 6pos∘ sing∘ ←ppp∘ adj∘ n.tatpu∘ *aśānta* (disturbed) ←4अ√शम् (to be calm); *kutaḥ:* (2.2); ***sukham*** (1nom∘ sing∘ ←n∘ *sukha* (happiness) 1.32) (2.66)

(§3) ***na*** **(no);** ***asti*** **(there is);** ***buddhiḥ:*** **(subj1∘ rational thinking, intuitive discrimination, soundness of mind, thoughtfullness);** ***ayuktasya*** **(of, for a person who is not equipped with discipline);** ***na*** **(there is no);** ***ća*** **(and);** ***ayuktasya*** **(↑);** ***bhāvanā*** **(subj∘ preception, imagination, thought, contemplation, feeling, faith);** ***na*** **(there is no);** ***ća*** **(and);** ***abhāvayataḥ:*** **(of, for one who is not keeping faith, for a faithless person);** ***śāntiḥ:*** **(subj2∘ peace);** ***aśāntasya*** **(of the unpeaceful person);** ***kutaḥ:*** **(subj∘3 from where? whence?);** ***sukham*** **(obj∘ the happiness)** (2.66)

(§4) asti na buddhiḥ: ayuktasya ća ayuktasya na bhāvanā ća abhāvayataḥ: na śāntiḥ: kutaḥ: sukham aśāntasya?

(§5) There is no rational thinking[252] for a person who is not equipped with discipline,[253] and for

---

[251] Elsewhere∘ *paryavatiṣṭhate* → is established, is set, is anchored, ...etc.

📖 तिष्ठते is a present tense, it is not a perfect tense or a ppp∘ → it becomes steady, it stadies, it stands steady, it establishes, it anchors, it settles down, it sets ...etc.

[252] Elsewhere∘ अयुक्तस्य → of the uncontrolled person, for the unsteady man, for the uncontrolled, to the unsteady, ...etc.

[253] Elsewhere∘ नास्ति बुद्धिः → there is no knowledge, there is no intellect, ...etc.

a person who is not disciplined there is no faith,[254] and for a faithless person[255] there is no peace. Whence (is) the happiness for the unpeaceful person? (2.66)

2.67 इन्द्रियाणां हि चरतां यन्मनोऽनुविधीयते ।
तदस्य हरति प्रज्ञां वायुर्नावमिवाम्भसि ।।

indriyāṇām hi ćaratām yanmano'nuvidhīyate,
tadasya harati prajñām vāyurnāvamivāmbhasi. (2.67)

(§1) इन्द्रियाणाम् हि चरताम् यत् मन: अनुविधीयते । तत् अस्य हरति प्रज्ञाम् वायु: नावम् इव अम्भसि । *indriyāṇām* (r० 24/6, 14/1) *hi ćaratām* (r० 14/1) *yat* (r० 12/2) *manaḥ:* (r० 15/1) *anuvidhīyate taṭ* (r० 8/2) *asya harati prajñām* (r० 14/1) *vāyuḥ:* (r० 16/8) *nāvam* (r० 8/18) *iva* (r० 1/1) *ambhasi*

(§2) *indriyāṇām* (2.8); *hi* (1.11); 🕮*ćaratām* (m० 6pos० plu० ←śatṛ० adj० *ćaraṭ* 2.64); **yaṭ** (n० 1nom० sing० ←pron० *yat* 1.45); *manaḥ:* (1nom० 1.30); 🕮*anuvidhīyate* (3rd-per० sing० pres० वर्तमान्-लट् ātmane० ←3०अनु-वि√धा (to put) 2.44); *tat* (1.10); *asya* (2.17); **harati** (3rd-per० sing० pres० वर्तमान्-लट् parasmai० ←1√ह (to take) 2.60); 🕮*prajñām* (2acc० sing० ←f० *prajñā* 2.11); 🕮**vāyuḥ:** (1nom० sing० ←m० **vāyu** (wind) ←2√वा (to move); 🕮*nāvam* (2acc० sing० ←f० *nau* (boat) ←6०√नुद् (to push); *iva* (1.30); 🕮*ambhasi* (7loc० sing० ←n० **ambhas** (water) ←1०√अम्भ् (to make sound) (2.67)

(§3) *indriyāṇām* (of the sense organs); *hi* (because) *ćaratām* (of the wandering; of the enjoying); *yaṭ* (adj०-subj1० that which); *manaḥ:* (subj1० the mind); *anuvidhīyate* (follows, becomes a slave); *taṭ* (adj०-subj० that, that mind); *asya* (his); *harati* (it carries away, it drives astray); *prajñām* (obj1० the judgement, discrimination, wisdom); *vāyuḥ:* (subj2० the wind); *nāvam* (obj2० a boat); *iva* (as); *ambhasi* (on the water) (2.67)

(§4) hi yaṭ manaḥ: anuvidhīyate ćaratām indriyāṇām taṭ harati asya prajñām iva vāyuḥ: nāvam ambhasi

(§5) Because,[256] that mind which becomes a slave of the wandering sense organs,[257] that mind

---

[254] Elsewhere० न भावना → nor is there meditation, nor is there any meditation, there is no meditation, nor there is meditation in him, no focus, ...etc.

[255] Elsewhere० अभावयत: → for the unmeditative person, of the unmeditative, ...etc.

[256] See the footnote in verse 2.15

[257] Elsewhere० *indriyāṇām ćaratām* → the roaming senses on which the mind focuses, by the wandering senses,...etc.

drives astray his wisdom, as the wind (drives astray) a boat on the water. (2.67)

2.68 तस्माद्यस्य महाबाहो निगृहीतानि सर्वशः ।
इन्द्रियाणीन्द्रियार्थेभ्यस्तस्य प्रज्ञा प्रतिष्ठिता ।।

tasmādyasya mahābāho nigṛhītāni sarvaśaḥ:,
indriyāṇīndriyārthebhyastasya prajñā pratiṣṭhitā. (2.68)

(§1) तस्मात् यस्य महाबाहो निगृहीतानि सर्वशः । इन्द्रियाणि इन्द्रियार्थेभ्यः तस्य प्रज्ञा प्रतिष्ठिता । *tasmāt* (r◦ 9/9) *yasya mahābāho nigṛhītāni sarvaśaḥ:* (r◦ 22/8) *indriyāṇi* (r◦ 24/7, 1/5) *indriyārthebhyaḥ:* (r◦ 18/1) *tasya prajñā pratiṣṭhitā*

(§2) *tasmāt* (1.37); *yasya* (2.61); *mahābāho* (2.26); 📖*nigṛhītāni* (n◦ 1nom◦ plu◦ ←ppp◦ adj◦ *nigṛhīta* (controlled) ←9◦नि√ग्रह् (to take); *sarvaśaḥ:* (1.18); *indriyāṇi* (2.60); *indriyārthebhyaḥ:* (2.58); *tasya* (1.12); *prajñā* (2.51); *pratiṣṭhitā* (2.57) (2.68)

(§3) *tasmāt* (therefore) *yasya* (whose); *mahābāho* (O Mahabāhu! O Arjuna!); *nigṛhītāni* (adj◦-subj1◦ restrained); *sarvaśaḥ:* (adv◦ from all sides); *indriyāṇi* (subj1◦ the sense organs); *indriyārthebhyaḥ:* (from the objects of the senses); *tasya* (his, of that person); *prajñā* (subj2◦ the discrimination, the judgement); *pratiṣṭhitā* (adj◦-subj2◦ established; steadfast) (2.68)

(§4) tasmāt mahābāho yasya indriyāṇi nigṛhītāni indriyārthebhyaḥ: sarvaśaḥ: tasya prajñā pratiṣṭhitā

(§5) Therefore,[258] O Arjuna! whose sense organs (are) restrained from the objects of the senses from all sides, his mind (is) steadfast (in *buddhi-yoga*). (2.68)

2.69 या निशा सर्वभूतानां तस्यां जागर्ति संयमी ।
यस्यां जाग्रति भूतानि सा निशा पश्यतो मुनेः ।।

yā niśā sarvabhūtānāṁ tasyāṁ jāgarti saṁyamī,
yasyāṁ jāgrati bhūtāni sā niśā paśyato muneḥ:. (2.69)

(§1) या निशा सर्वभूतानाम् तस्याम् जागर्ति संयमी । यस्याम् जाग्रति भूतानि सा निशा पश्यतः मुनेः । *yā niśā sarvabhūtānām* (r◦ 14/1) *tasyām* (r◦ 14/1) *jāgarti saṁyamī yasyām* (r◦ 14/1) *jāgrati bhūtāni sā niśā*

📖 इन्द्रियाणाम् and चरताम् are in the Possessive 6th case, not in Nominative 1st, Accusative 2nd case, or Instrumental (3d) case.

[258] See the footnote in verse 2.15

paśyataḥ: (r◦ 15/9) *mune* (r◦ 22/8)

(§2) ***yā*** (f◦ 1nom◦ sing◦ ←pron◦ *yad* 1.7); ***niśā*** (1nom◦ sing◦ ←f◦ *niśā* (obscurity) ←1◦√निश् (to be obscure, to concentrate); *sarva* (1.6); ***bhūtānām*** (6pos plu◦ ←n◦ *bhūta* 2.28); *tasyām* (f◦ 7loc◦ sing◦ ←pron◦ *tad* 1.2); *jāgarti* (3rd-per◦ sing◦ pres◦ वर्तमान्-लट् parasmai◦ ←2◦√जागृ (to stay awakw); *saṁyamī* (m◦ 1nom◦ sing◦ ←m◦ *saṁyamin* ←1◦सम्√यम् (to restrain); *yasyām* (f◦ 7loc◦ sing◦ ←pron◦ *yad* 1.7); *jāgrati* (3rd-per◦ plu◦ pres◦ वर्तमान्-लट् parasmai◦ -vi◦ ←2◦√जागृ (to stay awake); *bhūtāni* (2.28); ***sā*** (f◦ sing◦ ←pron◦ *tad* 1.2); *niśā* (↑); *paśyataḥ:* (m◦ 6pos◦ sing◦ ←śatṛ◦ adj◦ ***paśyat*** ←1◦√दृश् (to see); *muneḥ:* (6pos sing◦ ←m◦ *muni* 2.56) (2.69)

(§3) ***yā*** **(adj◦-subj1◦ that which);** ***niśā*** **(subj1◦ the darkness, obscurity);** ***sarva-bhūtānām*** **(of, for all beings);** ***tasyām*** **(in that);** ***jāgarti*** **(he stays sentient, awake, watchful, aware);** ***saṁyamī*** **(subj2◦ the disciplined person);** ***yasyām*** **(in which, about which);** ***jāgrati*** **(they stay awake, they are vigilant);** ***bhūtāni*** **(subj3◦ the beings);** ***sā*** **(adj◦-subj4◦ that);** ***niśā*** **(subj4◦ the night, darkness, obscurity);** ***paśyataḥ: muneḥ:*** **(for the quietly for fsdiscerning seer)** (2.69)

(§4) yā niśā sarva-bhūtānām tasyām saṁyamī jāgarti yasyām bhūtāni jāgrati sā niśā paśyataḥ: muneḥ:

(§5) That which (is) obscurity for all beings, in that the disciplined person stays sentient; about which the beings are vigilant,[259] that (is) the obscurity for the quietly discerning seer. (2.69)

2.70 आपूर्यमाणमचलप्रतिष्ठं समुद्रमापः प्रविशन्ति यद्वत् ।
तद्वत्कामा यं प्रविशन्ति सर्वे स शान्तिमाप्नोति न कामकामी ।।

āpūryamāṇamacalapratiṣṭhaṁ samudramāpaḥ: praviśanti yadvat,
tadvatkāmā yaṁ praviśanti sarve sa śāntimāpnoti na kāmakāmi. (2.70)

(§1) आपूर्यमाणम् अचलप्रतिष्ठम् समुद्रमापः प्रविशन्ति यद्वत् । यद्वत् कामाः यम् प्रविशन्ति सर्वे सः शान्तिम् आप्नोति न कामकामी । *āpūryamāṇam* (r◦ 8/16, 24/3) *acalapratiṣtham* (r◦ 14/1) *samudram* (r◦ 8/17) *āpaḥ:* (r◦ 22/3) *praviśanti yadvat* (r◦ 1/10) *tadvat* (r◦ 10/5) *kāmāḥ:* (r◦ 20/14) *yam* (r◦ 14/1) *praviśanti sarve saḥ:* (r◦ 21/2) *śāntim* (r◦ 8/17) *āpnoti na kāmakāmī*

(§2) *āpūryamāṇam* (m◦ 2acc◦ sing◦ ←śānac◦ adj◦ *āpūryamāṇa* (becoming full) ←3◦आ√पॄ (to fill); *acalapratiṣtham* (m◦ 2acc◦ sing◦ ←bahuvrī◦ adj◦ *acala-pratiṣtha,* अचला प्रतिष्ठा यस्य (standing still) ←adj◦ *acala* 2.24 + f◦ ***pratiṣtā*** ←ppp◦ adj◦ *pratiṣtha* ←1◦प्रति√स्था (to stay); ***samudram*** (2acc◦ sing◦ ←m◦ *samudra*

---

[259] For a clear understanding of the difference between जागर्ति and जाग्रति, see the 'A Critical Dictionary of the Gītā,' by the same author.

(ocean) ←7◦सम्√उन्द् to make wet); *āpaḥ:* (1nom◦ 2.23); ***praviśanti*** (3rd-per◦ plu◦ pres◦ वर्तमान्-लट् parasmai◦ ←6◦प्र√विश् (to enter); *yadvat* (time indicating ind◦ (as) ←pron◦ *yad* 1.7 + suffix *vat* 2.29); *tadvat* (time indicating ind◦ (so) ←pron◦ *tad* 1.2); *kāmāḥ:* (1nom◦ plu◦ ←m◦ *kāma* 1.22); *yam* (2.15); *praviśanti* (↑); *sarve* (1.6); *saḥ:* (1.13); ***śāntim*** (2acc◦ sing◦ ←f◦ *śānti* 2.66); 🕮***āpnoti*** (3rd-per◦ sing◦ pres◦ वर्तमान्-लट् parasmai◦ ←5◦√आप् (to attain, get); *na* (1.30); 🕮*kāmakāmī* (m◦ 1nom◦ sing◦ ←bahuvrī◦ *kāma-kāmin*, कामानां कामी । कामनानां कामी । ←m◦ *kāma* 1.22 + adj◦ *kāmin* ←1◦√कम् (to desire) (2.70)

(§3) *āpūrya-māṇam* (adj1◦-obj1◦ the one that is filling completely, that is becoming full); *aćalapratiṣṭham* (adj2◦-obj1◦ the one that is ever unmoving and standing still); *samudram* (obj1◦ to the ocean); *āpaḥ:* (subj1◦ the waters); *praviśanti* (they enter, they flow into); *yadvat* (as); *tadvat* (in that manner); *kāmāḥ:* (subj2◦ the desires); *yam* (obj2◦ whom); *praviśanti* (they encounter); *sarve* (adj◦-subj2◦ all); *saḥ:* (subj3◦ he); *śāntim* (obj3◦ peace); *āpnoti* (he attains); *na* (not); *kāmakāmī* (subj4◦ the yearner of the passions; desirer of desires) (2.70)

(§4) yadvat āpaḥ: praviśanti samudram āpūrya-māṇam aćalapratiṣṭham tadvat yam sarve kāmāḥ: praviśanti saḥ: āpnoti śāntim na kāmakāmī

(§5) As the waters flow into the ocean that is filling completely[260] (but) ever unmoving and standing still; in the same manner, he whom all desires encounter,[261] (he) attains peace; not the yearner of the passions. (2.70)

2.71 विहाय कामान्यः सर्वान्पुमांश्चरति निःस्पृहः ।
निर्ममो निरहङ्कारः स शान्तिमधिगच्छति ।।

vihāya kāmānyaḥ: sarvānpumāṁśćarati niḥ:spṛhaḥ:,
nirmamo nirahaṅkāraḥ: sa śāntimadhigaćchati. (2.71)

(§1) विहाय कामान् यः सर्वान् पुमान् चरति निःस्पृहः । निर्ममः निरहङ्कारः सः शान्तिम् अधिगच्छति । ***vihāya kāmān*** (r◦ 13/17) ***yaḥ:*** (r◦ 22/7) ***sarvān*** (r◦ 13/13) ***pumān*** (r◦ 13/6) ***ćarati niḥ:spṛhaḥ:*** (r◦ 22/8) ***nirmamaḥ:*** (r◦

---

[260] Elsewhere◦ *āpūrya-māṇam* → which is full (perfect tense), being filled (passive), filled from all sides (perfect), which becomes filled, ...etc.

🕮 आपूर्यमाण is not a perfect or habitual tense and it is not a passive or *parasmaipadī* adj◦. It is *ātmanepadī* present active participle adjective of the object ocean (समुद्रम्) to which all waters (from rivers and rains) are filling.

[261] Elsewhere◦ *kāmā yaṁ praviśanti* → a person who is not disturbed by (instrumental, passive) the desires, ...etc.

15/6) *nirahankārah:* (r◦ 22/7) *sah:* (r◦ 21/2) *śāntim* (r◦ 8/16) *adhigaććhati*

(§2) *vihāya* (2.22); *kāmān* (2.55); *yah:* (2.19); *sarvān* (1.27); *pumān* (1nom◦ sing◦ (person) ←m◦ *pum̐s* 2.62); *ćarati* (3rd-per◦ sing◦ pres◦ वर्तमान्-लट् parasmai◦ ←1◦√<u>चर्</u> (to move)); <u>***nih:sprhah:***</u> (m◦ 1nom◦ sing◦ ←adj◦ *nih:-sprha* ←10◦निर्√स्पृह् (to want)); <u>***nirmamah:***</u> (m◦ 1nom◦ sing◦ ←adj◦ n.tatpu◦ *nir-mama* (without my-ness) ←ind◦ *nir* 2.45 + pron◦ *mama* 1.7); <u>***nirahankārah:***</u> (m◦ 1nom◦ sing◦ ←adj◦ n.tatpu◦ *nir-ahankāra* ←m◦ <u>***ahankāra***</u> (I-ness) ←ind◦ *aham* ←5◦√अह् (to pervade) + adj◦ *kāra* 2.2); *sah:* (1.13); *śāntim* (2.70); *adhigaććhati* (2.64) (2.71)

(§3) *vihāya* (having kept away, renounced); *kāmān* (obj1◦ passions, desires); *yah:* (adj1◦-subj◦ who); *sarvān* (adj◦-obj1◦ all); *pumān* (subj◦ a person); *ćarati* (he lives; he carries on his life); *nih:sprhah:* (adj2◦-subj◦ free from desires); *nirmamah:* (adj3◦-subj◦ free from 'my'-ness); *nirahankārah:* (adj4◦-subj◦ he who is free from 'I'-ness *sah:* (adj5◦-subj◦ he); *śāntim* (obj2◦ peace); *adhigaććhati* (he attains) (2.71)

(§4) pumān nih:sprhah: nirmamah: nirahankārah: sah: yah: ćarati vihāya sarvān kāmān adhigaććhati śāntim

(§5) A person free from desires,[262] free from 'my'-ness (and) free from 'I'-ness, and carries on his life having kept away all passions, he attains peace. (2.71)

2.72 एषा ब्राह्मी स्थितिः पार्थ नैनां प्राप्य विमुह्यति ।
स्थित्वास्यामन्तकालेऽपि ब्रह्मनिर्वाणमृच्छति ।।

eṣā brāhmī sthitih: pārtha nainām prāpya vimuhyati,
sthitvāsyāmantakāle'pi brahmanirvāṇamrććhati. (2.72)

(§1) एषा ब्राह्मी स्थितिः पार्थ न एनाम् प्राप्य विमुह्यति । स्थित्वा अस्याम् अन्तकाले अपि ब्रह्मनिर्वाणम् ऋच्छति । *eṣā* (r◦ 25/2) *brāhmī sthitih:* (r◦ 22/3) *pārtha na* (r◦ 3/1) *enām* (r◦ 14/1) *prāpya vimuhyati sthitvā* (r◦ 1/3) *asyām* (r◦ 8/16) *antakāle* (r◦ 6/1) *api brahmanirvāṇam* (r◦ 8/21, 24/3) *rććhati*

(§2) *eṣā* (2.39); *brāhmī* (1nom◦ sing◦ ←taddhita◦ f◦ *brāhmī*, ब्रह्मणः या सा ←n◦ <u>***brahman***</u> ←1◦√<u>बृंह्</u> (to grow);

---

[262] Elsewhere◦ *nih:sprhah: nirmamah: nirahankārah:* → <u>lives free</u> from desires, <u>moves about without</u> attachment, <u>abandons</u> all desires, <u>lives devoid</u> of longing, <u>lives without</u> feeling of 'I' ...etc.

निःस्पृहः, निर्ममः and निरहङ्कारः are not adverbs, and therefore, can not be the adjectives of verb चरति (lives). They all are adjectives of m◦ noun पुमान् (nominative 1st case). Even if the word निःस्पृहः, निर्ममः and निरहङ्कारः come right after चरति, they must qualify पुमान्, not चरति ।

📖**sthitiḥ:** (1nom◦ sing◦ ←f◦ **sthiti** (state) ←1◦√स्था (to stay)); *pārtha* (1.15); *na* (1.30); *enām* (f◦ 2acc◦ sing◦ ←pron◦ *etad* 1.3); *prāpya* (2.57); 📖*vimuhyati* (3rd-per◦ sing◦ pres◦ वर्तमान्-लट् parasmai◦ ←4◦वि√मुह् (to be deluded) 2.13); 📖*sthitvā* (ipp◦ ind◦ ←1◦√स्था (to stay)); *asyām* (f◦ 7loc◦ sing◦ ←pron◦ *idam* 1.10); 📖**antakāle** (m◦ 7loc◦ sing◦ ←tatpu◦ *anta-kāla*, अन्तस्य काल: (at the end) ←m◦ *anta* 2.16 + m◦ **kāla** ←1◦√कल् (to count)); *api* (1.26); **brahmanirvāṇam** (2acc◦ sing◦ ←m◦ *brahma-nirvāṇa* ←tatpu◦ ब्रह्मण: निर्वाणम् ←n◦ *brahman* ↑ + m◦ **nirvāṇa** (final release) ←2◦निर्√वा (to move)); 📖 **ṛcchati** (3rd-per◦ sing◦ pres◦ वर्तमान्-लट् parasmai◦ ←6◦√ऋच्छ् (to go) (2.72)

(§3) *eṣā* (adj1◦-subj◦ this); *brāhmī* (adj2◦-subj◦ brahmic, pertaining to *brahma*); *sthitiḥ:* (subj◦ the state); *pārtha* (O Pārtha! O Arjuna!); *na* (does not); *enām* (adj◦-obj1◦ this, to this state); *prāpya* (having attained); *vimuhyati* (one confuses, baffles); *sthitvā* (having established); *asyām* (in it); *antakāle* (at the last moment); *api* (even); *brahmanirvāṇam* (obj2◦ oneness, unision with *brahma*); *ṛcchati* (one attains) (2.72)

(§4) pārtha eṣā sthitiḥ: brāhmī prāpya enām na vimuhyati sthitvā asyām api antakāle ṛcchati brahmanirvāṇam

(§5) O Arjuna! this (is) the *brahmic* state. Having attained this,[263] one does not beffle.[264] Having established[265] in it even at the last moment, one attains unision with *brahma*.[266] (2.72)

इति श्रीमद्भगवद्गीतासूपनिषत्सु ब्रह्मविद्यायां योगशास्त्रे

---

[263] Here, स्थितिम् is the object (obj1◦), though not actually mentioned, but it is understood.

[264] Elsewhere◦ *vimuhyati* → is deluded, is confused, is ever confused, ...etc.

📖 deluded is a ppp◦ adjective. विमुह्यति is लट् present tense → he confuses, he baffles, he errs ...etc.

[265] Elsewhere◦ *sthitvā* → being established, situated ...etc.

📖 'Being' indicates present existence. स्थित्वा is a past participle gerund attached to a subordinate action that is already completed, before the primary verb (ऋच्छति) begins. Therefore, स्थित्वा = after establishing he attains, having established he attains, first establishes and then after that he attains ...etc.

[266] Elsewhere◦ *brahmanirvāṇam* → nirvāṇa of Brahman, Beatitude of Brahman, felicity of Brahman, ...etc.

📖 ब्रह्मनिर्वाणम् n◦ noun, being a तत्पुरुष-समास:, the last word निर्वाणम् is the primary target of expression in this word. This तत्पुरुष compound word is not taking about ब्रह्म, the secondary word, but it is aiming at निर्वाणम्, the primary operative. निर्वाणम् n◦ is final liberation, dissolution, extinction, death; i.e. emancipation from worldly existence and reunion with external bliss. And thus, ब्रह्मनिर्वाणम् n◦ (nominative subject or accusative object) is reunion with ब्रह्म । The operative word is निर्वाणम् reunion, reunion with, libreration to.

श्रीकृष्णार्जुनसंवादे साङ्ख्ययोगो नाम द्वितीयोऽध्यायः ।

iti śrīmadbhagavadgītāsūpaniṣatsu brahmavidyāyām̐ yogaśāstre

śrīkṛṣṇārjunasam̐vāde sāṅkhyayogo nāma dvitīyo'dhyāyaḥ:.

(§1) *iti śrīmadbhagavadgītāsu* (r◦ 1/8) *upaniṣatsu brahmavidyāyām̐* (r◦ 14/1) *yogaśāstre śrīkṛṣṇārjunasam̐vāde sāṅkhyayogaḥ:* (r◦ 15/6) *nāma dvitīyaḥ:* (r◦ 15/1) *adhyāyaḥ:* (r◦ 22/8)

(§2) *iti* (1.25); *śrīmadbhagavadgītāsu* (f◦ 7loc◦ plu◦ tatpu◦ *śrīmad-bhagavad-gītā* ←adj◦ *śrīmat* 6.41 + adj◦ *bhagavat* 10.14 + f◦ *gītā* ←5◦√गै (to sing); *upaniṣatsu* (7loc◦ plu◦ ←f◦ *upaniṣad* ←6◦उप–नि√सद् (to sit); *brahmavidyāyām̐* (f◦ 7loc◦ sing◦ ←tatpu◦ *brahma-vidyā,* ब्रह्मणः विद्या ←n◦ *brahman* 2.72 + *vidyā* 5.18); *yogaśāstre* (n◦ 7loc◦ sing◦ ←tatpu◦ *yoga-śāstra,* योगानां शास्त्रम् । योगस्य शास्त्रम् ।←m◦ *yoga* 2.39 + n◦ *śāstra* 15.20); *śrīkṛṣṇārjunasam̐vāde* (m◦ 7loc◦ sing◦ ←tatpu◦ *śrī-kṛṣṇārjuna-sam̐vāda,* श्रीकृष्णस्य च अर्जुनस्य च संवादः ←adj◦ *śrī* 10.34 + m◦ prop◦ *kṛṣṇa* 1.28 + m◦ prop◦ *arjuna* 1.4 + m◦ *sam̐vāda* 18.70); *sāṅkhyayogaḥ:* (m◦ 1nom◦ sing◦ ←tatpu◦ *sāṅkhya-yoga,* ←prop◦ *sāṅkhya* ←2◦सम्√ख्या (to declare) + m◦ *yoga* 2.39); *nāma* (1nom◦ sing◦ ←n◦ *nāman* ←1◦√म्ना (to remember); *dvitīyaḥ:* (m◦ 1nom◦ sing◦ ←num◦ adj◦ *dvitīya* ←1◦√द्रु (to hinder); *adhyāyaḥ:* (1nom◦ sing◦ ←m◦ *adhyāya* ←1◦अधि√इ (to enter, come, go))

(§3) ***iti*** **(thus);** ***śrīmadbhagavadgītāsu upaniṣatsu*** **(among the upaniṣads of the Śrīmad-Bhagavadgītā);** ***brahmavidyāyām̐*** **(of the knowledge of self, knowledge of self realization, yoga of the eternal wisdom);** ***yogaśāstre*** **(in the science of** ***yoga*****);** ***śrīkṛṣṇārjunasam̐vāde*** **(in the dialogue between Śrī Kṛṣṇa and Arjuna);** ***sāṅkhyayogaḥ:*** **(adj1◦-**subj◦ **Sāṅkhya-yoga);** ***nāma*** **(called, named);** ***dvitīyaḥ:*** **(adj2◦-**subj◦ **the second);** ***adhyāyaḥ:*** (subj◦ **discourse; chapter)**

(§4) śrīmadbhagavadgītāsu upaniṣatsu yogaśāstre brahmavidyāyām̐ iti dvitīyaḥ: adhyāyaḥ: nāma sāṅkhyayogaḥ: śrīkṛṣṇārjunasam̐vāde

(§5) Among the upaniṣads of the Śrīmad-Bhagavadgītā, in the science of '*yoga* of self realization,' thus (is) the second discourse called *sāṅkhyayoga,* in the dialogue between Śrī Kṛṣṇa and Arjuna.

CHAPTER 3

tṛtīyo'adhyāyaḥ:

तृतीयोऽध्यायः ।

karmayogaḥ:

कर्मयोगः ।

THE YOGA OF DUTY[267]

Arjuna said (arjuna uvāća अर्जुन उवाच ।)

Arjuna's saṁskṛt words :

3.1 ज्यायसी चेत्कर्मणस्ते मता बुद्धिर्जनार्दन ।
तत्किं कर्मणि घोरे मां नियोजयसि केशव ।।

jyāyasī ćetkarmaṇaste matā buddhirjanārdana,
tatkiṁ karmaṇi ghore māṁ niyojayasi keśava. (3.1)

(§1) ज्यायसी चेत् कर्मण: ते मता बुद्धि: जनार्दन । तत् किम् कर्मणि घोरे माम् नियोजयसि केशव । *tṛtīyaḥ:* (r◦ 15/1) *adhyāyaḥ:* (r◦ 22/8). *karmayogaḥ:* (r◦ 22/8). *arjunaḥ:* (r◦ 19/4) *uvāća. jyāyasī ćet* (r◦ 10/5) *karmaṇaḥ:* (r◦ 18/1) *te matā buddhiḥ:* (r◦ 16/6) *janārdana taṭ* (r◦ 10/5) *kiṃ* (r◦ 14/1) *karmaṇi* (r◦ 24/7) *ghore māṃ* (r◦ 14/1) *niyojayasi keśava.* (3.1)

(§2) *tṛtīyaḥ:* (m◦ 1nom◦ sing◦ ←sequence indicating num◦ adj◦ *tṛtīya* ←adj◦ *tri* 2.45); *adhyāyaḥ:* (1nom◦ sing◦ ←m◦ *adhyāya* ←1◦अधि√इ). *karmayogaḥ:* (m◦ 1nom◦ sing◦ ←m◦ *karma-yoga* 3.3↓). *arjunaḥ:* (1.28); *uvāća* (1.25). (3.1)

📖*jyāyasī* (f◦ 1nom◦ sing◦ ←comparative adj◦ *jyā* (ज्यादेश:) with the kṛt suffix *iyaṣ* (इयस्) = ***jyāyaṣ*** (better, best) ←9◦√ज्या); *ćeṭ* (2.33); ***karmaṇaḥ:*** (5abl◦ sing◦ ←n◦ *karmaṇ* 1.15); *te* (ablative 2.34); 📖***matā***

---

[267] Elsewhere◦ *karmayogaḥ:* → The Yoga of Action, The Action Yoga, Yoga of Direct Action, ...etc.

📖 कर्मयोग: = निष्कामकर्मयोग: = The obdience of conduct without desire in its fruit, *niṣ-kāma-karma-yoga* (*niṣ* = without; *kāma* = *kāmanā, kāmanā* in fruit, desire in the result; *karma* = righteous conduct; *yoga* = attachment to a discipline, obdience). Therefore, ***karmayogaḥ:*** **= niṣkāma-karma-yoga = the discipline of renunciation of the desire** (निष्काम) **in the fruit of *karma* = the yoga of performing one's duty (what ought to be done by a person at a given moment and place)**

(1nom∘ sing∘ ←f∘ *matā* ←ppp∘ adj∘ *mata* (considered) ←1∘√मन्); *buddhiḥ:* (समबुद्धिः 2.39); *janārdana* (1.36); *tat̨* (3.1); *kim̨* (1.1); *karmaṇi* (2.47); 🕮*ghore* (n∘ 7loc∘ sing∘ ←adj∘ **ghora** (grave) ←6∘√घुर्); *mām̨* (1.46); 🕮*niyojayasi* (2nd-per∘ sing∘ pres∘ वर्तमान्–लट् parasmai∘ caus∘ ←7∘नि√युज्); *keśava* (1.31) (3.1)

(§3) *tṛtīyaḥ:* (adj∘-subj∘ the third); *adhyāyaḥ:* (subj∘ chapter). *karmayogaḥ:* (*karma-yoga*). *arjunaḥ:* (subj∘ Arjuna); *uvāća* (said).

jyāyasī (adj∘ subj∘ superior); *ćet̨* (if); *karmaṇaḥ:* (than *karma*); *te matā* (adj∘-subj∘ the one you considered, you described); *buddhiḥ:* (subj∘ the sama-buddhi, the equanimous thinking, equanimity, the buddhi-yoga); *janārdana* (O Janardana! O Kṛṣṇa!); *tat̨ kim̨* (adv∘ then why?); *karmaṇi-ghore* (in the grave work); *mām̨* (obj∘ to me, me); *niyojayasi* (you are causing to engage); *keśava* (O Keśava! O Kṛṣṇa!) (3.1)

(§4) tṛtīyaḥ: adhyāyaḥ:. karmayogaḥ:. arjunaḥ: uvāća. janārdana! ćet̨ te matā buddhiḥ: jyāyasī karmaṇaḥ: tat̨ keśava kim̨ niyojayasi mām̨ ghore karmaṇi?

(§5) The third chapter, the Yoga of Duty. Arjuna said : O Kṛṣṇa! if, the equanimous thinking[268] you described (is) superior than *niṣkāma-karma,*[269] then O Kṛṣṇa! why are you causing me to engage[270] in the grave work? (3.1)

3.2 **व्यामिश्रेणेव वाक्येन बुद्धिं मोहयसीव मे ।**
तदेकं वद निश्चित्य येन श्रेयोऽहमाप्नुयाम् ।।
vyāmiśreṇeva vākyena buddhiṁ mohayasīva me,
tadekaṁ vada niśćitya yena śreyo'hamāpnuyām̨. (3.2)

(§1) व्यामिश्रेण इव वाक्येन बुद्धिम् मोहयसि इव मे । तत् एकम् वद निश्चित्य येन श्रेयः अहम् आप्नुयाम् । *vyāmiśreṇa* (r∘ 24/1, 2/1) *iva vākyena buddhim̨* (r∘ 14/1) *mohayasi* (r∘ 1/5) *iva me tat̨* (r∘ 8/9) *ekam̨* (r∘ 14/1) *vada niśćitya yena śreyaḥ:* (r∘ 15/1) *aham̨* (r∘ 8/17) *āpnuyām̨* (r∘ 14/2)

(§2) 🕮*vyāmiśreṇa* (3inst∘ sing∘ ←adj∘ *vyāmiśra* (mixed) ←10∘वि–आ√मिश्र्); *iva* (1.30); 🕮*vākyena* (3inst∘ sing∘ ←n∘ *vākya* (speech) 1.21); ***buddhim̨*** (2acc∘ sing∘ ←f∘ *buddhi* (thinking) 1.23); 🕮*mohayasi* (2nd-per∘

---

[268] Elsewhere∘ *buddhiḥ:* → intelligence, intuitive determination, understanding, knowkedge, wisdom ...etc.

🕮 As explained earlier in the shloka 2.50, in the first half of the 2nd chapter of the Gita on *buddhi-yoga*, the *samabuddhi*, the equanimous thinking, the *buddhi-yoga*, the equanimity of thinking ...etc. are at many places referred simply as *buddhi*. Any intelligent person is not automatically a *buddhiyogi*.

[269] Elsewhere∘ *karmanaḥ:* → than the fruitive work, action ...etc.

[270] Elsewhere∘ *niyojayasi* → you want, thou urge, dost thou urge me ...etc.

sing◦ pres◦ वर्तमान्-लट् parasmai◦ caus◦ ←4◦√मुह्); *iva* (1.30); *me* (1.21); *tat* (2.7); ***ekam*** (*adv*◦ or n◦ 2acc◦ sing◦ ←adj◦ *eka* (one) 2.41); *vada* (2nd-per◦ sing◦ imperative◦ निवेदनार्थ-लोट् parasmai◦ ←1◦√वद्); 📖*niścitya* (lyp◦ past-participle ind◦ ←5◦निर्√चि); *yena* (2.17); *śreyaḥ:* (better 1.31); *aham* (1.22); 📖*āpnuyām* (1st-per◦ sing◦ potential◦ विधि◦ parasmai◦ ←5◦√आप्) (3.2)

(§3) *vyāmiśreṇa* (with a mixed); *iva* (as if, so to speak, like); *vākyena* (with speech); *buddhim* (obj1◦ mind, thinking); *mohayasi* (you are causing to confuse); *iva* (as if); *me* (my); *tat* (obj2◦ that); *ekam* (adj◦-obj2◦ only one); *vada* (please tell me); *niścitya* (certainly); *yena* (by which); *śreyaḥ:* (obj3◦ better); *aham* (subj◦ I); *āpnuyām* (I would attain) (3.2)

(§4) vākyena iva vyāmiśreṇa mohayasi iva me buddhim vada niścitya tat ekam yena aham āpnuyām śreyaḥ:

(§5) With like a mixed[271] speech you are causing, as if, to confuse my mind.[272] Please tell me certainly that only one by which I would attain better. (3.2)

The Lord said (śrībhagavānuvāca श्रीभगवानुवाच ।)

3.3 लोकेऽस्मिन्द्विविधा निष्ठा पुरा प्रोक्ता मयानघ ।
ज्ञानयोगेन साङ्ख्यानां कर्मयोगेन योगिनाम् ।।
loke'smindvividhā niṣṭhā purā proktā mayānagha,
jñānayogena sāṅkhyānām karmayogena yoginām. (3.3)

(§1) लोके अस्मिन् द्विविधा निष्ठा पुरा प्रोक्ता मया अनघ! ज्ञानयोगेन साङ्ख्यानाम् कर्मयोगेन योगिनाम् । *śrībhagavān* (r◦ 8/14) *uvāca. loke* (r◦ 6/1) *asmin* (r◦ 13/11) *dvividhā niṣṭhā purā proktā mayā* (r◦ 1/3) *anagha jñānayogena sāṅkhyānām* (r◦ 14/1) *karmayogena yoginām* (r◦ 14/2)

(§2) *śrībhagavān* (2.2); *uvāca* (1.25). *loke* (2.5); *asmin* (1.22); 📖*dvividhā* (f◦ 1nom◦ sing◦ ←mode indicating num◦ adj◦ *dvividha* (twofold) ←adj◦ *dvi* (two) 1.7 + m◦ ***vidha*** (kind) ←6◦**√विध्**); 📖***niṣṭhā*** (1nom◦ sing◦ ←f◦ ***niṣṭhā*** (faith) ←1◦नि√स्था); 📖***purā*** (adv◦ ind◦ (previously) ←6◦√पुर्); 📖*proktā* (f◦ 1nom◦ sing◦ ←ppp◦ adj◦ ***prokta*** (told) ←2◦प्र√**वच्**); *mayā* (1.22); ***anagha*** (m◦ 8voc◦ sing◦ ←n.bahuvrī◦ 📖*anagha*, नास्ति अघम् यस्य ←n◦ 📖***agha*** (sin) ←10◦**√अघ्**); *jñānayogena* (m◦ 3inst◦ sing◦ ←tatpu◦ prop◦ *jñāna-yoga*, कर्मण: कर्तृपदस्य संन्यासस्य बुद्धे: च समत्वस्य च ज्ञानयो: योग: ←n◦ 📖***jñāna*** ←9◦√ज्ञा + m◦ *yoga* 2.39); *sāṅkhyānām* (m◦ 6pos◦ plu◦ ←adj◦ *sāṅkhya* 2.39); ***karmayogena*** (m◦ 3inst◦ sing◦ ←tatpu◦ ***karma-yoga***, निष्कामकर्मण: योग: ←n◦ *karman* 1.15 + m◦ *yoga* 2.39); ***yoginām*** (6pos plu◦ ←m◦ or adj◦ ***yogin*** ←4◦√युज्) (3.3)

---

[271] Elsewhere◦ व्यामिश्रेण → perplexing, conflicting, equivocal ...etc.

[272] Elsewhere◦ बुद्धिम् → intelligence, understanding, intellect.

(§3) *śrībhagavān* (subj◦ the Lord); *uvāća* (said). *loke* (in the world); *asmin* (in this); *dvividhā* (adj◦-obj◦ twofold, of two kinds); *niṣṭhā* (obj◦ faith, discipline); *purā* (in older times, previously); *proktā* (told); *mayā* (subj◦ by me); *anagha* (O Anagha! O Sinless! O Arjuna!); *jñānayogena* (with the discipline of knowledge of renunciation of authorship of karma, with the *Sāṅkhya-yoga*); *sāṅkhyānām* (for the *Sānkhya-yogīs*); *karmayogena* (with the descipline of work without desire in its fruit, with *niṣkāma-karma*); *yoginām* (for the *karma-yogīs*) (3.3)

(§4) śrībhagavān uvāća. anagha purā loke asmin dvividhā niṣṭhā proktā mayā jñānayogena sāṅkhyānām karmayogena yoginām

(§5) The Lord said, O Arjuna! in older times, in this world, twofold faith[273] (was) told by me. With the discipline of knowledge of renunciation of authorship of karma,[274] for the Sānkhya-

---

[273] Elsewhere◦ द्विविधा निष्ठा → there are two classes of men, two-fold way of life ...etc.

[274] Elsewhere◦ *jñānayogena* → by empirical knowledge, by knowledge of reality, philosophical speculation, by yoga of knowledge, by the path of knowledge, by knowledge-yoga, by knowledge of self realization, by knowledge of self, by knowledge of brahman ...etc.

📖 The Lord anciently had told two ways of performing a duty. (i) by renouncing the authorship and doing a righteous deed with equanimous mind; and (ii) by not desiring the fruit of a righteous undertaking. NOTE : It does not mean renouncing the fruit itself, but it means renouncing the motive, intention, objective, aim, purpose, want, covet, yearning, longing, hunger, thirst, crave or desire behind whatever the fruit that may accrue in the future.

Jñānayoga is not the yoga of intelligence, knowledge, wisdom, speculation, or intuition. For, just because a person is intelligent, learned, wise, speculative or intuitive, he is not a jñānayogi. He is a *vidvān*. Also, a person who knows what is 'self,' reality or brahma is not called a *jnānayogi*. He is a *brahmajñānī, ātmajñānī*, brahmavetta or brahmajña. Giving up averything is not a *sanyāsa*. Person who has ran away from a righteous work is not a *sanyāsī* or *sanyāsayogī* or *sāṅkhyayogī*.

Similarly, *karmayoga* is not the yoga of 'action.' Neither any or every action belongs to *karmayoga*, nor an active or busy person is a *karmayogī*. A thief, murderer, criminal, cheat, thug or a selfish person is not a *karmayogī*, no matter how active or busy he may be.

Therefore, (i) Doer of a righteous deed knowing (having jñāna) that he is not the author of it but the guṇas are the author and he is merely an instrument, is a *jñānayogī*. (ii) Renounciation of this authorship is *sanyāsa* of the *sanyāsī, sanyāsayogī* or *sāṅkhyayogī*. (iii) Doer of a righteous action with an equanimous mind (*sama*-buddhi) for loss or gain therein is a *buddhiyogī*. (iv) Doer of a righteous action without desire (niṣ-kāma) for its fruit is a *yogī, karmayogī or niṣkāmakarmayogī*.

yogīs;[275] (and) with the descipline of *niṣkāma-karma*[276] for the *karma-yogīs*.[277] (3.3)

3.4 न कर्मणामनारम्भान्नैष्कर्म्यं पुरुषोऽश्नुते ।
न च संन्यसनादेव सिद्धिं समधिगच्छति ।।

na karmaṇāmanārambhānnaiṣkarmyaṁ puruṣo'śnute,
na ća sannyasanādeva siddhiṁ samadhigaććhti. (3.4)

(§1) न कर्मणाम् अनारम्भात् नैष्कर्म्यम् पुरुष: अश्नुते । न च संन्यसनात् एव सिद्धिम् समधिगच्छति । *na karmaṇām* (r∘ 24/6, 8/16) *anārambhāt* (r∘ 12/1) *naiṣkarmyam* (r∘ 14/1) *puruṣaḥ:* (r∘ 15/1) *aśnute na ća sannyasanāt* (r∘ 8/9) *eva* (r∘ 1.1) *siddhim* (r∘ 14/1) *samadhigaććhati*

(§2) *na* (1.30); ***karmaṇām*** (6pos plu∘ ←n∘ *karman* 1.15); *anārambhāt* (5abl∘ sing∘ ←n.tatpu∘ *anārambha* ←negative affix *na* (न) 1.30, or *an* (अन्) 3.31 + m∘ 🕮***ārambha*** (undertaking) ←1∘आ√रभ्); *naiṣkarmyam* (2acc∘ sing∘ ←n∘ n.tatpu∘ ***naiṣkarmya*** (selfless duty) ←*niṣ* + 8∘√कृ); *puruṣaḥ:* (2.21); 🕮***aśnute*** (3rd-per∘ sing∘ pres∘ वर्तमान्-लट् ātmane∘ ←9∘√अश्); *na* (1.30); *ća* (1.1); 🕮*sannyasanāt* (5abl∘ sing∘ ←n∘ *sannyasana* (renunciation) ←2∘सम्-नि√अस्); *eva* (1.1); 🕮***siddhim*** (2acc∘ sing∘ ←f∘ *siddhi* (success) 2.48); 🕮*samadhigaććhati* (3rd-per∘ sing∘ pres∘ वर्तमान्-लट् parasmai∘ ←1∘सम्-अधि√गम् 2.51) (3.4)

(§3) *na* (neither); *karmaṇām* (of the *karmas*); *anārambhāt* (from the abstinence of, from the non-commencement of); *naiṣkarmyam* (obj1∘ selfless *karma*); *puruṣaḥ:* (subj∘ man); *aśnute* (he enjoys); *na ća* (nor); *sannyasanāt* (from renunciation); *eva* (alone); *siddhim* (obj2∘ success, completion); *samadhigaććhati* (he attains) (3.4)

(§4) anārambhāt karmaṇām puruṣaḥ: na aśnute naiṣkarmyam na ća sannyasanāt eva samadhigaććhati siddhim

(§5) From the abstinence of *karmas* man neither enjoys selfless *karma*[278] nor from renunciation

---

[275] Elsewhere∘ *sāṅkhyānām* → for the men of realization, for the men of contemplation, for the men of knowledge, for the discerning ...etc.

[276] Elsewhere∘ *karmayogena* → by devotional service, of yoga by action, that of works, path of work, action-yoga ...etc.

🕮 कर्मयोगेन → With a conduct without desire in its fruit = निष्कामकर्मयोगेन ।

[277] Elsewhere∘ *yoginām* → others, to the active, of the *Yogīs*, for men of action, ...etc.

[278] Elsewhere∘ नैष्कर्म्य → freedom from reaction, freedom from from action, inactivity, non-action ...etc.

🕮 see नैष्कर्म्य-सिद्धिं परमाम् in 18.49. If नैष्कर्म्य is non-activity, non-action or inaction, it would be same as अकर्म । And then attainment of परम-सिद्धि: in नैष्कर्म्य (18.49 नैष्कमर्य-सिद्धिं परमां अधिगच्छति) would mean attainment of perfectly nothing, nothing perfectly, absolute inactivity or supreme inaction. It will negate

alone he attains success.[279] **(3.4)**

3.5 **न हि कश्चित्क्षणमपि जातु तिष्ठत्यकर्मकृत् ।**
कार्यते ह्यवशः कर्म सर्वः प्रकृतिजैर्गुणैः ॥

na hi kaścitkṣaṇamapi jātu tiṣṭhatyakarmakṛt,
kāryate hyavaśaḥ: karma sarvaḥ: prakṛtijairguṇaiḥ:. **(3.5)**

(§1) न हि कश्चित् क्षणम् अपि जातु तिष्ठति कर्मकृत् । कार्यते हि अवशः कर्म सर्वः प्रकृतिजैः गुणैः । *na hi kaścit* (r◦ 10/5) *kṣaṇam* (r◦ 8/16, 24/3) *api jātu tiṣṭhati* (r◦ 4/1) *akarmakṛt* (r◦ 23/1) *kāryate hi* (r◦ 4/1) *avaśaḥ:* (r◦ 22/1) *karma sarvaḥ:* (r◦ 22/3) *prakṛtijaiḥ:* (r◦ 16/11) *guṇaiḥ:* (r◦ 22/8)

(§2) *na* (1.30); *hi* (1.11); *kaścit* (2.17); 📖*kṣaṇam* (2acc◦ sing◦ ←m◦ or n◦ *kṣaṇa* (moment) ←6√क्षण्); *api* (1.26); *jātu* (ever 2.12); 📖**tiṣṭhati** (3rd-per◦ sing◦ pres◦ वर्तमान्-लट् parasmai◦ ←1◦√**स्था**); *akarmakṛt* (adj◦ n.tatpu◦ *akarma-kṛt* ←n◦ *karma* 2.49 + affix *kṛt* ←8√कृ); *kāryate* (3rd-per◦ sing◦ pres◦ वर्तमान्-लट् ātmane◦ caus◦ ←8◦√कृ); *hi* (1.11); 📖***avaśaḥ:*** (adv◦ ←m◦ *vaśa* (control) 2.61); *karma* (2.49); ***sarvaḥ:*** (m◦ 1nom◦ sing◦ ←pron◦ *sarva* (all) 1.6); ***prakṛtijaiḥ:*** (m◦ 3inst◦ plu◦ ←adj◦ ***prakṛti-ja*** ←bahuvrī◦ प्रकृत्या जन्म यस्य ←f◦ ***prakṛti*** ←8प्र√कृ + n◦ *janman* (birth) 2.27 or m◦ *ja* 1.7); ***guṇaiḥ:*** (3inst◦ plu◦ ←m◦ *guṇa* 2.45) **(3.5)**

(§3) *na* (no); *hi* (because); *kaścit* (subj1◦ anyone, one); *kṣaṇam* (obj1◦ a moment, for a moment); *api* (even, also); *jātu* (ever); *tiṣṭhati* (stays, remains); *akarmakṛt* (adj◦-subj◦ without doing anything); *kāryate* (is made to do, is driven); *hi* (because); *avaśaḥ:* (helplessly); *karma* (obj2◦ to karma); *sarvaḥ:*

---

what is said in the next shloka : there is no such thing as inactivity or inaction (न हि कश्चित् क्षणम् अपि जातु तिष्ठति कर्मकृत् ।).

[279] Elsewhere◦ सिद्धिम् → perfection

📖 see सिद्धिम् in 4.12.

NOTE : Siddhi is not 'perfection. 'If सिद्धि is perfection, then सिद्धि-परमा (in 18.49) would be a super perfection or beyond perfection, and संसिद्धिम् (in 3.20) would be perfectly perfect and असिद्धिम् would be imperfectly perfect, and then परमसिद्धि and संसिद्धि would be beyond *brahma*, the words which all are meaningless. Same is true for verses 12.10 and 16.23. For the notes on सिद्धिः (accomplishment), साध्य (accomplished), साध्यः (the accomplished one), साधित (accomplished, proven), सिद्ध (ready), सिद्धता (readyness), सिद्धार्थ (one who has accomplished the goal), ...etc. (see सिद्धानाम् in 7.3 below↓)

In Gita, only *brahma* is perfect, nothing else is perfect. 'Perfection' is परिपूर्णता, सम्पूर्णता, सर्वसम्पन्नता, अन्यूनता, निर्दोषत्वम् and 'Siddhi' is success (साधना), accomplishment सफलता, यशः, अर्थसिद्धिः, सिद्धार्थता, कृतार्थता, राद्धिः ।

(obj3◦ everyone - collective); *prakṛtijaiḥ: guṇaiḥ:* (subj2◦ by the *guṇas* born of nature, with naturally born guṇas, with inborn guṇas) (3.5)

(§4) hi na kaśćit jātu tiṣṭhati api kṣaṇam akarmakṛt hi avaśaḥ: sarvaḥ: kāryate karma prakṛtijaiḥ: guṇaiḥ:

(§5) Because,[280] no one ever remains even for a moment without doing anything. Because helplessly everyone is driven to *karma*[281] by the guṇas born of nature. (3.5)

3.6 **कर्मेन्द्रियाणि संयम्य य आस्ते मनसा स्मरन् ।**
इन्द्रियार्थान्विमूढात्मा मिथ्याचारः स उच्यते ।।

karmendriyāṇi saṁyamya ya āste manasā smaran,
indriyārthānvimūḍhātmā mithyāćāraḥ: sa ućyate. (3.6)

(§1) कर्मेन्द्रियाणि संयम्य यः आस्ते मनसा स्मरन् । इन्द्रियार्थान् विमूढात्मा मिथ्याचारः सः उच्यते ।।*karmendriyāṇi* (r◦ 24/7) *saṁyamya yaḥ:* (r◦ 19/1) *āste manasā smaran* (r◦ 23/1) *indriyārthān* (r◦ 13/19) *vimūḍhātmā mithyāćāraḥ:* (r◦ 22/7) *saḥ:* (r◦ 21/2) *ućyate*

(§2) *karmendriyāṇi* (n◦ 2acc◦ plu◦ कर्मणाम् इन्द्रियाणि ←tatpu◦ ***karmendriya*** ←n◦ *karman* 1.15 + n◦ *indriya* (organ) 2.8); 🕮*saṁyamya* (2.61); *yaḥ:* (2.19); ***āste*** (3rd-per◦ sing◦ pres◦ वर्तमान्-लट् ātmane◦ ←2◦√आस्); ***manasā*** (3inst◦ sing◦ ←n◦ *manas* (mind) 1.30); 🕮***smaran*** (m◦ 1nom◦ sing◦ ←śatṛ◦ adj◦ *smart* ←1√स्मृ); *indriyārthān* (m◦ 2acc◦ plu◦ ←tatpu◦ *indriyārtha* (sense) 2.58); 🕮*vimūḍhātmā* (m◦ 1nom◦ sing◦ ←bahuvrī◦

---

[280] Elsewhere◦ *hi* → indeed, certainly, truly, verily ...etc.

🕮 The translators who do not fully appreciate the foundation of Hindu ethos, do flatly treat the word हि as a filler word with meaningless expression such as indeed, certainly, truly, verily ...etc. However, otherwise, हि is a very important key word in the Gītā, as She is, in any ohter Hindu scripture. In the Gītā it invirably means 'because.' This word (along with *tasmāt* तस्मात्) actually separates the Hindu Scriptures from all other religious and dogmatic texts where reasoning has no place and no importance.

हि (because) always has तस्मात् (therefore) associated or understood with it. The Gītā, like any other typical Hindu scripture, is based on questioning, reasoning, understanding, seeing and then believing. In (2.14) the Lord says 'O Arjuna! you endure the pain and pleasures ...' not because I say so, but (2.15) 'because (हि) the self-controlled person is equanimous to pain and pleasures... therefore (तस्मात्) you endure them .'

NOTE : Everywhere in Gītā, while giving any advice, the reasoning is given with expressions हि and (or) तस्मात् । By flatly translating हि and तस्मात् as 'indeed,' you take away this beautiful and unique quality of the Gītā and turn it into a dogmatic and ritualistic blind faith, which it is not. See the footnote in verse 2.15

[281] Elsewhere◦ कर्म → karman

vimūḍhātman, विमूढ: आत्मा यस्य ←ppp∘ adj∘ 📖*__vimūḍha__* ←4वि√मुह् + m∘ *ātman* 2.41); 📖*mithyācāraḥ:* (m∘ 1nom∘ sing∘ ←bahuvrī∘ *mithyācāra* (hypocrite) मिथ्या आचर: यस्य ←adj∘ 📖*__mithyā__* ←1√मिष् + m∘ *ācāra* ←1आ√चर्); *saḥ:* (1.13); *ucyate* (2.25) (3.6)

(§3) *karmendriyāṇi* (obj1∘ the organs of karma) *saṁyamya* (having restrained) *yaḥ:* (subj∘ he who); *āste* (sits, stays, remains); *manasā* (with mind); *smaran* (adj1∘-subj∘ thinking of); *indriyārthān* (obj2∘ the objects of the sense organs, the *viṣayas*); *vimūḍhātmā* (adj2∘-subj∘ fool, foolish person); *mithyācāraḥ:* (adj3∘-subj∘ a hypocrite. a phony); *saḥ:* (adj4∘-subj∘ he, that); *ucyate* (is said to be, is called) (3.6)

(§4) saṁyamya karmendriyāṇi yaḥ: āste smaran indriyārthān manasā saḥ: vimūḍhātmā ucyate mithyācāraḥ:

(§5) Having restrained[282] the organs of *karma,*[283] he who sits thinking of the objects of the sense organs with mind, that foolish person is called a hypocrite. (3.6)

3.7 यस्त्विन्द्रियाणि मनसा नियम्यारभतेऽर्जुन ।
कर्मेन्द्रियै: कर्मयोगमसक्त: स विशिष्यते ।।

yastvindriyāṇi manasā niyamyārabhate'rjuna,
karmendriyaiḥ: karmayogamasaktaḥ: sa viśiṣyate. (3.7)

(§1) य: तु इन्द्रियाणि मनसा नियम्य आरभते अर्जुन । कर्मेन्द्रियै: कर्मयोगम् असक्त: स: विशिष्यते । *yaḥ:* (r∘ 18/1) *tu* (r∘ 4/8) *indriyāṇi* (r∘ 24/7) *manasā niyamya* (r∘ 1/2) *ārabhate* (r∘ 6/1) arjuna karmendriyaiḥ: (r∘ 22/1) *karmayogam* (r∘ 8/16) *asaktaḥ:* (r∘ 22/7) *saḥ:* (r∘ 21/2) *viśiṣyate*

(§2) *yaḥ:* (2.19); *tu* (1.2); *indriyāṇi* (2.58); *manasā* (3.6); 📖*__niyamya__* (lyp∘ past-participle ind∘ ←1∘नि√यम्); *ārabhate* (3rd-per∘ sing∘ pres∘ वर्तमान्-लट् ātmane∘ ←1∘आ√रभ्); *arjuna* (2.2); *karmendriyaiḥ:* (3inst∘ plu∘ ←n∘ *karmendriya* 3.6); *karmayogam* (2acc∘ sing∘ ←m∘ *karmayoga* 3.3); 📖*__asaktaḥ:__* (m∘ 1nom∘ sing∘ ←ppp∘ adj∘ n.tatpu∘ *__asakta__* (unattached) ←1∘अ√सञ्ज्); *saḥ:* (1.13); 📖*__viśiṣyate__* (3rd-per∘ sing∘ pres∘ वर्तमान्-लट् ātmane∘ ←7∘वि√शिष्) (3.7)

---

[282] Elsewhere∘ संयम्य → one who restrains, outwordly controls ...etc.

[283] Elsewhere∘ कर्मेन्द्रियाणि → senses of action, senses, organs of action ...etc.

📖 *karmendriyāṇi*, five organs of functioning are called कर्मेन्द्रियाणि, namely : hands, feet, mouth and the organs of excretion and reproduction. Other five, the sense organs, *jñānendriyāṇi* (ज्ञानेन्द्रियाणि) aer : ear, nose, eyes, skin and tongue. All ten are organs of ten types of actions, five function or work actions and five sense actions.

(§3) *yaḥ:* (adj1◦-subj◦ he who); *tu* (however); *indriyāṇi* (obj◦ the organs); *manasā* (with mind); *niyamya* (having restrained); *ārabhate* (he engages in); *arjuna* (O Arjuna!); *karmendriyaiḥ:* (with the organs of karma); *karmayogam̩* (obj◦ the *karmayoga, the niṣkāma-karma-yoga*);[284] *asaktaḥ:* (adj2◦-subj◦ unfettered, unattached person); *saḥ:* (subj◦ he, that); *viśiṣyate* (he excels) (3.7)

(§4) tu arjuna yaḥ: niyamya indriyāṇi manasā ārabhate karmayogam̩ karmendriyaiḥ: saḥ: asaktaḥ: viśiṣyate

(§5) However, O Arjuna! he who, having restrained the organs[285] with mind, engages in the *niṣkāma-karma-yoga*[286] with the organs of *karma*, that unfettered person excels. (3.7)

3.8 **नियतं कुरु कर्म त्वं कर्म ज्यायो ह्यकर्मणः ।**
शरीरयात्रापि च ते न प्रसिद्ध्येदकर्मणः ।।
niyataṁ kuru karma tvaṁ karma jyāyo hyakarmaṇaḥ:,
śarīrayātrāpi ća te na prasiddhyedakarmaṇaḥ:. (3.8)

(§1) नियतम् कुरु कर्म त्वम् कर्म ज्यायः हि अकर्मणः । शरीरयात्रा अपि च ते न प्रसिद्ध्येत् अकर्मणः । *niyatam̩* (r◦ 14/1) *kuru karma tvam̩* (r◦ 14/1) *karma jyāyaḥ:* (r◦ 15/14) *hi* (r◦ 4/1) *akarmaṇaḥ:* (r◦ 22/8) *śarīrayātrā* (r◦ 1/3) *api ća te na prasiddhyet̩* (r◦ 8/2) *akarmaṇaḥ:* (r◦ 22/8)

(§2) 🕮***niyatam̩*** (n◦ 2acc◦ sing◦ ←adj◦ *niyata* 1.44); *kuru* (2.48); ***karma*** (2acc◦ sing◦ ←*karman̩* 2.49); *tvam̩* (2.11); *karma* (2.49); 🕮*jyāyaḥ:* (n◦ 1nom◦ sing◦ ←comparitive adj◦ *jyāyas̩* 3.1); *hi* (1.11);

---

[284] Elsewhere◦ *karmayogam̩* → devotion, path of work, path of action, performance of action, ...etc.

[285] Elsewhere◦ इन्द्रियाणि नियम्य → tries to control the active senses, controls the organs, who controls the senses ...etc.

[286] Elsewhere◦ कर्मयोगम् असक्तः सः → begins karma-yoga without attachment, remaining unattached undertakes the yoga of action, commences Karma Yoga without attachment, engages in Karma-Yoga unattached with organs of action ...etc.

🕮 कर्मयोगमसक्तः is not a समासः between कर्मयोग and असक्तः (कर्मयोगासक्तः). It is a संधिः between two separately connected words कर्मयोगम् (Accusative 2nd case) and असक्तः (Nominative 1st case). कर्मेन्द्रियम् is qualified by कर्मेन्द्रियैः (यः कर्मेन्द्रियैः कर्मयोगम् आरभते । यः subject, कर्मेन्द्रियैः instrument, कर्मयोगम् accusative object, आरभते verb) and adj◦ असक्तः qualifies सः (असक्तः सः विषिष्यते । असक्तः nominative adjective of nominative subj◦, सः nominative subj◦ विषिष्यते verb). NOTE : असक्तः is not an adverb either, so it can not qualify आरभते e.g. he begins without attachment ...etc. Therefore, it could not be कर्मयोगम् असक्तः विषिष्यते or असक्तः आरभते ।

PLEASE REMEMBER : If one observes which ones are the subjects and objects; and their corresponding adjectives; and verbs and their adverbs in each *shloka*, such errors do not occur.

akarmaṇaḥ: (5abl◦ sing◦ ←n◦ *akarmaṇ* 2.47); 🕮*śarīrayātrā* (f◦ 1nom◦ sing◦ ←tatpu◦ *śarīra-yātrā* (livelyhood) शरीरस्य यात्रा । शरीरस्य निर्वाहः । ←n◦ *śarīra* 1.29 + f◦ *yātrā* ←2◦√या); *api* (1.26); *ća* (1.1); *te* (2.34); *na* (1.30); 🕮*prasiddhyeṭ* (3rd-per◦ sing◦ potential◦ विधि◦ parasmai◦ ←4◦प्र√सिध्); *akarmaṇaḥ:* (↑) (3.8)

(§3) *niyataṃ* (= *vihitaṃ* adj◦-obj◦ priscribbed, enjoined); *kuru* (please do); *karma* (obj◦ *karma*, duty, the duties - collective); *tvaṃ* (subj1◦ you); *karma* (subj2◦ karma, duty); *jyāyaḥ:* (adj◦-subj2◦ is better); *hi* (because); *akarmaṇaḥ:* (than *akarma*, than not performing the duties); *śarīrayātrā* (subj3◦ journey of life); *api ća* (also); *te* (your); *na* (not); *prasiddhyeṭ* (may be accomplished); *akarmaṇaḥ:* (without *karma*) (3.8)

(§4) tvaṃ kuru niyataṃ karma hi karma jyāyaḥ: akarmaṇaḥ: te śarīrayātrā api ća na prasiddhyeṭ akarmaṇaḥ:

(§5) (O Arjuna!) You please do the priscribed duty;[287] because[288] *karma* is better than not performing duty.[289] Your journey of life[290] also may not be accomplished without *karma*. (3.8)

3.9 **यज्ञार्थात्कर्मणोऽन्यत्र लोकोऽयं कर्मबन्धनः ।**
तदर्थं कर्म कौन्तेय मुक्तसङ्गः समाचर ॥
yajñārthātkarmaṇo'nyatra loko'yaṁ karmabandhanaḥ:,
tadarthaṁ karma kaunteya muktasaṅgaḥ: samāćara. (3.9)

(§1) यज्ञार्थात् कर्मणः अन्यत्र लोकः अयम् कर्मबन्धनः । तदर्थम् कर्म कौन्तेय मुक्तसङ्गः समाचर । *yajñārthāṭ* (r◦ 10/5) *karmaṇaḥ:* (r◦ 15/1) *anyatra lokaḥ:* (r◦ 15/1) *ayaṃ* (r◦ 14/1) *karmabandhanaḥ:* (r◦ 22/8) *tadarthaṃ* (r◦ 14/1) *karma kaunteya muktasaṅgaḥ:* (r◦ 22/7) *samāćara*

(§2) *yajñārthāṭ* (m◦ 5abl◦ sing◦ ←tatpu◦ *yajñārtha*, यज्ञस्य अर्थः ←m◦ 🕮***yajña*** ←1◦√यज् + m◦ *artha* 1.7); *karmaṇaḥ:* (3.1); *anyatra* (place or time indicating ind◦ ←4◦√अन्); 🕮***lokaḥ:*** (1nom◦ sing◦ ←m◦ *loka* 2.5); *ayaṃ* (2.19); *karmabandhanaḥ:* (m◦ 1nom◦ sing◦ ←bahuvrī◦ ***karma-bandhana***, कर्म बन्धनम् यस्य सः ←n◦ *karmaṇ* 1.15 + n◦ *bandhana* (bondage) ←1◦√बन्ध्); 🕮*tadarthaṃ* (m◦ 2acc◦ sing◦ ←tatpu◦ *tadartha*, (thus) तस्य

---

[287] Elsewhere◦ कर्म → action.

🕮 see footnote in verse 2.47

[288] See footnote in verse 3.5

[289] Elsewhere◦ अकर्मणः → to inaction, than inaction, ...etc.

🕮 अकर्म is not 'inaction.' There is no such thing as 'inaction.' Inaction is also an 'action' of doing a thing which appears like 'doing nothing.' For details please see footmote in verse 6.1.

[290] Elsewhere◦ शरीरयात्रा → maintainance of ones physical body, maintainance of the body, maintainance of your body, preservation of ones. body ...etc.

अर्थ: ←*tat* 1.10 + m∘ *artha* 1.7); *karma* (3.8); *kaunteya* (2.14); 📖*muktasaṅgaḥ:* (m∘ 1nom∘ sing∘ ←bahuvrī∘ **mukta-saṅga**, (detached) मुक्त: सङ्गात् य: ←adj∘ 📖**mukta** (free) ←6∘√मुच् + m∘ *saṅga* (attachment) 2.47); 📖**samācara** (2nd-per∘ sing∘ imperative∘ उपदेशार्थ-लोट् parasmai∘ ←1∘सम्-आ√चर्) **(3.9)**

(§3) *yajñārthāt* (from the point of view of sacrifice, for the sake of relinquishment, for the sake of austerity); *karmaṇaḥ:* (from the karma); *anyatra* (aside from, other than, except when); *lokaḥ:* (subj1∘ world); *ayam* (adj∘-subj1∘ this); *karmabandhanaḥ:* (adj2∘-subj1∘ that which is bound by *karma*); *tadartham* (for that reason, therefore); *karma* (obj∘ karma); *kaunteya* (O Kaunteya! O Arjuna!); *muktasaṅgaḥ:* (adj∘-subj2∘ freed from the bondage of); *samācara* (you please act! perform! accomplish!) **(3.9)**

(§4) ayam lokaḥ: karmabandhanaḥ: anyatra yajñārthāt kaunteya tadartham samācara karma muktasaṅgaḥ: karmaṇaḥ:

(§5) This world is bound by *karma*,[291] except when performed for the sake of austerity. O Arjuna!, therefore,[292] you please perform *karma*, freed from the bondage of the *karma*. **(3.9)**

3.10 सहयज्ञा: प्रजा: सृष्ट्वा पुरोवाच प्रजापति: ।
अनेन प्रसविष्यध्वमेष वोऽस्त्विष्टकामधुक् ।।

sahayajñāḥ: prajāḥ: sṛṣṭvā purovāca prajāpatiḥ:,
anena prasaviṣyadhvameṣa vo'stviṣṭakāmadhuk. **(3.10)**

(§1) सहयज्ञा: प्रजा: सृष्ट्वा पुरा उवाच प्रजापति: । अनेन प्रसविष्यध्वम् एष: व: अस्तु इष्टकामधुक् । *sahayajñāḥ:* (r∘ 22/3) *prajāḥ:* (r∘ 22/7) *sṛṣṭvā purā* (r∘ 2/4) *uvāca prajāpatiḥ:* (r∘ 22/8) *anena prasaviṣyadhvam* (r∘ 8/22) *eṣa* (r∘ 25/1, 21/1) *vaḥ:* (r∘ 15/1) *astu* (r∘ 4/8) *iṣṭakāmadhuk*

(§2) *sahayajñāḥ:* (m∘ 1nom∘ plu∘ ←s-sbahuvrī∘ *saha-yajña*, यज्ञेन सह ←m∘ *yajña* 3.9 + adj∘ *saha* (together with) 1.22); **prajāḥ:** (2acc∘ plu∘ ←f∘ 📖*prajā* (subjects) ←4∘प्र√जन्); 📖*sṛṣṭvā* (ipp∘ ind∘ ←1∘√सृ); *purā* (3.3); *uvāca* (1.25); **prajāpatiḥ:** (m∘ 1nom∘ sing∘ ←bahuvrī∘ *prajā-pati* (creator of subjects) प्रजाया: पति: य: ←f∘ *prajā* ↑ + m∘ *pati* 1.18); *anena* (m∘ 3inst∘ sing∘ ←pron∘ *idam* 1.10); *prasaviṣyadhvam* (2nd-per∘ plu∘ -conditional∘ ātmane∘ ←5∘प्र√सू); *eṣa* (m∘ 1nom∘ sing∘ ←pron∘ *etad* 1.3); *vaḥ:* (6pos plu∘ ←pron∘ *yuṣmad*

---

[291] Elsewhere∘ लोक: अयम् कर्मबन्धन: → causes bondage, are causes of human bondage, man is bound by his actions, this man becomes bound by actions, all those actions bind a person ...etc.

📖 *karmabandhanaḥ* is not a verb. It is Nominative case m∘ adjective of m∘ noun लोक:, same as the m∘ pronoun अयम् (अयं लोक: this world), NOT this man, or this person, but this world.

[292] See the footnote in verse 2.15

1.3); *astu* (2.47); *iṣṭakāmadhuk* (f∘ 1nom∘ sing∘ ←bahuvrī∘ *iṣṭa-kāmadhuk*, इष्टान् कामान् दोग्धि या ←ppp∘ adj∘ 📖**iṣṭa** ←1∘√इष् + m∘ *kāma* 1.22 + 3rd-per∘ sing∘ pres∘ वर्तमान्-लट् parasmai∘ *dogdhi* ←2∘√दुह्) (3.10)

(§3) *sahayajñāḥ:* (with yajñās); *prajāḥ:* (obj∘ the progenies, families of beings); *sṛṣṭvā* (having produced, having evolved); *purā* (at olden time); *uvāća* (said); *prajāpatiḥ:* (subj∘ Lord of the beings, Lord Bahmā); *anena* (with this); *prasaviṣyadhvam* (may you prosper); *vaḥ:* (your); *astu* (may it be); *iṣṭakāmadhuk* (wish-granter, wish-fulfiller) (3.10)

(§4) sṛṣṭvā prajāḥ: sahayajñāḥ: prajāpatiḥ: uvāća anena prasaviṣyadhvam astu vaḥ: iṣṭakāmadhuk

(§5) Having evolved the progenies beings with *yajñās*, Lord Bahmā said, "with this may you prosper (and) may it be your wish-granter." (3.10)

3.11 देवान्भावयतानेन ते देवा भावयन्तु वः ।
परस्परं भावयन्तः श्रेयः परमवाप्स्यथ ॥

devānbhāvayatānena te devā bhāvayantu vaḥ:,
parasparaṁ bhāvayantaḥ: śreyaḥ: paramavāpsyatha. (3.11)

(§1) देवान् भावयत अनेन ते देवाः भावयन्तु वः । परस्परम् भावयन्तः श्रेयः परम् अवाप्स्यथ । *devān* (r∘ 13/15) *bhāvayata* (r∘ 1/1) *anena te devāḥ:* (r∘ 20/12) *bhāvayantu vaḥ:* (r∘ 22/8) *parasparam* (r∘ 14/1) *bhāvayantaḥ:* (r∘ 22/5) *śreyaḥ:* (r∘ 22/3) *param* (r∘ 8/16) *avāpsyatha*

(§2) 📖***devān*** (2acc∘ plu∘ ←adj∘ or m∘ ***deva*** (god) ←4∘√दिव्); 📖*bhāvayata* (2nd-per∘ plu∘ imperative∘ उपदेशार्थ-लोट् parasmai∘ caus∘ ←1∘√भू); *anena* (3.10); *te* (1.33); ***devāḥ:*** (1nom∘ plu∘ ←m∘ *deva* ↑); 📖*bhāvayantu* (3rd-per∘ plu∘ imperative∘ सद्भावार्थ-लोट् parasmai∘ caus∘ ←1∘√भू); ***vaḥ:*** (2acc∘ plu∘ ←pron∘ *yuṣmad* 1.3); 📖***parasparam*** (2acc∘ sing∘ ←adj∘ ***paraspara*** = *paraḥ: paraḥ:* (mutual) ←m∘ 1nom∘ sing∘ ←adj∘ *para* 2.3); *bhāvayantaḥ:* (1nom∘ plu∘ ←śatṛ∘ adj∘ *bhāvayat* 2.66); *śreyaḥ:* (2acc∘ 1.31); *param* (2acc∘ 2.59); *avāpsyatha* (2nd-per∘ plu∘ fut2∘ लृट् भविष्य∘ parasmai∘ ←5∘अव√आप्) (3.11)

(§3) *devān* (obj1∘ the deities); *bhāvayata* (may you foster, may you cherish, may you please); *anena* (with this, with this *yajña*); *te* (adj∘-subj∘ those); *devāḥ:* (subj∘ deities); *bhāvayantu* (may they foster); *vaḥ:* (obj2∘ you); *parasparam* (obj3∘ one another, each other); *bhāvayantaḥ:* (while fostering); *śreyaḥ:* (obj3∘ welfare); *param* (adj∘-obj4∘ supreme); *avāpsyatha* (you shall attain) (3.11)

(§4) anena bhāvayata devān te devāḥ: bhāvayantu vaḥ: bhāvayantaḥ: parasparam avāpsyatha param śreyaḥ:

(§5) **With this, may you cherish[293] the deities (and) those deities may foster you; while fostering[294] each other, you shall attain[295] supreme welfare.** (3.11)

3.12 **इष्टान्भोगान्हि वो देवा दास्यन्ते यज्ञभाविताः ।**
तैर्दत्तानप्रदायैभ्यो यो भुङ्क्ते स्तेन एव सः ।।
iṣṭānbhogānhi vo devā dāsyante yajñabhāvitāḥ:,
tairdattānapradāyaibhyo yo bhuṅkte stena eva saḥ:. (3.12)

(§1) इष्टान् भोगान् हि वः देवाः दास्यन्ते यज्ञभाविताः । तैः दत्तान् अप्रदाय एभ्यः यः भुङ्क्ते स्तेनः एव सः । *iṣṭān* (r∘ 13/15) *bhogān* (r∘ 13/21) *hi vaḥ:* (r∘ 15/4) *devāḥ:* (r∘ 20/8) *dāsyante yajñabhāvitāḥ:* (r∘ 22/8) *taiḥ:* (r∘ 16/11) *dattān* (r∘ 8/11) *apradāya* (r∘ 3/1) *ebhyaḥ:* (r∘ 15/10) *yaḥ:* (r∘ 15/8) *bhuṅkte stenaḥ:* (r∘ 19/7) *eva saḥ:* (r∘ 22/8)

(§2) 🕮***iṣṭān*** (m∘ 2acc∘ plu∘ ←adj∘ *iṣṭa* (desired) 3.10); *bhogān* (2.5); *hi* (1.11); *vaḥ:* (3.11); *devāḥ:* (3.11); *dāsyante* (3rd-per∘ plu∘ fut2∘ लृट् भविष्य∘ ātmane∘ ←3∘√दा); *yajñabhāvitāḥ:* (1nom∘ plu∘ ←tatpu∘ *yajña-bhāvita*, यज्ञेन भावितः ←m∘ *yajña* 3.9 + ppp∘ caus∘-adj∘ 🕮***bhāvita*** ←1∘√भू); ***taiḥ:*** (m∘ or n∘ 3inst∘ plu∘ ←pron∘ *tad* 1.2); *dattān* (m∘ 2acc∘ plu∘ ←ppp∘ adj∘ ***datta*** (given) ←3∘√दा); *apradāya* (lyp∘ past-participle ind∘ ←3∘अ-प्र√दा); ***ebhyaḥ:*** (m∘ or n∘ 4dat∘ plu∘ ←pron∘ *idam* 1.10); *yaḥ:* (2.19); ***bhuṅkte*** (3rd-per∘ sing∘ pres∘ वर्तमान्-लट् ātmane∘ ←7∘√भुज्); 🕮*stenaḥ:* (1nom∘ sing∘ ←m∘ *stena* (thief) ←10∘√स्तेन्); *eva* (1.1); *saḥ:* (1.13) (3.12)

(§3) *iṣṭān* (adj∘-obj∘ desired); *bhogān* (obj1∘ wishes, pleasures); *hi* (because); *vaḥ:* (to you); *devāḥ:* (subj1∘ the deities); *dāsyante* (they will give, fulfill); *yajñabhāvitāḥ:* (pleased with *yajña*s); *taiḥ:* (by them); *dattān* (obj2∘ given); *apradāya* (without offering it); *ebhyaḥ:* (to them); *yaḥ:* (adj1∘-subj2∘ he who, who); *bhuṅkte* (consumes); *stenaḥ:* (adj2∘-subj2∘ a thief); *eva* (only); *saḥ:* (subj2∘ he) (3.12)

(§4) hi devāḥ: yajñabhāvitāḥ: dāsyante vaḥ: iṣṭān bhogān yaḥ: bhuṅkte dattān taiḥ: apradāya ebhyaḥ: saḥ: eve stenaḥ:

---

[293] Elsewhere∘ भावयत → entertain, multiply, nourish...etc.

[294] Elsewhere∘ भावयन्तः → by fostering, by co-operation, as a result of entertainment ...etc.

[295] Elsewhere∘ श्रेयः परम् अवाप्स्यथ → prosperity will reigh for all, may you attain the supreme good ...etc.

🕮 The subject of this clause (श्रेयः परम् अवाप्स्यथ) is 'you' plural. श्रेयः is not the subject. श्रेयः is not in Nominative 1st case. Here श्रेयः is the object in Accusative 2nd case singular. Also, अवाप्स्यथ is a लृट् future tense verb. It is not potential mood. Potential mood is आप्नुयात ।

(§5) Because,[296] the deities pleased with the *yajñas,*[297] will give you desired wishes. He who consumes (all) given by them, without offering it to them, (is) only a thief.
(3.12)

3.13 यज्ञशिष्टाशिनः सन्तो मुच्यन्ते सर्वकिल्बिषैः ।
भुञ्जते ते त्वघं पापा ये पचन्त्यात्मकारणात् ।।
yajñaśiṣṭāśinaḥ: santo mućyante sarvakilbiṣaiḥ:,
bhuñjate te tvaghaṁ pāpā ye paćantyātmakāraṇāṭ. (3.13)

(§1) यज्ञशिष्टाशिनः सन्तः मुच्यन्ते सर्वकिल्बिषैः । भुञ्जते ते तु अघम् पापाः ये पचन्ति आत्मकारणात् । *yajñaśiṣṭāśinaḥ:* (r◦ 22/7) *santaḥ:* (r◦ 15/9) *mućyante sarvakilbiṣaiḥ:* (r◦ 22/8) *bhuñjate te tu* (r◦ 4/6) *agham* (r◦ 14/1) *pāpāḥ:* (r◦ 20/14) *ye paćanti* (r◦ 4/2) *ātmakāraṇāṭ*

(§2) *yajñaśiṣṭāśinaḥ:* (m◦ 1nom◦ plu◦ ←bahuvrī◦ *yajña-śiṣṭāśin*, यज्ञस्य शिष्टम् अश्नाति यः ←m◦ *yajña* 3.9 + ppp◦ adj◦ ***śiṣṭa*** (leftover) ←7◦√शिष् + adj◦ ***āśin*** (consumer) ←m◦ *āśa* ←9◦√अश्); 🕮*santaḥ:* (a rightwous person 1nom◦ plu◦ ←m◦ śatṛ◦ adj◦ *sat* ←2◦√अस्, 1◦√सन्); 🕮***mućyante*** (3rd-per◦ plu◦ pres◦ वर्तमान्-लट् ātmane◦ ←6◦√मुच्); *sarvaiḥ:* (15.15); *kilbiṣaiḥ:* (3inst◦ plu◦ ←n◦ ***kilbiṣa*** (sin) ←6◦√किल्); *bhuñjate* (3rd-per◦ plu◦ pres◦ वर्तमान्-लट् ātmane◦ ←7◦√भुज्); *te* (1.33); *tu* (1.2); 🕮*agham* (2acc◦ sing◦ ←n◦ *agha* (sin) 3.3); 🕮*pāpāḥ:* (1nom◦ plu◦ ←m◦ *pāpa* (sin) 1.36); *ye* (1.7); *paćanti* (3rd-per◦ plu◦ pres◦ वर्तमान्-लट् parasmai◦ ←1◦√पच्); 🕮*ātmakāraṇāṭ* (n◦ 5abl◦ sing◦ ←tatpu◦ *ātma-kāraṇa*, आत्मनः कारणम् ←m◦ *ātman* (self) 2.41 + n◦ ***karaṇa*** (purpose) ←8◦√कृ) (3.13)

(§3) *yajñaśiṣṭāśinaḥ:* (adj◦-subj1◦ those who partake of the remainder of the yajña); *santaḥ:* (subj1◦ righteous, virtuous, *sattvic* -people); *mućyante* (they are freed, liberated, released); *sarvaiḥ:* (from all); *kilbiṣaiḥ:* (from sins); *bhuñjate* (they incur, they earn); *tu* (but); *agham* (obj◦ sin); *pāpāḥ:* (subj2◦ the evil ones, the sinners); *ye* (adj◦-subj2◦ those who); *paćanti* (they cook); *ātmakāraṇāṭ* (for their own sake) (3.13)

(§4) yajñaśiṣṭāśinaḥ: santaḥ: mućyante sarvaiḥ: kilbiṣaiḥ: tu ye pāpāḥ: paćanti ātmakāraṇāṭ bhuñjate agham

(§5) Those righteous people who partake of the remainder of the *yajña,*[298] they are freed from all

---

[296] See footnote in verse 3.5

[297] Elsewhere◦ यज्ञभाविताः देवाः → the gods brought into being by sacrifice, being nourished, being entertained by the sacrifices ...etc.

[298] Elsewhere◦ *yajñaśiṣṭāśinaḥ:* → by becoming partakers of, because they eat, ... etc.

🕮 अशिनः is adjective of सन्ताः ।

sins; but those evil ones, who cook for their own sake, they incur sin.[299] (3.13)

3.14 अन्नाद्भवन्ति भूतानि पर्जन्यादन्नसम्भवः ।
यज्ञाद्भवति पर्जन्यो यज्ञः कर्मसमुद्भवः ।।

annādbhavanti bhūtāni parjanyādannasambhavaḥ:,
yajñādbhavati parjanyo yajñaḥ: karmasamudbhavaḥ:; (3.14)

(§1) अन्नात् भवन्ति भूतानि पर्जन्यात् अन्नसम्भवः । यज्ञात् भवति पर्जन्यः यज्ञः कर्मसमुद्भवः । *annāt* (r◦ 9/8) *bhavanti bhūtāni parjanyāt* (r◦ 8/2) *annasambhavaḥ:* (r◦ 22/8) *yajñāt* (r◦ 9/8) *bhavati parjanyaḥ:* (r◦ 15/10) *yajñaḥ:* (r◦ 22/1) *karmasamudbhavaḥ:* (r◦ 22/8)

(§2) *annāt* (5abl◦ sing◦ ←n◦ 🕮**anna** (food) ←2◦√अद्); ***bhavanti*** (3rd-per◦ plu◦ pres◦ वर्तमान्-लट् parasmai◦ ←1◦√भू); 🕮*bhūtāni* (2.28); *parjanyāt* (5abl◦ sing◦ ←m◦ ***parjanya*** (rain) ←1◦√पृष्); *annasambhavaḥ:* (m◦ 1nom◦ sing◦ ←tatpu◦ *anna-sambhava*, अन्नस्य सम्भवः ←n◦ *anna* 3.14 + m◦ 🕮***sambhava*** (rise) ←1◦सम्√भू); ***yajñāt*** (5abl◦ sing◦ ←m◦ 🕮*yajña* 3.9); *bhavati* (1.44); 🕮*parjanyaḥ:* (1nom◦ sing◦ ←m◦ *parjanya* ↑); ***yajñaḥ:*** (1nom◦ sing◦ ←m◦ *yajña* 3.9); *karmasamudbhavaḥ:* (m◦ 1nom◦ sing◦ ←bahuvrī◦ *karma-samudbhava*, कर्मणः समुद्भवः यस्य ←n◦ *karman* 1.15 + m◦ 🕮***samudbhava*** (coming forth) ←1◦सम्-उद्√भू)

(§3) *annāt* (from the basic five elements महाभूतानि and the three *guṇas* गुणाः); *bhavanti* (they come to be); *bhūtāni* (subj1◦ the beings living and non-living भूतानि); *parjanyāt* (from the shower of the nature सृष्टेः वृष्ट्याः); *annasambhavaḥ:* (subj2◦ the rise of elements and *Guṇas*); *yajñāt* (from *yajña*, the *prakṛti*, सृष्टिः); *bhavati* (comes to be); *parjanyaḥ:* (subj3◦ the *shower of elements* सृष्टैः वृष्टिः); *yajñaḥ:* (subj4◦ *yajña*); *karmasamudbhavaḥ:* (adj◦-subj4◦ comes from *karma* कर्म, यज्ञकर्म, सृजनकर्म, ब्रह्मणः सृजनकर्म) (3.14)

(§4) annāt bhūtāni bhavanti parjanyāt annasambhavaḥ: yajñāt parjanyaḥ: bhavati yajñaḥ: karmasamudbhavaḥ:

(§5) From the (i) basic five elements (पञ्चभूतानि) and the three *guṇas* (गुणत्रयम्)[300] the beings (living

---

[299] Elsewhere◦ अघं भुञ्जते → they eat sin, they are the consumers of sin, eat their own impurity ... etc.

[300] Elsewhere◦ अन्नात् भवन्ति भूतानि → living beings subsist on food (locative), the beings live on food, beings are evolved from food (ppp◦), ... etc.

🕮 Three things to remember : (i) अन्नात् is Ablative (5th) case, It is not Locative (7th) case, (ii) The verb is भवन्ति । The verb is not जीवन्ति, उपजीवन्ति , अनुजीवन्ति or अवलम्बन्ति । and (iii) भूतानि does not mean only the living beings, but it includes liveing as well as non-living beings. भूतानि means all beings.

and non-living (भूतानि) come to be;[301] from (ii) the shower of the nature (सृष्टेर्वृष्ट्याः), the rise of the elements and *Guṇas* (पञ्चभूतानि च गुणाः); (iii) from *yajña* (सृष्टिः) the shower of the nature (सृष्टैः वृष्टिः) (iv) *yajña* (सृष्टिः) comes to be from *karma* (ब्रह्मणः सृजनकर्मणः); (3.14)

3.15 कर्म ब्रह्मोद्भवं विद्धि ब्रह्माक्षरसमुद्भवम् ।
तस्मात्सर्वगतं ब्रह्म नित्यं यज्ञे प्रतिष्ठितम् ।।
karma brahmodbhavaṁ viddhi brahmākṣarasamudbhavaṃ,
tasmātsarvagataṁ brahma nityaṁ yajñe pratiṣṭhitaṃ. (3.15)

(§1) कर्म ब्रह्मोद्भवम् विद्धि ब्रह्म अक्षरसमुद्भवम् । तस्मात् सर्वगतम् ब्रह्म नित्यम् यज्ञे प्रतिष्ठितम् । *karma brahmodbhavaṃ* (r∘ 14/1) *viddhi brahma* (r∘ 1/1) *akṣarasamudbhavaṃ* (r∘ 14/2) *tasmāt̩* (r∘ 10/7) *sarvagataṃ* (r∘ 14/1) *brahma nityaṃ* (r∘ 14/1) *yajñe pratiṣṭhitaṃ* (r∘ 14/2)

(§2) *karma* (*sṛjana-karma* 2acc∘ 3.8); *brahmodbhavaṃ* (n∘ 2acc∘ sing∘ ←bahuvrī∘ *brahmodbhava*, ब्रह्मणः उद्भवः यस्य ←n∘ *brahman* 2.72 + m∘ 🕮**udbhava** (coming forth) ←1∘उद्√भू); *viddhi* (2.17); **brahma** (2acc∘ sing∘ ←n∘ *brahman* 2.72); *akṣarasamudbhavaṃ* (n∘ 2acc∘ sing∘ ←bahuvrī∘ *akṣara-samudbhava*, अक्षरात् समुद्भवः यस्य ←n.tatpu∘ adj∘ or n∘ 🕮**akṣara** (eternal) यत् न क्षरति न क्षीयते वा ←1अ√क्षर् + m∘ *samudbhava* 3.14); *tasmāt̩* (1.37); 🕮***sarvagataṃ*** (n∘ 1nom∘ sing∘ ←ppp∘ adj∘ *sarvagata* (all-pervading) 2.24); *brahma* (1nom∘ ↑); *nityaṃ* (2.21); ***yajñe*** (7loc∘ sing∘ ←m∘ *yajña* 3.9); 🕮*pratiṣṭhitaṃ* (n∘ 1nom∘ sing∘ ←adj∘ *pratiṣṭhitaṃ* 2.57) (3.15)

(§3) *karma* (obj1∘ *karma* कर्म, यज्ञकर्म, सृजनकर्म); *brahmodbhavaṃ* (adj∘-obj1∘ arising from natural laws, the all-pervading natural laws, the *brahma* ब्रह्म, वेदः, सृष्टेः नियमाः); *viddhi* (you please know - to be!); *brahma* (obj2∘ the veda, the natural laws); *akṣarasamudbhavaṃ* (adj∘-obj2∘ emanated from the the eternal Brahmā, ब्रह्मा); *tasmāt̩* (therefore); *sarvagataṃ* (adj1∘-subj∘ the omnipresent natural laws); *brahma* (subj∘ brahma); *nityaṃ* (eternally); *yajñe* (in yajña, सृष्टौ, सृष्ट्याम्); *pratiṣṭhitaṃ* (adj2∘-subj∘ established) (3.15)

(§4) karma brahmodbhavaṃ viddhi brahma akṣarasamudbhavaṃ tasmāt̩ sarvagataṃ brahma nityaṃ pratiṣṭhitaṃ yajñe.

(§5) You please know (v) *karma* (सृजनकर्म) to be arising from *brahma* (ब्रह्माणः),[302] and (vi) the *veda*

---

[301] Elsewhere∘ अन्नात् भवन्ति → beings are evolved from food (ppp∘), ... etc.

[302] Elsewhere∘ ब्रह्म → in संकृत ब्रह्म in English brahman

(सृष्टेः नियमाः) to be from the eternal Brahmā.[303] Therefore,[304] (vii) the omnipresent natural laws (सर्वगताः सृष्टेः नियमाः) are eternally present in the *yajña* (सृष्टिः).

(3.15)

3.16 एवं प्रवर्तितं चक्रं नानुवर्तयतीह यः ।
अघायुरिन्द्रियारामो मोघं पार्थ स जीवति ।।
evam̦ pravartitam̦ ćakramț nānuvartayatīha yaḥ:,
aghāyurindriyārāmo mogham̦ pārtha sa jīvati. (3.16)

(§1) एवम् प्रवर्तितम् चक्रम् न अनुवर्तयति इह यः । अघायुः इन्द्रियारामः मोघम् पार्थ स जीवति । *evam̦* (r◦ 14/1) *pravartitam̦* (r◦ 14/1) *ćakram̦* (r◦ 14/1) *na* (r◦ 1/1) *anuvartayati* (r◦ 1/5) *iha yaḥ:* (r◦ 22/8) *aghāyuḥ:* (r◦ 16/3) *indriyārāmaḥ:* (r◦ 15/9) *mogham̦* (r◦ 14/1) *pārtha saḥ:* (r◦ 21/2) *jīvati*

(§2) *evam̦* (1.24); 🕮*pravartitam̦* (n◦ 2acc◦ sing◦ ←ppp◦ adj◦ caus◦*pravartita* (set in motion) ←4◦प्र√वृत्); *ćakram̦* (2acc◦ sing◦ ←n◦ ***ćakra*** (wheal) ←8◦√कृ); *na* (1.30); *anuvartayati* (3rd-per◦ sing◦ pres◦ वर्तमान्-लट् parasmai◦ caus◦ ←4◦अनु√वृत्); *iha* (2.5); *yaḥ:* (2.19); 🕮*aghāyuḥ:* (m◦ 1nom◦ sing◦ ←bahuvrī◦ *aghāyu*, अघम् आयुः यस्य ←n◦ *agha* (sin) 3.3 + n◦ ***āyu*** or ***āyuș*** (life) ←2◦आ√इण्); *indriyārāmaḥ:* (m◦ 1nom◦ sing◦ ←bahuvrī◦ *indriyārāma*, इद्रियेषु आरामः यस्य ←n◦ *indriya* 2.8 + m◦ ***ārāma*** (indulgence) ←1◦आ√रम्); 🕮*mogham̦* (adv◦ ind◦ or 2acc◦ sing◦ ←adj◦ ***mogha*** (futile) ←4◦√मुह्); *pārtha* (1.25); *saḥ:* (1.13); *jīvati* (3rd-per◦ sing◦ pres◦ वर्तमान्-लट् parasmai◦ ←1◦√जीव्) (3.16)

(§3) *evam̦* (in this manner); *pravartitam̦* (adj◦-obj◦ set in motion); *ćakram̦* (obj◦ the wheel); *na* (does not); *anuvartayati* (he causes to be adopted); *iha* (here, in this world); *yaḥ:* (adj1◦-subj◦ he who); *aghāyuḥ:* (adj2◦-subj◦ he whose life is sinful, the sinful person); *indriyārāmaḥ:* (adj3◦-subj◦ who is indulgent of senses, the indulgent person); *mogham̦* (in vain); *pārtha* (O Pārtha! O Arjuna!); *saḥ:* (subj◦ he, that person); *jīvati* (lives) (3.16)

(§4) yaḥ: na anuvartayati ćakram̦ pravartitam̦ evam̦ iha pārtha saḥ: aghāyuḥ: indriyārāmaḥ: jīvati mogham̦

(§5) He who does not cause to be adopted[305] the wheel (of nature) set in motion,[306] in this

---

[303] Elsewhere◦ ब्रह्माक्षरसमुद्भवम् → brahma risen from the Imperishable Brahman, Brahman comes from the Imperishable, Brahma springs from the Imperishable, Brahman originates from the Imperishable ...etc.

[304] See the footnote in verse 2.15

[305] Elsewhere◦ *na anuvartayati* → who does not help to turn, who does not cause to turn, ...etc.

🕮 (i) अनुवर्तयति is a causative verb, it means the subject is not doing the action but the action is caused to

manner in this world, O Arjuna! that sinful (and) indulgent person lives in vain. (3.16)

3.17 यस्त्वात्मरतिरेव स्यादात्मतृप्तश्च मानवः ।
आत्मन्येव च सन्तुष्टस्तस्य कार्यं न विद्यते ।।

yastvātmaratireva syādātmatṛptaśća mānavaḥ:,
ātmanyeva ća santuṣṭastasya kāryaṁ na vidyate. (3.17)

(§1) यः तु आत्मरतिः एव स्यात् आत्मतृप्तः च मानवः । आत्मनि एव च सन्तुष्टः तस्य कार्यम् न विद्यते । *yaḥ:* (r◦ 18/1) *tu* (r◦ 4/6) *ātmaratiḥ:* (r◦ 16/1) *eva syāt* (r◦ 8/3) *ātmatṛptaḥ:* (r◦ 17/1) *ća mānavaḥ:* (r◦ 22/8) *ātmani* (r◦ 4/4) *eva ća santuṣṭaḥ:* (r◦ 18/1) *tasya kāryam* (r◦ 14/1) *na vidyate*

(§2) *yaḥ:* (2.19); *tu* (1.2); 🕮*ātmaratiḥ:* (m◦ 1nom◦ sing◦ ←bahuvrī◦ *ātma-rati*, आत्मनि रतिः यस्य ।←m◦ *ātman* 2.41 + f◦ ***rati*** ←adj◦ *rata* (enjoyer) 2.42); *eva* (1.1); *syāt* (1.36); 🕮*ātmatṛptaḥ:* (m◦ 1nom◦ sing◦ ←bahuvrī◦ *ātma-tṛpta*, आत्मनि तृप्तः यः ।←m◦ *ātman* 2.41 + ppp◦ adj◦ 🕮***tṛpta*** (contented) ←4◦√तृष्); *ća* (1.1); 🕮***mānavaḥ:*** (m◦ 1nom◦ sing◦ ←taddhita◦ ***mānava*** (person) मनोः अपत्यम् ←4◦√मन्); *ātmani* (2.55); *eva* (1.1); *ća* (1.1); 🕮***santuṣṭaḥ:*** (m◦ 1nom◦ sing◦ ←ppp◦ adj◦ ***santuṣṭa*** (contented) ←4◦सम्√तुष् 2.55); *tasya* (1.12); ***kāryam*** (n◦ 1nom◦ sing◦ ←n◦ or pot◦ adj◦ ***kārya*** (duty) ←8◦√कृ); *na* (1.30); *vidyate* (2.16) (3.17)

(§3) *yaḥ:* (adj1◦-subj1◦ he who); *tu* (and); *ātmaratiḥ:* (adj2◦-subj1◦ he who is joyful in himself); *eva* (only); *syāt* (he may be); *ātmatṛptaḥ:* (adj3◦-subj1◦ contented in himself); *ća* (and); *mānavaḥ:* (subj1◦ the person); *ātmani* (in himself); *eva* (only); *ća* (and); *santuṣṭaḥ:* (adj4◦-subj1◦ satisfied); *tasya* (for him); *kāryam* (Pot. adj◦-sub2◦ ought to be done, to be done, duty); *na* (subj2◦ nothing); *vidyate* (exists, remains)

(§4) tu yaḥ: syāt ātmaratiḥ: eva ātmatṛptaḥ: ća mānavaḥ: ātmani eva ća santuṣṭaḥ: tasya kāryam na vidyate

(§5) And, the person who may be[307] joyful in himself only, (and) contented[308] in himself only, and

---

happen through the subject. (ii) The wheel is already set in motion (ppp◦ प्रवर्तितम्) by the law of nature, the subject is not causing, aiding or helping it to turn. It turns even without the help or aid by the subject, it will not stop without his help or conforming. He can not stop it either. What the subject can do is to adpot, follow or conform to the law of nature that is turning the wheel or that set the wheel in motion.

[306] Elsewhere◦ प्रवर्तितम् → revolving

🕮 प्रवर्तित is a ppp◦ = set. But, "revolving" is gerund or Present Continuous Tense.

[307] Elsewhere◦ *syāt* → remains, is ...etc.

[308] Elsewhere◦ आत्मतृप्तः → self-illuminated, self-realization, whose satisfaction is in ...etc.

satisfied in himself only, for him nothing remains to be done.

(3.17)

3.18 नैव तस्य कृतेनार्थो नाकृतेनेह कश्चन ।

न चास्य सर्वभूतेषु कश्चिदर्थव्यपाश्रयः ।।

naiva tasya kṛtenārtho nākṛteneha kaśćana,

na ćāsya sarvebhūteṣu kaśćidarthavyapāśrayaḥ:. (3.18)

(§1) न एव तस्य कृतेन अर्थः न अकृतेन इह कश्चन । न च अस्य सर्वभूतेषु कश्चित् अर्थव्यपाश्रयः । *na* (r◦ 3/1) *eva tasya kṛtena* (r◦ 1/1) *arthaḥ:* (r◦ 15/6) *na* (r◦ 1/1) *akṛtena* (r◦ 2/1) *iha kaśćana na ća* (r◦ 1/1) *asya sarvabhūteṣu* (r◦ 25/5) *kaśćiṭ* (r◦ 8/2) *arthavyapāśrayaḥ:* (r◦ 22/8)

(§2) *na* (1.30); *eva* (1.1); *tasya* (1.12); *kṛtena* (n◦ 3inst◦ sing◦ ←adj◦ *kṛta* 1.35); *arthaḥ:* (2.46); *na* (1.30); *akṛtena* (n◦ 3inst◦ sing◦ ←n.tatpu◦ ppp◦ adj◦ ***a-kṛta*** (not-done) ←adj◦ *kṛta* 1.35); *iha* (2.5); ***kaśćana*** (pron◦ *kiṃ* 1.1 + indeclinable affix *ćana* 2.47); *na* (1.30); *ća* (1.1); *asya* (2.17); ***sarvabhūteṣu*** (सर्वेषु भूतेषु 7loc◦ plu◦ ←pron◦ *sarva* 1.6 + n◦ *bhūta* (being) 2.28); *kaśćiṭ* (2.17); *arthavyapāśrayaḥ:* (m◦ 1nom◦ sing◦ ←bahuvrī◦ *artha-vyapāśraya*, अर्थः व्यपाश्रयः यस्य ←m◦ *artha* 1.7 + m◦ ***vyapāśraya*** (dependence) ←1◦वि–अप्–आ√श्रि) (3.18)

(§3) *na eva* (there is no); *tasya* (his, for him); *kṛtena* (by doing); *arthaḥ:* (subj◦ purpose); *na* (not); *akṛtena* (by not doing); *iha* (here, in this world); *kaśćana* (anyone, anything); *na* (not, nor); *ća* (and); *asya* (of it, of him, for him); *sarvabhūteṣu* (in all beings, in any of the beings); *kaśćiṭ* (any); *arthavyapāśrayaḥ:* (subj◦ self-serving objective, dependence that serves self-purpose) (3.18)

(§4) tasya na eva arthaḥ: kṛtena na akṛtena kaśćana iha ća na asya kaśćiṭ arthavyapāśrayaḥ: sarvabhūteṣu

(§5) For him there is no purpose (fulfilled) by doing not by ot doing anything in this world; nor for him (there is) any self-serving objective in any of the beings. (3.18)

3.19 तस्मादसक्तः सततं कार्यं कर्म समाचर ।

असक्तो ह्याचरन्कर्म परमाप्नोति पूरुषः ।।

tasmādasaktaḥ: satataṁ kāryaṁ karma samāćara,

asakto hyāćarankarma paramāpnoti pūruṣaḥ:. (3.19)

(§1) तस्मात् असक्तः सततम् कार्यम् कर्म समाचर । असक्तः हि आचरन् कर्म परम् आप्नोति पूरुषः । *tasmāṭ* (r◦ 8/2) *asaktaḥ:* (r◦ 22/7) *satataṃ* (r◦ 14/1) *kāryaṃ* (r◦ 14/1) *karma samāćara* (r◦ 23/1) *asaktaḥ:* (r◦ 15/14) *hi* (r◦ 4/2) *āćaraṇ* (r◦ 13/9) *karma paraṃ* (r◦ 8/17) *āpnoti puruṣaḥ:* (r◦ 22/8)

(§2) *tasmāt* (1.37); *asaktaḥ:* (3.7); 🕮***satatam*** (adv◦ ind◦ ←adj◦ ***satata*** (always) ←8◦सम्√तन्); *kāryam* (n◦ 2acc◦ sing◦ ←adj◦ *kārya* (duty) 3.17); *karma* (3.8); *samāćara* (3.9); *asaktaḥ:* (3.7); *hi* (1.11); *āćaran* (m◦ 1nom◦ sing◦ ←śatṛ◦ adj◦ ***āćarat*** (performing) ←1◦आ√चर्); *karma* (2.49); *param* (2.59); *āpnoti* (2.70); *pūruṣaḥ:* (1nom◦ sing◦ ←m◦ *pūruṣa* ←*puruṣa* (person) 2.15) (3.19)

(§3) *tasmāt* (therefore); *asaktaḥ:* (adj1◦-subj1◦ unattached); *satatam* (always, constantly); *kāryam* (adj◦-obj1◦ that ought to be performed); *karma* (obj1◦ the duty); *samāćara* (you please perform! refers to subj◦); *asaktaḥ:* (adj1◦-subj1◦ unattached); *hi* (because); *āćaran* (adj2◦-subj1◦ while performing); *karma* (obj1◦ karma, duty); *param* (obj2◦ the Supreme, the highest); *āpnoti* (attains); *pūruṣaḥ:* (subj2◦ a person) (3.19)

(§4) tasmāt asaktaḥ: samāćara satatam karma kāryam hi āćaran karma asaktaḥ: pūruṣaḥ: āpnoti param

(§5) Therefore,[309] unattached, you please always perform the duty that ought to be performed; because[310] while performing[311] duty unattached, a person attains the highest (state). (3.19)

3.20 कर्मणैव हि संसिद्धिमास्थिता जनकादय: ।
लोकसङ्ग्रहमेवापि सम्पश्यन्कर्तुमर्हसि ।।
karmaṇaiva hi saṁsiddhimāsthitā janakādayaḥ:,
lokasaṅgrahmevāpi sampaśyankartumarhasi. (3.20)

(§1) कर्मणि एव हि संसिद्धिम् आस्थिता: जनकादय: । लोकसङ्ग्रहम् एव अपि सम्पश्यन् कर्तुम् अर्हसि । *karmaṇā* (r◦ 24/4, 3/3) *eva hi saṁsiddhim* (r◦ 8/17) *āsthitāḥ:* (r◦ 20/7) *janakādayaḥ:* (r◦ 22/8) *lokasaṅgraham* (r◦ 8/22) *eva* (r◦ 1/1) *api sampaśyan* (r◦ 13/9) *kartum* (r◦ 8/16) *arhasi*

(§2) ***karmaṇā*** (3inst◦ sing◦ ←n◦ *karman* 1.15); *eva* (1.1); *hi* (1.11); 🕮***saṁsiddhim*** (2acc◦ sing◦ ←f◦ ***saṁsiddhi*** (success) ←ind◦ *sam* 1.1 + f◦ *siddhi* 2.48); 🕮*āsthitāḥ:* (m◦ 1nom◦ plu◦ ←ppp◦ adj◦ ***āsthita*** (attained) ←ind◦ *ā* (आ) 2.14 ←5◦√आप् + adj◦ *sthita* 1.14); *janakādayaḥ:* (m◦ 1nom◦ plu◦ ←bahuvrī◦ *janakādaya*, जनक: आदि: येषाम् ←m◦ prop◦ *Janaka* ←adj◦ *janaka* ←4◦√जन् + adj◦ *ādi* 2.28); ***lokasaṅgraham*** (m◦ 2acc◦ sing◦ ←tatpu◦ *loka-saṅgraha*, लोकस्य सङ्ग्रह: ←m◦ *loka* 2.5 + m◦ ***saṅgraha*** (people) ←1◦सम्√ग्रह्); *eva* (1.1); *api* (1.26); *sampaśyan* (m◦ 1nom◦ sing◦ ←ind◦ *sam* 1.1 + adj◦ *paśyat* 2.69); *kartum* (1.45); *arhasi* (2.25) (3.20)

---

[309] See the footnote in verse 2.15

[310] See footnote in verse 3.5

[311] Elsewhere◦ आचरन् → by performing, one who perform actions, by performing actions while unattached ...etc.

🕮 आचरत् is a śatṛ gerund adj.

(§3) *karmaṇā* (by karma, by *niṣkāka-karma*, by duty); *eva* (only); *hi* (because); *saṁsiddhiṃ* (obj1◦ to supreme success); *āsthitāḥ:* (adj◦-subj1◦ established in, attained); *janakādayaḥ:* (subj1◦ King Janaka and others following him); *lokasaṅgrahaṃ* (obj2◦ welfare of the people, world); *eva api* (also); *sampaśyan* (adj◦-subj2◦ while considering, looking at); *kartuṃ arhasi* (subj2◦ you ought to perform) (3.20)

(§4) hi janakādayaḥ: āsthitāḥ: saṁsiddhiṃ karmaṇā eva sampaśyan lokasaṅgrahaṃ eva api kartuṃ arhasi

(§5) Because[312] King Janaka and others following him attained supreme success[313] by *karma* only, (therefore,) while considering welfare of the people, you also ought to perform (*karma*). (3.20)

3.21 यद्यदाचरति श्रेष्ठस्तत्तदेवेतरो जनः ।
स यत्प्रमाणं कुरुते लोकस्तदनुवर्तते ।।
yadyadācarati śreṣṭhastattadevetaro janaḥ:,
sa yatpramāṇaṁ kurute lokastadanuvartate. (3.21)

(§1) यत् यत् आचरति श्रेष्ठः तत् तत् एव इतरः जनः । सः यत् प्रमाणम् कुरुते लोकः तत् अनुवर्तते । *yat* (r◦ 9/9) *yat* (r◦ 8/3) *ācarati śreṣṭhaḥ:* (r◦ 18/1) *tat* (r◦ 1/10) *tat* (r◦ 8/9) *eva* (r◦ 2/1) *itaraḥ:* (r◦ 15/3) *janaḥ:* (r◦ 22/8) *saḥ:* (r◦ 21/2) *yat* (r◦ 10/6) *pramāṇaṃ* (r◦ 14/1, 24/3) *kurute lokaḥ:* (r◦ 18/1) *tat* (r◦ 8/2) *anuvartate*

(§2) ***yat*** (n◦ 2acc◦ sing◦ ←pron◦ *yad* 1.45); *yat* (1.45); ***ācarati*** (3rd-per◦ sing◦ pres◦ वर्तमान्-लट् parasmai◦ ←1◦आ√चर्); 🕮*śreṣṭhaḥ:* (m◦ 1nom◦ sing◦ ←superlative adj◦ ***śreṣṭha*** (noble) ←1◦√**शंस्**); *tat* (2.7); *tat* (1.10); *eva* (1.1); *itaraḥ:* (m◦ 1nom◦ sing◦ ←pron◦ adj◦ *itara* ←1◦√तॄ); *janaḥ:* (1nom◦ sing◦ collective noun ←m◦ *jana* (person) 1.28); *saḥ:* (1.13); *yat* (1.45); 🕮**pramāṇaṃ** (2acc◦ sing◦ ←n◦ *pramāṇa* (standard) ←3◦प्र√मा); ***kurute*** (3rd-per◦ sing◦ pres◦ वर्तमान्-लट् ātmane◦ ←8◦√कृ); *lokaḥ:* (3.9); *tat* (1.10); *anuvartate* (3rd-per◦ sing◦ pres◦ वर्तमान्-लट् ātmane◦ ←4◦अनु√**वृत्**) (3.21)

(§3) *yat yat* (obj1◦ whatever); *ācarati* (does); *śreṣṭhaḥ:* (subj1◦ a noble person); *tat tat* (adj1◦-obj1◦ that); *eva* (alone); *itaraḥ:* (adj◦-subj2◦ other); *janaḥ:* (subj2◦ people); *saḥ:* (adj◦-subj1◦ he); *yat* (adj1◦-obj2◦ whatever); *pramāṇaṃ* (obj2◦ standard); *kurute* (he sets, he does); *lokaḥ:* (subj3◦ the world, people

---

[312] See footnote in verse 3.5

[313] Elsewhere◦ संसिद्धिम् → perfection, complete perfection, ...etc.

🕮 see footnote in 3.4

collective); *taț* (adj2∘-obj2∘ that); *anuvartate* (follows, adopts) (3.21)

(§4) yaț yaț śreṣṭhaḥ: āćarati taț eva itaraḥ: janaḥ: yaț pramāṇam saḥ: kurute taț lokaḥ: anuvartate

(§5) Whatever a noble person does, that alone other people (do); whatever standard he sets, that the world adopts. (3.21)

3.22 **न मे पार्थास्ति कर्तव्यं त्रिषु लोकेषु किञ्चन ।**
नानवाप्तमवाप्तव्यं वर्त एव च कर्मणि ।।

na me pārthāsti kartavyaṁ triṣu lokeṣu kiñćana,
nānavāptamavāptavyaṁ varta eva ća karmaṇi. (3.22)

(§1) न मे पार्थ अस्ति कर्तव्यम् त्रिषु लोकेषु किञ्चन । न अनवाप्तम् अवाप्तव्यम् वर्ते एव च कर्मणि । *na me pārtha* (r∘ 1/1) *asti kartavyaṃ* (r∘ 14/1) *triṣu* (r∘ 25/5) *lokeṣu* (r∘ 25/5) *kiñćana na* (r∘ 1/1) *anavāptaṃ* (r∘ 8/16) *avāptavyaṃ* (r∘ 14/1) *varte* (r∘ 5/4) *eva ća karmaṇi*

(§2) *na* (1.30); *me* (1.21); *pārtha* (1.25); *asti* (2.40); 🕮*kartavyaṃ* (1nom∘ sing∘ ←pass∘ -deriv∘ -pot∘ adj∘ ***kartavya*** (duty) ←8∘√कृ); *triṣu* (m∘ 7loc∘ plu∘ ←adj∘ *tri* 2.45); *lokeṣu* (7loc∘ plu∘ ←m∘ *loka* (world) 2.5); *kiñćana* (pron∘ *kiṃ* 1.1 + ind∘ *ćana* 2.47); *anavāptaṃ* (1nom∘ sing∘ ←ppp∘ adj∘ *an-avāpta* ←10∘अन्-अव√आप्); *avāptavyaṃ* (1nom∘ sing∘ ←pass∘ -pot∘ adj∘ adj∘ *avāptavya* ←अव्√आप्); *varte* (1st-per∘ sing∘ pres∘ वर्तमान्-लट् ātmane∘ ←4∘√वृत्); *eva* (1.1); *ća* (1.1); *karmaṇi* (2.47) (3.22)

(§3) *na* (not); *me* (for me); *pārtha* (O Pārtha! O Arjuna!); *asti* (is, there is); *kartavyaṃ* (adj1∘-subj1∘ ought to be done); *triṣu* (in the three); *lokeṣu* (in the worlds); *kiñćana* (subj1∘ anything); *anavāptaṃ* (adj2∘-subj1∘ unattained); *avāptavyaṃ* (adj3∘-subj1∘ to be attained, attainable, worth attaining) *varte* (subj2∘ I stay); *eva* (only); *ća* (and); *karmaṇi* (in karma, in duty) (3.22)

(§4) pārtha asti na kiñćana kartavyaṃ anavāptaṃ ća avāptavyaṃ me triṣu lokeṣu varte karmaṇi eva

(§5) O Arjuna! there is nothing ought to be done, unattained and to be attained, for me in the three worlds; (yet) I stay in *karma* only. (3.22)

3.23 **यदि ह्यहं न वर्तेयं जातु कर्मण्यतन्द्रितः ।**
मम वर्त्मानुवर्तन्ते मनुष्याः पार्थ सर्वशः ।।

yadi hyahaṁ na varteyaṁ jātu karmaṇyatandritaḥ:,
mama vartmānuvartante manuṣyāḥ: pārtha sarvaśaḥ:. (3.23)

(§1) यदि हि अहम् न वर्तेयम् जातु कर्मणि अतन्द्रितः । मम वर्त्म अनुवर्तन्ते मनुष्याः पार्थ सर्वशः । *yadi hi* (r∘ 4/1) *ahaṃ* (r∘ 14/1) *na varteyaṃ* (r∘ 14/1) *jātu karmaṇi* (r∘ 24/7, 4/1) *atandritaḥ:* (r∘ 22/8) *mama vartma* (r∘ 1/1) *anuvartante manuṣyāḥ:* (r∘ 22/3) *pārtha sarvaśaḥ:* (r∘ 22/8)

(§2) *yadi* (if 1.38); *hi* (1.11); *ahaṃ* (1.22); *na* (1.30); *varteyaṃ* (1nom∘ sing∘ potential∘ विधि∘ parasmai∘ ←4∘√वृत्); *jātu* (ever 2.12); *karmaṇi* (2.47); 🕮*atandritaḥ:* (adv∘ ←n.tatpu∘ ppp∘ adj∘ *atandrita* (non-stop) ←f∘ 🕮*tandri* ←1∘√तन्द्र्); *mama* (1.7); 🕮***vartma*** (2acc∘ sing∘ ←n∘ ***vartman*** (path) ←4∘√वृत्); ***anuvartante*** (3rd-per∘ plu∘ pres∘ वर्तमान्-लट् ātmane∘ ←4∘अनु√वृत् 3.21); ***manuṣyāḥ:*** (1nom∘ plu∘ ←m∘ *manuṣya* (prople) 1.44); *pārtha* (1.25); *sarvaśaḥ:* (1.18) (3.23)

(§3) *yadi* (if); *hi* (because); *ahaṃ* (subj1∘ I); *na* (not); *varteyaṃ* (I should stay) *jātu* (ever); *karmaṇi* (in karma); *atandritaḥ:* (steadily, tirelessly); *mama* (my); *vartma* (obj∘ path); *anuvartante* (they follow); *manuṣyāḥ:* (subj2∘ people); *pārtha* (O Pārtha! O Arjuna!); *sarvaśaḥ:* (in every way) (3.23)

(§4) hi yadi ahaṃ jātu na varteyaṃ karmaṇi atandritaḥ: pārtha manuṣyāḥ: anuvartante mama vartma sarvaśaḥ:

(§5) Because,[314] if I ever should not stay in *karma* tirelessly, O Arjuna! people (would) follow my path in every way. (3.23)

3.24 उत्सीदेयुरिमे लोका न कुर्यां कर्म चेदहम् ।
सङ्करस्य च कर्ता स्यामुपहन्यामिमाः प्रजाः ।।
utsīdeyurime lokā na kuryāṃ karma ćedahaṃ,
saṅkarasya ća kartā syāmupahanyāmimāḥ: prajāḥ:. (3.24)

(§1) उत्सीदेयुः इमे लोकाः न कुर्याम् कर्म चेत् अहम् । सङ्करस्य च कर्ता स्याम् उपहन्याम् इमाः प्रजाः । *utsīdeyuḥ:* (r∘ 16/3) *ime lokāḥ:* (r∘ 20/10) *na kuryāṃ* (r∘ 14/1) *karma ćeṭ* (r∘ 8/2) *ahaṃ* (r∘ 14/2) *saṅkarasya ća kartā syāṃ* (r∘ 8/20) *upahanyāṃ* (r∘ 8/18) *imāḥ:* (r∘ 22/3) *prajāḥ:* (r∘ 22/8)

(§2) *utsīdeyuḥ:* (3rd-per∘ plu∘ potential∘ विधि∘ parasmai∘ ←6∘उद्√सद्); *ime* (1.33); ***lokāḥ:*** (1nom∘ plu∘ ←m∘ *loka* (people) 2.5); *na* (1.30); *kuryāṃ* (1st-per∘ sing∘ potential∘ विधि∘ parasmai∘ ←8∘√कृ); *karma* (3.8); *ćeṭ* (2.33); *ahaṃ* (1.22); 🕮*saṅkarasya* (6pos sing∘ ←m∘ *saṅkara* (admixture) 1.42); *ća* (1.1); 🕮***kartā*** (m∘ 1nom∘ sing∘ ←adj∘ ***kartṛ*** (causer) ←8∘√कृ); ***syāṃ*** (1st-per∘ sing∘ potential∘ विधि∘ parasmai∘ ←2∘√अस्); *upahanyāṃ* (1nom∘ sing∘ potential∘ विधि∘ parasmai∘ ←2∘उप√हन्); ***imāḥ:*** (f∘ 2acc∘ plu∘ ←pron∘ *idaṃ* 1.10); *prajāḥ:* (2acc∘ 3.10) (3.24)

(§3) *utsīdeyuḥ:* (they would be ruined); *ime* (adj∘-subj1∘ these); *lokāḥ:* (subj1∘ people); *na* (not); *kuryāṃ* (I would perform); *karma* (obj1∘ karma); *ćeṭ* (if); *ahaṃ* (subj2∘ I); *saṅkarasya* (of confusion); *ća* (and); *kartā* (adj∘-subj2∘ the causer, doer); *syāṃ* (I would be); *upahanyāṃ* (I would destroy); *imāḥ:*

[314] See footnote in verse 3.5

(adj∘-obj2∘ these); *prajāḥ:* (obj2∘ people) (3.24)

(§4) ćet aham na kuryām karma ime lokāḥ: utsīdeyuḥ: ća syām kartā saṅkarasya upahanyām imāḥ: prajāḥ:

(§5) If I would not perform *karma*, these people would be ruined; I would be the causer of confusion[315] (and) I would destroy these people. (3.24)

3.25 सक्ताः कर्मण्यविद्वांसो यथा कुर्वन्ति भारत ।
कुर्याद्विद्वांस्तथाऽसक्तश्चिकीर्षुर्लोकसङ्ग्रहम् ।।
saktāḥ: karmaṇyavivdām̐so yathā kurvanti bhārata,
kuryādvidvām̐stathā'saktaśćikīrṣurlokasaṁgraham. (3.25)

(§1) सक्ताः कर्मणि अविद्वांसः यथा कुर्वन्ति भारत । कुर्यात् विद्वान् तथा असक्तः चिकीर्षुः लोकसङ्ग्रहम् । *saktāḥ:* (r∘ 22/1) *karmaṇi* (r∘ 24/7, 4/1) *avidvām̐saḥ:* (r∘ 15/10) *yathā kurvanti bhārata kuryāt* (r∘ 9/11) *vidvān* (r∘ 13/7) *tathā* (r∘ 1/3) *asaktaḥ:* (r∘ 17/1) *ćikīrṣuḥ:* (r∘ 16/8, 25/4) *lokasaṅgraham* (r∘ 14/2)

(§2) *saktāḥ:* (1nom∘ plu∘ ←ppp∘ adj∘ ***sakta*** (attached) ←1∘√सञ्ज्); *karmaṇi* (2.47); 📖*avidvām̐saḥ:* (1nom∘ plu∘ n.tatpu∘ ←adj∘ ***vidvas*** (wise) ←2∘√विद्); *yathā* (1.11); ***kurvanti*** (3rd-per∘ plu∘ pres∘ वर्तमान्-लट् parasmai∘ ←8∘√कृ); *bhārata* (1.24); *kuryāt* (3rd-per∘ sing∘ potential∘ विधि∘ parasmai∘ ←8∘√कृ); 📖***vidvān*** (m∘ 1nom∘ sing∘ ←adj∘ *vidvas* ↑); *tathā* (1.8); *asaktaḥ:* (3.7); 📖*ćikīrṣuḥ:* (1nom∘ sing∘ ←desi∘ adj∘ *ćikīrṣu* (desirous) 1.23 ←8∘√कृ); *lokasaṅgraham* (3.20) (3.25)

(§3) *saktāḥ:* (adj∘-subj1∘ attached); *karmaṇi* (in karma); *avidvām̐saḥ:* (subj1∘ the ignorant people); *yathā* (as); *kurvanti* (they act); *bhārata* (O Bhārata! O Arjuna!); *kuryāt* (he should perform); *vidvān* (subj2∘ a wise person); *tathā* (so); *asaktaḥ:* (adj-subj2∘ unattached); *ćikīrṣuḥ:* (adj2∘-subj2∘ desiring); *lokasaṅgraham* (obj∘ welfare of the people, the world) (3.25)

(§4) yathā avidvām̐saḥ: kurvanti saktāḥ: karmaṇi bhārata tathā vidvān ćikīrṣuḥ: lokasaṅgraham kuryāt asaktaḥ:

(§5) As the ignorant people act attached[316] in *karma*, O Arjuna! so a wise person, desiring welfare

---

[315] Elsewhere∘ सङ्करस्य → of unwanted population, admixture of castes, confusion of castes, intermingling of castes, confusion of species, discorded life ...etc. (castes, see footnote in 1.41)

[316] Elsewhere∘ *saktāḥ:* → being attached, from attachment to, with attachment ...etc.

📖 सक्ताः is not a gerund noun, instrumental case or ablative case. It is a nominative past participle plural adjective of the plural subject अविद्वांसः । Exactly same is true for the ppp∘ adjective *asaktaḥ:* (असक्तः) of the noun विद्वान् in this śloka.

of the people, should perform, (but) unattached. (3.25)

3.26 न बुद्धिभेदं जनयेदज्ञानां कर्मसङ्गिनाम् ।
जोषयेत्सर्वकर्माणि विद्वान्युक्तः समाचरन् ।।

na buddhibhedaṁ janayedajñānāṁ karmasaṅginām̦,
joṣayetsarvakarmāṇi vidvānyuktaḥ: samāćaran̦. (3.26)

(§1) न बुद्धिभेदम् जनयेत् अज्ञानाम् कर्मसङ्गिनाम् । जोषयेत् सर्वकर्माणि विद्वान् युक्तः समाचरन् । *na buddhibhedam̦* (r◦ 14/1) *janayeț* (r◦ 8/2) *ajñānām̦* (r◦ 14/1) *karmasaṅginām̦* (r◦ 14/2) *joṣayeț* (r◦ 10/7) *sarvakarmāṇi* (r◦ 24/7) *vidvān̦* (r◦ 13/17) *yuktaḥ:* (r◦ 22/7) *samāćaran̦*

(§2) *na* (1.30); *buddhibhedam̦* (m◦ 2acc◦ sing◦ ←tatpu◦ *buddhi-bheda* बुद्धेः भेदम् ←f◦ *buddhi* (thinking) 1.23 + m◦ 📖***bheda*** (conflict) ←7◦√भिद्); *janayeț* (3rd-per◦ sing◦ potential◦ विधि◦ parasmai◦ caus◦ ←4◦√जन्); *ajñānām̦* (m◦ 6pos◦ plu◦ ←n.bahuvrī◦ adj◦ ***a-jña*** ←adj◦ ***jña*** = *jnānin̦* (knower) ←9◦√ज्ञा); *karmasaṅginām̦* (m◦ 6pos◦ plu◦ ←bahuvrī◦ ***karma-saṅgin̦***, कर्मणि सङ्गः यस्य ←n◦ *karman̦* 1.15 + adj◦ *saṅgin̦* (attached) ←1◦√सञ्ज्); *joṣayeț* (3rd-per◦ sing◦ potential◦ विधि◦ parasmai◦ caus◦ ←6◦√जुष्); ***sarvakarmāṇi*** (सर्वाणि कर्माणि n◦ 1nom◦ 2acc◦ plu◦ *sarvāṇi* 2.30 *karmāṇi* 2.48); *vidvān̦* (3.25); *yuktaḥ:* (2.39); *samāćaran̦* (1nom◦ sing◦ ←śatṛ◦ adj◦ *samāćaraț* ←1◦सम्–आ√चर् 3.9) (3.26)

(§3) *na* (not); *buddhibhedam̦* (obj1◦ controversy, dispute, conflict in the thinking, in the mind); *janayeț* (they should cause); *ajñānām̦* (people ignorant of the *jñānayoga*); *karmasaṅginām̦* (of the ones attached to karma, of these attached to *sakāma-karma*); *joṣayeț* (he should cause them to be encouraged, he should inspire them); *sarvakarmāṇi* (obj2◦ to do all karmas, righteous deeds); *vidvān̦* (subj◦ the wise person); *yuktaḥ:* (adj1◦-subj◦ disciplined); *samāćaran̦* (adj2◦-subj◦ while performing properly) (3.26)

(§4) vidvān̦ na janayeț buddhibhedam̦ ajñānām̦ karmasaṅginām̦ joṣayeț sarvakarmāṇi samāćaran̦ yuktaḥ:

(§5) The wise person should not cause conflict[317] in the thinking of people ignorant of the *jñānayoga*, attached to *sakāma-karma*. He should inspire them to be encouraged to do all righteous deeds,[318] while (himself) performing properly disciplined. (3.26)

3.27 प्रकृतेः क्रियमाणानि गुणैः कर्माणि सर्वशः ।
अहङ्कारविमूढात्मा कर्ताऽहमिति मन्यते ।।

prakṛteḥ: kriyamāṇāni guṇaiḥ: karmāni sarvaśaḥ:,

---

[317] Elsewhere◦ न बुद्धिभेदम् जनयेत् → should not induce them to stop work, should not deter their mind ...etc.

[318] Elsewhere◦ जोषयेत्सर्वकर्माणि → make them follow the way of action, lead them to action, ...etc.

ahaṅkāravimūḍhātmā kartā'hamiti manyate. (3.27)

(§1) प्रकृते: क्रियमाणानि गुणै: कर्माणि सर्वश: । अहङ्कारविमूढात्मा कर्ता अहम् इति मन्यते । *prakṛteḥ:* (r◦ 22/1) *kriyamāṇāni guṇaiḥ:* (r◦ 22/1) *karmāṇi* (r◦ 24/7) *sarvaśaḥ:* (r◦ 22/8) *ahaṅkāravimūḍhātmā kartā* (r◦ 1/3) *ahaṃ* (r◦ 8/18) *iti manyate*

(§2) ***prakṛteḥ:*** (6pos sing◦ ←f◦ *prakṛti* 3.5); ***kriyamāṇāni*** (n◦ 1nom◦ plu◦ ←śānac◦ adj◦ *kriyamāṇa* ←8◦√कृ); *guṇaiḥ:* (3.5); ***karmāṇi*** (1nom◦ plu◦ ←n◦ *karman* 2.48); *sarvaśaḥ:* (1.18); *ahaṅkāravimūḍhātmā* (m◦ 1nom◦ sing◦ ←bahuvrī◦ *ahaṅkāra-vimūḍhātman*, अहङ्कारेण विमूढ: आत्मा यस्य स: ←m◦ *ahaṅkāra* (ego) 2.71 + adj◦ *vimūḍha* (deluded) 3.6 + m◦ *ātman* 2.41); *kartā* (3.24); *ahaṃ* (1.22); *iti* (1.25); *manyate* (2.19) (3.27)

(§3) *prakṛteḥ:* (of the *prakṛti,* of the inborn nature); *kriyamāṇāni* (adj◦-obj◦ while done, being performed); *guṇaiḥ:* (subj1◦ by the guṇas, by the three attributes); *karmāṇi* (obj◦ the karmas); *sarvaśaḥ:* (wholely); *ahaṅkāravimūḍhātmā* (adj◦-subj2◦ he who is deluded by 'I'-ness, the ego); *kartā* (subj3◦ the doer); *ahaṃ* (subj2◦ I am); *iti* (thus, as); *manyate* (he thinks) (3.27)

(§4) karmāṇi sarvaśaḥ: kriyamāṇāni guṇaiḥ: prakṛteḥ: ahaṅkāravimūḍhātmā manyate iti ahaṃ kartā

(§5) The *karmas* wholely[319] being performed[320] by the *guṇas* of the inborn nature, (but) he who is deluded by the 'I'-ness[321] thinks as, 'I am the doer.' (3.27)

3.28 तत्त्ववित्तु महाबाहो गुणकर्मविभागयो: ।
गुणा गुणेषु वर्तन्त इति मत्वा न सज्जते ।।

tattvavittu mahābāho guṇakarmavibhāgayoḥ:,
guṇā guṇeṣu vartante iti matvā na sajjate. (3.28)

---

[319] Elsewhere◦ *sarvaśaḥ:* → all kinds of (activities), all (actions), all kinds of (work), all (*karma*) ...etc.

📖 सर्वश: is not an adjective of plural noun कर्माणि । It is an adverb qualifying the शानच् adjective क्रियमाणानि । Therefore, सर्वश: = wholely, sloely, entirely, in every way - being performed (by the *guṇas* गुणै:)

[320] Elsewhere◦ क्रियमाणानि → are performed, that are performed actuality, carried out, perform, are done, are wrought, ...etc.

[321] Elsewhere◦ *ahaṅkāravimūḍhātmā* → the spirit soul bewildered by the false ego thinks, the self deluded by egotism thinketh ...etc.

📖 Here, the spirit or soul is not doing the thinking. Also, the soul (आत्मा) is अविकार्य ever unaffected. In the *bahūvrihi samāsa* of अहङ्कारविमूढात्मा, the person (external to the components of this *samāsa*), the possessor of the ātmā, is the subject, (qualified by the adjective अहङ्कारविमूढात्मा), and the performer the verb मन्यते ।

(§1) तत्त्ववित् तु महाबाहो गुणकर्मविभागयोः । गुणाः गुणेषु वर्तन्ते इति मत्वा न सज्जते । *tattvaviṭ* (r◦ 1/10) *tu mahābāho guṇakarmavibhāgayoḥ:* (r◦ 22/8) *guṇāḥ:* (r◦ 24/5, 20/6) *guṇeṣu* (r◦ 25/5) *vartante* (r◦ 5/2) *iti matvā na sajjate*

(§2) 📖***tattvaviṭ*** (m◦ 1nom◦ sing◦ ←adj◦ *tattva-viṭ* तत्त्वं वेत्ति यः ←n◦ *tattva* (reality) 2.16 + adj◦ *viḍ* (knower) 3.29); *tu* (1.2); *mahābāho* (2.26); *guṇakarmavibhāgayoḥ:* (m◦ 6pos◦ 7loc◦ dual◦ ←tatpu◦ *guṇa-karma-vibhāga*, गुणानाम् च विभागः कर्मणाम् च विभागः ←m◦ *guṇa* 2.45 + n◦ *karmaṇ* 1.15 + m◦ ***vibhāga*** (respective role) ←1◦वि√भज्); ***guṇāḥ:*** (1nom◦ plu◦ ←m◦ *guṇa* (one of the three attributes) 2.45); *guṇeṣu* (7loc◦ plu◦ ←m◦ *guṇa* 2.45); ***vartante*** (3rd-per◦ plu◦ pres◦ वर्तमान्–लट् ātmane◦ ←4◦√वृत्); *iti* (1.25); 📖***matvā*** (ipp◦ ind◦ ←4◦√मन्); *na* (1.30); *sajjate* (3rd-per◦ sing◦ pres◦ वर्तमान्–लट् ātmane◦ ←1◦√सञ्ज्) (3.28)

(§3) *tattvaviṭ* (subj1◦ the knower of the reality, knower of true principle, knower of the truth); *tu* (however); *mahābāho* (O Mahābāhu! O Arjuna!); *guṇakarmavibhāgayoḥ:* (of the respective roles of guṇas and karmas, in the modes of attributes and functions of nature); *guṇāḥ:* (subj2◦ the attributes, the guṇas); *guṇeṣu* (in the sphere of the guṇas); *vartante* (they function, operate, act; exist, remain, abide); *iti* (thus, that); *matvā* (having understood); *na* (does not); *sajjate* (he gets impeded, bound) (3.28)

(§4) tu mahābāho tattvaviṭ guṇakarmavibhāgayoḥ: matvā iti guṇāḥ: vartante guṇeṣu sajjate na

(§5) However, O Arjuna! the knower of the reality of the respective roles of *guṇas* and *karmas*, (and) having understood that the *guṇas* operate in the sphere of the *guṇas*, he does not get impeded. (3.28)

3.29 **प्रकृतेर्गुणसम्मूढाः सज्जन्ते गुणकर्मसु ।**
तानकृत्स्नविदो मन्दान्कृत्स्नविन्न विचालयेत् ।।
prakṛterguṇasammuḍhāḥ: sajjante guṇakarmasu,
tānakṛtsnavido mandānkṛtsnavinna vićālayeṭ. (3.29)

(§1) प्रकृतेः गणसम्मूढाः सज्जन्ते गुणकर्मसु । तान् अकृत्स्नविदः मन्दान् कृत्स्नविद् न विचालयेत् । *prakṛteḥ:* (r◦ 16/10) *guṇasammuḍhāḥ:* (r◦ 22/7) *sajjante guṇakarmasu tāṇ* (r◦ 8/11) *akṛtsnavidaḥ:* (r◦ 15/9) *mandāṇ* (r◦ 13/9) *akṛtsnaviḍ* (r◦ 12/1) *na vićālayeṭ*

(§2) *prakṛteḥ:* (3.27); *guṇasammuḍhāḥ:* (m◦ 1nom◦ plu◦ ←tatpu◦ *guṇa-sammuḍha*, गुणैः सम्मूढः ←m◦ *guṇa* 2.45 + ppp◦ adj◦ *sammūḍha* 2.7); *sajjante* (3rd-per◦ plu◦ pres◦ वर्तमान्–लट् ātmane◦ ←1◦√सञ्ज् 3.28); *guṇakarmasu* (n◦ 7loc◦ plu◦ dvandva◦ गुणेषु च कर्मसु च; tatpu◦ गुणानाम् कर्मसु । ←m◦ *guṇa* 2.45 + n◦ *karmaṇ* 1.15); *tāṇ* (1.7); *akṛtsnavidaḥ:* (m◦ 2acc◦ plu◦ n.tatpu◦ ←adj◦ ***kṛtsna-viḍ*** (wise) ←adj◦ *kṛtsna* 1.40 +

adj∘ ***vid*** ←2∘√विद्); 🕮*mandān* (m∘ 2acc∘ plu∘ ←adj∘ *mand* ←1∘√मन्द्); 🕮*kṛtsnavid* (1nom∘ sing∘ ←m∘ *kṛtsnavid* ↑); *na* (1.30); *vićālayet* (3rd-per∘ sing∘ potential∘ विधि∘ parasmai∘ caus∘ ←1∘वि√चल्) (3.29)

(§3) *prakṛteḥ:* (of the prakṛti, of nature); *guṇasammuḍhāḥ:* (sub1∘ those who are confused about the guṇas); *sajjante* (they get attached, bound, shackled); *guṇakarmasu* (in the karmas performed by the guṇas of prakṛti); *tān* (adj1∘-obj∘ to those); *akṛtsnavidaḥ:* (obj∘ to those who do not understand the whole truth); *mandān* (adj2∘-obj∘ fools, dullards); *kṛtsnavid* (subj2∘ he who understands fully well, the wise); *na* (not); *vićālayet* (they should cause to waver) (3.29)

(§4) guṇasammuḍhāḥ: prakṛteḥ: sajjante guṇakarmasu akṛtsnavidaḥ: tān mandān kṛtsnavid na vićālayet

(§5) Those who are confused about the *guṇas* of the *prakṛti,* they get attached to the *karmas* performed by the *guṇas.* To those who do not understand the whole truth, to those fools, he who understands fully well[322] should not cause them to waver. (3.29)

3.30 मयि सर्वाणि कर्माणि संन्यस्याध्यात्मचेतसा ।
निराशीर्निर्ममो भूत्वा युद्ध्यस्व विगतज्वरः ।।
mayi sarvāṇi karmāṇi sannyasyādhyātmaćetasā,
nirāśīrnirmamo bhūtvā yauddhyasva vigatajvaraḥ:. (3.30)

(§1) मयि सर्वाणि कर्माणि संन्यस्य अध्यात्मचेतसा । निराशीः निर्ममः भूत्वा युद्ध्यस्व विगतज्वरः । *mayi sarvāṇi* (r∘ 24/7) *karmāṇi* (r∘ 24/7) *sannyasya* (r∘ 1/1) *adhyātma ćetasā nirāśīḥ:* (r∘ 16/7) *nirmamaḥ:* (r∘ 15/8) *bhūtvā yuddhyasva vigatajvaraḥ:* (r∘ 22/8)

(§2) ***mayi*** (7loc∘ sing∘ ←pron∘ *asmad* 1.7); *sarvāṇi* (2.30); *karmāṇi* (2.48); ***sannyasya*** (lyp∘ past-participle ind∘ ←2∘सम्-नि√अस्); *adhyātma-ćetasā* (n∘ 3inst∘ sing∘ ←tatpu∘ *adhyātma-ćetas,* अध्यात्मनि चेतः ←adj∘ ***adhyātma*** (self aware) ←ind∘ *adhi* ←3∘√धा + m∘ *ātman* 2.41 + n∘ *ćetas* 1.38); 🕮***nirāśīḥ:*** (m∘ 1nom∘ sing∘ (indifferent) ←ind∘ *nir* 2.45 + adj∘ *āśin* 3.13); *nirmamaḥ:* (2.71); *bhūtvā* (2.20); *yuddhyasva* (2.18); 🕮*vigatajvaraḥ:* (m∘ 1nom∘ sing∘ ←bahuvrī∘ adj∘ *vigata-jvara,* विगतः ज्वरः यस्य ←adj∘ *vigata* (departed) 2.56 + m∘ 🕮*jvara* (grief) ←1∘√ज्वर्) (3.30)

(§3) *mayi* (in me, to me); *sarvāṇi* (adj∘-obj∘ all); *karmāṇi* (obj∘ krmas); *sannyasya* (having dedicated, relinquished); *adhyātma-ćetasā* (with self awareness); *nirāśīḥ:* (adj1∘-subj∘ indiffernt to the fruit, without desire for fruit); *nirmamaḥ:* (adj2∘-subj∘ unattached to 'my'-ness); *bhūtvā* (being, having

---

[322] Elsewhere∘ कृत्स्नविद् → man of perfect knowledge, he who knows everything ...etc.

become); *yuddhyasva* (subj◦ you fight!); *vigatajvaraḥ:* (adj◦-subj◦ grief departed, griefless, free from regret) (3.30)

(§4) sannyasya sarvāṇi karmāṇi mayi adhyātma-ćetasā bhūtvā nirāśīḥ: nirmamaḥ: vigatajvaraḥ: yuddhyasva

(§5) Having dedicated all *krmas* to me with self-awareness,[323] having become indiffernt to the fruit,[324] unattached to 'my'-ness,[325] (and) griefless you fight! (3.30)

3.31 ये मे मतमिदं नित्यमनुतिष्ठन्ति मानवाः ।
श्रद्धावन्तोऽनसूयन्तो मुच्यन्ते तेऽपि कर्मभिः ।।

ye me matamidaṁ nityamanutiṣṭhanti mānavāḥ:,
śraddhāvanto'nasūyanto mućyante te'pi karmabhiḥ:. (3.31)

(§1) ये मे मतम् इदं नित्यम् अनुतिष्ठन्ति मानवाः । श्रद्धावन्तः अनसूयन्तः मुच्यन्ते ते अपि कर्मभिः । *ye me matam* (r◦ 8/18) *idam* (r◦ 14/1) *nityam* (r◦ 8/16) *anutiṣṭhanti mānavāḥ:* (r◦ 22/8) *śraddhāvantaḥ:* (r◦ 15/1) *anasūyantaḥ:* (r◦ 15/9) *mućyante te* (r◦ 6/1) *api karmabhiḥ:* (r◦ 22/8)

(§2) *ye* (1.7); *me* (1.21); 🕮***matam*** (2acc◦ sing◦ ←n◦ *mata* (opinion) 2.35); *idam* (1.10); *nityam* (2acc◦ n◦ adj◦ 2.21); ***anutiṣṭhanti*** (3rd-per◦ plu◦ pres◦ वर्तमान्-लट् parasmai◦ ←1◦अनु√स्था); *mānavāḥ:* (1nom◦ plu◦ ←m◦ *mānava* 3.7); 🕮*śraddhāvantaḥ:* (m◦ 1nom◦ plu◦ ←adj◦ ***śraddhāvat*** ←f◦ ***śraddhā*** (faith) ←3◦श्रत्√धा + taddhita◦ affix *vat* 1.5); 🕮*anasūyantaḥ:* (m◦ 1nom◦ plu◦ ←n.tatpu◦ *anasūyat* ←negative prefix ***an*** (अन्) + śatṛ◦ adj◦ ***asūyat*** ←2◦√असू); *mućyante* (3.13); *te* (1.33); *api* (1.26); ***karmabhiḥ:*** (3inst◦ plu◦ ←n◦ *karman* 1.15) (3.31)

(§3) *ye* (adj1◦-subj◦ those who); *me* (my); *matam* (obj◦ opinion); *idam* (adj1◦-obj◦ this); *nityam* (adj2◦-obj◦ eternal); *anutiṣṭhanti* (they follow, abide by); *mānavāḥ:* (subj◦ people); *śraddhāvantaḥ:* (adj2◦-subj◦ faithful); *anasūyantaḥ:* (adj3◦-subj◦ the ones who are unenvious); *mućyante* (they become unattached); *te* (adj4◦-subj◦ they); *api* (also); *karmabhiḥ:* (with the karmas) (3.31)

(§4) ye anutiṣṭhanti me idam nityam matam te śraddhāvantaḥ: anasūyantaḥ: mānavāḥ: mućyante karmabhiḥ: api

---

[323] अध्यात्मचेतसा → for defination of अध्यात्म, see verse 8.1

[324] Elsewhere◦ निराशी → giving up hope, hopeless, without hope ...etc.

[325] Elsewhere◦ निर्मम: → free from egoism, free from selfishness ...etc.

🕮 egoism is अहंकार: 'I-ness,' and निर्मम, नि:मम, न मम is devoid of मम 'my-ness,' detachment from things considered as 'mine,' but not necessarily only the material possessions, but including such abstract and non-abstract attachments as 'my' wife, 'my' children, 'my' house, 'my' name, 'my' fame ...etc. also.

(§5) Those who follow my this eternal opinion,[326] those faithful (and) unenvious people become unattached with the *karmas* also. (3.31)

3.32 ये त्वेतदभ्यसूयन्तो नानुतिष्ठन्ति मे मतम् ।
सर्वज्ञानविमूढांस्तान्विद्धि नष्टानचेतसः ।।

ye tvetadabhyasūyanto nānutiṣṭhanti me matam,
sarvajñānavimūḍhānstānviddhi naṣṭānaćetasaḥ:. (3.32)

(§1) ये तु एतत् अभ्यसूयन्तः न अनुतिष्ठन्ति मे मतम् । सर्वज्ञानविमूढान् तान् विद्धि नष्टान् अचेतसः । *ye tu* (r◦ 4/9) *etat* (r◦ 8/2) *abhyasūyantaḥ:* (r◦ 15/6) *na* (r◦ 1/1) *anutiṣṭhanti me matam* (r◦ 14/2) *sarvajñānavimūḍhān* (r◦ 13/7) *tān* (r◦ 13/19) *viddhi naṣṭān* (r◦ 8/11) *aćetasaḥ:* (r◦ 22/8)

(§2) *ye* (1.7); *tu* (1.2); *etat* (2.6); 🕮*abhyasūyantaḥ:* (1nom◦ plu◦ ←śatṛ◦ adj◦ *abhyasūyat* (sneering) ←ind◦ *abhi* ←2◦√भा + adj◦ *asūyat* 3.31); *na* (1.30); *anutiṣṭhanti* (3.31); *me* (1.21); *matam* (3.31); 🕮*sarvajñānavimūḍhān* (m◦ 2acc◦ plu◦ ←bahuvrī◦ *sarva-jñāna-vimūḍha*, सर्वस्मिन् ज्ञाने विमूढः यः ←pron◦ *sarva* 1.6 + n◦ *jñāna* 3.3 + adj◦ *vimūḍha* (deluded) 3.6); *tān* (1.7); *viddhi* (2.17); 🕮*naṣṭān* (m◦ 2acc◦ plu◦ ←adj◦ *naṣṭa* (wretched) 1.40); 🕮***aćetasaḥ:*** (m◦ 2acc◦ plu◦ n.bahuvrī◦ *aćetasa* (mindless) नास्ति चेतः यस्य सः ←n◦ *ćetas* 1.38) (3.32)

(§3) *ye* (adj◦-subj◦ those who); *tu* (however); *etat* (adj◦-obj1◦ this, this opinion); *abhyasūyantaḥ:* (subj◦ those sneering at); *na* (do not); *anutiṣṭhanti* (they follow, abide by); *me* (my); *matam* (obj1◦ opinion); *sarvajñānavimūḍhān* (obj2◦ to those who are ignorant of all knowledge); *tān* (adj1◦-obj2◦ them, to those); *viddhi* (you please know - to be); *naṣṭān* (adj2◦-obj2◦ to those wretched ones); *aćetasaḥ:* (adj3◦-obj2◦ mindless) (3.32)

(§4) tu ye abhyasūyantaḥ: me matam na anutiṣṭhanti etat viddhi sarvajñānavimūḍhān tān naṣṭān aćetasaḥ:

(§5) However, those who, sneering at my opinion, do not abide by this (opinion), you please know those ignorant of all knowledge (and the) wretched ones to be mindless.
(3.32)

---

[326] Elsewhere◦ ये मे मतम् इदं नित्यम् अनुतिष्ठन्ति → those men who always practice this teaching, constantly follow, ever abide in this teaching, follow this teaching faithfully, constantly precice, abide ever in this teaching, ...etc.

🕮 Rather than अनुतिष्ठन्ति नित्यम् more logical is मतम् नित्यम्, नित्यम् मतम् । Lord's मतम् teaching is नित्यम् eternal. Therefore, it is ये अनुतिष्ठन्ति मे नित्यं मतम् ।

3.33 सदृशं चेष्टते स्वस्याः प्रकृतेर्ज्ञानवानपि ।
प्रकृतिं यान्ति भूतानि निग्रहः किं करिष्यति ।।

sadṛśaṁ ćeṣṭate svasyāḥ: prakṛterjñānavānapi,
prakṛtiṁ yānti bhūtāni nigrahaḥ: kiṁ kariṣyati. (3.33)

(§1) सदृशम् चेष्टते स्वस्याः प्रकृतेः ज्ञानवान् अपि । प्रकृतिम् यान्ति भूतानि निग्रहः किम् करिष्यति । *sadṛśam̦* (r◦ 14/1) *ćeṣṭate svasyāḥ:* (r◦ 22/3) *prakṛteḥ:* (r◦ 16/10) *jñānavān̦* (r◦ 8/11) *api prakṛtim̦* (r◦ 14/1) *yānti bhūtāni nigrahaḥ:* (r◦ 22/1) *kim̦* (r◦ 14/1) *kariṣyati* (r◦ 25/6)

(§2) 🕮***sadṛśam̦*** (adv◦ ←adj◦ ***sadṛśa*** (accordingly) ←1◦√दृश्); *ćeṣṭate* (3rd-per◦ sing◦ pres◦ वर्तमान्-लट् ātmane◦ ←1◦√चेष्ट्); *svasyāḥ:* (6pos◦ f◦ sing◦ ←pron◦ *sva* 1.28); *prakṛteḥ:* (3.27); 🕮***jñānavān̦*** (m◦ 1nom◦ sing◦ ←adj◦ ***jñānavaț*** (wise) ←n◦ *jñāna* 3.3 + affix *vaț* 1.5); *api* (1.26); ***prakṛtim̦*** (2acc◦ sing◦ ←f◦ *prakṛti* 3.5); ***yānti*** (3rd-per◦ plu◦ pres◦ वर्तमान्-लट् parasmai◦ ←2◦√या); *bhūtāni* (2.28); 🕮***nigrahaḥ:*** (1nom◦ sing◦ ←m◦ ***nigraha*** (control) ←9◦नि√ग्रह्); *kim̦* (1.1); *kariṣyati* (3rd-per◦ sing◦ fut2◦ लृट् भविष्य◦ parasmai◦ -v-t◦ ←8◦√कृ) (3.33)

(§3) *sadṛśam̦* (according to); *ćeṣṭate* (he acts); *svasyāḥ:* (his own); *prakṛteḥ:* (according to nature); *jñānavān̦* (subj1◦ the wise person); *api* (also); *prakṛtim̦* (obj◦ to nature); *yānti* (they go, follow, abide); *bhūtāni* (subj2◦ the beings); *nigrahaḥ:* (subj3◦ the restraint); *kim̦* (what?); *kariṣyati* (will do) (3.33)

(§4) jñānavān̦ ćeṣṭate sadṛśam̦ svasyāḥ: prakṛteḥ: bhūtāni api yānti prakṛtim̦ kim̦ nigrahaḥ: kariṣyati

(§5) The wise person acts according to his own nature (and) the beings also follow (their) nature, (then) what the restraint will do? (3.33)

3.34 इन्द्रियस्येन्द्रियस्यार्थे रागद्वेषौ व्यवस्थितौ ।
तयोर्न वशमागच्छेत्तौ ह्यस्य परिपन्थिनौ ।।

indriyasyendriyasyārthe rāgadveṣau vyavasthitau,
tayorna vaśamāgaććhettau hyasya paripanthinau. (3.34)

(§1) इन्द्रियस्य इन्द्रियस्य अर्थे रागद्वेषौ व्यवस्थितौ । तयोः न वशम् आगच्छेत् तौ हि अस्य परिपन्थिनौ । *indriyasya* (r◦ 2/1) *indriyasya* (r◦ 1/1) *arthe rāgadveṣau vyavasthitau tayoḥ:* (r◦ 16/12) *na vaśam̦* (r◦ 8/17) *āgaććheț* (r◦ 1/10) *tau hi* (r◦ 4/1) *asya paripanthinau*

(§2) ***indriyasya*** (6pos sing◦ ←n◦ *indriya* 2.8); 🕮*indriyasya-arthe* (1.9); 🕮***rāgadveṣau*** (m◦ 1nom◦ dual◦ ←dvandva◦ रागः च द्वेषः च ←m◦ *rāga* (attachment) 2.64 + m◦ *dveṣa* (aversion) 2.64); ***vyavasthitau*** (m◦ 1nom◦ dual◦ ←adj◦ *vyavasthita* (seated) 1.20); ***tayoḥ:*** (m◦ or n◦ 6pos◦ dual◦ ←pron◦ *tad̦* 1.2); *na* (1.30); 🕮***vaśam̦*** (2acc◦ sing◦ ←m◦ *vaśa* (control) 2.61); *āgaććheț* (3rd-per◦ sing◦ potential◦ विधि◦ parasmai◦ ←1◦आ√गम्); *tau*

(2.19); *hi* (1.11); *asya* (2.17); 🕮*paripanthinau* (m∘ 1nom∘ dual∘ ←m∘ *paripanthin̦* ←prefix∘ *pari* 1.29 + adj∘ *panthin̦* (adversary) ←1∘√पथ्) (3.34)

(§3) *indriyasya* (of the organs); *indriyasyārthe* (in the sense objects, in the *viṣayas*); *rāgadveṣau* (subj∘ passion and aversion); *vyavasthitau* (adj1∘-subj∘ rooted, seated) *tayoḥ:* (of these two); *na* (not); *vaśam̦* (obj∘ under the control, under subjugation); *āgaććheț* (one should come); *tau* (adj2∘-subj∘ these both); *hi* (because); *asya* (one's); *paripanthinau* (adj3∘-subj∘ two adversaries in the path) (3.34)

(§4) rāgadveṣau vyavasthitau indriyasyārthe indriyasya āgaććheț na vaśam̦ tayoḥ: hi tau asya paripanthinau

(§5) Passion and aversion (are) rooted[327] in the sense objects of the organs. One should not come under subjugation of these two, because[328] these both (are) one's two adversaries in the path. (3.34)

3.35 श्रेयान्स्वधर्मो विगुणः परधर्मात्स्वनुष्ठितात् ।
स्वधर्मे निधनं श्रेयः परधर्मो भयावहः ।।
śreyānsvadharmo viguṇaḥ: paradharmātsvanuṣṭhitāț,
svadharme nidhanaṁ śreyaḥ: paradharmo bhayāvahaḥ:. (3.35)

(§1) श्रेयान् स्वधर्मः विगुणः परधर्मात् स्वनुष्ठितात् । स्वधर्मे निधनम् श्रेयः परधर्मः भयावहः । *śreyān̦* (r∘ 13/20) *svadharmaḥ:* (r∘ 15/13) *viguṇaḥ:* (r∘ 22/3) *paradharmāț* (r∘ 10/7) *svanuṣṭhitāț* (r∘ 23/1) *svadharme nidhanam̦* (r∘ 14/1) *śreyaḥ:* (r∘ 22/3) *paradharmaḥ:* (r∘ 15/8) *bhayāvahaḥ:* (r∘ 22/8)

(§2) ***śreyān̦*** (m∘ 1nom∘ sing∘ ←comparative adj∘ *śreyaș* 1.31); ***svadharmaḥ:*** (1nom∘ sing∘ ←m∘ *sva-dharma* 2.31); 🕮***viguṇaḥ:*** (m∘ 1nom∘ sing∘ ←bahuvrī∘ *viguṇa* (defect) विगतः विपरितः वा गुणः यस्य ←m. *guṇa* 2.45); ***paradharmāț*** (m∘ 5abl∘ sing∘ ←tatpu∘ ***para-dharma*** ←adj∘ *para* 2.3 + m∘ *dharma* 1.1); ***svanuṣṭhitāț*** (5abl∘ sing∘ ←ppp∘ adj∘ *svanuṣṭhita* (well performed) ←1∘सु–अनु√स्था); *svadharme* (7loc∘ sing∘ ←m∘ *svadharma* 2.31); 🕮*nidhanam̦* (1nom∘ sing∘ ←n∘ *nidhana* (death) 2.28); 🕮*śreyaḥ:* (nom∘ 2.5); *paradharmaḥ:* (1nom∘ sing∘ ←m∘ *paradharma* ↑); 🕮*bhayāvahaḥ:* (m∘ 1nom∘ sing∘ ←adj∘ *bhayāvaha* ←m∘ *bhaya* (fear) 2.35 + adj∘ *āvaha* (causer) ←1∘आ√वह्) (3.35)

(§3) *śreyān̦* (adj1∘-subj1∘ better); *svadharmaḥ:* (subj1∘ our own duty); *viguṇaḥ:* (adj2∘-subj1∘ without good qualities, imperfect); *paradharmāț* (than others' duty, than the duty prescribed for other's);

---

[327] Elsewhere∘ *vyavasthitau* → they abide, they have, are natural ...etc.

🕮 व्यवस्थितौ is not a verb. It is a dual Past Passive Participle ppp∘ adjective of dual m∘ noun रागद्वेषौ ।

[328] See footnote in verse 3.5

svanuṣṭhitāt (than well performed); *svadharme* (in our own duty); *nidhanam* (subj2◦ death); *śreyaḥ:* (adj◦-subj2◦ better); *paradharmaḥ:* (subj3◦ duty prescribed for others, suitable for others); *bhayāvahaḥ:* (adj◦-subj3◦ dangerous) (3.35)

(§4) svadharmaḥ: viguṇaḥ: śreyān paradharmāt svanuṣṭhitāt nidhanam svadharme śreyaḥ: paradharmaḥ: bhayāvahaḥ:

(§5) Our own duty, (even) without good qualities, (is) better than well performed duty prescribed for others. Death in our own duty (is) better. Duty prescribed for others' (is) dangerous. (3.35)

Arjuna said (arjuna uvāća अर्जुन उवाच ।)

3.36 अथ केन प्रयुक्तोऽयं पापं चरति पूरुषः ।
अनिच्छन्नपि वार्ष्णेय बलादिव नियोजितः ।।

atha kena prayukto'yam pāpam ćarati pūruṣaḥ:,
aniććhnnapi vārṣṇeya balādiva niyojitaḥ:. (3.36)

(§1) अथ केन प्रयुक्तः अयम् पापम् चरति पूरुषः । अनिच्छन् अपि वार्ष्णेय बलात् इव नियोजितः । *arjunaḥ:* (r◦ 19/4) *uvāća. atha kena prayuktaḥ:* (r◦ 15/1) *ayam* (r◦ 14/1) *pāpam* (r◦ 14/1) *ćarati pūruṣaḥ:* (r◦ 22/8) *aniććhan* (r◦ 13/1) *api vārṣṇeya balāt* (r◦ 8/4) *iva niyojitaḥ:* (r◦ 22/8)

(§2) *arjunaḥ:* (1.28); *uvāća* (1.25). *atha* (1.20); *kena* (m◦ or n◦ 3inst◦ sing◦ ←pron◦ *kim* 1.1); 📖*prayuktaḥ:* (1nom◦ sing◦ ←ppp◦ adj◦ *prayukta* ←4◦प्र√युज्); *ayam* (2.19); *pāpam* (sin 2.33); *ćarati* (2.71); *pūruṣaḥ:* (3.19); *aniććhan* (m◦ 1nom◦ sing◦ ←śatṛ◦ adj◦ *aniććhat* ←ind◦ negative prefix *an* (अन्) 3.31 + ←śatṛ◦ adj◦ *iććhat* ←6◦√इष्); *api* (1.26); *vārṣṇeya* (1.41); 📖*balāt* (adv◦ or 5abl◦ sing◦ ←n◦ *bala* (compelled) 1.10); *iva* (1.30); 📖*niyojitaḥ:* (1nom◦ sing◦ ←ppp◦ adj◦ *niyojita* (appointed) ←4◦नि√युज्)

(§3) *arjunaḥ:* (subj◦ Arjuna); *uvāća* (said). *atha* (now, now then); *kena* (by what?); *prayuktaḥ:* (adj1◦-subj◦ impelled, compelled); *ayam* (adj2◦-subj◦ this, a); *pāpam* (obj◦ sin); *ćarati* (does, commits); *pūruṣaḥ:* (subj◦ a person); *aniććhan* (adj3◦-subj◦ while undesiring) *api* (even); *vārṣṇeya* (O Vārṣṇeya! O Kṛṣṇa!); *balāt* (adv◦ forcibly); *iva* (as if); *niyojitaḥ:* (adj4◦-subj◦ appointed, engaged, compelled) (3.36)

(§4) atha vārṣṇeya prayuktaḥ: kena ayam pūruṣaḥ: ćarati pāpam api aniććhan iva niyojitaḥ: balāt

(§5) Now then, O Kṛṣṇa! impelled by what a person commits sin, even while undesiring,[329] as if

---

[329] Elsewhere◦ *aniććhan* → involuntarily, unwillingly, reluctantly (adv◦)

📖 अनिच्छन् is not an adverb. It is (m◦ present passive participle) adjective of m◦ noun पूरुषः अनिच्छन् = while compelled forcibly? (3.36)

The Lord said (śrībhagavānuvāća श्रीभगवानुवाच ।)

3.37 काम एष क्रोध एष रजोगुणसमुद्भवः ।
महाशनो महापाप्मा विद्ध्येनमिह वैरिणम् ।।

kāma eṣa krodha eṣa rajoguṇasamudbhavaḥ:,
mahāśano mahāpāpmā viddhyenamiha vairiṇaṃ. (3.37)

(§1) कामः एषः क्रोधः एषः रजोगुणसमुद्भवः । महाशनः महापाप्मा विद्धि एनम् इह वैरिणम् । *śrībhagavāṇ* (r◦ 8/14) *uvāća. kāmaḥ:* (r◦ 19/7) *eṣa* (r◦ 25/1, 21/1) *krodhaḥ:* (r◦ 19/7) *eṣa* (r◦ 25/1, 21/1) *rajoguṇasamudbhavaḥ:* (r◦ 22/8) *mahāśanaḥ:* (r◦ 15/9) *mahāpāpmā viddhi* (r◦ 4/4) *enaṃ* (r◦ 8/18) *iha vairiṇaṃ* (r◦ 14/2, 24/3)

(§2) *śrībhagavāṇ* (12.2↓); *uvāća* (1.25). *kāmaḥ:* (craving 2.62); *eṣa* (3.10); *krodhaḥ:* (anger 2.62); *eṣa* (3.10); *rajoguṇasamudbhavaḥ:* (m◦ 1nom◦ sing◦ ←bahuvrī◦ *rajoguṇa-samudbhava,* रजसः गुणात् समुद्भवः यस्य ←n◦ ***rajaṣ*** ←4◦√रञ्ज् + m◦ *guṇa* 2.45 + m◦ *samudbhava* (rise) 3.14); 🕮*mahāśanaḥ:* (m◦ 1nom◦ sing◦ ←bahuvrī◦ *mahāśana* (insatiable) महान् अशनम् यस्य ←adj◦ *mahā* (great) 1.3 + n◦ *aśana* (apetite) ←9◦√अश्); 🕮*mahāpāpmā* (m◦ 1nom◦ sing◦ ←s-karm◦ *mahāpāpman,* महान् पाप्मा ←adj◦ *mahā* 1.3 + m◦ ***pāpmaṇ*** (sinner) ←1◦√पा); *viddhi* (2.17); *enaṃ* (2.19); *iha* (2.5); 🕮*vairiṇaṃ* (2acc◦ sing◦ ←m◦ ***vairiṇ*** (enemy) ←10◦√वीर्) (3.37)

(§3) *śrībhagavāṇ* (The Lord); *uvāća* (said). *kāmaḥ:* (subj1◦ desire, craving); *eṣa* (adj◦-subj1◦ this); *krodhaḥ:* (subj2◦ anger); *eṣa* (adj◦-subj2◦ this); *rajoguṇasamudbhavaḥ:* (adj◦-subj1◦ born out of the *guṇa* of *rajas*); *mahāśanaḥ:* (adj2◦-subj1◦ ever insatiable, ever hungry); *mahāpāpmā* (adj3◦-subj1◦ very sinful); *viddhi* (you please know!); *enaṃ* (adj◦-obj◦ this); *iha* (here, in this world); *vairiṇaṃ* (obj◦ an enemy) (3.37)

(§4) eṣa kāmaḥ: rajoguṇasamudbhavaḥ: mahāśanaḥ: mahāpāpmā eṣa krodhaḥ: viddhi enaṃ vairiṇaṃ iha

(§5) The Lord said : This craving, born out of the guṇa of rajas, ever insatiable (and) very sinful (is) this anger. You please know this craving (to be) an enemy[330] in this world. (3.37)

3.38 धूमेनाव्रियते वह्निर्यथादर्शो मलेन च ।

- unwilling, undesiring, being reluctant. बलात् (forcibly) is adv◦ नियोजितः is ppp◦ Thus, केन प्रयुक्तः अनिच्छन् पूरुषः – बलात् इव नियोजितः – पापम् चरति?

[330] Elsewhere◦ विद्धि एनम् वैरिणम् → They should be known as enemies

यथोल्बेनावृतो गर्भस्तथा तेनेदमावृतम् ।।

dhūmenāvriyate vahniryathādarśo malena ća,

yatholbenāvṛto garbhastathā tenedamāvṛtam. (3.38)

(§1) धूमेन आव्रियते वह्निः यथा आदर्शः मलेन च । यथा उल्बेन आवृतः गर्भः तथा तेन इदम् आवृतम् । *dhūmena* (r◦ 1/2) *āvriyate vahniḥ:* (r◦ 16/6) *yathā* (r◦ 1/4) *ādarśaḥ:* (r◦ 15/9) *malena ća yathā* (r◦ 2/4) *ulbena* (r◦ 1/2) *āvṛtaḥ:* (r◦ 15/2) *garbhaḥ:* (r◦ 18/1) *tathā tena* (r◦ 2/1) *idam* (r◦ 8/17) *āvṛtam* (r◦ 14/2)

(§2) 🕮***dhūmena*** (3inst◦ sing◦ ←m◦ ***dhūma*** (smoke) ←1◦√धू); 🕮*āvriyate* (3rd-per◦ sing◦ pres◦ वर्तमान्-लट् ātmane◦ ←10◦आ√वृ); 🕮*vahniḥ:* (1nom◦ sing◦ ←m◦ *vahni* (fire) ←1◦√वह्); *yathā* (1.11); 🕮*ādarśaḥ:* (1nom◦ sing◦ ←m◦ *ādarśa* (mirror) ←1◦आ√दृश्); 🕮*malena* (3inst◦ sing◦ ←n◦ or m◦ ***mala*** (dust) ←1◦√मल्); ća (1.1); *yathā* (1.11); 🕮*ulbena* (3inst◦ sing◦ ←n◦ *ulba* (placenta) ←4◦√उच्); 🕮*āvṛtaḥ:* (m◦ 1nom◦ sing◦ ←ppp◦ adj◦ ***āvṛta*** (covered) ←1◦आ√वृ); 🕮*garbhaḥ:* (1nom◦ sing◦ ←m◦ ***garbha*** (foetus) ←10◦√गृ); *tathā* (1.8); ***tena*** (m◦ or n◦ 3inst◦ sing◦ ←pron◦ *tad* 1.2); *idam* (n◦ 1.10); 🕮***āvṛtam*** (n◦ 1nom◦ sing◦ ←adj◦ *āvṛta* ↑)

(3.38)

(§3) *dhūmena* (subj1◦ with smoke); *āvriyate* (it gets covered); *vahniḥ:* (obj1◦ fire); *yathā* (as, just as); *ādarśaḥ:* (obj2◦ a mirror); *malena* (subj2◦ with dust, by dirt); *ća* (and); *yathā* (as, just as); *ulbena* (subj3◦ with placenta, by amnion); *āvṛtaḥ:* (adj◦-obj3◦ covered); *garbhaḥ:* (obj3◦ the foetus, the embryo); *tathā* (so); *tena* (adj1◦-subj4◦ by that, by that craving); *idam* (obj4◦ this, this wisdom, this knowledge); *āvṛtam* (adj◦-obj4◦ covered) (3.38)

(§4) yathā vahniḥ: āvriyate dhūmena ādarśaḥ: malena ća yathā garbhaḥ: āvṛtaḥ: ulbena tathā idam āvṛtam tena

(§5) Just as fire gets covered with smoke; a mirror with dust (and) just as the foetus covered with placenta,[331] so (is) this wisdom[332] covered[333] by that craving.[334]

---

[331] Elsewhere◦ उल्बेन → by the womb.

[332] Elsewhere◦ इदम् → the living entity, the universe, the intelligence ...etc.

🕮 Please note, that इदम् is a neuter gender pronominal adjective. For further clarification of this 'इदम्,' verify it in the next shloka ज्ञानम् आवृत्य 3.40

[333] Elsewhere◦ (i) *āvriyate* → it is covered; (ii) *āvṛtaḥ:* → it is covered *āvṛtam* → (iii) it is covered ...etc.

🕮 Please note, that (i) *āvriyate* (आव्रियते) is a verb → it gets covered; (ii) *āvṛtaḥ:* (आवृतः) ppp◦ m◦ adjective (covered); and (iii) *āvṛtam* (आवृतम्) is nominative ppp◦ n◦ adjective (covered). See the substitute words शब्दपर्यायाः given above↑

(3.38)

3.39 आवृतं ज्ञानमेतेन ज्ञानिनो नित्यवैरिणा ।
कामरूपेण कौन्तेय दुष्पूरेणानलेन च ।।

āvṛtaṁ jñānametena jñānino nityavairiṇā,
kāmarūpeṇa kaunteya duṣpūreṇānalena ća. (3.39)

(§1) आवृतम् ज्ञानम् एतेन ज्ञानिनः नित्यवैरिणा । कामरूपेण कौन्तेय दुष्पूरेण अनलेन च । *āvṛtam* (r∘ 14/1) *jñānam* (r∘ 8/22) *etena jñāninaḥ:* (r∘ 15/6) *nityavairiṇā* (r∘ 24/4) *kāmarūpeṇa* (r∘ 24/1) *kaunteya duṣpūreṇa* (r∘ 24/1) *analena ća*

(§2) 🕮*āvṛtam* (3.38); 🕮***jñānam*** (1nom∘ sing∘ ←n∘ *jñāna* 3.3); ***etena*** (m∘ or n∘ 3inst∘ sing∘ ←pron∘ *etad* 1.3); ***jñāninaḥ:*** (6pos sing∘ ←m∘ 🕮***jñānin*** ←9∘√ज्ञा); *nityavairiṇā* (m∘ 3inst∘ sing∘ ←s-karm∘ *nitya-vairin* ←ind∘ *nitya* 2.18 + m∘ *vairin* (enemy) 3.37); *kāma-rūpeṇa* (m∘ 3inst∘ sing∘ ←bahuvrī∘ ***kāma-rūpa,*** कामम् रूपम् यस्य ←n∘ *kāma* 1.22 + n∘ 🕮***rūpa*** (form) ←4∘√रूप्); *kaunteya* (2.14); 🕮*duṣpūreṇa* (m∘ 3inst∘ sing∘ ←adj∘ ***duṣpūra*** (insatiable) ←ind∘ ***duṣ*** ←5∘√दु + m∘ *pūra* ←6∘√पुर्); *analena* (m∘ 3inst∘ sing∘ ←n.tatpu∘ ***anala*** (fire) ←1∘√अल्); *ća* (1.1) (3.39)

(§3) *āvṛtam* (adj∘-obj1∘ covered, enveloped); *jñānam* (obj∘ knowledge, wisdom); *etena* (adj1∘-subj∘ by this, by this craving, by this desire, by this kāma); *jñāninaḥ:* (of the wise); *nityavairiṇā* (adj2∘-subj∘ by formidable enemy); *kāma-rūpeṇa* (adj3∘-subj∘ by that which is in the form of desire, craving, lust); *kaunteya* (O Kaunteya! O Arjuna!); *duṣpūreṇa-analena* (adj4∘-subj∘ by insatiable fire); ća (and) (3.39)

(§4) kaunteya āvṛtam jñānam jñāninaḥ: etena nityavairiṇā kāma-rūpeṇa ća duṣpūreṇa analena

(§5) O Arjuna! enveloped (is) wisdom of the wise by this formidable enemy[335] in the form of desire and insatiable fire.[336] (3.39)

---

[334] Elsewhere∘ तेन → by it.

[335] Elsewhere∘ *nityavairiṇā* → by eternal enemy, eternal foe ...etc.

🕮 If the enemy is eternal, then it is indestructible. Whereas in verse 3.41 in this chapter Lord Kṛṣṇa says, भरतर्षभ! पाप्मानं प्रजहि ह्येनम् (O Arjuna! destroy this sinful enemy); and in 3.43 जहि शत्रुं महाबाहो! (O Arjuna! destroy this enemy). It means, neither the origin of this enemy (शत्रुः) is eternal (शाश्वतः) nor the end is eternal. This enemy is not eternal but it is destructible, though it is formidable or constant (नित्यः).

[336] Elsewhere∘ एतेन नित्यवैरिणा कामरूपेण दुष्पूरेण अनलेन च → enemy known as desire which is insatiable like fire, ...insatiable like fire, which is an insatiable fire, which is like an insatiable fire, this insatiable fire of desire

3.40 इन्द्रियाणि मनो बुद्धिरस्याधिष्ठानमुच्यते ।
एतैर्विमोहयत्येष ज्ञानमावृत्य देहिनम् ।।

indriyāṇi mano buddhirasyādhiṣṭhānamucyate,
etairvimohayatyeṣa jñānamāvṛtya dehinam. (3.40)

(§1) इन्द्रियाणि मनः बुद्धिः अस्य अधिष्ठानम् उच्यते । एतैः विमोहयति एषः ज्ञानम् आवृत्य देहिनम् । *indriyāṇi* (r◦ 24/7) *manaḥ:* (r◦ 15/7) *buddhiḥ:* (r◦ 16/1) *asya* (r◦ 1/1) *adhiṣṭhānam* (r◦ 8/20) *ucyate* (r◦ 23/1) *etaiḥ:* (r◦ 16/11) *vimohayati* (r◦ 4/4) *eṣaḥ:* (r◦ 25/1, 21/1) *jñānam* (r◦ 8/17) *āvṛtya dehinam* (r◦ 14/2)

(§2) *indriyāṇi* (2.60); *manaḥ:* (1.30); *buddhiḥ:* (2.39); *asya* (2.17); 🕮***adhiṣṭhānam*** (1nom◦ sing◦ ←n◦ *adhiṣṭhāna* (seat) ←1◦अधि√स्था); *ucyate* (2.25); *etaiḥ:* (1.43); *vimohayati* (3rd-per◦ sing◦ pres◦ वर्तमान्-लट् parasmai◦ caus◦ ←4◦वि√मुह् 3.2); *eṣaḥ:* (3.10); ***jñānam*** (2acc◦ sing◦ ←n◦ *jñāna* 3.39); 🕮***āvṛtya*** (lyp◦ past-participle ind◦ ←1◦आ√वृ); ***dehinam*** (2acc◦ sing◦ ←m◦ *dehin* (embodied) 2.13) (3.40)

(§3) *indriyāṇi* (subj1◦ the organs); *manaḥ:* (subj2◦ mind); *buddhiḥ:* (subj3◦ intellect); *asya* (of this, of this enemy); *adhiṣṭhānam* (subj4◦ governance, seat, abode); *ucyate* (is called); *etaiḥ:* (through these); *vimohayati* (he causes to delude); *eṣaḥ:* (subj5◦ this, this enemy); *jñānam* (obj1◦ the knowledge, the wisdom); *āvṛtya* (covering, having covered); *dehinam* (obj2◦ the embodied being) (3.40)

(§4) indriyāṇi manaḥ: buddhiḥ: ucyate adhiṣṭhānam asya etaiḥ: āvṛtya jñānam eṣaḥ: vimohayati dehinam

(§5) The organs, mind (and) intellect is[337] (collectively) called an abode of this enemy. Through these, having covered the wisdom, this (enemy) causes to delude embodied being. (3.40)

3.41 तस्मात्त्वमिन्द्रियाण्यादौ नियम्य भरतर्षभ ।
पाप्मानं प्रजहि ह्येनं ज्ञानविज्ञाननाशनम् ।।

tasmāttvamindriyāṇyādau niyamya bharatarṣabha,
pāpmānaṁ prajahi hyenaṁ jñānavijñānanāśanam. (3.41)

(§1) तस्मात् त्वम् इन्द्रियाणि आदौ नियम्य भरतर्षभ । पाप्मानम् प्रजहि हि एनम् ज्ञानविज्ञाननाशनम् । *tasmāt* (r◦ 1/10) *tvam* (r◦ 8/18) *indriyāṇi* (r◦ 24/7, 4/2) *ādau niyamya bharatarṣabha pāpmānam* (r◦ 14/1) *prajahi hi* (r◦

---

which is the constant foe of the wise, which is insatiable as a flame ...etc.

🕮 एतेन, नित्यवैरिणा, कामरूपेण and दुष्पुरेण अनलेन are all Instrumental case adjectives of the subject *vairin* वैरिन्. They all should point to the subject वैरिणा, in Instrumental case, for a Sanskrit passive voice construction.

[337] Elsewhere◦ उच्यते → are said to be, are declared to be, are called, are the sittings ...etc.

🕮 Note that *ucyate* (उच्यते, is called) is a singular verb. and अधिष्ठानम् (an abode) is a singular subject.

4/4) *enam* (r∘ 14/1) *jñānavijñānanāśanam* (r∘ 14/2)

(§2) *tasmāt* (1.37); *tvam* (2.11); *indriyāṇi* (2.58); ***ādau*** (m∘ 7loc∘ sing∘ ←adj∘ *ādi* (first) 2.28); *niyamya* (3.7); 📖***bharatarṣabha*** (m∘ 8voc∘ sing∘ ←bahuvrī∘ *bharatarṣabha*, भरतानाम् ऋषभः यः ←m∘ -taddhita∘ *bharata*, दुश्यन्तस्य च शकुन्तलायाः च गोत्रापत्यम् + m∘ *ṛṣabha* (bull) ←6∘√ऋष्); *pāpmānam* (2acc∘ sing∘ ←m∘ *pāpman* (sinner) 3.37); *prajahi* (2nd-per∘ sing∘ imperative∘ आज्ञार्थ-लोट् parasmai∘ ←2∘प्र√हन्); *hi* (1.11); *enam* (2.19); *jñānavijñānanāśanam* (m∘ 2acc∘ sing∘ ←bahuvrī∘ *jñāna-vijñāna-nāśana*, ज्ञानस्य च विज्ञानस्य च नाशनः यः ←n∘ *jñāna* 3.3 + n∘ 📖***vijñāna*** ←9∘वि√ज्ञा + adj∘ ***nāśana*** (destroyer) ←3∘√नश्) (3.41)

(§3) *tasmāt* (therefore); *tvam* (subj∘ you); *indriyāṇi* (obj1∘ sense organs); *ādau* (first); *niyamya* (having restrained); *bharatarṣabha* (O Bharatarṣabha! O Arjuna!); *pāpmānam* (adj1∘-obj2∘ the sinful); *prajahi* (you please destroy!); *hi enam* (obj2∘ this, this enemy); *jñānavijñānanāśanam* (adj2∘-obj2∘ the destroyer of wisdom and knowledge) (3.41)

(§4) tasmāt bharatarṣabha ādau niyamya indriyāṇi tvam prajahi enam pāpmānam hi jñānavijñānanāśanam

(§5) Therefore,[338] O Arjuna! first, having restrained sense organs, you please destroy this enemy, the sinful destroyer of knowledge and wisdom.[339] (3.41)

3.42 इन्द्रियाणि पराण्याहुरिन्द्रियेभ्यः परं मनः ।
मनसस्तु परा बुद्धिर्यो बुद्धेः परतस्तु सः ।।[340]
ndriyāṇi parāṇyāhurindriyebhyaḥ: paraṁ manaḥ:,
manasastu parā bhddhiryo buddheḥ: paratastu saḥ:. (3.42)

(§1) इन्द्रियाणि पराणि आहुः इन्द्रियेभ्यः परम् मनः । मनसः तु परा बुद्धिः यः बुद्धेः परतः तु सः । *indriyāṇi* (r∘ 24/7) *parāṇi* (r∘ 24/7, 4/2) *āhuḥ:* (r∘ 16/3) *indriyebhyaḥ:* (r∘ 22/3) *param* (r∘ 14/1) *manaḥ:* (r∘ 22/8) *manasaḥ:* (r∘ 18/1) *tu parā buddhiḥ:* (r∘ 16/6) *yaḥ:* (r∘ 15/7) *buddheḥ:* (r∘ 22/3) *parataḥ:* (r∘ 18/1) *tu saḥ:* (r∘ 22/8)

(§2) *indriyāṇi* (1nom∘ 2.58); 📖*parāṇi* (n∘ 1nom∘ plu∘ ←adj∘ *para* 2.3); 📖***āhuḥ:*** (3rd-per∘ plu∘ pres∘

---

[338] See the footnote in verse 2.15

[339] Elsewhere∘ विज्ञान → self-realization, Self-realization, dissimination, knowledge of Sakāra Brahma or manifest Divinity.

[340] इन्द्रियेभ्यः परा ह्यर्था अर्थेभ्यश्च परं मनः । मनसस्तु परा बुद्धिर्बुद्धेरात्मा महान्परः ।। (kathopaniṣad 1.3.10)
Subtler than the (Sense) Organs are their Senses; Subtler than the Senses is the Mind; Subtler than the Mind is the Thinking; and Subtler than the Thinking is the Supreme ātmā.

वर्तमान्-लट् parasmai◦ ←2◦√ब्रू, 5√आह); *indriyebhyaḥ:* (5abl◦ plu◦ ←n◦ *indriya* 2.8); *paraṃ* (1nom◦ 2.12); *manaḥ:* (1nom◦ 1.30); *manasaḥ:* (5abl◦ sing◦ ←n◦ *manaṣ* 1.30); *tu* (1.2); ***parā*** (f◦ 1nom◦ sing◦ ←adj◦ *para* (superior) 2.3); *buddhiḥ:* (2.39); *yaḥ:* (2.19); ***buddheḥ:*** (5abl◦ sing◦ ←f◦ *buddhi* (thinking) 1.23); *parataḥ:* (comparative ind◦ *parataṣ* (more superior) ←n◦ *para* ←3◦√पृ); *tu* (1.2); *saḥ:* (1.13) (3.42)

(§3) *indriyāṇi* (subj1◦ sense organs); *parāṇi* (adj◦-subj1◦ higher, superior); *āhuḥ:* (they say); *indriyebhyaḥ:* (than the organs); *paraṃ* (adj◦-subj2◦ superior); *manaḥ:* (subj2◦ mind); *manasaḥ:* (than the mind); *tu* (and); *parā* (adj◦-subj3◦ superior); *buddhiḥ:* (subj3◦ intellect); *yaḥ:* (adj1◦-subj4◦ he who); *buddheḥ:* (than the intellect, than the thinking); *parataḥ:* (higher); *tu* (indeed); *saḥ:* (subj4◦ he, that, that ātmā) (3.42)

(§4) āhuḥ: indriyāṇi parāṇi paraṃ indriyebhyaḥ: manaḥ: parā manasaḥ: buddhiḥ: yaḥ: parataḥ: buddheḥ: tu saḥ:

(§5) They say[341] (that) sense organs (are) superior. Superior than the organs (is) mind. Superior than mind (is) intellect.[342] And, he who (is) higher than the intellect, (is) indeed that ātmā. (3.42)

3.43 **एवं बुद्धेः परं बुद्ध्वा संस्तभ्यात्मानमात्मना ।**
जहि शत्रुं महाबाहो कामरूपं दुरासदम् ॥
evaṃ buddheḥ: paraṁ buddhvā saṁstabhyātmānamātmanā,
jahi śatruṁ mahābāho kāmarūpaṁ durāsadaṃ. (3.43)

(§1) एवम् बुद्धेः परम् बुद्ध्वा संस्तभ्य आत्मानम् आत्मना । जहि शत्रुम् महाबाहो कामरूपम् दुरासदम् । *evaṃ* (r◦ 14/1) *buddheḥ:* (r◦ 22/3) *paraṃ* (r◦ 14/1) *buddhvā saṁstabhya* (r◦ 1/2) *ātmānaṃ* (r◦ 8/17) *ātmanā jahi śatruṃ* (r◦ 14/1) *mahābāho kāmarūpaṃ* (r◦ 14/1) *durāsadaṃ* (r◦ 14/2)

(§2) *evaṃ* (1.24); *buddheḥ:* (3.42); *paraṃ* (2acc◦ 2.59); ***buddhvā*** (ipp◦ ind◦ ←1◦√बुध्); 📖*saṁstabhya* (lyp◦ past-participle ind◦ ←9◦सम्√स्तम्भ्); ***ātmānam*** (2acc◦ sing◦ ←m◦ *ātmaṇ* 2.41); *ātmanā* (2.55); ***jahi*** (2nd-per◦ sing◦ imperative◦ आज्ञार्थ-लोट् parasmai◦ ←2◦√हन् 3.41); 📖*śatruṃ* (2acc◦ sing◦ ←m◦ ***śatru*** (enemy) ←1◦√शद्); *mahābāho* (2.26); *kāmarūpaṃ* (m◦ 2acc◦ sing◦ ←bahuvrī◦ *kāma-rūpa* 3.39); 📖*durāsadaṃ* (m◦ 2acc◦ sing◦ ←adj◦ *durāsada* (formidable) ←ind◦ *duṛ* 1.2 + m◦ *āsada* ←6◦आ√सद्) (3.43)

(§3) *evaṃ* (in this manner); *buddheḥ:* (obj1◦ *paraṃ* (obj1◦ that which is superior to intellect); *buddhvā* (having known, having understood); *saṁstabhya* (having restrained); *ātmānaṃ* (obj2◦ yourself);

---

[341] Elsewhere◦ आहुः → It is said that, are said to be, ...etc.

[342] Elsewhere◦ बुद्धिः → reason, intelligence ...etc.

ātmanā (by yourself); *jahi* (you please destroy!); *śatrum* (obj3◦ the enemy); *mahābāho* (O Mahābāho! O Arjuna!); *kāmarūpam* (adj1◦-obj3◦ that which is in the form of lust); *durāsadam* (adj2◦-obj3◦ that which is the formidable, which is unparallel) (3.43)

(§4) mahābāho evam buddhvā param buddheḥ: saṁstabhya ātmānam ātmanā jahi durāsadam śatrum kāmarūpam

(§5) O Arjuna! in this manner, having understood that (ātmā) which is superior[343] to the intellect, (and) having restrained yourself by yourself, you please destroy the formidable enemy that is in the form of lust. (3.43)

इति श्रीमद्भगवद्गीतासूपनिषत्सु ब्रह्मविद्यायां योगशास्त्रे
श्रीकृष्णार्जुनसंवादे कर्मयोगो नाम तृतीयोऽध्यायः ।।

iti śrīmadbhagavadgītāsūpaniṣatsu brahmavidyāyām yogaśāstre
śrīkṛṣṇārjunasaṁvāde karmayogo nāma tṛtīyo'dhyāyaḥ:.

(§1) *iti śrīmadbhagavadgītāsu* (r◦ 1/8) *upaniṣatsu brahmavidyāyām* (r◦ 14/1) *yogaśāstre śrīkṛṣṇārjunasaṁvāde karmayogaḥ:* (r◦ 15/6) *nāma tṛtīyaḥ:* (r◦ 15/1) *adhyāyaḥ:* (r◦ 22/8)

(§2) *iti* (1.25); *śrīmadbhagavadgītāsu* (f◦ 7loc◦ plu◦ tatpu◦ *śrīmad-bhagavad-gītā* ←adj◦ *śrīmat* 6.41 + adj◦ *bhagavat* 10.14 + f◦ *gītā* ←5◦√गै); *upaniṣatsu* (7loc◦ plu◦ ←f◦ *upaniṣad* ←6◦उप-नि√सद्); *brahmavidyāyām* (f◦ 7loc◦ sing◦ ←tatpu◦ *brahma-vidyā*, ब्रह्मण: विद्या ←n◦ *brahman* 2.72 + *vidyā* 5.18); *yogaśāstre* (n◦ 7loc◦ sing◦ ←tatpu◦ *yoga-śāstra*, योगानाम् शास्त्रम् । योगस्य शास्त्रम् । ←m◦ *yoga* 2.39 + n◦ *śāstra* 15.20); *śrīkṛṣṇārjunasaṁvāde* (m◦ 7loc◦ sing◦ ←tatpu◦ *śrī-kṛṣṇārjuna-saṁvāda*, श्रीकृष्णस्य च अर्जुनस्य च संवाद: ←adj◦ *śrī* 10.34 + m◦ prop◦ *kṛṣṇa* 1.28 + m◦ prop◦ *arjuna* 1.4 + m◦ *saṁvāda* 18.70); *karmayogo* (m◦ 1nom◦ sing◦ ←tatpu◦ *karma-yoga*, निष्कामकर्मण: योग: ←prop◦ *karman* 1.15 + m◦ *yoga* 2.39); *nāma* (1nom◦ sing◦ ←n◦ *nāman* ←1◦√म्ना); *tṛtīyaḥ:* (m◦ 1nom◦ sing◦ ←num◦ adj◦ *tṛtīya* ←adj◦ *tri* 2.45); *adhyāyaḥ:* (1nom◦ sing◦ ←m◦ *adhyāya* ←1◦अधि√इ)

(§3) *iti* (thus); *śrīmadbhagavadgītāsu upaniṣatsu* (among the upaniṣads of the Śrīmad-Bhagavadgītā); *brahmavidyāyām* (of the eternal wisdoms); *yogaśāstre* (in the science of Yoga); *śrīkṛṣṇārjunasaṁvāde* (in the dialogue between Śrī Kṛṣṇa and Arjuna); *karmayogaḥ:* (adj◦1-subj◦ karma-yoga); *nāma* (called); *tṛtīyaḥ:* (adj◦2-subj◦ the third); *adhyāyaḥ:* (subj◦ discourse; chapter)

(§4) śrīmadbhagavadgītāsu upaniṣatsu yogaśāstre brahmavidyāyām iti tṛtīyaḥ adhyāyaḥ: nāma karmayogo

---

[343] Elsewhere◦ बुद्धे: परं बुद्ध्वा → understanding the self as, knowing Him as, knowing oneself to be, ...etc.

(§5) Among the upaniṣads of the Śrīmad-Bhagavadgītā, in the science of yoga of self realization, thus (is) the third discourse called *karma-yogaḥ:*, in the dialogue between Śrī Kṛṣṇa and Arjuna. (3.43)

CHAPTER 4

ćaturtho'adhyāyaḥ:

चतुर्थोऽध्यायः ।

jñāna-karma-sannyāsa-yogaḥ:

ज्ञानकर्मसंन्यासयोगः ।

THE YOGA OF KNOWLEDGE,[344] CONDUCT AND RENUNCIATION

The Lord said (śrībhagavānuvāća श्रीभगवानुवाच ।)

4.1 इमं विवस्वते योगं प्रोक्तवानहमव्ययम् ।
विवस्वान्मनवे प्राह मनुरिक्ष्वाकवेऽब्रवीत् ।।
imaṁ vivasvate yogaṁ proktavānahamavyayam,
vivasvānmanave prāha manurikṣvākave'bravīt. (4.1)

(§1) इमम् विवस्वते योगम् प्रोक्तवान् अहम् अव्ययम् । विवस्वान् मनवे प्राह मनुः इक्ष्वाकवे अब्रवीत् । *ćaturthaḥ:* (r◦ 15/1) *adhyāyaḥ:* (r◦ 22/8). *jñānakarmasannyāsayogaḥ:* (r◦ 22/8). *śrībhagavān̦* (r◦ 8/14) *uvāća. imam̦* (r◦ 14/1) *vivasvate yogam̦* (r◦ 14/1) *proktavān̦* (r◦ 8/11) *aham̦* (r◦ 8/16) *avyayam̦* (r◦ 14/2) *vivasvān̦* (r◦ 13/16) *manave prāha manuḥ:* (r◦ 16/3) *ikṣvākave* (r◦ 6/1) *abravīț*

(§2) *ćaturthaḥ:* (m◦ 1nom◦ sing◦ ←sequence indicating num◦ adj◦ *ćaturtha* ←adj◦ *ćatur̦* 7.16↓); *adhyāyaḥ:* (1nom◦ sing◦ ←m◦ *adhyāya* ←1◦अधि√इ). *jñānakarmasannyāsayogaḥ:* (m◦ 1nom◦ sing◦ ←tatpu◦ *jñāna-karma-sannyāsa-yoga*, समत्वस्य ज्ञानस्य, निष्कामस्य च कर्मस्य, सङ्गस्य च संन्यासस्य, योगः ←n◦ *jñāna* 3.3 + n◦ *karman̦* 1.15 + m◦ *sannyāsa* 5.1 + m◦ *yoga* 2.39). *śrībhagavān̦* (2.2); *uvāća* (1.25).

imam̦ (1.28); *vivasvate* (4dat◦ sing◦ ←m◦ prop◦ ***vivasvaț***); *yogam̦* (2.53); 🕮***proktavān̦*** (m◦ 1nom◦

[344] Knowledge = Knowledge of Equanimity.

sing◦ ←pap◦ past◦-act◦-participle *proktavat̩* ←2◦प्र√वच् 3.3); *aham̩* (1.22); 🕮*avyayam̩* (indestructible 2acc◦ 2.21); *vivasvān̩* (1nom◦ sing◦ ←m◦ *vivasvat̩* ↑); *manave* (4dat◦ sing◦ ←m◦ prop◦ *manu* 1.44); *prāha* (3rd-per◦ sing◦ pres◦ पूर्णकालवाचक-लट् parasmai◦ ←2◦प्र√अह्); *manuḥ:* (1nom◦ sing◦ ←m◦ *manu* 1.44); *ikṣvākave* (4dat◦ sing◦ ←m◦ prop◦ *ikṣvāku); abravīt̩* (1.2) (4.1)

(§3) *ćaturthaḥ:* (adj◦-subj◦ fourth); *adhyāyaḥ:* (subj◦ chapter). *jñāna-karma-sannyāsayogaḥ:* (The yoga encompassing knowledge of equanimity, relinquishment of desire in fruit, and renunciation of attachment. The yoga of working with indifference, without desiring the fruit, and renunciation of doership). *śrībhagavān̩* (subj◦ the Lord); *uvāća* (said). *imam̩* (adj1◦-obj◦ this); *vivasvate* (to Vivasvat); *yogam̩* (obj◦ yoga); *proktavān̩* (told); *aham̩* (subj1◦ I); *avyayam̩* (adj2◦-obj◦ prestine, unalterable, immortal, indestructible); *vivasvān̩* (subj2◦ Vivasvat); *manave* (to Manu); *prāha* (he told); *manuḥ:* (subj3◦ Manu); *ikṣvākave* (to Ikṣvāku); *abravīt̩* (he told) (4.1)

(§4) ćaturthaḥ: adhyāyaḥ:. jñānakarmasannyāsayogaḥ:. śrībhagavān̩ uvāća. aham̩ proktavān̩ imam̩ avyayam̩ yogam̩ vivasvate vivasvān̩ prāha manave manuḥ: abravīt̩ ikṣvākave

(§5) Fourth chapter. The yoga encompassing knowledge of equanimity, relinquishment of desire in fruit and renunciation of attachment.[345] Lord Kṛshṇa said : I told this indestructible yoga to Vivasvat, Vivasvat told (it) to Manu, (and) Manu told (it) to Ikṣvāku. (4.1)

4.2 **एवं परम्पराप्राप्तमिमं राजर्षयो विदुः ।**
स कालेनेह महता योगो नष्टः परन्तप ।।
evaṁ parmparāprāptamiṁ rājarṣayo viduḥ:,
sa kāleneha mahtā yogo naṣṭaḥ: parantapa. (4.2)

(§1) एवम् परम्पराप्राप्तम् इमम् राजर्षयः विदुः । सः कालेन इह महता योगः नष्टः परन्तप । *evam̩* (r◦ 14/1) *parmparāprāptam̩* (r◦ 8/18) *imam̩* (r◦ 14/1) *rājarṣayaḥ:* (r◦ 15/13) *viduḥ:* (r◦ 22/8) *saḥ:* (r◦ 21/2) *kālena* (r◦ 2/1) *iha mahtā yogaḥ:* (r◦ 15/6) *naṣṭaḥ:* (r◦ 22/3) *parantapa*

(§2) *evam̩* (1.24); *parmparāprāptam̩* (m◦ 2acc◦ sing◦ ←tatpu◦ *parmparā-prāpta,* परम्परया प्राप्तम् ←f◦ 🕮*parmparā* (succession) ←3◦√पॄ + ppp◦ adj◦ 🕮***prāpta*** (attained) ←5◦प्र√आप्); *imam̩* (1.28); 🕮***rājarṣayaḥ:*** (m◦ 1nom◦ plu◦ ←tatpu◦ *rājarṣi* (royal sage) ऋषिषु राट् ←m◦ ***ṛṣi*** ←6◦√ऋष् + m◦ *rāj* ←1◦√राज्); ***viduḥ:*** (3rd-per◦ plu◦ pres◦ वर्तमान्-लट् parasmai◦ ←2◦√विद्); *saḥ:* (1.13); ***kālena*** (3inst◦ sing◦ ←m◦ *kāla* (time) 2.72); *iha* (2.5); *mahtā* (m◦ 3inst◦ sing◦ ←adj◦ *mahat̩* (great) 1.3); *yogaḥ:* (2.48); 🕮***naṣṭaḥ:*** (m◦ 1nom◦ sing◦ ←adj◦ *naṣṭa* =

---

[345] Elsewhere◦ *jñānakarmasannyāsayogaḥ:* → knowledge and renunciation of actions; the yoga of renunciation of action in knowledge; yoga of knowledge, the way of knowledge, action and renunciation ...etc.

vismṛta (forgotten) 1.40); *parantapa* (2.3) (4.2)

(§3) *evam* (in this manner); *parmparāprāptam* (adj1◦-obj◦ acquired through the system of teacher-to-pupil succession); *imam* (adj2◦-obj◦ this, this yoga); *rājarṣayaḥ:* (subj1◦ the great sages); *viduḥ:* (they learn, they are learning; in present context - they were learning); *saḥ:* (adj1◦-subj2◦ that); *kālena* (with time, with the passage of time); *iha* (in this world); *mahtā* (with long); *yogaḥ:* (subj2◦ yoga); *naṣṭaḥ:* (adj2◦-subj2◦ forgotten, disappeared, lost); *parantapa* (O Parantapa! O Arjuna!) (4.2)

(§4) parmparāprāptam evam rājarṣayaḥ: viduḥ: imam parantapa mahtā kālena saḥ: yogaḥ: naṣṭaḥ: iha

(§5) Acquired through the system of teacher-to-pupil succession in this manner, the great sages[346] (were) learning this yoga. O Arjuna! with long passage of time that yoga disappeared[347] in this world. (4.2)

4.3 स एवायं मया तेऽद्य योगः प्रोक्तः पुरातनः ।
भक्तोऽसि मे सखा चेति रहस्यं ह्येतदुत्तमम् ।।

sa evāyaṁ mayā te'dya yogaḥ: proktaḥ: purātanaḥ:,
bhakto'si me sakhā ćeti rahasyaṁ hyetaduttamam. (4.3)

(§1) सः एव अयम् मया ते अद्य योगः प्रोक्तः पुरातनः । भक्तः असि मे सखा च इति रहस्यम् हि एतत् उत्तमम् । *saḥ:* (r◦ 21/2) *eva* (r◦ 1/1) *ayam* (r◦ 14/1) *mayā te* (r◦ 6/1) *adya yogaḥ:* (r◦ 22/3) *proktaḥ:* (r◦ 22/3) *purātanaḥ:* (r◦ 22/8) *bhaktaḥ:* (r◦ 15/1) *asi me sakhā ća* (r◦ 2/1) *iti rahasyam* (r◦ 14/1) *hi* (r◦ 4/4) *etaṭ* (r◦ 8/6) *uttamam* (r◦ 14/2)

---

[346] Elsewhere◦ *rājarṣayaḥ:* → royal sages.

📖 The prefix राज- from the verb root √राज् (to be eminent) imperts the quality of being being best of its kind. Therefore, राज- not necessarily mean royal or kingly, but the great (महा) in any sense. eg. in Gītā, राजविद्या is superior knowledge, not royal education (not knowledge of king, but king of knowledges); राजगुह्य is supreme secret, not royal secret (not secert of king, but king of secrets) ...etc. महर्षयः would not be royal sages (not the sages of the kings, but the kings of sages)

[347] Elsewhere◦ *naṣṭaḥ:* → perished, destroyed, decayed ...etc.

📖 In 4.1 Bhagavān said इमं योगम् अव्ययम् । If the *yoga* is eternal, how can it be perished, destroyed or decayed? It can not. It will be a contradiction. Thus, नष्ट = स्मृतः नष्टः is forgotten, lost from people's mind, disappeared from public ..etc. That is, it is not present in people's dealings, but is everpresent eternally. An eternal thing can be lost. It can be forgotten or it can disappear and then it can again remembered or it can reappear in public.But, it is not lost.

(§2) *saḥ:* (1.13); *eva* (1.1); *ayaṃ* (2.19); *mayā* (1.22); *te* (1.7); ***adya*** (today, time indicating ind◦ ←2◦√अद्); *yogaḥ:* (2.48); ***proktaḥ:*** (m◦ 1nom◦ sing◦ ←adj◦ *prokta* (told) 3.3); 🕮*purātanaḥ:* (m◦ 1nom◦ sing◦ ←adj◦ *purātana* ←6◦√पुर्); 🕮***bhaktaḥ:*** (1nom◦ sing◦ ←m◦ ***bhakta*** (devotee) ←ppp◦ adj◦ ***bhakta*** (devoted) ←1◦√भज्); ***asi*** (2nd-per◦ sing◦ pres◦ वर्तमान्-लट् parasmai◦ ←2◦√अस्); *me* (1.21); 🕮***sakhā*** (1nom◦ sing◦ ←m◦ *sakhi* (companion) 1.26); *ća* (1.1); *iti* (1.25); 🕮*rahasyaṃ* (2acc◦ sing◦ ←n◦ *rahasya* (secret) ←1◦√रम्); *hi* (1.11); *etaṭ* (2.3); 🕮***uttamaṃ*** (n◦ 1nom◦ 2acc◦ sing◦ ←adj◦ *uttama* (the best) 1.7) (4.3)

(§3) *saḥ:* (adj◦-obj◦ that); *eva* (itself); *ayaṃ* (adj2◦-obj◦ this, the one just referred); *mayā* (subj1◦ by me); *te* (to you); *adya* (today); *yogaḥ:* (obj◦ yoga); *proktaḥ:* (adj3◦-obj◦ told); *purātanaḥ:* (adj4◦-obj◦ ancient); *bhaktaḥ:* (adj1◦-subj2◦ devotee); *asi* (subj2◦ you are); *me* (my); *sakhā* (adj2◦-subj2◦ dear, dear friend); *ća* (and); *iti* (thus, so); *rahasyaṃ* (obj2◦ secret); *hi* (because); *etaṭ* (adj1◦-obj2◦ this); *uttamaṃ* (adj2◦-obj2◦ supreme) (4.3)

(§4) saḥ: purātanaḥ: yogaḥ: eva ayaṃ proktaḥ: te mayā adya hi asi me bhaktaḥ: ća sakhā iti etaṭ uttamaṃ rahasyaṃ

(§5) That ancient yoga itself, the one just referred, (is being) told to you by me today, because[348] you are my devotee and dear friend, so this supreme secret.[349] (4.3)

Arjuna said (arjuna uvāća अर्जुन उवाच ।)

4.4 **अपरं भवतो जन्म परं जन्म विवस्वतः ।**
कथमेतद्विजानीयां त्वमादौ प्रोक्तवानिति ।।
aparaṁ bhavato janma paraṁ janma vivasvataḥ:,
kathametadvijānīyāṁ tvamādau proktavāniti. (4.4)

(§1) अपरम् भवतः जन्म परम् जन्म विवस्वतः । कथम् एतत् विजानीयाम् त्वम् आदौ प्रोक्तवान् इति । *arjunaḥ:* (r◦ 19/4) *uvāća. aparaṃ* (r◦ 14/1) *bhavataḥ:* (r◦ 15/3) *janma paraṃ* (r◦ 14/1) *janma vivasvataḥ:* (r◦ 22/8) *kathaṃ* (r◦ 8/22) *etaṭ* (r◦ 9/11) *vijānīyāṃ* (r◦ 14/1) *tvaṃ* (r◦ 8/17) *ādau proktavāṇ* (r◦ 8/13) *iti*

(§2) *arjunaḥ:* (1.47); *uvāća* (1.25). 🕮*aparaṃ* (m◦ 1nom◦ sing◦ ←adj◦ *apara* (recent) 2.22); ***bhavataḥ:*** (m◦ 6pos◦ sing◦ ←pron◦ *bhavaṭ* 1.8); *janma* (birth 1nom◦ 2.27); *paraṃ* (1nom◦ sing◦ ←adj◦ *para* 2.59); *janma* (2.27); *vivasvataḥ:* (m◦ 6pos◦ sing◦ ←prop◦ *vivasvaṭ* 4.1); 🕮*kathaṃ* (how? 1.37); *etaṭ* (2.6); *vijānīyāṃ* (1st-per◦ sing◦ potential◦ विधि◦ parasmai◦ ←9◦वि√ज्ञा); *tvaṃ* (2.11); *ādau* (3.41); *proktavāṇ* (4.1); *iti* (1.25)

---

[348] See footnote in verse 3.5

[349] Elsewhere◦ *etat rahasyaṃ uttamaṃ* → it is the supreme secret, this secret is supreme, this is supreme secret, this is a profound secret ...etc.

(4.4)

(§3) *arjunaḥ:* (subj◦ Arjuna); *uvāća* (said). *aparaṃ* (adj◦-subj1◦ m◦ recent, not distant, newer); *bhavataḥ:* (your); *janma* (subj1◦ birth); *paraṃ* (adj◦-subj2◦ earlier, distant, ancient); *janma* (subj2◦ birth); *vivasvataḥ:* (of Vivasvat); *kathaṃ* (how? how then?); *etaṭ* (this); *vijānīyāṃ* (may I understand); *tvaṃ* (subj3◦ you); *ādau* (before, in ancient time); *proktavāṇ* (told); *iti* (that) (4.4)

(§4) arjunaḥ: uvāća. bhavataḥ: janma aparaṃ, janma vivasvataḥ: paraṃ, kathaṃ vijānīyāṃ etaṭ iti tvaṃ proktavāṇ ādau

(§5) Arjuna said; Your birth (is) recent, (and) birth of Vivasvat (was) ancient, how then may I understand this that you told (it) in ancient time? (4.4)

The Lord said (śrībhagavānuvāća श्रीभगवानुवाच ।)

4.5 बहूनि मे व्यतीतानि जन्मानि तव चार्जुन ।
तान्यहं वेद सर्वाणि न त्वं वेत्थ परन्तप ।।

bahūni me vyatītāni janmāni tava ćārjuna,
tānyahaṁ veda sarvāṇi na tvaṁ vettha parantapa. (4.5)

(§1) बहूनि मे व्यतीतानि जन्मानि तव च अर्जुन । तानि अहम् वेद सर्वाणि न त्वम् वेत्थ परन्तप । *śrībhagavāṇ* (r◦ 8/14) *uvāća. bahūni me vyatītāni janmāni tava ća* (r◦ 1/1) *arjuna tāni* (r◦ 4/1) *ahaṃ* (r◦ 14/1) *veda sarvāṇi* (r◦ 24/7) *na tvaṃ* (r◦ 14/1) *vettha parantapa*

(§2) *śrībhagavāṇ* (2.2); *uvāća* (1.25). 🕮***bahūni*** (n◦ 1nom◦ plu◦ ←adj◦ *bahu* (many) 1.9); *me* (1.21); 🕮*vyatītāni* (n◦ 1nom◦ plu◦ ←ppp◦ adj◦ *vyatīta* (passed) ←1◦वि–अति√इ); *janmāni* (1nom◦ plu◦ ←n◦ *janmaṇ* (birth) 2.27); *tava* (1.3); *ća* (1.1); *arjuna* (2.2); *tāni* (2.61); *ahaṃ* (1.22); ***veda*** (1st-per◦ sing◦ -present perfect◦ parasmai◦ ←2◦√विद्); *sarvāṇi* (2acc◦ 2.30); *na* (1.30); *tvaṃ* (2.11); ***vettha*** (2nd-per◦ sing◦ pres◦ वर्तमान्–लट् parasmai◦ ←2◦√विद्); *parantapa* (2.3) (4.5)

(§3) *śrībhagavāṇ* (the Lord); *uvāća* (said). *bahūni* (adj1◦-subj1◦ many); *me* (adj2◦-subj1◦ my, of mine); *vyatītāni* (adj3◦-subj1◦ passed); *janmāni* (subj◦ births); *tava* (adj4◦-subj1◦ your); *ća* (and); *arjuna* (O Arjuna!); *tāni* (adj1◦obj◦ them, to them); *ahaṃ* (subj2◦ I); *veda* (I know); *sarvāṇi* (adj2◦-obj◦ all); *na* (not); *tvaṃ* (subj3◦ you); *vettha* (you do know); *parantapa* (O Parantapa! O Arjuna!) (4.5)

(§4) śrībhagavāṇ uvāća. arjuna! vyatītāni bahūni janmāni me ća tava; ahaṃ veda tāni sarvāṇi, parantapa! tvaṃ na vettha

(§5) The Lord said, O Arjuna! passed[350] (are) many births of mine (and) your. I know them all, (but) O Arjuna! you do not know (them or that). (4.5)

4.6 अजोऽपि सन्नव्ययात्मा भूतानामीश्वरोऽपि सन् ।
प्रकृतिं स्वामधिष्ठाय सम्भवाम्यात्ममायया ।।
ajo'pi sannavyayātmā bhūtānāmīśvaro'pi san,
prakṛtiṁ svāmadhiṣṭhāya sambhavāmyātmamāyayā. (4.6)

(§1) अजः अपि सन् अव्ययात्मा भूतानाम् ईश्वरः अपि सन् । प्रकृतिम् स्वाम् अधिष्ठाय सम्भवामि आत्ममायया । *ajaḥ:* (r∘ 15/1) *api san* (r∘ 13/1) *avyayātmā bhūtānām* (r∘ 8/19) *īśvaraḥ:* (r∘ 15/1) *api san* (r∘ 23/1) *prakṛtim* (r∘ 14/1) *svām* (r∘ 8/16) *adhiṣṭhāya sambhavāmi* (r∘ 4/2) *ātmamāyayā*

(§2) 🕮*ajaḥ:* (2.20); *api* (1.26); ***san*** (1nom∘ sing∘ ←adj∘ *sat* 2.16); 🕮*avyayātmā* (1nom∘ sing∘ ←bahuvrī∘ *avyayātman*, अव्ययः आत्मा यस्य ←adj∘ *avyaya* (immutable) 2.17 + m∘ *ātman* 2.41); *bhūtānām* (2.69); 🕮***īśvaraḥ:*** (1nom∘ sing∘ ←m∘ ***īśvara*** (lord) ←2∘√ईश्); *api* (1.26); *san* (↑); *prakṛtim* (3.33); 🕮***svām*** (f∘ 2acc∘ sing∘ ←pron∘ *sva* (own) 1.28); 🕮***adhiṣṭhāya*** (lyp∘ past-participle ind∘ ←1∘अधि√स्था); 🕮***sambhavāmi*** (1st-per∘ sing∘ pres∘ वर्तमान्-लट् parasmai∘ ←1∘सम्√भू); 🕮*ātmamāyayā* (f∘ 3inst∘ sing∘ ←tatpu∘ *ātma-māyā*, आत्मनः माया ←m∘ *ātman* 2.41 + f∘ 🕮***māyā*** (pleasure) ←3∘√मा) (4.6)

(§3) *ajaḥ:* (adj1∘-subj∘ birthless); *api* (although, even); *san* (adj2∘-subj∘ while being); *avyayātmā* (adj3∘-subj∘ immutable); *bhūtānām* (of the beings); *īśvaraḥ:* (subj∘ Lord); *api* (even); *san* (adj2∘-subj∘ while being); *prakṛtim* (obj∘ *prakṛti,* nature); *svām* (adj∘-obj∘ my own); *adhiṣṭhāya* (riding on); *sambhavāmi* (I come to being, I become, I incarnate); *ātmamāyayā* (with my own will, pleasure) (4.6)

(§4) api san ajaḥ: api san avyayātmā īśvaraḥ: bhūtānām adhiṣṭhāya svām prakṛtim sambhavāmi ātmamāyayā

(§5) Even while being birthless[351] (and) even while being immutable Lord of the beings, riding

---

[350] Elsewhere∘ *bahūni me janmāni vyatītāni* → many births are taken by me, many births have been left behind by me, many births I have passed, I have passed through many lives, many lives of mine have passed ...etc.

🕮 Note that, व्यतीतानि is not a verb, it is not a passive voice, मे is not Nominative case and thus I am not the subject (doer) and जन्मानि is not the object (2nd case). जन्मानि is the subject (1st case), व्यतितानि is adj∘ of जन्मानि (1st case) and मे has only external सम्बन्धः (6th case relationship) with जन्मानि । मे has no direct relationship with the verb व्यतितनि in this śloka.

[351] Elsewhere∘ *ajaḥ:* → unborn, not born ...etc.

🕮 Adjective 'unborn' is attached to one that is yet to be born, not yet born or not born (eg. an unborn child). Adjective अज is attached to the one that is born, but not from a womb or not by a normal birth

on my own nature I come to being with my own will. (4.6)

4.7 **यदा यदा हि धर्मस्य ग्लानिर्भवति भारत ।**
अभ्युत्थानमधर्मस्य तदात्मानं सृजाम्यहम् ।।
yadā yadā hi dharmasya glānirbhavati bhārata,
abhyutthānamadharmasya tadātmānaṁ sṛjāmyahaṃ. (4.7)

(§1) यदा यदा हि धर्मस्य ग्लानिः भवति भारत । अभ्युत्थानम् अधर्मस्य तत् आत्मानम् सृजामि अहम् । *yadā yadā hi dharmasya glāniḥ:* (r◦ 16/6) *bhavati bhārata* (r◦ 23/1) *abhyutthānaṃ* (r◦ 8/16) *adharmasya tadā* (r◦ 1/4) *ātmānaṃ* (r◦ 14/1) *sṛjāmi* (r◦ 4/1) *ahaṃ* (r◦ 14/2)

(§2) *yadā* (2.52); *yadā* (2.52); *hi* (1.11); 🕮*dharmasya* (2.40); 🕮*glāniḥ:* (1nom◦ sing◦ ←f◦ *glāni* (downfall) ←1◦√ग्लै); *bhavati* (1.44); *bhārata* (1.24); 🕮*abhyutthānaṃ* (1nom◦ sing◦ ←n◦ *abhyutthāna* (surge) ←1◦अभि–उद्√स्था); 🕮*adharmasya* (6pos sing◦ ←m◦ *adharma* (unrighteousness) 1.40); *tadā* (1.2); *ātmānaṃ* (3.43); ***sṛjāmi*** (1st-per◦ sing◦ pres◦ वर्तमान्–लट् parasmai◦ ←6◦√सृज्); *ahaṃ* (1.22) (4.7)

(§3) *yadā yadā* (whenever); *hi* (verily); *dharmasya* (of righteousness); *glāniḥ:* (subj◦ downfall); *bhavati* (it becomes, occurs); *bhārata* (O Bhārata! O Arjuna!); *abhyutthānaṃ* (subj2◦ predominaance, surge); *adharmasya* (of unrighteousness); *tadā* (at that time); *ātmānaṃ* (myself); *sṛjāmi* (I bring forth, manifest, incarnate); *ahaṃ* (I) (4.7)

(§4) bhārata yadā yadā glāniḥ: dharmasya abhyutthānaṃ adharmasya bhavati tadā ahaṃ hi sṛjāmi ātmānaṃ

(§5) O Arjuna! whenever downfall of righteousness[352] (and) surge of unrighteousness occurs,[353] at that time I verily incarnate myself. (4.7)

4.8 **परित्राणाय साधूनां विनाशाय च दुष्कृताम् ।**

---

process. Originally this word was coined to describe Brahmā, who was born, not to Mahālakṣmi's womb, but to Mahāviṣṇu, the *puruṣa*, through his navel. So, Brahmā ब्रह्मा (the personified or manifest *Brahm*a ब्रह्म), born from Viṣṇu, is अजः (birthless, without normal birth through a womb). In Gīta, though Kṛṣṇa is born to Devaki to assume the human *avatāra* (अवतारः), the divinity, that takes birth through आत्ममाया of Viṣṇu, and that is behind that human form अवतारः, is अजः ।

[352] Elsewhere◦ *dharmasya* → of religion, of religious practice ...etc.

[353] Elsewhere◦ *glāniḥ: bhavati* → righteousness is on the decline.

🕮 In this śloka धर्मः and अधर्मः are not subjects. ग्लानिः (downfall) and अभ्युत्थानम् (surge) are the subjects performing the verb भवति, which comes from root √भू to become, occur.

धर्मसंस्थापनार्थाय सम्भवामि युगे युगे ।।

paritrāṇāya sādhūnāṁ vināśāya ća duṣkṛtām,

dharmasaṁsthāpanārthāya sambhavāmi yuge yuge. **(4.8)**

(§1) परित्राणाय साधूनाम् विनाशाय च दुष्कृताम् । धर्मसंस्थापनार्थाय सम्भवामि युगे युगे । *paritrāṇāya sādhūnām* (r◦ 14/1) *vināśāya ća duṣkṛtām* (r◦ 14/2) *dharmasaṁsthāpanārthāya sambhavāmi yuge yuge*

(§2) 🕮*paritrāṇāya* (4dat◦ sing◦ ←n◦ *paritrāṇa* (protection) ←1◦परि√त्रै); 🕮*sādhūnām* (6pos plu◦ ←m◦ or adj◦ ***sādhu*** (gentleman) ←5◦√साध्); *vināśāya* (4dat◦ sing◦ ←m◦ *vināśa* (destruction) 2.17); *ća* (1.1); 🕮*duṣkṛtām* (6pos plu◦ ←m◦ ***duṣkṛt*** (evil doer) ←ind◦ *dus* 3.39 + adj◦ *kṛta* 1.35); *dharmasaṁsthāpanārthāya* (m◦ 4dat◦ sing◦ ←tatpu◦ m◦ *dharma-saṁsthāpanārtha,* धर्मस्य संस्थापनस्य अर्थः ←m◦ *dharma* (righteousness) 1.1 + f◦ *saṁsthāpanā* or n◦ *saṁsthāpana* (re-establishment) ←1◦सम्√स्था + m◦ *artha* 1.9); 🕮*sambhavāmi* (4.6); ***yuge*** (7loc◦ sing◦ ←n◦ ***yuga*** (age) ←4◦√युज्); *yuge* (↑) **(4.8)**

(§3) *paritrāṇāya* (for the protection); *sādhūnām* (of the righteous people); *vināśāya* (for the destruction); *ća* (and); *duṣkṛtām* (of unrighteous people); *dharmasaṁsthāpanārthāya* (for the re-establishment of righteousness); *sambhavāmi* (I incarnate, I come into being); *yuge yuge* (from time to time, from age to age) **(4.8)**

(§4) paritrāṇāya sādhūnām vināśāya duṣkṛtām ća dharmasaṁsthāpanārthāya sambhavāmi yuge yuge

(§5) For the protection of the righteous people, for the destruction of unrighteous people and for the re-establishment of righteousness,[354] I incarnate from age to age. (4.8)

4.9 **जन्म कर्म च मे दिव्यमेवं यो वेत्ति तत्त्वतः ।**

त्यक्त्वा देहं पुनर्जन्म नैति मामेति सोऽर्जुन ।।

janma karma ća me divyamevaṁ yo vetti tattvataḥ:,

tyaktvā dehaṁ punarjanma naiti māmeti so'rjuna. **(4.9)**

(§1) जन्म कर्म च मे दिव्यम् एवम् यः वेत्ति तत्त्वतः । त्यक्त्वा देहम् पुनर्जन्म न एति माम् एति सः अर्जुन । *janma karma ća me divyam* (r◦ 8/22) *evam* (r◦ 14/1) *yaḥ:* (r◦ 15/13) *vetti tattvataḥ:* (r◦ 22/8) *tyaktvā deham* (r◦ 14/1) *punarjanma na* (r◦ 3/1) *eti mām* (r◦ 8/22) *eti saḥ:* (r◦ 15/1) *arjuna*

(§2) *janma* (2acc◦ 2.27); *karma* (2acc◦ 3.8); *ća* (1.1); *me* (1.21); *divyam* (n◦ 2acc◦ sing◦ ←adj◦ *divya* (divine) 1.14); *evam* (1.24); *yaḥ:* (2.19); *vetti* (2.19); 🕮***tattvataḥ:*** (adv◦ ind◦ ←n◦ *tattva* (truth) 2.16);

---

[354] Elsewhere◦ धर्मसंस्थापनार्थाय → for the establishment of religion, for the firm establishment of religion, for the sake of the consolidation of the position of religion ...etc.

tyaktvā (1.33); 🕮**deham** (2acc∘ sing∘ ←m∘ or n∘ *deha* (body) 2.13); ***punarjanma*** (n∘ 2acc∘ sing∘ ←tatpu∘ *punar-janman* (re-birth) = recurrence indicating ind∘ ***punar*** or in writing mode '***punaḥ:***' (again) + n∘ *janman* (birth) 2.27); *na* (1.30); 🕮**eti** (3rd-per∘ sing∘ pres∘ वर्तमान्-लट् parasmai∘ ←2∘√इ); *mām* (1.46); *eti* (↑); *saḥ:* (1.13); *arjuna* (2.2) (4.9)

(§3) *janma* (obj1∘ birth); *karma* (obj2∘ function, work); *ća* (and); *me* (my); *divyam* (adj∘-obj2 divine); *evam* (adv∘ that, such, like this, in this manner, as described earlier); *yaḥ:* (adj∘-subj∘ he who); *vetti* (he knows); *tattvataḥ:* (truly); *tyaktvā* (having left); *deham* (obj3∘ the body); *punarjanma* (obj4∘ rebirth); *na* (not); *eti* (he attains); *mām* (obj5∘ me); *eti* (he attains); *saḥ:* (subj∘ he); *arjuna* (O Arjuna!) (4.9)

(§4) arjuna yaḥ: vetti tattvataḥ: me evam janma ća divyam karma, saḥ:, tyaktvā deham, na eti punarjanma, eti mām

(§5) O Arjuna! he who knows truly that my birth and function (are) divine, he, having left the body, does not attain rebirth, he attains me. (4.9)

4.10 **वीतरागभयक्रोधा मन्मया मामुपाश्रिताः ।**
बहवो ज्ञानतपसा पूता मद्भावमागताः ।।
vītarāgabhayakrodhā manmayā māmupāśritāḥ:,
bahavo jñānatapasā pūtā madbhāvamāgatāḥ:. (4.10)

(§1) वीतरागभयक्रोधाः मन्मयाः मामुपाश्रिताः । बहवः ज्ञानतपसा पूता मद्भावम् आगताः । *vītarāgabhayakrodhāḥ:* (r∘ 20/13) *manmayāḥ:* (r∘ 20/13) *mām* (r∘ 8/20) *upāśritāḥ:* (r∘ 22/8) *bahvaḥ:* (r∘ 15/3) *jñānatapasā pūtāḥ:* (r∘ 20/13) *madbhāvam* (r∘ 8/17) *āgatāḥ:* (r∘ 22/8)

(§2) *vītarāgabhayakrodhāḥ:* (nom∘ plu∘ ←m∘ *vīta-rāga-bhaya-krodha* 2.56); *manmayāḥ:* (m∘ 1nom∘ plu∘ ←adj∘ taddhita∘ *manmaya* ←pron∘ *mama* or *mat* ←pron∘ *asmad* 1.7 + taddhitaa forming suffix, adj∘ ***maya*** (full of) ←1∘√मय्); *mām* (1.46); 🕮***upāśritāḥ:*** (m∘ 1nom∘ plu∘ ←ppp∘ adj∘ *upāśrita* (sheltered) ←1∘उप-आ√श्रि); *bahvaḥ:* (1.9); *jñānatapasā* (n∘ 3inst∘ sing∘ ←tatpu∘ *jñāna-tapas*, ज्ञानस्य तपसः ←n∘ *jñāna* 3.3 + n∘ ***tapas*** ←1∘√तप्); 🕮*pūtāḥ:* (m∘ 1nom∘ plu∘ ←ppp∘ adj∘ ***pūta*** (cleansed) ←1∘√पू); ***madbhāvam*** (m∘ 2acc∘ sing∘ ←bahuvrī∘ ***madbhāva***, मयि भावः यस्य ←pron∘ *mat* 1.9 + m∘ *bhāva* (natre) 2.7); ***āgatāḥ:*** (m∘ 1nom∘ plu∘ ←ppp∘ adj∘ ***āgata*** (attained) ←1∘आ√गम्) (4.10)

(§3) *vītarāgabhayakrodhāḥ:* (adj1∘-subj∘ those whose attachment, fear and anger have gone away, those who have become free from attachment, fear and anger); *manmayāḥ:* (adj2∘-subj∘ those who are full of Me, those who are fully engrossed in me); *mām* (obj1∘ to me); *upāśritāḥ:* (adj3∘-subj∘ those who are dedicated, those who have taken - for shelter) *bahvaḥ:* (adj4◦-subj◦ many); *jñānatapasā* (with the austerity of knowledge); *pūtāḥ:* (adj4◦-subj◦ those who are purified); *madbhāvam̨* (obj2◦ my true nature); *āgatāḥ:* (adj5◦-subj◦ those who have attained) (4.10)

(§4) vītarāgabhayakrodhāḥ: manmayāḥ: upāśritāḥ: mām̨ pūtāḥ: jñānatapasā bahvaḥ: āgatāḥ: madbhāvam̨

(§5) Those whose attachment, fear and anger have gone away; those who are fully engrossed in me; those who are dedicated[355] to me; those who are purified with the austerity of knowledge; many who have attained[356] my true nature; (4.10)

4.11 ये यथा मां प्रपद्यन्ते तांस्तथैव भजाम्यहम् ।
मम वर्त्मानुवर्तन्ते मनुष्याः पार्थ सर्वशः ।।

ye yathā māṁ prapadyante tānstathaiva bhajāmyaham̨,
mama vartmānuvartante manuṣyāḥ: pārtha sarvaśaḥ:. (4.11)

(§1) ये यथा माम् प्रपद्यन्ते तान् तथा एव भजामि अहम् । मम वर्त्म अनुवर्तन्ते मनुष्याः पार्थ सर्वशः । *ye yathā mām̨* (r◦ 14/1) *prapadyante tān̨* (r◦ 13/7) *tathā* (r◦ 3/3) *eva bhajāmi* (r◦ 4/1) *aham̨* (r◦ 14/2) *mama vartma* (r◦ 1/1) *anuvartante manuṣyāḥ:* (r◦ 22/3) *pārtha sarvaśaḥ:* (r◦ 22/8)

(§2) *ye* (1.7); *yathā* (1.11); *mām̨* (1.46); 🕮***prapadyante*** (3rd-per◦ plu◦ pres◦ वर्तमान्-लट् ātmane◦ ←4◦प्र√पद्); *tān̨* (1.7); *tathā* (1.8); *eva* (1.1); 🕮*bhajāmi* (1st-per◦ sing◦ pres◦ वर्तमान्-लट् parasmai◦ ←1◦√भज्); *aham̨* (1.22); *mama* (1.7); *vartma* (2acc◦ 3.23); *anuvartante* (3.23); *manuṣyāḥ:* (3.23); *pārtha* (1.25); *sarvaśaḥ:* (1.18) (4.11)

(§3) *ye* (subj1◦ they, they who); *yathā* (as); *mām̨* (obj1◦ me); *prapadyante* (they serve, they approech); *tān̨* (obj2◦ to them); *tathā* (in that manner, so); *eva* (only); *bhajāmi* (I reward, I favour); *aham̨* (subj2◦ I); *mama* (my); *vartma* (obj3◦ path); *anuvartante* (they follow); *manuṣyāḥ:* (subj3◦ men, people); *pārtha* (O Pārtha! O Arjuna!); *sarvaśaḥ:* (in every way) (4.11)

(§4) yathā ye prapadyante mām̨ tathā eva aham̨ bhajāmi tān̨ pārtha manuṣyāḥ: anuvartante mama vartma sarvaśaḥ:

(§5) As they approach me, in that manner only I accept them. O Arjuna! people follow my path in

---

[355] Elsewhere◦ *māmupāśritāḥ:* → taking refuge in Me, who had taken refuge in Me ...etc.

🕮 उपाश्रित is a ppp◦ adjective of the subject, it is not a gerund, it is not a past perfect tense. → उपाश्रित, those who have taken refuge me for their shelter.

[356] Note that आगता: is an adjective, like other four adjectives. It is not a perfect tense.

every way. (4.11)

4.12 काङ्क्षन्तः कर्मणां सिद्धिं यजन्त इह देवताः ।
क्षिप्रं हि मानुषे लोके सिद्धिर्भवति कर्मजा ।।
kāṅkṣantaḥ: karmaṇāṁ siddhiṁ yajanta iha devatāḥ:,
kṣipraṁ hi mānuṣe loke siddhirbhavati karmajā. (4.12)

(§1) काङ्क्षन्तः कर्मणाम् सिद्धिम् यजन्तः इह देवताः । क्षिप्रम् हि मानुषे लोके सिद्धिः भवति कर्मजा । *kāṅkṣantaḥ:* (r∘ 22/1) *karmaṇām* (r∘ 24/6, 14/1) *siddhim* (r∘ 14/1) *yajante* (r∘ 5/2) *iha devatāḥ:* (r∘ 22/8) *kṣipram* (r∘ 14/1) *hi mānuṣe loke siddhiḥ:* (r∘ 16/6) *bhavati karmajā*

(§2) *kāṅkṣantaḥ:* (m∘ 1nom∘ plu∘ ←śatṛ∘ adj∘ *kāṅkṣat* ←1∘√कांक्ष्); *karmaṇām* (3.4); *siddhim* (3.4); ***yajante*** (3rd-per∘ plu∘ pres∘ वर्तमान्-लट् ātmane∘ ←1∘√यज्); *iha* (2.5); *devatāḥ:* (2acc∘ plu∘ ←f∘ 🕮***devatā*** (deity) ←4∘√दिव्); 🕮**kṣipram** (adv∘ ind∘ ←6∘√क्षिप्); *hi* (1.11); *mānuṣe* (m∘ 7loc∘ sing∘ ←adj∘ ***mānuṣa*** ←m∘ *manuṣya* 1.44); *loke* (2.5); *siddhiḥ:* (1nom∘ sing∘ ←f∘ *siddhi* (success) 2.48); *bhavati* (1.44); *karmajā* (1nom∘ sing∘ ←f∘ bahuvrī∘ *karma-jā,* कर्मे जायते या ←adj∘ *karmaja* 2.51) (4.12)

(§3) *kāṅkṣantaḥ:* (subj1∘ desiring, those who desire, those who are desiring); *karmaṇām* (of karmas); *siddhim* (obj1∘ the success, fruition, fulfillment); *yajante* (they worship); *iha* (here, in this world); *devatāḥ:* (obj2∘ deities, godheads); *kṣipram* (soon); *hi* (because); *mānuṣe* (in that which belongs to mankind); *loke* (in the world); *siddhiḥ:* (subj2∘ the success, accomplishment, fruition, fulfillment); *bhavati* (it becomes, comes to be); *karmajā* (adj∘-subj2∘ that which is born of karma) (4.12)

(§4) kāṅkṣantaḥ: siddhim karmaṇām yajante devatāḥ: iha hi loke mānuṣe siddhiḥ: karmajā bhavati kṣipram

(§5) Those who are desiring the fulfillment[357] of *karmas*, they worship godheads in this world; because,[358] in the world which belongs to mankind, the success born of *karma* comes to be soon. (4.12)

4.13 चातुर्वर्ण्यं मया सृष्टं गुणकर्मविभागशः ।
तस्य कर्तारमपि मां विद्धयकर्तारमव्ययम् ।।

---

[357] Elsewhere∘ सिद्धिः → perfection.

🕮 In the language of the Gītā, only *brahma* is perfect, nothing else is perfect. Perfection = परिपूर्णता, अन्यूनता । Therefore, सिद्धिः = success, fruition, fulfullment, accomplishment. See the word सिद्धि is translated is 'success' in verse 18.13 by all authors.

[358] See footnote in verse 3.5

ćāturvarṇyaṁ mayā sṛṣṭaṁ guṇakarmavibhāgaśaḥ:,
tasya kartāramapi māṁ viddhyakartāramavyayam. (4.13)

(§1) चातुर्वर्ण्यम् मया सृष्टम् गुणकर्मविभागशः । तस्य कर्तारम् अपि माम् विद्धि अकर्तारम् अव्ययम् । *ćāturvarṇyam* (r∘ 14/1) *mayā sṛṣṭam* (r∘ 14/1) *guṇakarmavibhāgaśaḥ:* (r∘ 22/8) *tasya kartāram* (r∘ 8/16) *api mām* (r∘ 14/1) *viddhi* (r∘ 4/1) *akartāram* (r∘ 8/16) *avyayam* (r∘ 14/2)

(§2) *ćāturvarṇyam* (1nom∘ sing∘ ←taddhita∘ the system that arose from *ćaturvarṇa* ←dvigu∘ n∘ *ćaturvarṇa*, चतुर्णाम् वर्ण्यानाम् समाहारः ←adj∘ *ćātur* (four) ←1∘√चत् + pot∘ adj∘ *varṇya* (class) ←10√वर्ण्); *mayā* (1.22); 🕮*sṛṣṭam* (n∘ 1nom∘ sing∘ ←ppp∘ adj∘ **sṛṣṭa** (organized) ←6∘√सृज्); 🕮*guṇakarmavibhāgaśaḥ:* (adv∘ ind∘ गुणानाम् च कर्मणाम् च विभागशः ←m∘ *guṇa* 2.45 + n∘ *karman* 1.15 + m∘ *vibhāga* 3.28); *tasya* (1.12); ***kartāram*** (2acc∘ sing∘ ←m∘ *kartṛ* 3.24); *api* (1.26); *mām* (1.46); *viddhi* (2.17); ***a-kartāram*** (2acc∘ sing∘ n.tatpu∘ ←m∘ *kartṛ* ↑); *avyayam* (2.21) (4.13)

(§3) *ćāturvarṇyam* (obj1∘ the system that is based on four classes, the four fold class order); *mayā* (subj∘ by me); *sṛṣṭam* (adj∘-obj1∘ made, organized, classified); *guṇakarmavibhāgaśaḥ:* (according to the modes of the *guṇas* and *karmas* of the beings); *tasya* (of that); *kartāram* (adj1∘-obj2∘ to the doer, author); *api* (even); *mām* (obj2∘ to me); *viddhi* (you please know); *a-kartāram* (adj2∘-obj2∘ non-doer); *avyayam* (adj3∘-obj2∘ eternal) (4.13)

(§4) ćāturvarṇyam sṛṣṭam mayā guṇakarmavibhāgaśaḥ: api kartāram tasya mām viddhi avyayam akartāram

(§5) The system that is based on four classes[359] (is) classified[360] by me according to the modes of

---

[359] Elsewhere∘ *ćāturvarṇyam* → the four castes, the fourflod caste ...etc.

🕮 वर्ण is not a caste. वर्णः (√वृ to describe) is a discription or class (based ones' own inborne nature स्वभावः). It is not जातयः मया सृष्टाः । The caste is जातिः (√जा to be born). The classes are four, and natural. Lord kṛṣṇa did not make castes (जातयः). The castes are man-made, artificial, post-birth and unlimited in number. They are outlawed by the Hindus. It is a matter of pity that even the Hindu writers are deluded into following who blindly or purposefully equate वर्णः with जातिः । Also, note that the word is not वर्णाः (four classes), it is तद्धित word वर्ण्यम्, the description or system that is based on वर्ण, nature and duties of each individual. It is चातुर्वर्ण्यम् not चातुर्वणम् ।

[360] Elsewhere∘ *sṛṣṭam* → was created, has been created ...etc.

🕮 सृष्टं is not a past tense ot any other tense, सृष्ट is not a verb. It is a ppp∘ adjective of the noun चातुर्वण्यम् । Also, they are not "created" from scratch, but rather they already existed in the population in the form of *guṇas*, and they are organized or classified into four groups of people according to their inborn *guṇas iand karmas* (गुणकर्मविभागशः). Remember, everyting always existed (नासतो विद्यते भावः) in some form of other.

the guṇas and ***karmas*** of the beings. Even to the doer of that, to me, you please know (to be) eternal non-doer.[361] (4.13)

4.14 न मां कर्माणि लिम्पन्ति न मे कर्मफले स्पृहा ।
इति मां योऽभिजानाति कर्मभिर्न स बध्यते ।।

na māṁ karmāṇi limpanti na me karmaphale spṛhā,
iti māṁ yo'bhijānāti karmabhirna sa badhyate. (4.14)

(§1) न माम् कर्माणि लिम्पन्ति न मे कर्मफले स्पृहा । इति माम् यः अभिजानाति कर्मभिः न सः बध्यते । *na mām* (r∘ 14/1) *karmāṇi* (r∘ 24/7) *limpanti na me karmaphale spṛhā* (r∘ 23/1) *iti mām* (r∘ 14/1) *yaḥ:* (r∘ 15/1) *abhijānāti karmabhiḥ:* (r∘ 16/6) *na saḥ:* (r∘ 21/2) *badhyate*

(§2) *na* (1.30); *mām* (1.46); *karmāṇi* (3.27); 🕮*limpanti* (3rd-per∘ plu∘ pres∘ वर्तमान्-लट् parasmai∘ ←6∘√लिप्); *na* (1.30); *me* (1.21); *karmaphale* (n∘ 7loc∘ sing∘ ←tatpu∘ ***karma-phala***, कर्मणः फलम् ←n∘ *karman* 1.15 + n∘ *phala* (fruit) 2.43); ***spṛhā*** (f∘ 1nom∘ sing∘ ←f∘ *spṛhā* 2.56); *iti* (1.25); *mām* (1.46); *yaḥ:* (2.19); ***abhijānāti*** (3rd-per∘ sing∘ pres∘ वर्तमान्-लट् parasmai∘ ←9∘अभि√ज्ञा); *karmabhiḥ:* (3.31); *na* (1.30); *saḥ:* (1.13); 🕮*badhyate* (3rd-per∘ sing∘ pres∘ वर्तमान्-लट् ātmane∘ ←9∘√बन्ध्) (4.14)

(§3) *na* (do not); *mām* (obj∘ me); *karmāṇi* (subj1∘ the karmas); *limpanti* (they taint, defile, soil, pollute); *na* (do not); *me* (my, I have); *karmaphale* (in the fruit of the karma); *spṛhā* (subj2∘ desire); *iti* (in this manner); *mām* (obj∘ me); *yaḥ:* (adj∘-subj3∘ he who); *abhijānāti* (he understands); *karmabhiḥ:* (by karmas); *na* (is not); *saḥ:* (subj3∘ he); *badhyate* (he gets dound) (4.14)

(§4) karmāṇi na limpanti mām me na spṛhā karmaphale yaḥ: abhijānāti mām iti saḥ: na badhyate karmabhiḥ:

(§5) The *karmas* do not defile me (and) I do not have desire in the fruit of the *karma*, he who understands me in this manner he does not get bound by *karmas*. (4.14)

4.15 एवं ज्ञात्वा कृतं कर्म पूर्वैरपि मुमुक्षुभिः ।

Nothing is new or created from nothing. And for this reason, the doer of this "classification" is a "non-doer or non-creator." He is merely an organizer, like Veda-Vyasa for the Vedas. This is what the Lord is saying.

[361] Elsewhere∘ अकर्तारम् → a non-agent, actionless, incapable of action ...etc.

🕮 The accusative (2nd case) adjective कर्तारम् (m∘ nominative 1st case कर्ता) comes from the root √कृ (to do) + कृत् suffix तृच् of which only तृ gets added. It imparts the meaning of doer of that root verb. Therefore, √कृ + तृच् = √कृ + तृ = कर्तृ → Nom∘ कर्ता, Acc∘ कर्तारम् adj∘ the doer, one who does the verb √कृ । अकर्तारम् → non-doer.

कुरु कर्मैव तस्मात्त्वं पूर्वैः पूर्वतरं कृतम् ।।

evam̱ jñātvā kṛtam̐ karma pūrvairapi mumukṣubhiḥ:,

kuru karmaiva tasmāttvam̐ paūrvaiḥ: pūrvataram̐ kṛtam̱. (4.15)

(§1) एवम् ज्ञात्वा कृतम् कर्म पूर्वैः अपि मुमुक्षुभिः । कुरु कर्म एव तस्मात् त्वम् पूर्वैः पूर्वतरम् कृतम् । *evam̱* (r◦ 14/1) *jñātvā kṛtam̱* (r◦ 14/1) *karma pūrvaiḥ:* (r◦ 16/4) *api mumukṣubhiḥ:* (r◦ 22/8) *kuru karma* (r◦ 3/1) *eva tasmāṯ* (r◦ 1/10) *tvam̱* (r◦ 14/1) *pūrvaiḥ:* (r◦ 22/3) *pūrvataram̱* (r◦ 14/1) *kṛtam̱* (r◦ 14/2)

(§2) *evam̱* (1.24); 📖***jñātvā*** (ipp◦ ind◦ ←9◦√ज्ञा); ***kṛtam̱*** (n◦ 1nom◦ sing◦ ←adj◦ *kṛta* (performed) 1.35); *karma* (1nom◦ 2.49); 📖***pūrvaiḥ:*** (m◦ 3inst◦ plu◦ ←adj◦ ***pūrva*** (ancient) ←10◦√पूर्व्); *api* (1.26); 📖*mumukṣubhiḥ:* (3inst◦ plu◦ ←desi◦ adj◦ *mumukṣu* ←6◦√मुच्); *kuru* (2.48); *karma* (2acc◦ 3.8); *eva* (1.1); *tasmāṯ* (1.37); *tvam̱* (2.11); *pūrvaiḥ:* (↑); *pūrvataram̱* (1nom◦ sing◦ *pūrvatara* (earlier) ←adj◦ *pūrva* ↑ + comparitive affix *tara* तर 1.46); *kṛtam̱* (1nom◦ 4.15) (4.15)

(§3) *evam̱* (in this manner); *jñātvā* (having known); *kṛtam̱* (adj◦-obj1◦ done); *karma* (obj1◦ karma, what ought to ne done); *pūrvaiḥ:* (adj◦-subj1◦ by the ones existing in the past, by the ancient); *api* (also); *mumukṣubhiḥ:* (subj1◦ by the seekers of liberation); *kuru* (you please do perform); *karma* (obj2◦ karma, what ought to ne done); *eva* (only); *tasmāṯ* (therefore); *tvam̱* (subj2◦ you); *pūrvaiḥ:* (subj3◦ by the ones existing in the past); *pūrvataram̱* (adj1◦-obj3◦ done in earlier times); *kṛtam̱* (adj◦-obj3◦ done) (4.15)

(§4) jñātvā evam̱ karma kṛtam̱ pūrvaiḥ: mumukṣubhiḥ: tasmāṯ tvam̱ api kuru karma eva kṛtam̱ pūrvaiḥ: pūrvataram̱

(§5) Having known in this manner, what ought to be done (was) done in the past by the seekers of liberation. Therefore,[362] you also please perform only what ought to ne done,[363] (as) done by the ones existing in the past in earlier times. (4.15)

4.16 किं कर्म किमकर्मेति कवयोऽप्यत्र मोहिताः ।

तत्ते कर्म प्रवक्ष्यामि यज्ज्ञात्वा मोक्ष्यसेऽशुभात् ।।

kim̐ karma kimakarmeti kavayo‘pyatra mohitāḥ:,

tatte karma pravakṣāmi yajjñātvā mokṣase‘śubhāṯ. (4.16)

(§1) किम् कर्म किम् अकर्म इति कवयः अपि यत्र मोहिताः । तत् ते कर्म प्रवक्ष्यामि यत् ज्ञात्वा मोक्ष्यसे अशुभात् । *kim̱* (r◦ 14/1) *karma kim̱* (r◦ 8/16) *akarma* (r◦ 2/1) *iti kavayaḥ:* (r◦ 15/1) *api* (r◦ 4/1) *atra mohitāḥ:* (r◦ 22/8)

---

[362] See the footnote in verse 2.15

[363] Elsewhere कर्म → action, actions, work ...etc.

taṭ (r∘ 1/10) *te karma pravakṣāmi yaṭ* (r∘ 11/2) *jñātvā mokṣase* (r∘ 6/1) *aśubhāṭ*

(§2) *kiṃ* (1nom∘ 2.36); *karma* (1nom∘ 2.49); *kiṃ* (1nom∘ 1.1); ***akarma*** (1nom∘ sing∘ ←n∘ *akarmaṇ* 2.47); *iti* (1.25); 📖***kavayaḥ:*** (1nom∘ plu∘ m∘ ***kavi*** (wise person) ←1∘√कव्); *api* (1.26); *atra* (1.4); 📖*mohitāḥ:* (m∘ 1nom∘ plu∘ ←ppp∘ adj∘ caus∘*mohita* (deluded) ←4∘√मुह्); *taṭ* (2.7); *te* (1.7); *karma* (2acc∘ 2.49); ***pravakṣāmi*** (1nom∘ sing∘ fut2∘ लृट् भविष्य∘ parasmai∘ ←2∘प्र√वच्); *yaṭ* (3.21); *jñātvā* (4.15); ***mokṣase*** (2nd-per∘ sing∘ fut2∘ लृट् भविष्य∘ ātmane∘ ←2∘√मुच्); ***aśubhāṭ*** (5abl∘ sing∘ ←adj∘ *āśubha* (evil) 2.57) (4.16)

(§3) *kiṃ* (what is?); *karma* (subj1∘ karma); *kiṃ* (what is?); *akarma* (subj2∘ akarma); *iti* (thus); *kavayaḥ:* (subj3∘ the wise); *api* (also); *atra* (in this matter); *mohitāḥ:* (adj∘-subj3∘ deluded, confused, confounded); *taṭ* (adj1∘-obj∘ that); *te* (to you); *karma* (obj∘ karma); *pravakṣāmi* (I shall explain); *yaṭ* (adj2∘-obj∘ which); *jñātvā* (having known); *mokṣase* (you shall attain freedom); *aśubhāṭ* (from evil) (4.16)

(§4) kiṃ karma kiṃ akarma iti atra kavayaḥ: api mohitāḥ: pravakṣāmi te taṭ karma yaṭ jñātvā mokṣase aśubhāṭ

(§5) What is *karma*? (and) what is *akarma*? Thus, in this matter, the wise (are) also confounded. I shall explain you that *karma*, which having known, you shall attain freedom from evil (of ignorance). (4.16)

4.17 कर्मणो ह्यपि बोद्धव्यं बोद्धव्यं च विकर्मणः ।
अकर्मणश्च बोद्धव्यं गहना कर्मणो गतिः ।।

karmaṇo hyapi boddhavyaṁ boddahvyaṁ ća vikarmaṇaḥ:,
akarmaṇaśća boddhavyaṁ gahanā karmaṇo gatiḥ:. (4.17)

(§1) कर्मणः हि अपि बोद्धव्यम् बोद्धव्यम् च विकर्मणः । अकर्मणः च बोद्धव्यम् गहना कर्मणः गतिः । *karmaṇaḥ:* (r∘ 15/14, 24/2) *hi* (r∘ 4/1) *api boddhavyaṃ* (r∘ 14/1) *boddhavyaṃ* (r∘ 14/1) *ća vikarmaṇaḥ:* (r∘ 22/8, 24/2) *akarmaṇaḥ:* (r∘ 17/1) *ća boddhavyaṃ* (r∘ 14/1) *gahanā karmaṇaḥ:* (r∘ 15/2, 24/2) *gatiḥ:* (r∘ 22/8)

(§2) *karmaṇaḥ:* (3.1); *hi* (1.11); *api* (1.26); 📖***boddhavyaṃ*** (1nom∘ sing∘ ←pass∘ -pot∘ adj∘ adj∘ *boddhavya* (ought to be known) ←1∘√बुध्); *boddhavyaṃ* (↑); *ća* (1.1); *vikarmaṇaḥ:* (6pos sing∘ ←n∘ *vikarmaṇ* (forbidden act) विगतम् वा विपरितम् वा विरुद्धम् वा निषिद्धम् वा कर्म ←8∘वि√कृ); ***akarmaṇaḥ:*** (6pos sing∘ ←n∘ *akarmaṇ* (undutiful) 2.47); *ća* (1.1); *boddhavyaṃ* (↑); *gahanā* (f∘ 1nom∘ sing∘ ←adj∘ *gahana* (deep) ←10∘√गह्); ***karmaṇaḥ:*** (6pos sing∘ ←n∘ *karmaṇ* 1.15); 📖***gatiḥ:*** (1nom∘ sing∘ ←f∘ *gati* (course) 2.43) (4.17)

(§3) *karmaṇaḥ:* (of karma, of doing); *hi* (because); *api* (also); *boddhavyaṃ* (adj∘-obj1∘ ought to be known); *boddhavyaṃ* (adj∘-obj2∘ ought to be known); *ća* (and); *vikarmaṇaḥ:* (of opposite *karma*, of doing opposite); *akarmaṇaḥ:* (of *akarma*, of not-doing); *ća* (and); *boddhavyaṃ* (adj∘-obj3∘ ought to be known); 📖*gahanā* (adj∘-subj4∘ profound); *karmaṇaḥ:* (of *karma*); *gatiḥ:* (subj4∘ the state, course) (4.17)

(§4) karmaṇaḥ: (tattvam) boddhavyaṃ ća vikarmaṇaḥ: boddhavyaṃ ća akarmaṇaḥ: api boddhavyaṃ, hi gahanā gatiḥ: karmaṇaḥ:

(§5) (The course) of doing ought to be known, and of doing opposite ought to be known, and of not-doing also ought to be known; because[364] profound (is) the course[365] of *karma*. (4.17)

4.18 कर्मण्यकर्म यः पश्येदकर्मणि च कर्म यः ।
स बुद्धिमान्मनुष्येषु स युक्तः कृत्स्नकर्मकृत् ।।
karmaṇyakarma yaḥ: paśyedakaramṇi ća karma yaḥ:,
sa buddhimānmanuṣyeṣu sa yuktaḥ: kṛtsnakarmakṛt. (4.18)

(§1) कर्मण्यि अकर्म यः पश्येत् अकर्मणि च कर्म यः । स बुद्धिमान् मनुष्येषु सः युक्तः कृत्स्नकर्मकृत् । *karmaṇi* (r∘ 24/7, 4/1) *akarma yaḥ:* (r∘ 22/3) *paśyet* (r∘ 8/2) *akarmaṇi* (r∘ 24/7) *ća karma yaḥ:* (r∘ 22/8) *saḥ:* (r∘ 21/2) *buddhimān* (r∘ 13/16) *manuṣyeṣu* (r∘ 25/5) *saḥ:* (r∘ 21/2) *yuktaḥ:* (r∘ 22/1) *kṛtsnakarmakṛt*

(§2) *karmaṇi* (2.47); *akarma* (2acc∘ sing∘ ←n∘ *akarman* 4.16); *yaḥ:* (2.19); *paśyet* (3rd-per∘ sing∘ potential∘ विधि∘ parasmai∘ ←1∘√दृश्); *akarmaṇi* (2.47); *ća* (1.1); *karma* (2.49); *yaḥ:* (2.19); *saḥ:* (1.13); 📖***buddhimān*** (m∘ 1nom∘ sing∘ ←taddhita∘ adj∘ ***buddhimat*** (wise) ←1∘√बुध्); ***manuṣyeṣu*** (7loc∘ plu∘ ←m∘ *manuṣya* (person) 1.44); *saḥ:* (1.13); *yuktaḥ:* (2.39); *kṛtsnakarmakṛt* (m∘ 1nom∘ sing∘ ←ppp∘ bahuvrī∘ adj∘ *kṛtsna-karma-kṛt*, कृत्स्नम् कर्म करोति यः ←adj∘ *kṛtsna* 1.40 + n∘ *karman* 1.15 + adj∘ affix कृत् *kṛt*) (4.18)

(§3) *karmaṇi* (in karma); *akarma* (obj1∘ akarma); *yaḥ:* (adj1∘-subj∘ he who); *paśyet* (he may see, perceive); *akarmaṇi* (in akarma); *ća* (and); *karma* (obj2∘ karma); *yaḥ:* (adj2∘-subj∘ he who); *saḥ:* (subj1∘ he, that person); *buddhimān* (adj3∘-subj∘ wise); *manuṣyeṣu* (in men, among men); *saḥ:* (adj4∘-subj∘ he, that person); *yuktaḥ:* (adj5∘-subj∘ equipped, disciplined); *kṛtsnakarmakṛt* (adj6∘-subj∘ while doing everything) (4.18)

---

[364] See footnote in verse 3.5

[365] The गतिः of *karma* is subj1∘; the गतिः of *vikarma* is subj2∘; the गतिः of *akarma* is subj3∘; the *gahanā gatiḥ* (गहना गतिः) of any karma is subj4∘

(§4) yaḥ: paśyet akarma karmaṇi ća yaḥ: karma akarmaṇi saḥ: buddhimān manuṣyeṣu saḥ: yuktaḥ: kṛtsnakarmakṛt

(§5) He who may perceive *akarma* in *karma* and he who (may perceive) *karma* in *akarma,* that person (is) wise among men, that person (is) disciplined,[366] while doing everything. (4.18)

4.19 यस्य सर्वे समारम्भाः कामसङ्कल्पवर्जिताः ।
ज्ञानाग्निदग्धकर्माणं तमाहुः पण्डितं बुधाः ।।
yasya sarve samārambhāḥ: kāmasaṅkalpavarjitāḥ:,
jñānāgnidagdhakarmāṇaṁ tamāhuḥ: paṇḍitaṁ budhāḥ:. (4.19)

(§1) यस्य सर्वे समारम्भाः कामसङ्कल्पवर्जिताः । ज्ञानाग्निदग्धकर्माणम् तम् आहुः पण्डितम् बुधाः । *yasya sarve samārambhāḥ:* (r◦ 22/1) *kāmasaṅkalpavarjitāḥ:* (r◦ 22/8) *jñānāgnidagdhakarmāṇam* (r◦ 14/1, 24/3) *tam* (r◦ 8/17) *āhuḥ:* (r◦ 22/3) *paṇḍitam* (r◦ 14/1) *budhāḥ:* (r◦ 22/8)

(§2) *yasya* (2.61); *sarve* (1.6); *samārambhāḥ:* (1nom◦ plu◦ ←m◦ *samārambha* (undertaking) ←1◦सम्-आ√रम्भ्); *kāmasaṅkalpavarjitāḥ:* (m◦ 1nom◦ plu◦ ←tatpu◦ *kāma-saṅkalpa-varjita,* कामैः च सकल्पैः च वर्जितः ←n◦ *kāma* (desire) 1.22 + m◦ ***saṅkalpa*** (craving) ←1◦सम्√कृप् + ppp◦ adj◦ ***varjita*** (devoid) ←2◦√वृज्); *jñānāgnidagdhakarmāṇam* (m◦ 2acc◦ sing◦ ←bahuvrī◦ *jñānāgni-dagdha-karman,* ज्ञानस्य अग्निना दग्धानि कर्माणि यस्य सः ←n◦ *jñāna* 3.3 + m◦ ***agni*** (fire) ←1◦√अङ्ग् + ppp◦ adj◦ *dagdha* (purified) ←1◦√दह् + n◦ *karman* 1.15); *tam* (2.1); *āhuḥ:* (3.42); *paṇḍitam* (2acc◦ sing◦ ←m◦ *paṇḍita* 2.11); ***budhāḥ:*** (m◦ 1nom◦ plu◦ ←adj◦ or m◦ ***budha*** (pundit) ←1◦√बुध्) (4.19)

(§3) *yasya* (adj1◦ he whose); *sarve* (adj1◦-subj1◦ all); *samārambhāḥ:* (subj1◦ undertakings); *kāmasaṅkalpavarjitāḥ:* (adj2◦-subj1◦ those which are devoid of craving and desire); *jñānāgnidagdhakarmāṇam* (obj◦ he whose karmas are purified with the fire of knowledge); *tam* (adj1◦-obj◦ to him); *āhuḥ:* (they call); *paṇḍitam* (adj2◦-obj◦ a paṇḍita, pundit); *budhāḥ:* (subj2◦ the wise people) (4.19)

(§4) yasya sarve samārambhāḥ: kāmasaṅkalpavarjitāḥ: jñānāgnidagdhakarmāṇam tam budhāḥ: āhuḥ: paṇḍitam

(§5) He, whose all undertakings are devoid of craving and desire (and) whose *karmas* are purified with the fire of knowledge, to him the wise people call[367] a *pundit.*

---

[366] Elsewhere युक्तः → poised, devout, yogin, Yogi, a yogi, ...etc.

[367] Elsewhere◦ *āhuḥ: paṇḍitam budhāḥ:* → is called wise by the sages, the wise have called a sage, he is said by

(4.19)

4.20 त्यक्त्वा कर्मफलासङ्गं नित्यतृप्तो निराश्रयः ।
कर्मण्यभिप्रवृत्तोऽपि नैव किञ्चित्करोति सः ।।
tyaktvā karmaphalāsangaṁ nityatṛpto niarāśrayaḥ:,
karmaṇyabhipravṛtto'pi naiva kiñcitkaroti saḥ:. (4.20)

(§1) त्यक्त्वा कर्मफलासङ्गं नित्यतृप्तः निराश्रयः । कर्मण्यि अभिप्रवृत्तः अपि न एव किञ्चित् करोति सः । *tyaktvā karmaphalāsangam* (r◦ 14/1) *nityatṛptaḥ:* (r◦ 15/6) *niarāśrayaḥ:* (r◦ 22/8) *karmaṇi* (r◦ 24/7, 4/1) *abhipravṛttaḥ:* (r◦ 15/1) *api na* (r◦ 3/1) *eva kiñcit* (r◦ 10/5) *karoti saḥ:* (r◦ 22/8)

(§2) *tyaktvā* (1.33); *karmaphalāsangam* (m◦ 2acc◦ sing◦ ←tatpu◦ *karma-phalāsanga*, कर्मणः फलस्य आसङ्गः ←n◦ *karman* 1.15 + n◦ *phala* 2.43 + m◦ 🕮*āsanga* (attachment) ←1◦आ√सञ्ज्); *nityatṛptaḥ:* (m◦ 1nom◦ sing◦ ←bahuvrī◦ adj◦ *nitya-tṛpta* ←ind◦ *nitya* 2.18 + adj◦ *tṛpta* (contented) 3.17); 🕮*niarāśrayaḥ:* (m◦ 1nom◦ sing◦ ←n.bahuvrī◦ *niarāśraya*, नास्ति आश्रयः यस्य ←ind◦ *nir* 2.45 + m◦ ***āśraya*** (shelter) ←1◦आ√श्रि); *karmaṇi* (2.47); *abhipravṛttaḥ:* (1nom◦ sing◦ ←ppp◦ adj◦ *abhipravṛtta* (engaged) ←4◦अभि-प्र√वृत्); *api* (1.26); *na* (1.30); *eva* (1.1); 🕮***kiñcit*** (pron◦ *kim* 1.1 + ind◦ *cit* 2.17); ***karoti*** (3rd-per◦ sing◦ pres◦ वर्तमान्-लट् parasmai◦ ←8◦√कृ); *saḥ:* (1.13) (4.20)

(§3) *tyaktvā* (having renounced, having given up); *karmaphalāsangam* (obj◦ attachment to desire in the fruit of karma); *nityatṛptaḥ:* (adj1◦-subj◦ he who is always contented); *niarāśrayaḥ:* (adj2◦-subj◦ he who is not dependent); *karmaṇi* (in karma); *abhipravṛttaḥ:* (adj3◦-subj◦ engaged); *api* (even, also); *na eva kiñcit* (not anything); *karoti* (he does do); *saḥ:* (subj◦ he) (4.20)

(§4) tyaktvā karmaphalāsangam nityatṛptaḥ: niarāśrayaḥ: saḥ: api abhipravṛttaḥ: karmaṇi karoti na eva kiñcit

(§5) Having renounced attachment to desire in the fruit of *karma,*[368] he who is always contented,

---

sages to be ...etc.

🕮 बुधाः आहुः is वर्तमान्-लट् present tense in active voice, and therefore subject बुधाः in Nominative (1st) case and object पण्डितम् is in accusative (2nd) case. If you make it a Sanskrit passive construction, then the subject would be बुधैः in Instrumental (3rd) case and object would be पण्डितः in Nominative (1st case). ppp◦ सः बोधितः he is called, they have called ते अबोधन् ।

[368] Elsewhere◦ त्यक्त्वा कर्मफलासङ्गम् → renouncing the attachment for action and its fruit, having abandoned attachment for the fruit of action, having renounced attachment to action and its fruits, renouncing the attachment for action and its fruit, given up attachment to the fruits of actions...etc.

🕮 कर्मफलासङ्गम् does not indicate renunciation of the Action and or its Fruit. As the nishkama-yoga says, it

he who is not dependent, he, even engaged in *karma*, (in fact) does not do anything (he is not the author of any deed). (4.20)

4.21 निराशीर्यतचित्तात्मा त्यक्तसर्वपरिग्रहः ।
शारीरं केवलं कर्म कुर्वन्नाप्नोति किल्बिषम् ॥
nirāśīryataćittātmā tyaktasarvaparigrahaḥ:,
śārīraṁ kevalaṁ karma kurvannāpnoti kilbiṣam. (4.21)

(§1) निराशीः यतचित्तात्मा त्यक्तसर्वपरिग्रहः । शारीरम् केवलम् कर्म कुर्वन् न आप्नोति किल्बिषम् । *nirāśīḥ:* (r∘ 16/7) *yataćittātmā tyaktasarvaparigrahaḥ:* (r∘ 22/8) *śārīram* (r∘ 14/1) *kevalam* (r∘ 14/1) *karma kurvan* (r∘ 1/11) *na* (r∘ 1/2) *āpnoti kilbiṣam* (r∘ 14/2)

(§2) *nirāśīḥ:* (3.30); ***yataćittātmā*** (m∘ 1nom∘ sing∘ ←bahuvrī∘ *yata-ćittātman*, यतम् चित्तम् च आत्मा च यस्य ←ppp∘ adj∘ ***yata*** (restrained) ←1∘√यत् + n∘ ***ćitta*** (mind) ←1∘√चित् + m∘ *ātman* (heart) 2.41); *tyaktasarvaparigrahaḥ:* (m∘ 1nom∘ sing∘ ←bahuvrī∘ *tyakta-sarva-parigraha*, त्यक्ताः सर्वे परिग्रहाः येन ←adj∘ *tyakta* (detached) 1.9 + pron∘ *sarva* 1.6 + m∘ 🕮***parigraha*** (belonging) ←9∘परि√ग्रह); ***śārīram*** (taddhita∘ adv∘ ind∘ ←adj∘ *śarīra* (body) 1.29); 🕮***kevalam*** (ind∘ ←adj∘ adv∘ ***kevala*** (only) ←1∘के√वल्); *karma* (3.8); ***kurvan*** (1nom∘ sing∘ ←śatṛ∘ adj∘ *kurvat* ←8∘√कृ); *na* (1.30); *āpnoti* (2.70); ***kilbiṣam*** (2acc∘ sing∘ ←n∘ *kilbiṣa* (sin) 3.13) (4.21)

(§3) *nirāśīḥ:* (adj1∘-subj∘ he who is indifferent); *yataćittātmā* (adj2∘-subj∘ he whose mind and heart are restrained); *tyaktasarvaparigrahaḥ:* (adj3∘-subj∘ he who has detached himself from all matters of belonging); *śārīram* (bodily); *kevalam* (only); *karma* (obj1∘ karma); *kurvan* (adj4∘-subj∘ performing, while doing); *na* (no); *āpnoti* (he incures); *kilbiṣam* (obj2∘ sin) (4.21)

(§4) nirāśīḥ: yataćittātmā tyaktasarvaparigrahaḥ: kurvan karma kevalam śārīram āpnoti na kilbiṣam

(§5) He who is indifferent, he whose mind and heart are restrained, he who has detached himself from all matters of belonging, (he) while performing *karma* only bodily, he incures no sin. (4.21)

4.22 यदृच्छालाभसन्तुष्टो द्वन्द्वातीतो विमत्सरः ।
समः सिद्धावसिद्धौ च कृत्वापि न निबद्धयते ॥
yadṛććhālābhasantuṣṭo dvandvātīto vimatsaraḥ:,
samaḥ: siddhāvasiddhau ća kṛtvāpi na niabaddhyate. (4.22)

---

is the renunciation of the "DESIRE" (काम, कामना in the words निष्काम, निष्कामना) for the fruit. Not the renunciation of action or its fruit. It is the common mistake found in many Gita translations.

(§1) यदृच्छालाभसन्तुष्टः द्वन्द्वातीतः विमत्सरः । समः सिद्धौ असिद्धौ च कृत्वा अपि न निबद्ध्यते ।
yadṛććhālābhasantuṣṭaḥ: (r◦ 15/4) *dvandvātītaḥ:* (r◦ 15/13) *vimatsaraḥ:* (r◦ 22/8) *samaḥ:* (r◦ 22/7) *siddhau* (r◦ 5/5) *asiddhau ća kṛtvā* (r◦ 1/3) *api na nibaddhyate*

(§2) *yadṛććhālābhasantuṣṭaḥ:* (m◦ 1nom◦ sing◦ ←tatpu◦ *yadṛććhā-lābha-santuṣṭa,* यदृच्छया लाभेन सन्तुष्टः ←f◦ *yadṛććhā* (own accord) 2.32 + m◦ *lābha* (gain) 2.38 + adj◦ *santuṣṭa* (satisfied) 3.17); *dvandvātītaḥ:* (1nom◦ sing◦ ←tatpu◦ *dvandvātīta,* द्वंद्वान् अतीतः ←n◦ 🕮*dvandva* (duality) 2.45 + ppp◦ adj◦ ***atīta*** (indifferent) ←1◦अति√इ); 🕮*vimatsaraḥ:* (m◦ 1nom◦ sing◦ ←bahuvrī◦ *vimatsara* (envyless) विगतः मत्सरः यस्य ←adj◦ *vigata* (gone) 2.56 + m◦ *matsara* (envy) ←1◦**√मद्**); *samaḥ:* (equanimous 2.48); 🕮*siddhau* (7loc◦ sing◦ ←f◦ *siddhi* (success) 2.48); 🕮*asiddhau* (7loc◦ sing◦ ←n.tatpu◦ *a-siddhi* (failure) 2.48); *ća* (1.1); *kṛtvā* (2.38); *api* (1.26); *na* (1.30); ***nibaddhyate*** (3rd-per◦ sing◦ pres◦ वर्तमान्-लट् ātmane◦ ←1◦नि√**बध्**) (4.22)

(§3) *yadṛććhālābhasantuṣṭaḥ:* (adj1◦-subj◦ he who is happy with whatever comes to him on its own accord); *dvandvātītaḥ:* (adj2◦-subj◦ he who is indiffernt to the opposites, pairs of opposites); *vimatsaraḥ:* (adj3◦-subj◦ he whose envy has gone away); *samaḥ:* (adj4◦-subj◦ he who is equanimous, indifferent); *siddhau* (in success); *asiddhau* (in failure); *ća* (and); *kṛtvā* (having done, having performed karma); *api* (also); *na* (not); *nibaddhyate* (he is bound) (4.22)

(§4) yadṛććhālābhasantuṣṭaḥ: dvandvātītaḥ: vimatsaraḥ: samaḥ: siddhau ća asiddhau kṛtvā api na nibaddhyate

(§5) He who is happy with whatever comes to him on its own accord,[369] he who is indiffernt to the pairs of opposites,[370] he whose envy has gone away, he who is equanimous in success and in

---

[369] Elsewhere◦ *yadṛććhālābhasantuṣṭaḥ:* → remaining satisfied with ...etc.

🕮 सन्तुष्टः is not a gerund or active present participle (◦ing). यदृच्छालाभसन्तुष्टः is बहुव्रीहि adjective of the subject, formed from ppp◦ सन्तुष्टः ।

[370] Elsewhere◦ *dvandvātītaḥ:* → transcending the dualities, having transcended the dualities, free from duality ...etc.)

🕮 द्वंद्वातीतः is not a gerund. अतीत is not free from, it is not having transcended, it is not transcending. अतीत is a ppp◦ adj◦ → one who has transcended, passed beyond, crossed gone over, surpassed, crossed over (अतिक्रान्तः, उत्क्रान्त, अत्ययीत, लंघितः, अन्तरितः); Also, द्वंद्व is not a duality. Duality is द्वैत, see footnote in 5.25.

(i) द्वंद्व is n◦ from adj◦ द्वि (द्वौ द्वौ सहाभिव्यक्तौ । द्वि-शब्दस्य द्वित्वं two opposites, a pair of opposites. Gītā has many examples of such pairs). द्वंद्व-समासः, however, is exception. It does not always include a pair of opposites, but then it does not always include only two objects either.

(ii) द्वैत is duality. It means relating to two, but not necessarily a pair of opposites. In upanishads it refers to the philosophy upheld by those who believe that *brahma* has created the word, thereby admitting that *brahma* is

failure, having performed *karma* also he is not bound.

(4.22)

4.23 गतसङ्गस्य मुक्तस्य ज्ञानावस्थितचेतस: ।
यज्ञायाचरत: कर्म समग्रं प्रविलीयते ।।

gatasaṅgasya muktasya jñānāvasthitaćetasaḥ:,
yajñāyāćarataḥ: karma samagraṁ pravilīyate. (4.23)

(§1) गतसङ्गस्य मुक्तस्य ज्ञानावस्थितचेतस: । यज्ञाय आचरत: कर्म समग्रम् प्रविलीयते । *gatasaṅgasya muktasya jñānāvasthitaćetasaḥ:* (r◦ 22/8) *yajñāya* (r◦ 1/2) *āćarataḥ:* (r◦ 22/1) *karma samagram̦* (r◦ 14/1) *pravilīyate*

(§2) 📖*gatasaṅgasya* (m◦ 6pos◦ sing◦ ←bahuvrī◦ *gata-saṅga,* गत: सङ्ग: यस्य ←adj◦ *gata* (gone) 2.11 + m◦ *saṅga* (attachment) 2.47); 📖*muktasya* (m◦ 6pos◦ sing◦ ←adj◦ *mukta* (free) 3.9); *jñānāvasthitaćetasaḥ:* (m◦ 1nom◦ sing◦ ←bahuvrī◦ *jñānāvasthita-ćetaș,* ज्ञाने अवस्थितम् चेत: यस्य ←n◦ *jñāna* (wisdom) 3.3 + adj◦ *avasthita* 1.11 + n◦ *ćetaș* (mind) 1.38); *yajñāya* (4dat◦ sing◦ ←m◦ *yajña* 3.9); *āćarataḥ:* (m◦ 1nom◦ sing◦ ←śatṛ◦ adj◦ *āćaraț* 3.19); *karma* (2.49); 📖***samagram̦*** (adv◦ ind◦ ←adj◦ ***samagra*** (whole) ←10◦सम√ग्रह); *pravilīyate* (3rd-per◦ sing◦ pres◦ वर्तमान्-लट् ātmane◦ ←4◦प्र-वि√ली) (4.23)

(§3) *gatasaṅgasya* (of him whose attachment has gone away, of him who is free from attachment); *muktasya* (of him who is unfettered); *jñānāvasthitaćetasaḥ:* (of him whose mind is established in wisdom); *yajñāya* (for the sake of *yajña,* for the sake of austerity, for the sake of offering); *āćarataḥ:* (adj◦-subj◦ while performing, he who is performing); *karma* (karma); *samagram̦* (all); *pravilīyate* (it dissolves) (4.23)

(§4) gatasaṅgasya muktasya jñānāvasthitaćetasaḥ: āćarataḥ: karma yajñāya samagram̦ pravilīyate

(§5) Of him whose attachment has gone away, of him who is unfettered, of him whose mind is established in wisdom, while performing *karma* for the sake of austerity, all (his *karma*) dissolves.[371] (4.23)

---

separate (duality) from the creation. Counter to this theory of duality, the Monism (अद्वैतम्), asserts that *brahma* IS everything (ब्रह्मैव जगत्त्रयम्), there is no duality between *brahma* and universe (अद्वैतब्रह्म), and thus, the universe is not a 'creation' but evolution, transformation, personification or manifestation of *brahma.*

(iii) द्वैध is a तद्धित word from द्विध (ind◦ द्वि+धाच् in two ways).

[371]प्रविलीयते, dissolves from the bondage and authorship.

4.24 ब्रह्मार्पणं ब्रह्म हविर्ब्रह्माग्नौ ब्रह्मणा हुतम् ।
ब्रह्मैव तेन गन्तव्यं ब्रह्मकर्मसमाधिना ।।

brahmārpaṇaṁ brahma havirbrahmāgnau brahmaṇā hutam,
brahmaiva tena gantavyaṁ brahmakarmasamādhinā. (4.24)

(§1) ब्रह्मार्पणम् ब्रह्म हविः ब्रह्माग्नौ ब्रह्मणा हुतम् । ब्रह्म एव तेन गन्तव्यम् ब्रह्मकर्मसमाधिना । *brahma* (r◦ 1/1) *arpaṇam* (r◦ 14/1, 24/3) *brahma haviḥ:* (r◦ 16/6) *brahmāgnau brahmaṇā* (r◦ 24/4) *hutam* (r◦ 14/2) *brahma* (r◦ 3/1) *eva tena gantavyam* (r◦ 14/1) *brahmakarmasamādhinā*

(§2) *brahma* (1nom◦ sing◦ ←n◦ *brahman* 3.15); *arpaṇam* (2acc◦ sing◦ ←n◦ ***arpaṇa*** (offering) ←1◦√ऋ); *brahma* (3.15); 🕮*haviḥ:* (1nom◦ sing◦ ←n◦ *haviṣ* (oblation) ←3◦√हु); *brahmāgnau* (m◦ 7loc◦ sing◦ ←tatpu◦ *brahmāgni*, ब्रह्मणः अग्निः ←n◦ *brahman* 2.72 + m◦ *agni* (fire) 4.19); *brahmaṇā* (3inst◦ sing◦ ←n◦ *brahman* 2.72); ***hutam*** (n◦ 1nom◦ sing◦ ←ppp◦ adj◦ *huta* (offered) ←3◦√हु); *brahma* (3.15); *eva* (1.1); *tena* (3.38); 🕮*gantavyam* (n◦ 1nom◦ sing◦ ←pass◦ -pot◦ adj◦ adj◦ *gantavya* (to be attained) ←1◦√गम्); *brahmakarmasamādhinā* (m◦ 3inst◦ sing◦ ←bahuvrī◦ *brahma-karma-samādhin*, ब्रह्मकर्मणि समाधिस्थः यः ←n◦ *brahman* 2.72 + n◦ *karman* 1.15 + f◦ *samādhi* (contemplation) 2.44) (4.24)

(§3) *brahma* (subj1◦ brahma); *arpaṇam* (adj◦-subj1◦ the offering); *brahma* (subj1◦ brahma); *haviḥ:* (adj2◦-subj1◦ the oblation); *brahmāgnau* (in the fire of brahma); *brahmaṇā* (by brahma); *hutam* (adj3◦-subj1◦ poured); *brahma* (obj◦ brahma); *eva* (only); *tena* (adj1◦-subj2◦ by him); *gantavyam* (adj◦-obj◦ to be attained, ought to be attained); *brahmakarmasamādhinā* (subj2◦ by him who contemplates brahma in his *karma*) (4.24)

(§4) brahma arpaṇam brahma haviḥ: brahmāgnau hutam brahmaṇā brahma eva gantavyam tena brahmakarmasamādhinā

(§5) *Brahma* (is) the offering; *brahma* (is) the oblation in the fire of *brahma,* poured by *brahma. Brahma* (is) only to be attained by him who contemplates *brahma* in his *karma.*[372] (4.24)

4.25 दैवमेवापरे यज्ञं योगिनः पर्युपासते ।
ब्रह्माग्नावपरे यज्ञं यज्ञेनैवोपजुह्वति ।।

daivamevāpare yajñaṁ yoginaḥ: paryupāsate,
brahmāgnāvapare yajñaṁ yajñenaivopajuhvati. (4.25)

---

[372] *brahma* (obj◦); *eva tena* (adj◦-subj◦); *gantavyam* (adj◦-obj◦); *brahmakarmasamādhinā* (subj), because it is a Sanskrit passive construction.

(§1) दैवम् एव अपरे यज्ञम् योगिनः पर्युपासते । ब्रह्माग्नौ अपरे यज्ञम् यज्ञेन एव उपजुह्वति । *daivam̦* (r∘ 8/22) *eva* (r∘ 1/1) *apare yajñam̦* (r∘ 14/1) *yoginah̦:* (r∘ 22/3) *paryupāsate brahmāgnau* (r∘ 5/5) *apare yajñam̦* (r∘ 14/1) *yajñena* (r∘ 3/1) *eva* (r∘ 2/2) *upajuhvati*

(§2) 🕮***daivam̦*** (2acc∘ sing∘ ←n∘ taddhita∘ *daiva* (divinity) ←n∘ or m∘ ***deva*** (god) ←4∘√दिव्); *eva* (1.1); ***apare*** (m∘ 1nom∘ plu∘ ←pron∘ adj∘ *apara* (other) 2.22); ***yajñam̦*** (2acc∘ sing∘ ←m∘ *yajña* 3.9); ***yoginah̦:*** (1nom∘ plu∘ ←m∘ *yogin̦* 3.3); ***paryupāsate*** (3rd-per∘ plu∘ pres∘ वर्तमान्–लट् ātmane∘ ←2∘परि–**उप√अस्**); *brahmāgnau* (4.24); *apare* (↑); *yajñam̦* (↑); ***yajñena*** (3inst∘ sing∘ ←m∘ *yajña* 3.9); *eva* (1.1); *upajuhvati* (3rd-per∘ plu∘ pres∘ वर्तमान्–लट् parasmai∘ ←3∘उप√हु 4.25) (4.25)

(§3) *daivam̦* (adj∘-obj1∘ pertaining to the deities); *eva* (only); *apare* (adj∘-subj1∘ other); *yajñam̦* (obj1∘ *yajña, austerity*); *yoginah̦:* (subj1∘ yogīs); *paryupāsate* (they perform, they perform worship, they worship); *brahmāgnau* (in the fire of brahma); *apare* (adj∘-subj2∘ other, some other yogīis); *yajñam̦* (obj2∘ yajña); *yajñena* (by offering); *eva* (only); *upajuhvati* (they perform, they perform yajña) (4.25)

(§4) apare yoginah̦: paryupāsate yajñam̦ daivam̦ eva apare upajuhvati yajñam̦ eva yajñena brahmāgnau

(§5) Other *yogīs* perform *yajña* pertaining to the deities only. Some other *yogīs* perform *yajña* only by offering in the fire of brahma. (4.25)

4.26 श्रोत्रादीनीन्द्रियाण्यन्ये संयमाग्निषु जुह्वति ।
शब्दादीन्विषयानन्य इन्द्रियाग्निषु जुह्वति ।।
śrotrādīnīndriyāṇyanye sam̐yamāgniṣu juhvati,
śabdādīnviṣayānanya indriyāgniṣu juhvati. (4.26)

(§1) श्रोत्रादीनि इन्द्रियाणि अन्ये संयमाग्निषु जुह्वति । शब्दादीन् विषयान् अन्ये इन्द्रियाग्निषु जुह्वति । *śrotrādīni* (r∘ 1/5) *indriyāṇi* (r∘ 4/1, 24/8) *anye sam̐yamāgniṣu* (r∘ 25/5) *juhvati śabdādīn̦* (r∘ 13/19) *viṣayān̦* (r∘ 8/11) *anye* (r∘ 5/2) *indriyāgniṣu* (r∘ 25/5) *juhvati*

(§2) *śrotrādīni* (n∘ 2acc∘ plu∘ ←bahuvrī∘ *śrotrādin̦*, श्रोत्रम् आदिः यस्य तत् ←n∘ ***śrotra*** (hearing) ←1∘√श्रु + m∘ or adj∘ *ādi* 2.28); *indriyāṇi* (2.58); *anye* (1.9); *sam̐yamāgniṣu* (m∘ 7loc∘ plu∘ ←tatpu∘ *sam̐yamāgni*, संयमरूपम् अग्निः ←m∘ ***sam̐yama*** (restraint) ←1∘सम्√यम् + m∘ *agni* 4.19); ***juhvati*** (3rd-per∘ plu∘ pres∘ वर्तमान्–लट् parasmai∘ ←3∘√हु 4.25); ***śabdādīn̦*** (m∘ 2acc∘ plu∘ ←bahuvrī∘ *śabdādi*, शब्दः आदि यस्य ←m∘ *shabda* (speech) 1.13 + adj∘ *ādi* 2.28); *viṣayān̦* (2.62); *anye* (1.9); *indriyāgniṣu* (m∘ 7loc∘ plu∘ ←tatpu∘ *indriyāgni*, इन्द्रियरूपम् अग्निः ←n∘ *indriya* 2.8 + m∘ *agni* 4.19); *juhvati* (↑) (4.26)

(§3) *śrotrādīni* (adj∘-obj1∘ hearing etc.); *indriyāṇi* (obj1∘ sense organs); *anye* (subj1∘ other, other yogīs); *saṁyamāgniṣu* (in the fire of restraint); *juhvati* (they offer); *śabdādīn* (adj∘-obj2∘ speech etc.); *viṣayān* (obj2∘ sense objects); *anye* (subj2∘ other, some other yogīs); *indriyāgniṣu* (in the fire of organs); *juhvati* (they offer) (4.26)

(§4) anye juhvati indriyāṇi śrotrādīni saṁyamāgniṣu anye juhvati viṣayān śabdādīn indriyāgniṣu

(§5) Other *yogīs* offer sense organs (such as) hearing etc. in the fire of restraint. Some other *yogīs* offer sense objects (such as) speech etc. in the fire of organs. (4.26)

4.27 सर्वाणीन्द्रियकर्माणि प्राणकर्माणि चापरे ।
आत्मसंयमयोगाग्नौ जुह्वति ज्ञानदीपिते ।।
sarvāṇīndriyakarmāṇi prāṇakarmāṇi ćāpare,
ātmasaṁyamayogāgnau juhvati jñānadīpite. (4.27)

(§1) सर्वाणि इन्द्रियकर्माणि प्राणकर्माणि चापरे । आत्मसंयमयोगाग्नौ जुह्वति ज्ञानदीपिते । *sarvāṇi* (r∘ 24/7, 1/5) *indriyakarmāṇi* (r∘ 24/7) *prāṇakarmāṇi* (r∘ 24/7) *ća* (r∘ 1/1) *apare* (r∘ 23/1) *ātmasaṁyamayogāgnau juhvati jñānadīpite*

(§2) *sarvāṇi* (2.30); *indriyakarmāṇi* (n∘ 2acc∘ plu∘ ←tatpu∘ *indriya-karma*, इन्द्रियस्य कर्म ←n∘ *indriya* 2.8 + n∘ *karman* 1.15); *prāṇakarmāṇi* (n∘ 2acc∘ plu∘ ←tatpu∘ *prāṇa-karma*, प्राणस्य कर्म ←m∘ *prāṇa* (life breath) 1.33 + n∘ *karman* 1.15); *ća* (1.1); *apare* (4.25); *ātmasaṁyamayogāgnau* (m∘ 7loc∘ sing∘ ←tatpu∘ *ātma-saṁyama-yogāgni*, आत्मनः संयमस्य योगाग्निः ←m∘ *ātman* 2.41 + m∘ *saṁyama* (control) *4.26* + f∘ *yogāgni*, योगस्य अग्नि ←m∘ *yoga* 2.39 + m∘ *agni* 4.19); *juhvati* (4.26); *jñānadīpite* (7loc∘ sing∘ ←tatpu∘ *jñāna-dīpita*, ज्ञानेन दीपितः ←m∘ *jñāna* 3.3 + ppp∘ adj∘ *dīpita* (enlightened) ←4∘√दीप्) (4.27)

(§3) *sarvāṇi* (adj∘-obj1∘ all); *indriyakarmāṇi* (obj1∘ functions of organs); *prāṇakarmāṇi* (obj2∘ functions of life breath); *ća* (and); *apare* (subj1∘ other, other yogīs); *ātmasaṁyamayogāgnau* (in the fire of self-restraint); *juhvati* (they offer); *jñānadīpite* (in the one that is enlightened by knowledge) (4.27)

(§4) apare juhvati sarvāṇi indriyakarmāṇi ća prāṇakarmāṇi ātmasaṁyamayogāgnau jñānadīpite

(§5) Other *yogīs* offer all functions of organs and functions of life breath, in the fire of self-restraint that is enlightened by knowledge. (4.27)

4.28 द्रव्ययज्ञास्तपोयज्ञा योगयज्ञास्तथापरे ।
स्वाध्यायज्ञानयज्ञाश्च यतयः संशितव्रताः ।।
dravyayajñāstapoyajñā yogayajñāstathāpare,
svādhyāyajñānayajñāśća yatayaḥ: saṁśitavratāḥ:. (4.28)

(§1) द्रव्ययज्ञा: तपोयज्ञा: योगयज्ञा: तथा अपरे । स्वाध्यायज्ञानयज्ञा: च यतय: संशितव्रता: । *dravyayajñāḥ:* (r∘ 18/1) *tapoyajñāḥ:* (r∘ 20/14) *yogayajñāḥ:* (r∘ 18/1) *tathā* (r∘ 1/3) *apare svādhyāyajñānayajñāḥ:* (r∘ 17/1) *ćа* *yatayaḥ:* (r∘ 22/7) *saṁśitavratāḥ:* (r∘ 22/8)

(§2) *dravyayajñāḥ:* (m∘ 1nom∘ plu∘ ←bahuvrī∘ *dravya-yajña,* द्रव्येण यज्ञ: यस्य ←n∘ ***dravya*** (material thing) ←1∘√द्रु + m∘ *yajña* 3.9); *tapoyajñāḥ:* (m∘ 1nom∘ plu∘ ←bahuvrī∘ *tapoyajña,* तपसा यज्ञ: यस्य ←n∘ *tapaṣ* (penance) 4.10 + m∘ *yajña* 3.9); *yogayajñāḥ:* (m∘ 1nom∘ plu∘ ←bahuvrī∘ *yoga-yajña,* योगेन यज्ञ: यस्य ←m∘ *yoga* 2.39 + m∘ *yajña* 3.9); *tathā* (1.8); *apare* (4.25); *svādhyāyajñānayajñāḥ:* (m∘ 1nom∘ plu∘ ←bahuvrī∘ *svādhyāya-jñāna-yajña,* स्वाध्यायेन च ज्ञानेन च यज्ञा: यस्य ←m∘ ***svādhyāya*** (study of scriptures) ←1∘सु–अधि√इ + n∘ *jñāna* 3.3 + m∘ *yajña* 3.9); *ća* (1.1); ***yatayaḥ:*** (1nom∘ plu∘ ←m∘ ***yati*** ←1∘√यत्); *saṁśitavratāḥ:* (m∘ 1nom∘ plu∘ ←bahuvrī∘ *saṁśita-vrata,* संशितम् व्रतम् यस्य ←ppp∘ adj∘ *saṁśita* (firm) ←4∘सम्√शो + n∘ or m∘ ***vrata*** (resolve) ←1∘√वृ) (4.28)

(§3) *dravyayajñāḥ:* (subj1∘ those whose *yajña* is offering of material things); *tapoyajñāḥ:* (subj2∘ those whose *yajña* is through penances); *yogayajñāḥ:* (subj3∘ those whose *yajña* is through the practice of yoga); *tathā* (as well as); *apare* (adj∘-subj1-5∘ other, other yogīs); *svādhyāyajñānayajñāḥ:* (subj4∘ those whose yajña is through the study of scriptures); *ća* (and); *yatayaḥ:* (subj5∘ the ascetics); *saṁśitavratāḥ:* (adj∘-subj5∘ the ones whose resolve is firm, the ones with severe vows, the ones with acute observance) (4.28)

(§4) tathā apare dravyayajñāḥ: tapoyajñāḥ: yogayajñāḥ: svādhyāyajñānayajñāḥ: ća yatayaḥ: saṁśitavratāḥ:

(§5) As well as other yogīs, those whose *yajña* is offering of material things,[373] those whose *yajña* is through penances, those whose *yajña* is through the practice of yoga, those whose yajña is through the knowledge of scriptures (and) the ascetics whose resolve is firm; (4.28)

---

[373] Elsewhere∘ *dravyayajñāḥ:* → sacrificing one's possessions, by sacrficing their possession, (some) perform sacrifice with material possessions, (others) are performers of sacrifices through wealth, (others) again offer wealth, (some) offer as sacrifice their material possessions ...etc.

📖 द्रव्ययज्ञा: is masculine, plural, बहूव्रीहि adjective. It is not a तत्पुरुष–समास: । Therefore, this *samāsa* neither refer to द्रव्यम् nor to यज्ञा:, but it is an adjective of THOSE WHO ... (m∘ plu∘ nominative). It does not denote a verb such as : some perform, as others are, others offer, some offer etc. It is not a gerundive : sacrificing etc. The same is also true for the ohter four बहूव्रीहि adjectives *tapoyajñāḥ:, yogayajñāḥ:, svādhyāyajñānayajñāḥ:* and *saṁśitavratāḥ:* in this śloka.

4.29 अपाने जुह्वति प्राणं प्राणेऽपानं तथापरे ।
प्राणापानगती रुद्ध्वा प्राणायामपरायणाः ॥

apāne juhvati prāṇaṁ prāṇe'pānaṁ tathāpare,
prāṇāpānagatī ruddhvā prāṇāyāmaparāyaṇāḥ:. (4.29)

(§1) *apāne juhvati prāṇam* (r◦ 14/1, 24/3) *prāṇe* (r◦ 24/9, 6/1) *apānam* (r◦ 14/1) *tathā* (r◦ 1/3) *apare prāṇāpānagatī ruddhvā prāṇāyāmaparāyaṇāḥ:* (r◦ 24/5, 22/8)

(§2) *apāne* (m◦ 7loc◦ sing◦ ←n.tatpu◦ ***apāna*** (exhalation) अधोगच्छति इति ←4◦अप्√अन्); *juhvati* (4.26); ***prāṇam*** (life breath) (2acc◦ sing◦ ←m◦ *prāṇa* 1.33); *prāṇe* (7loc◦ sing◦ ←m◦ *prāṇa* 1.33); *apānam* (2acc◦ sing◦ ←m◦ *apāna* ↑); *tathā* (1.8); *apare* (4.25); *prāṇāpānagatī* (f◦ 2acc◦ dual◦ ←tatpu◦ *prāṇāpāna-gatī*, प्राणस्य च अपानस्य च गती ←m◦ *prāṇa* 1.33 + m◦ *apāna* ↑ + f◦ *gati* (rate, flow) 2.43); 🕮*ruddhvā* (ipp◦ ind◦ ←7◦√रुध्); *prāṇāyāmaparāyaṇāḥ:* (m◦ 1nom◦ plu◦ ←bahuvrī◦ *prāṇāyāma-parāyaṇa*, प्राणस्य आयामम् परायणम् यस्य ←m◦ *prāṇa* 1.33 + m◦ *āyāma* ←1◦आ√यम् + n◦ ***parāyaṇa*** (devotee) ←adj◦ *para* 2.3 + n◦ *ayana* 1.11) (4.29)

(§3) *apāne* (in exhalation); *juhvati* (they offer, perform the offering of, they offer in yajña); *prāṇam* (obj1◦ inhalation, incoming breath); *prāṇe* (in inhalation); *apānam* (obj2◦ exhalation, outgoing breath); *tathā* (as well as); *apare* (adj◦-subj◦ other, other yogīs); *prāṇāpānagatī* (obj◦ the flow of inhalation and exhalation); *ruddhvā* (having restrained, restraining); *prāṇāyāmaparāyaṇāḥ:* (subj◦ those who are devoted to the practice of breath control) (4.29)

(§4) apare prāṇāyāmaparāyaṇāḥ: juhvati prāṇam apāne tathā apānam prāṇe ruddhvā prāṇāpānagatī

(§5) Other *yogīs,* who are devoted to the practice of breath control,[374] perform the offering of inhalation in exhalation as well as exhalation in inhalation, restraining the flow of inhalation and exhalation. (4.29)

4.30 अपरे नियताहाराः प्राणान्प्राणेषु जुह्वति ।
सर्वेऽप्येते यज्ञविदो यज्ञक्षपितकल्मषाः ॥

apare niyatāhārāḥ: prāṇānprāṇeṣu juhvati,

---

[374] प्रणायाम defined : (Pātañjalayogasūtram 2.49) तस्मिन्सति श्वासप्रश्वासयोर्गतिविच्छेदः प्राणायामः ।

* तस्मिन् सति = तस्य सिद्धौ; श्वास-प्रश्वासयोः = श्वासस्य च प्रश्वासस्य (उच्छ्वासस्य, निःश्वासस्य) च; गति-विच्छेदः = गतेः (चलनस्य, सरणस्य, वेगस्य) विच्छेदः (वियोगः, लवनम्); 'प्राणायामः' इति उच्यते । In attainment of flow of the incoming and outgoing breaths, their regulation is called *prāṇayamaḥ:*. (See "Learning Yoga Sūtras of Patañjali" by Ratnakar Narale; Pustak Bharati Publications)

sarve'pyete yajñavido yajñakṣapitakalmaṣāḥ:. (4.30)

(§1) अपरे नियताहारा: प्राणान् प्राणेषु जुह्वति । सर्वे अपि एते यज्ञविद: यज्ञक्षपितकल्मषा: । *apare niyatāhārāḥ:* (r◦ 22/3) *prāṇān* (r◦ 13/13) *prāṇeṣu* (r◦ 25/5) *juhvati sarve* (r◦ 6/1) *api* (r◦ 4/4) *ete yajñavidaḥ:* (r◦ 15/10) *yajñakṣapitakalmaṣāḥ:* (r◦ 22/8)

(§2) *apare* (4.25); *niyatāhārāḥ:* (m◦ 1nom◦ plu◦ ←bahuvrī◦ *niyatāhāra* (moderate eater) नियत: आहार: यस्य ←adj◦ *niyata* 1.44 + m◦ *āhāra* 2.59); *prāṇān* (1.33); *prāṇeṣu* (7loc◦ plu◦ ←m◦ *prāṇa* 1.33); *juhvati* (4.26); *sarve* (1.6); *api* (1.26); *ete* (1.23); *yajñavidaḥ:* (m◦ 1nom◦ plu◦ ←adj◦ *yajña-vida* ←m◦ *yajña* 3.9 + adj◦ *viḍ* 3.29); *yajñakṣapitakalmaṣāḥ:* (m◦ 1nom◦ plu◦ ←bahuvrī◦ *yajña-kṣapita-kalmaṣa*, यज्ञै: क्षपितम् कल्मषम् यस्य ←m◦ *yajña* 3.9 + ppp◦ adj◦ *kṣapita* (diminished) ←6◦√क्षि + n◦ 🕮**kalmaṣa** (sin) ←3◦कर्म√सो)

(4.30)

(§3) *apare* (adj◦-subj◦ other, other yogīs); *niyatāhārāḥ:* (subj◦ those who have regulated their food); *prāṇān* (obj◦ inhalations); *prāṇeṣu* (in inhalatios); *juhvati* (they offer, they offer in yajña); *sarve* (adj1◦-subj◦ all); *api* (also, even); *ete* (adj2◦-subj◦ these, these yogīs); *yajñavidaḥ:* (subj◦ the knowers of yajñas); *yajñakṣapitakalmaṣāḥ:* (adj3◦-subj◦ the ones whose sins are destroyed or diminished through yajñas) (4.30)

(§4) api apare niyatāhārāḥ: juhvati prāṇān sarve ete yajñavidaḥ: yajñakṣapitakalmaṣāḥ:

(§5) Also, other *yogīs,* who have regulated their food,[375] offer in *yajña* inhalations in inhalatios. All these *yogīs,* (are) the knowers of *yajñas* (and) whose sins are destroyed or diminished through *yajñas.*[376] (4.30)

4.31 यज्ञशिष्टामृतभुजो यान्ति ब्रह्म सनातनम् ।
नायं लोकोऽस्त्ययज्ञस्य कुतोऽन्य: कुरुसत्तम ।।
yajñaśiṣṭāmṛtabhujo yānti brahma sanātanam,
nāyaṁ loko'styayajñasya kuto'nyaḥ: kurusattama. (4.31)

---

[375] Elsewhere◦ *niyatāhārāḥ:* → having their food regulated, restricting their food, having controlled eating ...etc.

🕮 नियताहारा: is not a gerund or a verb. It is a बहूव्रीहि adjective, as explained in the footnote of śloka 4.28 above. It is therefore a m◦ plural adj◦ → THOSE WHO have resrticted or regulated their eating.

[376] Elsewhere◦ *yajñakṣapitakalmaṣāḥ:* → become cleansed of sinful reactions, have their sins destroyed, having their sins destroyed ...etc.

🕮 यज्ञक्षपितकल्मषा: is not a verb or gerund. It is a बहूव्रीहि adjective, as seen in the footnote of śloka 4.28 above. It is thus plural adj◦ → THOSE WHOSE sins are diminished through *yajña.*

(§1) यज्ञशिष्टामृतभुजः यान्ति ब्रह्म सनातनम् । न अयम् लोकः अस्ति अयज्ञस्य कुतः अन्यः कुरुसत्तम । *yajñaśiṣṭāmṛtabhujaḥ:* (r∘ 15/10) *yānti brahma sanātanaṃ* (r∘ 14/2) *na* (r∘ 1/1) *ayaṃ* (r∘ 14/1) *lokaḥ:* (r∘ 15/1) *asti* (r∘ 4/1) *ayajñasya kutaḥ:* (r∘ 15/1) *anyaḥ:* (r∘ 22/1) *kurusattama*

(§2) *yajñaśiṣṭāmṛtabhujaḥ:* (m∘ 1nom∘ plu∘ ←bahuvrī∘ *yajña-śiṣṭāmṛta-bhuj,* यज्ञस्य शिष्टम् अमृतम् भुनक्ति यः ←m∘ *yajña* 3.9 + adj∘ *śiṣṭa* 3.13 + n∘ *amṛta* (sacred food) 2.15 + adj∘ *bhuj* or 1st-per∘ sing∘ pres∘ वर्तमान्-लट् parasmai∘ *bhunakti* ←7∘√भुज्); *yānti* (3.33); *brahma* (3.15); ***sanātanaṃ*** (n∘ 2acc∘ sing∘ ←adj∘ *sanātana* (beginingIsss and endless) 1.40); *na* (1.30); *ayaṃ* (2.19); *lokaḥ:* (3.9); *asti* (2.40); *ayajñasya* (m∘ 6pos∘ sing∘ ←n.bahuvrī∘ *a-yajña* ←1∘अ√यज्); *kutaḥ:* (2.2); *anyaḥ:* (2.29); *kurusattama* (m∘ 8voc∘ sing∘ ←bahuvrī∘ *kuru-sattama,* कुरूषु सत्तमः यः ←prop∘ *kuru* 1.1 + superlative adj∘ ***sattama*** (most righteous) ←adj∘ *saṭ* 2.16 + superlative suffix तम) (4.31)

(§3) *yajñaśiṣṭāmṛtabhujaḥ:* (subj1∘ those who partake the remaining *prasāda* sacred food of the *yajña*); *yānti* (they attain); *brahma* (obj∘ brahma); *sanātanaṃ* (adj∘-obj∘ that which has no begining and no end; the eternal); *na* (not); *ayaṃ* (adj∘-subj2∘ this); *lokaḥ:* (subj2∘ world); *asti* (is); *ayajñasya* (of or for him - who does not observe yajña, for the non-performer of yajña); *kutaḥ:* (how? how then?); *anyaḥ:* (adj∘-subj3∘ the other, the other world, the next world); *kurusattama* (O Kurusattama! O Best of the Kurus! O Arjuna!) (4.31)

(§4) yajñaśiṣṭāmṛtabhujaḥ: yānti sanātanaṃ brahma kurusattama ayajñasya ayaṃ lokaḥ: asti na, kutaḥ: anyaḥ:?

(§5) Those who partake the remaining *prasāda* sacred food of the *yajña,* they attain the eternal *brahma.* O Arjuna! of him, who does not observe *yajña,* (even) this world is not;[377] how could then the next world (be his)? (4.31)

4.32 **एवं बहुविधा यज्ञा वितता ब्रह्मणो मुखे ।**
कर्मजान्विद्धि तान्सर्वानेवं ज्ञात्वा विमोक्ष्यसे ।।
evaṁ bahuvidhā yajñā vitatā brahmaṇo mukhe,
karmajānviddhi tānsarvānevaṁ jñātvā vimokṣyase. (4.32)

(§1) एवम् बहुविधाः यज्ञाः विततः ब्रह्मणः मुखे । कर्मजान् विद्धि तान् सर्वान् एवम् ज्ञात्वा विमोक्ष्यसे । *evaṃ* (r∘ 14/1) *bahuvidhāḥ:* (r∘ 20/14) *yajñāḥ:* (r∘ 20/17) *vitatāḥ:* (r∘ 20/11) *brahmaṇaḥ:* (r∘ 15/9) *mukhe karmajāṇ* (r∘ 13/19) *viddhi tāṇ* (r∘ 13/20) *sarvāṇ* (r∘ 8/15) *evaṃ* (r∘ 14/1) *jñātvā vimokṣase*

(§2) *evaṃ* (1.24); *bahuvidhāḥ:* (m∘ 1nom∘ plu∘ ←adj∘ *bahu-vidha* ←adj∘ *bahu* 1.9 + m∘ *vidha* 3.3);

---

[377] Elsewhere∘ This world ceases to exist ...etc.

yajñāḥ: (1nom◦ plu◦ ←m◦ *yajña* 3.9); 🕮*vitatāḥ:* (m◦ 1nom◦ plu◦ ←ppp◦ adj◦ *vitata* (spread) ←8◦वि√तन्); 🕮***brahmaṇaḥ:*** (6pos sing◦ ←n◦ *brahman* 2.72); *mukhe* (7loc◦ sing◦ ←n◦ *mukha* 1.29); *karmajān* (m◦ 2acc◦ plu◦ ←adj◦ *karma-ja* 2.51); *viddhi* (2.17); *tān* (1.7); *sarvān* (1.27); *evam* (1.24); *jñātvā* (4.15); *vimokṣase* (2nd-per◦ sing◦ fut2◦ लृट् भविष्य◦ ātmane◦ ←6◦वि√मुच्) (4.32)

(§3) *evam* (in this manner, thus); *bahuvidhāḥ:* (adj1◦-subj◦ those of many kinds, many kinds of); *yajñāḥ:* (subj◦ *yajñas*, austerities); *vitatāḥ:* (adj2◦-subj◦ spread); *brahmaṇaḥ:* (of the brahma; of the Veda); *mukhe* (in the speech, in the words); *karmajān* (adj1◦-obj◦ born out of karma, *sakāma* karma, with the desire of attaining *moksha*); *viddhi* (you please know); *tān* (obj◦ to them, to those *yajñas*); *sarvān* (adj2◦-obj◦ to all); *evam* (in this way); *jñātvā* (having known); *vimokṣase* (you will attain liberation)[378] (4.32)

(§4) evam bahuvidhāḥ: yajñāḥ: vitatāḥ: mukhe brahmaṇaḥ: viddhi sarvān tān karmajān jñātvā vimokṣase

(§5) In this manner, many kinds of *yajñas (are)* spread in the words of the *veda*. You please know all); *tān* (to be) born out of (*sakāma*)karma. Having known in this way, you will attain liberation.[379] (4.32)

4.33 श्रेयान्द्रव्यमयाद्यज्ञाज्ज्ञानयज्ञः परन्तप ।
सर्वं कर्माखिलं पार्थ ज्ञाने परिसमाप्यते ।।
śreyāndravyamayādyajñājjñānayajñaḥ: parantapa,
sarvaṁ karmākhilaṁ pārtha jñāne parisamāpyate. (4.33)

(§1) श्रेयान् द्रव्यमयात् यज्ञात् ज्ञानयज्ञः परन्तप । सर्वम् कर्म अखिलम् पार्थ ज्ञाने परिसमाप्यते । *śreyān* (r◦ 13/11) *dravyamayāt* (r◦ 9/9) *yajñāt* (r◦ 11/2) *jñānayajñaḥ:* (r◦ 22/3) *parantapa sarvam* (r◦ 14/1) *karma* (r◦ 1/1) *akhilam* (r◦ 14/1) *pārtha jñāne parisamāpyate*

(§2) *śreyān* (3.35); *dravyamayāt* (n◦ 5abl◦ sing◦ ←taddhita◦ adj◦ *dravya-maya* ←n◦ *dravya* (physical matter) 4.28 + adj◦ *maya* 4.10); *yajñāt* (3.14); *jñānayajñaḥ:* (m◦ 1nom◦ sing◦ ←tatpu◦ ***jñāna-yajña,*** ज्ञानस्य यज्ञः ←n◦ *jñāna* 3.3 + m◦ *yajña* 3.9); *parantapa* (2.3); *sarvam* (n◦ 1nom◦ sing◦ ←pron◦ *sarva* 1.6); *karma* (1nom◦ 2.49); ***akhilam*** (adv◦ ←adj◦ n.tatpu◦ *akhila* (whole) ←6◦√खिल्); *pārtha* (1.25); *jñāne* (7loc◦ sing◦ ←n◦

---

[378] liberation, from the bondage of karma.

[379] Elsewhee◦ *vimokṣase* → thou shalt be liberated, you shall be freed, thou shalt be released, thou shalt be freed, you shall be liberated ...etc.

🕮 विमोक्षसे is a simple present tense (लट्) verb, in active voice, ātmanepadī, performed by second person subject त्वम् (you) → you will attain ..., but not, 'you (object) will be liberated' by the third person subject.

jñāna 3.3); 🕮*parisamāpyate* (ind◦ prefix *pari* (परि) 1.29 + 3rd-per◦ sing◦ pres◦ वर्तमान्-लट् ātmane◦ ←5◦सम्√आप्) (4.33)

(§3) *śreyān* (adj◦-subj◦ better); *dravyamayāt* (than the one consisting of the offerings of meterial things); *yajñāt* (than the yajña); *jñānayajñaḥ:* (the yajña consisting of the offerings of wisdom, knowledge); *parantapa* (O Parantapa! O Arjuna!); *sarvam* (adj◦-subj2◦ the whole); *karma* (subj2◦ karma); *akhilam* (entirely); *pārtha* (O Pārtha! O Arjuna!); *jñāne* (in the knowledge); *parisamāpyate* (it eventually concludes, ends) (4.33)

(§4) parantapa jñānayajñaḥ: śreyān dravyamayāt yajñāt pārtha sarvam karma parisamāpyate jñāne akhilam

(§5) O Arjuna! the *yajña* consisting of the offerings of knowledge (is) better than the *yajña* consisting of the offerings of meterial things. Because,) O Arjuna! the whole *karma* eventually concludes[380] in the knowledge entirely. (4.33)

4.34 तद्विद्धि प्रणिपातेन परिप्रश्नेन सेवया ।
उपदेक्ष्यन्ति ते ज्ञानं ज्ञानिनस्तत्त्वदर्शिनः ।।
tadviddhi praṇipātena paripraśnena sevayā,
upadekṣyanti te jñānaṁ jñāninastattvadarśinaḥ:. (4.34)

(§1) तत् विद्धि प्रणिपातेन परिप्रश्नेन सेवया । उपदेक्ष्यन्ति ते ज्ञानम् ज्ञानिनः तत्त्वदर्शिनः । *tat* (r◦ 9/11) *viddhi praṇipātena paripraśnena sevayā* (r◦ 23/1) *upadekṣyanti te jñānam* (r◦ 14/1) *jñāninaḥ:* (r◦ 18/1) *tattvadarśinaḥ:* (r◦ 22/8)

(§2) *tat* (2.7); *viddhi* (2.17); 🕮*praṇipātena* (3inst◦ sing◦ ←m◦ *praṇipāta* (humble submission) ←1◦प्र-नि√पत्); *paripraśnena* (3inst◦ sing◦ ←m◦ *praśna* (question) ←6◦√प्रच्छ् + prefix ind◦ *pari* 1.29); 🕮*sevayā* (3inst◦ sing◦ ←f◦ ***sevā*** (servitude) ←1◦**√सेव्**); *upadekṣyanti* (3rd-per◦ plu◦ fut2◦ लृट् भविष्य◦ parasmai◦ ←6◦उप**√दिश्**); *te* (1.7); *jñānam* (2acc◦ 3.40); *jñāninaḥ:* (3.39); 🕮*tattvadarśinaḥ:* (m◦ 1nom◦ plu◦ ←adj◦ *tattva-darśin* (truth seer) 2.16) (4.34)

---

[380] Elsewhere◦ *karma parisamāpyate* → all action is comprehended..., all actions culminate ..., all works culminate ..., all sacrifices of work culminate ...etc.

🕮 The verb परिसमाप्यते is not used in passive voice. Neither the subject कर्म, nor the verb परिसमाप्यते, is plural. Here, the pronominal adjective सर्वम् qualifies the collective singular subject कर्म, and therefore, its verb परिसमाप्यते is also singular. Thus, सर्वं कर्म परिसमाप्यते → the whole *karma* concludes, ends. Same as प्रविलीयते in 4.23

(§3) *taṭ* (adj∘-obj∘ that); *viddhi* (you please know, understand); *praṇipātena* (by humble submission, by prostrating yourself); *paripraśnena* (by asking right questions); *sevayā* (by servitude, by waiting on); *upadekṣyanti* (they will advise, instruct); *te* (you); *jñānaṃ* (obj∘ knowledge); *jñāninaḥ:* (subj∘ the wise men); *tattvadarśinaḥ:* (adj∘-subj∘ the seers of reality, perceivers of truth) (4.34)

(§4) viddhi taṭ jñānaṃ praṇipātena paripraśnena sevayā jñāninaḥ: tattvadarśinaḥ: upadekṣyanti te

(§5) You please understand that knowledge by humble submission, by asking right questions (and) by waiting on (them); the wise men, the seers of reality, will instruct you. (4.34)

4.35 यज्ज्ञात्वा न पुनर्मोहमेवं यास्यसि पाण्डव ।
येन भूतान्यशेषेण द्रक्ष्यस्यात्मन्यथो मयि ।।[381]
yajjñātvā na punarmohamevaṁ yāsyasi pāṇḍva,
yena bhūtānyaśeṣeṇa drakṣyasyātmanyatho mayi. (4.35)

(§1) यत् ज्ञात्वा न पुनर् मोहम् एवम् यास्यसि पाण्डव । येन भूतानि अशेषेण द्रक्ष्यसि आत्मनि अथ: मयि । *yaṭ* (r∘ 11/2) *jñātvā na punarmohaṃ* (r∘ 8/22) *evaṃ* (r∘ 14/1) *yāsyasi pāṇḍava yena bhūtāni* (r∘ 4/1) *aśeṣeṇa* (r∘ 24/1) *drakṣyasi* (r∘ 4/2) *ātmani* (r∘ 4/1) *athaḥ:* (r∘ 15/9) *mayi*

(§2) *yaṭ* (3.21); *jñātvā* (4.15); *na* (1.30); ***punaḥ:*** = *punaṛ* (again 4.9); ***mohaṃ*** (2acc∘ sing∘ ←m∘ *moha* (delusion) 2.52); *evaṃ* (1.24); *yāsyasi* (2.35); ***pāṇḍava*** (8voc∘ sing∘ ←m∘ *pāṇḍava* 1.1); *yena* (2.17); *bhūtāni* (2.30); 🕮***aśeṣeṇa*** (3inst∘ sing∘ ←adj∘ n.tatpu∘ ***aśeṣa*** (completely) ←7∘अ√शिष्); *drakṣyasi* (2nd-per∘ sing∘ fut2∘ लृट् भविष्य∘ parasmai∘ ←1∘√दृश्); *ātmani* (2.55); *athaḥ:* (time indicating ind∘ = मङ्गलम्, आनन्तयम्, समुच्चय:, कात्स्र्नम्, अधिकार:, संशय:, विकल्प:, आदय: अर्था: ←*atha* 1.20); *mayi* (3.30) (4.35)

(§3) *yaṭ* (adj∘-obj1∘ which); *jñātvā* (having known); *na* (not); *punaṛ* (again); *mohaṃ* (obj2∘ delusion); *evaṃ* (like this); *yāsyasi* (you will attain, you will fall into); *pāṇḍava* (O Pāṇḍava! O Arjuna!); *yena* (by which); *bhūtāni* (obj3∘ the beings); *aśeṣeṇa* (wholely, fully); *drakṣyasi* (you will see, you will perceive); *ātmani* (in yourself); *athaḥ:* (as well as); *mayi* (in me) (4.35)

(§4) jñātvā yaṭ pāṇḍava na yāsyasi mohaṃ evaṃ punaṛ yena drakṣyasi bhūtāni aśeṣeṇa ātmani athaḥ: mayi

(§5) Having known which, O Arjuna! you will not fall into delusion like this again (and) by which

---

[381] अहं वा सर्वभूतेषु सर्वभूतान्यथो मयि । इति ज्ञानं तथैस्तस्य न त्यागो न ग्रहो लय: ।। (aṣṭāvakragītā 6.4)
सर्वभूतेषु चात्मानं सर्वभूतानि चात्मनि । मुनेजनित आश्चयइ ममत्वमनुवर्तते ।। (aṣṭāvakragītā 3.5)
सर्वभूतेषु चात्मानं सर्वभूतानि चात्मनि । विज्ञाय निरहंकारो निर्ममस्त्वं सुखी भव: ।। (aṣṭāvakragītā 15.8)

you will perceive the beings wholely[382] in yourself as well as in me. (4.35)

4.36 अपि चेदसि पापेभ्य: सर्वेभ्य: पापकृत्तम: ।
सर्वं ज्ञानप्लवेनैव वृजिनं सन्तरिष्यसि ।।

api ćedasi pāpebhyaḥ: sarvebhyaḥ: pāpakṛttamaḥ:,
sarvaṁ jñānaplavenaiva vṛjinaṁ santariṣyasi. (4.36)

(§1) अपि चेत् असि पापेभ्य: सर्वेभ्य: पापकृत्तम: । सर्वम् ज्ञानप्लवेन एव वृजिनम् सन्तरिष्यसि । *api ćet* (r◦ 8/2) *asi pāpebhyaḥ:* (r◦ 22/7) *sarvebhyaḥ:* (r◦ 22/3) *pāpakṛttamaḥ:* (r◦ 22/8) *sarvam* (r◦ 14/1) *jñānaplavena* (r◦ 3/1) *eva vṛjinam* (r◦ 14/1) *santariṣyasi*

(§2) *api ćet* (even if 1.26, 2.33); *asi* (4.3); 🕮*pāpebhyaḥ:* (m◦ 5abl◦ plu◦ ←n◦ or adj◦ *pāpa* (sinner) ←adj◦ ***pāpin*** (sinner) ←1◦√पा); *sarvebhyaḥ:* (5abl◦ plu◦ ←m◦ pron◦ *sarva* (all) 1.6); *pāpakṛttamaḥ:* (m◦ 1nom◦ sing◦ ←ppp◦ -superlative adj◦ *pāpakṛt-tama* (most sinful) ←n◦ pāpa 1.36 + adj◦ *kṛt* 2.50 + suffix *tama* (most) 1.7); *sarvam* (2.17); *jñānaplavena* (3inst◦ sing◦ ←tatpu◦ *jñāna-plava* (boat of jñāna-yoga) ज्ञानस्य प्लव: ←n◦ *jñāna* (jñānayoga) 3.3 + m◦ 🕮*plava* (boat) ←1◦√प्लु); *eva* (1.1); 🕮*vṛjinam* (2acc◦ sing◦ ←n◦ *vṛjina* ←2◦√वृज्); *santariṣyasi* (2nd-per◦ sing◦ fut2◦ लृट् भविष्य◦ parasmai◦ ←1◦सम्√तृ) (4.36)

(§3) *api* (even); *ćet* (if); *asi* (you are); *pāpebhyaḥ:* (than the sinful people); sarvebhyaḥ: (than all); *pāpakṛttamaḥ:* (adj◦-subj◦ the most sinful); *sarvam* (adj◦-obj◦ all); *jñānaplavena* (with the boat of knowledge); *eva* (only); *vṛjinam* (obj◦ sin, evil); *santariṣyasi* (you will cross over, you will transcend) (4.36)

(§4) api ćet asi pāpakṛttamaḥ: sarvebhyaḥ: pāpebhyaḥ: santariṣyasi sarvam vṛjinam jñānaplavena eva

(§5) Even if you are the most sinful than all sinful people, you will transcend all evil with the boat of *jñānayoga*[383] only. (4.36)

4.37 यथैधांसि समिद्धोऽग्निर्भस्मसात्कुरुतेऽर्जुन ।
ज्ञानाग्नि: सर्वकर्माणि भस्मसात्कुरुते तथा ।।

yathaidhaṁsi samiddho'gnirbhasmasātkurute'rjuna,

---

[382] Elsewhere◦ *bhūtāni aśeṣeṇa* → all beings, all living beings, all existences, entire creation, the whole of the creation, all bhutas ...etc.

🕮 अशेषेण is not an adjective qualifying the noun भूतानि । It is an adverb qualifying the verb द्रक्ष्यसि । Thus, *bhūtānyaśeṣeṇa drakṣyasi* → you will wholly see the beings.

[383] Elsewhere◦ *jñāna* → knowledge.

jñānāgniḥ: sarvakarmāṇi bhasmasātkurute tathā. (4.37)

(§1) यथा एधांसि समिद्धः अग्निः भस्मसात् कुरुते अर्जुन । ज्ञानाग्निः सर्वकर्माणि भस्मसात् कुरुते तथा । *yathā* (r◦ 3/3) *edhāṁsi samiddhaḥ:* (r◦ 15/1) *agniḥ:* (r◦ 16/6) *bhasmasāt̜* (r◦ 10/5) *kurute* (r◦ 6/1) *arjuna jñānāgniḥ:* (r◦ 22/7) *sarvakarmāṇi* (r◦ 24/7) *bhasmasāt̜* (r◦ 10/5) *kurute tathā*

(§2) *yathā* (as, 1.11); 📖*edhāṁsi* (2acc◦ plu◦ ←n◦ *edhas̜* (fuel) ←7◦√इन्ध्); 📖*samiddhaḥ:* (m◦ 1nom◦ sing◦ ←ppp◦ adj◦ *samiddha* (kindled) ←7◦सम्√इन्ध्); ***agniḥ:*** (1nom◦ sing◦ ←m◦ *agni* (fire) 4.19); ***bhasmasāt̜*** (adv◦ ind◦ ←adj◦ *bhasman̜* (ashes) ←3◦√भस्); *kurute* (3.21); *arjuna* (2.2); *jñānāgniḥ:* (f◦ 1nom◦ m◦ ←tatpu◦ *jñānāgni* (fire of jñāna) ज्ञानरूपम् अग्निः 4.19); *sarvakarmāṇi* (3.26); *bhasmasāt̜* (↑); *kurute* (3.21); *tathā* (1.8) (4.37)

(§3) *yathā* (just as); *edhāṁsi* (obj1◦ the wood, fuel, firewood); *samiddhaḥ:* (adj◦-subj1◦ the kindled); *agniḥ:* (subj1◦ fire); *bhasmasāt-kurute* (it reduces to ashes); *arjuna* (O Arjuna!); *jñānāgniḥ:* (subj2◦ the fire of knowledge, the fire of wisdom); *sarvakarmāṇi* (obj2◦ all karmas); *bhasmasāt-kurute* (it reduces to ashes); *tathā* (similarly) (4.37)

(§4) yathā samiddhaḥ: agniḥ: bhasmasāt̜ kurute edhāṁsi tathā arjuna jñānāgniḥ: bhasmasāt̜ kurute sarvakarmāṇi

(§5) Just as the kindled fire reduces[384] the fuel to ashes, similarly, O Arjuna! the fire of *jñānayoga* reduces all *karmas* to ashes. (4.37)

4.38 न हि ज्ञानेन सदृशं पवित्रमिह विद्यते ।
तत्स्वयं योगसंसिद्धः कालेनात्मनि विन्दति ।।

na hi jñānena sadṛśaṁ pavitramiha vidyate,
tatsvayaṁ yogasaṁsiddhaḥ: kālenātmani vindati. (4.38)

(§1) न हि ज्ञानेन सदृशम् पवित्रम् इह विद्यते । तत् स्वयम् योगसंसिद्धः कालेन आत्मनि विन्दति । *na hi jñānena sadṛśam̜* (r◦ 14/1) *pavitram̜* (r◦ 8/18) *iha vidyate tat̜* (r◦ 10/7) *svayam̜* (r◦ 14/1) *yogasaṁsiddhaḥ:* (r◦ 22/1) *kālena* (r◦ 1/2) *ātmani vindati*

(§2) *na* (1.30); *hi* (1.11); ***jñānena*** (3inst◦ sing◦ ←n◦ *jñāna* 3.3 + *sadṛśam̜* 3.33, *jñānena-sadṛśam̜* adv◦); 📖***pavitram̜*** (n◦ 1nom◦ sing◦ ←adj◦ *pavitra* (holy) ←1◦√पू); *iha* (2.5); *vidyate* (2.16); *tat̜* (2.7); ***svayam̜*** (adv◦

---

[384] Elsewhere◦ *bhasmasāt̜* → is reduced to ashes, burnt ...etc.

📖 भस्मस्तात् is not an adjective. It is an ind◦ adverb → to the state of ashed. Being an adv◦ it forms a phrase with verb √कृ or verb √भू । (1) भस्मस्तात्-कृ → to reduce to ashed and (2) भस्मसाद्-भू → to be reduced to ashed, to become ashes. In this verse, the verb भस्मसात्-कृ is used → it reduces to ashes. Same as प्रविलीयते in 4.23

ind∘ ←1∘सु√अय्); 🕮*yogasaṁsiddhaḥ:* (m∘ 1nom∘ sing∘ ←tatpu∘ *yoga-saṁsiddha,* योगे संसिद्धः ←m∘ *yoga* 2.39 + ppp∘ adj∘ ***samsiddha*** ←4∘सम्√सिध्); *kālena* (4.2); *ātmani* (2.55); 🕮***vindati*** (3rd-per∘ sing∘ -pres.parasmai∘ ←6∘√**विद्** to attain) (4.38)

(§3) *na* (there is nothing); *hi* (because); *jñānena-sadṛśaṃ* (like *jñānayoga,* wisdom); *pavitraṃ* (adj∘-subj∘ sacred, sanctified; purifying); *iha* (here, in this world); *vidyate* (it exists); *taṭ* (adj∘-obj∘ that, that wisdom); *svayaṃ* (himself); *yogasaṁsiddhaḥ:* (adj∘-subj2∘ the accomplished person); *ātmani* (in himself); *kālena* (with time); *vindati* (he attains) (4.38)

(§4) hi na pavitraṃ jñānena-sadṛśaṃ vidyate iha yogasaṁsiddhaḥ: svayaṃ vindati taṭ ātmani kālena

(§5) Because,[385] there is nothing purifying like *jñānayoga* exists in this world, the accomplished[386] person himself attains[387] that wisdom in himself with time.

4.39 श्रद्धावाँल्लभते ज्ञानं तत्परः संयतेन्द्रियः ।
ज्ञानं लब्ध्वा परां शान्तिमचिरेणाधिगच्छति ।।
śraddhāvāṁllabhate jñānaṁ tatparḥ: saṁyatendriyaḥ:,
jñānaṁ labdhvā parāṁ śāntimaćireṇādhigaćchati. (4.39)

(§1) श्रद्धावान् लभते ज्ञानम् तत्परः संयतेन्द्रियः । ज्ञानम् लब्ध्वा पराम् शान्तिम् अचिरेण अधिगच्छति । *śraddhāvāṇ* (r∘ 13/8) *labhate jñānaṃ* (r∘ 14/1) *tatparaḥ:* (r∘ 22/7) *saṁyatendriyaḥ:* (r∘ 22/8) *jñānaṃ* (r∘ 14/1) *labdhvā parāṃ* (r∘ 14/1) *śāntiṃ* (r∘ 8/16) *aćireṇa* (r∘ 24/1, 1/1) *adhigaćchati*

(§2) 🕮***śraddhāvāṇ*** (1nom∘ sing∘ ←adj∘ *śraddhāvaṭ* (faithful) 3.31); 🕮***labhate*** (3rd-per∘ sing∘ pres∘ वर्तमान्-लट् ātmane∘ ←1∘√लभ् 2.32); *jñānaṃ* (2acc∘ 3.40); *tatparaḥ:* (1nom∘ sing∘ ←adj∘ ***tatpara*** ←pron∘ *taḍ* 1.2 + adj∘ *para* 2.3); *saṁyatendriyaḥ:* (m∘ 1nom∘ sing∘ ←bahuvrī∘ *saṁyatendriya,* संयतानि इन्द्रियाणि यस्य ←ppp∘ adj∘ ***saṁyata*** (restrained) ←1∘सम्√यम् + n∘ *indriya* 2.8); *jñānaṃ* (↑); 🕮***labdhvā*** (ipp∘ ind∘ ←1∘√लभ्); ***parāṃ*** (2acc∘ sing∘ ←f∘ adj∘ *parā* 1.27); *śāntiṃ* (2.70); 🕮*aćireṇa* (adv∘ ind∘ ←adj∘ ***ćira*** ←5∘√चि); *adhigaćchati* (2.64) (4.39)

(§3) *śraddhāvāṇ* (subj∘ he who is possessed with faith, one who is devoted); *labhate* (he attains);

---

[385] See footnote in verse 3.5

[386] Elsewhere∘ संसिद्धः → perfected.

🕮 सिद्धिः = f∘ accomplishment, संसिद्धः = m∘ ppp∘ accomplished.

[387] Elsewhere∘ *vindati* → finds.

🕮 see how this verb is translated in ślokas 4.4, 5.21, 18.45 and 18.46 in the same books that you may have.

jñānam̥ (obj1∘ knowledge, wisdom); *tatparaḥ:* (= *tat-parāyaṇaḥ:* adj1∘-subj∘ for whom there is no higher goal, for whom this is the highest goal); *sam̃yatendriyaḥ:* (adj2∘-subj∘ he who has restrained his sense organs; he who has senses under control); *jñānam̥* (obj2∘ wisdom); *labdhvā* (having obtained, having earned); *parām̥* (adj∘-obj3∘ supreme); *śāntim̥* (obj3∘ peace); *aćireṇa* (soon); *adhigaććhati* (he attains) (4.39)

(§4) śraddhāvān̥ tatparaḥ: sam̃yatendriyaḥ: labhate jñānam̥ jñānam̥ labdhvā jñānam̥ aćireṇa adhigaććhati parām̥ śāntim̥

(§5) He who is possessed with faith, for whom this is the highest goal, he who has senses under control, he attains wisdom. Having earned wisdom, he soon attains supreme peace. (4.39)

4.40 **अज्ञश्चाश्रद्दधानश्च संशयात्मा विनश्यति ।**
नायं लोकोऽस्ति न परो न सुखं संशयात्मनः ।।
ajñaśćāśraddadhānaśća sam̃śayātmā vinaśyati,
nāyam̐ loko'sti na paro na sukham̐ sam̃śayātmanaḥ:. (4.40)

(§1) अज्ञः च अश्रद्दधानः च संशयात्मा विनश्यति । न अयम् लोकः अस्ति न परः न सुखम् संशयात्मनः । *ajñaḥ:* (r∘ 17/1) *ća* (r∘ 1/1) *aśraddadhānaḥ:* (r∘ 17/1) *ća sam̃śayātmā vinaśyati na* (r∘ 1/1) *ayam̥* (r∘ 14/1) *lokaḥ:* (r∘ 15/1) *asti na paraḥ:* (r∘ 15/6) *na sukham̥* (r∘ 14/1) *sam̃śayātmanaḥ:* (r∘ 22/8)

(§2) 🕮*ajñaḥ:* (m∘ 1nom∘ sing∘ ←adj∘ *ajña* (ignorant) 3.26); *ća* (1.1); 🕮*aśraddadhānaḥ:* (m∘ 1nom∘ sing∘ ←n.bahuvrī∘ ***a-śraddadhāna*** (faithless) ←negative affix (अ) 1.10 + ind∘ *śraṭ* ←9∘√श्री + deriv∘ adj∘ *dadāna* ←1∘√दा); *ća* (1.1); 🕮*sam̃śayātmā* (m∘ 1nom∘ sing∘ ←bahuvrī∘ ***sam̃śayātman̥***, संशयः आत्मा यस्य । संशयितुं शीलं यस्य । ←m∘ ***sam̃śaya*** (doubt) ←1∘सम्√शी + m∘ *ātman̥* 2.41); 🕮***vinaśyati*** (3rd-per∘ pres∘ वर्तमान्-लट् parasmai∘ ←4∘वि√नश्); *na* (1.30); *ayam̥* (2.19); *lokaḥ:* (3.9); *asti* (2.40); *na* (1.30); *paraḥ:* (3.11); *na* (1.30); ***sukham̥*** (1nom∘ 2acc∘ sing∘ or adv∘ ←n∘ *sukha* (happiness) 1.32); *sam̃śayātmanaḥ:* (m∘ 6pos∘ sing∘ ←bahuvrī∘ *sam̃śayātman̥* ↑)

(§3) *ajñaḥ:* (subj1∘ ignorant, he who is ingorant of this wisdom); *ća* (and); *aśraddadhānaḥ:* (adj1∘-subj1∘ he who is non-believer, faithless); *ća* (and); *sam̃śayātmā* (adj2∘-subj1∘ he who is possessed with doubt); *vinaśyati* (he perishes); *na* (neither); *ayam̥* (adj∘-subj2∘ this); *lokaḥ:* (subj2∘ world); *asti* (is); *na* (nor); *paraḥ:* (subj3∘ the other, the other world); *na* (nor); *sukham̥* (subj4∘ happiness); *sam̃śayātmanaḥ:* (for the one who is possessed with doubt) (4.40)

(§4) ajñaḥ: ća aśraddadhānaḥ: ća sam̃śayātmā vinaśyati; na ayam̥ lokaḥ: na paraḥ: na sukham̥ asti sam̃śayātmanaḥ:

(§5) He who is ingorant of this knowledge and he who is non-believer and he who is possessed with doubt, he perishes. Neither this world, nor the other world, nor happiness is for the one who is possessed with doubt.[388] (4.40)

4.41 योगसंन्यस्तकर्माणं ज्ञानसञ्छिन्नसंशयम् ।
आत्मवन्तं न कर्माणि निबध्नन्ति धनञ्जय ।।

yogasannyastakarmāṇaṁ jñānasaṁćchinnasaṁśayam,
ātmavantaṁ na karmāṇi nibadhnanti dhanañjaya. (4.41)

(§1) योगसंन्यस्तकर्माणम् ज्ञानसञ्छिन्नसंशयम् । आत्मवन्तम् न कर्माणि निबध्नन्ति धनञ्जय । *yogasannyastakarmāṇam̦* (r◦ 14/1, 24/3) *jñānasaṁćchinnasaṁśayam̦* (r◦ 14/2) *ātmavantam̦* (r◦ 14/1) *na karmāṇi* (r◦ 24/7) *nibadhnanti dhanañjaya*

(§2) *yogasannyastakarmāṇam̦* (m◦ 2acc◦ sing◦ ←bahuvrī◦ *yoga-sannyasta-karman̦*, योगेन संन्यस्तं कर्म येन ←m◦ *yoga* 2.39 + ppp◦ adj◦ 📖***sannyasta*** (renounced) ←2◦सम्-नि√अस् + n◦ *karman̦* 1.15); *jñānasaṁćchinnasaṁśayam̦* (m◦ 2acc◦ sing◦ ←bahuvrī◦ *jñāna-saṁćchinna-saṁśaya*, ज्ञानेन संच्छिन्नः संशयः यस्य ←n◦ *jñāna* 3.3 + ppp◦ adj◦ 📖*saṁćchinna* ←सम्√छिद् + m◦ *saṁśaya* 4.40); 📖*ātmavantam̦* (m◦ 2acc◦ sing◦ ←adj◦ *ātmavaț* 1.5); *na* (1.30); *karmāṇi* (3.27); *nibadhnanti* (3rd-per◦ plu◦ pres◦ वर्तमान्-लट् parasmai◦ ←class9◦ नि√बध्); *dhanañjaya* (2.48) (4.41)

(§3) *yogasannyastakarmāṇam̦* (adj1◦-obj◦ to him he who has renounced *sakāma-karmas* with practice of *yoga*); *jñānasaṁćchinnasaṁśayam̦* (adj2◦-obj◦ to him who has cut down his doubts with *jñana, jñānayoga,* this wisdom); *ātmavantam̦* (adj3◦-obj◦ to him who is self-possessed); *na* (do not); *karmāṇi* (subj◦ *karmas*); *nibadhnanti* (they fetter, they bind, they bind with attachment); *dhanañjaya* (O Arjuna!) (4.41)

(§4) yogasannyastakarmāṇam̦ jñānasaṁćchinnasaṁśayam̦ ātmavantam̦ dhanañjaya karmāṇi na nibadhnanti

---

[388] Elsewhere◦ *na ayam̦ lokaḥ: na paraḥ: na sukham̦ asti saṁśayātmanaḥ:* → (1) for the doubting self there is happiness neither in this world nor in the next ...etc. (2) The doubting self has neither this world, nor the next, nor the happiness.

📖 (1) In this verse, अयं-लोकः and परः are not in Locative (7th) case. अयं लोकः, परः लोकः and सुखम् are all in Nominative (1st) case, and therefore, the subjects, each performing the verb अस्ति । (2) The doubting self (संशयात्मनः) is not the subject; and this world (अयं लेकः), the next (परः) and happiness (सुखं) are not the objects. संशयात्मनः is the Possessice case. अयं लोकः, परः and सुखम् are the subjects, the performers of the verb अस्ति ।

(§5) To him he who has renounced the *sakāma-karmas* with the practice of *yoga,*[389] to him who has cut down his doubts with *jñana,* to him who is self-possessed, O Arjuna! *karmas* do not bind with attachment. (4.41)

4.42 तस्मादज्ञानसम्भूतं हृत्स्थं ज्ञानासिनात्मनः ।
छित्त्वैनं संशयं योगमातिष्ठोत्तिष्ठ भारत ।।
tasmādajñānasambhūtaṁ hṛtsthaṁ jñānāsinātmanaḥ:,
ćhitvainaṁ saṁśayaṁ yogamātiṣṭhottiṣṭha bhārata. (4.42)

(§1) तस्मात् ज्ञानसम्भूतम् हृत्स्थम् ज्ञानासिना आत्मनः । छित्त्वा एनम् संशयम् योगम् आतिष्ठ उत्तिष्ठ भारत । *tasmāt* (r∘ 8/2) *ajñānasambhūtam* (r∘ 14/1) *hṛtstham* (r∘ 14/1) *jñānāsinā* (r∘ 1/4) *ātmanaḥ:* (r∘ 22/8) *ćhittvā* (r∘ 3/3) *enam* (r∘ 14/1) *saṁśayam* (r∘ 14/1) *yogam* (r∘ 8/17) *ātiṣṭha* (r∘ 2/2) *uttiṣṭha bhārata*

(§2) *tasmāt* (1.37); 🕮*ajñānasambhūtam* (m∘ 2acc∘ sing∘ ←bahuvrī∘ *ajñāna-sambhūta,* अज्ञानात् सम्भूतः यः ←n∘ 🕮**ajñāna** ←9∘अ√ज्ञा + deriv∘ adj∘ *sambhūta* ←1∘सम्√भू); 🕮*hṛtstham* (m∘ 2acc∘ sing∘ ←tatpu∘ adj∘ *hṛtstha,* हृदि स्थितः ←n∘ ***hṛd*** (heart) ←1∘√हृ + ppp∘ adj∘ *sthita* 1.14 or *stha* 2.45); *jñānāsinā* (m∘ 3inst∘ sing∘ ←tatpu∘ *jñānāsi,* ज्ञानस्य असिः ←n∘ *jñāna* 3.3 + m∘ *asi* ←2∘√अस्); ***ātmanaḥ:*** (5abl∘ or 6pos∘ sing∘ ←m∘ *ātman* 2.41); 🕮***ćhittvā*** (ipp∘ ind∘ ←7∘√छिद्); *enam* (2.19); ***saṁśayam*** (2acc∘ sing∘ ←m∘ *saṁśaya* (doubt) 4.40); *yogam* (2.53); *ātiṣṭha* (2nd-per∘ sing∘ imperative∘ निमन्त्रणार्थ–लोट् parasmai∘ ←1∘आ√स्था); *uttiṣṭha* (2.3); *bhārata* (2.14) (4.42)

(§3) *tasmāt* (therefore); *ajñānasambhūtam* (adj1∘-obj1∘ that which is born out of ignorance); *hṛtstham* (adj2∘-obj1∘ that which has arisen in the heart); *jñānāsinā* (with the sword of jñāna); *ātmanaḥ:* (your); *ćhittvā* (having cut down); *enam* (adj3∘-obj1∘ this); *saṁśayam* (obj1∘ doubt); *yogam* (obj2∘ to yoga); *ātiṣṭha* (you please be fixed to, established); *uttiṣṭha* (you please stand up!); *bhārata* (O Bhārata! O Arjuna!) (4.42)

(§4) tasmāt ćhittvā jñānāsinā enam saṁśayam ajñānasambhūtam ātmanaḥ: hṛtstham bhārata ātiṣṭha yogam uttiṣṭha

(§5) Therefore,[390] having cut down with the sword of *jñāna,* this doubt which is born out of ignorance in your heart, O Arjuna! you please be fixed to *yoga* (and) please stand up! (4.42)

---

[389] Elsewhere∘ *yogasannyastakarmāṇam* → renouncing the fruits of his actions, has renounced action in Yoga, with work absolved in yoga, hath renounced action by yoga, renounced all works by yoga ...etc.

[390] See the footnote in verse 2.15

इति श्रीमद्भगवद्गीतासूपनिषत्सु ब्रह्मविद्यायां योगशास्त्रे
श्रीकृष्णार्जुनसंवादे ज्ञानकार्मसंन्यासयोगो नाम चतुर्थोऽध्यायः ।।

iti śrīmadbhagavadgītāsūpaniṣatsu brahmavidyāyāṁ yogaśāstre
śrīkṛṣṇārjunasaṁvāde jñānakarmasannyāsayogo nāma ćaturtho‘dhyāyaḥ:

(§1) *iti śrīmadbhagavadgītāsu* (r◦ 1/8) *upaniṣatsu brahmavidyāyām̧* (r◦ 14/1) *yogaśāstre śrīkṛṣṇārjunasaṁvāde jñānakarmasannyāsayogaḥ:* (r◦ 15/6) *nāma ćaturthaḥ:* (r◦ 15/1) *adhyāyaḥ:* (r◦ 22/8)

(§2) *iti* (1.25); *śrīmadbhagavadgītāsu* (f◦ 7loc◦ plu◦ tatpu◦ *śrīmad-bhagavad-gītā* ←adj◦ *śrīmaṭ* 6.41↓ + adj◦ *bhagavaṭ* 10.14↓ + f◦ *gītā* ←5◦√गै); *upaniṣatsu* (7loc◦ plu◦ ←f◦ *upaniṣaḍ* ←6◦उप-नि√सद्); *brahmavidyāyām̧* (f◦ 7loc◦ sing◦ ←tatpu◦ *brahma-vidyā*, ब्रह्मण: विद्या ←n◦ *brahman̥* 2.72↓ + *vidyā* 5.18↓); *yogaśāstre* (n◦ 7loc◦ sing◦ ←tatpu◦ *yoga-śāstra*, योगानाम् शास्त्रम् । योगस्य शास्त्रम् । ←m◦ *yoga* 2.39↓ + n◦ *śāstra* 15.20↓); *śrīkṛṣṇārjunasaṁvāde* (m◦ 7loc◦ sing◦ ←tatpu◦ *śrī-kṛṣṇārjuna-saṁvāda*, श्रीकृष्णस्य च अर्जुनस्य च संवाद: ←adj◦ *śrī* 10.34↓ + m◦ prop◦ *kṛṣṇa* 1.28 + m◦ prop◦ *arjuna* 1.4 + m◦ *saṁvāda* 18.70↓); *jñānakarmasannyāsayogaḥ:* (m◦ 1nom◦ sing◦ ←tatpu◦ *jñāna-karma-sannyāsa-yoga*, समत्वस्य ज्ञानस्य निष्कामस्य च कर्मस्य सङ्गस्य च संन्यासस्य योग: ←n◦ *jñāna* 3.3 + n◦ *karman̥* 1.15 + m◦ *sannyāsa* 5.1 + m◦ *yoga* 2.39); *nāma* (1nom◦ sing◦ ←n◦ *nāman̥* ←1◦√म्ना); *ćaturthaḥ:* (m◦ 1nom◦ sing◦ ←sequence indicating num◦ adj◦ *ćaturtha* ←adj◦ *ćatur̥* 7.16↓); *adhyāyaḥ:* (1nom◦ sing◦ ←m◦ *adhyāya* ←1◦अधि√इ)

(§3) *iti* (thus); *śrīmadbhagavadgītāsu upaniṣatsu* (among the upaniṣads of the Śrīmad-Bhagavadgītā); *brahmavidyāyām̧* (of the eternal wisdoms); *yogaśāstre* (in the science of Yoga); *śrīkṛṣṇārjunasaṁvāde* (in the dialogue between Śrī Kṛṣṇa and Arjuna); *jñānakarmasannyāsayogaḥ:* (adj1◦-subj◦ the *yoga* of the knowledge of equanimity, conduct of *karma* without desire in its fruit and renunciation of attachment); *nāma* (called); *ćaturthaḥ:* (adj◦2-subj◦ the fourth); *adhyāyaḥ:* (subj◦ discourse; chapter)

(§4) śrīmadbhagavadgītāsu upaniṣatsu yogaśāstre brahmavidyāyām̧ iti ćaturthaḥ: adhyāyaḥ: nāma jñānakarmasannyāsayogaḥ: śrīkṛṣṇārjunasaṁvāde

(§5) Among the upaniṣads of the Śrīmad-Bhagavadgītā, in the science of Yoga of self realization, thus (is) the fourth discourse called jñāna-karma-sannyāsa-yogaḥ: in the dialogue between Śrī Kṛṣṇa and Arjuna.

CHAPTER 5

pañćamo'dhyāyaḥ:

पञ्चमोऽध्याय: ।

karma-sannyāsa-yogaḥ:

कर्मसंन्यासयोग: ।

THE YOGA OF CONDUCT AND RENUNCIATION

Arjuna said (arjuna uvāća अर्जुन उवाच ।)

5.1 संन्यासं कर्मणां कृष्ण पुनर्योगं च शंससि ।
यच्छ्रेय एतयोरेकं तन्मे ब्रूहि सुनिश्चितम् ।।
sannyāsaṁ karmaṇām kṛṣṇa punaryogaṁ ća śaṁsasi,
yaććhreya etayorekaṁ tanme brūhi suniśćitam. (5.1)

(§1) संन्यासम् कर्मणाम् कृष्ण पुनर् योगम् च शंससि । यत् श्रेय: एतयो: एकं तत् मे ब्रूहि सुनिश्चितम् । *pañćamaḥ:* (r◦ 15/1) *adhyāyaḥ:* (r◦ 22/8). *karmasannyāsayogaḥ:* (r◦ 22/8). *arjunaḥ:* (r◦ 19/4) *uvāća. sannyāsaṃ* (r◦ 14/1) *karmaṇāṃ* (r◦ 24/6, 14/1) *kṛṣṇa punar yogaṃ* (r◦ 14/1) *ća śaṁsasi yaṭ* (r◦ 11/4) *śreyaḥ:* (r◦ 19/7) *etayoḥ:* (r◦ 16/5) *ekaṃ* (r◦ 14/1) *taṭ* (r◦ 12/2) *me bruhi suniśćitaṃ* (r◦ 14/2)

(§2) *pañćamaḥ:* (m◦ 1nom◦ sing◦ ←sequence indicating num◦ adj◦ *pañćama* 18.14); *adhyāyaḥ:* (1nom◦ sing◦ ←m◦ *adhyāy*←1◦अधि√इ). *karmasannyāsayogaḥ:* (m◦ 1nom◦ sing◦ ←tatpu◦ *karma-sannnyāsa-yoga*, कर्तृत्वस्य संन्यासस्य योग: ←n◦ *karmaṇ* 1.15 + m◦ *sannyāsa*↓ + m◦ *yoga* 2.39). *arjunaḥ:* (1.28); *uvāća* (1.25).

📖***sannyāsaṃ*** (2acc◦ sing◦ ←m◦ ***sannyāsa*** (renunciation) ←2◦सम्–नि√अस्); *karmaṇāṃ* (3.4); *kṛṣṇa* (1.28); *punaṛ* (4.9); 📖*yogaṃ* (2.53); *ća* (1.1); 📖*śaṁsasi* (2nd-per◦ sing◦ pres◦ वर्तमान्–लट् parasmai◦ ←1◦√शंस्); *yaṭ* (2.67); *śreyaḥ:* (2.5); *etayoḥ:* (m◦ or n◦ 6pos◦ dual◦ ←pron◦ *etad* 1.3); *ekaṃ* (3.2); *taṭ* (2.7); *me* (1.21); *bruhi* (2.7); 📖*suniśćitaṃ* (adv◦ (certainly) or n◦ 2acc◦ sing◦ ←adj◦ *suniśćita* (certain) ←ind◦ ***su*** ←1◦√सु + adj◦ *niśćita* (certain) 2.7) (5.1)

(§3) *pañćamaḥ:* (adj◦-subj◦ the fifth); *adhyāyaḥ:* (subj◦ chapter). *karmasannyāsayogaḥ:* (the yoga of renunciation of the authorship of karma). *arjunaḥ:* (Arjuna); *uvāća* (said). *sannyāsaṃ-karmaṇāṃ* (obj1◦ renunciation of karmas, renunciation of the authorship of karmas); *kṛṣṇa* (O Kṛṣṇa!); *punaṛ* (again, then); *yogaṃ* (obj2◦ yoga, karmayoga, renunciation of the desire in the fruit of the karmas); *ća* (and); *śaṁsasi* (you are praising, you praise); *yaṭ* (subj◦ which); *śreyaḥ:* (adj1◦-subj◦ better); *etayoḥ:* (in these two); *ekam̧* (adj2◦-subj◦ one); *taţ* (obj◦ that); *me* (me); *bruhi* (you please tell); *suniśćitam̧* (decisively, certainly) (5.1)

(§4) pañćamaḥ: adhyāyaḥ:. karmasannyāsayogaḥ:. arjunaḥ: uvāća. kṛṣṇa śaṁsasi sannyāsam̧ karmaṇām̧ ća punaŗ yogam̧ bruhi me suniśćitam̧ etayoḥ: taţ yaţ ekam̧ śreyaḥ:

(§5) The fifth chapter; The *yoga* of renunciation of the authorship of *karma;*[391] Arjuna said. O Kṛṣṇa! you are praising renunciation of the authorship of *karmas* and then the renunciation of the desire in the fruit of *karmas*. You please tell me decisively, in these two which one (is) better. (5.1)

The Lord Said (śrībhagavānuvāća श्रीभगवानुवाच ।)

5.2 **संन्यासः कर्मयोगश्च निःश्रेयसकरावुभौ ।**
तयोस्तु कर्मसंन्यासात्कर्मयोगो विशिष्यते ।।
sannyāsaḥ: karmayogāśća niḥ:śreyasakarāvubhau,
tayostu karmasannyāsātkarmayogo viśiṣyate. (5.2)

(§1) संन्यास: कर्मयोग: च नि:श्रेयसकरौ उभौ । तयो: तु कर्मसंन्यासात् कर्मयोग: विशिष्यते । *śrībhagavāņ* (r◦ 8/14) *uvāća. sannyāsaḥ:* (r◦ 22/1) *karmayogaḥ:* (r◦ 17/1) *ća niḥ:śreyasakarau* (r◦ 5/7) *ubhau tayoḥ:* (r◦ 18/1) *tu karmasannyāsāţ* (r◦ 10/5) *karmayogaḥ:* (r◦ 15/13) *viśiṣyate*

(§2) *śrībhagavāņ* (2.2); *uvāća* (1.25). 📖**sannyāsaḥ:** (1nom◦ sing◦ ←m◦ *sannyāsa* (renunciation) 5.1); ***karmayogaḥ:*** (1nom◦ sing◦ ←m◦ *karma-yoga* 3.3); *ća* (1.1); *niḥ:śreyasakarau* (m◦ 1nom◦ dual◦ ←adj◦ *niḥ:śreyasakara* ←ind◦ *niş* 2.45 + taddhita◦ *śreyasakara* (benefit giver) ←adj◦ *śreyaş* 1.31 + affix *kara* कर 2.2); *ubhau* (2.19); *tayoḥ:* (3.34); *tu* (1.2); *karmasannyāsāţ* (m◦ 5abl◦ sing◦ ←tatpu◦ *karma-sannyāsa*, कर्मण: कर्तृत्वस्य संन्यास: ←n◦ *karmaņ* 1.15 + m◦ *sannyāsa* 5.1); *karmayogaḥ:* (↑); *viśiṣyate* (3.7) (5.2)

(§3) *śrībhagavāņ* (The Lord); *uvāća* (said). *sannyāsaḥ:* (subj1◦ *sannyasayoga*, yoga of renunciation of 'authorship' of karma); *karmayogaḥ:* (subj2◦ karmayoga, niṣkāma-karmayoga, renunciation of the 'desire' in the fruit of karma); *ća* (and); *niḥ:śreyasakarau* (causers of great bliss, the givers of great benefit); *ubhau* (both); *tayoḥ:* (among these two); *tu* (however); *karmasannyāsāţ* (than renunciation of the authorship karma); *karmayogaḥ:* (sobj2◦ karmayoga, renunciation of the desire in the fruit of the karma); *viśiṣyate* (it excels) (5.2)

(§4) śrībhagavāņ uvāća. sannyāsaḥ: ća karmayogaḥ: ubhau niḥ:śreyasakarau tu tayoḥ: karmayogaḥ: viśiṣyate karmasannyāsāţ

---

[391] Elsewhere◦ *karmasannyāsayogaḥ:* → yoga of renunciation of action, yoga of renunciation of actions, yoga of rununciation ...etc.

(§5) The Lord said : *Sannyasayoga* (renunciation of the authorship of karma)[392] and *karmayoga* (renunciation of the desire in the fruit of karma)[393] both[394] (are) the givers of great benefit. However, among these two, the *karmayoga* excels the *Sannyasayoga.* (5.2)

5.3 ज्ञेयः स नित्यसंन्यासी यो न द्वेष्टि न काङ्क्षति ।
निर्द्वन्द्वो हि महाबाहो सुखं बन्धात्प्रमुच्यते ।।
jñeyaḥ: sa nityasannyāsī yo na dveṣṭi na kāṅkṣati,
nirdvandvo hi mahābāho sukhaṁ bandhātpramucyate. (5.3)

(§1) ज्ञेयः स नित्यसंन्यासी यः न द्वेष्टि न काङ्क्षति । निर्द्वन्द्वः हि महाबाहो सुखम् बन्धात् प्रमुच्यते । *jñeyaḥ:* (r◦ 22/7) *saḥ:* (r◦ 21/2) *nityasannyāsī yaḥ:* (r◦ 15/6) *na dveṣṭi na kāṅkṣati nirdvandvaḥ:* (r◦ 15/14) *hi mahābāho sukham* (r◦ 14/1) *bandhāt* (r◦ 10/6) *pramucyate*

(§2) 🕮***jñeyaḥ:*** (m◦ 1nom◦ sing◦ ←adj◦ *jñeya* 1.39); *saḥ:* (1.13); *nityasannyāsī* (m◦ 1nom◦ sing◦ ←ind◦ *nitya* 2.18 + m◦ 🕮***sannyāsin*** ←2◦सम्–नि√अस्); *yaḥ:* (2.19); *na* (1.30); *dveṣṭi* (2.57); *na* (1.30); 🕮***kāṅkṣati*** (3rd-per◦ sing◦ pres◦ वर्तमान्–लट् parasmai◦ ←1◦√कांक्ष्); *nirdvandvaḥ:* (2.45); *hi* (1.11); *mahābāho* (2.26); 🕮***sukham*** (adv◦ ←n◦ *sukha* (happiness) 1.32); *bandhāt* (5abl◦ sing◦ ←m◦ *bandha* (bondage) 1.27); ***pramucyate*** (3rd-per◦ sing◦ pres◦ वर्तमान्–लट् ātmane◦ ←6◦प्र√मुच्) (5.3)

(§3) *jñeyaḥ:* (adj1◦-subj◦ ought to be known); *saḥ:* (subj◦ he); *nityasannyāsī* (adj2◦-subj◦ a 'nitya-sannyāsī"); *yaḥ:* (adj3◦-subj◦ he who); *na* (does not); *dveṣṭi* (he does hate); *na* (nor); *kāṅkṣati* (he

---

[392] Elsewhere◦ *sannyāsaḥ:* → renunciation, renunciation of works, renunciation of work, renunciation of actions ...etc.

[393] Elsewhere◦ *karmayogaḥ:* → performance of action, work in devotion, yoga of action ...etc.

[394] Elsewhere◦ संन्यासः कर्मयोगः च → Renunciation and Yoga through action both, Yoga of renunciation and Yoga of action, Renunciation of action and Karmayoga both, Both renunciation and performance of action, Renunciation and performance of action both, Renunciation of work and work in devotion both, The yoga of Knowledge and Yoga of Action both, ...etc.

🕮 In Gita, if संन्यासः, संन्यासयेगः or सांख्ययोगः had meant 'renunciation of action' and कर्मयोगः or निष्कामकर्मयोगः or योगः had meant 'performance of action,' then the next verse (5.4) which says साङ्ख्ययोगौ पृथग्बालाः प्रवदन्ति न पण्डिताः would not conform with this verse. Because, एकम् अपि आस्थितः सम्यक् उभयोः विन्दते फलम् । Same is further clarified in verse 5.5 also. In Gita, संन्यासः, संन्यासयेगः or सांख्ययोगः is renunciation of the 'authorship' of karma (न एव किञ्चित करोमि इति मन्येत 5.8). It is NOT 'renunciation of action,' it is शारीरं केवलं कर्म कुर्वन् 4.21 पश्यन् शृण्वन् ...उन्मिशन् निमिषन् अपि इन्द्रियाणि इन्द्रियार्थेषु वर्तन्ते इति धारयन् 5.9. This is संन्यासः, संन्यासयेगः or सांख्ययोगः in Gita. कायेन मनसा बुद्धया केवलैः इन्द्रियैः सङ्गं त्यक्त्वा योगिनः कर्म कुर्वन्ति 5.11

desires, he covets); *nirdvandvaḥ:* (adj4◦-subj◦ he who is indifferent to pairs of diametric qualities); *hi* (because); *mahābāho* (O Mahābāho! O Arjuna!); *sukham* (easily); *bandhāt* (from bondage, from attachment); *pramućyate* (he becomes free) (5.3)

(§4) saḥ: yaḥ: na dveṣṭi na kāṅkṣati jñeyaḥ: nityasannyāsī hi mahābāho nirdvandvaḥ: sukham pramućyate bandhāt

(§5) He who does not hate nor he covets (is) ought to be known (as) a 'nityasannyāsī.'[395] Because,[396] O Arjuna! he who is indifferent to pairs of diametric qualities[397] easily becomes free from attachment. (5.3)

5.4 **साङ्ख्ययोगौ पृथग्बालाः प्रवदन्ति न पण्डिताः ।**
एकमप्यास्थितः सम्यगुभयोर्विन्दते फलम् ।।
sāṅkhyayogau pṛthagbālāḥ: pravadanti na paṇḍitāḥ:,
ekamapyāsthitaḥ: samyagubhayorvindate phalam. (5.4)

(§1) साङ्ख्ययोगौ पृथग्बालाः प्रवदन्ति न पण्डिताः । एकम् अपि आस्थितः सम्यक् उभयोः विन्दते फलम् । *sāṅkhyayogau pṛthak* (r◦ 9/1) *bālāḥ:* (r◦ 22/3) *pravadanti na paṇḍitāḥ:* (r◦ 22/8) *ekam* (r◦ 8/16) *api* (r◦ 4/2) *āsthitaḥ:* (r◦ 22/7) *samyak* (r◦ 8/1) *ubhayoḥ:* (r◦ 16/12) *vindate phalam* (r◦ 14/2)

(§2) *sāṅkhyayogau* (m◦ 1nom◦ dual◦ ←dvandva◦ सांख्यः च योगः च । संन्यासः च कर्मयोगः च । संन्यासयोगः च निष्कामकर्मयोगः च । कर्मणः कर्तृत्वस्य संन्यासस्य योगः कर्मणः च फलस्य कामनायाः त्यागस्य योगः । ←m◦ *sāṅkhya* 2.39 + m◦ *yoga* 2.39); *pṛthak* (1.18); *bālāḥ:* (m◦ 1nom◦ plu◦ ←adj◦ *bāla* (amateur) ←1◦√बल्); *pravadanti* (2.42); *na* (1.30); *paṇḍitāḥ:* (2.11); *ekam* (adv◦ 3.2); *api* (1.26); 🕮***āsthitaḥ:*** (m◦ 1nom◦ plu◦ ←adj◦ *āsthita* 3.20); 🕮***samyak*** (adv◦ ind◦ ←adj◦ *samyać* or *samyañć* (proper) ←1◦सम्√अञ्च्); *ubhayoḥ:* (1.21); 🕮*vindate*

---

[395] Elsewhere◦ *nityasannyāsī* → eternal remouncer, constant renouncer, man of constant renunciation, constant Sanyasin ...etc.

🕮 नित्यसंन्यासी being the 'title' or 'label' attached to such a *yogi*, it may well be used as such (like 'योगी'), instead of approximate English translation.

[396] See footnote in verse 3.5

[397] Elsewhere◦ *nirdvandvaḥ:* → free from pairs of opposites, without the pairs of opposites, free from duality.

🕮 One is never truly 'free' from opposites such as loss and gain, life and death, heat and cold, because they do occur to him and he does experience them, for they are inevitable. But, what he can do is to be 'indifferent' to them.

Also, a duality not necessarily have to be opposite, e.g. in द्वैतवादः 'brahma and creation' is a duality (द्वैतम्), but not an opposite or a diametric pair (द्वंद्व). See footnote in 4.22↑

(3rd-per◦ sing◦ pres◦ वर्तमान्-लट् ātmane◦ ←6◦√विद् 4.38); *phalam̦* (2.51) (5.4)

(§3) *sān̐khyayogau* (subj1◦ *sān̐khya-yoga* and *karma-yoga*, the renunciation of 'authorship' of karma and the renunciation of 'desire' in the fruit of karma); *pr̥thak̦* (separate, distinct, different); *bālāḥ:* (subj2◦ those who are childish); *pravadanti* (they say); *na* (but, but not); *paṇḍitāḥ:* (subj3◦ the ones who are learned, wise); *ekam̦* (in one); *api* (even); *āsthitaḥ:* (adj◦-subj4◦ he who is established); *samyak̦* (properly, duly); *ubhayoḥ:* (of both); *vindate* (he attains); *phalam̦* (obj◦ fruit) (5.4)

(§4) bālāḥ: pravadanti sān̐khyayogau pr̥thak̦ na paṇḍitāḥ: āsthitaḥ: samyak̦ api ekam̦ vindate phalam̦ ubhayoḥ:

(§5) Those who are childish they say *sān̐khya-yoga* (the renunciation of 'authorship' of karma) and *karma-yoga* (the renunciation of 'desire' in the fruit of karma) are different, but not the ones who are learned. He who is properly established even in one, he attains fruit of both. (5.4)

5.5 **यत्साङ्ख्यैः प्राप्यते स्थानं तद्योगैरपि गम्यते ।**
एकं साङ्ख्यं च योगं च यः पश्यति स पश्यति ।।
yatsān̐khyaiḥ: prāpyate sthānam̐ tadyogairapi gamyate,
ekam̐ san̐khyam̐ ća yogam̐ ća yaḥ: paśyati sa paśyati. (5.5)

(§1) यत् साङ्ख्यैः प्राप्यते स्थानम् तत् योगैः अपि गम्यते । एकम् साङ्ख्यम् च योगम् च यः पश्यति सः पश्यति । *yaț* (r◦ 10/7) *sān̐khyaiḥ:* (r◦ 22/3) *prāpyate sthānam̦* (r◦ 14/1) *taț* (r◦ 9/9) *yogaiḥ:* (r◦ 16/4) *api gamyate* (r◦ 23/1) *ekam̦* (r◦ 14/1) *san̐khyam̦* (r◦ 14/1) *ća yogam̦* (r◦ 14/1) *ća yaḥ:* (r◦ 22/3) *paśyati saḥ:* (r◦ 21/2) *paśyati*

(§2) *yaț* (2.67); *sān̐khyaiḥ:* (= sān̐khyāćāribiḥ:, m◦ 3inst◦ plu◦ ←adj◦ *sān̐khya* 2.39); 🕮*prāpyate* (3rd-per◦ sing◦ pres◦ वर्तमान्-लट् ātmane◦ ←5◦प्र√आप्); ***sthānam̦*** (1nom◦ sing◦ ←n◦ ***sthāna*** (place) ←1◦√स्था); *taț* (1.10); *yogaiḥ:* (= yogāćāribiḥ:, 3inst◦ plu◦ ←m◦ *yoga* 2.39); *api* (1.26); *gamyate* (3rd-per◦ sing◦ pres◦ वर्तमान्-लट् ātmane◦ ←1◦√गम्); *ekam̦* (adv◦ 3.2); *san̐khyam̦* (m◦ 2acc◦ sing◦ ←adj◦ *sān̐khya* 2.39); *ća* (1.1); *yogam̦* (2.53); *ća* (1.1); *yaḥ:* (2.19); *paśyati* (2.29); *saḥ:* (1.13); 🕮*paśyati* (2.29) (5.5)

(§3) *yaț* (adj◦-obj◦ that which); *sān̐khyaiḥ:* (subj1◦ by the sān̐khyāyogīs, by the yogīs who do not take the 'authorship' for karma, the yogīs who believe that they 'do' not do the karmas, but the karmas are 'done' by them);[398] *prāpyate* (it is attained); *sthānam̦* (obj1◦ place, state); *taț* (adj2◦-obj1◦ that, that place); *yogaiḥ:* (subj2◦ by karmayogīs); *api* (also); *gamyate* (it is attained); *ekam̦* (adj◦-obj2,3◦ one, as

---

[398] Elsewhere◦ *sān̐khyaiḥ:* → by men of knowledge, by men of renunciation, by means of analytical study ...etc.

🕮 In Gita, *sān̐khyāyogīs* = the yogīs who believe that they do not 'do' the karmas, but the karmas are 'done' by them as said in 4.21 and in 5.8-9 and 5.11. Please the footnote in 5.3

one); *saṅkhyaṃ* (obj2◦ sāṅkhyayoga); *ća* (and); *yogaṃ* (obj3◦ karmayoga); *ća* (and); *yaḥ:* (adj1◦-subj3◦ he who); *paśyati* (he sees, perceives); *saḥ:* (subj3◦ he); *paśyati* (he sees, perceives) (5.5)

(§4) sthānaṃ yaṭ prāpyate sāṅkhyaiḥ: taṭ yogaiḥ: gamyate api , ća yaḥ: paśyati saṅkhyaṃ ća yogaṃ ekaṃ, saḥ: paśyati

(§5) That place which is attained by the *sāṅkhyāyogīs,* that place is attained by *karmayogīs* [399] also. And, he who perceives *sāṅkhyayoga* and *karmayoga* as one, he perceives. (5.5)

5.6 संन्यासस्तु महाबाहो दुःखमाप्तुमयोगतः ।
योगयुक्तो मुनिर्ब्रह्म नचिरेणाधिगच्छति ।।

sannyāsastu mahābāho duḥ:khamāptumayogataḥ:,
yogayukto munirbrahma naćireṇādhigaććhati. (5.6)

(§1) संन्यासः तु महाबाहो दुःखम् आप्तुम् अयोगतः । योगयुक्तः मुनिः ब्रह्म नचिरेण अधिगच्छति । *sannyāsaḥ:* (r◦ 18/1) *tu mahābāho duḥ:khaṃ* (r◦ 8/17) *āptuṃ* (r◦ 8/16) *ayogataḥ:* (r◦ 22/8) *yogayuktaḥ:* (r◦ 15/9) *muniḥ:* (r◦ 16/6) *brahma naćireṇa* (r◦ 24/1, 1/1) *adhigaććhati*

(§2) *sannyāsaḥ:* (5.2); *tu* (1.2); *mahābāho* (2.26); 🕮***duḥ:khaṃ*** (adv◦ or 1nom◦ sing◦ ←n◦ *duḥ:kha* (difficulty) 2.14); 🕮***āptuṃ*** (inf◦ ind◦ ←5◦√आप्); *ayogataḥ:* (m◦ 5abl◦ sing◦ ←n.tatpu◦ śatṛ◦ adj◦ *ayogaṭ* ←4◦अ√युज्); 🕮*yogayuktaḥ:* (m◦ 1nom◦ sing◦ ←tatpu◦ *yoga-yukta,* योगेन युक्तः ←m◦ *yoga* 2.39 + adj◦ *yukta* 1.14); *muniḥ:* (2.56); *brahma* (2acc◦ 3.15); 🕮*naćireṇa* (adv◦ ind◦ ←n.tatpu◦ ***naćira*** (quickly) न चिरः ←adj◦ *ćira* (long time) 4.39); *adhigaććhati* (2.64) (5.6)

(§3) *sannyāsaḥ:* (subj1◦ sannyāsa, sannyasayoga, sāṅkhyayoga); *tu* (however); *mahābāho* (O Mahābāho! O Arjuna!); *duḥ:khaṃ* (adj◦-subj1◦ painful, difficult); *āptuṃ* (for attaining, to attain); *ayogataḥ:* (without karmayoga); *yogayuktaḥ:* (adj◦-subj2◦ he who is equipped with karmayoga); *muniḥ:* (subj2◦ the muni, the yogī); *brahma* (obj◦ brahma); *naćireṇa* (quickly, in a short time); *adhigaććhati* (he attains) (5.6)

(§4) tu mahābāho sannyāsaḥ: duḥ:khaṃ āptuṃ ayogataḥ: muniḥ: yogayuktaḥ: adhigaććhati brahma naćireṇa

(§5) However, O Arjuna! *sāṅkhyayoga* (is) difficult to attain without *karmayoga.* The *muni* who is equipped with karmayoga, attains *brahma* in a short time. (5.6)

5.7 योगयुक्तो विशुद्धात्मा विजितात्मा जितेन्द्रियः ।
सर्वभूतात्मभूतात्मा कुर्वन्नपि न लिप्यते ।।

---

[399] Elsewhere◦ *yogaiḥ:* → by men of action, by the devotional service, by action yogis ...etc.

yogayukto viśuddhātmā vijitātmā jitendriyaḥ:,
sarvabhūtātmabhūtātmā kurvannapi na lipyate. (5.7)

(§1) योगयुक्तः विशुद्धात्मा विजितात्मा जितेन्द्रियः । सर्वभूतात्मभूतात्मा कुर्वन् अपि न लिप्यते । *yogayuktaḥ:* (r◦ 15/13) *viśuddhātmā vijitātmā jitendriyaḥ:* (r◦ 22/8) *sarvabhūtātmabhūtātmā kurvan* (r◦ 13/1) *api na lipyate*

(§2) *yogayuktaḥ:* (5.6); 🕮*viśuddhātmā* (m◦ 1nom◦ sing◦ ←bahuvrī◦ *viśuddhātman*, विशुद्धः आत्मा यस्य ←ppp◦ adj◦ ***viśuddha*** (cleansed) ←4◦वि√शुध् + m◦ *ātman* 2.41); *vijitātmā* (m◦ 1nom◦ sing◦ ←bahuvrī◦ *vijitātman*, विजितः आत्मा यस्य ←ppp◦ adj◦ ***vijita*** (won) ←1◦वि√जि + m◦ *ātman* 2.41); 🕮*jitendriyaḥ:* (m◦ 1nom◦ sing◦ ←bahuvrī◦ *jitendriya*, जितानि इन्द्रियाणि येन ←ppp◦ adj◦ ***jita*** (won) ←1◦√जि + n◦ *indriya* 2.8); 🕮*sarvabhūtātmabhūtātmā* (m◦ 1nom◦ sing◦ ←bahuvrī◦ *sarva-bhūtātma-bhūtātman*, सर्वेषाम् भूतानाम् आत्मभूतः आत्मा यस्य ←pron◦ *sarva* 1.6 + n◦ *bhūta* 2.28 + ppp◦ adj◦ *ātmabhūta* ←1◦आत्म√भू + m◦ *ātman* 2.41); *kurvan* (4.21); *api* (1.26); *na* (1.30); 🕮*lipyate* (3rd-per◦ sing◦ pres◦ वर्तमान्-लट् ātmane◦ ←6◦√लिप्) (5.7)

(§3) *yogayuktaḥ:* (adj1◦-subj◦ he who is equipped with *karmayoga*); *viśuddhātmā* (adj2◦-subj◦ he who has cleansed his inner self, he who is chaste); *vijitātmā* (adj3◦-subj◦ he who has conquered his self, he who is self controlled); *jitendriyaḥ:* (adj4◦-subj◦ he who has controlled his sense organs); *sarvabhūtātmabhūtātmā* (adj5◦-subj◦ he who is one with all beings); *kurvan* (adj6◦-subj◦ while doing, while performing karma); *api* (also); *na lipyate* (he does not covet) (5.7)

(§4) yogayuktaḥ: viśuddhātmā vijitātmā jitendriyaḥ: sarvabhūtātmabhūtātmā kurvan api na lipyate

(§5) He who is equipped with *karmayoga,* he who has cleansed his inner self, he who is self controlled, he who has controlled his sense organs, he who is one with all beings,[400] he, while performing *karma* also does not covet. (5.7)

5.8 नैव किञ्चित्करोमीति युक्तो मन्येत तत्त्ववित् ।
पश्यञ्शृण्वन्स्पृशञ्जिघ्रन्नश्नन्गच्छन्स्वपञ्श्वसन् ।।
naiva kiñcitkaromīti yukto manyeta tattvavit,
paśyañśṛṇvanspṛśañjighrannaśnangacchansvapañśvasan; (5.8)

(§1) न एव किञ्चित् करोमि इति युक्तः मन्येत तत्त्ववित् । पश्यन् शृण्वन् स्पृशन् जिघ्रन् अश्नन् गच्छन् स्वपन् श्वसन् । *na* (r◦ 3/1) *eva kiñcit* (r◦ 10/5) *karomi* (r◦ 1/5) *iti yuktaḥ:* (r◦ 15/9) *manyeta tattvavit* (r◦ 23/1) *paśyan* (r◦

[400] Elsewhere◦ *sarvabhūtātmabhūtātmā* → who is dear to everyone and everyone is dear to him, the self of the selves of all beings, whose self becomes the self of all beings ...etc.

11/5) *śṛṇvan* (r◦ 13/20) *spṛśan* (r◦ 11/3) *jighran* (r◦ 13/1) *aśnan* (r◦ 13/10) *gaććhan* (r◦ 13/20) *svapan* (r◦ 11/5) *śvasan;*

(§2) *na* (1.30); *eva* (1.1); *kiñćit* (a bit, 4.20); *karomi* (1st-per◦ sing◦ pres◦ वर्तमान्-लट् parasmai◦ ←8◦√कृ); *iti* (1.25); *yuktaḥ:* (equipped, 2.39); 🕮*manyeta* (3rd-per◦ sing◦ potential◦ विधि◦ parasmai◦ ←4◦√मन्); *tattvavit* (3.28); ***paśyan*** (1nom◦ sing◦ ←adj◦ *paśyat* 2.69); *śṛṇvan* (1nom◦ sing◦ ←śatṛ◦ adj◦ ***śṛṇvat*** ←9◦√शृ); *spṛśan* (1nom◦ sing◦ ←śatṛ◦ adj◦ *spṛśat* ←6◦√स्पृश्); *jighran* (1nom◦ sing◦ ←śatṛ◦ adj◦ *jighrat* ←1◦√घ्रा); *aśnan* (1nom◦ sing◦ ←śatṛ◦ adj◦ ***aśnat*** ←5◦√अश्); *gaććhan* (1nom◦ sing◦ ←śatṛ◦ adj◦ *gaććhat* ←1◦√गम्); *svapan* (1nom◦ sing◦ ←śatṛ◦ adj◦ *svapat* ←2◦√स्वप्); *śvasan* (1nom◦ sing◦ ←śatṛ◦ adj◦ *śvasat* ←2◦√श्वस्); (5.8)

(§3) *na* (do not); *eva* (even); *kiñćit* (a little); *karomi* (I do); *iti* (so); *yuktaḥ:* (subj◦ he who is equipped with sāṅkhyayoga); *manyeta* (he may think); *tattvavit* (adj1◦-subj◦ the truth knower); *paśyan* (adj2◦-subj◦ while seeing); *śṛṇvan* (adj3◦-subj◦ while listening); *spṛśan* (adj4◦-subj◦ while touching); *jighran* (adj5◦-subj◦ while smelling); *aśnan* (adj6◦-subj◦ while eating); *gaććhan* (adj7◦-subj◦ while walking); *svapan* (adj8◦-subj◦ while sleeping); *śvasan* (adj9◦-subj◦ while breathing); (5.8)

(§4) karomi na eva kiñćit iti tattvavit yuktaḥ: manyet paśyan śṛṇvan spṛśan jighran aśnan gaććhan svapan śvasan;

(§5) I do not do even a little (I am not the author of the karma), so the truth knower, who is equipped with sāṅkhyayoga (the yoga of renouncing authorship of karma) may think while seeing, while listening, while touching, while smelling, while eating, while walking, while sleeping, while breathing; (5.8)

5.9 -प्रलपन्विसृजन्गृह्णन्नुन्मिषन्निमिषन्नपि ।
इन्द्रियाणीन्द्रियार्थेषु वर्तन्त इति धारयन् ।।
-pralapanvisṛjangṛhṇannunmiṣannimiṣannapi,
indriyāṇīndriyārtheṣu vartanta iti dhārayan. (5.9)

(§1) प्रलपन् विसृजन् गृह्णन् उन्मिषन् निमिषन् अपि । इन्द्रियाणि इन्द्रियार्थेषु वर्तन्ते इति धारयन् । *pralapan* (r◦ 13/19) *visṛjan* (r◦ 13/10) *gṛhṇan* (r◦ 13/4) *unmiṣan* (r◦ 13/3) *nimiṣan* (r◦ 13/1) *api* (r◦ 23/1) *indriyāṇi* (r◦ 24/7, 1/5) *indriyārtheṣu* (r◦ 25/5) *vartante* (r◦ 5/2) *iti dhārayan*

(§2) *pralapan* (1nom◦ sing◦ ←śatṛ◦ adj◦ *pralapat* ←1◦प्र√लप्); *visṛjan* (1nom◦ sing◦ ←śatṛ◦ adj◦ *visṛjat* ←6◦√सृज्); *gṛhṇan* (1nom◦ sing◦ ←śatṛ◦ adj◦ *gṛhṇat* ←9◦√ग्रह्); *unmiṣan* (1nom◦ sing◦ ←śatṛ◦ adj◦ *unmiṣat* ←6◦उद्√मिष्); *nimiṣan* (1nom◦ sing◦ ←śatṛ◦ adj◦ *nimiṣat* ←6◦नि√मिष्); *api* (1.26); *indriyāṇi* (inom◦ 2.60);

indriyārtheṣu (n◦ 7loc◦ plu◦ ←tatpu◦ *indriyārtha* 2.58); *vartante* (3.28); *iti* (1.25); ***dhārayan̦*** (1nom◦ sing◦ ←śatṛ◦ adj◦ *dhārayaț* ←1◦√धृ) (5.9)

(§3) *pralapan̦* (adj10◦-subj1◦ while talking); *visṛjan̦* (adj11◦-subj1◦ while excreting); *gṛhṇan̦* (adj12◦-subj1◦ while taking); *unmiṣan̦* (adj13◦-subj1◦ while opening the eyes); *nimiṣan̦* (adj14◦-subj1◦ while closing the eyes); *api* (and also); *indriyāṇi* (subj2◦ the organs); *indriyārtheṣu* (in their senses objects); *vartante* (they function); *iti* (so, that); *dhārayan̦* (adj15◦-subj1◦ while thinking, believing) (5.9)

(§4) pralapan̦ visṛjan̦ gṛhṇan̦ unmiṣan̦ api nimiṣan̦ dhārayan̦ iti indriyāṇi vartante indriyārtheṣu

(§5) ...while talking, while excreting, while taking, while opening the eyes and also while closing the eyes, believing that the organs function in their senses objects. (5.9)

5.10 **ब्रह्मण्याधाय कर्माणि सङ्गं त्यक्त्वा करोति यः ।**
लिप्यते न स पापेन पद्मपत्रमिवाम्भसा ।। (5.10)
brahmaṇyādhāya karmāṇi saṅgaṁ tyaktvā karoti yaḥ:,
lipyate na sa pāpena padmapatramivāmbhasā.

(§1) ब्रह्मणि आधाय कर्माणि सङ्गम् त्यक्त्वा करोति यः । लिप्यते न सः पापेन पद्मपत्रम् इव अम्भसा । *brahmaṇi* (r◦ 24/7, 4/2) *ādhāya karmāṇi* (r◦ 24/7) *saṅgam̦* (r◦ 14/1) *tyaktvā karoti yaḥ:* (r◦ 22/8) *lipyate na saḥ:* (r◦ 21/2) *pāpena padmapatram̦* (r◦ 8/18) *iva* (r◦ 1/1) *ambhasā*

(§2) *brahmaṇi* (7loc◦ sing◦ ←n◦ *brahman̦* 2.72); *ādhāya* (lyp◦ past-participle ind◦ ←3◦आ√धा); *karmāṇi* (2acc◦ 2.48); *saṅgam̦* (2.48); *tyaktvā* (1.33); *karoti* (4.20); *yaḥ:* (2.19); *lipyate* (5.7); *na* (1.30); *saḥ:* (1.13); *pāpena* (3inst◦ sing◦ ←n◦ *pāpa* (sin) 1.36); *padmapatram̦* (n◦ 1nom◦ sing◦ ←tatpu◦ *padma-patra*, पद्मस्य पत्रम् ←n◦ *padma* ←4◦√पद् + n◦ *patra* ←1◦√पत्); *iva* (1.30); *ambhasā* (3inst◦ sing◦ ←n◦ *ambhaș* (water) 2.67) (5.10)

(§3) *brahmaṇi* (in brahma); *ādhāya* (dedicating); *karmāṇi* (obj1◦ the karmas); *saṅgam̦* (obj2◦ attachment); *tyaktvā* (having renounced); *karoti* (he does, he does karma); *yaḥ:* (subj1◦ he who); *lipyate* (he gets besmeared); *na* (does not); *saḥ:* (obj3◦ he); *pāpena* (subj2◦ with sin); *padmapatram̦* (obj4◦ the leaf of lotus); *iva* (just as); *ambhasā* (subj3◦ with water) (5.10)

(§4) ādhāya karmāṇi brahmaṇi tyaktvā saṅgam̦ yaḥ: karoti saḥ: na lipyate pāpena iva padmapatram̦ ambhasā

(§5) Dedicating the *karmas* in *brahma* (and) having renounced attachment, he who does *karma,* he does not get besmeared with sin, just as the leaf of lotus with water. (5.10)

5.11 कायेन मनसा बुद्ध्या केवलैरिन्द्रियैरपि ।
योगिनः कर्म कुर्वन्ति सङ्गं त्यक्त्वात्मशुद्धये ।।

kāyena manasā buddhyā kevalairindriyairapi,
yoginaḥ: karma kurvanti saṅgaṁ tyaktvātmaśuddhaye. (5.11)

(§1) कायेन मनसा बुद्ध्या केवलैः इन्द्रियैः अपि । योगिनः कर्म कुर्वन्ति सङ्गं त्यक्त्वात्मशुद्धये । *kāyena manasā buddhyā kevalaiḥ:* (r∘ 16/4) *indriyaiḥ:* (r∘ 16/4) *api yoginaḥ:* (r∘ 22/1) *karma kurvanti saṅgaṃ* (r∘ 14/1) *tyaktvā* (r∘ 1/4) *ātmaśuddhaye*

(§2) 🕮*kāyena* (3inst∘ sing∘ ←m∘ ***kāya*** (body) ←5∘√चि); *manasā* (3.6); *buddhyā* (2.39); 🕮*kevalaiḥ:* (m∘ 3inst∘ plu∘ ←adj∘ *kevala* 4.21); *indriyaiḥ:* (2.64); *api* (1.26); *yoginaḥ:* (4.25); *karma* (2acc∘ 3.8); *kurvanti* (3.25); *saṅgaṃ* (2.48); *tyaktvā* (1.33); 🕮*ātmaśuddhaye* (f∘ 4dat∘ sing∘ ←tatpu∘ *ātma-śuddhi,* आत्मनः शुद्धिः ←n∘ *ātman* 2.41 + f∘ ***śuddhi*** (purification) ←4∘√शुध्)

(§3) *kāyena* (with body); *manasā* (with mind); *buddhyā* (with intellect); *kevalaiḥ:* (only with); *indriyaiḥ:* (with organs); *api* (and); *yoginaḥ:* (subj∘ the yogīs); *karma* (obj1∘ karma); *kurvanti* (they perform); *saṅgaṃ* (obj2∘ attachment); *tyaktvā* (having renounced, having kept aside); *ātmaśuddhaye* (for internal purification, for self purification) (5.11)

(§4) saṅgaṃ tyaktvā yoginaḥ: kurvanti karma kevalaiḥ: kāyena manasā buddhyā api indriyaiḥ: ātmaśuddhaye

(§5) Attachment having kept aside, the yogīs perform *karma* only with body, mind, intellect and organs, for self purification. (5.11)

5.12 युक्तः कर्मफलं त्यक्त्वा शान्तिमाप्नोति नैष्ठिकीम् ।
अयुक्तः कामकारेण फले सक्तो निबद्ध्यते ।।

yuktaḥ: karmaphalaṁ tyaktvā śāntimāpnoti naiṣṭhikiṃ,
ayuktaḥ: kāmakāreṇa phale sakto nibadhyate. (5.12)

(§1) युक्तः कर्मफलम् त्यक्त्वा शान्तिम् आप्नोति नैष्ठिकीम् । अयुक्तः कामकारेण फले सक्तः निबद्ध्यते । *yuktaḥ:* (r∘ 22/1) *karmaphalaṃ* (r∘ 14/1) *tyaktvā śāntiṃ* (r∘ 8/17) *āpnoti naiṣṭhikiṃ* (r∘ 14/2) *ayuktaḥ:* (r∘ 22/1) *kāmakāreṇa* (r∘ 24/1) *phale saktaḥ:* (r∘ 15/6) *nibaddhyate*

(§2) *yuktaḥ:* (2.39); ***karmaphalaṃ*** (n∘ 2acc∘ sing∘ ←tatpu∘ *karma-phala* 4.14); *tyaktvā* (1.33); *śāntiṃ* (2.70); *āpnoti* (2.70); 🕮*naiṣṭhikiṃ* (f∘ 2acc∘ sing∘ ←taddhita∘ adj∘ *naiṣṭhika* (supreme) ←f∘ *niṣṭhā* (faith) 3.3); 🕮***ayuktaḥ:*** (m∘ 1nom∘ sing∘ ←adj∘ *ayukta* (unequipped) 2.66); *kāmakāreṇa* (3inst∘ sing∘ ←tatpu∘ *kāma-kāra,* कामस्य कारः । कामस्य कारकः । कामस्य कारणम् । कामस्य कामना । ←m∘ *kāma* 1.22 + adj∘ *kāra* 2.2); *phale* (7loc∘ sing∘ ←n∘ *phala* 2.43); *saktaḥ:* (1nom∘ sing∘ ←adj∘ *sakta* 3.25); *nibaddhyate* (4.22)

(5.12)

(§3) *yuktaḥ:* (subj◦ he who is equipped with yoga, he who is equipped with niṣkāma-karma-yoga); *karmaphalam̧* (obj1◦ desire in the fruit of karma); *tyaktvā* (having renounced); *ṡāntim̧* (obj2◦ peace); *āpnoti* (he attains); *naiṣṭhikim̧* (adj◦-obj2◦ everlasting, supreme); *ayuktaḥ:* (subj2◦ he who is not equipped with niṣkāma-karma-yoga); *kāmakāreṇa* (with desire); *phale* (in fruit); *saktaḥ:* (adj◦-subj2◦ he who is attached; he who is attached to the desire in the fruit); *nibaddhyate* (he gets fettered)

(5.12)

(§4) yuktaḥ: tyaktvā karmaphalam̧ āpnoti naiṣṭhikim̧ ṡāntim̧ ayuktaḥ: saktaḥ: kāmakāreṇa phale nibaddhyate

(§5) He who is equipped with *niṣkāma-karma-yoga,*[401] he, having renounced[402] desire in the fruit of *karma,*[403] attains everlasting[404] peace. He who is not equipped with *niṣkāma-karma-yoga,*[405] he who is attached to the desire in the fruit, he gets fettered. (5.12)

5.13 सर्वकर्माणि मनसा संन्यस्यास्ते सुखं वशी ।
नवद्वारे पुरे देही नैव कुर्वन्न कारयन् ।।
sarvakarmāṇi manasā sannyasyāste sukham̊ vaṡī,
navadvāre pure dehī naiva kurvanna kārayaņ. (5.13)

(§1) सर्वकर्माणि मनसा संन्यस्य आस्ते सुखम् वशी । नवद्वारे पुरे देही न एव कुर्वन् न कारयन् । *sarvakarmāṇi* (r◦ 24/7) *manasā sannyasya* (r◦ 1/2) *āste sukham̧* (r◦ 14/1) *vaṡī navadvāre pure dehī na* (r◦ 3/1) *eva kurvaņ* (r◦ 1/11) *na kārayaņ*

(§2) *sarvakarmāṇi* (3.26); *manasā* (3.6); *sannyasya* (3.36); *āste* (3.6); *sukham̧* (4.40); 📖*vaṡī* (m◦ 1nom◦ sing◦ ←adj◦ *vaṡiņ* (self-controlled) ←2◦√वश्); *navadvāre* (n◦ 7loc◦ sing◦ ←dvigu◦ *nava-dvāra*, नवानाम् द्वाराणाम् समाहारा: ←adj◦ *navaņ* (nine) ←2◦√नु + n◦ *dvāra* (gate) 2.32); *pure* (7loc◦ sing◦ ←n◦ *pura* ←5◦√पॄ); 📖*dehī* (2.22); *na* (1.30); *eva* (1.1); *kurvaņ* (4.21); *na* (1.30); *kārayaņ* (1nom◦ sing◦ ←ṡatṛ◦ adj◦

---

[401] Elsewhere◦ *yuktaḥ* → the desireless person, well-poised, the steadily devoted soul, the harmonised one, harmonised man, the steady minded one, the soul earnest ...etc.

[402] Elsewhere◦ *tyaktvā* → gives up, offers, offering to God, abandoning, because he offers, ...etc.

[403] Elsewhere◦ *karmaphalam̧* → the fruit of action, fruits of action, fruit of actions, result of all activities, idea of the fruit of action, the fruits of works ...etc.

[404] Elsewhere◦ *naiṣṭhikim̧* → born of discipline, born of steadfastness, unaduletrated, well-founded ...etc.

[405] Elsewhere◦ *ayuktaḥ* → unbalanced one, non-harmonised one, one who works with selfish motive, one who is not in union with the Divine, he whose soul is not in union with the Divine, non-yogi, ...etc.

caus∘*kārayaṭ* ←8∘√कृ) (5.13)

(§3) *sarvakarmāṇi* (obj∘ all karmas); *manasā* (with mind); *sannyasya* (having renounced); *āste* (he stays); *sukham* (happily); *vaśī* (adj1∘-subj∘ he who has controlled himself, the self controlled); *navadvāre* (in the - with nine gates); *pure* (in the city); *dehī* (subj∘ the embodied person); *na* (neither); *eva* (even); *kurvan* (adj2∘-subj∘ doing karma); *na* (nor); *kārayan* (adj3∘-subj∘ causing to be done, perfprmed) (5.13)

(§4) dehī vaśī sannyasya sarvakarmāṇi manasā āste sukham pure navadvāre na eva kurvan na kārayan

(§5) **The embodied person,**[406] **he who has controlled himself,**[407] **having renounced all *karmas* with mind, he stays happily in the city, with nine gates,**[408] **neither even performing *karma* nor causing to be performed.** (5.13)

5.14 न कर्तृत्वं न कर्माणि लोकस्य सृजति प्रभुः ।
     न कर्मफलसंयोगं स्वभावस्तु प्रवर्तते ॥

     na kartṛtvam na karmāṇi lokasya sṛjati prabhuḥ:,
     na karmaphalasam̐yogam svabhāvastu pravartate. (5.14)

(§1) न कर्तृत्वम् न कर्माणि लोकस्य सृजति प्रभु: । न कर्मफलसंयोगम् स्वभावस्तु प्रवर्तते । *na kartṛtvam* (r∘ 14/1) *na karmāṇi* (r∘ 24/7) *lokasya sṛjati prabhuḥ*: (r∘ 22/8) *na karmaphalasam̐yogam* (r∘ 14/1) *svabhāvaḥ*: (r∘ 18/1) *tu pravartate*

(§2) *na* (1.30); 📖*kartṛtvam* (2acc∘ sing∘ ←n∘ *kartṛtva* ←8∘√कृ); *na* (1.30); *karmāṇi* (2acc∘ 2.48); *lokasya* (6pos sing∘ ←m∘ *loka* (people) 2.5); *sṛjati* (3rd-per∘ sing∘ pres∘ वर्तमान्-लट् parasmai∘ ←6∘√सृज्); *prabhuḥ*: (1nom∘ sing∘ ←m∘ **prabhu** (lord) ←1∘प्र√भू); *na* (1.30); *karmaphalasam̐yogam* (m∘ 2acc∘ sing∘ ←tatpu∘ *karma-phala-sam̐yoga*, कर्मण: च फलस्य च संयोग: ←n∘ *karman* 1.15 + n∘ *phala* 2.43 + m∘ *sam̐yoga* (association) ←4∘सम्√युज्); 📖*svabhāvaḥ*: (1nom∘ sing∘ ←m∘ *svabhāva* (nature) 2.7); *tu* (1.2); *pravartate* (3rd-per∘ sing∘ pres∘ वर्तमान्-लट् ātmane∘ ←1∘प्र√वृत् 3.28) (5.14)

---

[406] Elsewhere∘ *dehī* → the embodied soul, the atman, the self, the indweler ...etc.

📖 Remember, here in this verse, the *dehī* has qualifications attached, such as सर्वकर्माणि-मनसा-संन्यस्य, etc. which are inapplicable to ātmā, and are applicable only to an embodied person.

[407] Elsewhere∘ *vaśī* → sovereign dweller, the ruler, having mastry, lord ...etc.

[408] अस्थिपूर्णं नवद्वारं रक्तमांसावलेपनम् (yogavāsiṣṭha 27.12) The dwelling, that this body is, has bones for its pillars, blood and flessh for its mortar and nine entrances for its doors and windoews.

(§3) *na* (does not); *kartṛtvaṃ* (obj1◦ the authorship, the doership); *na* (nor); *karmāṇi* (obj2◦ the karmas); *lokasya* (of one, of a person, of anyone); *sṛjati* (he brings forth); *prabhuḥ:* (subj1◦ the Lord); *na* (nor); *karmaphalasaṁyogaṃ* (obj3◦ the association of *karma* with its fruit); *svabhāvaḥ:* (subj2◦ one's own nature); *tu* (however); *pravartate* (it reflects) (5.14)

(§4) prabhuḥ: na sṛjati kartṛtvaṃ na karmāṇi lokasya na karmaphalasaṁyogaṃ tu svabhāvaḥ: pravartate

(§5) The Lord does not bring forth the authorship (of *karmas*), nor the *karmas* nor the association of the fruit of *karma* of anyone, however, one's own nature reflects (them). (5.14)

5.15 नादत्ते कस्यचित्पापं न चैव सुकृतं विभुः ।
अज्ञानेनावृतं ज्ञानं तेन मुह्यन्ति जन्तवः ॥
nādatte kasyaćitpāpaṁ na ćaiva sukṛtaṁ vibhuḥ:,
ajñānenāvṛtaṁ jñānaṁ tena muhyanti jantavaḥ:. (5.15)

(§1) नादत्ते कस्यचित् पापम् न च एव सुकृतम् विभुः । अज्ञानेन आवृतम् ज्ञानम् तेन मुह्यन्ति जन्तवः । *na* (r◦ 1/2) *ādatte kasyaćiṭ* (r◦ 10/6) *pāpaṃ* (r◦ 14/1) *na ća* (r◦ 3/1) *eva sukṛtaṃ* (r◦ 14/1) *vibhuḥ:* (r◦ 22/8) *ajñānena* (r◦ 1/2) *āvṛtaṃ* (r◦ 14/1) *jñānaṃ* (r◦ 14/1) *tena muhyanti jantavaḥ:* (r◦ 22/8)

(§2) *na* (1.30); *ādatte* (3rd-per◦ sing◦ pres◦ वर्तमान्-लट् ātmane◦ ←3◦आ√दा); *kasyaćiṭ* (6pos sing◦ ←m◦ or n◦ pron◦ *kaśćiṭ* 2.17); *pāpaṃ* (1.36); *na* (1.30); *ća* (1.1); *eva* (1.1); 🕮*sukṛtaṃ* (2acc◦ sing◦ ←n◦ *sukṛta* (good deed) 2.50); 🕮*vibhuḥ:* (1nom◦ sing◦ ←m◦ ***vibhu*** (lord) ←1◦वि√भू); 🕮*ajñānena* (n◦ 3inst◦ sing◦ ←n.tatpu◦ *a-jñāna* (ignorance) 4.42); *āvṛtaṃ* (3.38); *jñānaṃ* (3.39); *tena* (3.38); 🕮*muhyanti* (3rd-per◦ plu◦ pres◦ वर्तमान्-लट् parasmai◦ ←4◦√मुह् 2.13); 🕮*jantavaḥ:* (1nom◦ plu◦ ←m◦ *jantu* (being) ←4◦√जन्)
(5.15)

(§3) *na* (does not); *ādatte* (he incurs, he receives); *kasyaćiṭ* (of anyone); *pāpaṃ* (obj1◦ sin, the punishment for bad deeds); *na* (not); *ća* (and); *eva* (even); *sukṛtaṃ* (obj2◦ *puṇyam,* the reward for good deeds); *vibhuḥ:* (subj1◦ the Lord); *ajñānena* (by ignorance); *āvṛtaṃ* (adj◦-subj2◦ the one that is covered); *jñānaṃ* (subj2◦ the wisdom, knowledge); *tena* (by that); *muhyanti* (they are deluded); *jantavaḥ:* (obj3◦ the beings) (5.15)

(§4) vibhuḥ: na ādatte pāpaṃ kasyaćiṭ ća na eva sukṛtaṃ jñānaṃ āvṛtaṃ ajñānena tena jantavaḥ: muhyanti

(§5) The Lord does not incur sin of anyone, and not even the reward for good deeds. The wisdom, that is covered by ignorance, with that the beings are deluded.[409] (In other words : The beings are

---

[409] Elsewhere◦ tena jantavaḥ: muhyanti → therefore living beings are deluded, hence it is that beings are...,

deluded by the jñana that is covered by the ignorance.)

(5.15)

5.16 ज्ञानेन तु तदज्ञानं येषां नाशितमात्मनः ।

तेषामादित्यवज्ज्ञानं प्रकाशयति तत्परम् ।।

jñānena tu tadjñānaṁ yeṣāṁ nāśitamātmanaḥ:,

teṣāmādityavajjñānaṁ prakāśayati tatparam. (5.16)

(§1) ज्ञानेन तु तत् अज्ञानम् येषाम् नाशितम् आत्मनः । तेषाम् आदित्यवत् ज्ञानम् प्रकाशयति तत्-परम् । *jñānena tu tat* (r◦ 8/2) *ajñānam* (r◦ 14/1) *yeṣām* (r◦ 25/3, 14/1) *nāśitam* (r◦ 8/17) *ātmanaḥ:* (r◦ 22/8) *teṣām* (r◦ 25/3, 8/17) *ādityavat* (r◦ 11/2) *jñānam* (r◦ 14/1) *prakāśayati tat param* (r◦ 14/2)

(§2) *jñānena* (4.38); *tu* (1.2); *tat* (1.10); ***ajñānam*** (1nom◦ sing◦ ←n◦ *ajñāna* (ignorance) 4.42); *yeṣām* (1.33); 🕮*nāśitam* (1nom◦ sing◦ ←ppp◦ adj◦ caus◦*nāśita* (destroyed) ←3◦√नश्); *ātmanaḥ:* (4.42); ***teṣām*** (m◦ 6pos◦ plu◦ ←pron◦ *tad* 1.2); *ādityavat* (ind◦ ←m◦ ***āditya*** (sun) ←3◦न√दा + affix indicating simile *vat* 2.29); *jñānam* (1nom◦ 3.39); 🕮***prakāśayati*** (3rd-per◦ sing◦ pres◦ वर्तमान्-लट् parasmai◦ caus◦ ←1◦प्र√काश्); ***tatparam*** (= pron◦ 2acc◦ *tat* 1.10 + adj◦ 2acc◦ *param* 2.12) (5.16)

(§3) *jñānena* (subj1◦ with the knowledge, wisdom); *tu* (but); *tat* (adj1◦-obj1◦ that); *ajñānam* (obj1◦ ignorance); *yeṣām* (of whom); *nāśitam* (adj2◦-obj1◦ that which is destroyed, that which is removed); *ātmanaḥ:* (of ātmā); *teṣām* (their); *ādityavat* (adj1◦-subj2◦ like the Sun); *jñānam* (subj2◦ wisdom); *prakāśayati* (it causes to perceive, it brings to discernment, it reveals); *tat* (adj2◦-subj◦ that); *param* (obj2◦ the Supreme) (5.16)

(§4) tu yeṣām tat ajñānam nāśitam jñānena ātmanaḥ:, teṣām tat jñānam ādityavat prakāśayati param

(§5) But, of whom that ignorance is destroyed with the knowledge of *ātmā*, their that wisdom like the Sun, reveals[410] the Supreme. (5.16)

---

beings are bewildered because of... ...etc.

🕮 तेन is not an adverb such as : therefore, thus, hence or because. Remember, it is the subject in a Sanskrit passive (कर्मणि) voice. Thus the subject is तेन is in 3rd Instrumental case; जन्तवः are object (in 1st Nominative case); and the verb मुह्यन्ति is plural, following the object. तेन (आवृतेन ज्ञानेन) मुह्यन्ति जन्तवः । In active voice, the subject would be तद् (ज्ञानम् nominative) and the object would be जन्तवान् (accusative). तद् (आवृतम् ज्ञानम्) मुह्यति जन्तवान् । प्रयोगे कर्मवाच्यस्य तृतीया स्यात्तु कर्तरि, कर्मणि प्रथमा चैव, क्रिया कर्मानुसारिणी ।

[410] Elsewhere◦ *ādityavat jñānaṁ prakāśayati tatparam* → lights up the Supreme self like the sun (adv◦), causes the Supreme to shine like the sun (adv◦) ...etc.

5.17 तद्बुद्धयस्तदात्मानस्तन्निष्ठास्तत्परायणाः ।
गच्छन्त्यपुनरावृत्तिं ज्ञाननिर्धूतकल्मषाः ।।
tadbuddhayastadātmānastanniṣṭhāstatparāyaṇāḥ:,
gaććhantyapunarāvṛttiṁ jñānanirdhutakalmaṣāḥ:. (5.17)

(§1) तद्बुद्धयः तदात्मानः तन्निष्ठाः तत्परायणाः । गच्छन्ति अपुनरावृत्तिम् ज्ञाननिर्धूतकल्मषाः । *tadbuddhayaḥ:* (r◦ 18/1) *tadātmānaḥ:* (r◦ 18/1) *tanniṣṭhāḥ:* (r◦ 18/1) *tatparāyaṇāḥ:* (r◦ 24/5, 22/8) *gaććhanti* (r◦ 4/1) *apunarāvṛttim* (r◦ 14/1) *jñānanirdhutakalmaṣāḥ:* (r◦ 22/8)

(§2) *tadbuddhayaḥ:* (m◦ 1nom◦ plu◦ ←bahuvrī◦ *tadbuddhi,* तस्मिन् बुद्धिः यस्य सः ←pron◦ *tad* 1.2 + 1nom◦ sing◦ ←f◦ *buddhi* (thinking) 1.23); *tadātmānaḥ:* (m◦ 1nom◦ plu◦ ←bahuvrī◦ *tadātman,* तस्मिन् आत्मा यस्य ←pron◦ *tat* 1.10 + m◦ *ātman* 2.41); *tanniṣṭhāḥ:* (m◦ 1nom◦ plu◦ ←bahuvrī◦ *tanniṣṭha,* तस्मिन् परायणता यस्य । तस्मिन् निष्ठा यस्य ←pron◦ *tad* 1.2 + f◦ *niṣṭhā* (faith) 3.3); *tatparāyaṇāḥ:* (m◦ 1nom◦ plu◦ ←bahuvrī◦ *tat-parāyaṇa,* तत् परमम् अयनम् यस्य ←adj◦ *tatpara* 4.39 + n◦ *ayana* 1.11); *gaććhanti* (2.51); *apunarāvṛttim* (2acc◦ sing◦ n.tatpu◦ ←f◦ 📖*punarāvṛtti* ←ind◦ *a* 1.10 + ind◦ *punar* (again) 4.9 + f◦ ***āvṛtti*** (birth) ←1◦आ√वृत्); *jñānanirdhutakalmaṣāḥ:* (m◦ 1nom◦ plu◦ ←bahuvrī◦ *jñāna-nirdhuta-kalmaṣa,* ज्ञानेन निर्धूतानि कल्मषाणि यस्य ←n◦ *jñāna* 3.3 + adj◦ 📖*nirdhuta* (cleansed) ←1◦निर्√धू + n◦ *kalmaṣa* (sin) 4.30)
(5.17)

(§3) *tadbuddhayaḥ:* (adj1◦-subj◦ they whose mind is in THAT); *tadātmānaḥ:* (adj2◦-subj◦ they whose soul is in THAT); *tanniṣṭhāḥ:* (adj3◦-subj◦ they whose faith is in THAT); *tatparāyaṇāḥ:* (adj4◦-subj◦ they who are devoted to THAT); *gaććhanti* (they attain); *apunarāvṛttim* (obj◦ non-returning, no rebirth); *jñānanirdhutakalmaṣāḥ:* (adj5◦-subj◦ they whose sins are washed away with wisdom) (5.17)

📖 Is आदित्यवत् an adjective, (आदित्यवत् ज्ञानम्), or is it an adverb (आदित्यवत् प्रकाशयति?). The Supreme is अक्षरं immutable, and thus can not be altered, enhanced or enlightened. The Supreme is already self-illuminated more than thousand suns (Gītā 11.12). The तद्धित suffix वत् when added to a noun, produces an adjective or a derivative noun suggesting possession of the quality contained by that noun. eg. धन + वत् = धनवत्, the possessor of धनम् । The वत् suffix is also added to a substantive to form a *taddhita* word to denote a likeness or resemblence, and then it means - like that noun. आदित्य + वत् = आदित्यवत् like the आदित्य ।

Here प्रकाशयति means : it reveal, makes known, (प्र√काश् to bring to light, bring to knowledge, reveal; as प्रकाशितं पुस्तकम् means the book that is revealed, brought to light, made known, released to public for information; not the book that is illuminated or enlightened). Therefore, आदित्यवत् ज्ञानम् = The knowledge, bright like the Sun; प्रकाशयति तत्परम् = (it) reveals the Supreme to the *yogī.*

(§4) tadbuddhayaḥ: tadātmānaḥ: tanniṣṭhāḥ: tatparāyaṇāḥ: jñāna-nirdhuta -kalmaṣāḥ: gaććhanti a-punarāvṛttim̥

(§5) They whose mind is in THAT, they whose soul is in THAT, they whose faith is in THAT, they who are devoted to THAT, they whose sins are washed away with wisdom, they attain no rebirth. (5.17)

5.18 विद्याविनयसम्पन्ने ब्राह्मणे गवि हस्तिनि ।
शुनि चैव श्वपाके च पण्डिताः समदर्शिनः ।।

vidyāvinayasampanne brāhmaṇe gavi hastini,
śuni ćaiva śvapāke ća paṇḍitaḥ: samadarśinaḥ:. (5.18)

(§1) विद्याविनयसम्पन्ने ब्राह्मणे गवि हस्तिनि । शुनि च एव श्वपाके च पण्डिताः समदर्शिनः । *vidyāvinayasampanne brāhmaṇe* (r◦ 24/9) *gavi hastini śuni ća* (r◦ 3/1) *eva śvapāke ća paṇḍitāḥ:* (r◦ 22/7) *samadarśinaḥ:* (r◦ 22/8)

(§2) *vidyāvinayasampanne* (m◦ 7loc◦ sing◦ ←ppp◦ adj◦ *vidyā-vinaya-sampanna,* विद्यया च विनयेन च सम्पन्नः ←f◦ 🕮***<u>vidyā</u>*** (knowledge) ←2◦√विद् + m◦ 🕮*vinaya* (humility) ←1◦वि√नी + ppp◦ adj◦ 🕮*sampanna* (enriched) ←4◦सम्√पद्); *brāhmaṇe* (7loc◦ sing◦ ←m◦ *brāhmaṇa* 2.46); *gavi* (7loc◦ sing◦ ←f◦ *go* (cow) ←1◦√गम्); *hastini* (7loc◦ sing◦ ←m◦ *hastin̥* (elephant) ←1◦√हस्); *śuni* (7loc◦ sing◦ ←m◦ śvan̥ (dog) ←1◦√श्वि); ća (1.1); *eva* (1.1); *śvapāke* (7loc◦ sing◦ ←m◦ *śvapāka* (pariah) ←1◦√श्वि); ća (1.1); *paṇḍitāḥ:* (2.11); 🕮*samadarśinaḥ:* (m◦ 1nom◦ plu◦ ←adj◦ *sama-darśin̥* (indifferent) ←1◦सम्√दृश्) (5.18)

(§3) *vidyāvinayasampanne* (in him who is endowed with knowledge and humility); *brāhmaṇe* (in a brāhmaṇa, in one who is knower of brahma, in one who is knower of the veda); *gavi* (in a cow); *hastini* (in an elephant); *śuni* (in a dog); *ća* (and); *eva* (also); *śvapāke* (in one who eats dog's meat, in a pariah); *ća* (and); *paṇḍitāḥ:* (subj◦ the wise people); *samadarśinaḥ:* (adj◦-subj◦ equaminous) (5.18)

(§4) paṇḍitāḥ: samadarśinaḥ: vidyāvinayasampanne brāhmaṇe gavi hastini ća śuni ća eva śvapāke

(§5) The wise people (are) equaminous in him who is endowed with knowledge and humility, in one who is knower of the *veda,* in a cow, in an elephant and in a dog and also in a pariah. (5.18)

5.19 इहैव तैर्जितः सर्गो येषां साम्ये स्थितं मनः ।
निर्दोषं हि समं ब्रह्म तस्माद्ब्रह्मणि ते स्थिताः ।।

ihaiva tairjitaḥ: sarga yeṣāṁ sāmye sthitaṁ manaḥ:,
nirdoṣaṁ hi samaṁ brahma tasmādbrahmaṇi te sthitāḥ:. (5.19)

(§1) इह एव तः जितः सर्गः येषाम् साम्ये स्थितम् मनः । निर्दोषम् हि समम् ब्रह्म तस्मात् ब्रह्मणि ते स्थिताः । *iha* (r◦ 3/1) *eva taiḥ:* (r◦ 16/11) *jitaḥ:* (r◦ 22/7) *sargaḥ:* (r◦ 15/10) *yeṣām* (r◦ 25/3, 14/1) *sāmye sthitam* (r◦ 14/1) *manaḥ:* (r◦ 22/8) *nirdoṣam* (r◦ 14/1) *hi samam* (r◦ 14/1) *brahma tasmāt* (r◦ 9/7) *brahmaṇi* (r◦ 24/7) *te sthitāḥ:* (r◦ 22/8)

(§2) *iha* (2.5); *eva* (1.1); *taiḥ:* (3.12); 🕮***jitaḥ:*** (m◦ 1nom◦ sing◦ ←adj◦ *jita* (won) 5.7); *sargaḥ:* (1nom◦ sing◦ ←m◦ ***sarga*** (birth) ←6◦√सृज्); *yeṣām* (1.33); *sāmye* (7loc◦ sing◦ ←n◦ ***sāmya*** (equanimity) ←1◦√सम्); ***sthitam*** (n◦ 1nom◦ sing◦ ←adj◦ *sthita* (established) 1.14); *manaḥ:* (1nom◦ 1.30); 🕮*nirdoṣam* (n◦ 1nom◦ sing◦ ←adj◦ *nirdoṣa* (spotless) ←ind◦ *nir* 2.45 + m◦ *doṣa* 1.38); *hi* (1.11); 🕮***samam*** (n◦ 1nom◦ sing◦ ←adj◦ *sama* (equal) 1.4); *brahma* (4.24); *tasmāt* (1.37); *brahmaṇi* (5.10); *te* (1.33); *sthitāḥ:* (m◦ 1nom◦ plu◦ ←adj◦ *sthita* (established) 1.14) (5.19)

(§3) *iha* (here, in this world); *eva* (even); *taiḥ:* (subj1◦ by them); *jitaḥ:* (adj◦-obj◦ conquered); *sargaḥ:* (obj◦ birth); *yeṣām* (of whom); *sāmye* (in equanimity); *sthitam* (adj◦-subj2◦ established); *manaḥ:* (subj2◦ the mind); *nirdoṣam* (adj1◦-subj3◦ free from defects; perfect); *hi* (because); *samam* (adj2◦-subj3◦ harmonious); *brahma* (subj3◦ brahma); *tasmāt* (therefore); *brahmaṇi* (in brahma); *te* (adj1◦-subj1◦ they); *sthitāḥ:* (adj2◦-subj1◦ established) (5.19)

(§4) sargaḥ: jitaḥ: taiḥ: eva iha yeṣām manaḥ: sthitam sāmye hi brahma nirdoṣam samam tasmāt te sthitāḥ: brahmaṇi

(§5) Birth (is) conquered by them, even in this world, of whom the mind (is) established in equanimity; because,[411] *brahma*[412] (is) perfect[413] (and) harmonious. Therefore,[414] they (are) established in *brahma*. (5.19)

5.20 न प्रहृष्येत्प्रियं प्राप्य नोद्विजेत्प्राप्य चाप्रियम् ।
स्थिरबुद्धिरसम्मूढो ब्रह्मविद्ब्रह्मणि स्थितः ।।
na prahṛṣyetpriyaṁ prāpya nodvijetprāpya ćāpriyam,
sthirabuddhirasammūḍho brahmavidbrahmaṇi sthitaḥ:. (5.20)

(§1) न प्रहृष्येत् प्रियम् प्राप्य न उद्विजेत् प्राप्य च अप्रियम् । स्थिरबुद्धिः असम्मूढः ब्रह्मवित् ब्रह्मणि स्थितः । *na prahṛṣyet* (r◦ 10/6) *priyam* (r◦ 14/1) *prāpya na* (r◦ 2/2) *udvijet* (r◦ 10/6) *prāpya ća* (r◦ 1/1) *apriyam* (r◦ 14/2)

---

[411] See footnote in verse 3.5

[412] Elsewhere◦ *brahma* → God.

[413] Elsewhere◦ निर्दोषम् → flawless, spotless, faultless, guiltless, incorruptible, ever equanimous ...etc.

[414] See the footnote in verse 2.15

sthirabuddhiḥ: (r◦ 16/1) *asammūḍhaḥ:* (r◦ 15/7) *brahmavit̨* (r◦ 9/7) *brahmaṇi* (r◦ 24/7) *sthitaḥ:* (r◦ 22/8)

(§2) *na* (1.30); *prahṛṣyet̨* (3rd-per◦ sing◦ potential◦ विधि◦ parasmai◦ ←4◦प्र√हृष्); *priyam̨* (n◦ 2acc◦ sing◦ ←adj◦ *priya* (desirable) 1.23); *prāpya* (2.57); *na* (1.30); *udvijet̨* (3rd-per◦ sing◦ potential◦ विधि◦ ātmane◦ ←6◦उद्√विज्); *prāpya* (2.57); *ća* (1.1); *apriyam̨* (n◦ 2acc◦ sing◦ ←n.bahuvrī◦ adj◦ ***a-priya*** (undesirable) ←adj◦ *priya* 1.23); *sthirabuddhiḥ:* (m◦ 1nom◦ sing◦ ←bahuvrī◦ *sthira-buddhi*, स्थिरा बुद्धिः यस्य ←adj◦ *sthira* (stable) 1.16 + f◦ *buddhi* (thinking) 1.23); ***a-sammūḍhaḥ:*** (m◦ 1nom◦ sing◦ n.tatpu◦ ←adj◦ *sammūḍha* (deluded) 2.7); *brahmavit̨* (m◦ 1nom◦ sing◦ ←bahuvrī◦ adj◦ *brahma-viḍ*, ब्रह्म वेत्ति यः ←n◦ *brahman̨* 2.72 + adj◦ *viḍ* 3.29); *brahmaṇi* (5.10); ***sthitaḥ:*** (m◦ 1nom◦ sing◦ ←adj◦ *sthita* 1.14) (5.20)

(§3) *na* (not); *prahṛṣyet̨* (he may rejoice); *priyam̨* (obj1◦ desirable); *prāpya* (having received); *na* (not); *udvijet̨* (he may become dejected); *prāpya* (having received); *ća* (and); *apriyam̨* (obj2◦ undesirable); *sthirabuddhiḥ:* (adj1◦-subj◦ he whose thinking is firm); *asammūḍhaḥ:* (adj2◦-subj◦ he who is not deluded); *brahmavit̨* (subj◦ the knower of brahma); *brahmaṇi* (in brahma); *sthitaḥ:* (adj3◦-subj◦ established) (5.20)

(§4) brahmavit̨ sthitaḥ: brahmaṇi sthirabuddhiḥ: asammūḍhaḥ: na prahṛṣyet̨ prāpya priyam̨ ća na udvijet̨ prāpya apriyam̨

(§5) The knower of *brahma*, established in *brahma*, he whose thinking is firm, he who is not deluded, he may not rejoice[415] having received desirable, and he may not become dejected having received undesirable. (5.20)

5.21 बाह्यस्पर्शेष्वसक्तात्मा विन्दत्यात्मनि यत्सुखम् ।
स ब्रह्मयोगयुक्तात्मा सुखमक्षयमश्नुते ।।
bāhyasparśeṣvasaktātmā vindatyātmani yatsukham̨,
sa brahmayogayuktātmā sukhamakṣayamaśnute. (5.21)

(§1) बाह्यस्पर्शेषु असक्तात्मा विन्दति आत्मनि यत् सुखम् । सः ब्रह्मयोगयुक्तात्मा सुखम् अक्षयम् अश्नुते । *bāhyasparśeṣu* (r◦ 25/5, 4/6) *asaktātmā vindati* (r◦ 4/2) *ātmani yat̨* (r◦ 10/7) *sukham̨* (r◦ 14/2) *saḥ:* (r◦ 21/2) *brahmayogayuktātmā sukham̨* (r◦ 8/16) *akṣayam̨* (r◦ 8/16) *aśnute*

(§2) *bāhyasparśeṣu* (m◦ 7loc◦ plu◦ ←tatpu◦ *bāhya-sparśa*, बाह्यः स्पर्शः ←adj◦ ***bāhya*** (external) ←1◦√वह् +

---

[415] Elsewhere◦ *na prahṛṣyet̨* → rejoices not, does not rejoice, ...etc.

प्रहृष्येत् is not a present tense (लट्). It is a potential mood (विधि) → he may not rejoice. The same is true for *na udvijet̨* → he grieves not.

m◦ *sparśa* (contact) 2.14 ←10◦√स्पर्श्); *asaktātmā* (m◦ 1nom◦ sing◦ ←bahuvrī◦ *asaktātman* (unattached person) असक्तः आत्मा यस्य ←adj◦ *asakta* (unattached) 3.7 + m◦ *ātman* 2.41); *vindati* (4.38); *ātmani* (2.55); *yat* (2.31); 📖**sukham** (2acc◦ sing◦ ←n◦ *sukha* (happiness) 1.32); *saḥ:* (1.13); *brahmayogayuktātmā* (m◦ 1nom◦ sing◦ ←bahuvrī◦ *brahmayoga-yuktātman*, ब्रह्मणि योगेन युक्तः आत्मा यस्य ←n◦ *brahman* 2.72 + adj◦ *yukta* (equipped) 1.14 + m◦ *yoga* 2.39 + m◦ *ātman* 2.41); *sukham* (2.66); *akṣayam* (n◦ 2acc◦ sing◦ ←adj◦ 📖**akṣaya** (everlasting) ←6◦अ√क्षि); *aśnute* (3.4) (5.21)

(§3) *bāhyasparśeṣu* (in the external contacts, sensationions); *asaktātmā* (adj1◦-subj◦ he who has no attachment, on interest); *vindati* (he attains); *ātmani* (in himself); *yat* (adj◦-obj1◦ that, which); *sukham* (obj1◦ happiness); *saḥ:* (subj◦ he); *brahmayogayuktātmā* (adj2◦-subj◦ through *yoga* he who is one with brahma); *sukham* (obj2◦ happiness); *akṣayam* (adj◦-obj2◦ everlasting); *aśnute* (he enjoys) (5.21)

(§4) asaktātmā bāhyasparśeṣu vindati yat sukham ātmani brahmayogayuktātmā saḥ: aśnute akṣayam sukham

(§5) He who has no interest in the external sensationions, he attains that happiness in himself through *yoga*, he who is one with *brahma*, enjoys everlasting happiness.

(5.21)

5.22 **ये हि संस्पर्शजा भोगा दुःखयोनय एव ते ।**

आद्यन्तवन्तः कौन्तेय न तेषु रमते बुधः ।।

ye hi saṁsparśajā bhogā duḥ:khayonaya eva te,

ādyantavantaḥ: kaunteya na teṣu ramate budhaḥ:. (5.22)

(§1) ये हि संस्पर्शजाः भोगाः दुःखयोनयः एव ते । आद्यन्तवन्तः कौन्तेय न तेषु रमते बुधः । *ye hi saṁsparśajāḥ:* (r◦ 20/12) *bhogāḥ:* (r◦ 20/8) *duḥ:khayonayaḥ:* (r◦ 19/7) *eva te* (r◦ 23/1) *ādyantavantaḥ:* (r◦ 22/1) *kaunteya na teṣu* (r◦ 25/5) *ramate budhaḥ:* (r◦ 22/8)

(§2) *ye* (1.7); *hi* (1.11); *saṁsparśajāḥ:* (m◦ 1nom◦ plu◦ ←bahuvrī◦ *saṁsparśaja*, संस्पर्शात् जायते यः ←m◦ 📖***saṁsparśa*** ←6◦सम्√स्पृश् + m◦ *ja* 1.7); *bhogāḥ:* (1.33); *duḥ:khayonayaḥ:* (m◦ 1nom◦ plu◦ ←bahuvrī◦ *duḥ:khayoni*, दुःखस्य योनिः यः ←n◦ *duḥ:kha* (sorrow) 2.14 + m◦ or f◦ 📖***yoni*** (womb) ←2◦√यु); *eva* (1.1); *te* (1.33); *ādyantavantaḥ:* (m◦ 1nom◦ plu◦ ←bahuvrī◦ *ādyantavat*, आदिवत् च अन्तवत् च यः ←adj◦ or m◦ ***ādya*** (beginning) ←3◦आ√दा + adj◦ *antavat* 1.5); *kaunteya* (2.14); *na* (1.30); *teṣu* (2.62); 📖***ramate*** (3rd-per◦ sing◦ pres◦ वर्तमान्-लट् ātmane◦ ←1◦√रम्); *budhaḥ:* (m◦ 1nom◦ sing◦ ←adj◦ *budha* (wise person) 4.19)

(5.22)

(§3) *ye* (adj1◦-subj1◦ which); *hi* (because); *saṁsparśajāḥ:* (adj2◦-subj1◦ the ones that arise from external sensations); *bhogāḥ:* (subj1◦ the elations, pleasures); *duḥ:khayonayaḥ:* (adj3◦-subj1◦ those which are the wombs of suffering, sorrow); *eva* (only); *te* (adj4∘-subj1∘ they); *ādyantavantaḥ:* (adj5∘-subj∘ the ones with beginning and end); *kaunteya* (O Kaunteya! O Arjuna!); *na* (does not); *teṣu* (in them); *ramate* (they indulge); *budhaḥ:* (subj2∘ the wise, a wise peerson) (5.22)

(§4) hi bhogāḥ: ye saṁsparśajāḥ: duḥ:khayonayaḥ: eva te ādyantavantaḥ: kaunteya budhaḥ: na ramate teṣu

(§5) Because[416] the elations which arise from external sensations are the wombs of suffering only (and) they (are) the ones with beginning and end;[417] O Arjuna! a wise peerson does not indulge in them. (5.22)

5.23 **शक्नोतीहैव यः सोढुं प्राक्शरीरविमोक्षणात् ।**
कामक्रोधोद्भवं वेगं स युक्तः स सुखी नरः ।।
śaknotīhaiva yaḥ: soḍhuṁ prākśarīravimokṣaṇāt,
kāmakrodhodbhavaṁ vegaṁ sa yuktaḥ: sa sukhī naraḥ:. (5.23)

(§1) शक्नोति इह एव यः सोढुम् प्राक्शरीरविमोक्षणात् । कामक्रोधोद्भवम् वेगम् सः युक्तः सः सुखी नरः । *śaknoti* (r∘ 1/5) *iha* (r∘ 3/1) *eva yaḥ:* (r∘ 22/7) *soḍhum* (r∘ 14/1) *prāk* (r∘ 10/3) *śarīravimokṣaṇāt* (r∘ 23/1) *kāmakrodhodbhavam* (r∘ 14/1) *vegam* (r∘ 14/1) *saḥ:* (r∘ 21/2) *yuktaḥ:* (r∘ 22/7) *saḥ:* (r∘ 21/2) *sukhī naraḥ:* (r∘ 22/8)

(§2) *śaknoti* (3rd-per∘ sing∘ pres∘ वर्तमान्-लट् parasmai∘ ←5∘√शक् 1.30); *iha* (2.5); *eva* (1.1); *yaḥ:* (2.19); 🕮**soḍhum** (inf∘ ind∘ ←1∘√सह्); *prāk* (time indicating ind∘ ←adj∘ *prāñca* ←1∘प्र√अञ्च्); *śarīravimokṣaṇāt* (5abl∘ sing∘ ←tatpu∘ *śarīra-vimokṣaṇa*, शरीरात् विमोक्षणम् ←n∘ *śarīra* 1.29 + n∘ 🕮*vimokṣaṇa* (departation) ←10∘वि√मोक्ष्); *kāmakrodhodbhavam* (m∘ 2acc∘ sing∘ ←bahuvrī∘ *kāma-krodhodbhava*, कामात् च क्रोधात् च उद्भवः यस्य ←n∘ *kāma* (desire) 1.22 + m∘ *krodha* (anger) 2.56 + m∘ *udbhava* (rise) 3.15); 🕮*vegam* (2acc∘ sing∘ ←m∘ vega (impulse) ←6∘√विज्); *saḥ:* (1.13); *yuktaḥ:* (5.12); *saḥ:* (1.13); 🕮**sukhī** (m∘ 1nom∘ sing∘ ←adj∘ *sukhin* (happy) ←10∘√सुख्); *naraḥ:* (person, 2.22) (5.23)

(§3) *śaknoti* (he is able); *iha* (here, in this world, in this life); *eva* (only, very); *yaḥ:* (adj1∘-subj∘ he who); *soḍhum* (for bearing, to endure, withstand, resist sustain, bear); *prāk śarīra-vimokṣaṇāt* (before death, before leaving the body, before departing the body); *kāmakrodhodbhavam* (adj∘-obj∘ the one

---

[416] See footnote in verse 3.5

[417] Elsewhere∘ *te ādyantavantaḥ:* → they have a beginning and an end, they have beginning and ending ...etc.

🕮 ते is not a verb, it is not a present tense; आद्यन्तवन्तः is not an object. ते and आद्यन्तवन्तः both are plural adjectives of noun भोगाः।

that is rooted in desire and anger, arising from desire and anger); *vegaṃ* (obj∘ the impulse); *saḥ:* (adj2∘-subj∘ he); *yuktaḥ:* (adj3∘-subj∘ the one who is disciplined with yoga); *saḥ:* (adj2∘-subj∘ he); *sukhī* (adj4∘-subj∘ the one who is happy); *naraḥ:* (subj∘ the person) (5.23)

(§4) naraḥ: yaḥ: śaknoti iha eva prāk śarīravimokṣaṇāt soḍhuṃ vegaṃ kāmakrodhodbhavaṃ saḥ: yuktaḥ: saḥ: sukhī

(§5) The person who is able in this very life, before leaving the body, to endure[418] the impulse arising from desire and anger, he is disciplined with yoga (and) he is happy. (5.23)

5.24 योऽन्तःसुखोऽन्तरारामस्तथान्तर्ज्योतिरेव यः ।
स योगी ब्रह्मनिर्वाणं ब्रह्मभूतोऽधिगच्छति ॥

yo'ntaḥ:sukho'ntarārāmastathāntarjyotireva yaḥ:,
sa yogī brahmanirvāṇaṃ brahmabhūto'dhigacchati. (5.24)

(§1) यः अन्तःसुखः अन्तराराम: तथा अन्तर्ज्योति: एव यः । सः योगी ब्रह्मनिर्वाणम् ब्रह्मभूतः अधिगच्छति । *yaḥ:* (r∘ 15/1) *antaḥ:sukhaḥ:* (r∘ 15/1) *antarārāmaḥ:* (r∘ 18/1) *tathā* (r∘ 1/3) *antarjyotiḥ:* (r∘ 16/1) *eva yaḥ:* (r∘ 22/8, 22/7) *saḥ:* (r∘ 21/2) *yogī brahmanirvāṇaṃ* (r∘ 14/1, 24/3) *brahmabhūtaḥ:* (r∘ 15/1) *adhigacchati*

(§2) *yaḥ:* (2.19); 🕮*antaḥ:sukhaḥ:* (m∘ 1nom∘ sing∘ ←bahuvrī∘ *antaḥ:-sukha*, अन्तरंगं सुखेन यस्य सः ←ind∘ *antaḥ* (internal) 2.16 + n∘ *sukha* (happiness) 3.32); 🕮*antarārāmaḥ:* (m∘ 1nom∘ sing∘ ←bahuvrī∘ *antarārāma*, अन्तः आरामः यस्य सः ←ind∘ ***antar*** (internal) ←4∘√अन् + m∘ *ārāma* 3.16); *tathā* (1.8); 🕮*antarjyotiḥ:* (m∘ 1nom∘ sing∘ ←bahuvrī∘ *antarjyoti*, अन्तरंगे ज्योतिः यस्य सः ←ind∘ *antar* 6.47 0r ind∘ ***ante*** + n∘ ***jyotis*** (illumination) ←1∘√द्युत्); *eva* (1.1); *yaḥ:* (2.19); *saḥ:* (1.13); 🕮***yogī*** (1nom∘ sing∘ ←m∘ or adj∘ *yogin* 3.3); *brahmanirvāṇaṃ* (2acc∘ 2.72); 🕮***brahmabhūtaḥ:*** (m∘ 1nom∘ sing∘ ←adj∘ ***brahma-bhūta*** ←n∘ *brahma* 3.15 + ppp∘ adj∘ 🕮*bhūta* (being) ←1∘√भू); *adhigacchati* (2.64) (5.24)

(§3) *yaḥ:* (adj1∘-subj∘ he who); *antaḥ:sukhaḥ:* (adj2∘-subj∘ he whose happiness is within); *antarārāmaḥ:* (adj3∘-subj∘ he whose delight is within); *tathā* (as well as); *antarjyotiḥ:* (adj4∘-subj∘ he who is illuminated from within); *eva* (only); *yaḥ:* (adj1∘-subj∘ he who); *saḥ:* (adj5∘-subj∘ that); *yogī* (subj∘ yogī); *brahmanirvāṇaṃ* (obj∘ reunion with brahma); *brahmabhūtaḥ:* (adj6∘-subj∘ he who has become one being with brahma, he who is one with brahma); *adhigacchati* (he attains) (5.24)

(§4) yaḥ: antaḥ:sukhaḥ: antarārāmaḥ: tathā antarjyotiḥ: eva yaḥ: brahmabhūtaḥ: saḥ: yogī adhigacchati brahmanirvāṇaṃ

---

[418] Elsewhere∘ *soḍhuṃ* → to resist.

(§5) He whose happiness is within, he whose delight is within, as well as he who is illuminated from within, he who has become one with *brahma*, only that *yogī*[419] attains reunion with *brahma*.[420] (5.24)

5.25 लभन्ते ब्रह्मनिर्वाणमृषयः क्षीणकल्मषाः ।
छिन्नद्वैधा यतात्मानः सर्वभूतहिते रताः ।।
labhante brahmanirvāṇamṛṣayaḥ: kśīṇakalmaṣāḥ:,
ćhinnadvaidhā yatātmānaḥ: sarvabhūtahite ratāḥ:. (5.25)

(§1) लभन्ते ब्रह्मनिर्वाणम् ऋषयः क्षीणकल्मषाः । छिन्नद्वैधाः यतात्मानः सर्वभूतहिते रताः । *labhante brahmanirvāṇam* (r∘ 8/21, 24/3) *ṛṣayaḥ:* (r∘ 22/1) *kśīṇakalmaṣāḥ:* (r∘ 22/8) *ćhinnadvaidhāḥ:* (r∘ 20/14) *yatātmānaḥ:* (r∘ 22/7) *sarvabhūtahite ratāḥ:* (r∘ 22/8)

(§2) *labhante* (2.32); *brahmanirvāṇam* (2.72); 🕮***ṛṣayaḥ:*** (1nom∘ plu∘ ←m∘ *ṛṣi* (sage) 4.2); 🕮*kśīṇakalmaṣāḥ:* (m∘ 1nom∘ plu∘ ←bahuvrī∘ *kśīṇa-kalmaṣa*, क्षीणानि कल्मषाणि यस्य । क्षिणानि पापानि यस्य । ←ppp∘ adj∘ 🕮***kśīṇa*** (attuned) ←6∘√क्षि + n∘ *kalmaṣa* (sin) 4.30); 🕮*ćhinnadvaidhāḥ:* (m∘ 1nom∘ plu∘ ←bahuvrī∘ *ćhinna-dvaidha*, छिन्नम् द्वैधम् यस्य ←ppp∘ adj∘ 🕮***ćhinna*** (cut away) ←7∘√छिद् 4.41 + n∘ *dvaidha* (doubt) ←1∘√द्व); 🕮*yatātmānaḥ:* (m∘ 1nom∘ plu∘ ←bahuvrī∘ ***yatātmān***, यतः आत्मा यस्य ←adj∘ *yata* (restrained) 4.21 + m∘ *ātman* (self) 2.41); ***sarvabhūtahiteratāḥ:*** (m∘ 7loc∘ plu∘ ←bahuvrī∘ *sarva-bhūta-hite-rata*, सर्वेषाम् भूतानाम् हिते रतः यः ←pron∘ *sarva* 1.6 + n∘ *bhūta* 2.28 + n∘ *hita* (benefit) ←ppp∘ adj∘ ***hita*** ←5∘√हि or 3∘√धा) 🕮***ratāḥ:*** (m∘ 1nom∘ plu∘ ←adj∘ *rata* (engaged) 2.42) (5.25)

(§3) *labhante* (they attain); *brahmanirvāṇam* (obj∘ reunion with brahma); *ṛṣayaḥ:* (subj∘ sages); *kśīṇakalmaṣāḥ:* (adj1∘-subj∘ those whose sins have been attenuated, waned away); *ćhinnadvaidhāḥ:* (adj2∘-subj∘ those whose doubts are cut away); *yatātmānaḥ:* (adj3∘-subj∘ those who are self-restrained, self-controlled); *sarvabhūtahiteratāḥ:* (adj4∘-subj∘ those who are engaged in the welfare of all beings, those who take delight in the welfare of all beings) (5.25)

(§4) ṛṣayaḥ: kśīṇakalmaṣāḥ: ćhinnadvaidhāḥ: yatātmānaḥ: sarvabhūtahiteratāḥ: labhante brahmanirvāṇam

(§5) Those sages whose sins have been attenuated, whose doubts are cut away,[421] who are self-

---

[419] Elsewhere∘ योगी → yogin

[420] ब्रह्मनिर्वाणम् → this word has appeared in 5.24, 25 and 26. For explanation, please see footnote in 2.72

[421] Elsewhere∘ *ćhinnadvaidhāḥ:* → beyond the dualities, free from doubts; doubts have been cut away, whose doubts have been dispelled, ...etc.

controlled, who are engaged in the welfare of all beings, they attain reunion with ***brahma.*** **(5.25)**

5.26 कामक्रोधवियुक्तानां यतीनां यतचेतसाम् ।
अभितो ब्रह्मनिर्वाणं वर्तते विदितात्मनाम् ॥
kāmakrodhaviyuktānāṁ yatīnāṁ yataćetasām̧,
abhito brahmanirvāṇaṁ vartate viditātmanām̧. **(5.26)**

(§1) कामक्रोधवियुक्तानाम् यतीनाम् यतचेतसाम् । अभितः ब्रह्मनिर्वाणम् वर्तते विदितात्मनाम् । *kāmakrodhaviyuktānām̧* (r∘ 14/1) *yatīnām̧* (r∘ 14/1) *yataćetasām̧* (r∘ 14/2) *abhitaḥ:* (r∘ 15/7) *brahmanirvāṇam̧* (r∘ 14/1, 24/3) *vartate viditātmanām̧* (r∘ 14/2)

(§2) *kāmakrodhaviyuktānām̧* (m∘ 6pos∘ plu∘ ←bahuvrī∘ *kāma-krodha-viyukta*, कामात् च क्रोधात् च वियुक्तः यः ←n∘ *kāma* (desire) 1.22 + m∘ *krodha* (anger) 2.56 + adj∘ *viyukta* (freed) 2.64); *yatīnam̧* (6pos plu∘ ←m∘ *yati* (auster) 4.28); *yataćetasām̧* (m∘ 6pos∘ plu∘ ←bahuvrī∘ *yata-ćetaş*, यतः चेतः यस्य ←adj∘ *yata* (controlled) 4.21 + n∘ *ćetaş* 1.38); 📖*abhitaḥ:* (= ind∘ *abhitaş* (near) ←2∘√भा); 📖*brahmanirvāṇam̧* (2.72); ***vartate*** (3rd-per∘ sing∘ pres∘ वर्तमान्-लट् ātmane∘ ←1∘√वृत् 3.28); 📖*viditātmanām̧* (m∘ 6pos∘ plu∘ ←bahuvrī∘ *viditātmaņ*, विदितः आत्मा यस्य ←ppp∘ adj∘ *vidita* (realized) ←2∘√विद् + m∘ *ātmaņ* 2.41) **(5.26)**

(§3) *kāmakrodhaviyuktānām̧* (of those who are free from craving and indignation); *yatīnam̧* (of those who are abstemious); *yataćetasām̧* (of those who are of austere mind); *abhitaḥ:* (near, close); *brahmanirvāṇam̧* (subj∘ reunion with brahma); *vartate* (it is, it exists); *viditātmanām̧* (of those who are

---

📖 छिन्न (cut) is past participle adjective, from root √छिद् (to cut), it means removal, cutting away, destruction etc. छिन्न is not a present or past tense of any kind. It qualifies the plural noun द्वैधाः, to form this बहुव्रीहिः समासः । द्वैधः being m∘ he who has doubts. Many times this word द्वैध, double mind, is confused or mistaken as द्वंद्व, pair of opposites; or द्वैत the duality.

(1) द्वैध is a तद्धित word from द्विध (ind∘ द्वि+धाच् in two ways).

(2) द्वंद्व is n∘ from adj∘ द्वि (द्वौ द्वौ सहाभिव्यक्तौ । द्वि-शब्दस्य द्वित्वं two opposites, a pair of opposites. Gītā has many examples of such pairs). द्वंद्व-समासः, however, is exception. It does not always include a pair of opposites, but then it does not always include only two objects either. (3) द्वैत (duality) means relating to two, but not necessarily a pair of opposites. In upanishads it refers to the philosophy upheld by those who believe that *brahma* has created the world, thereby admitting that *brahma* is separate (duality) from the creation. Counter to this 'theory of duality,' the Monism (अद्वैतम्), asserts that *brahma* IS everything (ब्रह्मैव जगत्सर्वं), there is no duality between *brahma* and universe (अद्वैतब्रह्म), and thus, the universe is not a 'creation' but evolution, transformation, personification or manifestation of *brahma.*

self realised) (5.26)

(§4) kāmakrodhaviyuktānām̐ yatīnam̐ yataćetasām̐ viditātmanām̐ brahmanirvāṇam̐ vartate

(§5) Of those who are free from craving and indignation, of those who are abstemious, of those who are of austere mind, of those who are self realised, reunion with *brahma* is near. (5.26)

5.27 **स्पर्शान्कृत्वा बहिर्बाह्यांश्चक्षुश्चैवान्तरे भ्रुवोः ।**
प्राणापानौ समौ कृत्वा नासाभ्यन्तरचारिणौ ।।
sparśānkṛtvā bahirbāhyām̐śćakṣuśćaivāntare bhruvoḥ:,
prāṇāpānau samau kṛtvā nāsābhyantaraćāriṇau. (5.27)

(§1) स्पर्शान् कृत्वा बहिः बाह्यान् चक्षुः च एव अन्तरे भ्रुवोः । प्राणापानौ समौ कृत्वा नासाभ्यन्तरचारिणौ । *sparśān̐* (r∘ 13/9) *kṛtvā bahiḥ:* (r∘ 16/6) *bāhyān̐* (r∘ 13/6) *ćakṣuḥ:* (r∘ 17/1) *ća* (r∘ 3/1) *eva* (r∘ 1/1) *antare bhruvoḥ:* (r∘ 22/8) *prāṇāpānau samau kṛtvā nāsābhyantaraćāriṇau*

(§2) *sparśān̐* (2acc∘ plu∘ ←m∘ 🕮*sparśa* (contact) 2.14); *kṛtvā* (2.38); ***bahiḥ:*** (= ind∘ *bahiṣ̐* (outside) ←1∘√वह्); *bāhyān̐* (m∘ 2acc∘ plu∘ ←adj∘ *bāhya* (external) 5.21); 🕮***ćakṣuḥ:*** (2acc∘ sing∘ ←n∘ ***ćakṣuṣ̐*** (eye) ←2∘**√चक्ष्**); *ća* (1.1); *eva* (1.1); *antare* (7loc∘ sing∘ ←n∘ *antara* (inside) 2.13); ***bhruvoḥ:*** (6pos∘ dual∘ ←f∘ *bhrū* (eyebrow) ←1∘√भ्रम्); *prāṇāpānau* (m∘ 2acc∘ dual∘ ←dvandva∘ प्राणं च अपानं च ←m∘ *prāṇa* (in-breath) 1.33 + m∘ *apāna* (out-breath) 4.29); *samau* (m∘ 2acc∘ dual∘ ←adj∘ *sama* (equal) 1.4); *kṛtvā* (2.38); *nāsābhyantaraćāriṇau* (m∘ 2acc∘ dual∘ ←tatpu∘ *nāsābhyantara-ćārin̐*, नासयोः अभ्यन्तरे चारी ←f∘ 🕮*nāsa* (nostril) ←1∘**√नास्** + adj∘ 🕮*abhyantara* (within) ←अभि√अन् + adj∘ 🕮***ćārin̐*** (moving) ←1∘√चर्) (5.27)

(§3) *sparśān̐* (obj1∘ contacts, sensations); *kṛtvā* (having done, having kept); *bahiḥ:* (outside); *bāhyān̐* (adj∘-obj1∘ the external); *ćakṣuḥ:* (obj2∘ the gaze, the vision); *ća* (and); *eva* (also); *antare* (between); *bhruvoḥ:* (between the two eyebrows); *prāṇāpānau* (obj3∘ the inhalation and axhalation); *samau* (adj1∘-obj3∘ both equal); *kṛtvā* (having done, having kept, making); *nāsābhyantaraćāriṇau* (adj2∘-obj3∘ moving within the two nostrils) (5.27)

(§4) bāhyān̐ sparśān̐ kṛtvā bahiḥ: ća ćakṣuḥ: eva antare bhruvoḥ: ća kṛtvā prāṇāpānau nāsābhyantaraćāriṇau samau

(§5) The external sensations having kept outside; the gaze (having kept) between the two eyebrows; and having kept the inhalation and exhalation moving within the two nostrils, both equal;[422] (5.27)

---

[422] Elsewhere∘ *samau* → equally, suspending ...etc.

5.28 यतेन्द्रियमनोबुद्धिर्मुनिर्मोक्षपरायणः ।
विगतेच्छाभयक्रोधो यः सदा मुक्त एव सः ॥
yatendriyamanobuddhirmunirmokṣaparāyaṇaḥ:,
vigatećchābhayakrodho yaḥ: sadā mukta eva saḥ:. (5.28)

(§1) यतेन्द्रियमनोबुद्धिः मुनिः मोक्षपरायणः । विगतेच्छाभयक्रोधः यः सदा मुक्तः एव सः । *yatendriyamanobuddhiḥ:* (r◦ 16/6) *muniḥ:* (r◦ 16/6) *mokṣaparāyaṇaḥ:* (r◦ 22/8, 24/2) *vigatećchābhayakrodhaḥ:* (r◦ 15/10) *yaḥ:* (r◦ 22/7) *sadā muktaḥ:* (r◦ 19/7) *eva saḥ:* (r◦ 22/8)

(§2) *yatendriyamanobuddhiḥ:* (m◦ 1nom◦ sing◦ ←bahuvrī◦ *yatendriya-manobuddhi,* यतानि इन्द्रियाणि च मनः च बुद्धिः च यस्य ←adj◦ *yata* (restrained) 4.21 + n◦ *indriya* (organ) 2.8 + n◦ *manas* (mind) 1.30 + f◦ *buddhi* (thinking) 1.23); *muniḥ:* (2.56); *mokṣaparāyaṇaḥ:* (m◦ 1nom◦ sing◦ ←bahuvrī◦ *mokṣa-parāyaṇa,* मोक्षः परायणम् यस्य ←m◦ 🕮***moksa*** (liberation) ←10◦√मोक्ष् + n◦ *parāyaṇa* (departure) 4.29); *vigatećchābhayakrodhaḥ:* (m◦ 1nom◦ sing◦ ←bahuvrī◦ *vigatećchā-bhaya-krodha,* विगताः इच्छा च भयम् च क्रोधः च यस्य ←adj◦ *vigata* (gone) 2.56 + f◦ 🕮***ićchā*** (desire) ←1◦√इष् + n◦ *bhaya* (fear) 2.35 + m◦ *krodha* (anger) 2.56); *yaḥ:* (2.19); *sadā* (1.40); ***muktaḥ:*** (m◦ 1nom◦ sing◦ ←adj◦ *mukta* (freed) 3.9); *eva* (1.1); *saḥ:* (1.13) (5.28)

(§3) *yatendriyamanobuddhiḥ:* (adj1◦-subj◦ he who has restrained his organs, mind and thinking); *muniḥ:* (subj◦ the muni, the yogī); *mokṣaparāyaṇaḥ:* (subj2◦-subj◦ he whose highest aim is reunion with brahma); *vigatećchābhayakrodhaḥ:* (adj3◦-subj◦ he whose craving, fear and indignation have gone away); *yaḥ:* (adj4◦-subj◦ he who); *sadā* (for ever, always); *muktaḥ:* (adj5◦-subj◦ he who is not bound by attachemnt, he who is liberated, freed); *eva* (and); *saḥ:* (adj6◦-subj◦ he, that) (5.28)

(§4) muniḥ: yaḥ: yatendriyamanobuddhiḥ: mokṣaparāyaṇaḥ: eva vigatećchābhayakrodhaḥ: saḥ: muktaḥ: sadā

(§5) The muni who has restrained his organs, mind and thinking;[423] whose highest aim is reunion with *brahma;* and whose craving, fear and indignation have gone away; he is not bound by attacmhent, for ever. (5.28)

🕮 समौ is not an adverb or a gerund. It is an adjective.

[423] Elsewhere◦ यतेन्द्रियमनोबुद्धिः → whose intelligence is controlled, controlling intellect ...etc.

🕮 To be a युक्तः, one need not control his intelligence and become less intelligent or unintelligent or extra intelligent, but only the thinking needs to be under control. यतेन्द्रियबुद्धिः is not a तत्पुरुष-समासः, it is बहुव्रीहि-समासः । Therfore, this *sāmāsic* word is not refering to बुद्धिः (intelligence or intellect), but to He WHO has controlled his thinking ...

5.29 भोक्तारं यज्ञतपसां सर्वलोकमहेश्वरम् ।
सुहृदं सर्वभूतानां ज्ञात्वा मां शान्तिमृच्छति ।।

bhoktāraṁ yajñatapasāṁ sarvalokamaheśvaram,
suhṛdaṁ sarvabhūtānāṁ jñātvā māṁ śāntimṛcchati. (5.29)

(§1) भोक्तारम् यज्ञतपसाम् सर्वलोकमहेश्वरम् । सुहृदम् सर्वभूतानाम् ज्ञात्वा माम् शान्तिम् ऋच्छति । *bhoktāram* (r∘ 14/1) *yajñatapasām* (r∘ 14/1) *sarvalokamaheśvaram* (r∘ 14/2) *suhṛdam* (r∘ 14/1) *sarvabhūtānām* (r∘ 14/1) *jñātvā mām* (r∘ 14/1) *śāntim* (r∘ 8/21) *ṛcchati*

(§2) *bhoktāram* (m∘ 2acc∘ sing∘ ←adj∘ 📖***bhoktṛ*** (realiser) ←7∘√भुज्); *yajñatapasām* (n∘ 6pos∘ plu∘ ←dvandva∘ यज्ञानाम् च तपसाम् च ←m∘ *yajña* 3.9 + n∘ *tapas* (austerity) 4.10); *sarvalokamaheśvaram* (m∘ 2acc∘ sing∘ ←tatpu∘ *sarva-loka-maheśvara*, सर्वेषाम् लोकानाम् महेश्वरः ←pron∘ *sarva* (all) 1.6 + m∘ *loka* (beings collective) 2.5 + adj∘ *mahā* (great) 1.3 + m∘ *īśvara* (lord) 4.6); 📖*suhṛdam* (2acc∘ sing∘ ←m∘ *suhṛd* (wellwisher) 1.26); *sarva* (1.6); *bhūtānām* (2.69); *jñātvā* (4.15); *mām* (1.46); *śāntim* (2.70); *ṛcchati* (2.72) (5.29)

(§3) *bhoktāram* (adj1∘-obj1∘ the relisher); *yajñatapasām* (of the yajñas and austerities); *sarvalokamaheśvaram* (adj2∘-obj1∘ the Great Lord of all beings); *suhṛdam* (adj3∘-obj1∘ the friend); *sarvabhūtānām* (of all beings); *jñātvā* (having known); *mām* (obj1∘ to me, me); *śāntim* (obj2∘ peace); *ṛcchati* (he attains, one attains) (5.29)

(§4) jñātvā mām sarvalokamaheśvaram bhoktāram yajñatapasām suhṛdam sarvabhūtānām ṛcchati śāntim

(§5) Having known me,[424] the Great Lord of all beings, the relisher of the *yajñas* and austerities, the friend of all beings, one attains peace. (5.29)

इति श्रीमद्भगवद्गीतासूपनिषत्सु ब्रह्मविद्यायां योगशास्त्रे
श्रीकृष्णार्जुनसंवादे कर्मसन्यासयोगो नाम पञ्चमोऽध्यायः ।।

iti śrīmadbhagavadgītāsūpaniṣatsu brahmavidyāyāṁ yogaśāstre
śrīkṛṣṇārjunasaṁvāde karmasannyāsayogo nāma pañcamo'dhyāyaḥ:.

(§1) *iti śrīmadbhagavadgītāsu* (r∘ 1/8) *upaniṣatsu brahmavidyāyām* (r∘ 14/1) *yogaśāstre śrīkṛṣṇārjuna-saṁvāde karmasannyāsayogaḥ:* (r∘ 15/6) *nāma pañcamaḥ:* (r∘ 15/1) *adhyāyaḥ:* (r∘ 22/8)

(§2) *iti* (1.25); *śrīmadbhagavadgītāsu* (f∘ 7loc∘ plu∘ tatpu∘ *śrīmad-bhagavad-gītā* ←adj∘ *śrīmat* 6.41 +

---

[424] Elsewhere∘ ज्ञात्वा माम् → Having known Me as, knowing Me as, He who knows Me as, knowing Me to be...

📖 See the explanation in footnote-1 in 2.21, **The difference is this :** (i)... (ii)...

adj∘ *bhagavat̩* 10.14 + f∘ *gītā* ←5∘√गै); *upaniṣatsu* (7loc∘ plu∘ ←f∘ *upaniṣad̩* ←6∘उप-नि√सद्); *brahmavidyāyām̩* (f∘ 7loc∘ sing∘ ←tatpu∘ *brahma-vidyā*, ब्रह्मण: वि‍ा ←n∘ *brahman̩* 2.72 + *vidyā* 5.18); *yogaśāstre* (n∘ 7loc∘ sing∘ ←tatpu∘ *yoga-śāstra*, योगानाम् शास्त्रम् । योगस्य शास्त्रम् । ←m∘ *yoga* 2.39 + n∘ *śāstra* 15.20); *śrīkṛṣṇārjunasam̐vāde* (m∘ 7loc∘ sing∘ ←tatpu∘ *śrī-kṛṣṇārjuna-sam̐vāda*, श्रीकृष्णस्य च अर्जुनस्य च संवाद: ←adj∘ *śrī* 10.34 + m∘ prop∘ *kṛṣṇa* 1.28 + m∘ prop∘ *arjuna* 1.4 + m∘ *sam̐vāda* 18.70); *karmannnyāsayogaḥ:* (m∘ 1nom∘ sing∘ ←tatpu∘ *karma-sannnyāsa-yoga*, कर्तृत्वस्य संन्यासस्य योग: ←n∘ *jñāna* 3.3 + n∘ *karman̩* 1.15 + m∘ *sannyāsa* 5.1 + m∘ *yoga* 2.39); *nāma* (1nom∘ sing∘ ←n∘ *nāman̩* ←1∘√म्ना); *pañćamaḥ:* (m∘ 1nom∘ sing∘ ←sequence indicating num∘ adj∘ *pañćama* ←adj∘ *pañća* 13.6↓); *adhyāyaḥ:* (1nom∘ sing∘ ←m∘ *adhyāya* ←1∘अधि√इ)

(§3) *iti* (thus); *śrīmadbhagavadgītāsu upaniṣatsu* (among the upaniṣads of the Śrīmad-Bhagavadgītā); *brahmavidyāyām̩* (of the eternal wisdoms); *yogaśāstre* (in the science of Yoga); *śrīkṛṣṇārjunasam̐vāde* (in the dialogue between Śrī Kṛṣṇa and Arjuna); *karmasannyāsayogaḥ:* (adj∘1-subj∘ the *yoga* of renunciation of authorship of karma); *nāma* (called); *pañćamaḥ:* (adj2∘-subj∘ the fifth); *adhyāyaḥ:* (subj∘ discourse; chapter)

(§4) śrīmadbhagavadgītāsu upaniṣatsu yogaśāstre brahmavidyāyām̩ iti pañćamaḥ adhyāyaḥ: nāma karmasannyāsayogaḥ: śrīkṛṣṇārjunasam̐vāde

(§5) Among the upaniṣads of the Śrīmad-Bhagavadgītā, in the science of Yoga of self realization, thus (is) the fifth discourse called karma-sannyāsa-yogaḥ: in the dialogue between Śrī Kṛṣṇa and Arjuna.

CHAPTER 6

ṣaṣṭho'dhyāyaḥ:

षष्ठोऽध्याय: ।

ātmasam̐yama-yogaḥ:

आत्मसंयमयोग: ।

THE YOGA OF SELF CONTROL

The Lord said (śrībhagavānuvāća श्रीभगवानुवाच ।)

6.1 अनाश्रितः कर्मफलं कार्यं कर्म करोति यः ।
स संन्यासी च योगी च न निरग्निर्न चाक्रियः ।।

anāśritaḥ: karmaphalaṁ kāryaṁ karma karoti yaḥ:,
sa sannyāsī ća yogī ća na niragnirna ćākriyaḥ:. (6.1)

(§1) अनाश्रितः कर्मफलम् कार्यम् कर्म करोति यः । सः संन्यासी च योगी च न निरग्निः न च अक्रियः । *ṣaṣṭhaḥ:* (r◦ 15/1) *adhyāyaḥ:. ātmasam̐yamayogaḥ:* (r◦ 22/8). *śrībhagavān̦* (r◦ 8/14) *uvāća. anāśritaḥ:* (r◦ 22/1) *karmaphalam̦* (r◦ 14/1) *kāryam̦* (r◦ 14/1) *karma karoti yaḥ:* (r◦ 22/8, 22/7) *saḥ:* (r◦ 21/2) *sannyāsī ca yogī ca na niragniḥ:* (r◦ 16/6) *na ća* (r◦ 1/1) *akriyaḥ:* (r◦ 22/8)

(§2) *ṣaṣṭhaḥ:* (m◦ 1nom◦ sing◦ ←sequence indicating num◦ adj◦ *ṣaṣṭha* → 15.7 ↓); *adhyāyaḥ:* (1nom◦ sing◦ ←m◦ *adhyāya* ←1◦अधि√इ). *ātmasam̐yamayogaḥ:* (m◦ 1nom◦ sing◦ ←tatpu◦ *ātma-sam̐yama-yoga*, आत्मनः संयमस्य योगः ←m◦ *ātman̦* 2.41 + m◦ *sam̐yama* 4.26 + m◦ *yoga* 2.39). *śrībhagavān̦* (2.2); *uvāća* (1.25).

🕮*anāśritaḥ:* (m◦ 1nom◦ sing◦ ←ppp◦ adj◦ *anāśrita* (independent) ←1◦अन्–आ√श्रि); *karmaphalam̦* (2acc◦ 5.12); *kāryam̦* (3.19); *karma* (2acc◦ 3.8); *karoti* (4.20); *yaḥ:* (2.19); *saḥ:* (1.13); *sannyāsī* (1nom◦ sing◦ ←m◦ *sannyāsin̦* (ascetic) 5.3); *ća* (1.1); *yogī* (5.24); *ća* (1.1); *na* (1.30); 🕮*niragniḥ:* (m◦ 1nom◦ sing◦ ←n.bahuvrī◦ *niragni*, अग्निहोत्रस्य अग्नेः अज्वलनं सहते यः । अग्नये न यजति यः । यज्ञः नास्ति जीवनं यस्य । तप्तं नास्ति जीवनं यस्य । ←negative affix *nir̦* (निर्) 2.45 + m◦ *agni* 4.19); *na* (1.30); *ća* (1.1); 🕮*akriyaḥ:* (m◦ 1nom◦ sing◦ ←adj◦ n.bahuvrī◦ *a-kriya* नास्ति क्रिया यस्मिन् ←f◦ *kriyā* (duty) 1.42) (6.1)

(§3) *ṣaṣṭhaḥ:* (adj◦-subj◦ the sixth); *adhyāyaḥ:* (subj◦ chapter). *ātmasam̐yamayogaḥ:* (the yoga of self-restraint). *śrībhagavān̦* (The Lord); *uvāća* (he said). *anāśritaḥ:* (adj1◦-subj◦ he who is not dependent upon-); *karmaphalam̦* (obj1◦ the fruit of karma); *kāryam̦* (adj◦-obj2◦ duty, the work that ought to be done); *karma* (obj2◦ work); *karoti* (he performs, he does); *yaḥ:* (adj2◦-subj◦ he who); *saḥ:* (subj◦ he); *sannyāsī* (adj3◦-subj◦ he who is an ascetic, sanyāsī[425]); *ća* (and); *yogī* (adj4◦-subj◦ he who is disciplined); *ća* (and); *na* (not); *niragniḥ:* (adj1◦-subj2◦ he who does not worship with a fire; he who does not perform yajña, he who does not perform austerity, he who is not austere); *na* (not); *ća* (and); *akriyaḥ:* (adj2◦-subj2◦ he who does not perform his duty) (6.1)

(§4) ṣaṣṭhaḥ: adhyāyaḥ:. ātmasam̐yamayogaḥ:. śrībhagavān̦ uvāća. anāśritaḥ: karmaphalam̦ yaḥ: karoti karma kāryam̦ saḥ: sannyāsī ća yogī ća (saḥ:) na ća niragniḥ: na ća akriyaḥ:

---

[425] Elsewhere◦ संन्यासी → sanyasin

(§5) Sixth Chapter. The yoga of self-restraint.[426] The Lord said : He who is not dependent upon the fruit of *karma* (but) he who performs the work that ought to be done, he is an ascetic and he is disciplined and he is not un-austere[427] and he is not non-perform his duty.[428] (6.1)

In other words : An ascetic is he who is not dependent upon the fruit of *karma,* performs the work that ought to be done and he who is disciplined. He is not a ascetic who is not austere and who does not perform his duty.

6.2 **यं संन्यासमिति प्राहुर्योगं तं विद्धि पाण्डव ।**
न ह्यसंन्यस्तसङ्कल्पो योगी भवति कश्चन ।।
yaṁ sannyāsamiti prāhuryogaṁ taṁ viddhi pāṇḍva,
na hyasannyastasaṅkalpo yogī bhavati kaśćana. (6.2)

(§1) यम् संन्यासम् इति प्राहुः योगम् तम् विद्धि पाण्डव । न हि असंन्यस्तसङ्कल्पः योगी भवति कश्चन । *yam* (r◦ 14/1) *sannyāsam* (r◦ 8/18) *iti prāhuḥ:* (r◦ 16/8) *yogam* (r◦ 14/1) *tam* (r◦ 14/1) *viddhi pāṇḍava na hi* (r◦ 4/1)

---

[426] PLEASE BE AWARE THAT : In most English Translations **सः न निरग्निर्न चाक्रियः (सः न च निरग्निः न च अक्रियः)** has been translated exactly opposite to what is said in Sanskrit shloka by Krishna.

[427] (Elsewhere◦ *niragniḥ:* → he who gives up fire, he who does not keep a fire, he who lights no fire, he who is without sacred fire ...etc.)

[428] Elsewhere◦ *akriyaḥ:* → he who remains without action, is actionless; performs no rites, without rites, who fails to perform sacred rites ...etc.

📖 (i) actionless → in 3.5 the Lord says न कश्चित् क्षणम् अपि जातु तिष्ठति अकर्मकृत् । no one ever stays without *karma* even for a fraction of a moment; it therefore means that there is no such thing as actionlessness. Remember, in 4.18 the Lord says (अकर्मणि कर्म यः पश्येत सः बुद्धिमान् मनुष्येषु) he who sees *karma* in *akarma* is wise among men. Actionlessness, i.e. not doing anything, is also act of 'doing' that which may be perceived or misunderstood as nothing. Because, at places doing, saying or thinking of nothing is the action more important than doing something. For example, in meditation, thinking of nothing is the actionlessness (*akarma*) necessary to be performed. At a right time and place, keeping mouth shut is the actionlessness (*akarma*) that is wiser to perform than the action of opening the mouth. When in sleep, what one may call actionlessness is the *akarma* that is the right action than performing the action of sleep-walking. Actionlessness (क्रियाशून्यता) is a misnomer for not doing required *karma.* Because actionlessness can never be performed by anyone. In 3.8 the Lord has said शरीरयात्रा न प्रसिध्येत् अकर्मणः, anybody's life can go on without performing at least something every moment. In what one misunderstands as actionlessness, the actions of breathing, growing up, seeing, hearing, touching, sitting, standing or sleeping are always going on unavoidably.

(ii) In *kriyaḥ* → क्रियः and कार्य should not include only the rites, but all duties.

asannyastasaṅkalpaḥ: (r◦ 15/10) *yogī bhavati kaśćana*

(§2) *yam* (2.15); 🕮*sannyāsam* (5.1); *iti* (1.25); 🕮***prāhuḥ:*** (3rd-per◦ plu◦ pres◦ लट् वर्त◦ parasmai◦ ←5◦प्र√अह, 2√ब्रू); 🕮*yogam* (2.53); *tam* (2.1); *viddhi* (2.17); *pāṇḍava* (4.35); *na* (1.30); *hi* (1.11); 🕮*asannyastasaṅkalpaḥ:* (m◦ 1nom◦ sing◦ ←bahuvrī◦ *a-sannyasta-saṅkalpa*, न संन्यस्ताः सङ्कल्पाः येन । न संन्यस्तः सङ्कल्पः येन ←adj◦ *sannyasta* (renounced) 4.41 + m◦ *saṅkalpa* (desire) 4.19); *yogī* (5.24); *bhavati* (1.44); *kaśćana* (3.18) (6.2)

(§3) *yam* (adj1◦-obj◦ that which); *sannyāsam* (obj◦ sannyāsa, renunciation, renunciation of authorship of karma);[429] *iti* (as); *prāhuḥ:* (they say. they call); *yogam* (adj2◦-obj◦ yoga, niṣkāmakarmayoga, renunciation of the desire in the fruit of karma);[430] *tam* (adj3◦-obj◦ that); *viddhi* (you please know); *pāṇḍava* (O Pāṇḍava! O Arjuna!); *na* (not, does not); *hi* (because); *asannyastasaṅkalpaḥ:* (adj◦-subj◦ he who has not renounced desires); *yogī* (subj2◦ a yogī); *bhavati* (he becomes); *kaśćana* (anyone, one) (6.2)

(§4) yam prāhuḥ: iti sannyāsam viddhi tam yogam hi pāṇḍava na kaśćana asannyastasaṅkalpaḥ: bhavati yogī

(§5) That which they say as *sannyāsa,* you please know that (to be) *yoga.* Because,[431] O Arjuna! one who has not renounced desires does not become a *yogī.* (6.2)

6.3 आरुरुक्षोर्मुनेर्योगं कर्म कारणमुच्यते ।
योगारूढस्य तस्यैव शमः कारणमुच्यते ।।
āruruksormuneryogaṁ karma kāraṇamućyate,
yogārūḍhasya tasyaiva śamaḥ: kāraṇamućyate. (6.3)

(§1) आरुरुक्षः मुनेः योगम् कर्म कारणम् उच्यते । योगारूढस्य तस्य एव शमः कारणम् उच्यते । *āruruksoḥ:* (r◦ 16/12) *muneḥ:* (r◦ 16/10) *yogam* (r◦ 14/1) *karma karaṇam* (r◦ 8/20, 24/3) *ućyate yogāruḍhasya tasya* (r◦ 3/1) *eva śamaḥ:* (r◦ 22/1) *kāraṇam* (r◦ 8/20, 24/3) *ućyate*

(§2) *āruruksoḥ:* (m◦ 6pos◦s. sing◦ ←parasmai◦ des◦ ◦adj◦ *āruruksu* (desiring ascendance) ←1◦आ√रुह); *muneḥ:* (2.69); *yogam* (2.53); *karma* (2.49); 🕮***kāraṇam*** (1nom◦ sing◦ ←n◦ *kāraṇa* (cause) 3.13); *ućyate* (2.25);

---

[429] (Elsewhere◦ *nsannyāsa* संन्यास → the abandonment of all action as well as its fruit, desire for sens gratification ...etc.)

[430] (Elsewhere◦ *yoga* योग → which consists in performance of action, the abandonment, disciplined activity, linking oneself with the Supreme ...etc.)

[431] See footnote in verse 3.5

📖*yogārūḍhasya* (m◦ 6pos◦ sing◦ ←bahuvrī◦ ***yogārūḍha,*** योगे आरूढ: य: ←m◦ *yoga* 2.39 + ppp◦ adj◦ **ārūḍha** (ascended) ←1◦आ√रुह्); *tasya* (1.12); *eva* (1.1); 📖***śamaḥ:*** (1nom◦ sing◦ ←m◦ ***śama*** (tranquality) ←4◦√शम्); *karaṇam* (↑); *ućyate* (2.25) (6.3)

(§3) *āruruksoḥ:* (for him who desires to ascend); *muneḥ:* (for a muni, for an ascetic); *yogam* (obj1◦ yoga, karmayoga); *karma* (subj1◦ karma, niṣkāmakarma); *kāraṇam* (subj2◦ the cause, the reason); *ućyate* (it is called); *yogārūḍhasya* (for him who has ascended the yoga, for the yogī); *tasya* (for that, for that yogī); *eva* (too, also, and); *śamaḥ:* (subj4◦ tranquility); *karaṇam* (subj4◦ the cause, the reason); *ućyate* (it is called) (6.3)

(§4) muneḥ: āruruksoḥ: yogam karma ućyate kāraṇam eva yogārūḍhasya tasya śamaḥ: ućyate karaṇam

(§5) For an ascetic who desires to ascend *yoga, niṣkāmakarma*[432] is called the cause; and him who has ascended the *yoga* for that *yogī,* tranquility is called the cause.

(6.3)

6.4 यदा हि नेन्द्रियार्थेषु न कर्मस्वनुषज्जते ।
सर्वसङ्कल्पसंन्यासी योगारूढस्तदोच्यते ।।

yadā hi nendriyārtheṣu na karmasvanuṣajjate,
sarvasaṅkalpasannyāsī yogārūḍhastadoćyate. (6.4)

(§1) यदा हि न इन्द्रियार्थेषु न कर्मषु अनुषज्जते । सर्वसङ्कल्पसंन्यासी योगारूढ: तदा उच्यते । *yadā hi na* (r◦ 2/1) *indriyārtheṣu* (r◦ 25/5) *na karmasu* (r◦ 4/6) *anuṣajjate sarvasaṅkalpasannyāsī yogārūḍhaḥ:* (r◦ 18/1) *tadā* (r◦ 2/4) *ućyate*

(§2) *yadā* (2.52); *hi* (1.11); *na* (1.30); *indriyārtheṣu* (5.9); *na* (1.30); *karmasu* (2.50); 📖***anuṣajjate*** (3rd-per◦ sing◦ pres◦ वर्तमान्-लट् ātmane◦ ←1◦अनु√सञ्ज्) *sarvasaṅkalpasannyāsī* (m◦ 1nom◦ sing◦ ←tatpu◦ *sarva-saṅkalpa-sannyāsin,* सर्वेषाम् सङ्कल्पानाम् संन्यासी ←pron◦ *sarva* 1.6 + m◦ 📖*saṅkalpa* (desire) 4.19 + m◦ *sannyāsin* 5.3); *yogārūḍhaḥ:* (m◦ 1nom◦ sing◦ ←adj◦ *yogārūḍha* 6.3); *tadā* (1.2); *ućyate* (2.25)

(6.4)

(§3) *yadā* (when); *hi* (because); *na* (neither); *indriyārtheṣu* (in the objects of the sense organs); *na* (nor); *karmasu* (in the karmas); *anuṣajjate* (he is shackled) *sarvasaṅkalpasannyāsī* (subj◦ the ascetic who vowed to renounce all desires); *yogārūḍhaḥ:* (adj◦-subj◦ yogāruḍha, the one who has ascended yoga); *tadā* (then); *ućyate* (he is called)

---

[432] (Elsewhere◦ *karma* → action, work, performance of duties ...etc.)

(§4) hi yadā anuṣajjate na indriyārtheṣu na karmasu tadā sarvasaṅkalpasannyāsī ucyate yogārūḍhaḥ:

(§5) Because,[433] when he is neither shackled in the objects of the sense organs nor in the *karmas*, then the ascetic who has vowed to renounce all desires, is called *yogārūḍha*, 'the one who has ascended yoga.' (6.4)

6.5 उद्धरेदात्मनात्मानं नात्मानमवसादयेत् ।
आत्मैव ह्यात्मनो बन्धुरात्मैव रिपुरात्मनः ।।
uddharedātmanātmānaṁ nātmānamavasādayet,
ātmaiva hyātmano bandhurātmaiva ripurātmanaḥ:. (6.5)

(§1) उद्धरेत् आत्मना आत्मानम् न आत्मानम् अवसादयेत् । आत्मा एव हि आत्मनः बन्धुः आत्मा एव रिपुः आत्मनः । *uddharet* (r◦ 8/3) *ātmanā* (r◦ 1/4) *ātmānam* (r◦ 14/1) *na* (r◦ 1/2) *ātmānam* (r◦ 8/16) *avasādayet* (r◦ 23/1) *ātmā* (r◦ 3/3) *eva hi* (r◦ 4/2) *ātmanaḥ:* (r◦ 15/7) *bandhuḥ:* (r◦ 16/3) *ātmā* (r◦ 3/3) *eva ripuḥ:* (r◦ 16/3) *ātmanaḥ:* (r◦ 22/8)

(§2) *uddharet* (3rd-per◦ sing◦ potential◦ विधि◦ parasmai◦ ←1◦उद्√धृ); *ātmanā* (2.55); *ātmānam* (3.43); *na* (1.30); *ātmānam* (↑); *avasādayet* (3rd-per◦ sing◦ potential◦ विधि◦ parasmai◦ caus◦ ←6◦अव√सद्); ***ātmā*** (1nom◦ sing◦ ←m◦ *ātman* (oneself) 2.41); *eva* (1.1); *hi* (1.11); *ātmanaḥ:* (4.42); 📖***bandhuḥ:*** (1nom◦ sing◦ ←m◦ *bandhu* 1.27); *ātmā* (↑); *eva* (1.1); 📖*ripuḥ:* (1nom◦ sing◦ ←m◦ *ripu* ←1◦√रप्); *ātmanaḥ:* (4.42) (6.5)

(§3) *uddharet* (one should uplift); *ātmanā* (by himself); *ātmānam* (obj◦ himself); *na* (not); *ātmānam* (obj◦ himself); *avasādayet* (one should degrade himself); *ātmā* (subj1◦ ātmā, he himself); *eva* (only); *hi* (because); *ātmanaḥ:* (of himself, his); *bandhuḥ:* (subj2◦ friend); *ātmā* (subj1◦ *ātmā,* he himself); *eva* (and); *ripuḥ:* (subj3◦ enemy); *ātmanaḥ:* (of himself, his) (6.5)

(§4) uddharet ātmanā ātmānam na ātmānam avasādayet ātmā eva hi ātmanaḥ: bandhuḥ: ātmā eva ripuḥ: ātmanaḥ:

(§5) One should uplift himself by himself. One should not degrade himself. Because,[434] only he himself (is) his friend, and he himself (is) his enemy. (6.5)

6.6 बन्धुरात्मात्मनस्तस्य येनात्मैवात्मना जितः ।
अनात्मनस्तु शत्रुत्वे वर्तेतात्मैव शत्रुवत् ।।

---

[433] See footnote in verse 3.5

[434] See footnote in verse 3.5

bandhurātmātmanastasya yenātmaivātmanā jitaḥ:,
anatmanastu śatrutve vartetātmaiva śatruvaṭ. (6.6)

(§1) बन्धुः आत्मा आत्मनः तस्य येन आत्मा एव आत्मना जितः । अनात्मनः तु शत्रुत्वे वर्तेत् आत्मा एव शत्रुवत् । *bandhuḥ:* (r◦ 16/3) *ātmā* (r◦ 1/4) *ātmanaḥ:* (r◦ 18/1) *tasya yena* (r◦ 1/2) *ātmā* (r◦ 3/3) *eva* (r◦ 1/2) *ātmanā jitaḥ:* (r◦ 22/8) *anātmanaḥ:* (r◦ 18/1) *tu śatrutve varteta* (r◦ 1/2) *ātmā* (r◦ 3/3) *eva śatruvaṭ*

(§2) *bandhuḥ:* (6.5); *ātmā* (6.5); *ātmanaḥ:* (4.42); *tasya* (1.12); *yena* (2.17); *ātmā* (6.5); *eva* (1.1); *ātmanā* (2.55); *jitaḥ:* (5.19); *anatmanaḥ:* (m◦ 6pos◦ sing◦ ←n.bahuvrī◦ *anātman*, नास्ति आत्मा यस्य ←n◦ *ātman* 2.41); *tu* (1.2); *śatrutve* (7loc◦ sing◦ ←n◦ *śatrutva* ←m◦ *śatru* 3.43); *varteta* (3rd-per◦ sing◦ potential◦ विधि◦ ātmane◦ ←1◦√वृत्); *ātmā* (6.5); *eva* (1.1); 🕮*śatruvaṭ* (m◦ *śatru* (enemy) 3.43 + affix *vaṭ* 2.29) (6.6)

(§3) *bandhuḥ:* (subj1◦ friend); *ātmā* (subj2◦ ātmā, he himself, his own self); *ātmanaḥ:* (of himself, his); *tasya* (his); *yena* (subj3◦ by whom); *ātmā* (obj◦ ātmā,[435] he himself, his own self); *eva* (only); *ātmanā* (by himself); *jitaḥ:* (adj◦-obj◦ the one that is conquered, is won); *anatmanaḥ:* (of the unconquered self); *tu* (however); *śatrutve* (in hostility); *varteta* (it behaves); *ātmā* (subj3◦ ātmā, he himself, his own self); *eva* (only); *śatruvaṭ* (like an enemy) (6.6)

(§4) yena ātmā jitaḥ: ātmanā eva ātmanaḥ: ātmā tasya bandhuḥ: tu anatmanaḥ: ātmā varteta eva śatrutve śatruvaṭ

(§5) By whom his own self is won by himself only, his own self (is) his friend; however, of the unconquered self, his own self behaves only in hostility like an enemy. (6.6)

6.7 **जितात्मनः प्रशान्तस्य परमात्मा समाहितः ।**
शीतोष्णसुखदुःखेषु तथा मानापमानयोः ।।
jitātmanaḥ: praśāntasya paramātmā samāhitaḥ:,
śītoṣṇasukhaduḥ:kheṣu tathā mānāpamānayoḥ:. (6.7)

(§1) जितात्मनः प्रशान्तस्य परमात्मा समाहितः । शीतोष्णसुखदुःखेषु तथा मानापमानयोः । *jitātmanaḥ:* (r◦ 22/3) *praśāntasya paramātmā samāhitaḥ:* (r◦ 22/8) *śītoṣṇasukhaduḥ:kheṣu* (r◦ 25/5) *tathā mānāpamānayoḥ:* (r◦ 22/8)

(§2) *jitātmanaḥ:* (m◦ 6pos◦ sing◦ ←bahuvrī◦ 🕮***jitātman***, जितः आत्मा यस्य ←adj◦ *jita* (won) 5.7 + m◦ *ātman*

---

[435] Elsewhere◦ आत्मा → atman

(oneself) 241); *praśāntasya* (m◦ 6pos◦ sing◦ ←s.pārdi bah◦ ppp◦ adj◦ 🕮**praśānta** (tranquil) ←4◦प्र√शम्); **paramātmā** (m◦ 1nom◦ sing◦ ←bahuvrī◦ *paramātman* (supreme-self) परम: आत्मा यस्य ←adj◦ *parama* (supreme) 1.17 + m◦ *ātman* (self) 2.41); 🕮*samāhitaḥ:* (m◦ 1nom◦ sing◦ ←ppp◦ adj◦ *samāhita* (reposed) ←3◦सम–आ√धा); **śītoṣṇasukhaduḥ:kheṣu** (7loc◦ plu◦ ←dvandva◦ शीतेषु च उष्णेषु च सुखेषु च दुःखेषु च 2.14); *tathā* (1.8); **mānāpamānayoḥ:** (7loc◦ dual◦ ←dvandva◦ माने च अपमाने च ←m◦ **māna** (respect) ←4◦√मन् + m◦ n.tatpu◦ *apamāna* (dishonour) ←4◦अप√मन्) (6.7)

(§3) *jitātmanaḥ:* (of him who has won himself); *praśāntasya* (of that tranquil person); *paramātmā* (subj◦ the supreme-self); *samāhitaḥ:* (adj◦-subj◦ reposed, the self-composed); *śītoṣṇasukhaduḥ:kheṣu* (in heat and in cold and in pleasure and in pain); *tathā* (as well as); *mānāpamānayoḥ:* (in honour and in dishonour) (6.7)

(§4) parmātmā praśāntasya jitātmanaḥ: samāhitaḥ: śītoṣṇasukhaduḥ:kheṣu tathā mānāpamānayoḥ:

(§5) The supreme-self of that tranquil person who has won himself (is) self-composed in heat and in cold and in pleasure and in pain as well as in honour and in dishonour. (6.7)

6.8 **ज्ञानविज्ञानतृप्तात्मा कूटस्थो विजितेन्द्रियः ।**
युक्त इत्युच्यते योगी समलोष्टाश्मकाञ्चनः ।।[436]
jñānavijñānatṛptātmā kūṭastho vijitendriyaḥ:,
yukta ityucyate yogī samaloṣṭāśmakāñcanaḥ:. (6.8)

(§1) ज्ञानविज्ञानतृप्तात्मा कूटस्थः विजितेन्द्रियः । युक्तः इति उच्यते योगी समलोष्टाश्मकाञ्चनः । *jñānavijñānatṛptātmā kūṭasthaḥ:* (r◦ 15/13) *vijitendriyaḥ:* (r◦ 22/8) *yuktaḥ:* (r◦ 19/2) *iti* (r◦ 4/3) *ucyate yogī samaloṣṭāśmakāñcanaḥ:* (r◦ 22/8)

(§2) *jñānavijñānatṛptātmā* (m◦ 1nom◦ sing◦ ←bahuvrī◦ *jñāna-vijñāna-tṛptātman*, ज्ञानेन च विज्ञानेन च तृप्तः आत्मा यस्य ←m◦ *jñāna* 3.3 + n◦ *vijñāna* (science, practical experience) 3.41 + adj◦ 🕮*tṛpta* (contented) 3.17 + m◦ *ātman* 2.41); 🕮**kūṭasthaḥ:** (m◦ 1nom◦ sing◦ ←adj◦ **kūṭastha** (unshaken) ←6◦√कूट्); 🕮*vijitendriyaḥ:* (m◦ 1nom◦ sing◦ ←bahuvrī◦ *vijitendriya*, विजितानि इन्द्रियाणि यस्य ←adj◦ *vijita* (won) 5.7 + n◦ *indriya* (organ) 2.8); *yuktaḥ:* (2.39); *iti* (1.25); *ucyate* (2.25); *yogī* (5.24); **samaloṣṭāśmakāñcanaḥ:** (m◦ 1nom◦ sing◦ ←bahuvrī◦ *sama-loṣṭāśma-kāñcana*, समानि लोष्टम् च अश्मा च काञ्चनम् च यस्मै ←adj◦ *sama* (equal) 1.4 + m◦ or n◦ *loṣṭa*

---

[436] निर्ममः शोभते धीरः समलोष्टाश्मकाञ्चनः । सुभिन्नहृदयग्रन्थिर्विनिधूतरजस्तमः ।। (aṣṭāvakragītā 18.88)

(clod) ←1∘√लोष्ट् + m∘ *aśman* (stone) ←9∘√अश् + n∘ *kāñćana* (gold) ←1∘√काञ्च्) (6.8)

(§3) *jñānavijñānatṛptātmā* (adj1∘-obj∘ he who is self content with the knowledge-of-self and with practical-experience); *kūṭasthaḥ:* (adj2∘-obj∘ seated at the apex, he who is rock seated, he whose faith is unshaken); *vijitendriyaḥ:* (adj3∘-obj∘ he who has conquered his sense organs); *yuktaḥ:* (adj4∘-obj∘ yukta, he who is equipped with yoga, he who is disciplined); *iti* (as); *ućyate* (obj∘ = yogī, yogī is **called** by people); *yogī* (obj∘ yogī); *samaloṣṭāśmakāñćanaḥ:* (adj5∘-obj∘ he for whom clod of soil, a stone and gold are all same, he who is indifferent to a clod of soil, a stone and a piece of gold) (6.8)

(§4) jñānavijñānatṛptātmā kūṭasthaḥ: vijitendriyaḥ: yuktaḥ: samaloṣṭāśmakāñćanaḥ: ućyate iti yogī

(§5) He who is self content with the knowledge-of-self and with practical-experience; he whose faith is unshaken; he who has conquered his sense organs; he who is equipped with yoga; he who is indifferent to a clod of soil, a stone and a piece of gold, he is called as *yogī.* (6.8)

6.9 **सुहृन्मित्रार्युदासीनमध्यस्थद्वेष्यबन्धुषु ।**
साधुष्वपि च पापेषु समबुद्धिर्विशिष्यते ॥
suhṛnmitrāryudāsīnamadhyasthadveṣyabandhuṣu,
sādhuṣvapi ća pāpeṣu samabuddhirviśiṣyate. (6.9)

(§1) सुहृद्-मित्र-अरि-उदासीन-मध्यस्थ-द्वेष्य-बन्धुषु । साधुषु अपि च पापेषु समबुद्धिः विशिष्यते । *suhṛd* (r∘ 12/3) *mitra* (r∘ 1/1) *ari* (r∘ 4/3) *udāsīna madhyastha dveṣya bandhuṣu* (r∘ 25/5) *sādhuṣu* (r∘ 25/5, 4/6) *api ća pāpeṣu* (r∘ 25/5) *samabuddhiḥ:* (r∘ 16/6) *viśiṣyate*

(§2) *suhṛtsu-mitreṣu-ariṣu-udāsīneṣu-madhyastheṣu-dveṣyeṣu-bandhuṣu* (m∘ 7loc∘ plu∘ dvandva∘ सुहृत्सु च मित्रेषु च अरिषु च उदासिनेषु च मध्यस्थेषु च द्वेष्येषु च बन्धुषु च ←m∘ *suhṛd* (wellwisher) 1.26 + m∘ *mitra* (friend) 1.38 + m∘ *ari* (enemy) 2.4 + deriv∘ 📖***udāsīna*** or adj∘ **udāsin** (indefferent) ←2∘उद्√आस् + m∘ 📖*madhyastha* ←*madhya* (middle) 1.21 + adj∘ *stha* (seated) 2.45 + m∘ ***dveṣya*** (hateful) ←2∘√द्विष् + m∘ *bandhu* (kinsman) 1.27); *sādhuṣu* (7loc∘ plu∘ ←m∘ *sādhu* (sage) 4.8); *api* (1.26); *ća* (1.1); *pāpeṣu* (7loc∘ plu∘ ←m∘ *pāpa* (sinful) 1.36); 📖*sama-buddhiḥ:* (m∘ 1nom∘ sing∘ ←bahuvrī∘ ***sama-buddhi***, समा बुद्धिः यस्य ←adj∘ *sama* (equanimous) 1.4 + f∘ *buddhi* (thinking) 1.23); *viśiṣyate* (excels, 3.7) (6.9)

(§3) *suhṛtsu-mitreṣu-ariṣu-udāsīneṣu-madhyastheṣu-dveṣyeṣu-bandhuṣu* (in the well-wishers, the friends, the foes, the indifferent, the neutrals, the hatefuls, the kinsmen); *sādhuṣu* (in the righteous people); *api* (also, as well as); *ća* (and); *pāpeṣu* (in the sinful people, the unrighteous people); *samabuddhiḥ:* (subj∘ he who has equanimous mind); *viśiṣyate* (he excels) (6.9)

(§4) samabuddhiḥ: suhṛtsu-mitreṣu-ariṣu-udāsīneṣu-madhyastheṣu-dveṣyeṣu-bandhuṣu api sādhuṣu ća pāpeṣu viśiṣyate

(§5) He who has equanimous mind in the well-wishers, the friends, the foes, the indifferent, the neutrals, the hatefuls, the kinsmen, as well as in the righteous people and the unrighteous people, he excels. (6.9)

6.10 योगी युञ्जीत सततमात्मानं रहसि स्थित: ।
एकाकी यतचित्तात्मा निराशीरपरिग्रह: ।।
yogī yuñjīta satatamātmānaṁ rahasi sthitaḥ:,
ekākī yataćittātmā nirāśīraparigrahaḥ:. (6.10)

(§1) योगी युञ्जीत सततम् आत्मानम् रहसि स्थित: । एकाकी यतचित्तात्मा निराशी: अपरिग्रह: । *yogī yuñjīta satataṃ* (r◦ 8/17) *ātmānaṃ* (r◦ 14/1) *rahasi sthitaḥ:* (r◦ 22/8) *ekākī yataćittātmā nirāśīḥ:* (r◦ 16/2) *aparigrahaḥ:* (r◦ 22/8)

(§2) *yogī* (5.24); *yuñjīta* (3rd-per◦ sing◦ potential◦ विधि◦ ātmane◦ ←7◦√युज्); *satataṃ* (3.19); *ātmānaṃ* (3.43); 🕮*rahasi* (7loc◦ sing◦ ←n◦ *rahaṣ* (solitude) ←1◦√रम्); *sthitaḥ:* (5.20); 🕮*ekākī* (m◦ 1nom◦ sing◦ ←adj◦ *ekākiṇ* (alone) ←1◦√इ); *yataćittātmā* (4.21); *nirāśīḥ:* (indifferent 3.30); 🕮*a-parigrahaḥ:* (m◦ 1nom◦ sing◦ n.tatpu◦ ←m◦ *parigraha* (greed) 4.21) (6.10)

(§3) *yogī* (subj◦ the yogī); *yuñjīta* (he should concentrate, he should meditate); *satataṃ* (always); *ātmānaṃ* (obj◦ himself); *rahasi* (in solitude); *sthitaḥ: ekākī* (adj1◦-subj◦ alone, remained alone); *yataćittātmā* (adj2◦-subj◦ he who is disciplined); *nirāśīḥ:* (adj3◦-subj◦ he who is non-covetous); *aparigrahaḥ:* (adj4◦-subj◦ he who has no desire of acquiring, he who has no greed) (6.10)

(§4) yogī yataćittātmā nirāśīḥ: aparigrahaḥ: yuñjīta ātmānaṃ satataṃ rahasi sthitaḥ: ekākī

(§5) The yogī, who is disciplined, who is non-covetous, who has no desire of acquiring, he should meditate himself always in solitude, alone. (6.10)

6.11 शुचौ देशे प्रतिष्ठाप्य स्थिरमासनमात्मन: ।
नात्युच्छ्रितं नातिनीचं चैलाजिनकुशोत्तरम् ।।
śućau deśe pratiṣṭhāpya sthiramāsanamātmanaḥ:,
nātyuććhritaṁ nātinīćaṁ ćailājinakuśottaraṃ; (6.11)

(§1) शुचौ देशे प्रतिष्ठाप्य स्थिरम् आसनम् आत्मन: । न अति उच्छ्रितम् न अति नीचम् चैलाजिनकुशोत्तरम् । *śućaudeśe pratiṣṭhāpya sthiraṃ* (r◦ 8/17) *āsanaṃ* (r◦ 8/17) *ātmanaḥ:* (r◦ 22/8) *na* (r◦ 1/1) *atyuććhritaṃ* (r◦ 14/1) *na* (r◦ 1/1) *atinīćaṃ* (r◦ 14/1) *ćailājinakuśottaraṃ* (r◦ 14/2)

(§2) *śućau* (m∘ 7loc∘ sing∘ ←adj∘ ***śući*** (clean) ←1∘√शुच्); ***deśe*** (7loc∘ sing∘ ←m∘ ***deśa*** (place) ←6∘√दिश्); *pratiṣṭhāpya* (caus∘lyp∘ past-participle ind∘ ←1∘प्रति√स्था + णिच्); ***sthiram*** (n∘ 2acc∘ sing∘ ←adj∘ *sthira* (steady) 1.16); *āsanam* (2acc∘ sing∘ ←n∘ ***āsana*** (seat) ←2∘√आस्); *ātmanaḥ:* ((one's) 4.42); *na* (1.30); *atyuććhritam* (n∘ 2acc∘ sing∘ ←ind∘ indicating degree ***ati*** (very) ←1∘√अत् + ppp∘ adj∘ 🕮*uććhrita* (high) ←1∘उद्√श्रि); *na* (1.30); *atinīćam* (n∘ 2acc∘ sing∘ ←ind∘ *ati* ↑ + adj∘ 🕮*nīća* (low) ←5∘नि-ई√चि); *ćailājinakuśottaram* (n∘ 2acc∘ sing∘ ←bah∘ *ćailājina-kuśottara,* चैलम् च अजिनम् च कुशाः च उत्तरम् यस्मिन् ←n∘ *ćaila* (cloth) ←1∘**√चेल्** + n∘ *ajina* (deer skin) ←7∘**√अज्** + m∘ *kuśa* (grass) ←1∘कु√शी + adj∘ or n∘ 🕮***uttara*** (top) ←1∘उद्√तॄ) (6.11)

(§3) *śućau* (in clean); *deśe* (in a place); *pratiṣṭhāpya* (having caused to be placed, having placed); *sthiram* (adj1∘-obj∘ steady); *āsanam* (obj∘ seat); *ātmanaḥ:* (one's); *na* (neither); *atyuććhritam* (adj2∘-obj∘ the one that is too high, very elevated); *na* (nor); *atinīćam* (adj3∘-obj∘ too low, very deep); *ćailājinakuśottaram* (adj4∘-obj∘ the one that has the last layer of *kuśa* grass, followed by a deer skin and then a white cloth) (6.11)

(§4) pratiṣṭhāpya ātmanaḥ: sthiram āsanam ćailājinakuśottaram śućau deśe na atyuććhritam na atinīćam

(§5) Having placed one's steady seat that has the last layer of *kuśa* grass, followed by a deer skin and then a white cloth, in a clean place, that is neither too high nor too low; (6.11)

6.12 **तत्रैकाग्रं मनः कृत्वा यतचित्तेन्द्रियक्रियः ।**
उपविश्यासने युञ्ज्याद्योगमात्मविशुद्धये ।।
tatraikāgarṁ manaḥ: kṛtvā yataćittendriyakriyaḥ:,
upaviśyāsane yuñjyādyogamātmaviśuddhaye. (6.12)

(§1) तत्र एकाग्रम् मनः कृत्वा यतचित्तेन्द्रियक्रियः । उपविश्य आसने युञ्ज्यात् योगम् आत्मविशुद्धये । *tatra* (r∘ 3/1) *ekāgarm* (r∘ 14/1) *manaḥ:* (r∘ 22/1) *kṛtvā yataćittendriyakriyaḥ:* (r∘ 22/8) *upaviśya* (r∘ 1/2) *āsane yuñjyāt* (r∘ 9/9) *yogam* (r∘ 8/17) *ātmaviśuddhaye*

(§2) *tatra* (1.26); *ekāgarm* (n∘ 2acc∘ sing∘ ←bahuvrī∘ 🕮***ekāgar*** (one pointed) एकम् अग्रम् यस्य तत् ←adj∘ *eka* (one) 2.41 + n∘ ***agra*** (point) ←1∘√अङ्ग्); ***manaḥ:*** (2acc∘ sing∘ ←n∘ *manaṣ* (mind) 1.30); *kṛtvā* (2.38); *yataćittendriyakriyaḥ:* (m∘ 1nom∘ sing∘ ←bahuvrī∘ *yata-ćittendriya-kriya,* यताः चित्तस्य च इन्द्रियाणाम् च क्रियाः यस्य ←adj∘ *yata* (united) 4.21 + n∘ *ćitta* (mind) 4.21 + n∘ *indriya* (organ) 2.8 + f∘ *kriyā* (activity) 1.42); *upaviśya* (lyp∘ past-participle ind∘ ←6∘उप√विश्); *āsane* (7loc∘ sing∘ ←n∘ *āsana* (seat) 6.11); *yuñjyāt* (3rd-per∘ sing∘ potential∘ विधि∘ parasmai∘ ←7∘√युज् 6.10); *yogam* (2.53); *ātmaviśuddhaye* (f∘ 4dat∘ sing∘ ←tatpu∘ *ātma-viśuddhi,* आत्मनः विशुद्धिः ←m∘ *ātman* 2.41 + f∘ 🕮***viśuddhi*** (purification) ←4∘वि√शुध् 5.11)

(6.12)

(§3) *tatra* (there, on that seat); *ekāgarm̩* (adj∘-obj∘ one pointed, concentrated); *manaḥ:* (obj1∘ the mind); *kṛtvā* (having made); *yatacittendriyakriyaḥ:* (subj∘ he who has controlled the activities of mind and sense organs); *upaviśya* (having seated); *āsane* (on the seat); *yuñjyāt̩* (he should attach); *yogam̩* (obj2∘ to yoga); *ātmaviśuddhaye* (for self-purification, for his own purification) (6.12)

(§4) tatra upaviśya āsane kṛtvā manaḥ: ekāgarm̩ yatacittendriyakriyaḥ: yuñjyāt̩ yogam̩ ātmaviśuddhaye

(§5) There, having seated on that seat, having made the mind one pointed, he who has controlled the activities of mind and sense organs,[437] he should attach[438] (himself) to yoga for his own purification. (6.12)

6.13 समं कायशिरोग्रीवं धारयन्नचलं स्थिर: ।
सम्प्रेक्ष्य नासिकाग्रं स्वं दिशश्चानवलोकयन् ।।

samaṁ kāyaśirogrīvaṁ dhārayannacalaṁ sthiraḥ:,
samprekṣya nāsikāgraṁ svaṁ diśaścānavalokayan̩. (6.13)

(§1) समम् कायशिरोग्रीवम् धारयन् अचलम् स्थिर: । सम्प्रेक्ष्य नासिकाग्रम् स्वम् दिश: च अनवलोकयन् । *samam̩* (r∘ 14/1) *kāyaśirogrīvam̩* (r∘ 14/1) *dhārayan̩* (r∘ 13/1) *acalam̩* (r∘ 14/1) *sthiraḥ:* (r∘ 22/8) *samprekṣya nāsikāgram̩* (r∘ 14/1) *svam̩* (r∘ 14/1) *diśaḥ:* (r∘ 17/1) *ca* (r∘ 1/1) *anavalokayan̩*

(§2) 🕮***samam*** (2acc∘ sing∘ ←adj∘ *sama* (straight) 5.19); *kāyaśirogrīvam̩* (2acc∘ sing∘ ←dvandva∘ कायम् च शिर: च ग्रीवम् च ←m∘ or m∘ *kāya* (body) 5.11 + n∘ *śīras* (head) ←9∘√शॄ + m∘ *grīva* = *graiva* =f∘ *grīvā* (neck)

---

[437] Elsewhere∘ *ekāgram manaḥ: kṛtvā yatacittendriyakriyaḥ:* → making the mind one-pointed and restraining the activities of...; making the mind one-pointed and restraining the thinking...; by controlling his mind..and fixing the mind on one point ...; concentrating the mind and controlling the functions of the mine...; making the mind one-pointed and controlling his thought...; making the mind one-pointed and keeping the actions of... etc.

🕮 In एकाग्रम् मन: कृत्वा यतचित्तेन्द्रियक्रिय:, the participle **कृत्वा can only qualify the objective (Accusative 2nd case) मन: only. It can not qualify the m∘ subject (Nominative 1st case) यतचित्तेन्द्रियक्रिय:** । Here, मन: कृत्वा and यतचित्तेन्द्रियक्रिय: are two independent claues. मन: कृत्वा and यतचित्तेन्द्रियक्रिय: कृत्वा are not two connected actions. मन: कृत्वा is an action, but **यतचित्तेन्द्रियक्रिय: is not an action. It is a m. noun**. यतचित्तेन्द्रियक्रिय: is not a तत्पुरुष-समास: and therefore **it is not a feminine क्रिया action**. यतचित्तेन्द्रियक्रिय: is a बहुव्रीहि-समास: denoting m∘ adj∘ HE WHO has performed the....क्रिया ।

[438] Elsewhere∘ *yuñjyāt̩* → let him practise.

←9∘√गॄ); *dhārayan̡* (5.9); ***aćalam̡*** (2acc∘ sing∘ ←n.tatpu∘ adj∘ *aćala* (steady) 2.24); ***sthirah̤:*** (m∘ 1nom∘ sing∘ ←adj∘ *sthira* (steady) 1.16); *sampreks̤ya* (lyp∘ past-participle ind∘ ←1∘सम्–प्र–√ईक्ष्); *nāsikāgram̡* (n∘ 2acc∘ sing∘ ←tatpu∘ *nāsikāgra* (tip of nose) नासिकाया: अग्रम् ←f∘ *nāsikā* (nose) ←1∘√नास् + n∘ *agra* (tip) 6.12); *svam̡* (n∘ 2acc∘ sing∘ ←adj∘ *sva* (own) 1.28); ***diśah̤:*** (2acc∘ plu∘ ←f∘ *diś* (direction) ←6∘√दिश्); *ća* (1.1); *anavalokayan̡* (1nom∘ sing∘ n.tatpu∘ ←śatr̤∘ adj∘ *anavalokayat̡* (looking) ←1∘अन्–अव√लोक्) (6.13)

(§3) *samam̡* (adj1∘-obj1∘ straight); *kāyaśirogrīvam̡* (obj1∘ the body, head and neck - collective); *dhārayan̡* (adj1∘-subj∘ while holding); *aćalam̡* (adj2∘-obj1∘ still, motionless); *sthirah̤:* (adj2∘-subj∘ steady, being steady);[439] *sampreks̤ya* (seeing with a concentrated focus); *nāsikāgram̡* (obj2∘ the tip of nose); *svam̡* (his); *diśah̤:* (obj3∘ to the directions, here and there); *ća* (and); *anavalokayan̡* (adj3∘-subj∘ while not looking) (6.13)

(§4) dhārayan̡ kāyaśirogrīvam̡ samam̡ aćalam̡ sthirah̤: sampreks̤ya svam̡ nāsikāgram̡ ća anavalokayan̡ diśah̤:

(§5) While holding the body, head and neck straight (and) still; being steady;[440] seeing the tip of his nose with a concentrated focus; and while not looking here and there;

(6.13)

6.14 प्रशान्तात्मा विगतभीर्ब्रह्मचारिव्रते स्थितः ।
मनः संयम्य मच्चित्तो युक्त आसीत मत्परः ।।
praśāntātmā vigatabhīrbrahmaćārivrate sthitah̤:,
manah̤: sam̐yamya maććitto yukta āsīta matparh̤:. (6.14)

(§1) प्रशान्तात्मा विगतभी: ब्रह्मचारिव्रते स्थित: । मन: संयम्य मच्चित्त: युक्त: आसीत मत्पर: । *praśāntātmā*

---

[439] NOTE: m∘ स्थिर: can not be an adjective∘ of the n∘ object कायशिरोग्रीवम् । This object has only two n∘ adj∘ (समं and अचलम्) in this verse. स्थिर: is m∘ adjective of the m∘ subject *yogī.* It is not स्थिरम्, it is स्थिर: ।

[440] Elsewhere∘ *samam̐ kāyaśirogrīvam̐ dhārayannaćalam̐ sthirah̤:* → holding the body, head and neck erect, motionless and steady; let him firmly hold the body body, head and neck erect and still; holding the body, head and neck erect, immovably steady; ...etc.

📖 In समं कायशिरोग्रीवं धारयन्नचलं स्थिर:, n∘ अचलं and m∘ स्थिर: can not be the adjectives of one and the same subject. Please note that n∘ समम् and n∘ अचलम् are two adjectives (not adverbs) of the collective object (Accusative 2nd case) n∘ कायशिरोग्रीवम् । Also, as said in the previous footnote, स्थिर: is the m∘ adjective of m∘ subject (Nominative 1st. case) and thus can not qualify the n∘ Accusative object कायशिरोग्रीवम्, unless it was n∘ स्थिरम् । The m∘ adj∘ स्थिर: qualifies the m∘ subject *yogī,* which is not actually mentioned in the verse.

vigatabhīḥ: (r◦ 16/7) *brahmaćārivrate sthitaḥ:* (r◦ 22/8) *manaḥ:* (r◦ 22/7) *saṁyamya maććittaḥ:* (r◦ 15/10) *yuktaḥ:* (r◦ 19/1) *āsīta matparaḥ:* (r◦ 22/8)

(§2) 🕮*praśāntātmā* (m◦ 1nom◦ sing◦ ←bahuvrī◦ *praśāntātman,* प्रशान्तः आत्मा यस्य ←adj◦ *praśānta* (tranquil) 6.7 + m◦ *ātman* (oneself) 2.41); 🕮*vigatabhīḥ:* (m◦ 1nom◦ sing◦ ←bahuvrī◦ *vigatabhī* (unafraid) विगता भीः यस्य ←adj◦ *vigata* (gone) 2.56 + f◦ ***bhī*** (fear) ←3◦√भी); *brahmaćārivrate* (7loc◦ sing◦ ←n◦ tatpu◦ *brahmaćāri-vrata,* ब्रह्मचारिणः व्रतम् ←adj◦ or m◦ *brahmaćārin* (chastity) ←1◦√बृंह् + adj◦ *ćārin* 5.27 + n◦ *vrata* (austerity) 4.28); *sthitaḥ:* (5.20); *manaḥ:* (2acc◦ 6.12); *saṁyamya* (2.61); ***maććittaḥ:*** (m◦ 1nom◦ sing◦ ←bahuvrī◦ ***maććitta,*** मयि चित्तम् यस्य ←pron◦ *mat* (me) 1.9 + n◦ *ćitta* (mind) 4.21); *yuktaḥ:* (2.39); *āsīta* (2.54); *matparaḥ:* (2.61) (6.14)

(§3) *praśāntātmā* (adj1◦-subj◦ he who is tranquil); *vigatabhīḥ:* (adj2◦-subj◦ he whose fear has gone away); *brahmaćārivrate* (in the austerity of chastity); *sthitaḥ:* (adj3◦-subj◦ he who is established); *manaḥ:* (obj◦ mind); *saṁyamya* (having controlled); *maććittaḥ:* (adj4◦-subj◦ he whose heart is fixed in me); *yuktaḥ:* (adj5◦-subj◦ disciplined, he who is disciplined); *āsīta* (he should sit); *matparaḥ:* (adj6◦-subj◦ he who is *matparayaṇaḥ:*, he for whom I am the highest goal) (6.14)

(§4) praśāntātmā vigatabhīḥ: sthitaḥ: brahmaćārivrate saṁyamya manaḥ: maććittaḥ: yuktaḥ: āsīta matparaḥ:

(§5) He who is tranquil, he whose fear has gone away, he who is established in the austerity of chastity having controlled (his) mind, he whose heart is fixed in me,[441] (and) he who is disciplined, he should sit (as) the one for whom I am the highest goal.[442] (6.14)

6.15 युञ्जन्नेवं सदात्मानं योगी नियतमानसः ।
शान्तिं निर्वाणपरमां मत्संस्थामधिगच्छति ॥
yuñjannevaṁ sadātmānaṁ yogī niyatamānasaḥ:,
śāntiṁ nirvāṇaparmāṁ matsaṁsthāmadhigaććhati. (6.15)

(§1) युञ्जन् एवम् सदा आत्मानम् योगी नियतमानसः । शान्तिम् निर्वाणपरमाम् मत्संस्थाम् अधिगच्छति । *yuñjan* (r◦ 13/5) *evam* (r◦ 14/1) *sadā* (r◦ 1/4) *ātmānam* (r◦ 14/1) *yogī niyatamānasaḥ:* (r◦ 22/8) *śāntim* (r◦ 14/1) *nirvāṇaparmām* (r◦ 14/1) *matsaṁsthām* (r◦ 8/16) *adhigaććhati*

---

[441] Elsewhere◦ *maććittaḥ:*→ thinking on Me, thinking of Me, thinking about Me ...etc.

🕮 मच्चित्तः is not a gerund or verb.

[442] Elsewhere◦ *matparaḥ:* → aspiring after Me, having Me..., should make Me the ultimate goal... etc.

🕮 मत्परः is not gerund or a potential mood.

(§2) ***yuñjan̦*** (1nom∘ sing∘ ←śatr̥∘ adj∘ parasmai∘ ***yuñjaț*** ←7∘√युज्); *evam̦* (1.24); *sadā* (1.40); *ātmānam̦* (3.43); *yogī* (5.24); 🕮*niyatamānasah̦:* (m∘ 1nom∘ sing∘ ←bahuvrī∘ *niyata-mānasa,* नियतम् मानसम् यस्य ←adj∘ *niyata* (disciplined) 1.44 + n∘ *mānasa* (mind) 1.47); *śāntim̦* (2.70); *nirvāṇaparmām̦* (f∘ 2acc∘ sing∘ ←bahuvrī∘ *nirvāṇa-parmā,* निर्वाणम् परमम् यस्या: ←adj∘ *nirvāṇam̦* (final liberation) 2.72 + adj∘ *parama* 1.17); *matsam̐sthām̦* (f∘ 2acc∘ sing∘ ←bahuvrī∘ adj∘ *mat-sam̐sthā,* मयि संस्था यस्या: ←pron∘ *maț* 1.9 + f∘ *sam̐sthā* (abiding) ←1∘सम्√स्था); *adhigaćchati* (2.64) (6.15)

(§3) *yuñjan̦* (adj1∘-subj∘ by connecting, while connecting, while concentrating on, while contemplating); *evam̦* (in this manner); *sadā* (always); *ātmānam̦* (obj∘ to himself, himself); *yogī* (subj∘ the yogī); *niyatamānasah̦:* (adj2∘-subj∘ he whose mind is disciplined); *śāntim̦* (obj2∘ the peace); *nirvāṇaparmām̦* (adj1∘-obj2∘ the one that culminates in the final liberation); *matsam̐sthām̦* (adj2∘-obj2∘ the one that abides in Me); *adhigaćchati* (he attains) (6.15)

(§4) yogī sadā niyatamānasah̦: evam̦ yuñjan̦ ātmānam̦ adhigaćchati śāntim̦ matsam̐sthām̦ nirvāṇaparmām̦

(§5) The yogī, whose mind is always disciplined in this manner by connecting himself,[443] he attains the peace that abides in Me (and) that culminates in the final liberation. (6.15)

6.16 नात्यश्नतस्तु योगोऽस्ति न चैकान्तमनश्नतः ।
न चाति स्वप्नशीलस्य जाग्रतो नैव चार्जुन ॥

nātyaśnatastu yogo‘sti na ćaikāntamanaśnatah̦:,
na ćāti svapnaśīlasya jāgrato naiva ćārjuna. (6.16)

(§1) न अत्यश्नत: तु योग: अस्ति न च एकान्तम् अनश्नत: । न च अति स्वप्नशीलस्य जाग्रत: न एव च अर्जुन । *na* (r∘ 1/1) *ati* (r∘ 4/1) *aśnatah̦:* (r∘ 18/1) *tu yogah̦:* (r∘ 15/1) *asti na ća* (r∘ 3/1) *ekāntam̦* (r∘ 8/16) *aśnatah̦:* (r∘ 22/8) *na ća* (r∘ 1/1) *ati svapnaśīlasya jāgratah̦:* (r∘ 15/6) *na* (r∘ 3/1) *eva ća* (r∘ 1/1) *arjuna*

(§2) *na* (1.30); *atyaśnatah̦:* (m∘ 6pos∘ sing∘ ←tatpu∘ *atyaśnaț* ←ind∘ *ati* (too much) 6.11 + adj∘ *aśnaț* (eating) 5.8); *tu* (1.2); *yogah̦:* (2.48); *asti* (2.40); *na* (1.30); *ća* (1.1); 🕮*ekāntam̦* (adv∘ ←adj∘ *eka* (one bit) 2.41); *aśnatah̦:* (m∘ 6pos∘ sing∘ n.tatpu∘ ←adj∘ *aśnaț* (eating) 5.8); *na* (1.30); *ća* (1.1); *ati* (6.11); *svapnaśīlasya* (m∘ 6pos∘ sing∘ ←bahuvrī∘ 🕮*svapna-śīla,* स्वप्तुम् शीलम् यस्य: स: ←m∘ ***svapna*** (sleep) ←2∘√स्वप् + n∘ *śīla* (heart) ←1∘√शील्); *jāgratah̦:* (m∘ 6pos∘ sing∘ ←śatr̥∘ adj∘ 🕮*jāgraț* (staying awake) ←2∘√जागृ); *na* (1.30); *eva*

---

[443] Elsewhere∘ *ātmānam̦* → of the body, mind and soul; with the self; of the self; by the self; in the self; to Me; ...etc.

🕮 आत्मानम् is Accusative 2nd case (आत्मानम्–आत्मानौ–आत्मन:), third person pronoun, he.

(1.1); ća (1.1); *arjuna* (2.2) (6.16)

(§3) *na* (not); *atyaśnataḥ:* (for him who eats too much);[444] *tu* (but); *yogaḥ:* (subj∘ yoga); *asti* (is); *na* (not); *ća* (and); *ekāntam* (too little); *aśnataḥ:* (for him who eats); *na* (not); *ća* (and); *ati* (too much); *svapnaśīlasya* (for him who sleeps too much); *jāgrataḥ:* (for him who stays awake); *na* (not); *eva* (also); *ća* (and); *arjuna* (O Arjuna!) (6.16)

(§4) tu arjuna yogaḥ: asti na atyaśnataḥ: ća na aśnataḥ: ekāntam ća na svapnaśīlasya ća eva na jāgrataḥ: ati

(§5) But, O Arjuna! *yoga* is not for him who eats too much; and not for him who eats too little; and not for him who sleeps too much; and also not for him who stays awake too much. (6.16)

6.17 युक्ताहारविहारस्य युक्तचेष्टस्य कर्मसु ।
युक्तस्वप्नावबोधस्य योगो भवति दुःखहा ।।
yuktāhāravihārasya yuktaćeṣṭasya karmasu,
yuktasvapnāvabodhasya yogo bhavati duḥ:khahā. (6.17)

(§1) युक्त–आहार–विहारस्य युक्त–चेष्टस्य कर्मसु । युक्त–स्वप्न–अवबोधस्य योगः भवति दुःखहा । *yuktāhāravihārasya yuktaćeṣtsya karmasu yuktasvapnāvabodhasya yogaḥ:* (r∘ 15/8) *bhavati duḥ:khahā*

(§2) *yuktāhāravihārasya* (for him m∘ 6pos∘ sing∘ ←bahuvrī∘ *yuktāhāra-vihāra*, युक्तः आहारः च विहारः च यस्य ←adj∘ *yukta* (disciplined) 1.14 + m∘ *āhāra* (eating) 2.59 + m∘ *vihāra* (pastime) ←3∘वि√हृ); *yuktaćeṣṭasya* (m∘ 6pos∘ sing∘ ←bahuvrī∘ *yukta-ćeṣṭa*, युक्ता चेष्टा यस्य ←adj∘ *yukta* 1.14 + f∘ *ćeṣṭā* (activity) ←1∘√चेष्ट्); *karmasu* (2.50); *yuktasvapnāvabodhasya* (m∘ 6pos∘ sing∘ ←bahuvrī∘ *yukta-svapnāvabodha*, युक्तम् स्वप्नम् च अवबोधः च यस्य ←adj∘ *yukta* 1.14 + n∘ *svapna* (sleep) 6.16 + m∘ *avabodha* (moving around) ←1∘अव√बुध्); *yogaḥ:* (2.48); *bhavati* (1.44); *duḥ:khahā* (1nom∘ sing∘ ←m∘ bah∘ adj∘ 🕮*duḥ:khahā* → *duh:kham* (grief) 5.6, v∘ *hanti* 2.19, pron∘ *yaḥ:* 2.19) (6.17)

(§3) *yuktāhāravihārasya* (for him whose eating and pastimes are disciplined);[445] *yuktaćeṣṭasya* (for

---

[444] Here, the Possessive case (of), when translated into English, appears as if it is a secondary Dative case (for), due to उपपदविभक्तिः । Same is true for the other three adjectives *ekāntamanaśnataḥ:*, *svapnaśīlasya* and *ati-jāgrataḥ;* in this verse and the three adjectives, *yuktāhāravihārasya, yuktaćeṣṭasya* and *yuktasvapnāvabodhasya* of the next verse.

[445] Remember, युक्त is a past passive participle → (he who is) disciplined.

🕮 We have used this adjective for युक्त–योगी in 6.8, the yogi who is disciplined; योगयुक्तः in 5.6, 5.7, 8.27; we have also used adj∘ युक्तः with similar meaning in 2.61 and 6.14 (युक्तः आसीत मत्परः); 4.18 (सः युक्तः), 5.8 (युक्तः

him whose activities are disciplined); *karmasu* (in karmas, in performing karmas); *yuktasvapnāvabodhasya* (for him whose sleeping and waking is disciplined); *yogaḥ:* (subj∘ yoga); *bhavati* (it becomes); *duḥ:khahāḥ:* (adj∘-subj∘ he who is the remover of grief, the one that removes suffering) (6.17)

(§4) yuktāhāravihārasya yuktaćeṣṭasya karmasu yuktasvapnāvabodhasya yogaḥ: bhavati duḥ:khahāḥ:

(§5) He whose eating and pastimes are disciplined, for him whose activities in performing karmas are disciplined, whose sleeping and waking is disciplined, for him *yoga* becomes the remover of grief. (6.17)

6.18 यदा विनियतं चित्तमात्मन्येवावतिष्ठते ।
निःस्पृहः सर्वकामेभ्यो युक्त इत्युच्यते तदा ।।

yadā viniyataṁ ćttamātmanyevāvatiṣṭhate,
niḥ:spṛhaḥ: sarvakāmebhyo yukta ityućyate tadā. (6.18)

(§1) यदा विनियतम् चित्तम् आत्मनि एव अवतिष्ठते । निःस्पृहः सर्वकामेभ्यः युक्तः इति उच्यते तदा । *yadā viniyataṃ* (r∘ 14/1) *ćittaṃ* (r∘ 8/17) *ātmani* (r∘ 4/4) *eva* (r∘ 1/1) *avatiṣṭhate niḥ:spṛhaḥ:* (r∘ 22/7) *sarvakāmebhyaḥ:* (r∘ 15/10) *yuktaḥ:* (r∘ 19/2) *iti* (r∘ 4/3) *ućyate tadā*

(§2) *yadā* (2.52); 🕮*viniyataṃ* (n∘ 1nom∘ sing∘ ←ppp∘ adj∘ *viniyata* ←adv∘ *niyata* (restrained) 1.44); ***ćittaṃ*** (1nom∘ sing∘ ←n∘ *ćitta* (mind) 4.21); *ātmani* (2.55); *eva* (1.1); *avatiṣṭhate* (3rd-per∘ sing∘ pres∘ वर्तमान्–लट् ātmane∘ ←1∘अव√स्था); *niḥ:spṛhaḥ:* (2.71); *sarvakāmebhyaḥ:* (सर्वेभ्यः कामेभ्यः m∘ 5abl∘ sing∘ ←pron∘ *sarva* 1.6 + m∘ *kāma* 1.22); *yuktaḥ:* (2.39); *iti* (1.25); *ućyate* (2.25); *tadā* (1.2)

(§3) *yadā* (when); *viniyataṃ* (adj∘-subj∘ the restrained); *ćittaṃ* (subj∘ mind); *ātmani* (in himself); *eva* (only); *avatiṣṭhate* (it abides, it rests); *niḥ:spṛhaḥ:* (adj1∘-subj2∘ one who is free from longing); *sarvakāmebhyaḥ:* (for all desires); *yuktaḥ:* (adj∘-obj∘ disciplined); *iti* (as); *ućyate* (he is called, he is called by people); *tadā* (then) (6.18)

(§4) yadā viniyataṃ ćittaṃ avatiṣṭhate eva ātmani niḥ:spṛhaḥ: sarvakāmebhyaḥ: tadā ućyate iti yuktaḥ:

(§5) When the restrained mind abides[446] only in himself (and he) is free from longing for all

---

मन्येत), 6.18 (युक्तः इति उच्यते तदा); and we will use it in next chapter 7.18 युक्तात्मा and 7.30 युक्तचेतसः ...and so on.

[446] Elsewhere∘ *avatiṣṭhate* → he is absorbed, mind is established ...etc.

🕮 The verb पर्यवतिष्ठते is not performed by he. The doer is by the mind. The mind is subject (Nominative

desires, then he is called as 'disciplined.' (6.18)

6.19 यथा दीपो निवातस्थो नेङ्गते सोपमा स्मृता ।
योगिनो यतचित्तस्य युञ्जतो योगमात्मनः ।।

yathā dīpo nivātastho neṅgate sopamā smṛtā,
yogino yataćittasya yuñjato yogamātmanaḥ:. (6.19)

(§1) यथा दीपः निवातस्थः न इङ्गते सा उपमा स्मृता । योगिनः यतचित्तस्य युञ्जतः योगम् आत्मनः । *yathā dīpaḥ:* (r◦ 15/6) *nivātasthaḥ:* (r◦ 15/6) *na* (r◦ 2/1) *iṅgate* *sā* (r◦ 2/4) *upamā*[447] *smṛtā yoginaḥ:* (r◦ 15/10) *yataćittasya yuñjataḥ:* (r◦ 15/10) *yogam̩* (r◦ 8/17) *ātmanaḥ:* (r◦ 22/8)

(§2) *yathā* (1.11); *dīpaḥ:* (1nom◦ sing◦ ←m◦ ***dīpa*** (lamp) ←4◦√दीप्); *nivātasthaḥ:* (m◦ 1nom◦ sing◦ ←ppp◦ adj◦ *nivāta-stha* (located in calm place) ←n◦ 🕮*nivāta* ←2◦नि√वा + adj◦ *stha* 2.45); *na* (1.30); ***iṅgate*** (3rd-per◦ sing◦ pres◦ वर्तमान्–लट् ātmane◦ ←1◦√इङ्ग्); *sā* (2.69); *upamā* (1nom◦ sing◦ ←f◦ 🕮***upamā*** (simile) ←3◦उप√मा); 🕮*smṛtā* (f◦ 1nom◦ sing◦ ←ppp◦ adj◦ ***smṛta*** (recalled) ←1◦√स्मृ); *yoginaḥ:* (4.25); *yataćittasya* (m◦ 6pos◦ sing◦ ←s-tat̩◦ *yata-ćitta,* यतम् चित्तम् ←adj◦ *yata* (restyrained) 4.21 + n◦ *ćitta* (mind) 4.21); *yuñjataḥ:* (m◦ 6pos◦ sing◦ ←adj◦ *yuñjat̩* 6.15); *yogam̩* (2.53); *ātmanaḥ:* (4.42) (6.19)

(§3) *yathā* (just as); *dīpaḥ:* (subj1◦ the lamp); *nivātasthaḥ:* (adj◦-subj1◦ located in a windless place); *na* (does not); *iṅgate* (it agitates, flickers); *sā* (adj1◦-subj2◦ that); *upamā* (subj2◦ simile, example); *smṛtā* (adj2◦-subj2◦ is known, remembered); *yoginaḥ:* (of yogī, for the yogī); *yataćittasya* (of disciplined mind); *yuñjataḥ:* (adj◦-subj3◦ while concentrating on, while performing); *yogam̩* (obj◦ yoga); *ātmanaḥ:* (of self, his own) (6.19)

(§4) yathā dīpaḥ: nivātasthaḥ: na iṅgate sā upamā smṛtā yoginaḥ: ātmanaḥ: yataćittasya yuñjataḥ: yogam̩

(§5) Just as the lamp located in a windless place[448] does not flicker, that[449] simile is known for

---

1st. case) for this verb. Also, पर्यवतिष्ठते is not a perfect tense, it is present (लट्) tense → it establishes.

[447] Elsewhere◦ *sopamā* → *saḥ upamā*

🕮 सोपमा is *sandhi* between सा + उपमा (स् + अ + उ = सो). But, सः + उपमा = स उपमा (see rules and the chart for visarga sandhi given in earlier chapter), not सोपमा. Moreover, सः is m◦ and उपमा is f◦

[448] Elsewhere◦ *nivātasthaḥ:* → in an airless palce, ...etc.

[449] Elsewhere◦ *sā* → this, it ...etc.

🕮 The pronoun तद् = he, she, that. The f◦ Nominative सा = she or that. The pronouns एतद् and इदम् = this, it. The f◦ Nominative of एतद् and इदम् would be एषा and इयम् ।

the *yogī* of self-disciplined mind,[450] while performing yoga.[451] (6.19)

6.20 यत्रोपरमते चित्तं निरुद्धं योगसेवया ।
यत्र चैवात्मनात्मानं पश्यन्नात्मनि तुष्यति ।।
yatroparamate ćttaṁ niruddhaṁ yogasevayā,
yatra ćaivātmanātmānaṁ paśyannātmani tuṣyati; (6.20)

(§1) यत्र उपरमते चित्तम् निरुद्धम् योगसेवया । यत्र च एव आत्मना आत्मानम् पश्यन् आत्मनि तुष्यति । *yatra* (r◦ 2/2) *uparamate ćittaṃ* (r◦ 14/1) *niruddhaṃ* (r◦ 14/1) *yogasevayā yatra ća* (r◦ 3/1) *eva* (r◦ 1/2) *ātmanā* (r◦ 1/4) *ātmānaṃ* (r◦ 14/1) *paśyaṇ* (r◦ 13/2) *ātmani tuṣyati*

(§2) ***yatra*** (place or time indicating ind◦ ←pron◦ *yad* 1.7); *uparamate* (3rd-per◦ sing◦ pres◦ वर्तमान्-लट् ātmane◦ ←1◦उप√रम्); *ćittaṃ* (6.18); 🕮*niruddhaṃ* (n◦ 1nom◦ sing◦ ←ppp◦ adj◦ *niruddha* (restrained) ←7◦नि√रुध्); *yogasevayā* (f◦ 3inst◦ sing◦ ←tatpu◦ *yoga-sevā*, योगस्य सेवा ←m◦ *yoga* 2.39 + f◦ *sevā* (practice) 4.34); *yatra* (↑); ća (1.1); *eva* (1.1); *ātmanā* (2.55); *ātmānaṃ* (3.43); *paśyaṇ* (5.8); *ātmani* (2.55); *tuṣyati* (3rd-per◦ sing◦ pres◦ वर्तमान्-लट् parasmai◦ ←1◦√तुष्) (6.20)

(§3) *yatra* (where, the state in which); *uparamate* (it quietens, it calms down, it comes to rest); *ćittaṃ* (subj1◦ the mind); *niruddhaṃ* (adj◦-subj1◦ the one that is restrained); *yogasevayā* (with practice of yoga); *yatra* (where, the state in which); *ća* (and); *eva* (also); *ātmanā* (by himself); *ātmānaṃ* (obj1◦ oneself, himself); *paśyaṇ* (adj◦-subj2◦ while seeing, the seer); *ātmani* (in himself); *tuṣyati* (he pleases) (6.20)

(§4) yatra ćittaṃ niruddhaṃ yogasevayā uparamate ća eva yatra paśyaṇ tuṣyati ātmānaṃ ātmanā ātmani

(§5) **The state[452] in which the mind, that is restrained with practice of *yoga*, comes to rest and also the state in which[453] the seer pleases himself by himself in himself;** (6.20)

---

[450] Elsewhre *yataćittasya* → of subdued thinking, of subdued mind ...etc.

[451] Elsewhere◦ translated like युञ्जतः योगम्-आत्मानम् ।

[452] The counter part of this यत्र (the state in which...) is not तत्र, but it is तम् (...to that state) which comes at the beginning of verse 6.23. The यम् that comes at the beginning of verse 6.22 is just a pronominal adjective for this यत्र । Thus these three verses are tied together. This यत्र (the state in which) is mentioned again in this verse, and again in the next verse.

[453] Elsewhere◦ *yatra* → when.

6.21 सुखमात्यन्तिकं यत्तद्बुद्धिग्राह्यमतीन्द्रियम् ।
वेत्ति यत्र न चैवायं स्थितश्चलति तत्त्वतः ।।

sukhamātyantikaṁ yattadbuddhigrāhyamatīndriyam,
vetti yatra na ćaivāyaṁ sthitasćalati tattvataḥ:. (6.21)

(§1) सुखम् आत्यन्तिकम् यत् तत् बुद्धिग्राह्यम् अतीन्द्रियम् । वेत्ति यत्र न च एव अयम् स्थितः चलति तत्त्वतः । *sukham̩* (r∘ 8/17) *ātyantikam̩* (r∘ 14/1) *yat̩* (r∘ 1/10) *tat̩* (r∘ 9/7) *buddhigrāhyam̩* (r∘ 8/16) *atīndriyam̩* (r∘ 14/2) *vetti yatra na ća* (r∘ 3/1) *eva* (r∘ 1/1) *ayam̩* (r∘ 14/1) *sthitaḥ:* (r∘ 17/1) *ćalati tattvataḥ:* (r∘ 22/8)

(§2) *sukham̩* (2acc∘ 5.13); 🕮*ātyantikam̩* (n∘ 2acc∘ sing∘ ←adj∘ taddhita∘ *ātyantika* (infinite) ←adj∘ *atyanta* (very much) ←10∘√अम्; *yat̩* (2acc∘ 2.67); *tat̩* (2acc∘ 1.10); *buddhigrāhyam̩* (n∘ 2acc∘ sing∘ ←pot∘ adj∘ *buddhi-grāhya*, बुद्ध्या ग्राह्यम् ←f∘ *buddhi* (thinking) 1.23 + pot∘ adj∘ *grāhya* (accessible) ←9∘√ग्रह्); *atīndriyam̩* (n∘ 2acc∘ sing∘ ←bahuvrī∘ adj∘ *atīndriya* (beyond senses) इन्द्रियेभ्यः अतीतम् यत् ←n∘ *indriya* (organ) 2.8 + ind∘ prefix *ati* 6.11); *vetti* (2.19); *yatra* (6.20); *na* (1.30); *ća* (1.1); *eva* (1.1); *ayam̩* (2.19); *sthitaḥ:* (5.20); *ćalati* (3rd-per∘ sing∘ pres∘ वर्तमान्–लट् parasmai∘ ←1∘√चल्); *tattvataḥ:* (5abl∘ 4.9) (6.21)

(§3) *sukham̩* (obj∘ the happiness); *ātyantikam̩* (adj1∘-obj∘ infinite); *yat̩* (adj2∘-obj∘ which); *tat̩* (adj3∘-obj∘ that, that happiness, that happy state); *buddhigrāhyam̩* (adj4∘-obj∘ accessible to mind, fathomable); *atīndriyam̩* (adj5∘-obj∘ beyond the realm of the sense organs, the one that transcends the senses); *vetti* (he knows, he perceives); *yatra* (subj∘ the state in which); *na* (does not); *ća* (and); *eva* (only); *ayam̩* (he); *sthitaḥ:* (adj∘-subj∘ one who is established); *ćalati* (he deviates, wavers, departs); *tattvataḥ:* (in reality; from the essence) (6.21)

(§4) tat̩ yatra vetti ātyantikam̩ sukham̩ yat̩ atīndriyam̩ ća eva buddhigrāhyam̩ sthitaḥ: ayam̩ na ćalati tattvataḥ:

(§5) That state, in which, he perceives infinite happiness which *(is)* beyond the realm of the sense organs[454] and only accessible to mind,[455] established[456] (in it) he does not deviate from the

---

[454] Elsewhere∘ *atīndriyam̩* → transcendental senses.

🕮 अतीन्द्रियम् is not about the senses, but about that which is beyond the senses (अतीतम्).

[455] Elsewhere∘ *buddhigrāhyam̩* → grasped by the intelligence, perceived by the intellect, perceived by intelligence, ..etc.

🕮 बुद्धिग्राह्य, is not a ppp∘. बुद्धिग्राह्य, बुद्धिग्रहणीय, and बुद्धिग्रहीतव्य are three potential participles that indicate that which can be grasped by thinking, which is perceivable by mind.

[456] Elsewhere∘ *sthitaḥ:* → having become steadfast.

🕮 स्थितः is ppp∘, having become is gerund स्थित्वा ।

essence. (6.21)

6.22 यं लब्ध्वा चापरं लाभं मन्यते नाधिकं ततः ।
यस्मिन्स्थितो न दुःखेन गुरुणापि विचाल्यते ।।
yaṁ labdhvā ćāparaṁ lābhaṁ manyate nādhikaṁ tataḥ:,
yasminsthito na duḥ:khena guruṇāpi vićālyate. (6.22)

(§1) यम् लब्ध्वा च अपरम् लाभम् मन्यते न अधिकम् ततः । यस्मिन् स्थितः न दुःखेन गुरुणा अपि विचाल्यते । *yam̦* (r◦ 14/1) *labdhvā ća* (r◦ 1/1) *aparam̦* (r◦ 14/1) *lābham̦* (r◦ 14/1) *manyate na* (r◦ 1/1) *adhikam̦* (r◦ 14/1) *tataḥ:* (r◦ 22/8) *yasmin̦* (r◦ 13/20) *sthitaḥ:* (r◦ 15/6) *na duḥ:khena guruṇā* (r◦ 24/4, 1/3) *api vićālyate*

(§2) *yam̦* (2.15); *labdhvā* (4.39); *ća* (1.1); *aparam̦* (4.4); *lābham̦* (2acc◦ sing◦ ←m◦ *lābha* (gain) 2.38); *manyate* (2.19); *na* (1.30); 📖*adhikam̦* (m◦ 2acc◦ sing◦ ←comparative adj◦ ***adhika*** (more) ←3◦न√धा); *tataḥ:* (1.13); ***yasmin̦*** (m◦ or n◦ 7loc◦ sing◦ ←pron◦ *yad* 1.7); *sthitaḥ:* (5.20); *na* (1.30); *duḥ:khena* (3inst◦ sing◦ ←n◦ *duḥ:kha* (sorrow) 2.14); 📖*guruṇā* (n◦ 3inst◦ sing◦ ←adj◦ *guru* (more) 2.5); *api* (1.26); ***vićālyate*** (3rd-per◦ sing◦ pres◦ वर्तमान्-लट् ātmane◦ caus◦ ←1◦√चल्) (6.22)

(§3) *yam̦* (obj1◦ which, that state which, that state); *labdhvā* (having achieved); *ća* (and); *aparam̦* (adj1◦-obj2◦ any other); *lābham̦* (obj2◦ gain); *manyate* (he considers); *na* (does not); *adhikam̦* (adj2◦-obj2◦ greater); *tataḥ:* (than that); *yasmin̦* (in which); *sthitaḥ:* (adj◦-subj◦ he who is established); *na* (not); *duḥ:khena* (by sorrow); *guruṇā* (by more profound, by a greater); *api* (also); *vićālyate* (he is caused to shake, he is shaken, he is disturbed) (6.22)

(§4) yam̦ labdhvā na manyate aparam̦ lābham̦ adhikam̦ tataḥ: ća sthitaḥ: yasmin̦ na vićālyate guruṇā duḥ:khena api

(§5) That state, having achieved, he does not consider any other gain greater than that; and established in which he is not shaken by more profound sorrow also. (6.22)

6.23 तं विद्याद्दुःखसंयोगवियोगं योगसंज्ञितम् ।
स निश्चयेन योक्तव्यो योगोऽनिर्विण्णचेतसा ।।
taṁ vidyādduḥ:khasaṁyogaviyogaṁ yogasañjñitam̦,
sa niśćayena yoktavyo yogo'nirviṇṇaćetasā. (6.23)

(§1) तम् विद्यात् दुःखसंयोगवियोगम् योगसंज्ञितम् । सः निश्चयेन योक्तव्यः योगः निर्विण्णचेतसा । *tam̦* (r◦ 14/1) *vidyāț* (r◦ 9/5) *duḥ:khasaṁyogaviyogam̦* (r◦ 14/1) *yogasañjñitam̦* (r◦ 14/2) *saḥ:* (r◦ 21/2) *niśćayena yoktavyaḥ:* (r◦ 15/10) *yogaḥ:* (r◦ 15/1) *anirviṇṇaćetasā*

(§2) *tam̦* (2.1); ***vidyāț*** (3rd-per◦ sing◦ potential◦ विधि◦ parasmai◦ ←2◦√विद्); *duḥ:khasaṁyogaviyogam̦*

(2acc◦ sing◦ ←tatpu◦ *duḥ:kha-saṁyoga-viyoga*, दुःखस्य संयोगात् वियोगः ←n◦ *duḥ:kha* (sorrow) 2.14 + m◦ *saṁyoga* (union) 5.14 + m◦ *viyoga* (severance) ←74वि√युज्); *yogasañjñitam̦* (2acc◦ sing◦ ←bahuvrī◦ *yoga-sañjñita* (called) योगः इति संज्ञितम् यः ←m◦ *yoga* 2.39 + ppp◦ adj◦ 🕮***sañjñita*** (known as) ←f◦ *sañjñā* 1.7); *saḥ:* (1.13); *niśćayena* (3inst◦ sing◦ ←m◦ *niśćaya* (determination) 2.37); 🕮*yoktavyaḥ:* (1nom◦ sing◦ ←pot◦ adj◦ *yoktavya* ←4◦√युज्); *yogaḥ:* (2.48); *a-nirviṇṇaćetasā* (3inst◦ sing◦ -s.ntaț◦ ←n◦ 🕮*nirviṇṇa-ćetaș*, निर्विण्णम् चेतः ←adj◦ *nirviṇṇa* (dejected) ←2◦निर्√विद् + n◦ *ćetaș* (mind) 1.38) (6.23)

(§3) *tam̦* (obj◦ that state); *vidyāț* (may be known as); *duḥ:khasaṁyogaviyogam̦* (adj1◦-obj◦ the state of union and severance from the contacts of sorrow); *yogasañjñitam̦* (adj2◦-obj◦ the one known as *yoga*); *saḥ:* (adj◦-subj2◦ that); *niśćayena* (with determination); *yoktavyaḥ:* (adj◦-subj2◦ ought to be practiced); *yogaḥ:* (subj2◦ yoga); *anirviṇṇaćetasā* (with undejected mind) (6.23)

(§4) tam̦ yogasañjñitam̦ vidyāț duḥ:khasaṁyogaviyogam̦ saḥ: yogaḥ: yoga yoktavyaḥ: a-nirviṇṇaćetasā niśćayena

(§5) That state,[457] the one known as *yoga* may be known as the state of union and severance from the contacts of sorrow. That *yoga* ought to be practiced with undejected mind (and) with determination. (6.23)

6.24 सङ्कल्पप्रभवान्कामांस्त्यक्त्वा सर्वानशेषतः ।
मनसैवेन्द्रियग्रामं विनियम्य समन्ततः ।।
ṡankalpaprabhavānkāmāṁstyaktvā sarvānaśeṣataḥ:,
manasaivendriyagrāmaṁ viniyamya samantataḥ:. (6.24)

(§1) सङ्कल्पप्रभवान् कामान् त्यक्त्वा सर्वान् अशेषतः । मनसा एव इन्द्रियग्रामम् विनियम्य समन्ततः । *ṡankalpaprabhavān̦* (r◦ 13/9) *kāmān̦* (r◦ 13/7) *tyaktvā sarvān̦* (r◦ 8/11) *aśeṣataḥ:* (r◦ 22/8) *manasā* (r◦ 3/3) *eva* (r◦ 2/1) *indriyagrāmam̦* (r◦ 14/1) *viniyamya samantataḥ:* (r◦ 22/8)

(§2) *ṡankalpaprabhavān̦* (m◦ 2acc◦ plu◦ ←bahuvrī◦ *ṡankalpa-prabhava*, सङ्कल्पात् प्रभवः यस्य ←m◦ *ṡankalpa* (desire) 4.19 + m◦ ***prabhava*** (mental state) ←1◦प्र√भू); *kāmān̦* (2.55); *tyaktvā* (1.33); *sarvān̦* (1.27); 🕮***aśeṣataḥ:*** (adv◦ ind◦ ←adj◦ *aśeṣa* (whole) 4.35); *manasā* (3.6); *eva* (1.1); ***indriyagrāmam̦*** (m◦ 2acc◦ sing◦ ←tatpu◦ *indriya-grāma*, इन्द्रियाणाम् ग्रामः ←n◦ *indriya* (organ) 2.8 + m◦ ***grāma*** (collective) ←1◦√ग्रस्); 🕮*viniyamya* (having restrained) (lyp◦ past-participle ind◦ ←1◦वि–नि√यम्); 🕮*samantataḥ:* (adv◦ ←bahuvrī◦ *samanta* (all over) सम्यक् अन्तः यत्र ←10◦सम्√अम्) (6.24)

---

[457] please see the connecting footnote in 6.20

(§3) *saṅkalpaprabhavān* (adj1∘-obj1∘ that arise out of mental resolve, vow, volition, will, desires); *kāmān* (obj1∘ cravings); *tyaktvā* (having given up, having renounced); *sarvān* (adj2∘-obj1∘ all); *aśeṣataḥ* (fully, wholly, without exception); *manasā* (by mind); *eva* (only); *indriyagrāmam* (obj2∘ all sense organs - clooective); *viniyamya* (having restrained); *samantataḥ* (from all sides) (6.24)

(§4) tyaktvā aśeṣataḥ sarvān kāmān saṅkalpaprabhavān viniyamya indriyagrāmam samantataḥ manasā eva;

(§5) Having given up wholly all cravings that arise out of volition, (and) having restrained all sense organs from all sides by mind only; (6.24)

6.25 शनै: शनैरुपरमेद्बुद्ध्या धृतिगृहीतया ।
आत्मसंस्थं मन: कृत्वा न किञ्चिदपि चिन्तयेत् ॥

śanaiḥ śanairuparamedbuddhyā dhṛtigṛhītayā,
ātmasaṁstham manaḥ kṛtvā na kiñćidapi ćintayeṭ. (6.25)

(§1) शनै: शनै: उपरमेत् बुद्ध्या धृतिगृहीतया । आत्मसंस्थम् मन: कृत्वा न किञ्चित् अपि चिन्तयेत् । *śanaiḥ* (r∘ 22/5) *śanaiḥ* (r∘ 16/4) *uparamet* (r∘ 9/7) *buddhyā dhṛtigṛhītayā* (r∘ 23/1) *ātmasaṁstham* (r∘ 14/1) *manaḥ* (r∘ 22/1) *kṛtvā na kiñćiṭ* (r∘ 8/2) *api ćintayeṭ*

(§2) 📖*śanaiḥ* (= adv∘ ind∘ *śanais* (slowly) ←1∘√शद्); *śanaiḥ* (↑); *uparameṭ* (3rd-per∘ sing∘ potential∘ विधि∘ parasmai∘ ←1∘उप√रम् 6.20); *buddhyā* (2.39); *dhṛtigṛhītayā* (f∘ 3inst∘ sing∘ ←tatpu∘ *dhṛti-gṛhītā*, धृत्या गृहीता ←f∘ 📖*dhṛti* (courage) ←1∘√धृ + f∘ ppp∘ adj∘ *gṛhītā* (held) ←9∘√ग्रह); *ātmasaṁstham* (n∘ 2acc∘ sing∘ ←tatpu∘ adj∘ *ātma-saṁstha*, आत्मनि संस्थम् ←m∘ *ātman* (oneself) 2.41+ adj∘ *saṁstha* (established) ←1∘सम्√स्था); *manaḥ* (1.30); *kṛtvā* (2.38); *na* (1.30); *kiñćiṭ* (4.20); *api* (1.26); *ćintayeṭ* (3rd-per∘ sing∘ potential∘ विधि∘ parasmai∘ caus∘ ←10∘√चिन्त्) (6.25)

(§3) *śanaiḥ śanaiḥ* (slowly slowly); *uparameṭ* (he may withraw, he may come to rest); *buddhyā* (with the thought); *dhṛtigṛhītayā* (by getting a grip on determination, courage); *ātmasaṁstham* (adj∘-obj∘ established in himself); *manaḥ* (obj∘ mind); *kṛtvā* (having made); *na* (not); *kiñćiṭ api* (about anything); *ćintayeṭ* (he should think) (6.25)

(§4) śanaiḥ śanaiḥ uparameṭ dhṛtigṛhītayā buddhyā kṛtvā manaḥ ātmasaṁstham na ćintayeṭ api kiñćiṭ

(§5) Slowly slowly he may withdraw, by getting a grip on determination (and) the <u>thought,</u>[458]

---

[458] Elsewhere∘ *buddhyā* → with the intellect, with the intelligence, by means of Reason ...etc.

having made the mind established in himself, he should not think about anything.[459] (6.25)

6.26 यतो यतो निश्चरति मनश्चञ्चलमस्थिरम् ।
ततस्ततो नियम्यैतदात्मन्येव वशं नयेत् ।।

yato yato niścarati manaścañcalamasthiram,
tatastato niyamyaitadātmanyeva vaśaṁ nayeta. (6.26)

(§1) यत: यत: निश्चरति मन: चञ्चलम् अस्थिरम् । तत: तत: नियम्य एतत् आत्मनि एव वशम् नयेत् । *yataḥ:* (r∘ 15/10) *yataḥ:* (r∘ 15/6) *niścarati manaḥ:* (r∘ 17/1) *cañcalam* (r∘ 8/16) *asthiram* (r∘ 14/2) *tataḥ:* (r∘ 18/1) *tataḥ:* (r∘ 15/6) *niyamya* (r∘ 3/1) *etat* (r∘ 8/3) *ātmani* (r∘ 4/4) *eva vaśam* (r∘ 14/1) *nayet*

(§2) 🕮***yataḥ:*** (from where) (ind∘ ←pron∘ *yad* 1.7); *yataḥ:* (↑); 🕮*niścarati* (3rd-per∘ sing∘ pres∘ वर्तमान्-लट् parasmai∘ ←1∘निर्√चर् 2.71); *manaḥ:* (1nom∘ 1.30); 🕮***cañcalam*** (n∘ 1nom∘ sing∘ ←adj∘ ***cañcala*** (restless) ←2∘चञ्च√ला); 🕮*asthiram* (unsteady) (n∘ 1nom∘ sing∘ n.tatpu∘ ←adj∘ *sthira* (steady) 1.16); *tataḥ:* (1.13); *tataḥ:* (1.13); *niyamya* (3.7); *etat* (2.3); *ātmani* (2.55); *eva* (1.1); *vaśam* (3.34); *nayet* (3rd-per∘ sing∘ potential∘ विधि∘ parasmai∘ ←1∘√नी) (6.26)

(§3) *yataḥ: yataḥ:* (from wherever, wheresover); *niścarati* (it wanders away); *manaḥ:* (subj∘ mind); *cañcalam* (adj∘-subj∘ the quick, the restless); *asthiram* (adj2∘-subj∘ unsteady); *tataḥ: tataḥ:* (from there, fromthence); *niyamya* (having restrained); *etat* (adj∘-obj∘ it); *ātmani* (in himself); *eva* (and); *vaśam* (under control); *nayet* (he should direct, he should bring) (6.26)

(§4) yataḥ: yataḥ: cañcalam asthiram manaḥ: niścarati tataḥ: tataḥ: niyamya etat ātmani eva nayet vaśam

(§5) Wherever[460] the quick[461] (and) unsteady mind wanders away, from there, having restrained it in himself, indeed he should bring (it) under control. (6.26)

6.27 प्रशान्तमनसं ह्येनं योगिनं सुखमुत्तमम् ।
उपैति शान्तरजसं ब्रह्मभूतमकल्मषम् ।।

---

[459] Elsewhere∘ *na cintayet kiñcit api* → let him not think of anything else.

🕮 It should be let him not think of anything. Because, adding adj∘ 'else' may mean let him think of somethings but not anything else. The ideal is, thinking nothing.

[460] Elsewhere∘ *yataḥ: yataḥ:* → whenever, whatsoever, whatever cause ...etc.

🕮 Remember, for this यत: यत: there is matching counter part तत: तत: (from there) in the next line.

[461] Elsewhere∘ *cañcalam* → moving, wavering, flickering ..etc.

🕮 चञ्चलं and अस्थिरं are not gerunds.

praśāntamanasaṁ hyenaṁ yoginaṁ sukhamuttamam,
upaiti śāntarajasaṁ brahmabhūtamakalmaṣam. (6.27)

(§1) प्रशान्तमनसम् हि एनम् योगिनम् सुखम् उत्तमम् । उपैति शान्तरजसम् ब्रह्मभूतम् अकल्मषम् । *praśāntamanasam* (r∘ 14/1) *hi* (r∘ 4/4) *enam* (r∘ 14/1) *yoginam* (r∘ 14/1) *sukham* (r∘ 8/20) *uttamam* (r∘ 14/2) *upaiti śāntarajasam* (r∘ 14/1) *brahmabhūtam* (r∘ 8/16) *akalmaṣam* (r∘ 14/2)

(§2) *praśāntamanasam* (m∘ 2acc∘ sing∘ ←bahuvrī∘ *praśānta-manas*, प्रशान्तम् मनः यस्य ←adj∘ *praśānta* (tranquil) 6.7 + n∘ *manas* (mind) 1.30); *hi* (1.11); *enam* (2.19); *yoginam* (2acc∘ sing∘ ←m∘ *yogin* 3.3); *sukham* (1nom∘ 2.66); *uttamam* (1nom∘ 4.3); ***upaiti*** (3rd-per∘ sing∘ pres∘ वर्तमान्–लट् parasmai∘ ←1∘उप√इ 4.9); *śāntarajasam* (m∘ 2acc∘ sing∘ ←bahuvrī∘ *śānta-rajasa*, शान्तम् रजः यस्य ←adj∘ *śānta* (quiet) ←4∘√शम् + n∘ *rajas* (rajo guṇa) 3.37); *brahmabhūtam* (m∘ 2acc∘ sing∘ ←adj∘ *brahma-bhūta* 5.24); 🕮*akalmaṣam* (m∘ 2acc∘ sing∘ n.tatpu∘ ←n∘ *kalmaṣa* 4.30) (6.27)

(§3) *praśāntamanasam* (adj1∘-obj∘ he whose mind is tranquil); *hi* (Because); *enam* (adj2∘-obj∘ to this); *yoginam* (obj∘ yogī); *sukham* (subj∘ happiness, peace); *uttamam* (adj∘-subj∘ the supreme); *upaiti* (it comes, it goes, it reaches); *śāntarajasam* (adj3∘-obj∘ he whose *rajo-guṇa* has subsided, he whose passions are subsided); *brahmabhūtam* (adj4∘-obj∘ he who has become one with brahma); *akalmaṣam* (adj5∘-subj∘ he who has become sinless) (6.27)

(§4) hi uttamam sukham upaiti enam yoginam praśāntamanasam śāntarajasam brahmabhūtam akalmaṣam

(§5) Because,[462] the supreme peace comes to this *yogī*[463] whose mind is tranquil, whose *rajo-guṇa* has subsided, who has become one with brahma (and) who has become sinless. (6.27)

6.28 युञ्जन्नेवं सदात्मानं योगी विगतकल्मषः ।
सुखेन ब्रह्मसंस्पर्शमत्यन्तं सुखमश्नुते ।।

yuñjannevaṁ sadātmānaṁ yogī vigatakalmaṣaḥ:,
sukhena brahmasaṁsparśamatyantaṁ sukhamaśnute. (6.28)

(§1) युञ्जन् एवम् सदा आत्मानम् योगी विगतकल्मषः । सुखेन ब्रह्मसंस्पर्शम् अत्यन्तम् सुखम् अश्नुते । *yuñjan* (r∘ 13/5) *evam* (r∘ 14/1) *sadā* (r∘ 1/4) *ātmānam* (r∘ 14/1) *yogī vigatakalmaṣaḥ:* (r∘ 22/8) *sukhena*

---

[462] See footnote in verse 3.5

[463] Elsewhere∘ The yogin...approaches the highest peace, the yogī...attains the highest perfection ...etc.

🕮 In this verse the योगिनं is not subject, it is the object (accusative), सुखं is the subject (nominative) performing the verb उपैति । In the next verse योगी is the subject performing the verb अश्नुते ।

brahmasaṁsparśaṃ (r◦ 8/16) *atyantaṃ* (r◦ 14/1) *sukhaṃ* (r◦ 8/16) *aśnute*

(§2) *yuñjaṇ* (6.15); *evaṃ* (1.24); *sadā* (1.40); *ātmānaṃ* (3.43); *yogī* (5.24); 🕮*vigatakalmaṣaḥ:* (m◦ 1nom◦ sing◦ ←bahuvrī◦ *vigata-kalmaṣa*, विगतम् कल्मषम् यस्य ←adj◦ *vigata* (gone) 2.56 + n◦ *kalmaṣa* (sin) 4.30); *sukhena* (3inst◦ sing◦ ←n◦ *sukha* (happiness) 1.32); *brahmasaṁsparśaṃ* (m◦ 2acc◦ sing◦ ←tatpu◦ *brahma-saṁsparśa*, ब्रह्मण: संस्पर्शम् ←n◦ *brahmaṇ* 2.72 + m◦ *saṁsparśa* (transcendence) 5.22); 🕮*atyantaṃ* (n◦ 2acc◦ sing◦ ←tatpu◦ adj◦ *atyanta* (infinite) अतिक्रान्त: अन्तम् ←10◦अति√अम्); *sukhaṃ* (2acc◦ 5.13); *aśnute* (3.4) (6.28)

(§3) *yuñjaṇ* (adj1◦-subj◦ while attaching, engagine, uniting); *evaṃ* (in this manner); *sadā* (always); *ātmānaṃ* (obj◦ himself); yogī (subj◦ the yogī); *vigatakalmaṣaḥ:* (adj2◦-subj◦ he whose sin has gone away); *sukhena* (easily); *brahmasaṁsparśaṃ* (adj1◦-obj2◦ to the transcendental contact of brahma); *atyantaṃ* (adj2◦-obj2◦ infinite, endless); *sukhaṃ* (obj2◦ the bliss, peace); *aśnute* (he enjoys) (6.28)

(§4) yogī vigatakalmaṣaḥ: sadā yuñjaṇ ātmānaṃ brahmasaṁsparśaṃ evaṃ sukhena aśnute atyantaṃ sukhaṃ

(§5) The yogī, whose sin has gone away, always while uniting himself to the transcendental contact of brahma, in this manner, easily he enjoys the infinite bliss.

(6.28)

6.29 **सर्वभूतस्थमात्मानं सर्वभूतानि चात्मनि ।**
ईक्षते योगयुक्तात्मा सर्वत्र समदर्शन: ।।

sarvabhūtasthamātmānaṁ sarvabhūtāni ćātmani,
īkṣate yogayuktātmā sarvatra samadarśanaḥ:. (6.29)

(§1) सर्वभूतस्थम् आत्मानम् सर्वभूतानि च आत्मनि । ईक्षते योगयुक्तात्मा सर्वत्र समदर्शन: । *sarvabhūtasthaṃ ātmānaṃ* (r◦ 14/1) *sarvabhūtāni ća* (r◦ 1/2) *ātmani* (r◦ 23/1) *īkṣate yogayuktātmā sarvatra samadarśanaḥ:* (r◦ 22/8)

(§2) *sarvabhūtasthaṃ* (n◦ 2acc◦ sing◦ ←bahuvrī◦ *sarva-bhūta-stha*, सर्वेषु भूतेषु स्थीयते तत् ←pron◦ *sarva* 1.6 + m◦ *bhūta* (being) 2.28 + adj◦ *stha* (seated) 2.45); *ātmānaṃ* (3.43); ***sarvabhūtāni*** (सर्वाणि भूतानि, 2acc◦ plu◦ ←pron◦ *sarva* 1.6 + n◦ *bhūta* 2.28); *ća* (1.1); *ātmani* (2.55); ***īkṣate*** (3rd-per◦ sing◦ pres◦ वर्तमान्-लट् ātmane◦ ←1◦√ईक्ष्); *yogayuktātmā* (m◦ 1nom◦ sing◦ ←bahuvrī◦ *yoga-yuktātmaṇ*, योगेन युक्त: आत्मा यस्य ←m◦ *yoga* 2.39 + adj◦ *yukta* (equipped) 1.14 + m◦ *ātmaṇ* 2.41); *sarvatra* (2.57); 🕮*samadarśanaḥ:* (1nom◦ sing◦ ←m◦ *samadarśana* (equanimity) ←1◦सम्√दृश्) (6.29)

(§3) *sarvabhūtasthaṃ* (adj◦-obj1◦ he who is seated in all beings, he who exists in all beings); *ātmānaṃ* (obj1◦ the ātmā, to the puroṣa); *sarvabhūtāni* (obj2◦ all beings); *ća* (and); *ātmani* (in himself); *īkṣate* (he perceives, he sees); *yogayuktātmā* (subj◦ he who is equipped with yoga); *sarvatra* (everywhere); *samadars̓anaḥ:* (adj◦-subj◦ he who has the outlook of equanimity) (6.29)

(§4) yogayuktātmā samadars̓anaḥ: īkṣate ātmānam̦ sarvabhūtastham̦ sarvatra c̓a sarvabhūtāni ātmani

(§5) He who is equipped with yoga (and) he who has the outlook of equanimity, he perceives the ātmā seated in all beings everywhere and all beings in himself. (6.29)

6.30 यो मां पश्यति सर्वत्र सर्वं च मयि पश्यति ।
तस्याहं न प्रणश्यामि स च मे न प्रणश्यति ।।

yo māṁ pas̓yati sarvatra sarvaṁ c̓a mayi pas̓yati,
tasyāhaṁ na praṇas̓yāmi sa c̓a me na praṇas̓yati. (6.30)

(§1) यः माम् पश्यति सर्वत्र सर्वम् च मयि पश्यति । तस्य अहम् न प्रणश्यामि सः च मे न प्रणश्यति । *yaḥ:* (r◦ 15/9) *mām̦* (r◦ 14/1) *pas̓yati sarvatra sarvam̦* (r◦ 14/1) *c̓a mayi pas̓yati tasya* (r◦ 1/1) *aham̦* (r◦ 14/1) *na praṇas̓yāmi saḥ:* (r◦ 17/1) *c̓a me na praṇas̓yati*

(§2) *yaḥ:* (2.19); *mām̦* (1.46); *pas̓yati* (2.29); *sarvatra* (2.57); *sarvam̦* (2.17); *c̓a* (1.1); *mayi* (3.30); *pas̓yati* (2.29); *tasya* (1.12); *aham̦* (1.22); *na* (1.30); 🕮*praṇas̓yāmi* (1st-per◦ sing◦ pres◦ वर्तमान्-लट् parasmai◦ ←4◦प्र√नश् 1.40); *saḥ:* (1.13); *c̓a* (1.1); *me* (1.21); *na* (1.30); *praṇas̓yati* (2.63) (6.30)

(§3) *yaḥ:* (subj1◦ he who); *mām̦* (obj1◦ me); *pas̓yati* (he perceives, he sees); *sarvatra* (everywhere); *sarvam̦* (obj2◦ everything); *c̓a* (and); *mayi* (in me); *pas̓yati* (he who perceives); *tasya* (of him, his); *aham̦* (subj2◦ I); *na* (do not); *praṇas̓yāmi* (I leave, I forsake, I desert); *saḥ:* (adj1◦-Subj1◦ he); *c̓a* (and); *me* (obj1◦ of me); *na* (does not); *praṇas̓yati* (he leaves, he lets go, he deserts) (6.30)

(§4) yaḥ: pas̓yati mām̦ sarvatra c̓a pas̓yati sarvam̦ mayi aham̦ na praṇas̓yāmi tasya c̓a saḥ: na praṇas̓yati me

(§5) He who perceives me everywhere and perceives everything in me, I do not let go of him and he does not let go of me.

6.31 सर्वभूतस्थितं यो मां भजत्येकत्वमास्थितः ।
सर्वथा वर्तमानोऽपि स योगी मयि वर्तते ।।

sarvabhūtasthitaṁ yo māṁ bhajatyekatvamāsthitaḥ:,
sarvathā vartamāno'pi sa yogī mayi vartate. (6.31)

(§1) सर्वभूतस्थितम् यः माम् भजति एकत्वम् आस्थितः । सर्वथा वर्तमानः अपि सः योगी मयि वर्तते । *sarvabhūtasthitam̦* (r◦ 14/1) *yaḥ:* (r◦ 15/9) *mām̦* (r◦ 14/1) *bhajati* (r◦ 4/4) *ekatvam̦* (r◦ 8/17) *āsthitaḥ:* (r◦ 22/8) *sarvathā vartamānaḥ:* (r◦ 15/1) *api saḥ:* (r◦ 21/2) *yogī mayi vartate*

(§2) *sarvabhūtasthitaṃ* (m◦ 2acc◦ sing◦ ←tatpu◦ *sarva-bhūta-sthita,* सर्वेषु भूतेषु स्थित: ←pron◦ *sarva* 1.6 + m◦ *bhūta* (being) 2.28 + adj◦ *sthita* (seated) 1.14); *yaḥ:* (2.19); *māṃ* (1.46); 🕮***bhajati*** (3rd-per◦ sing◦ pres◦ वर्तमान्-लट् parasmai◦ ←1◦√**भज्**); 🕮*ekatvaṃ* (adv◦ ←n◦ ***ekatva*** (focus) ←adj◦ *eka* 2.41); *āsthitaḥ:* (5.4); ***sarvathā*** (mode indicating ind◦ ←pron◦ *sarva* 1.6); ***vartamānaḥ:*** (1nom◦ sing◦ ←śānac◦ adj◦ ***vartamāna*** (living) ←1◦√वृत्); *api* (1.26); *saḥ:* (1.13); *yogī* (5.24); *mayi* (3.30); *vartate* (5.26) (6.31)

(§3) *sarvabhūtasthitaṃ* (adj◦-obj◦ he who abides in all beings); *yaḥ:* (adj1◦-subj◦ he who); *māṃ* (obj◦ me); *bhajati* (he worships, he serves); *ekatvaṃ* (in unity, in equanimity, in oneness); *āsthitaḥ:* (adj2◦-subj◦ established); *sarvathā* (in every which way); *vartamānaḥ:* (adj3◦-subj◦ being lived, making his living); *api* (even); *saḥ:* (adj4◦-subj◦ that); *yogī* (subj◦ yogī); *mayi* (in me); *vartate* (he abides) (6.31)

(§4) yaḥ: bhajati māṃ sarvabhūtasthitaṃ saḥ: yogī āsthitaḥ: ekatvaṃ vartate mayi api vartamānaḥ: sarvathā

(§5) He who worships Me, who abides in all beings, that *yogī* established in unity, abides in Me, even making his living[464] in every which way. (6.31)

6.32 आत्मौपम्येन सर्वत्र समं पश्यति योऽर्जुन ।
सुखं वा यदि वा दुःखं स योगी परमो मतः ।।
ātmaupamyena sarvatra samaṁ paśyati yo'rjuna,
sukhaṁ vā yadi vā duḥ:khaṁ sa yogī paramo mataḥ:. (6.32)

(§1) आत्मौपम्येन सर्वत्र समम् पश्यति य: अर्जुन । सुखम् वा यदि वा दु:खम् स: योगी परम: मत: । *ātmaupamyena sarvatra samaṃ* (r◦ 14/1) *paśyati yaḥ:* (r◦ 15/1) *arjuna sukhaṃ* (r◦ 14/1) *vā yadi vā duḥ:khaṃ* (r◦ 14/1) *saḥ:* (r◦ 21/2) *yogī paramaḥ:* (r◦ 15/9) *mataḥ:* (r◦ 22/8)

(§2) *ātmaupamyena* (n◦ 3inst◦ sing◦ ←bahuvrī◦ *ātmaupamya,* आत्मन: औपम्यम् ←m◦ *ātmaṇ* (own) 2.41 + adj◦ *aupamya* (comparison) ←f◦ *upamā* (simile) 6.19); *sarvatra* (2.57); *samaṃ* (2acc◦ 6.13); *paśyati* (2.29); *yaḥ:* (2.19); *arjuna* (2.2); *sukhaṃ* (5.13); *vā* (1.32); *yadi* (1.38); *vā* (1.32); *duḥ:khaṃ* (2acc◦ sing◦ ←n◦ *duh:kha* (sorrow) 2.14); *saḥ:* (1.13); *yogī* (5.24); *paramaḥ:* (m◦ 1nom◦ sing◦ ←adj◦ *parama* (supreme) 1.17); 🕮***mataḥ:*** (m◦ 1nom◦ sing◦ ←ppp◦ adj◦ ***mata*** (considered) ←8◦√मन्) (6.32)

(§3) *ātmaupamyena* (by comparison with himself); *sarvatra* (everywhere, everything); *samaṃ* (adj◦-

---

[464] Elsewhere◦ *sarvathā vartamānaḥ:* → no matter what he does, no matter how he appears to live, howsoever he may be active, in whatever condition he may be, whatever may be his mode of living ...etc.

🕮 वर्तमान is Present Active Participle formed form *ātmanepadī* root (1√वृत् to be, to live, to exist) of the first of the two groups of verbs, with मान (is being done) suffix. वर्तमान: → is being lived.

obj1,2◦ same); *paśyati* (he sees); *yaḥ:* (adj1◦-subj◦ he who); *arjuna* (O Arjuna!); *sukham̦* (obj1◦ pleasure); *vā yadi vā* (or); *duḥ:kham̦* (obj2◦ pain); *saḥ:* (adj2◦-subj◦ that); *yogī* (subj◦ yogī); *paramaḥ:* (adj3◦-subj◦ supreme); *mataḥ:* (adj4◦-subj◦ he is considered) (6.32)

(§4) ātmaupamyena yaḥ: paśyati sukham̦ vā-yadi-vā duḥ:kham̦ sarvatra samam̦ arjuna saḥ: yogī mataḥ: paramaḥ:

(§5) By comparison with himself, he who sees pleasure or pain everywhere same, O Arjuna! that yogī is considered supreme. (6.32)

Arjuna said (arjuna uvāća अर्जुन उवाच ।)

6.33 योऽयं योगस्त्वया प्रोक्तः साम्येन मधुसूदन ।
एतस्याहं न पश्यामि चञ्चलत्वात्स्थितिं स्थिराम् ।।
yo'yam̐ yogastvayā prokta: sāmyaena madhusūdana,
etasyāham̐ na paśyāmi ćañćalatvātsthitim̐ sthirām̦. (6.33)

(§1) य: अयम् योग: त्वया प्रोक्त: साम्येन मधुसूदन । एतस्य अहम् न पश्यामि चञ्चलत्वात् स्थितिम् स्थिराम् । *arjunaḥ:* (r◦ 19/4) *uvāća. yaḥ:* (r◦ 15/1) *ayam̦* (r◦ 14/1) *yogaḥ:* (r◦ 18/1) *tvayā proktaḥ:* (r◦ 22/7) *sāmyaena madhusūdana* (r◦ 23/1) *etasya* (r◦ 1/1) *aham̦* (r◦ 14/1) *na paśyāmi ćañćalatvāț* (r◦ 10/7) *sthitim̦* (r◦ 14/1) *sthirām̦* (r◦ 14/2)

(§2) *arjunaḥ:* (1.28); *uvāća* (1.25). *yaḥ:* (2.19); *ayam̦* (2.19); *yogaḥ:* (2.48); ***tvayā*** (3inst◦ sing◦ ←pron◦ *yuṣmad̦* 1.3); *proktaḥ:* (4.3); *sāmyaena* (3inst◦ sing◦ ←n◦ *sāmya* (equanimity) 5.19); *madhusūdana* (1.35); *etasya* (m◦ 6pos◦ sing◦ ←pron◦ *etad̦* 1.3); *aham̦* (1.22); *na* (1.30); *paśyāmi* (1.31); *ćañćalatvāț* (m◦ 5abl◦ sing◦ ←abstract noun *ćañćalatva* (unstability) ←adj◦ *ćañćala* 6.26); 🕮*sthitim̦* (2acc◦ sing◦ ←f◦ *sthiti* (state) 2.72); 🕮*sthirām̦* (f◦ 2acc◦ sing◦ ←adj◦ *sthira* (steady) 1.16) (6.33)

(§3) *arjunaḥ:* (subj◦ Arjuna); *uvāća* (said). *yaḥ:* (adj1◦-obj◦ which); *ayam̦* (adj2◦-obj◦ this); *yogaḥ:* (obj◦ yoga); *tvayā* (subj1◦ by you); *proktaḥ:* (adj3◦-obj◦ is told); *sāmyaena* (with equanimity); *madhusūdana* (O Madhusūdana!); *etasya* (of it, its); *aham̦* (subj2◦ I); *na* (do not); *paśyāmi* (I see); *ćañćalatvāț* (because of its unstable nature); *sthitim̦* (adj◦-obj2◦ state); *sthirām̦* (adj◦-obj2◦ stable) (6.33)

(§4) arjunaḥ: uvāća. ayam̦ yogaḥ: yaḥ: proktaḥ: tvayā sāmyaena madhusūdana aham̦ na paśyāmi etasya sthirām̦ sthitim̦ ćañćalatvāț

(§5) Arjuna said. This yoga which is told by you with equanimity,[465] O Kriṣṇa! I do not see its

[465] Elsewhere◦ *sāmyaena* → as evenness, as sameness, to be of the nature of equality, in the form of equanimity, of evenness, of equanimity ...etc.

permanent state because of capricious nature; (6.33)

6.34 चञ्चलं हि मनः कृष्ण प्रमाथि बलवद्दृढम् ।
तस्याहं निग्रहं मन्ये वायोरिव सुदुष्करम् ।।
ćañćalaṁ hi manaḥ: kṛṣṇa pramāthi balavaddṛḍham,
tasyāhaṁ nigrahaṁ manye vāyoriva suduṣkaram. (6.34)

(§1) चञ्चलम् हि मनः कृष्ण प्रमाथि बलवत् दृढम् । तस्य अहम् निग्रहम् मन्ये वायोः इव सुदुष्करम् । *ćañćalaṃ* (r∘ 14/1) *hi manaḥ:* (r∘ 22/1) *kṛṣṇa pramāthi balavat* (r∘ 9/5) *dṛḍhaṃ* (r∘ 14/2) *tasya* (r∘ 1/1) *ahaṃ* (r∘ 14/1) *nigrahaṃ* (r∘ 14/1) *manye vāyoḥ:* (r∘ 16/5) *iva suduṣkaraṃ* (r∘ 14/2)

(§2) *ćañćalaṃ* (6.26); *hi* (1.11); *manaḥ:* (1.30); *kṛṣṇa* (1.28); 🕮*pramāthi* (n∘ 1nom∘ sing∘ ←adj∘ *pramāthin* (exciting) 2.60); 🕮*balavat* (n∘ 1nom∘ sing∘ ←taddhita∘ adj∘ ***balavat*** (powerful) ←na∘ *bala* (power) 1.10 + affix *vatup* (possessor) 1.5); 🕮***dṛḍhaṃ*** (n∘ 1nom∘ sing∘ ←ppp∘ adj∘ ***dṛḍha*** (stubborn) ←4∘√दृह्); *tasya* (1.12); *ahaṃ* (1.22); 🕮*nigrahaṃ* (m∘ 2acc∘ sing∘ ←m∘ *nigraha* (control) 3.33); 🕮***manye*** (1st-per∘ sing∘ pres∘ वर्तमान्-लट् ātmane∘ ←4∘√मन्); *vāyoḥ:* (6pos sing∘ ←m∘ *vāyu* (wind) 2.67); *iva* (1.30); 🕮*suduṣkaraṃ* (n∘ 2acc∘ sing∘ ←adj∘ *suduṣkara* (very difficult) ←ind∘ *su* 5.1 + adj∘ *duṣkara* (difficult) ←8∘दुस्√कृ) (6.34)

(§3) *ćañćalaṃ* (adj1∘-subj1∘ unstable, uneasy); *hi* (because); *manaḥ:* (subj1∘ the mind); *kṛṣṇa* (O Kṛṣṇa!); *pramāthi* (adj2∘-subj1∘ exciting, agitating); *balavat* (adj3∘-subj1∘ powerful, strong); *dṛḍhaṃ* (adj4-subj1∘ unyielding, stubborn); *tasya* (its); *ahaṃ* (subj2∘ I); *nigrahaṃ* (obj∘ control); *manye* (I think, I consider); *vāyoḥ:-iva* (like the air); *suduṣkaraṃ* (adj∘-obj∘ difficult) (6.34)

(§4) hi kṛṣṇa manaḥ: ćañćalaṃ pramāthi balavat dṛḍhaṃ ahaṃ manye tasya nigrahaṃ suduṣkaraṃ vāyoḥ:-iva

(§5) Because,[466] O Kṛṣṇa! the mind (is) unstable, agitating, strong *(and)* stubborn, I consider its[467] control difficult like the air. (6.34)

The Lord said (śrībhagavānuvāća श्रीभगवानुवाच ।)

6.35 असंशयं महाबाहो मनो दुर्निग्रहं चलम् ।
अभ्यासेन तु कौन्तेय वैराग्येण च गृह्यते ।।
asaṁśayaṁ mahābāho mano durnigrahaṁ ćalam,

---

[466] See footnote in verse 3.5

[467] Elsewhere∘ *tasya nigraham...* → to subdue it, it is difficult to control, I deem it hard to control, ...etc.

🕮 तस्य is neither the subject nor the object, but merely a सम्बन्धः, 6th case, निग्रहं is not a verb (to control), it is the object (the control), of the subject अहं, verb मन्ये, and adj∘ of the obj∘ सुदुष्करम् (difficult). → I (subj∘) consider (verb∘) its (relation∘) control (obj∘) difficult.(adj∘)

abhyāsena tu kaunteya vairāgyeṇa ća gṛhyate. (6.35)

(§1) असंशयम् महाबाहो मनः दुर्निग्रहम् चलम् । अभ्यासेन तु कौन्तेय वैराग्येण च गृह्यते । *śrībhagavān̦* (r◦ 8/14) *uvāća. asam̐śayam̦* (r◦ 14/1) *mahābāho manaḥ:* (r◦ 15/4) *durnigraham̦* (r◦ 14/1) *ćalam̦* (r◦ 14/2) *abhyāsena tu kaunteya vairāgyeṇa* (r◦ 24/1) *ća gṛhyate*

(§2) *śrībhagavān̦* (2.2); *uvāća* (1.25). 🕮***asam̐śayam̦*** (ind◦ ←n.bahuvrī◦ ***a-sam̐śaya*** (no doubt) न संशयः यस्मात् ←ind◦ अ 1.10 + m◦ *sam̐śaya* (doubt) 4.40); *mahābāho* (2.26); *manaḥ:* (1.30); 🕮*durnigraham̦* (n◦ 1nom◦ sing◦ ←s-bahuvrī *dur-nigraha* (difficult to control) ←ind◦ *dur̦* (difficult) 1.2 + m◦ *nigraha* (control) 3.33); 🕮***ćalam̦*** (n◦ 1nom◦ sing◦ ←adj◦ *ćala* (unstable) ←1◦√चल्); 🕮*abhyāsena* (3inst◦ sing◦ ←m◦ ***abhyāsa*** (practice) ←2◦अभि√अस्); *tu* (1.2); *kaunteya* (2.14); 🕮*vairāgyeṇa* (3inst◦ sing◦ ←taddhita◦ n◦ ***vairāgya*** (detachment) ←m◦ *virāga* (detachment) ←4◦वि√रञ्ज्); ća (1.1); *gṛhyate* (3rd-per◦ sing◦ pres◦ वर्तमान्-लट् ātmane◦ ←9◦√ग्रह्) (6.35)

(§3) *śrībhagavān̦* (The Lord); *uvāća* (said). *asam̐śayam̦* (no doubt, undoubtedly, certainly); *mahābāho* (O Mahābāhu! O Arjuna!); *manaḥ:* (sub◦ the mind); *durnigraham̦* (adj1◦-subj◦ that which is difficult to control); *ćalam̦* (adj2◦-subj◦ unstable); *abhyāsena* (with practice); *tu* (but, however); *kaunteya* (O Kaunteya! O Arjuna!); *vairāgyeṇa* (with non-attachment, with detachment); *ća* (and); *gṛhyate* (it comes under grip, grasp, seize) (6.35)

(§4) śrībhagavān̦ uvāća. asam̐śayam̦ mahābāho manaḥ: ćalam̦ durnigraham̦ tu kaunteya abhyāsena ća vairāgyeṇa gṛhyate

(§5) The Lord said : No doubt, O Arjuna! the mind (is) unstable (and) difficult to control but, O Arjuna! with practice[468] and non-attachment it comes under grip.[469] (6.35)

6.36 असंयतात्मना योगो दुष्प्राप इति मे मतिः ।
वश्यात्मना तु यतता शक्योऽवाप्तुमुपायतः ।।

asam̐yatātmanā yogo duṣprāpa iti me matiḥ:,

---

[468] अभ्यासेन defined : (Pātañjalayogasūtram 1.12) अभ्यासवैराग्याभ्यां तन्निरोधः ।

* तत् = उपरोक्तस्य वृत्ति-पञ्चकस्य; निरोधः (अवरोधः, प्रतिबन्धः, निग्रहः); अभ्यास-वैराग्याभ्याम् = अभ्यासेन (नित्यव्यवहारेण, नित्यवृत्तिना) च वैराग्येण (विरक्तिना, अनासक्तिना) च शक्यते । See “Learning Yoga Sūtras of Patañjali” by Ratnakar Narale (Pustak Bharati Publications)

[469] Elsewhere◦ *gṛhyate* → it can be controlled, it is possible to curb, it can be brought under control, it is brought under centrol, it is restrained ...etc.

🕮 गृह्यते is not a *parasmaipadī* or potential verb.

vaśyātmanā tu yatatā śakyo'vāptumupāyataḥ:. (6.36)

(§1) असंयतात्मना योगो दुष्प्रापः इति मे मतिः । वश्यात्मना तु यतता शक्यः अवाप्तुम् उपायतः । *asaṁyatātmanā yogaḥ:* (r◦ 15/4) *duṣprāpaḥ:* (r◦ 19/2) *iti me matiḥ:* (r◦ 22/8) *vaśyātmanā tu yatatā śakyaḥ:* (r◦ 15/1) *avāptum̦* (r◦ 8/20) *upāyataḥ:* (r◦ 22/8)

(§2) *asaṁyatātmanā* (m◦ 3inst◦ sing◦ ←n.bahuvrī◦ *asaṁyatātman̦*, असंयतः आत्मा यस्य ←negative affix अ (not) 1.10 + adj◦ *saṁyata* (controlled) 4.39 + m◦ *ātman̦* (self) 2.41); *yogaḥ:* (2.48); 🕮*duṣprāpaḥ:* (m◦ 1nom◦ sing◦ ←adj◦ *duṣprāpa* (hard to attain) ←ind◦ *duș* (difficult) 3.39 + n◦ *prāpa* or *prāpaṇa* (attainment) ←5◦प्र√आप्); *iti* (1.25); *me* (1.21); ***matiḥ:*** (1nom◦ sing◦ ←f◦ ***mati*** (opinion) ←1◦√मन्); *vaśyātmanā* (m◦ 3inst◦ sing◦ ←bahuvrī◦ *vaśyātman̦*, वश्यः आत्मा यस्य ←adj◦ *vaśya* (controllable) ←2◦√वश् + m◦ *ātman̦* (oneself) 2.41); *tu* (1.2); *yatatā* (m◦ 3inst◦ sing◦ ←śatṛ◦ adj◦ *yataț* 2.60); 🕮***śakyaḥ:*** (m◦ 1nom◦ sing◦ ←pot◦ adj◦ ***śakya*** (possible) ←5◦√शक्); *avāptum̦* (inf◦ ind◦ ←10◦अव√आप्); 🕮*upāyataḥ:* (ind◦ ←m◦ *upāya* (remedy) ←1◦उप√अय् + affix- (तस्) *taș*) (6.36)

(§3) *asaṁyatātmanā* (subj◦by him who is not self-controlled); *yogaḥ:* (obj◦ the yoga); *duṣprāpaḥ:* (adj◦-obj1◦ difficult to attain); *iti* (so is); *me* (my); *matiḥ:* (subj2◦ opinion); *vaśyātmanā* (subj2◦ by him who is self-controled); *tu* (but); *yatatā* (adj◦-subj2◦ by him who is struggling); *śakyaḥ:* (adj◦-obj◦ possible); *avāptum̦* (to attain); *upāyataḥ:* (with proper means) (6.36)

(§4) yogaḥ: duṣprāpaḥ: asaṁyatātmanā tu śakyaḥ: avāptum̦ upāyataḥ: vaśyātmanā yatatā iti me matiḥ:

(§5) The yoga (is) difficult to attain by him who is not self-controlled, but (it is) possible to attain with proper means by him who is self-controled (and) who is struggling,[470] so is my opinion. (6.36)

Arjuna said (arjuna uvāća अर्जुन उवाच ।)

6.37 अयतिः श्रद्धयोपेतो योगाच्चलितमानसः ।
अप्राप्य योगसंसिद्धिं कां गतिं कृष्ण गच्छति ।।
ayatiḥ: śraddhayopeto yogāććalitamānasaḥ:,
aprāpya yogasaṁsiddhiṁ kaṁ gatiṁ kṛṣṇa gaććhati. (6.37)

(§1) अयतिः श्रद्धयोपेतः योगात् चलितमानसः । अप्राप्य योगसंसिद्धिम् काम् गतिम् कृष्ण गच्छति । *arjunaḥ:* (r◦ 19/4)

---

[470] Elsewhere◦ *yatatā* → attainable by striving through proper means, who strives by appropriate means, ...etc.

🕮 यतत् is a gerund adjective of the subject he (in passive voice), by him who is struggling.

uvāća. ayatiḥ: (r◦ 22/5) *śraddhayā* (r◦ 2/4) *upetaḥ:* (r◦ 15/10) *yogaṭ* (r◦ 11/1) *ćalitamānasaḥ:* (r◦ 22/8) *aprāpya yogasaṁsiddhiṃ* (r◦ 14/1) *kāṃ* (r◦ 14/1) *gatiṃ* (r◦ 14/1) *kṛṣṇa gaććhati*

(§2) *arjunaḥ:* (1.28); *uvāća* (1.25). 🕮*ayatiḥ:* (1nom◦ sing◦ n.bahuvrī◦ ←m◦ *yati* (disciplined person) 4.28); ***śraddhayā*** (3inst◦ sing◦ ←f◦ *śraddhā* (faith) 3.31); *upetaḥ:* (m◦ 1nom◦ sing◦ ←ppp◦ adj◦ ***upeta*** (equipped) ←1◦उप√इ); *yogaṭ* (5abl◦ sing◦ ←m◦ *yoga* 2.39); 🕮*ćalitamānasaḥ:* (m◦ 1nom◦ sing◦ ←bahuvrī◦ *ćalita-mānasa,* चलितम् मानसम् यस्य ←adj◦ *ćalita* (wavering) ←1◦√चल् + n◦ *mānasa* (mind) 1.47); ***aprāpya*** (negative prefix अ *a* + lyp◦ *prāpya* (havinf attained) 2.57); *yogasaṁsiddhiṃ* (f◦ 2acc◦ sing◦ ←tatpu◦ *yoga-saṁsiddhi,* योगस्य संसिद्धिः ←m◦ *yoga* 2.39 + f◦ *saṁsiddhi* (success) 3.20); *kāṃ* (f◦ 2acc◦ sing◦ ←pron◦ *kiṃ* 1.1); ***gatiṃ*** (2acc◦ sing◦ ←f◦ *gati* (state) 2.43); *kṛṣṇa* (1.28); ***gaććhati*** (3rd-per◦ sing◦ pres◦ वर्तमान्–लट् parasmai◦ ←1◦√गम् 2.51) **(6.37)**

(§3) *arjunaḥ:* (subj◦ Arjuna); *uvāća* (said). *ayatiḥ:* (adj1◦-subj◦ he who is not disciplined); *śraddhayā* (with faith); *upetaḥ:* (adj2◦-subj◦ he who is equipped) *yogaṭ* (from yoga); *ćalitamānasaḥ:* (adj3◦-subj◦ he whose mind is wavering, he whose mind is not stable); *aprāpya* (having not attained); *yogasaṁsiddhiṃ* (obj◦ attainment of yoga, success in yoga); *kāṃ* (adj◦-obj◦ which?); *gatiṃ* (obj◦ state); *kṛṣṇa* (O Kṛṣṇa!); *gaććhati* (he attains, he goes to) **(6.37)**

(§4) arjunaḥ: uvāća. kṛṣṇa ayatiḥ: upetaḥ: śraddhayā ćalitamānasaḥ: yogaṭ aprāpya yogasaṁsiddhiṃ kāṃ gatiṃ gaććhati

(§5) Arjuna said. O Kṛṣṇa! he who is not disciplined (but) he who is equipped with faith, he whose mind is wavering from *yoga* (he), having not attained success in yoga, which state he attains? (6.37)

6.38 कच्चिन्नोभयविभ्रष्टश्छिन्नाभ्रमिव नश्यति ।
अप्रतिष्ठो महाबाहो विमूढो ब्रह्मणः पथि ।।
kaććinnobhayavibhraṣṭaśćhinnābhramiva naśyati,
apratiṣṭho mahābāho vimūḍho brahmaṇaḥ: pathi. **(6.38)**

(§1) कच्चित् न उभयविभ्रष्टः छिन्न–अभ्रम् इव नश्यति । अप्रतिष्ठः महाबाहो विमूढः ब्रह्मणः पथि । *kaććiṭ* (r◦ 12/1) *na* (r◦ 2/2) *ubhayavibhraṣṭaḥ:* (r◦ 17/2) *ćhinnābhraṃ* (r◦ 8/18) *iva naśyati* (r◦ 23/1) *apratiṣṭhaḥ:* (r◦ 15/9) *mahābāho vimūḍhaḥ:* (r◦ 15/7) *brahmaṇaḥ:* (r◦ 22/3) *pathi*

(§2) ***kaććiṭ*** (ind◦ ←1◦√कम् + affix *ćiṭ* 2.17); *na* (1.30); *ubhayavibhraṣṭaḥ:* (m◦ 1nom◦ sing◦ ←tatpu◦ *ubhaya-vibhraṣṭa,* उभयतः विभ्रष्टः ←ind◦ *ubhayataṣ* (both sides) ←6◦√उभ् + ppp◦ adj◦ *vibhraṣṭa* (strayed) ←4◦वि√भ्रंश्); *ćhinnābhraṃ* (n◦ 1nom◦ sing◦ ←tatpu◦ *ćhinnābhra,* छिन्नम् अभ्रम् ←adj◦ *ćhinna* (scattered) 5.25 +

n∘ *abhra* (cloud) ←1∘√अभ्र्); *iva* (1.30); *naśyati* (3rd-per∘ sing∘ pres∘ वर्तमान्–लट् parasmai∘ ←4∘√नश् 2.63); 🕮*apratiṣṭhaḥ:* (m∘ 1nom∘ sing∘ n.tatpu∘ ←ppp∘ adj∘ ***pratiṣṭha*** (established) ←1∘प्रति√स्था); *mahābāho* (2.26); *vimūḍhaḥ:* (m∘ 1nom∘ sing∘ ←adj∘ *vimūḍha* (deluded) 3.6); *brahmaṇaḥ:* (4.32); *pathi* (irregular 7loc∘ sing∘ ←m∘ *pathin* (path) ←1∘√पथ्) (6.38)

(§3) *kaććit* (is it possible that); *na* (not); *ubhayavibhraṣṭaḥ:* (adj1∘-subj∘ strayed from both sides); *ćhinnābhram-iva* (like a scattered cloud); *naśyati* (he perishes); *apratiṣṭhaḥ:* (adj2-subj∘ un-established); *mahābāho* (O Mahābāhu! O Kṛṣṇa!); *vimūḍhaḥ:* (adj3∘-subj∘ confused, deluded); *brahmaṇaḥ:* (of brahma); *pathi* (in the path) (6.38)

(§4) mahābāho kaććit na apratiṣṭhaḥ: vimūḍhaḥ: pathi brahmaṇaḥ: ubhayavibhraṣṭaḥ: naśyati ćhinnābhram-iva

(§5) O Kṛṣṇa! is it not possible that, un-established *(and)* deluded in the path of *brahma*, strayed from both sides, he perishes like a scattered cloud? (6.38)

6.39 एतन्मे संशयं कृष्ण छेत्तुमर्हस्यशेषतः ।
त्वदन्यः संशयस्यास्य छेत्ता न ह्युपपद्यते ।।
etanme saṁśayaṁ kṛṣṇa ćhettumarhasyaśeṣataḥ:,
tvadanyaḥ: saṁśayasyāsya ćhettā na hyupapadyate. (6.39)

(§1) एतम् मे संशयम् कृष्ण छेत्तुम् अर्हसि अशेषतः । त्वदन्यः संशयस्य अस्य छेत्ता न हि उपपद्यते । *etam me saṁśayam* (r∘ 14/1) *kṛṣṇa ćhettum* (r∘ 8/16) *arhasi* (r∘ 4/1) *aśeṣataḥ:* (r∘ 22/8) *tvadanyaḥ:* (r∘ 22/7) *saṁśayasya* (r∘ 1/1) *asya ćhettā na hi* (r∘ 4/3) *upapadyate*

(§2) ***etam*** (m∘ 2acc∘ sing∘ ←pron∘ *etat* 2.3); *me* (1.21); *saṁśayam* (4.42); *kṛṣṇa* (1.28); *ćhettum* (inf∘ ind∘ ←7∘√छिद्); *arhasi* (2.25); *aśeṣataḥ:* (6.24); *tvadanyaḥ:* (m∘ 1nom∘ sing∘ ←adj∘ ***tvadanya*** (other than you) ←*pron*∘ sing∘ ***tvat*** ←pron∘ *yuṣmad* 3.1 + adj∘ *anya* (other) 1.9); 🕮*saṁśayasya* (6pos sing∘ ←m∘ *saṁśaya* (doubt) 4.40); *asya* (2.17); 🕮*ćhettā* (1nom∘ sing∘ ←m∘ *ćhettṛ* (remover) ←7∘√छिद्); *na* (1.30); *hi* (1.11); *upapadyate* (2.3) (6.39)

(§3) *etam* (m∘ adj∘-obj∘ this); *me* (my); *saṁśayam* (m∘ obj∘ doubt); *kṛṣṇa* (O Krishna); *ćhettum* (for removing, to remove); *arhasi* (you ought to); *aśeṣataḥ:* (fully); *tvadanyaḥ:* (adj∘-subj2∘ other than you); *saṁśayasya* (of the doubt); *asya* (of this); *ćhettā* (subj2∘ remover); *na* (not, no); *hi* (because); *upapadyate* (does exist, exists, there is) (6.39)

(§4) kṛṣṇa arhasi aśeṣataḥ: ćhettum me etam saṁśayam, hi tvadanyaḥ: upapadyate na ćhettā asya saṁśayasya

(§5) O Krishna! you ought to fully remove my this doubt, because[471] other than you there is no remover of this doubt. (6.39)

The Lord said (śrībhagavānuvāća श्रीभगवानुवाच ।)

6.40 पार्थ नैवेह नामुत्र विनाशस्तस्य विद्यते ।
न हि कल्याणकृत्कश्चिद्दुर्गतिं तात गच्छति ।।

pārtha naiveha nāmutra vināśastasya vidyate,
na hi kalyāṇakṛtkaśćiddurgatiṁ tāta gaćchati. (6.40)

(§1) पार्थ न एव इह न अमुत्र विनाशः तस्य विद्यते । न हि कल्याणकृत् कश्चित् दुर्गतिम् तात गच्छति । *śrībhagavān* (r◦ 8/14) *uvāća. pārtha na* (r◦ 3/1) *eva* (r◦ 2/1) *iha na* (r◦ 1/1) *amutra vināśaḥ:* (r◦ 18/1) *tasya vidyate na hi kalyāṇakṛt* (r◦ 10/5) *kaśćit* (r◦ 9/5) *durgatim* (r◦ 14/1) *tāta gaćchati*

(§2) *śrībhagavān* (2.2); *uvāća* (1.25). *pārtha* (1.25); *na* (1.30); *eva* (1.1); *iha* (2.5); *na* (1.30); 🕮*amutra* (other world) (ind◦ ←pron◦ *adas* ←4◦न√दस् 11.21↓); *vināśaḥ:* (1nom◦ sing◦ ←m◦ *vināśa* (downfall) 2.17); *tasya* (1.12); *vidyate* (2.16); *na* (1.30); *hi* (1.11); 🕮*kalyāṇakṛt* (n◦ 1nom◦ sing◦ ←adj◦ *kalyāṇa-kṛt* ←m◦ *kalyāṇa* (good deed) ←4◦कल्य√अण् + adj◦ affix कृत्); *kaśćit* (m◦ 2.17); 🕮*durgatim* (f◦ 2acc◦ sing◦ ←n.tatpu◦ *durgati* (downfall) ←ind◦ *dur* 1.2 + f◦ *gati* (state) 2.43); *tāta* (8voc◦ sing◦ ←m◦ *tāta* ←8◦√तन्); *gaćchati* (6.37)

(§3) *śrībhagavān* (The Lord); *uvāća* (said). *pārtha* (O Arjuna!); *na* (no); *eva* (certainly); *iha* (here, in this world); *na* (not); *amutra* (in the next world, hereafter); *vināśaḥ:* (subj1◦ ruin); *tasya* (his, for him); *vidyate* (there exists); *na* (no, does not); *hi* (because); *kalyāṇakṛt* (subj2◦ one who is engaged in good deeds for others); *kaśćit* (adj◦-subj2◦ anyone); *durgatim* (obj◦ a deplorable state, indigence); *tāta* (My Dear!) *gaćchati* (he goes, he ends up in) (6.40)

(§4) śrībhagavān uvāća pārtha eva na vidyate vināśaḥ: tasya iha na amutra hi tāta kaśćit kalyāṇakṛt na gaćchati durgatim

(§5) The Lord said : O Arjuna! certainly there exists no ruin for him in this world not in the next world; because,[472] My Dear! anyone who is engaged in good deeds for others, he does not end up in a deplorable state. (6.40)

6.41 प्राप्य पुण्यकृतां लोकानुषित्वा शाश्वतीः समाः ।
शुचीनां श्रीमतां गेहे योगभ्रष्टोऽभिजायते ।।

---

[471] See footnote in verse 3.5

[472] See footnote in verse 3.5

prāpya puṇyakṛtāṁ lokānuṣitvā śāśvatīḥ: samāḥ:,
śucīnāṁ śrīmatāṁ gehe yogabhraṣṭo'bhijāyate. (6.41)

(§1) प्राप्य पुण्यकृताम् लोकान् उषित्वा शाश्वती: समा: । शुचीनाम् श्रीमताम् गेहे योगभ्रष्ट: अभिजायते । *prāpya puṇyakṛtām* (r◦ 14/1) *lokān* (r◦ 8/14) *uṣitvā śāśvatīḥ:* (r◦ 22/7) *samāḥ:* (r◦ 22/8) *śucīnām* (r◦ 14/1) *śrīmatām* (r◦ 14/1) *gehe yogabhraṣṭaḥ:* (r◦ 15/1) *abhijāyate*

(§2) *prāpya* (2.57); 📖*puṇyakṛtām* (m◦ 6pos◦ plu◦ ←śatṛ◦ adj◦ *puṇya-kṛt*, n◦ or adj◦ ***puṇya*** (good deed) ←1◦√पू + adj◦ *kṛt* 1.35); ***lokān*** (2acc◦ plu◦ ←m◦ *loka* (world) 2.5); *uṣitvā* (ipp◦ ind◦ ←1◦√वस्); *śāśvatīḥ:* (f◦ 2acc◦ plu◦ ←adj◦ *śāśvatī* (countless) ←1◦√शश्); *samāḥ:* (2acc◦ plu◦ ←f◦ *samā* (year) ←1◦√सम्); *śucīnām* (m◦ 6pos◦ plu◦ ←adj◦ *śuci* (pious) 6.11); 📖*śrīmatām* (m◦ 6pos◦ plu◦ ←adj◦ ***śrīmat*** (affluent) ←f◦ or adj◦ *śrī* 10.34); *gehe* (7loc◦ sing◦ ←n◦ *geha* (home) ←9◦√ग्रह्); 📖*yogabhraṣṭaḥ:* (m◦ 1nom◦ sing◦ ←tatpu◦ *yoga-bhraṣṭa*, योगात् भ्रष्ट: ←m◦ *yoga* 2.39 + adj◦ *bhraṣṭa* (fallen down) ←4◦√भ्रंश्); *abhijāyate* (2.62) (6.41)

(§3) *prāpya* (having attained); *puṇyakṛtām* (of the righteous); *lokān* (obj1◦ the worlds); *uṣitvā* (having dwelt, having lived, living); *śāśvatīḥ:* (adj◦-obj2◦ countless, many); *samāḥ:* (obj2◦ years); *śucīnām* (of the pious); *śrīmatām* (of the affluent, prosperous); *gehe* (in the dwelling); *yogabhraṣṭaḥ:* (subj◦ he who had fallen from the *yoga*); *abhijāyate* (he is born, he takes birth) (6.41)

(§4) prāpya lokān puṇyakṛtām uṣitvā śāśvatīḥ: samāḥ:, yogabhraṣṭaḥ: abhijāyate gehe śucīnām śrīmatām

(§5) Having attained the worlds of the righteous, (and) having lived (there) many years,[473] he who had fallen from the *yoga,* takes birth in the dwelling of the pious (and) prosperous. (6.41)

6.42 अथवा योगिनामेव कुले भवति धीमताम् ।
एतद्धि दुर्लभतरं लोके जन्म यदीदृशम् ।।
athavā yogināmeva kule bhavati dhīmatām,
etaddhi durlabhataraṁ loke janma yadīdṛśam. (6.42)

(§1) अथवा योगिनाम् एव कुले भवति धीमताम् । एतत् हि दुर्लभतरम् लोके जन्म यत् ईदृशम् । *athavā yoginām* (r◦

---

[473] Elsewhere◦ prāpya lokān puṇyakṛtām uṣitvā gehe śāśvatīḥ: samāḥ: (Attaining the worlds of meritorious, having dwelt for endless years in the dwelling of the rediant and the illustrious ... is born.)

📖 Note that (worlds) लोकान् is plural, (years) समा: is plural, but (in the dwelling) गेहे is singular and (he takes birth) अभिजायते is singular. "Having lived in the worlds for countless years in a house ...he is born" is improper expression of what Kṛṣṇa said in verse 6.41; specially, because (i) then the verb he is born has no address or object, and (ii) the next verse says अथवा कुले भवति (or the birth occurs in the family of...)

8/22) *eva kulebhavati dhīmatām̦* (r◦ 14/2) *etaț* (r◦ 9/12) *hi durlabhataram̦* (r◦ 14/1) *loke janma yaț* (r◦ 8/5) *īdṛśam̦* (r◦ 14/2)

(§2) ***athavā*** (or else) (option indicating ind◦ ←10√अर्थ्-वा); *yoginām̦* (3.3); *eva* (1.1); 📖*kule* (7loc◦ sing◦ ←n◦ *kula* (family) 1.38); *bhavati* (1.44); 📖*dhīmatām̦* (m◦ 6pos◦ plu◦ ←adj◦ *dhīmaț* (wise) 1.3); *etaț* (1nom◦ 2.3); *hi* (1.11); 📖*durlabhataram̦* (n◦ 1nom◦ sing◦ ←adj◦ *durlabha* (difficult to attain) ←1◦दुर्√लभ् + comparative affix (तर) *tara* 1.46); *loke* (2.5); *janma* (2.27); *yaț* (1.45); *īdṛśam̦* (2.32) (6.42)

(§3) *athavā* (or, else, or else); *yoginām̦* (of the yogīs); *eva* (also); *kule* (in the family); *bhavati* (becomes, takes birth); *dhīmatām̦* (of the wise, of the learned); *etaț* (this); *hi* (indeed); *durlabhataram̦* (adj1◦-subj◦ more difficult); *loke* (in this world); *janma* (subj◦ birth); *yaț -īdṛśam̦* (adj2◦-subj◦ such like this is) (6.42)

(§4) athavā eva bhavati kule dhīmatām̦ yoginām̦, hi loke etaț janma yaț-īdṛśam̦ durlabhataram̦

(§5) Or else, (his birth) also becomes in the family of the learned *yogīs*. Indeed, in this world birth such like this is more difficult. (6.42)

6.43 तत्र तं बुद्धिसंयोगं लभते पौर्वदेहिकम् ।
यतते च ततो भूयः संसिद्धौ कुरुनन्दन ।।
tatra taṁ buddhisaṁyogaṁ labhate paurvadehikam̦,
yatate ća tato bhūyaḥ: saṁsiddhau kurunandana. (6.43)

(§1) तत्र तम् बुद्धिसंयोगम् लभते पौर्वदेहिकम् । यतते च ततः भूयः संसिद्धौ कुरुनन्दन । *tatra tam̦* (r◦ 14/1) *buddhisaṁyogam̦* (r◦ 14/1) *labhate paurvadehikam̦* (r◦ 14/2) *yatate ća tataḥ:* (r◦ 15/8) *bhūyaḥ:* (r◦ 22/7) *saṁsiddhau kurunandana*

(§2) *tatra* (1.26); *tam̦* (2.1); *buddhisaṁyogam̦* (m◦ 2acc◦ sing◦ ←tatpu◦ *buddhi-saṁyoga*, बुद्ध्याः or बुद्धेः संयोगः ←f◦ *buddhi* (thinking) 1.23 + m◦ *saṁyoga* (accretion) 5.14); *labhate* (4.39); *paurvadehikam̦* (m◦ 2acc◦ sing◦ ←taddhita◦ *paurva-dehika* ←adj◦ *pūrva* (prior) 4.15 + adj◦ *dehik* (bodied) ←2◦√दिह्); *yatate* (3rd-per◦ sing◦ pres◦ वर्तमान्-लट् ātmane◦ ←1◦√यत्); *ća* (1.1); *tataḥ:* (1.13); *bhūyaḥ:* (2.20); *saṁsiddhau* (7loc◦ sing◦ ←f◦ *saṁsiddhi* (success) 3.20); *kurunandana* (2.41) (6.43)

(§3) *tatra* (there); *tam̦* (adj1◦-obj◦ that); *buddhisaṁyogam̦* (obj◦ accretion of - knowledge); *labhate* (he attains); *paurvadehikam̦* (adj2◦-obj◦ from the previous birth); *yatate* (he strives); *ća* (and); *tataḥ:* (thereafter); *bhūyaḥ:* (again); *saṁsiddhau* (towards success); *kurunandana* (O Arjuna!) (6.43)

(§4) tatra labhate tam̦ buddhisaṁyogam̦ paurvadehikam̦ ća kurunandana tataḥ: bhūyaḥ: yatate saṁsiddhau.

(§5) There he attains accretion of that knowledge from the previous birth; and, O Arjuna! thereafter he again strives towards success (in yoga). (6.43)

6.44 **पूर्वाभ्यासेन तेनैव ह्रियते ह्यवशोऽपि सः ।**
जिज्ञासुरपि योगस्य शब्दब्रह्मातिवर्तते ।।
pūrvābhyāsena tenaiva hriyate hyavaśo'pi saḥ:,
jijñāsurapi yogasya śabdabrahmātivartate. (6.44)

(§1) पूर्वाभ्यासेन तेन एव ह्रियते हि अवशः अपि सः । जिज्ञासुः अपि योगस्य शब्दब्रह्म अतिवर्तते । *pūrvābhyāsena tena* (r◦ 3/1) *eva hriyate hi* (r◦ 4/1) *avaśaḥ:* (r◦ 15/1) *api saḥ:* (r◦ 22/8) *jijñāsuḥ:* (r◦ 16/3) *api yogasya śabdabrahma* (r◦ 1/1) *ativartate*

(§2) *pūrvābhyāsena* (m◦ 3inst◦ sing◦ ←tatpu◦ *pūrvābhyāsa*, पूर्वेण अभ्यासः ←adj◦ *pūrva* (prior) 4.15 + m◦ *abhyāsa* (practice) 6.35); *tena* (3.38); *eva* (1.1); *hriyate* (3rd-per◦ sing◦ pres◦ वर्तमान्–लट् ātmane◦ caus◦ ←1◦√हृ); *hi* (1.11); *avaśaḥ:* (3.5); *api* (1.26); *saḥ:* (1.13); 🕮***jijñāsuḥ:*** (m◦ 1nom◦ sing◦ ←desi◦ adj◦ *jijñāsā* (curiosity) ←9◦√ज्ञा); *api* (1.26); *yogasya* (6pos sing◦ ←m◦ *yoga* 2.39); *śabdabrahma* (1nom◦ sing◦ ←n◦ *śabda-brahman*, ब्रह्मणः शब्दः ←m◦ *shabda* 1.13 + n◦ *brahman* 2.72); 🕮***ativartate*** (3rd-per◦ sing◦ pres◦ वर्तमान्–लट् ātmane◦ ←1◦अति√वृत्) (6.44)

(§3) *pūrvābhyāsena* (with practice); *tena* (by that); *eva* (alone); *hriyate* (he is carried ahead); *hi* (because); *avaśaḥ:* (adv◦ helplessly); *api* (also); *saḥ:* (he); *jijñāsuḥ:* (desirous of knowledge); *api* (even); *yogasya* (of *yoga*); *śabdabrahma* (vedic recitation, the performance of *vedic* rituals); *ativartate* (goes beyond) (6.44)

(§4) hi pūrvābhyāsena tena eva hriyate avaśaḥ: api jijñāsuḥ: yogasya saḥ: api ativartate śabdabrahma

(§5) Because,[474] with that practice alone he is carried ahead helplessly. Also, desirous of knowledge of *yoga,* he goes even beyond the performance of *vedic* rituals. (6.44)

6.45 **प्रयत्नाद्यतमानस्तु योगी संशुद्धकिल्बिषः ।**
अनेकजन्मसंसिद्धस्ततो याति परां गतिम् ।।
prayatnādyatamānastu yogī saṁśuddhakilbiṣaḥ:,
anekajanmasaṁsiddhastato yāti parāṁ gatim. (6.45)

(§1) प्रयत्नात् यतमानः तु योगी संशुद्धकिल्बिषः । अनेकजन्मसंसिद्धः ततो याति पराम् गतिम् । *prayatnāt* (r◦ 9/9) *yatamānaḥ:* (r◦ 18/1) *tu yogī saṁśuddhakilbiṣaḥ:* (r◦ 22/8) *anekajanmasaṁsiddhaḥ:* (r◦ 18/1) *tataḥ:* (r◦

[474] See footnote in verse 3.5

15/10) *yāti parām* (r◦ 14/1) *gatim* (r◦ 14/2)

(§2) 🕮*prayatnāt* (5abl◦ sing◦ ←m◦ *prayatna* (effort) ←1◦प्र√यत्); 🕮*yatamānaḥ:* (m◦ 1nom◦ sing◦ ←śānac◦ adj◦ *yatamāna* (striving person) ←1◦√यत्); *tu* (1.2); *yogī* (5.24); *saṁśuddhakilbiṣaḥ:* (m◦ 1nom◦ sing◦ ←bahuvrī◦ *saṁśuddha-kilbiṣa*, संशुद्धम् किल्बिषम् यस्य ←ppp◦ adj◦ *saṁśuddha* (purified) ←4◦सम्√शुध् + *kilbiṣa* (sin) 3.13); *anekajanmasaṁsiddhaḥ:* (m◦ 1nom◦ sing◦ ←tatpu◦ *aneka-janma-saṁsiddha*, अनेकैः जन्मभिः संसिद्धः ←n.tatpu◦ ***aneka*** (many) ←adj◦ *eka* (one) 2.41 + n◦ *janman* (birth) 2.27 + adj◦ *samsiddha* (successful) 4.38); *tataḥ:* (1.13); ***yāti*** (3rd-per◦ sing◦ pres◦ वर्तमान्–लट् parasmai◦ ←2◦√या 3.33); *parām* (4.39); *gatim* (6.37) (6.45)

(§3) *prayatnāt* (from efforts); *yatamānaḥ:* (adj1◦-subj◦ the striving); *tu* (however); *yogī* (subj◦ *yogī*); *saṁśuddhakilbiṣaḥ:* (adj2◦-subj◦ purified of the sins); *anekajanmasaṁsiddhaḥ:* (ppp◦ adj3◦-subj◦ successful through many births); *tataḥ:* (thereafter); *yāti* (he attains); *parām* (adj◦-obj◦ the supreme); *gatim* (obj◦ state) (6.45)

(§4) tu prayatnāt yatamānaḥ: yogī saṁśuddhakilbiṣaḥ: anekajanmasaṁsiddhaḥ: tataḥ: yāti parām gatim

(§5) However, from efforts the striving[475] *yogī,* purified of the sins (and) successful through many births, thereafter attains the supreme state. (6.45)

6.46 तपस्विभ्योऽधिको योगी ज्ञानिभ्योऽपि मतोऽधिकः ।
कर्मिभ्यश्चाधिको योगी तस्माद्योगी भवार्जुन ।।

tapasvibhyo'dhiko yogī jñānibhyo'pi mato'dhikaḥ:,
karmibhyaśćādhiko yogī tasmādyogī bhavārjuna. (6.46)

(§1) तपस्विभ्यः अधिकः योगी ज्ञानिभ्यः अपि मतः अधिकः । कर्मिभ्यः च अधिकः योगी तस्मात् योगी भव अर्जुन । *tapasvibhyaḥ:* (r◦ 15/1) *adhikaḥ:* (r◦ 15/10) *yogī jñānibhyaḥ:* (r◦ 15/1) *api mataḥ:* (r◦ 15/1) *adhikaḥ:* (r◦ 22/8) *karmibhyaḥ:* (r◦ 17/1) *ća* (r◦ 1/1) *adhikaḥ:* (r◦ 15/10) *yogī tasmāt* (r◦ 9/9) *yogī bhava* (r◦ 1/1) *arjuna*

(§2) *tapasvibhyaḥ:* (5abl◦ plu◦ ←m◦ ***tapasvin*** (ascetic) ←1◦√तप्); 🕮***adhikaḥ:*** (m◦ 1nom◦ sing◦ ←adj◦ *adhika* (more) 6.22); *yogī* (5.24); *jñānibhyaḥ:* (5abl◦ plu◦ ←m◦ *jñānin* (*jnāna-yogi, Sankhya sannyasī*) 3.39); *api* (1.26);

---

[475] Elsewhere◦ *yatamānaḥ:* → who practices assiduously, who strives with assiduity engages himself, Yogin who strives with assiduity, who practices yoga with constant attention, who diligently takes up the practice, ...etc.

🕮 यतमान is a not a Present tense. It is an *ātmanepadī* gerund Present Participle adjective. e.g. practicing, striving. taking up ...etc.

mataḥ: (6.32); *adhikaḥ:* (↑); *karmibhyaḥ:* (5abl∘ plu∘ ←m∘ *karmin* ←8∘√कृ); *ćа* (1.1); *adhikaḥ:* (↑); *yogī* (5.24); *tasmāt* (1.37); *yogī* (5.24); *bhava* (2.45); *arjuna* (2.2) (6.46)

(§3) *tapasvibhyaḥ:* (than the ascetics); *adhikaḥ:* (better, greater, superior); *yogī* (the yogī, the *karmayogī*, the *niṣkāmakarmayogī*); *jñānibhyaḥ:* (than the *jñānīs*, the *sāṅkhyasannyāsīs*); *api* (also); *mataḥ:* (regarded as); *adhikaḥ:* (superior); *karmibhyaḥ:* (than the *sakāmakarmīs*); *ća* (and); *adhikaḥ:* (superior); *yogī* (a yogī); *tasmāt* (therefore); *yogī* (a yogī); *bhava* (you be); *arjuna* (O Arjuna!) (6.46)

(§4) yogī mataḥ: adhikaḥ: tapasvibhyaḥ: api adhikaḥ: jñānibhyaḥ: ća yogī adhikaḥ: karmibhyaḥ: tasmāt arjuna bhava yogī

(§5) The *niṣkāmakarmayogī* (is) regarded as superior than the ascetics, also superior than the *sāṅkhyasannyāsīs*[476] and a *niṣkāmakarmayogī* is regarded as superior than the *sakāmakarmīs*, therefore,[477] O Arjuna! you be a *niṣkāmakarmayogī*. (6.46)

6.47 योगिनामपि सर्वेषां मद्गतेनान्तरात्मना ।
श्रद्धावान्भजते यो मां स मे युक्ततमो मतः ।।
yogināmapi sarveṣām madgatenāntarātmanā,
śraddhāvānbhajate yo mām sa me yuktatamo mataḥ:. (6.47)

(§1) योगिनाम् अपि सर्वेषाम् मद्गतेन अन्तरात्मना । श्रद्धावान् भजते यः माम् सः मे युक्ततमः मतः । *yoginām* (r∘ 8/16) *api sarveṣām* (r∘ 25/3, 14/1) *madgatena* (r∘ 1/1) *antarātmanā śraddhāvān* (r∘ 13/15) *bhajate yaḥ:* (r∘ 15/9) *mām* (r∘ 14/1) *saḥ:* (r∘ 21/2) *me yuktatamaḥ:* (r∘ 15/9) *mataḥ:* (r∘ 22/8)

(§2) *yoginām* (3.3); *api* (1.26); *sarveṣām* (1.25); *madgatena* (m∘ 3inst∘ sing∘ ←tatpu∘ *madgata*, मयि गतम् ←pron∘ *mat* 1.9 + f∘ *gati* 2.43); *antarātmanā* (3inst∘ sing∘ ←m∘ ***antarātman*** (mind) ←ind∘ *antara* ←2∘अन्त√रा or ind∘ *antar* (5.24); + n∘ *ātman* 2.41); *śraddhāvān* (4.39); 🕮***bhajate*** (3rd-per∘ sing∘ pres∘ वर्तमान्-लट् ātmane∘ ←1∘√भज् 6.31); *yaḥ:* (2.19); *mām* (1.46); *saḥ:* (1.13); *me* (1.21); 🕮*yuktatamaḥ:* (m∘ 1nom∘ sing∘ ←superlative adj∘ ***yukta-tama*** ←adj∘ *yukta* (equipped) 1.14 + affix *tama* (most) 1.7); *mataḥ:* (6.32) (6.47)

(§3) *yoginām* (among the *yogīs*); *api* (also); *sarveṣām* (among all); *madgatena* (fixed on me); *antarātmanā* (by mind); *śraddhāvān* (adj1∘-obj∘ the faithful); *bhajate* (adores); *yaḥ:* (adj2∘-obj∘ who); *mām* (obj∘ me); *saḥ:* (obj∘ he); *me* (subj∘ for me, by me); *yuktatamaḥ:* (adj3∘-obj∘ best disciplined, best

---

[476] Elsewhere∘ *jñānibhyaḥ* → than men of knowledge, men of wisdom, those versed in sacred lore, than the wise, the learned, ...etc.

🕮 ज्ञान, ज्ञानयोग, ज्ञानी, योग, योगी see 3.3

[477] See the footnote in verse 2.15

equipped with yoga); *mataḥ:* (adj4◦-obj◦ thought, considered) (6.47)

(§4) api sarveṣāṃ yogināṃ śraddhāvān yaḥ: madgatena antarātmanā bhajate māṃ me saḥ: mataḥ: yuktatamaḥ:

(§5) Also among all *yogīs* the faithful who, fixed on me by mind, adores me, by me he (is) considered best equipped with yoga.[478] (6.47)

ति श्रीमद्भगवद्गीतासूपनिषत्सु ब्रह्मविद्यायां योगशास्त्रे
श्रीकृष्णार्जुनसंवाद आत्मसंयमयोगो नाम षष्ठोऽध्यायः ।।

iti śrīmadbhagavadgītāsūpaniṣatsu brahmavidyāyāṁ yogaśāstre
śrīkṛṣṇārjunasam̃vād ātmasam̃yamayogo nāma ṣaṣṭho'dhyāyaḥ:.

(§1) *iti śrīmadbhagavadgītāsu* (r◦ 1/8) *upaniṣatsu brahmavidyāyāṃ* (r◦ 14/1) *yogaśāstre śrīkṛṣṇārjunasam̃vāde* (r◦ 5/1) *ātmasam̃yamayogaḥ:* (r◦ 15/6) *nāma ṣaṣṭhaḥ:* (r◦ 15/1) *adhyāyaḥ:* (r◦ 22/8)

(§2) *iti* (1.25); *śrīmadbhagavadgītāsu* (f◦ 7loc◦ plu◦ tatpu◦ *śrīmad-bhagavad-gītā* ←adj◦ *śrīmaṭ* 6.41 + adj◦ *bhagavaṭ* 10.14 + f◦ *gītā* ←5◦√गै); *upaniṣatsu* (7loc◦ plu◦ ←f◦ *upaniṣaḍ* ←6◦उप-नि√सद्); *brahmavidyāyāṃ* (f◦ 7loc◦ sing◦ ←tatpu◦ *brahma-vidyā,* ब्रह्मणः विद्या ←n◦ *brahmaṇ* 2.72 + *vidyā* 5.18); *yogaśāstre* (n◦ 7loc◦ sing◦ ←tatpu◦ *yoga-śāstra,* योगानाम् शास्त्रम् । योगस्य शास्त्रम् । ←m◦ *yoga* 2.39 + n◦ *śāstra* 15.20); *śrīkṛṣṇārjunasam̃vāde* (m◦ 7loc◦ sing◦ ←tatpu◦ *śrī-kṛṣṇārjuna-sam̃vāda,* श्रीकृष्णस्य च अर्जुनस्य च संवादः ←adj◦ *śrī* 10.34 + m◦ prop◦ *kṛṣṇa* 1.28 + m◦ prop◦ *arjuna* 1.4 + m◦ *sam̃vāda* 18.70); *ātmasam̃yamayogaḥ:* (m◦ 1nom◦ sing◦ ←tatpu◦ *kātma-sam̃yama-yoga,* आत्मसंयमयोग, आत्मनः संयमस्य योगः ←prop◦ *ātman* 2.41 + m◦ *sam̃yama* 4.26 + m◦ *yoga* 2.39); *nāma* (1nom◦ sing◦ ←n◦ *nāmaṇ* ←1◦√म्ना); *ṣaṣṭhaḥ:* (m◦ 1nom◦ sing◦ ←num◦ adj◦ *ṣaṣṭa* 15.7); *adhyāyaḥ:* (1nom◦ sing◦ ←m◦ *adhyāya* ←1◦अधि√इ)

(§3) *iti* (thus); *śrīmadbhagavadgītāsu upaniṣatsu* (among the upaniṣads of the Śrīmad-Bhagavadgītā); *brahmavidyāyāṃ* (of the eternal wisdoms); *yogaśāstre* (in the science of Yoga); *śrīkṛṣṇārjunasam̃vāde* (in the dialogue between Śrī Kṛṣṇa and Arjuna); *ātmasam̃yamayogaḥ:* (adj1◦-subj◦ called ātmasam̃yamayoga); *nāma* (called); *ṣaṣṭhaḥ:* (adj2◦-subj◦ the sixth); *adhyāyaḥ:* (subj◦ discourse; chapter)

(§4) śrīmadbhagavadgītāsu upaniṣatsu yogaśāstre brahmavidyāyāṃ iti ṣaṣṭhaḥ: adhyāyaḥ: nāma ātmasam̃yamayogaḥ śrīkṛṣṇārjunasam̃vāde

(§5) Among the upaniṣads of the Śrīmad-Bhagavadgītā, in the science of yoga of self realization,

---

[478]युक्तः, see 2.61, 6.8, 5.8 and 5.12

thus (is) the sixth discourse called ātma-saṁyama-yoga, in the dialogue between Śrī Kṛṣṇa and Arjuna.

CHAPTER 7

saptamo'dhyāyaḥ:

सप्तमोऽध्यायः ।

jñānavijñānayogaḥ:

ज्ञानविज्ञानयोगः ।

THE YOGA OF KNOWLEDGE AND SCIENCE[479]

The Lord said (śrībhagavānuvāca श्रीभगवानुवाच ।)

7.1 **मय्यासक्तमनाः पार्थ योगं युञ्जन्मदाश्रयः ।**
असंशयं समग्रं मां यथा ज्ञास्यसि तच्छृणु ।।

mayyāsaktamanāḥ: pārtha yogaṁ yuñjanmadāśrayaḥ:,
asaṁśayaṁ samagraṁ māṁ yathā jñāsyasi tacchṛṇu. (7.1)

(§1) मयि आसक्तमनाः पार्थ योगम् युञ्जन् मदाश्रयः । असंशयम् समग्रम् माम् यथा ज्ञास्यसि तत् शृणु । *saptamaḥ:* (r◦ 15/1) *adhyāyaḥ:* (r◦ 22/8). *jñānavijñānayogaḥ:* (r◦ 22/8). *śrībhagavān* (r◦ 8/14) *uvāca. mayi* (r◦ 4/2) *āsaktamanāḥ:* (r◦ 22/3) *pārtha yogam* (r◦ 14/1) *yuñjan* (r◦ 13/16) *madāśrayaḥ:* (r◦ 22/8) *asaṁśayam* (r◦ 14/1) *samagram* (r◦ 14/1) *mām* (r◦ 14/1) *yathā jñāsyasi tat* (r◦ 11/4) *śṛṇu*

(§2) *saptamaḥ:* (m◦ 1nom◦ sing◦ ←sequence indicating num◦ adj◦ *saptama* ←adj◦ *saptan* 10.6 ↓); *adhyāyaḥ:* (1nom◦ sing◦ ←m◦ *adhyāya* ←अधि√इ). *jñānavijñānayogaḥ:* (m◦ 1nom◦ sing◦ ←tatpu◦ *jñāna-vijñāna-yoga,* ज्ञानस्य च विज्ञानस्य च योगः ←n◦ *jñāna* 3.3 + n◦ 🕮*vijñāna* 3.41 + m◦ *yoga* 2.39). *śrībhagavān* (2.2); *uvāca* (1.25).

mayi (3.30); *āsaktamanāḥ:* (m◦ 1nom◦ sing◦ ←bahuvrī◦ *āsakta-manas,* आसक्तम् मनः यस्य ←adj◦ ***āsakta*** (unattached) ←आ√सञ्ज् + n◦ *manas* 1.30); *pārtha* (1.25); *yogam* (2.53); *yuñjan* (6.15); *madāśrayaḥ:* (m◦

[479] Elsewhere◦ *jñānavijñānayogaḥ:* → 'Realisation of the Lord by Meditation,' 'The way of Knowledge and Realization,' 'God and the World,' 'Knowledge of the Absolute,' ...etc.

1nom◦ sing◦ ←bahuvrī◦ *madāśraya,* अहम् आश्रय: यस्य ←pron◦ *mat* 1.9 + m◦ *āśraya* (shelter) 4.20); *asaṁśayam* (adv◦ 6.35); *samagram* (adv◦ fully 4.23); *mām* (1.46); *yathā* (1.11); *jñāsyasi* (2nd-per◦ sing◦ fut2◦ लृट् भविष्य◦ parasmai◦ ←class9◦ √ज्ञा); *tat* (2.7); *śṛṇu* (2.39) (7.1)

(§3) *saptamaḥ:* (adj◦-subj◦ The seventh); *adhyāyaḥ:* (subj◦ cahpter). *jñānavijñānayogaḥ:* (jñāna-vijñāna-yoga, the yoga of Knowledge and Wisdom, yoga of knowledge and science). *śrībhagavān* (The Lord); *uvāća* (said). *mayi* (on me); *āsaktamanāḥ:* (with mind focused, heart attached); *pārtha* (O Partha, O Arjuna!); *yogam* (yoga); *yuñjan* (while concentrating on, while contemplating); *madāśrayaḥ:* (taken shelter in me); *asaṁśayam* (undoubdedly); *samagram* (fully); *mām* (me); *yathā* (how); *jñāsyasi* (you will understand); *tat* (adj◦-obj◦ to that); *śṛṇu* (please listen) (7.1)

(§4) saptamaḥ: adhyāyaḥ: jñānavijñānayogaḥ:. śrībhagavān uvāća. āsaktamanāḥ: mayi madāśrayaḥ: yuñjan yogam yathā jñāsyasi mām asaṁśayam pārtha śṛṇu tat samagram

(§5) The seventh cahpter. *jñāna-vijñāna-yoga.* The Lord said : With (your) mind focused on me, taken shelter in me (and) while concentrating[480] on *yoga,* how you will understand me undoubdedly (and) fully, O Arjuna! please listen to that. (7.1)

7.2 ज्ञानं तेऽहं सविज्ञानमिदं वक्ष्याम्यशेषतः ।
यज्ज्ञात्वा नेह भूयोऽन्यज्ज्ञातव्यमवशिष्यते ।।
jñānaṁ te'haṁ savijñānamidaṁ vakṣyāmyaśeṣataḥ:,
yajjñātvā neha bhūyo'nyajjñātavyamavaśiṣyate. (7.2)

(§1) *jñānam* (r◦ 14/1) *te* (r◦ 6/1) *aham* (r◦ 14/1) *savijñānam* (r◦ 8/18) *idam* (r◦ 14/1) *vakṣyāmi* (r◦ 4/1) *aśeṣataḥ:* (r◦ 22/8) *yat* (r◦ 11/2) *jñātvā na* (r◦ 2/1) *iha bhūyaḥ:* (r◦ 15/1) *anyat* (r◦ 11/2) *jñātavyam* (r◦ 8/16) *avaśiṣyate*

(§2) *jñānam* (3.40); *te* (1.7); *aham* (1.22); *savijñānam* (n◦ 2acc◦ sing◦ ←bahuvrī◦ *sa-vijñāna,* विज्ञानेन सह ←n◦ *vijñāna* (practical experience) 3.41 + adj◦ *saha* (with) 1.22); *idam* (Subj◦ 1.10); ***vakṣyāmi*** (1st-per◦ sing◦ fut2◦ लृट् भविष्य◦ parasmai◦ ←class2◦ √वच्); *aśeṣataḥ:* (6.24); *yat* (3.21); *jñātvā* (4.15); *na* (1.30); *iha* (2.5); *bhūyaḥ:* (2.20); *anyat* (2.31); *jñātavyam* (n◦ 1nom◦ sing◦ ←pot◦ adj◦ *jñātavya* (ought to be known) ←9√ज्ञा); *avaśiṣyate* (3rd-per◦ sing◦ pres◦ वर्तमान्–लट् ātmane◦ ←class7◦ अव√शिष्) (7.2)

---

[480] Elsewhere◦ *yuñjan* → by practicing (instrumental◦), with your mind concentrated, ...etc.

📖 युञ्जन् is Gerund, Present Active Participle of parasmaipadi verb √युज्, it denotes happening of one action WHILE other action occurs. It is not Instrumental Case, denoting an action caused 'by' or 'with the help of' other verb or thing.

(§3) *jñānaṃ* (obj1◦ knowledge); *te* (to you, you); *ahaṃ* (I); *savijñānaṃ* (with wisdom, with science, with practical-experience); *idaṃ* (adj◦-obj1◦ this); *vakṣyāmi* (I will explain); *aśeṣataḥ:* (fully); *yaṭ* (which); *jñātvā* (having understood); *na* (not); *iha* (in this world); *bhūyaḥ:* (again, any thing more); *anyaṭ* (adj1◦-obj2◦ other); *jñātavyaṃ* (adj2◦-obj2◦ worth knowing, ought to be known); *avaśiṣyate* (it remains, does remain) (7.2)

(§4) ahaṃ vakṣyāmi te idaṃ jñānaṃ aśeṣataḥ: savijñānaṃ yaṭ jñātvā bhūyaḥ: na anyaṭ jñātavyaṃ avaśiṣyate iha

(§5) I will explain you this knowledge[481] fully with (its) science, which having understood, nothing more other worth knowing remains in this world. (7.2)

7.3 मनुष्याणां सहस्त्रेषु कश्चिद्यतति सिद्धये ।
यततामपि सिद्धानां कश्चिन्मां वेत्ति तत्त्वतः ।।
manuṣyāṇām sahasreṣu kaśċidyatati siddhaye,
yatatāmapi siddhānām kaśċinmām vetti tattvataḥ:. (7.3)

(§1) *manuṣyāṇāṃ* (r◦ 24/6, 14/1) *sahasreṣu* (r◦ 25/5) *kaśċiṭ* (r◦ 9/9) *yatati siddhaye yatatāṃ* (r◦ 8/16) *api siddhānāṃ* (r◦ 14/1) *kaśċiṭ* (r◦ 12/2) *māṃ* (r◦ 14/1) *vetti tattvataḥ:* (r◦ 22/8)

(§2) *manuṣyāṇāṃ* (1.44); *sahasreṣu* (7loc◦ plu◦ ←adj◦ ***sahasra*** (thousand) ←√हस्); *kaśċiṭ* (2.17); 🕮*yatati* (3rd-per◦ sing◦ pres◦ वर्तमान्–लट् parasmai◦ ←class1◦ √यत् 6.43); ***siddhaye*** (4dat◦ sing◦ ←f◦ *siddhi* (success) 2.48); *yatatāṃ* (m◦ 6pos◦ sing◦ ←adj◦ *yataṭ* 2.60); *api* (1.26); 🕮***siddhānāṃ*** (6pos plu◦ ←m◦ ***siddha*** (accomplished) ←√सिध्); *kaśċiṭ* (2.17); *māṃ* (1.46); *vetti* (2.19); *tattvataḥ:* (4.9) (7.3)

(§3) *manuṣyāṇāṃ* (among the men); *sahasreṣu* (in thousands); *kaśċiṭ* (adj◦-subj1◦ someone); *yatati* (struggles, strives); *siddhaye* (for success); *yatatāṃ* (among the struggling ones); *api* (also); *siddhānāṃ* (of the successful ones, of the accomplished ones); *kaśċiṭ* (adj◦-subj2◦ someone); *māṃ* (obj◦ me); *vetti* (understands); *tattvataḥ:* (truly, in principle) (7.3)

(§4) manuṣyāṇāṃ sahasreṣu kaśċiṭ yatati siddhaye yatatāṃ siddhānāṃ api kaśċiṭ vetti māṃ tattvataḥ:

(§5) Among the thousands of men someone strives for success; among the struggling successful

---

[481] Elsewhere◦ *idaṃ jñānaṃ* → about this knowledge, that knowledge ...etc.

🕮 इदम् ज्ञामन् = this knowledge. There is a big difference between 'this knowledge' and 'about this knowledge.' e.g. reading 'about' the Gita is quite different from reading the Gita.

ones[482] also (only) someone understands me in principle. (7.3)

7.4 भूमिरापोऽनलो वायुः खं मनो बुद्धिरेव च ।
अहङ्कार इतीयं मे भिन्ना प्रकृतिरष्टधा ।।
bhūmirāpo‘nalo vāyuḥ: khaṁ mano buddhireva ća,
ahaṅkāra itīyaṁ me bhinnā prakṛtiraṣṭadhā. (7.4)

(§1) *bhūmiḥ:* (r◦ 16/1) *āpaḥ:* (r◦ 15/1) *analaḥ:* (r◦ 15/13) *vāyuḥ:* (r◦ 22/2) *khaṃ* (r◦ 14/1) *manaḥ:* (r◦ 15/7) *buddhiḥ:* (r◦ 16/1) *eva ća ahaṅkāraḥ:* (r◦ 19/2) *iti* (r◦ 1/5) *iyaṃ* (r◦ 14/1) *me bhinnā prakṛtiḥ:* (r◦ 16/1) *aṣṭadhā*

(§2) *bhūmiḥ:* (1nom◦ sing◦ ←f◦ *bhūmi* (earth) 2.8); *āpaḥ:* (water, 2.23); *analaḥ:* (1nom◦ sing◦ ←m◦ *anala* (fire) 3.39); *vāyuḥ:* (wind, 2.67); *khaṃ* (1nom◦ sing◦ ←n◦ ***kha*** (sky) ←√खर्व्); *manaḥ:* (1.30); *buddhiḥ:* (thinking) (2.39); *eva* (1.1); *ća* (1.1); ***ahaṅkāraḥ:*** (1nom◦ sing◦ ←m◦ *ahaṅkāra* (self-sense) 2.71); *iti* (1.25); ***iyaṃ*** (f◦ 1nom◦ sing◦ ←pron◦ *idaṃ* (this) 1.10); *me* (1.21); *bhinnā* (f◦ 1nom◦ sing◦ ←ppp◦ adj◦ *bhinna* (varied) ←√भिद्); ***prakṛtiḥ:*** (1nom◦ sing◦ ←f◦ *prakṛti* (nature) 3.5); *aṣṭadhā* (adv◦ ind◦ ←adj◦ *aṣṭa* or ***aṣṭaṇ*** (eight) ←√अश्) (7.4)

(§3) *bhūmiḥ:* (subj1◦ the earth, the gravity); *āpaḥ:* (subj2◦ water, the liquidity); *analaḥ:* (subj3◦ fire, the energy); *vāyuḥ:* (subj4◦ air, the fluidity); *khaṃ* (subj5◦ sky, the space); *manaḥ:* (subj6◦ the mind, the intellect); *buddhiḥ:* (subj7◦ thinking, the preception); *eva ća* (as well as); *ahaṅkāraḥ:* (subj8◦ self-sense, consciousness); *iti* (so, thus); *iyaṃ* (adj1◦-subj9◦ this, this is); *me* (my); *bhinnā* (adj2◦-Subj9◦ varied); *prakṛtiḥ:* (subj9◦ nature); *aṣṭadhā* (adj3◦-subj9◦ eightfold) (7.4)

(§4) bhūmiḥ: āpaḥ: analaḥ: vāyuḥ: khaṃ manaḥ: buddhiḥ: eva ća ahaṅkāraḥ: iti iyaṃ me aṣṭadhā bhinnā prakṛtiḥ:

(§5) The gravity, the liquidity, the energy, the fluidity, the space, the intellect, the preception as well as the consciousness,[483] thus is my eighfold varied[484] nature;
(7.4)

---

[482] Elsewhere◦ *siddhānāṃ* → among those who are perfect, amomgst those who are perfect, of the perfected ones, those who have achieved perfection, amongst those that are perfect, ...etc

📖 “among those who are perfect ...” If those all have achieved perfection and are perfect, then why only one “perfect” man understands Kṛṣṇa?

[483] Elsewhere◦ *ahaṅkāraḥ:* → egoism, ego, egoity, egotism, ...etc

[484] Elsewhere◦ *bhinnā* → divided, split, division, divided in to categories, kinds of elements, separated, ...etc.

7.5 अपरेयमितस्त्वन्यां प्रकृतिं विद्धि मे पराम् ।
जीवभूतां महाबाहो ययेदं धार्यते जगत् ।।

apareyamitastvanyāṃ prakṛtiṃ viddhi me parām,
jīvabhūtāṃ mahābāho yayedaṃ dhāryate jagat. (7.5)

(§1) *aparā* (r॰ 2/3) *iyaṃ* (r॰ 8/18) *itaḥ:* (r॰ 18/1) *tu* (r॰ 4/6) *anyāṃ* (r॰ 14/1) *prakṛtiṃ* (r॰ 14/1) *viddhi me parām* (r॰ 14/2) *jīvabhūtāṃ* (r॰ 14/1) *mahābāho yayā* (r॰ 2/3) *idaṃ* (r॰ 14/1) *dhāryate jagat*

(§2) *aparā* (f॰ 1nom॰ sing॰ ←adj॰ *apara* (inferior) 2.22); *iyaṃ* (7.4); **_itaḥ:_** (ind॰ *itas* ←pron॰ *idaṃ* 1.10); *tu* (1.2); *anyāṃ* (f॰ 2acc॰ sing॰ ←adj॰ *anya* (other) 1.9); *prakṛtiṃ* (3.33); *viddhi* (2.17); *me* (1.21); *parāṃ* (4.39); *jīvabhūtāṃ* (f॰ 2acc॰ sing॰ ←s-karm॰ **_jīva-bhūta_** (living being) ←m॰ **_jīva_** (jife) ←√जीव् + m॰ *bhūta* (being) 2.28); *mahābāho* (2.26); *yayā* (2.39); *idaṃ* (1.10); *dhāryate* (pass॰ 3rd-per॰ sing॰ pres॰ वर्तमान्-लट् ātmane॰ caus॰ ←class1॰ √धृ); **_jagat_** (1nom॰ sing॰ ←n॰ **_jagat_** (world) ←√गम्) (7.5)

(§3) *aparā* (adj1॰-subj1॰ 1inferior); *iyaṃ* (adj2॰-subj1॰ this); *itaḥ:* (than this); *tu* (however); *anyāṃ* (adj1॰-obj1॰ other); *prakṛtiṃ* (obj॰ nature); *viddhi* (please know); *me* (my); *parāṃ* (adj2॰-obj1॰ higher, superior); *jīvabhūtāṃ* (adj3॰-obj1॰ the life giving); *mahābāho* (O Mahabahu! O Arjuna!); *yayā* (by which); *idaṃ* (adj॰-obj2॰ this); *dhāryate* (is borne);[485] *jagat* (obj3॰ universe, world) (7.5)

(§4) iyaṃ aparā tu anyāṃ itaḥ: mahābāho viddhi me parāṃ prakṛtiṃ yayā jīvabhūtāṃ idaṃ jagat dhāryate

(§5) This (is my) inferior (nature), however, other than this O Arjuna! please know my life giving higher nature by which this universe is borne.[486] (7.5)

7.6 एतद्योनीनि भूतानि सर्वाणीत्युपधारय ।
अहं कृत्स्नस्य जगतः प्रभवः प्रलयस्तथा ।।

etadyonīni bhūtāni sarvāṇītyupadhāraya,
ahaṃ kṛtsnasya jagataḥ: prabhavaḥ: pralayastathā. (7.6)

(§1) *etadyonīni bhūtāni sarvāṇi* (r॰ 24/7, 1/5) *iti* (r॰ 4/3) *upadhāraya* (r॰ 23/1) *ahaṃ* (r॰ 14/1) *kṛtsnasya jagataḥ:* (r॰ 22/3) *prabhavaḥ:* (r॰ 22/3) *pralayaḥ:* (r॰ 18/1) *tathā*

(§2) *etadyonīni* (n॰ 1nom॰ plu॰ ←bahuvrī॰ adj॰ *etadyonīṃ*, एषा योनिः यस्य तत् ←pron॰ *etat* 2.3 + f॰ *yonī* 5.22); *bhūtāni* (1nom॰ 2.28); **_sarvāṇi_** (1nom॰ sing॰ ←n॰ *bhūta* (being) 2.30); *iti* (1.25); 📖**_upadhāraya_**

---

[485] Elsewhere॰ *dhāryate* → is sustained, is upheld...etc

[486] Elsewhere॰ *yayā dhāryate* → that which consists of, consisting of, comprising, which comprises, is converted into, ...etc.

(2nd-per◦ sing◦ imperative◦ लोट् parasmai◦ caus◦ ←class1◦ √धृ); *ahaṃ* (1.22); *kṛtsnasya* (6pos sing◦ ←adj◦ *kṛtsna* 1.40); *jagataḥ:* (6pos sing◦ ←n◦ *jagaṭ* (world) 7.5); 🕮***prabhavaḥ:*** (origin) (1nom◦ sing◦ ←m◦ *prabhava* 6.24); 🕮***pralayaḥ:*** (1nom◦ sing◦ ←m◦ ***pralaya*** (dissolution) ←प्र√ली); *tathā* (1.8) (7.6)

(§3) *etadyonīni* (adj1◦-subj◦ born in this womb); *bhūtāni* (subj◦ the beings born in this womb); *sarvāṇi* (adj2◦-subj◦ all); *iti* (thus, that); *upadhāraya* (please understand, bare in your mind); *ahaṃ* (subj2◦ I am); *kṛtsnasya* (of all, of the entire); *jagataḥ:* (of the universe); *prabhavaḥ:* (adj◦-subj2◦ the origine); *pralayaḥ:* (adj2◦-subj2◦ the dissolution); *tathā* (as well as) (7.6)

(§4) upadhāraya iti sarvāṇi bhūtāni etadyonīni ahaṃ prabhavaḥ:tathā pralayaḥ: kṛtsnasya jagataḥ:

(§5) Please bare in your mind that all the beings are born in this womb. I am the origine as well as the dissolution of the entire universe. (7.6)

7.7 मत्तः परतरं नान्यत्किञ्चिदस्ति धनञ्जय ।
मयि सर्वमिदं प्रोतं सूत्रे मणिगणा इव ।।
mattaḥ: parataraṁ nānyatkiñćidasti dhanañjaya,
mayi sarvamidaṁ protaṁ sūtre maṇigańā iva. (7.7)

(§1) *mattaḥ:* (r◦ 22/3) *parataraṃ* (r◦ 14/1) *na* (r◦ 1/1) *anyaṭ* (r◦ 10/5) *kiñćiṭ* (r◦ 8/2) *asti dhanañjaya mayi sarvaṃ* (r◦ 8/18) *idaṃ* (r◦ 14/1) *protaṃ* (r◦ 14/1) *sūtre maṇigańāḥ:* (r◦ 24/5, 20/3) *iva*

(§2) ***mattaḥ:*** (pronominal ind◦ ←5abl◦ sing◦ pron◦ *maṭ* 1.9); 🕮*parataraṃ* (n◦ 1nom◦ sing◦ ←adj◦ *para* (superior) 2.3 + comparative affix *tara* (more) 1.46); *na* (1.30); *anyaṭ* (2.31); *kiñćiṭ* (4.20); *asti* (2.40); *dhanañjaya* (2.48); *mayi* (3.30); *sarvaṃ* (2.17); *idaṃ* (1.10); 🕮*protaṃ* (n◦ 1nom◦ sing◦ ←ppp◦ adj◦ *prota* ←प्र√वे); *sūtre* (7loc◦ sing◦ ←n◦ ***sūtra*** (string) ←√सूत्र्); *maṇigańāḥ:* (m◦ 1nom◦ plu◦ ←tatpu◦ *maṇi-gańa*, मणीनाम् गण: ←m◦ or f◦ *maṇi* (bead) ←√मण् + collective noun m◦ ***gaṇa*** (group) ←√गण्); *iva* (1.30) (7.7)

(§3) *mattaḥ:* (than me); *parataraṃ* (adj◦-subj1◦ superior); *na* (does not); *anyaṭ* (adj2◦-subj1◦ other); *kiñćiṭ* (subj1◦ anything); *asti* (exist, there is); *dhanañjaya* (O Dhanañjaya! O Arjuna!); *mayi* (in me); *sarvaṃ* (adj1◦-subj2◦ all); *idaṃ* (subj2◦ this); *protaṃ* (obj2◦-subj2◦ is strung); *sūtre* (on a srting); *maṇigańāḥ:* (subj3◦ the pearls, the beads); *iva* (like) (7.7)

(§4) na asti kiñćiṭ anyaṭ parataraṃ mattaḥ: dhanañjaya mayi sarvaṃ idaṃ protaṃ iva maṇigańāḥ: sūtre

(§5) There does not exist anything other superior than me. O Arjuna! in me all this is strung like the pearls on a srting. (7.7)

7.8 रसोऽहमप्सु कौन्तेय प्रभास्मि शशिसूर्ययोः ।
प्रणवः सर्ववेदेषु शब्दः खे पौरुषं नृषु ।।

raso'hamapsu kaunteya prabhā'smi śaśisūryayoḥ:,
praṇavaḥ: sarvavedeṣu śabdaḥ: khe pauruṣaṁ nṛṣu; (7.8)

(§1) *rasaḥ:* (r◦ 15/1) *aham* (r◦ 8/16) *apsu kaunteya prabhā* (r◦ 1/3) *asmi śaśisūryayoḥ:* (r◦ 22/8) *praṇavaḥ:* (r◦ 22/7) *sarvavedeṣu* (r◦ 25/5) *śabdaḥ:* (r◦ 22/2) *khe pauruṣam* (r◦ 14/1) *nṛṣu* (r◦ 25/5)

(§2) 🕮*rasaḥ:* (2.59); *aham* (1.22); *apsu* (7loc◦ plu◦ ←f◦ collective noun *ap* (water) ←√आप्); *kaunteya* (2.14); 🕮*prabhā* (1nom◦ sing◦ ←f◦ *prabhā* (radiance) ←प्र√भा); ***asmi*** (1st-per◦ sing◦ pres◦ वर्तमान्-लट् parasmai◦ ←class2◦ √अस्); *śaśisūryayoḥ:* (m◦ 6pos◦ dual◦ ←dvandva◦ शशिनः च सूर्यस्य च ←m◦ ***śaśin*** (moon) ←√शश् + m◦ ***sūrya*** (sun) ←√सृ); *praṇavaḥ:* (1nom◦ sing◦ ←m◦ *praṇav* (Om) ←प्र√नू); *sarvavedeṣu* (सर्वेषु वेदेषु, m◦ 7loc◦ plu◦ ←pron◦ *sarva* 1.6 + m◦ *veda* 2.42); *śabdaḥ:* (1.13); *khe* (7loc◦ sing◦ ←n◦ *kha* (sky) 7.4); 🕮*pauruṣam* (1nom◦ sing◦ ←taddhita◦ adj◦ *pauruṣa* (virility) ←m◦ *puruṣa* 2.15); *nṛṣu* (7loc◦ plu◦ ←m◦ ***nṛ*** (man) ←√नी) (7.8)

(§3) *rasaḥ:* (subj◦-comp1◦[487] the liquidity); *aham* (subj◦ I); *apsu* (in the water); *kaunteya* (O Kaunteya! O Arjuna!); *prabhā* (subj◦-comp2◦ the radiance); *asmi* (am); *śaśisūryayoḥ:* (in the moon and the sun); *praṇavaḥ:* (subj◦-comp3◦ the sacred mono-syllable *om*); *sarvavedeṣu* (in all the vedas); *śabdaḥ:* (subj◦-comp4◦ the sound); *khe* (in the sky); *pauruṣam* (subj◦-comp5◦ the virility); *nṛṣu* (in the men) (7.8)

(§4) kaunteya aham asmi rasaḥ: apsu prabhā śaśisūryayoḥ: praṇavaḥ: sarvavedeṣu śabdaḥ: khe pauruṣam nṛṣu

(§5) O Arjuna! I am the liquidity[488] in the water, the radiance in the moon and the sun, the sacred mono-syllable *om*[489] in all the vedas, the sound in the sky (and) the virility in the men; (7.8)

7.9 पुण्यो गन्धः पृथिव्यां च तेजश्चास्मि विभावसौ ।
जीवनं सर्वभूतेषु तपश्चास्मि तपस्विषु ।।

puṇyo gandhaḥ: pṛthivyaṁ ća tejaśćāsmi vibhāvasau,
jīvanaṁ sarvabhūteṣu tapaśćāsmi tapasviṣu; (7.9)

---

[487] **subj◦-comp◦** = Subject Compliment. The sub◦-comp◦ is the Predicate Noun that links the subject with the verb. In this case the verb is √अस् to be.

[488] PLEASE NOTE : **In the use of the verb 'to be' (√as, √अस्), the subj◦-comp assumes Nominative (1st) case** (e.g. रसः, गन्धः ...etc.), **even in Active voice**.

[489] Elsewhere◦ *praṇava* → the Word Power, Aum, Syllable Aum...etc.

(§1) *puṇyaḥ:* (r◦ 15/2) *gandhaḥ:* (r◦ 22/3) *pṛthivyam̧* (r◦ 14/1) *ća tejaḥ:* (r◦ 17/1) *ća* (r◦ 1/1) *asmi vibhāvasau jīvanam̧* (r◦ 14/1) *sarvabhūteṣu* (r◦ 25/5) *tapaḥ:* (r◦ 17/1) *ća* (r◦ 1/1) *asmi tapasviṣu* (r◦ 25/5)

(§2) 🕮*puṇyaḥ:* (m◦ 1nom◦ sing◦ ←adj◦ *puṇya* (sacred) 6.41); 🕮*gandhaḥ:* (1nom◦ sing◦ ←m◦ ***gandha*** (fragrance) ←√गन्ध्); ***pṛthivyam̧*** (7loc◦ sing◦ ←f◦ *pṛthivī* (earth) 1.18); *ća* (1.1); 🕮***tejaḥ:*** (1nom◦ sing◦ ←n◦ ***tejaş*** (brilliance) ←√तिज्); *ća* (1.1); *asmi* (7.8); *vibhāvasau* (7loc◦ sing◦ ←m◦ *vibhāvasu* (fire) ←वि√भास्); 🕮*jīvanam̧* (1nom◦ sing◦ ←n◦ *jīvana* (life) ←√जीव्); *sarvabhūteṣu* (3.18); 🕮***tapaḥ:*** (1nom◦ sing◦ ←n◦ (austerity) *tapaş* 4.10); *ća* (1.1); *asmi* (7.8); *tapasviṣu* (7loc◦ plu◦ ←m◦ *tapasviņ* (ascetic) 6.46) (7.9)

(§3) *puṇyaḥ:* (adj◦-subj◦-comp6◦ the sacred); *gandhaḥ:* (subj◦-comp6◦ fragrance); *pṛthivyam̧* (in the earth); *ća* (and); *tejaḥ:* (subj◦-comp7◦ the brilliance); *ća* (and); *asmi* (subj◦ I am); *vibhāvasau* (in the fire); *jīvanam̧* (subj◦-comp8◦ life); *sarvabhūteṣu* (in all the beings); *tapaḥ:* (subj◦-comp9◦ the austerity); *ća* (and); *asmi* (I am); *tapasviṣu* (in the ascetics) (7.9)

(§4) ća asmi puṇyaḥ: gandhaḥ: pṛthivyam̧ ća tejaḥ: vibhāvasau jīvanam̧ sarvabhūteṣu ća asmi tapaḥ: tapasviṣu

(§5) And, I am the sacred fragrance in the earth and the brilliance in the fire, the life in all the beings, and I am the austerity[490] in the ascetics; (7.9)

7.10 बीजं मां सर्वभूतानां विद्धि पार्थ सनातनम् ।
बुद्धिर्बुद्धिमतामस्मि तेजस्तेजस्विनामहम् ।।
bījaṁ māṁ sarvabhūtānāṁ viddhi pārtha sanātanam̧,
buddhirbuddhimatāmasmi tejastejasvināmaham̧; (7.10)

(§1) *bījam̧* (r◦ 14/1) *mām̧* (r◦ 14/1) *sarvabhūtānām̧* (r◦ 14/1) *viddhi pārtha sanātanam̧* (r◦ 14/2) *buddhiḥ:* (r◦ 16/6) *buddhimatām̧* (r◦ 8/16) *asmi tejaḥ:* (r◦ 18/1) *tejasvinām̧* (r◦ 8/16) *aham̧* (r◦ 14/2)

(§2) 🕮***bījam̧*** (2acc◦ sing◦ ←n◦ ***bīja*** (seed) ←वि√जन्); *mām̧* (1.46); *sarva* (1.6); *bhūtānām̧* (2.69); *viddhi* (2.17); *pārtha* (1.25); *sanātanam̧* (2acc◦ 4.31); *buddhiḥ:* (2.39); *buddhimatām̧* (m◦ 6pos◦ plu◦ ←adj◦ *buddhimaţ* 4.18); *asmi* (7.8); *tejaḥ:* (1nom◦ 7.9); ***tejasvinām̧*** (6pos plu◦ ←m◦ *tejasviņ* (splendid) ←√तिज्);

---

[490]तप: = क्रियायोग: defined : (Pātañjalayogasūtram 2.1) तप: स्वाध्यायेश्वरप्रणिधानानि क्रियायोग: ।

* तप-स्वाध्याय-ईश्वर-प्रणिधानानि = तप: (स्वधर्मस्य स्वगुणानुसारेण सर्वदा पालनम्) स्वाध्याय: (शास्त्राभ्यास:) ईश्वर-प्रणिधानं (ईश्वरं प्रति श्रद्धा, निष्ठा, भक्ति:) च 'क्रियायोग:' इति उच्यते ।) The discipline of austerity of performing righteous actions according to one's own inborn nature, study of scriptures and devotion to God is called *'kriyā-yoga.'* See "*Learning Yoga Sūtras of Patañjali*" by Ratnakar Narale.

ahaṃ (1.22) (7.10)

(§3) *bījaṃ* (In this verse and in the following verse, the subj∘-comp is used as obj∘ obj10∘ the seed); *māṃ* (me); *sarva* (all); *bhūtānāṃ* (of the beings); *viddhi* (know, you please know); *pārtha* (O Partha! O Arjuna!); *sanātanaṃ* (the adj∘-obj10∘ beginingless and the endless); *buddhiḥ:* (obj11∘ thinking); *buddhimatāṃ* (of the thinkers, of the thoughtful); *asmi* (am); *tejaḥ:* (obj12∘ the splendor); *tejasvināṃ* (of the splendid); *ahaṃ* (subj∘ I) (7.10)

(§4) pārtha viddhi māṃ sanātanaṃ bījaṃ sarva bhūtānāṃ ahaṃ asmi buddhiḥ: buddhimatāṃ tejaḥ: tejasvināṃ;

(§5) (And), O Arjuna! you please know me, the beginingless and the endless seed of all beings. I am the thinking of the thinkers (and) the splendor of the splendid; (7.10)

7.11 **बलं बलवतामस्मि कामरागविवर्जितम् ।**
धर्माविरुद्धो भूतेषु कामोऽस्मि भरतर्षभ ॥
balaṁ balavatāmasmi kāmarāgavivarjitaṃ,
dharmāviruddho bhūteṣu kāmo'smi bharatarṣabha. (7.11)

(§1) *balaṃ* (r∘ 14/1) *balavatāṃ* (r∘ 8/16) *asmi kāmarāgavivarjitaṃ* (r∘ 14/2) *dharmāviruddhaḥ:* (r∘ 15/8) *bhūteṣu* (r∘ 25/5) *kāmaḥ:* (r∘ 15/1) *asmi bharatarṣabha*

(§2) 🕮*balaṃ* (power, strength) (1nom∘ 1.10); *balavatāṃ* (m∘ 6pos∘ plu∘ ←adj∘ *balavaṭ* (strong) 6.34); *asmi* (7.8); *kāmarāgavivarjitaṃ* (n∘ 1nom∘ sing∘ ←bahuvrī∘ adj∘ *kāma-rāga-vivarjita*, कामेन च रागेण च विवर्जितम् यत् तत् ←m∘ *kāma* (desire) 1.22 + m∘ *rāga* (attachment) 2.56 + ppp∘ adj∘ 🕮***vivarjita*** (gone) ←वि√वृज् 4.19); *dharmāviruddhaḥ:* (m∘ 1nom∘ sing∘ ←bahuvrī∘ *dharmāviruddha*, धर्मेण अविरुद्धः यः ←m∘ *dharma* (righteousness) 1.1 + negative affix अ *a* 1.10 + adj∘ *viruddha* (opposite) ←वि√रुध्); ***bhūteṣu*** (7loc∘ plu∘ ←m∘ *bhūta* 2.28); *kāmaḥ:* (2.62); *asmi* (7.8); *bharatarṣabha* (3.41) (7.11)

(§3) *balaṃ* (obj11∘ the strength); *balavatāṃ* (of the strong); *asmi* (subj∘ I am); *kāmarāgavivarjitaṃ* (adj∘-obj11∘ without desire and attachment); *dharmāviruddhaḥ:* (adj∘-obj12∘ not opposite to righteousness, that is consistant with righteousness); *bhūteṣu* (in the beings); *kāmaḥ:* (obj12∘ the desire); *asmi* (I am); *bharatarṣabha* (O Bharatarṣabha! O Arjuna!) (7.11)

(§4) bharatarṣabha balavatāṃ asmi balaṃ kāmarāgavivarjitaṃ asmi kāmaḥ: dharmāviruddhaḥ: bhūteṣu;

(§5) O Arjuna! of the strong I am the strength that is without desire and attachment[491] (and) I am

---

[491] Elsewhere∘ *kāmarāgavivarjitaṃ* → I am free from passion and attachment.

🕮 Note that कामरागविवर्जितम् is the adj∘ of n∘ noun बलम् (obj11∘), it is not qualifying m∘ subject अहम् (i.e.

the desire that is consistant with righteousness in the beings; (7.11)

7.12 ये चैव सात्त्विका भावा राजसास्तामसाश्च ये ।
मत्त एवेति तान्विद्धि न त्वहं तेषु ते मयि ।।
ye ćaiva sāttvikā bhāvā rājasāstāmasāśća ye,
matta eveti tānviddhi na tvahaṁ teṣu te mayi. (7.12)

(§1) *ye ća* (r◦ 3/1) *eva sāttvikāḥ:* (r◦ 20/12) *bhāvāḥ:* (r◦ 20/15) *rājasāḥ:* (r◦ 18/1) *tāmasāḥ:* (r◦ 17/1) *ća ye mattaḥ:* (r◦ 19/7) *eva* (r◦ 2/1) *iti tān̦* (r◦ 13/19) *viddhi na tu* (r◦ 4/6) *aham̦* (r◦ 14/1) *teṣu* (r◦ 25/5) *te mayi*

(§2) *ye* (1.7); *ća* (1.1); *eva* (1.1); ***sāttvikāḥ:*** (m◦ 1nom◦ plu◦ ←taddhita◦ adj◦ ***sāttvika*** (righteous) ←n◦ *saț* 2.16); *bhāvāḥ:* (1nom◦ plu◦ ←m◦ *bhāva* (nature) 2.16); ***rājasāḥ:*** (m◦ 1nom◦ plu◦ ←taddhita◦ adj◦ ***rājasa*** ←n◦ *rajaș* 3.37); ***tāmasāḥ:*** (m◦ 1nom◦ plu◦ ←taddhita◦ adj◦ ***tāmasa*** ←n◦ ***tamaș*** ←√तम्); *ća* (1.1); *ye* (1.7); *mattaḥ:* (7.7); *eva* (1.1); *iti* (1.25); *tān̦* (1.7); *viddhi* (2.17); *na* (1.30); *tu* (1.2); *aham̦* (1.22); *teṣu* (2.62); *te* (1.33); *mayi* (3.30) (7.12)

(§3) *ye* (adj1◦-subj1◦ those which are); *ća* (and); *eva* (even); *sāttvikāḥ:* (adj2◦-subj1◦ righteous, endowed with the attribute of *sattva*); *bhāvāḥ:* (subj1◦ states of beings); *rājasāḥ:* (adj2◦-subj1◦ those endowed with the attribute of *rajas*); *tāmasāḥ:* (adj3◦-subj1◦ endowed with the attribute of *tamas*); *ća* (and); *ye* (those which are); *mattaḥ:* (from me); *eva* (only); *iti* (thus, so); *tān̦* (them); *viddhi* (know to be); *na* (not); *tu* (but); *aham̦* (subj2◦ I am); *teṣu* (in them); *te* (adj4-subj1◦ they); *mayi* (in me) (7.12)

(§4) bhāvāḥ: ye sāttvikāḥ: ća rājasāḥ: ća eva ye tāmasāḥ: viddhi tān̦ mattaḥ: eva iti tu aham̦ na teṣu te mayi

(§5) Those states of beings, which are endowed with the attribute of *sattva* and those endowed with the attribute of *rajas* and even those which are endowed with the attribute of *tamas,* know them to be from me only so, but I am not in them, they (are) in me. (7.12)

7.13 त्रिभिर्गुणमयैर्भावैरेभिः सर्वमिदं जगत् ।
मोहितं नाभिजानाति मामेभ्यः परमव्ययम् ।।
tribhirguṇamayairbhāvairebhiḥ: sarvamidaṁ jagaț,
mohitaṁ nābhijānāti māmebhyaḥ: paramavyayam̦. (7.13)

(§1) *tribhiḥ:* (r◦ 16/6) *guṇamayaiḥ:* (r◦ 16/11) *bhāvaiḥ:* (r◦ 16/4) *ebhiḥ:* (r◦ 22/7) *sarvam̦* (r◦ 8/18)

Krishṇa).

idaṃ (r∘ 14/1) *jagaṭ* (r∘ 23/1) *mohitaṃ* (r∘ 14/1) *na* (r∘ 1/1) *abhijānāti māṃ* (r∘ 8/22) *ebhyaḥ:* (r∘ 22/3) *paraṃ* (r∘ 8/16) *avyayaṃ* (r∘ 14/2)

(§2) ***tribhiḥ:*** (m∘ 3inst∘ ←adj∘ *tri* (three) 2.45); *guṇamayaiḥ:* (m∘ 3inst∘ plu∘ ←taddhita∘ adj∘ ***guṇamaya*** ←m∘ *guṇa* (attribute) 2.45 + adj∘ *maya* (endowed with) 4.10); *bhāvaiḥ:* (3inst∘ plu∘ ←m∘ *bhāva* (nature) 2.7); ***ebhiḥ:*** (m∘ 3inst∘ plu∘ ←pron∘ *idaṃ* (this) 1.10); *sarvaṃ* (2.17); *idaṃ* (1.10); *jagaṭ* (7.5); *mohitaṃ* (1nom∘ sing∘ ←adj∘ *mohita* 4.16); *na* (1.30); *abhijānāti* (4.14); *māṃ* (1.46); *ebhyaḥ:* (3.12); *paraṃ* (2acc∘ 2.59); *avyayaṃ* (2acc∘ 2.21) (7.13)

(§3) *tribhiḥ:* (with the three); *guṇamayaiḥ:* (endowed with atteibutes); *bhāvaiḥ:* (with the states of beings); *ebhiḥ:* (with these); *sarvaṃ* (adj1∘-subj∘ all, whole); *idaṃ* (adj2∘-subj∘ this); *jagaṭ* (subj∘ world); *mohitaṃ* (adj3∘-subj∘ deluded); *na* (does not); *abhijānāti* (understand); *māṃ* (obj∘ me); *ebhyaḥ:* (than these); *paraṃ* (adj1∘-obj∘ transcendental, beyond); *avyayaṃ* (adj2∘-obj∘ eternal) (7.13)

(§4) idaṃ sarvaṃ jagaṭ mohitaṃ tribhiḥ: bhāvaiḥ: ebhiḥ: guṇamayaiḥ: na abhijānāti māṃ paraṃ ebhyaḥ: avyayaṃ

(§5) This whole world, deluded by the three states of beings endowed with these atteibutes, does not understand me (who is) beyond them (and) eternal. (7.13)

7.14 दैवी ह्येषा गुणमयी मम माया दुरत्यया ।
मामेव ये प्रपद्यन्ते मायामेतां तरन्ति ते ।।

daivī hyeṣā guṇamayī mama māyā duratyayā,
māmeva ye prapadyante māyāmetāṁ taranti te. (7.14)

(§1) *daivī hi* (r∘ 4/4) *eṣā* (r∘ 25/2) *guṇamayī mama māyā duratyayā māṃ* (r∘ 8/22) *eva ye prapadyante māyāṃ* (r∘ 8/22) *etāṃ* (r∘ 14/1) *taranti te*

(§2) 🕮***daivī*** (f∘ 1nom∘ sing∘ ←taddhita∘ adj∘ ***daivin*** (divine) ←n∘ *deva* (god) 4.25); *hi* (1.11); *eṣā* (2.39); *guṇamayī* (f∘ 1nom∘ sing∘ ←adj∘ *guṇamaya* 7.13); *mama* (1.7); *māyā* (4.6); 🕮*durtyayā* (f∘ 1nom∘ sing∘ ←adj∘ *durtyayā* (unfathomable) ←दुर्-अति√इ); *māṃ* (1.46); *eva* (1.1); *ye* (1.7); *prapadyante* (4.11); *māyāṃ* (2acc∘ sing∘ ←f∘ *māyā* 4.6); *etāṃ* (1.3); 🕮***taranti*** (3rd-per∘ plu∘ pres∘ वर्तमान्-लट् parasmai∘ ←class1∘ √तॄ); *te* (1.33) (7.14)

(§3) *daivī* (adj1∘-subj∘ divine); *hi* (because); *eṣā* (adj2∘-subj∘ this); *guṇamayī* (adj3∘-subj∘ endowed with the three attributes); *mama* (adj4∘-subj∘ my, of mine); *māyā* (subj∘ *māyā*, power, pleasure); *duratyayā* (adj5∘-subj∘ difficult to fathom); *māṃ* (me); *eva* (only); *ye* (adj∘-subj2∘ those who); *prapadyante* (they approach, they take refuge in); *māyāṃ* (obj∘ the *māya*); *etāṃ* (adj∘-obj∘ this); *taranti* (they cross over);

te (subj2∘ they)

(7.14)

(§4) hi eṣā daivī māyā mama guṇamayī duratyayā ye prapadyante mām̐ eva te taranti etām̐ māyām̐

(§5) Because[492] this divine *māyā* of mine, endowed with the three attributes, (is) difficult to fathom, (therefore) those who take refuge in me only they cross over this *māyā*. (7.14)

7.15 न मां दुष्कृतिनो मूढाः प्रपद्यन्ते नराधमाः ।
माययाऽपहृतज्ञाना आसुरं भावमाश्रिताः ।।

na māṁ duṣkṛtino mūḍhāḥ: prapadyante narādhamāḥ:,
māyayā'pahṛtajñānā āsuraṁ bhāvamāśritāḥ:. (7.15)

(§1) *na mām̐* (r∘ 14/1) *duṣkṛtinaḥ:* (r∘ 15/9) *mūḍhāḥ:* (r∘ 22/3) *prapadyante narādhamaḥ:* (r∘ 22/8) *māyayā* (r∘ 1/3) *apahṛtajñānāḥ:* (r∘ 20/2) *āsuram̐* (r∘ 14/1) *bhāvam̐* (r∘ 8/17) *āśritāḥ:* (r∘ 22/8)

(§2) *na* (1.30); *mām̐* (1.46); 🕮*duṣkṛtinaḥ:* (1nom∘ plu∘ ←m∘ *duṣkṛtin̐* (evil doer) ←ind∘ *duṣ̐* (evil) 3.39 + adj∘ *kṛtin̐* (doer) ←√कृ); 🕮***mūḍhāḥ:*** (1nom∘ plu∘ ←m∘ or ppp∘ adj∘ ***mūḍha*** (deluded) ←√मुह); *prapadyante* (4.11); 🕮*narādhamāḥ:* (m∘ 1nom∘ plu∘ ←bahuvrī∘ ***narādhama*** (base person) नरेषु अधमः यः ←m∘ *nara* (person) 1.5 + adj∘ ***adhama*** (mean) ←√अव्); ***māyayā*** (3inst∘ sing∘ ←f∘ *māyā* (delusion) 4.6); *apahṛtajñānāḥ:* (m∘ 1nom∘ plu∘ ←bahuvrī∘ *apahṛta-jñāna*, अपहृतम् ज्ञानम् यस्य ←adj∘ *apahṛta* (deprived) 2.44 + n∘ *jñāna* 3.3); 🕮***āsuram̐*** (m∘ 2acc∘ sing∘ ←adj∘ ***āsura*** (demonic) ←आ√अस्); ***bhāvam̐*** (2acc∘ sing∘ ←m∘ *bhāva* (nature) 2.7); 🕮***āśritāḥ:*** (m∘ 1nom∘ plu∘ ←ppp∘ adj∘ ***āśrita*** (sheltered) ←आ√श्रि) (7.15)

(§3) *na* (do not); *mām̐* (me); *duṣkṛtinaḥ:* (adj1∘-subj∘ the evil doers); *mūḍhāḥ:* (adj2-subj∘ foolish); *prapadyante* (they take for refuge); *narādhamāḥ:* (subj∘ mean people, vile people); *māyayā* (by *māyā*, through delusion); *apahṛtajñānāḥ:* (adj3∘-subj∘ those deprived of wisdom); *āsuram̐* (adj∘-obj∘ demonic); *bhāvam̐* (obj∘ state of being); *āśritāḥ:* (adj4∘-subj∘ taken recourse to) (7.15)

(§4) duṣkṛtinaḥ: mūḍhāḥ: narādhamāḥ: apahṛtajñānāḥ: māyayā āśritāḥ: āsuram̐ bhāvam̐ na mām̐ prapadyante

(§5) The evil doer foolish vile people, deprived of wisdom through delusion (and) taken recourse to demonic state of being, do not take me for refuge. (7.15)

7.16 चतुर्विधा भजन्ते मां जनाः सुकृतिनोऽर्जुन ।
आर्त्तो जिज्ञासुरर्थार्थी ज्ञानी च भरतर्षभ ।।

[492] See footnote in verse 3.5

ćaturvidhā bhajante māṁ janāḥ: sukṛtino‘rjuna,
ārtto jijñāsurarthārthī jñānī ća bharatarṣabha; (7.16)

(§1) *ćaturvidhā* (20.12) *bhajante māṃ* (r◦ 14/1) *janāḥ:* (r◦ 22/7) *sukṛtinaḥ:* (r◦ 15/1) *arjuna* (r◦ 23/1) *ārttaḥ:* (r◦ 15/3) *jijñāsuḥ:* (r◦ 16/3) *arthārthī jñānī ća bharatarṣabha;*

(§2) *ćaturvidhāḥ:* (m◦ 1nom◦ plu◦ ←adj◦ ***ćatur-vidha*** ←num◦ adj◦ ***ćatur*** (four) ←√चत् + m◦ *vidha* (kind) 3.3); 📖***bhajante*** (3rd-per◦ plu◦ pres◦ वर्तमान्-लट् ātmane◦ ←class1◦ √भज् 6.31); *māṃ* (1.46); ***janāḥ:*** (1nom◦ plu◦ ←m◦ *jana* (people) 1.28); *sukṛtinaḥ:* (1nom◦ plu◦ ←m◦ *sukṛtin* (righteous) ←सु√कृ); *arjuna* (2.2); *ārttaḥ:* (m◦ 1nom◦ sing◦ ←ppp◦ adj◦ *ārtta* (suffering) ←आ√ऋ); 📖*jijñāsuḥ:* (6.44); *arthārthī* (m◦ 1nom◦ sing◦ ←adj◦ *arthārthin* (wealth seeker) ←√अर्थ्); ***jñānī*** (m◦ 1nom◦ sing◦ ←adj◦ *jñānin* (*buddhiyogī,* selfless) 3.39); *ća* (1.1); *bharatarṣabha* (3.41); (7.16)

(§3) *ćaturvidhāḥ:* (adj1◦-subj◦ four types of); *bhajante* (worship); *māṃ* (me); *janāḥ:* (subj◦ persons); *sukṛtinaḥ:* (adj2◦-subj◦ righteous); *arjuna* (O Arjuna!); *ārttaḥ:* (adj3◦-subj◦ one who is suffering); *jijñāsuḥ:* (adj4◦-subj◦ one who is curious, desirous of knowledge); *arthārthī* (adj5◦-subj◦ one who is desirous of wealth); *jñānī* (adj6◦-subj◦ one who is equipped with the discipline of equanimity and selflessness)*ća* (and); *bharatarṣabha* (O Arjuna!); (7.16)

(§4) arjuna ćaturvidhāḥ: sukṛtinaḥ: janāḥ: bhajante māṃ ārttaḥ: jijñāsuḥ: arthārthī ća jñānī bharatarṣabha;

(§5) O Arjuna! four types of righteous persons worship me : (i) the one who is suffering, (ii) the one who is desirous of knowledge, (iii) the one who is desirous of wealth and (iv) the one who is equipped with the discipline of equanimity and selflessness,[493] O Arjuna! (7.16)

7.17 तेषां ज्ञानी नित्ययुक्त एकभक्तिर्विशिष्यते ।
प्रियो हि ज्ञानिनोऽत्यर्थमहं स च मम प्रियः ।।

teṣāṁ jñānī nityayukta ekabhaktirviśiṣyate,
priyo hi jñānino‘tyarthamahaṁ sa ća mama priyaḥ:; (7.17)

(§1) *teṣāṃ* (r◦ 25/3, 14/1) *jñānī nityayuktaḥ:* (r◦ 19/7) *ekabhaktiḥ:* (r◦ 16/6) *viśiṣyate* (r◦ 25/8) *priyaḥ:*

---

[493] Elsewhere◦ *jñānī* → knowledgable, the wise, intelligent, the man of wisdom, learned man, the wise man, the man of knowledge, one in full knowledge, one who is searching for knowledge, the man imbued with wisdom ...etc.

📖 For the explanation of the terms *jñāna, jñanayoga, jñānī* and *jñānavān,* in reference to the Gītā, please see Q2 of the Introductory Essay in the Volume I of this book.

(r◦ 15/14) *hi jñāninaḥ:* (r◦ 15/1) *atyarthaṃ* (r◦ 8/16) *ahaṃ* (r◦ 14/1) *saḥ:* (r◦ 21/2) *ća mama priyaḥ:* (r◦ 22/8);

(§2) *teṣāṃ* (5.16); *jñānī* (7.16); 🕮*nityayuktaḥ:* (m◦ 1nom◦ sing◦ ←s-karm◦ ***nitya-yukta***, नित्येन युक्तः ←adj◦ *nitya* (ever) 2.18 + adj◦ *yukta* (equipped) 1.14); *ekabhaktiḥ:* (m◦ 1nom◦ sing◦ ←bahuvrī◦ *eka-bhakti*, एकस्मिन् भक्तिः यस्य ←adj◦ *eka* (one pointed) 2.41 + f◦ 🕮***bhakti*** (devotion) ←√भज्); *viśiṣyate* (3.7); 🕮***priyaḥ:*** (m◦ 1nom◦ sing◦ ←adj◦ *priya* (dear) 1.23); *hi* (1.11); *jñāninaḥ:* (6pos◦ sing◦ ←m◦ *jñānin* 3.39); 🕮*atyarthaṃ* adv◦ ind◦ (very) ←अति√अर्थ्); *ahaṃ* (1.22); *saḥ:* (1.13); *ća* (1.1); *mama* (1.7); *priyaḥ:* (↑); (7.17)

(§3) *teṣāṃ* (of these, of these four types of people); *jñānī* (adj6◦-subj◦ the jñānī, one who is equipped with the discipline of equanimity with selflessness); *nityayuktaḥ:* (adj7◦-subj◦ he who is ever-equipped with the discipline of equanimity with selflessness); *ekabhaktiḥ:* (adj8◦-subj◦ one who has one-pointed faith, one whose faith is focused); *viśiṣyate* (excels); *priyaḥ:* (adj9◦-subj◦ dear); *hi* (because); *jñāninaḥ:* (of his or to him who is endowed with the discipline of equanimity with selflessness); *atyarthaṃ* (very); *ahaṃ* (subj3◦ I am); *saḥ:* (adj10◦-subj◦ he is); *ća* (and); *mama* (to me); *priyaḥ:* (adj11◦-subj◦ dear); (7.17)

(§4) teṣāṃ jñānī viśiṣyate hi nityayuktaḥ: ekabhaktiḥ: saḥ: jñāninaḥ: atyarthaṃ priyaḥ: mama ća ahaṃ priyaḥ:;

(§5) ...of these four types of people, the one who is equipped with the discipline of equanimity with selflessness excels because[494] he, who is ever equipped with the discipline of equanimity with selflessness, has one-pointed faith. He, who is endowed with the discipline of equanimity with selflessness, is very dear to me and I am dear to him; (7.17)

7.18 उदाराः सर्व एवैते ज्ञानी त्वात्मैव मे मतम् ।
आस्थितः स हि युक्तात्मा मामेवानुत्तमां गतिम् ।।
udārāḥ: sarva evaite jñānī tvātmaiva me matam,
āsthitaḥ: sa hi yuktātmā māmevānuttamām gatim; (7.18)

(§1) *udārāḥ:* (r◦ 22/7) *sarve* (r◦ 5/4) *eva* (r◦ 3/1) *ete jñānī tu* (r◦ 4/7) *ātmā* (r◦ 3/3) *eva me matam* (r◦ 14/2) *āsthitaḥ:* (r◦ 22/7) *saḥ:* (r◦ 21/2) *hi yuktātmā mām* (r◦ 8/22) *eva* (r◦ 1/1) *anuttamāṃ* (r◦ 14/1) *gatiṃ* (r◦ 14/2);

(§2) 🕮*udārāḥ:* (m◦ 1nom◦ plu◦ ←adj◦ *udāra* (noble) ←उद्–आ√रा); *sarve* (1.6); *eva* (1.1); *ete* (1.23); *jñānī*

[494] See footnote in verse 3.5

(7.16); *tu* (1.2); *ātmā* (6.5); *eva* (1.1); *me* (1.21); *matam̧* (adv◦ 3.31); *āsthitaḥ:* (5.4); *saḥ:* (1.13); *hi* (1.11); *yuktātmā* (m◦ 1nom◦ sing◦ ←bahuvrī◦ *yuktātman̦*, युक्तः आत्मा यस्य ←adj◦ *yukta* 1.14 + n◦ *ātman̦* 2.41); *mām̧* (1.46); *eva* (1.1); *anuttamām̧* (2acc◦ sing◦ ←f◦ 📖*anuttamā* ←adj◦ *uttama* (best) 1.7); *gatim̧* (6.37); (7.18)

(§3) *udārāḥ:* (adj12◦-subj◦ virtuous, noble); *sarve* (adj13◦-subj◦ all, all four); *eva* (indeed); *ete* (adj14◦-subj◦ these); *jñānī* (adj6◦-subj◦ he who is equipped with the discipline of equanimity with selflessness); *tu* (but); *ātmā* (adj15◦-subj◦ self); *eva* (very, indeed); *me* (my); *matam̧* (thought to be); *āsthitaḥ:* (adj16◦-subj◦ stable, established); *hi* (because); *yuktātmā* (adj17◦-subj◦ disciplined, equipped person); *mām̧* (to me); *eva* (only, alone); *anuttamām̧* (supreme); *gatim̧* (state, recourse); (7.18)

(§4) sarve ete eva udārāḥ: tu jñānī matam̧ me eva ātmā hi āsthitaḥ: yuktātmā anuttamām̧ gatim̧ mām̧ eva;

(§5) ...all these these four (are) indeed virtuous, but he who is equipped with the discipline of equanimity with selflessness (is) thought to be my very self, because[495] (this) stable (and) disciplined person (considers) supreme recourse to me[496] alone;

(7.18)

7.19 बहूनां जन्मनामन्ते ज्ञानवान्मां प्रपद्यते ।
वासुदेवः सर्वमिति स महात्मा सुदुर्लभः ।।
bahūnām̐ janmanāmante jñānavānmām̐ prapadyate,
vāsudevaḥ: sarvamiti sa mahātmā sudurlabhaḥ:. (7.19)

(§1) *bahūnām̧* (r◦ 14/1) *janmanām̧* (r◦ 8/16) *ante jñānavān̦* (r◦ 13/16) *mām̧* (r◦ 14/1) *prapadyate vāsudevaḥ:* (r◦ 22/7) *sarvam̧* (r◦ 8/18) *iti saḥ:* (r◦ 21/2) *mahātmā sudurlabhaḥ:* (r◦ 22/8).

(§2) *bahūnām̧* (n◦ 6pos◦ plu◦ ←adj◦ *bahu* (many) 1.9); *janmanām̧* (6pos plu◦ ←n◦ *janman̦* (birth) 2.27); ***ante*** (7loc◦ sing◦ ←adj◦ or m◦ 📖*anta* (end) 2.16); *jñānavān̦* (3.33); *mām̧* (1.46); *prapadyate* (3rd-per◦ sing◦

---

[495] See footnote in verse 3.5

[496] Elsewhere◦ *āsthitaḥ: saḥ mām anuttamām̐ gatim* → abides in Me; established in Me, the highest goal; mind fully established in Me; his mind concentrated on me, has taken refuge in me; in Me alone as the supreme goal, is fixed on Me, the highest Path ...etc.

📖 (i) *āsthitaḥ: saḥ* is the subject in Nominative (1st) case; mind is not the subject; *āsthitaḥ:* is ppp◦ adjective of the subject *saḥ*. (ii) *mām anuttamām̐ gatim* is not in Locative (7th) case, it is in Accusative (2nd) case, as it is the object of the subject *āsthitaḥ: saḥ*.

pres∘ वर्तमान्-लट् ātmane∘ ←class4∘ प्र√पद्); ***vāsudevaḥ:*** (m∘ 1nom∘ sing∘ ←prop∘ -taddhita∘ ***vāsudeva***, वसूनाम् देवस्य गोत्रापत्यम् ←m∘ *vāsu* or ***vasu*** (deity) ←√वस् + m∘ *deva* 3.11); *sarvam* (4.33); *iti* (1.25); *saḥ:* (1.13); 🕮**mahātmā** (m∘ 1nom∘ sing∘ ←m∘ **mahātman**, महान् आत्मा यस्य ←adj∘ *mahā* 1.3 + m∘ *ātman* 2.41); 🕮*sudurlabhaḥ:* (m∘ 1nom∘ sing∘ ←ind∘ *su* 5.1 + adj∘ *durlabha* 6.42). (7.19)

(§3) *bahūnām* (of many); *janmanām* (of births); *ante* (at the end); *jñānavān* (adj18∘-subj∘ he who is equipped with the discipline of equanimity with selflessness); *mām* (to me, me); *prapadyate* (approaches); *vāsudevaḥ:* (adj∘subj2∘ Vāsudeva, the Lord); *sarvam* (adv∘ altogether, all); *iti* (thus, as); *saḥ:* (adj19∘-subj∘ that, such, he); *mahātmā* (adj20∘-subj∘ a great soul); *sudurlabhaḥ:* (adj21∘-subj∘ rare). (7.19)

(§4) ante janmanām jñānavān prapadyate mām iti vāsudevaḥ: sarvam iti saḥ: mahātmā sudurlabhaḥ:.

(§5) At the end of many births he who is equipped with the discipline of equanimity with selflessness approaches me as the Lord (is) all. Such a great soul (is) rare. (7.19)

7.20 **कामैस्तैस्तैर्हृतज्ञानाः प्रपद्यन्तेऽन्यदेवताः ।**
तं तं नियममास्थाय प्रकृत्या नियताः स्वया ।।
kāmaistaistairhṛtajñānāḥ: prapadyante'nyadevatāḥ:,
taṁ taṁ niyamamāsthāya prakṛtyā niyatāḥ: svayā. (7.20)

(§1) *kāmaiḥ:* (r∘ 18/1) *taiḥ:* (r∘ 18/1) *taiḥ:* (r∘ 16/11) *hṛtajñānāḥ:* (r∘ 22/3) *prapadyante* (r∘ 6/1) *anyadevatāḥ:* (r∘ 22/8) *tam* (r∘ 14/1) *tam* (r∘ 14/1) *niyamam* (r∘ 8/17) *āsthāya prakṛtyā niyatāḥ:* (r∘ 22/7) *svayā*

(§2) *kāmaiḥ:* (3inst∘ plu∘ ←m∘ *kāma* (desire) 1.22); *taiḥ:* (3.12); *taiḥ:* (3.12); 🕮*hṛtajñānāḥ:* (m∘ 1nom∘ plu∘ ←bahuvrī∘ *hṛta-jñāna*, हृतम् ज्ञानम् यस्य ←ppp∘ adj∘ *hṛta* (overpowered) ←√हृ + n∘ *jñāna* (thinking) 3.3); *prapadyante* (4.11); *anyadevatāḥ:* (f∘ 1nom∘ plu∘ ←s-karm∘ *anya-devatā*, अन्या देवता ←adj∘ *anya* (other) 1.9 + f∘ *devatā* (deity) 4.12); *tam* (2.1); *tam* (2.1); 🕮*niyamam* (2acc∘ sing∘ ←m∘ *niyama* (ever) ←नि√यम्); *āsthāya* (lyp∘ past-participle ind∘ ←आ√स्था); *prakṛtyā* (3inst∘ sing∘ ←f∘ *prakṛti* (nature) 3.5); *niyatāḥ:* (f∘ 1nom∘ plu∘ ←adj∘ *niyata* (ever) 1.44); *svayā* (f∘ 3inst∘ sing∘ ←pron∘ *sva* (own) 1.28) (7.20)

(§3) *kāmaiḥ:* (by the desires); *taiḥ: taiḥ:* (by whichever those, by various); *hṛtajñānāḥ:* (those whose equanimous thinking is overpowered); *prapadyante* (approach, take recourse to); *anyadevatāḥ:* (other deities); *tam tam* (to those various); *niyamam* (rite, rites collectively); *āsthāya* (having ordained, ordaining); *prakṛtyā* (by nature); *niyatāḥ:* (prescribed, specific); *svayā* (by their own) (7.20)

(§4) hṛtajñānāḥ: taiḥ: taiḥ: kāmaiḥ: prapadyante niyatāḥ: anyadevatāḥ: āsthāya svayā prakṛtyā tam tam niyamam̦

(§5) Those whose equanimous thinking[497] is overpowered by various desires, approach other specific deities[498] ordaining their own nature to those various rites (collectively). (7.20)

7.21 यो यो यां यां तनुं भक्तः श्रद्धयार्चितुमिच्छति ।
तस्य तस्याचलां श्रद्धां तामेव विदधाम्यहम् ।।
yo yo yām̐ yām̐ tanum̐ bhaktaḥ: śraddhayārćitumiććhati,
tasya tasyāćalām̐ śraddhām̐ tāmeva vidadhāmyaham̦ (7.21)

(§1) *yo yo yām̦* (r∘ 14/1) *yām̦* (r∘ 14/1) *tanum̦* (r∘ 14/1) *bhaktaḥ:* (r∘ 22/5) *śraddhayā* (r∘ 1/3) *arćitum̦* (r∘ 8/18) *iććhati tasya tasya* (r∘ 1/1) *aćalām̦* (r∘ 14/1) *śraddhām̦* (r∘ 14/1) *tām̦* (r∘ 8/22) *eva vidadhāmi* (r∘ 4/1) *aham̦* (r∘ 14/2)

(§2) *yaḥ:* (2.19); *yaḥ:* (2.19); *yām̦* (2.42); *yām̦* (2.42); 🕮***tanum̦*** (2acc∘ sing∘ ←f∘ *tanu* (body) ←√तन्); *bhaktaḥ:* (4.3); *śraddhayā* (6.37); *arćitum̦* (inf∘ ind∘ ←√अर्च्); *iććhati* (3rd-per∘ sing∘ pres∘ वर्तमान्-लट् parasmai∘ ←class6∘ √इष् 1.35); *tasya* (1.12); *tasya* (1.12); 🕮*aćalām̦* (f∘ 2acc∘ sing∘ ←adj∘ *aćala* (firm) 2.24); *śraddhām̦* (2acc∘ sing∘ ←f∘ *śraddhā* (devotion) 3.31); ***tām̦*** (f∘ 2acc∘ sing∘ ←pron∘ *tad̦* 1.2); *eva* (1.1); *vidadhāmi* (1st-per∘ sing∘ pres∘ वर्तमान्-लट् parasmai∘ ←class3∘ वि√धा); *aham̦* (1.22) (7.21)

(§3) *yaḥ: yaḥ:* (adj1∘-subj1∘ whoever); *yām̦ yām̦* (adj∘-obj1∘ whatever); *tanum̦* (obj1∘ body, outward form, manifestation); *bhaktaḥ:* (subj∘ devotee); *śraddhayā* (with faith, with devotion); *arćitum̦* (to worship, to adore); *iććhati* (wishes, wants); *tasya tasya* (of that each devotee); *aćalām̦* (adj1∘-obj2∘ firm); *śraddhām̦* (obj2∘ faith); *tām̦* (adj2∘-obj2∘ that, that faith); *eva* (only); *vidadhāmi* (I make, confer);

---

[497] Elsewhere∘ *jñānam* → intelligence, knowledge, discrimination, capacity of discrimination, mind, minds, wisdom, ...etc.

[498] Elsewhere∘ (प्रपद्यन्ते अन्यदेवताः नियमम् आस्थाय) प्रकृत्या नियताः स्वया → being prompted by their own nature, being swayed by their own nature, according to their own nature, constrained by their own material nature, according to their own nature, led by their own nature, influenced by their own nature, ruled by their own nature, ...etc.

🕮 (i) In प्रकृत्या नियताः स्वया, the Instrumental (3rd) case स्वया is the adjective∘ of Instrumental (3rd) case प्रकृत्या । Nominative (1st) case plural∘ नियताः has no relationship with singular∘ प्रकृत्या and and singular∘ स्वया । fem∘ plural∘ नियताः (prescribed, specified) is the f∘ plu∘ adjective∘ of f∘ plu∘ Nominative case subject अन्यदेवताः । (ii) नियताः is not an adverb∘

ahaṃ (subj2◦ I) (7.21)

(§4) yaḥ: yaḥ: bhaktaḥ: iććhati arćitum yāṃ yāṃ tanuṃ śraddhayā ahaṃ vidadhāmi aćalāṃ eva tāṃ śraddhāṃ tasya tasya

(§5) Whichever devotee wishes to worship whichever manifestation with devotion, I make firm only that faith[499] of that each devotee; (7.21)

7.22 स तया श्रद्धया युक्तस्तस्याराधनमीहते ।
लभते च ततः कामान्मयैव विहितान्हि तान् ।।
sa tayā śraddhayā yuktastasyārādhanamīhate,
labhate ća tataḥ: kāmānmayaiva vihitānhi tān; (7.22)

(§1) *saḥ:* (r◦ 21/2) *tayā śraddhayā yuktaḥ:* (r◦ 18/1) *tasya* (r◦ 1/2) *ārādhanaṃ* (r◦ 8/19) *īhate labhate ća tataḥ:* (r◦ 22/1) *kāmān* (r◦ 13/16) *mayā* (r◦ 3/3) *eva vihitān* (r◦ 13/21) *hi tān*

(§2) *saḥ:* (1.13); *tayā* (2.44); *śraddhayā* (6.37); *yuktaḥ:* (2.39); *tasya* (1.12); 📖*ārādhanaṃ* (2acc◦ sing◦ ←n◦ *ārādhana* (adoration) ←आ√राध्); *īhate* (3rd-per◦ sing◦ pres◦ वर्तमान्-लट् ātmane◦ ←class1◦ √ईह्); *labhate* (4.39); *ća* (1.1); *tataḥ:* (1.13); *kāmān* (2.55); *mayā* (1.22); *eva* (1.1); *vihitān* (m◦ 2acc◦ plu◦ ←ppp◦ adj◦ 📖***vihita*** (prescribed) ←वि√धा); *hi* (1.11); *tān* (1.7) (7.22)

(§3) *saḥ:* (adj◦-subj1◦ he); *tayā* (with that); *śraddhayā* (faith); *yuktaḥ:* (adj2◦-subj1◦ equipped); *tasya* (his); *ārādhanaṃ* (obj3◦ adoration, object of adoration); *īhate* (he seeks); *labhate* (he attains); *ća* (and, and thus); *tataḥ:* (from it, from thence); *kāmān* (obj4◦ desires); *mayā* (subj2◦ by me); *eva* (only); *vihitān* (the ordained, prescribed); *hi* (because); *tān* (adj◦-obj4◦ those) (7.22)

(§4) hi yuktaḥ: tayā śraddhayā saḥ: īhate tasya ārādhanaṃ ća tataḥ: labhate tān kāmān vihitān mayā eva

(§5) ...because,[500] equipped with that faith, he seeks his object of adoration and thus, from it he attains those desires[501] (as) ordained by me only; (7.22)

---

[499] Elsewhere◦ *tāṃ* → on him, to that particular deity ...etc.

📖 ताम् is the pronominal f◦ adj◦ of the f◦ object◦ श्रद्धाम्. It does not qualify or relate to the m◦ भक्तः (devotee) or to f◦ तनुम् (deity).

[500] See footnote in verse 3.5

[501] Elsewhere◦ *saḥ labhate tān vihitān kāmān* → but they are actually bestowed up on him by none but Myself, But in actuality these benefits are bestowed by Me alone, Because those desires are decreed by Me, whatever he gets is indeed granted by me, which are being actually ordained by Me, ...etc.

7.23 अन्तवत्तु फलं तेषां तद्भवत्यल्पमेधसाम् ।
देवान्देवयजो यान्ति मद्भक्ता यान्ति मामपि ।।

antavattu phalaṁ teṣāṁ tadbhavatyalpamedhasām,
devāndevayajo yānti madbhaktā yānti māmapi. (7.23)

(§1) *antavaṭ* (r◦ 1/10) *tu phalaṃ* (r◦ 14/1) *teṣāṃ* (r◦ 253, 14/1) *taṭ* (r◦ 9/8) *bhavati* (r◦ 4/1) *alpamedhasāṃ* (r◦ 14/2) *devāṇ* (r◦ 13/11) *devayajaḥ:* (r◦ 15/10) *yānti madbhaktāḥ:* (r◦ 20/14) *yānti māṃ* (r◦ 8/16) *api*

(§2) *antavaṭ* (n◦ 1nom◦ sing◦ ←adj◦ *antavaṭ* 2.18); *tu* (1.2); 🕮***phalaṃ*** (1nom◦ sing◦ n◦ *phala* (fruit) 2.51); *teṣāṃ* (5.16); *taṭ* (1.10); *bhavati* (1.44); *alpamedhasāṃ* (m◦ 6pos◦ plu◦ ←bahuvrī◦ *alpa-medhaṣ,* अल्पा मेधा यस्य ←adj◦ 🕮***alpa*** (short) ←√अल् + m◦ *medhaṣ* ←f◦ 🕮***medhā*** (thinking) ←√मेधृ); *devāṇ* (3.11); *devayajaḥ:* (m◦ 1nom◦ plu◦ ←tatpu◦ देवयज् *deva-yaj,* देवानाम् यजी ←m◦ *deva* (deity) 3.11 + m◦ *yajī* (worshipper) ←adj◦ ***yajiṇ*** ←√यज्); *yānti* (3.33); *madbhaktāḥ:* (m◦ 1nom◦ plu◦ ←tatpu◦ ***madbhakta***, मम भक्तः ←pron◦ *maṭ* (my) 1.9 + m◦ *bhakta* (devotee) 4.3); *yānti* (3.33); *māṃ* (1.46); *api* (1.26) (7.23)

(§3) *antavaṭ* (adj1◦-subj1◦ having an end, impermament, temporary); *tu* (indeed, but); ***phalaṃ*** (subj1◦ fruit); *teṣāṃ* (of those); *taṭ* (adj2◦-subj◦ that); *bhavati* (becomes); *alpamedhasāṃ* (of the ones with narrow thinking, mediocre mind, little understanding, of the ignorant people); *devāṇ* (obj1◦ to the deities); *devayajaḥ:* (subj2◦ the worshippers of the deities); *yānti* (go, attain); *madbhaktāḥ:* (subj3◦ my devotees); *yānti* (attain); *māṃ* (obj2◦ me); *api* (and) (7.23)

(§4) taṭ phalaṃ teṣāṃ alpamedhasāṃ tu bhavati antavaṭ devayajaḥ: yānti devāṇ api madbhaktāḥ: yānti māṃ

(§5) That fruit of the faith of those ignorant people[502] indeed is temporary. The worshippers of the deities go to the deities and my devotees attain me. (7.23)

7.24 अव्यक्तं व्यक्तिमापन्नं मन्यन्ते मामबुद्धयः ।
परं भावमजानन्तो ममाव्ययमनुत्तमम् ।।

avyaktaṁ vyaktimāpannaṁ manyante māmabuddhayaḥ:,
paraṁ bhāvamajānanto mamāvyayamanuttamaṃ. (7.24)

(§1) *avyaktaṃ* (r◦ 14/1) *vyaktiṃ* (r◦ 8/17) *āpannaṃ* (r◦ 14/1) *manyante māṃ* (r◦ 8/16) *abuddhayaḥ:*

🕮 In सः लभते तान् विहितान् कामान्, the Accusative (2nd) case adj◦ तान् qualifies the Accisative object◦ विहितान् कामान् । of the subject सः verb लभते ।.

[502] Elsewhere◦ अल्पमेधसाम् → of small intellegence, of small intellect ...etc.

(r◦ 22/8) *paraṃ* (r◦ 14/1) *bhāvaṃ* (r◦ 8/16) *ajānantaḥ:* (r◦ 15/9) *mama* (r◦ 1/1) *avyayaṃ* (r◦ 8/16) *anuttamaṃ* (r◦ 14/2)

(§2) ***avyaktaṃ*** (m◦ 2acc◦ sing◦ ←adj◦ *avyakta* (unmanifest) 2.25); 🕮***vyaktiṃ*** (2acc◦ sing◦ ←f◦ ***vyakti*** (manifest) ←वि√अञ्ज्); 🕮*āpannaṃ* (2acc◦ sing◦ ←ppp◦ adj◦ ***āpanna*** (attained, assumed) ←आ√पद्); *manyante* (3rd-per◦ plu◦ pres◦ वर्तमान्–लट् ātmane◦ ←class4◦ √मन् 2.19); *māṃ* (1.46); *abuddhayaḥ:* (1nom◦ plu◦ ←m◦ n.bahuvrī◦ *abuddhi* नास्ति बुद्धिः यस्य सः ←f◦ *buddhi* (thinking) 2.39); *paraṃ* (2.59); *bhāvaṃ* (7.15); 🕮***ajānantaḥ:*** (m◦ 1nom◦ plu◦ ←śatṛ◦ adj◦ ***ajānaṭ*** (ignorant) ←अ√ज्ञा); *mama* (1.7); *avyayaṃ* (2.21); *anuttamaṃ* (m◦ 2acc◦ sing◦ ←n.bahuvrī◦ adj◦ *anuttamam* (paramount) 7.18, न उत्तमः यस्मात् ←adj◦ *uttama* (supreme) 1.7) (7.24)

(§3) *avyaktaṃ* (adj1◦-obj1◦ the unmanifest, unpersonified); *vyaktiṃ āpannaṃ* (adj2◦-obj1◦ one who is individual person, one who is born); *manyante* (they think, they imagine); *māṃ* (obj1◦ me, to me); *abuddhayaḥ:* (subj◦ the ignorant people); *paraṃ* (adj1◦-obj2◦ supreme); *bhāvaṃ* (obj2◦ nature, existence); *ajānantaḥ:* (not understanding); *mama* (my); *avyayaṃ* (adj2◦-obj2◦immutable); *anuttamaṃ* (adj3◦-obj2◦ paramount) (7.24)

(§4) abuddhayaḥ: ajānantaḥ: mama avyaktaṃ avyayaṃ anuttamaṃ paraṃ bhāvaṃ manyante māṃ āpannaṃ vyaktiṃ

(§5) The ignorant people, not understanding my supreme, unmanifest, immutable (and) paramount nature, think me (as) one who is an individual person.[503] (7.24)

7.25 नाहं प्रकाशः सर्वस्य योगमायासमावृतः ।
मूढोऽयं नाभिजानाति लोको मामजमव्ययम् ।।
nāhaṃ prakaśaḥ: savrvasya yogamāyāsamāvṛtaḥ:,
mūḍho'yaṃ nābhijānāti loko māmajamavyayaṃ. (7.25)

(§1) *na* (r◦ 1/1) *ahaṃ* (r◦ 14/1) *prakaśaḥ:* (r◦ 22/7) *sarvasya yogamāyāsamāvṛtaḥ:* (r◦ 22/8) *mūḍhaḥ:* (r◦ 15/1) *ayaṃ* (r◦ 14/1) *na* (r◦ 1/1) *abhijānāti lokaḥ:* (r◦ 15/9) *māṃ* (r◦ 8/16) *ajaṃ* (r◦ 8/16) *avyayaṃ* (r◦ 14/2)

(§2) *na* (1.30); *ahaṃ* (1.22); 🕮***prakaśaḥ:*** (1nom◦ sing◦ ←m◦ ***prakaśa*** (revelation) ←प्र√काश्); *sarvasya*

---

[503] Elsewhere◦ अव्यक्तं व्यक्तिमापन्नं मन्यन्ते मामबुद्धयः → Unintelligent men...think that I, ...was impersonal before and have now assumed this personality; The unmanifest has attained manifestation, so do men of samll intelligence think of Me; ...etc.

(2.30); *yogamāyāsamāvṛtaḥ:* (m∘ 1nom∘ sing∘ ←tatpu∘ *yoga-māyā-samāvṛta*, योगस्य मायया समावृत: ←m∘ *yoga* 2.39 + f∘ *māyā* (charm) 4.6 + ppp∘ adj∘ 🕮**samāvṛta** (covered) ←सम्-आ√वृ); *mūḍhaḥ:* (1nom∘ sing∘ ←m∘ *mūḍha* (deluded) 7.15); *ayaṃ* (2.19); *na* (1.30); *abhijānāti* (4.14); *lokaḥ:* (3.9); *māṃ* (1.46); *ajaṃ* (2.21); *avyayaṃ* (2.21) (7.25)

(§3) *na* (not); *ahaṃ* (subj1∘ I am); *prakaśaḥ:* (m∘ a revelation, an experience; adj1∘-subj1∘ visible, manifest); *sarvasya* (of all, for all); *yogamāyāsamāvṛtaḥ:* (adj2∘-subj1∘ covered with the charm of yoga); *mūḍhaḥ:* (adj1∘-subj2∘ deluded); *ayaṃ* (adj2∘-subj2∘ this); *na* (does not); *abhijānāti* (understand); *lokaḥ:* (subj2∘ world); *māṃ* (obj∘ me); *ajaṃ* (adj1∘-obj∘ the birthless); *avyayaṃ* (adj2∘-obj∘ immutable) (7.25)

(§4) yogamāyāsamāvṛtaḥ: ahaṃ na prakaśaḥ: sarvasya ayaṃ mūḍhaḥ: lokaḥ: na abhijānāti ajaṃ avyayaṃ māṃ

(§5) Covered with the charm of yoga,[504] I am not a revelation for everyone. This deluded world does not understand the birthless[505] immutable me.[506] (7.25)

7.26 वेदाहं समतीतानि वर्तमानानि चार्जुन ।
भविष्याणि च भूतानि मां तु वेद न कश्चन ।।

vedāhaṃ samatītāni vartamānāni ćārjuna,
bhaviṣyāṇi ća bhūtāni māṃ tu veda na kaśćana. (7.26)

(§1) *veda* (r∘ 1/1) *ahaṃ* (r∘ 14/1) *samatītāni vartamānāni ća* (r∘ 1/1) *arjuna bhaviṣyāṇi* (r∘ 24/7) *ća*

---

[504] Elsewhere∘ योगमाया → creative power, creation illusion, myserious power, divine potency, internal potency, cosmic illusion, yoga magic ...etc.

[505] Elsewhere∘ अजम् → unborn.

🕮 Please see the explanation given for अज in the footnote in the verse 2.20, in Volume I

[506] Elsewhere∘ नाभिजानाति माम् → they do not know that I am unborn and immutable, do not know me unborn and immutable as I am, ...etc.

🕮 In the use of phrase 'I am,' the attached attributes have to be in Nominative (1st) case (i.e. अज:, अव्यय:), as the m∘ subject is. Here the Ajamą and Avyayamą are the Accusative (2nd) case adjectives of the Accusative case object 'माम्' Thus, it should NOT be 'they do not know that I am ...,' instead it should be, 'they do not know me, the ...'

The difference is this : (i) The first case, 'they do not know that I am...' indicates that I have only these two attributes. (ii) Whereas, in the second case : 'they do not know me,' (in addition to being) the possessor these two qualities, as well as all other attributes mentioned the chapters the Gita. See the '301 attributes of Krishna' given in Volume I.

bhūtāni māṃ (r◦ 14/1) *tu veda na kaśćana*

(§2) *veda* (4.5); *ahaṃ* (1.22); 📖*samatītāni* (n◦ 2acc◦ plu◦ ←ppp◦ adj◦ *samatīta* (past) ←सम्√इ); 📖*vartamānāni* (n◦ 2acc◦ plu◦ ←adj◦ *vartamāna* 6.31); *ća* (1.1); *arjuna* (2.2); *bhaviṣyāṇi* (n◦ 2acc◦ plu◦ ←adj◦ 📖*bhaviṣya* (future) ←√भू); *ća* (1.1); *bhūtāni* (2.30); *māṃ* (1.46); *tu* (1.2); *veda* (2.21); *na* (1.30); *kaśćana* (3.18) (7.26)

(§3) *veda* (I know); *ahaṃ* (subj1◦ I); *samatītāni* (adj1◦-obj1◦ past, those of the past); *vartamānāni* (adj2◦-obj1◦ present, those who are present); *ća* (and); *arjuna* (O Arjuna!); *bhaviṣyāṇi* (adj3◦-obj1◦ future, those who will be in the future); *ća* (and); *bhūtāni* (obj1◦ the beings); *māṃ* (obj2◦ me); *tu* (but); *veda* (knows); *na kaśćana* (subj2◦ no one, nobody) (7.26)

(§4) arjuna ahaṃ veda bhūtāni samatītāni ća vartamānāni ća bhaviṣyāṇi tu na kaśćana veda māṃ

(§5) O Arjuna! I know the beings of the past and those who are present and those who will be in the future, but nobody knows me. (7.26)

7.27 इच्छाद्वेषसमुत्थेन द्वन्द्वमोहेन भारत ।
सर्वभूतानि सम्मोहं सर्गे यान्ति परन्तप ।।

iććhādveṣasamutthena dvandvamohena bhārata,
sarvabhūtāni sammohaṁ sarge yānti parantapa; (7.27)

(§1) *iććhādveṣasamutthena dvandvamohena bhārata sarvabhūtāni sammohaṃ* (r◦ 14/1) *sarge yānti parantapa*

(§2) *iććhādveṣasamutthena* (m◦ 3inst◦ sing◦ ←bahuvrī◦ *iććhā-dveṣa-samuttha*, इच्छाया: च द्वेषात् समुत्थ: य: ←f◦ *iććhā* (desire) 5.28 + m◦ *dveṣa* (revulsion) 2.64 + ppp◦ adj◦ 📖*samuttha* (rise) ←सम्–उद्√स्था); *dvandvamohena* (m◦ 3inst◦ sing◦ ←tatpu◦ *dvandva-moha*, द्वंद्वस्य मोह: ←n◦ *dvandva* (duality) 2.45 + m◦ *moha* (delusion) 2.52); *bhārata* (1.24); ***sarvabhūtāni*** (1nom◦ sing◦ 6.29); *sammohaṃ* (2acc◦ sing◦ ←m◦ *sammoha* 2.63); ***sarge*** (7loc◦ sing◦ ←m◦ *sarga* (beginning) 5.19); *yānti* (3.33); *parantapa* (2.3) (7.27)

(§3) *iććhādveṣasamutthena* (because of the rise of the desires and revulsion); *dvandvamohena* (as a result of the delusion caused by the pairs of opposites); *bhārata* (O Arjuna!); *sarvabhūtāni* (subj◦ all beings); *sammohaṃ* (obj◦ aberration); *sarge* (at the outset, at the beginning); *yānti* (develop, acquire); *parantapa* (O Arjuna!) (7.27)

(§4) bhārata iććhādveṣasamutthena dvandvamohena sarvabhūtāni yānti sammohaṃ sarge parantapa

(§5) O Arjuna! because of the rise of the desires and revulsion, as a result of the delusion caused by the pairs of opposites, O Arjuna! all beings develop aberration at the outset; (7.27)

7.28 येषां त्वन्तगतं पापं जनानां पुण्यकर्मणाम् ।
ते द्वन्द्वमोहनिर्मुक्ता भजन्ते मां दृढव्रताः ।।

yeṣāṁ tvantagataṁ pāpaṁ janānāṁ puṇyakarmaṇām,
te dvandvamohanirmuktā bhajante māṁ dṛḍhavratāḥ:. (7.28)

(§1) *yeṣām* (r◦ 25/3, 14/1) *tu* (r◦ 4/6) *antagatam* (r◦ 14/1) *pāpam* (r◦ 14/1) *janānām* (r◦ 14/1) *puṇyakarmaṇām* (r◦ 24/6, 14/2) *te dvandvamohanirmuktāḥ:* (r◦ 20/12) *bhajante mām* (r◦ 14/1) *dṛḍhavratāḥ:* (r◦ 22/8)

(§2) *yeṣām* (1.33); *tu* (1.2); 🕮*antagatam* (n◦ 1nom◦ sing◦ ←pass◦ past◦ adj◦ s-karm◦ *anta-gata*, अन्तम् गतम् ←m◦ *anta* (end) 2.16 + adj◦ *gata* (gone) 2.11); *pāpam* (sin, 1nom◦ 1.36); *janānām* (6pos plu◦ ←m◦ *jana* 1.28); 🕮***puṇyakarmaṇām*** (m◦ 6pos◦ plu◦ ←bahuvrī◦ *puṇya-karman*, पुण्यम् कर्म यस्य ←adj◦ *puṇya* (righteous deed) 6.41 + n◦ *karman* 1.15); *te* (1.33); *dvandvamohanirmuktāḥ:* (m◦ 1nom◦ plu◦ ←tatpu◦ *dvandva-moha-nirmukta*, द्वंद्वानाम् मोहात् निर्मुक्तः ←n◦ *dvandva* (duality) 2.45 + m◦ *moha* (delusion) 2.52 + ppp◦ adj◦ *nirmukta* (freed) ←निर्√मुच्); *bhajante* (7.16); *mām* (1.46); 🕮***dṛḍhavratāḥ:*** (m◦ 1nom◦ plu◦ ←bahuvrī◦ *dṛḍha-vrata*, दृढम् व्रतम् यस्य ←adj◦ *dṛḍha* (firm) 6.34 + n◦ or m◦ *vrata* (austerity) 4.28) (7.28)

(§3) *yeṣām* (of those -- whose); *tu* (but); *antagatam* (adj◦-subj1◦ has ended, is undone, nullified, quashed, repealed, annuled, cancelled, terminated, dissolved); *pāpam* (subj1◦ sin); *janānām* (of people); *puṇyakarmaṇām* (of righteous); *te* (adj1-subj2◦ they); *dvandvamohanirmuktāḥ:* (adj2◦-subj2◦ freed from or indifferent to the attachment to the delusion caused by pairs of opposites); *bhajante* (worship); *mām* (obj1◦ me); *dṛḍhavratāḥ:* (subj2◦ people of firm resolve) (7.28)

(§4) tu yeṣām puṇyakarmaṇām janānām dṛḍhavratāḥ: pāpam antagatam dvandvamohanirmuktāḥ: te bhajante mām

(§5) But, those righteous people of firm resolve[507] whose sin has ended, those people freed from the attachment to the delusion caused by pairs of opposites, they worship me. (7.28)

---

[507] Elsewhere◦ भजन्ते मां दृढव्रताः → they worship me with firm resolve, worship Me with firm resolve, worship Me with a firm resolve in every way, worship Me remaining steadfast in their vows, they engage themselves in My service with determination, ...etc.

🕮 दृढव्रताः is not Instrumentsl (3rd) case adverb qualifying the verb भजन्ते. It is not a gerund also. Here, दृढव्रताः (the people of firm resolve) is the Nominative (1st) case plural◦ adjective◦ of the Nominative plu◦ subject ते (they). येषां जनानां … **ते दृढव्रताः** भजन्ते माम् ।

7.29 जरामरणमोक्षाय मामाश्रित्य यतन्ति ये ।
ते ब्रह्म तद्विदुः कृत्स्नमध्यात्मं कर्म चाखिलम् ।।

jarāmaraṇamokṣāya māmāśritya yatanti ye,
te brahma tadviduḥ: kṛtsnamadhyātmaṁ karma ćākhilam; (7.29)

(§1) *jarāmaraṇamokṣāya mām̩* (r◦ 8/17) *āśritya yatanti ye te brahma tat̩* (r◦ 9/11) *viduḥ:* (r◦ 22/1) *kṛtsnam̩* (r◦ 8/16) *adhyātmam̩* (r◦ 14/1) *karma ća* (r◦ 1/1) *akhilam̩* (r◦ 14/2)

(§2) *jarāmaraṇamokṣāya* (m◦ 4dat◦ sing◦ ←tatpu◦ *jarā-maraṇa-mokṣa,* जरायाः च मरणात् च मोक्षः ←f◦ *jarā* (old age) 2.13 + n◦ *maraṇa* (death) 2.34 + m◦ *mokṣa* (liberation) 5.28); *mām̩* (1.46); ***āśritya*** (lyp◦ past-participle ind◦ ←आ√श्रि); *yatanti* (3rd-per◦ plu◦ pres◦ वर्तमान्–लट् parasmai◦ ←class1◦ √यत् 6.43); *ye* (1.7); *te* (1.33); *brahma* (3.15); *tat̩* (2.7); *viduḥ:* (4.2); *kṛtsnam̩* (adv◦ 1.40); ***adhyātmam̩*** (n◦ 2acc◦ sing◦ ←adj◦ *adhyātma* (knowledge of self) 3.30); *karma* (3.8); *ća* (1.1); *akhilam̩* (4.33) (7.29)

(§3) *jarāmaraṇamokṣāya* (for liberation old age and death); *mām̩* (obj1◦ me); *āśritya* (depending on me, having taken refuge in); *yatanti* (strive); *ye* (subj◦ those who); *te* (adj1◦-subj◦ they); *brahma* (obj2◦ brahma); *tat̩* (adj◦-obj2◦ THAT); *viduḥ:* (they know, understand); *kṛtsnam̩* (fully); *adhyātmam̩* (obj3◦ realization of the presence of brahma in oneself, understanding *ātmā* and *anātmā* अनात्मा*;* = *dehī* and *deha*); *karma* (obj4◦ *karma*); *ća* (and); *akhilam̩* (adj◦-obj4◦ all) (7.29)

(§4) ye āśritya mām̩ yatanti jarāmaraṇamokṣāya te viduḥ: tat̩ brahma kṛtsnam̩ adhyātmam̩ ća akhilam̩ karma

(§5) Those who, depending on me, strive for liberation old age and death, they understand THAT *brahma* fully (and they have) realization of the presence of brahma in oneself[508] and (and they understand) all *karma*; (7.29)

7.30 साधिभूताधिदैवं मां साधियज्ञं च ये विदुः ।
प्रयाणकालेऽपि च मां ते विदुर्युक्तचेतसः ।।

sādhibhūtādhidaivaṁ māṁ sādhiyajñaṁ ća ye viduḥ:,
prayāṇakāle'pi ća māṁ te viduryuktaćetasaḥ:. (7.30)

(§1) *sādhibhūtādhidaivam̩* (r◦ 14/1) *mām̩* (r◦ 14/1) *sādhiyajñam̩* (r◦ 14/1) *ća ye viduḥ:* (r◦ 22/8) *prayāṇakāle* (r◦ 6/1) *api ća mām̩* (r◦ 14/1) *te viduḥ:* (r◦ 16/8) *yuktaćetasaḥ:* (r◦ 22/8)

(§2) *sādhibhūtādhidaivam̩* (m◦ 2acc◦ sing◦ ←bahuvrī◦ *sādhibhūtādhidaiva,* अधिभूतेन च अधिदैवेन च सह

[508] Elsewhere◦ (i) यतन्ति = endavouring to; (ii) ते ब्रह्म तद्विदुः = they are actually Brahman; (iii) अध्यात्म = individual Self; (iv) कर्म चाखिलम् = all kinds of action; ...etc.

←ind◦ *saha* 1.22 + n◦ -taddhita◦ ***adhibhūta*** ←अधि√भू + n◦ -taddhita◦ ***adhidaiva*** ←अधि√दिव्); *mām̥* (1.46); *sādhiyajñam̥* (m◦ 2acc◦ sing◦ ←bahuvrī◦ *sādhiyajña,* अधियज्ञेन सह ←ind◦ *saha* 1.22 + m◦ ***adhiyajña*** ←अधि√यज्); *ćа* (1.1); *ye* (1.7); *viduḥ:* (4.2); ***prayāṇakāle*** (m◦ 7loc◦ sing◦ ←tatpu◦ *prayāṇa-kāla,* प्रयाणस्य कालः ←m◦ *prayāṇa* (exit, departure) ←प्र√या + m◦ *kāla* (time) 2.72); *api* (1.26); *ća* (1.1); *mām̥* (1.46); *te* (1.33); *viduḥ:* (4.2); *yuktaćetasaḥ:* (m◦ 1nom◦ plu◦ ←bahuvrī◦ *yukta-ćetas̥,* युक्तम् चेतः यस्य ←adj◦ *yukta* (equipped) 1.14 + n◦ *ćetas̥* (mind) 1.38) (7.30)

(§3) *sādhibhūtādhidaivam̥* (together with the adhibhuta and adhidaiva, with the context of the beings and the divinity); *mām̥* (obj1◦ me); *sādhiyajñam̥* (with the context of austerity);[509] *ća* (and); *ye* (adj1◦-subj◦ those who); *viduḥ:* (they know); *prayāṇakāle* (at the time of the final departure); *api* (also); *ća* (and); *mām̥* (obj1◦ me); *te* (adj2-subj◦ they); *viduḥ:* (know); *yuktaćetasaḥ:* (subj◦ they whose minds are disciplined) (7.30)

(§4) ća ye viduḥ: mām̥ sādhibhūtādhidaivam̥ ća sādhiyajñam̥ te yuktaćetasaḥ: viduḥ: mām̥ prayāṇakāle api

(§5) And those who know me, together with the beings and the divinity and with the context of austerity, they whose minds are disciplined, know me at the time of the final departure also. (7.30)

इति श्रीमद्भगवद्गीतासूपनिषत्सु ब्रह्मविद्यायां योगशास्त्रे
श्रीकृष्णार्जुनसंवादे ज्ञानविज्ञानयोगो नाम सप्तमोऽध्यायः ।।

iti śrīmadbhagavadgītāsūpaniṣatsu brahmavidyāyām̐ yogaśāstre
śrīkr̥ṣṇārjunasam̐vāde jñānavijñānayogo nāma saptamo'dhyāyaḥ:.

(§1) *iti śrīmadbhagavadgītāsu* (r◦ 1/8) *upaniṣatsu brahmavidyāyām̥* (r◦ 14/1) *yogaśāstre śrīkr̥ṣṇārjunasam̐vāde jñānavijñānayogaḥ:* (r◦ 15/6) *nāma saptamaḥ:* (r◦ 15/1) *adhyāyaḥ:* (r◦ 22/8)

(§2) *iti* (1.25); *śrīmadbhagavadgītāsu* (f◦ 7loc◦ plu◦ tatpu◦ *śrīmad-bhagavad-gītā* ←adj◦ *śrīmat̥* 6.41 + adj◦ *bhagavat̥* 10.14 + f◦ *gītā* ←5◦√गै); *upaniṣatsu* (7loc◦ plu◦ ←f◦ *upaniṣad̥* ←6◦उप-नि√सद्); *brahmavidyāyām̥* (f◦ 7loc◦ sing◦ ←tatpu◦ *brahma-vidyā,* ब्रह्मणः विद्या ←n◦ *brahman̥* 2.72 + *vidyā* 5.18); *yogaśāstre* (n◦ 7loc◦ sing◦ ←tatpu◦ *yoga-śāstra,* योगानाम् शास्त्रम् । योगस्य शास्त्रम् । ←m◦ *yoga* 2.39 + n◦ *śāstra* 15.20); *śrīkr̥ṣṇārjunasam̐vāde* (m◦ 7loc◦ sing◦ ←tatpu◦ *śrī-kr̥ṣṇārjuna-sam̐vāda,* श्रीकृष्णस्य च अर्जुनस्य च संवादः ←adj◦ *śrī* 10.34 + m◦ prop◦ *kr̥ṣṇa* 1.28 + m◦ prop◦ *arjuna* 1.4 + m◦ *sam̐vāda* 18.70); *jñānavijñānayogaḥ:* (m◦ 1nom◦ sing◦ ←tatpu◦ *jñānavijñānayoga,* ज्ञानविज्ञानयोग, ज्ञानस्य च विज्ञानस्य च योगः ←n◦ *jñāna* 3.3 + n◦ vijñāna 3.41 + m◦ *yoga* 2.39); *nāma* (1nom◦ sing◦ ←n◦ *nāman̥* ←1◦√म्ना); *saptamaḥ:*

---

[509] Elsewhere◦ साधियज्ञ = in the region of sacrifice, One that govern all sacrifices, as Adhiyajna, for the unmanifest Divinity dwelling in the heart of all beings as their witness, ...etc.

(m◦ 1nom◦ sing◦ ←num◦ adj◦ *sapta* 10.6); *adhyāyaḥ:* (1nom◦ sing◦ ←m◦ *adhyāya* ←1◦अधि√इ)

(§3) *iti* (thus); *śrīmadbhagavadgītāsu upaniṣatsu* (among the upaniṣads of the Śrīmad-Bhagavadgītā); *brahmavidyāyām* (of the eternal wisdoms); *yogaśāstre* (in the science of Yoga); *śrīkṛṣṇārjunasaṁvāde* (in the dialogue between Śrī Kṛṣṇa and Arjuna); *jñānavijñānayogaḥ:* (adj1◦-subj◦ (called jñānavijñānayoga); *nāma* (called); *saptamaḥ:* (adj2◦-subj◦ the seventh); *adhyāyaḥ:* (subj◦ discourse; chapter)

(§4) śrīmadbhagavadgītāsu upaniṣatsu yogaśāstre brahmavidyāyām iti saptamaḥ: adhyāyaḥ: nāma jñānavijñānayogaḥ: śrīkṛṣṇārjunasaṁvāde

(§5) Among the upaniṣads of the Śrīmad-Bhagavadgītā, in the science of yoga of self realization, thus (is) the seventh discourse called jñāna-vijñāna-yoga, in the dialogue between Śrī Kṛṣṇa and Arjuna.

CHAPTER 8

aṣṭamo'dhyāyaḥ:

अष्टमोऽध्याय: ।

akṣarabrahmayogaḥ:

अक्षरब्रह्मयोग: ।

YOGA OF COMPREHENDING THE IMMUTABLE BRAHMA[510]

Arjuna said (arjuna uvāća अर्जुन उवाच ।)

8.1 **किं तद्ब्रह्म किमध्यात्मं किं कर्म पुरुषोत्तम ।**
अधिभूतं च किं प्रोक्तमधिदैवं किमुच्यते ।।
kiṁ tadbrahma kimadhyātmaṁ kiṁ karma puruśottama,

[510] Elsewhere◦ अक्षरब्रह्मयोग: → the Yoga of the Imperishable Brahman, The Yoga of Imperishable Brahman, The Course of Cosmic Evolution, ...etc.

📖 In the tatpu◦ *samasa* of अक्षर-ब्रह्म-योग, the word अक्षर-ब्रह्म is not in Possessive (6th) case for the ब्रह्म is not the possessor of the *yoga*, but is the object◦ of the discipline pertaining to (understanding, or rather trying to understand) the अक्षरं (immutable) and अचिन्त्यं (incomprehensible) ब्रह्म (*brahma*).

adhibhūtaṁ ća kiṁ proktamadhidaivaṁ kimućyate; (8.1)

(§1) *aṣṭamḥ:* (r◦ 15/1) *adhyāyaḥ:* (r◦ 22/8). *akṣarabrahmayogaḥ:* (r◦ 22/8). *arjunaḥ:* (r◦ 19/4) *uvāća. kim̦* (r◦ 14/1) *taț* (r◦ 9/7) *brahma kim̦* (r◦ 8/16) *adhyātmam̦* (r◦ 14/1) *kim̦* (r◦ 14/1) *karma puruśottama* (r◦ 23/1) *adhibhūtam̦* r◦ 14/1) *ća kim̦* (r◦ 14/1) *proktam̦* (r◦ 8/16) *adhidaivam̦* (r◦ 14/1) *kim̦* (r◦ 8/20) *ućyate*

(§2) *aṣṭamḥ:* (m◦ 1nom◦ sing◦ ←sequence indicating num◦ adj◦ *aṣṭam* ←adj◦ *aṣṭan̦* ←√अश्); *adhyāyaḥ:* (1nom◦ sing◦ ←m◦ *adhyāya* ←अधि√इ). *akṣarabrahmayogaḥ:* (m◦ 1nom◦ sing◦ ←tatpu◦ *akṣara-brahma-yoga*, अक्षरं ब्रह्म आकलनस्य योगः ←adj◦ *akṣara* 3.15 + n◦ *brahman̦* 2.72 + m◦ *yoga* 2.39). *arjunaḥ:* (1.28); *uvāća* (1.25).

kim̦ (2.36); *taț* (1nom◦ 1.10); *brahma* (1nom◦ 3.15); *kim̦* (↑); *adhyātmam̦* (7.29); *kim̦* (↑); *karma* (1 nom◦ 2.49); ***puruśottama*** (m◦ 8voc◦ sing◦ ←bahuvrī◦ ***puruśottama***, पुरुषेषु उत्तमः यः ←m◦ *puruṣa* (the immutable person) 2.15 + adj◦ *uttama* (best) 1.7); ***adhibhūtam̦*** (1nom◦ sing◦ ←n◦ *adhibhūta* 7.30); *ća* (1.1); *kim̦* (↑); ***proktam̦*** (called) ; *adhidaivam̦* (adhidaiva); *kim̦* (what is); *ućyate* (is called) (8.1)

(§3) *aṣṭamḥ:* (adj1-subj◦ the eighth); *adhyāyaḥ:* (subj◦ chapter); *akṣarabrahmayogaḥ:* (adj2◦-subj◦ akṣarabrahmayoga, the yoga of comprehending or realizing the immutable *brahma*). *arjunaḥ:* (subj◦ Arjuna); *uvāća* (said);

kim̦ (what is); *taț* (adj2◦-obj1◦ THAT); *brahma* (obj1◦ *brahma*); *kim̦* (what); *adhyātmam̦* (obj2◦ adhyatma, substratum or receptacle of the self, realization of the presence of brahma in oneself, understanding ātmā and unātmā, comprehending dehī and deha);[511] *kim̦* (what); *karma* (obj3◦ karma); *puruśottama* (O Śrī Krishṇa!); *adhibhūtam̦* (obj4◦ adhibhūtam̦, the substratum or receptacle of the beings);[512] *ća* (and); *kim̦* (what is); *proktam̦* (adj1◦-obj1-5◦ is called); *adhidaivam̦* (obj5◦ adhidaivam̦, the substratum or receptacle of the divinity);[513] *kim̦* (what is); *ućyate* (is called) (8.1)

(§4) aṣṭamḥ: adhyāyaḥ: akṣarabrahmayogaḥ: arjunaḥ: uvāća puruśottama kim̦ taț brahma kim̦ proktam̦

---

[511] Elsewhere◦ अध्यात्म = that which exists in the individual plane, the Self, the Supreme Self, Spirit, the Individual Self, aggregate of elements of the individual self, ...etc.

[512] Elsewhere◦ अधिभूतम् = that which exists in the physical plane, the knowledge of the Elements, the inner essence of Elemental beings, the domain of the elements, the material manifestation, the physical region, the matter, My mutable nature, ...etc.

[513] Elsewhere◦ अधिदैवम् = that which is said to be existing in the divine plane, the demigods, Supreme God, the Shining Ones, Divine Intelligence, the divine region, the inner essence of Divine beings, the Supreme Divine Agent itself, ...etc.

adhyātmaṃ kiṃ karma kiṃ adhibhūtaṃ ća kiṃ ućyate adhidaivaṃ

(§5) The Eighth Chapter; 'the *yoga* of comprehending the immutable *brahma*.' Arjuna said : O Śrī Krishṇa! "what is called THAT *brahma*; what is called *adhyātma*; what is *karma*; what is *adhibhūtam* and what is called *adhidaivam?"* (8.1)

8.2 अधियज्ञः कथं कोऽत्र देहेऽस्मिन्मधुसूदन ।
प्रयाणकाले च कथं ज्ञेयोऽसि नियतात्मभिः ।।
adhiyajñaḥ: kathaṁ ko'tra dehe'sminmadhusūdana,
prayāṇakāle ća kathaṁ jñeyo'si niyatātmabhiḥ:. (8.2)

(§1) *adhiyajñaḥ:* (r∘ 22/1) *kathaṃ* (r∘ 14/1) *kaḥ:* (r∘ 15/1) *atra dehe* (r∘ 6/1) *asmiṇ* (r∘ 13/16) *madhusūdana prayāṇakāle ća kathaṃ* (r∘ 14/1) *jñeyaḥ:* (r∘ 15/1) *asi niyatātmabhiḥ:* (r∘ 22/8)

(§2) ***adhiyajñaḥ:*** (adhiyajña, यस्य प्रभुत्त्वेन यज्ञः अधिकृतः सः = यज्ञाधिकारी; adhi = अधिकारी); *kathaṃ* (1.37); ***kaḥ:*** (who? m∘ 1nom∘ sing∘ ←pron∘ *kiṃ* (what?) 1.1); *atra* (1.4); *dehe* (2.13); *asmiṇ* (1.22); *madhusūdana* (1.35); *prayāṇakāle* (7.30); *ća* (1.1); *kathaṃ* (1.37); *jñeyaḥ:* (5.3); *asi* (4.3); *niyatātmabhiḥ:* (3inst∘ plu∘ ←bahuvrī∘ *niyatātmaṇ*, नियतः आत्मा यस्य ←adj∘ *niyata* (disciplined) 1.44 + m∘ *ātmaṇ* (self, person) 2.41) (8.2)

(§3) *adhiyajñaḥ:* (subj1∘ adhiyajña, the presider of the austerity, the presider of the yajña);[514] *kathaṃ* (adv∘ how); (and) *kaḥ:* (adj∘-subj1∘ who is); *dehe* (in the body); *asmiṇ* (in this); *atra* (here); *madhusūdana* (O Śrī Krishṇa!); *prayāṇakāle* (at the time of the final departure); *ća* (and); *kathaṃ* (how); *jñeyaḥ:* (adj∘-obj∘ to be perceived); *asi* (obj∘ you are, are you); *niyatātmabhiḥ:* (subj2∘ by the disciplined selves) (8.2)

(§4) madhusūdana kathaṃ kaḥ:adhiyajñaḥ: atra asmiṇ dehe ća prayāṇakāle kathaṃ asi jñeyaḥ: niyatātmabhiḥ:

(§5) O Śrī Kṛṣṇa! "how (and) who is the presider of the austerity here in this body? And at the time of the final departure, how are you (the *adhiyajña*) to be perceived by the disciplined selves?" (8.2)

The Lord said (śrībhagavānuvāća श्रीभगवानुवाच ।)

---

[514] Elsewhere∘ अधियज्ञः = the region of sacrifice, the unmanifest Divinity dwelling in the heart of all beings as their witness, Lord of Sacrifice, the inner entity of sacrifice, the Entity concerned with sacrifice, the domain (part) of sacrifice, knowledge of sacrifice, Chief Sacrifice, the deity presiding over sacrifice, ...etc.

8.3 अक्षरं ब्रह्म परमं स्वभावोऽध्यात्ममुच्यते ।
भूतभावोद्भवकरो विसर्गः कर्मसंज्ञितः ।।

akṣaraṁ brahma paramaṁ svabhāvo‘dhyātmamućyate,
bhūtabhāvodbhavakaro visargaḥ: karmasañjñitaḥ:. (8.3)

(§1) *śrībhagavān̦* (r◦ 8/14) *uvāća. akṣaram̦* (r◦ 14/1) *brahma paramam̦* (r◦ 14/1) *svabhāvaḥ:* (r◦ 15/1) *adhyātmam̦* (r◦ 8/20) *ućyate bhūtabhāvodbhavakaraḥ:* (r◦ 15/13) *visargaḥ:* (r◦ 22/1) *karmasañjñitaḥ:* (r◦ 22/8)

(§2) *śrībhagavān̦* (2.2); *uvāća* (1.25). ***akṣaram̦*** (n◦ 1nom◦ sing◦ ←adj◦ or n◦ *akṣara* (immutable) 3.15); *brahma* (1nom◦ 4.24); ***paramam̦*** (n◦ 1nom◦ sing◦ ←adj◦ *parama* (supreme) 1.17); *svabhāvaḥ:* (5.14); *adhyātmam̦* (7.29); *ućyate* (2.25); *bhūtabhāvodbhavakaraḥ:* (m◦ 1nom◦ sing◦ ←tatpu◦ adj◦ *bhūta-bhāvodbhava-kara,* भूतानाम् भावस्य उद्भवकरः ←m◦ *bhūta* (being) 2.28 + m◦ *bhāva* (nature) 2.7 + m◦ *udbhava* (becoming) 3.15 + adj◦ *kāra* 2.2); *visargaḥ:* (1nom◦ sing◦ ←m◦ *visarga* (origin) ←वि√सृज्); *karmasañjñitaḥ:* (m◦ 1nom◦ sing◦ ←bahuvrī◦ *karma-sañjñita,* कर्म संज्ञा यस्य ←n◦ *karman̦* 1.15 + f◦ *sañjñā* (definition) 1.7)
(8.3)

(§3) *śrībhagavān̦* (The Lord); *uvāća* (said). *akṣaram̦* (adj1◦-obj1◦ the immutable); *brahma* (obj1◦ brahma); *paramam̦* (adj2◦-obj1◦ the Supreme, the absolute, the perfect); *svabhāvaḥ:* (obj2◦ understanding one’s own existance, substratum or receptacle of the self, realization of the presence of *brahma* in oneself, understanding one’s own *ātmā,* comprehending *dehī* in one’s *deha*); *adhyātmam̦* (adj◦-obj2◦ *adhyatma*); *ućyate* (is called); *bhūta-bhāva-udbhava-karaḥ:* (adj1◦-obj3◦ the causer of the nature of the beings); *visargaḥ:* (obj3◦ the beginning, the initiation, the actuation, the activation that is); *karmasañjñitaḥ:* (adj2◦-obj3◦ is called *karma*) (8.3)

(§4) śrībhagavān̦ uvāća akṣaram̦ paramam̦ brahma svabhāvaḥ: ućyate adhyātmam̦ visargaḥ: bhūta-bhāva-udbhava-karaḥ: karmasañjñitaḥ:

(§5) The Lord said : The immutable absolute (is called) *brahma*; understanding one’s own existance is called *adhyatma*; (and) the activation that is the causer of the nature of the beings is called *karma*. (8.3)

8.4 अधिभूतं क्षरो भावः पुरुषश्चाधिदैवतम् ।
अधियज्ञोऽहमेवात्र देहे देहभृतां वर ।।

adhibhūtaṁ kṣaro bhāvaḥ: puruṣaśćādhidaivatam̦,
adhiyajño‘hamevātra dehe dehabhṛtāṁ vara. (8.4)

(§1) *adhibhūtam̧* (r◦ 14/1) *kṣaraḥ:* (r◦ 15/8) *bhāvaḥ:* (r◦ 22/3) *puruṣaḥ:* (r◦ 17/1) *ća* (r◦ 1/1) *adhidaivatam̧* (r◦ 14/2) *adhiyajñaḥ:* (r◦ 15/1) *aham̧* (r◦ 8/22) *eva* (r◦ 1.1) *atra dehe dehabhṛtām̧* (r◦ 14/1) *vara*

(§2) *adhibhūtam̧* (1nom◦ 8.1); 🕮***kṣaraḥ:*** (m◦ 1nom◦ sing◦ ←adj◦ ***kṣara*** (mutable) ←√क्षर्); *bhāvaḥ:* (2.7); *puruṣaḥ:* (2.21); *ća* (1.1); *adhidaivatam̧* (1nom◦ sing◦ ←n◦ *adhidaivata* ←अधि√दिव्); *adhiyajñaḥ:* (8.2); *aham̧* (1.22); *eva* (1.1); *atra* (1.4); *dehe* (2.13); *dehabhṛtām̧-vara* (m◦ 8voc◦ sing◦ ←bahuvrī◦ *dehabhṛtām̧-vara,* देहेषु विभृतेषु वर: य: ←n◦ *deha* (body) 2.13 ←adj◦ ***vibhṛta*** (borne) ←वि√भृ + adj◦ 🕮***vara*** (superior) ←√वृ) (8.4)

(§3) *adhibhūtam̧* (adj1◦-subj1◦ *adhibhūtam̧,* the substratum or receptacle of the beings); *kṣaraḥ:* (adj2◦-subj1◦ the mutable); *bhāvaḥ:* (subj1◦ nature); *puruṣaḥ:* (subj2◦ puruṣaḥ, the divine catalist for the life of the living beings);[515] *ća* (and); *adhidaivatam̧* (adj◦-subj2◦ *adhidaivatam̧,* the presiding divinity); *adhiyajñaḥ:* (adj◦-subj3◦ adhiyajñaḥ, the substratum or receptacle of the austerity); *aham̧* (subj3◦ I am); *eva* (only, indeed); *atra* (here); *dehe* (in the body); *dehabhṛtām̧-vara* (O Arjuna!) (8.4)

(§4) dehabhṛtām̧-vara kṣaraḥ: bhāvaḥ: adhibhūtam̧ puruṣaḥ: adhidaivatam̧ ća aham̧ eva adhiyajñaḥ: atra dehe

(§5) **O Arjuna! (i) the mutable nature (is) *adhibhūtam̧;* (ii) Puruṣa, the presiding divinity; the divine catalist for the life of the living beings (is) *adhidaivatam̧,* and (iii) I am *adhiyajñaḥ,* the presiding divinity, here in the body.** (8.4)

8.5 अन्तकाले च मामेव स्मरन्मुक्त्वा कलेवरम् ।
य: प्रयाति स मद्भावं याति नास्त्यत्र संशय: ।।
antakāle ća māmeva smaranmuktvā kalevaram̧,
yaḥ: prayāti sa madbhāvam̊ yāti nāstyatra sam̊śayaḥ:. (8.5)

(§1) *antakāle ća mām̧* (r◦ 8/22) *eva smaraņ* (r◦ 13/16) *muktvā kalevaram̧* (r◦ 14/2) *yaḥ:* (r◦ 22/3) *prayāti saḥ:* (r◦ 21/2) *madbhāvam̧* (r◦ 14/1) *yāti na* (r◦ 1/1) *asti* (r◦ 4/1) *atra sam̊śayaḥ:* (r◦ 22/8)

(§2) *antakāle* (2.72); *ća* (1.1); *mām̧* (1.46); *eva* (1.1); *smaraņ* (3.6); *muktvā* (ipp◦ ind◦ ←√मुच्); 🕮***kalevaram̧*** (2acc◦ sing◦ ←m◦ or n◦ *kalevara* (body) ←√कल्); *yaḥ:* (2.19); ***prayāti*** (3rd-per◦ sing◦ pres◦ वर्तमान्-लट् parasmai◦ ←class2◦ प्र√या 2.22); *saḥ:* (1.13); *madbhāvam̧* (4.10); *yāti* (6.45); *na* (1.30); *asti* (2.40); *atra* (1.4); 🕮***sam̊śayaḥ:*** (1nom◦ sing◦ ←m◦ *sam̊śaya* (doubt) 4.40) (8.5)

(§3) *antakāle* (at the last moment, until the last breath); *ća* (and); *mām̧* (obj1◦ me); *eva* (only); *smaraņ*

---

[515] Elsewhere◦ पुरुष: = the cosmic spirit, the cosmic Being, the Person, the Soul, the universal form...etc.

(adj1◦-subj1◦ remembering, while remembering); *muktvā* (having left); *kalevaram̹* (obj1◦ the body); *yaḥ:* (adj◦-subj1◦ he who); *prayāti* (departs); *saḥ:* (subj1◦ he); *madbhāvam̹* (obj2◦ my nature); *yāti* (attains); *na* (no); *asti* (is, there is); *atra* (in this, here); *sam̐śayaḥ:* (subj2◦ doubt) (8.5)

(§4) ća yaḥ: antakāle smaran̹ mām̹ eva prayāti kalevaram̹ muktvā saḥ: yāti madbhāvam̹ atra asti na sam̐śayaḥ:

(§5) And he who, until last breath (i.e. always)[516] remembering[517] me only,[518] departs having left[519] the body, he attains my nature; in this there is no doubt. (8.5)

8.6 यं यं वाऽपि स्मरन्भावं त्यजत्यन्ते कलेवरम् ।
तं तमेवैति कौन्तेय सदा तद्भावभावितः ।।
yam̐ yam̐ vā‘pi smarnbhāvam̐ tyajatyante kalevaram̹
tam̐ tamevaiti kaunteya sadā tadbhāvabhāvitaḥ:. (8.6)

(§1) *yam̹* (r◦ 14/1) *yam̹* (r◦ 14/1) *vā* (r◦ 1/3) *api smaran̹* (r◦ 13/15) *bhāvam̹* (r◦ 14/1) *tyajati* (r◦ 4/1) *ante kalevaram̹* (r◦ 14/2) *tam̹* (r◦ 14/1) *tam̹* (r◦ 8/22) *eva* (r◦ 3/1) *eti kaunteya sadā tadbhāvabhāvitaḥ:*

---

[516] Elsewhere◦ अन्तकाले ... → at the time of death, gives up his body and departs...; at the time of death, anyone who departs...; at the time of death, leaving the body, goes forth...; at the hour of death...; at the time of death, sheds off his body...; thinking of Me even at the time of death...; goeth forth thinking up on Me only at the time of the end, at the end of his life, quits his body...; at the time of death remembers me alone; ...etc.

🕮 अन्तकाले does NOT literally mean ‘only at the time of death or at the last moment,’ but it means ‘remember me all the time, keep me in your thought all the time, always think of me’ so that it does not matter when you breathe last, I will be in your last thought. For, you never know which one is your last breath. So, do not try to remember to remember me when your death arrives, because no one knows for sure, when the death is coming and you may not have time to remember to remember me, or at that time different xxx words may come in your xxx mouth.

[517] Elsewhere◦ स्मरन् → remembers, thinks, ...etc.

🕮 स्मरन् is not a verb or present tense. It is a present continuous participle adjective of the subject यः ।

[518] Elsewhere◦ माम् एव स्मरन् → thinking upon Me only at the time of the end, ...etc.

🕮 (i) The above constructions are alright other than that they may pose a double meaning. (ii) Also, there is difference in : “remembering me only at the last moment” and remembering Me alone at the last mpment.” Please see 8.7 सवषु कालेषु ।

[519] Elsewhere◦ मुक्त्वा कलेवरम् → sheds off his body, leaves the body, gives up his body, by giving up the body, quits his body, quitting his body, ...etc.

🕮 मुक्त्वा is not a verb or present tense. It is an indeclinable past participle gerundive, ‘having left or leaving.’

(r◦ 22/8)

(§2) *yaṃ* (2.15); *yaṃ* (2.15); *vā* (1.32); *api* (1.26); *smaraṇ* (3.6); *bhāvaṃ* (7.15); *tyajati* (3rd-per◦ sing◦ pres◦ वर्तमान्-लट् parasmai◦ ←class1◦ √त्यज्); *ante* (7.20); *kalevaraṃ* (8.5); *taṃ* (2.1); *taṃ* (2.1); *eva* (1.1); *eti* (4.9); *kaunteya* (2.14); *sadā* (1.40); *tadbhāvabhāvitaḥ:* (m◦ 1nom◦ sing◦ caus◦ ←tatpu◦ *tadbhāva-bhāvita*, तेन भावेन भावित: ←n◦ pron◦ *taṭ* (that) 1.10 + m◦ *bhāva* (thought) 2.7 + adj◦ *bhāvita* (engrossed) 3.12) (8.6)

(§3) *yaṃ yaṃ* (adj◦-obj1◦ whichever); *vā api* (moreover); *smaraṇ* (recollecting, thinking of); *bhāvaṃ* (obj1◦ thought, state of being); *tyajati* (he leaves, one leaves); *ante* (at the end); *kalevaraṃ* (subj2◦ the body); *taṃ taṃ eva* (adj2◦-obj1◦ that very state of being); *eti* (he attains); *kaunteya* (O Arjuna!); *sadā* (always); *tadbhāvabhāvitaḥ:* (adj◦-subj◦ engrossed in that thought) (8.6)

(§4) kaunteya vā api smaraṇ yaṃ yaṃ bhāvaṃ tyajati kalevaraṃ ante sadā tadbhāvabhāvitaḥ: eti taṃ taṃ eva

(§5) O Arjuna! moreover, thinking of whichever state of being one leaves the body at the end, always engrossed in that thought, he attains that very state of being. (8.6)

8.7 **तस्मात्सर्वेषु कालेषु मामनुस्मर युध्य च ।**
मय्यर्पितमनोबुद्धिर्मामेवैष्यस्यसंशयम् ।।
tasmātsarveṣu kāleṣu māmanusmara yuddhya ća,
mayyarpitamanobuddhirmāmevaiṣyasyasaṁśayaṃ. (8.7)

(§1) *tasmāṭ* (r◦ 10/7) *sarveṣu* (r◦ 25/5) *kāleṣu* (r◦ 25/5) *māṃ* (r◦ 8/16) *anusmara yuddhya ća mayi* (r◦ 4/1) *arpitamanobuddhiḥ:* (r◦ 16/6) *māṃ* (r◦ 8/22) *eva* (r◦ 3/1) *eṣyasi* (r◦ 4/1) *asaṁśayaṃ* (r◦ 14/2)

(§2) *tasmāṭ* (1.37); *sarveṣu* (1.11); ***kāleṣu*** (7loc◦ plu◦ ←m◦ *kāla* (time) 2.72); *māṃ* (1.46); *anusmara* (2nd-per◦ sing◦ imperative◦ उपदेशार्थ-लोट् parasmai◦ ←class1◦ अनु√स्मृ); *yuddhya* (2nd-per◦ sing◦ imperative◦ सङ्केतार्थ-लोट् parasmai◦ ←class4◦ √युध्); *ća* (1.1); *mayi* (3.30); ***arpitamanobuddhiḥ:*** (m◦ 1nom◦ sing◦ ←bahuvrī◦ *arpita-manobuddhi*, अर्पिते मन: च बुद्धि: च यस्य ←adj◦ 📖*arpita* (devoted) ←√ऋ + n◦ *manaṣ* (mind) 1.30 + f◦ *buddhi* (thinking) 1.23); *māṃ* (1.46); *eva* (1.1); ***eṣyasi*** (2nd-per◦ sing◦ fut2◦ लृट् भविष्य◦ parasmai◦ ←class2◦ √इ); *asaṁśayaṃ* (6.35) (8.7)

(§3) *tasmāṭ* (Therefore); *sarveṣu kāleṣu* (at every moment, all times); *māṃ* (obj◦ me); *anusmara* (think of); *yuddhya* (fight); *ća* (and); *mayi* (in me); *arpitamanobuddhiḥ:* (devoted your mind and thought); *māṃ* (to me); *eva* (alone); *eṣyasi* (you will attain); *asaṁśayaṃ* (no doubt) (8.7)

(§4) tasmāṭ sarveṣu kāleṣu anusmara māṃ ća yuddhya arpitamanobuddhiḥ: mayi asaṁśayaṃ eṣyasi māṃ eva

(§5) Therefore,[520] at every moment think of me and (thus) fight. 'Devoted your mind and thought[521] in me,' you will no doubt[522] attain me alone. (8.7)

8.8 अभ्यासयोगयुक्तेन चेतसा नान्यगामिना ।
परमं पुरुषं दिव्यं याति पार्थानुचिन्तयन् ।।
abhyāsayogayuktena ćetasā nānyagāminā,
paramaṁ puruṣaṁ divyaṁ yāti pārthānućintayan. (8.8)

(§1) *abhyāsayogayuktena ćetasā nānyagāminā paramam* (r∘ 14/1) *puruṣam* (r∘ 14/1) *divyam* (r∘ 14/1) *yāti pārtha* (r∘ 1/1) *anućintayan*

(§2) *abhyāsayogayuktena* (m∘ 3inst∘ sing∘ ←tatpu∘ *abhyāsa-yoga-yuktam*, अभ्यासस्य योगेन युक्तम् ←m∘ *abhyāsa* (practice) 6.35 + m∘ *yoga* (disciplind) 2.39 + adj∘ *yukta* (equipped) 1.14); ***ćetasā*** (3inst∘ sing∘ ←n∘ *ćetas* (mind) 1.38); *nānyagāminā* (n∘ 3inst∘ sing∘ ←adj∘ tatpu∘ 🕮*nānya-gāmin*, न अन्यगामिन् ←negative ind∘ *na* (1.30) + adj∘ *anya* (other) 1.9 + adj∘ *gāmin* (deviated) ←√गम्); *paramam* (2acc∘ sing∘ ←adj∘ *parama* (supreme) 8.3); *puruṣam* (2.15); *divyam* (4.9); *yāti* (6.45); *pārtha* (1.25); *anućintayan* (1nom∘ sing∘ ←śatṛ∘ adj∘ caus∘*anućintayat* ←अनु√चिन्त्) (8.8)

(§3) *abhyāsayogayuktena ćetasā* (with mind that is equipped with the discipline of practice); *nānyagāminā* (with undeviated); *paramam* (adj1∘-obj∘ the supreme); *puruṣam* (obj∘ purusha); *divyam* (adj2∘-obj∘ divine); *yāti* (one attains); *pārtha* (O Arjuna!); *anućintayan* (contemplating, meditating) (8.8)

(§4) pārtha anućintayan nānyagāminā abhyāsayogayuktena ćetasā yāti paramam divyam puruṣam

(§5) O Arjuna! contemplating with undeviated mind, that is equipped with the discipline of

---

[520] See the footnote in verse 2.15

[521] Elsewhere∘ अर्पितमनोबुद्धिः → by dedicating your mind and **intellect**, Thy mind and **intelligence**, with mind and **reason**, with your mind and reason, with mind and **understanding**, with your mind and intellect, when thy mind and **understanding**, with your activities dedicated, ...etc.

🕮 अर्पितमनोबुद्धिः is a bahuvrīhi m∘ adjective of Arjuna derived from ppp∘ adj∘ अर्पित, therefore, as the definition of bahuvrīhi samāsa tells us, मय्यर्पितमनोबुद्धिः does not qualify mind, your mind or thy mind. Also, मय्यर्पितमनोबुद्धिः is not Instrumental case or a gerund to say with your mind, when your mind, by dedicating your mind etc. It is Nominative case m∘ adjective of Nominative case m∘ subject of the verb एष्यसि (you will attain).

[522] Elsewhere∘ असंशयम् → there is no doubt about this, there is no doubt that, ...etc.

🕮 असंशयम् is an adverb of the verb एष्यसि (you will attain). असंशयम् एष्यसि ।

practice, one attains the supreme divine ***purusha.*** (8.8)

8.9 कविं पुराणमनुशासितारमणोरणीयांसमनुस्मरेद्यः ।
सर्वस्य धातारमचिन्त्यरूपमादित्यवर्णं तमसः परस्तात् ।।
kaviṁ purāṇamanuśāsitāramaṇoraṇiyaṁsamanusmaredyaḥ:,
sarvasya dhātāramaćintyarūpamādityavarṇaṁ tamasaḥ: parstāt̩; (8.9)

(§1) *kavim̩* (r∘ 14/1) *purāṇam̩* (r∘ 8/16, 24/3) *anuśāsitāram̩* (r∘ 8/16) *aṇoḥ:* (r∘ 16/5) *aṇiyām̐sam̩* (r∘ 8/16) *anusmaret̩* (r∘ 9/9) *yaḥ:* (r∘ 22/8) *sarvasya dhātāram̩* (r∘ 8/16) *aćintyarūpam̩* (r∘ 8/17) *ādityavarṇam̩* (r∘ 14/1) *tamasaḥ:* (r∘ 22/3) *parstāt̩;*

(§2) 🕮*kavim̩* (2acc∘ sing∘ ←m∘ *kavi* (omniscient) 4.16); 🕮*purāṇam̩* (m∘ 2acc∘ sing∘ ←adj∘ *purāṇa* (primeval) 2.20); 🕮*anuśāsitāram̩* (m∘ 2acc∘ sing∘ ←adj∘ *anuśāsitṛ* (atomic) ←अनु√शास्); *aṇoḥ:* (5abl∘ sing∘ ←m∘ or adj∘ **aṇu** (atom) ←√अण्); 🕮*aṇiyām̐sam̩* (m∘ 2acc∘ sing∘ ←comparative adj∘ *aṇīyām̐s̩* (minuscle) ←adj∘ *aṇu* ↑); *anusmaret̩* (3rd-per∘ sing∘ potential∘ विधि∘ parasmai∘ ←class1∘ अनु√स्मृ 8.7); *yaḥ:* (2.19); *sarvasya* (2.30); 🕮*dhātāram̩* (2acc∘ sing∘ ←m∘ ***dhātṛ*** (supporter) ←√धा); *aćintyarūpam̩* (m∘ 2acc∘ sing∘ ←bahuvrī∘ *aćintya-rūpa*, अचिन्त्यम् रूपम् यस्य ←adj∘ *aćintya* (unthinkable) 2.25 + n∘ *rūpa* 3.39); *ādityavarṇam̩* (m∘ 2acc∘ sing∘ ←bahuvrī∘ *āditya-varṇam*, आदित्यवत् वर्णः यस्य ←m∘ *āditya* (sun) 5.16 + m∘ *varṇa* (colour) 1.41); ***tamasaḥ:*** (5abl∘ sing∘ ←n∘ *tamas̩* (darkness) 7.12); 🕮*parstāt̩* (beyond) (ind∘ ←adj∘ *para* 2.3 + 5abl∘ sing∘ *stāt̩* ←adj∘ *asta* ←√अस्); (8.9)

(§3) *kavim̩* (adj1∘-obj∘ the Omniscient); *purāṇam̩* (adj2∘-obj∘ the Primeval); *anuśāsitāram̩* (adj3∘-obj∘ the Sovereign Ruler); *aṇoḥ: aṇiyām̐sam̩* (adj4∘-obj∘ the Minuscule than an atom, the Minutest of the minute); *anusmaret̩* (should, may meditate up on); *yaḥ:* (he who); *sarvasya* (of all); *dhātāram̩* (adj5∘-obj∘ the Supporter); *aćintyarūpam̩* (adj6∘-obj∘ the Unimaginable, he whose form can not be imagined); *ādityavarṇam̩* (adj7∘-obj∘ the Refulgent as the sun); *tamasaḥ: parstāt̩* (adj8∘-obj∘ the One beyond darkness); (8.9)

(§4) yaḥ: anusmaret̩ kavim̩ purāṇam̩ anuśāsitāram̩ aṇoḥ: aṇiyām̐sam̩ dhātāram̩ sarvasya aćintyarūpam̩ ādityavarṇam̩ tamasaḥ: parstāt̩ ;

(§5) He who may[523] meditate up on the Omniscient, the Primeval, the Sovereign Ruler, the

[523] Elsewhere∘ अनुस्मरेत् यः → He who meditates on, He who thinketh, He who contemplates on, Who so meditates, He who meditates at ...etc.

🕮 अनुस्मरेत् is Potential mood विधि∘, not a habitual Present tense.

Minuscule than an atom, the Supporter of all, the Unimaginable, the Refulgent as the sun, the One beyond darkness; (8.9)

8.10 प्रयाणकाले मनसाऽचलेन भक्त्या युक्तो योगबलेन चैव ।
भ्रुवोर्मध्ये प्राणमावेश्य सम्यक् स तं परं पुरुषमुपैति दिव्यम् ।।

prayaṇakāle manasā'ćalena bhaktyā yukto yogabalena ćaiva,
bhruvormadhye prāṇamāveśya samyaksa taṁ paraṁ puruṣamupaiti divyaṃ.
(8.10)

(§1) *prayāṇakāle manasā* (r∘ 1/3) *aćalena bhaktyā yuktaḥ:* (r∘ 15/10) *yogabalena ća* (r∘ 3/1) *eva bhruvaoḥ:* (r∘ 16/12) *madhye prāṇaṃ* (r∘ 8/17, 24/3) *āveśya samyak̩* (r∘ 10/4) *saḥ:* (r∘ 21/2) *taṃ* (r∘ 14/1) *paraṃ* (r∘ 14/1) *puruṣaṃ* (r∘ 8/20) *upaiti divyaṃ* (r∘ 14/2)

(§2) *prayāṇakāle* (7.30); *manasā* (3.6); 🕮*aćalena* (n∘ 3inst∘ sing∘ ←adj∘ *aćala* (steady) 2.24); ***bhaktyā*** (3inst∘ sing∘ ←f∘ *bhakti* (devotion) 7.17); *yuktaḥ:* (2.39); *yogabalena* (n∘ 3inst∘ sing∘ ←tatpu∘ *yoga-bala*, योगस्य बलम् ←m∘ *yoga* 2.39 + n∘ *bala* (strength) 1.10); *ća* (1.1); *eva* (1.1); *bhruvaoḥ:* (5.27); *madhye* (1.21); *prāṇaṃ* (4.29); ***āveśya*** (lyp∘ past-participle ind∘ caus∘ ←आ√विश्); *samyak̩* (5.4); *saḥ:* (1.13); *taṃ* (2.1); *paraṃ* (2acc∘ 2.59); *puruṣaṃ* (2.15); *upaiti* (6.27); *divyaṃ* (4.9)(8.10)

(§3) *prayāṇakāle* (at the moment of the last journey); *manasā* (with mind); *aćalena* (non wandering, undeviated, steady); *bhaktyā* (with devotion); *yuktaḥ:* (equipped); *yogabalena* (with the strength of yoga); *ća* (and); *eva* (as well as); *bhruvaoḥ:* (the two eyebrows); *madhye* (in the middle of); *prāṇaṃ* (obj1∘ the life breath); *āveśya* (having held, having brought); 🕮*samyak̩* (properly); *saḥ:* (he, one); *taṃ* (adj1∘-obj2∘ that); *paraṃ* (adj2∘-obj2∘ supreme); *puruṣaṃ* (obj2∘ purusha); *upaiti* (attains); *divyaṃ* (adj3∘-obj2∘ divine)(8.10)

(§4) prayāṇakāle āveśya prāṇaṃ madhye bhruvaoḥ: samyak̩ manasā aćalena ća bhaktyā eva yuktaḥ: yogabalena saḥ: upaiti taṃ paraṃ divyaṃ puruṣaṃ

(§5) At the moment of the last journey, having held the life breath in the middle of the two eyebrows properly with undeviated mind and devotion as well as equipped with the strength of *yoga*, one attains that Supreme Divine *purusha*.(8.10)

8.11 यदक्षरं वेदविदो वदन्ति विशन्ति यद्यतयो वीतरागाः ।
यदिच्छन्तो ब्रह्मचर्यं चरन्ति तत्ते पदं सङ्ग्रहेण प्रवक्ष्ये ।।

yadakṣaraṁ vedavido vadanti viśanti yadyatayo vītarāgāḥ:,
yadićchanto brahmaćaryaṁ ćaranti tatte padaṁ saṅgraheṇa pravakṣye.

(8.11)

(§1) *yat̜* (r◦ 8/2) *akṣaram̜* (r◦ 14/1) *vedavidaḥ:* (r◦ 15/13) *vadanti viśanti yat̜* (r◦ 9/9) *yatayaḥ:* (r◦ 15/13) *vītarāgāḥ:* (r◦ 22/8) *yat̜* (r◦ 8/4) *iććhantaḥ:* (r◦ 15/7) *brahmaćaryam̜* (r◦ 14/1) *ćaranti tat̜* (r◦ 1/10) *te padam̜* (r◦ 14/1) *saṅgraheṇa* (r◦ 24/1) *pravakṣye*

(§2) *yat̜* (3.21); *akṣaram̜* (8.3); *vedavidaḥ:* (m◦ 1nom◦ plu◦ ←tatpu◦ *veda-vid̜* ←m◦ *veda* 2.42 + adj◦ *vid̜* (learned) 3.29); *vadanti* (3rd-per◦ plu◦ pres◦ वर्तमान्–लट् parasmai◦ ←class1◦ √vad̜ 2.29); ***viśanti*** (3rd-per◦ plu◦ pres◦ वर्तमान्–लट् parasmai◦ ←class6◦ √विश् 2.70); *yat̜* (1.45); *yatayaḥ:* (4.28); 🕮*vītarāgāḥ:* (m◦ 1nom◦ plu◦ ←bahuvrī◦ *vīta-rāga* (unattached) वीत: राग: यस्य 2.56); *yat̜* (1.45); *iććhantaḥ:* (m◦ 1nom◦ plu◦ ←śatṛ◦ adj◦ *iććhat̜* (desiring) ←√इष्); 🕮***brahmaćaryam̜*** (2acc◦ sing◦ ←n◦ *brahmaćarya* (celibacy) ←√बृंह्); *ćaranti* (3rd-per◦ plu◦ pres◦ वर्तमान्–लट् parasmai◦ ←class1◦ √चर् 2.71); *tat̜* (2.7); *te* (1.7); *padam̜* (state, 2.51); 🕮*saṅgraheṇa* (ind◦ adv◦ or 3inst◦ sing◦ ←m◦ *saṅgraha* (collection) 3.20); *pravakṣye* (1st-per◦ sing◦ fut2◦ लृट् भविष्य◦ ātmane◦ ←class2◦ प्र√वच् 4.16) (8.11)

(§3) *yat̜* (adj1◦-obj1◦ that which); *akṣaram̜* (adj2◦-obj1◦ Immutable); *vedavidaḥ:* (subj◦ the knowers of the vedas); *vadanti* (call); *viśanti* (sit in, enter); *yat̜* (adj1◦-obj1◦ which); *yatayaḥ:* (the ascetics); *vītarāgāḥ:* (freed from attachment); *yat̜* (adj1◦-obj1◦ which); *iććhantaḥ:* (adj3◦-obj1◦ aspiring); *brahmaćaryam̜* (obj2◦ celibacy); *ćaranti* (they practice); *tat̜* (adj4◦-obj1◦ that); *te* (you, to you); *padam̜* (obj1◦ state, step, place); *saṅgraheṇa* (= अशेषत: adv◦ collectively, without remainder, fully, wholly, entirely, completely); *pravakṣye* (I shall tell) (8.11)

(§4) pravakṣye te tat̜ saṅgraheṇa padam̜ yat̜ vedavidaḥ: vadanti akṣaram̜ yat̜ yatayaḥ: vītarāgāḥ: viśanti iććhantaḥ: yat̜ ćaranti brahmaćaryam

(§5) I shall tell you wholly[524] (of) that state,[525] which the knowers of the *vedas* call Immutable, which the ascetics freed from attachment sit in, aspiring which they practice celibacy. (8.11)

8.12 सर्वद्वाराणि संयम्य मनो हृदि निरुध्य च ।
मूर्ध्न्याधायात्मनः प्राणमास्थितो योगधारणाम् ।।

sarvadvārāṇi saṁyamya mano hṛdi nirudhya ća,
mūrdhnyādhāyātmanaḥ: prāṇamāsthito yogadhāraṇām̜; (8.12)

---

[524] Elsewhere◦ अशेषेण → briefly, in brief, with brevity, in short, succinctly, ...etc.

🕮 अ–शेष = without-remainder, entirely.

[525] Elsewhere◦ पदम् → goal, Goal ...etc.

(§1) *sarvadvārāṇi* (r◦ 24/7) *sam̃yamya manaḥ:* (r◦ 15/14) *hṛdi nirudhya ća mūrdhni* (r◦ 4/2) *ādhāya* (r◦ 1/2) *ātmanaḥ:* (r◦ 22/3) *prāṇaṃ* (r◦ 8/17, 24/3) *āsthitaḥ:* (r◦ 15/10) *yogadhāraṇāṃ* (r◦ 24/6, 14/2);

(§2) *sarvadvārāṇi* (सर्वाणि द्वाराणि, n◦ 2acc◦ plu◦ tatpu◦ ←pron◦ *sarva* (all) 1.6 + n◦ *dvāra* (door) 2.32); *sam̃yamya* (2.61); *manaḥ:* (2acc◦ 6.12); ***hṛdi*** (7loc◦ sing◦ ←n◦ *hṛd* 4.42); *nirudhya* (lyp◦ past-participle ind◦ ←नि√रुध् 6.20); *ća* (1.1); *mūrdhni* (7loc◦ sing◦ ←m◦ *mūrdhan* (neck, head) ←√मुर्व्); *ādhāya* (5.10); *ātmanaḥ:* (4.42); *prāṇaṃ* (4.29); *āsthitaḥ:* (5.4); *yogadhāraṇāṃ* (f◦ 2acc◦ sing◦ ←tatpu◦ *yoga-dhāraṇā*, योगस्य धारणा ←m◦ *yoga* 2.39 + f◦ *dhāraṇā* (posture) ←√धृ); (8.12)

(§3) *sarvadvārāṇi* (obj1◦ all gates); *sam̃yamya* (having brought under control); *manaḥ:* (obj2◦ the mind); *hṛdi* (in the heart); *nirudhya* (having confined); *ća* (and); *mūrdhni* (in the head); *ādhāya* (having placed); *ātmanaḥ:* (adj◦-obj3◦ one's); *prāṇaṃ* (obj3◦ life breath); *āsthitaḥ:* (adj◦-subj◦ established, seated); *yogadhāraṇāṃ* (obj4◦ in the posture, position, attitude of yoga); (8.12)

(§4) sam̃yamya sarvadvārāṇi nirudhya manaḥ: hṛdi ādhāya ātmanaḥ: prāṇaṃ mūrdhni ća āsthitaḥ: yogadhāraṇāṃ

(§5) Having brought all gates (of the body) under control,[526] having confined the mind in the heart, having placed one's life breath in the head and (thus) seated in the posture of yoga; (8.12)

8.13 ओमित्येकाक्षरं ब्रह्म व्याहरन्मामनुस्मरन् ।
यः प्रयाति त्यजन्देहं स याति परमां गतिम् ॥
omityekākṣaraṁ brahma vyāharanmāmanusmaraṇ,
yaḥ: prayāti tyajandehaṁ sa yāti paramāṁ gatiṃ. (8.13)

(§1) *oṃ* (r◦ 8/18) *iti* (r◦ 4/4) *ekākṣaraṃ* (r◦ 14/1) *brahma vyāharaṇ* (r◦ 13/16) *māṃ* (r◦ 8/16) *anusmaraṇ* (r◦ 23/1) *yaḥ:* (r◦ 22/3) *prayāti tyajaṇ* (r◦ 13/11) *dehaṃ* (r◦ 14/1) *saḥ:* (r◦ 21/2) *yāti paramāṃ* (r◦ 14/1) *gatiṃ* (r◦ 14/2)

(§2) ***oṃ*** (ind◦ ←√अव्); *iti* (1.25); *ekākṣaraṃ* (n◦ 2acc◦ sing◦ ←tatpu◦ *ekākṣara*, एकम् यस्य अक्षरम्, *eka* (one) 2.41 + n◦ *akṣara* (indivisible letter) 3.15); *brahma* (3.15); 🕮*vyāharaṇ* (1nom◦ sing◦ ←śatṛ◦ adj◦ *vyāharaṭ* ←वि-आ√हृ); *māṃ* (1.46); 🕮*anusmaraṇ* (1nom◦ sing◦ ←śatṛ◦ adj◦ *anusmaraṭ* (uttering) ←अनु√स्मृ); *yaḥ:* (2.19); *prayāti* (8.5); *tyajaṇ* (1nom◦ sing◦ ←śatṛ◦ adj◦ *tyajaṭ* (leaving) ←त्यज्); *dehaṃ* (4.9); *saḥ:* (1.13); *yāti* (6.45); ***paramāṃ*** (f◦ 2acc◦ sing◦ ←adj◦ *parama* (supreme) 1.17); *gatiṃ* (state, 6.37) (8.13)

---

[526] Elsewhere◦ निरुध्य → Having closed all the gates (senses), Having closed all the doors of the senses, ...etc.

🕮 gates = input /output entrances or openings.

(§3) *oṃ* (adj◦1-obj◦ om, ॐ) *iti* (thus); *ekākṣaram* (adj2◦-obj◦ the monosyllable); *brahma* (obj◦ brahma);[527] *vyāharan* (adj1◦-subj◦ uttering, while uttering); *mām* (obj2◦ me); *anusmaran* (adj2◦-subj◦ thinking of); *yaḥ:* (adj3◦-subj◦ he who); *prayāti* (departs, dies); *tyajan* (adj4◦-subj◦ leaving); *deham* (obj3◦ body); *saḥ:* (subj◦ he); *yāti* (attains); *paramām* (adj◦-obj4◦ supreme); *gatim* (obj4◦ state) (8.13)

(§4) oṃ iti vyāharan ekākṣaram brahma anusmaran mām yaḥ: prayāti tyajan deham saḥ: yāti paramām gatim

(§5) *oṃ* thus uttering the monosyllable brahma, thinking of me, he who departs leaving (his) body, he attains supreme state. (8.13)

8.14 अनन्यचेताः सततं यो मां स्मरति नित्यशः ।
तस्याहं सुलभः पार्थ नित्ययुक्तस्य योगिनः ।।
ananyaćetāḥ: satatam yo mām smarati nityaśaḥ:,
tasyāham sulabhaḥ: pārtha nityayuktasya yoginaḥ:. (8.14)

(§1) *ananyaćetā:* (r◦ 22/7) *satatam* (r◦ 14/1) *yaḥ:* (r◦ 15/9) *mām* (r◦ 14/1) *smarati nityaśaḥ:* (r◦ 22/8) *tasya* (r◦ 1/1) *aham* (r◦ 14/1) *sulabhaḥ:* (r◦ 22/3) *pārtha nityayuktasya yoginaḥ:* (r◦ 22/8)

(§2) 🕮*ananyaćetāḥ:* (m◦ 1nom◦ sing◦ ←bahuvrī◦ *ananya-ćetas*, नास्ति अन्यस्मिन् चेतः यस्य ←adj◦ ***ananya*** (one pointed) ←अन्√अन् + n◦ *ćetas* 1.38); *satatam* (3.19); *yaḥ:* (2.19); *mām* (1.46); *smarati* (3rd-per◦ sing◦ pres◦ वर्तमान्-लट् parasmai◦ ←class1◦ √स्मृ); *nityaśaḥ:* (mode indicating adv◦ ind◦ ←adj◦ *nitya* (constant) 2.18); *tasya* (1.12); *aham* (1.22); 🕮*sulabhaḥ:* (m◦ 1nom◦ sing◦ ←adj◦ *sulabha* (easy to attain) ←सु√लभ्); *pārtha* (1.25); *nityayuktasya* (m◦ 6pos◦ sing◦ ←adj◦ *nitya-yukta* 7.17); *yoginaḥ:* (6pos sing◦ ←m◦ *yogin* 3.3) (8.14)

(§3) *ananyaćetāḥ:* (adj◦-subj1◦ he who has one pointd, focused mind); *satatam* (always); *yaḥ:* (subj1◦ he who); *mām* (obj◦ me); *smarati* (remembers); *nityaśaḥ:* (constantly); *tasya* (his, for him, for that); *aham* (subj2◦ I am); *sulabhaḥ:* (easy to attain); *pārtha* (O Arjuna!); *nityayuktasya* (adj2◦-subj1◦ ever equipped); *yoginaḥ:* (adj3◦-subj1◦ yogī) (8.14)

(§4) pārtha tasya nityayuktasya yoginaḥ: ananyaćetāḥ: satatam yaḥ: smarati mām nityaśaḥ: aham sulabhaḥ:

(§5) O Arjuna! for that ever equipped yogī, who has one pointd focused mind, he who remembers me constantly, I am easy to attain. (8.14)

8.15 मामुपेत्य पुनर्जन्म दुःखालयमशाश्वतम् ।
नाप्नुवन्ति महात्मानः संसिद्धिं परमां गताः ।।

---

[527] Elsewhere◦ ब्रह्म → In Sanskrit ब्रह्म and in English brahman, Brahman ...etc. Why?

māmupetya punarjanma duḥ:khālayamaśāśvatam,
nāpnuvanti mahātmānaḥ: saṁsiddhiṁ paramāṁ gatāḥ:. (8.15)

(§1) *mām* (r◦ 8/20) *upetya punarjanma duḥ:khālayam* (r◦ 8/16) *aśāśvatam* (r◦ 14/2) *na* (r◦ 1/2) *āpnuvanti mahātmānaḥ:* (r◦ 22/7) *saṁsiddhim* (r◦ 14/1) *paramām* (r◦ 14/1) *gatāḥ:* (r◦ 22/8)

(§2) *mām* (1.46); 🕮***upetya*** (lyp◦ past-participle ind◦ ←उप√इ); *punarjanma* (4.9); *duḥ:khālayam* (n◦ 2acc◦ sing◦ ←tatpu◦ *duḥ:khālaya*, दुःखानाम् आलयम् ←n◦ *duḥ:kha* (sorrow) 2.14 + n◦ 🕮***ālaya*** (home) ←आ√ली); *aśāśvatam* (n◦ 2acc◦ sing◦ ←adj◦ n.tatpu◦ *a-śāśvata* ←अ√शस्); *na* (1.30); *āpnuvanti* (3rd-per◦ plu◦ pres◦ वर्तमान्–लट् parasmai◦ ←class10◦ √आप्); ***mahātmānaḥ:*** (m◦ 1nom◦ plu◦ ←m◦ *mahātman* 7.19); *saṁsiddhim* (3.20); *paramām* (8.13); *gatāḥ:* (m◦ 1nom◦ plu◦ ←adj◦ *gata* (gone, accomplished) 2.11) (8.15)

(§3) *mām* (obj1◦ me); *upetya* (having attained); *punarjanma* (obj2◦ rebirth); *duḥ:khālayam* (adj1◦-obj2◦ the abode of sorrows); *aśāśvatam* (adj2◦-obj2◦ the impermanent); *na* (do not); *āpnuvanti* (get); *mahātmānaḥ:* (subj◦ the great souls); *saṁsiddhim* (obj3◦ success); *paramām* (adj◦-obj3◦ supreme); *gatāḥ:* (adj◦-subj◦ who have accomplish) (8.15)

(§4) upetya mām mahātmānaḥ: gatāḥ: paramām saṁsiddhim na āpnuvanti aśāśvatam punarjanma duḥ:khālayam

(§5) Having attained[528] me, the great souls, who have accomplish supreme success,[529] do not get the impermanent rebirth (which is) the abode of sorrows. (8.15)

8.16 **आब्रह्मभुवनाल्लोकाः पुनरावर्तिनोऽर्जुन ।
मामुपेत्य तु कौन्तेय पुनर्जन्म न विद्यते ।।**
ābrahmabhuvanāllokāḥ: punarāvartino'rjuna,
māmupetya tu kaunteya punarjanma na vidyate. (8.16)

(§1) *ābrahmabhuvanāt* (r◦ 11/6) *lokāḥ:* (r◦ 22/3) *punarāvartinaḥ:* (r◦ 15/1) *arjuna mām* (r◦ 8/20) *upetya tu kaunteya punarjanma na vidyate*

(§2) *ābrahmabhuvanāt* (n◦ 5abl◦ sing◦ ←tatpu◦ *ābrahma-bhuvana*, आब्रह्मणः भुवनम् ←ind◦ *ā* आ 3.20 + m◦

---

[528] Elsewhere◦ उपेत्य → have realized, ...etc.

[529] Elsewhere◦ संसिद्धिं परमाम् → highest perfection, supreme perfection ...etc.

🕮 Are there such things as lower, lowest, moderate, higher and supreme perfections. Perfaction is itself superlative and needs no adjective. Only thing that is perfect is brahma (सं-परि-पूर्ण ब्रह्म).

brahman 2.72 + n◦ *bhuvana* (realm) ←√भू); *lokāḥ:* (3.24); *punarāvartinaḥ:* (m◦ 1nom◦ plu◦ ←adj◦ *punarāvartin* ←ind◦ *punar* (again) 4.9 + adj◦ *āvartin* (taking birth) ←आ√वृत्); *arjuna* (2.2); *mām* (1.46); *upetya* (8.15); *tu* (1.2); *kaunteya* (2.14); *punarjanma* (4.9); *na* (1.30); *vidyate* (2.16) (8.16)

(§3) *ābrahmabhuvanāt* (up to brahma's realm); *lokāḥ:* (subj◦ the worlds); *punarāvartinaḥ:* (adj◦-subj1◦ subject to successive rebirths); *arjuna* (O Arjuna!); *mām* (obj◦ me); *upetya* (having attained); *tu* (however); *kaunteya* (O Arjuna!); *punarjanma* (subj2◦ rebirth); *na* (does not); *vidyate* (exist, occure) (8.16)

(§4) arjuna lokāḥ: ābrahmabhuvanāt punarāvartinaḥ: tu kaunteya upetya mām punarjanma na vidyate

(§5) O Arjuna! the worlds up to brahma's realm (are) subject to successive rebirths. However, O Arjuna! having attained me, rebirth does not occure.[530] (8.16)

8.17 सहस्रयुगपर्यन्तमहर्यद्ब्रह्मणो विदुः ।
रात्रिं युगसहस्रान्तां तेऽहोरात्रविदो जनाः ।।
sahasrayugaparyantamaharyadbrahmaṇo viduḥ:,
rātriṁ yugasahasrāntāṁ te'horātravido janāḥ:. (8.17)

(§1) *sahasrayugaparyantam* (r◦ 8/16) *ahan*[531] *yat* (r◦ 9/7) *brahmaṇaḥ:* (r◦ 15/13) *viduḥ:* (r◦ 22/8) *rātrim* (r◦ 14/1) *yugasahasrāntām* (r◦ 14/1) *te* (r◦ 6/1) *ahorātravidaḥ:* (r◦ 15/3) *janāḥ:* (r◦ 22/8)

(§2) *sahasrayugaparyantam* (m◦ 2acc◦ sing◦ ←bahuvrī◦ *sahasra-yuga-paryantam*, सहस्राणि युगानि पर्यन्तः यस्य ←adj◦ *sahasra* (thousand) 7.3 + n◦ *yuga* (age) 4.8 + m◦ 🕮*paryanta* ←परि√अय्); ***ahahar*** (1nom◦ sing◦ ←n◦ *ahan* (day) न जहाति परिवर्तमानत्वात् इति ←√हा । word अहन् changes to अहर्); *yat* (1.45); *brahmaṇaḥ:* (4.32); *viduḥ:* (4.2); *rātrim* (2acc◦ sing◦ ←f◦ ***rātri*** (night) ←√रा); *yugasahasrāntām* (2acc◦ sing◦ ←bahuvrī◦ f◦ *yuga-sahasrāntā*, युगानाम् सहस्रेण अन्तः यस्याः ←n◦ *yuga* 4.8 + adj◦ *sahasra* (thousand) 7.3 + m◦ *anta* (end) 2.16); *te* (1.33); *ahorātravidaḥ:* (m◦ 1nom◦ plu◦ ←bahuvrī◦ *ahorātravid*, अहः च रात्रिम् च वेत्ति यः ←n◦ *aha* ↑ + f◦ *rātri* ↑ + adj◦ *vid* (knower) 3.29); *janāḥ:* (7.16) (8.17)

(§3) *sahasrayugaparyantam* (adj◦-obj1◦ which extends up to one thousand *yugas*); *ahahar* (obj1◦ the

---

[530] Elsewhere◦ पुनर्जन्म न विद्यते → one never takes rebirth, one never takes birth again, rebieth is not found, he knoweth birth no more, ...etc.

🕮 In पुनर्जन्म न विद्यते, 'he' or 'one' is not the subject, the subject is पुनर्जन्म in Nominative case. पुनर्जन्म is the doer of the verb विद्यते ।

[531] In Samasa अहन् becomes अह, अहस् or अहर् ।

day); *yaṭ* (which); *brahmaṇaḥ:* (of brahmā); *viduḥ:* (know); *rātrim̩* (obj2◦ the night); *yugasahasrāntām̩* (adj◦-obj2◦ which extends up to one thousand *yugas*); *te* (adj◦-subj◦ they); *ahorātravidaḥ:* (adj2◦-subj◦ knowers of the day and night, those who know day and night); *janāḥ:* (subj◦ the people) (8.17)

(§4) janāḥ: ahorātravidaḥ: te viduḥ: ahaḥar brahmaṇaḥ: yaṭ sahasrayugaparyantam̩ rātrim̩ yugasahasrāntām̩

(§5) The people who know day and night, they know the day of brahmā[532] which extends up to one thousand *yugas* (and) a night which extends up to one thousand *yugas*. (8.17)

8.18 अव्यक्ताद्व्यक्तयः सर्वाः प्रभवन्त्यहरागमे ।
रात्र्यागमे प्रलीयन्ते तत्रैवाव्यक्तसंज्ञके ।।
avyaktādvyaktayaḥ: sarvāḥ: prabhavantyaharāgame,
rātryāgame pralīyante tatraivāvyaktasañjñake. (8.18)

(§1) *avyaktāṭ* (r◦ 9/11) *vyaktayaḥ:* (r◦ 22/7) *sarvāḥ:* (r◦ 22/3) *prabhavanti* (r◦ 4/1) *aharāgame rātryāgame pralīyante tatra* (r◦ 3/1) *eva* (r◦ 1/1) *avyaktasañjñake*

(§2) ***avyaktāṭ*** (5abl◦ sing◦ ←adj◦ *avyakta* (unequipped) 2.25); *vyaktayaḥ:* (1nom◦ plu◦ ←f◦ *vyakti* (person, personification) 7.24); ***sarvāḥ:*** (f◦ 1nom◦ plu◦ ←pron◦ *sarva* 1.6); ***prabhavanti*** (f◦ 3rd-per◦ plu◦ pres◦ वर्तमान्–लट् parasmai◦ ←class1◦ प्र√भू); ***aharāgame*** (7loc◦ sing◦ ←tatpu◦ *aharāgama*, अहः आगमः ←n◦ *ahan̩* (day) 8.17 + m◦ *āgama* (arrival) 2.14); ***rātryāgame*** (m◦ 7loc◦ sing◦ ←tatpu◦ *rātryāgama*, रात्र्या आगमः ←f◦ (night) *rātri* 8.17 + m◦ (arrival) *āgama* 2.14); 🕮*pralīyante* (f◦ 3rd-per◦ plu◦ pres◦ वर्तमान्–लट् ātmane◦ ←class4◦ प्र√ली); *tatra* (1.26); *eva* (1.1); *avyaktasañjñake* (7loc◦ sing◦ ←bahuvrī◦ *avyakta-sañjñaka*, "अव्यक्त" इति संज्ञा यस्य ←adj◦ *avyakta* (unpersonified) 2.25 + adj◦ *sañjñaka* (called) ←सम्√ज्ञा–क) (8.18)

(§3) *avyaktāṭ* (from the unmanifest, from the unpersonified); *vyaktayaḥ:* (subj◦ personifications); *sarvāḥ:* (adj◦-subj◦ all); *prabhavanti* (arise, originate, take birth); *aharāgame* (at the commencement of

---

[532] Elsewhere◦ सहस्रयुगपर्यन्तम् अहः रात्रिं युगसहस्रान्ताम् → Those who know that the day of Brahma lasts a thousand Yugas and that his night lasts..., Those who know that the day of Brahma is of...thousand ages and that the night is..., Those who know that the day of Brahma is a thousand yugas long and that his night lasts..., know that the day of Brahma is a...thousand yugas long and that the night is..., They who know that the day of Brahmā extends as far as a thoudand yugas and that the night of Brahma ends only in a thousand... etc.

🕮 In सहस्रयुगपर्यन्तम् अहः रात्रिं युगसहस्रान्ताम्, the अहः and रात्रिम् are not the subjects in Nominative 1st case. They are the objects in 2nd Accusative 2nd case. And thus, the translation of Krishṇa's words must treat them as objects, not as subjects.

the day); *rātryāgame* (at the commencement of night); *pralīyante* (they dissolve); *tatra eva* (there itself); *avyaktasañjñake* (in the name of unmanifest, unpersonified) (8.18)

(§4) sarvāḥ: vyaktayaḥ: avyaktāt prabhavanti aharāgame rātryāgame pralīyante tatra eva avyaktasañjñake

(§5) All personifications originate from the unpersonified at the commencement of the day; (and) at the commencement of night they dissolve there itself, in the name of unpersonified. (8.18)

8.19 भूतग्रामः स एवायं भूत्वा भूत्वा प्रलीयते ।

रात्र्यागमेऽवशः पार्थ प्रभवत्यहरागमे ।।

bhūtagrāmaḥ: sa evāyaṁ bhūtvā bhūtvā pralīyate,

rātryāgame'vaśaḥ: pārtha prabhavatyaharāgame; (8.19)

(§1) *bhūtagrāmaḥ:* (r◦ 22/7) *saḥ:* (r◦ 21/2) *eva* (r◦ 1/1) *ayaṃ* (r◦ 14/1) *bhūtvā bhūtvā pralīyate rātryāgame* (r◦ 6/1) *avaśaḥ:* (r◦ 22/3) *pārtha prabhavati* (r◦ 4/1) *aharāgame;*

(§2) *bhūtagrāmaḥ:* (m◦ 1nom◦ sing◦ ←tatpu◦ ***bhūta-grāma***, भूतानाम् ग्रामः ←m◦ *bhūta* (being) 2.28 + m◦ *grāma* (group) 6.24); *saḥ:* (1.13); *eva* (1.1); *ayaṃ* (2.19); *bhūtvā* (2.20); *bhūtvā* (2.20); *pralīyate* (3rd-per◦ sing◦ pres◦ वर्तमान्–लट् ātmane◦ ←class4◦ प्र√ली see 8.18); *rātryāgame* (8.18); *avaśaḥ:* (3.5); *pārtha* (1.25); *prabhavati* (3rd-per◦ sing◦ pres◦ वर्तमान्–लट् parasmai◦ ←class1◦ प्र√भू 8.18); *aharāgame* (8.18);

(§3) *bhūtagrāmaḥ:* (subj◦ aggregate of beings); *saḥ:* (adj1◦-subj◦ that); *eva* (also, too, again); *ayaṃ* (adj2◦-subj◦ this); *bhūtvā bhūtvā* (having come in to being again and again, having personified again and again); *pralīyate* (it dissolves, merges back into unmanifest); *rātryāgame* (at the arrivel of night); *avaśaḥ:* (helplessly); *pārtha* (O Arjuna!); *prabhavati* (it reappears, it personifies, it manifests); *aharāgame* (at the arrival of day); (8.19)

(§4) ayaṃ bhūtagrāmaḥ: bhūtvā bhūtvā pralīyate rātryāgame avaśaḥ: pārtha saḥ: eva prabhavati aharāgame;

(§5) This aggregate of beings having come in to being again and again, merges back[533] helplessly into unmanifest at the arrivel of night. O Arjuna! that again manifests at the arrival of day; (8.19)

8.20 परस्तस्मात्तु भावोऽन्योऽव्यक्तोऽव्यक्तात्सनातनः ।

यः स सर्वेषु भूतेषु नश्यत्सु न विनश्यति ।।

parastasmāttu bhāvo'nyo'vyakto'vyaktātsanātanaḥ:,

---

[533] Elsewhere◦ प्रलीयते → annihilated, destroyed, ...etc.

yaḥ: sa sarveṣu bhūteṣu naśyatsu na vinaśyati. (8.20)

(§1) *paraḥ:* (r◦ 18/1) *tasmāt* (r◦ 1/10) *tu bhāvaḥ:* (r◦ 15/1) *anyaḥ:* (r◦ 15/1) *avyaktaḥ:* (r◦ 15/1) *avyaktāt* (r◦ 10/7) *sanātanaḥ:* (r◦ 22/8) *yaḥ:* (r◦ 22/7) *saḥ:* (r◦ 21/2) *sarveṣu* (r◦ 25/5) *bhūteṣu* (r◦ 25/5) *naśyatsu na vinaśyati*

(§2) *paraḥ:* (4.40); *tasmāt* (m◦ 5abl◦ sing◦ ←pron◦ *tad* 1.2); *tu* (1.2); *bhāvaḥ:* (2.16); *anyaḥ:* (2.29); *avyaktaḥ:* (2.25); *avyaktāt* (8.18); *sanātanaḥ:* (2.24); *yaḥ:* (2.19); *saḥ:* (1.13); *sarveṣu* (1.11); *bhūteṣu* (7.11); *naśyatsu* (m◦ 7loc◦ plu◦ ←śatṛ◦ adj◦ *naśyat* (dissolving) ←√नश्); *na* (1.30); *vinaśyati* (4.40) (8.20)

(§3) *paraḥ:* (adj1◦-subj◦ beyond, higher); *tasmāt* (than that); *tu* (However); *bhāvaḥ:* (subj◦ principle, nature); *anyaḥ:* (adj2◦-suj◦ another); *avyaktaḥ:* (adj3◦-subj◦ unmanifest); *avyaktāt* (than unmanifest); *sanātanaḥ:* (adj4◦-subj◦ primaeval, one that has no beginning and no end); *yaḥ:* (adj5◦-subj◦ that which); *saḥ:* (adj6◦-subj◦ that); *sarveṣu bhūteṣu* (in all beings); *naśyatsu* (in the dissolution of, in the death of); *na vinaśyati* (does not dissolve, does not die) (8.20)

(§4) tu paraḥ: tasmāt avyaktāt saḥ: anyaḥ: sanātanaḥ: avyaktaḥ: bhāvaḥ: yaḥ: na vinaśyati naśyatsu sarveṣu bhūteṣu

(§5) However, higher than that unmanifest, (there is) that another primaeval unmanifest principle which does not dissolve on the dissolution of all beings. (8.20)

8.21 अव्यक्तोऽक्षर इत्युक्तस्तमाहुः परमां गतिम् ।
यं प्राप्य न निवर्तन्ते तद्धाम परमं मम ।।

avyakto'kṣara ityuktastamāhuḥ: paramāṁ gatim,
yaṁ prāpya na nivartante taddhāma paramaṁ mama. (8.21)

(§1) *avyaktaḥ:* (r◦ 15/1) *akṣaraḥ:* (r◦ 19/2) *iti* (r◦ 4/3) *uktaḥ:* (r◦ 18/1) *tam* (r◦ 8/17) *āhuḥ:* (r◦ 22/3) *paramām* (r◦ 14/1) *gatim* (r◦ 14/2) *yam* (r◦ 14/1) *prāpya na nivartante tat* (r◦ 9/6) *dhāma paramam* (r◦ 14/1) *mama*

(§2) *avyaktaḥ:* (2.25); 🕮***akṣaraḥ:*** (1nom◦ sing◦ n.tatpu◦ ←adj◦ *kṣara* (mutable) 8.4); *iti* (1.25); *uktaḥ:* (1.24); *tam* (2.1); *āhuḥ:* (3.42); *paramām* (8.13); *gatim* (6.37); *yam* (2.15); *prāpya* (2.57); *na* (1.30); 🕮***nivartante*** (3rd-per◦ plu◦ pres◦ वर्तमान्–लट् ātmane◦ ←class1◦ नि√वृत् 2.59); *tat* (1.10); 🕮***dhāma*** (1nom◦ sing◦ ←n◦ *dhāman* (abode) ←√धा); *paramam* (8.3); *mama* (1.7) (8.21)

(§3) *avyaktaḥ:* (adj1◦-obj1◦ Unmanifest); *akṣaraḥ:* (adj2◦-obj1◦ immutable); *iti* (thus); *uktaḥ:* (adj3◦-obj1◦ is called); *tam* (adj4◦-obj1◦ to that); *āhuḥ:* (they call); *paramām* (adj◦-obj2◦ supreme); *gatim* (obj2◦

state,); *yam̜* (adj◦5-obj1◦ what); *prāpya* (having attained); *na nivartante* (one does not return back); *tat̜* (n◦ adj1◦-subj◦ that); *dhāma* (n◦ subj◦ abode); *paramam̜* (n◦ adj2◦-subj◦ supreme); *mama* (mine); (8.21)

(§4) yam̜ uktaḥ: avyaktaḥ: akṣaraḥ: iti tam̜ āhuḥ: paramām̜ gatim̜ prāpya na nivartante tat̜ paramam̜ dhāma mama

(§5) What is called Unmanifest (and) Immutable thus, to that they call supreme state, having attained (that), one does not return back. That supreme abode (is) mine.[534]

(8.21)

8.22 पुरुषः स परः पार्थ भक्त्या लभ्यस्त्वनन्यया ।
यस्यान्तःस्थानि भूतानि येन सर्वमिदं ततम् ।।

puruṣaḥ: sa paraḥ: pārtha bhaktyā labhyastvananyayā,
yasyāntaḥ:sthāni bhūtāni yena sarvamidaṁ tatam̜. (8.22)

(§1) *puruṣaḥ:* (r◦ 22/7) *saḥ:* (r◦ 21/2) *paraḥ:* (r◦ 22/3) *pārtha bhaktyā labhyaḥ:* (r◦ 18/1) *tu* (r◦ 4/6) *ananyayā yasya* (r◦ 1/1) *antaḥ:sthāni bhūtāni yena sarvam̜* (r◦ 8/18) *idam̜* (r◦ 14/1) *tatam̜* (r◦ 14/2)

(§2) *puruṣaḥ:* (2.21); *saḥ:* (1.13); *paraḥ:* (3.11); *pārtha* (1.25); *bhaktyā* (8.10); *labhyaḥ:* (m◦ 1nom◦ sing◦ ←pot◦ adj◦ 🕮*labhya* ←√लभ्); *tu* (1.2); ***ananyayā*** (f◦ 3inst◦ sing◦ ←adj◦ *ananya* (one pointed) 8.14); *yasya* (2.61); *antaḥ:sthāni* (n◦ 1nom◦ plu◦ ←ind◦ *antaḥ:stha* (seated within) अन्ते स्थितम् ←ind◦ *ante* (5.24) + adj◦ *sthita* (1.14); *bhūtāni* (1nom◦ 2.28); *yena* (2.17); *sarvam̜* (2.17); *idam̜* (1.10); *tatam̜* (2.17) (8.22)

(§3) *puruṣaḥ:* (m◦ obj1◦ purusha); *saḥ:* (adj1◦-obj1◦ that); *paraḥ:* (adj2◦-obj1◦ supreme); *pārtha* (O Arjuna!); *bhaktyā* (with devotion, dedication); *labhyaḥ:* (adj3◦-obj1◦ attainable); *tu* (now); *ananyayā* (with one pointed); *yasya* (whose, whom); *antaḥ:sthāni* (adj◦-subj1◦ situated in); *bhūtāni* (n◦ subj1◦ the

---

[534] In various translations, five important things to observe while translating and understanding this verse properly are :

(i) आहुः (they say) is not a past tense or a passive verb, e.g. is called, said to be;

(ii) उक्तः is ppp◦ passive particeple adjective of अव्यक्तोऽक्षरः

(iii) and therefore, in passive construction, both these adj◦ अव्यक्तः अक्षरः are in Nominative case.

(iv) the n◦ pronoun तत् does not qualify f◦ परमां गतिम्, it qualifies n◦ obj-2◦ धाम, thus, not - 'that (supreme state परमां गतिम्)' is my abode, but 'that supreme abode' धाम परमम् is mine ...etc.

(v) in यं प्राप्य, the m◦ pronominal adjective यम् does not qualify f◦ परमां गतिम् । It qualifies m◦ अव्यक्तोऽक्षरः । प्राप्य is a ल्यबन्त gerund, having attained (the परमां गतिम्), not Present Ternse - those who attain it, or he who attains it.

beings); *yena* (m◦ subj2◦ by whom); *sarvaṃ* (adj1◦-obj2◦ all); *idaṃ* (n◦ obj◦ this); *tataṃ* (n◦ adj2◦-obj2◦ THAT) (8.22)

(§4) tu pārtha saḥ: paraḥ: puruṣaḥ: antaḥ:sthāni yasya bhūtāni yena sarvaṃ idaṃ tataṃ labhyaḥ: ananyayā bhaktyā

(§5) Now, O Arjuna! that[535] supreme *purusha,* situated[536] in whom (are) the beings, by whom all this (is) THAT,[537] (is) attainable with one pointed devotion. (8.22)

8.23 यत्र काले त्वनावृत्तिमावृत्तिं चैव योगिनः ।
प्रयाता यान्ति तं कालं वक्ष्यामि भरतर्षभ ।।

yatra kāle tvanāvṛttimāvṛttiṁ ćaiva yoginaḥ:,
prayātā yānti taṁ kālaṁ vakṣyāmi bharatarṣabha. (8.23)

(§1) *yatra kāle tu* (r◦ 4/6) *anāvṛttiṃ* (r◦ 8/17) *āvṛttiṃ* (r◦ 14/1) *ća* (r◦ 3/1) *eva yoginaḥ:* (r◦ 22/8) *prayātāḥ:* (r◦ 20/14) *yānti taṃ* (r◦ 14/1) *kālaṃ* (r◦ 14/1) *vakṣyāmi bharatarṣabha*

(§2) *yatra* (6.20); ***kāle*** (7loc◦ sing◦ ←m◦ *kāla* (time) 2.72); *tu* (1.2); 🕮***anāvṛttiṃ*** (2acc◦ sing◦ n.tatpu◦ ←f◦ *āvṛtti* (birth) 5.17); *āvṛttiṃ* (2acc◦ sing◦ ←f◦ *āvṛtti* (birth) 5.17); *ća* (1.1); *eva* (1.1); *yoginaḥ:* (4.25); *prayātāḥ:* (m◦ 1nom◦ plu◦ ←ppp◦ adj◦ 🕮*prayāta* (departed) ←प्र√या); *yānti* (3.33); *taṃ* (2.1); *kālaṃ* (2acc◦ sing◦ ←m◦ *kāla* (time) 2.72); *vakṣyāmi* (7.2); *bharatarṣabha* (3.41) (8.23)

(§3) *yatra kāle* (that time at which); *tu* (now); *anāvṛttiṃ* (obj1◦ non-rebirth); *āvṛttiṃ* (obj2◦ rebirth); *ća eva* (as well as); *yoginaḥ:* (subj◦ yogīs); *prayātāḥ:* (adj◦-subj◦ the departed); *yānti* (attain); *taṃ* (adj◦-obj2◦ that); *kālaṃ* (obj2◦ time); *vakṣyāmi* (I shall tell); *bharatarṣabha* (O Arjuna!) (8.23)

(§4) bharatarṣabha tu vakṣyāmi yatra kāle prayātāḥ: yoginaḥ: yānti anāvṛttiṃ ća eva taṃ kālaṃ āvṛttiṃ

(§5) O Arjuna! now I shall tell (you) that time at which the departed[538] yogīs attain non-rebirth

---

[535] Elsewhere◦ सः → This

[536] Elsewhere◦ यस्यान्तस्थानि → in whom all beings reside, within whom all beings dewll, who is substrate of whatever exists, in whom all existances abide, in whom abide all existence, ...etc.

🕮 अन्तस्थानि, अन्तस्थ, or स्थ is not a Present tense verb, it is a ppp◦ past passive participle adjective of the n◦ noun भूतानि ।

[537] Elsewhere◦ ततम् → pervaded ...etc.

🕮 See the footnote in 2.17

[538] Elsewhere◦ प्रयाताः → going forth (present participle), passing away (क्त्वा), departing in death (क्त्वा), by

as well as that time (at which they attain) rebirth. (8.23)

8.24 अग्निर्ज्योतिरहः शुक्लः षण्मासा उत्तरायणम् ।
तत्र प्रयाता गच्छन्ति ब्रह्म ब्रह्मविदो जनाः ।।
agnirjyotirahaḥ: śuklaḥ: ṣaṇmāsā uttarāyaṇam,
tatra prayātā gaćchanti brahma brahmavido janāḥ:. (8.24)

(§1) *agniḥ:* (r◦ 16/6) *jyotiḥ:* (r◦ 16/1) *ahaḥ:* (r◦ 22/5) *śuklaḥ:* (r◦ 22/6) *ṣaṇmāsāḥ:* (r◦ 20/4) *uttarāyaṇam* (r◦ 14/2, 24/3) *tatra prayātāḥ* (r◦ 20/6) *gaćchanti brahma brahmavidaḥ:* (r◦ 15/3) *janāḥ:* (r◦ 22/8)

(§2) *agniḥ:* (4.37); ***jyotiḥ:*** (1nom◦ sing◦ ←n◦ *jyotiṣ* (brightness) 5.21); *ahaḥ:* (1nom◦ sing◦ ←n◦ *ahan* (day) 8.17); *śuklaḥ:* (m◦ 1nom◦ sing◦ ←adj◦ ***śukla*** ←√शुच्); ***ṣaṇmāsāḥ:*** (1nom◦ plu◦ ←m◦ *ṣaṇmāsa* (six months) ←adj◦ *ṣaṣ*, in nominative case- *ṣaṭ* or *ṣaḍ* (six) ←√सो + m◦ ***māsa*** (month) ←√मस्); *uttarāyaṇam* (1nom◦ sing◦ ←n◦ tatpu◦ *uttarāyaṇa*, उत्तरायाः अयनम् ←f◦ *uttarā* ←adj◦ *uttara* (north) 6.11 + n◦ *ayana* (gate) 1.11) *tatra* (1.26); *prayātāḥ* (8.23); *gaćchanti* (2.51); *brahma* (2acc◦ 3.15); *brahmavidaḥ:* (1nom◦ plu◦ ←bahuvrī◦ *brahma-vida*, ब्रह्म वेत्ति यः ←n◦ *brahman* 2.72 + adj◦ *vid* 3.29); *janāḥ:* (7.16) (8.24)

(§3) *agniḥ:* (fire God, the Sun); *jyotiḥ:* (brightness of the sky); *ahaḥ:* (the day time); *śuklaḥ:* (the bright lunar fortnight); *ṣaṇmāsāḥ:* (the six months of); *uttarāyaṇam* (the Northern solstic, northward travel of the Sun) *tatra* (there, in these periods, in the presence of); *prayātāḥ* (adj◦-subj◦ departed); *gaćchanti* (go); *brahma* (obj◦ to brahma); *brahmavidaḥ:* (adj2◦-subj◦ those who are the knowers of brahma); *janāḥ:* (subj◦ the people) (8.24)

(§4) janāḥ: brahmavidaḥ: prayātāḥ tatra agniḥ: jyotiḥ: ahaḥ: śuklaḥ: ṣaṇmāsāḥ: uttarāyaṇam gaćchanti brahma

(§5) The people who are the knowers of brahma, departed[539] during the presence of the Sun,

---

departing at which (क्त्वा), at which departing (क्त्वा), departing at which (क्त्वा), when yogins depart (present◦), the yogis depart (pres◦), after departing (क्त्वा), in what time departing (क्त्वा), departing when (क्त्वा), the time which yogins departing (present participle), ...etc.

📖 प्रयात is a ppp◦ past paassive participle adjective of योगिनः, it is not क्त्वा gerund. present participle or present tense verb. प्रयाताः = departed, same usgae in verse 8.24.

[539] Elsewhere◦ प्रयाताः → when they die, proceeding along it after death, passing away, then going forth, then departing, departing at which, at which departing, on their departure, ...etc.

📖 प्रयाताः is a ppp◦ past paassive participle adjective of जनाः, it is not क्त्वा gerund. present participle or

brightness of the sky, the day time, the bright lunar fortnight, the six months of northward travel of the Sun, go to brahma. (8.24)

8.25 धूमो रात्रिस्तथा कृष्णः षण्मासा दक्षिणायनम् ।
तत्र चान्द्रमसं ज्योतिर्योगी प्राप्य निवर्तते ।।
dhūmo rātristathā kṛṣṇaḥ: ṣaṇmāsā dakṣiṇāyanam̦,
tatra ćāndramasaṁ jyotiryogī prāpya nivartate. (8.25)

(§1) *dhūmaḥ:* (r◦ 15/11) *rātriḥ:* (r◦ 18/1) *tathā kṛṣṇaḥ:* (r◦ 22/6) *ṣaṇmāsāḥ:* (r◦ 20/8) *dakṣiṇāyanam̦* (r◦ 14/2) *tatra ćāndramasam̦* (r◦ 14/1) *jyotiḥ:* (r◦ 16/6) *yogī prāpya nivartate*

(§2) *dhūmaḥ:* (1nom◦ sing◦ ←m◦ *dhūma* (smoke) 3.38); *rātriḥ:* (1nom◦ sing◦ ←f◦ *rātri* (night) 8.17); *tathā* (1.8); ***kṛṣṇaḥ:*** (m◦ 1nom◦ sing◦ ←adj◦ *kṛṣṇa* (moment) 1.28); *ṣaṇmāsāḥ:* (8.24); *dakṣiṇāyanam̦* (1nom◦ sing◦ ←tatpu◦ n◦ *dakṣiṇāyana,* दक्षिणायाः अयनम् ←f◦ *dakṣiṇā* ←adj◦ *dakṣiṇa* (souht) ←√दक्ष् + n◦ *ayana* (gate) 1.11); *tatra* (1.26); *ćāndramasam̦* (n◦ 2acc◦ sing◦ ←adj◦ *ćāndramas* (moon) ←√चन्द्); *jyotiḥ:* (acc◦ 8.24); *yogī* (5.24); *prāpya* (2.57); *nivartate* (2.59) (8.25)

(§3) *dhūmaḥ:* (cloud, a cloudy day); *rātriḥ:* (the night time); *tathā* (as well as); *kṛṣṇaḥ:* (the dark lunar fortnight); *ṣaṇmāsāḥ:* (the six months of); *dakṣiṇāyanam̦* (the Southern solstic, southward travel of the Sun); *tatra* (there, in these periods); *ćāndramasam̦* (obj◦ the Moon); *jyotiḥ:* (beam, light); *yogī* (subj◦ yogī);[540] *prāpya* (having attained); *nivartate* (returns back) (8.25)

(§4) dhūmaḥ: rātriḥ: kṛṣṇaḥ: tathā ṣaṇmāsāḥ: dakṣiṇāyanam̦ tatra yogī prāpya ćāndramasam̦ jyotiḥ: nivartate

(§5) A cloudy day, the night time, the dark lunar fortnight, as well as the six months of the southward travel of the Sun, in these periods (departed) yogī, having attained the lunar beam, returns back. (8.25)

8.26 शुक्लकृष्णे गती ह्येते जगतः शाश्वते मते ।
एकया यात्यनावृत्तिमन्ययावर्तते पुनः ।।
śuklakṛṣṇe gatī hyete jagataḥ: śāśvate mate,
ekayā yātyanāvṛttimanyayāvartate punaḥ:. (8.26)

(§1) *śuklakṛṣṇe* (r◦ 24/9) *gatī hi* (r◦ 4/4) *ete jagataḥ:* (r◦ 22/5) *śāśvate mate* (r◦ 23/1) *kayā yāti* (r◦ 4/1) *anāvṛttim̦* (r◦ 8/16) *anyayā* (r◦ 1/4) *āvartate punaḥ:* (r◦ 22/8)

---

present tense verb. प्रयाताः = departed, see the footnote in verse 8.23.

[540] Elsewhere◦ योगी → In Sanskrit योगी, In English *yogin.* Why?

(§2) *śuklakṛṣṇe* (f∘ 1nom∘ dual∘ ←dvandva∘ शुक्ला च कृष्णा च ←adj∘ *śukla* 8.24 + adj∘ *kṛṣṇa* (moment) 1.28); *gatī* (1nom∘ dual∘ ←f∘ *gati* (state) 2.43); *hi* (1.11); *ete* (f∘ 2acc∘ dual∘ ←pron∘ *etad* (this) 1.3); *jagataḥ:* (7.6); *śāśvate* (f∘ 1nom∘ dual∘ ←adj∘ *śāśvata* (perpetual) 1.43); *mate* (1nom∘ dual∘ ←f∘ *matā* (known) ←n∘ 📖 *mata* 2.35); *ekayā* (f∘ 3inst∘ sing∘ ←num∘ adj∘ *eka* (one) 2.41); *yāti* (6.45); *anāvṛttim* (8.23); *anyayā* (f∘ 3inst∘ sing∘ ←adj∘ *anya* (other) 1.9); *āvartate* (3rd-per∘ sing∘ pres∘ वर्तमान्-लट् ātmane∘ ←class1∘ आ√वृत्); *punaḥ:* (= ind∘ *punar* (again) 4.9) (8.26)

(§3) *śuklakṛṣṇe* (adj1∘-subj∘ bright and dark); *gatī* (subj∘ two states); *hi* (because); *ete* (adj2∘-subj∘ these); *jagataḥ:* (of the world, for the world); *śāśvate* (f∘ adj∘3-subj∘ perpetual); *mate* (f∘ adj4-subj∘ known); *ekayā* (f∘ by one); *yāti* (he goes); *anāvṛttim* (to non-rebirth); *anyayā* (f∘ by other); *āvartate* (he takes birth); *punaḥ:* (adv∘ again) (8.26)

(§4) hi ete śuklakṛṣṇe gatī mate śāśvate jagataḥ: ekayā yāti anāvṛttim anyayā āvartate punaḥ:

(§5) Because[541] these two bright and dark states (are) known perpetual for the world, by one he goes to non-rebirth (and) by other he takes birth again. (8.26)

8.27 नैते सृती पार्थ जानन्योगी मुह्यति कश्चन ।
तस्मात्सर्वेषु कालेषु योगयुक्तो भवार्जुन ॥

naite sṛtī pārtha jānanyogī muhyati kaśćan,
tasmātsarveṣu kāleṣu yogayukto bhavārjuna. (8.27)

(§1) *na* (r∘ 3/1) *ete sṛtī pārtha jānan* (r∘ 13/17) *yogī muhyati kaśćana tasmāt* (r∘ 10/7) *sarveṣu* (r∘ 25/5) *kāleṣu* (r∘ 25/5) *yogayuktaḥ:* (r∘ 15/8) *bhava* (r∘ 1/1) *arjuna*

(§2) *na* (1.30); *ete* (2acc∘ 8.26); *sṛtī* (1nom∘ dual∘ ←f∘ *sṛti* (state) ←√सृ); *pārtha* (1.25); *jānan* (m∘ 1nom∘ sing∘ ←śatṛ∘ adj∘ *jānat* ←√ज्ञा); *yogī* (5.24); *muhyati* (2.13); *kaśćana* (3.18); *tasmāt* (1.37); *sarveṣu* (1.11); *kāleṣu* (8.7); *yogayuktaḥ:* (5.6); *bhava* (2.45); *arjuna* (2.2) (8.27)

(§3) *na* (is not); *ete* (f∘ adj∘-obj∘ these two); *sṛtī* (f∘ obj∘ two states); *pārtha* (O Arjuna!); *jānan* (adj1∘-subj∘ while knowing); *yogī* (subj∘ yogī); *muhyati* (is deluded); *kaśćana* (m∘ adj2∘-subj∘ a, any); *tasmāt* (therefore); *sarveṣu kāleṣu* (at all times); *yogayuktaḥ:* (equipped with yoga); *bhava* (you be); *arjuna* (O Arjuna!) (8.27)

(§4) pārtha jānan ete sṛtī kaśćana yogī na muhyati tasmāt arjuna sarveṣu kāleṣu bhava yogayuktaḥ:

---

[541] See footnote in verse 3.5

(§5) **O Arjuna! while knowing[542] these two states a yogī is not is deluded, therefore,[543] O Arjuna! at all times you be equipped with yoga.** (8.27)

8.28 वेदेषु यज्ञेषु तपःसु चैव दानेषु यत्पुण्यफलं प्रदिष्टम् ।
अत्येति तत्सर्वमिदं विदित्वा योगी परं स्थानमुपैति चाद्यम् ।।

vedeṣu yajñeṣu tapaḥ:su ćaiva dāneṣu yatpuṇyaphalaṁ pradiṣṭam,
atyeti tatsarvamidaṁ viditvā yogī paraṁ sthānamupaiti ćādyam. (8.28)

(§1) *vedeṣu* (r◦ 25/5) *yajñeṣu* (r◦ 25/5) *tapaḥ:su ća* (r◦ 3/1) *eva dāneṣu* (r◦ 25/5) *yat* (r◦ 10/6) *puṇyaphalam* (r◦ 14/1) *pradiṣṭam* (r◦ 14/2) *atyeti tat* (r◦ 10/7) *sarvam* (r◦ 8/18) *idam* (r◦ 14/1) *viditvā yogī param* (r◦ 14/1) *sthānam* (r◦ 8/20) *upaiti ća* (r◦ 1/2) *ādyam* (r◦ 14/2)

(§2) *vedeṣu* (2.46); *yajñeṣu* (7loc◦ plu◦ ←m◦ *yajña* 3.9); *tapaḥ:su* (7loc◦ plu◦ ←m◦ *tapas* (austerity) 4.10); *ća* (1.1); *eva* (1.1); *dāneṣu* (7loc◦ plu◦ ←n◦ 🕮***dāna*** (charity) ←√दा); *yat* (2acc◦ 3.21); *puṇyaphalam* (n◦ 1nom◦ sing◦ ←tatpu◦ *puṇya-phala*, पुण्यस्य फलम् ←n◦ *puṇya* (good deed) 6.41 + n◦ *phala* (fruit) 2.43); *pradiṣṭam* (n◦ 1nom◦ sing◦ ←ppp◦ adj◦ *pradiṣṭa* (ordained) ←प्र√दिश्); *atyeti* (3rd-per◦ sing◦ pres◦ वर्तमान्-लट् parasmai◦ ←class2◦ अति√इ); *tat* (2acc◦ 2.7); *sarvam* (2acc◦ 2.17); *idam* (2acc◦ 1.10); *viditvā* (2.25); *yogī* (5.24); *param* (2acc◦ 2.12); 🕮*sthānam* (2acc◦ sing◦ ←n◦ *sthāna* 5.5); *upaiti* (6.27); *ća* (1.1); ***ādyam*** (n◦ 2acc◦ sing◦ ←adj◦ *ādya* (primal) 5.22) (8.28)

(§3) *vedeṣu* (in the vedas); *yajñeṣu* (in the yajñas); *tapaḥ:su* (in the tapas, in the austerities); *ća* (and); *eva* (also); *dāneṣu* (in the charities);[544] *yat* (adj1◦-obj1◦ which is); *puṇyaphalam* (obj1◦ the fruit of one's good deeds); *pradiṣṭam* (adj2◦-obj1◦ told, ordained, ascribed); *atyeti* (goes beyond); *tat* (adj3◦-obj1◦ that); *sarvam* (adj4◦-obj1◦ all); *idam* (adj◦-obj2◦ this); *viditvā* (having known); *yogī* (subj◦ the yogī); *param* (adj1◦-obj3◦ supreme); *sthānam* (obj3◦ state, place); *upaiti* (he attains); *ća* (and); *ādyam* (adj2◦-

---

[542] Elsewhere◦ जानन् योगी → yogi who knows, yogins who know, yogin who knows, yogin knowing these two, ...etc.

🕮 जानन् is not a present tense verb or a ppp◦ past passive participle. It is a present participle gerund (जानत्) m◦ adjective of m◦ noun योगी ।

[543] See the footnote in verse 2.15

[544] Elsewhere◦ वेदेषु यज्ञेषु तपःसु चैव दानेषु → with regard to the vedas, sacrifices...; declared regarding the Vedas, sacrifices,...; accruing from the study of the Vedas, sacrifices...; declared to acrue from the study of the Vedas...; attached to the study of the Vedas...; proclaimed regarding the Vedas...; assigned to the the study of the Vedas...; such as study of the Vedas, performance of sacrifices...; derived from studying vedas, performing austere sacrifices...etc.

obj3◦ primal) (8.28)

(§4) viditvā idaṃ yogī atyeti sarvaṃ puṇyaphalaṃ pradiṣṭaṃ vedeṣu yajñeṣu tapaḥ:su eva dāneṣu ća upaiti taṭ sthānaṃ yaṭ ādyaṃ ća paraṃ

(§5) Having known this, the yogī goes beyond all the fruit of one's good deeds ascribed in the[545] vedas, in the yajñas, in the tapas, also in the charities and he attains that place which is primal and supreme. (8.28)

ति श्रीमद्भगवद्गीतासूपनिषत्सु ब्रह्मविद्यायां योगशास्त्रे
श्रीकृष्णार्जुनसंवादे अक्षरब्रह्मयोगो नाम अष्टमोऽध्यायः ।।

iti śrīmadbhagavadgītāsūpaniṣatsu brahmavidyāyām̐ yogaśāstre
śrīkṛṣṇārjunasam̐vāde akṣarabrahmayogo nāma aṣṭamo'dhyāyaḥ:.

(§1) *iti śrīmadbhagavadgītāsu* (r◦ 1/8) *upaniṣatsu brahmavidyāyāṃ* (r◦ 14/1) *yogaśāstre śrīkṛṣṇārjunasam̐vāde* (r◦ 6/1) *akṣarabrahmayogaḥ:* (r◦ 15/6) *nāma* (r◦ 1/1) *aṣṭamaḥ:* (r◦ 15/1) *adhyāyaḥ:* (r◦ 22/8)

(§2) *iti* (1.25); *śrīmadbhagavadgītāsu* (f◦ 7loc◦ plu◦ tatpu◦ *śrīmad-bhagavad-gītā* ←adj◦ *śrīmaṭ* 6.41 + adj◦ *bhagavaṭ* 10.14 + f◦ *gītā* ←5◦√गै); *upaniṣatsu* (7loc◦ plu◦ ←f◦ *upaniṣaḍ* ←6◦उप–नि√सद्); *brahmavidyāyāṃ* (f◦ 7loc◦ sing◦ ←tatpu◦ *brahma-vidyā*, ब्रह्मणः विद्या ←n◦ *brahmaṇ* 2.72 + *vidyā* 5.18); *yogaśāstre* (n◦ 7loc◦ sing◦ ←tatpu◦ *yoga-śāstra*, योगानाम् शास्त्रम् । योगस्य शास्त्रम् । ←m◦ *yoga* 2.39 + n◦ *śāstra* 15.20); *śrīkṛṣṇārjunasam̐vāde* (m◦ 7loc◦ sing◦ ←tatpu◦ *śrī-kṛṣṇārjuna-sam̐vāda*, श्रीकृष्णस्य च अर्जुनस्य च संवादः ←adj◦ *śrī* 10.34 + m◦ prop◦ *kṛṣṇa* 1.28 + m◦ prop◦ *arjuna* 1.4 + m◦ *sam̐vāda* 18.70); *akṣarabrahmayogaḥ:* (m◦ 1nom◦ sing◦ ←tatpu◦ *akṣarabrahmayoga* अक्षरब्रह्मणः ज्ञानस्य योगः ←n◦ *akṣara* 8.21 + brahma 3.15 + m◦ *yoga* 2.39); *nāma* (1nom◦ sing◦ ←n◦ *nāmaṇ* ←1◦√म्ना); *aṣṭamaḥ:* (m◦ 1nom◦ sing◦ ←num◦ adj◦ *aṣṭa* 7.4); *adhyāyaḥ:* (1nom◦ sing◦ ←m◦ *adhyāya* ←1◦अधि√इ)

(§3) *iti* (thus); *śrīmadbhagavadgītāsu upaniṣatsu* (among the upaniṣads of the Śrīmad-Bhagavadgītā); *brahmavidyāyāṃ* (of the eternal wisdoms); *yogaśāstre* (in the science of Yoga); *śrīkṛṣṇārjunasam̐vāde* (in the dialogue between Śrī Kṛṣṇa and Arjuna); (adj1◦-subj◦ (called akṣarabrahmayoga); *nāma* (called); *aṣṭamaḥ:* (adj2◦-subj◦ the eighth); *adhyāyaḥ:* (subj◦ discourse; chapter)

(§4) śrīmadbhagavadgītāsu upaniṣatsu yogaśāstre brahmavidyāyāṃ iti aṣṭamaḥ: adhyāyaḥ: nāma akṣarabrahmayogaḥ: śrīkṛṣṇārjunasam̐vāde

[545] Elsewhere◦ दानम् → gifts, ...etc.

(§5) Among the upaniṣads of the Śrīmad-Bhagavadgītā, in the science of yoga of self realization, thus (is) the eighth discourse called akṣara-brahma-yoga, in the dialogue between Śrī Kṛṣṇa and Arjuna.

CHAPTER 9

navamao'dhyāyaḥ:
नवमोऽध्याय: ।

rājavidyārājaguhyayogaḥ:
राजविद्याराजगुह्ययोग: ।

YOGA OF THE MOST MYSTERIOUS KNOWLEDGE

The Lord said (śrībhagavānuvāca श्रीभगवानुवाच ।)

9.1 इदं तु ते गुह्यतमं प्रवक्ष्याम्यनसूयवे ।
ज्ञानं विज्ञानसहितं यज्ज्ञात्वा मोक्ष्यसेऽशुभात् ।।
idaṁ tu te guhyatamaṁ pravakṣyāmyanasūyave,
jñānaṁ vijñānasahitaṁ yajjñātvā mokṣyase'śubhāt. (9.1)

(§1) *navamaḥ:* (r◦ 15/1) *adhyāyaḥ:* (r◦ 22/8). *rājavidyārājaguhyayogaḥ:* (r◦ 22/8). *śrībhagavān* (r◦ 8/14) *uvāca. idam* (r◦ 14/1) *tu te guhyatamam* (r◦ 14/1) *pravakṣāmi* (r◦ 4/1) *anasūyave jñānam* (r◦ 14/1) *vijñānasahitam* (r◦ 14/1) *yat* (r◦ 11/2) *jñātvā mokṣase* (r◦ 6/1) *aśubhāt*

(§2) *navamaḥ:* (m◦ 1nom◦ sing◦ ←sequence indicating num◦ adj◦ नवम् ←num◦ *navan* 5.13); *adhyāyaḥ:* (1nom◦ sing◦ ←m◦ *adhyāya* ←अधि√इ). *rājavidyārājaguhyayogaḥ:* (m◦ 1nom◦ sing◦ ←tatpu◦ *rāja-vidyā-rāja-guhya-yoga,* राजविद्याया: च राजगुह्यस्य च योग: ←f◦ *rāja-vidyā* 9.2 + n◦ *rāja-guhya* 9.2 + m◦ *yoga* 2.39). *śrībhagavān* (2.2); *uvāca* (1.25).

idam (2acc◦ 1.10); *tu* (1.2); *te* (1.7); ***guhyatamam*** (2acc◦ sing◦ ←adj◦ *guhyatama* (most secret) ←n◦ 📖***guhya*** (secret) ←√गुह् + superlative affix *tama* (most) 1.7); *pravakṣāmi* (4.16); *anasūyave* (m◦ 4dat◦ sing◦ ←n.bahuvrī◦ ***anasūyu*** (unsuspicious) ←m◦ *asūya* ←√असू); *jñānam* (2acc◦ 3.40); *vijñānasahitam* (2acc◦ sing◦ ←sah.bahuvrī◦ *vijñāna-sahita,* विज्ञानेन सहितम् यत् ←n◦ *vijñāna* 3.41 + adj◦ ***sahita*** (with) ←√सह्); *vijñāna* 3.41); *yat* (2acc◦ 3.21); *jñātvā* (4.15); *mokṣase* (4.16); *aśubhāt* (4.16) (9.1)

(§3) *navamaḥ:* (adj◦-subj◦ ninth); *adhyāyaḥ:* (subj◦ chapter). *rājavidyārājaguhyayogaḥ:* (the discipline of supreme knowledge and the supreme secret). *śrībhagavān* (the Lord); *uvāca* (said). *idam* (adj◦1-obj◦ this); *tu* (now); *te* (to you, for you); *guhyatamam* (adj2◦-obj◦ most secret, most mysterious); *pravakṣāmi* (I shall tell); *anasūyave* (for Arjuna); *jñānam* (obj◦ knowledge); *vijñānasahitam* (adj3◦-obj◦ with science, with realization); *yat* (adj4◦-obj which); *jñātvā* (having known, having learned); *mokṣase* (you shall attain liberation); *aśubhāt* (from evil) (9.1)

(§4) navamaḥ: adhyāyaḥ:. rājavidyārājaguhyayogaḥ:. śrībhagavān uvāca. tu pravakṣāmi te anasūyave idam guhyatamam jñānam vijñānasahitam yat jñātvā mokṣase aśubhāt

(§5) Ninth Chapter. The discipline of supreme knowledge and the supreme secret. The Lord said : Now, for you Arjuna, I shall reveal this most mysterious knowledge with realization, which having known you shall attain liberation from evil. (9.1)

9.2 राजविद्या राजगुह्यं पवित्रमिदमुत्तमम् ।
प्रत्यक्षावगमं धर्म्यं सुसुखं कर्तुमव्ययम् ।।
rājavidyā rājaguhyaṁ pavitramidamuttamam,
pratyakṣāvagamaṁ dharmyaṁ susukhaṁ kartumavyayam. (9.1)

(§1) *rājavidyā rājaguhyam* (r◦ 14/1) *pavitram* (r◦ 8/18) *idam* (r◦ 8/20) *uttamam* (r◦ 14/2) *pratyakṣāvagamam* (r◦ 14/1) *dharmyam* (r◦ 14/1) *susukham* (r◦ 14/1) *kartum* (r◦ 8/16) *avyayam* (r◦ 14/2)

(§2) *rājavidyā* (f◦ 1nom◦ sing◦ ←tatpu◦ ***rāja-vidyā***, राजा वा राज्ञी वा विद्यायाम् ←m◦ *rājā* (king, queen) 1.2 + *vidyā* (knowledge) 5.18); *rājaguhyam* (n◦ 1nom◦ sing◦ ←tatpu◦ ***rāja-guhya***, राजा गुह्यानाम् ←n◦ *guhya* (secret) 9.1 + m◦ *rājā* (king) 1.2); *pavitram* (see 4.38); *idam* (1.10); *uttamam* (4.3); *pratyakṣāvagamam* (n◦ 1nom◦ sing◦ ←bahuvrī◦ *pratyakṣāvagama*, प्रत्यक्षेण अवगमः यस्य तत् ←adj◦ *pratyakṣa* (practical) ←प्रति√अक्ष् + m◦ *avagama* ←अव√गम्); *dharmyam* (see 2.33); 🕮*susukham* (n◦ 1nom◦ sing◦ ←ind◦ *su* (very) 5.1 + adv◦ *sukha* (easy) 1.32); *kartum* (1.45); ***avyayam*** (n◦ 1nom◦ sing◦ ←adj◦ *avyaya* (eternal) 2.21)

(§3) *rājavidyā* (subj◦ supreme knowledge); *rājaguhyam* (adj1◦-subj◦ most mysterious); *pavitram* (adj2◦-subj◦ sacred, sanctified); *idam* (adj3◦-subj◦ this); *uttamam* (adj4◦-subj◦ ultimate); *pratyakṣāvagamam* (adj5◦-subj◦ practical); *dharmyam* (adj6◦-subj◦ righteous); *susukham* (adj7◦-subj◦ pleasent, easy); *kartum* (to follow, to practice); *avyayam* (adj8◦-subj◦ eternal)

(§4) idam rājavidyā rājaguhyam uttamam pavitram avyayam dharmyam pratyakṣāvagamam susukham kartum

(§5) This most mysterious knowledge (is) ultimate, sacred, eternal, righteous,[546] practical (and) easy to follow.

9.3 अश्रद्दधानाः पुरुषा धर्मस्यास्य परन्तप ।
अप्राप्य मां निवर्तन्ते मृत्युसंसारवर्त्मनि ।।
aśraddadhānāḥ: puruṣā dharmasyāsya parantapa,
aprāpya māṁ nivartante mṛtyusaṁsāravartmani. (9.2)

(§1) *aśraddadhānāḥ:* (r◦ 22/3) *puruṣāḥ:* (r◦ 20/9) *dharmasya* (r◦ 1/1) *asya parantapa* (r◦ 23/1) *aprāpya māṃ* (r◦ 14/1) *nivartante mṛtyusaṁsāravartmani*

(§2) *aśraddadhānāḥ:* (m◦ 1nom◦ plu◦ ←n.bahuvrī◦ adj◦ *a-śraddadhāna* 4.40); *puruṣāḥ:* (1nom◦ plu◦ ←m◦ *puruṣa* 2.15); *dharmasya* (2.40); *asya* (2.17); *parantapa* (2.3); *aprāpya* (6.37); *māṃ* (1.46); *nivartante* (8.21); *mṛtyusaṁsāravartmani* (n◦ 7loc◦ sing◦ ←tatpu◦ *mṛtyu-saṁsāra-vartmaṇ*, मृत्यमयस्य संसारस्य वर्त्म ←m◦ *mṛtyu* (death) 2.27 + m◦ 🕮**saṁsāra** (world) ←सम्√सृ + n◦ *vartmaṇ* (path, cycle) 3.23) (9.2)

(§3) *aśraddadhānāḥ:* (adj◦-subj◦ not having faith in); *puruṣāḥ:* (subj◦ the people); *dharmasya* (of righteous conduct); *asya* (of this, in this); *parantapa* (O Arjuna!); *aprāpya* (not having attained); *māṃ* (me); *nivartante* (return); *mṛtyusaṁsāravartmani* (in the world typified with the cycles of birth and death) (9.2)

(§4) parantapa puruṣāḥ: the people aśraddadhānāḥ: asya dharmasya aprāpya māṃ nivartante mṛtyusaṁsāravartmani

(§5) O Arjuna! the people faithless in this righteous conduct,[547] not having attained me, return in the world typified with the cycles of birth and death. (9.2)

9.4 मया ततमिदं सर्वं जगदव्यक्तमूर्तिना ।
मत्स्थानि सर्वभूतानि न चाहं तेष्ववस्थितः ।।
mayā tatamidaṁ sarvaṁ jagadavyaktamūrtinā,
matsthāni sarvabhūtāni na ćahaṁ teṣvavasthitaḥ:. (9.4)

(§1) *mayā tataṃ* (r◦ 8/18) *idaṃ* (r◦ 14/1) *sarvaṃ* (r◦ 14/1) *jagaṭ* (r◦ 8/2) *avyaktamūrtinā matsthāni sarvabhūtāni na ća* (r◦ 1/1) *ahaṃ* (r◦ 14/1) *teṣu* (r◦ 25/5, 4/6) *avasthitaḥ:* (r◦ 22/8)

---

[546] Elsewhere◦ धर्म्यम् → perfection of religion, perfection of Dharma, unopposed to Dharma ...etc.

[547] Elsewhere◦ धर्मस्य → in Self-knowledge, of religion, towards the process of religion, ...etc.

(§2) *mayā* (1.22); *tatam̹* (1nom∘ 2.17); *idam̹* (1nom∘ 1.10); *sarvam̹* (1nom∘ 2.17); *jagat̹* (1npm∘ 7.5); *avyaktamūrtinā* (3inst∘ sing∘ ←bahuvrī∘ *avyakta-mūrti*, अव्यक्ता मूर्तिः यस्य ←adj∘ *avyakta* (unpersonified) 2.25 + f∘ 🕮**mūrti** (form) ←√मुर्च्छ्); ***matsthāni*** (1nom∘ plu∘ ←bahuvrī∘ *matstha* (rooted in me) मयि स्थीयते तत् ←pron∘ *mayi* 3.30 + adj∘ *stha* 2.45); *sarvabhūtāni* (6.29); *na* (1.30); *ćа* (1.1); *aham̹* (1.22); *teṣu* (2.62); ***avasthitaḥ:*** (m∘ 1nom∘ sing∘ ←ppp∘ adj∘ *avasthita* (rooted) 1.11) (9.4)

(§3) *mayā* (subj1∘ by me); *tatam̹* (obj1∘ THAT); *idam̹* (adj1∘-obj2∘ this); *sarvam̹* (adj2∘-obj2∘ whole, all); *jagat̹* (obj2∘ world); *avyaktamūrtinā* (adj1∘-subj1∘ by unmanifest, by unpersonified); *matsthāni* (adj∘-subj2∘ rooted in me); *sarvabhūtāni* (subj2∘ all beings); *na* (not); *ća* (and); *aham̹* (subj1∘ I); *teṣu* (in them); *avasthitaḥ:* (adj2∘-subj1∘ rooted) (9.4)

(§4) idam̹ sarvam̹ jagat̹ tatam̹ mayā avyaktamūrtinā sarvabhūtāni matsthāni ća na aham̹ avasthitaḥ: teṣu

(§5) This whole world (is) THAT[548] by unpersonified me. All beings (are) rooted[549] in me and I (am) not rooted in them. (9.4)

9.5 **न च मत्स्थानि भूतानि पश्य मे योगमैश्वरम् ।**
भूतभृन्न च भूतस्थो ममात्मा भूतभावनः ।।
na ća matsthāni bhūtāni paśya me yogamaiśvaram̹,
bhūtabhṛnna ća bhūtastho mamātmā bhūtabhāvanaḥ:. (9.5)

(§1) *na ća matsthāni bhūtāni paśya me yogam̹* (r∘ 8/23) *aiśvaram̹* (r∘ 14/2) *bhūtabhṛt̹* (r∘ 12/1) *na ća bhūtasthaḥ:* (r∘ 15/9) *mama* (r∘ 1/2) *ātmā bhūtabhāvanaḥ:* (r∘ 22/8)

(§2) *na* (1.30); *ća* (1.1); *matsthāni* (2acc∘ sing∘ ←adj∘ *matsthāni* (rooted in me) 9.4); *bhūtāni* (2.30); *paśya* (1.3); *me* (1.21); *yogam̹* (2.53); 🕮***aiśvaram̹*** (m∘ 2acc∘ sing∘ ←adj∘ *aiśvar* (divine) ←√ईश्); *bhūtabhṛt̹*

---

[548] Elsewhere∘ मया ततम् इदम् → I pervade all this, this is pervaded by Me, By Me this is pervaded ...etc.

🕮 ततम् is not a verb. It is a ppp∘ adj∘ by which (येन) this everything is THAT (ततम्). Thus, That does not 'pervade,' it, but everything 'IS' that. When I am (or THAT is) everything, how can I (or THAT) pervade myself (itself). If I did, then I will be separate from It and That, and I will not be That, and That will not be It, and then तत्सर्वम्, सर्वं खल्विदं ब्रह्म, प्रज्ञानं ब्रह्म, तत्त्वमसि, अहं ब्रह्मास्मि, अयमात्मा ब्रह्म... will not hold good. See footnote in 2.17

[549] Elsewhere∘ मत्स्थानि → abide in Me, take abode in Me, have root in Me, all beings exist in Me, all beings are in me, all beings rest on the idea within Me, All beings dwell in Me, ...etc.

🕮 मत्स्थानि is not a verb or a Present tense. It is a ppp∘ adj∘ qualifying the subject भूतानि । "I am not rooted in them," see Gita 7.12 for the same statement.

(1nom◦ sing◦ ←tatpu◦ adj◦ *bhūta-bhṛt̖*, भूतानि विभ्रति इति ←n◦ *bhūta* (being) 2.28 + śatṛ◦ adj◦ *bhṛt̖* or *vibhrat̖* (source) ←√भृ 2.54); *na* (1.30); *ća* (1.1); *bhūtasthaḥ:* (1nom◦ sing◦ ←tatpu◦ adj◦ *bhūtastha* (rooted in beings) भूतेषु स्थीयते इति ←n◦ *bhūta* (being) 2.28 + adj◦ *stha* (rooted) 2.45); *mama* (1.7); *ātmā* (6.5); *bhūtabhāvanaḥ:* (m◦ 1nom◦ sing◦ ←bahuvrī◦ adj◦ ***bhūta-bhāvana,*** भूतानि भावयति यः ←n◦ *bhūta* (being) 2.28 + adj◦ or m◦ *bhāvana* (sustainer) ←√भू) (9.5)

(§3) *na* (not); *ća* (and); *matsthāni* (adj◦-obj1◦ rooted in me); *bhūtāni* (obj1◦ the beings); *paśya* (please see, behold); *me* (my); *yogam̖* (obj2◦ yoga); *aiśvaram̖* (adj◦-obj2◦ divine); *bhūtabhṛt̖* (adj1◦-subj◦ the source of the beings); *na* (not); *ća* (and); *bhūtasthaḥ:* (adj2◦-subj◦ rooted in the beings); *mama* (my); *ātmā* (subj◦ self); *bhūtabhāvanaḥ:* (adj3◦-subj◦ the sustainer of the beings) (9.5)

(§4) paśya me aiśvaram̖ yogam̖ ća na bhūtāni matsthāni mama ātmā bhūtabhṛt̖ ća bhūtabhāvanaḥ: na bhūtasthaḥ:

(§5) Please behold my divine yoga and not the beings rooted in me.[550] My self, the source of the beings and the sustainer of the beings (is) not rooted in the beings.
(9.5)

9.6 यथाकाशस्थितो नित्यं वायुः सर्वत्रगो महान् ।
तथा सर्वाणि भूतानि मत्स्थानीत्युपधारय ।।
yathākāśasthito nityaṁ vāyuḥ: sarvatrago mahān̖,
tathā sarvāṇi bhūtāni matsthānītyupadhāraya. (9.6)

(§1) *yathā* (r◦ 1/4) *ākāśasthitaḥ:* (r◦ 15/6) *nityam̖* (r◦ 14/1) *vāyuḥ:* (r◦ 22/7) *sarvatragaḥ:* (r◦ 15/9) *mahān̖* (r◦ 23/1) *tathā sarvāṇi* (r◦ 24/7) *bhūtāni matsthāni* (r◦ 1/5) *iti* (r◦ 4/3) *upadhāraya*

---

[550] Elsewhere◦ न मत्स्थानि भूतानि पश्य मे योगम् → beings do not abide in Me, behold My majestic power; the beings do not dewll in Me, behold My divine mystery, Nor are the beings in me, so behold my divine mystery; everything that is created does not rest in Me, behold My mystic opulence; Nor have beings root in Me, behold My sovereign Yoga; Nor do the beings dwell in Me, behold My divine yoga; all those beings abide not in Me, but behold the wonderful power; Neither do beings exist in Me, behold My divine Yoga; ...etc.

📖 The above translations are exactly opposite of what Krishṇa has said in the previous verse (as well as in the next verse). The error or contradiction in these translations occurs obviously because मत्स्थानि is wrongly translated as a verb and भूतानि as its subject. In fact, Krishṇa has used मत्स्थानि as the ppp◦ Accusative (2nd) case adjective of the Accusative object भूतानि । Thus, what Krishṇa said is simply पश्य मे योगम्, न मत्स्थानि भूतानि = behold my yoga, not the (object) beings (ppp◦ adjective) rooted in me.

(§2) *yathā* (1.11); *ākāśasthitaḥ:* (m◦ 1nom◦ sing◦ ←adj◦ tatpu◦ *ākāśa-sthita,* आकाशे स्थित: ←n◦ 🕮***ākāśa*** (sky) ←आ√काश् + adj◦ *sthita* (rooted) 1.14); *nityam* (2.21); *vāyuḥ:* (2.67); *sarvatragaḥ:* (m◦ 1nom◦ sing◦ ←bahuvrī◦ ***sarvatra-ga,*** सर्वत्र गच्छति य: ←ind◦ *sarvatra* (omni, everywhere) 2.57 + adj◦ *gaćchati* 6.37); ***mahān*** (1nom◦ sing◦ ←adj◦ *mahat* (great) 1.3); *tathā* (1.8); *sarvāṇi* (2.30); *bhūtāni* (2.28); *matsthāni* (9.4); *iti* (1.25); *upadhāraya* (7.6) (9.6)

(§3) *yathā* (just as); *ākāśasthitaḥ:* (adj1◦-subj◦ rooted in the sky, space); *nityam* (adv◦ universal, perpetual, eternal, timeless); *vāyuḥ:* (subj◦ wind, air); *sarvatragaḥ:* (adj2◦-subj◦ omnipresent); *mahān* (adj3◦-subj◦ the lofty); *tathā* (just so, so are); *sarvāṇi* (adj1◦-subj2◦ all); *bhūtāni* (subj2◦ beings); *matsthāni* (adj2◦-subj2◦ rooted in me); *iti* (thus); *upadhāraya* (you please understand) (9.6)

(§4) yathā mahān sarvatragaḥ: vāyuḥ: ākāśasthitaḥ: nityam tathā sarvāṇi bhūtāni matsthāni iti upadhāraya

(§5) Just as the lofty omnipresent air rooted[551] in the space (is) universal, so are all beings rooted[552] in me, thus you please understand. (9.6)

9.7 सर्वभूतानि कौन्तेय प्रकृतिं यान्ति मामिकाम् ।
कल्पक्षये पुनस्तानि कल्पादौ विसृजाम्यहम् ।।
sarvabhūtāni kaunteya prakṛtim yānti māmikām,
kalpakṣaye punastāni kalpādau visṛjāmyaham. (9.7)

(§1) *sarvabhūtāni kaunteya prakṛtim* (r◦ 14/1) *yānti māmikām* (r◦ 14/2) *kalpakṣaye punaḥ:* (r◦ 18/1) *tāni kalpādau visṛjāmi* (r◦ 4/1) *aham* (r◦ 14/2)

(§2) *sarvabhūtāni* (6.29); *kaunteya* (2.14); *prakṛtim* (3.33); *yānti* (3.33); *māmikām* (2acc◦ sing◦ ←f◦ adj◦ *māmikā* (my) ←m◦ adj◦ *māmaka* 1.1); *kalpakṣaye* (m◦ 7loc◦ sing◦ ←tatpu◦ *kalpa-kṣaya,* कल्पस्य क्षय: ←m◦ ***kalpa*** (age, eon) ←√क्लृप् + m◦ *kṣaya* (dissolution, end) 1.38); *punaḥ:* (4.35); *tāni* (2.61); *kalpādau* (m◦ 7loc◦ sing◦ ←tatpu◦ *kalpādi,* कल्पस्य आदि: ←m◦ *kalpa* ↑ + m◦ *ādi* (begining) 2.28); ***visṛjāmi*** (1st-per◦ sing◦ pres◦ वर्तमान्-लट् parasmai◦ ←class4◦ वि√सृज् 4.7 ↑); *aham* (1.22) (9.7)

---

[551] Elsewhere◦ आकाशस्थित: → rests in the sky, abides, remains, *dwells,* is ever present, ...etc.

🕮 आकाशस्थित: is not a Presrnt tense or a verb. It is ppp◦ adjective of the m◦ subject वायु: ।

[552] Elsewhere◦ मत्स्थानि भूतानि → beings dwell in Me, beings exist in Me, beings rest in Me, beings abide in Me, things abide in me, existences abide in Me, ...etc.

🕮 मत्स्थानि is not a Presrnt tense or a verb. It is ppp◦ adjective of the n◦ subject भूतानि । Please see the footnotes in 9.4 and 9.5

(§3) *sarvabhūtāni* (subj1◦ all beings); *kaunteya* (O Arjuna!); *prakṛtiṃ* (obj1◦ nature, being); *yānti* (come into, merge into, dissolve into); *māmikāṃ* (adj◦-obj1◦ my); *kalpakṣaye* (at the end of the a *kalpa* cycle); *punaḥ:* (and again); *tāni* (adj◦-obj2◦ them); *kalpādau* (at the begining of the *kalpa* cycle); *visṛjāmi* (I evolve); *ahaṃ* (subj2◦ I)

(§4) kaunteya sarvabhūtāni yānti māmikāṃ prakṛtiṃ kalpakṣaye punaḥ: ahaṃ visṛjāmi tāni kalpādau

(§5) O Arjuna! all beings dissolve into my *prakriti*[553] at the end of the a *kalpa* cycle; and again I evolve them at the begining of the *kalpa* cycle. (9.7)

9.8 प्रकृतिं स्वामवष्टभ्य विसृजामि पुनः पुनः ।
भूतग्राममिमं कृत्स्नमवशं प्रकृतेर्वशात् ।।
prakṛtiṁ svāmavaṣṭabhya visṛjāmi punaḥ: punaḥ:,
bhūtagrāmamimaṁ kṛtsnamavaśaṁ prakṛtervaśāt. (9.8)

(§1) *prakṛtiṃ (r◦ 14/1) svāṃ* (r◦ 8/16) *avaṣṭabhya visṛjāmi punaḥ:* (r◦ 22/3) *punaḥ:* (r◦ 22/8) *bhūtagrāmaṃ* (r◦ 8/18) *imaṃ* (r◦ 14/1) *kṛtsnaṃ* (r◦ 8/16) *avaśaṃ* (r◦ 14/1) *prakṛteḥ:* (r◦ 16/10) *vaśāṭ*

(§2) 📖*prakṛtiṃ* (3.33); *svāṃ* (4.6); 📖***avaṣṭabhya*** (lyp◦ past-participle ind◦ ←अव√स्तम्भ्); *visṛjāmi* (9.7); *punaḥ:* (4.35); *punaḥ:* (4.35); ***bhūtagrāmaṃ*** (2acc◦ sing◦ ←m◦ *bhūta-grāma* (the beings) 8.19); *imaṃ* (1.28); *kṛtsnaṃ* (1.40); 📖*avaśaṃ* (2acc◦ sing◦ ←adj◦ *avaśa* (helpless) 3.5); *prakṛteḥ:* (3.27); *vaśāṭ* (5abl◦ sing◦ ←m◦ *vaśa* (control) 2.61)

(§3) *prakṛtiṃ* (obj1◦ *prakriti,* nature); *svāṃ* (adj◦-obj1◦ my own); *avaṣṭabhya* (having regulated, governed); *visṛjāmi* (I bring forth); *punaḥ: punaḥ:* (again and again); *bhūtagrāmaṃ* (obj2◦ mass of beings); *imaṃ* (adj1◦-obj2◦ this); *kṛtsnaṃ* (adj2◦-obj2◦ entire); *avaśaṃ* (adj3◦-obj2◦ helpless); *prakṛteḥ:* (of the prakriti); *vaśāṭ* (from, because of the power) (9.8)

(§4) avaṣṭabhya svāṃ prakṛtiṃ punaḥ: punaḥ: visṛjāmi imaṃ kṛtsnaṃ bhūtagrāmaṃ avaśaṃ vaśāṭ prakṛteḥ:

(§5) Having regulated my own *prakriti,* again and again I bring forth this entire mass of beings (which is) helpless because of the power of the *prakriti.* (9.8)

9.9 न च मां तानि कर्माणि निबध्नन्ति धनञ्जय ।
उदासीनवदासीनमसक्तं तेषु कर्मसु ।।
na ća māṁ tāni karmāṇi nibadhnati dhanañjaya,

---

[553] Elsewhere◦ प्रकृतिम् → nature, material nature, cosmic nature, the prime cause, ...etc.

udāsīnavadāsīnamasaktaṁ teṣu karmasu. (9.9)

(§1) *na ća mām̦* (r◦ 14/1) *tāni karmāṇi* (r◦ 24/7) *nibadhnanti dhanañjaya* (r◦ 23/1) *udāsīnavaț* (r◦ 8/3) *āsīnam̦* (r◦ 8/16) *asaktam̦* (r◦ 14/1) *teṣu* (r◦ 25/5) *karmasu*

(§2) *na* (1.30); *ća* (1.1); *mām̦* (1.46); ***tāni*** (1nom◦ plu◦ ←pron◦ *tad̦* (that) 1.2); *karmāṇi* (1nom◦ 3.27); ***nibadhnanti*** (3rd-per◦ plu◦ pres◦ वर्तमान्-लट् parasmai◦ ←class9◦ नि√बध् 4.41); *dhanañjaya* (2.48); ***udāsīnavaț*** (adv◦ ←adj◦ *udāsin̦* (indifferent) 6.9 + affix (वत्) *vaț* 2.29); *āsīnam̦* (m◦ 2acc◦ sing◦ ←deriv◦ adj◦ ***āsīna*** (seated) ←√आस्); ***asaktam̦*** (2acc◦ sing◦ ←adj◦ *asakta* (unattached) 3.7); *teṣu* (2.62); *karmasu* (2.50) (9.9)

(§3) *na* (not); *ća* (and); *mām̦* (obj◦ me); *tāni* (adj◦-subj◦ those); *karmāṇi* (subj◦ karmas, functions); *nibadhnanti* (bind); *dhanañjaya* (O Arjuna!); *udāsīnavaț* (adj1-obj◦ the one who is indifferent); *āsīnam̦* (adj2◦-obj◦ seated); *asaktam̦* (adj3◦-obj◦ unattached); *teṣu* (in those); *karmasu* (in karmas, deeds, functions) (9.9)

(§4) dhanañjaya tāni karmāṇi na nibadhnanti mām̦ udāsīnavaț ća āsīnam̦ asaktam̦ teṣu karmasu

(§5) O Arjuna! those functions do not[554] bind me, the one who is seated indifferent,[555] and unattached[556] in those karmas. (9.9)

9.10 मयाध्यक्षेण प्रकृतिः सूयते सचराचरम् ।
हेतुनानेन कौन्तेय जगद्विपरिवर्तते ।।
mayādhyakṣeṇa prakṛtiḥ: sūyate saćarāćaram̦,
hetunānena kaunteya jagadviparivartate. (9.10)

(§1) *mayā* (r◦ 1/3) *adhyakṣeṇa* (r◦ 24/1) *prakṛtiḥ:* (r◦ 22/7) *sūyate saćarāćaram̦* (r◦ 14/2) *hetunā* (r◦ 1/3) *anena kaunteya jagaț* (r◦ 9/11) *viparivartate*

(§2) *mayā* (1.22); 📖*adhyakṣeṇa* (3inst◦ sing◦ ←m◦ *adhyakṣa* (director) ←अधि√अक्ष्); *prakṛtiḥ:* (7.4); 📖*sūyate* (3rd-per◦ sing◦ pres◦ वर्तमान्-लट् ātmane◦ ←class4◦ √सू); *saćarāćaram̦* (n◦ 1nom◦ 2acc◦ sing◦ ←bahuvrī◦ *sa-ćarāćaram̦*, चरेण च अचरेण च सह यत् ←ind◦ *sa* 7.30 + adj◦ ***ćara*** (moving) ←√car̦ + n.bahuvrī◦

---

[554] Elsewhere◦ न निबध्नन्ति → can not bind Me, ...etc.

[555] Elsewhere◦ उदासीनवत् → unconcerned, detached, I sit indifferently ...etc.

[556] Elsewhere◦ असक्तम् → I remain unattached, without attraction, ...etc.

📖 असक्तम् is not a Presrnt tense or a verb. It is ppp◦ adjective of the m◦ object माम् ।

acara (non-moving) ←अ√चर्); *hetunā* (3inst∘ sing∘ ←m∘ *hetu* 1.35); *anena* (3.10); *kaunteya* (2.14); *jagat* (7.5); 🕮*viparivartate* (3rd-per∘ sing∘ pres∘ वर्तमान्–लट् ātmane∘ ←class1∘ वि–परि√वृत् 3.28) (9.10)

(§3) *mayā adhyakṣeṇa* (directed by me); *prakṛtiḥ:* (subj1∘ the prakriti); *sūyate* (evolves, brings forth, gives birth); *sacarācaram* (obj∘ the world with moving and non-moving beings); *hetunā* (by the reason); *anena* (by this); *kaunteya* (O Arjuna!); *jagat* (subj2∘ the world); *viparivartate* (rotates, truns in cycles, transforms in cycles) (9.10)

(§4) kaunteya mayā adhyakṣeṇa prakṛtiḥ: sūyate sacarācaram anena hetunā jagat viparivartate

(§5) O Arjuna! directed by me the prakriti brings forth the world, with moving and non-moving beings; by this reason the world transforms in cycles. (9.10)

9.11 अवजानन्ति मां मूढा मानुषीं तनुमाश्रितम् ।
परं भावमजानन्तो मम भूतमहेश्वरम् ।।
avajānanti māṁ mūḍhā mānuṣīṁ tanumāśritam,
paraṁ bhāvamajānanto mama bhūtamaheśvaram; (9.11)

(§1) *avajānanti mām* (r∘ 14/1) *mūḍhāḥ:* (r∘ 20/13) *mānuṣīm* (r∘ 14/1) *tanum* (r∘ 8/17) *āśritam* (r∘ 14/2) *param* (r∘ 14/1) *bhāvam* (r∘ 8/16) *ajānantaḥ:* (r∘ 15/9) *mama bhūtamaheśvaram* (r∘ 14/2);

(§2) *avajānanti* (3rd-per∘ plu∘ pres∘ वर्तमान्–लट् parasmai∘ ←class9∘ अव√ज्ञा); *mām* (1.46); *mūḍhāḥ:* (7.15); *mānuṣīm* (f∘ 2acc∘ sing∘ ←adj∘ *mānuṣa* (person) 4.12); *tanum* (7.21); *āśritam* (m∘ 2acc∘ sing∘ ←adj∘ *āśrita* (sheltered) 7.15); *param* (2.59); *bhāvam* (7.15); *ajānantaḥ:* (7.24); *mama* (1.7); *bhūtamaheśvaram* (m∘ 2acc∘ sing∘ ←tatpu∘ *bhūta-maheśvara*, भूतानाम् महान् ईश्वरः ←m∘ *bhūta* (being) 2.28 + adj∘ *mahā* (great) 1.3 + m∘ *īśvara* (lord) 4.6); (9.11)

(§3) *avajānanti* (disregard); *mām* (obj∘ me); *mūḍhāḥ:* (subj1∘ the foolish people); *mānuṣīm tanum āśritam* (adj1∘-obj∘ the one who has taken human body); *param bhāvam ajānantaḥ:* (adj1∘-subj∘ not knowing supreme nature); *mama* (my); *bhūtamaheśvaram* (adj2∘-obj∘ the Great Lord of the Beings); (9.11)

(§4) mama param bhāvam ajānantaḥ: mūḍhāḥ: avajānanti mām bhūtamaheśvaram mānuṣīm tanum āśritam ;

(§5) Not knowing my supreme nature, the foolish people disregard me, the Great Lord of the Beings who has taken[557] human body; (9.11)

---

[557] Elsewhere∘ मानुषिं तनुम् आश्रितम् → When I assume human form, when I assume in human form, having

9.12 मोघाशा मोघकर्माणो मोघज्ञाना विचेतसः ।
राक्षसीमासुरीं चैव प्रकृतिं मोहिनीं श्रिताः ॥

moghāśā moghakarmaṇo moghajñānā vićetasaḥ:,
rākṣasīmāsurīṁ ćaiva prakṛtiṁ mohinīṁ śritāḥ:; (9.12)

(§1) *moghāśāḥ:* (r◦ 20/13) *moghakarmaṇaḥ:* (r◦ 15/9, 24/2) *moghajñānāḥ:* (r◦ 20/17) *vićetasaḥ:* (r◦ 22/8) *rākṣasīṃ* (r◦ 8/17) *āsurīṃ* (r◦ 14/1) *ća* (r◦ 3/1) *eva prakṛtiṃ* (r◦ 14/1) *mohinīṃ* (r◦ 14/1) *śritāḥ:* (r◦ 22/8);

(§2) *moghāśāḥ:* (m◦ 1nom◦ plu◦ ←bahuvrī◦ *moghāśā*, मोघाः आशाः यस्य ←adj◦ *mogha* (vain) 3.16 + f◦ 📖***āśā*** (hope) ←आ√अश्); *moghakarmaṇaḥ:* (m◦ 1nom◦ plu◦ ←bahuvrī◦ *mogha-karman*, मोघानि कर्माणि यस्य ←adj◦ *mogha* (vain) 3.16 + n◦ *karman* 1.15); *moghajñānāḥ:* (m◦ 1nom◦ plu◦ ←bahuvrī◦ *mogha-jñāna*, मोघम् ज्ञानम् यस्य ←adj◦ *mogha* (vain) 3.16 + n◦ *jñāna* 3.3); *vićetasaḥ:* (m◦ 1nom◦ plu◦ ←bahuvrī◦ *vićetas*, (improper mind) विपरितम् विरुद्धम् विगतम् वा चेतः यस्य ←prefix◦ *vi* (improper) , indicating negation ←√वा + n◦ *ćetas* (mind, thinking) 1.38); *rākṣasīṃ* (2acc◦ sing◦ ←f◦ adj◦ *rākṣasī* (demonic) ←√रक्ष्); ***āsurīṃ*** (2acc◦ sing◦ ←f◦ adj◦ ***āsurī*** (demonic) ←आ√अस्); *ća* (1.1); *eva* (1.1); *prakṛtiṃ* (3.33); *mohinīṃ* (2acc◦ sing◦ ←f◦ adj◦ *mohinī* (deluding, deceptive) ←√मुह्); *śritāḥ:* (m◦ 1nom◦ plu◦ ←ppp◦ adj◦ *śrita* (possessed) ←√श्रि); (9.12)

(§3) *moghāśāḥ:* (adj2◦-subj1◦ the ones with vain hopes); *moghakarmaṇaḥ:* (adj3◦-subj1◦ the ones with vain deeds); *moghajñānāḥ:* (adj4◦-subj1◦ the ones with vain knowledge); *vićetasaḥ:* (adj5◦-subj1◦ the ones with improper thinking); *rākṣasīṃ* (demonic); *āsurīṃ* (devilish); *ća* (and); *eva* (as well as); *prakṛtiṃ* (disposition, nature); *mohinīṃ* (deceptive); *śritāḥ:* (adj6◦-subj1◦ the ones who have taken, possessed); (9.12)

(§4) ća moghāśāḥ: moghakarmaṇaḥ: moghajñānāḥ: vićetasaḥ: eva śritāḥ: rākṣasīṃ āsurīṃ mohinīṃ prakṛtiṃ

(§5) and the ones with vain hopes, the ones with vain deeds, the ones with vain knowledge, the ones with improper thinking, as well as the ones who have possessed[558] demonic, devilish,

---

assumed this form, ...etc.

📖 अश्रित is not a Presrnt tense, gerund or a conditional mood. It is ppp◦ adjective of the m◦ object माम् ।

[558] Elsewhere◦ श्रिताः → they become verily possessed, partaking of, they continue to be, partaking of the, taking to, partaking verily of the, they have embreced, they have resorted to, they abide in, ...etc.

📖 श्रिताः is not a Presrnt tense or gerund. It is one of the six adjectives attached to the subj1◦ मूढाः mentioned in the previous verse 9.11 (the other five are भावमजानन्तः, मोघाशाः, मोघकर्माणाः, मोघज्ञानाः and विचेतसः). One must notice that, the present verse 9.12 is continuation of verse 9.11 and 9.12 has only the adjectives of the subhect

deceptive disposition; (9.12)

9.13 महात्मानस्तु मां पार्थ दैवीं प्रकृतिमाश्रिताः ।
भजन्त्यनन्यमनसो ज्ञात्वा भूतादिमव्ययम् ॥

mahātmānastu māṁ pārtha daivīṁ prakṛtimāśritāḥ:,
bhajantyananyamanaso jñātvā bhūtādimavyayam; (9.13)

(§1) *mahātmānaḥ:* (r◦ 18/1) *tu mām* (r◦ 14/1) *pārtha daivīm* (r◦ 14/1) *prakṛtim* (r◦ 8/17) *āśritāḥ:* (r◦ 22/8) *bhajanti* (r◦ 4/1) *ananyamanasaḥ:* (r◦ 15/3) *jñātvā bhūtādim* (r◦ 8/16) *avyayam* (r◦ 14/2);

(§2) *mahātmānaḥ:* (8.15); *tu* (1.2); *mām* (1.46); *pārtha* (1.25); ***daivīm*** (f◦ 2acc◦ sing◦ ←adj◦ taddhita◦ *daivī* (divine) 7.14); *prakṛtim* (3.33); *āśritāḥ:* (7.15); ***bhajanti*** (3rd-per◦ plu◦ pres◦ वर्तमान्-लट् parasmai◦ ←class1◦ √भज् 6.46); *ananyamanasaḥ:* (m◦ 1nom◦ sing◦ ←bahuvrī◦ *ananya-manas*, अनन्यम् मनः यस्य ←adj◦ *ananya* (one pointed) 8.14 + n◦ *manas* (mind) 1.30); *jñātvā* (4.15); *bhūtādim* (m◦ 2acc◦ sing◦ ←tatpu◦ *bhūtādi* (thinking) भूतानाम् आदिः ←m◦ *bhūta* (being) 2.28 + m◦ *ādi* (origin) 2.28); *avyayam* (eternal, 2.21);
(9.13)

(§3) *mahātmānaḥ:* (subj2◦ the great people); *tu* (however,); *mām* (obj◦ me); *pārtha* (O Arjuna!); *daivīm* (divine); *prakṛtim* (nature, disposition); *āśritāḥ:* (adj1◦-subj2◦ the ones possessed with); *bhajanti* (they worship); *ananyamanasaḥ:* (adj2◦-subj2◦ the ones with one pointed mind); *jñātvā* (having known); *bhūtādim* (adj1◦-obj◦ origin of the beings); *avyayam* (adj2◦-obj◦ the eternal); (9.13)

(§4) tu pārtha mahātmānaḥ: āśritāḥ: daivīm prakṛtim ananyamanasaḥ: bhajanti mām jñātvā avyayam bhūtādim;

(§5) However, O Arjuna! the great people, possessed with[559] divine nature, the ones with one pointed mind, they worship me having known (me), the eternal origin of the beings; (9.13)

9.14 सततं कीर्तयन्तो मां यतन्तश्च दृढव्रताः ।

(मूढाः) mentioned in verse 9.11, otherwise the errors as seen in above translations occur. Also note that, the next verse 9.13 and 9.14 are continuation of verses 9.11- 9.12

[559] Elsewhere◦ प्रकृतिमाश्रिताः → having taken shelter of, partaking of, abiding in celestial nature, partaking the nature of the Devas, partaking of My divine nature, taking to the divine nature, resorting to divine nature, who abide in divine nature, ...etc.

📖 प्रकृतिमाश्रिताः is not a Presrnt tense or gerund. It is one of the seven adjectives (प्रकृतिमाश्रिताः, अनन्यमनसः, कीर्तयन्तः, यतन्तः, दृढव्रताः, नमस्यन्तः and नित्ययुक्ता, mentioned in the verses 9.13 and 9.14) qualifying the subj2◦ महात्मानः ।

नमस्यन्तश्च मां भक्त्या नित्ययुक्ता उपासते ।।

satataṁ kīrtayanto māṁ yatantaśća dṛḍhavratāḥ:,
namasyantaśća māṁ bhaktyā nityayuktā upāsate; (9.14)

(§1) *satataṃ* (r∘ 14/1) *kīrtayantaḥ:* (r∘ 15/9) *māṃ* (r∘ 14/1) *yatantaḥ:* (r∘ 17/1) *ća dṛḍhavratāḥ:* (r∘ 22/8) *namasyantaḥ:* (r∘ 17/1) *ća māṃ* (r∘ 14/1) *bhaktyā nityayuktāḥ:* (r∘ 20/4) *upāsate;*

(§2) *satataṃ* (3.19); *kīrtayantaḥ:* (m∘ 1nom∘ plu∘ ←caus∘śatṛ∘ adj∘ *kīrtayaṭ* ←√कृत्); *māṃ* (1.46); ***yatantaḥ:*** (m∘ 1nom∘ plu∘ ←*śatṛ* adj∘ *yataṭ* (striving) 2.60); *ća* (1.1); *dṛḍhavratāḥ:* (7.28); *namasyantaḥ:* (m∘ 1nom∘ plu∘ ←śatṛ∘ adj∘ *namasyaṭ* (prostrating) ←√नम्); *ća* (1.1); *māṃ* (1.46); *bhaktyā* (8.10); ***nityayuktāḥ:*** (1nom∘ plu∘ ←m∘ *nityayukta* (ever equipped) 7.17); ***upāsate*** (3rd-per∘ plu∘ pres∘ वर्तमान्-लट् ātmane∘ ←class2∘ उप√अस् 4.25); (9.14)

(§3) *satataṃ* (always); *kīrtayantaḥ:* (ipp∘ adj∘3∘-subj2∘ glorifying, those who glorify); *māṃ* (obj∘ me); *yatantaḥ:* (adj4∘-subj2∘ the striving ones); *ća* (and); *dṛḍhavratāḥ:* (adj5∘-subj2∘ the ones whose vows are severe); *namasyantaḥ:* (ipp∘ adj6∘-subj2∘ saluting me, the ones who bow to me); *ća* (and); *māṃ* (adj∘-obj∘ me); *bhaktyā* (with devotion); *nityayuktāḥ:* (adj7∘-subj2∘ the ones who are ever equipped with yoga); *upāsate* (they worship); (9.14)

(§4) ća satataṃ kīrtayantaḥ: māṃ yatantaḥ: dṛḍhavratāḥ: nityayuktāḥ: ća namasyantaḥ: upāsate māṃ bhaktyā ;

(§5) **and, those who always glorify me, the striving ones, the ones whose vows are severe, the ones who are ever equipped with yoga and ones who bow to me they worship me with devotion;** (9.14)

9.15 ज्ञानयज्ञेन चाप्यन्ये यजन्तो मामुपासते ।
एकत्वेन पृथक्त्वेन बहुधा विश्वतोमुखम् ।।

jñānayajñena ćāpyanye yajantao māmupāsate,
ekatvena pṛthaktvena bahudhā viśvatomukhaṃ. (9.15)

(§1) *jñānayajñena ća* (r∘ 1/1) *api* (r∘ 4/1) *anye yajantaḥ:* (r∘ 15/9) *māṃ* (r∘ 8/20) *upāsate* (r∘ 23/1) *ekatvena pṛthaktvena bahudhā viśvatomukhaṃ* (r∘ 14/2)

(§2) ***jñānayajñena*** (m∘ 3inst∘ sing∘ ←tatpu∘ *jñāna-yajña* 4.33); *ća* (1.1); *api* (1.26); *anye* (1.9); *yajantaḥ:* (m∘ 1nom∘ plu∘ ←śatṛ∘ adj∘ *yajaṭ* (performing austerity) ←√यज्); *māṃ* (1.46); *upāsate* (9.14); *ekatvena* (adv∘ ←3inst∘ sing∘ n∘ *ekatva* (focus) 6.31); ***pṛthaktvena*** (adv∘ ←3inst∘ sing∘ n∘ *pṛthaktva* (diverted) ←√प्रथ्); 🕮***bahudhā*** (diverse adv∘ num∘ ind∘ ←√बंह); ***viśvatomukhaṃ*** (m∘ 2acc∘ sing∘ ←bahuvrī∘ ***viśvatomukha***, विश्वत: मुखम् यस्य ←ind∘ *viśvataṣ* (omniscient) ←√विश् + n∘ *mukha* (face, vision) 1.29) (9.15)

(§3) *jñānayajñena* (with austerity of *jñānayoga*); *ća* (and); *api* (also); *anye* (subj3◦ other people); *yajantaḥ:* (adj◦-subj3◦ performing austerity); *mām̨* (obj◦ me); *upāsate* (worship); *ekatvena* (adv◦ with, in one form); *pr̥thaktvena* (with, in many forms); *bahudhā* (adv◦ in various ways); *viśvatomukham̨* (adj◦-obj◦ the Omniscient) (9.15)

(§4) ća api anye yajantaḥ: upāsate viśvatomukham̨ mām̨ jñānayajñena ekatvena pr̥thaktvena bahudhā

(§5) and also, other people performing austerity, worship the Omniscient me, with the austerity of *jñānayoga*[560] in one form (or) in many forms, in various ways. (9.15)

9.16 अहं क्रतुरहं यज्ञः स्वधाहमहमौषधम् ।
मन्त्रोऽहमहमेवाज्यमहमग्निरहं हुतम् ।।
ahaṁ kraturahaṁ yajñaḥ: svadhāhamahamauṣadham̨,
mantro'hamahamevājyamahamagnirahaṁ hutam̨; (9.16)

(§1) *aham̨* (r◦ 14/1) *kratuḥ:* (r◦ 16/3) *aham̨* (r◦ 14/1) *yajñaḥ:* (r◦ 22/7) *svadhā* (r◦ 1/3) *aham̨* (r◦ 8/16) *aham̨* (r◦ 8/25) *auṣadham̨* (r◦ 14/2) *mantraḥ:* (r◦ 15/1) *aham̨* (r◦ 8/16) *aham̨* (r◦ 8/22) *eva* (r◦ 1/2) *ājyam̨* (r◦ 8/16) *aham̨* (r◦ 8/16) *agniḥ:* (r◦ 16/1) *aham̨* (r◦ 14/1) *hutam̨* (r◦ 14/2)

(§2) *aham̨* (1.22); *kratuḥ:* (1nom◦ sing◦ ←m◦ *kratu* (offering) ←√कृ); *aham̨* (1.22); *yajñaḥ:* (3.14); *svadhā* (1nom◦ sing◦ ←f◦ *svadhā* (oblation) ←√स्वद्); *aham̨* (1.22); *aham̨* (1.22); *auṣadham̨* (1nom◦ sing◦ ←n◦ *auṣadha* (herb) ←ओष√धा); *mantraḥ:* (1nom◦ sing◦ ←m◦ ***mantra*** (chant) ←√मन्त्र्); *aham̨* (1.22); *aham̨* (1.22); *eva* (1.1); *ājyam̨* (1nom◦ sing◦ ←n◦ *ājya* (offering) ←आ√अञ्ज्); *aham̨* (1.22); *agniḥ:* (4.37); *aham̨* (1.22); *hutam̨* (4.24) (9.16)

(§3) *aham̨* (subj◦ I am); *kratuḥ:* (subj◦-comp1◦[561] the offering of *kratu*); *aham̨* (subj◦ I am); *yajñaḥ:* (subj◦-comp2◦ the austerity); *svadhā* (subj◦-comp3◦◦ the oblation of *svadha* offered to ancestors); *aham̨* (subj◦ I am); *aham̨* (I am); *auṣadham̨* (subj◦-comp4◦ the offering of herbs); *mantraḥ:* (subj◦-comp5◦ the vedic chant, spell); *aham̨* (I am); *aham̨* (I am); *eva* (also); *ājyam̨* (subj◦-comp6◦the offering of clarified butter); *aham̨* (I am); *agniḥ:* (subj◦-comp7◦ the fire of the yajña); *aham̨* (I am); *hutam̨* (subj◦-comp8◦ everything else that is offered as oblation) (9.16)

(§4) aham̨ kratuḥ: aham̨ yajñaḥ: aham̨ svadhā aham̨ auṣadham̨ aham̨ mantraḥ: aham̨ ājyam̨ aham̨ agniḥ: aham̨

---

[560] For explanation on "subj◦-comp◦" see footnote in 7.8

[561] Elsewhere◦ ज्ञानयज्ञेन → with sacrifice of knowledge, through the knowledge-sacrifice, by the knowledge sacrifice, with the wisdom sacrifice, by the wisdom-sacrifice, with the sacrifice of wisdom, by cultivation of knowledge, ...etc.

eva hutam

(§5) I am the (i) offering of *kratu*, I am (ii) the austerity, I am (iii) the oblation of *svadhā* offered to ancestors, I am (iv) the offering of herbs, I am (v) the vedic chant, I am (vi) the offering of clarified butter, I am (vii) the fire of the *yajña*, I am also (viii) everything else that is offered as oblation; (9.16)

9.17 पिताहमस्य जगतो माता धाता पितामहः ।
वेद्यं पवित्रमोङ्कार ऋक्साम यजुरेव च ।।
pitāhamasya jagato mātā dhātā pitāmahaḥ:,
vedyaṁ pavitramoṁkāra ṛksāma yajureva ća; (9.17)

(§1) *pitā* (r◦ 1/3) *aham* (r◦ 8/16) *asya jagataḥ:* (r◦ 15/9) *mātā dhātā pitāmahaḥ:* (r◦ 22/8) *vedyam* (r◦ 14/1) *pavitram* (r◦ 8/24) *oṁkāraḥ:* (r◦ 19/6) *ṛk* (r◦ 10/4) *sāma yajuḥ:* (r◦ 16/3) *eva ća*

(§2) ***pitā*** (1nom◦ sing◦ ←m◦ *pitṛ* (father) 1.12); *aham* (1.22); *asya* (2.17); *jagataḥ:* (7.6); *mātā* (1nom◦ sing◦ ←f◦ *mātṛ* (mother) 1.26); *dhātā* (1nom◦ sing◦ ←m◦ *dhātṛ* (supporter) 8.9); *pitāmahaḥ:* (1.12); ***vedyam*** (2acc◦ sing◦ ←pot◦ adj◦ 🕮**vedya** (knowable) ←√विद्); *pavitram* (4.38); *oṁkāraḥ:* (ॐकार: = ind◦ om ॐ ← ←√अव्); *ṛk* (m◦ 1nom◦ sing◦ ←prop◦ *ṛk* ←√ऋच्); *sāma* (m◦ 1nom◦ sing◦ ←prop◦ ***sāman*** (Samaveda) ←√saae); *yajuḥ:* (n◦ 1nom◦ sing◦ ←prop◦ *yajus* (Yajurveda) ←√यज्); *eva* (1.1); *ća* (1.1) (9.17)

(§3) *pitā* (subj◦-comp9◦ the father); *aham* (I am); *asya* (of this); *jagataḥ:* (of the world); *mātā* (subj◦-comp10◦ the mother); *dhātā* (subj◦-comp11◦ the supported, the nourisher); *pitāmahaḥ:* (subj◦-comp12◦ the grandfather); *vedyam* (subj◦-comp13◦ the knowable); *pavitram oṁkāraḥ:* (subj◦-comp14◦ the monosyllable of om); *ṛk* (subj◦-comp15◦ the rigveda); *sāma* (subj◦-comp16◦ the *samāveda*); *yajuḥ:* (subj◦-comp17◦ the yajurveda); *eva ća* (as well as) (9.17)

(§4) asya jagataḥ: aham pitā mātā dhātā pitāmahaḥ: vedyam pavitram oṁkāraḥ: ṛk sāma yajuḥ: eva ća

(§5) Of this world, I am (ix) the father, (x) the mother, (xi) the supported, (xii) the grandfather, (xiii) the knowable, (xiv) the sacred monosyllable of om, (xv) the rigveda, (xvi) the *sāmaveda*, as well as (xvii) the *yajurveda*; (9.17)

9.18 गतिर्भर्ता प्रभुः साक्षी निवासः शरणं सुहृत् ।
प्रभवः प्रलयः स्थानं निधानं बीजमव्ययम् ।।
gatirbhartā prabhuḥ: sākṣī nivāsaḥ: śaraṇaṁ suhṛt,
prabhavaḥ: pralayaḥ: sthānaṁ nidhānaṁ bījamavyayam. (9.18)

(§1) *gatiḥ:* (r◦ 16/6) *bhartā prabhuḥ:* (r◦ 22/7) *sākṣī nivāsaḥ:* (r◦ 22/5) *śaraṇam* (r◦ 14/1, 24/3) *suhṛt*

(r◦ 23/1) *prabhavaḥ:* (r◦ 22/3) *pralayaḥ:* (r◦ 22/7) *sthānaṃ* (r◦ 14/1) *nidhānaṃ* (r◦ 14/1) *bījaṃ* (r◦ 8/16) *avyayaṃ* (r◦ 14/2)

(§2) *gatiḥ:* (4.17); 📖***bhartā*** (1nom◦ sing◦ ←m◦ ***bhartṛ*** (sustainer) ←√Ba◦); *prabhuḥ:* (5.14); *sākṣī* (1nom◦ sing◦ ←m◦ *sākṣin* (witness) ←सह्√अक्ष्); 📖*nivāsaḥ:* (1nom◦ sing◦ ←m◦ ***nivāsa*** (abode) ←नि√वस्); 📖*śaraṇaṃ* (1nom◦ sing◦ ←n◦ *śaraṇa* (refuge) 2.49); *suhṛt* (1nom◦ sing◦ ←m◦ *suhṛt* ←√हृ); *prabhavaḥ:* (7.6); *pralayaḥ:* (7.6); *sthānaṃ* (5.5); 📖***nidhānaṃ*** (1nom◦ sing◦ ←n◦ *nidhāna* (treasure) ←नि√धा); *bījaṃ* (7.10); *avyayaṃ* (9.2) (9.18)

(§3) *gatiḥ:* (subj◦-comp18◦ the state, destination); *bhartā* (subj◦-comp19◦ the master, sustainer); *prabhuḥ:* (subj◦-comp20◦ the Lord); *sākṣī* (subj◦-comp21◦ the witness, the overseer); *nivāsaḥ:* (subj◦-comp22◦ the abode); *śaraṇaṃ* (subj◦-comp23◦ the refuge); *suhṛt* (subj◦-comp24◦ the well wisher); *prabhavaḥ:* (subj◦-comp25◦ the evolution, origination); *pralayaḥ:* (subj◦-comp26◦ the dissolution); *sthānaṃ* (subj◦-comp27◦ foundation, place); *nidhānaṃ* (subj◦-comp28◦ the treasure); *bījaṃ* (subj◦-comp29◦ the seed); *avyayaṃ* (adv◦ the imperishable) (9.18)

(§4) aham gatiḥ: bhartā prabhuḥ: sākṣī nivāsaḥ: śaraṇaṃ suhṛt prabhavaḥ: pralayaḥ: sthānaṃ nidhānaṃ avyayaṃ bījaṃ

(§5) I am (xviii) the destination, (xix) the sustainer, (xx) the Lord, (xxi) the overseer, (xxii) the abode, (xxiii) the refuge, (xxiv) the well wisher, (xxv) the evolution, (xxvi) the dissolution, (xxvii) the foundation, (xxviii) the treasure, (as well as) (xxix) the imperishable seed; (9.18)

9.19 तपाम्यहमहं वर्षं निगृह्णाम्युत्सृजामि च ।
अमृतं चैव मृत्युश्च सदसच्चाहमर्जुन ।।
tapāmyahamahaṁ varṣaṁ nigṛhṇāmyutsṛjāmi ća,
amṛtaṁ ćaiva mṛtyuśća sadasaććāhamarjuna. (9.19)

(§1) *tapāmi* (r◦ 4/1) *ahaṃ* (r◦ 8/16) *ahaṃ* (r◦ 14/1) *varṣaṃ* (r◦ 14/1) *nigṛhṇāmi* (r◦ 4/3) *utsṛjāmi ća* (r◦ 23/1) *amṛtaṃ* (r◦ 14/1) *ća* (r◦ 3/1) *eva mṛtyuḥ:* (r◦ 17/1) *ća sat* (r◦ 8/2) *asat* (r◦ 11/1) *ća* (r◦ 1/1) *ahaṃ* (r◦ 8/16) *arjuna*

(§2) *tapāmi* (1nom◦ sing◦ pres◦ वर्तमान्-लट् parasmai◦ ←class1◦ √तप्); *ahaṃ* (1.22); *ahaṃ* (↑); 📖*varṣaṃ* (1nom◦ sing◦ ←n◦ *varṣa* ←√वृष्); *nigṛhṇāmi* (1st-per◦ sing◦ pres◦ वर्तमान्-लट् parasmai◦ ←class9◦ नि√ग्रह् or √ग्रभ्); *utsṛjāmi* (1nom◦ sing◦ pres◦ वर्तमान्-लट् parasmai◦ ←class6◦ उद्√सृज् 4.7); *ća* (1.1); 📖***amṛtaṃ*** (1nom◦ sing◦ ←n◦ *amṛta* (nectar of immortality) 2.15); *ća* (1.1); *eva* (1.1); *mṛtyuḥ:* (2.27); *ća* (1.1); *sat* (be, being 2.16); ***asat*** (1nom◦ sing◦ ←adj◦ *asat* (non-being) 2.16); *ća* (1.1); *ahaṃ* (1.22); *arjuna* (2.2) (9.19)

(§3) *tapāmi* (I radiate warmth); *aham̦* (I); *aham̦* (I); *varṣam̦* (obj◦ rain); *nigṛhṇāmi* (I withhold); *utsṛjāmi* (I shower); *ća* (and); *amṛtam̦* (subj◦-comp30◦ the immortality); *ća* (and); *eva* (also); *mṛtyuḥ:* (subj◦-comp31◦ the death); *ća* (and); *saț* (subj◦-comp32◦ the being); *asaț* (subj◦-comp33◦ the non-being); *ća* (and); *aham̦* (I am); *arjuna* (O Arjuna!) (9.19)

(§4) ća arjuna aham̦ tapāmi aham̦ nigṛhṇāmi ća utsṛjāmi varṣam̦ aham̦ amṛtam̦ ća mṛtyuḥ: eva saț ća asat

(§5) **and, O Arjuna! I radiate warmth. I withhold and shower rain. I am (xxx) the immortality and (xxxi) the death, also (xxxii) the being and (xxxiii) the non-being.** (9.19)

9.20 त्रैविद्या मां सोमपाः पूतपापा यज्ञैरिष्ट्वा स्वर्गतिं प्रार्थयन्ते ।
ते पुण्यमासाद्य सुरेन्द्रलोकमश्नन्ति दिव्यान्दिवि देवभोगान् ।।

traividyā māṁ somapāḥ: pūtapāpā yajñairiṣṭvā svargatiṁ prārthayante,
te puṇyamāsādya surendralokamaśnanti divyāndivi devabhogān̦. (9.20)

(§1) *traividyāḥ:* (r◦ 20/13) *mām̦* (r◦ 14/1) *somapāḥ:* (r◦ 22/3) *pūtapāpāḥ:* (r◦ 20/14) *yajñaiḥ:* (r◦ 16/4) *iṣṭvā svargatim̦* (r◦ 14/1) *prārthayante te puṇyam̦* (r◦ 8/17) *āsādya surendralokam̦* (r◦ 8/16) *aśnanti divyān̦* (r◦ 13/11) *divi devabhogān̦*

(§2) 🕮*traividyāḥ:* (m◦ 1nom◦ plu◦ ←bahuvrī◦ *trai-vidya*, तिस्त्रः विद्याः यस्य ←always pleural num◦ adj◦ *tri* (three) 2.45 + *vidyā* (vedic knowledge) 5.18); *mām̦* (1.46); *somapāḥ:* (m◦ 1nom◦ sing◦ ←bahuvrī◦ adj◦ *somapā*, सोमम् पिबति इति ←m◦ ***soma*** (nectar) ←√sau + 3rd-per◦ sing◦ pres◦ वर्तमान्–लट् parasmai◦ v◦ *pibati* ←class1◦ √पा); *pūtapāpāḥ:* (m◦ 1nom◦ plu◦ ←bahuvrī◦ *pūta-pāpa*, पूतम् पापम् यस्य ←adj◦ *pūta* (cleansed) 4.10 + n◦ *pāpa* (sin) 1.36); *yajñaiḥ:* (3inst◦ plu◦ ←m◦ *yajña* 3.9); *iṣṭvā* (ipp◦ ind◦ ←√इष्); *svargatim̦* (2acc◦ sing◦ ←tatpu◦ *svargati* (supreme state) स्वर्गस्य गतिः ←ind◦ *svar̦* (heavenly) ←**√sva◦** + f◦ *gati* (state) 2.43); *prārthayante* (3rd-per◦ plu◦ pres◦ वर्तमान्–लट् ātmane◦ ←class10◦ प्र√अर्थ्); *te* (1.33); 🕮***puṇyam̦*** (2acc◦ sing◦ ←n◦ *puṇya* (good deed) 6.41); *āsādya* (lyp◦ past-participle ind◦ ←आ√सद्); *surendralokam̦* (m◦ 2acc◦ 1st-per◦ ←tatpu◦ *surendra-loka*, सुरेन्द्रस्य लोकः ←m◦ *sura* (god) 2.8 + adj◦ ***indra*** (lord) ←√इन्द् + m◦ *loka* (world) 2.5); *aśnanti* (3rd-per◦ plu◦ pres◦ वर्तमान्–लट् parasmai◦ ←class9◦ √अश् 3.4); ***divyān̦*** (m◦ 2acc◦ plu◦ ←adj◦ *divya* (divine) 1.14); ***divi*** (7loc◦ sing◦ ←f◦ *diva* (heaven) ←√दिव्); *devabhogān̦* (m◦ 2acc◦ plu◦ ←tatpu◦ *deva-bhoga*, देवस्य भोगः ←m◦ *deva* (god) 3.11 + m◦ *bhoga* (pleasure) 1.32) (9.20)

(§3) *traividyāḥ:* (adj1◦-subj◦ those who have studied three vedas); *mām̦* (obj◦ me); *somapāḥ:* (adj2◦-subj◦ those who drink *soma* nectar); *pūtapāpāḥ:* (adj3◦-subj◦ those whose sins are washed away); *yajñaiḥ:* (by austerities); *iṣṭvā* (having aspired); *svargatim̦* (obj1◦ supreme state); *prārthayante* (they pray); *te* (subj◦ they); *puṇyam̦* (adj◦-obj2◦ sacred); *āsādya* (having attained); *surendralokam̦* (obj2◦ the heaven); *aśnanti* (they enjoy); *divyān̦* (adj◦-obj3◦ divine); *divi* (in the heaven); *devabhogān̦* (obj3◦ the celestial pleasures) (9.20)

(§4) traividyāḥ: somapāḥ: pūtapāpāḥ: yajñaiḥ: te iṣṭvā svargatim̦ prārthayante mām̦ āsādya puṇyam̦ surendralokam̦ aśnanti divyān̦ devabhogān̦ divi

(§5) Those who have studied three vedas, those who drink soma nectar, those whose sins are washed away by austerities, they, having aspired[562] supreme state, pray me (and) having attained the sacred heaven, they enjoy the divine celestial pleasures in the heaven. (9.20)

9.21 ते तं भुक्त्वा स्वर्गलोकं विशालं क्षीणे पुण्ये मर्त्यलोकं विशन्ति ।
एवं त्रयीधर्ममनुप्रपन्नाः गतागतं कामकामा लभन्ते ।।
te taṁ bhuktvā svargalokaṁ viśālaṁ kṣīṇe puṇye martyalokaṁ viśanti,
evaṁ trayīdharmamanuprapannāḥ: gatāgataṁ kāmakāmā labhante.
(9.21)

(§1) *te tam̦* (r◦ 14/1) *bhuktvā svargalokam̦* (r◦ 14/1) *viśālam̦* (r◦ 14/1) *kṣīṇe* (r◦ 24/9) *puṇye martyalokam̦* (r◦ 14/1) *viśanti* (r◦ 23/1) *evam̦* (r◦ 14/1) *trayīdharmam̦* (r◦ 8/16) *anuprapannāḥ:* (r◦ 20/6) *gatāgatam̦* (r◦ 14/1) *kāmakāmāḥ:* (r◦ 20/16) *labhante*

(§2) *te* (1.33); *tam̦* (2.1); *bhuktvā* (ipp◦ ind◦ ←√भुज्); *svargalokam̦* (m◦ 2acc◦ sing◦ ←tatpu◦ *svarga-loka*, स्वर्गस्य लोकः ←m◦ *svarga* (heaven) 2.2 + m◦ *loka* (world) 2.5); *viśālam̦* (m◦ 2acc◦ sing◦ ←adj◦ 📖**viśāla** (vast) ←वि√शाल्); *kṣīṇe* (m◦ 7loc◦ sing◦ ←adj◦ *kṣīṇa* (diminished) 5.25); *puṇye* (m◦ 7loc◦ sing◦ ←n◦ *puṇya* (merit) 6.41); *martyalokam̦* (m◦ 2acc◦ sing◦ ←tatpu◦ *martya-loka* (earth) मर्त्यानाम् लोकः ←adj◦ 📖**martya** (death ridden) ←√ma◦ + m◦ *loka* (world) 2.5); *viśanti* (8.11); *evam̦* (1.24); *trayīdharmam̦* (m◦ 2acc◦ sing◦ ←tatpu◦ *trayī-dharma*, त्रय्याः धर्मः ←f◦ *trayī* (three vedas) ←√तॄ + m◦ *dharma* (rituals) 1.1); *anuprapannāḥ:* (m◦ 1nom◦ plu◦ ←ppp◦ adj◦ *anuprapanna* (deloted) ←अनु-प्र√पद् 2.7); *gatāgatam̦* (m◦ 2acc◦ sing◦ ←bah◦ गतम् च आगतम् च यत् तत् ←adj◦ *gata* (gone, dead) 2.11 + adj◦ *āgata* (came, born) 4.10); *kāmakāmāḥ:* (m◦ 1nom◦ plu◦ ←bahuvrī◦ *kāma-kāma*, कामानाम् कामः यस्य ←m◦ *kāma* (desire) 1.22); *labhante* (2.32) (9.21)

(§3) *te* (adj1◦-subj◦ they); *tam̦* (adj1◦-obj1◦ that); *bhuktvā* (having enjoyed); *svargalokam̦* (obj1◦ heaven); *viśālam̦* (adj2◦-obj1◦ vast); *kṣīṇe puṇye* (on the exhaustion of *puṇya*); *martyalokam̦* (obj2◦ the

---

[562] Elsewhere◦ इष्ट्वा स्वर्गतिम् → seek to go to heaven, seek acces to heaven, aspire for heavenly planets, pray for heavenly goals, pray for goal of heaven, pray for way to heaven, pray for attainment of heaven, pray for admission to heaven, pray for access to heaven, ...etc.

📖 इष्ट्वा is not a Presrnt tense. It is a क्त्वा ind◦ participle gerund = having desired.

mortal world); *viśanti* (they return to); *evaṃ* (in this way, thus); *trayīdharmaṃ* (obj3◦ the rituals priscribed in the four *vedas*); *anuprapannāḥ:* (adj2◦-subj◦ those who are devoted to); *gatāgataṃ* (obj4◦ temporary thing, temporal life); *kāmakāmāḥ:* (adj3◦-subj◦ those who desire pleasures); *labhante* (they attain) (9.21)

(§4) te bhuktvā taṃ viśālaṃ svargalokaṃ kśīṇe puṇye viśanti martyalokaṃ evaṃ anuprapannāḥ: trayīdharmaṃ kāmakāmāḥ: labhante gatāgataṃ

(§5) They, having enjoyed that vast heaven, on the exhaustion of *puṇya* they return to the mortal world. In this way, those who are devoted[563] to the rituals priscribed in the four[564] *vedas* (and) desire pleasures, they attain temporal life. (9.21)

9.22 **अनन्याश्चिन्तयन्तो मां ये जनाः पर्युपासते ।**
तेषां नित्याभियुक्तानां योगक्षेमं वहाम्यहम् ।।
ananyāśćintayanto māṁ ye janāḥ: paryupāsate,
teṣāṁ nityābhiyuktānāṁ yogakṣemaṁ vahāmyahaṃ; (9.22)

(§1) *ananyāḥ:* (r◦ 17/1) *ćintayantaḥ:* (r◦ 15/9) *māṃ* (r◦ 14/1) *ye janāḥ:* (r◦ 22/3) *paryupāsate teṣāṃ* (r◦ 25/3, 14/1) *nityābhiyuktānāṃ* (r◦ 14/1) *yogakṣemaṃ* (r◦ 14/1) *vahāmi* (r◦ 4/1) *ahaṃ* (r◦ 14/2)

(§2) *ananyāḥ:* (m◦ 1nom◦ plu◦ ←adj◦ *ananya* (one pointed) 8.14); *ćintayantaḥ:* (m◦ 1nom◦ plu◦ ←śatṛ◦ adj◦ *ćintayat* (contemplating) ←√चिन्त्); *māṃ* (1.46); *ye* (1.7); *janāḥ:* (7.16); *paryupāsate* (4.25); *teṣāṃ* (5.16); *nityābhiyuktānāṃ* (6pos plu◦ ←m◦ *nityābhiyukta*, ←ind◦ *nitya* (ever) 2.18 + adj◦ *abhiyukta* (equipped)

---

[563] Elsewhere◦ त्रयीधर्मम् अनुप्रपन्नाः → conforming to the law, those who follow, following the virtues, adhering to the principles, who take refuge in the religion, those who have recourse to, following the Dharma, ...etc.

📖 अनुप्रपन्नाः is not a gerund or a Presrnt tense. It is a plural क्त ppp◦ adjective of subject ते ।

[564] Elsewhere◦ त्रयीधर्मम् → three vedas.

📖 लिखितम् अस्ति "ऋग्यजुसामशब्दाम् अर्थविषये जनाः सम्भ्रान्ताः इति ज्ञापयति सायणः सिद्धान्यपक्षनिरूपणावसरे । ऋक् इति शब्दः ऋग्वेदम् । सामान्याः लौकिकाः तु ऋक्शब्दात् ऋग्वेदमात्रम् एव गृह्णन्ति एवमेव यजुस्सामादिविषये अपि । अतः एव त्रयी-शब्दात् त्रयः वेदाः । वस्तुतः वेदमन्त्राः त्रिविधाः - ऋचः यजूंषि साम्नानि चेति । जैमिनिः तेषां लक्षणं वदति ऋक् यत्र अर्थवशेन पादव्यवस्था । गीतिषु सामाख्या । शेषे यजुश्शब्दः इति । एवं समस्ते वेदवाङ्मये त्रिप्रकाराः एव मन्त्राः सन्ति । यत्र यत्र त्रयी इति शब्दः श्रूयते तत्र **त्रिप्रकारमन्त्राणाम् एव निर्देशः भवति** । अथर्ववेदे अपि त्रिप्रकारकाः मन्त्राः सन्ति । एवं त्रयी इति पदं मन्त्रप्रकारसमूहं निर्दिशति वेदाः कति इति निरूपयितुम् उद्युक्तं पदं न तत् । चत्वारः वेदाः त्रिप्रकारकाः वेदमन्त्राः । उभयोपि भेदः अस्ति । त्रयी इति पदं तु द्वितीयम अंशम् -त्रिप्रकारकाः वेदमन्त्राः इत्येतम् अंशम्- निरूपयति । एतत् अजानन्तः केचन पामराः त्रयीपदेन त्रयः वेदाः उच्यन्ते, न तु अथर्ववेदः, इति वदन्ति । अमरकोशस्य सुधाव्याख्यानस्य टिप्पणी वदति- आथर्वणस्तु त्रय्यनुवादः एव इति स्वामी -इति । त्रयी इति पदस्य यथा तथैव अन्येषां बहूनाम् अपि पदानाम् अन्यार्थकल्पनं दृश्यते लोके । अल्पज्ञत्वम् एव प्रायः अत्र कारणम् ।"

←अभि√युज्); *yogakṣemam̩* (2acc◦ sing◦ dvandva◦ योगम् च क्षेमम् च ←m◦ *yoga* (maintainance) 2.39 + m◦ or n◦ *kṣema* (protection) 1.46); *vahāmi* (1st-per◦ sing◦ pres◦ वर्तमान्–लट् parasmai◦ ←class1◦ √वह्); *aham̩* (1.22) (9.22)

(§3) *ananyāḥ:* (adj1◦-subj1◦ those whose devotion is one pointed); *ćintayantaḥ:* (adj2◦-subj1◦ the ones who are contemplating on); *mām̩* (obj1◦ me); *ye* (adj3◦-subj1◦ those who); *janāḥ:* (subj1◦ people); *paryupāsate* (they worship); *teṣām̩* (of those); *nityābhiyuktānām̩* (of the ever equipped people); *yogakṣemam̩* (obj2◦ maintainance and protection); *vahāmi* (I perform); *aham̩* (subj2◦ I) (9.22)

(§4) ye janāḥ: ananyāḥ: ćintayantaḥ: mām̩ paryupāsate teṣām̩ nityābhiyuktānām̩ vahāmi aham̩ yogakṣemam̩

(§5) Those people whose devotion is one pointed, the ones who are contemplating on me, they worship (me). Of those ever equipped people, I perform maintainance and protection; (9.22)

9.23 येऽप्यन्यदेवताभक्ता यजन्ते श्रद्धयान्विताः ।
तेऽपि मामेव कौन्तेय यजन्त्यविधिपूर्वकम् ।।
ye'pyanyadevatā bhaktā yajante śraddhayānvitāḥ:,
te'pi māmeva kaunteya yajantyavidhipūrvakam̩. (9.23)

(§1) *ye* (r◦ 6/1) *api* (r◦ 4/1) *anyadevatāḥ:* (r◦ 20/12) *bhaktāḥ:* (r◦ 20/14) *yajante śraddhayā* (r◦ 1/3) *anvitāḥ:* (r◦ 22/8) *te* (r◦ 6/1) *api mām̩* (r◦ 8/22) *eva kaunteya yajanti* (r◦ 4/1) *avidhipūrvakam̩* (r◦ 14/2)

(§2) *ye* (1.7); *api* (1.26); *anyadevatāḥ:-bhaktāḥ:* (m◦ 1nom◦ plu◦ ←tatpu◦ *anya-devatā-bhakata*, अन्यानाम् देवतानाम् भक्तः ←adj◦ *anya* (other) 1.9 + f◦ *devatā* (deity) 4.12 + m◦ *bhakta* (devotee) 4.3); *yajante* (4.12); *śraddhayā* (6.37); ***anvitāḥ:*** (m◦ 1nom◦ plu◦ ←ppp◦ adj◦ 🕮***anvita*** (endowed with) ←अनु√इण्); *te* (1.33); *api* (1.26); *mām̩* (1.46); *eva* (1.1); *kaunteya* (2.14); *yajanti* (3rd-per◦ plu◦ pres◦ वर्तमान्–लट् parasmai◦ ←class1◦ √यज् 4.12); 🕮***avidhipūrvakam̩*** (adv◦ ind◦ ←ind◦ अ 1.10 + m◦ ***vidhi*** (priscription) ←वि√धा + adj◦ ***pūrvak*** (according to) ←√पूर्व्) (9.23)

(§3) *ye* (adj◦-subj◦ those who); *api* (also); *anyadevatāḥ: bhaktāḥ:* (subj◦ devotees of other gods); *yajante* (worship); *śraddhayā anvitāḥ:* (adj◦-subj◦ endowed with faith); *te* (adj◦-subj◦ they); *api* (also); *mām̩* (obj◦ me); *eva* (only); *kaunteya* (O Arjuna!); *yajanti* (worship); *avidhipūrvakam̩* (adv◦ erroneously, improperly) (9.23)

(§4) api kaunteya ye anyadevatāḥ: bhaktāḥ: anvitāḥ: śraddhayā yajante te api yajanti mām̩ eva avidhipūrvakam̩.

(§5) also, O Arjuna! those devotees of other gods, endowed with faith, who worship, they also worship me only, (but) improperly. (9.23)

9.24 अहं हि सर्वयज्ञानां भोक्ता च प्रभुरेव च ।
न तु मामभिजानन्ति तत्त्वेनातश्च्यवन्ति ते ।।

aham hi sarvayajñānām bhoktā ća prabhureva ća,
na tu māmabhijānanti tattvenātasćyavanti te. (9.24)

(§1) *aham* (r◦ 14/1) *hi sarvayajñānām* (r◦ 14/1) *bhoktā ća prabhuḥ:* (r◦ 16/3) *eva ća na tu mām* (r◦ 8/16) *abhijānanti tattvena* (r◦ 1/1) *ataḥ:* (r◦ 17/1) *ćyavanti te*

(§2) *aham* (1.22); *hi* (1.11); *sarvayajñānām* (सर्वेषाम् यज्ञानाम्, m◦ 1nom◦ plu◦ ←pron◦ *sarva* 1.6 + m◦ *yajña* 3.9); ***bhoktā*** (m◦ 1nom◦ sing◦ ←adj◦ *bhoktṛ* (acceptor) 5.29); *ća* (1.1); *prabhuḥ:* (5.14); *eva* (1.1); *ća* (1.1); *na* (1.30); *tu* (1.2); *mām* (1.46); *abhijānanti* (3rd-per◦ plu◦ pres◦ वर्तमान्-लट् parasmai◦ ←class9◦ अभि√ज्ञा 4.14); ***tattvena*** (3inst◦ sing◦ ←n◦ *tattva* (reality) 2.16); *ataḥ:* (2.12); *ćyavanti* (3rd-per◦ plu◦ pres◦ वर्तमान्-लट् parasmai◦ ←class1◦ √च्यु); *te* (1.33) (9.24)

(§3) *aham* (subj1◦ I am); *hi* (because); *sarvayajñānām* (of all austerities); *bhoktā* (adj1◦-subj1◦ the acceptor); *ća* (and); *prabhuḥ:* (adj2◦-subj1◦ the governor, autuhrity); *eva* (also); *ća* (and); *na* (do not); *tu* (but); *mām* (obj◦ me); *abhijānanti* (they understand); *tattvena* (in reality); *ataḥ:* (therefore); *ćyavanti* (they fall, go down); *te* (subj2◦ they) (9.24)

(§4) ća aham bhoktā ća eva prabhuḥ: sarvayajñānām tu hi na abhijānanti mām tattvena ataḥ: te ćyavanti

(§5) And, I am the acceptor[565] and also the autuhrity of all austerities, but because[566] they do not understand me in reality, therefore,[567] they go down. (9.24)

9.25 यान्ति देवव्रता देवान्पितृन्यान्ति पितृव्रताः ।
भूतानि यन्ति भूतेज्या यान्ति मद्याजिनोऽपि माम् ।।

yānti devavratā devānpitṛ́nyānti pitṛvratāḥ:,
bhūtāni yānti bhūtejyā yānti madyājino'pi mām. (9.25)

(§1) *yānti devavratāḥ:* (r◦ 20/8) *devān* (r◦ 13/13) *pitṛ́n* (r◦ 13/17) *yānti pitṛvratāḥ:* (r◦ 22/8) *bhūtāni yānti bhūtejyāḥ:* (r◦ 20/14) *yānti madyājinaḥ:* (r◦ 15/1) *api mām* (r◦ 14/2)

(§2) *yānti* (3.33); *devavratāḥ:* (m◦ 1nom◦ plu◦ ←bahuvrī◦ *deva-vrata*, देवेभ्यः व्रतम् यस्य ←m◦ *deva* (deity)

---

[565] Bhoktā → enjoyer.

[566] See footnote in verse 3.5

[567] See the footnote in verse 2.15

3.11 + n◦ *vrata* (austerity) 4.28); *devān* (3.11); *pitṝn* (1.26); *yānti* (3.33); *pitṛvratāḥ:* (m◦ 1nom◦ plu◦ ←bahuvrī◦ *pitṛ-vratāḥ:*, पितृभ्य: व्रतम् यस्य ←m◦ *pitṛ* (forefather) 1.12 + n◦ *vrata* (austerity) 4.28); *bhūtāni* (2.30); *yānti* (3.33); *bhūtejyāḥ:* (m◦ 1nom◦ plu◦ ←bahuvrī◦ *bhūtejya*, भूतेभ्य: इज्या यस्य ←m◦ *bhūta* (being) 2.28 + f◦ ***ijyā*** (worship) ←√यज्); *yānti* (3.33); *madyājinaḥ:* (m◦ 1nom◦ plu◦ ←bahuvrī◦ ***madyājin*** (my worshipper) माम् यजति य: ←pron◦ *mat* (me) 1.9 + m◦ *yajin* (worshipper) 7.23); *api* (1.26); *mām* (1.46) (9.25)

(§3) *yānti* (attain); *devavratāḥ:* (subj1◦ the worshippers of the gods); *devān* (obj1◦ gods); *pitṝn* (obj2◦ forefathers, ancestors); *yānti* (attain); *pitṛvratāḥ:* (subj2◦ the worshippers of the ancestors); *bhūtāni* (obj3◦ the beings, the spirits); *yānti* (attain); *bhūtejyāḥ:* (subj3◦ the worshippers of the beings); *yānti* (attain); *madyājinaḥ:* (subj4◦ my devotees); *api* (also, and); *mām* (obj4◦ me) (9.25)

(§4) devavratāḥ: yānti devān pitṛvratāḥ: yānti pitṝn bhūtejyāḥ: yānti bhūtāni api madyājinaḥ: yānti mām

(§5) (i) The worshippers of the gods attain gods; (ii) the worshippers of the ancestors attain ancestors; (iii) the worshippers of the beings attain the beings, and (iv) my devotees attain me. (9.25)

9.26 पत्रं पुष्पं फलं तोयं यो मे भक्त्या प्रयच्छति ।
तदहं भक्त्युपहृतमश्नामि प्रयतात्मन: ।।
patraṁ puṣpaṁ phalaṁ toyaṁ yo me bhaktyā prayaćchati,
tadahaṁ bhaktyupahṛtamaśnāmi prayatātmanaḥ:. (9.26)

(§1) *patram* (r◦ 14/1) *puṣpam* (r◦ 14/1) *phalam* (r◦ 14/1) *toyam* (r◦ 14/1) *yaḥ:* (r◦ 15/9) *me bhaktyā prayaćchati tat* (r◦ 8/2) *aham* (r◦ 14/1) *bhaktyupahṛtam* (r◦ 8/16) *aśnāmi prayatātmanaḥ:* (r◦ 22/8)

(§2) 🕮*patram* (2acc◦ sing◦ ←n◦ *patra* (leaf) 5.10); 🕮*puṣpam* (2acc◦ sing◦ ←n◦ *puṣpa* (flower) ←√पुष्प्); 🕮*phalam* (fruit, 2.51); 🕮*toyam* (2acc◦ sing◦ ←n◦ *toya* (water) ←√तु); *yaḥ:* (2.19); *me* (1.21); *bhaktyā* (8.10); *prayaćchati* (3rd-per◦ sing◦ pres◦ वर्तमान्-लट् parasmai◦ ←class1◦ प्र√यम्); *tat* (2.7); *aham* (1.22); *bhaktyupahṛtam* (2acc◦ sing◦ ←tatpu◦ adj◦ *bhaktyupahṛta*, भक्त्या उपहृतम् यत् ←adj◦ *bhakti* (devotion) 7.17 + ppp◦ adj◦ *upahṛta* (offered) ←उप√हृ); *aśnāmi* (1st-per◦ sing◦ pres◦ वर्तमान्-लट् parasmai◦ ←class9◦ √अश् 3.4); *prayatātmanaḥ:* (m◦ 6pos◦ sing◦ ←bahuvrī◦ *prayatātman*, प्रयत: आत्मा यस्य ←ppp◦ adj◦ *prayata* (austere) ←प्र√यम् + m◦ *ātman* (person, self) 2.41) (9.26)

(§3) *patram* (obj1◦ a leaf); *puṣpam* (obj2◦ a flower); *phalam* (obj3◦ a fruit); *toyam* (obj4◦ water); *yaḥ:* (subj1◦ whoever); *me* (obj5◦ me); *bhaktyā* (with devotion); *prayaćchati* (offers); *tat* (adj1◦-obj1-4◦ that); *aham* (subj2◦ I); *bhaktyupahṛtam* (adj2◦-obj1-4◦ offered with devotion); *aśnāmi* (I accept); *prayatātmanaḥ:* (of the austere, ascetic person) (9.26)

(§4) yaḥ: prayacchati me bhaktyā patram puṣpam phalam toyam aham aśnāmi tat prayatātmanaḥ: bhaktyupahṛtam

(§5) Whoever offers me with devotion - a leaf, a flower, a fruit, (or) water, I accept that, of the ascetic person,[568] offered[569] with devotion. (9.26)

9.27 यत्करोषि यदश्नासि यज्जुहोषि ददासि यत् ।
यत्तपस्यसि कौन्तेय तत्कुरुष्व मदर्पणम् ।।
yatkaroṣi yadaśnāsi yajjuhoṣi dadāsi yat
yattapasyasi kaunteya tatkuruṣva madarpaṇam. (9.27)

(§1) *yat* (r◦ 10/5) *karoṣi* (r◦ 25/4) *yat* (r◦ 8/2) *aśnāsi yat* (r◦ 11/2) *juhoṣi* (r◦ 25/4) *dadāsi yat* (r◦ 23/1) *yat* (r◦ 1/10) *tapasyasi kaunteya tat* (r◦ 10/5) *kuruṣva* (r◦ 25/11) *madarpaṇam* (r◦ 14/2, 24/3)

(§2) *yat* (3.21); *karoṣi* (2nd-per◦ sing◦ pres◦ वर्तमान्-लट् parasmai◦ ←class8◦ √कृ 4.20); *yat* (1.45); *aśnāsi* (2nd-per◦ sing◦ pres◦ वर्तमान्-लट् parasmai◦ ←class9◦ √दा); *yat* (3.21); *juhoṣi* (2nd-per◦ sing◦ pres◦ वर्तमान्-लट् parasmai◦ ←class3◦ √hu 4.26); *dadāsi* (2nd-per◦ sing◦ pres◦ वर्तमान्-लट् parasmai◦ ←class3◦ √दा 2.43); *yat* (↑); *yat* (↑); *tapasyasi* (3rd-per◦ -pre sing◦ ←noun used as root, n◦ *tapas* 4.10); *kaunteya* (2.14); *tat* (2acc◦ 2.7); *kuruṣva* (2nd-per◦ sing◦ imperative◦ लोट् ātmane◦ ←class8◦√कृ); *madarpaṇam* (n◦ 2acc◦ sing◦ ←pron◦ *mat* 1.9 + n◦ *arpaṇa* (an offering) 4.24) (9.27)

(§3) *yat* (adj1◦-obj◦ that which, whatever); *karoṣi* (you do, you perform); *yat* (adj1◦-obj◦ whatever); *aśnāsi* (you eat, consume); *yat* (adj1◦-obj◦ whatever); *juhoṣi* (you offer); *dadāsi* (you give); *yat* (adj1◦-obj◦ whatever); *yat* (adj1◦-obj◦ whatever); *tapasyasi* (you abstain, austerity you perform); *kaunteya* (O Arjuna!); *tat* (adj2◦-obj◦ that); *kuruṣva* (you do, you perform); *madarpaṇam* (adj3◦-obj◦ as an offering to me) (9.27)

(§4) kaunteya yat karoṣi yat aśnāsi yat juhoṣi yat dadāsi yat tapasyasi tat kuruṣva madarpaṇam

(§5) O Arjuna! whatever you do, whatever you consume, whatever you offer, whatever you give,

---

[568] Elsewhere◦ भक्त्युपहृतम् → offering of love, pious offering, ...etc.

📖 In भक्ति-उपहृत, उपहृत is a ppp◦ adjective of that which offered (with devotion).

[569] Elsewhere◦ प्रयतात्मन: → of the pure-hearted man, from pure hearted, of the pure of heart, of the pure in heart, by the pure in heart, by the pure-minded, of the pure minded one, from one in pure consciousness, whose self is pure, disinterested devotee of the sinless mind, ...etc.

📖 In प्र-यत-आत्मन:, यत (auster) is ppp◦ adjective indicating the austere or ascetic character of the devotee.

whatever austerity you perform, that you should do as an offering to me. (9.27)

9.28 शुभाशुभफलैरेवं मोक्ष्यसे कर्मबन्धनैः ।
संन्यासयोगयुक्तात्मा विमुक्तो मामुपैष्यसि ।।
śubhāśubhaphalairevaṁ mokṣyase karmabandhanaiḥ:,
sannyāsayogayuktātmā vimukto māmupaiṣyasi. (9.28)

(§1) *śubhāśubhaphalaiḥ:* (r∘ 16/4) *evaṃ* (r∘ 14/1) *mokṣase karmabandhanaiḥ:* (r∘ 22/8) *sannyāsayogayuktātmā vimuktaḥ:* (r∘ 15/9) *māṃ* (r∘ 8/20) *upaiṣyasi*

(§2) *śubhāśubhaphalaiḥ:* (n∘ 3inst∘ plu∘ ←bahuvrī∘ *śubhāśubha-phala*, शुभम् च अशुभम् च फलानि यस्य ←adj∘ *śubha* (auspicious) 2.57 + adj∘ *aśubha* (unauspicious) 2.57 + n∘ *phala* 2.43); *evaṃ* (1.24); *mokṣase* (4.16); *karmabandhanaiḥ:* (n∘ 3inst∘ ←plu∘ tatpu∘ *karma-bandhana* 3.9); *sannyāsayogayuktātmā* (m∘ 1nom∘ sing∘ ←bahuvrī∘ *sannyāsa-yoga-yuktātmaṇ,* संन्यासेन च योगेन च युक्तः आत्मा यस्य ←m∘ *sannyāsa* (Sankhya) 5.1 + m∘ *yoga* 2.39 + adj∘ *yukta* (equipped) 1.14 + m∘ *ātmaṇ* 2.41); 📖***vimuktaḥ:*** (m∘ 1nom∘ sing∘ ←ppp∘ adj∘ ***vimukta*** (freed) ←वि√मुच्); *māṃ* (1.46); *upaiṣyasi* (2nd-per∘ sing∘ fut2∘ लृट् भविष्य∘ parasmai∘ ←class2∘ उप√इण्) (9.28)

(§3) *śubhāśubhaphalaiḥ:* (by the auspicious as well as unauspicious fruits, by the good or bad results); *evaṃ* (in this manner); *mokṣase* (you will become free); *karmabandhanaiḥ:* (by the bonds of attachment to the objects of karmas); *sannyāsayogayuktātmā* (adj1∘-subj∘ equipped with *sanyāsayoga*); *vimuktaḥ:* (adj2∘-subj∘ released, let go); *māṃ* (obj∘ me); *upaiṣyasi* (you will reach, you will attain) (9.28)

(§4) sannyāsayogayuktātmā vimuktaḥ: karmabandhanaiḥ: śubhāśubhaphalaiḥ: evaṃ mokṣase upaiṣyasi māṃ

(§5) Equipped with *sanyāsayoga* (and) released by[570] the bonds of attachment to the objects of karmas by their auspicious as well as unauspicious fruits, you will become free (and) in this manner you will attain me.[571] (9.28)

---

[570] Elsewhere∘ शुभाशुभफलैः कर्मबन्धनैः विमुक्तः सन्यासयोगयुक्तात्मा (भवान्) → from bondage of..., from the bonds of..., etc.

📖 Things to remember in these words of Lord Krishṇa are : शुभाशुभफलैः and कर्मबन्धनैः are in Instrumental (3rd) case, they are not in Ablative (5th) case, and विमुक्तः-सन्यासयोगयुक्तात्मा-भवान् is in Nominative (1st) case. Therefore, the idea is that, when one is fettered by the bonds of attachments, then he is released by them and he becomes free. The bonds are the subject, doing the act of binding or releasing the person.

[571] Elsewhere∘ विमुक्तः मामुपैष्यसि → thou shalt come unto Me when set free, you will be liberated and come to Me, becoming free you will attain Me, being free, thou shalt become free and attain to Me, ...etc.

9.29 समोऽहं सर्वभूतेषु न मे द्वेष्योऽस्ति न प्रियः ।
ये भजन्ति तु मां भक्त्या मयि ते तेषु चाप्यहम् ।।

samo'haṁ sarvabhūteṣu na me dveṣyo'sti na priyaḥ:,
ye bhajanti tu māṃ bhaktyā mayi te teṣu ćāpyahaṃ. (9.29)

(§1) *samaḥ:* (r◦ 15/1) *ahaṃ* (r◦ 14/1) *sarvabhūteṣu* (r◦ 25/5) *na me dveṣyaḥ:* (r◦ 15/1) *asti na priyaḥ:* (r◦ 22/8) *ye bhajanti tu māṃ* (r◦ 14/1) *bhaktyā mayi te teṣu* (r◦ 25/5) *ća* (r◦ 1/1) *api* (r◦ 4/1) *ahaṃ* (r◦ 14/2)

(§2) *samaḥ:* (2.48); *ahaṃ* (1.22); *sarvabhūteṣu* (3.18); *na* (1.30); *me* (1.21); *dveṣyaḥ:* (m◦ 1nom◦ sing◦ ←adj◦ *dveṣya* 6.9); *asti* (2.40); *na* (1.30); *priyaḥ:* (7.17); *ye* (1.7); *bhajanti* (9.13); *tu* (1.2); *māṃ* (1.46); *bhaktyā* (8.10); *mayi* (3.30); *te* (1.33); *teṣu* (2.62); *ća* (1.1); *api* (1.26); *ahaṃ* (1.22) (9.29)

(§3) *samaḥ:* (adj◦-subj1◦ equanimous); *ahaṃ* (subj1◦ I am); *sarvabhūteṣu* (in all beings); *na* (no one); *me* (my, for me); *dveṣyaḥ:* (adj1◦-subj2◦ disliked); *asti* (there is); *na* (no one); *priyaḥ:* (adj2◦-subj2◦ preferred, liked); *ye* (adj1◦-subj3◦ those who); *bhajanti* (worship); *tu* (but); *māṃ* (obj◦ me); *bhaktyā* (with devotion); *mayi* (are in me); *te* (adj2◦-subj3◦ they); *teṣu* (in them); *ća* (and); *api* (also, and); *ahaṃ* (subj1◦ I am) (9.29)

(§4) ahaṃ samaḥ: sarvabhūteṣu me asti na dveṣyaḥ: ća na priyaḥ: tu ye bhajanti māṃ bhaktyā te mayi api ahaṃ teṣu

(§5) I am equanimous in all beings. For me there is no one disliked and no one is preferred; but those who worship me with devotion, they are in me and I am in them.
(9.29)

9.30 अपि चेत्सुदुराचारो भजते मामनन्यभाक् ।
साधुरेव स मन्तव्यः सम्यग्व्यवसितो हि सः ।।

api ćetsudurāćāro bhajate māmananyabhāk,
sādhureva sa mantavyaḥ: samyagvyavasito hi saḥ:. (9.30)

(§1) *api ćeṭ* (r◦ 10/7) *sudurāćāraḥ:* (r◦ 15/8) *bhajate māṃ* (r◦ 8/16) *ananyabhāk* (r◦ 23/1) *sādhuḥ:* (r◦ 16/3) *eva saḥ:* (r◦ 21/2) *mantavyaḥ:* (r◦ 22/7) *samyak* (r◦ 9/3) *vyavasitāḥ:* (r◦ 15/14) *hi saḥ:* (r◦ 22/8)

(§2) *api* (1.26); *ćeṭ* (2.33); *sudurāćāraḥ:* (m◦ 1nom◦ sing◦ ←bahuvrī◦ *sudurāćāra* (unrighteous person)

📖 विमुक्तः is not a Conditional moon, Gerund or a Future tense. It is the Nominative case ppp◦ adjective of the Nominative case subject योगयुक्तात्मा भवान् (माम् एवम् उपैष्यसि) ।

दुराचारेण सह यः ←adj∘ *saha* (with) 1.22 + ind∘ *dur̩* (bad) 1.2 + m∘ *āćāra* (behaviour) 3.6); *bhajate* (6.47); *mām̩* (1.46); *ananyabhāk̩* (1nom∘ sing∘ ←adj∘ *ananya-bhāj* (one pointed faith) ←adj∘ *ananya* (one pointed) 8.14 + m∘ *bhājaka* (worshipper) ←√भाज्); *sādhuḥ:* (1nom∘ sing∘ ←m∘ *sādhu* (righteous person) 4.8); *eva* (1.1); *saḥ:* (1.13); *mantavyaḥ:* (m∘ 1nom∘ sing∘ ←pot∘ adj∘ *manitavya* or *mantavya* (ought to be known) ←√मन्); *samyak̩* (proper, 5.4); *vyavasitāḥ:* (m∘ 1nom∘ sing∘ ←adj∘ *vyavasita* (resolved, of resolve) 1.45); *hi* (1.11); *saḥ:* (1.13) (9.30)

(§3) *api ćet̩* (even if); *sudurāćāraḥ:* (adj1∘-subj∘ an undeviated person); *bhajate* (worships); *mām̩* (obj∘ me); *ananyabhāk̩* (adj2∘-subj∘ of one pointed faith); *sādhuḥ:* (adj1∘-obj∘ righteous); *eva* (only); *saḥ:* (adj2∘-obj∘ he); *mantavyaḥ:* (adj3∘-obj∘ ought to be considered); *samyak̩* (adv∘ rightly); *vyavasitāḥ:* (adj4∘-obj∘ resolved); *hi* (because); *saḥ:* (adj2∘-obj∘ he) (9.30)

(§4) api ćet̩ sudurāćāraḥ: ananyabhāk̩ bhajate mām̩ saḥ: mantavyaḥ: sādhuḥ: eva hi saḥ: samyak̩ vyavasitāḥ:

(§5) Even if an undeviated person of one pointed faith[572] worships me, he ought to be considered righteous only, because[573] he (is) rightly resolved. (9.30)

9.31 क्षिप्रं भवति धर्मात्मा शश्वच्छान्तिं निगच्छति ।
कौन्तेय प्रतिजानीहि न मे भक्तः प्रणश्यति ।।

kṣipram̐ bhavati dharmātmā śaśvaććhāntim̐ nigaććhati,
kaunteya pratijānīhi na me bhaktaḥ: praṇaśyati. (9.31)

(§1) *kṣipram̩* (r∘ 14/1) *bhavati dharmātmā śaśvat̩* (r∘ 11/4) *śāntim̩* (r∘ 14/1) *nigaććhati kaunteya pratijānīhi na me bhaktaḥ:* (r∘ 22/3) *praṇaśyati*

(§2) *kṣipram̩* (4.12); *bhavati* (1.44); 📖*dharmātmā* (m∘ 1nom∘ sing∘ ←bahuvrī∘ *dharmātman̩* (righteous) धर्मे आत्मा यस्य ←m∘ *dharma* (righteousness) 1.1 + m∘ *ātman̩* (person) 2.41); *śaśvat̩* (ind∘ ←√शश्); *śāntim̩* (2.70); ***nigaććhati*** (3rd-per∘ sing∘ pres∘ वर्तमान्–लट् parasmai∘ ←class1∘ नि√गम् 2.51); *kaunteya* (2.14); *pratijānīhi* (2nd-per∘ sing∘ imperative∘ लोट् parasmai∘ ←class9∘ प्रति√ज्ञा); *na* (1.30); *me* (1.21); *bhaktaḥ:* (4.3); 📖*praṇaśyati* (2.63) (9.31)

---

[572] Elsewhere∘ अनन्यभाक् → with one-pointed devotion, with undivided devotion, if he is engaged in devotional service, with undivided heart, with exclusive devotion, to the exclusion of anybody elas, with undistracted devotion, with undeviated devotion, and none else, resorting to none else, ...etc.

📖 अनन्यभाक् is in Instrumental (3rd) case (अनन्यभाजा), it is not an adverb or gerund. अनन्यभाक् is m∘ Nominative (1st) case of adjective अनन्यभाज् (he who is of one-pointed faith) qualifying the Nominative subject सः । In this verse सम्यक् is the adverb that qualifyies the ppp∘ adjective व्यवसितः सः ।

[573] See footnote in verse 3.5

(§3) *kṣipram* (quickly, soon); *bhavati* (he becomes); *dharmātmā* (adj∘-subj∘ a righteous person); *śaśvat* (adv∘ for ever, always); *śāntim* (obj∘ peace, tranquility); *nigacchati* (he attains); *kaunteya* (O Arjuna); *pratijānīhi* (you please know it, be aware!); *na* (does not); *me* (my); *bhaktaḥ:* (subj∘ devotee); *praṇaśyati* (perish, perishes) (9.31)

(§4) kṣipram bhavati dharmātmā śaśvat nigacchati śāntim kaunteya pratijānīhi me bhaktaḥ: na praṇaśyati

(§5) Soon he becomes a righteous person. He attains tranquility for ever.[574] O Arjuna! be aware, my devotee does not perish. (9.31)

9.32 मां हि पार्थ व्यपाश्रित्य येऽपि स्युः पापयोनयः ।
स्त्रियो वैश्यास्तथा शूद्रास्तेऽपि यान्ति परां गतिम् ।।
mām hi pārtha vyapāśritya ye'pi syuḥ: pāpayonayaḥ:,
striyo vaiśyāstathā śūdrāstepi yānti parām gatim; (9.32)

(§1) *mām* (r∘ 14/1) *hi pārtha vyapāśritya ye* (r∘ 6/1) *api syuḥ:* (r∘ 22/3) *pāpayonayaḥ:* (r∘ 22/8) *striyaḥ:* (r∘ 15/13) *vaiśyāḥ:* (r∘ 18/1) *tathā śūdrāḥ:* (r∘ 18/1) *te* (r∘ 6/1) *api yānti parām* (r∘ 14/1) *gatim* (r∘ 14/2);

(§2) *mām* (1.46); *hi* (1.11); *pārtha* (1.25); *vyapāśritya* (lyp∘ past-participle ind∘ ←वि–अप–आ√श्रि); *ye* (1.7); *api* (1.26); *syuḥ:* (3rd-per∘ plu∘ potential∘ विधि∘ parasmai∘ ←class2∘ √अस्); 📖*pāpayonayaḥ:* (m∘ 1nom∘ plu∘ ←bahuvrī∘ *pāpa-yoni*, पापिनी योनिः यस्य ←adj∘ *pāpin* (sinful) 4.36 + f∘ *yoni* (womb) 5.22); *striyaḥ:* (1nom∘ plu∘ ←f∘ *strī* (woman) 1.41); *vaiśyāḥ:* (1nom∘ plu∘ ←m∘ ***vaiśya*** (treader) ←√विश्); *tathā* (1.8); *śūdrāḥ:* (1nom∘ plu∘ ←m∘ ***śūdra*** (worker) ←√शुच्); *te* (1.33); *api* (1.26); *yānti* (3.33); *parām* (4.39); *gatim* (6.37); (9.32)

(§3) *mām* (obj∘ me); *hi* (because); *pārtha* (O Arjuna!); *vyapāśritya* (taking for refuge, protection); *ye* (adj1∘-subj1-4∘ those people); *api* (even); *syuḥ:* (should they be); *pāpayonayaḥ:* (adj∘-subj1∘ those of low origin,); *striyaḥ:* (subj2∘ the women); *vaiśyāḥ:* (subj3∘ the members of the business class); *tathā* (as well as); *śūdrāḥ:* (subj4∘ the members of the service class); *te* (adj2∘-subj1-4∘ they); *api* (also); *yānti* (attain);

---

[574] Elsewhere∘ शश्वत् शान्तिम् निगच्छति →he attains everlasting peace, attains lasting peace, goeth to eternal peace, ...etc.

📖 शश्वत् being an indeclinable qualifier, preferably it should be treated as an adverb, even though in a poetic compound (सामासिक) construction use as an adjective is permitted. Therefore, for a prose translation, शन्तिं शश्वत् निगच्छति, शाश्वति शान्तिं निगच्छति, शाश्वतिकी शान्तिम् should be preferred over शाँत् शान्तिं निगच्छति ।

parām̧ (supreme); *gatim̧* (state); (9.32)

(§4) hi pārtha api (even); ye syuḥ: pāpayonayaḥ: striyaḥ: vaiśyāḥ: tathā śūdrāḥ: te api yānti parām̧ gatim̧ mām̧ vyapāśritya

(§5) Because,[575] O Arjuna! even those people, should they be - (i) of low origin, (ii) women, (iii) the members of the business class as well as (iv) the members of the service class,[576] - they also attain supreme state, taking me for refuge; (9.32)

9.33 किं पुनर्ब्राह्मणाः पुण्या भक्ता राजर्षयस्तथा ।
अनित्यमसुखं लोकमिमं प्राप्य भजस्व माम् ।।

kiṁ punarbrāhmaṇāḥ: puṇyā bhaktā rājarṣayastathā,
anityamasukhaṁ lokamimaṁ prāpya bhajasva mām̧. (9.33)

(§1) *kim̧* (r◦ 14/1) *punarbrāhmaṇāḥ:* (r◦ 24/5, 22/3) *puṇyāḥ:* (r◦ 20/12) *bhaktāḥ:* (r◦ 20/15) *rājarṣayaḥ:* (r◦ 18/1) *tathā* (r◦ 23/1) *anityam̧* (r◦ 8/16) *asukham̧* (r◦ 14/1) *lokam̧* (r◦ 8/18) *imam̧* (r◦ 14/1) *prāpya bhajasva mām̧* (r◦ 14/2)

(§2) *kim̧* (1.1); *punaŗ* (4.9); ***brāhmaṇāḥ:*** (m◦ 1nom◦ plu◦ ←adj◦ *brāhmaṇa* 2.46); *puṇyāḥ:* (m◦ 1nom◦ plu◦ ←adj◦ *puṇya* (pious) 6.41); ***bhaktāḥ:*** (1nom◦ plu◦ ←m◦ *bhakta* (devotee) 4.3); *rājarṣayaḥ:* (4.2); *tathā* (1.8); *anityam̧* (m◦ 2acc◦ sing◦ ←n.tatpu◦ *anitya* (transient) 2.14 ←adj◦ *nitya* (permanent) 2.18); *asukham̧* (m◦ 2acc◦ sing◦ ←n.tatpu◦ *asukha* (sorrowful) ←adj◦ *sukha* (happiness) 1.32); ***lokam̧*** (2acc◦ sing◦ ←m◦ *loka* (world) 2.5); *imam̧* (1.28); *prāpya* (2.57); *bhajasva* (2nd-per◦ sing◦ imperative◦ लोट् parasmai◦ ←class1◦ √भज् 4.11); *mām* (1.46) (9.33)

(§3) *kim̧ punaŗ* (then what, so do); *brāhmaṇāḥ:* (adj5◦-subj◦ the members of the *brahmaṇa* class); *puṇyāḥ:* (adj6◦-subj◦ the pious people); *bhaktāḥ:* (adj7◦-subj◦ the devoted people); *rājarṣayaḥ:* (adj8◦-subj◦ the great sages); *tathā* (as well as); *anityam̧* (adj1◦-obj1◦ transient, temporary); *asukham̧* (adj2◦-obj1◦ sorrowful, difficult); *lokam̧* (obj1◦ world); *imam̧* (adj3◦-obj1◦ this); *prāpya* (having acquired);

---

[575] See footnote in verse 3.5

[576] Elsewhere◦ स्यु: पापयोनय: स्त्रिय: वैश्या: तथा शूद्रा: ते अपि → even those who are born of sin - women, Vaiśyas, as also Sūdras - even they ...etc.

📖 Remember that स्त्रिय:, वैश्या:, and शूद्रा: are not the three adjectives of पापयोनय: । The पापयोनय:, स्त्रिय:, वैश्या: and शूद्रा: (along with the other four people ब्राह्मणा:, पुण्या:, भक्ता: and राजर्षय: mentioned in the next verse) are the four (six) adjectives of the subject ये । There is a fundamental difference in these two constructions, that can be understood only by those who understand the scriptures properly.

bhajasva (please worship, please serve); *mām* (obj2◦ me) (9.33)

(§4) kiṃ punaṛ brāhmaṇāḥ: puṇyāḥ: bhaktāḥ: tathā rājarṣayaḥ: prāpya imaṃ anityaṃ asukhaṃ lokaṃ bhajasva mām

(§5) So do (v) the members of the *brahmaṇa* class, (vi) the pious people, (vii) the devoted people, as well as (viii) the great sages? Having acquired this transient (and) sorrowful world, you should serve me. (9.33)

9.34 मन्मना भव मद्भक्तो मद्याजी मां नमस्कुरु ।
मामेवैष्यसि युक्त्वैवमात्मानं मत्परायणः ।।

manmanā bhava madbhakto madyājī māṃ namaskuru,
māmevaiṣyasi yuktvaivamātmānaṁ matparāyaṇaḥ:. (9.34)

(§1) *manmanāḥ:* (r◦ 20/12) *bhava madbhaktaḥ:* (r◦ 15/9) *madyājī māṃ* (r◦ 14/1) *namaskuru māṃ* (r◦ 8/22) *eva* (r◦ 3/1) *eṣyasi yuktvā* (r◦ 3/3) *evaṃ* (r◦ 8/17) *ātmānaṃ* (r◦ 14/1) *matparāyaṇaḥ:* (r◦ 22/8)

(§2) ***manmanāḥ:*** (m◦ 1nom◦ sing◦ ←bahuvrī◦ *manmanaṣ* (devoted to me) मयि मनः यस्य ←pron◦ *mat* (me) 1.9 + m◦ *manaṣ* (mind) 1.30); *bhava* (2.45); ***madbhaktaḥ:*** (m◦ 1nom◦ sing◦ ←tatpu◦ *madbhakta* (my devotee) 7.23); ***madyājī*** (m◦ 1nom◦ sing◦ ←adj◦ *madyājiṇ* (my worshipper) 9.25); *māṃ* (1.46); **namaskuru** (2nd-per◦ sing◦ imperative◦ लोट् parasmai◦ ←class8◦ √कृ); *māṃ* (1.46); *eva* (1.1); *eṣyasi* (8.7); *yuktvā* (ipp◦ ind◦ ←√युज्); *evaṃ* (1.24); *ātmānaṃ* (3.43); *matparāyaṇaḥ:* (m◦ 1nom◦ sing◦ ←bahuvrī◦ *mat-parāyaṇa*, मयि परायणः यः ←pron◦ *mat* (me) 1.9 + adj◦ *parāyaṇa* (of supreme aim) 4.29) (9.34)

(§3) *manmanāḥ:* (adj1◦-subj◦ the one whose mind is engrossed in me); *bhava* (you be, you should become); *madbhaktaḥ:* (adj2◦-subj◦ one who is devoted to me); *madyājī* (adj3◦-subj◦ one who worships me); *māṃ* (obj1◦ me); *namaskuru* (you pay respect to); *māṃ* (obj1◦ me); *eva* (only); *eṣyasi* (you will attain); *yuktvā* (having equipped); *evaṃ* (in this manner); *ātmānaṃ* (yourself); *matparāyaṇaḥ:* (adj4◦-subj◦ one for whom I am the supreme goal) (9.34)

(§4) bhava manmanāḥ: madbhaktaḥ: madyājī matparāyaṇaḥ: namaskuru māṃ eva yuktvā ātmānaṃ evaṃ eṣyasi māṃ

(§5) You should become the one whose mind is engrossed in me, one who is devoted to me, one who worships me, one for whom I am the supreme goal,[577] (and) you should pay respect to me

---

[577] Elsewhere◦ मत्परायणः → taking Me as the Supreme Goal, having me as supreme goal, having Me for the supreme goal, having Me as thy supreme goal, entirely depending on Me, accepting Me as the supreme Goal,

only. Having equipped yourself in this manner, you will attain me.

इति श्रीमद्भगवद्गीतासूपनिषत्सु ब्रह्मविद्यायां योगशास्त्रे
श्रीकृष्णार्जुनसंवादे राजविद्याराजगुह्ययोगो नाम नवमोऽध्याय: ।।

iti śrīmadbhagavadgītāsūpaniṣatsu brahmavidyāyāṁ yogaśāstre
śrīkṛṣṇārjunasaṁvāde rājavidyārājaguhyayogo nāma navamo'dhyāyaḥ:

(§1) *iti śrīmadbhagavadgītāsu* (r∘ 1/8) *upaniṣatsu brahmavidyāyāṃ* (r∘ 14/1) *yogaśāstre śrī-kṛṣṇārjunasaṁvāde rājavidyārājaguhyayogaḥ:* (r∘ 15/6) *nāma navamaḥ:* (r∘ 15/1) *adhyāyaḥ:* (r∘ 22/8)

(§2) *iti* (1.25); *śrīmadbhagavadgītāsu* (f∘ 7loc∘ plu∘ tatpu∘ *śrīmad-bhagavad-gītā* ←adj∘ *śrīmaṭ* 6.41 + adj∘ *bhagavaṭ* 10.14 + f∘ *gītā* ←5∘√गै); *upaniṣatsu* (7loc∘ plu∘ ←f∘ *upaniṣaḍ* ←6∘उप-नि√सद्); *brahmavidyāyāṃ* (f∘ 7loc∘ sing∘ ←tatpu∘ *brahma-vidyā*, ब्रह्मण: विद्या ←n∘ *brahmaṇ* 2.72 + *vidyā* 5.18); *yogaśāstre* (n∘ 7loc∘ sing∘ ←tatpu∘ *yoga-śāstra*, योगानाम् शास्त्रम् । योगस्य शास्त्रम् । ←m∘ *yoga* 2.39 + n∘ *śāstra* 15.20); *śrīkṛṣṇārjunasaṁvāde* (m∘ 7loc∘ sing∘ ←tatpu∘ *śrī-kṛṣṇārjuna-saṁvāda*, श्रीकृष्णस्य च अर्जुनस्य च संवाद: ←adj∘ *śrī* 10.34 + m∘ prop∘ *kṛṣṇa* 1.28 + m∘ prop∘ *arjuna* 1.4 + m∘ *saṁvāda* 18.70); *rājavidyārājaguhyayogaḥ:* (m∘ 1nom∘ sing∘ ←tatpu∘ *rājavidyārājaguhyayoga* राजविद्याया: च राजगुह्यस्य च योग: ←f∘ *rāja-vidyā* 9.2 + n∘ *rāja-guhya* 9.2 + m∘ *yoga* 2.39); *nāma* (1nom∘ sing∘ ←n∘ *nāmaṇ* ←1∘√म्ना); *navamaḥ:* (m∘ 1nom∘ sing∘ ←num∘ adj∘ *nava* 5.13); *adhyāyaḥ:* (1nom∘ sing∘ ←m∘ *adhyāya* ←1∘अधि√इ)

(§3) *iti* (thus); *śrīmadbhagavadgītāsu upaniṣatsu* (among the upaniṣads of the Śrīmad-Bhagavadgītā); *brahmavidyāyāṃ* (of the eternal wisdoms); *yogaśāstre* (in the science of Yoga); *śrīkṛṣṇārjunasaṁvāde* (in the dialogue between Śrī Kṛṣṇa and Arjuna); (adj1∘-subj∘ (called akṣarabrahmayoga); *nāma* (called); *aṣṭamaḥ:* (adj2∘-subj∘ the ninth); *adhyāyaḥ:* (subj∘ discourse)

(§4) śrīmadbhagavadgītāsu upaniṣatsu yogaśāstre brahmavidyāyāṃ iti navamaḥ: adhyāyaḥ: nāma rājavidyārājaguhyayogaḥ: śrīkṛṣṇārjunasaṁvāde

(§5) Among the upaniṣads of the *Śrīmad-Bhagavadgītā*, in the science of yoga of self realization, thus (is) the ninth discourse called rāja-vidyā-rāja-guhya-yogaḥ:, in the dialogue between Śrī Kṛṣṇa and Arjuna.

---

surrendered yourself to Me, with me as thy goal, with Me as thy Supreme Goal, with Me as supreme aim, ...etc.

📖 मत्परायण: is not a gerund, or Instrumental. मत्परायण: is one of the four Nominative (1st) case m∘ adjectives of the Subject त्वम्, other three being मन्मना:, मद्भक्त: and मद्याजी ।

CHAPTER 10

daśamao'dhyāyaḥ:
दशमोऽध्याय: ।

vibhūtiyogaḥ:
विभूतियोग: ।

THE YOGA OF DIVINE PERSONOFICATION

The Lord said (śrībhagavānuvāća श्रीभगवानुवाच ।)

10.1 भूय एव महाबाहो शृणु मे परमं वच: ।
यत्तेऽहं प्रीयमाणाय वक्ष्यामि हितकाम्यया ।।

bhūya eva mahābāho śṛṇu me paramaṁ vaćaḥ:,
yatte'haṁ prīyamāṇāya vakṣāmi hitakāmyayā. (10.1)

(§1) *daśamaḥ:* (rule◦ 15/1) *adhyāyaḥ:* (r◦ 22/8). *vibhūtiyogaḥ:* (r◦ 22/8). *śrībhagavān* (r◦ 8/14) *uvāća. bhūyaḥ:* (r◦ 19/7) *eva mahābāho śṛṇu me paramaṃ* (r◦ 14/1) *vaćaḥ:* (r◦ 22/8) *yaṭ* (r◦ 1/10) *te* (r◦ 6/1) *ahaṃ* (r◦ 14/1) *prīyamāṇāya vakṣyāmi hitakāmyayā*

(§2) *daśamaḥ:* (m◦ 1nom◦ sing◦ ←sequence indicating num◦ adj◦ *daśama* ←adj◦ *daśaṇ* 11.27 ↓); *adhyāyaḥ:* (1nom◦ sing◦ ←m◦ *adhyāya* ←अधि√इ). *vibhūtiyogaḥ:* (m◦ 1nom◦ sing◦ ←tatpu◦ *vibhūti-yoga*, भगवत: विभूतीनाम् योग: ←f◦ *vibhūti* 10.7 + m◦ *yoga* 2.39). *śrībhagavāṇ* (2.2); *uvāća* (1.25).

bhūyaḥ: (2.20); *eva* (1.1); *mahābāho* (2.26); *śṛṇu* (2.39); *me* (1.21); *paramaṃ* (8.8); *vaćaḥ:* (2.10); *yaṭ* (3.21); *te* (1.7); *ahaṃ* (1.22); *prīyamāṇāya* (m◦ 4dat◦ sing◦ ←śānać◦ adj◦ *prīyamāṇa* (beloved) ←√प्रि); *vakṣyāmi* (7.2); *hitakāmyayā* (3inst◦ sing◦ ←f◦ tatpu◦ *hita-kāmyā*, हितस्य काम्या ←adj◦ *hita* (benefut) 5.25 + adj◦ ***kāmya*** (desirous) ←√कम्) (10.1)

(§3) *daśamaḥ:* (adj◦-subj◦ the tenth); *adhyāyaḥ:* (subj◦ chapter). *vibhūtiyogaḥ:* (vibhūtiyoga). *śrībhagavāṇ* (subj◦ the Lord); *uvāća* (said). *bhūyaḥ: eva* (once again); *mahābāho* (O Arjuna!); *śṛṇu* (please listen); *me* (my); *paramaṃ* (adj1◦-obj◦ supreme); *vaćaḥ:* (obj◦ saying, word); *yaṭ* (adj2◦-obj◦ which); *te* (for you, you); *ahaṃ* (subj◦ I); *prīyamāṇāya* (to the loving, to the beloved); *vakṣyāmi* (I shall tell); *hitakāmyayā* (with the desire of your wellbeing) (10.1)

(§4) daśamaḥ: adhyāyaḥ:. vibhūtiyogaḥ: śrībhagavāṇ uvāća. mahābāho bhūyaḥ: eva śṛṇu me paramaṃ vaćaḥ: yaṭ ahaṃ vakṣyāmi prīyamāṇāya te hitakāmyayā .

(§5) The tenth chapter. vibhūtiyoga. The Lord said : O Arjuna! once again please listen my supreme saying, which I shall tell to the beloved you, with the desire of your wellbeing. (10.1)

10.2 न मे विदुः सुरगणाः प्रभवं न महर्षयः ।
अहमादिर्हि देवानां महर्षीणां च सर्वशः ।।

na me viduḥ: suragaṇāḥ: prabhavaṁ na maharṣayaḥ:,
ahamādirhi devānāṁ maharṣiṇāṁ ća sarvaśaḥ:. (10.2)

(§1) *na me viduḥ:* (r◦ 22/7) *suragaṇāḥ:* (r◦ 24/5, 22/3) *prabhavaṃ* (r◦ 14/1) *na maharṣayaḥ:* (r◦ 22/8) *ahaṃ* (r◦ 8/17) *ādiḥ:* (r◦ 16/6) *hi devānāṃ* (r◦ 14/1) *maharṣiṇāṃ* (r◦ 24/6, 14/1) *ća sarvaśaḥ:* (r◦ 22/8)

(§2) *na* (1.30); *me* (2.7); *viduḥ:* (4.2); *suragaṇāḥ:* (m◦ 1nom◦ plu◦ ←tatpu◦ *sura-gaṇa,* सुराणाम् गणः ←m◦ *sura* (god) 2.8 + m◦ *gaṇa* (class) 7.7); 📖*prabhavaṃ* (2acc◦ sing◦ ←m◦ *prabhava* (origin) 6.24); *na* (1.30); ***maharṣayaḥ:*** (m◦ 1nom◦ plu◦ ←s-karm◦ ***maharṣi,*** महान् ऋषिः ←adj◦ *mahā* (great) 1.3 + m◦ *ṛṣi* (sage) 4.2); *ahaṃ* (1.22); ***ādiḥ:*** (m◦ 1nom◦ sing◦ ←adj◦ *ādi* (begining) 2.28); *hi* (1.11); ***devānāṃ*** (6pos plu◦ ←m◦ *deva* (god) 3.11); ***maharṣiṇāṃ*** (6pos plu◦ ←m◦ *maharṣi* ↑); *ća* (1.1); *sarvaśaḥ:* (1.18) (10.2)

(§3) *na* (neither); *me* (my); *viduḥ:* (understand, know); *suragaṇāḥ:* (subj1◦ the gods); *prabhavaṃ* (obj◦ origin); *na* (nor); *maharṣayaḥ:* (subj2◦ the sages, the great sages); *ahaṃ* (subj3◦ I am); *ādiḥ:* (the begining, source); *hi* (because); *devānāṃ* (of the gods); *maharṣiṇāṃ* (of the great sages); *ća* (as well as); *sarvaśaḥ:* (in everywhich way) (10.2)

(§4) na suragaṇāḥ: na maharṣayaḥ: viduḥ: me prabhavaṃ hi sarvaśaḥ: ādiḥ: devānāṃ ća maharṣiṇāṃ

(§5) Neither the gods nor the sages know my origin. Because I am, in everywhich way, the source of the gods as well as of the sages. (10.2)

10.3 यो मामजमनादिं च वेत्ति लोकमहेश्वरम् ।
असम्मूढः स मर्त्येषु सर्वपापैः प्रमुच्यते ।।

yo māmajamanādiṁ ća vetti lokamaheśvaraṃ,
asammūḍhaḥ: sa martyeṣu sarvapāpaiḥ: pramuććyate. (10.3)

(§1) *yaḥ:* (r◦ 15/9) *māṃ* (r◦ 8/16) *ajaṃ* (r◦ 8/16) *anādiṃ* (r◦ 14/1) *ća vetti lokamaheśvaraṃ* (r◦ 14/2) *asammūḍhaḥ:* (r◦ 22/7) *saḥ:* (r◦ 21/2) *martyeṣu* (r◦ 22/7, 25/5) *sarvapāpaiḥ:* (r◦ 22/3) *pramućyate*

(§2) *yaḥ:* (2.19); *māṃ* (1.46); *ajaṃ* (2acc◦ 2.21); *anādiṃ* (m◦ 2acc◦ sing◦ ←n.bahuvrī◦ adj◦ ***anādi*** (beginingless) ←अन्-आ√दा); *ća (1.1); vetti* (2.19); *lokamaheśvaraṃ* (m◦ 2acc◦ sing◦ ←tatpu◦ *loka-maheśvara,* लोकस्य महान् ईश्वरः ←m◦ *loka* (beings) 2.5 + adj◦ *mahā* (great) 1.3 + m◦ *īśvara* (lord) 4.6); *asammūḍhaḥ:* (5.20); *saḥ:* (1.13); *martyeṣu* (7loc◦ plu◦ ←adj◦ *martya* (mortal) 9.21); *sarvapāpaiḥ:* (tatpu◦ सर्वैः पापैः m◦ 3inst◦

plu∘ ←pron∘ *sarva* (all) 1.6 + m∘ *pāpa* (sin) 1.36); *pramućyate* (5.3) (10.3)

(§3) *yaḥ:* (subj∘ he who); *mām̩* (obj∘ me); *ajam̩* (adj1∘-obj∘ the birthless); *anādim̩* (adj2∘-obj∘ the beginningless); *ća* (1.1); *vetti* (knows); *lokamahesvaram̩* (adj∘-obj∘ the great Lord of the beings); 🕮*asammūḍhaḥ:* (adj1∘-subj∘ non-deluded); *saḥ:* (adj2∘-subj∘ he, that person); *martyeṣu* (among the mortals); *sarvapāpaiḥ:* (from all his sins); *pramućyate* (he becomes free) (10.3)

(§4) yaḥ: vetti mām̩ ajam̩ anādim̩ ća lokamahesvaram̩ saḥ: asammūḍhaḥ: martyeṣu pramućyate sarvapāpaiḥ:

(§5) He who knows me[578] - the birthless[579] *anādim̩* the beginningless and the great Lord of the beings - that non-deluded person among the mortals, becomes free from all his sins. (10.3)

10.4 बुद्धिर्ज्ञानमसम्मोहः क्षमा सत्यं दमः शमः ।
सुखं दुःखं भवोऽभावो भयं चाभयमेव च ।।

buddhirjñānamasammohaḥ: kṣamā satyaṁ damaḥ: śamaḥ:,
sukhaṁ duḥ:khaṁ bhavo'bhāvo bhayaṁ ćābhayameva ća; (10.4)

(§1) *buddhiḥ:* (r∘ 16/6) *jñānam̩* (r∘ 8/16) *asammohaḥ:* (r∘ 22/1) *kṣamā satyam̩* (r∘ 14/1) *damaḥ:* (r∘ 22/5) *śamaḥ:* (r∘ 22/8) *sukham̩* (r∘ 14/1) *duḥ:kham̩* (r∘ 14/1) *bhavaḥ:* (r∘ 15/1) *abhāvaḥ:* (r∘ 15/8) *bhayam̩* (r∘ 14/1) *ća* (r∘ 1/1) *abhayam̩* (r∘ 8/22) *eva ća;*

(§2) *buddhiḥ:* (2.39); *jñānam̩* (3.39); 🕮*asammohaḥ:* (1nom∘ sing∘ n.tatpu∘ ←m∘ *sammoha* (delusion) 2.63); 🕮***kṣamā*** (1nom∘ sing∘ ←f∘ ***kṣamā*** (forgiveness) ←√क्षम्); 🕮***satyam̩*** (1nom∘ sing∘ ←n∘ or adj∘ ***satya*** (truth) ←adj∘ *sat̩* 2.16); 🕮***damaḥ:*** (1nom∘ sing∘ ←m∘ *dama* (control) ←√दम्); *śamaḥ:* (6.3); 🕮*sukham̩* (2.66);

---

[578] Elsewhere∘ यो माम् अजम् अनादिं च वेत्ति लोकमहेँरम् → He who knows Me as unborn and beginningless, as the Great Lord of the worlds; He who knows Me as unborn, as beginningless, as the Supreme God of all the worlds; He who knows Me as birthless and without beginning, and as the Great Lord of the Universe; ...etc.

🕮 **The difference is this :** If you say "he who kmows me as unborn, beginningless and great lord," you have to know that Lord has these three attribute to be free from sins; whereas if you say "he who knows Me--the unborn, beginningless and great lord--" it means that to be free from sins you have to fully know that Lord, whose three attributes are given here."

[579] Elsewhere∘ *ajaḥ:* → unborn.

🕮 Adjective 'unborn' is attached to one that is yet to be born, not yet born or not born (eg. an unborn child). Adjective अज is attached to the one that is born, but not from a womb or not by a normal birth process. Originally this word was coined to describe Brahmā, who was born, not to Mahālakṣmi's womb, but to Mahāviṣṇu, the *puruṣa*, through his navel. So, Brahmā ब्रह्मा (the personified or manifest Brahma ब्रह्म), born from Viṣṇu, is अजः । (see footnote in 2.20)

duḥ:khaṃ (1nom∘ sing∘ ←n∘ *duḥkha* (sorrow) 2.14); *bhavḥ:* (1nom∘ sing∘ ←m∘ ***bhava*** (evolution) ←√भू); *abhāvaḥ:* (2.16); ***bhayaṃ*** (1nom∘ 2acc∘ sing∘ ←n∘ *bhaya* (fear) 2.35); *ća* (1.1); ***abhayaṃ*** (fearlessness) (1nom∘ 2acc∘ sing∘ n.tatpu∘ ←n∘ *bhaya* (fear) 2.35); *eva* (1.1); *ća* (1.1); (10.4)

(§3) *buddhiḥ:* (subj1∘ thinking); *jñānaṃ* (subj2∘ knowledge); *asammohaḥ:* (subj3∘ non-delusion); *kṣamā* (subj4∘ forgiveness, forberance); *satyaṃ* (subj5∘ truth); *damaḥ:* (subj6∘ self control); *śamaḥ:* (subj6∘ calmness); *sukhaṃ* (subj7∘ happiness); *duḥ:khaṃ* (subj8∘ sorrow); *bhavḥ:* (subj9∘ evolution, birth); *abhāvaḥ:* (subj10∘ dissolution, death); *bhayaṃ* (subj11∘ fear); *ća* (and); *abhayaṃ* (subj12∘ fearlessness); *eva ća* (as well as); (10.4)

(§4) buddhiḥ: jñānaṃ asammohaḥ: kṣamā satyaṃ damaḥ: śamaḥ: sukhaṃ duḥ:khaṃ bhavḥ: abhāvaḥ: bhayaṃ ća abhayaṃ eva ća

(§5) Thinking, knowledge, non-delusion, forberance, truth, self control, calmness, happiness, sorrow, evolution and dissolution, fear as well as fearlessness; (10.4)

10.5 अहिंसा समता तुष्टिस्तपो दानं यशोऽयशः ।
भवन्ति भावा भूतानां मत्त एव पृथग्विधाः ।।
ahimsā samatā tuṣṭistapo dānaṁ yaśo‘yaśaḥ:,
bhavanti bhāvā bhūtānāṁ matta eva pṛthagvidhāḥ:. (10.5)

(§1) *ahimsā samatā tuṣṭiḥ:* (r∘ 18/1) *tapaḥ:* (r∘ 15/4) *dānaṃ* (r∘ 14/1) *yaśaḥ:* (r∘ 15/1) *ayaśaḥ:* (r∘ 22/8) *bhavanti bhāvāḥ:* (r∘ 20/12) *bhūtānāṃ* (r∘ 14/1) *mattaḥ:* (r∘ 19/7) *eva pṛthagvidhāḥ:* (r∘ 22/8)

(§2) ***ahimsā*** (non-violence) (1nom∘ sing∘ n.tatpu∘ ←f∘ ***himsā*** (violence) ←√हिंस्); *samatā* (1nom∘ sing∘ ←f∘ *samatā* (equanimity) ←adj∘ *sama* (equal) 1.4); *tuṣṭiḥ:* (1nom∘ sing∘ ←f∘ *tuṣṭi* (satisfaction) ←adj∘ *tuṣṭa* (satisfied) 2.55); *tapaḥ:* (7.9); **dānaṃ** (1nom∘ sing∘ ←n∘ *dāna* (charity) 8.28); ***yaśaḥ:*** (1nom∘ sing∘ ←n∘ ***yaśaṣ*** (success) ←√अस्); *ayaśaḥ:* (disappointment) (1nom∘ sing∘ n.tatpu∘ ←n∘ *yaśaṣ* ↑); *bhavanti* (3.14); *bhāvāḥ:* (7.12); *bhūtānāṃ* (2.69); *mattaḥ:* (same as ablative case *maṭ* 7.7); *eva* (1.1); *pṛthagvidhāḥ:* (m∘ 1nom∘ plu∘ ←bahuvrī∘ adj∘ ***pṛthagvidha*** (various) पृथक् विधाः यस्य ←ind∘ *pṛthak* (various) 1.18 + m∘ *vidha* (way) 3.3) (10.5)

(§3) *ahimsā* (subj13∘ non-violence); *samatā* (subj14∘ equanimity); *tuṣṭiḥ:* (aubj15∘ satisfaction, contentment); *tapaḥ:* (subj16∘ austerity); *dānaṃ* (subj17∘ charity); *yaśaḥ:* (subj18∘ achievement); *ayaśaḥ:* (subj19∘ disappointment); *bhavanti* (they become, spring, arise); *bhāvāḥ:* (subj20∘ dispositions); *bhūtānāṃ* (of the beings); *mattaḥ:* (from me); *eva* (only); *pṛthagvidhāḥ:* (adj∘-subj20∘ various) (10.5)

(§4) ahimsā samatā tuṣṭiḥ: tapaḥ: dānaṃ yaśaḥ: ayaśaḥ: pṛthagvidhāḥ: bhāvāḥ: bhūtānāṃ bhavanti mattaḥ: eva

(§5) non-violence, equanimity, contentment, austerity, charity, achievement, disappointment, (are) various dispositions of the beings that arise from me only. (10.5)

10.6 महर्षयः सप्त पूर्वे चत्वारो मनवस्तथा ।
मद्भावा मानसा जाता येषां लोक इमाः प्रजाः ।।
maharṣayaḥ: sapta pūrve ćatvāro manavastathā,
madbhāvāmānasā jātā yeṣām loka imāḥ: prajāḥ:. (10.6)

(§1) *maharṣayaḥ:* (r◦ 22/7) *sapta pūrve ćatvāraḥ:* (r◦ 15/9) *manavaḥ:* (r◦ 18/1) *tathā madbhāvāḥ:* (r◦ 20/13) *mānasāḥ:* (r◦ 20/7) *jātāḥ:* (r◦ 20/14) *yeṣāṃ* (r◦ 25/3, 14/1) *loke* (r◦ 5/2) *imāḥ:* (r◦ 22/3) *prajāḥ:* (r◦ 22/8)

(§2) *maharṣayaḥ:* (10.2); *sapta* (1nom◦ sing◦ ←num◦ adj◦ ***saptaṇ*** (seven) ←√सप्); *pūrve* (7loc◦ sing◦ ←adj◦ *pūrva* (ancient) 4.15); *ćatvārḥ:* (1nom◦ ←adj◦ *ćatuṛ* (four) 7.16); *manavaḥ:* (m◦ 1nom◦ plu◦ ←adj◦ *manu* 1.44); *tathā* (1.8); *madbhāvāḥ:* (m◦ 1nom◦ plu◦ ←bahu◦ मयि भावः येषां ते ←*bhāva* 4.10); *mānasāḥ:* (m◦ 1nom◦ plu◦ ←adj◦ *mānasa* (mind) 1.47); *jātāḥ:* (m◦ 1nom◦ plu◦ ←adj◦ *jāta* (born) 2.26); *yeṣāṃ* (1.33); *loke* (2.5); *imāḥ:* (3.24); *prajāḥ:* (see 3.10) (10.6)

(§3) *maharṣayaḥ:* (subj1◦ the great sages); *sapta* (adj◦-subj1◦ seven); *pūrve* (adj1◦-subj2◦ ancient); *ćatvārḥ:* (subj2◦ four sanatkumaras); *manavaḥ:* (subj3◦ manus, the fourteen manus); *tathā* (as well as); *madbhāvāḥ:* (adj◦-subj3◦ those who have faith in me, my devotees); *mānasāḥ: jātāḥ:* (born from mind); *yeṣāṃ* (whose); *loke* (in this world); *imāḥ:* (adj◦-sunj4◦ these); *prajāḥ:* (subj4◦ progenies) (10.6)

(§4) sapta maharṣayaḥ: pūrve ćatvārḥ: tathā madbhāvāḥ: mānasāḥ: jātāḥ: manavaḥ: yeṣāṃ imāḥ: prajāḥ: loke

(§5) The seven great sages, four ancient sanatkumaras,[580] as well as those my devotees the fourteen[581] manus born from mind, whose (are) these progenies in this world. (10.6)

---

[580] Elsewhere◦ चत्वारः → the four Manus, four ancient Manus, the four other sages, ...etc.

📖 Manus were fourteen, namely svāyambhūva, svāroćiśa, uttama, tāmasa, raivata, ćākṣuśa, vaivasvata, sāvarṇī, dakṣasāvarṇī, brahmasāvarṇī, dharmasāvarṇī, rući and bhauma. Four were the sanatkumaras, namely sanaka, sanandana, sanātana, sanatsujāta.

[581] Elsewhere◦ मद्भावाः → born from Me, from me origins, originating from me, born of Me, their beings in Me, their being in Me, ...etc.

📖 The word is मद्भावाः (मयि भावः येषाम्) not मद्भवाः (मयि भवः येषाम्) ।

10.7 एतां विभूतिं योगं च मम यो वेत्ति तत्त्वत: ।
सोऽविकम्पेन योगेन युज्यते नात्र संशय: ।।

etāṁ vibhutiṁ yogaṁ ća mama yo vetti tattvataḥ:,
so‘vikampena yogena yujyate nātra saṁśayaḥ:. (10.7)

(§1) *etāṃ* (r◦ 14/1) *vibhutiṃ* (r◦ 14/1) *yogaṃ* (r◦ 14/1) *ća mama yaḥ:* (r◦ 15/13) *vetti tattvataḥ:* (r◦ 22/8) *saḥ:* (r◦ 15/1) *avikampena yogena yujyate na* (r◦ 1/1) *atra saṁśayaḥ:* (r◦ 22/8)

(§2) *etāṃ* (1.3); ***vibhutiṃ*** (2acc◦ sing◦ ←f◦ ***vibhūti*** (divinity) ←वि√भू); *yogaṃ* (2.53); *ća* (1.1); *mama* (1.7); *yaḥ:* (2.19); *vetti* (2.19); *tattvataḥ:* (4.9); *saḥ:* (1.13); *avikampena* (3inst◦ sing◦ n.bahuvrī◦ ←bahuvrī◦ adj◦ *vikampa* (weavering) विशेषेण कम्प: यस्य ←वि√कम्प् 2.31); ***yogena*** (3inst◦ sing◦ ←m◦ *yoga* 2.39); ***yujyate*** (3rd-per◦ sing◦ pres◦ वर्तमान्-लट् ātmane◦ ←class7◦ √युज्); *na* (1.30); *atra* (1.4); *saṁśayaḥ:* (see 8.5) (10.7)

(§3) *etāṃ* (adj◦-obj1◦ this); *vibhutiṃ* (obj2◦ divinity); *yogaṃ* (obj2◦ yoga); *ća* (and); *mama* (my); *yaḥ:* (adj◦-subj1◦ he who); *vetti* (knows, understands); *tattvataḥ:* (in reality, in principle); *saḥ:* (subj1◦ he); *avikampena* (with unwavering); *yogena* (with discipline); *yujyate* (he gets established); *na* (there is no); *atra* (in this, in this matter); *saṁśayaḥ:* (subj2◦ doubt) (10.7)

(§4) yaḥ: vetti etāṃ vibhutiṃ ća mama yogaṃ tattvataḥ: saḥ: yujyate avikampena yogena atra na saṁśayaḥ:

(§5) He who understands this divinity and my yoga in principle, he engages[582] with unwavering with discipline, in this there is no doubt. (10.7)

10.8 अहं सर्वस्य प्रभवो मत्त: सर्वं प्रवर्तते ।
इति मत्वा भजन्ते मां बुधा भावसमन्विता: ।।

ahaṁ sarvasya prabhavo mattaḥ: sarvaṁ pravartate,
iti matvā bhajante māṁ budhā bhāvasamanvitāḥ:. (10.8)

(§1) *ahaṃ* (r◦ 14/1) *sarvasya prabhavaḥ:* (r◦ 15/9) *mattaḥ:* (r◦ 22/7) *sarvaṃ* (r◦ 14/1) *pravartate* (r◦ 23/1) *iti matvā bhajante māṃ* (r◦ 14/1) *budhāḥ:* (r◦ 20/12) *bhāvasamanvitāḥ:* (r◦ 22/8)

(§2) *ahaṃ* (1.22); *sarvasya* (2.30); *prabhavaḥ:* (7.6); *mattaḥ:* (7.7); *sarvaṃ* (2.17); *pravartate* (5.14); *iti*

---

[582] Elsewhere◦ युज्यते → he is harmonised, he is balanced, he is endowed with, is united, is engaged, will be endowed, ...etc.

📖 युज्यते is not a ppp◦ or a futire tense. युज्यते is आत्मनेपदी habitual Present tense → unites, establishes, engages, etc.

(1.25); *matvā* (3.28); *bhajante* (7.16); *mām̹* (1.46); *budhāḥ:* (see 4.19); *bhāvasamanvitāḥ:* (m◦ 1nom◦ plu◦ ←tatpu◦ adj◦ *bhāva-samanvita*, भावेन समन्वित: ←m◦ *bhāva* (faith) 2.7 + ppp◦ adj◦ ***samanvita*** (endowed) ←सम्–अनु√इ) (10.8)

(§3) *aham̹* (subj1◦ I am); *sarvasya* (of everything); *prabhavaḥ:* (subj2◦ the origin); *mattaḥ:* (from me); *sarvam̹* (subj3◦ everything); *pravartate* (originates); *iti* (thus); *matvā* (having understood); *bhajante* (they worship); *mām̹* (obj◦ me); *budhāḥ:* (subj3◦ wise people); *bhāvasamanvitāḥ:* (adj◦-subj3◦ the faithful people) (10.8)

(§4) aham̹ prabhavaḥ: sarvasya sarvam̹ pravartate mattaḥ: matvā iti bhāvasamanvitāḥ: bhajante mām̹

(§5) I am the origin of everthing; everything originates from me; having understood thus the faithful wise people worship me. (10.8)

10.9 मच्चित्ता मद्गतप्राणा बोधयन्तः परस्परम् ।
कथयन्तश्च मां नित्यं तुष्यन्ति च रमन्ति च ।।
maććittā madgataprāṇā bodhayantaḥ: parasparam̹,
kathayantasća māṁ nityaṁ tuṣyanti ća ramanti ća. (10.9)

(§1) *maććittāḥ:* (r◦ 20/13) *madgataprāṇāḥ:* (r◦ 24/5, 20/11) *bodhayantaḥ:* (r◦ 22/3) *parasparam̹* (r◦ 14/2) *kathayantaḥ:* (r◦ 17/1) *ća mām̹* (r◦ 14/1) *nityam̹* (r◦ 14/1) *tuṣyanti* (r◦ 25/7) *ća ramanti ća*

(§2) *maććittāḥ:* (1nom◦ plu◦ ←bahuvrī◦ m◦ *maććitta* (heart in me) 6.14 मयि चित्तं यस्य स:); *madgataprāṇāḥ:* (m◦ 1nom◦ plu◦ ←bahuvrī◦ *madgata-prāṇā*, माम् गत: प्राण: यस्य स: ←pron◦ *mat̹* (me) 1.9 + adj◦ *gata* (gone) 2.11 + m◦ *prāṇa* (life) 1.33); *bodhayantaḥ:* (m◦ 1nom◦ plu◦ ←śatṛ◦ adj◦ caus◦*bodhayat̹* (enlightening) ←√बुध्); *parasparam̹* (3.11); *kathayantaḥ:* (m◦ 1nom◦ plu◦ ←śatṛ◦ adj◦ ***kathayat̹*** (discussing) ←√कथ्); *ca* (1.1); *mām̹* (1.46); *nityam̹* (2.21); *tuṣyanti* (3rd-per◦ plu◦ pres◦ वर्तमान्–लट् parasmai◦ ←class1◦ √तुष् 6.20); *ća* (1.1); *ramanti* (3rd-per◦ plu◦ pres◦ वर्तमान्–लट् parasmai◦ ←class1◦ √रम् 5.22); *ća* (1.1) (10.9)

(§3) *maććittāḥ:* (adj1◦-subj◦ they whose hearts are in me); *madgataprāṇāḥ:* (adj2◦-subj◦ they whose lives are devoted to me); *bodhayantaḥ:* (adj3◦-subj◦ while enlightening); *parasparam̹* (adv◦ among each other); *kathayantaḥ:* (adj4◦-subj◦ while discussing); *ca* (and); *mām̹* (about me); *nityam̹* (always); *tuṣyanti* (they rejoice); *ća* (and); *ramanti* (they enjoy); *ća* (and) (10.9)

(§4) maććittāḥ: ca madgataprāṇāḥ: nityam̹ tuṣyanti ća ramanti bodhayantaḥ: parasparam̹ ća kathayantaḥ: mām̹

(§5) They, whose hearts are in me,[583] and they, whose lives are devoted to me,[584] they always rejoice and enjoy while enlightening among each other and while discussing about me. (10.9)

10.10 तेषां सततयुक्तानां भजतां प्रीतिपूर्वकम् ।
ददामि बुद्धियोगं तं येन मामुपयान्ति ते ।।
teṣām satatayuktānām bhajatām prītipūrvakam,
dadāmi buddhiyogam tam yena māmupayānti te. (10.10)

(§1) *teṣām̦* (r◦ 25/3, 14/1) *satatayuktānām̦* (r◦ 14/1) *bhajatām̦* (r◦ 14/1) *prītipūrvakam̦* (r◦ 14/2) *dadāmi buddhiyogam̦* (r◦ 14/1) *tam̦* (r◦ 14/1) *yena mām̦* (r◦ 8/20) *upayānti te*

(§2) *teṣām̦* (5.16); *satatayuktānām̦* (m◦ 6pos◦ plu◦ ←karmadhā◦ tatpu◦ 🕮***satata-yukta***, सतत: युक्त: ←ind◦ or adj◦ *satata* (ever) 3.14 + adj◦ *yukta* (equipped) 1.14); *bhajatām̦* (m◦ 6pos◦ plu◦ ←śatṛ◦ adj◦ *bhajaț* (worshipping) ←√भज्); 🕮*prītipūrvakam̦* (adv◦ ←f◦ *prīti* (love) 1.36 + adj◦ *pūrvak* (with) 9.23); ***dadāmi*** (1st-per◦ sing◦ pres◦ वर्तमान्-लट् parasmai◦ ←class3◦ √दा 2.43); ***buddhiyogam̦*** (2acc◦ sing◦ ←m◦ *buddhiyoga* 2.49); *tam̦* (2.1); *yena* (2.17); *mām̦* (1.46); *upayānti* (3rd-per◦ plu◦ pres◦ वर्तमान्-लट् parasmai◦ ←class2◦ उप√या 3.33); *te* (1.33) (10.10)

(§3) *teṣām̦* (for those); *satatayuktānām̦* (ever equipped); *bhajatām̦* (worshipping people); *prītipūrvakam̦* (affectionately, lovingly); *dadāmi* (I give); *buddhiyogam̦* (obj1◦ the yoga of equanimity); *tam̦* (adj◦-obj1◦ that, the one that I told previously); *yena* (by which); *mām̦* (obj2◦ to me); *upayānti* (they come, return); *te* (subj◦ they) (10.10)

(§4) teṣām̦ satatayuktānām̦ bhajatām̦ prītipūrvakam̦ dadāmi buddhiyogam̦ tam̦ yena te upayānti mām̦

(§5) For those ever equipped (and) worshipping people, I affectionately give[585] the yoga of

---

[583] Elsewhere◦ मच्चित्ता: → with their minds engrossed in Me, with their minds fixed on Me, their thoughts on Me, their thoughts are fixed in Me, with their minds and sensed directed to Me, ...etc.

🕮 मच्चित्त is not a *tatpurusha samasa* and, therefore, the primary operative of this word is not the minds, or the thoughts, but because it is a *bahuvrīhi samasa*, the target is 'they' (whose minds or thoughts are...).

[584] Elsewhere◦ मद्गतप्राणा: → with their lives dedicated to Me, their lives surrendered to Me, their lives are wholy given up to Me, with their life absorbed in Me, with their pranas fully absorbed in Me, with their lives are fully devoted to My service, their life rooted in Me, ...etc.

🕮 मद्गतप्राण is not a *tatpurusha samasa* and, therefore, the primary operative of this word is not the life or prana, but because it is a *bahuvrīhi samasa*, the target is 'they' (whose life or prana is...)

[585] Elsewhere◦ भजतां प्रीतिपूर्वकं ददामि → प्रीतिपूर्वकं भजतां ददामि to them who worship Me with love, ...etc.

equanimity, the one that I told previously, by which they return to me.

(10.10)

10.11 तेषामेवानुकम्पार्थमहमज्ञानजं तमः ।
नाशयाम्यात्मभावस्थो ज्ञानदीपेन भास्वता ॥

teṣāmevānukampārthamahamajñānajaṁ tamaḥ:,
nāśayāmyātmabhāvastho jñānadīpena bhāsvatā. (10.11)

(§1) *teṣāṃ* (r◦ 25/3, 8/22) *eva* (r◦ 1/1) *anukampārthaṃ* (r◦ 8/16) *ahaṃ* (r◦ 8/16) *ajñānajaṃ* (r◦ 14/1) *tamaḥ:* (r◦ 22/8) *nāśayāmi* (r◦ 4/2) *ātmabhāvasthaḥ:* (r◦ 15/3) *jñānadīpena bhāsvatā*

(§2) *teṣāṃ* (5.16); *eva* (1.1); *anukampārthaṃ* (s.avyayi◦ or m◦ 2acc◦ sing◦ ←tatpu◦ *anukampārtha*, अनुकम्पाया अर्थः ←f◦ 📖*anukampā* (compassion) ←अनु√कम्प् + m◦ *artha* (for) 1.7); *ahaṃ* (1.22); 📖***ajñānajaṃ*** (n◦ 2acc◦ sing◦ ←tatpu◦ *ajñāna-ja*, अज्ञानात् जातम् ←n◦ *ajñāna* (ignorance) 4.42 + m◦ *ja* (birth) 1.7); ***tamaḥ:*** (2acc◦ sing◦ ←n◦ *tamas* (darkness) 7.12); *nāśayāmi* (1st-per◦ sing◦ pres◦ वर्तमान्-लट् parasmai◦ caus◦ ←class4◦ √नश्); *ātmabhāvasthaḥ:* (m◦ 1nom◦ sing◦ ←ppp◦ adj◦ tatpu◦ *ātma-bhāvastha*, आत्मनः भावे स्थितः ←m◦ *ātman* (oneself) 2.41 + m◦ *bhāva* (nature) 2.7 + adj◦ *stha* (dewlling) 2.45); *jñānadīpena* (m◦ 3inst◦ sing◦ ←tatpu◦ *jñānadīpa* (lamp of knowledge) ज्ञानस्य दीपः ←n◦ *jñāna* (knowledge) 3.3 + m◦ *dīpa* (lamp) 6.19); 📖*bhāsvatā* (m◦ 3inst◦ sing◦ ←adj◦ or m◦ *bhāsvat* (bright) ←√भास्) (10.11)

(§3) *teṣāṃ* (for them); *eva* (only); *anukampārthaṃ* (out of compassion); *ahaṃ* (subj◦ I); *ajñānajaṃ* (born of ignorance); *tamaḥ:* (obj◦ the darkness); *nāśayāmi* (I remove); *ātmabhāvasthaḥ:* (dwelling in one's self, residing in one's self-consciousness); *jñānadīpena* (with the lamp of knowledge); *bhāsvatā* (with the luminous) (10.11)

(§4) teṣāṃ eva anukampārthaṃ ahaṃ ātmabhāvasthaḥ: nāśayāmi tamaḥ: ajñānajaṃ bhāsvatā jñānadīpena

(§5) For them, only out of compassion,[586] I residing in one's self-consciousness, remove the darkness born of ignorance with the luminous lamp of knowledge.

(10.11)

Arjuna said (arjuna uvāca अर्जुन उवाच ।)

10.12 परं ब्रह्म परं धाम पवित्रं परमं भवान् ।
पुरुषं शाश्वतं दिव्यमादिदेवमजं विभुम् ॥

paraṁ brahma paraṁ dhāma pavitraṁ paramaṁ bhavān,

---

[586] Elsewhere◦ तेषामेवानुकम्पार्थमहम् → Out of compassion for them alone, I, residing in their hearts ...etc.

puruṣaṁ śāśvataṁ divyamādidevamajaṁ vibhuṃ; (10.12)

(§1) *arjunaḥ:* (r◦ 19/4) *uvāća. paraṃ* (r◦ 14/1) *brahma paraṃ* (r◦ 14/1) *dhāma pavitraṃ* (r◦ 14/1) *paramaṃ* (r◦ 14/1) *bhavān* (r◦ 23/1) *puruṣaṃ* (r◦ 14/1) *śāśvataṃ* (r◦ 14/1) *divyaṃ* (r◦ 8/17) *ādidevaṃ* (r◦ 8/16) *ajaṃ* (r◦ 14/1) *vibhuṃ* (r◦ 14/2);

(§2) *arjunaḥ:* (1.28); *uvāća* (1.25). *paraṃ* (1nom◦ 4.4); *brahma* (1nom◦ 4.24); *paraṃ* (↑); *dhāma* (1nom◦ 8.21); *pavitraṃ* (1nom◦ 4.38); *paramaṃ* (1nom◦ 8.3); *bhavān* (1.8); *puruṣaṃ* (2acc◦ 2.15); ***śāśvataṃ*** (2acc◦ sing◦ ←adj◦ *śāśvata* (eternal) 1.43); *divyaṃ* (2acc◦ 4.9); *ādidevaṃ* (m◦ 2acc◦ sing◦ ←tatpu◦ ***ādideva*** ←adj◦ *ādi* (primal) 2.28 + m◦ *deva* (god) 3.11); *ajaṃ* (birthless 2acc◦ 2.21); *vibhuṃ* (2acc◦ sing◦ ←m◦ *vibhu* (the omnipresent one) 5.15); (10.12)

(§3) *arjunaḥ:* (subj◦ Arjuna); *uvāća* (said). *paraṃ brahma* (adj◦1-subj◦ the Supreme brahma); *paraṃ dhāma* (adj2◦-subj◦ the Supreme Abode, the Final Destination); *pavitraṃ paramaṃ* (adj3◦-subj◦ the Supreme Sanctifier); *bhavān* (subj◦ you are); *puruṣaṃ śāśvataṃ divyaṃ* (the Eternal Divine Person); *ādidevaṃ* (adj4◦-subj◦ the Primal God); *ajaṃ* (adj5◦-subj◦ the Birthless); *vibhuṃ* (adj6◦-subj◦ the Omnipresent); (10.12)

(§4) arjunaḥ: uvāća. bhavān paraṃ brahma paraṃ dhāma pavitraṃ paramaṃ puruṣaṃ śāśvataṃ divyaṃ ādidevaṃ ajaṃ vibhuṃ;

(§5) Arjuna said : You are the Supreme brahma, the Supreme Abode,[587] the Supreme Sanctifier, the Eternal Divine Person, the Primal God, the Birthless, the Omnipresent; (10.12)

10.13 **आहुस्त्वामृषय: सर्वे देवर्षिर्नारदस्तथा ।**
असितो देवलो व्यास: स्वयं चैव ब्रवीषि मे ।।
āhustvāmṛṣayaḥ: sarve devarṣirnāradastathā,
asito devalo vyāsaḥ: svayaṁ ća eva braviṣi me. (10.13)

(§1) *āhuḥ:* (r◦ 18/1) *tvāṃ* (r◦ 8/21) *ṛṣayaḥ:* (r◦ 22/7) *sarve devarṣiḥ:* (r◦ 16/6) *nāradaḥ:* (r◦ 18/1) *tathā* (r◦ 23/1) *asitaḥ:* (r◦ 15/4) *devalḥ:* (r◦ 15/13) *vyāsaḥ:* (r◦ 22/7) *svayaṃ* (r◦ 14/1) *ća* (r◦ 3/1) *eva braviṣi* (r◦ 25/4) *me*

(§2) *āhuḥ:* (3.42); *tvāṃ* (2.7); *ṛṣayaḥ:* (5.25); *sarve* (1.6); *devarṣiḥ:* (m◦ 1nom◦ sing◦ ←s-karm◦ ***devarṣi,*** देव: इव ऋषि: ←m◦ *deva* (god) 3.11 + m◦ *ṛṣi* (sage) 4.2); ***nāradaḥ:*** (1nom◦ sing◦ ←m◦ prop◦ ***nārada*** ←bahuvrī◦ नरेभ्य: धर्मम् दर्शयति य: ←aggregative n◦ *nāra* (men, collective noun); ←m◦ *nara* (person) 1.5 + √दा); *tathā*

[587] Elsewhere◦ परं धाम → the Supreme Light.

(1.8); *asitaḥ:* (1nom◦ sing◦ ←m◦ prop◦ n.tatpu◦ *asita* ←ppp◦ adj◦ *sita* ←√सो or √सि); *devalaḥ:* (1nom◦ sing◦ ←m◦ prop◦ *devala* ←m◦ *deva* 3.11 + √ला); ***vyāsaḥ:*** (1nom◦ sing◦ ←m◦ prop◦ ***vyāsa*** ←वि√अस्); *svayam* (4.38); *ća* (1.1); *eva* (1.1); *braviṣi* (2nd-per◦ sing◦ pres◦ वर्तमान्–लट् parasmai◦ ←class2◦ √ब्रू); *me* (2.7) (10.13)

(§3) *āhuḥ:* (They say, call); *tvām* (obj1◦ you); *ṛṣayaḥ:* (subj1◦ the sages); *sarve* (adj◦-subj1◦ all); *devarṣiḥ:* (adj◦-subj2◦ the divine sage); *nāradaḥ:* (subj2◦ Nārada); *tathā* (as well as); *asitaḥ:* (subj3◦ Asita); *devalaḥ:* (subj4◦ Devala); *vyāsaḥ:* (dubj5◦ Vyāsa muni); *svayam* (adv◦ yourself); *ća* (and); *eva* (so also); *braviṣi* (you are telling); *me* (obj2◦ me) (10.13)

(§4) sarve ṛṣayaḥ: tathā devarṣiḥ: nāradaḥ: asitaḥ: devalaḥ: ća vyāsaḥ: āhuḥ: tvām eva svayam braviṣi me

(§5) (Thus) all the sages as well as the divine sage, Nārada, Asita, Devala and Vyāsa muni call you. So also yourself you are telling me. (10.13)

10.14 सर्वमेतदृतं मन्ये यन्मां वदसि केशव ।
न हि ते भगवन्व्यक्तिं विदुर्देवा न दानवाः ।।

sarvametadṛtaṁ manye yanmāṁ vadasi keśava,
na hi te bhagavanvyaktiṁ vidurdevā na dānavāḥ:. (10.14)

(§1) *sarvam* (r◦ 8/22) *etat* (r◦ 8/8) *ṛtam* (r◦ 14/1) *manye yat* (r◦ 12/2) *mām* (r◦ 14/1) *vadasi keśava na hi te bhagavan* (r◦ 13/19) *vyaktim* (r◦ 14/1) *viduḥ:* (r◦ 16/8) *devāḥ:* (r◦ 20/10) *na dānavāḥ:* (r◦ 22/8)

(§2) *sarvam* (n◦ 2acc◦ 2.17); *etat* (2acc◦ 2.6); 🕮*ṛtam* (2acc◦ sing◦ ←n◦ or adj◦ *ṛta* ←√ऋ); *manye* (6.34); *yat* (3.21); *mām* (1.46); *vadasi* (2nd-per◦ sing◦ pres◦ वर्तमान्–लट् parasmai◦ ←class1◦ √वद्); *keśava* (1.31); *na* (1.30); *hi* (1.11); *te* (2.7); 🕮***bhagavan*** (8voc◦ sing◦ ←m◦ ***bhagavat*** ←√भज्); *vyaktim* (7.24); *viduḥ:* (4.2); *devāḥ:* (3.11); *na* (1.30); 🕮*dānavāḥ:* (1nom◦ plu◦ ←m◦ -taddhita◦ *dānava*, दनोः अपत्यम् ←f◦ prop◦ Danu, daughter of prajāpati Dakṣa, wife of Kaśyapa, sister of Aditi and Diti) (10.14)

(§3) *sarvam* (adj1◦obj1◦ all); *etat* (obj1◦ this); *ṛtam* (adj2◦-obj1◦ true); *manye* (I accept, I hold it to be); *yat* (adj3◦-obj1◦ which); *mām* (obj2◦ me); *vadasi* (you are telling); *keśava* (O Krṣṇa!); *na* (neither); *hi* (because); *te* (your); *bhagavan* (O Lord!); *vyaktim* (obj3◦ manifestation, personification); *viduḥ:* (understand); *devāḥ:* (subj1◦ the gods); *na* (nor); *dānavāḥ:* (subj2◦ the demigods, feinds, fairies, demons, imps, elves) (10.14)

(§4) keśava etat sarvam manye ṛtam yat vadasi mām hi bhagavan na devāḥ: na dānavāḥ: viduḥ: te vyaktim

(§5) O Krṣṇa! this all I hold it to be true which you are telling me; because, O Lord! neither the gods nor the demigods understand your personification. (10.14)

10.15 स्वयमेवात्मनात्मानं वेत्थ त्वं पुरुषोत्तम ।
भूतभावन भूतेश देवदेव जगत्पते ।।

svayamevātmanātmānaṁ vettha tvaṁ puruṣottama,
bhūtabhāvana bhūteśa devadeva jagatpate. (10.15)

(§1) *svayaṃ* (r◦ 8/22) *eva* (r◦ 1/2) *ātmanā* (r◦ 1/4) *ātmānaṃ* (r◦ 14/1) *vettha tvaṃ* (r◦ 14/1) *puruśottama bhūtabhāvana bhūteśa devadeva jagatpate*

(§2) *svayaṃ* (4.38); *eva* (1.1); *ātmanā* (2.55); *ātmānaṃ* (3.43); *vettha* (4.5); *tvaṃ* (2.11); *puruśottama* (8.1); *bhūtabhāvana* (m◦ 8voc◦ sing◦ ←bahuvrī◦ *bhūta-bhāvana* (being)-(originator) 9.5); *bhūteśa* (m◦ 8voc◦ sing◦ ←tatpu◦ *bhūteśa*, भूतानाम् ईश: ←m◦ *bhūta* (being) 2.28 + adj◦ *īśa* (god) 1.15); *devadeva* (m◦ 8voc◦ sing◦ ←tatpu◦ ***devadeva***, देवानाम् देव: ←m◦ *deva* (god) 3.11); *jagatpate* (m◦ 8voc◦ sing◦ ←bahuvrī◦ *jagat-pati*, जगत: पति: इव य: ←n◦ *jagaṭ* (world) 7.5 + m◦ *pati* (lord) 1.18) (10.15)

(§3) *svayaṃ* (you yourself); *eva* (only); *ātmanā* (by yourself); *ātmānaṃ* (obj◦ yourself); *vettha* (know); *tvaṃ* (adj◦-obj◦ yourself); *puruśottama* (O Kṛṣṇa!, O Sipreme Person!); *bhūtabhāvana* (O Originator of the beings!); *bhūteśa* (O Lord of the beings!); *devadeva* (O Lord of the Lords!); *jagatpate* (O Lord of the Universe!) (10.15)

(§4) puruśottama bhūteśa devadeva jagatpate eva svayaṃ vettha ātmānaṃ tvaṃ ātmanā

(§5) Oh Kṛṣṇa! Oh Originator of the beings! Oh Lord of the beings![588] Oh Lord of the Lords! Oh Lord of the Universe! only you know yourself by yourself. (10.15)

10.16 वक्तुमर्हस्यशेषेण दिव्या ह्यात्मविभूतय: ।
याभिर्विभूतिभिर्लोकानिमांस्त्वं व्याप्य तिष्ठसि ।।

vaktumarhasyaśeṣeṇa divyā hyātmavibhūtayaḥ:,
yābhirvibhūtibhirlokānimānstvaṁ vyāpya tiṣṭhasi. (10.16)

(§1) *vaktuṃ* (r◦ 8/16) *arhasi* (r◦ 4/1) *aśeṣeṇa* (r◦ 24/1) *divyā* (r◦ 20/18) *hi* (r◦ 4/2) *ātmavibhūtayaḥ:* (r◦ 22/8) *yābhiḥ:* (r◦ 16/6) *vibhūtibhiḥ:* (r◦ 16/6) *lokāṇ* (r◦ 8/13) *imāṇ* (r◦ 13/7) *tvaṃ* (r◦ 14/1) *vyāpya tiṣṭhasi*

(§2) *vaktuṃ* (inf◦ ind◦ ←√वच्); *arhasi* (2.25); *aśeṣeṇa* (4.35); ***divyāḥ*** (f◦ 1nom◦ plu◦ ←adj◦ *divya* (divine)

---

[588] Elsewhere◦ भूतभावन... → You are the originator of all beings, ...etc.

📖 पुरुषोत्तम भूतभावन भूतेश देवदेव and जगत्पते are all Vocative case addresses. They are Nominative (1st) case subjects.

1.14); *hi* (adv∘ 1.11); ***ātmavibhūtayaḥ:*** (f∘ 1nom∘ plu∘ ←tatpu∘ *ātma-vibhūti,* आत्मनः विभूति ←m∘ *ātman* (own) 2.41 + f∘ *vibhūti* (divinity) 10.7); *yābhiḥ:* (f∘ 3inst∘ plu∘ ←pron∘ *yad* 1.7); *vibhūtibhiḥ:* (3inst∘ plu∘ ←f∘ *vibhūti* (divinity) 10.7); *lokān* (6.41); ***imān*** (m∘ 2acc∘ plu∘ ←pron∘ *idam* (this) 1.10); *tvam* (2.11); *vyāpya* (lyp∘ past-participle ind∘ ←वि√आप्); *tiṣṭhasi* (2nd-per∘ sing∘ pres∘ वर्तमान्–लट् parasmai∘ ←class1∘ √स्था 3.5) (10.16)

(§3) *vaktum* (to tell, for telling); *arhasi* (you are apposite, fit, most suitable); *aśeṣeṇa* (fully); *divyāḥ* (adj∘-obj∘ divine); *hi* (because); *ātmavibhūtayaḥ:* (obj1∘ your own splendors); *yābhiḥ:* (by which); *vibhūtibhiḥ:* (the glories by which); *lokān* (obj2∘ three worlds); *imān* (adj∘-obj2∘ these); *tvam* (subj∘ you); *vyāpya* (having occupied, occupying); *tiṣṭhasi* (you stay, you exist) (10.16)

(§4) hi arhasi vaktum aśeṣeṇa ātmavibhūtayaḥ: divyāḥ vibhūtibhiḥ: yābhiḥ: tvam tiṣṭhasi vyāpya imān lokān

(§5) Indeed you are most suitable[589] to tell fully your own divine splendors, the glories by which you exist occupying these three worlds. (10.16)

10.17 कथं विद्यामहं योगिंस्त्वां सदा परिचिन्तयन् ।
केषु केषु च भावेषु चिन्त्योऽसि भगवन्मया ।।
kathaṁ vidyāmahaṁ yogiṁstvāṁ sadā paricintayan,
keṣu keṣu ca bhāveṣu cintyo'si bhagavanmayā. (10.17)

(§1) *katham* (r∘ 14/1) *vidyām* (r∘ 8/16) *aham* (r∘ 14/1) *yogin* (r∘ 13/7) *tvām* (r∘ 14/1) *sadā paricintayan* (r∘ 23.1) *keṣu* (r∘ 25/5) *keṣu* (r∘ 25/5) *ca bhāveṣu* (r∘ 25/5) *cintayḥ:* (r∘ 15/1) *asi bhagavan* (r∘ 13/16) *mayā*

(§2) 🕮*katham* (1.37); *vidyām* (1st-per∘ sing∘ potential∘ विधि∘ parasmai∘ ←class2∘ √विद्); *aham* (1.22); *yogin* (8voc∘ sing∘ ←m∘ *yogin* 3.3); *tvām* (2.7); *sadā* (1.40); *paricintayan* (1nom∘ sing∘ ←śatṛ∘ adj∘ caus∘ *paricintayat* (contemplating) ←परि√चिन्त्); ***keṣu*** (m∘ or n∘ 7loc∘ plu∘ ←pron∘ *kim* 1.1); *keṣu* (↑); *ca* (1.1); *bhāveṣu* (7loc∘ plu∘ ←m∘ *bhāva* (form) 2.7); 🕮*cintyaḥ:* (m∘ 1nom∘ sing∘ ←pot∘ adj∘ *cintya* (to be contemplated up on) ←√चिन्त्); *asi* (4.3); *bhagavan* (10.14); *mayā* (1.22) (10.17)

(§3) *katham* (how); *vidyām* (may I know); *aham* (subj1∘ I); *yogin* (O Kṛṣṇa!); *tvām* (obj1∘ you); *sadā* (always, constantly); *paricintayan* (adj∘-subj1∘ while contemplating); *keṣu keṣu* (in whichever); *ca*

---

[589] Elsewhere∘ वक्तुम् अर्हसि → Be pleased to speak, Please tell me, Deign to tell, Thou shouldst indeed tell, You should indeed tell, ...etc.

🕮 अर्हसि is not potential विधि∘ or imperative लोट्∘ । It is a simple Present tense.

(and); *bhāveṣu* (in forms); *ćintyaḥ:* (adj◦-obj2◦ ought to be contemplated on); *asi* (obj2◦ you); *bhagavan̦* (O Lord!); *mayā* (subj3◦ by me) (10.17)

(§4) katham̦ vidyām̦ aham̦ yogin̦ tvām̦ sadā parićintayan̦ keṣu keṣu ća bhāveṣu ćintyaḥ: asi bhagavan̦ mayā

(§5) O Krṣṇa! how may I know you, while constantly contemplating?[590] And O Lord! in whichever forms you ought to be contemplated on by me? (10.17)

10.18 **विस्तरेणात्मनो योगं विभूतिं च जनार्दन ।**
भूयः कथय तृप्तिर्हि शृण्वतो नास्ति मेऽमृतम् ।।
vistareṇātmano yogaṁ vibhūtiṁ ća janārdana,
bhūyaḥ: kathaya tṛptirhiś́ṛṇvato nāsti me'mṛtam̦. (10.18)

(§1) *vistareṇa* (r◦ 24/1, 1/2) *ātmanaḥ:* (r◦ 15/10) *yogam̦* (r◦ 14/1) *vibhutim̦* (r◦ 14/1) *ća janārdana bhūyaḥ:* (r◦ 22/1) *kathaya tṛptiḥ:* (r◦ 16/6) *hi ś́ṛṇvataḥ:* (r◦ 15/6) *na* (r◦ 1/1) *asti me* (r◦ 6/1) *amṛtam̦* (r◦ 14/2)

(§2) *vistareṇa* (3inst◦ sing◦ ←m◦ ***vistara*** (expansion) ←वि√स्तृ); *ātmanaḥ:* (4.42); *yogam̦* (2.53); *vibhutim̦* (10.7); *ća* (1.1); *janārdana* (1.36); 🕮*bhūyaḥ:* (2.20); *kathaya* (2nd-per◦ sing◦ imperative◦ निवेदनार्थ-लोट् parasmai◦ ←class10◦ √कथ्); *tṛptiḥ:* (1nom◦ sing◦ ←f◦ *tṛpti* (satisfaction) ←√तृप्); *hi* (1.11); *ś́ṛṇvataḥ:* (n◦ 6pos◦ sing◦ ←ś́atṛ◦ adj◦ *ś́ṛṇvaț* 5.8); *na* (1.30); *asti* (2.40); *me* (1.21); *amṛtam̦* (9.19) (10.18)

(§3) *vistareṇa* (elaborately, in details); *ātmanaḥ:* (your own); *yogam̦* (obj1◦ yoga); *vibhutim̦* (obj2◦ divine glory); *ća* (and); *janārdana* (O Krṣṇa!); *bhūyaḥ:* (further, again); *kathaya* (please narrate); *tṛptiḥ:* (subj◦ satiety, contentment); *hi* (because); *ś́ṛṇvataḥ:* (while listening); *na* (no); *asti* (there is); *me* (for me); *amṛtam̦* (obj◦ your nectar like sweet words) (10.18)

(§4) janārdana kathaya ātmanaḥ: yogam̦ ća vibhutim̦ bhūyaḥ: vistareṇa hi ś́ṛṇvataḥ: amṛtam̦ asti na tṛptiḥ: me

(§5) O Krṣṇa! please narrate your own yoga and divine glory again in details. Because,[591] while listening your nectar like sweet words, there is no contentment for me. (10.18)

---

[590] Elsewhere◦ सदा परिचिन्तयन् → by remaining ever-engaged in meditation, by constant mrditation, how shall I constantly think of you, by constantly meditating upon, through what process of continuous meditation, how shall I think of you, ...etc.

🕮 परिचिन्तयन् is not an Instrumental (3rd) case, or a simple future tense लृट् । It is a Nominative (1st) case Present Continuous Participle शतृ◦ adjective of the m◦ Subject Arjuna (अहम्), e.g. (i) meditating me; (ii) I, while contemplating.

[591] See footnote in verse 3.5

The Lord said (śrībhagavānuvāća श्रीभगवानुवाच ।)

10.19 हन्त ते कथयिष्यामि दिव्या ह्यात्मविभूतयः ।
प्राधान्यतः कुरुश्रेष्ठ नास्त्यन्तो विस्तरस्य मे ।।

hanta te kathayiṣyāmi divyā hi ātmavibhūtayaḥ:,
prādhānyataḥ: kuruśreṣṭha nāstyanto vistarasya me. (10.19)

(§1) *śrībhagavān̦* (r◦ 8/14) *uvāća. hanta te kathayiṣyāmi* (r◦ 25/9) *divyāḥ* (r◦ 20/18) *hi* (r◦ 4/2) *ātmavibhūtayaḥ:* (r◦ 22/8) *prādhānyataḥ:* (r◦ 22/1) *kuruśreṣṭha na* (r◦ 1/1) *asti* (r◦ 4/1) *antaḥ:* (r◦ 15/13) *vistarasya me*

(§2) *śrībhagavān̦* (2.2); *uvāća* (1.25). *hanta* (affirmative ind◦ (ok then!) ←√हन्); *te* (1.7); *kathayiṣyāmi* (1st-per◦ sing◦ fut2◦ लृट् भविष्य◦ parasmai◦ ←class10◦ √कथ् 2.34); *divyāḥ* (10.16); *hi* (1.11); *ātmavibhūtayaḥ:* (nom◦ 10.16); *prādhānyataḥ:* (adv◦ ind◦ ←n◦ *prādhānya* ←adj◦ *pradhāna* (main) ←पाट√धा); *kuruśreṣṭha* (m◦ 8voc◦ sing◦ ←bahuvrī◦ *kuru-śreṣṭha*, कुरुषु श्रेष्ठः यः ←m◦ *kuru* 1.1 + adj◦ *śreṣṭha* (best) 3.21); *na* (1.30); *asti* (2.40); *antaḥ:* (2.16); 🕮*vistarasya* (6pos sing◦ ←m◦ *vistara* (magnitude) 10.18); *me* (1.21) (10.19)

(§3) *śrībhagavān̦* (subj◦ The Lord); *uvāća* (said). *hanta* (alright then); *te* (you); *kathayiṣyāmi* (I shall tell); *divyāḥ* (adj◦-subj◦ divine); *hi* (because); *ātmavibhūtayaḥ:* (subj◦ my own glories); *prādhānyataḥ:* (mainly, according to importance); *kuruśreṣṭha* (O Arjuna!); *na asti* (there is no); *antaḥ:* (subj◦ end); *vistarasya* (of spread, magnitude, limit, extent); *me* (my) (10.19)

(§4) śrībhagavān̦ uvāća hanta kathayiṣyāmi te divyā ātmavibhūtayaḥ: prādhānyataḥ: hi kuruśreṣṭha na asti antaḥ: me vistarasya

(§5) The Lord said : Alright then! I shall tell you (about) my own divine glories according to importance;[592] because, O Arjuna! there is no end of my spread. (10.19)

---

[592] Elsewhere◦ प्राधान्यतः → glories such as are the most important, that are prominant, splendorous manifestations, conspicuous divine glories, principle divine glories, those which are prominent, prominent among My divine glories, My heavenly glories, main divine glories, ...etc.

🕮 प्राधान्यतः is not an adjective of the Nominatine (1st) case f◦ subject◦ आत्मविभूतयः । It is an adverb. It can not qualify a noun. It is qualifying the verb कथयिष्यामि । Also, NOTE that आत्मविभूतयः is not the object◦ (in Accusative 2nd case) of the verb कथयिष्यामि । Therefore, the construction should be, "I shall tell you about आत्मविभूतयः, the subject◦ in Nominative 1st case"

10.20 अहमात्मा गुडाकेश सर्वभूताशयस्थितः ।
अहमादिश्च मध्यं च भूतानामन्त एव च ।।

ahamātmā guḍākeśa sarvabhūtāśayasthitaḥ:,
ahamādiśća madhyaṁ ća bhūtānāmanta eva ća. (10.20)

(§1) *aham̩* (r◦ 8/17) *ātmā guḍākeśa sarvabhūtāśayasthitaḥ:* (r◦ 22/8) *aham̩* (r◦ 8/17) *ādiḥ:* (17.1) *ća madhyam̩* (r◦ 14/1) *ća bhūtānām̩* (r◦ 8/16) *antaḥ:* (r◦ 19/7) *eva ća*

(§2) *aham̩* (1.22); *ātmā* (6.5); ***guḍākeśa*** (m◦ 8voc◦ sing◦ ←bahuvrī◦ *guḍākeśa* 1.24); *sarvabhūtāśayasthitaḥ:* (m◦ 1nom◦ sing◦ ←tatpu◦ *sarva-bhūtāśaya-sthita*, सर्वेषाम् भूतानाम् आशये स्थितः ←pron◦ *sarva* 1.6 + m◦ *bhūta* (being) 2.28 + m◦ *āśaya* (heart, mind, essence) ←आ√शी + adj◦ *sthita* (resident) 1.14); *aham̩* (1.22); *ādiḥ:* (10.2); *ća* (1.1); ***madhyam̩*** (1nom◦ sing◦ ←adj◦ or n◦ *madhya* (middle) 1.21); *ća* (1.1); *bhūtānām̩* (2.69); *antaḥ:* (2.16); *eva* (1.1); *ća* (1.1) (10.20)

(§3) *aham̩* (I am); *ātmā* (subj1◦ the ātmā, the soul); *guḍākeśa* (O Arjuna!); *sarvabhūtāśayasthitaḥ:* (adj◦-subj◦ resident in the essence of all beings); *aham̩* (I am); *ādiḥ:* (subj2◦ the beginning); *ća* (and); *madhyam̩* (subj3◦ the middle state); *ća* (and); *bhūtānām̩* (of the beings); *antaḥ:* (subj4◦ the end); *eva ća* (as well as) (10.20)

(§4) guḍākeśa aham̩ ātmā sarvabhūtāśayasthitaḥ: ća aham̩ ādiḥ: ća madhyam̩ eva ća antaḥ: bhūtānām̩

(§5) O Arjuna! I am the ātmā[593] resident in the essence of all beings and I am the beginning and the middle state as well as the end of the beings. (10.20)

10.21 आदित्यानामहं विष्णुर्ज्योतिषां रविरंशुमान् ।
मरीचिर्मरुतामस्मि नक्षत्राणामहं शशी ।।

ādityānāmahaṁ viṣṇurjyotiṣāṁ raviraṁśumān,
marīćirmarutāmasmi nakṣatrāṇāmahaṁ śaśī. (10.21)

(§1) *ādityānām̩* (r◦ 8/16) *aham̩* (r◦ 14/1) *viṣṇuḥ:* (r◦ 16/8) *jyotiṣām̩* (r◦ 25/3, 14/1) *raviḥ:* (r◦ 16/1) *aṁśumān̩* (r◦ 23/1) *marīćiḥ:* (r◦ 16/6) *marutām̩* (r◦ 8/16) *asmi nakṣatrāṇām̩* (r◦ 24/6, 8/16) *aham̩* (r◦ 14/1) *śaśī*

(§2) *ādityānām̩* (6pos plu◦ ←m◦ *āditya* 5.16); *aham̩* (1.22); *viṣṇuḥ:* (m◦ 1nom◦ sing◦ ←prop◦ ***viṣṇu***

[593] Elsewhere◦ आत्मा → the self seated in the hearts, the universal Self seated in the heart, the Self residing in the mind, the self that resides in the minds, the Supersoul seated in the hearts, the self that dwells in the body, I am the ātman abiding in the heart, ...etc.

←√विष्); ***jyotiṣām*** (6pos plu◦ ←n◦ *jyotiṣ* 5.24); 🕮***raviḥ:*** (1nom◦ sing◦ ←m◦ *ravi* ←√रु); *aṁśumān* (1nom◦ sing◦ ←adj◦ *aṁśumat* ←√अंशु); *marīćiḥ:* (m◦ 1nom◦ sing◦ ←prop◦ *marīći* ←n◦ adj◦ *marīćin* ←√मृ); *marutām* (6pos plu◦ ←m◦ ***marut*** ←√मृ); *asmi* (7.8); *nakṣatrāṇām* (6pos plu◦ ←n◦ *nakṣatra* ←√नक्ष्); *aham* (1.22); 🕮*śaśī* (1nom◦ sing◦ ←m◦ *śaśin* 7.8) (10.21)

(§3) *ādityānām* (among the twelve āditya sons of Aditi); *aham* (I am); *viṣṇuḥ:* (subj5◦ Lord Vishnu); *jyotiṣām* (among the luminaries); *raviḥ:* (subj6◦ the sun); *aṁśumān* (adj◦-subj5◦ the radiant); *marīćiḥ:* (subj6◦ Marīchi); *marutām* (among the forty-nine *maruts*, the sons of Diti); *asmi* (I am); *nakṣatrāṇām* (among the lunar asterisms); *aham* (I am); *śaśī* (subj7◦ the moon, the asterism *abhijit*);
(10.21)

(§4) ādityānām aham viṣṇuḥ: jyotiṣām aṁśumān raviḥ: marutām asmi marīćiḥ: nakṣatrāṇām aham śaśī

(§5) Among the twelve āditya sons of Aditi I am Lord Vishnu, among the luminaries (I am) the radiant sun, among the forty-nine sons of Diti I am Marīchi, among the lunar asterisms I am the *abhijit*.[594] (10.21)

10.22 वेदानां सामवेदोऽस्मि देवानामस्मि वासवः ।
इन्द्रियाणां मनश्चास्मि भूतानामस्मि चेतना ।।
vedānāṁ sāmavedo'smi devānāmasmi vāsavaḥ:,
indriyāṇāṁ manaśćāsmi bhūtānāmasmi ćetanā. (10.22)

(§1) *vedānām* (r◦ 14/1) *sāmavedaḥ:* (r◦ 15/1) *asmi devānām* (r◦ 8/16) *asmi vāsavaḥ:* (r◦ 22/8) *indriyāṇām* (r◦ 24/6, 14/1) *manaḥ:* (r◦ 17/1) *ća* (r◦ 1/1) *asmi bhūtānām* (r◦ 8/16) *asmi ćetanā*

(§2) *vedānām* (6pos plu◦ ←m◦ *veda* 2.42); *sāmavedaḥ:* (m◦ 1nom◦ sing◦ ←prop◦ tatpu◦ *sāmaveda*, साम्नाम् वेदः ←m◦ *sāman* 9.17 + m◦ *veda* 2.42); *asmi* (7.8); *devānām* (10.2); *asmi* (7.8); 🕮*vāsavaḥ:* (1nom◦ sing◦ ←m◦ *vāsava* (Indra) ←√वस्); *indriyāṇām* (2.8); *manaḥ:* (1.30); *ća* (1.1); *asmi* (7.8); *bhūtānām* (2.69); *asmi* (7.8); 🕮***ćetanā*** (1nom◦ sing◦ ←f◦ *ćetanā* (life) ←√चित्) (10.22)

(§3) *vedānām* (among the vedas); *sāmavedaḥ:* (subj8◦ the Sama veda); *asmi* (I am); *devānām* (among the gods); *asmi* (I am); *vāsavaḥ:* (subj9◦ Lord Indra); *indriyāṇām* (among the organs); *manaḥ:* (subj10◦ the mind); *ća* (and); *asmi* (I am); *bhūtānām* (among the beings); *asmi* (I am); *ćetanā* (subj11◦ the life) (

---

[594] Elsewhere◦ अभिजित् → *Shrimadbhagavata* 11.16.27
संवत्सरोऽस्म्यनिमिषामृतूनां मधुमाधवौ ।
मासानां मार्गशीर्षोऽहं नक्षत्राणां तथाभिजित् ।।

10.22)

(§4) vedānāṃ asmi sāmavedaḥ: devānāṃ asmi vāsavaḥ: indriyāṇāṃ asmi manaḥ: ća bhūtānāṃ asmi ćetanā

(§5) Among the vedas I am the Sama veda, among the gods I am Lord Indra, among the organs I am the mind and of the beings I am the life.[595] (10.22)

10.23 रुद्राणां शङ्करश्चास्मि वित्तेशो यक्षरक्षसाम् ।
वसूनां पावकश्चास्मि मेरु: शिखरिणामहम् ।।
rudrāṇāṁ śaṅkaraśćāsmi vitteśo yakṣarakṣasāṃ,
vasūnāṁ pāvakaśćāsmi meruḥ: śikhariṇāmahaṃ. (10.23)

(§1) *rudrāṇāṃ* (r◦ 24/6, 14/1) *śaṅkaraḥ:* (r◦ 17/1) *ća* (r◦ 1/1) *asmi vitteśaḥ:* (r◦ 15/10) *yakṣarakṣasāṃ* (r◦ 14/2) *vasūnāṃ* (r◦ 14/1) *pāvakaḥ:* (r◦ 17/1) *ća* (r◦ 1/1) *asmi meruḥ:* (r◦ 22/5) *śikhariṇāṃ* (r◦ 24/6, 8/16) *ahaṃ* (r◦ 14/2)

(§2) *rudrāṇāṃ* (6pos plu◦ ←m◦ ***rudra*** (deity) ←√रुद्); *śaṅkaraḥ:* (m◦ 1nom◦ sing◦ ←prop◦ *śaṅkara* (shiva) ←शम्√कृ); *ća* (1.1); *asmi* (7.8); *vitteśaḥ:* (m◦ 1nom◦ sing◦ ←bahuvrī◦ *vitteśa*, वित्तस्य ईश: य: ←n◦ *vitta* (wealth) ←√विद् + adj◦ *īśa* (lord) 1.15); *yakṣarakṣasāṃ* (6pos plu◦ ←dvandva◦ यक्षाणाम् च रक्षसाम् च ←m◦ ***yakṣa*** (demigod) ←√यक्ष् + n◦ ***rakṣasa*** (imp) ←√रक्ष्); *vasūnāṃ* (6pos plu◦ ←m◦ *vasu* (wealth) 7.19); 🕮*pāvakaḥ:* (2.23); *ća* (1.1); *asmi* (7.8); *meruḥ:* (m◦ 1nom◦ sing◦ ←prop◦ or m◦ *meru* (mountaain) ←√मि); 🕮*śikhariṇāṃ* (m◦ 6pos◦ plu◦ ←bahuvrī◦ *śikhariṇ* (mountain) शिखराणि सन्ति यस्मिन् ←n◦ or m◦ *śikhara* (apex) ←f◦ *śikhā* ←√शी); *ahaṃ* (1.22) (10.23)

(§3) *rudrāṇāṃ* (among the eleven *rudra* sons of Aditi); *śaṅkaraḥ:* (subj12◦ Lord Shiva); *ća* (and); *asmi* (I am); *vitteśaḥ:* (subj13◦ Kubera); *yakṣarakṣasāṃ* (among the demigods and imps); *vasūnāṃ* (among the eight *vasu* sons of Aditi); *pāvakaḥ:* (subj14◦ the Agni); *ća* (and); *asmi* (I am); *meruḥ:* (subj15◦ the mountain Meru); *śikhariṇāṃ* (among the mountains); *ahaṃ* (I am) (10.23)

(§4) rudrāṇāṃ asmi śaṅkaraḥ: ća yakṣarakṣasāṃ asmi vitteśaḥ: vasūnāṃ ahaṃ pāvakaḥ: ća śikhariṇāṃ meruḥ:

(§5) Among the eleven *rudra* sons of Aditi I am Lord Shiva and among the demigods and imps I am Kubera, among the eight *vasu* sons of Aditi I am the Agni and among the mountains (I am) the mountain Meru. (10.23)

---

[595] Elsewhere◦ चेतना → intelligence, thought, consciousness, life-energy, ...etc.

10.24 पुरोधसां च मुख्यं मां विद्धि पार्थ बृहस्पतिम् ।
सेनानीनामहं स्कन्दः सरसामस्मि सागरः ।।

purodhasāṁ ća mukhyaṁ māṁ viddhi pārtha bṛhaspatim̧,
senānīnāmahaṁ skandaḥ: sarasāmasmi sāgaraḥ:. (10.24)

(§1) *purodhasām̧* (r◦ 14/1) *ća mukhyam̧* (r◦ 14/1) *mām̧* (r◦ 14/1) *viddhi pārtha bṛhaspatim̧* (r◦ 14/2) *senānīnām̧* (r◦ 8/16) *aham̧* (r◦ 14/1) *skandaḥ:* (r◦ 22/7) *sarasām̧* (r◦ 8/16) *asmi sāgaraḥ:* (r◦ 22/8)

(§2) *purodhasām̧* (m◦ 6pos◦ plu◦ ←m◦ *purodhaş* (proest) ←ind◦ *puraş* (front) ←√पूर्व् + √धा); *ća* (1.1); *mukhyam̧* (m◦ 2acc◦ sing◦ ←adj◦ ***mukhya*** (main) ←√खन्); *mām̧* (1.46); *viddhi* (2.17); *pārtha* (1.25); *bṛhaspatim̧* (m◦ 2acc◦ sing◦ ←tatpu◦ prop◦ *bṛhaspati,* बृहताम् वाचाम् पतिः ←adj◦ ***bṛhaţ*** (great) ←√बृह् + m◦ *pati* (lord) 1.18); *senānīnām̧* (6pos plu◦ ←m◦ *senānī* (commander) ←f◦ *senā* (army) 1.21); *aham̧* (1.22); *skandaḥ:* (m◦ 1nom◦ sing◦ ←prop◦ *Skanda* ←√स्कन्द्); *sarasām̧* (6pos plu◦ ←m◦ *saraş* (lake) ←√सृ); *asmi* (7.8); *sāgaraḥ:* (1nom◦ sing◦ ←m◦ ***sāgara*** (ocean) ←√गृ) (10.24)

(§3) *purodhasām̧* (among the divine priests); *ća* (and); *mukhyam̧* (adj◦-subj16◦ the chief priest); *mām̧* (obj◦ me); *viddhi* (know to be); *pārtha* (O Arjuna!); *bṛhaspatim̧* (obj16◦ Bṛhaspati); *senānīnām̧* (among the commanders-in-chiefs); *aham̧* (I am); *skandaḥ:* (subj17◦ Skanda); *sarasām̧* (among the bodies of water); *asmi* (I am); 🕮*sāgaraḥ:* (the ocean) (10.24)

(§4) pārtha purodhasām̧ mām̧ viddhi mukhyam̧ bṛhaspatim̧ senānīnām̧ aham̧ skandaḥ: ća sarasām̧ asmi sāgaraḥ:

(§5) O Arjuna! among the divine priests know me to be the chief priest Bṛhaspati, among the commanders-in-chiefs I am Skanda and among the bodies of water I am the ocean. (10.24)

10.25 महर्षीणां भृगुरहं गिरामस्म्येकमक्षरम् ।
यज्ञानां जपयज्ञोऽस्मि स्थावराणां हिमालयः ।।

maharṣiṇāṁ bhṛguraham̧ girāmasmyekamakṣaram̧,
yajñānāṁ japayajño'smi sthāvarāṇāṁ himālayaḥ:. (10.25)

(§1) *maharṣiṇām̧* (r◦ 24/6, 14/1) *bhṛguḥ:* (r◦ 16/3) *aham̧* (r◦ 14/1) *girām̧* (r◦ 8/16) *asmi* (r◦ 4/4) *ekam̧* (r◦ 8/16) *akṣaram̧* (r◦ 14/2) *yajñānām̧* (r◦ 14/1) *japayajñaḥ:* (r◦ 15/1) *asmi sthāvarāṇām̧* (r◦ 24/6, 14/1) *himālayaḥ:* (r◦ 22/8)

(§2) *maharṣiṇām̧* (10.2); *bhṛguḥ:* (m◦ 1nom◦ sing◦ ←prop◦ *Bhṛgu* ←√भ्रस्ज्); *aham̧* (1.22); *girām̧* (6pos plu◦ ←f◦ *gir* (speech) ←√गृ); *asmi* (7.8); *ekam̧* (1nom◦ sing◦ ←adj◦ *ek* (one) 3.2); *akṣaram̧* (n◦ 1nom◦ sing◦ ←adj◦ *akṣara* (immutable) 8.3); *yajñānām̧* (6pos plu◦ ←m◦ *yajña* 3.9); *japayajñaḥ:* (m◦ 1nom◦ sing◦ ←tatpu◦

japa-yajña, जपस्य यज्ञः ←m◦ *japa* (utterance) ←√जप् + m◦ *yajña* 3.9); *asmi* (7.8); *sthāvarāṇām̦* (m◦ 6pos◦ plu◦ ←adj◦ ***sthāvara*** (steady) ←√स्था); *himālayaḥ:* (m◦ 1nom◦ sing◦ ←prop◦ *Himālaya* ←adj◦ *hima* (ice, snow) ←√हि + n◦ *ālaya* (stirehouse) 8.15) (10.25)

(§3) *maharṣiṇām̦* (among the great sages); *bhṛguḥ:* (subj18◦ sage Bhṛgu); *aham̦* (I am); *girām̦* (among the utterances); *asmi* (I am); *ekam̦ akṣaram̦* (subj19◦ the monosyllable of om̦); *yajñānām̦* (among the austerities); *japayajñaḥ:* (subj20◦ the Japayajña); *asmi* (I am); *sthāvarāṇām̦* (among the immovables); *himālayaḥ:* (subj21◦ the Himālaya) (10.25)

(§4) maharṣiṇām̦ aham̦ bhṛguḥ: girām̦ asmi ekam̦ akṣaram̦ yajñānām̦ asmi japayajñaḥ: sthāvarāṇām̦ himālayaḥ:

(§5) Among the great sages I am sage Bhṛgu, among the utterances I am the monosyllable of om̦, among the austerities I am the *japayajña*, among the immovables I am the Himālaya. (10.25)

10.26 **अश्वत्थः सर्ववृक्षाणां देवर्षीणां च नारदः ।**
गन्धर्वाणां चित्ररथः सिद्धानां कपिलो मुनिः ।।
aśvatthaḥ: sarvavṛkṣāṇāṁ devarṣīṇāṁ ća nāradaḥ:,
gandharvāṇāṁ ćitrarathaḥ: siddhānāṁ kapilo muniḥ:. (10.26)

(§1) *aśvatthaḥ:* (r◦ 22/7) *sarvavṛkṣāṇām̦* (r◦ 24/6, 14/1) *devarṣīṇām̦* (r◦ 24/6, 14/1) *ća nāradaḥ:* (r◦ 22/8) *gandharvāṇām̦* (r◦ 24/6, 14/1) *ćitrarathaḥ:* (r◦ 22/7) *siddhānām̦* (r◦ 14/1) *kapilaḥ:* (r◦ 15/9) *muniḥ:* (r◦ 22/8)

(§2) *aśvatthaḥ:* (1nom◦ sing◦ ←m◦ n.tatpu◦ ***aśvattha,*** न श्वः चिरम् तिष्ठति इति *ficus religiosa* Pīpal tree or Banyan Tree←√स्था); *sarvavṛkṣāṇām̦* (सर्वेषाम् वृक्षाणाम् 6pos◦ plu◦ ←pron◦ *sarva* (all) 1.6 + m◦ 🕮*vṛkṣa* (tree) ←√वृश्च्); *devarṣīṇām̦* (6pos plu◦ ←m◦ *devarṣi* (divine sage) 10.13); *ća* (1.1); *nāradaḥ:* (10.13); *gandharvāṇām̦* (6pos plu◦ ←m◦ ***gandharva*** (divine mucisian) ←गन्ध√अर्व); *ćitrarathaḥ:* (m◦ 1nom◦ sing◦ ←prop◦ *ćitraratha* ←√चि); *siddhānām̦* (7.3); *kapilaḥ:* (m◦ 1nom◦ sing◦ ←prop◦ *Kapila* ←√कम्प्); *muniḥ:* (2.56) (10.26)

(§3) *aśvatthaḥ:* (subj22◦ the ficus Pīpal tree); *sarvavṛkṣāṇām̦* (among the trees); *devarṣīṇām̦* (among the divine sages); *ća* (and); *nāradaḥ:* (subj23◦ Nārada); *gandharvāṇām̦* (among the divine musicians); *ćitrarathaḥ:* (subj24◦ Chitraratha; *siddhānām̦* (among the accomplished ones); *kapilaḥ:* (subj25◦ Kapila); *muniḥ:* (adj◦-subj25◦ sage) (10.26)

(§4) sarvavṛkṣāṇām̦ aśvatthaḥ: devarṣīṇām̦ nāradaḥ: gandharvāṇām̦ ćitrarathaḥ: ća siddhānām̦ muniḥ: kapilaḥ:

(§5) Among the trees I am the Pīpal tree, among the divine sages I am Nārada, among the divine musicians I am Chitraratha, and among the accomplished ones (I am) sage Kapila.

10.27 उच्चैःश्रवसमश्वानां विद्धि माममृतोद्भवम् ।
ऐरावतं गजेन्द्राणां नराणां च नराधिपम् ।।
uććaiḥ:śravasamaśvānāṁ viddhi māmamṛtodbhavaṃ,
airāvataṁ gajendrāṇāṁ narāṇāṁ ća narādhipaṃ. (10.27)

(§1) *uććaiḥ:śravasaṃ* (r◦ 8/16) *aśvānāṃ* (r◦ 14/1) *viddhi māṃ* (r◦ 8/16) *amṛtodbhavaṃ* (r◦ 14/2) *airāvataṃ* (r◦ 14/1) *gajendrāṇāṃ* (r◦ 24/6, 14/1) *narāṇāṃ* (r◦ 24/6, 14/1) *ća narādhipaṃ* (r◦ 14/2)

(§2) *uććaiḥ:śravasaṃ* (m◦ 2acc◦ sing◦ ←prop◦ *Uććaiḥ:śravas* ←उद्√चि); *aśvānāṃ* (6pos plu◦ ←m◦ 🕮*aśva* (horse) 1.8); *viddhi* (2.17); *māṃ* (1.46); *amṛtodbhavaṃ* (m◦ 2acc◦ sing◦ ←bahuvrī◦ *amṛtodbhava*, अमृतात् उद्भवः यस्य ←n◦ *amṛta* (nectar of immortality) 2.15 + m◦ *udbhava* (origin) 3.15); *airāvataṃ* (m◦ 2acc◦ sing◦ ←prop◦ *Airāvata* ←√इ); *gajendrāṇāṃ* (m◦ 6pos◦ plu◦ ←tatpu◦ *Gajendra*, गजानाम् इन्द्रः ←m◦ 🕮*gaja* (elephant) ←√गज् + adj◦ *indra* (lord) 9.20); *narāṇāṃ* (6pos plu◦ ←m◦ *nara* (person) 1.5); *ća* (1.1); *narādhipaṃ* (m◦ 2acc◦ sing◦ ←tatpu◦ *narādhipa*, नराणाम् अधिपः ←m◦ *nara* (person) 1.5 + m◦ *adhipa* (king) 2.8) (10.27)

(§3) *uććaiḥ:śravasaṃ* (subj26◦ Uććaiḥśravasa); *aśvānāṃ* (among the horses); *viddhi* (know - to be); *māṃ* (obj◦ me); *amṛtodbhavaṃ* (adj◦-subj26◦ the one born from the nectar of immortality); *airāvataṃ* (subj27◦ Airāvata); *gajendrāṇāṃ* (among the great elephants); *narāṇāṃ* (among the men); *ća* (and);

(§4) aśvānāṃ viddhi māṃ uććaiḥ:śravasaṃ amṛtodbhavaṃ gajendrāṇāṃ airāvataṃ ća narāṇāṃ narādhipaṃ

(§5) Among the horses know me to be Uććaiḥśravasa, the one born from the nectar of immortality; among the great elephants (I am) Airāvata, and among the men (I am) the king. (10.27)

10.28 आयुधानामहं वज्रं धेनूनामस्मि कामधुक् ।
प्रजनश्चास्मि कन्दर्पः सर्पाणामस्मि वासुकिः ।।
āyudhānāmahaṁ vajraṁ dhenūnāmasmi kāmadhuk,
prajanaśćāsmi kandarpaḥ: sarpāṇāmasmi vāsukiḥ:. (10.28)

(§1) *āyudhānāṃ* (r◦ 8/16) *ahaṃ* (r◦ 14/1) *vajraṃ* (r◦ 14/1) *dhenūnāṃ* (r◦ 8/16) *asmi kāmadhuk* (r◦ 23/1) *prajanaḥ:* (r◦ 17/1) *ća* (r◦ 1/1) *asmi kandarpaḥ:* (r◦ 22/7) *sarpāṇāṃ* (r◦ 24/6, 8/16) *asmi vāsukiḥ:* (r◦ 22/8)

(§2) *āyudhānāṃ* (6pos plu◦ ←m◦ or n◦ 🕮***āyudha*** (weapon) ←आ√युध्); *ahaṃ* (1.22); 🕮*vajraṃ* (1nom◦ sing◦ ←n◦ *vajra* (thunderbolt) ←√वज्); *dhenūnāṃ* (6pos plu◦ ←f◦ 🕮*dhenu* (cow) ←√धे); *asmi* (7.8); *kāmadhuk*

(f∘ 1nom∘ sing∘ ←bahuvrī∘ *Kāmadhuk̦*, कामान् दोग्धि या 3.10); *parjanaḥ:* (1nom∘ sing∘ ←m∘ *parjana* (impregnation) ←पा√जन्); *ća* (1.1); *asmi* (7.8); *kandarpaḥ:* (m∘ 1nom∘ sing∘ ←bahuvrī∘ *Kandarpa* ←pron∘ *kam̦* 2.21 + m∘ ***darpa*** (ego) ←√दृप्); *sarpāṇām̦* (6pos plu∘ ←m∘ 🕮*sarpa* (snake) ←√सृप्); *asmi* (7.8); *vāsukiḥ:* (m∘ 1nom∘ sing∘ ←prop∘ taddhita∘ *Vāsuki* ←m∘ *vasuka* ←वसु√कै) (10.28)

(§3) *āyudhānām̦* (among weapons); *aham̦* (I am); *vajram̦* (subj28∘ the thunderbolt); *dhenūnām̦* (among cows); *asmi* (I am); *kāmadhuk̦* (subj29∘ Kamadhenu, the wish granting cow); *parjanaḥ:* (adj∘-subj30∘ the impregnator); *ća* (and); *asmi* (I am); *kandarpaḥ:* (subj30∘ Kandarpa); *sarpāṇām̦* (among the snakes); *asmi* (I am); *vāsukiḥ:* (subj31∘ Vāsuki) (10.28)

(§4) āyudhānām̦ aham̦ vajram̦ dhenūnām̦ asmi kāmadhuk̦ sarpāṇām̦ asmi vāsukiḥ: ća asmi kandarpaḥ: parjanaḥ: the impregnator

(§5) Among weapons I am the thunderbolt; among cows I am Kamadhenu, the wish granting cow; among the snakes I am Vāsuki; and I am Kandarpa, the impregnator.

(10.28)

10.29 **अनन्तश्चास्मि नागानां वरुणो यादसामहम् ।**
पितॄणामर्यमा चास्मि यमः संयमतामहम् ।।

anantaśćāsmi nāgānām̦ varuṇo yādasāmaham̦,
pitṛṇāmaryamā ćāsmi yamaḥ: sam̐yamatāmaham̦. (10.29)

(§1) *anantaḥ:* (r∘ 17/1) *ća* (r∘ 1/1) *asmi nāgānām̦* (r∘ 14/1) *varuṇaḥ:* (r∘ 15/10) *yādasām̦* (r∘ 14/2) *aham̦* (r∘ 14/1) *pitṛṇām̦* (r∘ 24/6, 8/16) *aryamā ća* (r∘ 1/1) *asmi yamaḥ:* (r∘ 22/7) *sam̐yamatām̦* (r∘ 8/16) *aham̦* (r∘ 14/2)

(§2) *anantaḥ:* (m∘ 1nom∘ sing∘ ←prop∘ or adj∘ *ananta* 2.41); ća (1.1); *asmi* (7.8); *nāgānām̦* (6pos plu∘ ←m∘ *nāga* (cobra) ←न√अग्); ***varuṇaḥ:*** (1nom∘ sing∘ ←m∘ *varuṇa* (lord of waters) ←√वृ); *yādasām̦* (6pos plu∘ ←n∘ *yādaș* (aquatics) ←√या); *aham̦* (1.22); *pitṛṇām̦* (6pos plu∘ ←m∘ *pitṛ* (forefather) 1.26); *aryamā* (1nom∘ sing∘ ←m∘ prop∘ *Aryaman̦* ←√मा); ća (1.1); *asmi* (7.8); ***yamaḥ:*** (m∘ 1nom∘ sing∘ ←prop∘ *Yama* ←√यम्); *sam̐yamatām̦* (m∘ 6pos∘ plu∘ ←śatṛ∘ adj∘ *sam̐yamaț* ←सम्√यम्); *aham̦* (1.22) (10.29)

(§3) *anantaḥ:* (subj32∘ Ananta, the Viṣṇu's eternal throne); ća (and); *asmi* (I am); *nāgānām̦* (among the cobras); *varuṇaḥ:* (subj33∘ Varuṇa, the Lord of waters); *yādasām̦* (among the aquatics); *aham̦* (I am); *pitṛṇām̦* (among the predecessors, antecedents); *aryamā* (subj34∘ Aryamā); ća (and); *asmi* (I am); *yamaḥ:* (subj35∘ Yama, the Lord of Death); *sam̐yamatām̦* (among the controllers); *aham̦* (I am)

(10.29)

(§4) nāgānām̦ asmi anantaḥ: ća yādasām̦ aham̦ varuṇaḥ: pitṛṇām̦ asmi aryamā ća sam̐yamatām̦ aham̦ yamaḥ:

(§5) Among the cobras I am Ananta, the Viṣṇu's eternal throne; and among the aquatics I am Varuṇa, the Lord of waters; among the predecessors I am Aryamā' and among the controllers I am Yama, the Lord of Death. (10.29)

10.30 प्रह्लादश्चास्मि दैत्यानां कालः कलयतामहम् ।
मृगाणां च मृगेन्द्रोऽहं वैनतेयश्च पक्षिणाम् ।।
prahlādaśćāsmi daityānām kālaḥ: kalayatāmaham,
mṛgāṇām ća mṛgendro'ham vainateyaśća pakṣiṇām. (10.30)

(§1) *prahlādaḥ:* (r◦ 17/1) *ća* (r◦ 1/1) *asmi daityānām* (r◦ 14/1) *kālaḥ:* (r◦ 22/1) *kalayatām* (r◦ 8/16) *aham* (r◦ 14/2) *mṛgāṇām* (r◦ 24/6, 14/1) *ća mṛgendraḥ:* (r◦ 15/1) *aham* (r◦ 14/1) *vainateyaḥ:* (r◦ 17/1) *ća pakṣiṇām* (r◦ 24/6, 14/2)

(§2) *prahlādaḥ:* (m◦ 1nom◦ sing◦ ←prop◦ *prahlādaḥ:* ←m◦ *hlāda* (joy) ←√ह्लाद्); ća (1.1); *asmi* (7.8); *daityānām* (m◦ 6pos◦ plu◦ ←taddhita◦ *daitya*, दितेः अपत्यम् ←f◦ *Diti* ←√दो); ***kālaḥ:*** (1nom◦ sing◦ ←m◦ *kāla* (time) 2.72); *kalayatām* (6pos plu◦ ←śatṛ◦ adj◦ *kalayat* (counting) ←√कल्); *aham* (1.22); *mṛgāṇām* (6pos plu◦ ←m◦ 🕮***mṛga*** (animal) ←√मृग्); ća (1.1); *mṛgendraḥ:* (m◦ 1nom◦ sing◦ ←bahuvrī◦ *mṛgendra* (lion) मृगाणाम् इन्द्रः यः ←m◦ *mṛga* ↑ + *indra* (lord) 9.20); *aham* (1.22); *vainateyaḥ:* (m◦ 1nom◦ sing◦ ←taddhita◦ *Vainateya*, विनतायाः अपत्यम् ←f◦ *vinatā* ←वि√नम्); ća (1.1); *pakṣiṇām* (6pos plu◦ ←m◦ 🕮*pakṣin* (bird) ←√पक्ष्) (10.30)

(§3) *prahlādaḥ:* (subj36◦ Prahlāda); *ća* (and); *asmi* (I am); *daityānām* (among the pious sons of Diti); *kālaḥ:* (subj37◦ the Time); *kalayatām* (among the reconers); *aham* (I am); *mṛgāṇām* (among the beasts, animals); ća (and); *mṛgendraḥ:* (subj38◦ the lion); *aham* (I am); *vainateyaḥ:* (subj 39◦ Vainateya, the vehicle of Lord Vishṇu); ća (and); *pakṣiṇām* (among the flyers) (10.30)

(§4) daityānām asmi prahlādaḥ: ća kalayatām aham kālaḥ: ća mṛgāṇām aham mṛgendraḥ: ća pakṣiṇām vainateyaḥ:

(§5) Among the pious sons of Diti I am Prahlāda; and among the reconers I am the Time; and among the beasts I am the lion; and among the flyers[596] I am Vainateya, the vehicle of Lord Vishṇu. (10.30)

10.31 पवनः पवतामस्मि रामः शस्त्रभृतामहम् ।

---

[596] Elsewhere◦ पक्षिणाम् → of the birds.

🕮 Here, पक्षिः is not just the अण्डजः or अण्डदः, but the flyer in the sky खगः (उड़ने उड़ानेवाला खग), the carrier vehicle in the sky खयानम् of Viṣṇu, ...etc.

झषाणां मकरश्चास्मि स्रोतसामस्मि जाह्नवी ।।

pavanaḥ: pavatāmasmi rāmaḥ: śastrabhṛtāmaham,

jhaṣāṇām makaraśćāsmi srotasāmasmi jāhnavī. (10.31)

1) *pavanaḥ:* (r∘ 22/3) *pavatāṃ* (r∘ 8/16) *asmi rāmaḥ:* (r∘ 22/5) *śastrabhṛtāṃ* (r∘ 8/16) *ahaṃ* (r∘ 14/2) *jhaṣāṇāṃ* (r∘ 24/6, 14/1) *makaraḥ:* (r∘ 17/1) *ća* (r∘ 1/1) *asmi srotasāṃ* (r∘ 8/16) *asmi jāhnavī*

(§2) 📖*pavanaḥ:* (1nom∘ sing∘ ←m∘ *pavana* (wind) ←√पू); *pavatāṃ* (6pos plu∘ ←śatṛ∘ adj∘ *pavat* (purifying) ←√पू); *asmi* (7.8); *rāmaḥ:* (m∘ 1nom∘ sing∘ ←prop∘ *Rāma* ←√रम्); *śastrabhṛtāṃ* (m∘ 6pos∘ plu∘ ←tatpu∘ *śastrabhṛt*, शस्त्राणि बिभ्रति इति ←n∘ *śastra* (weapon) 1.9 + śatṛ∘ adj∘ ***vibhrat*** (bearing) ←√भृ); *ahaṃ* (1.22); *jhaṣāṇāṃ* (6pos plu∘ ←m∘ 📖*jhaṣa* (aquatic animal) ←√झष्); 📖*makaraḥ:* (1nom∘ sing∘ ←m∘ *makara* (alligator) ←म√कृ); ća (1.1); *asmi* (7.8); *srotasāṃ* (6pos plu∘ ←n∘ 📖*srotaṣ* (river) ←√स्रु); *asmi* (7.8); *jāhnavī* (Gaṅgā, f∘ 1nom∘ sing∘ ←taddhita∘ *Jāhnavī*, जह्नोः पुत्री ←m∘ *jahnu*, son of Suhotra, the Ajmiḍh king ←√हा) (10.31)

(§3) *pavanaḥ:* (subj40∘ the wind); *pavatāṃ* (among purifiers); *asmi* (I am); *rāmaḥ:* (subj41∘ Lord Rāma); *śastrabhṛtāṃ* (among the weapon bearers); *ahaṃ* (I am); *jhaṣāṇāṃ* (among the aquatic animals); *makaraḥ:* (subj42∘ the Alligator); *ća* (and); *asmi* (I am); *srotasāṃ* (among the water flows); *asmi* (I am); *jāhnavī* (subj43∘ the river Gangā, Ganges) (10.31)

(§4) pavatāṃ asmi pavanaḥ: śastrabhṛtāṃ ahaṃ rāmaḥ: jhaṣāṇāṃ asmi makaraḥ: ća srotasāṃ asmi jāhnavī

(§5) Among purifiers I am the wind; among the weapon bearers I am Lord Rāma; among the aquatic animals I am the Alligator; and among the water flows I am the river Gangā. (10.31)

10.32 सर्गाणामादिरन्तश्च मध्यं चैवाहमर्जुन ।

अध्यात्मविद्या विद्यानां वादः प्रवदतामहम् ।।

sargāṇāmādirantaśća madhyam ćaivāhamarjuna,

adhyātmavidyā vidyānām vādaḥ: pravadatāmahaṃ. (10.32)

(§1) *sargāṇāṃ* (r∘ 24/6, 8/17) *ādiḥ:* (r∘ 16/1) *antaḥ:* (r∘ 17/1) *ća madhyaṃ* (r∘ 14/1) *ća* (r∘ 3/1) *eva* (r∘ 1/1) *ahaṃ* (r∘ 8/16) *arjuna* (r∘ 23/1) *adhyātmavidyā vidyānāṃ* (r∘ 14/1) *vādaḥ:* (r∘ 22/3) *pravadatāṃ* (r∘ 8/16) *ahaṃ* (r∘ 14/2)

(§2) *sargāṇāṃ* (6pos plu∘ ←m∘ *sarga* (evolution) 5.19); *ādiḥ:* (10.2); *antaḥ:* (2.16); ća (1.1); *madhyaṃ* (10.20); *ća* (1.1); *eva* (1.1); *ahaṃ* (1.22); *arjuna* (2.2); *adhyātmavidyā* (f∘ 1nom∘ sing∘ ←tatpu∘ *adhyātma-vidyā*, अध्यात्मनः विद्या ←adj∘ *adhyātma* (knowledge of self) 3.30 + f∘ *vidyā* (knowledge) 5.18); *vidyānāṃ* (6pos plu∘ ←f∘ *vidyā* (knowledge) 5.18); *vādaḥ:* (1nom∘ sing∘ ←m∘ *vāda* 2.11); *pravadatāṃ* (m∘ 6pos∘ plu∘ ←śatṛ∘ adj∘ *pravadat* (arguing) ←प्र√वद्); *ahaṃ* (1.22) (10.32)

(§3) *sargāṇām* (among the evolutionary things, entities); *ādiḥ:* (subj44◦ the beginning); *antaḥ:* (subj45◦ the end); *ća* (and); *madhyam* (subj46◦ the middle state); *ća eva* (as well as); *aham* (I am); *arjuna* (O Arjuna!); *adhyātmavidyā* (subj47◦ the science of the self); *vidyānām* (among the sciences); *vādaḥ:* (subj48◦ the oration, logic); *pravadatām* (of the orators, of the logicians); *aham* (I am) (10.32)

(§4) arjuna sargāṇām aham ādiḥ: madhyam ća eva antaḥ: vidyānām aham adhyātmavidyā ća vādaḥ: pravadatām

(§5) O Arjuna! among the evolutionary entities I am the beginning, the middle state as well as the end; among the sciences I am the science of the self and (Iam) the logic of the logicians. (10.32)

10.33 **अक्षराणामकारोऽस्मि द्वन्द्वः सामासिकस्य च ।**
अहमेवाक्षयः कालो धाताहं विश्वतोमुखः ।।

akṣarāṇāmakāro'smi dvandvaḥ: sāmāsikasya ća,
ahamevākṣayaḥ: kālo dhātāhaṁ viśvatomukhaḥ:. (10.33)

(§1) *akṣarāṇām* (r◦ 24/6, 8/16) *akāraḥ:* (r◦ 15/1) *asmi dvandvaḥ:* (r◦ 22/7) *sāmāsikasya ća* (r◦ 23/1) *aham* (r◦ 8/22) *eva* (r◦ 1/1) *akṣayaḥ:* (r◦ 22/1) *kālaḥ:* (r◦ 15/5) *dhātā* (r◦ 1/3) *aham* (r◦ 14/1) *viśvatomukhaḥ:* (r◦ 22/8)

(§2) *akṣarāṇām* (6pos plu◦ ←n◦ *akṣara* (immutable) 3.15); *akāraḥ:* (1nom◦ sing◦ ←m◦ *akāra* (letter a) ←vowel "अ" + adj◦ *kāra* 2.2); *asmi* (7.8); *dvandvaḥ:* (m◦ 1nom◦ sing◦ ←prop◦ *dvandva* (dual compound) द्वंद्वः समासः ←√द्वु); *sāmāsikasya* (6pos sing◦ ←taddhita◦ adj◦ *sāmāsika* (dual) ←m◦ ***samāsa*** (compound word) ←सम्√अस्); *ća* (1.1); *aham* (1.22); *eva* (1.1); *akṣayaḥ:* (m◦ 1nom◦ sing◦ ←adj◦ *akṣaya* (perpetual) 5.21); *kālaḥ:* (10.30); *dhātā* (9.17); *aham* (1.22); *viśvatomukhaḥ:* (m◦ 1nom◦ sing◦ ←bahuvrī◦ *viśvatomukha* (omniscient) 9.15) (10.33)

(§3) *akṣarāṇām* (among the indeclanable characters, the alphabet); *akāraḥ:* (subj49◦ the character a); *asmi* (I am); *dvandvaḥ:* (subj50◦ the Aggregative Compound); *sāmāsikasya* (among the compound words, composite words); *ća* (and); *aham* (I am); *eva* (also); *akṣayaḥ:* (adj◦-subj51◦ the perpetual, eternal); *kālaḥ:* (subj51◦ Time); *dhātā* (subj52◦ Sustainer); *aham* (I am); *viśvatomukhaḥ:* (adj◦-subj52◦ the omniscient) (10.33)

(§4) akṣarāṇām asmi akāraḥ: sāmāsikasya aham dvandvaḥ: ća aham akṣayaḥ: kālaḥ: eva viśvatomukhaḥ: dhātā

(§5) Among the indeclanable characters I am the character a, among the composite words I am the Aggregative Compound and I am the perpetual Time also (I am) the omniscient

Sustainer. (10.33)

10.34 मृत्युः सर्वहरश्चाहमुद्भवश्च भविष्यताम् ।
कीर्तिः श्रीर्वाक्च नारीणां स्मृतिर्मेधा धृतिः क्षमा ॥

mṛtyuḥ: sarvaharaśćāhamudbhavaśća bhaviṣyatām,
kīrti śrīrvākća nārīṇām smṛtirmedhā dhṛtiḥ: kṣamā. (10.34)

(§1) *mṛtyuḥ:* (r◦ 22/7) *sarvaharaḥ:* (r◦ 17/1) *ća* (r◦ 1/1) *aham* (r◦ 8/20) *udbhavaḥ:* (r◦ 17/1) *ća bhaviṣyatām* (r◦ 14/2) *kīrtiḥ:* (r◦ 22/5) *śrīḥ:* (r◦ 16/7) *vāk* (r◦ 10/1) *ća nārīṇām* (r◦ 24/6, 14/1) *smṛtiḥ:* (r◦ 16/6) *medhā dhṛtiḥ:* (r◦ 22/1) *kṣamā*

(§2) 📖*mṛtyuḥ:* (2.27); *sarvaharaḥ:* (1nom◦ sing◦ ←m◦ *sarva-hara*, सर्वम् हरति इति ←pron◦ *sarva* (all) 1.6 + adj◦ *hara* (take away) ←√हृ); ća (1.1); *aham* (1.22); *udbhavaḥ:* (1nom◦ sing◦ ←m◦ *udbhava* (origin) 3.15); ća (1.1); *bhaviṣyatām* (6pos sing◦ ←śatṛ◦ adj◦ *bhaviṣyat* (to be in the future) ←√भू); 📖*kīrtiḥ:* (1nom◦ sing◦ ←f◦ *kīrti* (fame) 2.2); 📖***śrīḥ:*** (1nom◦ sing◦ ←f◦ *śrī* (prosperity) ←√श्री); 📖*vāk* (1nom◦ sing◦ *vāk* or *vāg* (speech) ←f◦ *vāk* ←√वच्); ća (1.1); *nārīṇām* (6pos plu◦ ←f◦ *nārī* (woman) ←√नृ); 📖***smṛtiḥ:*** (1nom◦ sing◦ ←f◦ *smṛti* (cognizance) 2.63); 📖*medhā* (1nom◦ sing◦ ←f◦ *medhā* (intelligence) 7.23); ***dhṛtiḥ:*** (1nom◦ sing◦ ←f◦ *dhṛti* (courage) 6.25); *kṣamā* (10.4) (10.34)

(§3) *mṛtyuḥ:* (subj53◦ Death); *sarvaharaḥ:* (adj◦-subj53◦ the all-devouring); *ća* (and); *aham* (I am); *udbhavaḥ:* (subj54◦ the Birth); *ća* (and); *bhaviṣyatām* (of those that are to be); *kīrtiḥ:* (subj55◦ the fame); *śrīḥ:* (subj56◦ prosperity); *vāk* (subj57◦ oration, eloquence); *ća* (and); *nārīṇām* (of the wonem); *smṛtiḥ:* (subj58◦ cognizance); *medhā* (subj59◦ intelligence); *dhṛtiḥ:* (subj60◦ courage); *kṣamā* (subj61◦ forgivrness) (10.34)

(§4) aham udbhavaḥ: ća sarvaharaḥ: mṛtyuḥ: bhaviṣyatām ća kīrtiḥ: śrīḥ: vāk smṛtiḥ: medhā dhṛtiḥ: ća kṣamā nārīṇām

(§5) I am the Birth of those that ate to be and (I am) the all-devouring Death. (I am) the fame, prosperity, eloquence, cognizance, intelligence, courage and forgivrness of the wonem. (10.34)

10.35 बृहत्साम तथा साम्नां गायत्री छन्दसामहम् ।
मासानां मार्गशीर्षोऽहमृतूनां कुसुमाकरः ॥

bṛhatsāma tathā sāmnām gāyatrī ćhandasāmaham,
māsānām mārgaśīrṣo'hamṛtūnām kusumākaraḥ:. (10.35)

(§1) *bṛhatsāma tathā sāmnām* (r◦ 14/1) *gāyatrī ćhandasām* (r◦ 8/16) *aham* (r◦ 14/2) *māsānām* (r◦ 14/1) *mārgaśīrṣaḥ:* (r◦ 15/1) *aham* (r◦ 8/21) *ṛtūnām* (r◦ 14/1) *kusumākaraḥ:* (r◦ 22/8)

(§2) *bṛhatsāma* (n◦ 1nom◦ sing◦ ←prop◦ tatpu◦ *bṛhat-sāman* ←adj◦ *bṛhaṭ* (great) 10.24 + n◦ *sāman* (verse of the Sama-veda) 9.17); *tathā* (1.8); *sāmnām* (6pos plu◦ ←n◦ *sāman* (Sama-veda) 9.17); *gāyatrī* (f◦ 1nom◦ sing◦ ←bahuvrī◦ *Gāyatrī*, गायन्तम् त्रायते या ←m◦ *gāya* (song) ←√गै + adj◦ *trāyate* 2.40; for *gāyatrī mantra-* please see at the end of this chapter ↓); *ćhandasām* (6pos plu◦ ←n◦ ***ćhandas*** (meter) ←√छन्द्); *aham* (1.22); *māsānām* (6pos plu◦ ←n◦ *māsa* (month) 8.24); *mārgaśīrṣaḥ:* (1nom◦ sing◦ ←prop◦ *Mārgaśīrṣa* ←√मृग्); *aham* (1.22); *ṛtūnām* (6pos plu◦ ←m◦ *ṛtu* (season) ←√ऋ); 🕮*kusumākaraḥ:* (1nom◦ sing◦ ←bahuvrī◦ *Kusumākara*, कुसुमानाम् आकर: ←n◦ *kusuma* (flower) ←√कुस् + m◦ *ākara* (soorehouse) ←आ√कृ) (10.35)

(§3) *bṛhatsāma* (subj62◦ the Bṛhatsāma); *tathā* (also); *sāmnām* (among the hyms of the Sāmaveda); *gāyatrī* (subj63◦ the Gāyatri metre); *ćhandasām* (among the poetic metres; *aham* (I am); *māsānām* (of the twelve months of the year); *mārgaśīrṣaḥ:* (subj64◦ the month of Mārgaśīrṣa); *aham* (I am); *ṛtūnām* (among the six seasons of the year); *kusumākaraḥ:* (adj◦-subj64◦ the flowering Spring season) (10.35)

(§4) sāmnām aham bṛhatsāma tathā ćhandasām gāyatrī māsānām aham mārgaśīrṣaḥ: ṛtūnām kusumākaraḥ:

(§5) Among the hyms of the Sāmaveda I am the Bṛhatsāma, also among the poetic metres I am the Gāyatri metre of the twelve months of the year I am the month of Mārgaśīrṣa among the six seasons of the year (I am) the flowering Spring season.

(10.35)

10.36 द्यूतं छलयतामस्मि तेजस्तेजस्विनामहम् ।
जयोऽस्मि व्यवसायोऽस्मि सत्त्वं सत्त्ववतामहम् ।।
dyūtaṁ ćhalayatāmasmi tejastejasvināmaham,
jayo'smi vyavasāyosmi satvaṁ satvavatāmaham. (10.36)

(§1) *dyūtam* (r◦ 14/1) *ćhalayatām* (r◦ 8/16) *asmi tejaḥ:* (r◦ 18/1) *tejasvinām* (r◦ 8/16) *aham* (r◦ 14/2) *jayaḥ:* (r◦ 15/1) *asmi vyavasāyaḥ:* (r◦ 15/1) *asmi sattvam* (r◦ 14/1) *satvavatām* (r◦ 8/16) *aham* (r◦ 14/2)

(§2) *dyūtam* (1nom◦ sing◦ ←n◦ *dyūta* (gamble) ←√दिव्); *ćhalayatām* (m◦ 6pos◦ plu◦ ←śatṛ◦ adj◦ *ćhalayaṭ* (deceiving) ←√छल्); *asmi* (7.8); *tejaḥ:* (7.9); *tejasvinām* (7.10); *aham* (1.22); 🕮*jayaḥ:* (1nom◦ sing◦ ←m◦ *jaya* (victory) 1.8); *asmi* (7.8); ***vyavasāyaḥ:*** (1nom◦ sing◦ ←m◦ *vyavasāya* (resolution) 2.41); *asmi* (7.8); ***sattvam*** (1nom◦ sing◦ ←n◦ *sattva* (truth) 2.15); *satvavatām* (6pos plu◦ ←śatṛ◦ adj◦ *satvavaṭ* (truthful) ←√अस्); *aham* (1.22) (10.36)

(§3) *dyūtam* (subj65◦ the Game of luck); *ćhalayatām* (among the deceits); *asmi* (I am); *tejaḥ:* (subj66◦ the Brilliance); *tejasvinām* (of the brilliant); *aham* (I am); *jayaḥ:* (subj67◦ the Victory); *asmi* (I am);

vyavasāyaḥ: (subj68◦ the Resolution);[597] *asmi* (I am); *sattvaṃ* (subj69◦ the Truth); *satvavatāṃ* (of the truthful); *ahaṃ* (I am) (10.36)

(§4) ćhalayatāṃ asmi dyūtaṃ ahaṃ tejaḥ: tejasvināṃ asmi jayaḥ: ahaṃ vyavasāyaḥ: asmi sattvaṃ satvavatāṃ

(§5) Among the deceits I am the Game of luck. I am the Brilliance of the brilliant. I am the Victory. I am the Resolution. I am the Truth of the truthful. (10.36)

10.37 वृष्णीनां वासुदेवोऽस्मि पाण्डवानां धनञ्जयः ।
मुनीनामप्यहं व्यासः कवीनामुशना कविः ॥
vṛṣṇināṁ Vasudevo'smi pāṇḍavānāṁ dhanañjaya,
munīnāmapyahaṁ vyāsaḥ: kavīnāmuśanā kaviḥ:. (10.37)

(§1) *vṛṣṇināṃ* (r◦ 14/1) *Vāsudevaḥ:* (r◦ 15/1) *asmi pāṇḍavānāṃ* (r◦ 14/1) *dhanañjayaḥ:* (r◦ 22/8) *munīnāṃ* (r◦ 8/16) *api* (r◦ 4/1) *ahaṃ* (r◦ 14/1) *vyāsaḥ:* (r◦ 22/1) *kavīnāṃ* (r◦ 8/20) *uśanā kaviḥ:* (r◦ 22/8)

(§2) *vṛṣṇināṃ* (6pos plu◦ ←prop◦ *Vṛṣṇi* 1.41); *Vāsudevaḥ:* (7.19); *asmi* (7.8); *pāṇḍavānāṃ* (6pos plu◦ ←m◦ *Pāṇḍava* 1.1); *dhanañjayaḥ:* (1.15); *munīnāṃ* (6pos plu◦ ←m◦ *muni* (sage) 2.56); *api* (1.26); *ahaṃ* (1.22); *vyāsaḥ:* (10.13); *kavīnāṃ* (6pos plu◦ ←m◦ *kavi* (erudite) 4.16); *uśanā* (1nom◦ sing◦ ←m◦ prop◦ *Uśanaṣ* ←√वश्); *kaviḥ:* (1nom◦ sing◦ ←m◦ *kavi* (learned) 4.16) (10.37)

(§3) *vṛṣṇināṃ* (among the Vṛṣṇī kinfolk, clan); *Vāsudevaḥ:* (subj70◦ Vāsudeva, Vishṇu); *asmi* (I am); *pāṇḍavānāṃ* (among the Paṇḍavas); *dhanañjayaḥ:* (subj71◦ Arjuna); *munīnāṃ* (among the sages); *api* (also); *ahaṃ* (I am); *vyāsaḥ:* (subj 72◦ the sage Vyāsa); *kavīnāṃ* (among the erudite); *uśanā* (subj73◦ Uśanā); *kaviḥ:* (adj◦-subj73◦ the learned) (10.37)

(§4) vṛṣṇināṃ asmi Vāsudevaḥ: pāṇḍavānāṃ dhanañjayaḥ: api munīnāṃ ahaṃ vyāsaḥ: kavīnāṃ kaviḥ: uśanā

(§5) Among the Vṛṣṇī kinfolk I am Vāsudeva; among the Paṇḍavas (Iam) Arjuna. Also among the sages I am the sage Vyāsa; among the erudite (I am) the learned Uśanā. (10.37)

10.38 दण्डो दमयतामस्मि नीतिरस्मि जिगीषताम् ।
मौनं चैवास्मि गुह्यानां ज्ञानं ज्ञानवतामहम् ॥
daṇḍo damayatāmasmi nītirasmi jigīṣatām,
maunaṁ ćaivāsmi guhyānāṁ jñānaṁ jñānavatāmahaṃ. (10.38)

(§1) *daṇḍaḥ:* (r◦ 15/4) *damayatāṃ* (r◦ 8/16) *asmi nītiḥ:* (r◦ 16/1) *asmi jigīṣatāṃ* (r◦ 14/2) *maunaṃ* (r◦

---

[597] For the meaning of व्यवसायः, व्यवसायामिका, अव्यवसायी → see verse 2.41

14/1) *ća* (r◦ 3/1) *eva* (r◦ 1/1) *asmi guhyānām̦* (r◦ 14/1) *jñānam̦* (r◦ 14/1) *jñānavatām̦* (r◦ 8/16) *aham̦* (r◦ 14/2)

(§2) 🕮*daṇḍah̦:* (1nom◦ sing◦ ←m◦ *daṇḍa* (punishment, rule) ←√दण्ड्); *damayatām̦* (m◦ 6pos◦ plu◦ ←śatr̥◦ adj◦ *damayaț* (ruler) ←√दम्); *asmi* (7.8); 🕮***nītih̦:*** (1nom◦ sing◦ ←f◦ *nīti* (morality) ←√नी); *asmi* (7.8); *jigīṣatām̦* (m◦ 6pos◦ plu◦ ←śatr̥◦ -desi◦ adj◦ *jigīṣaț* (seeking) ←√जि); 🕮***maunam̦*** (n◦ 1nom◦ sing◦ ←tatpu◦ taddhita◦ *mauna,* मुने: भाव: ←m◦ *muni* (sage) 2.56 + m◦ *bhāva* (nature) 2.7); *ća* (1.1); *eva* (1.1); *asmi* (7.8); *guhyānām̦* (6pos plu◦ ←n◦ *guhya* (secret) 9.1); *jñānam̦* (3.39); *jñānavatām̦* (6pos plu◦ ←adj◦ *jñānavaț* (knowledgeable) 3.33); *aham̦* (1.22) (10.38)

(§3) *daṇḍah̦:* (subj74◦ the Scepture, Punishment); *damayatām̦* (of the rulers); *asmi* (I am); *nītih̦:* (subj75◦ righteousness, morality); *asmi* (I am); *jigīṣatām̦* (of those seek justice); *maunam̦* (subj◦ 76◦ taciturnity, silence); *ća eva* (and); *asmi* (I am); *guhyānām̦* (of the secrets); *jñānam̦* (subj77◦ knowledge); *jñānavatām̦* (of the knowledgeable); *aham̦* (I am) (10.38)

(§4) asmi daṇḍah̦: damayatām̦ asmi nītih̦: jigīṣatām̦ asmi maunam̦ guhyānām̦ ća eva aham̦ jñānam̦ jñānavatām̦

(§5) I am the Scepture of the rulers; I am morality of those seek justice; I am silence of the secrets and I am knowledge of the knowledgeable. (10.38)

10.39 यच्चापि सर्वभूतानां बीजं तदहमर्जुन ।
न तदस्ति विना यत्स्यान्मया भूतं चराचरम् ।।
yaććāpi sarvabhūtānāṁ bījaṁ tadahamarjuna,
na tadasti vinā yatsyānmayā bhūtaṁ ćarāćaram̦. (10.39)

(§1) *yaț* (r◦ 11/1) *ća* (r◦ 1/1) *api sarvabhūtānām̦* (r◦ 14/1) *bījam̦* (r◦ 14/1) *taț* (r◦ 8/2) *aham̦* (r◦ 8/16) *arjuna na taț* (r◦ 8/2) *asti vinā yaț* (r◦ 10/7) *syāț* (r◦ 12/2) *mayā bhūtam̦* (r◦ 14/1) *ćarāćaram̦* (r◦ 14/2)

(§2) *yaț* (1nom◦ 2.67); *ća* (1.1); *api* (1.26); *sarva* (1.6); *bhūtānām̦* (2.69); *bījam̦* (seed, 7.10); *taț* (1nom◦ 1.10); *aham̦* (1.22); *arjuna* (2.2); *na* (1.30); *taț* (1.10); *asti* (2.40); *vinā* (without, absence indicating ind◦ *vi* 9.12 + negative ind◦ *nā* (not) ←√नह्); *yaț* (1.45); *syāț* (1.36); *mayā* (1.22); *bhūtam̦* (1nom◦ sing◦ ←n◦ *bhūta* 2.28); 🕮***ćarāćaram̦*** (n◦ 1nom◦ sing◦ ←dvandva◦ चरम् च अचरम् च ←adj◦ *ćara* (movable) 9.10 + *a-ćara* (non-movable) 9.10) (10.39)

(§3) *yaț ća api* (and whatsoever is); *sarva bhūtānām̦* (of all beings); *bījam̦* (subj 78◦ the seed); *taț* (that); *aham̦* (I am); *arjuna* (O Arjuna!); *na* (nothing); *asti* (there is); *vinā* (without); *yaț* (which); *syāț* (may be); *mayā* (by me); *bhūtam̦* (being); *ćarāćaram̦* (moving as well as non-moving. (10.39)

(§4) arjuna yaț ća api bījam̦ sarva bhūtānām̦ taț aham̦. asti na ćarāćaram̦ bhūtam̦ taț yaț syāț vinā mayā

(§5) **And, O Arjuna! whatsoever is the seed of all beings that I am. There is no moving as well as non-moving being that which may be without me.** (10.39)

10.40 नान्तोऽस्ति मम दिव्यानां विभूतीनां परन्तप ।
एष तूद्देशतः प्रोक्तो विभूतेर्विस्तरो मया ।।

nānto'sti mama divyānāṁ vibhūtīnāṁ parantapa,
eṣa tūddeśataḥ: prokto vibhūtervistaro mayā. (10.40)

(§1) *na* (r◦ 1/1) *antaḥ:* (r◦ 15/1) *asti mama divyānām̦* (r◦ 14/1) *vibhūtīnām̦* (r◦ 14/1) *parantapa* (r◦ 23/1) *eṣaḥ:* (r◦ 25/1, 21/1) *tu* (r◦ 1/8) *uddeśataḥ:* (r◦ 22/3) *proktaḥ:* (r◦ 15/13) *vibhūteḥ:* (r◦ 16/10) *vistaraḥ:* (r◦ 15/9) *mayā*

(§2) *na* (1.30); *antaḥ:* (end, 2.16); *asti* (2.40); *mama* (1.7); *divyānām̦* (6pos plu◦ ←adj◦ *divya* (divine) 1.14); *vibhūtīnām̦* (6pos plu◦ ←f◦ *vibhūti* (divinity) 10.7); *parantapa* (2.3); *eṣaḥ:* (3.10); *tu* (1.2); 🕮*uddeśataḥ:* (adv◦ ind◦ ←n◦ *uddeśa* (example) ←उद्√दिश्); *proktaḥ:* (4.3); *vibhūteḥ:* (6pos sing◦ ←f◦ *vibhūti* (divinity) 10.7); *vistaraḥ:* (1nom◦ sing◦ ←m◦ *vistara* (spread) 10.18); *mayā* (1.22) (10.40)

(§3) *na* (no); *antaḥ:* (subj1◦ end); *asti* (there is); *mama* (my); *divyānām̦* (divine); *vibhūtīnām̦* (manifestations); *parantapa* (O Arjuna!); *eṣaḥ:* (adj◦-obj◦ this); *tu* (however); *uddeśataḥ:* (by way of, for the purpose of illustration); *proktaḥ:* (stated); *vibhūteḥ:* (of manifestations); *vistaraḥ:* (obj◦ expanse); *mayā* (subj2◦ by me) (10.40)

(§4) parantapa asti na antaḥ: mama divyānām̦ vibhūtīnām̦ tu eṣaḥ: vistaraḥ: vibhūteḥ: proktaḥ: mayā uddeśataḥ:

(§5) **O Arjuna! there is no end (to) my divine manifestations, however, this expanse of (my) manifestations (is) stated by me for the purpose of illustration (only).** (10.40)

10.41 यद्यद्विभूतिमत्सत्त्वं श्रीमदूर्जितमेव वा ।
तत्तदेवावगच्छ त्वं मम तेजोंऽशसम्भवम् ।।

yadyadvibhūtimatsatvaṁ śrīmadūrjitameva vā,
tattadevāvagaćcha tvaṁ mama tejo'm̐śasambhavam̦. (10.41)

(§1) *yaț* (r◦ 9/9) *yaț* (r◦ 9/11) *vibhūtimaț* (r◦ 10/7) *sattvam̦* (r◦ 14/1) *śrīmaț* (r◦ 8/7) *ūrjitam̦* (r◦ 8/22) *eva vā taț* (r◦ 1/10) *taț* (r◦ 8/9) *eva* (r◦ 1/1) *avagaćcha tvam̦* (r◦ 14/1) *mama tejaḥ:* (r◦ 15/1) *am̐śasambhavam̦* (r◦ 14/2)

(§2) *yaț* (1.45); *yaț* (1.45); *vibhūtimaț* (n◦ 1nom◦ sing◦ ←adj◦ *vibhūtimaț* (divine) ←f◦ *vibhūti* (divinity) 10.7 + affix *maț* (possessed of) ←वि√भू); *sattvam̦* (essence, 10.36); *śrīmaț* (n◦ 1nom◦ sing◦ ←adj◦ *śrīmaț* (lofty) 6.41);

📖*ūrjitam̧* (n∘ 1nom∘ sing∘ ←adj∘ ppp∘ *ūrjita* (mighty) ←√ऊर्ज्); *eva* (1.1); *vā* (1.32); *taţ* (1nom∘ 2.7); *taţ* (↑); *eva* (1.1); *avagac̀cha* (2nd-per∘ sing∘ imperative∘ उपदेशार्थ–लोट् parasmai∘ ←class1∘ अव√गम् 9.2); *tvam̧* (2.11); *mama* (1.7); *tejo'm̃s'asambhavam̧* (m∘ 2acc∘ sing∘ ←bahuvrī∘ *tejaḩ:-am̃s'a-sambhava*, तेजसः अंशात् सम्भवः यस्य ←m∘ *tejaş* (splendor) 7.9 + m∘ ***ams'a*** (fractiom) ←√अंश् + m∘ *sambhava* (manifestation) 3.14) (10.41)

(§3) *yaţ yaţ* (whatever); *vibhūtimaţ* (adj1∘-subj∘ divine); *sattvam̧* (subj∘ existance); *s'rīmaţ* (adj2∘-subj∘ glorious, oppulant); *ūrjitam̧* (adj3∘-subj∘ mighty, powerful); *eva* (and); *vā* (or); *taţ taţ* (obj∘ that everything); *eva* (only); *avagac̀cha* (you please know); *tvam̧* (you); *mama* (my); *tejo'm̃s'asambhavam̧* (adj∘-obj∘ a manifestation of a fraction of my splendor) (10.41)

(§4) yaţ yaţ vibhūtimaţ s'rīmaţ eva vā ūrjitam̧ sattvam̧ avagac̀cha tvam̧ taţ taţ mama tejo'm̃s'asambhavam̧ eva

(§5) Whatever (is) divine, glorious and or mighty existance, you please know that everything (to be) a manifestation[598] of a fraction of my splendor only. (10.41)

10.42 **अथवा बहुनैतेन किं ज्ञातेन तवार्जुन ।**
विष्टभ्याहमिदं कृत्स्नमेकांशेन स्थितो जगत् ।।
athavā bahunaitena kiṁ jñātena tavārjuna,
viṣṭbhyāhamidaṁ kr̥tsnamekām̃s'ena sthito jagaţ. (10.42)

(§1) *athavā bahunā* (r∘ 3/3) *etena kim̧* (r∘ 14/1) *jñātena tava* (r∘ 1/1) *arjuna viṣṭbhya* (r∘ 1/1) *aham̧* (r∘ 8/18) *idam̧* (r∘ 14/1) *kr̥tsnam̧* (r∘ 8/22) *ekām̃s'ena sthitaḩ:* (r∘ 15/3) *jagaţ*

(§2) *athavā* (or, 6.42); *bahunā* (m∘ 3inst∘ sing∘ ←adj∘ *bahu* (much) 1.9); *etena* (3.39); *kim̧* (1.1); *jñātena* (m∘ 3inst∘ sing∘ ←ppp∘ adj∘ *jñāta* (known) ←√ज्ञा); *tava* (1.3); *arjuna* (2.2); *viṣṭbhya* (lyp∘ past-participle ind∘ ←वि√स्तम्भ्); *aham̧* (1.22); *idam̧* (1.10); *kr̥tsnam̧* (entire, 1.40); *ekām̃s'ena* (m∘ 3inst∘ sing∘ ←tatpu∘ *ekām̃s'a*, एकस्य अंशः ←adj∘ *eka* (one) 2.41 + m∘ *ams'a* (fraction) 10.41); *sthitaḩ:* (5.20); *jagaţ* (7.5) (10.42)

(§3) *athavā* (or else, on the other hand); *bahunā* (with much, with excessive, with extensive); *etena* (with this); *kim̧* (what); *jñātena* (by known); *tava* (for you); *arjuna* (O Arjuna!); *viṣṭbhya* (having

---

[598] Elsewhere∘ अंशसंभवम् → He originates from (Present tense verb∘), to go forth from (Present∘ verb∘), have manifested from (ppp∘), having a part of (gerund), spring from (Present∘ verb∘), have sprung from (plu∘ ppp∘), to have sprung but from (ppp∘), is born of (sing∘ ppp∘), ...etc.

📖 अंशसंभवम् is not a verb, gerund or ppp∘ of any kind. अंशसंभवः is a Nominative case noun subject∘ composed of a *tatpurusha samāsa* m∘ अंश + m∘ संभवः (अंशात् संभवः = manifestation from a fraction). And, अंशसंभवम् is the Accusative (2nd) case object of that m∘ noun अंशसंभवः ।

supported safely); *aham* (subj◦ I); *idam* (adj1◦-obj◦ this); *kṛtsnam* (adj2◦-obj◦ entire); *ekāṁśena* (with one bit); *sthitaḥ:* (adj◦-subj◦ stay, stay put, remain); *jagat* (obj◦ universe) (10.42)

(§4) arjuna athavā kiṁ tava etena bahunā jñātena ahaṁ sthitaḥ: viṣṭbhya idaṁ kṛtsnaṁ jagat ekāṁśena

(§5) O Arjuna! on the other hand, what (avail is) for you with this much[599] known?[600] I remain, having sustained[601] this entire universe with one bit (of myself). (10.42)

इति श्रीमद्भगवद्गीतासूपनिषत्सु ब्रह्मविद्यायां योगशास्त्रे
श्रीकृष्णार्जुनसंवादे विभूतियोगो नाम दशमोऽध्यायः ।।

iti śrīmadbhagavadgītāsūpaniṣatsu brahmavidyāyāṁ yogaśāstre
śrīkṛṣṇārjunasaṁvāde vibhūtiyogo nāma daśamo'dhyāyaḥ:.

(§1) *iti śrīmadbhagavadgītāsu* (r◦ 1/8) *upaniṣatsu brahmavidyāyām* (r◦ 14/1) *yogaśāstre śrīkṛṣṇārjunasaṁvāde vibhūtiyogaḥ:* (r◦ 15/6) *nāma daśamaḥ:* (r◦ 15/1) *adhyāyaḥ:* (r◦ 22/8)

(§2) *iti* (1.25); *śrīmadbhagavadgītāsu* (f◦ 7loc◦ plu◦ tatpu◦ *śrīmad-bhagavad-gītā* ←adj◦ *śrīmat* 6.41 + adj◦ *bhagavat* 10.14 + f◦ *gītā* ←5◦√गै); *upaniṣatsu* (7loc◦ plu◦ ←f◦ *upaniṣad* ←6◦उप-नि√सद्); *brahmavidyāyām* (f◦ 7loc◦ sing◦ ←tatpu◦ *brahma-vidyā*, ब्रह्मणः विद्या ←n◦ *brahman* 2.72 + *vidyā* 5.18); *yogaśāstre* (n◦ 7loc◦ sing◦ ←tatpu◦ *yoga-śāstra*, योगानाम् शास्त्रम् । योगस्य शास्त्रम् । ←m◦ *yoga* 2.39 + n◦ *śāstra* 15.20); *śrīkṛṣṇārjunasaṁvāde* (m◦ 7loc◦ sing◦ ←tatpu◦ *śrī-kṛṣṇārjuna-saṁvāda*, श्रीकृष्णस्य च अर्जुनस्य च संवादः ←adj◦ *śrī* 10.34 + m◦ prop◦ *kṛṣṇa* 1.28 + m◦ prop◦ *arjuna* 1.4 + m◦ *saṁvāda* 18.70); *vibhūtiyogaḥ:* (m◦ 1nom◦ sing◦ ←tatpu◦ *vibhūtiyoga*, विभूतियोग, विभूतेः योगः ← f◦ *vibhutiḥ* 10.16 + m◦ *yoga* 2.39); *nāma* (1nom◦ sing◦ ←n◦ *nāman* ←1◦√म्ना); *daśamaḥ:* (m◦ 1nom◦ sing◦ ←num◦ adj◦ *daśa* 13.5); *adhyāyaḥ:* (1nom◦ sing◦ ←m◦ *adhyāya* ←1◦अधि√इ)

---

[599] Elsewhere◦ बहुना एतेन ज्ञातेन → knowing this extensively (adv◦), knowing this in detail (adv◦), ...etc.

📖 बहुना is not an adverb, and thus it is not qualifying the verb √ज्ञा (knowing), it is a an Instrumental (3rd) case adj◦ qualifying the n◦ Instrumental case pronoun एतेन । बहुना एतेन = with this much.

[600] Elsewhere◦ एतेन ज्ञातेन → knowing this, (gerund), knowledge of all these details, extensive knowledge (noun◦ ज्ञानेन); detailed knowledge, should you know of all these (pot◦), to know all these (infintive), ...etc.

📖 ज्ञातेन is not a gerund, noun, pot◦ or infinitive. It is Instrumental (3rd) case inflection of the n◦ ppp◦ adjective ज्ञात (known) qualifying the neuter gender peonoun एतेन । It is not qualifying बहुना (all these details).

[601] Elsewhere◦ विष्टभ्य → I support (present◦), I pervade, ...etc.

📖 विष्टभ्य is not a Present tense verb.

(§3) *iti* (thus); *śrīmadbhagavadgītāsu upaniṣatsu* (among the upaniṣads of the Śrīmad-Bhagavadgītā); *brahmavidyāyāṃ* (of the eternal wisdoms); *yogaśāstre* (in the science of Yoga); *śrīkṛṣṇārjunasaṁvāde* (in the dialogue between Śrī Kṛṣṇa and Arjuna); *vibhūtiyogaḥ:* (adj∘1-subj∘ vibhūti-yoga); *nāma* (called); *daśamaḥ:* (adj∘2-subj∘ the tenth); *adhyāyaḥ:* (subj∘ discourse; chapter)

(§4) śrīmadbhagavadgītāsu upaniṣatsu yogaśāstre brahmavidyāyāṃ iti daśamaḥ: adhyāyaḥ: nāma vibhūtiyogaḥ: śrīkṛṣṇārjunasaṁvāde

(§5) Among the upaniṣads of the Śrīmad-Bhagavadgītā, in the science of yoga of self realization, thus (is) the tenth discourse called vibhūti-yogaḥ:, in the dialogue between Śrī Kṛṣṇa and Arjuna.

CHAPTER 11

ekādaśo'dhyāyaḥ:

एकादशोऽध्यायः ।

viśvarūpadarśanayogaḥ:

विश्वरूपदर्शनयोगः ।

THE YOGA OF UNIVERSAL MANIFESTATION

Arjuna said (arjuna uvāca अर्जुन उवाच ।)

11.1 मदनुग्रहाय परमं गुह्यमध्यात्मसंज्ञितम् ।
यत्त्वयोक्तं वचस्तेन मोहोऽयं विगतो मम ।।

madanugrahāya paramaṁ guhyamadhyātmasañjñitam,
yattvayoktaṁ vacastena moho'yaṁ vigato mama. **(11.1)**

(§1) *ekādaśaḥ:* (r∘ 15/1) *adhyāyaḥ:* (r∘ 22/8). *viśvarūpadarśanayogaḥ:* (r∘ 22/8). *arjunaḥ:* (r∘ 19/4) *uvāca. madanugrahāya paramaṃ* (r∘ 14/1) *guhyaṃ* (r∘ 8/16) *adhyātmasañjñitaṃ* (r∘ 14/2) *yaṭ* (r∘ 1/10) *tvayā* (r∘ 2/4) *uktaṃ* (r∘ 14/1) *vacaḥ:* (r∘ 18/1) *tena mohaḥ:* (r∘ 15/1) *ayaṃ* (r∘ 14/1) *vigataḥ:* (r∘ 15/9) *mama*

(§2) *ekādaśaḥ:* (m∘ 1nom∘ sing∘ ←sequence indicating num∘ adj∘ *ekādaśa* ←adj' *eka* 2.41 + adj∘ *daśa* 13.6); *adhyāyaḥ:* (1nom∘ sing∘ ←m∘ *adhyāya* ←अधि√इ). *viśvarūpadarśanayogaḥ:* (m∘ 1nom∘ sing∘ ←tatpu∘ *viśva-rūpa-darśana-yoga,* विश्वरूपस्य दर्शनस्य योगः ←n∘ *viśvarūpa* 11.16 + n∘ *darśana* 11.10 + m∘ *yoga* 2.39). *arjunaḥ:* (1.28); *uvāca* (1.25).

madanugrahāya (m∘ 4dat∘ sing∘ ←tatpu∘ *madanugraha,* मम अनुग्रहः ←pron∘ *maṭ* (me) 1.9 + m∘ *anugraha* (compassion) ←अनु√ग्रह्); *paramaṃ* (1nom∘ 8.8); ***guhyaṃ*** (1nom∘ sing∘ ←n∘ *guhya* (secret) 9.1); *adhyātmasañjñitaṃ* (n∘ 1nom∘ sing∘ ←ppp∘ adj∘ *adhyātma-sañjñita,* अध्यात्मात् संज्ञितम् ←n∘ *adhyātma* (knowledge of self) 3.30 + adj∘ *sañjñita* (known) 6.23); *yaṭ* (1nom∘ 2.67); *tvayā* (6.33); ***uktaṃ*** (n∘ 1nom∘ sing∘ ←adj∘ *ukta* (said) 1.24); *vaćaḥ:* (2.10); *tena* (3.38); ***mohaḥ:*** (1nom∘ sing∘ ←m∘ *moha* (delusion) 2.52); *ayaṃ* (2.19); 🕮*vigataḥ:* (1nom∘ sing∘ ←adj∘ *vigata* (gone) 2.56); *mama* (1.7) (11.1)

(§3) *ekādaśaḥ:* (adj∘-subj∘ the eleventh); *adhyāyaḥ:* (subj∘ chapter). *viśvarūpadarśanayogaḥ:* (m∘ viśva-rūpa-darśana-yoga). *arjunaḥ:* (Subj∘ Arjuna); *uvāća* (said).

madanugrahāya (for a favor to me, out of compassion for me); *paramaṃ* (adj1∘-obj∘ supreme); *guhyaṃ* (adj2∘-obj∘ secret); *adhyātmasañjñitaṃ* (adj3∘-obj∘ called 'adhyātatma,' called 'substratum or receptacle of the self,' called 'realization of the presence of brahma in oneself,' called 'understanding ātmā and unātmā,' called 'comprehending dehī and deha'); *yaṭ* (adj4∘-subj which); *tvayā* (subj1∘ by you); *uktaṃ* (adj5∘-obj∘ told); *vaćaḥ:* (obj∘ speech); *tena* (by that); *mohaḥ:* (subj2∘ delusion); *ayaṃ* (adj∘-subj2∘ this); *vigataḥ:* (adj3∘-subj2∘ gone away); *mama* (my, of mine) (11.1)

(§4) ekādaśaḥ: adhyāyaḥ:. viśvarūpadarśanayogaḥ:. arjunaḥ: uvāća . ayaṃ mohaḥ: mama vigataḥ: tena paramaṃ guhyaṃ adhyātmasañjñitaṃ yaṭ vaćaḥ:-uktaṃ tvayā madanugrahāya

(§5) The eleventh chapter. viśva-rūpa-darśana-yoga. Arjuna said :

This delusion of mine (has) gone away by that supreme secret called 'adhyātatma,' which (is) told by you out of compassion for me. (11.1)

11.2 भवाप्ययौ हि भूतानां श्रुतौ विस्तरशो मया ।

त्वत्तः कमलपत्राक्ष माहात्म्यमपि चाव्ययम् ।।

bhavāpyayau hi bhūtānāṁ śrutau vistaraśo mayā,

tvattaḥ: kamalapatrākṣa māhātmyamapi ćāvyayaṃ; (11.2)

(§1) *bhavāpyayau hi bhūtānāṃ* (r∘ 14/1) *śrutau vistaraśaḥ:* (r∘ 15/9) *mayā tvattaḥ:* (r∘ 22/1) *kamalapatrākṣa māhātmyaṃ* (r∘ 8/16) *api ća* (r∘ 1/1) *avyayaṃ* (r∘ 14/2);

(§2) *bhavāpyayau* (m∘ 1nom∘ dual∘ ←dvandva∘ भवः च अप्ययः च ←m∘ *bhava* (evolution) 10.4 + m∘ *apyaya* (dissolution) ←अपि√इण्); *hi* (1.11); *bhūtānāṃ* (2.69); *śrutau* (m∘ 1nom∘ dual∘ ←adj∘ *śruta* 2.52); *vistaraśaḥ:* (mode indicating adv∘ ind∘ ←m∘ *vistara* (expansion) 10.18); *mayā* (1.22); *tvattaḥ:* (adv∘ ind∘ ←pron∘ *tvaṭ* (from you) 6.39); *kamalapatrākṣa* (m∘ 8voc∘ sing∘ ←bahuvrī∘ *kamala-patrākṣa,* कमलपत्रस्य इव अक्षिणी यस्य ←n∘ ***kamala*** (lotus) ←कम्√अल् + n∘ *patra* (leaf) 5.10 + n∘ 🕮***akṣi*** (eye) ←√अक्ष्); 🕮*māhātmyaṃ* (n∘ 1nom∘ sing∘ ←adj∘ *māhātmya* (greatness) ←महा√अत्); *api* (1.26); *ća* (1.1); *avyayaṃ* (9.2); (11.2)

(§3) *bhavāpyayau* (obj◦ the evolution and the dissolution, the origine and the end); *hi* (because); *bhūtānām̦* (of beings); *śrutau* (adj◦-obj◦ heard); *vistaraśaḥ:* (comprehensively); *mayā* (by me); *tvattaḥ:* (from you); *kamalapatrākṣa* (O Lord Kṛṣṇa!); *māhātmyam̦* (obj◦ greatness); *api ća* (as well as); *avyayam̦* (adj◦-obj2◦ eternal, perpetual); (11.2)

(§4) hi tvattaḥ: kamalapatrākṣa śrutau vistaraśaḥ: mayā bhavāpyayau bhūtānām̦ api ća avyayam̦ māhātmyam̦;

(§5) Because,[602] from you O Lord Kṛṣṇa! heard comprehensively by me,[603] the evolution and the dissolution[604] of beings[605] as well as (your) eternal greatness;

(11.2)

11.3 एवमेतद्यथात्थ त्वमात्मानं परमेश्वर ।
द्रष्टुमिच्छामि ते रूपमैश्वरं पुरुषोत्तम ।।
evametadyathāttha tvamātmānaṁ parameśvara,
draṣṭumiććhāmi te rūpamaiśvaraṁ puruṣottama. (11.3)

(§1) *evam̦* (r◦ 8/22) *etaț* (r◦ 9/9) *yathā* (r◦ 1/4) *āttha tvam̦* (r◦ 8/17) *ātmānam̦* (r◦ 14/1) *parameśvara draṣṭum̦* (r◦ 8/18) *iććhāmi te rūpam̦* (r◦ 8/23) *aiśvaram̦* (r◦ 14/1) *puruśottama*

(§2) *evam̦* (1.24); *etaț* (2.3); *yathā* (1.11); *āttha* (= *bravīṣi,* 2nd-per◦ sing◦ pres◦ वर्तमान्-लट् parasmai◦ ←class2◦ √ब्रू or con◦1√अह्); *tvam̦* (2.11); *ātmānam̦* (3.43); *parameśvara* (m◦ 8voc◦ sing◦ ←bahuvrī◦ ***parameśvara*** (supreme lord) परम: ईश्वर: य: ←adj◦ *parama* (supreme) 1.17 + m◦ *īśvara* (lord) 4.6); ***draṣṭum̦*** (inf◦ ind◦ ←√दृश्); *iććhāmi* (1.35); te (2.7); 🕮***rūpam̦*** (2acc◦ sing◦ ←n◦ *rūpa* (form) 3.39); *aiśvaram̦* (9.5); *puruśottama* (8.1) (11.3)

(§3) *evam̦ etaț* (adj◦-obj1◦ thus this, so this); *yathā* (as); *āttha* (you are saying); *tvam̦* (subj◦ you); *ātmānam̦* (obj2◦ about yourself); *parameśvara* (O Lord Kṛṣṇna!); *draṣṭum̦* (to see); *iććhāmi* (I desire, I

---

[602] See the footnote in verse 3.5

हि is the most important word in this verse, and thus it needs to be translated thoughtfully. The 'because' at the beginning of this verse indicates its connection and continuation with the next verse which begins with 'thus' ...

[603] Elsewhere◦ श्रुतौ मया → I have heard (active◦), have been heard ...etc.

🕮 In श्रुतौ मया, श्रुतौ is not a verb, and मया is not an active voice. मया is used for passive voice and m◦ श्रुतौ is a ppp◦ adjective of m◦ nouns भवाप्ययौ ।

[604] Elsewhere◦ भवाप्ययौ → The production and destruction, origin and decay, birth and passing away, ...etc.

[605] Elsewhere◦ भूतानाम् → of every living entity, of things, ...etc.

want); *te* (your); *rūpaṃ* (obj3◦ form, figure, appearance, manifestation, expression); *aiśvaraṃ* (adj◦-obj3◦ divine); *puruśottama* (O Lord Kṛṣṇa!) (11.3)

(§4) parameśvara evaṃ etaṭ yathā tvaṃ āttha ātmānaṃ puruśottama iććhāmi draṣṭuṃ te aiśvaraṃ rūpaṃ

(§5) O Lord Kṛṣṇna! so this (is) as you are saying about yourself.[606] O Lord Kṛṣṇa! I desire to see your divine manifestation. (11.3)

11.4 मन्यसे यदि तच्छक्यं मया द्रष्टुमिति प्रभो ।
योगेश्वर ततो मे त्वं दर्शयात्मानमव्ययम् ।।

manyase yadi taććhkyaṁ mayā draṣṭumiti prabho,
yogeśvara tato me tvaṁ darśayātmānamavyayaṃ. (11.4)

(§1) *manyase yadi taṭ* (r◦ 11/4) *śakyaṃ* (r◦ 14/1) *mayā draṣṭuṃ* (r◦ 8/18) *iti prabho yogeśvara tataḥ:* (r◦ 15/9) *me tvaṃ* (r◦ 14/1) *darśaya* (r◦ 1/2) *ātmānaṃ* (r◦ 8/16) *avyayaṃ* (r◦ 14/2)

(§2) *manyase* (2.26); *yadi* (1.38); *taṭ* (1.10); ***śakyaṃ*** (n◦ 1nom◦ sing◦ ←adj◦ *śakya* (possible) 6.36); *mayā* (1.22); *draṣṭuṃ* (11.13); *iti* (1.25); ***prabho*** (8voc◦ sing◦ ←m◦ *prabhu* (lord) 5.14); *yogeśvara* (m◦ 8voc◦ sing◦ ←bahuvrī◦ ***yogeśvara*** (lord of yogas) योगस्य ईश्वरः यः ←m◦ *yoga* 2.39 + m◦ *īśvara* (lord) 4.6); *tataḥ:* (1.13); *me* (1.21); *tvaṃ* (2.11); ***darśaya*** (2nd-per◦ sing◦ imperative◦ निवेदनार्थ-लोट् parasmai◦ caus◦ ←class1◦ √दृश्); *ātmānaṃ* (3.43); *avyayaṃ* (2.21) (11.4)

(§3) *manyase* (you think); *yadi* (if); *taṭ* (adj1◦-obj◦ that); *śakyaṃ* (adj2◦-obj◦ possible); *mayā* (subj1◦ by me); *draṣṭuṃ* (to see); *iti* (adv◦ thus, that); *prabho* (O Lord Kṛṣṇa!); *yogeśvara* (O Lord Kṛṣṇa!); *tataḥ:* (then); *me* (to me, me); *tvaṃ* (subj2◦ you); *darśaya* (please reveal); *ātmānaṃ* (obj◦ your - self); *avyayaṃ* (adj3◦-obj◦ eternal) (11.4)

(§4) prabho yadi manyase iti mayā śakyaṃ draṣṭuṃ tataḥ: yogeśvara tvaṃ darśaya me taṭ avyayaṃ ātmānaṃ

(§5) O Lord Kṛṣṇa! if you think that by me (it is) possible to see, then O Lord Kṛṣṇa! you please

---

[606] Elsewhere◦ यथा आत्थ त्वम् आत्मानम् → as You have described Yourself, as Thou describest Thyself, as Thou sayest Thou Thyself, as thou hast declared Thyself, as You have declared Yourself, ...etc.

📖 त्वम् is the subject in Nominative (1st) case, आत्मानम् is object in Accusative (2nd) case. Therefore, आत्मान् can not qualify त्वम् । Thus, त्वम् आत्मानम् does not mean 'you yourself' (you = nominative, subject; yourself = nominative, adjective of subject). It means 'you about yourself' (you = nominative, subject; 'about yourself' = accusative, object). Also, आत्थ is not a Perfect tense or a Past tense. it is a Present tense, as shown above.

reveal me your that eternal self. (11.4)

The Lord said (śrībhagavānuvāća श्रीभगवानुवाच ।)

11.5 पश्य मे पार्थ रूपाणि शतशोऽथ सहस्रशः ।
नानाविधानि दिव्यानि नानावर्णाकृतीनि च ।।

paśya me pārtha rūpāṇi śataśo'tha sahasraśaḥ:,
nānāvidhāni divyāni nānāvarṇākṛtīni ća. (11.5)

(§1) *śrībhagavāṇ* (r◦ 8/14) *uvāća. paśya me pārtha rūpāṇi* (r◦ 24/7) *śataśaḥ:* (r◦ 15/1) *atha sahasraśaḥ:* (r◦ 22/8) *nānāvidhāni divyāni nānāvarṇākṛtīni ća*

(§2) *śrībhagavāṇ* (2.2); *uvāća* (1.25). *paśya* (1.3); *me* (1.21); *pārtha* (1.25); *rūpāṇi* (2acc◦ plu◦ ←n◦ *rūpa* (form) 3.39); *śataśaḥ:* (adv◦ ind◦ *śataśaṣ* ←num◦ adj◦ ***śata*** (hundred) ←दश दशत:); *atha* (1.20); *sahasraśaḥ:* (adv◦ ind◦ *sahasraśaṣ* ←adj◦ *sahasra* (thousand) 7.3); *nānāvidhāni* (n◦ 2acc◦ plu◦ ←adj◦ *nānā-vidha* ←adj◦ *nānā* (many) 1.9 + m◦ *vidha* (way) 3.3); *divyāni* (n◦ 2acc◦ plu◦ ←adj◦ *divya* (divine) 1.14); *nānāvarṇākṛtīni* (n◦ 2acc◦ plu◦ ←bahuvrī◦ adj◦ *nānā-varṇākṛti,* नाना वर्णानि च आकृतीनि च यस्य ←ind◦ *nānā* (various) 1.9 + m◦ *varṇa* (colour) 1.41 + f◦ *ākṛti* (form) ←आ√कृ); *ća* (1.1) (11.5)

(§3) *śrībhagavāṇ* (The Lord); *uvāća* (said). *paśya* (behold!); *me* (my); *pārtha* (O Arjuna!); *rūpāṇi* (obj◦ personifications); *śataśaḥ:* (a hundredfold); *atha* (as well as); *sahasraśaḥ:* (a thousandfold); *nānāvidhāni* (adj1◦-obj◦ of various kind); *divyāni* (adj2◦-obj◦ divine); *nānāvarṇākṛtīni* (adj3◦-obj◦ of various colours and forms); *ća* (and) (11.5)

(§4) śrībhagavāṇ uvāća pārtha paśya śataśaḥ: atha sahasraśaḥ: me rūpāṇi nānāvidhāni divyāni ća nānāvarṇākṛtīni

(§5) The Lord said : O Arjuna! behold, a hundredfold as well as a thousandfold, my personifications of various kind, divine and of various colours and forms. (11.5)

11.6 पश्यादित्यान्वसून्रुद्रानश्विनौ मरुतस्तथा ।
बहून्यदृष्टपूर्वाणि पश्याश्चर्याणि भारत ।।

paśyādityānvasūnrudrānaśvinau marutastathā,
bahūnyadṛṣṭapūrvāṇi paśyāśćaryāṇi bhārata. (11.6)

(§1) *paśya* (r◦ 1/2) *ādityāṇ* (r◦ 13/19) *vasūṇ* (r◦ 13/18) *rudrāṇ* (r◦ 8/11) *aśvinau marutaḥ:* (r◦ 18/1) *tathā bahūni* (r◦ 4/1) *adṛṣṭapūrvāṇi* (r◦ 24/7) *paśya* (r◦ 1/2) *āśćaryāṇi* (r◦ 24/7) *bhārata*

(§2) *paśya* (1.3); *ādityāṇ* (2acc◦ plu◦ ←m◦ *āditya* (sun) 5.16); *vasūṇ* (2acc◦ plu◦ ←m◦ *vasu* 7.19); *rudrāṇ* (2acc◦ plu◦ ←m◦ *rudra* 10.23); ***aśvinau*** (m◦ 2acc◦ dual◦ ←prop◦ *aśvin); **marutaḥ:*** (2acc◦ plu◦ ←m◦ *maruṭ*

10.21); *tathā* (1.8); *bahūni* (n◦ 2acc◦ plu◦ ←adj◦ *bahu* (many) 4.5); 🕮*adṛṣṭapūrvāṇi* (n◦ 2acc◦ plu◦ n.bahuvrī◦ ←adj◦ ***dṛṣṭapūrva***, दृष्टानि पूर्वम् ←adj◦ *dṛṣṭa* (seen) 2.16 + adj◦ *pūrva* (before) 4.15); *paśya* (1.3); *āścaryāṇi* (1nom◦ 2acc◦ plu◦ ←n◦ *āścarya* (wonder) 2.29); *bhārata* (1.24) (11.6)

(§3) *paśya* (see); *ādityān* (obj1◦ the adityas, the demigod sons of Aditi); *vasūn* (obj2◦ the vasus, the eight vasu sons of Aditi); *rudrān* (obj3◦ the eleven rudra sons of Aditi); *aśvinau* (the two Ashvinikumars); *marutaḥ:* (obj4◦ the forty-nine marut sons of Diti); *tathā* (as well as); *bahūni* (adj1◦-obj5◦ the beings); *adṛṣṭapūrvāṇi* (adj2◦-obj5◦ which are never seen before); *paśya* (see); *āścaryāṇi* (obj5◦ the wonders); *bhārata* (O Arjuna!) (11.6)

(§4) bhārata paśya ādityān vasūn rudrān aśvinau marutaḥ: tathā paśya bahūni āścaryāṇi adṛṣṭapūrvāṇi

(§5) O Arjuna! see the adityas, the vasus, the rudras, the *Ashvinikumars*, the maruts as well as see many wonders which are never seen before. (11.6)

11.7 इहैकस्थं जगत्कृत्स्नं पश्याद्य सचराचरम् ।
मम देहे गुडाकेश यच्चान्यद्द्रष्टुमिच्छसि ।।
ihaikasthaṁ jagatkṛtsnaṁ paśyādya saćarāćaram,
mama dehe guḍākeśa yaććānyaddraṣṭumiććhasi; (11.7)

(§1) *iha* (r◦ 3/1) *ekastham* (r◦ 14/1) *jagat* (r◦ 10/5) *kṛtsnam* (r◦ 14/1) *paśya* (r◦ 1/1) *adya saćarāćaram* (r◦ 14/2) *mama dehe guḍākeśa yat* (r◦ 11/1) *ća* (r◦ 1/1) *anyat* (r◦ 9/5) *draṣṭum* (r◦ 8/18) *iććhasi*

(§2) *iha* (2.5); 🕮***ekastham*** (n◦ 2acc◦ sing◦ ←adj◦ *eka-stha*, एके स्थितम् ←adj◦ *eka* (one) 2.41 + adj◦ *stha* (seated) 2.45); *jagat* (2acc◦ sing◦ ←n◦ *jagat* (world) 7.5); *kṛtsnam* (1.40); *paśya* (1.3); *adya* (4.3); *saćarāćaram* (9.10); *mama* (1.7); *dehe* (2.13); *guḍākeśa* (10.20); *yat* (2acc◦ 2.31); *ća* (1.1); *anyat* (n◦ 2acc◦ 2.31); *draṣṭum* (11.3); ***iććhasi*** (2nd-per◦ sing◦ pres◦ वर्तमान्-लट् parasmai◦ ←class6◦ √इष्) (11.7)

(§3) *iha* (here); *ekastham* (adj1◦-obj6◦ unified); *jagat* (obj6◦ the universe); *kṛtsnam* (adj2◦-obj6◦ whole); *paśya* (see); *adya* (today); *saćarāćaram* (adj03◦-obj6◦ with moving and non-moving); *mama* (my); *dehe* (in body); *guḍākeśa* (O Arjuna!); *yat* (adj1◦-obj7◦ that, which); *ća* (and); *anyat* (adj2◦-obj7◦ whaever else); *draṣṭum* (to see); *iććhasi* (you wish) (11.7)

(§4) guḍākeśa paśya dehe mama iha adya kṛtsnam ekastham saćarāćaram jagat ća anyat yat iććhasi draṣṭum

(§5) O Arjuna! see in my body, here today, the whole unified with moving and non-moving universe and whaever else that you wish to see; (11.7)

11.8 न तु मां शक्यसे द्रष्टुमनेनैव स्वचक्षुषा ।
दिव्यं ददामि ते चक्षुः पश्य मे योगमैश्वरम् ।।

na tu mām̐ śkyase draṣṭumanenaiva svaćakṣuṣā,
divyam̐ dadāmi te ćakṣuḥ: paśya me yogamaiśvaram. (11.8)

(§1) *na tu mām* (r◦ 14/1) *śakyase draṣṭum* (r◦ 8/16) *anena* (r◦ 3/1) *eva svaćakṣuṣā* (r◦ 25/2) *divyam* (r◦ 14/1) *dadāmi te ćakṣuḥ:* (r◦ 22/3) *paśya me yogam* (r◦ 8/23) *aiśvaram* (r◦ 14/2)

(§2) *na* (1.30); *tu* (1.2); *mām* (1.46); *śakyase* (2nd-per◦ sing◦ pres◦ वर्तमान्-लट् ātmane◦ ←class5◦ √शक्); *draṣṭum* (11.3); *anena* (3.10); *eva* (1.1); *svaćakṣuṣā* (3inst◦ sing◦ ←tatpu◦ *sva-ćakṣu* (own eye) ←adj◦ *sva* (own) 1.28 + n◦ *ćakṣus* (eye) 5.27); *divyam* (4.9); *dadāmi* (10.10); *te* (2.7); *ćakṣuḥ:* (5.27); *paśya* (1.3); *me* (1.21); *yogam* (2.53); *aiśvaram* (9.5) (11.8)

(§3) *na* (not); *tu* (however); *mām* (obj1◦ me); *śakyase* (you are able); *draṣṭum* (to see); *anena* (with this, with this present); *eva* (only); *svaćakṣuṣā* (with your own vision); *divyam* (adj◦-obj◦ divine); *dadāmi* (I am giving); *te* (you); *ćakṣuḥ:* (vision); *paśya* (see); *me* (my); *yogam* (obj3◦ yoga); *aiśvaram* (adj◦-obj3◦ celestial, divine) (11.8)

(§4) tu na śakyase draṣṭum mām eva anena svaćakṣuṣā dadāmi te divyam ćakṣuḥ: paśya me aiśvaram yogam

(§5) however, you are not able to see me only with this your own present vision.[607] I am giving you divine vision. See my celestial *yoga*. (11.8)

Sanjaya said (sañjaya uvāća सजय उवाच ।)

11.9 एवमुक्त्वा ततो राजन्महायोगेश्वरो हरिः ।
दर्शयामास पार्थाय परमं रूपमैश्वरम् ।।

evamuktvā tato rājanmahāyogeśvaro hariḥ:,
darśayāmāsa pārthāya paramam̐ rūpamaiśvaram; (11.9)

(§1) *sañjayaḥ:* (r◦ 19/4) *uvāća. evam* (r◦ 8/20) *uktvā tataḥ:* (r◦ 15/11) *rājan* (r◦ 13/16) *mahāyogeśvaraḥ:* (r◦ 15/14) *hariḥ:* (r◦ 22/8) *darśayāmāsa pārthāya paramam* (r◦ 14/1) *rūpam* (r◦ 8/23) *aiśvaram* (r◦ 14/2)

(§2) *sañjayaḥ:* (1.2); *uvāća* (1.25). *evam* (1.24); *uktvā* (1.47); *tataḥ:* (1.13); ***rājan*** (8voc◦ sing◦ ←m◦ *rājan* (king) 1.2); *mahāyogeśvaraḥ:* (m◦ 1nom◦ sing◦ ←bahuvrī◦ *mahā-yogeśvara,* योगस्य महान् ईश्वरः यः ←adj◦ *mahā* (great) 1.3 + m◦ *yoga* 2.39 + m◦ *īśvara* (lord) 4.6); *hariḥ:* (m◦ 1nom◦ sing◦ ←bahuvrī◦ ***hari***, हरति यः ←v◦ *harati* 2.67); ***darśayāmāsa*** (3rd-per◦ sing◦ past-perf◦ लिट् भूत◦ caus◦parasmai◦ ←1√दृश्); *pārthāya*

---

[607] Elsewhere◦ अनेन (स्व)चक्षुषा → with these thine eyes (plural◦), with these eyes, with these human eyes, ...etc.

📖 Lord Kṛṣṇa may not have given Arjuna new eyes, but new 'vision' (singular◦) in his eyes.

(4dat∘ sing∘ ←m∘ *pārtha* 1.26); *paramam̦* (2acc∘ 8.8); *rūpam̦* (2acc∘ 11.3); *aiśvaram̦* (2acc∘ 9.5) (11.9)

(§3) *sañjayaḥ:* (subj∘ Sañjaya); *uvāća* (said). *evam̦* (in this manner); *uktvā* (having spoken); *tataḥ:* (thereafter, then); *rājan̦* (O King Dhṛtarāṣṭra!); *mahāyogeśvaraḥ:* (adj∘-subj∘ the great lord of yoga); *hariḥ:* (subj∘ Hari, Kṛṣṇa); *darśayāmāsa* (showed); *pārthāya* (to Arjuna); *paramam̦* (adj1∘-obj1∘ supreme); *rūpam̦* (obj1∘ manifestation); *aiśvaram̦* (adj2∘-obj1∘ divine) (11.9)

(§4) sañjayaḥ: uvāća rājan̦ uktvā evam̦ tataḥ: hariḥ: mahāyogeśvaraḥ: darśayāmāsa paramam̦ aiśvaram̦ rūpam̦ pārthāya

(§5) Sañjaya said : O King Dhṛtarāṣṭra! having spoken in this manner, then Kṛṣṇa, the Great Lord of yoga, showed (his) supreme divine manifestation to Arjuna; (11.9)

11.10 अनेकवक्त्रनयनमनेकाद्भुतदर्शनम् ।
अनेकदिव्याभरणं दिव्यानेकोद्यतायुधम् ।।

anekavaktranayanamanekādbhutadarśanam̦,
anekadivyābharaṇaṁ divyānekodyatāyudham̦; (11.10)

(§1) *anekavaktranayanam̦* (r∘ 8/16) *anekādbhutadarśanam̦* (r∘ 14/2) *anekadivyābharaṇam̦* (r∘ 14/1, 24/3) *divyānekodyatāyudham̦* (r∘ 14/2)

(§2) *anekavaktranayanam̦* (n∘ 2acc∘ sing∘ ←bahuvrī∘ *aneka-vaktra-nayanam̦*, अनेकानि वक्त्राणि च नयनानि च यस्मै तत् ←adj∘ *aneka* (many) 6.45 + n∘ ***vaktra*** (mouth) ←√वच् + n∘ *nayana* (eye) ←√नी); *anekādbhutadarśanam̦* (n∘ 2acc∘ sing∘ ←bahuvrī∘ *anekādbhuta-darśana*, अनेकानि अद्भुतानि दर्शनानि यस्य तत् ←adj∘ *aneka* (many) 6.45 + adj∘ ***adbhuta*** (never before) ←√भा + n∘ ***darśana*** (sight) ←√दृश्); *anekadivyābharaṇam̦* (n∘ 2acc∘ sing∘ ←bahuvrī∘ *aneka-divyābharaṇa*, अनेकानि दिव्यानि आभरणानि यस्मै तत् ←adj∘ *aneka* (many) 6.45 + adj∘ *divya* (divine) 1.14 + n∘ *ābharaṇa* (ornament) ←आ√भृ); *divyānekodyatāyudham̦* (n∘ 2acc∘ sing∘ ←bahuvrī∘ *divyānekodyatāyudha*, दिव्यानि अनेकानि उद्यतानि आयुधानि यस्मिन् तत् ←adj∘ *divya* (divine) 1.14 + adj∘ *aneka* (many) 6.45 + adj∘ *udyata* (brandished) 1.45 + n∘ *āyudha* (weapon) 10.28) (11.10)

(§3) *anekavaktranayanam̦* (adj3∘-obj1∘ the one having many mouths and eyes); *anekādbhutadarśanam̦* (adj4∘-obj1∘ the one with many woudrful sights); *anekadivyābharaṇam̦* (adj5∘-obj1∘ the one with many divine ornaments); *divyānekodyatāyudham̦* (adj6∘-obj1∘ the one brandishing many celestial weapons); (11.10)

(§4) anekavaktranayanam̦ anekādbhutadarśanam̦ anekadivyābharaṇam̦ divyānekodyatāyudham̦

(§5) the one having many mouths and eyes, the one with many woudrful sights, *divyānekodyatāyudham̦* the one brandishing many celestial weapons; (11.10)

11.11 दिव्यमाल्याम्बरधरं दिव्यगन्धानुलेपनम् ।
सर्वाश्चर्यमयं देवमनन्तं विश्वतोमुखम् ।।

divyamālyāmbradharaṁ divyagandhānulepanam̦,
sarvāśćaryamayaṁ devamanantaṁ viśvatomukham̦. (11.11)

(§1) *divyamālyāmbradharam̦* (r◦ 14/1) *divyagandhānulepanam̦* (r◦ 14/2) *sarvāśćaryamayam̦* (r◦ 14/1) *devam̦* (r◦ 8/16) *anantam̦* (r◦ 14/1) *viśvatomukham̦* (r◦ 14/2)

(§2) *divyamālyāmbradharam̦* (n◦ 2acc◦ sing◦ ←bahuvrī◦ *divya-mālyāmbra-dhara*, दिव्यानि माल्यानि च अम्बराणि धृतम् यत् ←adj◦ *divya* (divine) 1.14 + adj◦ 🕮*mālya* (garland) ←√मा + n◦ 🕮*ambara* ←√अम्ब् + adj◦ ***dhara*** (bearer) ←√धृ); *divyagandhānulepanam̦* (n◦ 2acc◦ sing◦ ←bahuvrī◦ *divya-gandhānulepana*, दिव्यानि गन्धानि अनुलेपनानि यस्मै ←adj◦ *divya* (divine) 1.14 + m◦ *gandha* (fragrance) 7.9 + n◦ *anulepana* (covering) ←अनु√लिप्); *sarvāśćaryamayam̦* (n◦ 2acc◦ sing◦ ←bahuvrī◦ *sarvāśćaryamaya*, सर्वम् आश्चर्यमयम् यत् ←pron◦ *sarva* (all) 1.6 + adj◦ m◦ *āśćarya* (wonder) 2.29 + adj◦ *maya* (possessed of) 4.10); ***devam̦*** (2acc◦ sing◦ ←m◦ *deva* (god) 3.11); ***anantam̦*** (n◦ 2acc◦ sing◦ ←adj◦ *ananta* (infinite) 2.41); *viśvatomukham̦* (9.15) (11.11)

(§3) *divyamālyāmbradharam̦* (adj7-obj1◦ the one wearing many divine garlands and garments); *divyagandhānulepanam̦* (adj8◦-obj1◦ the one wearing many divine perfumes and scents); *sarvāśćaryamayam̦* (adj9◦-obj1◦ the all marvelous); *devam̦* (adj10-obj1◦ God); *anantam̦* (adj11◦-obj◦ infinite); *viśvatomukham̦* (adj12◦-obj1◦ the one seeing everything, Omniscient) (11.11)

(§4) divyamālyāmbradharam̦ divyagandhānulepanam̦ sarvāśćaryamayam̦ devam̦ anantam̦ viśvatomukham̦

(§5) the one wearing many divine garlands and garments,[608] the one wearing many divine perfumes and scents, the all marvelous, infinite, omniscient God. (11.11)

11.12 दिवि सूर्यसहस्रस्य भवेद्युगपदुत्थिता ।
यदि भाः सदृशी सा स्याद्भासस्तस्य महात्मनः ।।

divi sūryasahasrasya bhavedyugapadutthitā,
yadi bhāḥ: sadṛśī sā syādbhāsastasya mahātmana:. (11.12)

---

[608] Elsewhere◦ दिव्यमाल्याम्बरधरं → He wore celestial garlands and garments, ...etc.

🕮 दिव्यमाल्याम्बरधरम् is not the verb performed by he (m◦), but it is one of the twelve *bahuvrīhi* adjectives of the n◦ object◦ रूपम् mentioned in verse 11.9 previously. दिव्यमाल्याम्बरधरम् = the manifestation (रूपम्) that was wearing celestial garlands and garments ...etc.

(§1) *divi sūryasahasrasya bhavet̨* (r◦ 9/9) *yugapat̨* (r◦ 8/6) *utthitā yadi bhāḥ:* (r◦ 22/7) *sadṛśī sā syāt̨* (r◦ 9/8) *bhāsaḥ:* (r◦ 18/1) *tasya mahātmana:* (r◦ 22/8)

(§2) *divi* (9.20); *sūryasahasrasya* (m◦ 6pos◦ sing◦ ←tatpu◦ *sūrya-sahasra,* सूर्याणाम् सहस्त्र: ←m◦ *sūrya* (sun) 7.8 + adj◦ *sahasra* (thousand) 7.3); *bhavet̨* (1.46); 🕮*yugapat̨* (at once mode indicating ind◦ ←युग√पत्); *utthitā* (f◦ 1nom◦ sing◦ ←ppp◦ adj◦ ***utthita*** (rose) ←उद्√स्था); *yadi* (1.38); 🕮*bhāḥ:* (1nom◦ sing◦ ←f◦ *bhās̨* (effulgence, brightness) ←√भास्); *sadṛśī* (f◦ 1nom◦ sing◦ ←adj◦ *sadṛśa* (similar) 3.33); *sā* (2.69); *syāt̨* (1.36); ***bhāsaḥ:*** (6pos sing◦ ←f◦ *bhās̨* ↑); *tasya* (1.12); ***mahātmana:*** (6pos sing◦ ←m◦ *mahātman̨* 7.19) (11.12)

(§3) *divi* (in the sky); *sūryasahasrasya* (of thousands of suns); *bhavet̨* (should there be); *yugapat̨* (simultaneously); *utthitā* (adj◦-subj1◦ arisen); *yadi* (if); *bhāḥ:* (subj1◦ an effulgence); *sadṛśī* (adj3◦-subj1◦ similar to); *sā* (adj2◦-subj1◦ that, that effulgence); *syāt̨* (may become); *bhāsaḥ:* (subj2◦ of splendor); *tasya* (of that); *mahātmana:* (of Great Puruṣa, of the Supreme One) (11.12)

(§4) yadi bhāḥ: sūryasahasrasya bhavet̨ utthitā divi yugapat̨ sā syāt̨ sadṛśī bhāsaḥ: tasya mahātmana:

(§5) If an effulgence of thousands of suns should there be arisen[609] in the sky simultaneously, that effulgence may become similar to the splendor of that Supreme Puruṣa. (11.12)

11.13 तत्रैकस्थं जगत्कृत्स्नं प्रविभक्तमनेकधा ।
अपश्यद्देवदेवस्य शरीरे पाण्डवस्तदा ।।

tatraikasthaṁ jagatkṛtsnaṁ pravibhaktamanekadhā,
apaśyaddevadevasya śarīre pāṇḍvastadā. (11.13)

(§1) *tatra* (r◦ 3/1) *ekastham̨* (r◦ 14/1) *jagat̨* (r◦ 10/5) *kṛtsnam̨* (r◦ 14/1) *pravibhaktam̨* (r◦ 8/16) *anekadhā* (r◦ 23/1) *apaśyat̨* (r◦ 9/5) *devadevasya śarīre pāṇḍavaḥ:* (r◦ 18/1) *tadā*

(§2) *tatra* (1.26); *ekastham̨* (11.7); *jagat̨* (2acc◦ 11.7); *kṛtsnam̨* (1.40); 🕮*pravibhaktam̨* (n◦ 2acc◦ sing◦ ←ppp◦ adj◦ ***pravibhakta*** (differentiated) ←प्र–वि√भज्); *anekadhā* (mode indicating ind◦ ←adj◦ *aneka* (many) 6.45); *apaśyat̨* (1.26); *devadevasya* (6pos sing◦ ←m◦ *devadeva* 10.15); *śarīre* (1.29); *pāṇḍavaḥ:* (1.14); *tadā* (1.2) (11.13)

(§3) *tatra* (there); *ekastham̨* (adj1◦-obj◦ united); *jagat̨* (obj◦ universe); *kṛtsnam̨* (adj2◦-obj◦ entire, the

---

[609] Elsewhere◦ सूर्यसहस्त्रस्य भवेत् युगपत् उत्थिता यदि भा: → If a thousand suns were to blaze forth simultaneously, if they appear simultaneously, A thousand suns risen all at once, ...etc.

🕮 उत्थिता (f◦ singular) is not an adjective of suns (m◦ plural◦). उत्थिता (f◦ sing◦) is ppp◦ adjective of f◦ singular noun भा: । Other two adjectives of f◦ noun भा: in this verse are सा and सदृशी ।

whole); *pravibhaktam̜* (adj3∘-obj∘ differentiated); *anekadhā* (adv∘ diversely); *apaśyat̜* (he saw); *devadevasya* (of the Lord of the Lords, of Lord Kṛṣṇa); *śarīre* (in the body); *pāṇḍavaḥ:* (subj∘ Arjuna); *tadā* (at that time) (11.13)

(§4) tatra tadā pāṇḍavaḥ: apaśyat̜ kṛtsnam̜ anekadhā pravibhaktam̜ jagat̜ ekastham̜ śarīre devadevasya

(§5) There, at that time, Arjuna saw the whole diversely differentiated universe united in the body of Lord Kṛṣṇa. (11.13)

11.14 **ततः स विस्मयाविष्टो हृष्टरोमा धनञ्जयः ।**
प्रणम्य शिरसा देवं कृताञ्जलिरभाषत ।।
tataḥ: sa vismayāviṣṭo hṛṣṭaromā dhanañjayaḥ:,
praṇamya śirasā devaṁ kṛtāñjalirabhāṣata. (11.14)

(§1) *tataḥ:* (r∘ 22/7) *saḥ:* (r∘ 21/2) *vismayāviṣṭaḥ:* (r∘ 15/14) *hṛṣṭaromā dhanañjayaḥ:* (r∘ 22/8) *praṇamya śirasā devam̜* (r∘ 14/1) *kṛtāñjaliḥ:* (r∘ 16/1) *abhāṣata*

(§2) *tataḥ:* (1.13); *saḥ:* (1.13); *vismayāviṣṭaḥ:* (m∘ 1nom∘ sing∘ ←bahuvrī∘ adj∘ *vismayāviṣṭa*, विस्मयेन आविष्टः यः ←m∘ 🕮***vismaya*** (surprise) ←वि√स्मि + ppp∘ adj∘ *āviṣṭa* (taken over) 1.27); 🕮*hṛṣṭaromā* (m∘ 1nom∘ sing∘ ←bahuvrī∘ *hṛṣṭa-roman̜*, हृष्टानि रोमाणि यस्य ←ppp∘ adj∘ *hṛṣṭa* (happy, excited) ←√हृष् + n∘ *roman̜* (hair) 1.39); *dhanañjayaḥ:* (1.15); ***praṇamya*** (lyp∘ past-participle ind∘ ←प्र√नम्); *śirasā* (3inst∘ sing∘ ←n∘ 🕮***śiras̜*** (head) ←√श्रि); *devam̜* (11.11); ***kṛtāñjaliḥ:*** (m∘ 1nom∘ sing∘ ←bahuvrī∘ *kṛtāñjali* (folded hands) कृता अञ्जलिः येन ←adj∘ *kṛta* (done) 1.35 + f∘ *añjali* (palm) ←√अञ्ज्); *abhāṣata* (3rd-per∘ sing∘ -past-imper∘ लङ् भूत∘ parasmai∘ ←class1∘ √भाष्) (11.14)

(§3) *tataḥ:* (then); *saḥ:* (adj1∘-subj∘ he, that); *vismayāviṣṭaḥ:* (adj2∘-subj∘ he who was filled with awe, amazement); *hṛṣṭaromā* (adj3∘-subj∘ he whose hair stood on end); *dhanañjayaḥ:* (subj∘ Arjuna); *praṇamya śirasā* (bowing his head); *devam̜* (obj∘ to Lord Kṛṣṇna); *kṛtāñjaliḥ:* (adj4∘-subj∘ he who folded his hands); *abhāṣata* (he said) (11.14)

(§4) tataḥ: saḥ: dhanañjayaḥ: hṛṣṭaromā vismayāviṣṭaḥ: kṛtāñjaliḥ: praṇamya śirasā abhāṣata devam̜

(§5) Then, that Arjuna whose hair stood on end,[610] who was filled with awe, who folded his

---

[610] Elsewhere∘ विस्मयाविष्टः → with hairs standing on end, with the hair standing on end. with his hair standing on end, ...etc.

🕮 विस्मयाविष्टः is not an adverb or in Instrumental (3rd) case qualifying the verb अभाषत् । The ind∘ gerund प्रणम्य is qualifying the verb अभाषत् । As seen above, विस्मयाविष्टः is Nominative (1st) case m∘ ppp∘

hands,[611] bowing his head said to Lord Kṛṣnna. (11.14)

Arjuna said (arjuna uvāća अर्जुन उवाच ।)

11.15 **पश्यामि देवांस्तव देव देहे सर्वांस्तथा भूतविशेषसङ्घान् ।**
ब्रह्माणमीशं कमलासनस्थमृषींश्च सर्वानुरगांश्च दिव्यान् ।।

paśyāmi devāṁstava deva dehe sarvāṁstathā bhūtaviśeṣasaṅghān,
brahmāṇamīśaṁ kamalāsanasthamṛṣīṁśća sarvānuragāṁśća divyān.
(11.15)

(§1) *arjunaḥ:* (r∘ 19/4) *uvāća. paśyāmi devān* (r∘ 13/7) *tava deva dehe sarvān* (r∘ 13/7) *tathā bhūtaviśeṣasaṅghān* (r∘ 23/1) *brahmāṇam* (r∘ 8/19, 24/3) *īśam* (r∘ 14/1) *kamalāsanastham* (r∘ 8/21) *ṛṣīn* (r∘ 13/6) *ća sarvān* (r∘ 8/14) *uragān* (r∘ 13/6) *ća divyān*

(§2) *arjunaḥ:* (1.28); *uvāća* (1.25). *paśyāmi* (1.31); *devān* (3.11); *tava* (1.3); ***deva*** (8voc∘ sing∘ ←m∘ *deva* (god) 3.11); *dehe* (2.13); *sarvān* (1.27); *tathā* (1.8); *bhūtaviśeṣasaṅghān* (m∘ 2acc∘ plu∘ ←tatpu∘ *bhūta-viśeṣa-saṅgha*, भूतानाम् विशेषाणाम् सङ्घः ←n∘ *bhūta* (being) 2.28 + adj∘ *viśeṣa* (special, unusual) 2.43 + m∘ 🕮***saṅgha*** (group) ←सम्√हन्); *brahmāṇam* (2acc∘ sing∘ ←m∘ *brahman* 2.72); ***īśam*** (2acc∘ sing∘ ←m∘ *īśa* (god) 1.15); *kamalāsanastham* (2acc∘ sing∘ ←tatpu∘ *kamalāsana-stha*, कमलस्य आसने स्थितः ←n∘ *kamala* (lotus) 11.2 + n∘ *āsana* (seat) 6.11 + adj∘ *stha* (seated) 2.45); *ṛṣīn* (2acc∘ plu∘ ←m∘ *ṛṣi* (sage) 4.2); *ća* (1.1); *sarvān* (1.27); 🕮*uragān* (2acc∘ plu∘ ←m∘ *uraga* (snake) ←m∘ ***uras*** (snake) ←√ऋ + √गम्); *ća* (1.1); *divyān* (9.20) (11.15)

(§3) *arjunaḥ:* (subj∘ Arjuna); *uvāća* (said). *paśyāmi* (I see, I am seeing); *devān* (obj1∘ the gods); *tava* (your); *deva* (O Lord Kṛṣṇa!); *dehe* (in body); *sarvān* (adj∘-obj1-2∘ all); *tathā* (as well as); *bhūtaviśeṣasaṅghān* (obj2∘ groups of unusual beings); *brahmāṇam* (obj3∘ Brahmā); *īśam* (adj1∘-obj3∘ Lord); *kamalāsanastham* (adj2∘-obj3∘ seated in his seat in the lotus flower); *ṛṣīn* (obj4∘ the sages); *ća* (and); *sarvān* (adj1∘-obj4-5∘ all); *uragān* (obj5∘ serpents); *ća* (and); *divyān* (adj2∘-obj4-5∘ the divine) (11.15)

---

adjective that is qualifying the Nominative m∘ subject धनञ्जयः ।

[611] Elsewhere∘ कृताञ्जलिः → with folded hands, with hands folded, with palms joined, with joined palms, with a reverent gesture, ...etc.

🕮 कृताञ्जलिः is not an adverb or in Instrumental (3rd) case qualifying the verb अभाषत् । The ind∘ gerund प्रणम्य is qualifying the verb अभाषत् । Please note that कृताञ्जलिः is also a Nominative (1st) case m∘ ppp∘ adjective that is qualifying the Nominative m∘ subject धनञ्जयः ।

(§4) arjunaḥ: uvāća deva dehe tava paśyāmi sarvān devān tathā bhūtaviśeṣasaṅghān īśam brahmāṇam kamalāsanastham ća sarvān ṛṣīn ća divyān uragān

(§5) Arjuna said : O Lord Kṛṣṇa! in your body I am seeing all the gods as well as groups of unusual beings, Lord[612] Brahmā seated in his seat in the lotus flower, and all the sages and the divine serpents; (11.15)

11.16 अनेकबाहूदरवक्त्रनेत्रं पश्यामि त्वां सर्वतोऽनन्तरूपम् ।
नान्तं न मध्यं न पुनस्तवादिं पश्यामि विश्वेश्वर विश्वरूप ।।
anekabāhūdaravaktranetraṁ paśyāmi tvāṁ sarvato'nantarūpam,
nāntaṁ na madhyaṁ na punastavādiṁ paśyāmi viśveśvara viśvarūpa.
(11.16)

(§1) *anekabāhūdaravaktranetram* (r◦ 14/1) *paśyāmi tvām* (r◦ 14/1) *sarvataḥ:* (r◦ 15/1) *anantarūpam* (r◦ 14/2) *na* (r◦ 1/1) *antam* (r◦ 14/1) *na madhyam* (r◦ 14/1) *na punaḥ:* (r◦ 18/1) *tava* (r◦ 1/2) *ādim* (r◦ 14/1) *paśyāmi viśveśvara viśvarūpa*

(§2) *anekabāhūdaravaktranetram* (m◦ 2acc◦ sing◦ ←bahuvrī◦ *aneka-bāhūdara-vaktra-netra,* अनेकानि बाहवः च उदराणि च वक्त्राणि च नेत्राणि च यस्य ←adj◦ *aneka* (many) 6.45 + m◦ *bāhu* (arm) 1.18 + n◦ *udara* (stomach) 1.15 + n◦ *vaktra* (mouth) 11.10 n◦ ***netra*** (eye) ←√नी); *paśyāmi* (1.31); *tvām* (2.7); *sarvataḥ:* (2.46); *anantarūpam* (m◦ 2acc◦ sing◦ ←bahuvrī◦ ***ananta-rūpa***, अनन्तानि रूपाणि यस्य ←adj◦ *ananta* (infinite) 2.41 + n◦ *rūpa* (form) 3.39); *na* (1.30); *antam* (2acc◦ sing◦ ←m◦ *anta* (end) 2.16); *na* (1.30); *madhyam* (2acc◦ sing◦ ←m◦ *madhya* (middle) 10.20); *na* (1.30); *punaḥ:* (4.35); *tava* (1.3); *ādim* (2acc◦ sing◦ ←m◦ *ādi* (beginning) 2.28); *paśyāmi* (1.31); *viśveśvara* (m◦ 8voc◦ sing◦ ←bahuvrī◦ *viśveśvara,* विश्वस्य ईश्वरः यः ←n◦ ***viśva*** (world) ←√विश् + m◦ *īśvara* (lord) 4.6); *viśvarūpa* (m◦ 8voc◦ sing◦ ←bahuvrī◦ ***viśva-rūpa***, विश्वम् एव रूपम् यस्य ←n◦ *viśva* ↑ + m◦ *rūpa* (form) 3.39) (11.16)

(§3) *anekabāhūdaravaktranetram* (adj1◦-obj1◦ he who has many arms, bellies, mouths and eyes); *paśyāmi* (I am seeing); *tvām* (obj1◦ you); *sarvataḥ:* (all around); *anantarūpam* (adj2◦-obj1◦ he who has infinite form); *na* (do not); *antam* (obj2◦ the end); *na* (nor); *madhyam* (obj3◦ the median); *na* (nor); *punaḥ:* (even); *tava* (your); *ādim* (obj4◦ beginning); *paśyāmi* (I see); *viśveśvara* (O Lord of the Lords!); *viśvarūpa* (O Universal Being!) (11.16)

(§4) viśveśvara paśyāmi tvām anekabāhūdaravaktranetram sarvataḥ: anantarūpam viśvarūpa na paśyāmi tava

---

[612] Elsewhere◦ ईशम् → the Ruler, Lord Śiva, ...etc.

ādiṃ na madhyaṃ na punaḥ: antaṃ

(§5) O Lord of the Lords! I am seeing you,[613] who has many arms, bellies, mouths and eyes all around; (and) who has infinite form. O Universal Being! I do not see your beginning nor the median nor even the end; (11.17)

11.17 किरीटिनं गदिनं चक्रिणं च तेजोराशिं सर्वतो दीप्तिमन्तम् ।
पश्यामि त्वां दुर्निरीक्ष्यं समन्ताद्दीप्तानलार्कद्युतिमप्रमेयम् ।।

kirīṭinaṁ gadinaṁ ćakriṇaṁ ća tejorāśiṁ sarvataḥ: dīptimantaṃ,
paśyāmi tvāṁ durnirīkṣyam samantāddīptānalārkadyutimaprameyaṃ.
(11.17)

(§1) *kirīṭinaṃ* (r∘ 14/1) *gadinaṃ* (r∘ 14/1) *ćakriṇaṃ* (r∘ 14/1, 24/3) *ća tejorāśiṃ* (r∘ 14/1) *sarvataḥ:* (r∘ 15/4) *dīptimantaṃ* (r∘ 14/2) *paśyāmi tvāṃ* (r∘ 14/1) *durnirīkṣyaṃ* (r∘ 14/1) *samantāṭ* (r∘ 9/5) *dīptānalārkadyutiṃ* (r∘ 8/16) *aprameyaṃ* (r∘ 14/2)

(§2) ***kirīṭinaṃ*** (m∘ 2acc∘ sing∘ ←bah∘ *kirīṭin*, किरीटः अस्ति शिरषि यस्य ←m∘ 📖***kirīṭa*** (crown) ←√कृ); ***gadinaṃ*** (m∘ 2acc∘ sing∘ ←bah∘ *gadiṇ* गदा अस्ति हस्ते यस्य ←f∘ *gadā* (mace) ←√गद्); *ćakriṇaṃ* (m∘ 2acc∘ sing∘ ←bah∘ *ćakriṇ*, चक्रम् अस्ति हस्ते यस्य ←n∘ *ćakra* (wheal) 3.16); ca (1.1); *tejorāśiṃ* (m∘ 2acc∘ sing∘ ←tat∘ *tejorāśi*, तेजसः राशिः यस्मिन् सः ←m∘ *tejaṣ* (splendor) 7.9 + m∘ *rāśi* (heap) ←√अश्); *sarvataḥ:* (adv∘ adj∘ of adj∘ 2.46); *dīptimantaṃ* (m∘ 2acc∘ sing∘ ←śatṛ∘ adj∘ *dīptimaṭ* ←adj∘ 📖***dīpta*** (lit) ←√दीप्); *paśyāmi* (1.31); *tvāṃ* (2.7); *durnirīkṣyaṃ* (m∘ 2acc∘ sing∘ ←adj∘ *durnirīkṣya* (difficult to see) ←ind∘ *duṛ* (difficult) 1.2 + pot∘ adj∘ *nirīkṣya* (to be seen) ←निर्√ईक्ष्); ***samantāṭ*** (adv∘ ←adj∘ *samanta* (around) 6.24); *dīptānalārkadyutiṃ* (m∘ 2acc∘ sing∘ ←bah∘ *dīptānalārka-dyuti*, अनलस्य च अर्कस्य च इव दीप्तम् द्युतिः यस्य तत् ←m∘ or ppp∘ adj∘ *dīpta* (lit) ←√दीप् + m∘ *anala* (fire) 3.39 + m∘ *arka* (sun) ←√अर्च + f∘ *dyuti* (blaze) ←√द्युत्); 📖***aprameyaṃ*** (m∘ 2acc∘ sing∘ n.tatpu∘ ←adj∘ *prameya* (infinite) 2.18) (11.17)

(§3) *kirīṭinaṃ* (adj1∘-obj∘ he who is adroned with crown on his head); *gadinaṃ* (adj2∘-obj∘ he who is adorned with *gadā* in his hand); *ćakriṇaṃ* (adj3∘-obj∘ he who is adorned with *Sudarshan ćakra* in his hand); ca (and); *tejorāśiṃ* (aj4-obj∘ he who is adorned with mountain of splendor); *sarvataḥ:-dīptimantaṃ* (adj5∘-obj∘ he who is full of brilliance from all sides); *paśyāmi* (subj∘ I see); *tvāṃ* (obj∘ you); *durnirīkṣyaṃ* (adj6∘-obj∘ he who is difficult to observe); *samantāṭ* (on all sides);

---

[613] Elsewhere∘ पश्यामि त्वाम् → I see in Your body many many arms, bellies, mouths and eyes ...etc.

📖 in पश्यामि त्वां the 'arms, bellies, mouths and eyes' do not form the object of the subject I, they make up the *bahuvrīhi* adjective of the object 'you.'

dīptānalārkadyutiṃ (adj7◦-obj◦ he who is ablaze with fire and radiance of the sun); *aprameyaṃ* (adj8◦-obj◦ he who is infinite) (11.17)

(§4) paśyāmi tvāṃ kirīṭinaṃ gadinaṃ ćakriṇaṃ tejorāśiṃ sarvataḥ:-dīptimantaṃ durnirīkṣyaṃ dīptānalārkadyutiṃ samantāṭ ca aprameyaṃ

(§5) I see you, who is adroned with crown on his head,[614] who is adorned with *gadā* in his hand, who is adorned with *Sudarshan ćakra* in his hand, who is adorned with mountain of splendor, who is full of brilliance from all sides, who is difficult to observe, who is ablaze on all sides[615] with fire and radiance of the sun, and who is infinite. (11.17)

11.18 त्वमक्षरं परमं वेदितव्यं त्वमस्य विश्वस्य परं निधानम् ।
त्वमव्ययः शाश्वतधर्मगोप्ता सनातनस्त्वं पुरुषो मतो मे ।।

tvamakṣaraṁ paramaṁ veditavyaṁ tvamasya viśvasya paraṁ nidhānaṃ,
tvamavyayaḥ: śāśvatadharmagoptā sanātanastvaṁ puruṣo mato me.
(11.18)

(§1) *tvaṃ* (r◦ 8/16) *akṣaraṃ* (r◦ 14/1) *paramaṃ* (r◦ 14/1) *veditavyaṃ* (r◦ 14/1) *tvaṃ* (r◦ 8/16) *asya viśvasya paraṃ* (r◦ 14/1) *nidhānaṃ* (r◦ 14/2) *tvaṃ* (r◦ 8/16) *avyayaḥ:* (r◦ 22/5) *śāśvatadharmagoptā sanātanaḥ:* (r◦ 18/1) *tvaṃ* (r◦ 14/1) *puruṣaḥ:* (r◦ 15/9) *mataḥ:* (r◦ 15/9) *me*

(§2) *tvaṃ* (2.11); *akṣaraṃ* (1nom◦ 8.3); *paramaṃ* (n◦ 1nom◦ 8.3); *veditavyaṃ* (m◦ 1nom◦ sing◦ ←pot◦ adj◦ *veditavya* ←√विद्); *tvaṃ* (2.11); *asya* (2.17); ***viśvasya*** (6pos sing◦ ←n◦ *viśva* (universe) 11.16); *paraṃ* (1nom◦ 2.12); *nidhānaṃ* (1nom◦ 9.18); *tvaṃ* (2.11); ***avyayaḥ:*** (m◦ 1nom◦ sing◦ ←adj◦ *avyaya* (immutable) 2.17); *śāśvatdharmagoptā* (m◦ 1nom◦ sing◦ ←tatpu◦ *śāśvata-dharma-goptṛ*, शाश्वतस्य धर्मस्य गोप्ता ←adj◦ *śāśvata* (eternal) 1.43 + m◦ *dharma* (righteousness) 1.1 + adj◦ *goptṛ* (protector) ←√गुप्); *sanātanaḥ:* (2.24); *tvaṃ* (2.11); *puruṣaḥ:* (2.21); *mataḥ:* (m◦ 1nom◦ sing◦ ←ppp◦ adj◦ *mata* (thought) 6.32); *me* (1.21) (11.18)

---

[614] Elsewhere◦ किरीटिनम् → with helmetes, with varoius crowns, ...etc.

📖 किरीटिनम् is m◦ singular, Accusative (2nd) case *bahuvrīhi* adjective of Lord Krishṇa त्वाम् । Same is true for the other seven *bahuvrīhi* adjectives in this verse, namely : गदिनम्, चक्रिणम्, तेजोराशिम्, सर्वतो-दीप्तिमन्तम्, दुर्निरीक्ष्यंम्, दीप्तानलार्कद्युतिम् and अप्रमेयम् ।

[615] Elsewhere◦ समन्तात् दीप्तानलार्कद्युतिमप्रमेयम् → difficult to behold completely, I see this glowing from everywhere, difficult to look at from all sides, ...etc.

📖 समन्तात् is not qualifying दुर्निरीक्ष्यम् or पश्यामि । It is qualifying दीप्तानलार्कद्युतिमप्रमेयम् । All eight adjectives, including दुर्निरीक्ष्यम्, are the objects of पश्यामि ।

(§3) *tvam̦* (m◦ you); *akṣaram̦* (n◦ adj1◦-subj1◦ that which immutable); *paramam̦* (n◦ adj2◦-subj1◦ that which is supreme); *veditavyam̦* (m◦ adj3◦-subj1◦ that which is ought to be known); *tvam̦* (m◦ you); *asya* (of this); *viśvasya* (world); *param̦* (n◦ adj4◦-subj1◦ that which is highest);[616] *nidhānam̦* (subj1◦ the abode); *tvam̦* (m◦ subj2◦ you); *avyayaḥ:* (m◦ adj1◦-subj2◦ perpetual); *śāśvatdharmagoptā* (m◦ adj3◦-subj2◦ eternal protector of righteousness);[617] *sanātanaḥ:* (m◦ adj4◦-subj2◦ beginningless and endless); *tvam̦* (m◦ subj2◦ you); *puruṣaḥ:* (adj5◦-subj2◦ Supreme being); *mataḥ:* (subj3◦ opinion, belief); *me* (my) (11.18)

(§4) asya viśvasya tvam̦ akṣaram̦ paramam̦ param̦ nidhānam̦ veditavyam̦ tvam̦ avyayaḥ: tvam̦ śāśvatdharmagoptā tvam̦ sanātanaḥ: puruṣaḥ: me mataḥ:

(§5) Of this world, you (are) the immutable, supreme, (and) highest abode, which is ought to be known.[618] You (are) perpetual. You (are) eternal protector of righteousness. You (are) beginningless and endless Supreme being. (This is) my belief. (11.18)

11.19 **अनादिमध्यान्तमनन्तवीर्यमनन्तबाहुं शशिसूर्यनेत्रम् ।**
पश्यामि त्वां दीप्तहुताशवक्त्रं स्वतेजसा विश्वमिदं तपन्तम् ।।
anādimadhyāntamanantavīryamanantabāhuṁ śaśisūryanetram̦,
paśyāmi tvāṁ dīptahutāśavaktaraṁ svatejasā viśvamidaṁ tapantam̦.
(11.19)

(§1) *anādimadhyāntam̦* (r◦ 8/16) *anantavīryam̦* (r◦ 8/16) *anantabāhum̦* (r◦ 14/1) *śaśisūryanetram̦* (r◦ 14/2) *paśyāmi tvām̦* (r◦ 14/1) *dīptahutāśavaktarm̦* (r◦ 14/1) *svatejasā viśvam̦* (r◦ 8/18) *idam̦* (r◦ 14/1) *tapantam̦* (r◦ 14/2)

(§2) *anādimadhyāntam̦* (m◦ 2acc◦ sing◦ ←bahuvrī◦ *anādi-madhyānta*, नास्ति आदि: च मध्यम् च अन्त: च

---

[616] Elsewhere◦ परम् → most perfect, ...etc.

📖 परम् itself is a superlative adjective (उत्तमम्, पराकोटि:, पराकाष्टा) and does not take another adjective of degree of comparison, such as least, medium or most.

[617] Elsewhere◦ धर्मगोप्ता → Protector of religion, ...etc.

[618] Elsewhere◦ त्वम् अक्षरं परमं वेदितव्यं त्वमस्य विँास्य परं निधानम् → you are Immutable, ...etc.

📖 In त्वम् अक्षरं, परमं, वेदितव्यं, परं, निधानम् । त्वम् implies a masculine subject and निधानम् is a neuter gender subject. Therefore, these four neuter gender adjectives अक्षरम्, परमम्, वेदितव्यम् and परम्, can not qualify m◦ subject त्वम् । These four n◦ adjectives qualify the n◦ subject निधानम् । And for this very reason, next four adjectives अव्यय: शाँतधर्मगोप्ता, सनातन: and पुरुष: which qualify m◦ subject त्वम् are also shown masculine.

यस्य ←adj◦ *ādi* (beginning) 2.28 + n◦ *madhya* (middle) 1.21 + m◦ *anta* (end) 2.16); *anantavīryam̦* (m◦ 2acc◦ sing◦ ←bahuvrī◦ ***ananta-vīrya***, अनन्तम् वीर्यम् यस्य ←adj◦ *ananta* (infinite) 2.41 + n◦ *vīrya* (prowess) 1.5); *anantabāhum̦* (m◦ 2acc◦ sing◦ ←bahuvrī◦ *ananta-bāhu,* अनन्ताः बाहवः यस्य ←adj◦ *ananta* (countless) 2.41 + m◦ *bāhu* (arm) 1.18); *śaśisūryanetram̦* (2acc◦ sing◦ ←bahuvrī◦ *śaśi-sūrya-netra,* शशी च सूर्यः च नेत्रे यस्य ←m◦ *śaśin̦* (moon) 7.8 + m◦ *sūrya* (moon) 7.8 + n◦ *netra* (eye) 11.16); *paśyāmi* (1.31); *tvām̦* (2.7); *dīptahutāśavaktarm̦* (m◦ 2acc◦ sing◦ ←bahuvrī◦ *dīpta-hutāśa-vaktara,* दीप्तः हुताशनः इव वक्त्रम् यस्य ←adj◦ *dīpta* (lit) 11.17 + m◦ *hutāśana* (fire) ←√हु + n◦ *vaktra* (mouth) 11.10); *svatejaș* (n◦ 3inst◦ sing◦ ←tatpu◦ *sva-tejaș* ←adj◦ *sva* (own) 1.28 + n◦ *tejaș* (blaze) 7.9); ***viśvam̦*** (2acc◦ sing◦ ←n◦ *viśva* (universe) 11.16); *idam̦* (1.10); *tapantam̦* (m◦ 2acc◦ sing◦ ←śatr̥◦ adj◦ *tapaț* (burning) ←√तप्) (11.19)

(§3) *anādimadhyāntam̦* (adj1◦-obj◦ he who has no beginning, middle and end); *anantavīryam̦* (adj2◦-obj◦ he who is of infinite prowess); *anantabāhum̦* (adj3◦-obj◦ he who has infinite arms); *śaśisūryanetram̦* (adj4◦-obj◦ he who has sun and moon as his eyes); *paśyāmi* (subj◦ I see); *tvām̦* (obj◦ you); *dīptahutāśavaktarm̦* (adj5◦-obj◦ he whose mouth is blazing with flames); *svatejaș* (by his own radiance); *viśvam̦-idam̦-tapantam̦* (adj6◦-obj◦ he who is burning this world) (11.19)

(§4) paśyāmi tvām̦ anādimadhyāntam̦ anantavīryam̦ anantabāhum̦ śaśisūryanetram̦ dīptahutāśavaktarm̦ viśvam̦-idam̦-tapantam̦ svatejaș

(§5) I see you (as) who has no beginning, middle and end,[619] who is of infinite prowess, who has infinite arms, who has sun and moon as his eyes, whose mouth is blazing with flames (and who is burning this world by his own radiance. (11.19)

11.20 द्यावापृथिव्योरिदमन्तरं हि व्याप्तं त्वयैकेन दिशश्च सर्वाः ।
दृष्ट्वाऽद्भुतं रूपमुग्रं तवेदं लोकत्रयं प्रव्यथितं महात्मन् ।।

dyāvāpr̥thivyoridamantaraṁ hi vyāptaṁ tvayaikena diśaśća sarvāḥ:,
dr̥̣ṣṭvā‘dhbutaṁ rūpamugraṁ tavedaṁ lokatrayaṁ pravyathitaṁ mahātman̦.
(11.20)

(§1) *dyāvāpr̥thivyoḥ:* (r◦ 16/5) *idam̦* (r◦ 8/16) *antaram̦* (r◦ 14/1) *hi vyāptam̦* (r◦ 14/1) *tvayā* (r◦ 3/3) *ekena diśaḥ:* (r◦ 17/1) *ća sarvāḥ:* (r◦ 22/8) *dr̥ṣṭvā* (r◦ 1/3) *adhbutam̦* (r◦ 14/1) *rūpam̦* (r◦ 8/20) *ugram̦*

---

[619] Elsewhere◦ अनादिमध्यान्तम् अनन्तवीर्यम् अनन्तबाहुम् शशिसूर्यनेत्रम् पश्यामि → you are without origin, middle or end, ...etc.

📖 Here, ‘you’ does not indicate the subject. The subject is ‘I’ (पश्यामि). त्वाम् is object. अनादिमध्यान्तम् अनन्तवीर्यम्, अनन्तबाहुम्, शशिसूर्यनेत्रम्, दीप्तहुताशवक्त्रम् and तपन्तम् are the six adjectives of the object त्वाम् ।

(r◦ 14/1) *tava* (r◦ 2/1) *idam̧* (r◦ 14/1) *lokatrayam̧* (r◦ 14/1) *pravyathitam̧* (r◦ 14/1) *mahātmaņ*

(§2) *dyāvāpṛthivyoḥ:* (f◦ 6pos◦ dual◦ ←dvandva◦ द्यावया: च पृथिव्या: च ←f◦ *dyāvā* ←n◦ *dyu* (sky) ←√दिव् + f◦ *pṛthivī* (earth) 1.18); *idam̧* (nom◦ 1.10); ***antaram̧*** (1nom◦ sing◦ ←n◦ *antara* (space) 2.13); *hi* (1.11); *vyāptam̧* (n◦ 1nom◦ sing◦ ←ppp◦ adj◦ *vyāpta* (occupied) ←वि√आप्); *tvayā* (6.33); ***ekena*** (m◦ 3inst◦ sing◦ ←adj◦ ***eka*** (one) 2.41); *diśaḥ:* (6.13); *ća* (1.1); *sarvāḥ:* (8.18); *dṛṣṭvā* (1.2); 🕮***adhbutam̧*** (n◦ 2acc◦ sing◦ ←adj◦ *adbhuta* (never before) 11.10); *rūpam̧* (2acc◦ 11.3); *ugram̧* (n◦ 2acc◦ sing◦ ←adj◦ 🕮***ugra*** (dreadful) ←√उच्); *tava* (1.3); *idam̧* (2acc◦ 1.10); 🕮***lokatrayam̧*** (n◦ 1nom◦ sing◦ ←tatpu◦ ***loka-traya***, लोकानाम् त्रयम् ←m◦ *loka* (world) 2.5 + n◦ ***traya*** (trio) ←√तॄ); 🕮*pravyathitam̧* (n◦ 1nom◦ sing◦ ←ppp◦ adj◦ ***pravyathita*** ←प्र√व्यथ्); ***mahātmaņ*** (8voc◦ sing◦ ←m◦ *mahātmaņ* 7.19) (11.20)

(§3) *dyāvāpṛthivyoḥ:* (of the sky and the earth); *idam̧* (adj1◦-obj1◦ this); *antaram̧* (obj1◦ space, distance between); *hi* (because); *vyāptam̧* (adj2◦-obj1◦ occupied); *tvayā* (subj1◦ by you); *ekena* (adj◦-subj1◦ alone); *diśaḥ:* (obj2◦ directions); *ća* (and); *sarvāḥ:* (adj◦-obj2◦ all); *dṛṣṭvā* (having seen); *adhbutam̧* (adj1◦-obj3◦ which is never seen before); *rūpam̧* (obj3◦ form); *ugram̧* (adj2◦-obj3◦ dreadful); *tava* (your); *idam̧* (adj4◦-obj3◦ this); *lokatrayam̧* (subj2◦ whole of the three worlds); *pravyathitam̧* (adj◦-subj2◦ shaken up); *mahātmaņ* (O Lord Kṛṣṇa!) (11.20)

(§4) mahātmaņ hi sarvāḥ: diśaḥ:idam̧ antaram̧ dyāvāpṛthivyoḥ: vyāptam̧ tvayā ekena ća dṛṣṭvā tava ugram̧ rūpam̧ adhbutam̧ idam̧ lokatrayam̧ pravyathitam̧

(§5) O Lord Kṛṣṇa! because[620] all directions (and) this space between the sky and the earth (is) occupied by you[621] alone, and having seen your dreadful form which is never seen before, this whole of the three worlds (is) shaken up.[622] (11.20)

11.21 अमी हि त्वां सुरसङ्घा विशन्ति केचिद्भीताः प्राञ्जलयो गृणन्ति ।
स्वस्तीत्युक्त्वा महर्षिसिद्धसङ्घा स्तुवन्ति त्वा स्तुतिभिः पुष्कलाभिः ।।

amī hi tvām̐ surasaṅghā viśanti kećidbhītāḥ: prāñjalayo gṛṇanti,

---

[620] See footnote in verse 3.5

[621] Elsewhere◦ व्याप्तं त्वया → You spread throughout, ...etc.

🕮 Remember, it is not an active voice. It is a passive construction. The subject is not त्वम्, it is त्वया । Therefore, ppp◦ व्याप्तम् is used.

[622] Elsewhere◦ प्रव्यथितम् → three worlds are trembling (gerund), three worlds tremble (pr◦), triple worlds sink down (pr◦), ...etc.

🕮 प्रव्यथितम् is not a gerund or a Present tense verb. It is a ppp◦ adjective.

svastītyuktvā maharṣisiddhasaṅghā stuvanti tvāṁ stutibhiḥ: puṣkalābhiḥ:.

(11.21)

(1) *amī hi tvāṃ* (r◦ 14/1) *surasaṅghāḥ:* (r◦ 20/17) *viśanti kecit* (r◦ 9/8) *bhītāḥ:* (r◦ 22/3) *prāñjalayaḥ:* (r◦ 15/2) *gṛṇanti svasti* (r◦ 1/5) *iti* (r◦ 4/3) *uktvā maharṣisiddhasaṅghāḥ:* (r◦ 22/7) *stuvanti tvāṃ* (r◦ 14/1) *stutibhiḥ:* (r◦ 22/3) *puṣkalābhiḥ:* (r◦ 22/8)

(§2) ***amī*** (m◦ 1nom◦ plu◦ ←pron◦ ***adaṣ*** -this); *hi* (1.11); *tvāṃ* (2.7); *surasaṅghāḥ:* (m◦ 1nom◦ plu◦ ←tatpu◦ *sura-saṅgha*, सुराणाम् सङ्घः ←m◦ *sura* (god) 2.8 + m◦ *saṅgha* (group) 11.15); *viśanti* (8.11); ***kecit*** (1nom◦ plu◦ ←pron◦ *kaścit* (some) 2.17); 📖*bhītāḥ:* (m◦ 1nom◦ plu◦ ←ppp◦ adj◦ ***bhīta*** (afraid) ←√भी); *prāñjalayaḥ:* (m◦ 1nom◦ plu◦ ←bahuvrī◦ *prāñjali*, प्रबद्धा अञ्जलिः यस्य सः ←प्र√अञ्ज्); *gṛṇanti* (3rd-per◦ plu◦ pres◦ वर्तमान्–लट् parasmai◦ ←class9◦ √गॄ); *svasti* (exclamatory ind◦ ←सु√अस्); *iti* (1.25); *uktvā* (1.47); *maharṣisiddhasaṅghāḥ:* (m◦ 1nom◦ plu◦ ←tatpu◦ *maharṣi-siddha-saṅgha*, महर्षीणाम् च सिद्धानाम् च सङ्घः ←m◦ *maharṣi* 10.2 + m◦ *siddha* 7.3 + m◦ *saṅgha* 11.15); *stuvanti* (3rd-per◦ plu◦ pres◦ वर्तमान्–लट् parasmai◦ ←class2◦ √स्तु); *tvāṃ* (2.7); *stutibhiḥ:* (3inst◦ plu◦ ←f◦ 📖***stuti*** (praise) ←√स्तु); *puṣkalābhiḥ:* (f◦ 3inst◦ plu◦ ←adj◦ *puṣkala* (much) ←√पष्) (11.21)

(§3) *amī* (adj1◦-subj◦ those); *hi* (because); *tvāṃ* (obj◦ you); *surasaṅghāḥ:* (subj1◦ hordes of gods); *viśanti* (are entering); *kecit* (adj2◦-subj1◦ some); *bhītāḥ:* (struck with fear, scared); *prāñjalayaḥ:* (adj3◦-subj1◦ those with folded hands); *gṛṇanti* (are offering prayers); *svasti* ('peace be on you'); *iti* (thus); *uktvā* (saying); *maharṣisiddhasaṅghāḥ:* (subj2◦ hordes of the great sages); *stuvanti* (are praising); *tvāṃ* (obj◦ you); *stutibhiḥ:* (with praises, with hymns); *puṣkalābhiḥ:* (with many) (11.21)

(§4) hi bhītāḥ: amī surasaṅghāḥ: viśanti tvāṃ kecit prāñjalayaḥ: gṛṇanti uktvā svasti iti maharṣisiddhasaṅghāḥ: stuvanti tvāṃ puṣkalābhiḥ: stutibhiḥ:

(§5) Because[623] struck with fear, those hordes of gods are entering (in) you, some with folded hands are offering prayers saying 'peace be on you,' hordes of the great sages are praising you with many hymns. (11.21)

11.22 रुद्रादित्या वसवो ये च साध्या विश्वेऽश्विनौ मरुतश्चोष्मपाश्च ।
गन्धर्वयक्षासुरसिद्धसङ्घा वीक्षन्ते त्वां विस्मिताश्चैव सर्वे ।।

rudrādityā vasavo ye ca sādhyā viśve'śvinau marutaścoṣmapāśca,
gandharvayakṣāsurasiddhasaṅghā vīkṣante tvāṁ vismitāścaiva sarve.

(11.22)

---

[623] See footnote in verse 3.5

(§1) *rudrādityāḥ:* (r◦ 20/17) *vasavaḥ:* (r◦ 15/10) *ye ća sādhyāḥ:* (r◦ 20/17) *viśve* (r◦ 6/1) *aśvinau marutaḥ:* (r◦ 17/1) *ća* (r◦ 2/2) *uṣmapāḥ:* (r◦ 17/1) *ća gandharvayakṣāsurasiddhasaṅghāḥ:* (r◦ 20/17) *vīkṣante tvāṃ* (r◦ 14/1) *vismitāḥ:* (r◦ 17/1) *ća* (r◦ 3/1) *eva sarve*

(§2) 🕮*rudrādityāḥ:* (m◦ 1nom◦ plu◦ ←dvandva◦ रुद्राः च आदित्याः च ←m◦ *rudra* 10.23 + m◦ *āditya* 5.16); 🕮*vasavaḥ:* (1nom◦ plu◦ ←m◦ *vasu* 10.23); *ye* (1.7); *ća* (1.1); 🕮*sādhyāḥ:* (1nom◦ plu◦ ←m◦ *sādhya* ←√सिध्); *viśve,* an abbriaviation for *viśvedevāḥ* or *viśvadevāḥ:* (1nom◦ plu◦ ←bahuvrī◦ विश्वस्य देवाः ←n◦ *viśva* (universe) 11.16 + m◦ *deva* (god) 3.11, there are ten *viśvadevas,* see footnote); *aśvinau* (1nom◦ dual◦ ←m◦ *aśvina* 11.6); 🕮*marutaḥ:* (11.6); *ća* (1.1); *uṣmapāḥ:* (1nom◦ plu◦ ←m◦ or f◦ bahuvrī◦ *uṣma-pā,* उष्णम् पिबति यः ←adj◦ *uṣma* (conflagration) ←√उष् + adj◦ *pā* (drinker) ←√पा); *ća* (1.1); *gandharvayakṣāsurasiddhasaṅghāḥ:* (m◦ 1nom◦ plu◦ ←tatpu◦ *gandharva-yakṣāsura-siddha-saṅgha,* गन्धर्वाणाम् च यक्षानाम् च असुराणाम् च सिद्धानाम् च सङ्घः ←m◦ *gandharva* 10.26 + m◦ *yakṣa* 10.23 + m◦ n.tatpu◦ *asura* ←अ-सु√रा + m◦ *siddha* 7.3 + m◦ *saṅgha* (group) 11.15); *vīkṣante* (3rd-per◦ plu◦ pres◦ वर्तमान्-लट् ātmane◦ ←class1◦ वि√ईक्ष्); *tvāṃ* (2.7); 🕮*vismitāḥ:* (m◦ 1nom◦ plu◦ ←ppp◦ adj◦ *vismita* (surprised) ←वि√स्मि); *ća* (1.1); *eva* (1.1); *sarve* (m◦ 1nom◦ plu◦ ←pron◦ *sarva* (all) 1.6) (11.22)

(§3) *rudrādityāḥ:* (subj1◦ the eleven rudra sons and the twelve āditya sons of Aditi); *vasavaḥ:* (subj2◦ the eight vasu sons of Aditi); *ye* (those who); *ća* (and); *sādhyāḥ:* (subj3◦ the accomplished beings); *viśve* (subj4◦ the ten celestial deities); *aśvinau* (subj5◦ the two twin physicians of the gods, the two twin sons of the sun); *marutaḥ:* (subj6◦ the forty-nine marut sons of Aditi); *ća* (and); *uṣmapāḥ:* (subj7◦ the drinkers of the conflagration); *ća* (and); *gandharvayakṣāsurasiddhasaṅghāḥ:* (subj8◦ the hordes of the celestial musicians, the demigod attendents of Kubera, the evil spirits, and the accomplished beings); *vīkṣante* (are beholding); *tvāṃ* (obj◦ you); *vismitāḥ:* (adj◦-subj1-8◦ struck with wonder, surprised, taken aback, stunned); *ća eva* (as well as); *sarve* (all) (11.22)

(§4) ća ye vismitāḥ: rudrādityāḥ: vasavaḥ: sādhyāḥ: viśve aśvinau ća marutaḥ: ća uṣmapāḥ: ća eva sarve gandharvayakṣāsurasiddhasaṅghāḥ:

(§5) And those who are struck with wonder, the eleven rudra sons and the twelve āditya sons of Aditi, the eight vasu sons of Aditi, the accomplished[624] beings, the ten celestial deities, [625] the two

---

[624] Elsewhere◦ isaīa: → the perfected ones, the perfected souls, the perfected... etc.

🕮 See above for the various shades of the Sanskrit meanings of the word *'siddhāḥ:.'* Siddhi (सिद्धि) does not imply perfection, but it means 'accomplishment.' See footnote given in verse 4.12 for details.

[625] The ten all omnioresent viśvedevās :

twin physicians of the gods,[626] and the forty-nine marut sons of Aditi, and the drinkers of the conflagration,[627] as well as all the hordes of the celestial musicians,[628] the demigod attendents of Kubera,[629] the evil spirits,[630] and the accomplished beings are beholding you. (11.22)

11.23 रूपं महत्ते बहुवक्त्रनेत्रं महाबहो बहुबाहूरुपादम् ।
बहूदरं बहुदंष्ट्राकरालं दृष्ट्वा लोकाः प्रव्यथितास्तथाऽहम् ।।

rūpaṁ mahatte bahuvaktranetraṁ mahābāho bahubāhūrupādam,
bahūdaraṁ bahudaṁṣṭrākarālaṁ dṛṣṭvā lokāḥ: pravyathitāstathā'ham.
(11.23)

(§1) *rūpam* (r◦ 14/1) *mahat* (r◦ 1/10) *te bahuvaktranetram* (r◦ 14/1) *mahābāho bahubāhūrupādam* (r◦ 14/2) *bahūdaram* (r◦ 14/1) *bahudaṁṣṭrākarālam* (r◦ 14/1) *dṛṣṭvā lokāḥ:* (r◦ 22/3) *pravyathitāḥ:* (r◦ 18/1) *tathā* (r◦ 1/3) *aham* (r◦ 14/2)

(§2) *rūpam* (11.3); *mahat* (1.3); *te* (2.7); *bahuvaktranetram* (n◦ 2acc◦ sing◦ ←bahuvrī◦ *bahu-vaktra-netra*, बहुनि वक्त्राणि च नेत्राणि च यस्मिन् ←adj◦ *bahu* (arm) 1.9 + n◦ *vaktra* (mouth) 11.10 + n◦ *netra* (eye) 11.16); *mahābāho* (2.26); *bahubāhūrupādam* (n◦ 2acc◦ sing◦ ←bahuvrī◦ *bahu-bāhūru-pāda*, बहवः बाहवः च उरवः च पादाः च यस्मिन् ←adj◦ *bahu* (many) 1.9 + m◦ *bāhu* (arm) 1.18 + m◦ *uru* (chest) ←√ऋ + m◦ 📖***pāda*** (foot) ←√पद्); *bahūdaram* (n◦ 2acc◦ sing◦ ←bahuvrī◦ *bahūdara*, बहुनि उदराणि यस्मिन् ←adj◦ *bahu* (many) 1.9 + n◦ 📖*udara* (stomach) 1.15); *bahudaṁṣṭrākarālam* (n◦ 2acc◦ sing◦ ←bahuvrī◦ *bahu-daṁṣṭrā-karāla*, बहुभिः–बह्वीभिः

वसुः सत्यः क्रतुर्दक्षः कालः कामोधृतिः कुरुः ।
पुरूरवा माद्रवश्च विश्वेदेवाः प्रकीर्तिताः ।।

[626] The two Ashvini-kumaras :
त्वाष्ट्री तु सवितुर्भार्या वडवारूपधारिणी ।
असूयत महाभागा सान्तरीक्षेऽश्विनावुभौ ।।

[627] The uṣmapās :
ओषाञ्चकार कामाग्निर्दशवक्त्रमहर्निशम् ।

[628] The gandharvas :
पतङ्गो वाचं मनसा बिभर्ति तां गन्धर्वोऽवदाद्गर्भे ।
सोमं शौचं ददावासां गन्धर्वश्च शुभां गिरम् ।

[629] The yakṣas :
यक्षोत्तमा यक्षपतिं धनेशं रक्षन्ति वै प्रासगदादिहस्ताः ।

[630] The asuras :
सुराप्रतिग्रहाद्देवाः सुरा इत्यभिविश्रुताः ।
अप्रतिग्रहणात्तस्यादैतेयाश्चासुरास्तथा ।।

दंष्ट्राभि: करालम् यत् तत् ←adj◦ *bahu* (many) 1.9 + f◦ 🕮***daṁṣṭrā*** (jaw) ←√दंश् + f◦ adj◦ 🕮***karālā*** (fearful) ←कर–आ√ला); *dṛṣṭvā* (1.2); *lokāḥ:* (3.24); *pravyathitāḥ:* (m◦ 1nom◦ plu◦ ←adj◦ *pravyathita* (shaken) 11.20); *tathā* (1.8); *aham* (1.22) (11.23)

(§3) *rūpam* (obj◦ form); *mahat* (adj◦-obj◦ immense); *te* (your); *bahuvaktranetram* (adj1◦-obj◦ that which is with many mouths and eyes); *mahābāho* (O Lord Kṛṣṇa!); *bahubāhūrupādam* (adj2◦-obj◦ with numerous arms, thighs, and feet); *bahūdaram* (with many bellies); *bahudaṁṣṭrākarālam* (with countless fearful teeth); *dṛṣṭvā* (seeing); *lokāḥ:* (the three worlds); *pravyathitāḥ:* (shaken); *tathā* (as well as, so); *aham* (subj2◦ I am, am I) (11.23)

(§4) mahābāho dṛṣṭvā te mahat rūpam bahuvaktranetram bahubāhūrupādam bahūdaram bahudaṁṣṭrākarālam lokāḥ: pravyathitāḥ: tathā aham

(§5) O Lord Kṛṣṇa! seeing your immense form with many mouths and eyes, with numerous arms, thighs, and feet, with many bellies, (and) with countless fearful teeth, the three worlds(are) shaken[631] so am I. (11.23)

11.24 **नभःस्पृशं दीप्तमनेकवर्णं व्यात्ताननं दीप्तविशालनेत्रम् ।**
दृष्ट्वा हि त्वां प्रव्यथितान्तरात्मा धृतिं न विन्दामि शमं च विष्णो ॥

nabhaḥ:spṛśaṁ dīptamanekavarṇaṁ vyāttānanaṁ dīptaviśālanetram,
dṛṣṭvā hi tvāṁ pravyathitāntarātmā dhṛtiṁ na vindāmi śamaṁ ća viṣṇo;
(11.24)

(§1) *nabhaḥ:spṛśam* (r◦ 14/1) *dīptam* (r◦ 8/16) *anekavarṇam* (r◦ 14/1) *vyāttānanam* (r◦ 14/1) *dīptaviśālanetram* (r◦ 14/2) *dṛṣṭvā hi tvām* (r◦ 14/1) *pravyathitāntarātmā dhṛtim* (r◦ 14/1) *na vindāmi śamam* (r◦ 14/1) *ća viṣṇo;*

(§2) *nabhaḥ:spṛśam* (m◦ 2acc◦ sing◦ ←bahuvrī◦ *nabhaḥ:-spṛśa*, नभ: स्पृशति य: ←n◦ *nabhas* (sky) 1.19 + m◦ *sparśa* (touch) 2.14); *dīptam* (m◦ 2acc◦ sing◦ ←adj◦ *dīpta* (lit) 11.17); *anekavarṇam* (m◦ 2acc◦ sing◦ ←bahuvrī◦ *aneka-varṇa*, अनेके वर्णा: यस्य ←adj◦ *aneka* (many) 6.45 + m◦ *varṇa* (colour) 1.41); *vyāttānanam* (m◦ 2acc◦ sing◦ ←bahuvrī◦ *vyāttānana*, व्यात्तानि आननानि यस्य ←adj◦ ppp◦ 🕮*vyātta* (open) ←वि–आ√दा + n◦ 🕮*ānana* (mouth) ←आ√अन्); *dīptaviśālanetram* (m◦ 2acc◦ sing◦ ←bahuvrī◦ *dīpta-viśāla-netra*, दीप्तानि च विशालानि च नेत्राणि यस्य ←adj◦ *dīpta* (lit) 11.17 + adj◦ *viśālam* (big) 9.21 + n◦ *netra* (eye) 11.16); *dṛṣṭvā* (1.2);

---

[631] Elsewhere◦ दृष्ट्वा लोका: प्रव्यथिता: → are beholding You in wonder, the three words tremble and so do I, the three words are trembling, ...etc.

🕮 Remember, दृष्ट्वा is a past indeclinable क्त्वा participle, and प्रव्यथिता: is a ppp◦ adjective.

hi (1.11); *tvāṃ* (2.7); *pravyathitāntarātmā* (m∘ 1nom∘ sing∘ ←bahuvrī∘ *pravyathitāntarātmaṇ*, प्रव्यथितः अन्तरात्मा यस्य ←adj∘ *pravyathita* (shaken, terrified) 11.20 + m∘ *antarātmaṇ* (heart) 6.47); *dhṛtiṃ* (2acc∘ sing∘ ←f∘ *dhṛti* (courage) 6.25); *na* (1.30); *vindāmi* (1st-per∘ sing∘ pres∘ वर्तमान्-लट् parasmai∘ ←class6∘ √विद् 4.38); *śamaṃ* (2acc∘ sing∘ ←m∘ *śama* (peace) 6.3); *ća* (1.1); **viṣṇo** (m∘ 8voc∘ sing∘ ←prop∘ *Viṣṇu* 10.21); (11.24)

(§3) *nabhaḥ:spṛśaṃ* (adj1∘-obj1∘ that which is touching the sky); *dīptaṃ* (adj2∘-obj1∘ blazing); *anekavarṇaṃ* (adj3∘-obj1∘ that which has many colours); *vyāttānanaṃ* (adj4∘-obj1∘ open-mouthed); *dīptaviśālanetraṃ* (adj5∘-obj1∘ with fiery large eyes); *dṛṣṭvā* (having seen, seeing); *hi* (because); *tvāṃ* (obj1∘ you); *pravyathitāntarātmā* (adj1∘-subj∘ he who is terrified at heart); *dhṛtiṃ* (obj2∘ courage); *na* (do not); *vindāmi* (I get, I find); *śamaṃ* (obj3∘ peace); *ća* (and); *viṣṇo* (O Viṣṇu! O Lord Kṛṣṇa!); (11.24)

(§4) viṣṇo dṛṣṭvā tvāṃ nabhaḥ:spṛśaṃ dīptaṃ anekavarṇaṃ vyāttānanaṃ dīptaviśālanetraṃ hi pravyathitāntarātmā na vindāmi dhṛtiṃ ća śamaṃ;

(§5) O Lord Kṛṣṇa! seeing you (in the form)[632] that is touching the sky, blazing, that which has many colours, open-mouthed (and) with fiery large eyes, because[633] (I am) terrified at heart, I do not find courage and peace; (11.24)

11.25 दंष्ट्राकरालानि च ते मुखानि दृष्ट्वैव कालानलसन्निभानि ।
दिशो न जाने न लभे च शर्म प्रसीद देवेश जगन्निवास ।।

damṣṭrākarālāni ća te mukhāni dṛṣṭvaiva kālānalasannibhāni,
diśo na jāne na labhe ća śarma prasīda deveśa jagannivāsa. (11.25)

(§1) *damṣṭrākarālāni ća te mukhāni dṛṣṭvā* (r∘ 3/3) *eva kālānalasannibhāni diśaḥ:* (r∘ 20/10) *na jāne na labhe ća śarma prasīda deveśa jagannivāsa*

(§2) **damṣṭrākarālāni** (n∘ 2acc∘ plu∘ ←s-karm∘ **damṣṭrā-karāla**, दंष्ट्रा कराला ←f∘ *damṣṭrā* (jaw) *11.23* + adj∘

---

[632] Elsewhere∘ नभःस्पृशं दीप्तम् अनेकवर्णं व्यात्ताननं दीप्त-विशाल-नेत्रम् दृष्ट्वा त्वां → seeing You touching the skies ...etc.

📖 In नभःस्पृशं दीप्तमनेकवर्णं व्यात्ताननं दीप्तविशालनेत्रम् दृष्ट्वा त्वाम्, the adjectives नभःस्पृशम, दीप्तम्, अनेकवर्णम्, व्यात्ताननम्, दीप्तविशालनेत्रम् are neuter gender and can not qualify the pronoun त्वाम् which is masculine gender . Therefore, "in the form" a neuter gender phrase is understood to make a proper connection between the object and its five adjectives.

[633] See footnote in verse 3.5

karāla (dreadful) 11.23); *ća* (1.1); *te* (2.7); *mukhāni* (1nom◦ 2acc◦ plu◦ ←n◦ *mukha* (mouth) 1.29); *dṛṣṭvā* (1.2); *eva* (1.1); *kālānalasannibhāni* (n◦ 2acc◦ plu◦ ←tatpu◦ *kālānala-sannibha,* कालस्य अनलस्य संनिभम् ←m◦ *kāla* (dissolver) 2.72 + m◦ *anala* (fire) 3.39 + ind◦ *saṃ* (fully) 1.1 + adj◦ *nibha* (oblitrative) ←नि√भा); *diśaḥ:* (6.13); *na* (1.30); *jāne* (1st-per◦ sing◦ pres◦ वर्तमान्-लट् ātmane◦ ←class9◦ √ज्ञा); *na* (1.30); ***labhe*** (1st-per◦ sing◦ pres◦ वर्तमान्-लट् ātmane◦ ←class1◦ √लभ्); *ća* (1.1); *śarma* (2acc◦ sing◦ ←n◦ *śarman* (peace) ←√शॄ); ***prasīda*** (2nd-per◦ sing◦ imperative◦ निवेदनार्थ-लोट् parasmai◦ ←class6◦ प्र√सद्); 🕮***deveśa*** (m◦ 8voc◦ sing◦ ←bahuvrī◦ *deveśa,* देवानाम् ईशः यः ←m◦ *deva* (god) 3.11 + adj◦ *īśa* (lord) 1.15); ***jagannivāsa*** (m◦ 8voc◦ sing◦ ←bahuvrī◦ *jagannivāsa,* जगतः निवासः यः ←n◦ *jagat* (world) 7.5 + m◦ *nivāsa* (abode) 9.18)◦

(11.25)

(§3) *daṁṣṭrākarālāni* (adj1◦-obj1◦ those which are with fearful teeth); *ća* (and); *te* (your); *mukhāni* (obj1◦ mouths); *dṛṣṭvā* (having seen, seeing); *eva* (also); *kālānalasannibhāni* (adj2◦-obj1◦ those which are burning like obliterative fire at the dissolution of the world); *diśaḥ:* (obj2◦ the directions, the right ways); *na* (do not); *jāne* (I know); *na* (do not); *labhe* (I find); *ća* (and); *śarma* (obj3◦ peace); *prasīda* (please be pleased!); *deveśa* (O Lord of the Lords! O Lord Kṛṣṇa!); *jagannivāsa* (O Refuge of the World! O Lord Kṛṣṇa!)

(11.25)

(§4) jagannivāsa dṛṣṭvā te mukhāni daṁṣṭrākarālāni ća kālānalasannibhāni na jāne diśaḥ: ća na labhe śarma eva deveśa prasīda

(§5) O Lord Kṛṣṇa! having seen your mouths with fearful teeth and which are burning like obliterative fire at the dissolution of the world,[634] I do not know the right ways and I do not find peace also.[635] O Lord of the Lords! please be pleased!

(11.25)

11.26 अमी च त्वां धृतराष्ट्रस्य पुत्राः सर्वे सहैवावनिपालसङ्घैः ।
भीष्मो द्रोणः सूतपुत्रस्तथासौ सहास्मदीयैरपि योधमुख्यैः ।।

amī ća tvāṁ dhṛtarāṣṭrasya putrāḥ: sarve sahaivāvanipālasaṅghaiḥ:,
bhīṣmo droṇaḥ: sūtaputrastathāsau sahāsmadīyairapi yodhamukhyaiḥ:;

(11.26)

---

[634] Elsewhere◦ कालानल → time-fire, fires of time, Time's fire, fire of death, blazing deathlike, ...etc.

[635] Elsewhere◦ दिशो न जाने न लभे च शर्म → In all directions I am bewildered, ...etc.

🕮 Here दिशः is not an adverb of the verb जाने or the verb न लभे च शर्म । It is the object of the verb जाने ।

(§1) *amī ća tvām* (r∘ 14/1) *dhṛtarāṣṭrasya putrāḥ:* (r∘ 22/7) *sarve saha* (r∘ 3/1) *eva* (r∘ 1/1) *avanipālasaṅghaiḥ:* (r∘ 22/8) *bhīṣmaḥ:* (r∘ 15/4) *droṇaṃ* (r∘ 22/7) *sūtaputraḥ:* (r∘ 18/1) *tathā* (r∘ 1/3) *asau saha* (r∘ 1/1) *asmadīyaiḥ:* (r∘ 16/4) *api yodhamukhyaiḥ:* (r∘ 22/8);

(§2) *amī* (11.21); *ća* (1.1); *tvāṃ* (2.7); *dhṛtarāṣṭrasya* (6pos sing∘ ←m∘ *dhṛtarāṣṭra* 1.1); *putrāḥ:* (1.34); *sarve* (1.6); *saha* (1.22); *eva* (1.1); *avanipālsaṅghaiḥ:* (m∘ 3inst∘ plu∘ ←tatpu∘ *avanipāla-saṅgha* (kings) अवनेः पालानाम् सङ्घः ←f∘ *avani* (earth) ←√अव् + m∘ *pāla* (protectors) ←√पाल् + m∘ *saṅgha* (group) 11.15); *bhīṣmaḥ:* (1.8); *droṇaṃ* (m∘ 1nom∘ sing∘ ←prop∘ *Droṇa* 1.25); *sūtaputraḥ:* (m∘ 1nom∘ sing∘ ←bahuvrī∘ *sūta-putra* (Karṇa) सूतस्य पुत्रः ←m∘ *sūta* (charioteer) ←√सू + m∘ *putra* (son) 1.3); *tathā* (1.8); ***asau*** (m∘ 1nom∘ sing∘ ←pron∘ *adaṣ* 11.21); *saha* (1.22); *asmadīyaiḥ:* (m∘ 3inst∘ plu∘ ←adj∘ taddhita∘ *asmadīya* (our) अस्माकम् इदम् ←pron∘ *asmad* 1.7); *api* (1.26); *yodhamukhyaiḥ:* (m∘ 3inst∘ plu∘ ←tatpu∘ *yodha-mukhya*, योधानाम् मुख्यः ←m∘ 🕮***yodha*** (warrior) ←√युध् + adj∘ *mukhya* (leader) 10.24); (11.26)

(§3) *amī* (adj∘-subj∘ these); *ća* (and); *tvāṃ* (obj∘ you, to you, into you, into your); *dhṛtarāṣṭrasya* (of Dhṛtarāṣṭra); *putrāḥ:* (subj1∘ sons); *sarve* (adj∘-subj1∘ all); *saha* (along with); *eva* (also); *avanipālsaṅghaiḥ:* (with the hoards of the kings); *bhīṣmaḥ:* (subj2∘ Bhiṣmāchārya); *droṇaṃ* (subj3∘ Droṇāchārya); *sūtaputraḥ:* (subj4∘ Karṇa); *tathā* (as well as); *asau* (adj∘-subj4∘ this); *saha* (together with); *asmadīyaiḥ:* (with our); *api* (also); *yodhamukhyaiḥ:* (with chief warriors); (11.26)

(§4) sarve amī putrāḥ: dhṛtarāṣṭrasya saha avanipālsaṅghaiḥ: ća eva bhīṣmaḥ: droṇaṃ tathā asau sūtaputraḥ: saha asmadīyaiḥ: yodhamukhyaiḥ: api tvāṃ

(§5) All these sons of Dhṛtarāṣṭra along with the hoards of the kings and also Bhiṣmāchārya, Droṇāchārya as well as this Karṇa, together with our chief warriors also, into your; (11.26)

11.27 वक्त्राणि ते त्वरमाणा विशन्ति दंष्ट्राकरालानि भयानकानि ।
केचिद्विलग्ना दशनान्तरेषु सन्दृश्यन्ते चूर्णितैरुत्तमाङ्गैः ।।
vaktrāṇi te tvaramāṇā viśanti daṁṣṭrākarālāni bhayānakāni,
kećidvilagnā daśanāntareṣu saṁdṛśyante ćūrṇitairuttamāṅgaiḥ:.
(11.27)

(§1) *vaktrāṇi* (r∘ 24/7) *te tvaramāṇāḥ:* (r∘ 24/5, 20/17) *viśanti daṁṣṭrākarālāni bhayānakāni kećiṭ* (r∘ 9/11) *vilagnāḥ:* (r∘ 20/8) *daśanāntareṣu* (r∘ 25/5) *saṁdṛśyante ćūrṇitaiḥ:* (r∘ 16/4) *uttamāṅgaiḥ:* (r∘ 22/8)

(§2) ***vaktrāṇi*** (2acc∘ plu∘ ←n∘ *vaktra* (mouth) 11.10); *te* (2.7); *tvaramāṇāḥ:* (m∘ 1nom∘ plu∘ ←śānać∘ adj∘ *tvaramāṇa* (hastening) ←√त्वर्); *viśanti* (8.11); *daṁṣṭrākarālāni* (2acc∘ 11.23); *bhayānakāni* (n∘ 2acc∘ plu∘

←adj∘ *bhayānaka* (terrible) ←√भी); *kec̓it* (11.21); *vilagnāḥ:* (m∘ 1nom∘ plu∘ ←ppp∘ adj∘ *vilagna* (stuck) ←वि√लग् or √लस्); *das̓anāntareṣu* (n∘ 7loc∘ plu∘ ←tatpu∘ *das̓anāntara* (gap between teeth) दशनयोः अन्तरम् ←tatpu∘ ***das̓ana*** (tooth) ←√दंश् + n∘ *antara* (gap) 2.13); *saṁdṛs̓yante* (3rd-per∘ plu∘ pres∘ वर्तमान्-लट् ātmane∘ ←class1∘ सम्√दृश्); *c̓ūrṇitaiḥ:* (m∘ 3inst∘ plu∘ ←ppp∘ adj∘ *c̓ūrṇita* (chewed) ←√चूर्ण्); *uttamāṅgaiḥ:* (n∘ 3inst∘ plu∘ ←s-karm∘ *uttamāṅga* (head) उत्तमम् अङ्गम् ←adj∘ *uttama* (top) 1.7 + n∘ *aṅga* (organ) 2.58)

(11.27)

(§3) *vaktrāṇi* (obj∘ mouths); *te* (your); *tvaramāṇāḥ:* (adj∘-subj1-4∘ hastening they, they who are in a haste); *vis̓anti* (are entering); *daṁṣṭrākarālāni* (adj1∘-obj∘ with dreadful teeth); *bhayānakāni* (adj2∘-obj∘ fearful); *kec̓it* (adj∘-subj1-4∘ some); *vilagnāḥ:* (adj2∘-subj1-4∘ stuck); *das̓anāntareṣu* (in the gaps between teeth); *saṁdṛs̓yante* (appear); *c̓ūrṇitaiḥ:* (with crushed); *uttamāṅgaiḥ:* (with their heads)

(11.27)

(§4) tvaramāṇāḥ: vis̓anti te bhayānakāni vaktrāṇi daṁṣṭrākarālāni kec̓it saṁdṛs̓yante vilagnāḥ: das̓anāntareṣu c̓ūrṇitaiḥ: uttamāṅgaiḥ:

(§5) Hastening they[636] are entering your fearful mouths with dreadful teeth, some appear stuck[637] in the gaps between teeth with their crushed heads. (11.27)

11.28 यथा नदीनां बहवोऽम्बुवेगाः समुद्रमेवाभिमुखा द्रवन्ति ।
तथा तवामी नरलोकवीरा विशन्ति वक्त्राण्यभिविज्वलन्ति ।।

yathā nadīnāṁ bahavo‘mbuvegāḥ: samudramevābhimukhā dravanti,
tathā tavāmī naralokavīrā vis̓anti vaktrāṇyabhivijvalanti. (11.28)

(§1) *yathā nadīnāṃ* (r∘ 14/1) *bahvaḥ:* (r∘ 15/1) *ambuvegāḥ:* (r∘ 22/7) *samudraṃ* (r∘ 8/22) *eva* (r∘ 1/1) *abhimukhāḥ:* (r∘ 20/8) *dravanti tathā tava* (r∘ 1/1) *amī naralokavīrāḥ:* (r∘ 20/17) *vis̓anti vaktrāṇi* (r∘ 24/7, 4/1) *abhivijvalanti*

(§2) *yathā* (1.11); *nadīnāṃ* (6pos plu∘ ←f∘ *nadī* (river) ←√नद्); *bahvaḥ:* (1.9); *ambuvegāḥ:* (m∘ 1nom∘ plu∘ ←tatpu∘ *ambu-vega* (water current) अम्बोः वेगः ←n∘ *ambu* (water) ←√अम्ब् + m∘ *vega* (current) 5.23); *samudraṃ* (2.70); *eva* (1.1); *abhimukhāḥ:* (m∘ 1nom∘ plu∘ ←adj∘ *abhimukha* (facing) ←अभि√खन्); ***dravanti*** (3rd-per∘

---

[636] Elsewhere∘ त्वरमाणाः विशन्ति → rapidly enter, entering rapidly, are entering in a rush, are entering in a hurry, they are rushing, ...etc.

📖 त्वरमाणाः is not a verb or an adverb of the verb विशन्ति । It is the मान-शानच् adjective of subjects 1-4.

[637] Elsewhere∘ विलग्नाः → clinging, becoming attached, sticking, ...etc.

📖 विलग्नाः is not a gerund. It is a ppp∘ adjective of subjcts 1-4.

plu∘ pres∘ वर्तमान्-लट् parasmai∘ ←class1∘ √द्रु); *tathā* (1.8); *tava* (1.3); *amī* (11.21); *naralokavīrāḥ:* (m∘ 1nom∘ sing∘ ←tatpu∘ *nara-loka-vīra*, नराणाम् लोके वीर: ←m∘ *nara* (people) 1.5 + m∘ *loka* (world) 2.5 + adj∘ ***vīra*** (brave) ←√वीर्); *viśanti* (8.11); *vaktrāṇi* (11.27); *abhivijvalanti* (3rd-per∘ plu∘ pres∘ वर्तमान्-लट् parasmai∘ ←class1∘ अभि-वि√ज्वल्) (11.28)

(§3) *yathā* (as); *nadīnāṃ* (of the rivers); *bahvaḥ:* (adj∘-subj1∘ many); *ambuvegāḥ:* (subj1∘ water currents); *samudraṃ* (obj1∘ ocean); *eva* (only); *abhimukhāḥ:* (forward towards); *dravanti* (flow); *tathā* (similarly, so); *tava* (your); *amī* (adj∘-subj2∘ these); *naralokavīrāḥ:* (subj2∘ earthy warriors); *viśanti* (are entering); *vaktrāṇi* (obj2∘ mouths11.27); *abhivijvalanti* (adj∘-obj2∘ burning, blazing) (11.28)

(§4) yathā bahvaḥ: ambuvegāḥ: nadīnāṃ dravanti eva abhimukhāḥ: samudraṃ tathā amī naralokavīrāḥ: viśanti tava abhivijvalanti vaktrāṇi

(§5) As countless water currents of the rivers flow only forward towards ocean, similarly these earthy warriors are entering your burning mouths.[638] (11.28)

11.29 यथा प्रदीप्तं ज्वलनं पतङ्गा विशन्ति नाशाय समृद्धवेगाः ।
तथैव नाशाय विशन्ति लोकास्तवापि वक्त्राणि समृद्धवेगाः ।।
yathā pradīptaṁ jvalanaṁ pataṅgā viśanti nāśāya samṛddhavegāḥ:,
tathaiva nāśāya viśanti lokāstavāpi vaktrāṇi samṛddhavegāḥ:. (11.29)

(§1) *yathā pradīptaṃ* (r∘ 14/1) *jvalanaṃ* (r∘ 14/1) *pataṅgāḥ:* (r∘ 20/17) *viśanti nāśāya samṛddhavegāḥ:* (r∘ 22/8) *tathā* (r∘ 3/3) *eva nāśāya viśanti lokāḥ:* (r∘ 18/1) *tava* (r∘ 1/1) *api vaktrāṇi* (r∘ 24/7) *samṛddhavegāḥ:* (r∘ 22/8)

(§2) *yathā* (1.11); *pradīptaṃ* (n∘ 2acc∘ sing∘ ←ppp∘ adj∘ *pradīpta* (blazing) ←प्र√दीप् 11.24); *jvalanaṃ* (1nom∘ sing∘ ←n∘ *jvalana* (fire) ←√ज्वल्); *pataṅgāḥ:* (1nom∘ plu∘ ←m∘ *pataṅga* (moth) ←√पत्); *viśanti* (8.11); ***nāśāya*** (4dat∘ sing∘ ←m∘ *nāśa* (distruction) 2.40); ***samṛddhavegāḥ:*** (m∘ 1nom∘ plu∘ ←bahuvrī∘ *samṛddha-vega*, समृद्धः वेगः यस्य ←adj∘ ***samṛddha*** (rapid) ←सम्√ऋध् + m∘ *vega* (speed) 5.23); *tathā* (1.8); *eva* (1.1); *nāśāya* (↑); *viśanti* (8.11); *lokāḥ:* (3.24); *tava* (1.3); *api* (1.26); *vaktrāṇi* (11.27); *samṛddhavegāḥ:* (↑) (11.29)

---

[638] Elsewhere∘ नरलोकवीराः विशन्ति वक्त्राणि अभिविज्वलन्ति → warriors enter blazing into Your mouths, ...etc.

📖 अभिविज्वलन्ति is not a verb or an adjective of masculine Nominative (1st) case subject नरलोकवीराः । It is neuter gender Accusative (2nd) case Present Participle Adjective of the neuter Accusative object वक्त्राणि ।

(§3) *yathā* (as); *pradīptaṃ* (adj◦-obj1◦ blazing); *jvalanaṃ* (obj1◦ fire); *pataṅgāḥ:* (subj1◦ the moths); *viśanti* (enter); *nāśāya* (for their destruction); *samṛddhavegāḥ:* (adj◦-subj1◦ flying with rapid speed); *tathā* (similarly, so); *eva* (only); *nāśāya* (for their destruction); *viśanti* (are entering); *lokāḥ:* (subj2◦ these people); *tava* (your); *api* (also); *vaktrāṇi* (obj◦ mouths); *samṛddhavegāḥ:* (moving with rapid speed) (11.29)

(§4) yathā pataṅgāḥ: samṛddhavegāḥ: viśanti pradīptaṃ jvalanaṃ nāśāya tathā lokāḥ: samṛddhavegāḥ: viśanti tava vaktrāṇi api eva nāśāya

(§5) As the moths flying with rapid speed[639] enter blazing fire for their destruction; similarly, these people moving with rapid speed are entering your mouths also, only for their destruction. (11.29)

11.30 **लेलिह्यसे ग्रसमानः समन्ताल्लोकान्समग्रान्वदनैर्ज्वलद्भिः ।**
तेजोभिरापूर्य जगत्समग्रं भासस्तवोग्राः प्रतपन्ति विष्णो ।।

lelihyase grasamānaḥ: samantāllokānsamagrānvadanairjvaladbhiḥ:,
tejobhirāpūrya jagatsamagraṁ bhāsastavogrāḥ: pratapanti viṣṇo.
(11.30)

(§1) *lelihyase grasamānaḥ:* (r◦ 22/7) *samantāṭ* (r◦ 11/6) *lokāṇ* (r◦ 13/20) *samagrāṇ* (r◦ 13/19) *vadanaiḥ:* (r◦ 16/11) *jvaladbhiḥ:* (r◦ 22/8) *tejobhiḥ:* (r◦ 16/1) *āpūrya jagaṭ* (r◦ 10/7) *samagraṃ* (r◦ 14/1) *bhāsaḥ:* (r◦ 18/1) *tava* (r◦ 2/2) *ugrāḥ:* (r◦ 22/3) *pratapanti viṣṇo*

(§2) *lelihyase* (emphatic form of the verb *lihyase* is *lelihyase*. Noun m◦ *leliha* is used as a root to form the verb *lelihyase* ←2nd-per◦ sing◦ pres◦ वर्तमान्–लट् parasmai◦ ←class2◦ √लिह + यङ् –लुक्); *grasamānaḥ:* (m◦ 1nom◦ sing◦ ←śānac◦ adj◦ *grasamāna* (eating) ←1√ग्रस्); *samantāṭ* (11.17); *lokāṇ* (6.41); *samagrāṇ* (m◦ 2acc◦ plu◦ ←adj◦ *samagra* (all) 4.23); *vadanaiḥ:* (3inst◦ plu◦ ←n◦ *vadana* (mouth) ←√वद्); *jvaladbhiḥ:* (n◦ 3inst◦ plu◦ ←śatṛ◦ adj◦ *jvalaṭ* (burning) ←√ज्वल्); *tejobhiḥ:* (3inst◦ plu◦ ←n◦ *tejaṣ* (brilliance) 7.9); *āpūrya* (lyp◦ past-participle ind◦ ←आ√पॄ 2.70); *jagaṭ* (11.7); *samagraṃ* (4.23); *bhāsaḥ:* (11.12); *tava* (1.3); *ugrāḥ:* (f◦ 1nom◦ plu◦ ←adj◦ *ugra* (intense) 11.20); *pratapanti* (3rd-per◦ plu◦ pres◦ वर्तमान्–लट् parasmai◦ ←class1◦ प्र√तप् 9.19); *viṣṇo* (11.24) (11.30)

---

[639] Elsewhere◦ ज्वलनं पतङ्गा विशन्ति नाशाय समृद्धवेगाः → moths enter the blazing flame to their destruction with great speed, ...etc.

📖 समृद्धवेगाः is not an adjective of neuter Accusative (2nd) case singular object ज्वलनम् । It is pl◦ masculine adjective of the pl◦ m◦ subject पतङ्गा ।

(§3) *lelihyase* (you are constantly licking); *grasamānaḥ:* (adj◦-subj1◦ eating, while eating); *samantāt* (from all sides); *lokān* (obj1◦ these people); *samagrān* (adj◦-obj1◦ all); *vadanaiḥ:* (with mouths); *jvaladbhiḥ:* (with burning, flaming); *tejobhiḥ:* (with brilliance); *āpūrya* (adj1◦-obj2◦ having filled); *jagat* (obj2◦ world); *samagram* (adj2◦-obj2◦ the whole); *bhāsaḥ:* (subj2◦ light); *tava* (your); *ugrāḥ:* (adj◦-subj2◦ intense); *pratapanti* (is roasting); *viṣṇo* (O Lord Viṣṇu! O Lord Kṛṣṇa!) (11.30)

(§4) grasamānaḥ: lelihyase samagrān lokān samantāt jvaladbhiḥ: vadanaiḥ: viṣṇo tava ugrāḥ: bhāsaḥ: āpūrya samagram jagat pratapanti tejobhiḥ:

(§5) You, while eating,[640] are constantly licking all these people from all sides with (your) burning mouths. O Lord Kṛṣṇa! your intense light, having filled the whole world, is roasting (it) with brilliance. (11.30)

11.31 आख्याहि मे को भवानुग्ररूपो नमोऽस्तु ते देववर प्रसीद ।
विज्ञातुमिच्छामि भवन्तमाद्यं न हि प्रजानामि तव प्रवृत्तिम् ।।

ākhyāhi me ko bhavānugrarūpo namo'stu te devavara prasīda,
vijñātumicchāmi bhavantamādyaṁ na hi prajānāmi tava pravṛttim.
(11.31)

(§1) *ākhyāhi me kaḥ:* (r◦ 15/8) *bhavān* (r◦ 8/14) *ugrarūpaḥ:* (r◦ 15/6) *namaḥ:* (r◦ 15/1) *astu te devavara prasīda vijñātum* (r◦ 8/18) *icchāmi bhavantam* (r◦ 8/17) *ādyam* (r◦ 14/1) *na hi prajānāmi tava pravṛttim* (r◦ 14/2)

(§2) *ākhyāhi* (2nd-per◦ sing◦ imperative◦ निवेदनार्थ-लोट् parasmai◦ ←class2◦ आ√ख्या); *me* (1.21); *kaḥ:* (8.2); *bhavān* (1.8); 📖*ugrarūpaḥ:* (m◦ 1nom◦ sing◦ ←bahuvrī◦ *ugrarūp*, उग्रम् रूपम् यस्य ←adj◦ *ugra* (terrible) 11.20 + n◦ *rūpa* (form) 3.39); 📖**namaḥ:** (ind◦ ←m◦ *namas* (obeisance) ←√नम्); *astu* (2.47); *te* (2.7); 📖*devavara* (m◦ 8voc◦ sing◦ ←tatpu◦ *deva-vara*, देवेषु वरः ←m◦ *deva* (god) 3.11 + adj◦ *vara* (superior) 8.4); *prasīda* (11.25); *vijñātum* (inf◦ ind◦ ←वि√ज्ञा); *icchāmi* (1.35); *bhavantam* (m◦ 2acc◦ sing◦ ←adj◦ *bhavat* 1.8); *ādyam* (8.28); *na* (1.30); *hi* (1.11); *prajānāmi* (1st-per◦ sing◦ pres◦ वर्तमान्-लट् parasmai◦ ←class9◦

---

[640] Elsewhere◦ लेलिह्यसे ग्रसमानः समन्तात् लोकान् समग्रान् → Thou lickest swallowing from all sides all the worlds, Thou lickest up devouring all worlds on every side, You are licking devouring all worlds on every side, Swallowing through your blazing mouths, Devouring all worlds on every side with thy flaming mouths, You are devouring all the worlds by your blazing mouths and are licking them up, ...etc.

📖 ग्रसमानः is not a verb or an adjective of Accusative (2nd) case plural object लोकान् । It is Nominative (1st) case singular masculine adjective of the sg◦ m◦ subject 'You' embeded in the second person verb लेलिह्यसे । Also, therefore, the adverb समन्तात् is qualifying the verb लेलिहसे । It is not an adjective of the object लोकान् ।

प्र√ज्ञा); *tava* (1.3); *pravṛttiṃ* (2acc◦ sing◦ ←f◦ 🕮***pravṛtti*** (intention) ←प्र√वृत्) (11.31)

(§3) *ākhyāhi* (You please tell!); *me* (me); *kaḥ: bhavān̦* (who are you?); *ugrarūpaḥ:* (adj◦-subj◦ of terrible form); *namaḥ: astu* (obeisance be); *te* (to you); *devavara* (O Lord of the Lords! O Lord Kṛṣṇa!); *prasīda* (please be pleased!); *vijñātuṃ* (to know); *iććhāmi* (I desire, I want); *bhavantaṃ* (obj1◦ you); *ādyaṃ* (adj◦-obj1◦ the Primal One); *na* (do not); *hi* (because); *prajānāmi* (I clearly understand); *tava* (your); *pravṛttiṃ* (obj2◦ intention) (11.31)

(§4) ākhyāhi me kaḥ: bhavān̦ ugrarūpaḥ: namaḥ: astu te devavara prasīda hi na prajānāmi tava pravṛttiṃ iććhāmi vijñātuṃ bhavantaṃ ādyaṃ

(§5) You please tell! me who are you, of terrible form? Obeisance be to you, O Lord Kṛṣṇa! please be pleased! Because[641] I do not clearly understand your intention,[642] I desire to know You, the Primal One. (11.31)

The Lord said (śrībhagavānuvāća श्रीभगवानुवाच ।)

11.32 कालोऽस्मि लोकक्षयकृत्प्रवृद्धो लोकान्समाहर्तुमिह प्रवृत्तः ।
ऋतेऽपि त्वां न भविष्यन्ति सर्वे येऽवस्थिताः प्रत्यनीकेषु योधाः ।।

kālosmi lokakṣayakṛtpravṛddho lokānsamāhartumiha pravṛttaḥ:,
ṛte'pi tvāṁ na bhaviṣyanti sarve ye'vasthitāḥ: pratyanīkeṣu yodhāḥ:.
(11.32)

(§1) *śrībhagavān̦* (r◦ 8/14) *uvāća. kālaḥ:* (r◦ 15/1) *asmi lokakṣayakṛț* (r◦ 10/6) *pravṛddhaḥ:* (r◦ 15/12) *lokān̦* (r◦ 13/20) *samāhartuṃ* (r◦ 8/18) *iha pravṛttaḥ:* (r◦ 22/8) *ṛte* (r◦ 6/1) *api tvāṃ* (r◦ 14/1) *na bhaviṣyanti* (r◦ 25/7) *sarve ye* (r◦ 6/1) *avasthitaḥ:* (r◦ 22/3) *pratyanīkeṣu* (r◦ 25/5) *yodhāḥ:* (r◦ 22/8)

(§2) *śrībhagavān̦* (2.2); *uvāća* (1.25). *kālaḥ:* (10.30); *asmi* (7.8); *lokakṣayakṛț* (m◦ 1nom◦ sing◦ ←bahuvrī◦ *lokakṣaya-kṛț*, लोकानाम् क्षयः करोति यः ←m◦ *loka* (world) 2.5 + m◦ *kṣaya* (dissolution) 1.38 + verb◦ *karoti* 4.20 or adj◦ *kṛț* (doer) 1.35); *pravṛddhaḥ:* (m◦ 1nom◦ sing◦ ←ppp◦ adj◦ ***pravṛddha*** (bent up on) ←प्र√वृध्); *lokān̦* (6.41); *samāhartuṃ* (inf◦ ind◦ ←सम्-आ√हृ); *iha* (2.5); 🕮*pravṛttaḥ:* (m◦ 1nom◦ sing◦ ←adj◦ *pravṛtta* 1.20); *ṛte* (contrast indicating ind◦ ←√ऋ); *api* (1.26); *tvāṃ* (2.7); *na* (1.30); *bhaviṣyanti* (3rd-per◦ plu◦ fut2◦ लृट् भविष्य◦ parasmai◦ ←class1◦ √भू); *sarve* (1.6); *ye* (1.7); *avasthitaḥ:* (1.11); *pratyanīkeṣu* (m◦ 7loc◦ plu◦ ←tatpu◦ *pratyanīka* ←ind◦ *prati* (opposite) 2.43 + m◦ *anīka* (army) 1.2); *yodhāḥ:* (1nom◦ plu◦ ←m◦ *yodha*

---

[641] See footnote in verse 3.5

[642] Elsewhere◦ प्रवृत्तिम् → mission, working, actions, forthestreaming Life, doing, ...etc.

(warrior) 11.26) (11.32)

(§3) *śrībhagavān* (the Lord); *uvāća* (said). *kālaḥ:* (adj1∘-subj1∘ the Lord of death, the time of death, the destiny, the fate, the personification of the terminating principle); *asmi* (subj1∘ I am); *lokakṣayakṛt* (the dissolver of the beings, terminator of the beings); *pravrddhaḥ:* (adj2∘-subj1∘ the great); *lokān* (obj1∘ these people); *samāhartum* (to take away, to remove); *iha* (here); *pravṛttaḥ:* (adj3∘-subj1∘ bent upon, intent upon, engaged); *ṛte* (without); *api* (even); *tvām* (obj2∘ you); *na* (not); *bhaviṣyanti* (they will be, will remain); *sarve* (adj∘-subj2∘ all); *ye* (adj2∘-subj2∘ who, those who); *avasthitaḥ:* (adj3∘-subj2∘ stood, arrayed); *pratyanīkeṣu* (on the opposite side in the battle); *yodhāḥ:* (subj2∘ the warriors).
(11.32)

(§4) śrībhagavān uvāća asmi pravrddhaḥ: kālaḥ: lokakṣayakṛt pravṛttaḥ: iha samāhartum lokān yodhāḥ: ye sarve avasthitaḥ: pratyanīkeṣu na bhaviṣyanti api ṛte tvām

(§5) The Lord said : I am the great personification of the terminating principle, dissolver of the beings, engaged here to take away these people, the warriors who all (are) arrayed on the opposite side in the battle, they will not remain even without you. (11.32)

11.33 तस्मात्त्वमुत्तिष्ठ यशो लभस्व जित्वा शत्रून्भुङ्क्ष्व राज्यं समृद्धम् ।
मयैवैते निहताः पूर्वमेव निमित्तमात्रं भव सव्यसाचिन् ।।

tasmāttvamuttiṣṭha yaśo labhasva jitvā śatrūnbhuṅkṣva rājyaṁ samṛddham,
mayaivaite nihatāḥ: pūrvameva nimittamātraṁ bhava savyasāćin. (11.33)

(§1) *tasmāt* (r∘ 1/10) *tvam* (r∘ 8/20) *uttiṣṭha yaśaḥ:* (r∘ 15/12) *labhasva jitvā śatrūn* (r∘ 13.15) *bhuṅkṣva rājyam* (r∘ 14/1) *samṛddham* (r∘ 14/2) *mayā* (r∘ 3/3) *eva* (r∘ 3/1) *ete nihatāḥ:* (r∘ 22/3) *pūrvam* (r∘ 8/22) *eva nimittamātram* (r∘ 14/1) *bhava savyasāćin*

(§2) *tasmāt* (1.37); *tvam* (2.11); *uttiṣṭha* (2.3); *yaśaḥ:* (2acc∘ sing∘ ←n∘ *yaśaś* 10.5); *labhasva* (2nd-per∘ sing∘ imperative∘ उपदेशार्थ-लोट् ātmane∘ ←class1∘ √लभ्); *jitvā* (2.37); *śatrūn* (2acc∘ plu∘ ←m∘ *śatru* (enemy) 3.43); *bhuṅkṣva* (2nd-per∘ sing∘ imperative∘ उपदेशार्थ-लोट् ātmane∘ ←class7∘ √भुज्); *rājyam* (1.32); 🕮*samṛddham* (n∘ 2acc∘ sing∘ ←adj∘ *samṛddha* (rich) 11.29); *mayā* (1.22); *eva* (1.1); *ete* (1.23); *nihatāḥ:* (m∘ 1nom∘ plu∘ ←ppp∘ adj∘ *nihata* (slain) ←नि√हन्); *pūrvam* (adv∘ ←adj∘ *pūrva* (before) 4.15); *eva* (1.1); *nimittamātram* (adv∘ निमित्तस्य मात्रम् ←n∘ *nimitta* (occasion) 1.31 + exclusiveness indicating adj∘ *mātra* ←√मा); *bhava* (2.45); *savyasāćin* (m∘ 8voc∘ sing∘ ←bahuvrī∘ *savyasāćin*, सव्येन साचितुम् सामर्थ्यम् यस्मिन् ←adj∘ *savya* (left hand) ←√सू + adj∘ *sāćin* (fighter) ←√सच्) (11.33)

(§3) *tasmāt* (therefore); *tvam* (subj1∘ you); *uttiṣṭha* (please get up! rise up! stand up!); *yaśaḥ:* (obj1∘

victory); *labhasva* (atain); *jitvā* (having won); *śatrūn̦* (obj2◦ the enemies); *bhun̊kṣva* (please enjoy! utilize!); *rājyam̦* (obj3◦ the kingdom); *samṛddham̦* (afj◦-obj3◦ affluent, prosperous); *mayā* (subj2◦ by me); *eva* (only); *ete* (obj4◦ these, these enemies); *nihatāḥ:* (adj◦-obj4◦ killed); *pūrvam̦* (earlier, a while ago); *eva* (only); *nimittamātram̦* (just an occasion); *bhava* (please be!); *savyasāćin̦* (O Arjuna!) (11.33)

(§4) tasmāț savyasāćin̦ tvam̦ uttiṣṭha jitvā śatrūn̦ labhasva yaśaḥ: bhun̊kṣva samṛddham̦ rājyam̦ ete eva pūrvam̦ nihatāḥ: mayā bhava eva nimittamātram̦

(§5) Therefore[643] O Arjuna! you please rise up! Having won the enemies, atain victory (and) utilize! the affluent kingdom. These enemies (have been) only a while ago killed by me; (now) only be just an occasion. (11.33)

11.34 **द्रोणं च भीष्मं च जयद्रथं च कर्णं तथाऽन्यानपि योधवीरान् ।**
मया हतांस्त्वं जहि मा व्यथिष्ठा युद्धयस्व जेतासि रणे सपत्नान् ।।

droṇam̊ ća bhīṣmam̊ ća jayadratham̊ ća karṇam̊ tathā'nyānapi yodhavīrān̦,
mayā hatām̊stvam̊ jahi mā vyathiṣṭhā yudhyasva jetāsi raṇe sapatnān̦.
(11.34)

(§1) *droṇam̦* (r◦ 14/1, 24/3) *ća bhīṣmam̦* (r◦ 14/1) *ća jayadratham̦* (r◦ 14/1) *ća karṇam̦* (r◦ 14/1) *tathā* (r◦ 1/3) *anyān̦* (r◦ 8/11) *api yodhavīrān̦* (r◦ 23/1) *mayā hatān̦* (r◦ 13/7) *tvam̦* (r◦ 14/1) *jahi mā vyathiṣṭhāḥ:* (r◦ 20/14) *yuddhyasva jetāsi raṇe* (r◦ 24/9) *sapatnān̦*

(§2) *droṇam̦* (2.4); *ća* (1.1); *bhīṣmam̦* (1.11); *ća* (1.1); *jayadratham̦* (m◦ 2acc◦ sing◦ ←prop◦ *jayadratha); ća* (1.1); *karṇam̦* (m◦ 2acc◦ sing◦ ←prop◦ *karṇa* 1.8); *tathā* (1.8); *anyān̦* (m◦ 2acc◦ plu◦ ←adj◦ *anya* (other) 1.9); *api* (1.26); *yodhavīrān̦* (m◦ 2acc◦ plu◦ ←tatpu◦ *yodha-vīra*, योधानाम् वीरः ←m◦ *yodha* (warrior) 11.26 + adj◦ *vīra* (brave) 11.28); *mayā* (1.22); *hatān̦* (m◦ 2acc◦ plu◦ ←adj◦ *hata* (slain) 2.19); *tvam̦* (2.11); *jahi* (3.43); *mā* (2.3); *vyathiṣṭhāḥ:* (2nd-per◦ sing◦ ātmane◦ pastind◦ लुङ् भूत ←class1◦ √व्यथ्); *yuddhyasva* (2.18); *jetāsi* (2nd-per◦ sing◦ fut1◦ लुट् parasmai◦ ←class1◦ √जि); *raṇe* (1.46); *sapatnān̦* (2acc◦ plu◦ ←m◦ 🕮*sapatna* (enemy) 2.8) (11.34)

(§3) *droṇam̦* (obj1◦ Droṇa); *ća* (and); *bhīṣmam̦* (obj2◦ Bhīṣma); *ća* (and); *jayadratham̦* (obj3◦ Jayadratha); *ća* (and); *karṇam̦* (obj4◦ Karṇa); *tathā* (as well as); *anyān̦* (adj◦-obj5◦ the other); *api* (also); *yodhavīrān̦* (obj5◦ heroic warriors); *mayā* (subj1◦ by me); *hatān̦* (adj◦ obj1-5◦ killed); *tvam̦* (subj2◦ you); *jahi* (slay); *mā* (do not); *vyathiṣṭhāḥ:* (be perturbed); *yuddhyasva* (fight!); *jetāsi* (you will win); *raṇe* (on

[643] See the footnote in verse 2.15

the battlefield); *sapatnān̦* (obj6◦ the enemies) (11.34)

(§4) jahi droṇam̦ ća bhīṣmam̦ ća jayadratham̦ ća karṇam̦ tathā anyān̦ yodhavīrān̦ api hatān̦ mayā tvam̦ mā vyathiṣṭhāḥ: yuddhyasva jetāsi sapatnān̦ raṇe

(§5) Slay Droṇa and Bhīṣma and Jayadratha and Karṇa as well as the other heroic warriors also killed by me. You do not be perturbed. Fight! You will win the enemies on the battlefield. (11.34)

Sanjaya said (sañjaya uvāća सजय उवाच ।)

11.35 एतच्छ्रुत्वा वचनं केशवस्य कृताञ्जलिर्वेपमानः किरीटी ।
नमस्कृत्वा भूय एवाह कृष्णं सगद्गदं भीतभीतः प्रणम्य ।।
etaććhrutvā vaćanaṁ keśavasya kṛtāñjalirvepamānaḥ: kirīṭī,
namaskṛtvā bhūya evāha kṛṣṇaṁ sagadgadaṁ bhītabhītaḥ: praṇamya.
(11.35)

(§1) *sañjayaḥ:* (r◦ 19/4) *uvāća. etaț* (r◦ 11/4) *śrutvā vaćanam̦* (r◦ 14/1) *keśavasya kṛtāñjaliḥ:* (r◦ 16/6) *vepamānaḥ:* (r◦ 22/1) *kirīṭī namaskṛtvā bhūyaḥ:* (r◦ 19/7) *eva* (r◦ 1/2) *āha kṛṣṇam̦* (r◦ 14/1, 24/3) *sagadgadam̦* (r◦ 14/1) *bhītabhītaḥ:* (r◦ 22/3) *praṇamya*

(§2) *sañjayaḥ:* (1.2); *uvāća* (1.25). *etaț* (2.3); *śrutvā* (2.29); *vaćanam̦* (1.2); *keśavasya* (6pos sing◦ ←m◦ *keśava* 1.31); *kṛtāñjaliḥ:* (11.14); *vepamānaḥ:* (m◦ 1nom◦ sing◦ ←śānać◦ adj◦ *vepamāna* (shaking) ←√वेपृ); *kirīṭī* (m◦ 1nom◦ sing◦ ←bahuvrī◦ *kirīṭin,* किरीटः धारयति यः ←m◦ *kirīṭa* (crown) 11.17); *namaskṛtvā* (lyp◦ past-participle ind◦ ←नमस्√कृ); *bhūyaḥ:* (2.20); *eva* (1.1); *āha* (1.21); *kṛṣṇam̦* (m◦ 2acc◦ sing◦ ←prop◦ *kṛṣṇa* 1.28); *sagadgadam̦* (adv◦ ind◦ ←bahuvrī◦ adj◦ *sa-gadgadam̦,* गद्गदेन सह ←adj◦ *saha* (with) 1.22 + adj◦ 🕮*gadgada* (stutter) ←गद्√गद्); *bhītabhītaḥ:* (= *bhītaḥ: bhītaḥ:* ←m◦ 1nom◦ sing◦ *bhītaḥ:* (afraid) ←adj◦ *bhita* (afraid) 11.21); *praṇamya* (11.14) (11.35)

(§3) *sañjayaḥ:* (Sañjaya); *uvāća* (said). *etaț* (this); *śrutvā* (having); *vaćanam̦* (heard); *keśavasya* (of Śrī Kṛṣṇa); *kṛtāñjaliḥ:* (adj1◦-subj◦ he who has joined palms, one with folded hands); *vepamānaḥ:* (adj2◦-subj◦ trembling); *kirīṭī* (subj◦ Arjuna); *namaskṛtvā* (offering obeisance); *bhūyaḥ:* (again); *eva* (and); *āha* (said); *kṛṣṇam̦* (obj◦ to Śrī Kṛṣṇa); *sagadgadam̦* (stutteringly); *bhītabhītaḥ:* (adj3◦-subj◦ very much frightened); *praṇamya* (bowing down) (11.35)

(§4) sañjayaḥ: uvāća śrutvā vaćanam̦ etaț keśavasya kirīṭī kṛtāñjaliḥ: eva namaskṛtvā bhūyaḥ: praṇamya bhītabhītaḥ: āha sagadgadam̦ kṛṣṇam̦

(§5) **Sañjaya said : Having heard this[644] (utterance) of Śrī Kṛṣṇa, Arjuna with folded hands,[645] trembling, and offering obeisance[646] again bowing down very much frightened said stutteringly to Śrī Kṛṣṇa.** **(11.35)**

Arjuna said (arjuna uvāća अर्जुन उवाच ।)

11.36 **स्थाने हृषीकेश तव प्रकीर्त्या जगत्प्रहृष्यत्यनुरज्यते च ।**
रक्षांसि भीतानि दिशो द्रवन्ति सर्वे नमस्यन्ति च सिद्धसङ्घाः ।।
sthāne hṛṣīkeśa tava prakīrtyā jagatprahṛṣyatyanurajyate ća,
rakṣāṁsi bhītāni diśo dravanti sarve namasyanti ća siddhasaṁghāḥ:.
(11.36)

(§1) *arjunaḥ:* (r∘ 19/4) *uvāća. sthāne hṛṣīkeśa tava prakīrtyā jagat* (r∘ 10/6) *prahṛṣyati* (r∘ 25/6, 4/1) *anurajyate ća rakṣāṁsi bhītāni diśaḥ:* (r∘ 15/4) *dravanti sarve namasyanti ća siddhasaṁghāḥ:*

(§2) *arjunaḥ:* (1.28); *uvāća* (1.25). 🕮*sthāne* (rightly, adv∘ or 7loc∘ sing∘ ←n∘ *sthāna* 5.5); *hṛṣīkeśa* (8voc∘ sing∘ ←m∘ *Hṛṣīkeśa* 1.15); *tava* (1.3); *prakīrtyā* (3inst∘ sing∘ ←f∘ 🕮*prakīrti* (praise) ←प्र√कृत्); *jagat* (7.5); *prahṛṣyati* (3rd-per∘ sing∘ pres∘ वर्तमान्-लट् parasmai∘ ←class4∘ प्र√हृष्); *anurajyate* (3rd-per∘ sing∘ pres∘ वर्तमान्-लट् ātmane∘ ←class4∘ अनु√रञ्ज्); *ća* (1.1); *rakṣāṁsi* (1nom∘ plu∘ ←n∘ *rakṣasa* (demon) 10.23); *bhītāni* (n∘ 1nom∘ plu∘ ←adj∘ *bhita* (afraid) 11.21); *diśaḥ:* (6.13); *dravanti* (11.28); *sarve* (1.6); *namasyanti* (3rd-per∘ plu∘ fut2∘ लृट् भविष्य∘ parasmai∘ ←class1∘ √नम्); *ća* (1.1); *siddhasaṁghāḥ:* (m∘ 1nom∘ plu∘ ←tatpu∘ *siddha-saṁgha*, सिद्धानाम् सङ्घः ←m∘ *siddha* (ascetic) 7.3 + m∘ *saṅgha* (group) 11.15)
(11.36)

(§3) *arjunaḥ:* (Arjun); *uvāća* (said). *sthāne* (rightly); *hṛṣīkeśa* (O Śrī Kṛṣṇa!); *tava* (your); *prakīrtyā* (by praise); *jagat* (subj1∘ the world); *prahṛṣyati* (exults, becomes delighted, rejoices); *anurajyate* (becomes

---

[644] Elsewhere∘ एतत् → these words, thus, that speech, ...etc.

🕮 एतत् (= this) is a singular pronominal adjective of singular noun utterance.

[645] Elsewhere∘ कृताञ्जलिः → offered obeisances with folded hands, saluted with folded palms, bowed to Him with folded palms, saluted with folded hands, ...etc.

🕮 कृताञ्जलिः is not an adverb qualifying the verb offered, saluted or bowed. It is not adjective qualifying obeisances. It is m∘ singuler bahuvrīhi adjective of m∘ noun *kirīṭī* (Arjuna), he who was with his hands folded or palms joined.

[646] Elsewhere∘ नमस्कृत्वा → prostrating himself, ...etc.

🕮 Prostrating in the chariot? Remember, Arjuna and Śrī Kṛṣṇa both are still sitting on the chariot.

pleased); *ća* (and); *rakṣāṁsi* (subj2◦ demons); *bhītāni* (adj◦-subj2◦ the terrified); *diśaḥ:* (directions, in all directions); *dravanti* (they flee, they run amok); *sarve* (adj◦-subj3◦ all); *namasyanti* (shall bow); *ća* (and); *siddhasaṁghāḥ:* (subj3◦ hosts of ascetics) (11.36)

(§4) arjunaḥ: uvāća sthāne hṛṣīkeśa jagaṭ prahṛṣyati anurajyate prakīrtyā tava ća bhītāni rakṣāṁsi dravanti diśaḥ: ća sarve siddhasaṁghāḥ: namasyanti

(§5) Arjun said : Rightly O Śrī Kṛṣṇa! the world becomes delighted (and) becomes pleased by your praise, and the terrified demons run amok in all directions and all hosts of ascetics[647] shall bow[648] (to you); (11.36)

11.37 कस्माच्च ते न नमेरन्महात्मन् गरीयसे ब्रह्मणोऽप्यादिकर्त्रे ।
अनन्त देवेश जगन्निवास त्वमक्षरं सदसत्तत्परं यत् ।।
kasmāćća te na nameranmahātmangarīyase brahmaṇo'pyādikartre,
ananta deveśa jagannivāsa tvamakṣaraṁ sadasattatparaṁ yaṭ. (11.37)

(§1) *kasmāṭ* (r◦ 11/1) *ća te na nameraṇ* (r◦ 13/16) *mahātmaṇ* (r◦ 13/10) *garīyase brahmaṇaḥ:* (r◦ 15/1) *api* (r◦ 4/2) *ādikartre* (r◦ 23/1) *ananta deveśa jagannivāsa tvaṃ* (r◦ 8/16) *akṣaraṃ* (r◦ 14/1) *saṭ* (r◦ 8/2) *asaṭ* (r◦ 1/10) *tatparaṃ* (r◦ 14/1) *yaṭ*

(§2) *kasmāṭ* (m◦ or n◦ 5abl◦ sing◦ ←pron◦ *kiṃ* 1.1); *ća* (1.1); *te* (1.7); *na* (1.30); *nameraṇ* (3rd-per◦ plu◦ potential◦ विधि◦ ātmane◦ ←class1◦ √नम्); *mahātmaṇ* (11.20); *garīyase* (4dat◦ sing◦ ←adj◦ *garīyaṣ* (superior) 2.6); *brahmaṇaḥ:* (4.32); *api* (1.26); *ādikartre* (m◦ 4dat◦ sing◦ ←tatpu◦ *ādikartṛ* (progenitor) ←adj◦ *ādi* (beginning) 2.28 + adj◦ *kartṛ* (causer) 3.24); *ananta* (m◦ 8voc◦ sing◦ ←bahuvrī◦ adj◦ *ananta* (infinite) 2.41); *deveśa* (11.25); *jagannivāsa* (11.25); *tvaṃ* (2.11); *akṣaraṃ* (8.3); *saṭ* (2.16); *asaṭ* (9.19); *tatparaṃ* (5.16); *yaṭ* (1nom◦ 2.67) (11.37)

(§3) *kasmāṭ* (from what reason, wherefor, why?); *ća* (and); *te* (obj◦ to you); *na* (not); *nameraṇ* (should they bow); *mahātmaṇ* (O Great Puruśa! O Śrī Kṛṣṇa!); *garīyase* (greater); *brahmaṇaḥ:* (than brahmā); *api* (also); *ādikartre* (progenitor); *ananta* (O infinite One! O Śrī Kṛṣṇa!); *deveśa* (O Lord of the Lords! O Śrī Kṛṣṇa!); *jagannivāsa* (O Abode of the Universe! Śrī O Kṛṣṇa!); *tvaṃ* (subj◦ you); *akṣaraṃ* (adj1◦-

---

[647] Elsewhere◦ सिद्धाः → the perfected ones, the perfect beings, the perfecrted beings, perfected souls, ...etc.

📖 Only *brahma* is perfect, and nothing else (निर्दोषं ब्रह्म Gītā 5.19).

[648] Elsewhere◦ नमस्यन्ति → are bowing, are bowing down, perfected beings offer, perfected beings bow down, the siddhas bow down, siddhas bow, do reverence, pay their reverence, should bowd own, ...etc.

📖 नमस्यन्ति is not a present tense. It is a simple future tense.

subj◦ immutable); *sat̩* (adj2◦-subj◦ being); *asat̩* (adj3◦-subj◦ non-being); *tatparam̩* (beyond that); *yat̩* (whatever is) (11.37)

(§4) ćа mahātman̩ ananta kasmāt̩ na nameran̩ te garīyase ādikartre brahmaṇaḥ: api deveśa jagannivāsa tvam̩ akṣaram̩ sat̩ asat̩ yat̩ tatparam̩

(§5) And O Śrī Kṛṣṇa! O Infinite One! why should they not bow to you, the greater progenitor than brahmā[649] also. O Lord of the Lords! O Abode of the Universe! you (are) Immutable, Being, Non-being (and) whatever is beyond that. (11.37)

11.38 त्वमादिदेवः पुरुषः पुराणस्त्वमस्य विश्वस्य परं निधानम् ।
वेत्तासि वेद्यं च परं च धाम त्वया ततं विश्वमनन्तरूप ।।

tvamādidevaḥ: puruṣaḥ: purāṇastvamasya viśvasya paraṁ nidhānam̩,
vettāsi vedyaṁ ća paraṁ ća dhāma tvayā tataṁ viśvamanantarūpa;
(11.38)

(§1) *tvam̩* (r◦ 8/17) *ādidevaḥ:* (r◦ 22/3) *puruṣaḥ:* (r◦ 22/3) *purāṇaḥ:* (r◦ 18/1) *tvam̩* (r◦ 8/16) *asya viśvasya param̩* (r◦ 14/1) *nidhānam̩* (r◦ 14/2) *vettā* (r◦ 1/3) *asi vedyam̩* (r◦ 14/1) *ća param̩* (r◦ 14/1) *ća dhāma tvayā tatam̩* (r◦ 14/1) *viśvam̩* (r◦ 8/16) *anantarūpa;*

(§2) *tvam̩* (2.11); *ādidevaḥ:* (m◦ 1nom◦ sing◦ ←tatpu◦ *ādi-deva* (primal-god) 10.12); *puruṣaḥ:* (2.21); *purāṇaḥ:* (2.20); *tvam̩* (2.11); *asya* (2.17); *viśvasya* (11.18); *param̩* (4.4); *nidhānam̩* (9.18); *vettā* (m◦ 1nom◦ sing◦ ←adj◦ *vettṛ* ←√विद्); *asi* (4.3); *vedyam̩* (9.17); *ća* (1.1); *param̩* (2.12); *ća* (1.1); *dhāma* (8.21); *tvayā* (6.33); *tatam̩* (1nom◦ 2.17); ***viśvam̩*** (1nom◦ sing◦ ←n◦ *viśva* (universe) 11.19); *anantarūpa* (m◦ 8voc◦ sing◦ ←bahuvrī◦ *ananta-rūpa* (of inite-forms) 11.16); (11.38)

---

[649] Elsewhere◦ गिरियसे ब्रह्मण: अपि आदिकर्त्रे → you are the first Creator (1st) even of Brahmā (6th); are the progenitor (1st) of Brahmā himself (6th); Brahmā himself (1st) is less greater than Thou (5th); the Primal Cause (1st) even of Brahmā (6th); the Primal Cause (1st) even of Brahma (6th), greater (1st) than even brahma (5th), the Prime Creator (5th); O great one, greater even than Brahmā (7th), ...etc.

📖 All expressions shown above are incorrect. Remember, in this sholka, ते is (4th) Dative case, गरियसे is (4th) Dativa case, आदिकर्त्रे is (4th) Dative case and बैह्मण: is (5th) Ablative case. Therefore, ते गरियसे आदिकर्त्रे is one clause (in Dative case) which is compared with ब्रह्मण: in Ablative case. And after understanding this relationship properly, then it automatically falls in place as : कस्मात् न नमेरन् ते गरियसे आदिकर्त्रे ब्रह्मण:? (why should they not bow to you, the greater progenitor than brahmā). Now you know why the expressions such as, "the creator of brahma, greater than brahma, brahma is less grearter, O greatr even than brahma!, ...etc" are incorrect.

(§3) *tvam̦* (subj◦ you); *ādidevaḥ:* (adj1◦-subj◦ the primal deity); *puruṣaḥ: purāṇaḥ:* (adj2◦-subj◦ the primeval soul); *tvam̦* (subj◦ you); *asya* (of this); *viśvasya* (world); *param̦ nidhānam̦* (the supreme abode); *vettā* (adj3◦-subj◦ the knower); *asi* (are); *vedyam̦* (adj4◦-subj◦ knowable, fit to be known); *ća* (and); *param̦ ća dhāma* (and the supreme refuge); *tvayā* (subj◦ by you); *tatam̦* (THAT, THAT *brahma*); *viśvam̦* (the world); *anantarūpa* (O Infinite Form!); **(11.38)**

(§4) anantarūpa tvayā viśvam̦ tatam̦ tvam̦ asi ādidevaḥ: puruṣaḥ: purāṇaḥ: tvam̦ param̦ nidhānam̦ asya viśvasya vettā vedyam̦ ća param̦ ća dhāma;

(§5) O Infinite Form! by you the world is THAT *brahma*. You are the primal deity, the primeval soul; you are the supreme abode of this world; you are the knower and fit to be known[650] and you are the supreme refuge; (11.38)

11.39 वायुर्यमोऽग्निर्वरुणः शशाङ्कः प्रजापतिस्त्वं प्रपितामहश्च ।
नमो नमस्तेऽस्तु सहस्रकृत्वः पुनश्च भूयोऽपि नमो नमस्ते ।।
vāyuryamo‘gnirvaruṇaḥ: śaśāṅkaḥ: prajāpatistvam prapitāmahaśća,
namo namaste‘stu sahasrakṛtvaḥ: punaśća bhūyo‘pi namo namaste.
(11.39)

(§1) *vāyuḥ:* (r◦ 16/8) *yamaḥ:* (r◦ 15/1) *agniḥ:* (r◦ 16/6) *varuṇaḥ:* (r◦ 22/5) *śaśāṅkaḥ:* (r◦ 22/3) *prajāpatiḥ:* (r◦ 18/1) *tvam̦* (r◦ 14/1) *prapitāmahaḥ:* (r◦ 17/1) *ća namaḥ:* (r◦ 15/6) *namaḥ:* (r◦ 18/1) *te* (r◦ 6/1) *astu sahasrakṛtvaḥ:* (r◦ 22/3) *punaḥ:* (r◦ 17/1) *ća bhūyaḥ:* (r◦ 15/1) *api namaḥ:* (r◦ 15/6) *namaḥ:* (r◦ 18/1) *te*

(§2) *vāyuḥ:* (2.67); *yamaḥ:* (10.29); *agniḥ:* (4.37); *varuṇaḥ:* (10.29); ***śaśāṅkaḥ:*** (1nom◦ sing◦ ←m◦ *śaśāṅka* (moonशश्); *prajāpatiḥ:* (3.10); *tvam̦* (2.11); *prapitāmahaḥ:* (1nom◦ sing◦ ←m◦ *prapitāmaha* (great grandfather) 1.12); ca (1.1); *namaḥ: namaḥ:* (11.31); *te* (2.7); *astu* (2.47); *sahasrakṛtvaḥ:* (adv◦ ←num◦ adj◦ *sahasra* (thousandadj◦ *kṛt* 2.50); *punaḥ:* (4.35); *ca* (1.1); *bhūyaḥ:* (2.20); *api* (1.26); *namaḥ: namaḥ:* (11.31); *te* (2.7) **(11.39)**

(§3) *vāyuḥ:* (adj5◦-subj◦ the Lord of wind); *yamaḥ:* (adj6◦-subj◦ the Lors of Death); *agniḥ:* (adj7◦-subj◦ the Lord of fire); *varuṇaḥ:* (adj8◦-subj◦ the Lord of waters); *śaśāṅkaḥ:* (adj8◦-subj◦ the moom); *prajāpatiḥ:* (adj9◦-subj◦ the Lord of the creatures); *tvam̦* (subj◦ you are); *prapitāmahaḥ:* (adj9◦-subj◦ the

---

[650] Elsewhere◦ वेद्यम् → the object of knowledge (noun), known (ppp◦), ...etc.

📖 वेद्यम् is an pot. participle adjective which also means वेदितव्यम् and वेदनीयम् (to be known, knowable, fit to be known).

Great ancestor); ca (and); *namaḥ: namaḥ:* (obj∘ obeisances again and again); *te* (to you); *astu* (be); *sahasrakṛtvaḥ:* (a thousand times); *punaḥ:* (again); *ca* (and); *bhūyaḥ:* (again); *api* (and); *namaḥ: namaḥ:* (obj∘ obeisances); *te* (to you) (11.39)

(§4) tvam̧ vāyuḥ: yamaḥ: agniḥ: varuṇaḥ: śaśāṅkaḥ: prajāpatiḥ: ca prapitāmahaḥ: api te astu namaḥ: namaḥ: sahasrakṛtvaḥ: te namaḥ: namaḥ: punaḥ: ca bhūyaḥ:

(§5) You are the Lord of wind, the Lors of Death, the Lord of fire, the Lord of waters, the moom, the Lord of the creatures, and the Great ancestor; and to you[651] be obeisances again and again a thousand times; to you obeisances again and again.

(11.39)

11.40 नमः पुरस्तादथ पृष्ठतस्ते नमोऽस्तु ते सर्वत एव सर्व ।
अनन्तवीर्यामितविक्रमस्त्वं सर्वं समाप्नोषि ततोऽसि सर्वः ।।

namaḥ: purastādatha pṛṣṭhataste namo'stu te sarvata eva sarva,
anantavīryāmitavikramastvaṁ sarvaṁ samāpnoṣi tato'si sarvaḥ:.
(11.40)

(§1) *namaḥ:* (r∘ 22/3) *purastāţ* (r∘ 8/2) *atha pṛṣṭhataḥ:* (r∘ 18/1) *te namaḥ:* (r∘ 15/1) *astu te sarvataḥ:* (r∘ 19/7) *eva sarva* (r∘ 23/1) *anantavīrya* (r∘ 1/1) *amitavikramaḥ:* (r∘ 18/1) *tvam̧* (r∘ 14/1) *sarvam̧* (r∘ 14/1) *samāpnoṣi* (r∘ 25/4) *tataḥ:* (r∘ 15/1) *asi sarvaḥ:* (r∘ 22/8)

(§2) *namaḥ:* (11.31); *purastāţ* (ind∘ ←√पुर्); *atha* (1.20); *pṛṣṭhataḥ:* (ind∘ *pṛṣṭhataş* (from behind; *te* (1.7); *namaḥ:* (11.31); *astu* (2.47); *te* (1.7); *sarvataḥ:* (2.46); *eva* (1.1); *sarva* (voc∘ sing∘ proper noun ←pron∘ adj∘ *sarva* 1.6); *anantavīrya* (voc∘ sing∘ ←bahuvrī∘ *ananta-vīrya,* अनन्तवीर्यः यः ←adj∘ *ananta-vīrya* (infinie-prowesss) *amitavikramaḥ:* (m∘ 1nom∘ sing∘ ←bahuvrī∘ *amita-vikrama,* अमितविक्रमः यः ←adj∘ *amita* (boundless) ←√मा + m∘ *vikrama* (valor) ←वि√क्रम्); *tvam̧* (2.11); *sarvam̧* (2.17); *samāpnoṣi* (2nd-per∘ sing∘ pres∘ वर्तमान्-लट् parasmai∘ ←class5∘ सम्√आप् 2.70); *tataḥ:* (1.13); *asi* (4.3); *sarvaḥ:* (3.5) (11.40)

(§3) *namaḥ:* (obj∘ obeisance); *purastāţ* (from the front); *atha* (and, also); *pṛṣṭhataḥ:* (from back); *te* (to you); *namaḥ:* (obj∘ obeisance); *astu* (be); *te* (to you); *sarvataḥ:* (from all sides); *eva* (also); *sarva* (O All! O Everything); *anantavīrya* (voc∘ O Unbound in power!); *amitavikramaḥ:* (adj1∘-subj∘ of infinite power and infinite valor); *tvam̧* (subj∘ you are); *sarvam̧* (obj∘ everything); *samāpnoṣi* (you occupy,

---

[651] Elsewhere∘ नमः ते → I offer thousandsof adorations; I offer my, ...etc.

📖 नमः is not a verb.

pervade); *tataḥ:* (therefore); *asi* (you are); *sarvaḥ:* (adj2∘-subj∘ everything) (11.40)

(§4) sarva namaḥ: astu te purastāt atha pṛṣṭhataḥ: namaḥ: te sarvataḥ: eva tvam anantavīryāmitavikramaḥ: samāpnoṣi sarvam tataḥ: asi sarvaḥ:

(§5) O Everything![652] Obeisance be to you from the front[653] and from back; obeisance to you from all sides also. O Unbound in power![654] you are of infinite valor. You pervade[655] everything, therefore, you are everything. (11.40)

11.41 सखेति मत्वा प्रसभं यदुक्तं हे कृष्ण हे यादव हे सखेति ।
अजानता महिमानं तवेदं मया प्रमादात्प्रणयेन वापि ।।
sakheti matvā prasabhaṁ yaduktaṁ he kṛṣṇa he yādava he sakheti,
ajānatā mahimānaṁ tavedaṁ mayā pramādātpraṇayena vā'pi. (11.41)

(§1) *sakhā* (r∘ 2/3) *iti matvā prasabham* (r∘ 14/1) *yat* (r∘ 8/6) *uktam* (r∘ 14/1) *he kṛṣṇa he yādava he sakhe* (ārṣa exception to r∘ 5/2) *iti* (r∘ 23/1) *ajānatā mahimānam* (r∘ 14/1) *tava* (r∘ 2/1) *idam* (r∘ 14/1) *mayā pramādāt* (r∘ 10/6) *praṇayena vā* (r∘ 1/3) *api*

(§2) *sakhā* (4.3); *iti* (1.25); *matvā* (3.28); *prasabham* (2.60); *yat* (1nom∘ 2.67); *uktam* (1nom∘ 11.1); ***he*** (vocative ind∘ ←√हा); *kṛṣṇa* (1.28); *he* (↑); *yādava* (m∘ 8voc∘ sing∘ ←taddhita∘ *yādava*, यदोः गोत्रापत्यम् ←m∘

---

[652] Elsewhere∘ सर्व → because You are everything, ...etc.

📖 Here सर्व is a Vocative pronoun = O Everything! O Kṛṣṇna!

[653] Elsewhere∘ पुरस्तात् → in the East, before, from before,...etc.

📖 Here सर्व is a Vocative pronoun = O Everything! O Kṛṣṇna!

[654] Elsewhere∘ अनन्तवीर्य-अमितविक्रमः → You are possessed of infinite strength and infinite heroism; You are of infinite prowess, of immesurable valour, You are endowed with endless valour and limitless power; O infinite in might and infinite in prowess! O All, boundless in power and immesurable in strength! O All, Infinite in might and immesurable in strength! Your power is infinite and your energy is; You possess infinite prowess and immeasurable valor; Though, infinite in power and infinite in daring pervadest; ...etc.

📖 अनन्तवीर्य-अमितविक्रमः is only a sandhi between two grammatically different words अनन्तवीर्य! and अमितविक्रमः । It can not be a *dvandva-samasa* of these two uncompatible words, because अनन्तवीर्य! is in Vocative case and अमितविक्रमः is a Nominative case *bahuvrīhi* -adjective of the subject. Therefore, these two words can neither be connected together in habitual present tense (लट्), nor can be addressed together by conjunction 'and' to make a Vocative case.

[655] Elsewhere∘ समाप्नोषि → you are all-pervading, you have pervaded, ...etc.

📖 समाप्नोषि is not an adjective. It is a present tense लट् verb.

yadu ←√यज्); *he* (↑); *sakhe* (8voc◦ sing◦ ←m◦ *sakhi* (friend) 1.26); *iti* (1.25); *ajānatā* (3inst◦ sing◦ ←śatṛ◦ adj◦ *ajānat* (not-knowing) 7.24); *mahimānam* (2acc◦ sing◦ ←m◦ *mahiman* (greatness) ←√मह्); *tava* (1.3); *idam* (1.10); *mayā* (1.22); *pramādāt* (5abl◦ sing◦ ←m◦ 🕮**pramāda** (negligence) ←प्र√मद्); *praṇayena* (3inst◦ sing◦ ←m◦ *praṇaya* (affection) ←प्र√नी); *vā* (1.32); *api* (1.26) (11.41)

(§3) *sakhā* (obj1◦ a companion); *iti* (as); *matvā* (having thought of, thinking of); *prasabham* (adv◦ importunately, impetuously, presumptuously); *yat* (obj2◦ that which, whatever); *uktam* (adj◦-obj2◦ said); *he kṛṣṇa* (O Kṛṣṇa!); *he yādava* (O Yādava!); *he sakhe* (O Friend!); *iti* (as, thus); *ajānatā* (adv◦ inadvertently, unintentionally, not knowing); *mahimānam* (obj3◦ lordliness); *tava* (your, of yours); *idam* (adj◦-obj3◦ this); *mayā* (subj◦ by me); *pramādāt* (from, out of negligence); *praṇayena* (with affection) ; *vā* (or); *api* (also) (11.41)

(§4) ajānatā idam mahimānam tava yat uktam mayā iti he kṛṣṇa he yādava he sakhe pramādāt vā api praṇayena prasabham matvā iti sakhā

(§5) Not knowing this lordliness of yours, whatever (was) said[656] by me to you as, O Kṛṣṇa! O Yādava! O Friend! out of negligence or also with affection, presumptuously thinking of (you) as companion. (11.41)

11.42 यच्चावहासार्थमसत्कृतोऽसि विहारशय्यासनभोजनेषु ।
एकोऽथवाप्यच्युत तत्समक्षं तत्क्षामये त्वामहमप्रमेयम् ।।
yaććāvahāsārthamasatkṛto'si vihāraśayyāsanabhojaneṣu,
eko'thavāpyaćyuta tatsamakṣaṁ tatkṣāmaye tvāmahamaprameyam.
(11.42)

(§1) *yat* (r◦ 11/1) *ća* (r◦ 1/1) *avahāsārtham* (r◦ 8/16) *asatkṛtaḥ:* (r◦ 15/1) *asi vihāraśayyāsanabhojaneṣu* (r◦ 25/5, 23/1) *ekaḥ:* (r◦ 15/1) *athavā* (r◦ 1/3) *api* (r◦ 4/1) *aćyuta tatsamakṣam* (r◦ 14/1) *tat* (r◦ 10/5) *kṣāmaye tvām* (r◦ 8/16) *aham* (r◦ 8/16) *aprameyam* (r◦ 14/2)

(§2) *yat* (1nom◦ 2.67); *ća* (1.1); *avahāsārtham* (m◦ 2acc◦ sing◦ ←tatpu◦ *avahāsārtha*, अवहासस्य अर्थ: ←m◦ 🕮*avahāsa* (joke) ←अव√हस् + m◦ *artha* (for) 1.7); 🕮*asatkṛtaḥ:* (m◦ 1nom◦ sing◦ n.tatpu◦ ←ppp◦ adj◦ **asatkṛta** (ill treated) ←adj◦ *sat* 2.16 + adj◦ *kṛta* 1.35); *asi* (4.3); *vihāraśayyāsanabhojaneṣu* (n◦ 7loc◦ plu◦

---

[656] Elsewhere◦ (मया) उक्तम् → I have said, I have addressed, I have called, I may have said, I have spoken, ...etc.

🕮 उक्तम् is not a present tense verb, it is a past passive participle adjective of यत् 'whatever' in a passive construction.

←dvandva◦ विहारेषु च शय्यासु च आसनेषु च भोजनेषु च ←m◦ 📖*vihāra* (passtime) 6.17 + f◦ *śayyā* (sleep) ←√शी + n◦ *āsana* (sitting) 6.11 + n◦ ***bhojana*** (eating) ←√भुज्); ***ekaḥ:*** (adv◦ or m◦ 1nom◦ sing◦ ←adj◦ *eka* (one) 2.41); *athavā* (6.42); *api* (1.26); *aćyuta* (1.21); *tatsamakṣam* (adv◦ or ind◦ ←pron◦ *tat* 1.10 + ind◦ or adj◦ *samakṣa* ←सम्√अक्ष्); *tat* (2acc◦ 2.7); *kṣāmaye* (1st-per◦ sing◦ pres◦ वर्तमान्-लट् ātmane◦ caus◦ ←class1◦ √क्षम्); *tvām* (2.7); *aham* (1.22); *aprameyam* (11.17) (11.42)

(§3) *yat* (obj1◦ that); *ća* (and); *avahāsārtham* (adv◦ discourteously, disrespectfully); *asatkṛtaḥ:* (adj◦-obj2◦ ill treated); *asi* (obj2◦ you are); *vihāraśayyāsanabhojaneṣu* (during passtime, reposing, sitting together and at meals); *ekaḥ:* (in private, privately); *athavā* (or); *api* (also); *aćyuta* (O Kṛṣṇa!); *tatsamakṣam* (adv◦ in public, publicly); *tat* (obj1◦ that); *kṣāmaye* (request to please excuse me); *tvām* (to you, you); *aham* (subj◦ I); *aprameyam* (adj◦-obj2◦ the incomprehensible, the unfathomable) (11.42)

(§4) ća yat asi avahāsārtham asatkṛtaḥ: vihāraśayyāsanabhojaneṣu ekaḥ: athavā api aćyuta tatsamakṣam aham tvām aprameyam kṣāmaye tat

(§5) And that you are[657] discourteously ill treated (by me) during play, reposing, sitting together and at meals, in private or also in public. I request you, the unfathomable, to please excuse me that. (11.42)

11.43 पितासि लोकस्य चराचरस्य त्वमस्य पूज्यश्च गुरुर्गरीयान् ।
न त्वत्समोऽस्त्यभ्यधिकः कुतोऽन्यो लोकत्रयेऽप्यप्रतिमप्रभाव ।।

pitāsi lokasya ćarāćarasya tvamasya pūjyaśća gururgarīyān,
na tvatsamo'styabhyadhikaḥ: kuto'nyo lokatraye'pyapratimaprabhāva.
(11.43)

(§1) *pitā* (r◦ 1/3) *asi lokasya ćarāćarasya tvam* (r◦ 8/16) *asya pūjyaḥ:* (r◦ 17/1) *ća guruḥ:* (r◦ 16/8) *garīyān* (r◦ 23/1) *na tvatsamaḥ:* (r◦ 15/1) *asti* (r◦ 4/1) *abhyadhikaḥ:* (r◦ 22/1) *kutaḥ:* (r◦ 15/1) *anyaḥ:* (r◦ 15/12) *lokatraye* (r◦ 6/1) *api* (r◦ 4/1) *apratimaprabhāva*

(§2) *pitā* (9.17); *asi* (4.3); *lokasya* (5.14); *ćarāćarasya* (6pos sing◦ ←n◦ *ćarāćara* (moving and non-moving) 10.39); *tvam* (2.11); *asya* (2.17); *pūjyaḥ:* (m◦ 1nom◦ sing◦ ←pot◦ adj◦ *pūjya* (worthy of worship) ←√पूज्); *ća*

---

[657] Elsewhere◦ अवहासार्थम् असत्कृतः असि → You have been discourteously treated, You have been slighted in jest, I may have insulted you for jest, I may have insulted Thee for fun, disrespectful treatment has been shown, ...etc.

📖 असि is simple present tense of active voice लट् , for 2nd person (you are). Also, while अवहासार्थम् is discourteously, असत्कृतः is not 'treated' but it means 'ill-treated.'

(1.1); *guruḥ:* (1nom◦ sing◦ ←m◦ *guru* (mentor) 2.5); *garīyān̦* (m◦ 1nom◦ sing◦ ←comparitive adj◦ *garīyaș* (more venerable) 2.6); *na* (1.30); *tvatsamaḥ:* (m◦ 1nom◦ sing◦ ←adj◦ *tvat-sama* (like you) तव समः ←pron◦ *tvaț* (you) 6.39 + adj◦ *sama* (like) 1.4); *asti* (2.40); *abhyadhikaḥ:* (m◦ 1nom◦ sing◦ ←adj◦ -prādi samāsa *abhyadhika* (superior) अभितः अधिकः ←अभि√धा); *kutaḥ:* (2.2); *anyaḥ:* (2.29); *lokatraye* (n◦ 7loc◦ sing◦ ←tatpu◦ *loka-traya* (three worlds) 11.20); *api* (1.26); *apratimaprabhāva* (m◦ 8voc◦ sing◦ ←bahuvrī◦ *apratima-prabhāva*, अप्रतिमः प्रभावः यस्य सः कृष्णः ←adj◦ *apratima* (unmatched) ←अ–प्रति√मा + m◦ ***prabhāva*** (prowess) ←प्र√भू) (11.43)

(§3) *pitā* (adj1◦-subj◦ the father, guardian); *asi* (subj1◦ you are); *lokasya* (of this world); *ćarāćarasya* (of the moving and non-moving); *tvam̦* (subj1◦ you are); *asya* (for this eorld2.17); *pūjyaḥ:* (adj2◦-subj◦ worthy of worship); *ća* (and); *guruḥ:* (adj3◦-subj◦ mentor); *garīyān̦* (adj1◦-subj2◦ more venerable); *na* (no); *tvatsamaḥ:* (adj◦-subj2◦ like you); *asti* (subj2◦ there is anyone); *abhyadhikaḥ:* (adj3◦-subj2◦ superior); *kutaḥ:* (how? then how can there be); *anyaḥ:* (adj04◦-subj2◦ anyone else); *lokatraye* (in the three worlds); *api* (even, also1.26); *apratimaprabhāva* (O Lord Kr̥ṣṇna!) (11.43)

(§4) ćarāćarasya lokasya asi pitā asya tvam̦ garīyān̦ guruḥ: ća pūjyaḥ: apratimaprabhāva api lokatraye na asti tvatsamaḥ: kutaḥ: anyaḥ: abhyadhikaḥ:

(§5) Of this moving and non-moving world, you are the guardian. For this world you are more venerable, mentor and worthy of worship. O Lord Kr̥ṣṇna! even in the three worlds there is no one like you, then how can there be anyone else superior? (11.43)

11.44 तस्मात्प्रणम्य प्रणिधाय कायं प्रसादये त्वामहमीशमीड्यम् ।
पितेव पुत्रस्य सखेव सख्युः प्रियः प्रियायार्हसि देव सोढुम् ।।
tasmātpraṇamya praṇidhāya kāyaṁ prasādaye tvāmahamīśamīḍyam̦
piteva putrasya sakheva sakhyuḥ: priyaḥ: priyāyārhasi deva soḍhum̦
(11.44)

(§1) *tasmāț* (r◦ 10/6) *praṇamya praṇidhāya kāyam̦* (r◦ 14/1) *prasādaye tvām̦* (r◦ 8/16) *aham̦* (r◦ 8/19) *īśam̦* (r◦ 8/19) *īḍyam̦* (r◦ 14/2) *pitā* (r◦ 2/3) *iva putrasya sakhā* (r◦ 2/3) *iva sakhyuḥ:* (r◦ 22/3) *priyaḥ:* (r◦ 22/3) *priyāyaḥ:* (ārṣa exception to r◦ 20.1) *arhasi deva soḍhum̦* (r◦ 14/2)

(§2) *tasmāț* (1.37); *praṇamya* (11.14); *praṇidhāya* (lyp◦ past-participle ind◦ ←प्र–नि√धा); *kāyam̦* (2acc◦ sing◦ ←n◦ *kāya* (body) 5.11); *prasādaye* (1st-per◦ sing◦ pres◦ वर्तमान्–लट् ātmane◦ caus◦ ←class6◦ प्र√सद्); *tvām̦* (2.7); *aham̦* (1.22); *īśam̦* (11.15); *īḍyam̦* (2acc◦ sing◦ ←ppp◦ adj◦ *īḍya* (venerable) ←√ईड्); *pitā* (9.17); *iva* (1.30); *putrasya* (6pos sing◦ ←m◦ *putra* (son) 1.3); *sakhā* (4.3); *iva* (1.30); *sakhyuḥ:* (6pos sing◦ ←m◦ *sakhi* (friend) 1.26); *priyaḥ:* (7.17); *priyāyāḥ:* (*ārṣa* exception to rule 20.1 or here the understood form could be *priyāya*) ←f∘ sing∘ *priyāyā* (m∘ 4dat∘ sing∘ ←adj∘ *priya* (dear) 1.23); *arhasi* (2.25); *deva* (11.5); *soḍhuṃ* (5.23) (11.44)

(§3) *tasmāt* (therefore); *praṇamya* (bowing with reverence); *praṇidhāya* (prostrating); *kāyaṃ* (obj∘ the body); *prasādaye* (I ask for blessing); *tvāṃ* (obj2∘ you, to you); *ahaṃ* (subj1∘ I); *īśaṃ* (adj1∘-obj2∘ the Lord); *īḍyaṃ* (adj2∘-obj2∘ worthy of worship); *pitā* (subj2∘ a father); *iva* (as); *putrasya* (of a son, to a son); *sakhā* (subj3∘ a friend); *iva* (as); *sakhyuḥ:* (of a friend, to a friend); *priyaḥ:* (subj4∘ a lover); *priyāyāḥ:* (of a dear, to his dear); *arhasi* (you are worthy); *deva* (O Lord!); *soḍhuṃ* (for forgiving, to forgive)

(§4) tasmāt praṇidhāya praṇamya kāyaṃ ahaṃ prasādaye tvāṃ īśaṃ īḍyaṃ deva arhasi soḍhuṃ iva pitā putrasya sakhā sakhyuḥ: iva priyaḥ: priyāyāḥ: (11.44)

(§5) Therefore, prostrating (and) bowing the body with reverence, I ask for blessing to you, the Lord worthy of worship. O Lord! you are worthy for forgiving,[658] as a father to a son, a friend to a friend (and) as a lover to his dear. (11.44)

11.45 अदृष्टपूर्वं हृषितोऽस्मि दृष्ट्वा भयेन च प्रव्यथितं मनो मे ।
तदेव मे दर्शय देव रूपं प्रसीद देवेश जगन्निवास ।।

adṛṣṭapūrvaṁ hṛṣito'smi dṛṣṭvā bhayena ća pravyathitaṁ mano me,
tadeva me darśaya deva rūpaṁ prasīda deveśa jagannivāsa. (11.45)

(§1) *adṛṣṭapūrvaṃ* (r∘ 14/1) *hṛṣitaḥ:* (r∘ 15/1) *asmi dṛṣṭvā bhayena ća pravyathitaṃ* (r∘ 14/1) *manaḥ:* (r∘ 15/9) *me tat* (r∘ 8/9) *eva me darśaya deva rūpaṃ* (r∘ 14/1) *prasīda deveśa jagannivāsa*

(§2) *a-dṛṣṭapūrvaṃ* (n∘ 2acc∘ sing∘ n.bahuvrī∘ ←adj∘ *dṛṣṭa-pūrva* (seen-before) 11.6); *hṛṣitaḥ:* (m∘ 1nom∘ sing∘ ←ppp∘ adj∘ *hṛṣita* (joyful, delighted) ←√हृष्); *asmi* (7.8); *dṛṣṭvā* (1.2); *bhayena* (3inst∘ sing∘ ←n∘ *bhaya* (fear) 2.35); *ća* (1.1); *pravyathitaṃ* (perturbed, 1nom∘ 11.20); *manaḥ:* (1nom∘ 1.30); *me* (1.21); *tat* (4dat∘ 2.7); *eva* (1.1); *me* (2.7); *darśaya* (11.4); *deva* (11.15); *rūpaṃ* (2acc∘ 11.3); *prasīda* (11.25); *deveśa* (11.25); *jagannivāsa* (11.25) (11.45)

(§3) *a-dṛṣṭapūrvaṃ* (obj∘ something not seen before); *hṛṣitaḥ:* (adj∘-subj∘ delighted); *asmi* (subj∘ I am); *dṛṣṭvā* (having seen, seeing); *bhayena* (with fear); *ća* (and); *pravyathitaṃ* (adj∘-subj2∘ perturbed) *manaḥ:* (subj2∘ mind); *me* (my); *tat* (adj∘-obj3∘ that); *eva* (a suitable filler word); *me* (dat∘ me); *darśaya*

---

[658] Elsewhere∘ सोढुम् → bless Thou me, please tolerate, You should forgive me, Thou shouldst bear with me, Bear with me, Thou forgive me, You forgive me, ...etc.

📖 सोढुम् is not an imperative verb. It is an infinitive = for forgiving, to forgive.

(please reveal); *deva* (O Lord!); *rūpaṃ* (obj3◦ form); *prasīda* (please be gracious); *deveśa* (O Lord of the Lords!); *jagannivāsa* (O Abode of the World!) (11.45)

(§4) deva asmi hṛṣitaḥ: dṛṣṭvā a-dṛṣṭapūrvaṃ ća deveśa me manaḥ: pravyathitaṃ bhayena jagannivāsa prasīda darśaya me taṭ rūpaṃ

(§5) O Lord! I am delighted[659] seeing[660] something not seen before and O Lord of the Lords! my mind (is) perturbed with fear. O Abode of the World! please be gracious (and) please reveal me that original form. (11.45)

11.46 **किरीटिनं गदिनं चक्रहस्तमिच्छामि त्वां द्रष्टुमहं तथैव ।**
तेनैव रूपेण चतुर्भुजेन सहस्रबाहो भव विश्वमूर्ते ॥

kirīṭinaṃ gadinaṁ ćakrahastamiććhāmi tvāṁ dṛṣṭumahaṁ tathaiva,
tenaiva rūpeṇa ćaturbhujena sahasrabāho bhava viśvamūrte. (11.46)

(§1) *kirīṭinaṃ* (r◦ 14/1) *gadinaṃ* (r◦ 14/1) *ćakrahastaṃ* (r◦ 8/18) *iććhāmi tvāṃ* (r◦ 14/1) *draṣṭuṃ* (r◦ 8/16) *ahaṃ* (r◦ 14/1) *tathā* (r◦ 3/3) *eva tena* (r◦ 3/1) *eva rūpeṇa* (r◦ 24/1) *ćaturbhujena sahasrabāho bhava viśvamūrte*

(§2) *kirīṭinaṃ* (11.7); *gadinaṃ* (11.7); *ćakrahastaṃ* (m◦ 2acc◦ sing◦ ←bahuvrī◦ *ćakra-hastaṃ*, चक्रम् हस्ते यस्य ←n◦ *ćakra* (wheal) 3.16 + m◦ *hasta* (hand) 1.30); *iććhāmi* (1.35); *tvāṃ* (2.7); *draṣṭuṃ* (11.3); *ahaṃ* (1.22); *tathā* (1.8); *eva* (1.1); *tena* (3.38); *eva* (1.1); *rūpeṇa* (3inst◦ sing◦ ←n◦ *rūpa* 3.39); *ćaturbhujena* (3inst◦ sing◦ ←bahuvrī◦ *ćatur-bhuja*, चत्वारः भुजाः यस्य ←adj◦ *ćatuṛ* (four) 7.16 + m◦ *bhuja* (arm) ←√भुज्); *sahasrabāho* (m◦ 8voc◦ sing◦ ←bahuvrī◦ *sahasra-bāhu*, सहस्राणि बाहवः यस्य ←num◦ adj◦ *sahasra* (thousand) 7.3 + m◦ *bāhu* (arm) 1.18); *bhava* (2.45); *viśvamūrte* (m◦ 8voc◦ sing◦ ←bahuvrī◦ *viśva-mūrti*, विश्वम् एव मूर्तिः यस्य ←n◦ *viśva* (universe) 11.16 + f◦ *mūrti* (form) 9.4) (11.46)

(§3) *kirīṭinaṃ* (adj1◦-obj◦ wearing the diadem); *gadinaṃ* (adj2◦-obj◦ bearing the mace); *ćakrahastaṃ* (adj3◦-obj◦ bearing the *sudarśana ćakra*); *iććhāmi* (I desire); *tvāṃ* (obj◦ you); *draṣṭuṃ* (to see); *ahaṃ* (subj◦ I); *tathā eva* (like that alone, like before); *tena* (subj◦ with that); *eva* (only); *rūpeṇa* (with form); *ćaturbhujena* (with four-armed); *sahasrabāho* (O Kṛṣṇa! O Thousand armed one); *bhava* (please become); *viśvamūrte* (O Kṛṣṇa! O Universal form) (11.46)

---

[659] Elsewhere◦ हृषितः → My heart is glad...etc.

📖 हृषितः (m◦) is not an adjective of मनः (n◦). It is an adj◦ of m◦ subj◦ अस्मि

[660] Elsewhere◦ दृष्ट्वा → I have seen ...etc.

📖 दृष्ट्वा is not a verb. It is ipp◦ क्त्वा participle gerund.

(§4) sahasrabāho aham̦ iććhāmi tvām̦ draṣṭum̦ kirīṭinam̦ gadinam̦ ćakrahastam̦ viśvamūrte bhava tathā eva tena ćaturbhujena rūpeṇa eva

(§5) O Kṛṣṇa! I desire to see you wearing the diadem, bearing the mace (and) the *sudarśana ćakra;* O Kṛṣṇa! please become,[661] like before, with that four armed form only. (11.46)

The Lord said (śrībhagavānuvāća श्रीभगवानुवाच ।)

11.47 मया प्रसन्नेन तवार्जुनेदं रूपं परं दर्शितमात्मयोगात् ।
तेजोमयं विश्वमनन्तमाद्यं यन्मे त्वदन्येन न दृष्टपूर्वम् ।।

mayā prasannena tavārjunedaṁ rūpaṁ paraṁ darśitamātmayogāț,
tejomayaṁ viśvamanantamādyaṁ yanme tvadanyena na dṛṣṭapūrvam̦.
(11.47)

(§1) *śrībhagavān̦* (r◦ 8/14) *uvāća. mayā prasannena tava* (r◦ 1/1) *arjuna* (r◦ 2/1) *idam̦* (r◦ 14/1) *rūpam̦* (r◦ 14/1) *param̦* (r◦ 14/1) *darśitam̦* (r◦ 8/17) *ātmayogāț* (r◦ 1/10) *tejomayam̦* (r◦ 14/1) *viśvam̦* (r◦ 8/16) *anantam̦* (r◦ 8/17) *ādyam̦* (r◦ 14/1) *yaț* (r◦ 12/2) *me tvadanyena na dṛṣṭapūrvam̦* (r◦ 14/2)

(§2) *śrībhagavān̦* (2.2); *uvāća* (1.25). *mayā* (1.22); 🕮*prasannena* (m◦ 3inst◦ sing◦ ←adj◦ *prasanna* (pleased) 2.65); *tava* (1.3); *arjuna* (2.2); *idam̦* (1nom◦ 1.10); *rūpam̦* (1nom◦ sing◦ ←n◦ *rupa* (form) 11.3); *param̦* (1nom◦ 4.4); *darśitam̦* (n◦ 1nom◦ sing◦ ←ppp◦ adj◦ *darśita* (shown) ←√दृश्); 🕮*ātmayogāț* (m◦ 5abl◦ sing◦ ←tatpu◦ *ātma-yoga,* आत्मन: योग: ←m◦ *ātman̦* 2.41 + m◦ *yoga* 2.39); 🕮*tejomayam̦* (n◦ 1nom◦ sing◦ ←adj◦ taddhita◦ *tejomaya,* तेजसा मयम् ←n◦ *tejaṣ* (splendor) 7.9 + taddhitaa affix *maya* (possessed of) *); viśvam̦* (1nom◦ 11.38); *anantam̦* (1nom◦ 11.11); *ādyam̦* (1nom◦ sing◦ ←adj◦ *ādya* (primal) 8.28); *yaț* (1nom◦ 2.67); *me* (1.21); ***tvadanyena*** (m◦ 3inst◦ sing◦ ←adj◦ *tvadanya* (other than you) 6.39); *na* (1.30); *dṛṣṭapūrvam̦* (n◦ 1nom◦ sing◦ ←adj◦ *dṛṣṭa-pūrva* (seen-before) 11.6) (11.47)

(§3) *śrībhagavān̦* (Lord Kṛṣṇa); *uvāća* (said). *mayā* (subj◦ by me); *prasannena* (with pleasure); *tava* (for you, to you); *arjuna* (O Arjuna!); *idam̦* (adj◦-obj◦ this); *rūpam̦* (obj◦ form); *param̦* (adj2◦-obj◦ supreme); *darśitam̦* (adj3◦-obj◦ shown, manifested); *ātmayogāț* (with my *yoga*); *tejomayam̦* (adj4◦-obj◦ splendorous, effulgent*); viśvam̦* (adj5◦-obj◦ universal); *anantam̦* (adj6◦-obj◦ infinite); *ādyam̦* (adj6◦-obj◦ primal); *yaț* (adj7◦-obj◦ which); *me* (adj8◦-obj◦ my); *tvadanyena* (other than you anyone else); *na* (not);

---

[661] Elsewhere◦ भव → assume, resume, presume, take ...etc.

🕮 भव is an intransitive action performed by the subject on the subject = you become. Assume, resume, presume, take, etc. are transitive verbs, which are performed on an object other than subject. In most translations this (भव) verb is omitted.

dṛṣṭapūrvam (adj8∘-obj∘ seen before) (11.47)

(§4) śrībhagavān uvāća arjuna idam me param tejomayam viśvam anantam ādyam rūpam darśitam mayā ātmayogāt prasannena tava yat tvadanyena na dṛṣṭapūrvam

(§5) Lord Kṛṣṇa said : O Arjuna! this my supreme, splendorous, universal, infinite (and) primal form (is) shown by me with my *yoga* with pleasure for you, which other than you anyone else (has) not seen before. (11.47)

11.48 न वेदयज्ञाध्ययनैर्न दानैर्न च क्रियाभिर्न तपोभिरुग्रैः ।
एवंरूपः शक्य अहं नृलोके द्रष्टुं त्वदन्येन कुरुप्रवीर ।।
na vedayajñādhyayanairna dānairna ća kriyābhirna tapobhirugraiḥ:,
evaṁrūpaḥ: śakya ahaṁ nṛloke draṣṭuṁ tvadanyaena kurupravīra.
(11.48)

(§1) *na vedayajñādhyayanaiḥ:* (r∘ 16/11) *na dānaiḥ:* (r∘ 16/11) *na ća kriyābhiḥ:* (r∘ 16/6) *na tapobhiḥ:* (r∘ 16/1) *ugraiḥ:* (r∘ 22/8) *evam* (r∘ 14/1) *rūpaḥ:* (r∘ 22/5) *śakyaḥ:* (ārṣa exception to r∘ 15/1) *aham* (r∘ 14/1) *evam rūpaḥ: draṣṭum* (r∘ 14/1) *tvadanyena kurupravīra*

(§2) *na* (1.30); *vedayajñādhyayanaiḥ:* (n∘ 3inst∘ plu∘ dvandva∘ वेदैः च यज्ञैः च अध्ययनैः च ←m∘ *veda* 2.42 + m∘ *yajña* 3.9 + n∘ 🕮*adhyayana* ←अधि√इ); *na* (1.30); *dānaiḥ:* (3inst∘ plu∘ ←n∘ *dāna* (charity) 8.28); *na* (1.30); *ća* (1.1); *kriyābhiḥ:* (3inst∘ plu∘ ←f∘ *kriyā* (deed) 1.42); *na* (1.30); *tapobhiḥ:* (3inst∘ plu∘ ←n∘ *tapaṣ* (austerity) 4.10); *ugraiḥ:* (n∘ 3inst∘ plu∘ ←adj∘ *ugra* (severe) 11.20); *evam-rūpaḥ:* (m∘ 1nom∘ sing∘ ←bahuvrī∘ *evam rūpa*, एवम् रूपम् यस्य सः ←pron∘ *evam* (like this) 1.24 + n∘ *rūpa* (form) 3.39); *śakyaḥ:* (6.36); *aham* (1.22); 🕮*nṛloke* (m∘ 7loc∘ sing∘ ←tatpu∘ *nṛloka*, नृणाम् लोकः ←m∘ *nṛ* (people) 7.8 + m∘ *loka* (world) 2.5); *draṣṭum* (11.3); *tvadanyena* (11.47); *kurupravīra* (m∘ 8voc∘ sing∘ ←bahuvrī∘ *kuru-pravīra*, कुरुणाम् प्रवीरः यः ←m∘ *kuru* 1.1 + adj∘ *pravīra* (most brave) ←प्र√वीर्) (11.48)

(§3) *na* (not); *vedayajñādhyayanaiḥ:* (by reading the *vedas*, nor by performing *yajñas*, nor by studies); *na* (nor); *dānaiḥ:* (by charities); *na* (nor); *ća* (also); *kriyābhiḥ:* (by performing *karmas*); *na* (nor); *tapobhiḥ:* (by performing austerities); *ugraiḥ:* (severe); *evam-rūpaḥ:* (in such form); *śakyaḥ:* (adj∘-obj∘ possible, able); *aham* (obj∘ I am); *nṛloke* (in this human world); *draṣṭum* (for seeing, to be seen); *tvadanyena* (subj∘ by anyone else than you, by no one other than you); *kurupravīra* (O Arjuna!)
(11.48)

(§4) kurupravīra tvadanyena nṛloke aham śakyaḥ: draṣṭum evam-rūpaḥ: na vedayajñādhyayanaiḥ: na dānaiḥ: na ća kriyābhiḥ: na ugraiḥ: tapobhiḥ:

(§5) **O Arjuna! by no one other than you, in this human world, I am able to be seen in such form not by reading the *vedas,* nor by performing *yajñas,* nor by studies, nor by charities,[662] nor also by performing *karmas,* nor by performing severe austerities.**

(11.48)

11.49 मा ते व्यथा मा च विमूढभावो दृष्ट्वा रूपं घोरमीदृङ्ममेदम् ।
व्यपेतभीः प्रीतमनाः पुनस्त्वं तदेव मे रूपमिदं प्रपश्य ।।

ma te vyathā ma ća vimaūḍhabhāvo dṛṣṭvā rūpaṁ ghoramidṛṅmamedam,
vyapetabhīḥ: prītamanāḥ: punastvaṁ tadeva me rūpamidaṁ prapaśya.

(11.49)

(§1) *mā te vyathā mā ća vimaūḍhabhāvaḥ:* (r◦ 15/4) *dṛṣṭvā rūpaṃ* (r◦ 14/1) *ghoraṃ* (r◦ 8/19) *idṛk* (r◦ 9/2) *mama* (r◦ 2/1) *idaṃ* (r◦ 14/2) *vyapetabhīḥ:* (r◦ 22/3) *prītamanāḥ:* (r◦ 22/3) *punaḥ:* (r◦ 18/1) *tvaṃ* (r◦ 14/1) *taṭ* (r◦ 8/9) *eva me rūpaṃ* (r◦ 8/18) *idaṃ* (r◦ 14/1) *prapaśya*

(§2) *mā* (2.3); *te* (1.7); *vyathā* (1nom◦ sing◦ ←f◦ ***vyathā*** (hurt) ←√व्यथ्); *mā* (2.3); *ća* (1.1); *vimaūḍhabhāvaḥ:* (1nom◦ sing◦ ←tatpu◦ *vimaūḍha-bhāva,* विमूढः भावः ←adj◦ *vimūḍha* (deluded) 3.6 + m◦ *bhāva* (nature) 2.7); *dṛṣṭvā* (1.2); *rūpaṃ* (11.3); 🕮***ghoraṃ*** (n◦ 2acc◦ sing◦ ←adj◦ *ghora* (terrible) 3.1); *idṛk* (mode indicating ind◦ ←adj◦ ईदृश (such, like this) 2.32); *mama* (1.7); *idaṃ* (1.10); *vyapetabhīḥ:* (m◦ 1nom◦ sing◦ ←bahuvrī◦ *vyapeta-bhī,* व्यपेता भीः यस्य सः ←ppp◦ adj◦ *vyapeta* (gone) ←वि–अप√इ + f◦ *bhī* (fear) 6.14); 🕮*prītamanāḥ:* (m◦ 1nom◦ sing◦ ←bahuvrī◦ *prīta-manaṣ,* प्रीतम् मनः यस्य ←adj◦ *prīta* (joyful) ←√प्री + n◦ *manaṣ* (mind, heart) 1.30); *punaḥ:* (4.35); *tvaṃ* (2.11); *taṭ* (2acc◦ 2.7); *eva* (1.1); *me* (1.21); *rūpaṃ* (2acc◦ 11.3); *idaṃ* (1.10); *prapaśya* (2nd-per◦ sing◦ imperative◦ उपदेशार्थ–लोट् parasmai◦ ←class1◦ प्र√दृश् 1.3)

(11.49)

(§3) *mā* (don't, do not let - be); *te* (for you); *vyathā* (subj1◦ anguish, agitation, hurt); *mā* (don't, don't you be); *ća* (and); *vimaūḍhabhāvaḥ:* (adj1◦-subj2◦ duluded); *dṛṣṭvā* (seeing); *rūpaṃ* (obj◦ form); *ghoraṃ* (adj1◦-obj◦ terrible, horrible); *idṛk* (adj2-obj◦ like this one, such); *mama* (my); *idaṃ* (adj3◦-obj◦ this); *vyapetabhīḥ:* (adj2◦-subj2◦ fearless, one whose fear has gone away); *prītamanāḥ:* (adj3◦-subj2◦

---

[662] Elsewhere◦ दानैः → by gifts, ...etc.

🕮 The word दानम् can be considered in two ways, depending on one's point of view : (i) charity (given out of pity, compassion, mercy, forgiveness, kindness) दयालुत्वम्, त्यागः, भिक्षादानम्, वितरणम्, विश्राणनम् (ii) gift (given out of pleasure, gratification, joy, delight, liking) उपहारः, पारितोषकम्, उपग्राह्यम्, उपायनम्, उपहरणम्, अर्पणम् ।

cheerful, one whose heart is joyful); *punaḥ:* (again); *tvaṃ* (subj2◦ you, you be); *taṭ* (adj4-obj◦ that); *eva* (very); *me* (my, of mine); *rūpaṃ* (obj◦ form); *idaṃ* (adj3◦-obj◦ this, here it is); *prapaśya* (behold! see! look!) (11.49)

(§4) mā vyathā te ća mā vimaūḍhabhāvaḥ: dṛṣṭvā mama ghoraṃ rūpaṃ idṛk idaṃ tvaṃ vyapetabhīḥ: prītamanāḥ: prapaśya taṭ eva rūpaṃ me idaṃ punaḥ:

(§5) Do not let anguish be for you[663] and don't you be duluded seeing my terrible form such like this one. You be fearless (and) cheerful. Behold! that very form of mine, here it is again. (11.49)

Sanjaya said (sañjaya uvāća सजय उवाच ।)

11.50 **इत्यर्जुनं वासुदेवस्तथोक्त्वा स्वकं रूपं दर्शयामास भूयः ।**
आश्वासयामास च भीतमेनं भूत्वा पुनः सौम्यवपुर्महात्मा ।।

ityarjunaṁ vāsudevastathoktvā svakaṁ rūpaṁ darśayāmāsa bhūyahḥ:,
āśvāsayāmāsa ća bhītamenaṁ bhūtvā punaḥ: saumyavapurmahātmā.
(11.50)

(§1) *sañjayaḥ:* (r◦ 19/4) *uvāća. iti* (r◦ 4/1) *arjunaṃ* (r◦ 14/1) *vāsudevaḥ:* (r◦ 18/1) *tathā* (r◦ 2/4) *uktvā svakaṃ* (r◦ 14/1) *rūpaṃ* (r◦ 14/1) *darśayāmāsa bhūyaḥ:* (r◦ 22/8) *āśvāsayāmāsa ća bhītaṃ* (r◦ 8/22) *enaṃ* (r◦ 14/1) *bhūtvā punaḥ:* (r◦ 22/7) *saumyavapuḥ:* (r◦ 16/8) *mahātmā*

(§2) *sañjayaḥ:* (1.2); *uvāća* (1.25). *iti* (1.25); *arjunaṃ* (m◦ 2acc◦ sing◦ ←prop◦ *arjuna* 1.4); *vāsudevaḥ:* (7.19); *tathā* (1.8); *uktvā* (1.47); *svakaṃ* (m◦ 2acc◦ sing◦ ←adj◦ *svaka* (own) ←√स्वन्); *rūpaṃ* (11.3); *darśayāmāsa* (11.9); *bhūyaḥ:* (2.20); *āśvāsayāmāsa* (3rd-per◦ sing◦ past-perf◦ लिट् भूत◦ parasmai◦ caus◦ ←class2◦ आ√श्वस्); *ća* (1.1); *bhītaṃ* (m◦ 2acc◦ sing◦ ←adj◦ *bhīta* (afraid) 11.21); *enaṃ* (2.19); *bhūtvā* (2.20); *punaḥ:* (4.35); *saumyavapuḥ:* (n◦ 2acc◦ sing◦ ←tatpu◦ *saumya-vapuḥ:*, सौम्यम् वपुः ←adj◦ ***saumya*** (normal) ←√सु + n◦ *vapau* (body) ←√वप्); *mahātmā* (7.19) (11.50)

(§3) *sañjayaḥ:* (subj◦ Sañjaya); *uvāća* (said). *iti* (thus); *arjunaṃ* (obj1◦ to Arjuna); *vāsudevaḥ:* (subj◦ Kṛṣṇa, son of Vasudeva); *tathā* (like that, in that manner); *uktvā* (having spoken); *svakaṃ* (adj◦-obj2◦ his own); *rūpaṃ* (obj2◦ form); *darśayāmāsa* (revealed); *bhūyaḥ:* (again); *āśvāsayāmāsa* (consoled); *ća*

---

[663] Elsewhere◦ मा ते व्यथा → May you not have fear, Have no fear, be not afraid, Don't be terrified, Do not be afraid, You have been perturbed, Do not be agitated, be not agitated, May you not be faraid, ...etc.

📖 Remember, in मा ते व्यथा, the word व्यथा (anguish) is subject in Nominative (1st) case, it is not the object, it is not in Accusative (2nd) case, it is also not the ppp◦ adjective of ते । The word ते is in possessive (6th) case, so it is not the subject.

(and); *bhītaṃ* (adj1◦-obj1◦ the frightened Arjuna); *enaṃ* (= etam; adj2◦-obj1◦ this); *bhūtvā* (having become); *punaḥ:* (again); *saumyavapuḥ:* (adj1◦-subj◦ of normal body); *mahātmā* (adj2◦-subj◦ Kṛṣṇa, the great soul) (11.50)

(§4) sañjayaḥ: uvāća iti uktvā arjunaṃ tathā vāsudevaḥ: darśayāmāsa svakaṃ rūpaṃ bhūyaḥ: ća mahātmā āśvāsayāmāsa enaṃ bhītaṃ bhūtvā saumyavapuḥ: punaḥ:

(§5) Sañjaya said : Thus, having spoken to Arjuna in that manner, Kṛṣṇa revealed his own form again. And, Kṛṣṇa, the great soul consoled this frightened Arjuna, having become of normal body again. (11.50)

Arjuna said (arjuna uvāća अर्जुन उवाच ।)

11.51 **दृष्ट्वेदं मानुषं रूपं तव सौम्यं जनार्दन ।**
इदानीमस्मि संवृत्तः सचेताः प्रकृतिं गतः ।।
dṛṣṭvedaṁ mānuṣaṁ rūpaṁ tava saumyaṁ janardana,
idānīmasmi saṁvṛttaḥ: saćetāḥ: prakṛtiṁ gataḥ:. (11.51)

(§1) *arjunaḥ:* (r◦ 19/4) *uvāća. dṛṣṭvā* (r◦ 2/3) *idaṃ* (r◦ 14/1) *mānuṣaṃ* (r◦ 14/1) *rūpaṃ* (r◦ 14/1) *tava saumyaṃ* (r◦ 14/1) *janārdana* (r◦ 23/1) *idānīṃ* (r◦ 8/16) *asmi saṁvṛttaḥ:* (r◦ 22/7) *saćetāḥ:* (r◦ 22/3) *prakṛtiṃ* (r◦ 14/1) *gataḥ:* (r◦ 22/8)

(§2) *arjunaḥ:* (1.28); *uvāća* (1.25). *dṛṣṭvā* (1.2); *idaṃ* (1.10); *mānuṣaṃ* (n◦ 1nom◦ 2acc◦ sing◦ ←adj◦ *mānuṣa* (human) 4.12); *rūpaṃ* (11.3); *tava* (1.3); *saumyaṃ* (n◦ 1nom◦ 2acc◦ sing◦ ←adj◦ *saumya* (normal) 11.50); *janārdana* (1.36); ***idānīṃ*** (time indicating ind◦ ←pron◦ *idaṃ* (this) 1.10); *asmi* (7.8); 🕮*saṁvṛttaḥ:* (m◦ 1nom◦ sing◦ ←ppp◦ adj◦ *saṁvṛtta* (composed) ←सम्√वृत्); 🕮*saćetāḥ:* (1nom◦ sing◦ ←m◦ bahuvrī◦ *sa-ćetaṣ* (collected) ←स√चित्); 🕮*prakṛtiṃ* (3.33); *gataḥ:* (m◦ 1nom◦ sing◦ ←adj◦ *gata* (gone) 2.11)
(11.51)

(§3) *arjunaḥ:* (subj◦ Arjuna); *uvāća* (said). *dṛṣṭvā* (having seen); *idaṃ* (this); *mānuṣaṃ* (adj◦-obj◦ human); *rūpaṃ* (obj◦ form); *tava* (obj1◦-obj◦ your); *saumyaṃ* (obj2◦-obj◦ normal, mild, pleasant); *janārdana* (O Kṛṣṇa!); *idānīṃ* (now); *asmi* (subj◦ I am); *saṁvṛttaḥ:* (adj1◦-subj◦ composed); *saćetāḥ:* (adj2◦-subj◦ the one whose mind is restored, collected); *prakṛtiṃ-gataḥ:* (adj3◦-subj◦ restored to normal state) (11.51)

(§4) arjunaḥ: uvāća. janārdana dṛṣṭvā tava idaṃ saumyaṃ mānuṣaṃ rūpaṃ asmi idānīṃ saṁvṛttaḥ: saćetāḥ: prakṛtiṃ-gataḥ:

(§5) Arjuna said : O Kṛṣṇa! having seen your this normal human form, I am now composed and

restored to normal state. (11.51)

The Lord said (śrībhagavānuvāća श्रीभगवानुवाच ।)

11.52 सुदुर्दर्शमिदं रूपं दृष्टवानसि यन्मम ।
देवा अप्यस्य रूपस्य नित्यं दर्शनकाङ्क्षिणः ।।
sudurdarśamidaṁ rūpaṁ dṛṣṭavānasi yanmama,
devā apyasya rūpasya nityaṁ darśanākāṅkṣiṇaḥ:. (11.52)

(§1) *śrībhagavān̩* (r◦ 8/14) *uvāća. sudurdarśam̩* (r◦ 8/18) *idam̩* (r◦ 14/1) *rūpam̩* (r◦ 14/1) *dṛṣṭavān̩* (r◦ 8/11) *asi yat̩* (r◦ 12/2) *mama devāḥ:* (r◦ 20/1) *api* (r◦ 4/1) *asya rūpasya nityam̩* (r◦ 14/1) *darśanākāṅkṣiṇaḥ:* (r◦ 22/8)

(§2) *śrībhagavān̩* (2.2); *uvāća* (1.25). *sudurdarśam̩* (n◦ 2acc◦ sing◦ ←tatpu◦ *su-dur-darśa* ←ind◦ *su* (very) 5.1 + ind◦ *dur̩* (difficult) 1.2 + n◦ *darśa* (appearance) ←√दृश्); *idam̩* (2acc◦ 1.10); *rūpam̩* (2acc◦ 11.3); ***dṛṣṭavān̩*** (m◦ 1nom◦ sing◦ ←act◦ past◦ adj◦ *dṛṣṭavat̩* ←√दृश्); *asi* (4.3); *yat̩* (2acc◦ 1.45); *mama* (1.7); *devāḥ:* (3.11); *api* (1.26); *asya* (2.17); *rūpasya* (6pos sing◦ ←n◦ *rūpa* (form) 3.39); *nityam̩* (adv◦ 2.21); *darśanākāṅkṣiṇaḥ:* (m◦ 1nom◦ plu◦ ←tatpu◦ *darśanākāṅkṣin̩*, दर्शनस्य आकाङ्क्षी ←n◦ *darśana* (appearance) 11.10 + adj◦ 🕮*ākāṅkṣin̩* (desirous, eager) ←आ√कांक्ष्) (11.52)

(§3) *śrībhagavān̩* (Lord Kṛṣṇa); *uvāća* (said). *sudurdarśam̩* (adj1◦-obj◦ very rare to be seen); *idam̩* (adj2◦-obj◦ this); *rūpam̩* (obj◦ form); *dṛṣṭavān̩ asi* (adj◦-subj◦ you are witness); *yat̩* (of which); *mama* (adj3◦-obj◦ my, of mine); *devāḥ:* (subj2◦ the gods); *api* (also); *asya* (of this); *rūpasya* (form); *nityam̩* (always); *darśanākāṅkṣiṇaḥ:* (adj◦-subj2◦ eager to witness) (11.52)

(§4) śrībhagavān̩ uvāća idam̩ sudurdarśam̩ rūpam̩ mama yat̩ dṛṣṭavān̩ asi devāḥ: api nityam̩ darśanākāṅkṣiṇaḥ: asya rūpasya

(§5) Lord Kṛṣṇa said : This very rare to be seen form of mine, of which you are witness,[664] the gods (are) also always eager to witness this form. (11.52)

11.53 नाहं वेदैर्न तपसा न दानेन न चेज्यया ।
शक्य एवंविधो द्रष्टुं दृष्टवानसि मां यथा ।।
nāhaṁ vedairna tapasā na danena na ćejyayā,

---

[664] Elsewhere◦ दृष्टवान् असि → you have seen, you have just seen, you are now seeing, you have just beheld, thou hast seen, ...etc.

🕮 दृष्टवान् is not a past or present tense. It is participle adjective ot subject असि (you are) ।

śakya evam̃vidho dṛṣṭum̐ dṛṣṭavānasi mām̐ yathā. (11.53)

(§1) *na* (r∘ 1/1) *ahaṃ* (r∘ 14/1) *vedaiḥ:* (r∘ 16/11) *na tapasā na danena na ća* (r∘ 2/1) *ijyayā śakyaḥ:* (r∘ 19/7) *evaṃ* (r∘ 14/1) *vidhaḥ:* (r∘ 15/4) *draṣṭuṃ* (r∘ 14/1) *dṛṣṭvāṇ* (r∘ 8/11) asi māṃ (r∘ 14/1) *yathā*

(§2) *na* (1.30); *ahaṃ* (1.22); ***vedaiḥ:*** (3inst∘ plu∘ ←m∘ *veda* 2.42); *na* (1.30); *tapasā* (3inst∘ sing∘ ←n∘ *tapaṣ* (aausterity) 4.10); *na* (1.30); *danena* (3inst∘ sing∘ ←n∘ *dāna* (charity) 8.28); *na* (1.30); *ća* (1.1); *ijyayā* (3inst∘ sing∘ ←f∘ 📖*ijyā* (yajña) 9.25); *śakyaḥ:* (6.36); ***evam̃vidhaḥ:*** (m∘ 1nom∘ sing∘ ←bahuvrī∘ *evaṃ-vidha*, एवम् विधः यः ←pron∘ *evaṃ* (like this, such) 1.24 + m∘ *vidha* (way) 3.3); *draṣṭuṃ* (11.3); *dṛṣṭavāṇ* (m∘ adj∘ 11.52); *asi* (4.3); *māṃ* (1.46); *yathā* (1.11) (11.53)

(§3) *na* (not); *ahaṃ* (subj∘ I am); *vedaiḥ:* (through the *Vedas*); *na* (nor); *tapasā* (by austerity); *na* (nor); *danena* (by charity); *na* (nor); *ća* (and); *ijyayā* (by *yajña*); *śakyaḥ:* (adj∘-subj∘ possible, able); *evam̃vidhaḥ:* (in this way); *draṣṭuṃ* (for seeing); *dṛṣṭavāṇ asi* (you are witness); *māṃ* (obj∘ to me, to my form); *yathā* (as) (11.53)

(§4) yathā dṛṣṭavāṇ asi māṃ ahaṃ na śakyaḥ: draṣṭuṃ evam̃vidhaḥ: vedaiḥ: na tapasā na danena na ća ijyayā

(§5) As you are witness[665] to my form, I am not possible for seeing in this way, through the *Vedas,* nor by austerity, nor by charity,[666] (and) nor by *yajña.* (11.53)

11.54 भक्त्या त्वनन्यया शक्य अहमेवंविधोऽर्जुन ।
ज्ञातुं द्रष्टुं च तत्त्वेन प्रवेष्टुं च परन्तप ।।

bhaktyā tvananyayā śakya ahamevam̃vidho'rjuna,
jñātum̐ dṛṣṭum̐ ća tattvena praveṣṭum̐ ća parantapa. (11.54)

(§1) *bhaktyā tu* (r∘ 4/6) *ananyayā śakyaḥ:* (ārṣa exception to r∘ 15/1) *ahaṃ* (r∘ 8/22) *evaṃ* (r∘ 14/1) *vidha* (r∘ 15/1) *arjuna jñātuṃ* (r∘ 14/1) *draṣṭuṃ* (r∘ 14/1) *ća tattvena praveṣṭuṃ* (r∘ 14/1) *ća parantapa*

(§2) *bhaktyā* (8.10); *tu* (1.2); *ananyayā* (8.22); *śakyaḥ:* (6.36); *ahaṃ* (1.22); *evaṃ-vidhaḥ:* (11.53); *arjuna* (2.2); *jñātuṃ* (inf∘ ind∘ ←√ज्ञा); *draṣṭuṃ* (11.3); *ća* (1.1); *tattvena* (9.24); 📖*praveṣṭuṃ* (inf∘ ind∘ ←प्र√विश्); *ća* (1.1); *parantapa* (2.3) (11.54)

(§3) *bhaktyā* (by devotion); *tu* (however); *ananyayā* (one pointed); *śakyaḥ:* (adj1∘-subj∘ possible, able); *ahaṃ* (subj∘ I am); *evaṃ-vidhaḥ:* (adj2∘-subj∘ in this manner); *arjuna* (O Arjuna!); *jñātuṃ* (for knowing); *draṣṭuṃ* (for seeing); *ća* (and); *tattvena* (in principle); *praveṣṭuṃ* (for entering); *ća* (and);

---

[665] See footnote in 11.53

[666] See footnote in 11.49

parantapa (O Arjuna!) (11.54)

(§4) tu arjuna aham̧ śakyaḥ: jñātum̧ ća draṣṭum̧ evam̧-vidhaḥ: ća praveṣṭum̧ tattvena bhaktyā ananyayā parantapa

(§5) However, O Arjuna! I am possible for knowing and for seeing in this manner and for entering, in principle, by one pointed devotion, O Arjuna! (11.54)

11.55 मत्कर्मकृन्मत्परमो मद्भक्तः सङ्गवर्जितः ।
निर्वैरः सर्वभूतेषु यः स मामेति पाण्डव ।।
matkarmakṛnmatparamo madbhaktaḥ: saṅgavarjitaḥ:,
nirvairaḥ: sarvabhūteṣu yaḥ: sa māmeti pāṇḍva. (11.55)

(§1) *matkarmakṛt* (r◦ 12/2) *matparamaḥ:* (r◦ 15/9) *madbhaktaḥ:* (r◦ 22/7) *saṅgavarjitaḥ:* (r◦ 22/8) *nirvairaḥ:* (r◦ 22/7) *sarvabhūteṣu* (r◦ 25/5) *yaḥ:* (r◦ 22/7) *saḥ:* (r◦ 21/2) *mām̧* (r◦ 8/22) *eti pāṇḍava*

(§2) *matkarmakṛt* (m◦ 1nom◦ sing◦ ←tatpu◦ *mat-karma-kṛt*, मम वा मदर्थे वा कर्म करोति इति ←pron◦ *mat* 1.9 + n◦ *karman* 1.15 + adj◦ affix कृत् 2.50); *matparamaḥ:* (m◦ 1nom◦ sing◦ ←bahuvrī◦ ***mat-parama***, अहम् परमः यस्य सः । मयि परायणः यः । ←pron◦ *mat* 1.9 + adj◦ *parama* 1.17); *madbhaktaḥ:* (9.34); *saṅgavarjitaḥ:* (m◦ 1nom◦ sing◦ ←ppp◦ adj◦ tatpu◦ *saṅga-varjita*, सङ्गेन वर्जितः ←m◦ *saṅga* 2.47 + ppp◦ adj◦ *varjita* (without) 4.19); 📖*nirvairaḥ:* (m◦ 1nom◦ sing◦ ←n.bahuvrī◦ *nirvaira* (without ill feeling) ←ind◦ *nir* (without) 2.45 + n◦ taddhita◦ *vaira* (ill feeling) ←√वीर्); *sarvabhūteṣu* (3.18); *yaḥ:* (2.19); *saḥ:* (1.13); *mām̧* (1.46); *eti* (4.9); *pāṇḍava* (4.25) (11.55)

(§3) *matkarmakṛt* (adj1◦-subj◦ he who is working for my cause); *matparamaḥ:* (adj2◦-subj◦ he for whom I am the supreme aim); *madbhaktaḥ:* (adj3◦-subj◦ my devotee); *saṅgavarjitaḥ:* (adj4◦-subj◦ he who is dovoid of attachment); *nirvairaḥ:* (adj4◦-subj◦ he who has no ill feeling); *sarvabhūteṣu* (in all beings); *yaḥ:* (adj6◦-subj◦ he who); *saḥ:* (subj◦ he); *mām̧* (obj◦ me); *eti* (attains); *pāṇḍava* (O Arjuna!) (11.55)

(§4) pāṇḍava madbhaktaḥ: yaḥ: matkarmakṛt matparamaḥ: saṅgavarjitaḥ: nirvairaḥ: sarvabhūteṣu saḥ: eti mām̧

(§5) O Arjuna! my devotee who is working for my cause, he for whom I am the supreme aim, he who is dovoid of attachment he who has no ill feeling in all beings - he attains me. (11.55)

इति श्रीमद्भगवद्गीतासूपनिषत्सु ब्रह्मविद्यायां योगशास्त्रे
श्रीकृष्णार्जुनसंवादे विश्वरूपदर्शनयोगो नामैकादशोऽध्यायः ।।

iti śrīmadbhagavadgītāsūpaniṣatsu brahmavidyāyām̐ yogaśāstre śrīkṛṣṇārjunasaṁvāde viśvarūpadarśanayogo nāmaikādaśo'dhyāyaḥ:

(§1) *iti śrīmadbhagavadgītāsu* (r∘ 1/8) *upaniṣatsu brahmavidyāyām* (r∘ 14/1) *yogaśāstre śrīkṛṣṇārjunasaṁvāde viśvarūpadarśanayogaḥ:* (r∘ 15/6) *nāma* (r∘ 3/1) *ekādaśaḥ:* (r∘ 15/1) *adhyāyaḥ:* (r∘ 22/8)

(§2) *iti* (1.25); *śrīmadbhagavadgītāsu* (f∘ 7loc∘ plu∘ tatpu∘ *śrīmad-bhagavad-gītā* ←adj∘ *śrīmat* 6.41 + adj∘ *bhagavat* 10.14 + f∘ *gītā* ←5∘√गै); *upaniṣatsu* (7loc∘ plu∘ ←f∘ *upaniṣad* ←6∘उप-नि√सद्); *brahmavidyāyām* (f∘ 7loc∘ sing∘ ←tatpu∘ *brahma-vidyā,* ब्रह्मणः विद्या ←n∘ *brahman* 2.72 + *vidyā* 5.18); *yogaśāstre* (n∘ 7loc∘ sing∘ ←tatpu∘ *yoga-śāstra,* योगानाम् शास्त्रम् । योगस्य शास्त्रम् । ←m∘ *yoga* 2.39 + n∘ *śāstra* 15.20); *śrīkṛṣṇārjunasaṁvāde* (m∘ 7loc∘ sing∘ ←tatpu∘ *śrī-kṛṣṇārjuna-saṁvāda,* श्रीकृष्णस्य च अर्जुनस्य च संवादः ←adj∘ *śrī* 10.34 + m∘ prop∘ *kṛṣṇa* 1.28 + m∘ prop∘ *arjuna* 1.4 + m∘ *saṁvāda* 18.70); *viśvarūpadarśanayogaḥ:* (m∘ 1nom∘ sing∘ ←tatpu∘ *viśvarūpadarśanayoga,* विविश्वरूपदर्शनयोग, विश्वरूपस्य दर्शनस्य योगः ← n∘ *viśva-rūpa* विश्वात्मकम् रूपम् + n∘ *darśana* 11.52 + *yoga* 2.39); *nāma* (1nom∘ sing∘ ←n∘ *nāman* ←1∘√म्ना); *ekādaśaḥ:* (m∘ 1nom∘ sing∘ ←num∘ adj∘ eka 2.41 + *daśa* 13.5); *adhyāyaḥ:* (1nom∘ sing∘ ←m∘ *adhyāya* ←1∘अधि√इ)

(§3) *iti* (thus); *śrīmadbhagavadgītāsu upaniṣatsu* (among the upaniṣads of the Śrīmad-Bhagavadgītā); *brahmavidyāyām* (of the eternal wisdoms); *yogaśāstre* (in the science of Yoga); *śrīkṛṣṇārjunasaṁvāde* (in the dialogue between Śrī Kṛṣṇa and Arjuna); *viśvarūpadarśanayogaḥ:* (m∘ 1nom∘ sing∘ ←tatpu∘ *viśvarūpadarśanayoga,* विविश्वरूपदर्शनयोग, विश्वरूपस्य दर्शनस्य योगः ← n∘ *viśva-rūpa* विश्वात्मकम् रूपम् + n∘ *darśana* 11.52 + *yoga* 2.39); (adj∘1-subj∘ vibhūti-yoga); *nāma* (called); *ekādaśah* (adj∘2-subj∘ the eleventh); *adhyāyaḥ:* (subj∘ discourse; chapter)

(§4) śrīmadbhagavadgītāsu upaniṣatsu yogaśāstre brahmavidyāyām iti ekādaśaḥ: adhyāyaḥ: nāma viśvarūpadarśanayogaḥ: śrīkṛṣṇārjunasaṁvāde

(§5) Among the upaniṣads of the Śrīmad-Bhagavadgītā, in the science of yoga of self realization, thus (is) the eleventh discourse called viśvarūpa-darśana-yogaḥ:, in the dialogue between Śrī Kṛṣṇa and Arjuna.

CHAPTER 12

dvādaśo'dhyāyaḥ:

द्वादशोऽध्यायः ।

YOGA OF DEVOTION

bhaktiyogopanishat

भक्तियोगोपनिषत् ।

Arjuna said (arjuna uvāća अर्जुन उवाच ।)

12.1 **एवं सततयुक्ता ये भक्तास्त्वां पर्युपासते ।**
ये चाप्यक्षरमव्यक्तं तेषां के योगवित्तमाः ।।

evaṁ satatayuktā ye bhaktāstvāṁ paryupāsate,
ye ćāpyakṣaramavyaktaṁ teṣāṁ ke yogavittamāḥ:. (12.1)

(§1) एवम् सततयुक्ताः ये भक्ताः त्वाम् पर्युपासते । ये च अपि अक्षरम् अव्यक्तम् तेषाम् के योगवित्तमाः ।। *dvādaśaḥ:* (r◦ 15/1) *adhyāyaḥ:* (r◦ 22/8). *bhaktiyogaḥ:* (r◦ 22/8). *arjunaḥ:* (r◦ 19/4) *uvāća. evaṃ* (r◦ 14/1) *satatayuktāḥ:* (r◦ 20/14) *ye bhaktāḥ:* (r◦ 18/1) *tvāṃ* (r◦ 14/1) *paryupāsate ye ća* (r◦ 1/1) *api* (r◦ 4/1) *akṣaraṃ* (r◦ 8/16) *avyaktaṃ* (r◦ 14/1) *teṣāṃ* (r◦ 25/3, 14/1) *ke yogavittamāḥ:* (r◦ 22/8)

(§2) *dvādaśaḥ:* (m◦ 1nom◦ sing◦ ←sequence indicating num◦ adj◦ *dvādaśa* ←num◦ adj◦ *dvi* 1.7 + num◦ adj◦ *daśa* 13.6); *adhyāyaḥ:* (1nom◦ sing◦ ←m◦ *adhyāya* ←1◦अधि√इ (to enter, come, go). *bhaktiyogaḥ:* (m◦ 1nom◦ sing◦ ←tatpu◦ *bhakti-yoga* भक्तेः योगः 14.26). *arjunaḥ:* (1.28); *uvāća* (1.25). *evaṃ* (1.24); *satatayuktāḥ:* (m◦ 1nom◦ plu◦ ←s-karm◦ *satata-yukta* 10.10); *ye* (1.7); *bhaktāḥ:* (9.33); *tvāṃ* (2.7); *paryupāsate* (4.25); *ye* (1.7); *ća* (1.1); *api* (1.26); *akṣaraṃ* (8.3); *avyaktaṃ* (7.24); *teṣāṃ* (5.16); *ke* (m◦ 1nom◦ plu◦ ←pron◦ *kiṃ* 1.1); *yogavittamāḥ:* (m◦ 1nom◦ plu◦ ←bahuvrī◦ adj◦ *yoga-vittama*, योगस्य वित्तमः । योगाचरिषु वित्तमः । योगिषु वित्तमः । भक्तियोगिषु वित्तमः । भक्तियोगज्ञानिषु उत्तमः । भक्तियोगवेत्तासु उत्तमः । यः ←m◦ *yoga* 2.39 + superlative adj◦ *vittama* ←adj◦ *viḍ* 3.29 + affix *tama* 1.7) (12.1)

(§3) ***dvādaśaḥ:*** (adj◦-subj◦ twelfth) ***adhyāyaḥ:*** (subj◦ chapter) ***bhaktiyogaḥ:*** (bhakti-yoga; the Yoga of Devotion). ***arjunaḥ:*** (Arjuna) ***uvāća*** (said). ***evaṃ*** (in this manner) ***satatayuktāḥ:*** (adj1◦-subj1◦ ever-equipped, disciplined, steadfast) ***ye*** (adj2◦-subj1◦ those who) ***bhaktāḥ:*** (subj1◦ devotees) ***tvāṃ*** (obj1◦ you) ***paryupāsate*** (they worship) ***ye*** (subj2◦ those who) ***ća api*** (and) ***akṣaraṃ*** (adj1◦-obj2◦ the Indestructible) ***avyaktaṃ*** (obj2◦ the Unmanifest) ***teṣāṃ*** (among them, among those devotees) ***ke*** (adj1◦-subj1,2◦ who, who are?) 🕮***yogavittamāḥ:*** (adj1◦-subj1,2◦ the best knowers of the bhakti-yoga) (12.1)

(§4) satatayuktāḥ: ye bhaktāḥ: paryupāsate tvām̧ evam̧ ća api ye akṣaram̧ avyaktam̧ teṣām̧ ke yogavittamāḥ:

(§5) Those ever-equipped devotees who worship you in this manner, and those who (worship) the Indestructible Unmanifest (brahma) - among them who are the best knowers of the *bhakti-yoga*?[667] (12.1)

The Lord said (śrībhagavānuvāća श्रीभगवानुवाच ।)

12.2 मय्यावेश्य मनो ये मां नित्ययुक्ता उपासते ।
श्रद्धया परयोपेतास्ते मे युक्ततमा मताः ॥

mayyāveśya mano ye mām̐ nityayuktā upāsate,
śraddhayā parayopetāste me yuktatamāḥ: matāḥ:. (12.2)

(§1) मयि आवेश्य मनः ये माम् नित्ययुक्ताः उपासते । श्रद्धया परया उपेताः ते मे युक्ततमाः मताः ।।*śrībhagavāņ* (r◦ 8/14) *uvāća. mayi* (r◦ 4/2) *āveśya manaḥ:* (r◦ 15/10) *ye mām̧* (r◦ 14/1) *nityayuktāḥ:* (r◦ 20/4) *upāsate śraddhayā parayā* (r◦ 2/4) *upetāḥ:* (r◦ 18/1) *te me yuktatamāḥ:* (r◦ 20/13) *matāḥ:* (r◦ 22/8)

(§2) *śrībhagavāņ* (2.2); *uvāća* (1.25). *mayi* (3.30); *āveśya* (8.10); *manaḥ:* (2acc◦ 1.30); *ye* (1nom◦ 1.7); *mām̧* (1.46); *nityayuktāḥ:* (9.14); *upāsate* (9.14); *śraddhayā* (6.37); *parayā* (1.27); 📖*upetāḥ:* (m◦ 1nom◦ plu◦ ←adj◦ *upeta* 6.37); *te* (1.33); *me* (2.7); *yuktatamāḥ:* (m◦ 1nom◦ plu◦ ←adj◦ *yukta-tama* 6.47); *matāḥ:* (m◦ 1nom◦ plu◦ ←adj◦ *mata* 6.32) (12.2)

(§3) ***mayi*** (in me) ***āveśya*** (having ingressed; having anchored); ***manaḥ:*** (obj◦ mind) ***ye*** (subj◦ those who) ***mām̧*** (obj◦ me) ***nityayuktāḥ:*** (adj1◦-subj◦ the ever-equipped, disciplined, steadfast ones) ***upāsate*** (they worship) ***śraddhayā*** (with faith, with devotion) ***parayā*** (with supreme, deep) ***upetāḥ:*** (adj2◦-subj◦ diligent ones) ***te*** (adj3◦-subj◦ those) ***me*** (to me, for me, in my opinion) ***yuktatamāḥ:*** (adj4◦-subj◦ the best equipped) ***matāḥ:*** (adj5◦-subj◦ considered as) (12.2)

(§4) ye nityayuktāḥ: āveśya manaḥ: mayi upāsate mām̧ parayā śraddhayā me te upetāḥ: matāḥ: yuktatamāḥ:

---

[667] Elsewhere◦ *yogavittamāḥ:* → more perfect, have greater knowledge, better versed ...etc.

📖 तम् suffix attached to the verb √विद् produces a superlative adjective (most, greatest, best), where as the adjectives more, greater, better etc. are comparative expressions formed from the suffix तर । The verb √*viḑ* indicates knowledge, rather than perfection. Also, the adjective perfect implies superlative state not a comparative state. The thing is either imperfect or it is imperfect, but not less perfect or more perfect. The thing is 'imperfect' until it is perfect. For a Gītā student, the only thing that is 'perfect' is *brahma*.

(§5) Those steadfast ones, who, having ingressed[668] their mind in me, worship me with deep devotion, in my opinion those diligent ones (are) the ones who are considered as[669] the best equipped. (12.2)

12.3 ये त्वक्षरमनिर्देश्यमव्यक्तं पर्युपासते ।
सर्वत्रगमचिन्त्यं च कूटस्थमचलं ध्रुवम् ।।

ye tvakṣaramanirdeśyamavyaktaṁ paryupāsate,
sarvatragamaćintyaṁ ća kūṭasthamaćalaṁ dhruvam; (12.3)

(§1) ये तु अक्षरम् अनिर्देश्यम् अव्यक्तम पर्युपासते । सर्वत्रगम् अचिन्त्यम् च कूटस्थम् अचलम् ध्रुवम् ।। *ye tu* (r◦ 4/6) *akṣaram* (r◦ 8/16) *anirdeśyam* (r◦ 8/16) *avyaktam* (r◦ 14/1) *paryupāsate sarvatragam* (r◦ 8/16) *aćintyam* (r◦ 14/1) *ća kūṭastham* (r◦ 8/16) *aćalam* (r◦ 14/1); *dhruvam* (r◦ 14/2)

(§2) *ye* (1.7); *tu* (1.2); *akṣaram* (2acc◦ 8.3); 📖*anirdeśyam* (n◦ 2acc◦ sing◦ ←pot◦ adj◦ *anirdeśya* (explainable) न निर्देश्यम् ←ind◦ *a* 1.10 + 6◦निर्√दिश् (to point out); 📖*avyaktam* (2acc◦ 7.24); *paryupāsate* (4.25); 📖*sarvatragam* (n◦ 2acc◦ sing◦ ←adj◦ *sarvatraga* (omnipresent) 9.6); 📖*aćintyam* (n◦ 2acc◦ sing◦ ←pot◦ adj◦ *aćintya* 2.25); *ća* (1.1); 📖*kūṭastham* (n◦ 2acc◦ sing◦ ←ppp◦ adj◦ *kūṭastha* 6.8); *aćalam* (6.13); *dhruvam* (2acc◦ sing◦ ←adj◦ *dhṛva* 2.27) (12.3)

(§3) ***ye*** (subj◦ those who) ***tu*** (however) ***akṣaram*** (adj1◦-obj◦ the immutable) ***anirdeśyam*** (adj2◦-obj◦ inexplicable) ***avyaktam*** (adj3◦-obj◦ impersonal; unmanifest) ***paryupāsate*** (they worship) ***sarvatragam*** (adj4◦-obj◦ omnipresent) ***aćintyam*** (adj5◦-obj◦ inconceivable) ***ća*** (and) ***kūṭastham*** (adj6◦-obj◦ inaccessible) ***aćalam*** (adj7◦-obj◦ immovable) ***dhruvam*** (adj8◦-obj◦ invariable; steady) (12.3)

(§4) tu ye paryupāsate akṣaram anirdeśyam avyaktam sarvatragam aćintyam kūṭastham aćalam ća

---

[668] Elsewhwre◦ *āveśya* → those who fix, who have fixed, by fixing ...etc.

📖 आवेश्य is a past indeclinable lyp◦ gerundive, with a function of *having done.* It is applied when two actions are performed by the same person or persons, and second (the main) action is contingent upon completion of the first (the subordinate) action. In this case, the first action (√विश् to enter) is completed, i.e. first they are ingressed in me (perfect tense) and then begins main action of पर्युपासते (they worship).

[669] Elsewhere◦ *te me matāḥ:* → them do I consider, them I consider, I regard them, these in my opinion ...etc.

📖 *te* (स: तौ ते) those, (not - these or them); *me* (मे, आवाभ्याम्, अस्मभ्य:) to me, for me (not - by me, do I or I); *matāḥ:* (मत: मतौ मता:) a plural ppp◦ adjective of the subject devotees → the devotees who are regarded as ... (not - I consider; considered by me; or in my opinion). मता: is not a verb, it is a plural ppp◦ adjective. Thus, *te me matāḥ:* → for me, im my opinion, they are the ones who are regarded as ...

dhruvam̩;

(§5) However, those who worship the immutable, inexplicable, impersonal, omnipresent, inconceivable, inaccessible, immovable and invariable; (12.3)

12.4 सन्नियम्येन्द्रियग्रामं सर्वत्र समबुद्धयः ।
ते प्राप्नुवन्ति मामेव सर्वभूतहिते रताः ।।

sanniyamyendriyagrāmaṁ sarvatra samabuddhayaḥ:,
te prāpnuvanti māmeva sarvabhūtahite ratāḥ:. (12.4)

(§1) सन्नियम्य इन्द्रियग्रामम् सर्वत्र समबुद्धयः । ते प्राप्नुवन्ति माम् एव सर्वभूतहिते रताः ।। *sanniyamya* (r◦ 2/1) *indriyagrāmam̩* (r◦ 14/1) *sarvatra samabuddhayaḥ:* (r◦ 22/8) *te prāpnuvanti mām̩* (r◦ 8/22) *eva sarvabhūtahite ratāḥ:* (r◦ 22/8)

(§2) 🕮*sanniyamya* (lyp◦ past-participle ind◦ ←1◦सम्-नि√यम् (to restrain); *indriyagrāmam̩* (6.24); *sarvatra* (2.57); 🕮*samabuddhayaḥ:* (m◦ 1nom◦ plu◦ ←bahuvrī◦ *samabuddhi* (equanimity) 6.9); *te* (1.33); *prāpnuvanti* (3rd-per◦ plu◦ pres◦ वर्तमान्-लट् parasmai◦ ←5◦प्र√आप् (to attain, get); *mām̩* (1.46); *eva* (1.1); *sarvabhūtahite* (5.25); 🕮*ratāḥ:* (5.25) (12.4)

(§3) ***sanniyamya*** **(having controlled, controlling);** ***indriyagrāmam̩*** **(**obj◦ **the group of sense organs; all sense organs - collectively)** ***sarvatra*** **(from all sides; in all respects)** ***samabuddhayaḥ:*** **(adj1◦-**subj◦ **the ones with equanimous mind; the even minded);** ***te*** **(**subj◦ **they)** ***prāpnuvanti*** **(attain, they attain);** ***mām̩*** **(**obj◦ **me)** ***eva*** **(too; only)** ***sarvabhūtahite*** **(in the welfare of all beings)** ***ratāḥ:*** **(adj2◦-**subj◦ **those who are engaged)** (12.4)

(§4) samabuddhayaḥ: ratāḥ: sarvabhūtahite te eva sanniyamya indriyagrāmam̩ sarvatra prāpnuvanti mām̩

(§5) Those who possess equanimous mind[670] (and) are engaged in the welfare of all beings, they too, having controlled[671] all sense organs in all respects,[672] attain[673] me. (12.4)

---

[670] Elsewhere◦ *samabuddhayaḥ:* → with the cognition of sameness, being even-minded ...etc.

🕮 समबुद्धयः is not singular, instrumental case or a gerund. It is not a *tatpuruṣa samāsa*, and therefore, it does not refer to *buddhi*, mind or cognition. It is a plural *bahuvrīhi* adj◦ of those people who possess equanimous mind, the *buddhi-yogī*s, as already explained in the Chapter two 2.49.

[671] Elsewhere◦ *sanniyamya* → by controlling, by fully controlling, by restraining ...etc.

🕮 सन्नियम्य is a lyp◦ prefixed past participle adj◦ → having restrained, restraining. See the first footnote in 12.2

12.5 क्लेशोऽधिकतरस्तेषामव्यक्तासक्तचेतसाम् ।
अव्यक्ता हि गतिर्दुःखं देहवद्भिरवाप्यते ॥

kleśo'dhikatarasteṣāmavyaktāsaktacetasām,
avyaktā hi gatirduḥ:khaṁ dehavadbhiravāpyate. (12.5)

(§1) क्लेशः अधिकतरः तेषाम् व्यक्तासक्तचेतसाम् । अव्यक्ता हि गतिर्दुःखं देहवद्भिरवाप्यते ॥ *kleśaḥ:* (r◦ 15/1) *adhikataraḥ:* (r◦ 18/1) *teṣām* (r◦ 25/3, 8/16) *avyaktāsaktacetasām* (r◦ 14/2) *avyaktā hi gatiḥ:* (r◦ 16/6) *duḥ:kham* (r◦ 14/1) *dehavadbhiḥ:* (r◦ 16/1) *avāpyate*

(§2) 🕮*kleśaḥ:* (1nom◦ sing◦ ←m◦ ***kleśa*** ←4◦√क्लिश् (to be distressed); *adhikataraḥ:* (m◦ 1nom◦ sing◦ ←comparative adj◦ *adhika-tara* ←adj◦ *adhika* 6.22 + comparitive affix *tara* 1.46); *teṣām* (5.16); *avyaktāsaktacetasām* (m◦ 6pos◦ plu◦ ←bahuvrī◦ *avyaktāsakta-cetas*, अव्यक्ते आसक्तं चेतः यस्य ←adj◦ *avyakta* 2.25 + adj◦ *āsakta* 7.1 + n◦ *cetas* 1.38); 🕮*avyaktā* (f◦ 1nom◦ sing◦ ←adj◦ *avyakta* (unpersonified) 2.25); *hi* (1.11); 🕮*gatiḥ:* (4.17); 🕮*duḥ:kham* (adv◦ ind◦ (with difficulty) ←n◦ *duḥ:kha* 2.14); 🕮*dehavadbhiḥ:* (m◦ 3inst◦ plu◦ ←bahuvrī◦ *dehavat* ←m◦ *deha* 2.13 + taddhita◦ affix *vat* 1.5); *avāpyate* (3rd-per◦ sing◦ pres◦ वर्तमान्-लट् ātmane◦ ←5◦अव्√आप् (to attain, get) (12.5)

(§3) ***kleśaḥ:*** (subj1◦ the difficulty, the pain); ***adhikataraḥ:*** (adj◦-subj1◦ greater); ***teṣām*** (of those) ***avyaktāsaktacetasām*** (of those whose minds which are fixed on the Unmanifest) ***avyaktā*** (adj◦-obj◦ the imperceptible, the indiscernible); ***hi*** (because) ***gatiḥ:*** (obj◦ the state; the course; the refuge; the path) ***duḥ:kham*** (adv◦ with difficulty) ***dehavadbhiḥ:*** (subj◦ by the embodied ones; by the living beings); ***avāpyate*** (it is attained) (12.5)

(§4) kleśaḥ: teṣām avyaktāsaktacetasām adhikataraḥ: hi avyaktā gatiḥ: avāpyate duḥ:kham dehavadbhiḥ:

(§5) The pain[674] of those whose minds which are fixed on the Unmanifest, (is) greater;[675]

---

for lyp gerundive.

[672] Elsewhere◦ सर्वत्र समबुद्धयः → even-minded everywhere, sameness at all times, always being even-minded, functioning uniformly everywhere, regarding everything equally, ...etc.

[673] Elsewhere◦ *prāpnuvanti* → they come to, come unto, come in ...etc.

[674] क्लेशः (defination), अविद्यास्मितारागद्वेषाभिनिवेशाः क्लेशाः ॥ (pātañjalayogadarśanam 2.3)

[675] Elsewhere◦ *adhikataraḥ:* → very, very much, very hard ...etc. (as an adverb)

🕮 अधिकतरः is a comparative adjective of the noun क्लेशः । It is not an adverb.

because[676] the imperceptible[677] state is attained with difficulty by the embodied ones.[678] (12.5)

12.6 ये तु सर्वाणि कर्माणि मयि संन्यस्य मत्पराः ।
अनन्येनैव योगेन मां ध्यायन्त उपासते ।।

ye tu sarvāṇi karmāṇi mayi sannyasya matparāḥ:,
ananyenaiva yogena māṁ dhyāyanta upāsate; (12.6)

(§1) ये तु सर्वाणि कर्माणि मयि संन्यस्य मत्पराः । अनन्येन एव योगेन माम् ध्यायन्तः उपासते ।। *ye tu sarvāṇi* (r◦ 24/7) *karmāṇi* (r◦ 24/7) *mayi sannyasya matparāḥ:* (r◦ 22/8) *ananyena* (r◦ 3/1) *eva yogena mām̩* (r◦ 14/1) *dhyāyantaḥ:* (r◦ 19/4) *upāsate*

(§2) *ye* (1.7); *tu* (1.2); *sarvāṇi* (2.30); *karmāṇi* (2.48); *mayi* (3.30); *sannyasya* (3.30); *matparāḥ:* (m◦ 1nom◦ plu◦ ←bahuvrī◦ *matpara* 2.61); *ananyena* (m◦ 3inst◦ sing◦ ←adj◦ *ananya* (singular) 8.14); *eva* (1.1); *yogena* (10.7); *mām̩* (1.46); *dhyāyantaḥ:* (m◦ 1nom◦ plu◦ ←adj◦ *dhyāyat̩* 2.62); *upāsate* (9.14) (12.6)

(§3) *ye* (subj◦ those who) *tu* (however) *sarvāṇi* (adj◦-obj1◦ all) *karmāṇi* (obj1◦ *karmas*, works) *mayi* (in me) *sannyasya* (having relinquished, submitted, surrendeed) *matparāḥ:* (adj1◦-subj◦ those for whom I am the supreme goal); 🕮*ananyena* (with unwavering; with a singular) *eva* (only) *yogena* (with discipline; with the *bhakti*-yoga) *mām̩* (obj2◦ me) 🕮*dhyāyantaḥ:* (adj2◦-subj◦ while contemplating, while concentrating) *upāsate* (they worship) (12.6)

(§4) tu ye matparāḥ: sannyasya sarvāṇi karmāṇi mayi upāsate mām̩ dhyāyantaḥ: eva ananyena

---

[676] see the footnote in verse 2.15

[677] Elsewhere◦ *avyaktā* → toward the unmanifest, toward the unmanifested, path of unmanifest, goal of unmanifest, of the Unmanifest, अव्यक्त, अव्यक्तब्रह्म ...etc.

🕮 अव्यक्ता does not qualify the neuter noun unmanifest (ब्रह्म). It is a feminine adj◦ of the f◦ subject *gatiḥ:* (गतिः). A feminine adjective (अव्यक्ता) can not qualify the neuter noun (ब्रह्म, अव्यक्तब्रह्म, Unmanifest) that is referred in previous word *avyakta-āsakta-ćetasam̩* (अव्यक्त-आसक्त-चेतसाम् ।). These two expressions are separate form each other. There is no genitive or possessive relation between the adj◦ अव्यक्ता and the object गतिः । Both these words are in the Nominative case. Note that, in this Sanskrit passive voice, गतिः is the object (nominative 1st case) and देहवद्भिः is the subject (Instrumental 3rd case), Because, प्रयोगे कर्मवाच्यस्य तृतीया स्यात्तु कर्तरि (देहवद्भिः), कर्मणि प्रथमा (गतिः) चैव, क्रिया (अवाप्यते) कर्मानुसारिणि ।

[678] Elsewhere◦ *dehavadbhiḥ:* → for the embodied.

🕮 देहवद्भिः is not a Dative 4th case (for the embodied), it is Instrumental 3rd case subject = by the embodied (passive construction)

yogena;

(§5) However, those for whom I am the supreme goal,[679] having relinquished all *karmas* in me, they worship me while contemplating[680] only with a singular *bhakti-yoga.* (12.6)

12.7 तेषामहं समुद्धर्ता मृत्युसंसारसागरात् ।
भवामि नचिरात्पार्थ मय्यावेशितचेतसाम् ।।

teṣāmahaṁ samuddhartā mṛtyusaṁsārasāgarāt,
bhavāmi naćirātpārtha mayyāveśitaćetasām. (12.7)

(§1) तेषाम् अहम् समुद्धर्ता मृत्युसंसारसागरात् । भवामि नचिरात् पार्थ मयि आवेशितचेतसाम् ।। *teṣām* (r◦ 25/3, 8/16) *aham* (r◦ 14/1) *samuddhartā mṛtyusaṁsārasāgarāt* (r◦ 23/1) *bhavāmi naćirāt* (r◦ 10/6) *pārtha mayi* (r◦ 4/2) *āveśitaćetasām* (r◦ 14/2)

(§2) *teṣām* (5.16); *aham* (1.22); *samuddhartā* (m◦ 1nom◦ sing◦ ←bahuvrī◦ *samuddhartṛ* ←1◦सम्–उद्√धृ (to bear); *mṛtyusaṁsārasāgarāt* (m◦ 5abl◦ sing◦ ←tatpu◦ *mṛtyu-saṁsār- sāgara*, मृत्युमयस्य संसारस्य सागर: ←m◦ *mṛtyu* (death) 2.27 + m◦ *saṁsāra* (ocean) 9.3 + m◦ *sāgara* 10.24); *bhavāmi* (1st-per◦ sing◦ pres◦ वर्तमान्–लट् parasmai◦ ←1◦√भू (to be, become); *naćirāt* (adv◦ ←adj◦ *naćira* 5.6); *pārtha* (1.25); *mayi* (3.30); *āveśitaćetasām* (m◦ 6pos◦ plu◦ ←bahuvrī◦ *āveśita-ćetas*, आवेशितं चेत: यस्य ←ppp◦ adj◦ *āveśita* ←6◦आ√विश् (to enter) + n◦ *ćetas* 1.38) (12.7)

(§3) ***teṣām*** **(of them)** ***aham*** **(subj◦ I)** ***samuddhartā*** **(adj◦-subj◦ the deliverer, the one who delivers, up-lifts)** ***mṛtyusaṁsārasāgarāt*** **(from the mundane ocean beset with birth and death)** ***bhavāmi*** **(I become);** ***naćirāt*** **(adv◦ without delay; quickly);** ***pārtha*** **(O Pārtha! O Arjuna!);** ***mayi*** **(in me, on me)** ***āveśitaćetasām*** **(Of those whose minds are fixed, of those whose minds have entered)** (12.7)

(§4) āveśitaćetasām mayi pārtha teṣām aham naćirāt bhavāmi samuddhartā mṛtyusaṁsārasāgarāt

(§5) Of those, whose minds are fixed[681] on me, O Arjuna! I quickly[682] become[683] the deliverer[684]

---

[679] Elsewhere◦ *matparāḥ:* → regarding Me, being attached to Me ...etc.

मत्परा: is not a gerund or a verb. मत्परा: is an adjective of the subj◦ those who *ye* (ये) are मयि परायणा: ।

[680] Elsewhere◦ ध्यायन्त: → through meditation, meditate by thinking...etc.

[681] Elsewhere◦ *āveśita* → having fixed.

आवेशित is not a gerund, it is a ppp◦ adj◦ → the one that has entered.

[682] Elsewhere◦ *naćirāt* → swift deliverer.

नचिरात् is not an adjective, and therefore, it does not qualify the m◦ noun deliverer. It is an adverb, and thus,

from the mundane ocean beset with birth and death. (12.7)

12.8 मय्येव मन आधत्स्व मयि बुद्धिं निवेशय ।
निवसिष्यसि मय्येव अत ऊर्ध्वं न संशयः ।।

mayyeva mana ādhatsva mayi buddhiṁ niveśaya,
nivasiṣyasi mayyeva ata ūrdhvaṁ na saṁśayaḥ:. (12.8)

(§1) मयि एव मनः आधत्स्व मयि बुद्धिम् निवेशय । निवसिष्यसि मयि एव अतः ऊर्ध्वम् न संशयः ।। *mayi* (r◦ 4/4) *eva manaḥ:* (r◦ 19/1) *ādhatsva mayi buddhiṃ* (r◦ 14/1) *niveśaya nivasiṣyasi mayi* (r◦ 4/4) *eva* (ārsh exceprion to r◦ 1/1) *ataḥ:* (r◦ 19/5) *ūrdhvaṃ* (r◦ 14/1) *na saṁśayaḥ:* (r◦ 22/8)

(§2) *mayi* (3.30); *eva* (1.1); *manaḥ:* (2acc◦ 6.12); *ādhatsva* (2nd-per◦ sing◦ imperative◦ लोट् ātmane◦ ←3◦आ√धा (to put); *mayi* (3.30); *buddhiṃ* (3.2); *niveśaya* (2nd-per◦ sing◦ imperative◦ लोट् parasmai◦ caus◦ ←6◦नि√विश् (to enter); 🕮*nivasiṣyasi* (2nd-per◦ sing◦ fut2◦ लृट् भविष्य◦ parasmai◦ ←1◦नि√वस् (to stay); *mayi* (3.30); *eva* (1.1); *ataḥ:* (2.12); ***ūrdhvaṃ*** (adv◦ ←adj◦ ***ūrdhva*** (ahead) ←3◦उद्√हा (to go); *na* (1.30); *saṁśayaḥ:* (8.5) (12.8)

(§3) ***mayi*** (in me) ***eva*** (only) ***manaḥ:*** (obj1◦ mind) 🕮***ādhatsva*** (you please anchor) ***mayi*** (in me) ***buddhiṃ*** (obj2◦ the cognizance, understanding, contemplation, thinking, mind) ***niveśaya*** (you please place) 🕮***nivasiṣyasi*** (you will dwell, abide) ***mayi*** (on me) ***eva*** (only) ***ataḥ: ūrdhvaṃ*** (hereafter, henceforth) ***na*** (no) ***saṁśayaḥ:*** (subj◦ doubt) (12.8)

(§4) ādhatsva manaḥ: mayi eva niveśaya buddhiṃ mayi ataḥ: ūrdhvaṃ mayi eva na saṁśayaḥ:

(§5) You please anchor (your) mind in me only (and) you please place (your) contemplation on me, henceforth you will dwell in me, no doubt. (12.8)

12.9 अथ चित्तं समाधातुं न शक्नोषि मयि स्थिरम् ।
अभ्यासयोगेन ततो मामिच्छाप्तुं धनञ्जय ।।

---

it qualifies the verb भवामि → I quickly become.

[683] Elsewhere◦ *bhavāmi* → I shall be.

🕮 भवामि is not a future tense, it is वर्तमान्-लट् present tense from √भू (to become) → I become.

[684] Elsewhere◦ *ahaṁ samuddhartā* → I deliver, I shall be up-lifter, I quickly redeem, ...etc.

🕮 समुद्धर्ता is not a verb. समुद्धर्तु the deliverer, is a m◦ sing◦ nominative adjective of subject अहम्, the one who delivers from... If we say समुद्धर्ता = I deliver, then the verb भवामि has no connection. Therefore, it should be अहं समुद्धर्ता भवामि, I become the deliverer.

atha ćittaṁ samādhātuṁ na śaknoṣi mayi sthiram,
abhyāsayogena tato māmiććhāptuṁ dhanañjaya. (12.9)

(§1) अथ चित्तम् समाधातुम् न शक्नोषि मयि स्थिरम् । अभ्यासयोगेन ततः माम् इच्छ आप्तुम् धनञ्जय ।। ***atha ćittam̧*** (r∘ 14/1) ***samādhātum̧*** (r∘ 14/1) ***na śaknoṣi*** (r∘ 25/4) ***mayi sthiram̧*** (r∘ 14/2) ***abhyāsayogena tataḥ:*** (r∘ 15/9) ***mām̧*** (r∘ 8/18) ***iććha*** (r∘ 1/2) ***āptum̧*** (r∘ 14/1) ***dhanañjaya***

(§2) *atha* (1.7); *ćittam̧* (2acc∘ sing∘ ←n∘ *ćitta* 6.14); *samādhātum̧* (inf∘ ind∘ ←3∘सम्-आ√धा (to put); *na* (1.30); *śaknoṣi* (2nd-per∘ sing∘ pres∘ वर्तमान्-लट् parasmai∘ ←5∘√शक् (to be able); *mayi* (3.30); *sthiram̧* (adv∘ (steadily) adj∘ 6.11); *abhyāsayogena* (m∘ 3inst∘ sing∘ ←tatpu∘ *abhyāsa-yoga*, अभ्यासस्य योगः ←m∘ *abhyāsa* 6.35 + m∘ *yoga* 2.39); *tataḥ:* (1.13); *mām̧* (1.46); *iććha* (2nd-per∘ sing∘ imperative∘ उपदेशार्थ-लोट् parasmai∘ ←6∘√इष् (to desire) 2.49); *āptum̧* (5.6); *dhanañjaya* (2.48) (12.9)

(§3) *atha* (now; now if, in case, but if, if) *ćittam̧* (obj∘ mind) 📖*samādhātum̧* (for concentrating; to focus) *na* (not) *śaknoṣi* (you can, you are able) *mayi* (in me, on me) 📖*sthiram̧* (adv∘ unwaveringly, steadily) *abhyāsayogena* (with the *yoga* of continual practice) *tataḥ:* (then) *mām̧* (obj∘ me) *iććha* (you please desire) 📖*āptum̧* (for attaining, to attain) *dhanañjaya* (O Dhanañjaya! O Arjuna!) (12.9)

(§4) atha śaknoṣi na samādhātum̧ ćittam̧ sthiram̧ mayi tataḥ: dhanañjaya iććha āptum̧ mām̧ abhyāsayogena

(§5) O Arjuna! now if you are not able to focus (your) mind unwaveringly on me, then, you please desire to attain me with the *yoga* of continual practice. (12.9)

12.10 अभ्यासेऽप्यसमर्थोऽसि मत्कर्मपरमो भव ।
मदर्थमपि कर्माणि कुर्वन्सिद्धिमवाप्स्यसि ।।

abhyāse'pyasamartho'si matkarmaparamo bhava,
madarthamapi karmāṇi kurvansiddhimavāpsyasi. (12.10)

(§1) अभ्यासे अपि अयसमर्थः असि मत्कर्मपरमः भव । मदर्थम् अपि कर्माणि कुर्वन् सिद्धिम् अवाप्स्यसि ।। ***abhyāse*** (r∘ 6/1) ***api*** (r∘ 4/1) ***asamarthaḥ:*** (r∘ 15/1) ***asi matkarmaparamaḥ:*** (r∘ 15/8) ***bhava madartham̧*** (r∘ 8/16) ***api karmāṇi*** (r∘ 24/7) ***kurvaņ*** (r∘ 13/20) ***siddhim̧*** (r∘ 8/16) ***avāpsyasi***

(§2) *abhyāse* (7loc∘ sing∘ ←m∘ *abhyāsa* 6.35); *api* (1.26); 📖*asamarthaḥ:* (1nom∘ sing∘ n.tatpu∘ ←adj∘ *samartha* (able) 2.36); *asi* (4.3); *matkarmaparamaḥ:* (m∘ 1nom∘ sing∘ ←bahuvrī∘ *mat-karma-parama*, मम कर्म परमं यस्य ←pron∘ *maţ* 1.9 + n∘ *karmaņ* 1.15 + adj∘ *parama* 1.17); *bhava* (2.45); *madartham̧* (m∘ 2acc∘ sing∘ ←m∘ *madartha* 1.9); *api* (1.26); *karmāṇi* (2.48); *kurvaņ* (4.21); *siddhim̧* (success) (3.4); *avāpsyasi*

(2.33) (12.10)

(§3) ***abhyāse*** (in the continual practice) ***api*** (but however, but if, if; even, also) ***asamarthaḥ:*** (adj1∘-subj∘ unable, weak) ***asi*** (subj∘ you are) ***matkarmaparamaḥ:*** (adj2∘-subj∘ the one whose supreme goal is my service) ***bhava*** (you please be) ***madarthaṃ*** (for my service) ***api*** (even, also) ***karmāṇi*** (obj1∘ the ***karmas***) ***kurvaṇ*** (while performing); ***siddhiṃ*** (obj2∘ accomplishment, success) ***avāpsyasi*** (you will attain) (12.10)

(§4) api asi asamarthaḥ: abhyāse bhava matkarmaparamaḥ: api kurvaṇ karmāṇi madarthaṃ avāpsyasi siddhiṃ

(§5) But if you are weak in the continual practice, please be the one whose supreme goal is my service. (Because,) even while performing[685] the *karmas* for my service, you will attain success.[686] (12.10)

12.11 अथैतदप्यशक्तोऽसि कर्तुं मद्योगमाश्रितः ।
सर्वकर्मफलत्यागं ततः कुरु यतात्मवान् ।।

athaitadapyaśakto'si kartuṁ madyogamāśritaḥ:,
sarvakarmaphalatyāgaṁ tataḥ: kuru yatātmavāṇ. (12.11)

(§1) अथ एतत् अपि अयशक्तः असि कर्तुम् मद्योगम् आश्रितः । सर्वकर्मफलत्यागम् ततः कुरु यतात्मवान् ।। *atha* (r∘ 3/1) *etaṭ* (r∘ 8/2) *api* (r∘ 4/1) *aśaktaḥ:* (r∘ 15/1) *asi kartuṃ* (r∘ 14/1) *madyogaṃ* (r∘ 8/17) *āśritaḥ:* (r∘ 22/8) *sarvakarmaphalatyāgaṃ* (r∘ 14/1) *tataḥ:* (r∘ 22/1) *kuru yatātmavāṇ*

(§2) *atha* (1.7); *etaṭ* (2.6); *api* (1.26); 📖*aśaktaḥ:* (m∘ 1nom∘ sing∘ ←ppp∘ adj∘ *aśakta* (unable, weak) ←5∘अ√शक् (to be able); *asi* (4.3); *kartuṃ* (1.45); 📖*madyogaṃ* (m∘ 2acc∘ sing∘ ←tatpu∘ *madyoga*, मम योगः ←pron∘ *maṭ* 1.9 + m∘ *yoga* 2.39); ***āśritaḥ:*** (m∘ 1nom∘ sing∘ ←adj∘ *āśrita* 7.15); ***sarvakarmaphalatyāgaṃ*** (m∘ 2acc∘ sing∘ ←tatpu∘ *sarva-karma-phala-tyāga*, सर्वेषां कर्मणां फलानां वासनायाः त्यागः ←pron∘ *sarva* 1.6 + n∘ *karmaṇ* 1.15 + n∘ *phala* (desire of the fruit) 2.43 + m∘ ***tyāga*** (renunciation) ←1∘√त्यज् (to renounce); *tataḥ:* (1.13);

---

[685] Elsewhere∘ *kurvaṇ* → by doing, by performing ...etc. (instrumental∘)

📖 कुर्वन् is is present participle adj∘ = while doing, performing.

[686] Elsewhere∘ सिद्धिम् → perfection

📖 see सिद्धिम् in 4.12. Perfection may come, if at all, only after attaining success. Same is true for verses 3.4 and 16.23. In Gita, only *brahma* is perfect, nothing else. See the word सिद्धि is translated is 'success' in verses 18.13 and 18.26 in the same sources.

kuru (2.48); *yatātmavān̩* (m∘ 1nom∘ sing∘ ←adj∘ *yatātmavat̩* (self controlled) ←ind∘ *yat̩* ←1∘√यत् (to strive) + adj∘ *ātmavat̩* 1.5) (12.11)

(§3) ***atha*** **(now; now if, in case, but if, if)** ***etat̩*** **(obj1∘ this)** ***api*** **(also, even)** ***aśaktaḥ:*** **(adj1∘-subj∘ unable, weak)** ***asi*** **(you are)** ***kartum̩*** **(for doing, to do)** ***madyogam̩*** **(obj2∘ my yoga, my** ***bhakti-yoga*****);** ***āśritaḥ:*** **(adj2∘-subj∘ sheltered in);** ***sarvakarmaphalatyāgam̩*** **(obj3∘ renunciation of the desire in the fruit of all** ***karmas*****);** ***tataḥ:*** **(thereupon, then)** ***kuru*** **(you please do)** ***yatātmavān̩*** **(adj3∘-subj∘ self restrained);** (12.11)

(§4) atha api asi aśaktaḥ: kartum̩ etat̩ tataḥ: āśritaḥ: madyogam̩ yatātmavān̩ kuru sarvakarmaphalatyāgam̩

(§5) But if, you are unable to do even this, then, sheltered in[687] my *(bhakti) yoga*[688] (and) self restrained,[689] you please do renunciation of the desire[690] in the fruit of all *karmas (karma-yoga).* (

---

[687] Elsewhere∘ *āśritaḥ:* → taking refuge, having resorted ...etc.

📖 आश्रित is not a present participle gerund, it is past passive participle adj∘ → sheltered, one who has taken refuge; It is one of the two ppp∘ adjectives attached to Arjuna, मद्योगम्-आश्रित: and कर्तुम् अशक्त: असि ।

[688] *madyogaḥ:* → my yoga, my-bhakti-yoga, the yoga of devotion, the yoga for my devotee. 41-signs of a devotee (the subject of verse 12.20) are described in verses 12.13-20, some of which are similar to the signs of the स्थितप्रज्ञ: described in Chapter Two.

[689] Elsewhere∘ *yatātmavān̩* → with self control, with the self subdued, by becoming controlled ...etc.

📖 यतात्मवान् is not an Instrumental case noun, it is a Nominative case adjective attached to the subj∘ Arjuna.

[690] Elsewhere∘ *sarvakarmaphalatyāgam̩* → giving up all results of your work, abandoning the fruit of all actions, renounce the fruit ...etc.

📖 Every action, good as well as bad, has a fruit. Whether you want it or not, everyone gets it unevitably. You have no choice. The fruit of any work is a success or failure, which is abstract. It is unavoidable (अनिवार्य, अनतिक्रमणीय, अपरिहार्य अर्थ:) and not to be renounced. What one can, however, renounce is only the desire or the motive behind the fruit.

If you do सुकर्म, the fruit is पुण्यम्, which you will get, whether you want it or not, you can not renounce it. All you can do is renounce the desire for the fruit before doing that *su-karma.* If you do कुकर्म, the fruit is पापम्, which you can not abandon. If you do कुकर्म, then you can not renounce the fruit of it. If one could do it, there would be no such thing as sin or crime.

There is no such thing as renunciation or abandoning of the fruits of all actions. The Lord says, Arjuna! as a *kṣatriya,* perform the war as a duty, without looking at the future outcome (success or failure, the fruit) i.e. treat the loss or gain equal. But , after doing the duty, if you loose, enjoy the reward, i.e. the स्वर्ग (2.37↑) and if

12.11)

12.12 श्रेयो हि ज्ञानमभ्यासाज्ज्ञानाद्ध्यानं विशिष्यते ।
ध्यानात्कर्मफलत्यागस्त्यागाच्छान्तिरनन्तरम् ।।

śreyo hi jñānamabhyāsājjñānāddhyānaṃ viśiṣyate,
dhyānātkarmaphalatyāgastyāgāc̍c̍hāntiranantaram. (12.12)

(§1) श्रेयः हि ज्ञानम् अभ्यासात् ज्ञानात् ध्यानम् विशिष्यते । ध्यानात् कर्मफलत्यागः त्यागात् शान्तिः अनन्तरम् ।। *śreyaḥ:* (r◦ 15/14) *hi jñānam* (r◦ 8/16) *abhyāsāt* (r◦ 11/2) *jñānāt* (r◦ 9/6) *dhyānam* (r◦ 14/1) *viśiṣyate* (r◦ 25/8) *dhyānāt* (r◦ 10/5) *karmaphalatyāgaḥ:* (r◦ 18/1) *tyāgāt* (r◦ 11/4) *śāntiḥ:* (r◦ 16/1) *anantaram* (r◦ 14/2)

(§2) *śreyaḥ:* (2.5); *hi* (1.11); *jñānam* (3.39); ***abhyāsāt*** (5abl◦ sing◦ ←m◦ *abhyāsa* (practice) 6.35); *jñānāt* (5abl◦ sing◦ ←n◦ *jñāna* 3.3); *dhyānam* (1nom◦ sing◦ ←n◦ ***dhyāna*** (concentration) ←1◦√ध्यै (to meditate); *viśiṣyate* (3.7); *dhyānāt* (5abl◦ sing◦ ←n◦ *dhyāna* ↑); *karmaphalatyāgaḥ:* (m◦ 1nom◦ sing◦ ←tatpu◦ *karma-phala-tyāga*, कर्मफलस्य कामनायाः त्यागः ←n◦ *karma-phala* 4.14 + m◦ *tyāga* 12.11); *tyāgāt* (5abl◦ sing◦ ←m◦ *tyāga* 12.11); *śāntiḥ:* (2.67); *anantaram* (adj◦ or adv◦ ←n.bahuvrī◦ ***anantara*** (unending) नास्ति अन्तरं यस्मात्, निरन्तरम्, अखण्डम् ←4◦अन्√अन् (to move) (12.12)

(§3) ***śreyaḥ:*** (adj◦-subj1◦ better) ***hi*** (because) ***jñānam*** (subj1◦ knowledge) ***abhyāsāt*** (than practice) ***jñānāt*** (than knowledge) ***dhyānam*** (subj2◦ contemplation, concentration) ***viśiṣyate*** (it is superior) ***dhyānāt*** (than contemplation) ***karmaphalatyāgaḥ:*** (subj3◦ renunciation of the motive in the fruit of the karma) ***tyāgāt*** (from the renunciation of the motive in the fruit of karma) ***śāntiḥ:*** (subj4◦ peace) ***anantaram*** (adv◦ steadily, unceasingly; adj◦ everlasting) (12.12)

(§4) jñānam śreyaḥ: abhyāsāt dhyānam viśiṣyate jñānāt karmaphalatyāgaḥ: dhyānāt hi tyāgāt śāntiḥ: anantaram

(§5) Knowledge (is) better than practice; contemplation is superior than knowledge (and)

---

you win, enjoy the fruit of success and the reward of kingdom, do not abandon or renounce it (शत्रून् जीत्वा समृद्धं राज्यं भुङ्क्ष्व 11.33↑). What you must renounce is, not the fruit itself, but renounce the motive of victory before starting the duty and the desire for the reward (प्रतिफलम्) that may follow the sucess (फलम्).

NOTE :फलत्यागः is not a *sandhi* between two dictionary words फल and त्यागः । It is a *samāsa,* joining the words फलं and त्यागः with a logical defination. In Gita, फलत्यागः is not simply a त्यागः of फलम्, but it is logically the त्यागः of the desire (कामना) of फलम्, the result, i.e. निः-कामना-कर्म, निष्-काम-कर्म, निष्कामकर्म ।

renunciation of the motive in the fruit of the *karma* (is better) than contemplation. Because,[691] from the renunciation of the motive in the fruit of *karma*, (comes) everlasting prace; peace (comes) steadily.[692] (12.12)

12.13 अद्वेष्टा सर्वभूतानां मैत्रः करुण एव च ।
निर्ममो निरहङ्कारः समदुःखसुखः क्षमी ।।

advesṭā sarvabhūtānām maitraḥ: karuṇa eva ća,
nirmamo nirahankāraḥ: samaduḥ:khasukhaḥ: kṣamī; (12.13)

(§1) अद्वेष्टा सर्वभूतानाम् मैत्रः करुणः एव च । निर्ममः निरहङ्कारः समदुःखसुखः क्षमी ।। *advesṭā sarvabhūtānām* (r◦ 14/1) *maitraḥ:* (r◦ 22/1) *karuṇaḥ:* (r◦ 19/7) *eva ća nirmamaḥ:* (r◦ 15/6) *nirahankāraḥ:* (r◦ 22/7) *samaduḥ:khasukhaḥ:* (r◦ 22/1) *kṣamī*

(§2) *a-dvesṭā* (1nom◦ sing◦ ←m◦ *a-dvesṭṛ* ←2◦अ√द्विष् (to loath, dislike); *sarva* (1.6); *bhūtānām* (2.69); 📖*maitraḥ:* (m◦ 1nom◦ sing◦ ←adj◦ *maitra* ←m◦ *mitra* 1.38); *karuṇaḥ:* (m◦ 1nom◦ sing◦ ←adj◦ *karuṇa* ←8◦√कृ (to do); *eva* (1.1); *ća* (1.1); 📖*nirmamaḥ:* (2.71); *nirahankāraḥ:* (2.71); ***samaduḥ:khasukhaḥ:*** (m◦ 1nom◦ sing◦ ←bahuvrī◦ *sama-duḥ:kha-sukha* 2.15); *kṣamī* (m◦ 1nom◦ sing◦ ←adj◦ *kṣamin* (forgiving) ←1◦√क्षम् (to forgive) (12.13)

(§3) 📖***advesṭā*** (adj1◦-subj1◦ one who does not hate, one who is non-hater) ***sarva*** (all) ***bhūtānām*** (of beings) ***maitraḥ:*** (adj2◦-subj1◦ one who possesses feeling of friendliness) 📖***karuṇaḥ:*** (adj3◦-subj1◦ one

---

[691] See footnote in verse 2.15

[692] Elsewhere◦ *anantaram* → immediately, instantly, quickly, without delay ...etc.

📖 (1) If we say peace comes instantly or immediately, it means if you listen to the Lord, the peace will come immediately. If you don't listen then the peace will not come immediately. It will come with a delay or slowly.

(2) If we say peace comes steadily, it will mean that if you follow the *yoga*, then everlasting peace will come, it may not come instantly but it will come for ever. And, on the other hand, if you do not follow the *yoga*, the peace may come temporarily or it may possibly not come. What is the use of that peace which comes instantly but does not last, as against the one that comes with time but is everlasting? In fact, progress of the attainment of *karma-yoga* is slow and its result is realised even slowly but steadily, as you progress in success (सिद्धिः). When it truly takes a life time to attain the *nishkam-karmayoga,* how and at what point will you get the result instantly? Therefore, अनन्तरम् → अन् अन्तरम्, न खण्डम्, अखण्डम्, continuous, everlasting; unceasingly, steadily; but not विना-अन्तरम् quickly, instantly, immediately. Same meaning we have seen in in śloka 5.12 for the adj◦ नैष्ठिकीम् । (शान्तिम् आप्नोति नैष्ठिकीम् । he attains everlasting peace)

who is merciful) ***eva ćа*** (and) ***nirmamaḥ:*** (adj4◦-subj1◦ one who does not possess 'mine'-ness) **📖*nirahaṅkāraḥ:*** (adj5◦-subj1◦ one who does not possess 'I'-ness) ***samaduḥ:khasukhaḥ:*** (adj6◦-subj1◦ one who is equanimous to pain and pleasures) **📖*kṣamī*** (adj7◦-subj1◦ one who is forgiving;) (12.13)

(§4) adveṣṭā sarva bhūtānām maitraḥ: karuṇaḥ: samaduḥ:khasukhaḥ: kṣamī nirmamaḥ: eva ća nirahaṅkāraḥ:;

(§5) One who is non-hater of all beings, one who possesses feeling of friendliness, one who is merciful, one who is equanimous to pain and pleasures, one who is forgiving, one who does not possess 'mine'-ness and 'I'-ness; (12.13)

12.14 सन्तुष्टः सततं योगी यतात्मा दृढनिश्चयः ।
मय्यर्पितमनोबुद्धिर्यो मद्भक्तः स मे प्रियः ।।

santuṣṭaḥ: satataṁ yogī yatātmā dṛḍhaniśćayaḥ:,
mayyarpitamanobuddhiryo madbhaktaḥ: sa me priyah:; (12.14)

(§1) सन्तुष्टः सततम् योगी यतात्मा दृढनिश्चयः । मयि अर्पितमनोबुद्धिः यः मद्भक्तः सः मे प्रियः ।। ***santuṣṭaḥ:*** (r◦ 22/7) ***satataṃ*** (r◦ 14/1) ***yogī yatātmā dṛḍhaniśćayaḥ:*** (r◦ 22/8) ***mayi*** (r◦ 4/1) ***arpitamanobuddhiḥ:*** (r◦ 16/6) ***yaḥ:*** (r◦ 15/9) ***madbhaktaḥ:*** (r◦ 22/7) ***saḥ:*** (r◦ 21/2) ***me priyaḥ:*** (r◦ 22/8);

(§2) *santuṣṭaḥ:* (3.17); *satataṃ* (3.19); *yogī* (5.24); *yatātmā* (m◦ 1nom◦ sing◦ ←bahuvrī◦ *yatātmaṇ* 5.25); *dṛḍhaniśćayaḥ:* (m◦ 1nom◦ sing◦ ←bahuvrī◦ *dṛḍha-niśćaya*, दृढः निश्चयः यस्य ←adj◦ *dṛḍha* 6.34 + m◦ *niśćaya* 2.37); *mayi* (3.30); *arpitamanobuddhiḥ:* (8.7); *yaḥ:* (2.19); *madbhaktaḥ:* (9.34); *saḥ:* (1.13); *me* (1.21); *priyaḥ:* (7.17) (12.14)

(§3) ***santuṣṭaḥ:*** (adj8◦-subj1◦ he who is contented) ***satataṃ*** (adv◦ always) ***yogī*** (adj9◦-subj1◦ the yogi) ***yatātmā*** (adj10◦-subj1◦ he who is self-controlled) **📖*dṛḍhaniśćayaḥ:*** (adj11◦-subj1◦ he who is resolute); ***mayi*** (in me) ***arpitamanobuddhiḥ:*** (adj12◦-subj1◦ he who has devoted his mind) ***yaḥ:*** (adj◦-subj1◦ he who) ***madbhaktaḥ:*** (adj13◦-subj1◦ my devotee); ***saḥ:*** (adj14◦-subj1◦ he) ***me*** (for me) ***priyaḥ:*** (adj15◦-subj1◦ dear) (12.14)

(§4) yogī santuṣṭaḥ: satataṃ yatātmā dṛḍhaniśćayaḥ: arpitamanobuddhiḥ: mayi yaḥ: madbhaktaḥ: saḥ: priyaḥ: me;

(§5) The *yogi* who is always contented, he who is self-controlled, he who is resolute,[693] he who

---

[693] Elsewhere◦ *dṛḍhaniśćayaḥ:* → steady in meditation.

has devoted his mind and thought in me, (and) he who is my devotee,[694] - he (is) dear to me; (12.14)

12.15 यस्मान्नोद्विजते लोको लोकान्नोद्विजते च यः ।
हर्षामर्षभयोद्वेगैर्मुक्तो यः स च मे प्रियः ।।

yasmannodvijate loko lokānnodvijate ća yaḥ:,
harṣāmarṣabhayodvegairmukto yaḥ: sa ća me priyaḥ:; (12.15)

(§1) यस्मात् न उद्विजते लोकः लोकात् न उद्विजते च यः । हर्षामर्षभयोद्वेगैः मुक्तः यः सः च मे प्रियः ।। *yasmaṭ* (r◦ 12/1) *na* (r◦ 2/2) *udvijate lokaḥ:* (r◦ 15/12) *lokāṭ* (r◦ 12/1) *na* (r◦ 2/2) *udvijate ća yaḥ:* (r◦ 22/8) *harṣāmarṣabhayodvegaiḥ:* (r◦ 16/11) *muktaḥ:* (r◦ 15/10) *yaḥ:* (r◦ 22/7) *saḥ:* (r◦ 21/2) *ća me priyaḥ:* (r◦ 22/8)

(§2) ***yasmaṭ*** (m◦ or n◦ 5abl◦ sing◦ ←pron◦ *yaḍ* 1.7); *na* (1.30); ***udvijate*** (3rd-per◦ sing◦ pres◦ वर्तमान्-लट् ātmane◦ ←6◦उद्√विज् (to tremble) 5.20); *lokaḥ:* (3.9); *lokāṭ* (5abl◦ sing◦ ←m◦ *loka* 2.5); *na* (1.30); *udvijate* (↑); *ća* (1.1); *yaḥ:* (2.19); *harṣāmarṣabhayodvegaiḥ:* (3inst◦ plu◦ dvandva◦ हर्षेण च आमर्षेण च भयेन च उद्वेगेन च ←m◦ *harṣa* 1.12 (joy) + m◦ *āmarṣa* (pain) ←1◦आ√मृष् (to endure) + n◦ *bhaya* (fear) 2.35 + m◦ *udvega* (distress) 2.56); *muktaḥ:* (5.28); *yaḥ:* (2.19); *saḥ:* (1.13); *ća* (1.1); *me* (1.21); *priyaḥ:* (7.17) (12.15)

(§3) ***yasmaṭ*** **(from whom)** ***na*** **(not)** ***udvijate*** **(it is agitated, pertrubed)** ***lokaḥ:*** **(subj2◦ the world; people collective)** ***lokāṭ*** **(from people, from the world)** ***na*** **(not)** ***udvijate*** **(he is agitated)** ***ća*** **(and)** ***yaḥ:*** **(adj1◦-subj1◦ he who)** ***harṣāmarṣabhayodvegaiḥ:*** **(with pleasure, pain, fear and distress)** ***muktaḥ:*** **(adj16◦-subj1◦ he who has become detached)** ***yaḥ:*** **(adj1◦-subj1◦ he who)** ***saḥ:*** **(adj14◦-subj1◦ he)** ***ća*** **(and)** ***me*** **(for me)** ***priyaḥ:*** **(adj15◦-subj1◦ dear)** (12.15)

(§4) yasmaṭ lokaḥ: na udvijate ća yaḥ: na udvijate lokāṭ ća yaḥ: muktaḥ: harṣāmarṣabhayodvegaiḥ: saḥ: priyaḥ: me

(§5) From whom the world is not agitated, and he who is not agitated from the world, and he who has become detached with[695] pleasure, pain, fear and distress - he (is) dear to me; (12.15)

12.16 अनपेक्षः शुचिर्दक्ष उदासीनो गतव्यथः ।

---

[694] Elsewhere◦ *yaḥ madbhaktaḥ* → that devotee, he my devotee ...etc.

📖 यः (he who) → he who is मद्भक्तः (my devotee) सः मे प्रियः (he is dear to me). Not यः मे प्रियः or सः मद्भक्तः मे प्रियः ।

[695] Elsewhere◦ *udvegaiḥ mukth* → equipoised in, free from ...etc.

सर्वारम्भपरित्यागी यो मद्भक्तः स मे प्रियः ।।

anapekṣa śucirdakṣa udāsīno gatavyathaḥ:,

sarvārambhaparityāgī yo madbhaktaḥ: sa me priyaḥ:; (12.16)

(§1) अनपेक्षः शुचिर्दक्षः उदासीनः गतव्यथः । सर्वारम्भपरित्यागी यः मद्भक्तः सः मे प्रियः ।। *anapekṣaḥ:* (r◦ 22/5) *śuciḥ:* (r◦ 16/6) *dakṣaḥ:* (r◦ 19/4) *udāsīnaḥ:* (r◦ 15/2) *gatavyathaḥ:* (r◦ 22/8) *sarvārambhaparityāgī yaḥ:* (r◦ 15/9) *madbhaktaḥ:* (r◦ 22/7) *saḥ:* (r◦ 21/2) *me priyaḥ:* (r◦ 22/8)

(§2) 📖*anapekṣaḥ:* (m◦ 1nom◦ sing◦ ←n.bahuvrī◦ *anapekṣa* ←1◦अन्–अप√ईक्ष् (to see); 📖 *śuciḥ:* (m◦ 1nom◦ sing◦ ←adj◦ *śuci* 6.11); 📖*dakṣaḥ:* (m◦ 1nom◦ sing◦ ←adj◦ *dakṣa* (prompt) ←1◦√दक्ष् (to be prompt, be competent); *udāsīnaḥ:* (m◦ 1nom◦ sing◦ ←adj◦ *udāsīna* (indifferent) 6.9; *gatavyathaḥ:* (m◦ 1nom◦ sing◦ ←bahuvrī◦ *gata-vyatha*, गताः व्यथाः यस्य ←adj◦ *gata* 2.11 + f◦ *vyathā* 11.49); ***sarvārambhaparityāgī*** (m◦ 1nom◦ sing◦ ←tatpu◦ *sarvārambha-parityāgi*, सर्वेषाम् आरम्भाणाम् परित्यागी ←pron◦ *sarva* 1.6 + m◦ *ārambha* 3.4 + adj◦ ***parityāgin*** ←1◦परि√त्यज् (to renounce); *yaḥ:* (2.19); *madbhaktaḥ:* (9.34); *saḥ:* (1.13); *me* (1.21); *priyaḥ:* (7.17) (12.16)

(§3) ***anapekṣaḥ:*** (adj17◦-subj1◦ **he who does not expect anything from anyone)** ***śuciḥ:*** (adj18◦-subj1◦ **he who is pure)** ***dakṣaḥ:*** (adj19◦-subj1◦ **he who is peompt)** ***udāsīnaḥ:*** (adj20◦-subj1◦ **he who is indifferent)** ***gatavyathaḥ:*** (adj◦21-subj1◦ **he whose susceptibility to anguish has gone away)** ***sarvārambhaparityāgī*** (adj22◦-subj1◦ **he who relinquishes the attachment or authorship of anything that he undertakes, starts);** ***yaḥ:*** (adj1◦-subj◦ **he who)** ***madbhaktaḥ:*** (adj13◦-subj1◦ **he who is my devotee)** ***saḥ:*** (adj14◦-subj1◦ **he)** ***me*** (for me) ***priyaḥ:*** (adj15◦-subj1◦ **dear)** (12.16)

(§4) anapekṣaḥ: śuciḥ: dakṣaḥ: udāsīnaḥ: gatavyathaḥ: sarvārambhaparityāgī yaḥ: madbhaktaḥ: saḥ: priyaḥ: me;

(§5) He who he who does not expect anything from anyone,[696] he who is pure, he who is peompt, he who is indifferent, he whose susceptibility to anguish has gone away, he who relinquishes the attachment or authorship[697] of anything that he starts, and he who is my devotee he (is) dear to me; (12.16)

---

[696] Elsewhere◦ अनपेक्षः → Independent, He who has no wants, he who is free from wants, ...etc.

[697] Elsewhere◦ *sarvārambhaparityāgī* → renouncing, one who has renounced ...etc.

📖 The कृत् suffixes णिनि and घिनुण् when attached to a root they produce an adjective indicating → the one who does or the one who is doer of that verb or a possessor of that nature, e.g. √युज् + घिनुण् = योगिन् the performer of yoga or doer of yoga; the one who practices yoga; or the one who possesses a yogic nature.

12.17 यो न हृष्यति न द्वेष्टि न शोचति न काङ्क्षति ।
शुभाशुभपरित्यागी भक्तिमान्यः स मे प्रियः ।।

yo na hṛṣyati na dveṣṭi na śocati na kāṅkṣati,
śubhāśubhaparityāgī bhaktimānyaḥ: sa me priyaḥ:; (12.17)

(§1) यः न हृष्यति न द्वेष्टि न शोचति न काङ्क्षति । शुभाशुभपरित्यागी भक्तिमान्यः सः मे प्रियः ।। *yaḥ:* (r∘ 15/6) *na hṛṣyati* (r∘ 25/6) *na dveṣṭi na śocati na kāṅkṣati śubhāśubhaparityāgī bhaktimān* (r∘ 13/17) *yaḥ:* (r∘ 22/7) *saḥ:* (r∘ 21/2) *me priyaḥ:* (r∘ 22/8)

(§2) *yaḥ:* (2.19) *na* (1.30); *hṛṣyati* (3rd-per∘ sing∘ pres∘ वर्तमान्-लट् parasmai∘ ←1∘√**हृष्** (to be joyful); *na* (1.30); *dveṣṭi* (2.57); *na* (1.30); ***śocati*** (3rd-per∘ sing∘ pres∘ वर्तमान्-लट् parasmai∘ ←1∘√शुच् (to lament); *na* (1.30); *kāṅkṣati* (5.3); *śubhāśubhaparityāgī* (m∘ 1nom∘ sing∘ ←bahuvrī∘ *śubhāśubha-parityāgin*, शुभम् च अशुभम् च परित्यजति यः ←adj∘ *śubha* 2.57 + adj∘ *āśubha* 2.57 + adj∘ *parityāgin* (12.16); 🕮***bhaktimān*** (m∘ 1nom∘ sing∘ ←adj∘ *bhaktimat* ←1∘√भज् (to adore, worship); *yaḥ:* (2.19); *saḥ:* (1.13); *me* (1.21); *priyaḥ:* (7.17) (12.17)

(§3) *yaḥ:* (adj1∘-subj1∘ he who) *na* (neither) *hṛṣyati* (he gets filled with joy) *na* (not) *dveṣṭi* (he develops hate) *na* (not) *śocati* (he laments) *na* (not) *kāṅkṣati* (he goes after wants) *śubhāśubhaparityāgī* (adj23∘-subj∘ he who forsakes the sentiments in pleasant as well as unpleasent things); *bhaktimān* (adj24∘-subj1∘ he who is full of devotion) *yaḥ:* (adj1∘-subj1∘ he who) *saḥ:* (adj14∘-subj1∘ he) *me* (for me) *priyaḥ:* (adj15∘-subj1∘ dear) (12.17)

(§4) yaḥ na hṛṣyati na dveṣṭi na śocati na kāṅkṣati śubhāśubhaparityāgī yaḥ: bhaktimān saḥ priyaḥ me;

(§5) He who neither gets filled with joy not he develops hate, not he laments, not he goes after wants, he who forsakes the sentiments in pleasant as well as unpleasent things[698] (and) he who is full of devotion he (is) dear to me; (12.17)

12.18 समः शत्रौ च मित्रे च तथा मानापमानयोः ।
शीतोष्णसुखदुःखेषु समः सङ्गविवर्जितः ।।

samaḥ: śatrau ća mitre ća tathā mānāpamānayoḥ:,
śītoṣṇasukhaduḥ:kheṣu samaḥ: saṅgavivarjitaḥ:; (12.18)

---

[698] Elsewhere∘ *śubhāśubhaparityāgī* → renouncing good and evil...

🕮 One can not renounce good and evil that comes to you. But, what one can do only is to be indifferent to the sentiments of whatever good and evil comes to you. They are beyond your control.

(§1) समः शत्रौ च मित्रे च तथा मानापमानयोः । शीतोष्णसुखदुःखेषु समः सङ्गविवर्जितः ।। *samaḥ:* (r◦ 22/5) *śatrau ća mitre ća tathā mānāpamānayoḥ:* (r◦ 22/8) *śītoṣṇasukhaduḥ:kheṣu* (r◦ 25/5) *samaḥ:* (r◦ 22/7) *saṅgavivarjitaḥ:* (r◦ 22/8)

(§2) *samaḥ:* (2.48); *śatrau* (7loc◦ sing◦ ←m◦ *śatru* (enemy) 3.43); *ća* (1.1); *mitre* (7loc◦ sing◦ ←m◦ *mitra* (friend) 1.38); *ća* (1.1); *tathā* (1.8); *mānāpamānayoḥ:* (6.7); *śītoṣṇasukhaduḥ:kheṣu* (6.7); *samaḥ:* (2.48); *saṅgavivarjitaḥ:* (m◦ 1nom◦ sing◦ ←tatpu◦ *saṅga-vivarjita,* सङ्गात् विवर्जितः ←m◦ *saṅgaḥ:* (attachment) 2.47 + ppp◦ adj◦ *vivarjita* (freed) 7.11) (12.18)

(§3) ***samaḥ:*** (adj25-subj1◦ **equanimous; he who is equanimous or indifferent to)** ***śatrau*** **(between one who considers himself an enemy)** ***ća*** **(and)** ***mitre*** **(between one who considers him a friend)** ***ća*** **(and)** ***tathā*** **(as well as)** ***mānāpamānayoḥ:*** **(in honour and dishonour)** ***śītoṣṇasukhaduḥ:kheṣu*** **(in cold and warm feelings and in pleasure and pain)** ***samaḥ:*** (adj◦26-subj1◦ **he who is equanimous)** 📖***saṅgavivarjitaḥ:*** (adj27◦-subj1◦ **he who has freed himself from attachments)** (12.18)

(§4) samaḥ: śatrau ća mitre tathā mānāpamānayoḥ: ća samaḥ: śītoṣṇasukhaduḥ:kheṣu saṅgavivarjitaḥ:;

(§5) He who is equanimous between one who considers him an enemy and one who considers him a friend[699] as well as in honour and dishonour; and he who is equanimous in cold and warm feelings[700] and in pleasure and pain; he who has freed himself from attachments; (12.18)

12.19 तुल्यनिन्दास्तुतिर्मौनी सन्तुष्टो येन केनचित् ।
अनिकेतः स्थिरमतिर्भक्तिमान्मे प्रियो नरः ।।

tulyanindāstutirmaunī santuṣṭo yena kenaćit,
aniketaḥ: sthiramatirbhaktimānme priyo naraḥ:. (12.19)

(§1) तुल्यनिन्दास्तुतिर्मौनी सन्तुष्टः येन केनचित् । अनिकेतः स्थिरमतिः भक्तिमान् मे प्रियः नरः ।। *tulyanindāstutiḥ:* (r◦

---

[699] Elsewhere◦ शत्रौ च मित्रे च → your enemy and friend, to foe and friend, ...etc.

📖 Here the thing to remember is that 'you' should not be anyone's enemy and no one should be enemy to 'you.' Other people may think you an enemy or a friend, that is their way. That is not your way. 'Your' should be warm hearted (सुहृद्) to everyone regardless of whether he considers you a his friend or his enemy, and thus being equanimous, you can be समशत्रौ च मित्रे च । See answer to Question 11

[700] Elsewhere◦ शीतोष्णसुखदुःखेषु → cold and heat, cold and hot, winter and summer, cold and warmth, ...etc.

📖 Here शीत and उष्ण are not to be translated in their literal meanings. They mean : the cold and warm feelings, the good and bad times, favourable and unfavourable events, the ups and downs in the life, ...etc.

16/6) *maunī santuṣṭaḥ:* (r◦ 15/10) *yena kenacit* (r◦ 23/1) *aniketaḥ:* (r◦ 22/7) *sthiramatiḥ:* (r◦ 16/6) *bhaktimān* (r◦ 13/16) *me priyaḥ:* (r◦ 15/6) *naraḥ:* (r◦ 22/8)

(§2) *tulyanindāstutiḥ:* (m◦ 1nom◦ sing◦ ←bahuvrī◦ *tulya-nindā-stuti*, तुल्ये निन्दा च स्तुतिः च यस्य ←adj◦ ***tulya*** ←10◦√तुल् (to weigh) + f◦ ***nindā*** (criticism) ←1◦√निन्द् (to criticize)+ f◦ *stuti* (praise) 11.21); *maunī* (1nom◦ sing◦ ←m◦ *maunin* ←4◦√मन् (to think); *santuṣṭaḥ:* (3.17); *yena* (2.17); *kenacit* (3inst◦ sing◦ ←pron◦ *kaścit* 2.17); *aniketaḥ:* (m◦ 1nom◦ sing◦ ←bahuvrī◦ *a-niketa*, नास्ति निकेते आसक्ति यस्य सः ←negative affix *a* अ 1.10 + m◦ *niketa* ←1◦नि√कित् (to examine); *sthiramatiḥ:* (m◦ 1nom◦ sing◦ ←bahuvrī◦ *sthira-mati*, स्थिरा मतिः यस्य ←adj◦ *sthira* (steady) 1.16 + f◦ *mati* (mind) 6.36); *bhaktimān* (12.17); *me* (1.21); *priyaḥ:* (7.17); *naraḥ:* (2.22) (12.19)

(§3) ***tulyanindāstutiḥ:*** **(adj28◦-subj1◦ he who is equanimous to criticism and praises)** ***maunī*** **(adj29◦-subj1◦ he who is quiet)** ***santuṣṭaḥ:*** **(adj30◦-subj1◦ he who is contented);** ***yena kenacit*** **(with anything whatever may come)** ***aniketaḥ:*** **(adj31◦-subj1◦ one who is detached from his abode);** ***sthiramatiḥ:*** **(adj32◦-subj1◦ he whose mind is stable)** ***bhaktimān*** **(adj33◦-subj◦ he who is full of devotion)** ***me*** **(for me)** ***priyaḥ:*** **(adj15◦-subj◦ dear)** ***naraḥ:*** **(subj1◦ a person)** (12.19)

(§4) tulyanindāstutiḥ maunī santuṣṭaḥ yena kenacit aniketaḥ sthiramatiḥ: bhaktimān priyaḥ: naraḥ me;

(§5) He who is equanimous to criticism and praises, he who is quiet, he who is contented[701] with anything whatever may come, one who is detached from his abode,[702] he whose mind is stable (and) he who is full of devotion (is) a dear person to me; (12.19)

12.20 ये तु धर्म्यामृतमिदं यथोक्तं पर्युपासते ।
श्रद्दधाना मत्परमा भक्तास्तेऽतीव मे प्रियाः ।।

ye tu dharmyāmṛtamidaṁ yathoktaṁ paryupāsate,
śraddadhānā matparamā bhaktāste'tīva me priyaḥ:. (12.20)

---

[701] Elsewhere◦ *santuṣṭaḥ:* → content (noun or noun used as an adj◦)

📖 सन्तुष्ट is a past participle ppp◦ adj◦ → one who is contented, satisfied, not desiring anything more or different; where contented (सन्तुष्टः) is a pp◦ of content (सन्तोषः), the noun that is contained.

[702] *aniketaḥ:* अनिकेतः is not a person who has lost his home, sold his house, can not buy a house, or has become homeless, but a it is he who is detached from (unattached to) his abode. To be अनिकेतः is to take upone of the four stages (चतुराश्रमाः) in the life of a righteous person.

(§1) ये तु धर्म्यामृतम् इदम् यथोक्तम् पर्युपासते । श्रद्दधानाः मत्परमाः भक्ताः ते अतीव मे प्रियाः ।। *ye tu dharmyāmṛtam* (r∘ 8/18) *idam* (r∘ 14/1) *yathā* (r∘ 2/4) *uktam* (r∘ 14/1) *paryupāsate śraddadhānāḥ:* (r∘ 20/13) *matparamāḥ:* (r∘ 20/12) *bhaktāḥ:* (r∘ 18/1) *te* (r∘ 6/1) *atīva me priyaḥ:* (r∘ 22/8)

(§2) *ye* (1nom∘ 1.7); *tu* (1.2); *dharmyāmṛtam* (n∘ 2acc∘ sing∘ ←tatpu∘ *dharmyāmṛta*, धर्ममयम् अमृतम् ←adj∘ *dharmya* (righteous) or m∘ *dharma* 1.1 + n∘ *amṛta* (nectar) 2.15); *idam* (2acc∘ 1.10); *yathā* (1.11); *uktam* (2acc∘ 11.1); *paryupāsate* (4.25); *śraddadhānāḥ:* (1nom∘ plu∘ ←m∘ *śraddadhāna* (faithful) ←3∘श्रत्√धा (to put); *matparamāḥ:* (m∘ 1nom∘ plu∘ ←adj∘ *matparama* 11.55); *bhaktāḥ:* (9.33); *te* (1.33); *atīva* (extent indicating adv∘ ind∘ *atīva* ←1∘√अत् (to wander); *me* (1.21); *priyaḥ:* (m∘ 1nom∘ sing∘ ←adj∘ *priya* 1.23) (12.20)

(§3) ***ye*** (adj∘-subj2∘ those who) ***tu*** (certainly) ***dharmyāmṛtam*** (obj∘ the righteous, virtuous, pious nectar of immortality); ***idam*** (adj1∘-obj∘ this) ***yathā*** (in this manner) ***uktam*** (adj2∘-obj∘ described) ***paryupāsate*** (they revere) 🕮***śraddadhānāḥ:*** (adj∘1-subj2∘ those who are faithful); ***matparamāḥ:*** (adj2∘-subj2∘ those for whom I am the supreme goal); ***bhaktāḥ:*** (subj2∘ devotees) ***te*** (adj3∘-subj2∘ those) 🕮***atīva*** (adv∘ very) ***me*** (for me) ***priyaḥ:*** (adj3∘-subj2∘ dear) (12.20)

(§4) tu ye paryupāsate idam dharmyāmṛtam uktam yathā śraddadhānāḥ: matparamāḥ: te bhaktāḥ: atīva priyaḥ: me

(§5) Certainly, those who revere this pious nectar of immortality[703] described in this manner, those who are faithful,[704] those for whom I am the supreme goal,[705] those devotees (are) very dear for me. (12.20)

इति श्रीमद्भगवद्गीतासूपनिषत्सु ब्रह्मविद्यायां योगशास्त्रे

---

[703] Elsewhere∘ *dharmyāmṛtam* → immortal virtues, immortalwisdom, immortal dharma ...etc.

🕮 In this *karmadhāraya tatpuruṣa samāsa*, धर्म्य righteous, virtuous, pious is the adjective; and अमृतम्, the nectar of immortality, is the noun; not other way around. In this *sāmāsic* word *amṛtam* (the divine message) being the second (प्रधान) word, this compound word is referring to the *amṛta* of which *dharma* is a qualifier, not the other way around.

[704] Elsewhere∘ *śraddadhānāḥ:* → with faith.

🕮 श्रद्दधान is an adjective formed from ind∘ prefix श्रत् (faith, truth, belief) attached to the root √धा (to bear, hold; दधाति) श्रत् + √धा → adj∘ he who bears faith, the faithful. श्रद्दधानाः is Nominative case plural adjective, not the Instrumental case singular noun.

[705] Elsewhere∘ *matparamāḥ:* → holding, looking upon, making, taking, having taken Me ...etc.

🕮 मत्परमः is not a gerund or क्त्वा participle. It is a simple adj∘ → he, for whom I am परमः ।

श्रीकृष्णार्जुनसंवादे भक्तियोगो नाम द्वादशोऽध्यायः ।

iti śrīmadbhagavadgītāsūpaniṣatsu brahmavidyāyām̐ yogaśāstre

śrīkṛṣṇārjunasam̐vāde bhaktiyogo nāma dvādaśo'dhyāyaḥ:.

(§1) इति श्रीमद्भगवद्गीतासु उपनिषत्सु ब्रह्मविद्यायां योगशास्त्रे श्रीकृष्णार्जुनसंवादे भक्तियोगः नाम द्वादशः अध्यायः । *iti śrīmadbhagavadgītāsu* (r∘ 1/8) *upaniṣatsu brahmavidyāyām* (r∘ 14/1) *yogaśāstre śrīkṛṣṇārjunasam̐vāde bhaktiyogaḥ:* (r∘ 15/6) *nāma dvādaśaḥ:* (r∘ 15/1) *adhyāyaḥ:* (r∘ 22/8)

(§2) *iti* (1.25); *śrīmadbhagavadgītāsu* (f∘ 7loc∘ plu∘ tatpu∘ *śrīmad-bhagavad-gītā* ←adj∘ *śrīmat* 6.41 + adj∘ *bhagavat* 10.14 + f∘ *gītā* ←5∘√गै (to sing); *upaniṣatsu* (7loc∘ plu∘ ←f∘ *upaniṣad* ←6∘उप-नि√सद् (to sit); *brahmavidyāyām* (f∘ 7loc∘ sing∘ ←tatpu∘ *brahma-vidyā,* ब्रह्मणः विद्या ←n∘ *brahman* 2.72 + *vidyā* 5.18); *yogaśāstre* (n∘ 7loc∘ sing∘ ←tatpu∘ *yoga-śāstra,* योगानां शास्त्रम् । योगस्य शास्त्रम् । ←m∘ *yoga* 2.39 + n∘ *śāstra* 15.20); *śrīkṛṣṇārjunasam̐vāde* (m∘ 7loc∘ sing∘ ←tatpu∘ *śrī-kṛṣṇārjuna-sam̐vāda,* श्रीकृष्णस्य च अर्जुनस्य च संवादः ←adj∘ *śrī* 10.34 + m∘ prop∘ *kṛṣṇa* 1.28 + m∘ prop∘ *arjuna* 1.4 + m∘ *sam̐vāda* 18.70); *bhaktiyogaḥ:* (m∘ 1nom∘ sing∘ ←tatpu∘ *bhakti-yoga* भक्तेः योगः ←f∘ *bhakti* (devotion) 7.17 + m∘ *yoga* 2.39); *nāma* (1nom∘ sing∘ ←n∘ *nāman* ←1∘√म्ना (to remember); *dvādaśaḥ:* (m∘ 1nom∘ sing∘ ←num∘ adj∘ *dvādaśa* (twelfth) ←1∘√द्दृ (to hinder) + 1∘√दंश् (to hinder); *adhyāyaḥ:* (1nom∘ sing∘ ←m∘ *adhyāya* (chapter) ←1∘अधि√इ (to enter, come, go) (12.20)

(§3) *iti* (thus) *śrīmadbhagavadgītāsu upaniṣatsu* (among the upaniṣads of the Śrīmad-Bhagavadgītā) *brahmavidyāyām* (of the eternal wisdoms) *yogaśāstre* (in the science of Yoga) *śrīkṛṣṇārjunasam̐vāde* (in the dialogue between Śrī Kṛṣṇa and Arjuna) *bhaktiyogaḥ:* (Bhaktiyoga) *nāma* (called, named) *dvādaśaḥ:* (obj∘-subj∘ the twelfth) *adhyāyaḥ:* (subj∘ discourse; chapter) (12.20)

(§4) śrīmadbhagavadgītāsu upaniṣatsu yogaśāstre brahmavidyāyām iti dvādaśaḥ: adhyāyaḥ: nāma bhaktiyogaḥ: śrīkṛṣṇārjunasam̐vāde

(§5) Among the upaniṣads of the Śrīmad-Bhagavadgītā, in the science of Yoga of self realization, thus (is) the twelfth discourse called 'Bhaktiyoga,' in the dialogue between Śrī Kṛṣṇa and Arjuna.

CHAPTER 13

trayodaśo'dhyāyaḥ:

त्रयोदशोऽध्याय: ।

THE YOGA OF "THE BODY AND ITS KNOWER"[706]

kṣetrakṣetrajñavibhāgayogaḥ:

क्षेत्रक्षेत्रज्ञविभागयोग: ।

Arjuna said (arjuna uvāća अर्जुन उवाच ।)

Arjuna's saṁskṛt words :

13.1 प्रकृतिं पुरुषं चैव क्षेत्रं क्षेत्रज्ञमेव च । एतद्वेदितुमिच्छामि ज्ञानं ज्ञेयं च केशव ।।

prakṛtiṁ puruṣaṁ ćaiva kṣetraṁ kṣetrajñameva ća,

etadveditumiććhāmi jñānaṁ jñeyaṁ ća keśava. **(13.1)**

PLEASE NOTE :

(§1) = Analysis of the verse, with the 25 Sandhi Rules explained in Volume I,

(§2) = Grammatical analysis of each Sanskrit word with the rules given in Volume I,

(§3) = Plain grammatical English meaning of each Sanskrit word of the shloka based on the grammar given in Step §2. These exact English words to be used in step §5 below,

(§4) = Sanskrit words re-arranged in the order of English syntax,

(§5) = English meaning of the shloka, exactly as translated in step §3 above.

(§1) **Analysis of the verse, with the 25 Sandhi Rules explained in Volume I :**

trayodaśaḥ: (r◦ 15/1) *adhyāyaḥ:* (r◦ 22/8). *kṣetra-kṣetrajña-vibhāga-yogaḥ:* (r◦ 22/8). *arjunaḥ:* (r◦ 19/4) *uvāća. prakṛtiṃ* (r◦ 14/1) *puruṣaṃ* (r◦ 14/1) *ća* (r◦ 3/1) *eva kṣetraṃ* (r◦ 14/1) *kṣetrajñaṃ* (r◦ 8/22) *eva ća* (r◦ 23/1) *etaṭ* (r◦ 9/11) *veditum* (r◦ 8/18) *iććhāmi jñānaṃ* (r◦ 14/1) *jñeyaṃ* (r◦ 14/1) *ća keśava*

(§2) **Grammatical analysis of each Sanskrit word with the rules of grammar given in Vol. I :**

trayodaśaḥ: (m◦ 1nom◦ sing◦ ←sequence indicating num◦ adj◦ *trayodaśa* ←num◦ *tri* 2.45 + num◦ *daśa* 13.6); *adhyāyaḥ:* (1nom◦ sing◦ ←m◦ *adhyāya* ←अधि√इ). *kṣetrakṣetrajñavibhāgayogaḥ:* (m◦ 1nom◦ sing◦

---

[706] Elsewhere◦ *kṣetrakṣetrajñavibhāgayogaḥ:* → Nature, the Enjoyer and Consciousness; Matter and Spitit; Discrimination between Nature and Soul; ..etc.

←tatpu◦ *kṣetra-kṣetrajña-vibhāga-yoga,* क्षेत्रस्य च क्षेत्रज्ञस्य च विभागयोः योगः ←n◦ *kṣetra* 1.1 + m◦ *kṣetrakṣetrajña* 13.1 + m◦ *vibhāga* 3.28 + m◦ *yoga* 2.39). *arjunaḥ:* (1.28); *uvāća* (1.25). *prakṛtiṃ* (3.33); *puruṣaṃ* (2.15); *ća* (1.1); *eva* (1.1); *kṣetraṃ* (2acc◦ sing◦ ←n◦ *kṣetra* 1.1); *kṣetrajñaṃ* (m◦ 2acc◦ sing◦ ←bahuvrī◦ adj◦ or m◦ *kṣetrajña,* क्षेत्रम् जानाति यः ←n◦ *kṣetra* 1.1 + adj◦ *jña* 3.26); *eva* (1.1); *ća* (1.1); *etaṭ* (2acc◦ 2.6); 📖*veditum* (18.1); *iććhāmi* (1.35); *jñānaṃ* (2acc◦ 3.40); *jñeyaṃ* (2acc◦ 1.39); *ća* (1.1); *keśava* (1.31) (13.1)

(§3) **Plain grammatical English meaning of each one of the Sanskrit words of the shloka (exact same English words to be used in step 5 below) :**

trayodaśaḥ: (adj◦-subj◦ thirteenth); *adhyāyaḥ:* (subj◦ chapter). *kṣetrakṣetrajñavibhāgayogaḥ:* (yoga of Discrimination between the body and its knower). *arjunaḥ:* (subj◦ Arjun 1.28); *uvāća* (said 1.25).

prakṛtiṃ (obj1◦ prakṛti); *puruṣaṃ* (obj2◦ *puruṣa*); *ća* (and); *kṣetraṃ* (obj3◦ kṣetra, the body); *kṣetrajñaṃ* (obj4◦ kṣetrajña, the witness in the body); *eva* (as well as1.1); *etaṭ* (adj◦-obj1-4◦ this); *veditum* (to know); *iććhāmi* (I desire); *jñānaṃ* (obj5◦ jñāna); *jñeyaṃ* (obj6◦ jñeya); *ća* (and); *keśava* (O Kṛṣṇa!) (13.1)

(§4) **Sanskrit words re-arranged in the order of English syntax :**

trayodaśaḥ: adhyāyaḥ:. kṣetrakṣetrajñavibhāgayogaḥ:. arjunaḥ: uvāća. keśava iććhāmi veditum etaṭ prakṛtiṃ puruṣaṃ kṣetraṃ ća kṣetrajñaṃ eva jñānaṃ ća jñeyaṃ

(§5) English meaning of the shloka, exactly as translated in step (§3) above[707]

Thirteenth chapter. Yoga of Discrimination between the Body and the Witness in the body. Arjuna said. O Keshava![708] (Kṛṣṇa!) I desire[709] to know (what is) this[710] *prakṛti, puruṣa,*[711]

---

[707] The true meaning of an original verse, as it is, lies ONLY within Kṛṣṇa's and Vyāsa's Sanskṛt words, and nowhere else. It can only be obtained by understanding the original Saṁskṛt words and then deducting your own heartfelt meaning. There is no better way. Any translation or commentary is not a substitute. For your help, alternate Sanskṛt words are provided for most of the KEY WORDS. They are your second best guide.

PLEASE treat English meaning of Saṁskṛt text as an approximation only. Do not depend solely on translation and defeat the purpose of this book. Please use it only as a guide, if and when you need help. Giving the English translation is not within the objectives of this book, however, it is provided just to complete the step-by-step flow and proper termination of the process of explanation. Notwithstanding, to render an honest translation in step 5, care is taken to use the same English words given as meaning in step 3 above. It holds good for the entire book.

[708] elsewhere◦ केशव = Handsome haired one; Brahma-Vishṇu-Rudra, embodiment of Vedic Trinity,

kṣetra and *kṣetrajña* as well as *jñāna* and *jñeya*. (13.1)

The Lord said (śrībhagavānuvāća श्रीभगवानुवाच ।)

13.2 इदं शरीरं कौन्तेय क्षेत्रमित्यभिधीयते । एतद्यो वेत्ति तं प्राहु: क्षेत्रज्ञ इति तद्विद: ।।

idaṁ śarīraṁ kaunteya kṣetramityabhidhīyate,
etadyo vetti taṁ prāhuḥ: kṣetrajña iti tadvidaḥ:; (13.2)

(§1) *śrībhagavān* (r◦ 8/14) *uvāća. idam* (r◦ 14/1) *śarīram* (r◦ 14/1) *kaunteya kṣetram* (r◦ 8/18) *iti* (r◦ 4/1) *abhidhīyate* (r◦ 23/1) *etat* (r◦ 9/9) *yaḥ:* (r◦ 15/13) *vetti tam* (r◦ 14/1) *prāhuḥ:* (r◦ 22/1) *kṣetrajñaḥ:* (r◦ 19/2) *iti tadvidaḥ:* (r◦ 22/8);

(§2) *śrībhagavān* (2.2); *uvāća* (1.25) *idam* (1nom◦ 1.10); *śarīram* (1nom◦ sing◦ ←n◦ *śarīra* 1.29); *kaunteya* (2.14); ***kṣetram*** (1nom◦ sing◦ ←n◦ 🕮*kṣetra* 13.1); *iti* (1.25); 🕮*abhidhīyate* (3rd-per◦ sing◦ pres◦ वर्तमान्-लट् ātmane◦ ←class3◦ अभि√धा); *etat* (2acc◦ 2.3); *yaḥ:* (2.19); *vetti* (2.19); *tam* (2.1); *prāhuḥ:* (6.2); *kṣetrajñaḥ:* (m◦ 1nom◦ sing◦ ←adj◦ *kṣetrajña* 1.0); *iti* (1.25); *tadvidaḥ:* (m◦ 1nom◦ plu◦ ←bahuvrī◦ *tadvid*, तत् वेत्ति य: ←pron◦ *tat* 1.10 + adj◦ *vid* 3.29); (13.2)

(§3) *śrībhagavān* (Lord Kṛṣṇa); *uvāća* (said). *idam* (adj◦-subj1◦ this); *śarīram* (subj1◦ body); *kaunteya* (O Arjuna!); *kṣetram* (adj2◦-subj1◦ kṣetra); *iti abhidhīyate* (is called as); *etat* (adj1◦-obj1◦ this, as just said); *yaḥ:* (subj2◦ he who); *vetti* (knows); *tam* (obj2◦ to him); *prāhuḥ:* (they call); *kṣetrajñaḥ:* (adj2◦-subj2) knower of the *kṣetram*); *iti* (ind◦ as, thus); *tadvidaḥ:* (its knowers); (13.2)

(§4) śrībhagavān uvāća kaunteya idam śarīram iti abhidhīyate kṣetram yaḥ: vetti etat tam tadvidaḥ: prāhuḥ: iti kṣetrajñaḥ:;

(§5) Lord Kṛṣṇa said. O Arjuna! this body is called as *"kṣetram."* He who knows this, to him, its knowers call *"kṣetrajñaḥ:."* (13.2)

13.3 क्षेत्रज्ञं चापि मां विद्धि सर्वक्षेत्रेषु भारत ।
क्षेत्रक्षेत्रज्ञयोर्ज्ञानं यत्तज्ज्ञानं मतं मम ।।

🕮 केशव (क: + इश + √वा + इ) Astonished at the divine acts of child Kṛṣṇa (बाललीला:), the people of *vraj* Gokul, Mathura and Vṛndāvana exclaimed स: "क ईशो वा!" (*kaḥ īśḥ vā* "is he, God or what!") क: ईश: वा = केशवा, केशव

[709] elsewhere◦ वेदितुम इच्छामि् = I should kike to know.

[710] elsewhere◦ एतत् = these

🕮 एतत् is a singular n◦ adjective, refering to the statement "इदं शरीरं क्षेत्रमित्यिभिधीयते" - एतत् ।

[711] elsewhere◦ पुरुष = spirit, person, man, the enjoyer.

kṣetrajñaṁ ćāpi māṁ viddhi sarvakṣetreṣu bhārata,
kṣetrakṣetrajñayorjñānaṁ yattajjñānaṁ mataṁ mama. (13.3)

(§1) *kṣetrajñaṃ* (r◦ 14/1) *ća* (r◦ 1/1) *api māṃ* (r◦ 14/1) *viddhi sarvakṣetreṣu* (r◦ 25/5) *bhārata kṣetrakṣetrajñayoḥ:* (r◦ 16/12) *jñānaṃ* (r◦ 14/1) *yaṭ* (r◦ 1/10) *taṭ* (r◦ 11/2) *jñānaṃ* (r◦ 14/1) *mataṃ* (r◦ 14/1) *mama*

(§2) *kṣetrajñaṃ* (13.1); *ća* (1.1); *api* (1.26); *māṃ* (1.46); *viddhi* (2.17); *sarvakṣetreṣu* (सर्वेषु क्षेत्रेषु, n◦ 7loc◦ plu◦ tatpu◦ ←pron◦ *sarva* 1.6 + n◦ *kṣetra* 1.1); *bhārata* (1.24); *kṣetrakṣetrajñayoḥ:* (m◦ 6pos◦ dual◦ dvandva◦ क्षेत्रस्य च क्षेत्रज्ञस्य च ←n◦ *kṣetra* 1.1 + m◦ *kṣetrajña* 13.1); *jñānaṃ* (nom◦ 3.39); *yaṭ* (1.45); *taṭ* (1.10); *jñānaṃ* (nom◦ 3.39); *mataṃ* (7.18); *mama* (1.7) (13.3)

(§3) *kṣetrajñaṃ* (adj◦-obj◦ *kṣetrajña,* knower of being); *ća* (and); *api* (also); *māṃ* (obj◦ to me, me to be); *viddhi* (know, you please know); *sarvakṣetreṣu* (among all *kṣetras,* among all beings); *bhārata* (O Arjuna!); *kṣetrakṣetrajñayoḥ:* (of *kṣetra* and *kṣetrajña*); *jñānaṃ* (subj◦ knowledge); *yaṭ* (adj1◦-subj◦ that which is); *taṭ* (adj2-subj◦ that is); *jñānaṃ* (subj◦ knowledge); *mataṃ* (opinion); *mama* (my)

(§4) ća api bhārata viddhi māṃ kṣetrajñaṃ sarvakṣetreṣu. jñānaṃ yaṭ kṣetrakṣetrajñayoḥ: jñānaṃ taṭ mama mataṃ

(§5) and also, O Arjuna! you please know me to be "*kṣetrajña* among all *kṣetras*" (knower of all beings). Knowledge of *kṣetra* and *kṣetrajña,* is *jñāna* (knowledge), that is my opinion. (13.3)

13.4 तत्क्षेत्रं यच्च यादृक्च यद्विकारि यतश्च यत् ।
स च यो यत्प्रभावश्च तत्समासेन मे शृणु ।।
tatkṣetraṁ yaćća yādṛkća yadvikāri yataśća yaṭ,
sa ća yo yatprabhāvaśća tatsamāsena me śṛnu; (13.4)

(§1) *taṭ* (r◦ 10/5) *kṣetraṃ* (r◦ 14/1) *yaṭ* (r◦ 11/1) *ća yādṛk* (r◦ 10/1) *ća yadvikāri yataḥ:* (r◦ 17/1) *ća yaṭ* (r◦ 23/1) *saḥ:* (r◦ 21/2) *ća yaḥ:* (r◦ 15/10) *yatprabhāvaḥ:* (r◦ 17/1) *ća taṭ* (r◦ 10/7) *samāsena me śṛṇu;*

(§2) *taṭ* (1nom◦ 1.10); *kṣetraṃ* (1nom◦ 13.2); *yaṭ* (1nom◦ 2.67); *ća* (1.1); 🕮*yādṛk* (ind◦ ←pron◦ *yaḍ* 1.7); *ća* (1.1); *yadvikāri* (n◦ 1nom◦ sing◦ ←bahuvrī◦ *yadvikāriṇ,* यः विकारः यस्य तत् ←pron◦ *yaṭ* 1.45 + adj◦ *vikāriṇ* ←m◦ 🕮*vikāra* ←वि√कृ); *yataḥ:* (abl◦ 6.26); *ća* (1.1); *yaṭ* (1nom◦ 1.45); *saḥ:* (1.13); *ća* (1.1); *yaḥ:* (2.19); *yatprabhāvaḥ:* (m◦ 1nom◦ sing◦ ←tatpu◦ *yat-prabhāva,* यस्य प्रभावः ←pron◦ *yaṭ* 1.45 + m◦ 🕮*prabhāva* 11.43); *ća* (1.1); *taṭ* (2acc◦ 2.7); 🕮*samāsena* (adv◦ or 3inst◦ sing◦ ←m◦ *samāsa* 10.33); *me* (gen◦ 1.21); *śṛṇu* (2.39);

(§3) *taṭ* (adj1◦-subj1◦ that); *kṣetraṃ* (subj1◦ *kṣetra*); *yaṭ* (adj2◦-subj1◦ what, what it is); *ća* (and); *yādṛk* (ind∘ how, what is its nature); *ća* (and); *yadvikāri* (adj3∘-subj1∘ how it transforms); *yataḥ:* (from where, whence); *ća* (and); *yaṭ* (adj4∘-subj1∘ that); *saḥ:* (subj2∘ that); *ća* (and); *yaḥ:* (adj1∘-subj2∘ who, who is); *yatprabhāvaḥ:* (adj2∘-subj2∘ of what potential, influence he is); *ća* (and); *taṭ* (obj∘ that, it); *samāsena* (concisely); *me* (of me, from me); *śṛṇu* (please listen); (13.4)

(§4) ća, yaṭ taṭ kṣetraṃ ća yādṛk ća yataḥ: yaṭ ća yadvikāri; ća yaḥ: saḥ: yatprabhāvaḥ: śṛṇu taṭ samāsena me

(§5) and, what that *kṣetra* is, and what is its nature, and whence that is, and how it transforms; and who that (*kṣetrajña*) is, of what potential he is, (...etc.) please listen that concisely from me.

13.5 ऋषिभिर्बहुधा गीतं छन्दोभिर्विविधैः पृथक् ।
ब्रह्मसूत्रपदैश्चैव हेतुमद्भिर्विनिश्चितैः ।।
ṛṣibhirbahudhā gītaṁ ćhandobhirvividhaiḥ: pṛthak,
brahmasūtrapadaiśćaiva hetumadbhirviniśćitaiḥ:. (13.5)

(§1) *ṛṣibhiḥ:* (r∘ 16/6) *bahudhā gītaṃ* (r∘ 14/1) *ćhandobhiḥ:* (r∘ 16/6) *vividhaiḥ:* (r∘ 22/3) *pṛthak* (r∘ 23/1) *brahmasūtrapadaiḥ:* (r∘ 17/1) *ća* (r∘ 3/1) *eva hetumadbhiḥ:* (r∘ 16/6) *viniśćitaiḥ:* (r∘ 22/8)

(§2) *ṛṣibhiḥ:* (3inst∘ plu∘ ←m∘ *ṛṣi* 4.2); *bahudhā* (9.15); *gītaṃ* (n∘ 2acc∘ sing∘ ←ppp∘ adj∘ *gīta* ←√गै); *ćhandobhiḥ:* (3inst∘ plu∘ ←n∘ *ćhandaṣ* 10.35); *vividhaiḥ:* (n∘ 3inst∘ plu∘ ←bahuvrī∘ adj∘ 🕮*vividha* ←वि-वि√धा); *pṛthak* (1.18); *brahmasūtrapadaiḥ:* (n∘ 3inst∘ plu∘ ←tatpu∘ *brahmasūtra-pada*, ब्रह्मणः सूत्रस्य पदम् ←n∘ *brahmaṇ* 2.72 + n∘ *sūtra* 7.7 + n∘ *pada* 2.51 ←√पद्); *ća* (1.1); *eva* (1.1); *hetumadbhiḥ:* (3inst∘ plu∘ ←adj∘ *hetumaṭ* ←m∘ *hetu* 1.35); *viniśćitaiḥ:* (3inst∘ plu∘ ←ppp∘ adj∘ *viniśćita* ←ind∘ *vi* 1.4 + adj∘ *niśćita* 2.7) (13.5)

(§3) *ṛṣibhiḥ:* (subj∘ by the sages, seers); *bahudhā* (variously); *gītaṃ* (adj∘-obj∘ sung);[712] *ćhandobhiḥ:* (with meters); *vividhaiḥ:* (with various); *pṛthak* (distinct); *brahmasūtrapadaiḥ:* (with the hymns of *brahmasūtras*); *ća eva* (as well as); *hetumadbhiḥ:* (with reasons); *viniśćitaiḥ:* (with rational)

(§4) bahudhā gītaṃ ṛṣibhiḥ: brahmasūtrapadaiḥ: vividhaiḥ: ćhandobhiḥ: ća eva hetumadbhiḥ: pṛthak viniśćitaiḥ:

(§5) Variously sung by the seers, with the hymns of *brahmasūtras* with various meters as well as with distinct rational reasons. (13.5)

13.6 महाभूतान्यहङ्कारो बुद्धिरव्यक्तमेव च ।
इन्द्रियाणि दशैकं च पञ्च चेन्द्रियगोचराः ।।
mahābhūtānyahaṅkaro buddhirvyaktameva ća,

[712] The Object ("that") is mentioned in the previous verse 13.5; and is fully itemized in the following verses.

indriyāṇi daśaikaṁ ća pañća ćendriyagoćarāḥ:; (13.6)

(§1) *mahābhūtāni* (r◦ 4/1) *ahaṅkāraḥ:* (r◦ 15/7) *buddhiḥ:* (r◦ 16/1) *avyaktam̦* (r◦ 8/22) *eva ća* (r◦ 23/1) *indriyāṇi* (r◦ 24/7) *daśa* (r◦ 3/1) *ekam̦* (r◦ 14/1) *ća pañća ća* (r◦ 2/1) *indriyagoćarāḥ:* (r◦ 22/8);

(§2) *mahābhūtāni* (n◦ 1nom◦ plu◦ ←tatpu◦ *mahā-bhūta*, महान् भूतम् ←adj◦ *mahā* 1.3 + n◦ *bhūta* 2.28); *ahaṅkāraḥ:* (7.4); *buddhiḥ:* (2.39); *avyaktam̦* (7.24); *eva* (1.1); *ća* (1.1); *indriyāṇi* (2.60); *daśa* (1nom◦ sing◦ ←num◦ adj◦ *daśan̦* 11.27); *ekam̦* (10.25); *ća* (1.1); *pañća* (1nom◦ sing◦ ←ever pleural num◦ adj◦ *pañćan̦* ←√पञ्च्); *ća* (1.1); *indriyagoćarāḥ:* (m◦ 1nom◦ plu◦ ←adj◦ *indriya-goćara*, इन्द्रियाणाम् गोचर: ←n◦ *indriya* 2.8 + adj◦ *goćara* ←√गम्); (13.6)

(§3) *mahābhūtāni* (obj1◦ the five primary elements); *ahaṅkāraḥ:* (obj2◦ the self-consciousness, the i-ness); *buddhiḥ:* (obj3◦ the intellect, thinking); *avyaktam̦* (obj4◦ the Unpersonified, the Unmanifest); *eva ća* (as well as); *indriyāṇi* (obj5◦ the organs); *daśa* (adj◦-obj5◦ ten); *ekam̦* (the mind); *ća* (and); *pañća* (adj◦-obj6◦ the five); *ća* (and); *indriyagoćarāḥ:* (obj6◦ the senses tangible to the five sense organs); (13.6)

(§4) mahābhūtāni ahaṅkāraḥ: buddhiḥ: avyaktam̦ eva ća daśa indriyāṇi ća ekam̦ ća pañća indriyagoćarāḥ:;

(§5) The five Primary elements, the Self-consciousness, the Intellect, the Unpersonified (*ātmā*), as well as the ten Organs (five motor organs and five sense organs), and the Mind and the five Senses tangible to the five sense organs; (13.6)

13.7 इच्छा द्वेष: सुखं दु:खं सङ्घातश्चेतना धृति: ।
एतत्क्षेत्रं समासेन सविकारमुदाहृतम् ।।
iććhā dveṣaḥ: sukhaṁ duḥ:khaṁ saṅghātaśćetanā dhṛti,
etatkṣetraṁ samāsena savikāramudāhṛtam̦; (13.7)

(§1) *iććhā dveṣaḥ:* (r◦ 22/7) *sukham̦* (r◦ 14/1) *duḥ:kham̦* (r◦ 14/1) *saṅghātaḥ:* (r◦ 17/1) *ćetanā dhṛtiḥ:* (r◦ 22/8) *etaț* (r◦ 10/5) *kṣetram̦* (r◦ 14/1) *samāsena savikāram̦* (r◦ 8/20) *udāhṛtam̦* (r◦ 14/2);

(§2) *iććhā* (1nom◦ sing◦ ←f◦ *iććhā* 5.28); *dveṣaḥ:* (1nom◦ sing◦ ←m◦ *dveṣa* 2.64); *sukham̦* (2.66); *duḥ:kham̦* (1nom◦ 10.4); *saṅghātaḥ:* (1nom◦ sing◦ ←aggregative m◦ *saṅghāta* ←सम्√हन्); *ćetanā* (10.22); *dhṛtiḥ:* (10.34); *etaț* (1nom◦ 2.3); *kṣetram̦* (1nom◦ 13.2); *samāsena* (13.4); *savikāram̦* (n◦ 1nom◦ sing◦ ←s-sbahuvrī◦ *savikāra*, विकारेण सह ←m◦ *vikāra* 13.4 + adj◦ *saha* 1.22); *udāhṛtam̦* (n◦ 1nom◦ sing◦ ←ppp◦ adj◦ *udāhṛta* ←उद्–आ√हृ); (13.7)

(§3) *iććhā* (obj7◦ desire); *dveṣaḥ:* (obj8◦ revulsion); *sukham̦* (obj9◦ happiness); *duḥ:kham̦* (obj10◦ sorrow); *saṅghātaḥ:* (obj11◦ the sum of eleven elements); *ćetanā* (obj12◦ sentience); *dhṛtiḥ:* (obj13◦

fortitude, courage); *etaț* (adj1◦-obj1-13◦ this); *kṣetram̦* (obj◦ *kṣetra*); *samāsena* (concisely); *savikāram̦* (with its variations); *udāhṛtam̦* (adj2◦-obj1-13◦ exemplified); (13.7)

(§4) iććhā dveṣaḥ: sukham̦ duḥ:kham̦ saṅghātaḥ: ćetanā dhṛtiḥ: etaț savikāram̦ samāsena udāhṛtam̦ kṣetram̦

(§5) Desire, revulsion, happiness, sorrow, the sum of eleven elements, sentience, (and) fortitude; this, with its variations, (is) concisely exemplified (as) *kṣetram̦*. (13.7)

13.8 अमानित्वमदम्भित्वमहिंसा क्षान्तिरार्जवम् ।
आचार्योपासनं शौचं स्थैर्यमात्मविनिग्रहः ।।

amānitvamadambhitvamahiṁsā kṣāntirārjavam̦,
āćāryopāsanaṁ śaućaṁ sthairyamātmavinigrahaḥ:. (13.8)

(§1) *amānitvam̦* (r◦ 8/16) *adambhitvam̦* (r◦ 8/16) *ahimsā kṣāntiḥ:* (r◦ 16/1) *ārjavam̦* (r◦ 14/2) *āćāryopāsanam̦* (r◦ 14/1) *śaućam̦* (r◦ 14/1) *sthairyam̦* (r◦ 8/17) *ātmavinigrahaḥ:* (r◦ 22/8)

(§2) 🕮*amānitvam̦* (1nom◦ sing◦ ←n◦ *a-mānitva* ←n.bahuvrī◦ *amānin̦* ←m◦ *māna* 6.7); 🕮*adambhitvam̦* (1nom◦ sing◦ ←n◦ *a-dambhitva* ←adj◦ *adambhin̦* ←ind◦ A 1.10 + m◦ *dambha* ←√दम्भ्); 🕮*ahimsā* (10.5); 🕮*kṣāntiḥ:* (1nom◦ sing◦ ←f◦ *kṣānti* ←adj◦ *kṣānta* ←√क्षम्); 🕮*ārjavam̦* (1nom◦ sing◦ ←n◦ *ārjava* ←adj◦ *ṛju* ←√ऋज्); *āćāryopāsanam̦* (n◦ 1nom◦ sing◦ ←tatpu◦ *āćāryopāsana*, आचार्याणाम् उपासनम् ←m◦ 🕮*āćārya* 1.2 + n◦ 🕮*upāsana* ←उप√आस्); 🕮*śaućam̦* (n◦ 1nom◦ sing◦ ←n◦ *śauća* ←adj◦ *śući* 6.11); 🕮*sthairyam̦* (n◦ 1nom◦ sing◦ ←taddhita◦ n◦ *sthairya* ←adj◦ *sthira* 1.16); *ātmavinigrahaḥ:* (m◦ 1nom◦ sing◦ ←tatpu◦ *ātma-vinigraha*, आत्मनः विनिग्रहः ←m◦ *ātman̦* 2.41 + m◦ 🕮*vinigraha* ←वि-नि√ग्रह् 1.4, 3.33) (13.8)

(§3) *amānitvam̦* (obj1◦ humility); *adambhitvam̦* (obj2◦ honesty); *ahimsā* (obj3◦ non-violence); *kṣāntiḥ:* (subj4◦ patience); *ārjavam̦* (obj5◦ simplicity, rectitude); *āćāryopāsanam̦* (obj6◦ service to the tutor); *śaućam̦* (obj7◦ purity); *sthairyam̦* (obj8◦ stability); *ātmavinigrahaḥ:* (obj 9◦ self-control) (13.8)

(§4) amānitvam̦ adambhitvam̦ ahimsā kṣāntiḥ: ārjavam̦ āćāryopāsanam̦ śaućam̦ sthairyam̦ ātmavinigrahaḥ:

(§5) Humility, honesty, non-violence, patience, simplicity, service to the tutor, purity, stability, self-control; (13.8)

13.9 इन्द्रियार्थेषु वैराग्यमनहङ्कार एव च ।
जन्ममृत्युजराव्याधिदुःखदोषानुदर्शनम् ।।

indriyārtheṣu vairāgyamanahaṅkāra eva ća,
janmamṛtyujarāvyādhidu:khadoṣānudarśanam̦. (13.9)

(§1) *indriyārtheṣu* (r◦ 25/5) *vairāgyam* (r◦ 8/16) *anahaṅkāraḥ:* (r◦ 19/7) *eva ća janmamṛtyujarāvyādhidu:khadoṣānudarśanam* (r◦ 14/2)

(§2) *indriyārtheṣu* (5.9); *vairāgyam* (1nom◦ sing◦ ←n◦ *vairāgya* 6.35); *anahaṅkāraḥ:* (m◦ 1nom◦ sing◦ n.tatpu◦ ←m◦ *ahaṅkāra* 2.71); *eva* (1.1); *ća* (1.1); 🕮*janmamṛtyujarāvyādhidu:khadoṣānudarśanam* (n◦ 1nom◦ sing◦ ←tatpu◦ *janma-mṛtyu-jarā-vyādhi-du:kha -doṣānudarśana,* जन्मस्य च मृत्योः च जरायाः च व्याध्याः च दुःखस्य च दोषस्य च अनुदर्शनम् ←n◦ *janman* 2.27 + m◦ *mṛtyu* 2.27 + f◦ *jarā* 2.13 + f◦ *vyadhi* ←वि-आ√धा + n◦ *duḥ:kha* 2.14 + m◦ *doṣa* 1.38 + n◦ *anudarśana* ←अनु√दृश् 11.10) (13.9)

(§3) *indriyārtheṣu* (to the senses of organs); *vairāgyam* (obj10◦ non-attachment); *anahaṅkāraḥ:* (obj11◦ nonexistance of 'I'-ness); *eva ća* (as well as); *janma-mṛtyu-jarā-vyādhi-du:kha-doṣa-anudarśanam* (obj12◦ the understanding of the birth, the death, the ageing, the illness, the sorrow and the defects) (13.9)

(§4) vairāgyam indriyārtheṣu anahaṅkāraḥ: eva ća janma-mṛtyu-jarā-vyādhi-du:kha-doṣa-anudarśanam

(§5) Non-attachment to the senses of organs, nonexistance of 'I'-ness and the understanding of[713] (i) the birth, (ii) the death, (iii) the ageing, (iv) the illness, the (v) sorrow and (vi) the defects;[714] (13.9)

13.10 असक्तिरनभिष्वङ्गः पुत्रदारगृहादिषु ।
नित्यं च समचित्तत्वमिष्टानिष्टोपपत्तिषु ।।
asaktiranabhiṣvaṅgaḥ: putradāragṛhādiṣu,
nityam ća samaćittatvamiṣṭāniṣṭopapattiṣu. (13.10)

(§1) *asaktiḥ:* (r◦ 16/1) *anabhiṣvaṅgaḥ:* (r◦ 22/3) *putradāragṛhādiṣu* (r◦ 25/5) *nityam* (r◦ 14/1) *ća samaćittatvam* (r◦ 8/18) *iṣṭāniṣṭopapattiṣu*

(§2) 🕮*asaktiḥ:* (1nom◦ sing◦ ←f◦ *asakti* ←अ√सञ्ज्); 🕮*anabhiṣvaṅgaḥ:* (1nom◦ sing◦ n.tatpu◦ ←m◦

---

[713] See Patanjali 1.33 : मैत्रीकरुणामुदितोपेक्षाणां सुखदुःखपुण्यापुण्यविषयाणां भावनातश्चित्तप्रसादनम् = Purity of Mind occurs with the contemplation of such concerns as happiness, unhappiness, righteous consequence, unrighteous consequence, amity, compassion, joy, sorrow ...etc.

[714] elsewhere◦ जन्ममृत्युजराव्याधिदुःखदोषानुदर्शनम् → seeing the evil in...; keeping in view the evils of...; insight into the evil of...; preception of the evil of...; preception of evil in...; ...etc.

🕮 जन्ममृत्युजराव्याधिदुःखदोषानुदर्शनम् = जन्मस्य च मृत्योः च जरायाः च व्याध्याः च दुःखस्य च दोषस्य च अनुदर्शनम् । not जन्मस्य च मृत्योः च जरायाः च व्याध्याः च दुःखस्य दोषस्य अनुदर्शनम् । Also, अनुदर्शनम् is not a gerund, it is noun, subject3◦ of the six objects in that compound (समासिक) word.

abhiṣvaṅga ←अभि√स्वञ्ज्); *putra-dāra-gṛhādiṣu* (m◦ 7loc◦ plu◦ ←dvandva◦ पुत्रेषु च दारे च गृहे च आदौ च ←m◦ *putra* 1.3 + m◦ *dārā* ←√दृ + n◦ *gṛha* ←√ग्रह् + m◦ *ādi* 2.28); *nityam̧* (2.21); *ća* (1.1); 🕮*samaćittatvam̧* (1nom◦ sing◦ ←n◦ *sama-ćittatva* ←adj◦ *sama-ćitta* ←adj◦ *sama* 1.4 + n◦ *ćitta* 4.21); *iṣṭāniṣṭopapattiṣu* (f◦ 7loc◦ plu◦ ←tatpu◦ *iṣṭāniṣṭopapatti*, इष्टानाम् च अनिष्टानाम् च उपपत्तिः ←adj◦ *iṣṭa* 3.10 + adj◦ n.bahuvrī◦ 🕮*aniṣṭa* ←अन्√इष् + f◦ 🕮*upapatti* ←उप√पद्) (13.10)

(§3) *asaktiḥ:* (obj13◦ non-attachment); *anabhiṣvaṅgaḥ:* (obj14◦ non-bondage to, absence of feeling of 'my'-ness towards); *putra-dāra-gṛhādiṣu* (the children, wife, house, etc.); *nityam̧* (always); *ća* (and); *samaćittatvam̧* (obj15◦ indifference); *iṣṭāniṣṭopapattiṣu* (to the attainment of likes and dislikes) (13.10)

(§4) asaktiḥ: anabhiṣvaṅgaḥ: putra-dāra-gṛhādiṣu ća nityam̧ samaćittatvam̧ iṣṭāniṣṭopapattiṣu.

(§5) Non-attachment, absence of 'my'-ness towards the children, wife, house, etc.[715] and always indifference to the attainment of likes and dislikes; (13.10)

13.11 मयि चानन्ययोगेन भक्तिरव्यभिचारिणी ।
विविक्तदेशसेवित्वमरतिर्जनसंसदि ।।
mayi ćānanyayogena bhaktiravyabhićāriṇi,
viviktadeśasevitvamaratirjanasaṁsadi. (13.11)

(§1) *mayi ća* (r◦ 1/1) *ananyayogena bhaktiḥ:* (r◦ 16/1) *avyabhićāriṇi* (r◦ 24/8) *viviktadeśasevitvam̧* (r◦ 8/16) *aratiḥ:* (r◦ 16/6) *janasaṁsadi*

(§2) *mayi* (3.30); *ća* (1.1); *ananyayogena* (m◦ 3inst◦ sing◦ ←tatpu◦ *ananya-yoga*, अनन्यः योगः ←adj◦ *ananya* 8.14 + m◦ *yoga* 2.39); *bhaktiḥ:* (1nom◦ sing◦ ←f◦ *bhakti* 7.17); 🕮*avyabhićāriṇi* (f◦ 1nom◦ sing◦ ←adj◦ *a-vyabhićāriņ* ←अ–वि–अभि√चर्); *viviktadeśasevitvam̧* (n◦ 1nom◦ sing◦ ←tatpu◦ *vivikta-deśa-sevitva*, विविक्तस्य देशस्य सेवित्वम् ←ppp◦ adj◦ 🕮*vivikta* ←वि√विच् + m◦ *deśa* 6.11 + n◦ *sevitva* ←√सेव्); *a-ratiḥ:* (1nom◦ sing◦ n.bahuvrī◦ ←f◦ *rati* 3.17); *janasaṁsadi* (f◦ 7loc◦ sing◦ ←tatpu◦ *jana-saṁsaḑ*, जनानाम् संसद् ←m◦ *jana* 1.28 + f◦ 🕮*saṁsaḑ* ←सम्√सद्) (13.11)

---

[715] elsewhere◦ पुत्रदारगृहादिषु → to sons, wives, homes; non-identification with son, non-identification of self with son, ...etc.

🕮 (i) In this *dvandva samasa* आदिषु indicates a Locative case of more than two objects, but each item does not have to be plural. (ii) Generally, in a *subhashita* or *shloka*, the word पुत्र denotes a child or an offspring, not necessarily a son only.

(§3) *mayi* (in me); *ća* (and); *ananyayogena* (with one pointed allegiance, mind); *bhaktiḥ:* (obj16◦ devotion); *avyabhićāriṇi* (adj◦-obj16◦ unwavering); *viviktadeśasevitvaṃ* (obj17◦ inclination to solitude); *aratiḥ:* (obj18◦ non-indulgence); *janasaṁsadi* (in mass of people, crowd) (13.11)

(§4) ća avyabhićāriṇi bhaktiḥ: mayi ananyayogena viviktadeśasevitvaṃ aratiḥ: janasaṁsadi.

(§5) And, unwavering devotion in me with one pointed allegiance,[716] inclination to solitude, non-indulgence in crowd of people; (13.11)

13.12 अध्यात्मज्ञाननित्यत्वं तत्त्वज्ञानार्थदर्शनम् ।
एतज्ज्ञानमिति प्रोक्तमज्ञानं यदतोऽन्यथा ।।
adhyātmajñānanityatvaṁ tattvajñanārthadarśanaṃ,
etajjñānamiti proktamajñanaṁ yadato'nyathā. (13.12)

(§1) *adhyātmajñānanityatvaṃ* (r◦ 14/1) *tattvajñanārthadarśanaṃ* (r◦ 14/2) *etaṭ* (r◦ 11/2) *jñānaṃ* (r◦ 8/18) *iti proktaṃ* (r◦ 8/16) *ajñānaṃ* (r◦ 14/1) *yaṭ* (r◦ 8/2) *ataḥ:* (r◦ 15/1) *anyathā*

(§2) *adhyātmajñānanityatvaṃ* (n◦ 1nom◦ sing◦ ←tatpu◦ *adhyātma-jñāna-nityatva*, अध्यात्मस्य ज्ञाने नित्यत्वम् ←adj◦ *adhyātma* 3.30 + n◦ *jñāna* 3.3 + n◦ *nityatva* ←adj◦ *nitya* 2.18); *tattvajñanārthadarśanaṃ* (n◦ 1nom◦ sing◦ ←tatpu◦ *tattva-jñanārtha-darśana*, तत्त्वस्य ज्ञानस्य अर्थस्य दर्शनम् ←n◦ *tattva* 2.16 + n◦ *jñāna* 3.3 + m◦ *artha* 1.7 + n◦ *darśana* 11.10); *etaṭ* (2.3); *jñānaṃ* (1nom◦ 3.39); *iti* (1.25); *proktaṃ* (8.1); *ajñānaṃ* (1nom◦ 5.16); *yaṭ* (1nom◦ 2.67); *ataḥ:* (2.12); *anyathā* (option indicating ind◦ ←adj◦ *anya* 1.9) (13.12)

(§3) *adhyātmajñānanityatvaṃ* (obj19◦ ceaseless pursuit of self realization, being constantly in the contemplation on self realization); *tattvajñanārthadarśanaṃ* (obj20◦ experiencing the reality); *etaṭ* (this, all these twenty subjects); *jñānaṃ* (obj21◦ knowledge); *iti* (as); *proktaṃ* (is called); *ajñānaṃ* (non-knowledge, nescience, information, data); *yaṭ* (that which is); *ataḥ:* (than this); *anyathā* (other)

(§4) adhyātmajñānanityatvaṃ tattvajñanārthadarśanaṃ proktaṃ iti jñānaṃ yaṭ anyathā ataḥ: ajñānaṃ.

(§5) Ceaseless pursuit of self realization (and) experiencing the reality, all this is called as knowledge; that which is other than this (is) information. (13.12)

13.13 ज्ञेयं यत्तत्प्रवक्ष्यामि यज्ज्ञात्वामृतमश्नुते ।
अनादिमत्परं ब्रह्म न सत्तन्नासदुच्यते ।।

---

[716] elsewhere◦ अनन्ययोगेन → through the Yoga of non-separation; through exclusive attachment; in me with not other yoga, with single minded Yoga; by unalloyed devotional service; ...etc.

jñeyaṁ yattatpravakṣāmi yajjñātvāmṛtamaśnute,
anādimatparamaṁ brahma na sattannāsaducyate; (13.13)

(§1) *jñeyam* (r◦ 14/1) *yat* (r◦ 1/10) *tat* (r◦ 10/6) *pravakṣāmi yat* (r◦ 11/2) *jñātvā* (r◦ 1/3) *amṛtam* (r◦ 8/16) *aśnute* (r◦ 23/1) *anādimat* (r◦ 10/6) *param* (r◦ 14/1) *brahma na sat* (r◦ 1/10) *tat* (r◦ 12/1) *na* (r◦ 1/1) *asat* (r◦ 8/6) *ucyate*

(§2) *jñeyam* (2acc◦ 1.39); *yat* (1nom◦ 1.45); *tat* (2acc◦ 1.10); *pravakṣāmi* (4.16); *yat* (2acc◦ 1.45); *jñātvā* (4.15); 🕮*amṛtam* (2acc◦ 9.19); *aśnute* (3.4); *anādimat* (n◦ 1nom◦ sing◦ ←adj◦ *anādimat* ←adj◦ *anādi* 10.3 + taddhita◦ affix (मत्) *matup* 1.3); *param* (1nom◦ 2.12); *brahma* (1nom◦ 3.15); *na* (1.30); *sat* (1nom◦ 2.16); *tat* (1nom◦ 1.10); *na* (1.30); *asat* (1nom◦ 9.19); *ucyate* (2.25) (13.13)

(§3) *jñeyam* (obj1◦ the one that is ought to be known); *yat* (adj1-obj1◦ which); *tat* (adj2◦-subj1◦ that); *pravakṣāmi* (I shall explain); *yat* (adj1-obj1◦ which); *jñātvā* (having known); *amṛtam* (obj2◦ immortality); *aśnute* (one attains); *anādimat* (adj2◦-subj1◦ that which is beginingless, everpresent); *param* (adj3◦-subj1◦ supreme); *brahma* (subj1◦ *brahma, jñeyam*); *na* (neither); *sat* (adj4-subj1◦ being, existant); *tat* (adj5◦-subj1◦ that which is); *na* (nor); *asat* (adj6◦-subj1◦ non-being, non-existant); *ucyate* (called) (13.13)

(§4) pravakṣāmi tat yat jñeyam yat jñātvā aśnute amṛtam tat brahma anādimat param na ucyate sat na asat.

(§5) I shall explain (you) that which is ought to be known, which having known one attains immortality. That (*jñeyam* is) *brahma* which is everpresent (and) supreme. That which is neither called existant nor non-existant; (13.13)

13.14 सर्वत:पाणिपादं तत्सर्वतोऽक्षिशिरोमुखम् ।
सर्वत:श्रुतिमल्लोके सर्वमावृत्य तिष्ठति ।।
sarvataḥ: pāṇipādaṁ tatsarvato'kṣiśiromukham,
sarvataḥ: śrutimalloke sarvamāvṛtya tiṣṭhati; (13.14)

(§1) *sarvataḥ:* (r◦ 22/3) *pāṇipādam* (r◦ 14/1) *tat* (r◦ 10/7) *sarvataḥ:* (r◦ 15/1) *akṣiśiromukham* (r◦ 14/2) *sarvataḥ:* (r◦ 22/5) *śrutimat* (r◦ 11/6) *loke sarvam* (r◦ 8/17) *āvṛtya tiṣṭhati*

(§2) *sarvataḥ:pāṇipādam* (n◦ 1nom◦ sing◦ ←bahuvrī◦ *sarvataḥ:-pāṇi-pāda*, सर्वत: पाणय: च पादा: च यस्य तत् ←ind◦ *sarvataḥ:* 2.46 + m◦ *pāṇi* 1.46 + m◦ *pāda* 11.23); *tat* (1.10); *sarvato'kṣiśiromukham* (n◦ 1nom◦ sing◦ ←bahuvrī◦ *sarvato'kṣiśiromukha*, सर्वत: अक्षिणि च शिरांसि च मुखानि च यस्य ←ind◦ *sarvataḥ:* 2.46 + n◦ *akṣi* 11.2 + n◦ *śiras* 11.14 + n◦ *mukha* 1.29); *sarvataḥ:śrutimat* (n◦ ←bahuvrī◦ *sarvataḥ:-śrutimat*, सर्वत: श्रुति: यस्य ←ind◦ *sarvataḥ:* 2.46 + f◦ *śruti* 2.53 + taddhita◦ *matup* 1.3); *loke* (2.5); *sarvam* (2.17);

📖 *āvṛtya* (3.40); *tiṣṭhati* (3.5) (13.14)

(§3) *sarvataḥ:pāṇipādam̦* (adj7∘-subj1∘ that which has hands and feet from all sides; omnificent and omnipresent); *taț* (adj8∘-subj1∘ that, that jñeyam); *sarvato'kṣiśiromukham̦* (adj9∘-subj1∘ which has eyes, heads and mouths from all sides; omniscient and omnifarious and omnivorous); *sarvataḥ:śrutimaț* (adj10∘-subj1∘ which has ears from all sides; omnipotent, all knower); *loke* (in this world); *sarvam̦* (everything); *āvṛtya* (enveloping); *tiṣṭhati* (it stays) (13.14)

(§4) taț sarvataḥ:pāṇipādam̦ sarvato'kṣiśiromukham̦ sarvataḥ:śrutimaț tiṣṭhati loke āvṛtya sarvam̦.

(§5) That *jñeyam* (is) omnificent and omnipresent, omniscient, omnifarious and omnivorous and omnipotent. It[717] stays in this world enveloping[718] everything;

(13.14)

13.15 सर्वेन्द्रियगुणाभासं सर्वेन्द्रियविवर्जितम् ।
असक्तं सर्वभृच्चैव निर्गुणं गुणभोक्तृ च ।।

sarvendriyaguṇābhāsaṁ sarvendriyavivarjitam̦,
asaktaṁ sarvabhṛććaiva nirguṇaṁ guṇabhoktṛ ća; (13.15)

(§1) *sarvendriyaguṇābhāsam̦* (r∘ 14/1) *sarvendriyavivarjitam̦* (r∘ 14/2) *asaktam̦* (r∘ 14/1) *sarvabhṛț* (r∘ 11/1) *ća* (r∘ 3/1) *eva nirguṇam̦* (r∘ 14/1, 24/3) *guṇabhoktṛ ća*

(§2) *sarvendriyaguṇābhāsam̦* (n∘ 1nom∘ sing∘ ←bahuvrī∘ *sarvendriya-guṇābhāsa*, सर्वेषाम् इन्द्रियाणाम् गुणेषु आभास: यस्य ←pron∘ *sarva* 1.6 + n∘ *indriya* 2.8 + m∘ *guṇa* 2.45 + m∘ *ābhāsa* ←आ√भास्); *sarvendriyavivarjitam̦* (n∘ 1nom∘ sing∘ ←bahuvrī∘ *sarvendriya-vivarjita*, सर्वै: इन्द्रियै: विवर्जितम् यत् ←pron∘ *sarva* 1.6 + n∘ *indriya* 2.8 + adj∘ *vivarjita* 7.11); *asaktam̦* (9.9); *sarvabhṛț* (n∘ 1nom∘ sing∘ ←bahuvrī∘ adj∘ *sarva-bhṛt*, सर्वम् बिभर्ति यत् ←adj∘ *sarva* 1.6 + adj∘ *vibhraț* 10.31); *ća* (1.1); *eva* (1.1); *nirguṇam̦* (n∘ 1nom∘ sing∘ ←bahuvrī∘ adj∘ *nir-guṇa*, नास्ति गुणा: यस्मिन् तत् ←ind∘ *nir* 2.45 + m∘ *guṇa* 2.45); *guṇabhoktṛ* (n∘ 1nom∘ sing∘ ←bahuvrī∘ adj∘ *guṇa-bhoktṛ*, गुणान् भुनक्ति यत् ←m∘ *guṇa* 2.45 + adj∘ *bhoktṛ* 5.29); *ća* (1.1) (13.15)

---

[717] elsewhere∘ तत् → He ...etc.

📖 (i) तत् *jñeyam, brahma, the nirguṇabrahma* is a neuter gender word (that or it). It is not *brahmā, saguṇabrahmā,* a masculine gender (he) word.

[718] elsewhere∘ आवृत्य → pervading.

📖 Please see footnote ततम् in verse 2.17, in volume I of this book.

(§3) *sarvendriyaguṇābhāsam̦* (adj11∘-subj1∘ that which conveys perception of all senses of the organs); *sarvendriyavivarjitam̦* (adj12∘-subj1∘ that which is devoid of all organs); *asaktam̦* (adj13∘-subj1∘ that which is indifferent, unattached); *sarvabhṛț* (adj14∘-subj1∘ that which bears everything); *ća eva* (as well as); *nirguṇam̦* (adj15∘-subj1∘ that which is devoid of the three attributes); *guṇabhoktṛ* (adj16∘-subj1∘ that which perceives the attributes); *ća* (and) (13.15)

(§4) sarvendriyaguṇābhāsam̦ sarvendriyavivarjitam̦ asaktam̦ sarvabhṛț ća nirguṇam̦ ća eva guṇabhoktṛ

(§5) That which conveys perception of all senses of the organs (yet) which is devoid of all organs, that which is indifferent, that which bears everything and that which is devoid of the three attributes as well as which perceives the attributes; (13.15)

13.16 बहिरन्तश्च भूतानामचरं चरमेव च ।
सूक्ष्मत्वात्तदविज्ञेयं दूरस्थं चान्तिके च तत् ।।
bahirantaśća bhūtānāmaćaraṁ ćarameva ća,
sūkṣmatvāttadavijñeyaṁ dūrasthaṁ ćāntike ća taț (13.16)

(§1) *bahiḥ:* (r∘ 16/1) *antaḥ:* (r∘ 17/1) *ća bhūtānām̦* (r∘ 8/16) *aćaram̦* (r∘ 14/1) *ćaram̦* (r∘ 8/22) *eva ća sūkṣmatvāț* (r∘ 1/10) *taț* (r∘ 8/2) *avijñeyam̦* (r∘ 14/1) *dūrastham̦* (r∘ 14/1) *ća* (r∘ 1/1) *antike ća taț*

(§2) *bahiḥ:* (5.27); *antaḥ:* (2.16); *ća* (1.1); *bhūtānām̦* (2.69); *aćaram̦* (n∘ 1nom∘ sing∘ ←nbahuvrī∘ adj∘ *aćara* 9.10); *ćaram̦* (n∘ 1nom∘ sing∘ ←adj∘ *ćara* 9.10); *eva* (1.1); *ća* (1.1); *sūkṣmatvāț* (5abl∘ sing∘ ←n∘ *sūkṣmatva* ←adj∘ 🕮*sūkṣma* ←√सूच्); *taț* (1.10); *avijñeyam̦* (1nom∘ sing∘ n.tatpu∘ ←n∘ *avijñeya* ←अ-वि√ज्ञा); *dūrastham̦* (n∘ 1nom∘ sing∘ ←tatpu∘ *dūra-stha*, दूरे स्थियते इति, *adj∘ dūra* 2.49 + adj∘ *stha* 2.45); *ća* (1.1); *antike* (n∘ 7loc∘ plu∘ ←adj∘ *antika* ←√अन्त्); *ća* (1.1); *taț* (1.10) (13.16)

(§3) *bahiḥ:* (adj16∘-subj1∘ that which is outside); *antaḥ:* (inside); *ća* (and); *bhūtānām̦* (of the beings); *aćaram̦* (adj17∘-subj1∘ that which is immovable); *ćaram̦* (adj18∘-subj1∘ that which is movable); *eva ća* (as well as); *sūkṣmatvāț* (due to subtleness); *taț* (adj8∘-subj1∘ that *jñeyam*, that *brahma*); *avijñeyam̦* (adj19∘-subj1∘ that which is incomprehensible); *dūrastham̦* (adj20∘-subj1∘ that which is far); *ća* (as well as, yet); 🕮*antike* (near); *ća* (and); *taț* (adj8∘-subj1∘ that *jñeyam*, that *brahma*); (13.16)

(§4) bahiḥ: ća antaḥ: bhūtānām̦ aćaram̦ eva ća ćaram̦ taț avijñeyam̦ sūkṣmatvāț ća taț dūrastham̦ ća antike;

(§5) That which is outside and inside of the beings, that which is immovable as well as movable, that which is incomprehensible due to subtleness and that (is) *jñeyam* which is far yet near; (13.16)

13.17 अविभक्तं च भूतेषु विभक्तमिव च स्थितम् ।

भूतभर्तृ च तज्ज्ञेयं ग्रसिष्णु प्रभविष्णु च ।।

avibhaktaṁ ća bhūteṣu vibhaktamiva ća sthitam,

bhūtabhartṛ ća tajjneyaṁ grasiṣṇu prabhaviṣṇu ća; (13.17)

(§1) *avibhaktam* (r◦ 14/1) *ća bhūteṣu* (r◦ 25/5) *vibhaktam* (r◦ 8/18) *iva ća sthitam* (r◦ 14/2) *bhūtabhartṛ ća tat* (r◦ 11/2) *jñeyam* (r◦ 14/1) *grasiṣṇu prabhaviṣṇu ća*

(§2) 📖*a-vibhaktam* (n◦ 1nom◦ sing◦ n.tatpu◦ ←ppp◦ adj◦ *vibhakta* ←वि√भज्); *ća* (1.1); *bhūteṣu* (7.11); 📖*vibhaktam* (n◦ 1nom◦ 2acc◦ sing◦ n.tatpu◦ ←adj◦ *vibhakta* ↑); *iva* (1.30); *ća* (1.1); *sthitam* (5.19); *bhūtabhartṛ* (n◦ 1nom◦ sing◦ ←bahuvrī◦ *bhūta-bhartṛ*, भूतानाम् भर्ता यः ←m◦ *bhūta* 2.28 + m◦ *bhartṛ* 9.18); *ća* (1.1); *tat* (1.10); *jñeyam* (1.39); *grasiṣṇu* (n◦ 1nom◦ sing◦ ←bahuvrī◦ adj◦ *grasiṣṇu* ←n◦ *grasana* ←√ग्रस् + *kṛt* affix इष्णुच् *iṣṇu*, indicating possession of a property, skill or resplendence); *prabhaviṣṇu* (n◦ 1nom◦ sing◦ ←bahuvrī◦ *prabhaviṣṇu* ←m◦ *prabhava* 6.24 + affix *iṣṇu* ↑); *ća* (1.1)

(13.17)

(§3) *a-vibhaktam* (adj21◦-subj1◦ that which is uniform in all beings, that which connected through all beings); *ća* (and, and yet); *bhūteṣu* (in all beings); *vibhaktam* (adj22◦-subj1◦ dispersed, individualized); *iva* (as if); *ća* (and); *sthitam* (ppp. situated, existing); *bhūtabhartṛ* (adj23◦-subj1◦ that which is sustainer of all beings); *ća* (and); *tat* (adj8◦-subj1◦ that, that *jñeya*, that *brahma*); *jñeyam* (adj1◦-subj1◦ *jñeyam*); *grasiṣṇu* (adj21◦-subj1◦ that which assimilates); *prabhaviṣṇu* (adj21◦-subj1◦ that which brings forth beings); *ća* (and)

(13.17)

(§4) a-vibhaktam ća iva sthitam vibhaktam bhūteṣu ća bhūtabhartṛ ća tat jñeyam grasiṣṇu ća prabhaviṣṇu

(§5) That which is uniform in all beings and yet (it is) as if situated individualized in all beings, and (it is) that which is sustainer of all beings and that (is) *jñeyam* which assimilates and that which brings forth beings; (13.17)

13.18 ज्योतिषामपि तज्ज्योतिस्तमसः परमुच्यते ।

ज्ञानं ज्ञेयं ज्ञानगम्यं हृदि सर्वस्य विष्ठितम् ।।

jyotiṣāmapi tajjyotistamasaḥ: paramućyate,

jñānaṁ jñeyaṁ jñānagamyaṁ hṛdi sarvasya viṣṭhitam. (13.18)

(§1) *jyotiṣām* (r◦ 25/3, 8/16) *api tat* (r◦ 11/2) *jyotiḥ:* (r◦ 18/1) *tamasaḥ:* (r◦ 22/3) *param* (r◦ 8/20) *ućyate jñānam* (r◦ 14/1) *jñeyam* (r◦ 14/1) *jñānagamyam* (r◦ 14/1) *hṛdi sarvasya viṣṭhitam* (r◦ 14/2)

(§2) *jyotiṣām* (10.21); *api* (1.26); *tat* (1.10); 📖*jyotiḥ:* (8.24); *tamasaḥ:* (8.9); *param* (2.12); *ućyate*

(2.25); *jñānaṃ* (3.39); *jñeyaṃ* (1.39); *jñānagamyaṃ* (n◦ 1nom◦ sing◦ ←bahuvrī◦ adj◦ *jñāna-gamya*, ज्ञानेन गम्यते यत् ←n◦ *jñāna* 3.3 + pot◦ adj◦ *gamya* ←√गम्); *hṛdi* (8.12); *sarvasya* (2.30); *viṣṭhitaṃ* (n◦ 1nom◦ sing◦ ←prefix *vi* 1.4 + ppp◦ adj◦ *viṣṭhita* ←वि√स्था). (13.18)

(§3) *jyotiṣāṃ* (of the luminaries); *api* (even); *taṭ* (adj8◦-subj1◦ that *jñeyam,* that *brahma*); *jyotiḥ:* (adj26◦-subj1◦ light, luminance); *tamasaḥ: paraṃ* (adj27◦-subj1◦ beyond darkness, that which is bliss); *ućyate* (is called); *jñānaṃ* (adj28◦-subj1◦ wisdom); *jñeyaṃ* (adj1◦-subj1◦ that which ought to be known); *jñānagamyaṃ* (adj29◦-subj1◦ knowable); *hṛdi* (in the soul); *sarvasya* (of everyone); *viṣṭhitaṃ* (adj30◦-subj1◦ that which is situated). (13.18)

(§4) taṭ ućyate jyotiḥ: api jyotiṣāṃ tamasaḥ: paraṃ jñānaṃ jñeyaṃ jñānagamyaṃ viṣṭhitaṃ hṛdi sarvasya.

(§5) That *jñeyam* is called luminance even of the luminaries, that which is bliss, it is wisdom, that which ought to be known (and) knowable. It is that which is situated in the soul of everyone. (13.18)

13.19 इति क्षेत्रं तथा ज्ञानं ज्ञेयं चोक्तं समासत: ।
मद्भक्त एतद्विज्ञाय मद्भावायोपपद्यते ।।
iti kṣetraṁ tathā jñānaṁ jñeyaṁ ćoktaṁ samāsataḥ:,
madbhakta etadvijñāya madbhāvāyopapadyate. (13.19)

(§1) *iti kṣetraṃ* (r◦ 14/1) *tathā jñānaṃ* (r◦ 14/1) *jñeyaṃ* (r◦ 14/1) *ća* (r◦ 2/2) *uktaṃ* (r◦ 14/1) *samāsataḥ:* (r◦ 22/8) *madbhaktaḥ:* (r◦ 19/7) *etaṭ* (r◦ 9/11) *vijñāya madbhāvāya* (r◦ 2/2) *upapadyate*

(§2) *iti* (1.25); *kṣetraṃ* (1nom◦ 13.2); *tathā* (1.8); *jñānaṃ* (1nom◦ 3.39); *jñeyaṃ* (1nom◦ 1.39); *ća* (1.1); *uktaṃ* (1nom◦ 11.1); 🕮*samāsataḥ:* (adv◦ ind◦ ←m◦ *samāsa* 10.33); *madbhaktaḥ:* (9.34); *etaṭ* (2acc◦ 2.3); *vijñāya* (lyp◦ past-participle ind◦ ←वि√ज्ञा); *madbhāvāya* (m◦ 4dat◦ sing◦ ←tatpu◦ *madbhāva* 4.10); *upapadyate* (2.3) (13.19)

(§3) *iti* (thus); *kṣetraṃ* (obj1◦ the *kṣetraṃ*); *tathā* (and); *jñānaṃ* (obj2◦ *jñānaṃ*); *jñeyaṃ* (obj3◦ *jñeyaṃ*); *ća* (and); *uktaṃ* (spoken of); *samāsataḥ:* (adv◦ briefly); *madbhaktaḥ:* (subj1◦); *etaṭ* (collectively obj1-3◦ this); *vijñāya* (having understood); *madbhāvāya* (my nature); *upapadyate* (realizes) (13.19)

(§4) iti kṣetraṃ tathā jñānaṃ ća jñeyaṃ uktaṃ samāsataḥ: vijñāya etaṭ madbhaktaḥ: upapadyate madbhāvāya

(§5) Thus the *kṣetraṃ* and *jñānaṃ* and *jñeyaṃ* (are) spoken of briefly (by me). Having

understood this my devotee realizes my nature.[719] (13.19)

13.20 प्रकृतिं पुरुषं चैव विद्ध्यनादी उभावपि ।
विकारांश्च गुणांश्चैव विद्धि प्रकृतिसम्भवान् ।।
prakṛtiṁ puruṣaṁ ćaiva viddhyanādī ubhāvapi,
vikārāṁśća guṇāṁśćaiva viddhi prakṛtisambhavān̦. (13.20)

(§1) *prakṛtiṃ* (r◦ 14/1) *puruṣaṃ* (r◦ 14/1) *ća* (r◦ 3/1) *eva viddhi* (r◦ 4/1) *anādī* (r◦ 7/1) *ubhau* (r◦ 5/5) *api vikārān̦* (r◦ 13/6) *ća guṇān̦* (r◦ 13/6) *ća* (r◦ 3/1) *eva viddhi prakṛtisambhavān̦*

(§2) *prakṛtiṃ* (3.33); *puruṣaṃ* (2.15); *ća* (1.1); *eva* (1.1); *viddhi* (2.17); *anādī* (m◦ 2acc◦ dual◦ ←adj◦ *anādi* 10.3); *ubhau* (2acc◦ 2.19); *api* (1.26); *vikārān̦* (2acc◦ plu◦ ←m◦ *vikāra* 13.4); *ća* (1.1); *guṇān̦* (2acc◦ plu◦ ←m◦ *guṇa* 2.45); *ća* (1.1); *eva* (1.1); *viddhi* (2.17); *prakṛtisambhavān̦* (m◦ 2acc◦ plu◦ ←bahuvrī◦ *prakṛti-sambhava*, प्रकृते: सम्भव: यस्य ←f◦ *prakṛti* 3.5 + m◦ *sambhava* 3.14) (13.20)

(§3) *prakṛtiṃ* (obj1◦ *prakṛtiḥ*, the nature); *puruṣaṃ* (obj2◦ *puruṣa*, the life of living beings, the life principle); *ća eva* (as well as); *viddhi* (you please know); *anādī* (adj1◦-obj1-2◦ beginningless); *ubhau* (adj2◦-obj1-2◦ both); *api* (also); 🕮*vikārān̦* (obj3◦ the transformations); *ća* (and); *guṇān̦* (obj4◦ the three attributes); *ća eva* (as well as); *viddhi* (know); *prakṛtisambhavān̦* (adj1◦-obj3-4◦ born of the *prakṛtiḥ*) (13.20)

(§4) viddhi prakṛtiṃ ća eva puruṣa, ubhau anādī ća api viddhi vikārān̦ ća eva guṇān̦ prakṛtisambhavān̦

(§5) You please know *prakṛtiḥ*, the nature,[720] as well as *puruṣa*, the life of living beings,[721] both (to be) beginningless. And also know the transformations as well as the three attributes (to be) born of the *prakṛtiḥ*. (13.20)

13.21 कार्यकरणकर्तृत्वे हेतु: प्रकृतिरुच्यते ।
पुरुष: सुखदु:खानां भोक्तृत्वे हेतुरुच्यते ।।
kāryakaraṇakartṛtve hetuḥ: prakṛtirućyate,
puruṣaḥ: sukhaduḥ:khānāṁ bhoktṛtve heturućyate. (13.21)

---

[719] elsewhere◦ मद्भावायोपपद्यते → enters into My being, is fitted for My state, becomes fit for My state, approaches My state of being, attains to my being, becomes qualified for My State, becomes worthy of My State, ...etc.

[720] elsewhere◦ प्रकृति: → Matter, Material nature, ...etc.

[721] elsewhere◦ पुरुष: → the Individual soul, Spirit, the living entities, Person, Soul, ...etc.

(§1) *kāryakaraṇakartṛtve hetuḥ:* (r◦ 22/3) *prakṛtiḥ:* (r◦ 16/1) *ućyate puruṣaḥ:* (r◦ 22/7) *sukhaduḥ:khānāṃ* (r◦ 14/1) *bhoktṛtve hetuḥ:* (r◦ 16/3) *ućyate*

(§2) *kāryakaraṇakartṛtve* (n◦ 7loc◦ dual◦ ←tatpu◦ *kārya-karaṇa-kartṛtvam,* कार्याणाम् च करणानाम् च कर्तृत्वम् ←n◦ or adj◦ *kārya* 3.17 + n◦ *karaṇa* ←√कृ + n◦ *kartṛtva* ←adj◦ *kartṛ* 3.24); *hetuḥ:* (1nom◦ sing◦ ←m◦ *hetu* 1.35); *prakṛtiḥ:* (7.4); *ućyate* (2.25); *puruṣaḥ:* (2.21); *sukhduḥ:khānāṃ* (6pos plu◦ ←dvandva◦ सुखानाम् च दुःखानाम् च ←*sukha-duḥ:kha* 2.38); *bhoktṛtve* (7loc◦ sing◦ ←n◦ *bhoktṛtve* ←m◦ or adj◦ *bhoktṛ* 5.29); *hetuḥ:* (↑); *ućyate* (2.25) (13.21)

(§3) *kāryakaraṇakartṛtve* (in the matter of evolution, in the matter of evolution and the twenty four evolutes); *hetuḥ:* (adj◦-obj1◦ the cause); *prakṛtiḥ:* (obj1◦ the nature); *ućyate* (is called, is called by); *puruṣaḥ:* (obj2◦ the life of the living beings); *sukhduḥ:khānāṃ* (of the pains and pleasures); *bhoktṛtve* (in the matter of experience); *hetuḥ:* (adj◦-obj2◦ the cause); *ućyate* (is called) (13.21)

(§4) kāryakaraṇakartṛtve prakṛtiḥ: ućyate hetuḥ: bhoktṛtve sukhduḥ:khānāṃ puruṣaḥ: ućyate hetuḥ:

(§5) In the matter of evolution and the twenty four evolutes, the nature is called the cause. (And) in the matter of experience of the pains and pleasures, 'the life of the living beings' is called the cause. (13.21)

13.22 पुरुषः प्रकृतिस्थो हि भुङ्क्ते प्रकृतिजान्गुणान् ।
कारणं गुणसङ्गोऽस्य सदसद्योनिजन्मसु ।।
puruṣaḥ: prakṛtistho hi bhuṅkte prakṛtijānguṇāṇ,
kāraṇaṁ guṇasaṅgo'sya sadasadyonijanmasu. (13.22)

(§1) *puruṣaḥ:* (r◦ 22/3) *prakṛtisthaḥ:* (r◦ 15/14) *hi bhuṅkte prakṛtijāṇ* (r◦ 13/10) *guṇāṇ* (r◦ 23/1) *kāraṇaṃ* (r◦ 14/1, 24/3) *guṇasaṅgaḥ:* (r◦ 15/1) *asya sadasadyonijanmasu*

(§2) *puruṣaḥ:* (2.21); *prakṛtisthaḥ:* (m◦ 1nom◦ sing◦ ←tatpu◦ adj◦ *prakṛti-stha,* प्रकृतौ तिष्ठति इति ←f◦ *prakṛti* 3.5 + adj◦ *stha* 2.45); *hi* (1.11); *bhuṅkte* (3.12); *prakṛtijāṇ* (m◦ 2acc◦ plu◦ ←bahuvrī◦ adj◦ *prakṛti-ja* 3.5); *guṇāṇ* (13.20); *kāraṇaṃ* (6.3); *guṇasaṅgaḥ:* (m◦ 1nom◦ sing◦ ←tatpu◦ *guṇa-saṅga,* गुणस्य सङ्गः ←m◦ *guṇa* 2.45 + m◦ *saṅgaḥ:* 2.47); *asya* (2.17); *sadasadyonijanmasu* (7loc◦ plu◦ ←tatpu◦ *sadasadyoni-janmaṇ,* सत् च असत् च योन्योः जन्मनि ←adj◦ *saṭ* 2.16 + adj◦ *asaṭ* 2.16 + f◦ *yoni* 5.22 + n◦ *janmaṇ* 2.27) (13.22)

(§3) *puruṣaḥ:* (subj1◦ the *puruṣaḥ:,* the life of the living beings); *prakṛtisthaḥ:* (adj◦-subj1◦ seated in the *prakṛiti,* the nature); *hi* (because); *bhuṅkte* (experiences, witnesseses); *prakṛtijāṇ* (adj◦-obj1◦ born of *prakṛitiḥ*); *guṇāṇ* (obj1◦ the three attributes); *kāraṇaṃ* (adj◦-subj1◦ the cause); *guṇasaṅgaḥ:* (subj2◦

contact with the group of three *guṇas*); *asya* (adj∘-subj2∘ its); *sadasadyonijanmasu* (for the the righteous or unrighteous births) (13.22)

(§4) hi puruṣaḥ: prakṛtisthaḥ: bhuṅkte guṇān prakṛtijān asya guṇasaṅgaḥ: kāraṇam sadasadyonijanmasu

(§5) Because,[722] the *puruṣaḥ:*, seated[723] in the *prakṛti,* witnesseses the three attributes born of *prakṛtiḥ.* Its contact with the group of three *guṇas* (is) the cause for the[724] righteous or unrighteous births. (13.22)

13.23 उपद्रष्टानुमन्ता च भर्ता भोक्ता महेश्वरः ।
परमात्मेति चाप्युक्तो देहेऽस्मिन्पुरुषः परः ।।
upadraṣṭānumantā ća bhartā bhoktā maheśvaraḥ:,
paramātmeti ćāpyukto dehe'sminpuruṣaḥ: paraḥ:. (13.23)

(§1) *upadraṣṭā* (r∘ 1/3) *anumantā ća bhartā bhoktā maheśvaraḥ:* (r∘ 22/8) *parmātmā* (r∘ 2/3) *iti ća* (r∘ 1/1) *api* (r∘ 4/3) *uktaḥ:* (r∘ 15/4) *dehe* (r∘ 6/1) *asmin* (r∘ 13/13) *puruṣaḥ:* (r∘ 22/3) *paraḥ:* (r∘ 22/8)

(§2) *upadraṣṭā* (1nom∘ sing∘ ←m∘ *upadraṣṭṛ* ←उप√दृश्); *anumantā* (1nom∘ sing∘ ←m∘ *anumantṛ* ←अनु√मन्); *ća* (1.1); *bhartā* (9.18); *bhoktā* (9.24); *maheśvaraḥ:* (m∘ 1nom∘ sing∘ ←bahuvrī∘ *maheśvara,*

---

[722] elsewhere∘ हि → See the footnote in 2.16

[723] elsewhere∘ पुरुषः प्रकृतिस्थो → soul is seated, The soul while seated, Purusha **when** seated in, The living entity thus follows, **When** Purusha dwells within, ...etc.

📖 (i) पुरुषः प्रकृतिस्थः = प्रकृतिस्थः पुरुषः Remember, प्रकृतिस्थः is not a verb. प्रकृतिस्थः is the adjective of पुरुषः । Also, प्रकृतिस्थः is not a conditional expression 'when' or 'while.'

[724] elsewhere∘ गुणसङ्गोऽस्य → his birth, his births, its birth, its births, it attains births, he meets, birth of this soul, ...etc.

📖 (i) अस्य refers to गुणसङ्गः not to his/its/purusha's birth/births. पुरुषः does not have a birthday. पुरुषः is अजः । पुरुषः is अनादिः । पुरुषः is नित्यः । पुरुषः is शाश्वतः । पुरुषः is पुराणः । पुरुषः is सनातनः । पुरुषः न जायते म्रियते वा हन्यमाने शरीरे । पुरुषः is आत्मा । आत्मा is ब्रह्म । The so called 'birth' and 'deaths' (actually the transformation) is for शरीरम् । Not for पुरुषः । पुरुषः leaves the previous clothes and wears the new ones. The concept of his/its/purusha's birth/births is quite contrary to the teaching s of the Gītā. So are opposite the concepts of 'this' soul, 'that' soul, 'individual' soul, ...etc. They are not from Gita. They are from other scriptures. There is no such thing in Gita. Please read the 'Introductory Essay' at the begining of Chapter II of this book.
(ii) सदसद्योनिजन्मसु कारणं is for the births of भूतानि (beings), not for births of पुरुषः or आत्मा or soul or whatever one calls. Births are not for पुरुषः । See the above footnote.

महान् ईश्वरः यः ←adj∘ *mahaṭ* 1.3 + m∘ *īśvara* 4.6); *parmātmā* (6.7); *iti* (1.25); *ća* (1.1); *api* (1.26); *uktaḥ:* (1.24); *dehe* (2.13); *asmin̥* (1.22); *puruṣaḥ:* (2.21); *paraḥ:* (3.11) (13.23)

(§3) *upadraṣṭā* (adj1∘-obj∘ the witness, overseer); *anumantā* (adj2∘-obj∘ the proprietor); *ća* (and); *bhartā* (adj3∘-obj∘ the sustainer); *bhoktā* (adj4∘-obj∘ the relisher); *maheśvaraḥ:* (adj5∘-obj∘ the Great Lord); *parmātmā* (adj6∘-obj∘ *puruṣaḥ*); *iti* (as); *ća* (and); *api* (also); *uktaḥ:* (is called, is called by ... subject people); *dehe* (in the body); *asmin̥* (in this); *puruṣaḥ:* (obj1∘ *puruṣaḥ:,* the life of the living being); *paraḥ:* (adj7∘-obj∘ the supreme) (13.23)

(§4) asmin̥ dehe puruṣaḥ: uktaḥ: api iti upadraṣṭā anumantā ća bhartā bhoktā maheśvaraḥ: ća paraḥ: parmātmā

(§5) In this body the *puruṣaḥ* is also called as the overseer, the proprietor, and the sustainer, the relisher the Great Lord and the supreme *puruṣaḥ:*. (13.23)

13.24 य एवं वेत्ति पुरुषं प्रकृतिं च गुणैः सह ।
सर्वथा वर्तमानोऽपि न स भूयोऽभिजायते ॥
ya evaṁ vetti puruṣaṁ prakṛtiṁ ća guṇaiḥ: saha,
sarvathā vartamāno'pi na sa bhūyo'bhijāyate. (13.24)

(§1) *yaḥ:* (r∘ 19/7) *evam̥* (r∘ 14/1) *vetti puruṣam̥* (r∘ 14/1) *prakṛtim̥* (r∘ 14/1) *ća guṇaiḥ:* (r∘ 22/7) *saha sarvathā vartamānaḥ:* (r∘ 15/1) *api na saḥ:* (r∘ 21/2) *bhūyaḥ:* (r∘ 15/1) *abhijāyate*

(§2) *yaḥ:* (2.19); *evam̥* (1.24); *vetti* (2.19); *puruṣam̥* (2.15); *prakṛtim̥* (3.33); *ća* (1.1); *guṇaiḥ:* (3.5); *saha* (1.22); *sarvathā* (6.31); *vartamānaḥ:* (Present Active Participle 6.31); *api* (1.26); *na* (1.30); *saḥ:* (1.13); *bhūyaḥ:* (2.20); *abhijāyate* (2.62) (13.24)

(§3) *yaḥ:* (adj1∘-subj∘ he who); *evam̥* (in this manner, thus); *vetti* (knows); *puruṣam̥* (obj1∘ *puruṣaḥ*); *prakṛtim̥* (obj2∘ *prakṛtiḥ*); *ća* (and); *guṇaiḥ: saha* (with the three *guṇas*); *sarvathā* (in whatever way); *vartamānaḥ:* (living); *api* (even); *na* (does not); *saḥ:* (adj2∘-subj∘ he); *bhūyaḥ:* (again); *abhijāyate* (take birth) (13.24)

(§4) yaḥ: vetti puruṣam̥ ća prakṛtim̥ guṇaiḥ: saha evam̥ na abhijāyate saḥ: bhūyaḥ: api vartamānaḥ: sarvathā

(§5) He who knows *puruṣaḥ* and *prakṛtiḥ* with the three *guṇas* in this manner, he does not take birth again, even living[725] in whatever way. (13.24)

---

[725] elsewhere∘ वर्तमानः → he may live, he lives, he acts, he fares, he exists, he may be, ...etc.

📖 वर्तमानः is not a Verb or Potential or Conditional mood. It is Nominative case of the शानच आत्मनेपदी adjective वर्तमान, √वृत् + शानच् मुक् (मान) ।

13.25 ध्यानेनात्मनि पश्यन्ति केचिदात्मानमात्मना ।
अन्ये साङ्ख्येन योगेन कर्मयोगेन चापरे ।।

dhyānenātmani paśyanti kećidātmānamātmanā,
anye sāṁkhyena yogena karmayogena ćāpare; (13.25)

(§1) *dhyānena* (r∘ 1/2) *ātmani paśyanti kećit̩* (r∘ 8/3) *ātmānam̩* (r∘ 8/17) *ātmanā* (r∘ 23/1) *anye sāṁkhyena yogena karmayogena ća* (r∘ 1/1) *apare;*

(§2) *dhyānena* (3inst∘ sing∘ ←n∘ *dhyāna* 12.12); *ātmani* (2.55); *paśyanti* (1.38); *kećit̩* (11.21); *ātmānam̩* (3.43); *ātmanā* (2.55); *anye* (1.9); *sāṁkhyena* (n∘ 3inst∘ sing∘ ←adj∘ *sāṅkhya* 2.39); *yogena* (10.7); *karmayogena* (3.3); *ća* (1.1); *apare* (4.25); (13.25)

(§3) *dhyānena* (with *dhyāna-yoga,* with the help of *yoga* of concentration); *ātmani* (in themselves); *paśyanti* (see, realize, behold); *kećit̩* (subj1∘ some); *ātmānam̩* (obj∘ themselves); *ātmanā* (by themselves); *anye* (subj2∘); *sāṁkhyena yogena* (with *sāṁkhya-yoga,* with the *yoga* of renunciation of authorship); *karmayogena* (with *karma-yoga,* with the *yoga* of renunciation in the desire of fruit); *ća* (and); *apare* (subj3∘ some others); (13.25)

(§4) kećit̩ paśyanti ātmānam̩ ātmanā ātmani dhyānena anye sāṁkhyena yogena ća apare karmayogena;

(§5) Some realize themselves by themselves[726] in themselves[727] with the help of *yoga* of concentration; others with the *yoga* of renunciation of authorship and some others with the *yoga* of renunciation in the desire of fruit; (13.25)

13.26 अन्ये त्वेवमजानन्तः श्रुत्वान्येभ्य उपासते ।
तेऽपि चातितरन्त्येव मृत्युं श्रुतिपरायणाः ।।

anye tvevamajānantaḥ: śrutvānyebhya upāsate,
te'pi ćātitarantyeva mṛtyuṁ śrutiparāyaṇāḥ:. (13.26)

(§1) *anye tu* (r∘ 4/9) *evam̩* (r∘ 8/16) *ajānantaḥ:* (r∘ 22/5) *śrutvā* (r∘ 1/3) *anyebhyaḥ:* (r∘ 19/4) *upāsate te* (r∘ 6/1) *api ća* (r∘ 1/1) *atitaranti* (r∘ 4/4) *eva mṛtyum̩* (r∘ 14/1) *śrutiparāyaṇāḥ:* (r∘ 24/5, 22/8)

(§2) *anye* (1.9); *tu* (1.2); *evam̩* (1.24); *ajānantaḥ:* (7.24); *śrutvā* (2.29); *anyebhyaḥ:* (5abl∘ plu∘ ←adj∘ *anya* 1.9); *upāsate* (9.14); *te* (1.33); *api* (1.26); *ća* (1.1); *atitaranti* (3rd-per∘ plu∘ pres∘ वर्तमान्-लट्

[726] elsewhere∘ आत्मना → with the help of the internal organs, with the help of their refined and sharp intellect, by the mind, ...etc.

[727] elsewhere∘ आत्मनि → in the heart, in the mind, ...etc.

parasmai◦ ←class1◦ अति√तॄ 7.14); *eva* (1.1); *mṛtyuṃ* (2acc◦ sing◦ ←m◦ *mṛtyu* 2.27); *śrutiparāyaṇāḥ:* (m◦ 1nom◦ plu◦ ←bahuvrī◦ *śruti-parāyaṇa*, श्रुतिः परम् अयनम् यस्य ←f◦ *śruti* 2.53 + adj◦ *para* 2.3 + n◦ *ayana* 1.11)

(13.26)

(§3) *anye* (subj4◦ still others); *tu* (however); *evaṃ* (in this manner, thus); *ajānantaḥ:* (śatṛ◦ adj◦-subj4◦ not knowing); *śrutvā* (having heard); *anyebhyaḥ:* (from others); *upāsate* (worship, worship me); *te* (adj1◦-subj4◦ those); *api ća* (also); *atitaranti* (overcome); *eva* (even); *mṛtyuṃ* (death); *śrutiparāyaṇāḥ:* (adj2◦-subj4◦ those who are devoted to hearing) (13.26)

(§4) anye tu ajānantaḥ: evaṃ upāsate śrutvā anyebhyaḥ: te śrutiparāyaṇāḥ: api ća atitaranti eva mṛtyuṃ

(§5) Still others, however, not knowing thus, worship me having heard from others. Those who are devoted to hearing also overcome even death. (13.26)

13.27 यावत्सञ्जायते किञ्चित्सत्त्वं स्थावरजङ्गमम् ।
क्षेत्रक्षेत्रज्ञसंयोगात्तद्विद्धि भरतर्षभ ।।
yāvatsañjāyate kiñćitsattvaṁ sthāvarajaṅgamaṃ,
kṣetrakṣetrajñasam̃yogāttadviddhi bharatarṣabha. (13.27)

(§1) *yāvaṭ* (r◦ 10/7) *sañjāyate kiñćiṭ* (r◦ 10/7) *sattvaṃ* (r◦ 14/1) *sthāvarajaṅgamaṃ* (r◦ 14/2) *kṣetrakṣetrajñasam̃yogāṭ* (r◦ 1/10) *taṭ* (r◦ 9/11) *viddhi bharatarṣabha*

(§2) *yāvaṭ* (1.22); 📖*sañjāyate* (2.62); *kiñćiṭ* (4.20); *sattvaṃ* (10.36); *sthāvara-jaṅgamaṃ* (n◦ 1nom◦ sing◦ ←dvandva◦ स्थावरम् च जङ्गमम् च ←adj◦ *sthāvara* 10.25 + adj◦ *jaṅgama* ←√गम्); *kṣetrakṣetrajñasam̃yogāṭ* (m◦ 5abl◦ sing◦ ←tatpu◦ *kṣetra-kṣetrajña-sam̃yoga*, क्षेत्रस्य च क्षेत्रज्ञस्य च संयोगः ←n◦ *kṣetra* 1.1 + m◦ *kṣetrajña* 13.1 + m◦ *sam̃yoga* 5.14); *taṭ* (2acc◦ 2.7); *viddhi* (2.17); *bharatarṣabha* (3.41) (13.27)

(§3) *yāvaṭ* (whenever); *sañjāyate* (takes birth, evolves); *kiñćiṭ* (any); *sattvaṃ* (subj◦ being); *sthāvara-jaṅgamaṃ* (adj◦-subj◦ moving or non-moving); *kṣetrakṣetrajñasam̃yogāṭ* (as a result of the union of *kṣetra* and *kṣetrajña*); *taṭ* (obj◦ that. it); *viddhi* (know it to be); *bharatarṣabha* (O Arjuna!) (13.27)

(§4) bharatarṣabha yāvaṭ kiñćiṭ sthāvara-jaṅgamaṃ sattvaṃ sañjāyate moving or non-moving, taṭ viddhi kṣetrakṣetrajñasam̃yogāṭ.

(§5) O Arjuna! whenever any moving or non-moving being evolves, know it to be as a result of the union of *kṣetra* and *kṣetrajña*. (13.27)

13.28 समं सर्वेषु भूतेषु तिष्ठन्तं परमेश्वरम् ।

विनश्यत्स्वविनश्यन्तं यः पश्यति स पश्यति ।।

samaṁ sarveṣu bhūteṣu tiṣṭhantaṁ parameśvaraṃ,
vinaśyatsvavinaśyantaṁ yaḥ: paśyati sa paśyati. (13.28)

(§1) *samaṃ* (r∘ 14/1) *sarveṣu* (r∘ 25/5) *bhūteṣu* (r∘ 25/5) *tiṣṭhantaṃ* (r∘ 14/1) *parameśvaraṃ* (r∘ 14/2) *vinaśyatsu* (r∘ 4/6) *avinaśyantaṃ* (r∘ 14/1) *yaḥ:* (r∘ 22/3) *paśyati saḥ:* (r∘ 21/2) *paśyati*

(§2) *samaṃ* (adv∘ 5.19); *sarveṣu* (1.11); *bhūteṣu* (7.11); *tiṣṭhantaṃ* (m∘ 2acc∘ sing∘ ←śatṛ∘ adj∘ *tiṣṭhat* ←√स्था); *parameśvaraṃ* (m∘ 2acc∘ sing∘ ←bahuvrī∘ *parameśvar* 11.3); *vinaśyatsu* (m∘ 7loc∘ plu∘ ←śatṛ∘ adj∘ *vinaśyat* ←वि√नश्); *a-vinaśyantaṃ* (m∘ 2acc∘ sing∘ n.tatpu∘ ←adj∘ *vinaśyat* ↑); *yaḥ:* (2.19); *paśyati* (2.29); *saḥ:* (1.13); *paśyati* (2.29) (13.28)

(§3) *samaṃ* (equanimously); *sarveṣu* (in all); *bhūteṣu* (in beings); *tiṣṭhantaṃ* (adj1∘-obj∘ dwelling); *parameśvaraṃ* (obj∘ Great Lord); *vinaśyatsu* (in the perishable); *a-vinaśyantaṃ* (adj2∘-obj∘ the eternal); *yaḥ:* (adj∘-subj∘ he who); *paśyati* (sees); *saḥ:* (subj∘ he); *paśyati* (sees, understands) (13.28)

(§4) yaḥ: paśyati a-vinaśyantaṃ parameśvaraṃ tiṣṭhantaṃ samaṃ sarveṣu vinaśyatsu bhūteṣu saḥ: paśyati

(§5) He who sees the eternal Great Lord dwelling equanimously in all perishable beings, he understands. (13.28)

13.29 समं पश्यन्हि सर्वत्र समवस्थितमीश्वरम् ।
न हिनस्त्यात्मनात्मानं ततो याति परां गतिम् ।।

samaṁ paśyanhi sarvatra samavasthitamīśvaraṃ,
na hinastyātmanātmānaṁ tato yāti parāṁ gatiṃ. (13.29)

(§1) *samaṃ* (r∘ 14/1) *paśyaṇ* (r∘ 13/21) *hi sarvatra samavasthitaṃ* (r∘ 8/19) *īśvaraṃ* (r∘ 14/2) *na hinasti* (r∘ 4/2) *ātmanā* (r∘ 1/4) *ātmānaṃ* (r∘ 14/1) *tataḥ:* (r∘ 15/10) *yāti parāṃ* (r∘ 14/1) *gatiṃ* (r∘ 14/2)

(§2) *samaṃ* (adv∘ 6.13); *paśyaṇ* (5.8); *hi* (1.11); *sarvatra* (2.57); *samavasthitaṃ* (m∘ 2acc∘ sing∘ ←ppp∘ adj∘ *samavasthita* ←सम्-अव√स्था); *īśvaraṃ* (m∘ 2acc∘ sing∘ ←m∘ *īśvara* 4.6); *na* (1.30); *hinasti* (3rd-per∘ sing∘ pres∘ वर्तमान्-लट् parasmai∘ ←class7∘ √हिंस्); *ātmanā* (2.55); *ātmānaṃ* (3.43); *tataḥ:* (1.13); *yāti* (6.45); *parāṃ* (4.39); *gatiṃ* (6.37) (13.29)

(§3) *samaṃ* (equanimously); *paśyaṇ* (seeing); *hi* (because, for); *sarvatra* (everywhere); *samavasthitaṃ* (dwelling equanimously); *īśvaraṃ* (obj1∘ the Lord); *na hinasti* (he does not hurt); *ātmanā* (obj2∘ himself); *ātmānaṃ* (by himself); *tataḥ:* (thus); *yāti* (he attains); *parāṃ* (supreme); *gatiṃ* (obj3∘ state) (13.29)

(§4) hi samaṃ paśyan īśvaraṃ samavasthitaṃ sarvatra na hinasti ātmanā ātmānaṃ tataḥ: yāti parāṃ gatiṃ

(§5) For,[728] equanimously seeing the Lord dwelling equanimously everywhere, he does not hurt himself by himself, (and) thus he attains supreme state. (13.29)

13.30 प्रकृत्यैव च कर्माणि क्रियमाणानि सर्वशः ।
यः पश्यति तथात्मानमकर्तारं स पश्यति ।।

prakṛtyaiva ća karmāṇi kriyamāṇāni sarvaśaḥ:,
yaḥ: paśyati tathātmānamakartāraṁ sa paśyati. (13.30)

(§1) *prakṛtyā* (r◦ 3/3) *eva ća karmāṇi* (r◦ 24/7) *kriyamāṇāni sarvaśaḥ:* (r◦ 22/8) *yaḥ:* (r◦ 22/3) *paśyati tathā* (r◦ 1/4) *ātmānaṃ* (r◦ 8/16) *akartāraṃ* (r◦ 14/1) *saḥ:* (r◦ 21.2) *paśyati*

(§2) *prakṛtyā* (7.20); *eva* (1.1); *ća* (1.1); *karmāṇi* (1nom◦ 2.48); *kriyamāṇāni* (3.27); *sarvaśaḥ:* (1.18); *yaḥ:* (2.19); *paśyati* (2.29); *tathā* (1.8); *ātmānaṃ* (3.43); *akartāraṃ* (4.13); *saḥ:* (1.13); *paśyati* (2.29) (13.30)

(§3) *prakṛtyā* (subj1◦ by the *prakṛtiḥ*, by the three *guṇas* of the *prakṛtiḥ*); *eva* (only); *ća* (and); *karmāṇi* (obj1◦ the deeds, *karmas*); *kriyamāṇāni* (are performed); *sarvaśaḥ:* (wholely); *yaḥ:* (adj◦-subj2◦ he who); *paśyati* (sees, understands); *tathā* (similarly he sees, he considers); *ātmānaṃ* (obj2◦ to himself, himself); *akartāraṃ* (adj◦-obj2◦ non-doer); *saḥ:* (subj2◦ he); *paśyati* (understands) (13.30)

(§4) yaḥ: paśyati karmāṇi kriyamāṇāni sarvaśaḥ: prakṛtyā eva ća tathā ātmānaṃ akartāraṃ saḥ: paśyati

(§5) He who understands (that) *karmas* are performed wholely by the three *guṇas* of the *prakṛtiḥ* only, and similarly he considers himself[729] non-doer, he understands. (13.30)

13.31 यदा भूतपृथग्भावमेकस्थमनुपश्यति ।
तत एव च विस्तारं ब्रह्म सम्पद्यते तदा ।।

yadā bhūtapṛthagbhāvamekasthamanupaśyati,
tata eva ća vistāraṁ brahma sampadyate tadā. (13.31)

---

[728] elsewhere◦ हि → See the footnote in 2.16

[729] elsewhere◦ आत्मानम् → the Self, the Atman, ...etc.

📖 As the Lord said in 3.27 प्रकृतेः गुणैः क्रियमाणानि कर्माणि सर्वशः । अहङ्कारविमूढात्मा कर्ता अहम् इति मन्यते । and in shloka 5.8 किञ्चित् नैव करोमि । *Guṇas* of the *prakriti* are the doer, I am not the doer. See Volume II, Chapters 3 and 5. See shloka 14.23 गुणा वर्तन्ते इति एव (मत्वा) यः अवतिष्ठति ।

(§1) *yadā bhūtapṛthagbhāvam̥* (r◦ 8/22) *ekastham̥* (r◦ 8/16) *anupaśyati tataḥ:* (r◦ 19/7) *eva ća vistāram̥* (r◦ 14/1) *brahma sampadyate tadā*

(§2) *yadā* (2.52); *bhūtapṛthagbhāvam̥* (m◦ 2acc◦ sing◦ ←tatpu◦ 🕮*bhūta-pṛthagbhāva*, भूतानाम् पृथक् भाव: ←n◦ *bhūta* 2.28 + adj◦ *pṛthak* 1.18 + m◦ *bhāva* 2.7); *ekastham̥* (11.7); *anupaśyati* (3rd-per◦ sing◦ pres◦ वर्तमान्-लट् parasmai◦ ←class1◦ अनु√दृश् 2.29); *tataḥ:* (1.13); *eva* (1.1); *ća* (1.1); 🕮*vistāram̥* (m◦ 2acc◦ sing◦ ←m◦ *vistāra* ←वि√स्तृ); *brahma* (3.15); *sampadyate* (3rd-per◦ sing◦ pres◦ वर्तमान्-लट् ātmane◦ ←class4◦ सम्√पद्); *tadā* (1.2) (13.31)

(§3) *yadā* (when); *bhūtapṛthagbhāvam̥* (obj◦ the diversity in the nature of beings); *ekastham̥* (adj◦-obj◦ rooted in one); *anupaśyati one clearly unserstands*); *tataḥ:* (from that); *eva ća* (and, as well as); *vistāram̥* (the manifestations); *brahma* (*brahma*); *sampadyate* (attains, becomes one with); *tadā* (then, at that time) (13.31)

(§4) yadā anupaśyati bhūtapṛthagbhāvam̥ ekastham̥ eva vistāram̥ ća tataḥ: tadā sampadyate brahma

(§5) When one clearly unserstands the diversity in the nature of beings rooted in One, and the manifestations from That, then (he) becomes one with *brahma.* (13.31)

13.32 अनादित्वान्निर्गुणत्वात्परमात्मायमव्ययः ।
शरीरस्थोऽपि कौन्तेय न करोति न लिप्यते ।।

anāditvānnirguṇatvātparamātmāyamavyayaḥ:,
śarīrastho'pi kaunteya na karoti na lipyate. (13.32)

(§1) *anāditvāt̥* (r◦ 12/1) *nirguṇatvāt̥* (r◦ 10/6) *parmātmā* (r◦ 1/3) *ayam̥* (r◦ 8/16) *avyayaḥ:* (r◦ 22/8) *śarīrasthaḥ:* (r◦ 15/1) *api kaunteya na karoti na lipyate*

(§2) *anāditvāt̥* (5abl◦ sing◦ ←n◦ *anāditva* ←adj◦ *anādi* 10.3); *nirguṇatvāt̥* (5abl◦ sing◦ ←n◦ *nirguṇatva* ←adj◦ *nirguṇa* 13.15); *parmātmā* (6.7); *ayam̥* (2.19); *avyayaḥ:* (11.18); *śarīrasthaḥ:* (m◦ 1nom◦ sing◦ ←tatpu◦ adj◦ *śarīra-stha*, शरीरे तिष्ठति इति ←n◦ *śarīra* 1.29 + adj◦ *stha* 2.45); *api* (1.26); *kaunteya* (2.14); *na* (1.30); *karoti* (4.20); *na* (1.30); *lipyate* (5.7) (13.32)

(§3) *anāditvāt̥* (being beginningless); *nirguṇatvāt̥* (being attributeless); *parmātmā* (subj◦ *ātmā*); *ayam̥* (adj1◦-subj◦ this); *avyayaḥ:* (adj2◦-subj◦ immutable); *śarīrasthaḥ:* (adj3◦-subj◦ associated with the body); *api* (also); *kaunteya* (O Arjuna!); *na* (neither); *karoti* (does); *na* (nor); *lipyate* (attaches, sticks to the body) (13.32)

(§4) kaunteya anāditvāt̥ nirguṇatvāt̥ ayam̥ avyayaḥ: parmātmā ātmā śarīrasthaḥ: api na karoti na lipyate

(§5) **O Arjuna! being beginningless (and) being attributeless this immutable *ātmā* associated with the body also neither does nor sticks to the body.** (13.32)

13.33 यथा सर्वगतं सौक्ष्म्यादाकाशं नोपलिप्यते ।
सर्वत्रावस्थितो देहे तथात्मा नोपलिप्यते ।।

yathā sarvagataṁ saukṣmyādakaśaṁ nopalipyate,
sarvatrāvasthito dehe tathātmā nopalipyate. (13.33)

(§1) *yathā sarvagataṃ* (r∘ 14/1) *saukṣmyāṭ* (r∘ 8/3) *ākaśaṃ* (r∘ 14/1) *na* (r∘ 2/2) *upalipyate sarvatra* (r∘ 1/1) *avasthitaḥ:* (r∘ 15/4) *dehe tathā* (r∘ 1/4) *ātmā na* (r∘ 2/2) *upalipyate*

(§2) *yathā* (1.11); *sarvagataṃ* (nom∘ 3.15); *saukṣmyāṭ* (5abl∘ sing∘ ←n∘ taddhita∘ *saukṣmya* ←adj∘ *sūkṣma* 13.16); *ākaśaṃ* (1nom∘ sing∘ ←n∘ *ākāśa* 9.6); *na* (1.30); *upalipyate* (3rd-per∘ sing∘ pres∘ वर्तमान्-लट् ātmane∘ ←class6∘ उप√लिप् 5.7); *sarvatra* (2.57); *avasthitaḥ:* (9.4); *dehe* (2.13); *tathā* (1.8); *ātmā* (6.5); *na* (1.30); *upalipyate* (↑) (13.33)

(§3) *yathā* (just as); *sarvagataṃ* (adj1∘-subj1∘ the all occupying); *saukṣmyāṭ* (being subtle); *ākaśaṃ* (subj1∘ space); *na* (does not); *upalipyate* (stick, attach); *sarvatra* (everywhere); *avasthitaḥ:* (adj∘-subj2∘ present); *dehe* (in the body); *tathā* (so); *ātmā* (the *ātmā*); *na* (does not); *upalipyate* (stick) (13.33)

(§4) yathā sarvagataṃ ākaśaṃ saukṣmyāṭ na upalipyate tathā ātmā avasthitaḥ: sarvatra dehe na upalipyate

(§5) **Just as the all occupying space, being subtle, does not stick; so the *ātmā* present everywhere in the body, does not stick.** (13.33)

13.34 यथा प्रकाशयत्येकः कृत्स्नं लोकमिमं रविः ।
क्षेत्रं क्षेत्री तथा कृत्स्नं प्रकाशयति भारत ।।

yathā prakaśayatyekaḥ: kṛtsnaṁ lokamimaṁ raviḥ:,
kṣetraṁ kṣetrī tathā kṛtsnaṁ prakāśayati bhārata. (13.34)

(§1) *yathā prakāśayati* (r∘ 4/4) *ekaḥ:* (r∘ 22/1) *kṛtsnaṃ* (r∘ 14/1) *lokaṃ* (r∘ 8/18) *imaṃ* (r∘ 14/1) *raviḥ:* (r∘ 22/8) *kṣetraṃ* (r∘ 14/1) *kṣetrī tathā kṛtsnaṃ* (r∘ 14/1) *prakāśayati bhārata*

(§2) *yathā* (1.11); *prakāśayati* (5.16); *ekaḥ:* (11.42); *kṛtsnaṃ* (1.40); *lokaṃ* (9.33); *imaṃ* (1.28); *raviḥ:* (10.21); *kṣetraṃ* (13.1); *kṣetrī* (1nom∘ sing∘ ←m∘ *kṣetriṇ* ←√क्षि); *tathā* (1.8); *kṛtsnaṃ* (2acc∘ or adv∘ 1.40); *prakāśayati* (5.16); *bhārata* (1.24) (13.34)

(§3) *yathā* (just as); *prakāśayati* (enlightens); *ekaḥ:* (adj∘-subj∘ alone); *kṛtsnaṃ* (adj1∘-obj1∘ the whole);

lokaṃ (obj∘ world); *imaṃ* (adj2∘-obj1∘ this); *raviḥ:* (subj∘ the sun); *kṣetraṃ* (obj2∘ *kṣetraṃ*, body); *kṣetrī* (subj2∘ the *kṣetrī, ātmā*); *tathā* (so does); *kṛtsnaṃ* (adj∘-obj2∘ the whole); *prakāśayati* (enlightens, enlivens); *bhārata* (O Arjuna!) (13.34)

(§4) bhārata yathā raviḥ: ekaḥ: prakāśayati kṛtsnaṃ lokaṃ tathā imaṃ kṣetrī prakāśayati kṛtsnaṃ kṣetraṃ

(§5) O Arjuna! just as the sun alone illuminates the whole world, so does this *ātmā* enlivens the whole body. (13.34)

13.35 क्षेत्रक्षेत्रज्ञयोरेवमन्तरं ज्ञानचक्षुषा ।
भूतप्रकृतिमोक्षं च ये विदुर्यान्ति ते परम् ।।
kṣetrakṣetrajñayorevamantaraṁ jñānaćakṣuṣā,
bhūtaprakṛtimokṣaṁ ća ye viduryānti te paraṃ. (13.35)

(§1) *kṣetrakṣetrajñayoḥ:* (r∘ 16/5) *evaṃ* (r∘ 8/16) *antaraṃ* (r∘ 14/1) *jñānaćakṣuṣā* (r∘ 25/2) *bhūtaprakṛtimokṣaṃ* (r∘ 14/1) *ća ye viduḥ:* (r∘ 16/8) *yānti te paraṃ* (r∘ 14/2)

(§2) *kṣetrakṣetrajñayoḥ:* (13.3); *evaṃ* (1.24); *antaraṃ* (2acc∘ sing∘ ←n∘ *antara* 11.20); *jñānaćakṣuṣā* (n∘ 3inst∘ sing∘ ←tatpu∘ *jñāna-ćakṣus*, ज्ञानस्य चक्षुः ←n∘ *jñāna* 3.3 + n∘ *ćakṣus* 5.27); *bhūtaprakṛtimokṣaṃ* (m∘ 2acc∘ sing∘ ←tatpu∘ *bhūta-prakṛti-mokṣa*, भूतानाम् प्रकृतेः मोक्षः ←n∘ *bhūta* 2.28 + f∘ *prakṛti* 3.5 + m∘ *mokṣa* 5.28); *ća* (1.1); *ye* (1.7); *viduḥ:* (4.2); *yānti* (3.33); *te* (1.33); *paraṃ* (2acc∘ 2.59) (13.35)

(§3) *kṣetrakṣetrajñayoḥ:* (of the *kṣetra* and the *kṣetrajña,* between the body and the *ātmā*); *evaṃ* (thus); *antaraṃ* (obj1∘ the difference); *jñānaćakṣuṣā* (with the eye of wisdom); *bhūtaprakṛtimokṣaṃ* (obj2∘ the dissolution of the beings back to the *prakṛtiḥ*); *ća* (and); *ye* (adj∘-subj∘ they who); *viduḥ:* (understand, see); *yānti* (attain); *te* (subj∘ they); *paraṃ* (obj3∘ the Supreme, the supreme state) (13.35)

(§4) evaṃ ye viduḥ: antaraṃ kṣetrakṣetrajñayoḥ: ća bhūtaprakṛtimokṣaṃ jñānaćakṣuṣā te yānti paraṃ

(§5) Thus, they who see the difference between the body and the *ātmā* and the dissoulution of the beings back to[730] the *prakṛtiḥ,* with the eye of wisdom, they attain the Supreme. (13.35)

---

[730] elsewhere∘ भूतप्रकृतिमोक्षम् → release from Prakriti, annihilation of the matrix from, liberation from Prakṛti, liberation from the bondage, deliverance from, freedom from, ...etc.

📖 Remember, the definition of Prakṛtiḥ is "the perfect balance of the five *mahāhhūtās* and the three *guṇās*. The beings (living, non-living) are the *vikārās* (modifications) of this perfect balance. *Mokṣaḥ* is back to the perfect balance i.e. the *prakṛtiḥ* (nature), with disconnection of *ātmā.* Now, the *ātmā,* disconnected from the body (also called untainted), is *brahma.*

इति श्रीमद्भगवद्गीतासूपनिषत्सु ब्रह्मविद्यायां योगशास्त्रे
श्रीकृष्णार्जुनसंवादे क्षेत्रक्षेत्रज्ञविभागयोगो नाम त्रयोदशोऽध्याय: ।

iti śrīmadbhagavadgītāsūpaniṣatsu brahmavidyāyāṁ yogaśāstre
śrīkṛṣṇārjunasaṁvāde kṣetrakṣetrajñavibhāgayogo nāma trayodaśo'dhyāyaḥ:

(§1) *iti śrīmadbhagavadgītāsu* (r◦ 1/8) *upaniṣatsu brahmavidyāyāṃ* (r◦ 14/1) *yogaśāstre śrīkṛṣṇārjunasaṁvāde kṣetrakṣetrajñavibhāgayogaḥ:* (r◦ 15/6) *nāma trayodaśaḥ:* (r◦ 15/1) *adhyāyaḥ:* (r◦ 22/8)

(§2) *iti* (1.25); *śrīmadbhagavadgītāsu* (f◦ 7loc◦ plu◦ tatpu◦ *śrīmad-bhagavad-gītā* ←adj◦ *śrīmaṭ* 6.41↓ + adj◦ *bhagavaṭ* 10.14↓ + f◦ *gītā* ←5◦√गै); *upaniṣatsu* (7loc◦ plu◦ ←f◦ *upaniṣaḍ* ←6◦उप-नि√सद्); *brahmavidyāyāṃ* (f◦ 7loc◦ sing◦ ←tatpu◦ *brahma-vidyā*, ब्रह्मण: विद्या ←n◦ *brahmaṇ* 2.72↓ + *vidyā* 5.18↓); *yogaśāstre* (n◦ 7loc◦ sing◦ ←tatpu◦ *yoga-śāstra*, योगानाम् शास्त्रम् । योगस्य शास्त्रम् । ←m◦ *yoga* 2.39↓ + n◦ *śāstra* 15.20↓); *śrīkṛṣṇārjunasaṁvāde* (m◦ 7loc◦ sing◦ ←tatpu◦ *śrī-kṛṣṇārjuna-saṁvāda*, श्रीकृष्णस्य च अर्जुनस्य च संवाद: ←adj◦ *śrī* 10.34↓ + m◦ prop◦ *kṛṣṇa* 1.28 + m◦ prop◦ *arjuna* 1.4 + m◦ *saṁvāda* 18.70↓); *kṣetrakṣetrajñavibhāgayogaḥ:* (m◦ 1nom◦ sing◦ ←tatpu◦ *kṣetra-kṣetrajña-vibhāga-yoga,* क्षेत्रस्य च क्षेत्रज्ञस्य च विभागयो: योग: ←n◦ *kṣetra* 1.1 + m◦ *kṣetrakṣetrajña* 13.1 + m◦ *vibhāga* 3.28 + m◦ *yoga* 2.39); *nāma* (1nom◦ sing◦ ←n◦ *nāmaṇ* ←1◦√म्ना); *trayodaśaḥ:* (m◦ 1nom◦ sing◦ ←num◦ adj◦ *trayodaśa* ←1◦√तॄ); *adhyāyaḥ:* (1nom◦ sing◦ ←m◦ *adhyāya* ←1◦अधि√इ)

(§3) *iti* (thus); *śrīmadbhagavadgītāsu upaniṣatsu* (among the upaniṣads of Śrīmad-Bhagavadgītā); *brahmavidyāyāṃ* (of the eternal wisdoms); *yogaśāstre* (in the science of Yoga); *śrīkṛṣṇārjunasaṁvāde* (in the dialogue between Śrī Kṛṣṇa and Arjuna); *kṣetrakṣetrajñavibhāgayogaḥ:* (adj1◦-subj◦ kṣetra-kṣetrajña-vibhāga-yoga); *nāma* (called) *trayodaśaḥ:* (adj2◦-subj◦ thirteenth); *adhyāyaḥ:* (subj◦ discourse)

(§4) śrīmadbhagavadgītāsu upaniṣatsu yogaśāstre brahmavidyāyāṃ iti trayodaśaḥ: adhyāyaḥ: nāma kṣetrakṣetrajñavibhāgayogaḥ: śrīkṛṣṇārjunasaṁvāde

(§5) Among the upaniṣads of the Śrīmad-Bhagavadgītā, in the science of Yoga of self realization, thus (is) the thirteenth discourse called kṣetra-kṣetrajña-vibhāga-yogaḥ: in the dialogue between Śrī Kṛṣṇa and Arjuna.

CHAPTER 14

ćaturdaśo'dhyāyaḥ:

चतुर्दशोऽध्याय: ।

THE YOGA PERTAINING TO "THE THREE ATTRIBUTES"[731]

guṇatrayavibhāgayogaḥ:

गुणत्रयविभागयोग: ।

The Lord said (śrībhagavānuvāća श्रीभगवानुवाच ।)

14.1 परं भूय: प्रवक्ष्यामि ज्ञानानां ज्ञानमुत्तमम् ।
यज्ज्ञात्वा मुनय: सर्वे परां सिद्धिमितो गता: ।।

paraṁ bhūyaḥ: pravakṣyāmi jñānānāṁ jñānamuttamam,
yajjñātvā munayaḥ: sarve parāṁ siddhimito gatāḥ:; (14.1)

(§1) *ćaturdaśaḥ:* (r◦ 15/1) *adhyāyaḥ:* (r◦ 22/8). *guṇatrayavibhāgayogaḥ:* (r◦ 22/8). *śrībhagavān* (r◦ 8/14) *uvāća. param* (r◦ 14/1) *bhūyaḥ:* (r◦ 22/3) *pravakṣāmi jñānānām* (r◦ 14/1) *jñānam* (r◦ 8/20) *uttamam* (r◦ 14/2) *yat* (r◦ 11/2) *jñātvā munayaḥ:* (r◦ 22/7) *sarve parām* (r◦ 14/1) *siddhim* (r◦ 8/18) *itaḥ:* (r◦ 15/2) *gatāḥ:* (r◦ 22/8);

(§2) *ćaturdaśaḥ:* (m◦ 1nom◦ sing◦ ←sequence indicating num◦ adj◦ *ćaturdaśa* ←adj◦ *ćatur* 7.16 + adj◦ *daśa* 13.6); *adhyāyaḥ:* (1nom◦ sing◦ ←m◦ *adhyāya* ←अधि√इ). *guṇatrayavibhāgayogaḥ:* (m◦ 1nom◦ sing◦ ←tatpu◦ *guṇa-traya-vibhāga-yoga*, गुणानाम् त्रयस्य विभागस्य योग: ←m◦ *guṇa* 2.45 + n◦ *traya* 11.20 + m◦ *vibhāga* 3.28 + m◦ *yoga* 2.39). *śrībhagavān* (2.2); *uvāća* (1.25). *param* (2acc◦ 2.12); *bhūyaḥ:* (2.20); *pravakṣāmi* (4.16); *jñānānām* (6pos plu◦ ←n◦ *jñāna* 3.3); *jñānam* (2acc◦ 3.40); *uttamam* (2acc◦ 4.3); *yat* (2acc◦ 3.21); *jñātvā* (4.15); *munayaḥ:* (1nom◦ plu◦ ←m◦ *muni* 2.56); *sarve* (1.6); *parām* (4.39); *siddhim* (3.4); *itaḥ:* (7.5); *gatāḥ:* (8.15); (14.1)

(§3) *ćaturdaśaḥ:* (adj◦-subj◦ the fourteenth); *adhyāyaḥ:* (subj◦ chapter). *guṇatrayavibhāgayogaḥ:* (subj1◦ The yoga pertaining to the three attributes of the nature). *śrībhagavān* (subj◦ Lord Kṛṣṇa); *uvāća* (said). *param* (adj1◦-obj◦ supreme); *bhūyaḥ:* (again); *pravakṣāmi* (subj1◦ I shall tell); *jñānānām*

---

[731] Elsewhere◦ *guṇatrayavibhāgayogaḥ:* → The Yoga of Division of the Three Gunas, The separation of the Three Guṇas, The Mystical Father of All Beings, The Three Modes of Material Nature, ...etc.

(of all knowledges); *jñānam* (obj1◦ knowledge); *uttamam* (adj2◦-obj1◦ the best); *yat* (adj3◦-obj1◦ that which); *jñātvā* (having known); *munayaḥ:* (subj2◦ the sages); *sarve* (adj1◦-subj2◦ all); *parām* (adj◦-obj2◦ supreme); *siddhim* (obj2◦ state); *itaḥ:* (from this world); *gatāḥ:* (adj2◦-subj2◦ attained); (14.1)

(§4) ćaturdaśaḥ: adhyāyaḥ: guṇatrayavibhāgayogaḥ: śrībhagavān uvāća pravakṣāmi bhūyaḥ: param jñānam uttamam jñānānām yat jñātvā sarve munayaḥ: itaḥ: gatāḥ: parām siddhim

(§5) The fourteenth chapter. The *yoga* pertaining to the three attributes (*guṇas*) of the nature.

Lord Kṛṣṇa said : I shall tell (you) again that supreme knowledge, the best of all knowledges, which having known all the sages from this world attained supreme success;[732] (14.1)

14.2 इदं ज्ञानमुपाश्रित्य मम साधर्म्यमागताः ।
सर्गेऽपि नोपजायन्ते प्रलये न व्यथन्ति च ।।

idaṁ jñānamupāśritya mama sādharmyamāgatāḥ:,
sarge‘pi nopajāyante pralaye na vyathanti ća. (14.2)

(§1) *idam* (r◦ 14/1) *jñānam* (r◦ 8/20) *upāśritya mama sādharmyam* (r◦ 8/17) *āgatāḥ:* (r◦ 22/8) *sarge* (r◦ 6/1) *api na* (r◦ 2/2) *upajāyante pralaye na vyathanti ća*

(§2) *idam* (2acc◦ 1.10); *jñānam* (2acc◦ 3.39); *upāśritya* (lyp◦ past-participle ind◦ ←उप-आ√श्रि); *mama* (1.7); *sādharmyam* (n◦ 2acc◦ sing◦ ←taddhita◦ *sādharmya*, समानः धर्मः यस्य ←adj◦ *sadharman* ←adj◦ *sama* 1.4 + m◦ *dharma* 1.1); *āgatāḥ:* (4.10); *sarge* (7.27); *api* (1.26); *na* (1.30); *upajāyante* (3rd-per◦ plu◦ pres◦ वर्तमान्-लट् ātmane◦ ←class4◦ उप√जन् 2.62); *pralaye* (7loc◦ sing◦ ←m◦ *pralaya* 7.6); *na* (1.30); *vyathanti* (3rd-per◦ plu◦ pres◦ वर्तमान्-लट् parasmai◦ ←class1◦ √व्यथ् 2.15); *ća* (1.1) (14.2)

(§3) *idam* (adj◦-obj1◦ this); *jñānam* (obj1◦ knowledge); *upāśritya* (having taken for shelter); *mama sādharmyam* (obj2◦ unison with me); *āgatāḥ:* (adj◦-subj◦ attained); *sarge* (at evolution); *api* (also); *na* (they do not); *upajāyante* (take birth); *pralaye* (at dissolution); *na* (they do not); *vyathanti* (distress); *ća* (and) (14.2)

(§4) upāśritya idam jñānam āgatāḥ: mama sādharmyam sarge na upajāyante ća pralaye api na vyathanti

(§5) Having taken this knowledge for shelter, (they) attained unison with me. At evolution they

---

[732] elsewhere◦ परां सिद्धिम् → supreme perfection, high perfection, highest perfection, ...etc.

📖 Prefect is perfect. It does not have comparative or superlative degrees of comparison. A thing is either perfect, if not, it is imperfect. The imperfect has degrees of comparison. **Only *brahma* is perfect**, nothing else is perfect.

do not take birth and at dissolution also they do not distress. (14.2)

14.3 मम योनिर्महद्ब्रह्म तस्मिन्गर्भं दधाम्यहम् ।
सम्भवः सर्वभूतानां ततो भवति भारत ।।

mama yonirmahadbrahma tasmingarbhaṁ dadhāmyahaṃ,
sambhava: sarvabhūtānāṁ tato bhavati bhārata. (14.3)

(§1) *mama yoniḥ:* (r◦ 16/6) *mahaṭ* (r◦ 9/7) *brahma tasmiṇ* (r◦ 13/10) *garbhaṃ* (r◦ 14/1) *dadhāmi* (r◦ 4/1) *ahaṃ* (r◦ 14/2) *sambhavaḥ:* (r◦ 22/7) *sarvabhūtānāṃ* (r◦ 14/1) *tataḥ:* (r◦ 15/8) *bhavati bhārata*

(§2) *mama* (1.7); *yoniḥ:* (1nom◦ sing◦ ←f◦ *yoni* 5.22); *mahaṭ* (1nom◦ 1.3); *brahma* (1nom◦ 4.24); *tasmiṇ* (m◦ 7loc◦ sing◦ ←pron◦ *taḍ* 1.2); *garbhaṃ* (2acc◦ sing◦ ←m◦ *garbha* 3.38); *dadhāmi* (1st-per◦ sing◦ pres◦ वर्तमान्-लट् parasmai◦ ←class3◦ √धा); *ahaṃ* (1.22); *sambhavaḥ:* (1nom◦ sing◦ ←m◦ *sambhava* 3.14); *sarva* (1.6); *bhūtānāṃ* (2.69); *tataḥ:* (1.13); *bhavati* (1.44); *bhārata* (1.24) (14.3)

(§3) *mama* (my); *yoniḥ:* (subj1◦ womb); *mahaṭ* (adj◦-subj2◦ the great); *brahma* (subj2◦ *brahma*); *tasmiṇ* (in it, in that); *garbhaṃ* (obj◦ the seed); *dadhāmi* (sow); *ahaṃ* (subj3◦ I); *sambhavaḥ:* (subj4◦ origination, evolution, birth); *sarva-bhūtānāṃ* (of all beings); *tataḥ:* (from that); *bhavati* (occurs); *bhārata* (O Arjuna!) (14.3)

(§4) bhārata mahaṭ brahma mama yoniḥ: tasmiṇ ahaṃ dadhāmi garbhaṃ tataḥ: bhavati sambhavaḥ: sarva-bhūtānāṃ

(§5) O Arjuna! the great *brahma* (is) my womb. In it I sow the seed. From that occurs evolution of all beings. (14.3)

14.4 सर्वयोनिषु कौन्तेय मूर्तयः सम्भवन्ति याः ।
तासां ब्रह्म महद्योनिरहं बीजप्रदः पिता ।।

sarvayoniṣu kaunteya mūrtayaḥ: sambhavanti yāḥ:,
tāsāṁ brahma mahadyoniraham̐ bījapradaḥ: pitā. (14.4)

(§1) *sarvayoniṣu* (r◦ 25/5) *kaunteya mūrtayaḥ:* (r◦ 22/7) *sambhavanti yāḥ:* (r◦ 22/8) *tāsāṃ* (r◦ 14/1) *brahma mahaṭ* (r◦ 9/9) *yoniḥ:* (r◦ 16/1) *ahaṃ* (r◦ 14/1) *bījapradaḥ:* (r◦ 22/3) *pitā*

(§2) *sarvayoniṣu* (सर्वासु योनिषु 7loc◦ plu◦ ←pron◦ *sarva* 1.6 + f◦ *yoni* 5.22); *kaunteya* (2.14); *mūrtayaḥ:* (7loc◦ plu◦ ←f◦ *mūrti* 9.4); *sambhavanti* (3rd-per◦ plu◦ pres◦ वर्तमान्-लट् parasmai◦ ←class1◦ सम्√भू 4.6); *yāḥ:* (f◦ 1nom◦ plu◦ ←pron◦ *yaḍ* 1.7); *tāsāṃ* (f◦ 6pos◦ plu◦ ←pron◦ *taḍ* 1.2); *brahma* (1nom◦ 4.24); *mahaṭ* (1nom◦ 1.3); *yoniḥ:* (14.3); *ahaṃ* (1.22); *bījapradaḥ:* (m◦ 1nom◦ sing◦ ←tatpu◦ *bīja-prada*, बीजम् प्रददाति इति ←n◦ *bīja* 7.10 + m◦ *pradātṛ* ←प्र√दा); *pitā* (9.17) (14.4)

(§3) *sarvayoniṣu* (in all wombs); *kaunteya* (O Arjuna!); *mūrtayaḥ:* (subj∘ the beings); *sambhavanti* (take birth); *tāsām̦* (their); *brahma mahaṭ* (adj∘-subj2∘ the divine *brahma*); *yoniḥ:* (subj2∘ womb); *aham̦* (subj3∘ I, I am); *bījapradaḥ:* (adj∘-subj3∘ the seed giving); *pitā* (adj2∘-subj3∘ father) (14.4)

(§4) kaunteya mūrtayaḥ: sambhavanti sarvayoniṣu brahma mahaṭ tāsām̦ yoniḥ: aham̦ bījapradaḥ: pitā

(§5) O Arjuna! (for) the beings (that) take birth in all wombs, the divine *brahma* (is) their womb (and) I am the seed giving father. (14.4)

14.5 सत्त्वं रजस्तम इति गुणाः प्रकृतिसम्भवाः ।
निबध्नन्ति महाबाहो देहे देहिनमव्ययम् ।।
sattavaṁ rajastama iti guṇāḥ: prakṛtisambhavāḥ:,
nibadhnanti mahābāho dehe dehinamavyayam̦. (14.5)

(§1) *sattvam̦* (r∘ 14/1) *rajaḥ:* (r∘ 18/1) *tamaḥ:* (r∘ 19/2) *iti guṇāḥ:* (r∘ 24/5, 22/3) *prakṛtisambhavāḥ:* (r∘ 22/8) *nibadhnanti mahābāho dehe dehinam̦* (r∘ 8/16) *avyayam̦* (r∘ 14/2)

(§2) *sattvam̦* (10.36); *rajaḥ:* (1nom∘ sing∘ ←n∘ *rajaṣ* 3.37); ***tamaḥ:*** (1nom∘ sing∘ ←n∘ *tamaṣ* 10.11); *iti* (1.25); *guṇāḥ:* (3.28); *prakṛtisambhavāḥ:* (m∘ 1nom∘ plu∘ ←bahuvrī∘ *prakṛti-sambhava* 13.20); *nibadhnanti* (4.41); *mahābāho* (2.26); *dehe* (2.13); *dehinam̦* (3.40); *avyayam̦* (2.21) (14.5)

(§3) *sattvam̦* (adj1∘-subj1∘ the *sat-guṇa*); *rajaḥ:* (adj2∘-subj1∘ the *rajoguṇa*); *tamaḥ:* (adj3∘-subj1∘ the *tamoguṇa*); *iti* (namely); *guṇāḥ:* (subj∘ the *guṇas*, attributes); *prakṛtisambhavāḥ:* (adj4∘-subj1∘ born of *prakṛtiḥ*); *nibadhnanti* (bind, connect); *mahābāho* (O Arjuna!); *dehe* (with the body); *dehinam̦* (obj∘ embodied *ātmā*); *avyayam̦* (adj∘-obj∘ the immutable) (14.5)

(§4) mahābāho guṇāḥ: prakṛtisambhavāḥ: iti sattvam̦ rajaḥ: tamaḥ: nibadhnanti avyayam̦ dehinam̦ dehe

(§5) O Arjuna! the *guṇas* born of *prakṛtiḥ* namely the *sat-guṇa*, the *rajo-guṇa* (and) the *tamo-guṇa* connect the immutable embodied *ātmā* with the body. (14.5)

14.6 तत्र सत्त्वं निर्मलत्वात्प्रकाशकमनामयम् ।
सुखसङ्गेन बध्नाति ज्ञानसङ्गेन चानघ ।।
tatra sattvaṁ nirmalatvātprakāśakamanāmayam̦,
sukhasaṅgena badhnāti jñānasaṅgena ćānagha. (14.6)

(§1) *tatra sattvam̦* (r∘ 14/1) *nirmalatvāṭ* (r∘ 10/6) *prakāśakam̦* (r∘ 8/16) *anāmayam̦* (r∘ 14/2) *sukhasaṅgena badhnāti jñānasaṅgena ća* (r∘ 1/1) *anagha*

(§2) *tatra* (1.26); *sattvam̦* (10.36); *nirmalatvāṭ* (5abl∘ sing∘ ←n∘ *nirmalatva* ←adj∘ *nir-mala* ←ind∘ *nir̦*

2.45 + n◦ m◦ *mala* 3.38); *prakāśakam̦* (n◦ 1nom◦ sing◦ ←adj◦ *prakāśaka* ←प्र√काश्); *anāmayam̦* (1nom◦ sing◦ ←adj◦ *anāmaya* 2.51); *sukhasaṅgena* (m◦ 3inst◦ sing◦ ←tatpu◦ *sukha-saṅga*, सुखस्य सङ्गः ←n◦ *sukha* 1.32 + m◦ *saṅga* 2.47); *badhnāti* (3rd-per◦ sing◦ pres◦ वर्तमान्-लट् parasmai◦ ←class9◦ √बन्ध् 4.41); *jñānasaṅgena* (m◦ 3inst◦ sing◦ ←tatpu◦ *jñāna-saṅga*, ज्ञानस्य सङ्गः ←n◦ *jñāna* 3.3 + m◦ *saṅga* 2.47); *ća* (1.1); *anagha* (3.3) (14.6)

(§3) *tatra* (there, among them, among the three *guṇas*); *sattvam̦* (subj1◦ *satguṇa*); *nirmalatvāț* (due to its purity); *prakāśakam̦* (adj1◦-subj1◦ the enlightener); *anāmayam̦* (adj2◦-subj1◦ stainless); *sukhasaṅgena* (by its charm of happiness); *badhnāti* (it binds); *jñānasaṅgena* (by its magic of wisdom); *ća* (and); *anagha* (O Arjuna!) (14.6)

(§4) anagha tatra prakāśakam̦ anāmayam̦ sattvam̦ nirmalatvāț badhnāti sukhasaṅgena ća jñānasaṅgena

(§5) O Arjuna! among the three *guṇas*, the enlightener (and) stainless *satguṇa*, due to its purity it binds (us, the *sāttavic* embodied ones)[733] by[734] its charm of happiness and by its magic of wisdom. (14.6)

14.7 रजो रागात्मकं विद्धि तृष्णासङ्गसमुद्भवम् ।
तन्निबध्नाति कौन्तेय कर्मसङ्गेन देहिनम् ।।
rajo rāgātmakaṁ viddhi tr̥ṣṇāsaṅgasamudbhavam̦,
tannibadhnāti kaunteya karmasaṅgena dehinam̦. (14.7)

(§1) *rajaḥ:* (r◦ 15/11) *rāgātmakam̦* (r◦ 14/1) *viddhi tr̥ṣṇāsaṅgasamudbhavam̦* (r◦ 14/2) *taț* (r◦ 12/1) *nibadhnāti kaunteya karmasaṅgena dehinam̦* (r◦ 14/2)

(§2) ***rajaḥ:*** (2acc◦ sing◦ ←n◦ *rajaș* 14.5); *rāgātmakam̦* (n◦ 1nom◦ 2acc◦ sing◦ ←bahuvrī◦ adj◦ *rāgātmaka*, रागः आत्मा यस्य ←m◦ *rāga* 2.56 + adj◦ *ātmaka* ←n◦ *ātman̦* 2.41 + taddhita◦ affix *ak̦*, अक – कन् or क्वुन् indicating relating to or produced from); *viddhi* (2.17); *tr̥ṣṇāsaṅgasamudbhavam̦* (m◦ 2acc◦ sing◦ ←bahuvrī◦ *tr̥ṣṇā-saṅga-samudbhava*, तृष्णायाः च सङ्गात् च समुद्भवः यस्य ←f◦ *tr̥ṣṇa* ←√तृष् + m◦ *saṅga* 2.47 +

---

[733] NOTE : dehī (देही) = embodied one, embodied beings, us humans and animals. Not *ātmā* (or soul) in this context. See the footnote in verse 14.14 below.

[734] elsewhere◦ सुखसङ्गेन बध्नाति ज्ञानसङ्गेन च → it binds to happiness and knowledge, ...etc.

📖 In सुखसङ्गेन and ज्ञानसङ्गेन, (Instrumental 3rd case), सुखम् and ज्ञानम् are the 'instruments' of *sat-guṇa* **by which, by means of which or through which** it binds us, the embodied ones. सुखम् and ज्ञानम् are not the (Accusative 2nd case) 'objects' **to** which it binds.

Remember : The ātmā is अक्षरः, अविकारः and can not be bound or affected by anything and by anyone.

m∘ *samudbhava* 3.14); *taṭ* (1.10); *nibadhnāti* (3rd-per∘ sing∘ pres∘ वर्तमान्-लट् parasmai∘ ←class9∘ नि√बन्ध् 4.41); *kaunteya* (2.14); *karmasaṅgena* (m∘ 3inst∘ sing∘ ←tatpu∘ *karma-saṅga*, कर्मण: सङ्ग: ←n∘ *karmaṇ* 1.15 + m∘ *saṅga* 2.47); *dehinaṃ* (3.40) (14.7)

(§3) *rajaḥ:* (obj1∘ *rajoguṇa*); *rāgātmakaṃ* (adj1∘-obj1∘ stimulator of desire); *viddhi* (know it to be); *tṛṣṇāsaṅgasamudbhavaṃ* (adj2∘-obj1∘ born out of greed and attachment); *taṭ* (adj3∘-obj1∘ that); *nibadhnāti* (binds); *kaunteya* (O Arjuna!); *karmasaṅgena* (by the attraction to *karma*); *dehinaṃ* (obj2∘ the embodied one) (14.7)

(§4) kaunteya rajaḥ: tṛṣṇāsaṅgasamudbhavaṃ viddhi rāgātmakaṃ taṭ nibadhnāti dehinaṃ karmasaṅgena

(§5) O Arjuna! *rajo-guṇa,* born out of greed and attachment, know it to be stimulator of desire that binds the (*tāmasic*) embodied ones by the attraction to *karma.* (14.7)

14.8 तमस्त्वज्ञानजं विद्धि मोहनं सर्वदेहिनाम् ।
प्रमादालस्यनिद्राभिस्तन्निबध्नाति भारत ।।
tamastvajñānajaṁ viddhi mohanaṁ sarvadehinām,
pramādālasyanidrābhistannibadhnāti bhārata. (14.8)

(§1) *tamaḥ:* (r∘ 18/1) *tu* (r∘ 4/6) *ajñānajaṃ* (r∘ 14/1) *viddhi mohanaṃ* (r∘ 14/1) *sarvadehināṃ* (r∘ 14/2) *pramādālasyanidrābhiḥ:* (r∘ 18/1) *taṭ* (r∘ 12/1) *nibadhnāti bhārata*

(§2) *tamaḥ:* (10.11); *tu* (1.2); *ajñānajaṃ* (10.11); *viddhi* (2.17); 🕮*mohanaṃ* (n∘ 1nom∘ sing∘ ←adj∘ *mohana* ←√मुह्); *sarvadehināṃ* (सर्वेषाम् देहिनाम्, m∘ 6pos∘ plu∘ ←pron∘ *sarva* 1.6 + m∘ *dehiṇ* 2.13); *pramādālasyanidrābhiḥ:* (f∘ 3inst∘ plu∘ ←tatpu∘ or dvandva∘ प्रमादेन च आलस्येन च निद्रया च ←m∘ *pramāda* 11.41 + n∘ *ālasya* ←आ√लस् + f∘ *nidrā* ←√निन्द्); *taṭ* (1.10); *nibadhnāti* (14.7); *bhārata* (1.24) (14.8)

(§3) *tamaḥ:* (obj1∘ the *tamoguṇa*); *tu* (but, and); *ajñānajaṃ* (adj1∘-obj1∘ born out of ignorance); *viddhi* (know it to be); *mohanaṃ* (adj2∘-obj1∘ delusion); *sarvadehināṃ* (of all embodied ones, our); *pramādālasyanidrābhiḥ:* (by confusion, indolence and intoxication); *taṭ* (adj3∘-obj1∘ that, it); *nibadhnāti* (binds); *bhārata* (O Arjuna!) (14.8)

(§4) tu bhārata tamaḥ: ajñānajaṃ viddhi mohanaṃ sarvadehināṃ taṭ nibadhnāti pramādālasyanidrābhiḥ:

(§5) And, O Arjuna! the *tamo-guṇa,* born out of ignorance, know it to be delusion of all embodied ones that binds (us) by confusion, indolence and intoxication. (14.8)

14.9 सत्त्वं सुखे सञ्जयति रज: कर्मणि भारत ।

ज्ञानमावृत्य तु तम: प्रमादे सञ्जयत्युत ।।

sattavaṁ sukhe sañjayati rajaḥ: karmaṇi bhārata,
jñānamāvṛtya tu tamaḥ: pramāde sañjayatyuta. (14.9)

(§1) *sattvam̦* (r◦ 14/1) *sukhe sañjayati rajaḥ:* (r◦ 22/1) *karmaṇi* (r◦ 24/7) *bhārata jñānam̦* (r◦ 8/17) *āvṛtya tu tamaḥ:* (r◦ 22/3) *pramāde sañjayati* (r◦ 4/3) *uta*

(§2) *sattvam̦* (10.36); *sukhe* (7loc◦ sing◦ ←n◦ *sukha* 1.32); *sañjayati* (causative, 3rd-per◦ sing◦ pres◦ वर्तमान्-लट् parasmai◦ caus◦ ←class1◦ √सञ्ज्); *rajaḥ:* (14.5); *karmaṇi* (2.47); *bhārata* (1.24); *jñānam̦* (2acc◦ 3.40); *āvṛtya* (3.40); *tu* (1.2); *tamaḥ:* (14.5); *pramāde* (7loc◦ sing◦ ←m◦ *pramāda* 11.41); *sañjayati* (↑); *uta* (1.40) (14.9)

(§3) *sattvam̦* (subj1◦ the *sat-guṇa*); *sukhe* (in happiness, to happiness); *sañjayati* (causes one's attachment); *rajaḥ:* (subj2◦ the *rajoguṇa*); *karmaṇi* (in the *karma*); *bhārata* (O Arjuna!); *jñānam̦* (obj◦ thinking); *āvṛtya* (enveloping, covering, overpowering); *tu* (but, and); *tamaḥ:* (subj3◦ *tamoguṇa*); *pramāde* (in confusion, in inadvertence); *sañjayati* (causes attachment); *uta* (verily) (14.9)

(§4) bhārata sattvam̦ sañjayati sukhe rajaḥ: karmaṇi tu tamaḥ: tamoguṇaḥ āvṛtya jñānam̦ sañjayati uta pramāde

(§5) O Arjuna! the *sat-guṇa* causes one's attachment in happiness; the *rajoguṇa* in the *karma* and *tamoguṇa,* overpowering the thinking, causes attachment verily in inadvertence. (14.9)

14.10 रजस्तमश्चाभिभूय सत्त्वं भवति भारत ।
रज: सत्त्वं तमश्चैव तम: सत्त्वं रजस्तथा ।।

rajastamaśćābhibhūya sattvaṁ bhavati bhārata,
rajaḥ: sattvaṁ tamaśćaiva tamaḥ: sattvaṁ rajastathā. (14.10)

(§1) *rajaḥ:* (r◦ 18/1) *tamaḥ:* (r◦ 17/1) *ća* (r◦ 1/1) *abhibhūya sattvam̦* (r◦ 14/1) *bhavati bhārata rajaḥ:* (r◦ 22/7) *sattvam̦* (r◦ 14/1) *tamaḥ:* (r◦ 17/1) *ća* (r◦ 3/1) *eva tamaḥ:* (r◦ 22/7) *sattvam̦* (r◦ 14/1) *rajaḥ:* (r◦ 18/1) *tathā*

(§2) *rajaḥ:* (2acc◦ 14.5); *tamaḥ:* (2acc◦ 14.5); *ća* (1.1); *abhibhūya* (lyp◦ past-participle ind◦ ←अभि√भू); *sattvam̦* (1nom◦ 10.36); *bhavati* (1.44); *bhārata* (1.24); *rajaḥ:* (2acc◦ 14.5); *sattvam̦* (2acc◦ 10.36); *tamaḥ:* (1nom◦ 14.5); *ća* (1.1); *eva* (1.1); *tamaḥ:* (2acc◦ 14.5); *sattvam̦* (2acc◦ 10.36); *rajaḥ:* (1nom◦ 14.5); *tathā* (1.8) (14.10)

(§3) *rajaḥ:* (obj1◦ *rajoguṇa*); *tamaḥ:* (obj2◦ *tamoguṇa*); *ća* (and); *abhibhūya* (by overpowering, by subduing); *sattvam̦* (subj1◦ *sat-gunaḥ*); *bhavati* (becomes, becomes dominant, becomes active); *bhārata*

(O Arjuna!); *rajaḥ:* (obj1◦ *rajoguṇa*); *sattvam̩* (obj3◦ *sat-guṇa*); *tamaḥ:* (subj2◦ *tamoguṇa*); *ća eva* (and); *tamaḥ:* (obj2◦ *tamoguṇa*); *sattvam̩* (obj3◦ *sat-guṇa*); *rajaḥ:* (subj3◦ *rajoguṇa*); *tathā* (similarly) (14.10)

(§4) bhārata sattvam̩ bhavati abhibhūya rajaḥ: ća tamaḥ:; tamaḥ: rajaḥ: ća sattvam̩; eva rajaḥ: tamaḥ: sattvam̩ tathā

(§5) O Arjuna! *sat-guṇa* becomes dominant[735] by subduing *rajo-guṇa* and *tamoguṇa; tamo-guṇa* (becomes dominant by subduing) *rajo-guṇa* and *sat-guṇa;* similarly *rajo-guṇa* (becomes dominant by subduing) *tamo-guṇa* (and) *sat-guṇa.* (14.10)

14.11 सर्वद्वारेषु देहेऽस्मिन्प्रकाश उपजायते ।
ज्ञानं यदा तदा विद्याद्विवृद्धं सत्त्वमित्युत ।।
sarvadvāreṣu dehe'sminprakāśa upajāyate,
jñānaṁ yadā tadā vidyādvivṛddhaṁ sattvamityuta. (14.11)

(§1) *sarvadvāreṣu* (r◦ 25/5) *dehe* (r◦ 6/1) *asmin̩* (r◦ 13/13) *prakaśaḥ:* (r◦ 19/4) *upajāyate jñānam̩* (r◦ 14/1) *yadā tadā vidyāt̩* (r◦ 9/11) *vivṛddham̩* (r◦ 14/1) *sattvam̩* (r◦ 8/18) *iti* (r◦ 4/3) *uta*

(§2) *sarvadvāreṣu* (सर्वेषु द्वारेषु, 7loc◦ plu◦ ←pron◦ *sarva* 1.6 + n◦ *dvāra* 2.32); *dehe* (2.13); *asmin̩* (1.22); *prakaśaḥ:* (7.25); *upajāyate* (2.62); *jñānam̩* (2acc◦ 3.39); *yadā* (2.52); *tadā* (12); *vidyāt̩* (6.23); 🕮*vivṛddham̩* (n◦ 1nom◦ sing◦ ←ppp◦ adj◦ vivṛddha ←वि√वृध्); *sattvam̩* (1nom◦ 10.36); *iti* (1.25); *uta* (1.40) (14.11)

(§3) *sarvadvāreṣu* (in all nine gates); *dehe* (in the body); *asmin̩* (in this); *prakaśaḥ:* (subj1◦ enlightenment); *upajāyate* (generates, engenderes); *jñānam̩* (subj1◦ awareness, realization,

---

[735] elsewhere◦ भवति → increases, becomes increased, ...etc.

🕮 Many of my students also had this misunderstanding. They thus believe that a *guṇa* can be 'increased' (or decreased or removed) from the body. As illustrated and explained in the 'Introductory Essay' of Volume I, Chapter II of this book, every body and every particle of this universe (*prakṛti*) has the three guṇas in equal proportion. And that is the defination of the *prakṛti,* an exact equilibrium (in ratio of 1/3 each) of the three *guṇas.* Each body or perticle may however differ from each other only because this ratio of the dominance of the three *guṇas* is different in them. **YOU CAN NOT INCREASE ANY GUNA** IN THE BODY, BUT what you can do is **YOU CAN MAKE A GUNA DOMINANT OVER OTHER TWO** GUNAS, BY SUBDUING THE OTHER TWO GUNAS. In short, you can not increase the amount of the *guṇas* but you can alter their ratio. How do you subdue (or make active) any *guṇa*? Please read the Introductory essay.

discernment, comprehension); *yadā* (when); *tadā* (then); *vidyāt* (one should know); *vivṛddham* (adj3◦-subj2◦ has become dominant); *sattvam* (subj2◦ *sat-guṇa*); *iti uta* (that) (14.11)

(§4) yadā prakaśaḥ: jñānam upajāyate sarvadvāreṣu asmin dehe tadā vidyāt iti uta sattvam vivṛddham

(§5) When enlightenment in all nine gates generates[736] realization in this body, then one should know that *sat-guṇa* has become dominant. (14.11)

14.12 लोभः प्रवृत्तिरारम्भः कर्मणामशमः स्पृहा ।
रजस्येतानि जायन्ते विवृद्धे भरतर्षभ ।।
lobhaḥ: pravṛttirārambhaḥ: karmaṇāmaśamaḥ: spṛhā,
rajasyetāni jāyante vivṛddhe bharatarṣabha. (14.12)

(§1) *lobhaḥ:* (r◦ 22/3) *pravṛttiḥ:* (r◦ 16/1) *ārambhaḥ:* (r◦ 22/1) *karmaṇām* (r◦ 24/6, 8/16) *aśamaḥ:* (r◦ 22/7) *spṛhā rajasi* (r◦ 4/4) *etāni jāyante vivṛddhe bharatarṣabha*

(§2) *lobhaḥ:* (1nom◦ sing◦ ←m◦ *lobha* 1.38); *pravṛttiḥ:* (1nom◦ sing◦ ←f◦ *pravṛtti* 11.31); *ārambhaḥ:* (1nom◦ sing◦ ←m◦ *ārambha* 3.4); *karmaṇām* (3.4); *a-śamaḥ:* (1nom◦ sing◦ ←m◦ *śama* 6.3); *spṛhā* (2.56, 4.14); *rajasi* (7loc◦ sing◦ ←n◦ *rajas* 3.37); *etāni* (n◦ 1nom◦ 2acc◦ plu◦ ←pron◦ *etad* 1.3); *jāyante* (3rd-per◦ plu◦ pres◦ वर्तमान्-लट् ātmane◦ ←class4◦ √जन् 1.29); *vivṛddhe* (n◦ 7loc◦ sing◦ ←ppp◦ adj◦ *vivṛddha* 14.11); *bharatarṣabha* (3.41) (14.12)

---

[736] elsewhere◦ सर्वद्वारेषु देहे and प्रकाशः उपजायते ज्ञानं यदा → When at every gate in this body shoots up knowledge-wisdom, when wisdom-light streameth..., when the light of knowledge..., when light and discernment..., when light of wisdom shines forth..., when light of knowledge radiates..., when through all the sense-openings in this body..., when light of knowledge illuminates all the senses of the dody, when light of knowledge beams through all the gateways of the dody, when all the gates of the body are illuminated by knowledge, ...etc.

📖 (i) द्वारेषु and देहे do not have Possessive (6th case) or adjective-object relationship. It is not देहद्वारेषु possessive तत्पुरुषसमसः or द्वारेषु + देहेषु द्वन्द्वसमासः । These are two saparate Locative (7th case) nouns.

(ii) In प्रकाशः उपजायते ज्ञानं, the प्रकाशः (m◦) is not the adjective of ज्ञानं (n◦), because the genders of these two words are different. In प्रकाशः उपजायते ज्ञानं, प्रकाशः is subject, ज्ञानं is object उपजायते is verb (प्रकाशः ज्ञानं उपजायते). Therefore, an honest syntax, as Kṛṣṇa says, would be : यदा प्रकाशः सर्व-द्वारेषु अस्मिन् देहे ज्ञानं उपजायते, तदा सत्त्वम् विवृद्धं इति विद्यात् । यदा प्रकाशः (subject) सर्व-द्वारेषु अस्मिन् देहे ज्ञानं (object) उपजायते (verb), तदा सत्त्वम् विवृद्धं इति विद्यात् । Remember, it is प्रकाशः ज्ञानं उपजायते, not ज्ञानस्य प्रकाशः उपजायते ।

(iii) Please read the Introductory essay in Volume I of this book for the illustrated interrelationship between enlightenment in the nine gates and realization due to the dominant *sat-guṇa* in the body.

(§3) *lobhaḥ:* (suj1◦ greed); *pravṛttiḥ:* (suj2◦ predilection); *ārambhaḥ: karmaṇām* (suj3◦ indulgence of *karmas*); *a-śamaḥ:* (suj4◦ turbulence, disorder, instability); *spṛhā* (suj5◦ desire, hankering); *rajasi* (in *rajoguṇa*); *etāni* (suj1-5◦ these); *jāyante* (develop); *vivṛddhe* (in the predominance of); *bharatarṣabha* (O Arjuna!) (14.12)

(§4) bharatarṣabha vivṛddhe rajasi lobhaḥ: pravṛttiḥ: ārambhaḥ: karmaṇām a-śamaḥ: spṛhā etāni jāyante

(§5) O Arjuna! in the predominance of *rajo-guṇa* greed, predilection, indulgence of *karmas*, turbulence, desire, (etc.) these develop. (14.12)

14.13 अप्रकाशोऽप्रवृत्तिश्च प्रमादो मोह एव च ।
तमस्येतानि जायन्ते विवृद्धे कुरुनन्दन ।।
aprakāśo'pravṛttiśća pramādo moha eva ća,
tamasyetāni jāyante vivṛddhe kurunandana. (14.13)

(§1) *aprakaśaḥ:* (r◦ 15/1) *apravṛttiḥ:* (r◦ 17/1) *ća pramādaḥ:* (r◦ 15/9) *mohaḥ:* (r◦ 19/7) eva ća tamasi (r◦ 4/4) *etāni jāyante vivṛddhe kurunandana*

(§2) *a-prakaśaḥ:* (1nom◦ sing◦ n.tatpu◦ ←m◦ *prakaśa* 7.25); *a-pravṛttiḥ:* (1nom◦ sing◦ n.tatpu◦ ←f◦ *pravṛtti* 11.31); *ća* (1.1); *pramādaḥ:* (1nom◦ sing◦ ←m◦ *pramāda* 11.41); *mohaḥ:* (11.1); *eva* (1.1); *ća* (1.1); *tamasi* (7loc◦ sing◦ ←n◦ *tamaṣ* 7.12); *etāni* (14.12); *jāyante* (14.12); *vivṛddhe* (14.12); *kurunandana* (2.41) (14.13)

(§3) *a-prakaśaḥ:* (suj1◦ ignorance); *a-pravṛttiḥ:* (suj2◦ abhorrence); *ća* (and); *pramādaḥ:* (suj3◦ inadvertence); *mohaḥ:* (suj4◦ delusion); *eva ća* (and, also); *tamasi* (in the *tamoguṇa*); *etāni* (adj◦-suj1-4◦ these); *jāyante* (develop); *vivṛddhe* (in the predominance of); *kurunandana* (O Arjuna!) (14.13)

(§4) ća kurunandana vivṛddhe tamasi a-prakaśaḥ: a-pravṛttiḥ: pramādaḥ: eva ća mohaḥ: etāni jāyante

(§5) And, O Arjuna! in the predominance of *tamo-guṇa* ignorance, abhorrence, inadvertence and delusion, these develop. (14.13)

14.14 यदा सत्त्वे प्रवृद्धे तु प्रलयं याति देहभृत् ।
तदोत्तमविदां लोकानमलान्प्रतिपद्यते ।।
yada sattve pravṛddhe tu pralayaṁ yāti dehabhṛt,
tadottamavidāṁ lokānamalānpratipadyate. (14.14)

(§1) *yadā sattve pravṛddhe tu pralayam* (r◦ 14/1) *yāti dehabhṛt* (r◦ 23/1) *tadā* (r◦ 2/4) *uttamavidām* (r◦ 14/1) *lokān* (r◦ 8/11) *amalān* (r◦ 13/13) *pratipadyate*

(§2) *yadā* (2.52); *sattve* (7loc◦ sing◦ ←n◦ *sattva* 2.45); *pravṛddhe* (n◦ 7loc◦ sing◦ ←adj◦ *pravṛtta* 11.32); *tu* (1.2); *pralayam* (2acc◦ sing◦ ←m◦ *pralaya* 7.6); *yāti* (6.45); *dehabhṛt* (m◦ 1nom◦ sing◦ ←bahuvrī◦ *dehabhṛt*, देहम् विभ्रति यत् ←n◦ *deha* 2.13 + adj◦ *vibhṛta* 8.4); *tadā* (1.2); *uttamavidām* (m◦ 6pos◦ plu◦ ←bahuvrī◦ *uttama-vid*, उत्तमम् विन्दति यः ←adj◦ *uttama* 1.7 + adj◦ *vindati* 4.38); *lokān* (6.41); *amalān* (m◦ 2acc◦ plu◦ ←adj◦ *a-mala* ←अ√मल्); *pratipadyate* (3rd-per◦ sing◦ pres◦ वर्तमान्-लट् ātmane◦ ←class4◦ प्रति√पद्) (14.14)

(§3) *yadā* (when); *sattve* (in the *sat-guṇa*); *pravṛddhe* (in the predominance of); *tu* (but, and); *pralayam* (obj1◦ death); *yāti* (attains); *dehabhṛt* (= dehī, dehadhārī; suj1◦ an embodied being, a living being); *tadā* (then); *uttamavidām* (adj1◦-obj2◦ of those who know best, those who know the best that is to be known, wise); *lokān* (obj2◦ people); *amalān* (adj2◦-obj2◦ pure, chaste); *pratipadyate* (he attains, he reaches) (14.14)

(§4) tu yadā dehabhṛt yāti pralayam sattve tadā pratipadyate amalān lokān uttamavidām

(§5) And, when a living being[737] attains death in the predominance of the *sat-guṇa,* then he reaches those chaste people who know the best that is to be known.

(14.14)

14.15 रजसि प्रलयं गत्वा कर्मसङ्गिषु जायते ।
तथा प्रलीनस्तमसि मूढयोनिषु जायते ।।
rajasi pralayaṁ gatvā karmasaṅgiṣu jāyate,
tathā pralīnastamasi mūḍhayoniṣu jāyate. (14.15)

(§1) *rajasi pralayam* (r◦ 14/1) *gatvā karmasaṅgiṣu* (r◦ 25/5) *jāyate tathā pralīnaḥ:* (r◦ 18/1) *tamasi mūḍhayoniṣu* (r◦ 25/5) *jāyate*

(§2) *rajasi* (14.12); *pralayam* (14.14); *gatvā* (ipp◦ ind◦ ←√गम्); *karmasaṅgiṣu* (m◦ 7loc◦ plu◦ ←bahuvrī◦ *karma-saṅgin* 3.26); *jāyate* (1.29); *tathā* (1.8); *pralīnaḥ:* (m◦ 1nom◦ sing◦ ←ppp◦ adj◦ *pralīna* ←प्र√ली); *tamasi* (14.13); *mūḍhayoniṣu* (7loc◦ plu◦ ←f◦ tatpu◦ *mūḍha-yoni*, मूढा योनिः ←adj◦ *mūḍha* 7.15 + f◦ *yoni* 5.22); *jāyate* (1.29) (14.15)

(§3) *rajasi* (in the predominance of *rajoguṇa*); *pralayam* (obj1◦ death); *gatvā* (having attained);

---

[737] Please NOTE : The word देहभृत् = देही = देहधारी is variously used for (i) the one who is the dweller in the body i.e. ***ātmā*** (as in verses 2.22, 2.30 and 14.5); as well as for (ii) "the one who has body" i.e. a living being or embodied person (as in verses 2.59, 5.14, 14.14 and 14.20).

karmasaṅgiṣu (in the world of people attached to *karma*); *jāyate* (verb of subj1◦ he takes birth); *tathā* (similarly); *pralīnaḥ:* (subj2◦ he who died); *tamasi* (in the predominance of *tamoguṇa*); *mūḍhayoniṣu* (in the wombs for deluded people); *jāyate* (verb of subj2◦ he takes birth) (14.15)

(§4) gatvā pralayaṃ rajasi jāyate karmasaṅgiṣu tathā pralīnaḥ: tamasi jāyate mūḍhayoniṣu

(§5) Having attained[738] death in the predominance of *rajo-guṇa,* he takes birth in the world of people attached to *karma;* similarly, he who died[739] in the predominance of *tamo-guṇa,* he takes birth in the wombs for deluded people. (14.15)

14.16 कर्मणः सुकृतस्याहुः सात्त्विकं निर्मलं फलम् ।
रजसस्तु फलं दुःखमज्ञानं तमसः फलम् ।।
karmaṇaḥ: sukṛtasyāhuḥ: sāttvikaṁ nirmalaṁ phalaṃ,
rajasastu phalaṁ duḥ:khamajñānaṁ tamasaḥ: phalaṃ. (14.16)

(§1) *karmaṇaḥ:* (r◦ 22/7, 24/2) *sukṛtasya* (r◦ 1/2) *āhuḥ:* (r◦ 22/7) *sāttvikaṃ* (r◦ 14/1) *nirmalaṃ* (r◦ 14/1) *phalaṃ* (r◦ 14/2) *rajasaḥ:* (r◦ 18/1) *tu phalaṃ* (r◦ 14/1) *duḥ:khaṃ* (r◦ 8/16) *ajñānaṃ* (r◦ 14/1) *tamasaḥ:* (r◦ 22/4) *phalaṃ* (r◦ 14/2)

(§2) *karmaṇaḥ:* (3.1); *sukṛtasya* (6pos sing◦ ←n◦ *sukṛta* 2.50); *āhuḥ:* (3.42); *sāttvikaṃ* (n◦ 2acc◦ sing◦ ←adj◦ *sāttvika* 7.12); *nirmalaṃ* (n◦ 2acc◦ sing◦ ←adj◦ *nirmala* 14.6); *phalaṃ* (2.51); *rajasaḥ:* (6pos sing◦ ←n◦ *rajaṣ* 3.37); *tu* (1.2); *phalaṃ* (2.51); *duḥ:khaṃ* (2acc◦ 6.32); *ajñānaṃ* (2acc◦ 5.16); *tamasaḥ:* (8.9); *phalaṃ* (2acc◦ 2.51) (14.16)

(§3) *karmaṇaḥ:* (of the *karma*); *sukṛtasya* (of *puṇya*, of the righteous *karma*); *āhuḥ:* (they say that); *sāttvikaṃ* (adj1◦-subj1◦ virtuous); *nirmalaṃ* (adj2◦-subj1◦ clean, unadulterated, pure); *phalaṃ* (subj1◦ the fruit); *rajasaḥ:* (of the *rajasik karma*); *tu* (but, and); *phalaṃ* (subj2◦ the fruit); *duḥ:khaṃ* (adj1◦-

---

[738] elsewhere◦ प्रलयं गत्वा → When one dies, when a person *dies*, When the individual dies, when the embodied being dies, when he dies, He who goes to dissolution, if one *dies*, if it meets with death, if death occurs, ...etc.

📖 गत्वा is not a Present tense or a Potential mood (विध्यर्थः). It is simple Past participle gerund, meaning having done or doing something.

[739] elsewhere◦ प्रलीनः → When one dies, when a person *dies*, When the individual dies, when the embodied being dies, when he dies, He who goes to dissolution, if one *dies*, if it meets with death, if death occurs, ...etc.

📖 प्रलीन is not a Present tense or a Potential mood (विध्यर्थः). It is simple Past passive participle. adjective, meaning one who died.

subj2◦ painful, suffering, sorrow); *ajñānam̧* (adj1◦-subj3◦ ignorance); *tamasaḥ:* (of the *tamasik karma*); *phalam̧* (subj3◦ the fruit) (14.16)

(§4) āhuḥ: phalam̧ sukṛtasya karmaṇaḥ: sāttvikam̧ nirmalam̧ tu phalam̧ rajasaḥ: duḥ:kham̧ phalam̧ tamasaḥ: ajñānam̧

(§5) They say[740] that the fruit of the righteous *karma* (is) virtuous (and) clean, but the fruit of the *rajasik karma* (is) painful (and) the fruit of the *tamasik karma* (is) ignorance. (14.16)

14.17 सत्त्वात्सञ्जायते ज्ञानं रजसो लोभ एव च ।
प्रमादमोहौ तमसो भवतोऽज्ञानमेव च ।।
sattvātsañjāyate jñānaṁ rajaso lobha eva ća,
pramādamohau tamaso bhavato'jñanameva ća. (14.17)

(§1) *sattvāţ* (r◦ 10/7) *sañjāyate jñānam̧* (r◦ 14/1) *rajasaḥ:* (r◦ 15/12) *lobhaḥ:* (r◦ 19/7) *eva ća pramādamohau tamasaḥ:* (r◦ 15/8) *bhavataḥ:* (r◦ 15/1) *ajñānam̧* (r◦ 8/22) *eva ća*

(§2) *sattvāţ* (5abl◦ sing◦ ←n◦ *sattva* 2.45); *sañjāyate* (2.62); *jñānam̧* (1nom◦ 3.39); *rajasaḥ:* (14.16); *lobhaḥ:* (14.12); *eva* (1.1); *ća* (1.1); *pramādamohau* (m◦ 1nom◦ dual◦ ←dvandva◦ प्रमादः च मोहः च ←m◦ *pramāda* 11.41 + m◦ *moha* 2.52); *tamasaḥ:* (6pos◦ sing◦ ←n◦ *tamaş* 7.12); *bhavataḥ:* (3rd-per◦ dual◦ pres◦ वर्तमान्-लट् parasmai◦ ←class1◦ √भू); *ajñānam̧* (1nom◦ 5.16); *eva* (1.1); *ća* (1.1) (14.17)

(§3) *sattvāţ* (from the *sat-guṇa*); *sañjāyate* (develops); *jñānam̧* (subj1◦ wisdom, righteousness); *rajasaḥ:* (from the *rejoguṇa*); *lobhaḥ:* (subj2◦ greed); *eva ća* (and); *pramādamohau* (subj3-4◦ inadvertence and delusion); *tamasaḥ:* (from the *tamoguṇa*); *bhavataḥ:* (evolves, develop); *ajñānam̧* (subj5◦ ignorance); *eva ća* (and also) (14.17)

(§4) sattvāţ sañjāyate jñānam̧ rajasaḥ: lobhaḥ: eva ća tamasaḥ: bhavataḥ: pramādamohau eva ća ajñānam̧

(§5) righteousness evolves[741] from the *sat-guṇa,* greed (develops) from the *rejo-guṇ* and inadvertence, delusion and ignorance develop from *tamo-guṇa.*

---

[740] elsewhere◦ आहुः → is said to be, is declared to be, ...etc.

📖 आहुः is the action of subject, not the object. आहुः is Plural, not singular. आहुः is परस्मैपदी verb not आत्मनेपदी । आहुः is Active voice, not Passive. Please see verse 3.42 for more details on आहुः ।

[741] elsewhere◦ सत्त्वात्सञ्जायते ज्ञानम् → sattava promotes knowledge, goodness gives birth to knowledge ...etc.

📖 In सत्त्वात् सञ्जायते ज्ञानम्, the ज्ञानम् is subject, सत्त्वम् is not subject. ज्ञानम् is not object. सत्त्वात् has ablative function, it is not Nominative Subject of the verb सञ्जायते । If one observes which ones are the subjects and which ones are the objects and their adjectives in each *shloka*, such errors do not occur.

(14.17)

14.18 ऊर्ध्वं गच्छन्ति सत्त्वस्था मध्ये तिष्ठन्ति राजसा: ।
जघन्यगुणवृत्तिस्था अधो गच्छन्ति तामसा: ।।
ūrdhvaṁ gaććhanti sattvasthā madhye tiṣṭati rājasaḥ:,
jaghanyaguṇavṛttisthā adho gaććhanti tāmasāḥ:. (14.18)

(§1) *ūrdhvaṃ* (r◦ 14/1) *gaććhanti sattvasthāḥ:* (r◦ 20/13) *madhye tiṣṭati rajasāḥ:* (r◦ 22/8) *jaghanyaguṇavṛttisthāḥ:* (r◦ 20/1) *adhaḥ:* (r◦ 15/2) *gaććhanti tāmasāḥ:* (r◦ 22/8)

(§2) 🕮*ūrdhvaṃ* (12.8); *gaććhanti* (2.51); *sattvasthāḥ:* (m◦ 1nom◦ plu◦ ←bahuvrī◦ *sattva-stha*, सत्त्वे स्थास्यति य: ←n◦ *sattva* 2.45 + adj◦ *stha* 2.45); *madhye* (1.21); *tiṣṭati* (3rd-per◦ plu◦ pres◦ वर्तमान्–लट् parasmai◦ ←class1◦ √स्था); *rajasāḥ:* (7.12); *jaghanyaguṇavṛttisthāḥ:* (m◦ 1nom◦ plu◦ ←tatpu◦ adj◦ *jaghanya-guṇa-vṛtti-stha*, जघन्यस्य गुणस्य वृत्याम् स्थित: ←adj◦ *jaghanya* ←√हन् + m◦ *guṇa* 2.45 + f◦ *vṛtti* ←√वृत् + adj◦ *stha* 2.45); *adhaḥ:* (ind◦ *adhas* ←√धृ); *gaććhanti* (2.51); *tāmasāḥ:* (7.12) (14.18)

(§3) *ūrdhvaṃ* (up wards); *gaććhanti* (go); *sattvasthāḥ:* (subj1◦ those who are establishes in the preponderance of *sat-guṇa*); *madhye* (in the middle, in limbo); *tiṣṭati* (stay); *rajasāḥ:* (subj2◦ those who are establishes in the preponderance of *rajoguṇa*); *jaghanyaguṇavṛttisthāḥ:* (adj◦-subj3◦ the ones set in base attitude); *adhaḥ:* (downwards); *gaććhanti* (go); *tāmasāḥ:* (subj3◦ those who are establishes in the preponderance of *tamoguṇa*) (14.18)

(§4) sattvasthāḥ: gaććhanti ūrdhvaṃ rajasāḥ: tiṣṭati madhye tāmasāḥ: jaghanyaguṇavṛttisthāḥ: gaććhanti adhaḥ:

(§5) Those who are establishes in the preponderance of *sat-guṇa* go upwards; those who are establishes in the preponderance of *rajo-guṇa,* stay in limbo (and) those who are establishes in the preponderance of *tamo-guṇa,* the ones set in base attitude, go downwards. (14.18)

14.19 नान्यं गुणेभ्य: कर्तारं यदा द्रष्टानुपश्यति ।
गुणेभ्यश्च परं वेत्ति मद्भावं सोऽधिगच्छति ।।
nānyaṁ guṇebhyaḥ: kartāraṁ yadā draṣṭānupaśyati,
guṇebhyaśća paraṁ vetti madbhāvaṁ so'dhigaććhati. (14.19)

(§1) *na* (r◦ 1/1) *anyaṃ* (r◦ 14/1) *guṇebhyaḥ:* (r◦ 22/1) *kartāraṃ* (r◦ 14/1) *yadā draṣṭā* (r◦ 1/3) *anupaśyati guṇebhyaḥ:* (r◦ 17/1) *ća paraṃ* (r◦ 14/1) *vetti madbhāvaṃ* (r◦ 14/1) *saḥ:* (r◦ 15/1) *adhigaććhati*

(§2) *na* (1.30); *anyaṃ* (m◦ 2acc◦ sing◦ ←adj◦ *anya* 1.9); *guṇebhyaḥ:* (5abl◦ plu◦ ←m◦ *guṇa* 2.45);

kartāram̦ (4.13); *yadā* (2.52); *draṣṭā* (1nom∘ sing∘ ←m∘ *draṣṭṛ* ←√दृश्); *anupaśyati* (13.31); *guṇebhyaḥ:* (↑); *ća* (1.1); *param̦* (2acc∘ 2.59); *vetti* (2.19); *madbhāvam̦* (4.10); *saḥ:* (1.13); *adhigaććhati* (2.64) (14.19)

(§3) *na* (not); *anyam̦* (adj∘-obj1∘ other); *guṇebhyaḥ:* (than the three *guṇas*); *kartāram̦* (obj1∘ doer, the doer of the karmas); *yadā* (when); *draṣṭā* (an observer, a thinker, an observing person); *anupaśyati* (sees); *guṇebhyaḥ:* (than the three *guṇas*); *ća* (and); *param̦* (obj2∘ superior, that which is beyond); *vetti* (he understands); *madbhāvam̦* (obj3∘ my nature); *saḥ:* (subj1∘ he); *adhigaććhati* (realizes) (14.19)

(§4) na anyam̦ guṇebhyaḥ: kartāram̦ yadā draṣṭā anupaśyati guṇebhyaḥ: ća param̦ vetti madbhāvam̦ saḥ: adhigaććhati

(§5) When an observing person sees none other than the three *guṇas* (as) the doer of the *karmas* and (when) he understands that which is beyond the three *guṇas* (then) he realizes my nature. (14.19)

14.20 गुणानेतानतीत्य त्रीन्देही देहसमुद्भवान् ।
जन्ममृत्युजरादु:खैर्विमुक्तोऽमृतमश्नुते ।।
guṇānetānatītya trīndehī dehasamudbhavān̦,
janmamṛtyujarāduḥ:khairvimukto'mṛtamaśnute. (14.20)

(§1) *guṇān̦* (r∘ 8/15) *etān̦* (r∘ 8/11) *atītya trīn̦* (r∘ 13/11) *dehī dehasamudbhavān̦* (r∘ 23/1) *janmamṛtyujarāduḥ:khaiḥ:* (r∘ 16/11) *vimuktaḥ:* (r∘ 15/1) *amṛtam̦* (r∘ 8/16) *aśnute*

(§2) *guṇān̦* (13.20); *etān̦* (1.22); *atītya* (lyp∘ past-participle ind∘ ←अति√इ); *trīn̦* (m∘ 2acc∘ sing∘ ←always pleural num∘ adj∘ *tri* 2.45); *dehī* (2.22); *dehasamudbhavān̦* (m∘ 2acc∘ plu∘ ←bahuvrī∘ *deha-samudbhava*, देहे समुद्भव: यस्य that which arises in body ←m∘ *deha* 2.13 + m∘ *samudbhava* सम्-उद्√भू+अप् 3.14); *janma-mṛtyu-jarā -duḥ:khaiḥ:* (3inst∘ plu∘ ←dvandva∘ जन्मना च मृत्युना च जरया च दु:खेन च ←n∘ *janman̦* 2.27 + m∘ *mṛtyu* 2.27 + f∘ *jarā* 2.13 + n∘ *duḥ:kha* 2.14); *vimuktaḥ:* (9.28); *amṛtam̦* (9.19); *aśnute* (3.4) (14.20)

(§3) *guṇān̦* (obj1∘ *guṇas*); *etān̦* (adj1∘-obj1∘ these); *atītya* (being unaffected by, having crossed over, having brought under control); *trīn̦* (adj2∘-obj1∘ three); *dehī* (subj∘ the embodied one, the embodied living being); *dehasamudbhavān̦* (adj3∘-obj1∘ those which arise in the body); *janma-mṛtyu-jarā -duḥ:khaiḥ:* (from pain, old age, death and rebirth); *vimuktaḥ:* (adj∘-subj∘ freed); *amṛtam̦* (obj2∘ immortality); *aśnute* (enjoys) (14.20)

(§4) atītya etān̦ trīn̦ guṇān̦ dehasamudbhavān̦ dehī vimuktaḥ: janma-mṛtyu-jarā -duḥ:khaiḥ: aśnute amṛtam̦

(§5) **Having brought under control these three *guṇas,* which arise in the body,[742] the embodied living being,[743] freed from pain, old age, death and rebirth, enjoys immortality.** (14.20)

Arjuna said (arjuna uvāća अर्जुन उवाच ।)

14.21 कैर्लिङ्गैस्त्रीन्गुणानेतानतीतो भवति प्रभो ।
किमाचार: कथं चैतांस्त्रीन्गुणानतिवर्तते ।।

kairlingaistrīnguṇānetānatīto bhavati prabho,
kimāćāraḥ: katham ćaitaṁstringuṇānativartate. (14.21)

(§1) *arjunaḥ:* (r◦ 19/4) *uvāća. kaiḥ:* (r◦ 16/11) *lingaiḥ:* (r◦ 18/1) *trīṇ* (r◦ 13/10) *guṇāṇ* (r◦ 8/15) *etāṇ* (r◦ 8/11) *atītaḥ:* (r◦ 15/8) *bhavati prabho kimāćāraḥ:* (r◦ 22/1) *kathaṃ* (r◦ 14/1) *ća* (r◦ 3/1) *etāṇ* (r◦ 13/7) *trīṇ* (r◦ 13/10) *guṇāṇ* (r◦ 8/11) *ativartate*

(§2) *arjunaḥ:* (1.28); *uvāća* (1.25), *kaiḥ:* (1.22); *lingaiḥ:* (3inst◦ plu◦ ←m◦ *linga* ←√लिङ्ग्); *trīṇ* (14.20); *guṇāṇ* (13.20); *etāṇ* (1.22); *atītaḥ:* (m◦ 1nom◦ sing◦ ←adj◦ *atīta* 4.22); *bhavati* (1.44); *prabho* (11.4); *kimāćāraḥ:* (m◦ 1nom◦ sing◦ ←tatpu◦ *kim-āćāra,* किम् आचार: ←pron◦ *kiṃ* 1.1 + m◦ *āćāra* 3.6); *kathaṃ* (1.37); *ća* (1.1); *etāṇ* (1.22); *trīṇ* (14.20); *guṇāṇ* (13.20); *ativartate* (3rd-per◦ sing◦ pres◦ वर्तमान्-लट् ātmane◦ ←class1◦ अति√वृत् 3.28) (14.21)

---

[742] elsewhere◦ देहसमुद्भवान् → which are the origin of the body, out of which the body is evolved, associated with the material body, which are the source of the body, which are the cause of this body, ...etc.

📖 Quite contrary to "the *guṇas* are origin or source or cause of the body," what Lord Kṛṣṇa is saying is that "the *guṇas* which have origin (समुद्भव:) in the body..." The word देहसमुद्भव: is same बहुव्रीहि समास: as the words अक्षरसमुद्भवम् (arose from अक्षरम्), पर्जन्यादन्नसम्भव: (arose from पजृन्यम्) and कर्मसमुद्भव: (arose in karma) we studied in 3.14; रजोगुणसमुद्भव: (arose in रजोगुण:) we studied in 3.37; and तृष्णासङ्गसमुद्भवम् we studied in 14.7 (arose from तृष्णासङ्ग:). And, please note, these are the words of Lord Kṛṣṇa.

[743] elsewhere◦ देही → the embodied soul...attains immortality, the embodied self...,attains immortality, the dweller in the body...attains immortality, ...etc.

📖 Remember, the soul or the self or dweller *ātmā* does not attain birth or immortality. The soul or the self or dweller *ātmā* is immortal. Please refer to Verses : 2,20 (न जायते म्रियते वा, अजो नित्य: शाश्वतोऽयं पुराण:), 2.30 (देही नित्यं देहे), 10.20 (अहमत्मा), ...etc.

Therefore, please note that, as said in the footnote of verse 14.14, the word देही is used for (i) the one who is the dweller in the body i.e. ***ātmā*** (as in verses 2.22, 2.30 and 14.5); as well as for (ii) "the one who has body" i.e. a living being or embodied person (as in verses 5.14, 14.14 and 14.20). And thus, it becomes very easy to get mixed up, if the translator is not careful.

(§3) *arjunaḥ:* (subj∘ Arjuna); *uvāća* (said), *kaiḥ:* (by which, by what); *liṅgaiḥ:* (by signs); *trīn̖* (adj1∘-obj∘ three); *guṇān̖* (obj∘ *guṇas*); *etān̖* (adj2∘-obj∘ these); *atītaḥ:* (adj1∘-subj1∘ one who has crossed over, the one who has brought under his control); *bhavati* (is); *prabho* (O Lord!); *kimāćāraḥ:* (subj2∘ how his behaviour); *katham̖* (how, how does he); *ća* (and); *etān̖* (adj2∘-obj∘ these); *trīn̖* (adj1∘-obj∘ three); *guṇān̖* (obj∘ *guṇas*); *ativartate* (does he cross over, does he bring under his control) (14.21)

(§4) arjunaḥ: uvāća. prabho kaiḥ: liṅgaiḥ: etān̖ trīn̖ guṇān̖ atītaḥ: kimāćāraḥ: bhavati ća katham̖ ativartate etān̖ trīn̖ guṇān̖

(§5) Arjuna said : O Lord! by what signs is (recognized) one who has brought these three *guṇas* under his control? How his behaviour is? And how does he bring these three *guṇas* under his control? (14.21)

The Lord said (śrībhagavānuvāća श्रीभगवानुवाच ।)

14.22 प्रकाशं च प्रवृत्तिं च मोहमेव च पाण्डव ।
न द्वेष्टि सम्प्रवृत्तानि न निवृत्तानि काङ्क्षति ।।
prakāśaṁ ća pravṛttiṁ ća mohameva ća pāṇḍava,
na dveṣṭi sampravṛttāni na nivṛttāni kāṅkṣati. (14.22)

(§1) *śrībhagavān̖* (r∘ 8/14) *uvāća. prakāśam̖* (r∘ 14/1) *ća pravṛttim̖* (r∘ 14/1) *ća moham̖* (r∘ 8/22) *eva ća pāṇḍava na dveṣṭi sampravṛttāni na nivṛttāni kāṅkṣati*

(§2) *śrībhagavān̖* (2.2); *uvāća* (1.25). *prakāśam̖* (2acc∘ sing∘ ←m∘ *prakaśa* 7.25); *ća* (1.1); *pravṛttim̖* (11.31); *ća* (1.1); *moham̖* (4.35); *eva* (1.1); *ća* (1.1); *pāṇḍava* (4.35); *na* (1.30); *dveṣṭi* (2.57); *sampravṛttāni* (2acc∘ plu∘ ←n∘ *sampravṛtta* ←सम्-प्र√वृत्); *na* (1.30); *nivṛttāni* (n∘ 2acc∘ plu∘ ←ppp∘ adj∘ *nivṛtta* ←नि√वृत्); *kāṅkṣati* (5.3) (14.22)

(§3) *śrībhagavān̖* (subj∘ Lord Kṛṣṇa); *uvāća* (said). *prakāśam̖* (obj1∘ revelation, *sat-guṇa*); *ća* (and); *pravṛttim̖* (obj2∘ undertaking, *rajoguṇa*); *ća* (and); *moham̖* (obj3∘ delusion, *pramādaḥ, tamoguṇa*); *eva ća* (also); *pāṇḍava* (O Arjuna!); *na* (neither); *dveṣṭi* (he dislikes); *sampravṛttāni* (present); *na* (nor); *nivṛttāni* (departed, absent); *kāṅkṣati* (he desires, he longs for) (14.22)

(§4) śrībhagavān̖ uvāća pāṇḍava na dveṣṭi prakāśam̖ ća pravṛttim̖ ća moham̖ sampravṛttāni na eva ća kāṅkṣati nivṛttāni

(§5) Lord Kṛṣṇa said. O Arjuna! neither he dislikes revelation, and undertaking and delusion(when present) nor also longs for (when) absent.

Paraphrasing in other words :

Lord Kṛṣṇa said. O Arjuna! he is indifferent[744] to *sat-guṇa, rajo-guṇa* or *tamo-guṇa* if preponderant.[745] (14.22)

14.23 उदासीनवदासीनो गुणैर्यो न विचाल्यते ।
गुणा वर्तन्त इत्येव योऽवतिष्ठति नेङ्गते ।।
udāsīnavadāsīno guṇairyo na vićālyate,
guṇā vartanta ityeva yo'vatiṣṭhati neṅgate; (14.23)

(§1) *udasīnavaṭ* (r◦ 8/3) *āsīnaḥ:* (r◦ 15/2) *guṇaiḥ:* (r◦ 16/11) *yaḥ:* (r◦ 15/6) *na vićālyate guṇāḥ:* (r◦ 24/5, 20/17) *vartante* (r◦ 5/2) *iti* (r◦ 4/4) *eva yaḥ:* (r◦ 15/1) *avatiṣṭhati na* (r◦ 2/1) *iṅgate;*

(§2) *udasīnavaṭ* (9.9); *āsīnaḥ:* (m◦ 1nom◦ sing◦ ←adj◦ *āsīna* 9.9); *guṇaiḥ:* (3.5); *yaḥ:* (2.19); *na* (1.30); *vićālyate* (6.22); *guṇāḥ:* (3.28); *vartante* (3.28); *iti* (1.25); *eva* (1.1); *yaḥ:* (2.19); *avatiṣṭhati* (3rd-per◦ sing◦ pres◦ वर्तमान्-लट् parasmai◦ ←class1◦ अव√स्था); *na* (1.30); *iṅgate* (6.19); (14.23)

(§3) *udasīnavaṭ* (indifferent); *āsīnaḥ:* (adj1◦-subj1◦ remained, seated); *guṇaiḥ:* (by the three *guṇas*); *yaḥ:* (adj2◦-subj1◦ he who); *na* (does not); *vićālyate* (does not falter); *guṇāḥ:* (subj2◦ the *guṇas*); *vartante* (act, do the *karmas*); *iti* (thus, that); *eva* (only); *yaḥ:* (adj2◦-subj1◦ he who); *avatiṣṭhati* (remains undisturbed); *na* (does not); *iṅgate* (waver); (14.23)

(§4) udasīnavaṭ āsīnaḥ: guṇaiḥ: yaḥ: na vićālyate guṇāḥ: vartante iti eva yaḥ: avatiṣṭhati na iṅgate

(§5) He who, (i) remained[746] indifferent, does not falter by the three *guṇas;* (ii) he who (thinking) that the *guṇas* only act, remains undisturbed (and) does not waver; (14.23)

14.24 समदुःखसुखः स्वस्थः समलोष्टाश्मकाञ्चनः ।
तुल्यप्रियाप्रियो धीरस्तुल्यनिन्दात्मसंस्तुतिः ।।
samaduḥ:khasukhaḥ: svasthaḥ: samaloṣṭāśmakāñćnaḥ:,
tulyapriyāpriyo dhīrastulyanindātmasaṁstutiḥ:; (14.24)

(§1) *samaduḥ:khasukhaḥ:* (r◦ 22/7) *svasthaḥ:* (r◦ 22/7) *samaloṣṭāśmakāñćanaḥ:* (r◦ 22/8)

---

[744] Indifferent = न द्वेष्टि सम्प्रवृत्तानि न निवृत्तानि काङ्क्षति = उदासीनः, तटस्थः सः । See the next verse 14.23

[745] If preponderant = सम्प्रवृत्तानि निवृत्तानि वा ।

[746] elsewhere◦ आसीनः → sitting, remains, rests, sits, ...etc.

📖 Remember, आसीनः is not is gerund or a present tense. It is Past passive participle Adjective of the subject यः ।

tulyapriyāpriyaḥ: (r◦ 15/5) *dhīraḥ:* (r◦ 18/1) *tulyanindātmasaṁstutiḥ:* (r◦ 22/8);

(§2) *samaduḥ:khasukhaḥ:* (12.13); *svasthaḥ:* (m◦ 1nom◦ sing◦ ←bahuvrī◦ adj◦ *sva-stha,* स्वये स्थित: य: ←pron◦ adj◦ *sva* 1.28 + ppp◦ adj◦ *stha* 2.45); *samaloṣṭāśmakāñćanaḥ:* (6.8); *tulyapriyāpriyaḥ:* (m◦ 1nom◦ sing◦ ←bahuvrī◦ *tulya-priyāpriya,* प्रिय: च अप्रिय: च तुल्यौ यस्य ←adj◦ *tulya* 12.19 + adj◦ *priya* 1.23 + adj◦ *a-priya* 5.20); *dhīraḥ:* (2.13); *tulyanindātmasaṁstutiḥ:* (m◦ 1nom◦ sing◦ ←bahuvrī◦ *tulya-nindātma-saṁstuti,* तुल्ये निन्दा च आत्मन: संस्तुति: च यस्मै ←adj◦ *tulya* 12.19 + f◦ *nindā* 12.19 + n◦ *ātman* 2.41 + f◦ *saṁstuti* ←सम्√स्तु); (14.24)

(§3) *samaduḥ:khasukhaḥ:* (adj3◦-subj1◦ he who is indifferent to joy and sorrow); *svasthaḥ:* (adj4◦-subj1◦ he who is self contented); *samaloṣṭāśmakāñćanaḥ:* (adj5◦-subj1◦ he who is indifferent to a clod of soil, a stone and a piece of gold); *tulyapriyāpriyaḥ:* (adj6◦-subj1◦ he who is indifferent to pleasant and unpleasant); *dhīraḥ:* (adj7◦-subj1◦ he who is courageous, he who is stable); *tulyanindātmasaṁstutiḥ:* (adj8◦-subj1◦ he who is indifferent to his own praise or criticism); (14.24)

(§4) samaduḥ:khasukhaḥ: svasthaḥ: samaloṣṭāśmakāñćanaḥ: tulyapriyāpriyaḥ: dhīraḥ: tulyanindātmasaṁstutiḥ:

(§5) (And) (iii) he who is indifferent to joy and sorrow, (iv) he who is self contented, (v) he who is indifferent to a clod of soil, a stone and a piece of gold, (vi) he who is indifferent to pleasant and unpleasant, (vii) he who is stable, (viii) he who is indifferent to his own praise or criticism; (14.24)

14.25 मानापमानयोस्तुल्यस्तुल्यो मित्रारिपक्षयो: ।
सर्वारम्भपरित्यागी गुणातीत: स उच्यते ।।
mānāpamānayostulyastulyo mitrāripakṣayoḥ:,
sarvārambhaparityāgī guṇātītaḥ: sa ućyate. (14.25)

(§1) *mānāpamānayoḥ:* (r◦ 18/1) *tulyaḥ:* (r◦ 18/1) *tulyaḥ:* (r◦ 15/9) *mitrāripakṣayoḥ:* (r◦ 22/8) *sarvārambhaparityāgī guṇātītaḥ:* (r◦ 22/7) *saḥ:* (r◦ 21/2) *ućyate.*

(§2) *mānāpamānayoḥ:* (6.7); *tulyaḥ:* (m◦ 1nom◦ sing◦ ←adj◦ *tulya* 12.19); *tulyaḥ:* (↑); *mitrāri-pakṣayoḥ:* (m◦ 7loc◦ dual◦ ←dvandva◦ मित्रपक्षे च अरिपक्षे च ←m◦ *mitra* 1.38 + m◦ *ari* 2.4 + m◦ *pakṣa* ←√पक्ष्); *sarvārambhaparityāgī* (12.16); *guṇātītaḥ:* (m◦ 1nom◦ sing◦ ←adj◦ *guṇātīta,* गुणान् अतीत: ←m◦ *guṇa* 2.45 + adj◦ *atīta* 4.22); *saḥ:* (1.13); *ućyate* (2.25). (14.25)

(§3) *mānāpamānayoḥ: tulyaḥ:* (adj9◦-subj1◦ he who is indifferent to honour or insult); *tulyaḥ: mitrāri-pakṣayoḥ:* (adj10◦-subj1◦ he who is indifferent towards those people who consider him as a friend or foe); *sarvārambhaparityāgī* (adj11◦-subj1◦ he who relinquishes the attachment or authorship of anything that he undertakes); *guṇātītaḥ:* (adj12◦-subj1◦ guṇātīta, the one hwo who is unindifferent to the effects of the three *gunas*); *saḥ:* (subj1◦ he); *ućyate* (is called, he is known as). (14.25)

(§4) mānāpamānayoḥ: tulyaḥ: tulyaḥ: mitrāri-pakṣayoḥ: sarvārambhaparityāgī saḥ: he ućyate guṇātītaḥ:

(§5) (And) (ix) he who is indifferent to honour or insult, (x) he who is indifferent towards those people who consider him as a friend or foe, (xi) he who relinquishes the attachment or authorship of anything that he undertakes, (xii) he is known as *'guṇātīta,'* the one who is indifferent to the effects of the three *gunas*. (14.25)

14.26 मां च योऽव्यभिचारेण भक्तियोगेन सेवते ।
स गुणान्समतीत्यैतान्ब्रह्मभूयाय कल्पते ।।
māṁ ća yo'vyabhićāreṇa bhaktiyogena sevate,
sa guṇānsamatītyaitānbrahmabhūyāya kalpate. (14.26)

(§1) *mām* (r◦ 14/1) *ća yaḥ:* (r◦ 15/1) *avyabhićāreṇa* (r◦ 24/1) *bhaktiyogena sevate saḥ:* (r◦ 21/2) *guṇān* (r◦ 13/20) *samatītya* (r◦ 3/1) *etān* (r◦ 13/14) *brahmabhūyāya kalpate*

(§2) *mām* (1.46); *ća* (1.1); *yaḥ:* (2.19); *avyabhićāreṇa* (3inst◦ sing◦ n.tatpu◦ ←m◦ *a-vyabhićāra* ←वि-अभि√चर् 13.11); *bhaktiyogena* (m◦ 3inst◦ sing◦ ←tatpu◦ *bhakti-yoga*, भक्त्या: योग: ←f◦ *bhakti* 7.17 + m◦ *yoga* 2.39); *sevate* (3rd-per◦ sing◦ pres◦ वर्तमान्-लट् ātmane◦ ←class1◦ √सेव्); *saḥ:* (1.13); *guṇān* (13.20); *samatītya* (lyp◦ past-participle ind◦ ←सम्-अति√इ); *etān* (1.22); *brahmabhūyāya* (m◦ 4dat◦ sing◦ ←adj◦ tatpu◦ *brahma-bhūya*, ब्रह्मण: भूय: ←n◦ *brahmaṇaḥ:* 4.32 + n◦ *bhūya* ←√भू); *kalpate* (2.15) (14.26)

(§3) *mām* (obj1◦ me); *ća* (and); *yaḥ:* (adj◦-subj◦ he who); *avyabhićāreṇa* (with one pointed, with undeviated); *bhaktiyogena* (with *bhaktiyoga, yoga* of Devotion); *sevate* (worships, serves); *saḥ:* (subj◦ he); *guṇān* (obj2◦ three *guṇas*); *samatītya* (being unaffected by); *etān* (adj◦-obj2◦ these); *brahmabhūyāya* (for coming in unison with *brahma*); *kalpate* (he becomes fit) (14.26)

(§4) ća yaḥ: sevate mām avyabhićāreṇa bhaktiyogena saḥ: samatītya etān guṇān kalpate brahmabhūyāya

(§5) And, he who serves me with one pointed *bhaktiyoga,* he, being unaffected by these three *guṇas,* becomes fit for coming in unison with *brahma*. (14.26)

14.27 ब्रह्मणो हि प्रतिष्ठाहममृतस्याव्ययस्य च ।
शाश्वतस्य च धर्मस्य सुखस्यैकान्तिकस्य च ।।
brahmaṇo hi pratiṣṭāhamamṛtasyāvyayasya ća,
śāśvatasya ća dharmasya sukhasyaikāntikasya ća. (14.27)

(§1) *brahmaṇaḥ:* (r◦ 15/14) *hi pratiṣṭā* (r◦ 1/3) *ahaṃ* (r◦ 8/16) *amṛtasya* (r◦ 1/1) *avyayasya ća śāśvatasya ća dharmasya sukhasya* (r◦ 3/1) *aikāntikasya ća*

(§2) *brahmaṇaḥ:* (4.32); *hi* (1.11); *pratiṣṭā* (1nom◦ sing◦ ←f◦ *pratiṣṭā* 2.70); *ahaṃ* (1.22); *amṛtasya* (6pos sing◦ ←m◦ adj◦ *amṛta* 2.15); *avyayasya* (m◦ 2.17); *ća* (1.1); *śāśvatasya* (6pos sing◦ ←m◦ adj◦ *śāśvata* 1.43); *ća* (1.1); *dharmasya* (2.40); *sukhasya* (6pos sing◦ ←n◦ *sukha* 1.32); *aikāntikasya* (6pos sing◦ ←n◦ adj◦ taddhita◦ 🕮*aikāntika* ←num◦ adj◦ *eka* 2.41); *ća* (1.1) (14.27)

(§3) *brahmaṇaḥ:* (of *brahma*); *hi* (because, for); *pratiṣṭā* (adj◦-subj◦ abode); *ahaṃ* (subj◦ I am); *amṛtasya* (of the immortal); *avyayasya* (of the immutable); *ća* (and); *śāśvatasya* (of the eternal); *ća* (and); *dharmasya* (of the righteous); *sukhasya* (of the peace); *aikāntikasya* (of the absolute); *ća* (and) (14.27)

(§4) hi ahaṃ dharmasya pratiṣṭā amṛtasya ća avyayasya ća śāśvatasya brahmaṇaḥ: ća aikāntikasya sukhasya

(§5) Because,[747] I am the righteous abode of the immortal and the immutable and the eternal *brahma*, and of the absolute peace. (14.27)

इति श्रीमद्भगवद्गीतासूपनिषत्सु ब्रह्मविद्यायां योगशास्त्रे
श्रीकृष्णार्जुनसंवादे गुणत्रयविभागयोगो नाम चतुर्दशोऽध्यायः ।

iti śrīmadbhagavadgītāsūpaniṣatsu brahmavidyāyām̐ yogaśāstre
śrīkṛṣṇārjunasam̐vāde guṇatrayavibhāgayogo nāma ćaturdaśo'dhyāyaḥ:

(§1) *iti śrīmadbhagavadgītāsu* (r◦ 1/8) *upaniṣatsu brahmavidyāyāṃ* (r◦ 14/1) *yogaśāstre śrīkṛṣṇārjunasam̐vāde guṇatrayavibhāgayogaḥ:* (r◦ 15/6) *nāma ćaturdaśaḥ:* (r◦ 15/1) *adhyāyaḥ:* (r◦ 22/8)

(§2) *iti* (1.25); *śrīmadbhagavadgītāsu* (1.1); *upaniṣatsu* (1.1); *brahmavidyāyāṃ* (1.1); *yogaśāstre* (1.1); *śrīkṛṣṇārjunasam̐vāde* (1.1); *guṇatrayavibhāgayogaḥ:* (m◦ 1nom◦ sing◦ ←tatpu◦ *guṇatrayavibhāgayogaḥ:*, गुणानां त्रयाणां विभागस्य योगः ←n◦ *guṇa* 2.45 + m◦ *traya* 11.20 + m◦ *vibhāga* 3.28 + m◦ *yoga* 2.39); *nāma* (1.1); *chaturdaśaḥ:* (m◦ 1nom◦ sing◦ ←num◦ adj◦ *chaturdaśa* ←1◦√चत् + उरन्); *adhyāyaḥ:* (1nom◦ sing◦ ←m◦ *adhyāya* ←1◦अधि√इ)

(§3) *iti* (thus); *śrīmadbhagavadgītāsu upaniṣatsu* (among the upaniṣads of Śrīmad-Bhagavadgītā); *brahmavidyāyāṃ* (of the eternal wisdoms); *yogaśāstre* (in the science of Yoga); *śrīkṛṣṇārjunasam̐vāde* (in the dialogue between Śrī Kṛṣṇa and Arjuna); *guṇatrayavibhāgayogaḥ:* (adj1◦-subj◦ *guṇa-traya-vibhāga-yogaḥ:*); *nāma* (called) *chaturdaśaḥ:* (adj2◦-subj◦ fourteenth); *adhyāyaḥ:* (subj◦ discourse)

---

[747] elsewhere◦ हि → See the footnote in 2.16

(§4) śrīmadbhagavadgītāsu upaniṣatsu yogaśāstre brahmavidyāyām̩ iti chaturdaśaḥ: adhyāyaḥ: nāma guṇatrayavibhāgayogaḥ: śrīkṛṣṇārjunasam̐vāde

(§5) Among the upaniṣads of the Śrīmad-Bhagavadgītā, in the science of Yoga of self realization, thus (is) the fourteenth discourse called guṇa-traya-vibhāga-yogaḥ: in the dialogue between Śrī Kṛṣṇa and Arjuna.

CHAPTER 15

pañćadaśo'dhyāyaḥ:

पञ्चदशोऽध्यायः ।

THE YOGA PERTAINING TO "THE SUPREME BEING"

puruṣottamayogaḥ:

पुरुषोत्तमयोगः ।

The Lord said (śrībhagavānuvāća श्रीभगवानुवाच ।)

15.1 ऊर्ध्वमूलमधःशाखमश्वत्थं प्राहुरव्ययम् ।
छन्दांसि यस्य पर्णानि यस्तं वेद स वेदवित् ।।
ūrdhvamūlamadhaḥ:śākhamaśvastham̐ prāhurvyayam̩,
ćhandām̐si yasya parṇāni yastam̐ veda sa vedaviṭ. (15.1)

(§1) *pañćadaśaḥ:* (r◦ 15/1) *adhyāyaḥ:* (r◦ 22/8). *puruṣottamayogaḥ:* (r◦ 22/8). *śrībhagavāṇ* (r◦ 8/14) *uvāća. ūrdhvamūlaṃ* (r◦ 8/16) *adhaḥ:śākhaṃ* (r◦ 8/16) *aśvatthaṃ* (r◦ 14/1) *prāhuḥ:* (r◦ 16/3) *avyayaṃ* (r◦ 14/2) *ćhandām̐si yasya parṇāni yaḥ:* (r◦ 18/1) *taṃ* (r◦ 14/1) *veda saḥ:* (r◦ 21/2) *vedaviṭ*

(§2) *pañćadaśaḥ:* (m◦ 1nom◦ sing◦ ←sequence indicating num◦ adj◦ *pañćadaśa* ←num◦ adj◦ *pañća* 13.6 + num◦ adj◦ *daśa* 13.6); *adhyāyaḥ:* (1nom◦ sing◦ ←m◦ *adhyāya* ←अधि√इ). *puruṣottamayogaḥ:* (m◦ 1nom◦ sing◦ ←tatpu◦ *puruṣottama-yoga*, पुरुषोत्तमस्य योगः ←m◦ *puruśottama* 8.1 + m◦ *yoga* 2.39). *śrībhagavāṇ* (2.2); *uvāća* (1.25). *ūrdhvamūlaṃ* (m◦ 2acc◦ sing◦ ←bahuvrī◦ *ūrdhva-mūla*, ऊर्ध्वानि मूलानि यस्य ←adj◦ *ūrdhva* 12.8 + n◦ 🕮*mūla* ←√मूल्); *adhaḥ:śākhaṃ* (m◦ 2acc◦ sing◦ ←bahuvrī◦ *adhaḥ:-śākha*, अधाः शाखाः यस्य ←adj◦ *adhaṣ* 14.18 + f◦ *śākhā* 2.41); *aśvatthaṃ* (2acc◦ sing◦ ←m◦ *aśvattha* = *ficus religiosa* tree 10.26); *prāhuḥ:* (6.2); *avyayaṃ* (2.21); *ćhandām̐si* (1nom◦ plu◦ ←n◦ 🕮*ćhandaṣ* 10.35); *yasya* (2.61); *parṇāni* (1nom◦ plu◦ ←n◦ 🕮*parṇa* ←√पॄ or √पर्ण्); *yaḥ:* (2.19); *taṃ* (2.1); *veda* (2.21); *saḥ:* (1.13); *vedaviṭ*

(1nom∘ sing∘ ←bahuvrī∘ *veda-viț*, वेद: वेत्ति य: ←m∘ *veda* 2.42 + adj∘ *vetti* 2.19) **(15.1)**

(§3) *pañćadaśaḥ:* (adj∘-subj∘ fifteenth); *adhyāyaḥ:* (subj∘ chapter). *puruṣottamayogaḥ:* (the *puruṣottamayogaḥ*). *śrībhagavān* (subj∘ Lord Kṛṣṇa); *uvāća* (said).

ūrdhvamūlam (adj1∘-subj1∘ that which has its roots upwards); *adhaḥ:śākham* (adj2∘-subj1∘ that which has its branches downwards); *aśvattham* (subj1∘ Peepul tree); *prāhuḥ:* (they say that); *avyayam* (adj3∘-subj1∘ the eternal); *ćhandāṁsi yasya parṇāni* (adj4∘-subj1∘ that of which the *veda-ṛćās* are the leaves); *yaḥ:* (adj1∘-subj2∘ he who); *tam* (obj∘ that, that tree); *veda* (knows); *saḥ:* (subj2∘ he); *vedaviț* (adj2∘-subj2∘ the knower of the *veda*) **(15.1)**

(§4) pañćadaśaḥ: adhyāyaḥ: puruṣottamayogaḥ: śrībhagavān uvāća. prāhuḥ: avyayam aśvattham ūrdhvamūlam adhaḥ:śākham ćhandāṁsi yasya parṇāni yaḥ: veda tam saḥ: vedaviț

(§5) Fifteenth Chapter. The *puruṣottamayogaḥ*. Lord Kṛṣṇa said :

They say[748] that the eternal Pīpal[749] tree has its roots upwards, its branches downwards and the *veda-ṛćās* are its leaves. He who understands that tree,[750] he (is) the knower of the *veda*. **(15.1)**

15.2 अधश्चोर्ध्वं प्रसृतास्तस्य शाखा गुणप्रवृद्धा विषयप्रवाला: ।
अधश्च मूलान्यनुसन्ततानि कर्मानुबन्धीनि मनुष्यलोके ।।

adhaśćordhvam prasṛtāstasya śākhā guṇapravṛddhā viṣayapravālāḥ:,
adhaśća mūlānyanusantatāni karmānubandhīni manuṣyaloke. **(15.2)**

(§1) *adhaḥ:* (r∘ 17/1) *ća* (r∘ 2/2) *ūrdhvam* (r∘ 14/1) *prasṛtāḥ:* (r∘ 18/1) *tasya śākhāḥ:* (r∘ 20/6) *guṇapravṛddhāḥ:* (r∘ 20/17) *viṣayapravālāḥ:* (r∘ 22/8) *adhaḥ:* (r∘ 17/1) *ća mūlāni* (r∘ 4/1) *anusantatāni karmānubandhīni manuṣyaloke*

---

[748] elsewhere∘ आहु: → is said to be, is declared to be, ...etc.

📖 आहु: is the action of subject, not the object. आहु: is Plural, not singular. आहु: is परस्मैपदी verb not आत्मनेपदी । आहु: is Active voice, not Passive. Please see verse 3.42 for more details on आहु: । See also footnote in 14.16

[749] elsewhere∘ अश्वत्थ: → is Pīpal or Peepul, but not Banyan or Bargad.

[750] elsewhere∘ तम् → He who knows it, he who knoweth it, He who realises it, ...etc.

📖 Remember, In य: तं वेत्ति, the word is तम् not एतद् । The pronoun तम् is masculine adjective for the अश्वत्थ: tree, as also said in 15.3 अश्वत्थमेनम् । Thus, he who understands 'that eternal tree.' Not, he who knows 'that the tree is eternal.' See the first footnote in verse 2.21 in Volume I for more clarification of this point.

(§2) *adhaḥ:* (adv◦ 14.18); *ća* (1.1); *ūrdhvaṃ* (adv◦ 12.8); *prasṛtāḥ:* (f◦ 1nom◦ plu◦ ←ppp◦ adj◦ *prasṛta* ←प्र√सृ); *tasya* (1.12); *śākhāḥ:* (1nom◦ plu◦ ←f◦ 📖*śākhā* 2.41); *guṇapravṛddhāḥ:* (f◦ 1nom◦ plu◦ ←ppp◦ adj◦ *guṇa-pravṛddha*, गुणैः प्रवृद्धः ←m◦ *guṇa* 2.45 + adj◦ *pravṛddha* 11.32); *viṣayapravālāḥ:* (f◦ 1nom◦ plu◦ ←bahuvrī◦ *viṣaya-pravāla*, विषयाः प्रवालाः यस्य ←m◦ *viṣaya* 2.45 + m◦ *pravāla* or *prabāla* ←प्र√बल्); *adhaḥ:* (14.18); *ća* (1.1); *mūlāni* (1nom◦ plu◦ ←n◦ *mūla* 15.1); *anusantatāni* (n◦ 1nom◦ plu◦ ←ppp◦ adj◦ *anusantata* ←अनु-सम्-√तन्); *karmānubandhīni* (n◦ 1nom◦ plu◦ ←bahuvrī◦ *karmānubandhin*, कर्म अनुबन्धः यस्य ←n◦ *karman* 1.15 + m◦ *anubandha* ←अनु√बन्ध्); *manuṣyaloke* (m◦ 7loc◦ sing◦ ←tatpu◦ *manuṣya-loka*, मनुष्याणाम् लोकः ←m◦ *manuṣya* 1.44 + m◦ *loka* 2.5) (15.2)

(§3) *adhaḥ:* (adv◦ downwards); *ća* (and); *ūrdhvaṃ* (adv◦ upwards); *prasṛtāḥ:* (adj1◦-subj1◦ spread); *śākhāḥ:* (subj1◦ the branches); *guṇapravṛddhāḥ:* (adj2◦-subj1◦ which are nourished by the *guṇas*); *viṣayapravālāḥ:* (adj3◦-subj1◦ of which the shoots are the sense-objectss); *adhaḥ:* (adv◦ downwards); *ća* (and); *mūlāni* (subj2◦ the roots); *anusantatāni* (adj◦-subj2◦ extended, spread); *karmānubandhīni* (adj2◦-subj◦ which are the product of *karmas*); *manuṣyaloke* (in the earthy world) (15.2)

(§4) śākhāḥ: prasṛtāḥ: adhaḥ: ća ūrdhvaṃ guṇapravṛddhāḥ: ća viṣayapravālāḥ: mūlāni karmānubandhīni anusantatāni adhaḥ: manuṣyaloke

(§5) The branches (of this worldly eternal tree are) spread downwards and upwards, which are nourished by the *guṇas* and of which the shoots are the sense-objects. The roots, which are the product of *karmas* (are) spread downwards in the earthy world.

(15.2)

15.3 न रूपमस्येह तथोपलभ्यते नान्तो न चादिर्न च सम्प्रतिष्ठा ।
अश्वत्थमेनं सुविरूढमूलमसङ्गशस्त्रेण दृढेन छित्त्वा ।।

na rūpamasyeha tathopalabhyate nāntao na ćādirna ća sampratiṣṭhā,
aśvatthamenaṃ suvirūḍhamūlamasaṅgaśastreṇa dṛḍhena ćhittvā.

(15.3)

(§1) *na rūpaṃ* (r◦ 8/16) *asya* (r◦ 2/1) *iha tathā* (r◦ 2/4) *upalabhyate na* (r◦ 1/1) *antaḥ:* (r◦ 15/6) *na ća* (r◦ 1/2) *ādiḥ:* (r◦ 16/6) *na ća sampratiṣṭā* (r◦ 23/1) *aśvatthaṃ* (r◦ 8/22) *enaṃ* (r◦ 14/1) *suvirūḍhamūlaṃ* (r◦ 8/16) *asaṅgaśastreṇa* (r◦ 24/1) *dṛḍhena ćhittvā;*

(§2) *na* (1.30); *rūpaṃ* (n◦ 11.47); *asya* (2.17); *iha* (2.5); *tathā* (1.8); *upalabhyate* (3rd-per◦ sing◦ pres◦ वर्तमान्-लट् ātmane◦ ←class1◦ उप√लभ्); *na* (1.30); *antaḥ:* (2.16); *na* (1.30); *ća* (1.1); *ādiḥ:* (10.2); *na* (1.30); *ća* (1.1); 📖*sampratiṣṭā* (f◦ 1nom◦ sing◦ ←सम्-प्रति√स्था); *aśvatthaṃ* (15.1); *enaṃ* (2.19); *suvirūḍhamūlaṃ* (m◦ 2acc◦ sing◦ ←bahuvrī◦ *suvirūḍha-mūla,* सुविरूढानि मूलानि यस्य ←adj◦ *suvirūḍha* ←सु-वि√रुह् + n◦ *mūla* 15.1); *asaṅgaśastreṇa* (n◦ 3inst◦ sing◦ ←tatpu◦ *asaṅga-śastra,* असङ्गस्य शस्त्रम् ←n.tatpu◦ m◦ *asaṅga* ←अ√सञ्ज् + n◦ *śastra* 1.9); *dṛḍhena* (n◦ 3inst◦ sing◦ ←adj◦ *dṛḍha* 6.34); *ćhittvā* (4.42); (15.3)

(§3) *na* (not); *rūpaṃ* (subj1◦ form); *asya* (its); *iha* (in this world); *tathā* (in that way); *upalabhyate* (is perceived); *na* (nor); *antaḥ:* (subj2◦ end); *na* (nor); *ća* (and); *ādiḥ:* (subj3◦ the beginning); *na* (nor); *ća* (and); *sampratiṣṭā* (subj4◦ the continuity); *aśvatthaṃ* (obj1◦ *pīpal* tree); *enaṃ* (adj1◦-obj◦ this); *suvirūḍhamūlaṃ* (adj2◦-obj◦ of well developed root system); *asaṅgaśastreṇa* (with the weapon of non-attachment); *dṛḍhena* (with the unswerving); *ćhittvā* (having cut, having cut the attachment to); (15.3)

(§4) iha asya rūpaṃ na upalabhyate tathā na antaḥ: ća na ādiḥ: ća na sampratiṣṭā ćhittvā enaṃ aśvatthaṃ suvirūḍhamūlaṃ dṛḍhena asaṅgaśastreṇa

(§5) In this world its form is not perceived in that way; nor (its) end, and nor the beginning, and nor the continuity. Having cut the bondage[751] with this *pīpal* tree of well developed root system, with the unswerving weapon of non-attachment; (15.3)

15.4 ततः पदं तत्परिमार्गितव्यं यस्मिन्गता न निवर्तन्ति भूयः ।
तमेव चाद्यं पुरुषं प्रपद्ये यतः प्रवृत्तिः प्रसृता पुराणी ।।
tataḥ: padaṁ tatparimārgitavyaṁ yasmingatā na nivartanti bhūyaḥ:,

---

[751] elsewhere◦ छित्वा → felling, cutting, cutting down, Having cut asunder, having been cut down, one must cut down, Having severed, ...etc.

📖 (1) The word 'अश्वत्थः' suggests that there is only one worldly eternal tree for all mankind, which is अव्यक्तः invisible and अव्ययः eternal and can not be cut, partly or fully, by any weapon, however sharp, by anyone ever (as said in Gita 2.23 न छिन्दन्ति शस्त्राणि). Therefore, the theory of 'cuttingdown or felling the tree' theory is not proper.

(2) How can you cut asunder the Worldly Tree संसारवृक्षः of which you are a part. You will be cutting down yourself. Unless you are separate from the Worldly Tree.

(3) Nevertheless, if the word छित्वा means 'felling' or 'cutting down' the tree, after the first man cut it down (along with the *vedas* as its leaves and *purushottama* at its root), there should be no more tree left for anyone else to cut it. Unless, of course, there are as many 'अश्वत्थाः' trees in the *aśvattha*-forest, as many people ever took birth in the world. Most of the trees would have to be left un-cut by the people without *asang-shastra.* In that case Lord Kṛṣṇa would have said 'अश्वत्थाः'

(4) See Patanjali 2.11 : वृत्तयः ध्यान-हेयाः *vṛttayaḥ dhyāna-heyāḥ* = inherent afflictions of states of mind, should be terminated with the weapon of contemplation.

tameva ćādyam puruṣam prapadye yataḥ: pravṛttiḥ: prasṛtā purāṇī.
(15.4)

(§1) *tataḥ:* (r∘ 22/3) *padam̩* (r∘ 14/1) *tat̩* (r∘ 10/6) *parimārgitavyam̩* (r∘ 14/1) *yasmin̩* (r∘ 13/10) *gatāḥ:* (r∘ 20/10) *na nivartanti bhūyaḥ:* (r∘ 22/8) *tam̩* (r∘ 8/22) *eva ća* (r∘ 1/2) *ādyam̩* (r∘ 14/1) *puruṣam̩* (r∘ 14/1) *prapadye yataḥ:* (r∘ 22/3) *pravṛttiḥ:* (r∘ 22/3) *prasṛtā purāṇī*

(§2) *tataḥ:* (1.13); *padam̩* (1nom∘ sing∘ ←na∘ *pada* 2.51); *tat̩* (1nom∘ 1.10); *parimārgitavyam̩* (n∘ 1nom∘ 2acc∘ sing∘ ←pot∘ adj∘ *parimārgitavya* ←परि√मार्ग्); *yasmin̩* (6.22); *gatāḥ:* (8.15); *na* (1.30); 🕮*nivartanti* (3rd-per∘ plu∘ pres∘ वर्तमान्–लट् parasmai∘ ←class1∘ नि√वृत् 2.59); *bhūyaḥ:* (2.20); *tam̩* (2.1); *eva* (1.1); *ća* (1.1); *ādyam̩* (2acc∘ 8.28); *puruṣam̩* (2.15); *prapadye* (1st-per∘ sing∘ pres∘ वर्तमान्–लट् ātmane∘ ←class4∘ प्र√पद् 4.11); *yataḥ:* (6.26); *pravṛttiḥ:* (14.12); *prasṛtā* (f∘ 1nom∘ sing∘ ←ppp∘ adj∘ *prasṛta* 15.2); *purāṇī* (f∘ 1nom∘ sing∘ ←adj∘ *purāṇa* 2.20) (15.4)

(§3) *tataḥ:* (then, therafter); *padam̩* (obj1∘ place, state); *tat̩* (adj1∘-obj1∘ that); *parimārgitavyam̩* (adj2∘-obj1∘ that which is ought to be sought, seeked, investigated); *yasmin̩* (in which); *gatāḥ:* (subj1∘ the ones who have departed); *na nivartanti* (they do not return); *bhūyaḥ:* (again); *tam̩* (adj1∘-obj2∘ to him, to that); *eva* (only); *ća* (and); *ādyam̩* (adj2∘-obj2∘ primeval); *puruṣam̩* (obj2∘ the source of life); *prapadye* (I submit); *yataḥ:* (adv. from where, whence); *pravṛttiḥ:* (subj2∘ the evolution); *prasṛtā* (adj1∘-subj2∘ streamed forth, evolved); *purāṇī* (adj2∘-subj2∘ the primordial) (15.4)

(§4) tataḥ: tat̩ padam̩ parimārgitavyam̩ yasmin̩ gatāḥ: na nivartanti bhūyaḥ: ća prapadye eva tam̩ ādyam̩ puruṣam̩ yataḥ: purāṇī pravṛttiḥ: prasṛtā

(§5) Then, that state ought to be sought, in which the departed[752] do not return again. And, "I submit only to that primeval source of life whence the primordial evolution streamed forth." (15.4)

15.5 निर्मानमोहा जितसङ्गदोषा अध्यात्मनित्या विनिवृत्तकामाः ।
द्वन्द्वैर्विमुक्ताः सुखदुःखसंज्ञैर्गच्छन्त्यमूढाः पदमव्ययं तत् ।।
nirmānamohā jitasaṅgadoṣā adhyātmanityā vinivṛttakāmāḥ:,
dvandvairvimuktāḥ sukhaduḥ:khasañjñairgaććhantya mūḍhāḥ:
padamavyayam̩ tat; (15.5)

---

[752] elsewhere∘ गताः → having gone, going where, having attained, treading which, going whither, going where, reaching which, ...etc.

🕮 गताः is not an indeclinable gerund. It is plural adjective of the plural subject of the verb न निवर्तन्ति ।

(§1) *nirmānamohāḥ:* (r◦ 20/7) *jitasaṅgadoṣāḥ:* (r◦ 20/1) *adhyātmanityāḥ:* (r◦ 20/17) *vinivṛttakāmāḥ:* (r◦ 22/8) *dvandvaiḥ:* (r◦ 16/11) *vimuktāḥ:* (r◦ 22/7) *sukhaduḥ:khasañjñaiḥ:* (r◦ 16/11) *gaććhanti* (r◦ 4/1) *amūḍhāḥ:* (r◦ 22/3) *padam̥* (r◦ 8/16) *avyayam̥* (r◦ 14/1) *tat̥;*

(§2) *nirmānamohāḥ:* (m◦ 1nom◦ plu◦ ←bahuvrī◦ *nirmāna-moha,* मानः च मोहः च विगतौ यस्य ←ind◦ *nir̥* 2.45 + m◦ *māna* 6.7 + m◦ *moha* 2.52); *jitasaṅgadoṣāḥ:* (m◦ 1nom◦ plu◦ ←bahuvrī◦ *jita-saṅga-doṣa,* जितः सङ्गस्य दोषः यस्य ←ppp◦ adj◦ *jita* 5.7 + m◦ *saṅgaḥ:* 2.47 + m◦ *doṣa* 1.38); *adhyātmanityāḥ:* (m◦ 1nom◦ plu◦ ←bahuvrī◦ *adhyātma-nitya,* अध्यात्मनि नित्यरतः यः ←n◦ *adhyātma* 3.30 + adj◦ *nitya* 2.18); *vinivṛttakāmāḥ:* (m◦ 1nom◦ plu◦ ←bahuvrī◦ *vinivṛtta-kāma,* विनिवृत्ताः कामाः यस्य ←ppp◦ adj◦ *vinivṛtta* ←वि-नि√वृत् 14.22 + m◦ *kāma* 1.22); *dvandvaiḥ:* (3inst◦ plu◦ ←n◦ *dvandva* 2.45); *vimuktāḥ:* (m◦ 1nom◦ plu◦ ←ppp◦ adj◦ *vimukta* 9.28); *sukhaduḥ:khasañjñaiḥ:* (3inst◦ plu◦ ←bahuvrī◦ *sukha-duḥ:kha-sañjña,* सुखम् च दुःखम् च संज्ञे यस्य ←n◦ *sukha* 1.32 + n◦ *duḥ:kha* 2.14 + f◦ *sañjñā* 1.7); *gaććhanti* (2.51); *amūḍhāḥ:* (1nom◦ plu◦ n.tatpu◦ ←m◦ *mūḍha* 7.15); *padam̥* (2.51); *avyayam̥* (2acc◦ 2.21); *tat̥* (2acc◦ 2.7);

(15.5)

(§3) *nirmānamohāḥ:* (adj1◦-subj◦ those who are free from pride and delusion); *jitasaṅgadoṣāḥ:* (adj2◦-subj◦ those who have defeated the vice of attachment); *adhyātmanityāḥ:* (adj3◦-subj◦ those who are always immersed in study of scriptures); *vinivṛttakāmāḥ:* (adj4◦-subj◦ those who have retired from passions); *dvandvaiḥ: vimuktāḥ:* (adj5◦-subj◦ those who have turned away from or have become indifferent to the pairs of opposites); *sukhaduḥ:khasañjñaiḥ:* (such as happiness and sorrow etc.); *gaććhanti* (they attain); *amūḍhāḥ:* (adj6◦-subj◦ those non-deluded people); *padam̥* (obj◦ state, abode); *avyayam̥* (adj1◦-obj◦ immutable); *tat̥* (adj2◦-obj◦ that);

(15.5)

(§4) nirmānamohāḥ: jitasaṅgadoṣāḥ: adhyātmanityāḥ: vinivṛttakāmāḥ: dvandvaiḥ: vimuktāḥ: sukhaduḥ:khasañjñaiḥ: amūḍhāḥ: gaććhanti tat̥ avyayam̥ padam̥;

(§5) Those who are (i) free from pride and delusion, (ii) those who have defeated the vice of attachment, (iii) those who are always immersed in study of scriptures, (iv) those who have retired from passions, (v) those who have become indifferent to the pairs of opposites such as happiness and sorrow etc., (vi) those who are non-deluded, they attain that immutable abode; (15.5)

15.6 न तद्भासयते सूर्यो न शशाङ्को न पावकः ।
यद्गत्वा न निवर्तन्ते तद्धाम परमं मम ।।
na tadbhāsayate sūryo na śaśāṅko na pāvakaḥ:,
yadgatvā na nivartantae taddhāma paramaṁ mama. (15.6)

(§1) *na taṭ* (r◦ 9/8) *bhāsayate sūryaḥ:* (r◦ 15/6) *na śaśāṅkaḥ:* (r◦ 15/6) *na pāvakaḥ:* (r◦ 22/8) *yaṭ* (r◦ 9/4) *gatvā na nivartante taṭ* (r◦ 9/6) *dhāma paramaṃ* (r◦ 14/1) *mama*

(§2) *na* (1.30); *taṭ* (2acc◦ 1.10); *bhāsayate* (3rd-per◦ sing◦ pres◦ वर्तमान्-लट् ātmane◦ caus◦ ←class1◦ √भास्); *sūryaḥ:* (1nom◦ sing◦ ←m◦ *sūrya* 7.8); *na* (1.30); *śaśāṅkaḥ:* (11.39); *na* (1.30); *pāvakaḥ:* (2.23); *yaṭ* (2acc◦ 3.21); *gatvā* (14.15); *na* (1.30); *nivartante* (8.21); *taṭ* (1nom◦ 2.7); *dhāma* (1nom◦ 8.21); *paramaṃ* (1nom◦ 8.3); *mama* (1.7) (15.6)

(§3) *na* (neither); *taṭ* (adj2◦-obj◦ that, that abode, that self-illuminated abode); *bhāsayate* (causative : causes to shine, lights up); *sūryaḥ:* (subj1◦ the sun); *na* (nor); *śaśāṅkaḥ:* (subj2◦ the moon); *na* (nor); *pāvakaḥ:* (subj3◦ a fire); *yaṭ* (where); *gatvā* (having gone); *na* (one does not); *nivartante* (return, come back); *taṭ* (adj1◦-subj4◦ that); *dhāma* (subj4◦ abode); *paramaṃ* (adj2◦-subj4◦ supreme); *mama* (adj3◦-subj4◦ my)

(15.6)

(§4) taṭ na sūryaḥ: na śaśāṅkaḥ: na pāvakaḥ: bhāsayate yaṭ gatvā na nivartante taṭ mama paramaṃ dhāma

(§5) That self-illuminated abode (which) neither the sun nor the moon nor a fire causes to shine (and) where having gone one does not return, that (is) my supreme abode.

(15.6)

15.7 ममैवांशो जीवलोके जीवभूत: सनातन: ।
मन:षष्ठानीन्द्रियाणि प्रकृतिस्थानि कर्षति ।।
mamaivāṃśo jīvaloke jīvabhūtaḥ: sanātanaḥ:,
manaḥ:ṣaṣṭhānīndriyāṇi prakṛtisthāni karṣati. (15.7)

(§1) *mama* (r◦ 3/1) *eva* (r◦ 1/1) *aṃśaḥ:* (r◦ 15/3) *jīvaloke jīvabhūtaḥ:* (r◦ 22/7) *sanātanaḥ:* (r◦ 22/8) *manaḥ:ṣaṣṭhāni* (r◦ 1/5) *indriyāṇi* (r◦ 24/7) *prakṛtisthāni karṣati*

(§2) *mama* (1.7); *eva* (1.1); 📖*aṃśaḥ:* (1nom◦ sing◦ ←m◦ *aṃśa* 10.41); *jīvaloke* (m◦ 7loc◦ sing◦ ←tatpu◦ *jīva-loka*, जीवानाम् लोक: ←m◦ *jīva* 7.5 + m◦ *loka* 2.5); 📖*jīvabhūtaḥ:* (m◦ 1nom◦ sing◦ ←tatpu◦ *jīva-bhūta* 7.5); *sanātanaḥ:* (2.24); *manaḥ:ṣaṣṭhāni* (n◦ 2acc◦ plu◦ ←bahuvrī◦ *manaḥ:-ṣaṣṭha*, मन: षष्ठम् यस्य ←n◦ *manaṣ* 1.30 + adj◦ *ṣaṣṭha* ←√सो); *indriyāṇi* (2acc◦ 2.58); *prakṛtisthāni* (n◦ 2acc◦ plu◦ ←adj◦ *prakṛtistha* 13.22); *karṣati* (3rd-per◦ sing◦ pres◦ वर्तमान्-लट् parasmai◦ ←class6◦ √कृष्) (15.7)

(§3) *mama* (adj◦-subj◦ my, of mine); *eva* (merely); *aṃśaḥ:* (subj1◦ a tiny aspect, a fragment); *jīvaloke* (in the world of beings); *jīvabhūtaḥ:* (subj2◦ life of the living beings, the bhūtātmā, the ātmā); *sanātanaḥ:* (adj◦-subj2◦ the beginingless and endless); *manaḥ:ṣaṣṭhāni indriyāṇi* (obj◦ those five essences along with cognition as the sixth one); *prakṛtisthāni* (adj1◦-obj◦ which exist in the nature); *karṣati* (takes with it, draws with it) (15.7)

(§4) sanātanaḥ: jīvabhūtaḥ: eva aṁśaḥ: mama jīvaloke karṣati manaḥ:ṣaṣṭhāni indriyāṇi prakṛtisthāni

(§5) The beginingless and endless life of the living beings,[753] (that is) merely a tiny aspect of mine in the world of beings, draws with it those five essences, along with cognition as the sixth essence, which exist in the nature. (15.7)

15.8 शरीरं यदवाप्नोति यच्चाप्युत्क्रामतीश्वरः ।
गृहीत्वैतानि संयाति वायुर्गन्धानिवाशयात् ।।
śarīraṁ yadavāpnoti yaććāpyutkramatīśvaraḥ:,
gṛhītvaitāni saṁyāti vāyurgandhānivāśayāt; (15.8)

(§1) *śarīraṃ* (r◦ 14/1) *yaṭ* (r◦ 8/2) *avāpnoti yaṭ* (r◦ 11/1) *ća* (r◦ 1/1) *api* (r◦ 4/3) *utkramati* (r◦ 1/6) *īśvaraḥ:* (r◦ 22/8) *gṛhītvā* (r◦ 3/3) *etāni saṁyāti vāyuḥ:* (r◦ 16/8) *gandhāṇ* (r◦ 8/13) *iva* (r◦ 1/2) *āśayāṭ;*

(§2) *śarīraṃ* (2acc◦ sing◦ ←n◦ *śarīra* 3.8); *yaṭ* (2acc◦ 3.21); *avāpnoti* (3rd-per◦ sing◦ pres◦ वर्तमान्-लट् parasmai◦ ←class5◦ अव√आप्); *yaṭ* (↑); *ća* (1.1); *api* (1.26); *utkramati* (3rd-per◦ sing◦ pres◦ वर्तमान्-लट् parasmai◦ ←class1◦ उद्√क्रम्); *īśvaraḥ:* (4.6); *gṛhītvā* (ipp◦ ind◦ ←√ग्रह्); ***etāni*** (n◦ 2acc◦ plu◦ ←pron◦ *etaḍ* 1.3); *saṁyāti* (2.22); *vāyuḥ:* (2.67); *gandhāṇ* (2acc◦ plu◦ ←m◦ *gandha* 7.9); *iva* (1.30); *āśayāṭ* (5abl◦ sing◦ ←m◦ *āśaya* 10.20); (15.8)

(§3) *śarīraṃ* (obj1-2◦ the body); *yaṭ* (adj◦-obj1◦ which); *avāpnoti* (he assumes); *yaṭ* (adj◦-obj2◦ the one which); *ća api* (and); *utkramati* (he leaves); *īśvaraḥ:* (subj1◦ the Lord, the life of the living beings, the *bhūtātmā*, the *ātmā*); *gṛhītvā* (having taken with him); *etāni* (adj◦-obj2◦ these six senses); *saṁyāti* (carries away with it); *vāyuḥ:* (subj2◦ the wind); *gandhāṇ* (obj3◦ essences, fragrences); *iva* (as); *āśayāṭ* (from their sources); (15.8)

(§4) śarīraṃ yaṭ īśvaraḥ: avāpnoti ća api yaṭ utkramati gṛhītvā etāni iva vāyuḥ: saṁyāti gandhāṇ āśayāṭ

(§5) The body which[754] the *ātmā* assumes and the one which he leaves having taken with him these six essences,[755] as the wind carries away with it essences from their sources; (15.8)

---

[753] elsewhere◦ जीवभूतः → becoming, become, became, having become, transformed, has transformed into, ...individual soul, individual self, a living Spirit, embodied soul, living entities, a living soil, ...etc.

[754] elsewhere◦ यत् → When

[755] Six essences : please see (5) in the next verse 15.9).

15.9 श्रोत्रं चक्षुः स्पर्शनं च रसनं घ्राणमेव च ।
अधिष्ठाय मनश्चायं विषयानुपसेवते ।।
śrotraṁ ćakṣuḥ: sparśanaṁ ća rasanaṁ ghrāṇameva ća,
adhiṣṭhāya manaśćāyaṁ viṣayānupasevate. (15.9)

(§1) *śrotraṃ* (r◦ 14/1) *ćakṣuḥ:* (r◦ 22/7) *sparśanaṃ* (r◦ 14/1) *ća rasanaṃ* (r◦ 14/1) *ghrāṇaṃ* (r◦ 8/22, 24/3) *eva ća* (r◦ 23/1) *adhiṣṭhāya manaḥ:* (r◦ 17/1) *ća* (r◦ 1/1) *ayaṃ* (r◦ 14/1) *viṣayān* (r◦ 8/14) *upasevate*

(§2) *śrotraṃ* (2acc◦ sing◦ ←n◦ *śrotra* 4.26); *ćakṣuḥ:* (2acc◦ 5.27); *sparśanaṃ* (n◦ 2acc◦ sing◦ ←adj◦ *sparśana* ←√स्पर्श्); *ća* (1.1); *rasanaṃ* (n◦ 2acc◦ sing◦ ←adj◦ *rasana* ←√रस्); *ghrāṇaṃ* (n◦ 2acc◦ sing◦ ←adj◦ *ghrāṇa* ←√घ्रा); *eva* (1.1); *ća* (1.1); *adhiṣṭhāya* (participle 4.6); *manaḥ:* (2acc◦ 6.12); *ća* (1.1); *ayaṃ* (2.19); *viṣayān* (2.62); *upasevate* (3rd-per◦ sing◦ pres◦ वर्तमान्–लट् ātmane◦ ←class1◦ उप√सेव्)
(15.9)

(§3) *śrotraṃ* (obj1◦ the essence of hearing - not the actual ear itself); *ćakṣuḥ:* (obj2◦ the essence of sight - not the actual eyes themselves); *sparśanaṃ* (obj3◦ the essence of touch - not the actual skin itself); *ća* (and); *rasanaṃ* (obj4◦ the essence of taste - not the actual tongue itself); *ghrāṇaṃ* (obj5◦ the essence of smell - not the actual nose itself); *eva ća* (and); *adhiṣṭhāya* (carring with him, positioning with him); *manaḥ:* (obj6◦ the essence of intellect); *ća* (and); *ayaṃ* (subj◦ this, this *ātmā*); *viṣayān* (obj7◦ the sense objects); *upasevate* (facilitates) (15.9)

(§4) adhiṣṭhāya śrotraṃ ćakṣuḥ: sparśanaṃ ća rasanaṃ ća ghrāṇaṃ eva ća manaḥ: ayaṃ upasevate viṣayān

(§5) Positioning[756] with him the (i) essence of hearing,[757] the (ii) essence of sight, the (iii) essence of touch and the (iv) essence of taste and the (v) essence of smell and the (vi) essence of intellect, the *ātmā* facilitates[758] the sense objects. (15.9)

15.10 उत्क्रामन्तं स्थितं वापि भुञ्जानं वा गुणान्वितम् ।
विमूढा नानुपश्यन्ति पश्यन्ति ज्ञानचक्षुषः ।।
utkrāmantaṁ sthitaṁ vāpi bhuñjānaṁ vā guṇānvitam,

---

[756] elsewhere◦ अधिष्ठाय → presiding over, obtains, ...etc.

[757] elsewhere◦ श्रोत्रं चक्षुः स्पर्शनं रसनं घ्राणम् मनः → the ear, eyes, skin, tongue, nose, mind, the ears, the eyes, the organs of touch, taste and smell as well as the mind, a certain type of ear, eye, tongue, nose and sense of touch which are grouped about the mind, ...etc.

[758] elsewhere◦ उपसेवते → enjoys, experiencing, experiences,

vimūḍhā nānupaśyanti paśyanti jñānacakṣuṣaḥ:. (15.10)

(§1) *utkrāmantam̦* (r∘ 14/1) *sthitam̦* (r∘ 14/1) *vā* (r∘ 1/3) *api bhuñjānam̦* (r∘ 14/1) *vā guṇānvitam̦* (r∘ 14/2) *vimūḍhāḥ:* (r∘ 20/10) *na* (r∘ 1/1) *anupaśyanti paśyanti jñānacakṣuṣaḥ:* (r∘ 25/1, 22/8)

(§2) *utkrāmantam̦* (m∘ 2acc∘ sing∘ ←śatṛ∘ adj∘ *utkrāmaț* ←उद√क्रम्); *sthitam̦* (m∘ 2acc∘ sing∘ ←ppp∘ adj∘ *sthita* 5.19); *vā* (1.32); *api* (1.26); *bhuñjānam̦* (m∘ 2acc∘ sing∘ ←śatṛ∘ adj∘ *bhuñjāț* or *bhuñjāna* ←√भुज्); *vā* (1.32); *guṇānvitam̦* (m∘ 2acc∘ sing∘ ←ppp∘ adj∘ *guṇānvita* ←गुण–अनु√इ); *vimūḍhāḥ:* (m∘ 1nom∘ plu∘ ←adj∘ *vimūḍha* 3.6); *na* (1.30); *anupaśyanti* (3rd-per∘ plu∘ pres∘ वर्तमान्–लट् parasmai∘ ←class1∘ अनु√दृश् 6.30); *paśyanti* (1.38); *jñānacakṣuṣaḥ:* (m∘ 1nom∘ plu∘ ←tatpu∘ *jñāna-cakṣuṣ* 13.35) (15.10)

(§3) *utkrāmantam̦* (adj1∘-obj∘ while leaving); *sthitam̦* (adj2∘-obj∘ seated, while seated); *vā api* (or even); *bhuñjānam̦* (adj3∘-obj∘ while facilitating); *vā* (or); *guṇānvitam̦* (adj4∘-obj∘ associated with the three *guṇas*); *vimūḍhāḥ:* (subj1∘ a deluded person); *na* (does not); *anupaśyanti* (perceive); *paśyanti* (perceive); *jñānacakṣuṣaḥ:* (subj2∘ those with eye of knowledge, those with the inner eye) (15.10)

(§4) utkrāmantam̦ sthitam̦ vā bhuñjānam̦ vā api guṇānvitam̦ vimūḍhāḥ: na anupaśyanti jñānacakṣuṣaḥ:

(§5) While leaving (the body) or while seated (in the body) facilitating or even associated with the three *guṇas*, a deluded person does not perceive (the *ātmā*), as those with the inner eye perceive (him, the *ātmā*). (15.10)

15.11 यतन्तो योगिनश्चैनं पश्यन्त्यात्मन्यवस्थितम् ।
यतन्तोऽप्यकृतात्मानो नैनं पश्यन्त्यचेतसः ।।

yatanto yoginaścainaṁ paśyantyātmanyavasthitam̦,
yatanto'pyakṛtātmāno nainaṁ paśyantyacetasaḥ:. (15.11)

(§1) *yatantaḥ:* (r∘ 15/10) *yoginaḥ:* (r∘ 17/1) *ca* (r∘ 3/1) *enam̦* (r∘ 14/1) *paśyanti* (r∘ 4/2) *ātmani* (r∘ 4/1) *avasthitam̦* (r∘ 14/2) *yatantaḥ:* (r∘ 15/1) *api* (r∘ 4/1) *akṛtātmānaḥ:* (r∘ 15/6) *na* (r∘ 3/1) *enam̦* (r∘ 14/1) *paśyanti* (r∘ 4/1) *acetasaḥ:* (r∘ 22/8)

(§2) *yatantaḥ:* (9.14); *yoginaḥ:* (4.25); *ca* (1.1); *enam̦* (2.19); *paśyanti* (1.38); *ātmani* (2.55); *avasthitam̦* (m∘ 2acc∘ sing∘ ←ppp∘ adj∘ *avasthita* 1.11); *yatantaḥ:* (9.14); *api* (1.26); *akṛtātmānaḥ:* (m∘ 1nom∘ plu∘ ←bahuvrī∘ *a-kṛtātman̦*, न कृतः आत्मा यस्य ←ind∘ *na* 1.30 + adj∘ *kṛta* 1.35 + m∘ *ātman̦* 2.41); *na* (1.30); *enam̦* (↑); *paśyanti* (1.38); *acetasaḥ:* (3.32) (15.11)

(§3) *yatantaḥ:* (adj∘-subj1∘ the striving); *yoginaḥ:* (subj1∘ *yogis*); *ca* (and); *enam̦* (adj1∘-obj∘ this); *paśyanti* (do perceive); *ātmani* (in themselves); *avasthitam̦* (adj2∘-obj∘ seated); *yatantaḥ:* (adj1∘-subj2∘ striving); *api* (even); *akṛtātmānaḥ:* (adj2∘-subj2∘ the ones without self realization); *na* (do not); *enam̦* (adj1◦-obj◦ this *ātmā*); *paśyanti* (perceive); *aćetasaḥ:* (adj3◦-subj2◦ those devoid of spiritual mind) (15.11)

(§4) yatantaḥ: yoginaḥ: paśyanti enam̩ avasthitam̩ ātmani ća akṛtātmānaḥ: aćetasaḥ: api yatantaḥ: na paśyanti enam̩

(§5) The striving *yogis* do perceive this *ātmā* seated in themselves; and those without self realization, the ones devoid of spiritual mind,[759] even striving do not perecive this *ātmā*. (15.11)

15.12 यदादित्यगतं तेजो जगद्भासयतेऽखिलम् ।
यच्चन्द्रमसि यच्चाग्नौ तत्तेजो विद्धि मामकम् ।।
yadādityagataṁ tejo jagadbhāsayate‘khilam̩,
yaććandramasi yaććāgnau tattejo viddhi māmakam̩. (15.12)

(§1) *yat̩* (r◦ 8/3) *ādityagatam̩* (r◦ 14/1) *tejaḥ:* (r◦ 15/3) *jagat̩* (r◦ 9/8) *bhāsayate* (r◦ 6/1) *akhilam̩* (r◦ 14/2) *yat̩* (r◦ 11/1) *ćandramasi yat̩* (r◦ 11/1) *ća* (r◦ 1/1) *agnau tat̩* (r◦ 1/10) *tejaḥ:* (r◦ 15/13) *viddhi māmakam̩* (r◦ 14/2)

(§2) *yat̩* (1nom◦ 2.67); *ādityagatam̩* (n◦ 1nom◦ sing◦ ←adj◦ tatpu◦ *āditya-gata*, आदित्यम् गत: ←m◦ *āditya* 5.16 + adj◦ *gata* 2.11); *tejaḥ:* (1nom◦ 7.9); *jagat̩* (2acc◦ 11.7); *bhāsayate* (15.6); *akhilam̩* (4.33); *yat̩* (1nom◦ 1.45); *ćandramasi* (7loc◦ sing◦ ←m◦ *ćandramas̩* ←√चन्द्); *yat̩* (1nom◦ 1.45); *ća* (1.1); *agnau* (7loc◦ sing◦ ←m◦ *agni* 4.19); *tat̩* (2acc◦ 1.10); *tejaḥ:* (1nom◦ 7.9); *viddhi* (2.17); *māmakam̩* (n◦ 2acc◦ sing◦ ←adj◦ *māmaka* 1.1) (15.12)

(§3) *yat̩* (adj1◦-subj1◦ that which); *ādityagatam̩* (adj2◦-subj1◦ of the sun); *tejaḥ:* (subj1◦ radiance); *jagat̩* (obj1◦ the world); *bhāsayate* (illuminates); *akhilam̩* (adj◦-obj1◦ whole); *yat̩* (adj◦-subj2◦ that which); *ćandramasi* (in the moon); *yat̩* (adj◦-subj3◦ that which); *ća* (and); *agnau* (in the fire); *tat̩* (adj1◦-subj1-3 collective◦ that); *tejaḥ:* (subj1-3 collective◦ glow, illumination, radiance); *viddhi* (know it to be); *māmakam̩* (adj2◦-subj1-3 collective◦ mine) (15.12)

(§4) yat̩ tejaḥ: ādityagatam̩ bhāsayate akhilam̩ jagat̩ yat̩ ćandramasi yat̩ agnau tat̩ tejaḥ: viddhi māmakam̩.

(§5) That radiance of the sun which illuminates the whole world; that (glow) which (is) in the moon and that glow which (is) in the fire, know that illumination to be mine. (15.12)

---

[759] elsewhere◦ अचेतस: → diligent, unintelligent, those who have not purified their hearts, unperfected selves, ...etc.

15.13 गामाविश्य च भूतानि धारयाम्यहमोजसा ।
पुष्णामि चौषधी: सर्वा: सोमो भूत्वा रसात्मक: ।।
gāmāviśya ća bhūtāni dhārayāmyahamojasā,
puṣṇāmi ćauṣadhīḥ: sarvāḥ: somo bhūtvā rasātmakaṃ. (15.13)

(§1) *gāṃ* (r∘ 8/17) *āviśya ća bhūtāni dhārayāmi* (r∘ 4/1) *ahaṃ* (r∘ 8/24) *ojasā puṣṇāmi ća* (r∘ 3/2) *oṣadhīḥ:* (r∘ 22/7) *sarvāḥ:* (r∘ 22/7) *somaḥ:* (r∘ 15/8) *bhūtvā rasātmakaṃ* (r∘ 22/8)

(§2) *gāṃ* (2acc∘ sing∘ ←f∘ *gā* 1.32); *āviśya* (lyp∘ past-participle ind∘ ←आ√विश्); *ća* (1.1); *bhūtāni* (2acc∘ 2.30); *dhārayāmi* (1st-per∘ sing∘ pres∘ वर्तमान्–लट् parasmai∘ caus∘ ←class1∘ √धृ); *ahaṃ* (1.22); *ojasā* (3inst∘ sing∘ ←n∘ *ojaṣ* ←√उब्ज्); *puṣṇāmi* (1st-per∘ sing∘ pres∘ वर्तमान्–लट् parasmai∘ ←class9∘ √पुष्); *ća* (1.1); *oṣadhīḥ:* (2acc∘ plu∘ ←f∘ *oṣadhi* or *oṣadhī* ←ओष√धा 9.16); *sarvāḥ:* (8.18); *somaḥ:* (1nom∘ sing∘ ←m∘ *soma* 9.20); *bhūtvā* (2.20); *rasātmakaṃ* (m∘ 1nom∘ sing∘ ←adj∘ *rasātmaka* ←m∘ *rasa* 2.59 + adj∘ *ātmaka* 14.7) (15.13)

(§3) *gāṃ* (obj1∘ the earth); *āviśya* (having descended to); *ća* (and); *bhūtāni* (obj2∘ the beings); *dhārayāmi* (I support); *ahaṃ* (subj1∘ I); *ojasā* (with my power); *puṣṇāmi* (I nourish); *ća* (and); *oṣadhīḥ:* (obj3∘ vegetations, plants); *sarvāḥ:* (adj∘-obj3∘ all); *somaḥ:* (adj∘-subj1∘ the juice); *bhūtvā* (becoming); *rasātmakaṃ* (in the form of sap) (15.13)

(§4) ća āviśya gāṃ dhārayāmi ahaṃ bhūtāni ojasā ća puṣṇāmi sarvāḥ: oṣadhīḥ: bhūtvā somaḥ: rasātmakaṃ

(§5) And having descended to the earth I support the beings with (my) power and I nourish all vegetations becoming the juice in the form of sap. (15.13)

15.14 अहं वैश्वानरो भूत्वा प्राणिनां देहमाश्रित: ।
प्राणापानसमायुक्त: पचाम्यन्नं चतुर्विधम् ।।
ahaṁ vaiśvānaro bhūtvā prāṇināṁ dehamāśritaḥ:,
prāṇāpānasamāyuktaḥ: paćāmyannaṁ ćaturvidhaṃ. (15.14)

(§1) *ahaṃ* (r∘ 14/1) *vaiśvānaraḥ:* (r∘ 15/8) *bhūtvā prāṇināṃ* (r∘ 14/1) *dehaṃ* (r∘ 8/17) *āśritaḥ:* (r∘ 22/8) *prāṇāpānasamāyuktaḥ:* (r∘ 22/3) *paćāmi* (r∘ 4/1) *annaṃ* (r∘ 14/1) *ćaturvidhaṃ* (r∘ 14/2)

(§2) *ahaṃ* (1.22); *vaiśvānaraḥ:* (1nom∘ sing∘ ←m∘ taddhita∘ *vaiśvānara* or *viśvānara); bhūtvā* (2.20); *prāṇināṃ* (6pos plu∘ ←m∘ *prāṇiṇ* ←प्र√अन्); *dehaṃ* (4.9); *āśritaḥ:* (9.11); *prāṇāpānasamāyuktaḥ:* (m∘ 1nom∘ sing∘ ←tatpu∘ *prāṇāpāna-samāyukta,* प्राणेन च अपानेन च समायुक्त: ←m∘ *prāṇa* 1.33 + m∘ *apāna* 4.29 + ppp∘ adj∘ *samāyukta* ←सम्–आ√युज्); *paćāmi* (1st-per∘ sing∘ pres∘ वर्तमान्–लट् parasmai∘ ←class1∘ √पच्); *annaṃ* (2acc∘ sing∘ ←n∘ *anna* 3.14); *ćaturvidhaṃ* (n∘ 2acc∘ sing∘ ←dvigu∘ *ćatur-vidha* 7.16)

(15.14)

(§3) *ahaṃ* (subj◦ I); *vaiśvānaraḥ:* (adj1◦-subj1◦ the digestive force); *bhūtvā* (becoming); *prāṇināṃ* (of the living beingṣ); *dehaṃ* (obj1◦ body); *āśritaḥ:* (adj2◦-subj◦ sheltered in); *prāṇāpānasamāyuktaḥ:* (adj3◦-subj◦ equipped with incoming and outgoing air flows); *paćāmi* (I digest); *annaṃ* (obj2◦ the food); *ćaturvidhaṃ* (adj◦-obj2◦ of four kinds) (15.14)

(§4) bhūtvā vaiśvānaraḥ: āśritaḥ: dehaṃ prāṇināṃ prāṇāpānasamāyuktaḥ: ahaṃ paćāmi annaṃ ćaturvidhaṃ

(§5) Becoming the digestive force, sheltered[760] in the body of the living beings (and) equipped[761] with incoming and outgoing air flows, I digest the food four kinds.[762]

(15.14)

15.15 सर्वस्य चाहं हृदि सन्निविष्टो मत्तः स्मृतिर्ज्ञानमपोहनं च ।
वेदैश्च सर्वैरहमेव वेद्यो वेदान्तकृद्वेदविदेव चाहम् ।।
sarvasya ćāhaṁ hṛdi sanniviṣṭo mattaḥ: smṛtirjñānamapohanaṁ ća,
vedaiśća sarvairahameva vedyo vedāntakṛdvedavideva ćāhaṃ. (15.15)

(§1) *sarvasya ća* (r◦ 1/1) *ahaṃ* (r◦ 14/1) *hṛdi sanniviṣṭaḥ:* (r◦ 15/9) *mattaḥ:* (r◦ 22/7) *smṛtiḥ:* (r◦ 16/6) *jñānaṃ* (r◦ 8/16) *apohanaṃ* (r◦ 14/1) *ća vedaiḥ:* (r◦ 17/1) *ća sarvaiḥ:* (r◦ 16/4) *ahaṃ* (r◦ 8/22) *eva vedyaḥ:* (r◦ 15/13) *vedāntakṛt* (r◦ 9/11) *vedavit* (r◦ 8/9) *eva ća* (r◦ 1/1) *ahaṃ* (r◦ 14/2)

(§2) *sarvasya* (2.30); *ća* (1.1); *ahaṃ* (1.22); *hṛdi* (8.12); *sanniviṣṭaḥ:* (m◦ 1nom◦ sing◦ ←ppp◦ adj◦ *sanniviṣṭa* ←सम्–नि√विश्); *mattaḥ:* (7.7); *smṛtiḥ:* (10.34); *jñānaṃ* (1nom◦ 3.39); 🕮*apohanaṃ* (1nom◦ sing◦ ←n◦ *apohana* ←अप√ऊह्); *ća* (1.1); *vedaiḥ:* (11.52); *ća* (1.1); *sarvaiḥ:* (3inst◦ plu◦ ←pron◦ *sarva* 1.6); *ahaṃ* (1.22); *eva* (1.1); *vedyaḥ:* (1nom◦ sing◦ ←adj◦ *vedya* 9.17); *vedāntakṛt* (m◦ 1nom◦ sing◦ ←bahuvrī◦ *vedānta-kṛt*, वेदान्तः करोति यः ←m◦ *vedānta* ←√विद् + v◦ *karoti* 4.20); *vedavit* (15.1); *eva* (1.1); *ća* (1.1); *ahaṃ* (1.22) (15.15)

---

[760] elsewhere◦ आश्रितः → residing, abide, dwelling, entering, penetrating, abiding, ...etc.

🕮 आश्रितः is not a gerund or त्वान्त participle or present tense. It is one of the tow adjectives of वैश्वानरः

[761] elsewhere◦ समायुक्तः → in association with, joining with, having united with, becoming, become, mingling with, I join, ...etc.

🕮 Similarly, समायुक्तः is not a gerund or त्वान्त participle or present tense. It is one of the tow adjectives of वैश्वानरः

[762] foods of four kinds : (i) to be eaten by masticating, (ii) to be eaten by swallowing, (iii) to be eating by sucking, and (iv) to be eaten by licking.

(§3) *sarvasya* (of everyone); *ća* (and); *aham̧* (subj1◦ I am); *hr̥di* (in the heart); **(i)** *sannivis̩tah̩:* (adj◦-subj1◦ seated, situated); *mattah̩:* (from me); *smr̥tih̩:* (subj2◦ cognition; *jñānam̧* (subj3◦ knowledge); *apohanam̧* (subj4◦ reasoning); *ća* (and); *vedaih̩:* (through the *vedas*); *ća* (and); *sarvaih̩:* (all); *aham̧* (subj1◦ I); *eva* (also); **(ii)** *vedyah̩:* (adj1◦-subj1◦ knowable); **(iii)** *vedāntakr̥t̩* (adj2◦-subj1◦ the maker of the *vedanta*); **(iv)** *vedavit̩* (adj3◦-subj1◦ the knower of the veda); *eva ća* (as well as); *aham̧* (subj1◦ I am) (15.15)

(§4) sarvasya ća aham̧ hr̥di sannivis̩tah̩: mattah̩: smr̥tih̩: jñānam̧ apohanam̧ ća vedaih̩: ća sarvaih̩: aham̧ eva vedyah̩: aham̧ vedāntakr̥t̩ vedavit̩ eva ća

(§5) And I am seated in the heart of everyone.[763] From me (are) cognition, knowledge and reasoning. And I am knowable through all the *vedas*. Also, I am the maker of the *vedanta* as well as the knower of the *veda*. (15.15)

15.16 द्वाविमौ पुरुषौ लोके क्षरश्चाक्षर एव च ।
क्षर: सर्वाणि भूतानि कूटस्थोऽक्षर उच्यते ।।

dvāvimau purus̩au loke ks̩araśćāks̩ara eva ća,
ks̩arah̩: sarvāni bhūtāni kūt̩astho‘ks̩ara ućyate; (15.16)

(§1) *dvau* (r◦ 5/6) *imau purus̩au loke ks̩arah̩:* (r◦ 17/1) *ća* (r◦ 1/1) *aks̩arah̩:* (r◦ 19/7) *eva ća ks̩arah̩:* (r◦ 22/7) *sarvān̩i* (r◦ 24/7) *bhūtāni kūt̩asthah̩:* (r◦ 15/1) *aks̩arah̩:* (r◦ 19/4) *ućyate;*

(§2) *dvau* (1nom◦ dual◦ ←always dual num◦ adj◦ *dvi* 1.7); *imau* (m◦ 1nom◦ dual◦ ←pron◦ *idam̧* 1.10); *purus̩au* (1nom◦ dual◦ ←m◦ *purus̩a* 2.15); *loke* (2.5); *ks̩arah̩:* (8.4); *ća* (1.1); *aks̩arah̩:* (8.21); *eva* (1.1); *ća* (1.1); *ks̩arah̩:* (8.4); *sarvān̩i* (1nom◦ 2.30); *bhūtāni* (1nom◦ 2.30); *kūt̩asthah̩:* (6.8); *aks̩arah̩:* (8.21); *ućyate* (2.25); (15.16)

(§3) *dvau* (adj1◦-subj1-2◦ two); *imau* (adj2◦-subj1-2◦ these); *purus̩au* (subj1-2◦ the *purus̩as*); *loke* (in the world); *ks̩arah̩:* (adj3◦-subj1◦ the mutable); *ća* (and); *aks̩arah̩:* (adj3◦-subj2◦ immutable); *eva* (as well as); *ća* (and); *ks̩arah̩:* (adj3◦-subj1◦ the mutable); *sarvān̩i* (adj4◦-subj1◦ all); *bhūtāni* (subj1◦ the beings); *kūt̩asthah̩:* (adj4◦-subj2◦); *aks̩arah̩:* (adj3◦-subj2◦ the immutable); *ućyate* (is called); (15.16)

(§4) imau dvau purus̩au loke ks̩arah̩: eva aks̩arah̩: ća ks̩arah̩: sarvān̩i bhūtāni ća aks̩arah̩: ućyate kūt̩asthah̩:;

(§5) These two (are) the *purus̩as* in the world, the mutable as well as immutable. And, the

---

[763] elsewhere◦ अपोहनम् → memory loss, memory and knowledge loss, negation, forgetfulness, ...etc.

mutable (comprises) all the beings and the immutable is called the Supreme;[764] (15.16)

15.17 उत्तम: पुरुषस्त्वन्य: परमात्मेत्युदाहृत: ।
यो लोकत्रयमाविश्य बिभर्त्यव्यय ईश्वर: ।।

uttamaḥ: puruṣastvanyaḥ: paramātmetyudāhṛtaḥ:,
yo lokatrayamāviśya bibhartyavyaya īśvaraḥ:. (15.17)

(§1) *uttamaḥ:* (r◦ 22/3) *puruṣaḥ:* (r◦ 18/1) *tu* (r◦ 4/6) *anyaḥ:* (r◦ 22/3) *parmātmā* (r◦ 2/3) *iti* (r◦ 4/3) *udāhṛtaḥ:* (r◦ 22/8) *yaḥ:* (r◦ 15/12) *lokatrayaṃ* (r◦ 8/17) *āviśya bibharti* (r◦ 4/1) *avyayaḥ:* (r◦ 19/3) *īśvaraḥ:* (r◦ 22/8)

(§2) *uttamaḥ:* (m◦ 1nom◦ sing◦ ←adj◦ *uttama* 1.7); *puruṣaḥ:* (2.21); *tu* (1.2); *anyaḥ:* (2.29); *parmātmā* (6.7); *iti* (1.25); *udāhṛtaḥ:* (m◦ 1nom◦ sing◦ ←adj◦ *udāhṛta* 13.7); *yaḥ:* (2.19); *lokatrayaṃ* (11.20); *āviśya* (15.13); *bibharti* (3rd-per◦ sing◦ pres◦ वर्तमान्-लट् parasmai◦ ←class3◦ √भृ 10.31); *avyayaḥ:* (11.18); *īśvaraḥ:* (4.6) (15.17)

(§3) *uttamaḥ:* (adj1◦-subj3◦ most superior); *puruṣaḥ:* (subj3◦ *puruṣa*); *tu* (but); *anyaḥ:* (adj2◦-subj3◦ another); *parmātmā* (adj3◦-subj3◦ supreme-*ātmā, brahma*); *iti udāhṛtaḥ:* (adj4◦-subj3◦ known as); *yaḥ:* (adj5◦-subj3◦ who); *lokatrayaṃ* (obj◦ the three worlds); *āviśya* (descending); *bibharti* (supports); *avyayaḥ:* (adj6◦-subj3◦ the immutable); *īśvaraḥ:* (adj7◦-subj3◦ Lord) (15.17)

(§4) tu anyaḥ: uttamaḥ: puruṣaḥ: iti udāhṛtaḥ: parmātmā avyayaḥ: īśvaraḥ: yaḥ: āviśya bibharti lokatrayaṃ

(§5) but (there is) another, the most superior *puruṣa* known as supreme-*ātmā,* the immutable Lord, who having descended supports the three worlds.[765] (15.17)

15.18 यस्मात्क्षरमतीतोऽहमक्षरादपि चोत्तम: ।
अतोऽस्मि लोके वेदे च प्रथित: पुरुषोत्तम: ।।

yasmātkṣaramatīto'hamakṣrādapi ćottamaḥ:,
ato'smi loke vede ća prathitaḥ: puruṣottamaḥ:. (15.18)

(§1) *yasmaṭ* (r◦ 10/5) *kṣaraṃ* (r◦ 8/16) *atītaḥ:* (r◦ 15/1) *ahaṃ* (r◦ 8/16) *akṣrāṭ* (r◦ 8/2) *api ća* (r◦ 2/2) *uttamaḥ:* (r◦ 22/8) *ataḥ:* (r◦ 15/1) *asmi loke vede ća prathitaḥ:* (r◦ 22/3) *puruṣottamaḥ:* (r◦ 22/8)

---

[764] elsewhere◦ कूटस्थ: → Māyā, Māyā-illusion, imperishable, the unperturbed, embodied soul, ...etc.

📖 कूट (कूट् + अच्) = apex, mountain top, peak, summit, zenith, top, apogee, highest point; स्थ = seated.

[765] the three worlds : the heaven (स्वर्ग), the earth (पृथ्वी) and the hell (नरक).

(§2) *yasmat̨* (12.15); *kṣaram̨* (2acc∘ sing∘ ←adj∘ *kṣara* 8.4); *atītaḥ:* (14.20); *aham̨* (1.22); *akṣrāt̨* (5abl∘ sing∘ ←adj∘ *a-kṣara* 3.15); *api* (1.26); *ća* (1.1); *uttamaḥ:* (15.17); *ataḥ:* (2.12); *asmi* (7.8); *loke* (2.5); *vede* (7loc∘ sing∘ ←m∘ *veda* 2.42); *ća* (1.1); *prathitaḥ:* (1nom∘ sing∘ ←ppp∘ adj∘ *prathita* ←√प्रथ्); *puruṣottamaḥ:* (1nom∘ sing∘ ←bahuvrī∘ *puruśottama* 8.1) (15.18)

(§3) *yasmat̨* (because); *kṣaram̨* (adj∘-obj∘ the mutable); *atītaḥ:* (adj1∘-subj∘ exalted beyond, excelled); *aham̨* (subj∘ I am); *akṣrāt̨* (than the immutable); *api ća* (as well as) ; *uttamaḥ:* (adj2∘-subj∘ most superior); *ataḥ:* (therefore); *asmi* (I am); *loke* (in the world); *vede* (in the *veda*); *ća* (and); 🕮*prathitaḥ:* (adj3∘-subj∘ known); *puruṣottamaḥ:* (adj4∘-subj∘ the supreme among the three *purushas*) (15.18)

(§4) yasmat̨ aham̨ atītaḥ: kṣaram̨ api ća uttamaḥ: akṣrāt̨ ataḥ: asmi prathitaḥ: puruṣottamaḥ: loke ća vede.

(§5) Because[766] I am exalted beyond the mutable as well as superior than the immutable, therefore, I am known (as) the most supreme among the three[767] *purushas* in the world and in the *veda*.[768] (15.18)

15.19 यो मामेवमसम्मूढो जानाति पुरुषोत्तमम् ।
स सर्वविद्भजति मां सर्वभावेन भारत ।।

yo māmevamasammūḍho jānāti puruṣottamam̨,
sa sarvavidbhajati mām̐ sarvabhāvena bhārata. (15.19)

(§1) *yaḥ:* (r∘ 15/9) *mām̨* (r∘ 8/22) *evam̨* (r∘ 8/16) *asammūḍhaḥ:* (r∘ 15/3) *jānāti puruṣottamam̨* (r∘ 14/2) *saḥ:* (r∘ 21/2) *sarvavid̨* (r∘ 9/8) *bhajati mām̨* (r∘ 14/1) *sarvabhāvena bhārata*

(§2) *yaḥ:* (2.19); *mām̨* (1.46); *evam̨* (1.24); *asammūḍhaḥ:* (5.20); *jānāti* (3rd-per∘ sing∘ pres∘ वर्तमान्-लट् parasmai∘ ←class9∘ √ज्ञा 4.14); *puruṣottamam̨* (m∘ 2acc∘ sing∘ ←bahuvrī∘ *puruśottama* 8.1); *saḥ:* (1.13);

---

[766] See the footnote in verse 2.15

[767] elsewhere∘ पुरुषोत्तम: → supreme Being, the Supreme in all Beings, the Highest Spirit, Supreme Person, Supreme Self, Highest self, ...etc.

🕮 The discussion in the present verse is in continuation with the previous two verses 15.16-17, where it says द्वाविमौ पुरुषौ लोके and उत्तम: पुरुषस्त्वन्य:, thus, here पुरुषोत्तम: refers to (other than the two) the most superior (third) *purusha* in the three *purushas*, त्रिषु पुरुषेषु उत्तम: तृतीय: पुरुषोत्तम: । In Gita, there are only three *purushas*.

[768] elsewhere∘ वेदे → in the vedas, ...etc.

🕮 वेदे is singular. May be treated as a singular collective.

sarvavid (m∘ 1nom∘ sing∘ ←bahuvrī∘ *sarva-vit*, सर्वम् वेत्ति यः ←pron∘ *sarva* 1.6 + adj∘ *vid* 3.29); *bhajati* (6.31); *mām* (1.46); *sarvabhāvena* (सर्वेण भावेन m∘ 3inst∘ sing∘ ←pron∘ *sarva* 1.6 + m∘ *bhāva* 2.7); *bhārata* (1.24) (15.19)

(§3) *yaḥ:* (adj1∘-subj∘ he who); *mām* (adj1∘-obj∘ me); *evam* (in this manner); *asammūḍhaḥ:* (adj2∘-subj∘ undeluded person); *jānāti* (knows); *puruṣottamam* (adj2∘-obj∘ the most supreme among the three *purushas*); *saḥ:* (subj∘ he, that person); *sarvavid* (adj3∘-subj∘ that all-knowing person); *bhajati* (serves); *mām* (adj1∘-obj∘ me); *sarvabhāvena* (with full devotion); *bhārata* (O Arjuna!) (15.19)

(§4) bhārata evam yaḥ: jānāti mām puruṣottamam saḥ: asammūḍhaḥ: sarvavid bhajati mām sarvabhāvena

(§5) O Arjuna! in this manner, he who knows me, the most supreme among the three *purushas*, that undeluded[769] (and) all-knowing person[770] serves me with full devotion. (15.19)

15.20 इति गुह्यतमं शास्त्रमिदमुक्तं मयानघ ।
एतद्बुद्ध्वा बुद्धिमान्स्यात्कृतकृत्यश्च भारत ।।
iti guhyatamaṁ śāstramidamuktaṁ mayānagha,
etadbuddhvā buddhimānsyātkṛtakṛtyaśca bhārata. (15.20)

(§1) *iti guhyatamam* (r∘ 14/1) *śāstram* (r∘ 8/18) *idam* (r∘ 8/20) *uktam* (r∘ 14/1) *mayā* (r∘ 1/3) *anagha* (r∘ 23/1) *etat* (r∘ 9/7) *bhddhvā buddhimān* (r∘ 13/9) *syāt* (r∘ 10/5) *kṛtakṛtyaḥ:* (r∘ 17/1) *ća bhārata*

(§2) *iti* (1.25); *guhyatamam* (1nom∘ 9.1); *śāstram* (1nom∘ sing∘ ←n∘ *śāstra* ←√शास्); *idam* (1nom∘ 1.10); *uktam* (1nom∘ 11.1); *mayā* (1.22); *anagha* (3.3); *etat* (2acc∘ 2.6); *bhddhvā* (3.43); *buddhimān* (4.18); *kṛtakṛtyaḥ:* (m∘ 1nom∘ sing∘ ←bahuvrī∘ *kṛta-kṛtyaḥ:*, कृतम् कृत्यम् येन ←adj∘ *kṛta* 1.35 + n∘ or -pot∘ adj∘ *kṛtya* ←√कृ); *ća* (1.1); *bhārata* (1.24) (15.20)

(§3) *iti* (thus); *guhyatamam* (adj1∘-subj1∘ the most secret); *śāstram* (subj∘ science); *idam* (adj2∘-subj1∘ this); *uktam* (adj3∘-subj1∘ told); *mayā* (by me); *anagha* (O Arjuna!); *etat* (obj∘ this); *bhddhvā* (having understood); *buddhimān* (adj1∘-subj2∘ wise, a wise person); *syāt* (would be); *kṛtakṛtyaḥ:* (adj2∘-subj2∘

---

[769] elsewhere∘ असम्मूढः → being free from delusion, without doubting, being thus undeluded, ...etc.

📖 असम्मूढः is not a gerund. It is an ppp. adjective of subject he.

[770] elsewhere∘ स सर्वविद् → he is all-knowing, he knows all, he is the knower of everything, he knows everything, he is the knower of all, becomes all-knowing, ...etc.

📖 सर्वविद् is not a verb. It is 'he,' the all-knowing, as an adjective of subject 'he.'

accomplished, contended); *ća* (and); *bhārata* (O Arjuna!) (15.20)

(§4) anagha iti idam̱ guhyatamam̱ śāstram̱ uktam̱ mayā bhārata bhddhvā etaṯ syāt buddhimāṉ ća kṛtakṛtyaḥ:

(§5) O Arjuna! thus is the most secret science told[771] by me. O Arjuna! having understood this one would[772] be a wise and accomplished person.[773] (15.20)

इति श्रीमद्भगवद्गीतासूपनिषत्सु ब्रह्मविद्यायां योगशास्त्रे
श्रीकृष्णार्जुनसंवादे पुरुषोत्तमयोगो नाम पञ्चदशोऽध्यायः ।

iti śrīmadbhagavadgītāsūpaniṣatsu brahmavidyāyāṁ yogaśāstre
śrīkṛṣṇārjunasam̐vāde puruṣottamayogo nāma pañćadaśo'dhyāyaḥ:.

(§1) *iti śrīmadbhagavadgītāsu* (r◦ 1/8) *upaniṣatsu brahmavidyāyām̱* (r◦ 14/1) *yogaśāstre śrīkṛṣṇārjunasam̐vāde puruṣottamayogaḥ:* (r◦ 15/6) *nāma pañćadaśaḥ:* (r◦ 15/1) *adhyāyaḥ:* (r◦ 22/8)

(§2) *iti* (1.25); *śrīmadbhagavadgītāsu* (1.1); *upaniṣatsu* (1.1); *brahmavidyāyām̱* (1.1); *yogaśāstre* (1.1); *śrīkṛṣṇārjunasam̐vāde* (1.1); *puruṣottamayogaḥ:* (m◦ 1nom◦ sing◦ ←tatpu◦ *puruṣottamayogaḥ:* त्रिषु पुरुषेषु उत्तमस्य पुरुषस्य योगः ←n◦ *triṣu* 3.22 + m◦ *puruṣa* 2.15 + m◦ *uttama* 4.3 + m◦ *yoga* 2.39); *nāma* (1.1); *pañćadaśaḥ:* (m◦ 1nom◦ sing◦ ←num◦ adj◦ *pañća* 13.5 + *daśa* 13.5); *adhyāyaḥ:* (1.1)

(§3) *iti* (thus); *śrīmadbhagavadgītāsu upaniṣatsu* (among the upaniṣads of Śrīmad-Bhagavadgītā); *brahmavidyāyām̱* (of the eternal wisdoms); *yogaśāstre* (in the science of Yoga); *śrī-kṛṣṇārjuna-sam̐vāde* (in the dialogue between Śrī Kṛṣṇa and Arjuna); *puruṣottamayogaḥ:* (adj1◦-subj◦ *puruṣ-ottama-yogaḥ:*); *nāma* (called) *pañćadaśaḥ:* (adj2◦-subj◦ fifteenth); *adhyāyaḥ:* (subj◦ discourse)

(§4) śrīmadbhagavadgītāsu upaniṣatsu yogaśāstre brahmavidyāyām̱ iti pañćadaśaḥ: adhyāyaḥ: nāma guṇatrayavibhāgayogaḥ: śrīkṛṣṇārjunasam̐vāde

(§5) Among the upaniṣads of the Śrīmad-Bhagavadgītā, in the science of Yoga of self realization, thus (is) the fifteenth discourse called puruṣottama-yogaḥ: in the dialogue between Śrī Kṛṣṇa and Arjuna.

---

[771] elsewhere◦ उक्तम् → has been uttered, has been imparted, has been taught, I have imparted, ...etc.

[772] elsewhere◦ स्यात् → becomes, has, ...etc.

[773] elsewhere◦ कृतकृत्य → perfection, he will have fullfilled all his duties, his duties are accomplished ...etc.

CHAPTER 16

ṣoḍaśo'dhyāyaḥ:

षोडशोऽध्यायः ।

THE YOGA PERTAINING TO "THE DIVINE AND DEMONIC ATTITUDES"

daivāsurasampadvibhāgayogaḥ:

दैवासुरसंपद्विभागयोगः ।

The Lord said (śrībhagavānuvāća श्रीभगवानुवाच ।)

16.1 अभयं सत्त्वसंशुद्धिर्ज्ञानयोगव्यवस्थितिः ।
दानं दमश्च यज्ञश्च स्वाध्यायस्तप आर्जवम् ।।

abhayaṁ sattvasaṁśuddhirjñānayogavyavasthitiḥ:
dānaṁ damaśća yajñaśća svādhyāyastapa ārjavam; (16.1)

(§1) *ṣoḍaśaḥ:* (r◦ 15/1) *adhyāyaḥ:* (r◦ 22/8). *daivāsurasampadvibhāgayogaḥ:* (r◦ 22/8). *śrībhagavān* (r◦ 8/14) *uvāća*. *abhayam* (r◦ 14/1) *sattvasaṁśuddhiḥ:* (r◦ 16/6) *jñānayogavyavasthitiḥ:* (r◦ 22/8) *dānam* (r◦ 14/1) *damaḥ:* (r◦ 17/1) *ća yajñaḥ:* (r◦ 17/1) *ća svādhyāyaḥ:* (r◦ 18/1) *tapaḥ:* (r◦ 19/1) *ārjavam* (r◦ 14/2);

(§2) *ṣoḍaśaḥ:* (m◦ 1nom◦ sing◦ ←sequence indicating num◦ adj◦ *ṣoḍaśa* ←num◦ *ṣaṣṭha* 15.7 + num◦ *daśa* 13.6); *adhyāyaḥ:* (1nom◦ sing◦ ←m◦ *adhyāya* ←अधि√इ). *daivāsurasampadvibhāgayogaḥ:* (m◦ 1nom◦ sing◦ ←tatpu◦ *daivāsura-sampadvibhāga-yoga*, दैवी च आसुरी च सम्पदोः विभागस्य योगः ←adj◦ *daivī* 7.14 + adj◦ āsurī 9.12 + f◦ *sampad* 16.3 + m◦ *vibhāga* 3.28 + m◦ *yoga* 2.39). *śrībhagavān* (2.2); *uvāća* (1.25). *abhayam* (10.4); *sattvasaṁśuddhiḥ:* (f◦ 1nom◦ sing◦ ←tatpu◦ *sattva-saṁśuddhi*, सत्त्वस्य संशुद्धिः ←n◦ *sattva* 2.45 + f◦ *saṁśuddhi* ←सम्√शुध्); *jñānayogavyavasthitiḥ:* (f◦ 1nom◦ sing◦ ←tatpu◦ *jñāna-yoga-vyavasthiti*, ज्ञाने च योगे च व्यवस्थितिः ←n◦ *jñāna* 3.3 + m◦ *yoga* 2.39 + f◦ 🕮*vyavasthiti* ←वि–अव√स्था); *dānam* (10.5); *damaḥ:* (10.4); *ća* (1.1); *yajñaḥ:* (3.14); *ća* (1.1); *svādhyāyaḥ:* (1nom◦ sing◦ ←m◦ *svādhyāya* 4.28); *tapaḥ:* (7.9); *ārjavam* (13.8); (16.1)

(§3) *ṣoḍaśaḥ:* (adj◦-subj◦ the sixteenth); *adhyāyaḥ:* (subj◦ Chapter). *daivāsurasampadvibhāgayogaḥ:* (subj◦ the yoga pertaining to the divine and demonic attitudes). *śrībhagavān* (subj◦ lord kṛṣṇa); *uvāća* (said).

(i) *abhayam* (subj1◦ bravery, courage); **(ii)** *sattvasaṁśuddhiḥ:* (subj2◦ serenity of righteousness); **(iii)**

jñāna-yoga-vyavasthitiḥ: (subj3◦ steadfastness in the *jñanayoga*, commitment to the yoga of non-authorship); **(iv)** *dānam* (subj4◦ charity); **(v)** *damaḥ:* (subj5◦ self-control); *ća* (and); **(vi)** *yajñaḥ:* (subj6◦ austerity); *ća* (and); **(vii)** *svādhyāyaḥ:* (subj7◦ study of scriptures); **(viii)** *tapaḥ:* (subj8◦ asceticism); **(ix)** *ārjavam* (subj9◦ candor, straightforwardness); (16.1)

(§4) ṣoḍaśaḥ: adhyāyaḥ: daivāsurasampadvibhāgayogaḥ: śrībhagavān uvāća.

abhayam sattvasaṁśuddhiḥ: jñānayogavyavasthitiḥ: dānam damaḥ: ća yajñaḥ: ća svādhyāyaḥ: tapaḥ: ārjavam;

(§5) the sixteenth Chapter. The yoga pertaining to the divine and demonic attitudes. Lord Kṛṣṇa said : (i) Bravery, (ii) serenity of righteousness, (iii) commitment to the yoga of non-authorship,[774] (iv) charity, (v) self-control, and (vi) austerity, and (vii) study of scriptures, (viii) asceticism, (ix) straightforwardness; (16.1)

16.2 अहिंसा सत्यमक्रोधस्त्यागः शान्तिरपैशुनम् ।
दया भूतेष्वलोलुप्त्वं मार्दवं ह्रीरचापलम् ।।
ahimsā satyamakrodhastyāgaḥ: śāntirapaiśunam,
dayā bhūteṣvaloluptvaṁ mārdavaṁ hriraćāpalam; (16.2)

(§1) *ahimsā satyam* (r◦ 8/16) *akrodhaḥ:* (r◦ 18/1) *tyāgaḥ:* (r◦ 22/5) *śāntiḥ:* (r◦ 16/1) *apaiśunam* (r◦ 14/2) *dayā bhūteṣu* (r◦ 25/5, 4/6) *aloluptvam* (r◦ 14/1) *mārdavam* (r◦ 14/1) *hriḥ:* (r◦ 16/2) *aćāpalam* (r◦ 14/2);

(§2) *ahimsā* (10.5); *satyam* (10.4); 🕮*akrodhaḥ:* (1nom◦ sing◦ n.bahuvrī◦ नास्ति क्रोधः यस्य ←m◦ *krodha* 2.56); *tyāgaḥ:* (1nom◦ sing◦ ←m◦ *tyāga* 12.11); *śāntiḥ:* (2.67); 🕮*apaiśunam* (1nom◦ sing◦ n.tatpu◦ ←n◦ *a-paiśuna* ←अ–√पिश्); 🕮*dayā* (1nom◦ sing◦ ←f◦ *dayā* ←√दय्); *bhūteṣu* (7.11); 🕮*aloluptvam* (1nom◦ sing◦ ←n◦ *a-loluptva* ←ppp◦ adj◦ *lolupta* ←√लुप्); 🕮*mārdavam* (1nom◦ sing◦ ←n◦ *mārdava* ←√म्रद्); 🕮*hriḥ:* (1nom◦ sing◦ ←f◦ *hri* ←√ह्री); 🕮*aćāpalam* (1nom◦ sing◦ n.tatpu◦ ←n◦ *ćāpala* or *ćāpalya* ←√चुप्);

(16.2)

(§3) **(x)** *ahimsā* (subj10◦ non-violence); **(xi)** *satyam* (subj11◦ truthfulness); **(xii)** *akrodhaḥ:* (subj12◦

---

[774] elsewhere◦ ज्ञानयोगव्यवस्थितिः → persistence in knowledge and yoga, steadfastness in Yoga of knowledge, wise apportionment of knowledge and concentration, fixity in the Yoga of meditation, firmness in the yoga of intelligence, ...etc.

🕮 ज्ञानयोगः, please read the definitions of yogas of the Gita given in the answers to Q2 and Q9 in the 'Introductory Essay' of Chapter II, in Volume I of this book and understand various yogas clearly.

calmness); **(xiii)** *śāntiḥ:* (subj13∘ peace); **(xiv)** *apaiśunaṃ* (subj14∘ tranquility); **(xv)** *dayā* (subj15∘ mercy. kindness); *bhūteṣu* (for all creatures, animals); **(xvi)** *aloluptvaṃ* (subj16∘ non-covetousness); **(xvii)** *mārdavaṃ* (subj17∘ gentleness, softness); **(xviii)** *hriḥ:* (subj18∘ modesty, shame, humility); **(xix)** *aćāpalaṃ* (subj19∘ soundness, dependability);
(16.2)

(§4) ahimsā satyaṃ akrodhaḥ: śāntiḥ: apaiśunaṃ dayā bhūteṣu aloluptvaṃ mārdavaṃ hriḥ: aćāpalaṃ;

(§5) (x) non-violence, (xi) truthfulness, (xii) calmness, (xiii) peace, (xiv) tranquility, (xv) kindness for all creatures, (xvi) non-covetousness, (xvii) gentleness, (xviii) humility, (xix) dependability; (16.2)

16.3 तेजः क्षमा धृतिः शौचमद्रोहो नातिमानिता ।
भवन्ति सम्पदं दैवीमभिजातस्य भारत ।।
tejaḥ: kṣamā dhṛtiḥ: śaućamadroho nātimānitā,
bhavanti sampadaṁ daivīmabhijātasya bhārata. (16.3)

(§1) *tejaḥ:* (r∘ 22/1) *kṣamā dhṛtiḥ:* (r∘ 22/5) *śaućaṃ* (r∘ 8/16) *adrohaḥ:* (r∘ 15/6) *nātimānitā bhavanti sampadaṃ* (r∘ 14/1) *daivīṃ* (r∘ 8/16) *abhijātasya bhārata*

(§2) *tejaḥ:* (7.9); *kṣamā* (10.4); *dhṛtiḥ:* (10.34); *śaućaṃ* (13.8); 🕮*adrohaḥ:* (m∘ 1nom∘ sing∘ n.tatpu∘ ←m∘ *droha* 1.38); *nātimānitā* (f∘ 1nom∘ sing∘ ←adj∘ *nātimānita* ←negative ind∘ *na* 1.30 + ind∘ indicating degree *ati* 6.11 + ppp∘ adj∘ *mānita* ←√मान्); *bhavanti* (3.14); 🕮*sampadaṃ* (2acc∘ sing∘ ←f∘ sampaṭ or *sampaḍ* ←सम्√पद्); *daivīṃ* (9.13); *abhijātasya* (n∘ 6pos∘ sing∘ ←ppp∘ adj∘ *abhijāta* ←अभि√जन्); *bhārata* (1.24) (16.3)

(§3) **(xx)** *tejaḥ:* (subj19∘ aura, radiance); **(xxi)** *kṣamā* (subj20∘ forgiveness); **(xxii)** *dhṛtiḥ:* (subj20∘ courage); **(xxiii)** *śaućaṃ* (subj21∘ purity); **(xxiv)** *adrohaḥ:* (subj22∘ loyalty, faithfulness, non-treachery); **(xxv)** *nātimānitā* (subj22∘ modesty); *bhavanti* (are); *sampadaṃ* (subj26∘ the possession); *daivīṃ abhijātasya* (of the one who is born with divine nature); *bhārata* (O Arjuna!) (16.3)

(§4) tejaḥ: kṣamā dhṛtiḥ: śaućaṃ adrohaḥ: nātimānitā bhavanti sampadaṃ daivīṃ abhijātasya bhārata

(§5) (xx aura,[775] (xxi) forgiveness, (xxii) courage, (xxiii) purity, (xxiv) loyalty, (and) (xxv) modesty (is) the possession of the one who is born with divine nature, O Arjuna! (16.3)

16.4 दम्भो दर्पोऽभिमानश्च क्रोधः पारुष्यमेव च ।

[775] elsewhere∘ तेजः → Vigour.

अज्ञानं चाभिजातस्य पार्थ सम्पदमासुरीम् ।।

dambho darpo'bhimānaśća krodhaḥ: pāruṣyameva ća,

ajñānaṁ ćābhijātasya pārtha sampadamāsurīm. (16.4)

(§1) *dambhaḥ:* (r◦ 15/4) *darpaḥ:* (r◦ 15/1) *abhimānaḥ:* (r◦ 17/1) *ća krodhaḥ:* (r◦ 22/3) *pāruṣyam* (r◦ 8/22) *eva ća* (r◦ 23/1) *ajñānam* (r◦ 14/1) *ća* (r◦ 1/1) *abhijātasya pārtha sampadam* (r◦ 8/17) *āsurīm* (r◦ 14/2)

(§2) *dambhaḥ:* (1nom◦ sing◦ ←m◦ *dambha* 13.8); *darpaḥ:* (1nom◦ sing◦ ←m◦ *darpa* 10.28); 🕮*abhimānaḥ:* (1nom◦ sing◦ ←m◦ *abhimāna* ←अभि√मन्); *ća* (1.1); *krodhaḥ:* (2.62); 🕮*pāruṣyam* (1nom◦ sing◦ ←n◦ *pāruṣya* ←√पृ); *eva* (1.1); *ća* (1.1); *ajñānam* (5.16); *ća* (1.1); *abhijātasya* (16.3); *pārtha* (1.25); *sampadam* (16.3); *āsurīm* (9.12) (16.4)

(§3) **(i)** *dambhaḥ:* (subj1◦ false pretension); **(ii)** *darpaḥ:* (subj2◦ conceit); **(iii)** *abhimānaḥ:* (subj3◦ vanity); *ća* (and); **(iv)** *krodhaḥ:* (subj4◦ anger); **(v)** *pāruṣyam* (subj5◦ harshness, rudeness); *eva ća* (and, also); **(vi)** *ajñānam* (subj6◦ ignorance); *ća* (and); *abhijātasya* (one who is born with); *pārtha* (O Arjuna!); *sampadam* (subj7◦ wealth, possession); *āsurīm* (subj◦-subj7◦ demonic nature) (16.4)

(§4) ća pārtha dambhaḥ: darpaḥ: abhimānaḥ: krodhaḥ: ća pāruṣyam eva ća ajñānam sampadam abhijātasya āsurīm

(§5) And, O Arjuna! (i) false pretension, (ii) conceit, (iii) vanity, (iv) anger and (v) harshness and (vi) ignorance (is) the possession of one who is born with demonic nature. (16.4)

16.5 दैवी सम्पद्विमोक्षाय निबन्धायासुरी मता ।

मा शुचः सम्पदं दैवीमभिजातोऽसि पाण्डव ।।

daivī sampadvimokṣāya nibandhāyāsurī matā,

mā śućaḥ: sampadaṁ daivīmabhijāto'si pāṇḍava. (16.5)

(§1) *daivī sampaṭ* (r◦ 9/11) *vimokṣāya nibandhāya* (r◦ 1/2) *āsurī matā mā śućaḥ:* (r◦ 22/7) *sampadam* (r◦ 14/1) *daivīm* (r◦ 8/16) *abhijātaḥ:* (r◦ 15/1) *asi pāṇḍva*

(§2) *daivī* (7.14); *sampaṭ* (1nom◦ sing◦ ←f◦ *sampaṭ* or *sampaḍ* 16.3); *vimokṣāya* (4dat◦ sing◦ ←m◦ *vimokṣa* ←वि√मोक्ष्); *nibandhāya* (4dat◦ sing◦ ←m◦ *nibandha* ←नि√बन्ध्); *āsurī* (f◦ 1nom◦ sing◦ ←adj◦ *āsurī* 9.12); *matā* (3.1); *mā* (2.3); *śućaḥ:* (2nd-per◦ sing◦ ←class1◦ √शुच्); *sampadam* (16.3); *daivīm* (9.13); *abhijātaḥ:* (1nom◦ sing◦ ←adj◦ *abhijāta* 16.3); *asi* (4.3); *pāṇḍava* (4.35) (16.5)

(§3) *daivī* (adj1◦-subj1◦ the divine); *sampaṭ* (subj1◦ possession, nature); *vimokṣāya* (for emancipation); *nibandhāya* (for bondage); *āsurī* (subj2◦ the demonic nature); *matā* (thought to be); *mā śućaḥ:* (don't grieve); *sampadaṃ* (obj◦ wealth, possession, nature); *daivīṃ* (adj◦-obj◦ the divine); *abhijātaḥ:* (adj◦-subj3◦ the one who is born with); *asi* (subj3◦ you are); *pāṇḍava* (O Arjuna!) (16.5)

(§4) daivī sampaṭ matā vimokṣāya āsurī nibandhāya pāṇḍava mā śućaḥ: asi abhijātaḥ: daivīṃ sampadaṃ

(§5) The divine nature (is) thought to be[776] for emancipation (and) the demonic nature is for bondage. O Arjuna! don't grieve. You are born with the divine nature. (16.5)

16.6 द्वौ भूतसर्गौ लोकेऽस्मिन्दैव आसुर एव च ।
दैवो विस्तरशः प्रोक्त आसुरं पार्थ मे शृणु ।।
dvau bhūtasargau loke'smindaiva āsura eva ća,
daivo vistaraśaḥ: prokta āsuraṁ pārtha me śṛṇu. (16.6)

(§1) *dvau bhūtasargau loke* (r◦ 6/1) *asmiṇ* (r◦ 13/11) *daivaḥ:* (r◦ 19/1) *āsuraḥ:* (r◦ 19/7) *eva ća daivaḥ:* (r◦ 15/13) *vistaraśaḥ:* (r◦ 22/3) *proktaḥ:* (r◦ 19/1) *āsuraṃ* (r◦ 14/1) *pārtha me śṛṇu*

(§2) *dvau* (15.16); *bhūtasargau* (m◦ 1nom◦ dual◦ ←tatpu◦ *bhūta-sarga*, भूतानाम् सर्गः ←n◦ *bhūta* 2.28 + m◦ *sarga* 5.19); *loke* (2.5); *asmiṇ* (1.22); *daivaḥ:* (1nom◦ sing◦ ←n◦ taddhita◦ *daiva* 4.25); *āsuraḥ:* (m◦ 1nom◦ sing◦ ←adj◦ *āsura* 7.15); *eva* (1.1); *ća* (1.1); *daivaḥ:* (↑); *vistaraśaḥ:* (11.2); *proktaḥ:* (4.3); *āsuraṃ* (7.15); *pārtha* (1.25); *me* (1.21); *śṛṇu* (2.39) (16.6)

(§3) *dvau* (adj1-2◦-subj◦ two); *bhūtasargau* (subj1-2◦ evolutions of the beings); *loke asmiṇ* (in this world); *daivaḥ:* (subj1◦ the divine); *āsuraḥ:* (subj2◦ the demonic); *eva ća* (and); *daivaḥ:* (subj1◦ the divine); *vistaraśaḥ:* (in detail, at length); *proktaḥ:* (adj◦-subj1◦ told); *āsuraṃ* (obj◦ the demonic); *pārtha* (O Arjuna!); *me* (from me, of me); *śṛṇu* (hear, listen) (16.6)

(§4) pārtha dvau bhūtasargau loke asmiṇ daivaḥ: eva ća āsuraḥ: daivaḥ: proktaḥ: vistaraśaḥ: śṛṇu āsuraṃ me

(§5) O Arjuna! (there are) two evolutions[777] of the beings in this world, (i) the divine and (ii) the demonic. The divine (was) told (by me) at length. Now listen to the demonic nature from me. (16.6)

16.7 प्रवृत्तिं च निवृत्तिं च जना न विदुरासुराः ।
न शौचं नापि चाचारो न सत्यं तेषु विद्यते ।।
pravṛttiṁ ća nivṛttiṁ ća janā na vidurāsurāḥ:,

---

[776] elsewhere◦ मता → are for, gives, ...etc.

📖 मता is not a verb. It is feminine ppp. adjective of सम्पद्.

[777] elsewhere◦ भूतसर्गौ → creations, cerated beings, beings created, ...etc.

na śaućaṁ nāpi ćāćāro na satyaṁ teṣu vidyate. (16.7)

(§1) *pravṛttiṃ* (r◦ 14/1) *ća nivṛttiṃ* (r◦ 14/1) *ća janāḥ:* (r◦ 20/10) *na viduḥ:* (r◦ 16/3) *āsurāḥ:* (r◦ 22/8) *na śaućaṃ* (r◦ 14/1) *na* (r◦ 1/1) *api ća* (r◦ 1/2) *āćāraḥ:* (r◦ 15/6) *na satyaṃ* (r◦ 14/1) *teṣu* (r◦ 25/5) *vidyate*

(§2) *pravṛttiṃ* (11.31); *ća* (1.1); <u>*nivṛttiṃ*</u> (2acc◦ sing◦ ←f◦ *nivṛtti* ←नि√वृत्); *ća* (1.1); *janāḥ:* (7.16); *na* (1.30); *viduḥ:* (4.2); *āsurāḥ:* (m◦ 1nom◦ plu◦ ←adj◦ *āsura* 7.15); *na* (1.30); *śaućaṃ* (13.8); *na* (1.30); *api* (1.26); *ća* (1.1); *āćāraḥ:* (1nom◦ sing◦ ←m◦ *āćāra* 3.6); *na* (1.30); *satyaṃ* (10.4); *teṣu* (2.62); *vidyate* (2.16) (16.7)

(§3) *pravṛttiṃ* (obj1◦ right attitude to proceed ahead, what ought to be done); *ća* (and); *nivṛttiṃ* (obj2◦ what ought to be refrained from); *ća* (and); *janāḥ:* (subj1◦ people); *na* (do not); *viduḥ:* (understand, know); *āsurāḥ:* (adj1◦-subj1◦ the demonic); *na* (neither); *śaućaṃ* (subj2◦ purity, integrity); *na* (nor); *api ća* (and); *āćāraḥ:* (subj3◦ righteous behaviour); *na* (nor); *satyaṃ* (subj4◦truthfulness); *teṣu* (in them); *vidyate* (exists) (16.7)

(§4) āsurāḥ: janāḥ: na viduḥ: pravṛttiṃ ća nivṛttiṃ ća na śaućaṃ api ća na āćāraḥ: na satyaṃ vidyate teṣu

(§5) The demonic people do not understand what ought to be done and what ought to be refrained from, and neither integrity and nor righteous behaviour nor truthfulness exists in them. (16.7)

16.8 असत्यमप्रतिष्ठं ते जगदाहुरनीश्वरम् ।
अपरस्परसम्भूतं किमन्यत्कामहैतुकम् ।।
asatyamapratiṣṭhaṁ te jagadāhuranīśvaram,
aparasparasambhūtaṁ kimanyatkāmahaitukam. (16.8)

(§1) *asatyaṃ* (r◦ 8/16) *apratiṣṭhaṃ* (r◦ 14/1) *te jagat* (r◦ 8/3) *āhuḥ:* (r◦ 16/3) *anīśvaraṃ* (r◦ 14/2) *aparasparasambhūtaṃ* (r◦ 14/1) *kiṃ* (r◦ 8/16) *anyat* (r◦ 10/5) *kāmahaitukaṃ* (r◦ 14/2)

(§2) 🕮*asatyaṃ* (n◦ 2acc◦ sing◦ ←n.tatpu◦ *a-satya* ←n◦ *satya* 10.4); 🕮*apratiṣṭhaṃ* (n◦ 2acc◦ sing◦ ←n.tatpu◦ *a-pratiṣṭha* ←adj◦ *pratiṣṭha* 6.38); *te* (1.33); *jagat* (2acc◦ 7.5); *āhuḥ:* (3.42); 🕮*anīśvaraṃ* (2acc◦ sing◦ ←n.tatpu◦ *anīśvara* ←m◦ *īśvara* 4.6); *a-parasparasambhūtaṃ* (n◦ 2acc◦ sing◦ n.tatpu◦ ←adj◦ *paraspara-sambhūta*, परस्परेण सम्भूतम् ←adj◦ *paraspara* 3.11 + ppp◦ adj◦ *sambhūta* ←सम्√भू); *kiṃ* (2acc◦ 2.36); 🕮*anyat* (2acc◦ 2.31); *kāmahaitukaṃ* (n◦ 2acc◦ sing◦ ←bahuvrī◦ *kāma-haituka*, कामः हेतुः यस्य ←m◦ *kāma* 1.22 + taddhita◦ *haituka* ←m◦ *hetu* 1.35) (16.8)

(§3) *asatyaṃ* (adj1◦-subj1◦ fantastic, illusory); *apratiṣṭhaṃ* (adj2◦-subj1◦ without foundation, baseless);

te (subj2◦ they); *jagat̩* (subj1◦ the world); *āhuḥ:* (they call, say); *anīśvaram̩* (adj3◦-subj1◦ godless); *a-parasparasambhūtam̩* (adj4◦-subj1◦ arose without mutual cause and effect); *kim̩* (what); *anyat̩* (else); *kāmahaitukam̩* (adj5◦-subj1◦ for the purpose of passion) (16.8)

(§4) te āhuḥ: jagat̩ asatyam̩ apratiṣṭham̩ anīśvaram̩ a-parasparasambhūtam̩ kāmahaitukam̩ kim̩ anyat̩

(§5) They say the world (is) illusory, baseless, godless, (and) arose without mutual cause and effect for the purpose of passion, what else? (16.8)

16.9 एतां दृष्टिमवष्टभ्य नष्टात्मानोऽल्पबुद्धयः ।
प्रभवन्त्युग्रकर्माणः क्षयाय जगतोऽहिताः ।।

etām̐ dṛṣṭimavaṣṭabhya naṣṭātmāno'lpabuddhayaḥ:,
prabhavantyugrakarmāṇaḥ: kṣayāya jagato'hitāḥ:. (16.9)

(§1) *etām̩* (r◦ 14/1) *dṛṣṭim̩* (r◦ 8/16) *avaṣtbhya naṣṭātmānaḥ:* (r◦ 15/1) *alpabuddhayaḥ:* (r◦ 22/8) *prabhavanti* (r◦ 4/3) *ugrakarmāṇaḥ:* (r◦ 22/1, 24/2) *kṣayāya jagataḥ:* (r◦ 15/1) *ahitāḥ:* (r◦ 22/8)

(§2) *etām̩* (1.3); *dṛṣṭim̩* (2acc◦ sing◦ ←f◦ *dṛṣti* ←√दृश्); *avaṣtbhya* (9.8); *naṣṭātmānaḥ:* (m◦ 1nom◦ plu◦ ←bahuvrī◦ 🕮*naṣṭātman̩*, नष्टः आत्माः यस्य ←adj◦ *naṣta* 1.40 + m◦ *ātman̩* 2.41); 🕮*alpabuddhayaḥ:* (m◦ 1nom◦ plu◦ ←bahuvrī◦ *alpa-buddhi,* अल्पा बुद्धिः यस्य ←adj◦ *alpa* 7.23 + f◦ *buddhi* 1.23); *prabhavanti* (8.18); *ugrakarmāṇaḥ:* (m◦ 1nom◦ plu◦ ←bahuvrī◦ *ugra-karmān̩*, उग्राणि कर्माणि यस्य ←adj◦ *ugra* 11.20 + n◦ *karman̩* 1.15); *kṣayāya* (4dat◦ sing◦ ←m◦ *kṣaya* 1.38); *jagataḥ:* (7.6); *ahitāḥ:* (2.36) (16.9)

(§3) *etām̩* (adj◦-obj◦ this); *dṛṣṭim̩* (obj◦ vision, view); *avaṣtbhya* (holding, having held); *naṣṭātmānaḥ:* (adj1◦-subj◦ those people with depraved heart, the people with vile disposition); *alpabuddhayaḥ:* (adj2◦-subj◦ those short sighted people); *prabhavanti* (they take birth); *ugrakarmāṇaḥ:* (adj3◦-subj◦ those people of evil deeds); *kṣayāya* (for the destruction); *jagataḥ:* (of the world order); *ahitāḥ:* (subj◦-the enemies of mankind) (16.9)

(§4) avaṣṭbhya etām̩ dṛṣṭim̩ ahitāḥ: naṣṭātmānaḥ: alpabuddhayaḥ: ugrakarmāṇaḥ: prabhavanti kṣayāya jagataḥ:

(§5) Holding this vision, the demonic enemies of mankind, those people with vile disposition, those short sighted people, those people of evil deeds, they take birth[778] for the destruction of the

---

[778] elsewhere◦ प्रभवन्ति → wax strong, prove equal, engage in, become as, come forth as, rise up as, rise as, are born as, ...etc.

world order. (16.9)

16.10 कामममाश्रित्य दुष्पूरं दम्भमानमदान्विताः ।
मोहाद्गृहीत्वासद्ग्राहान्प्रवर्तन्तेऽशुचिव्रताः ।।
kāmamāśritya duṣpuraṁ dambhamānamadānvitaḥ:,
mohādgṛhītvāsadgrāhānpravartante'śućivratāḥ:; (16.10)

(§1) *kāmam̱* (r◦ 8/17) *āśritya duṣpuram̱* (r◦ 14/1) *dambhamānamadānvitaḥ:* (r◦ 22/8) *mohāṯ* (r◦ 9/4) *gṛhītvā* (r◦ 1/3) *asadgrāhāṉ* (r◦ 13/13) *pravartante* (r◦ 6/1) *aśućivratāḥ:* (r◦ 22/8)

(§2) *kāmam̱* (2acc◦ sing◦ ←m◦ *kāma* 1.22); *āśritya* (7.29); *duṣpuram̱* (m◦ 2acc◦ sing◦ ←adj◦ 📖*duṣpura* 3.39); *dambhamānamadānvitaḥ:* (m◦ 1nom◦ plu◦ ←tatpu◦ *dambha-māna-madānvita,* दम्भेन च मानेन च मदेन च अन्वितः ←m◦ *dambha* 13.8 + m◦ *māna* 6.7 + m◦ *mada* ←√मद् + ppp◦ adj◦ *anvita* 9.23); *mohāṯ* (5abl◦ sing◦ ←m◦ *moha* 2.52); *gṛhītvā* (15.8); *asadgrāhāṉ* (m◦ 2acc◦ plu◦ ←tatpu◦ 📖*asadgrāha,* असतः ग्राहः ←adj◦ *a-saṯ* 2.16 + m◦ *grāha* ←√ग्रह्); *pravartante* (3rd-per◦ plu◦ pres◦ वर्तमान्-लट् ātmane◦ ←class1◦ प्र√वृत्); *aśućivratāḥ:* (m◦ 1nom◦ plu◦ ←bahuvrī◦ *a-śući-vrata,* अशुचीनि व्रतानि यस्य ←adj◦ 📖*aśući* ←अ√शुच् + n◦ *vrata* 4.28); (16.10)

(§3) *kāmam̱* (obj◦ passion); *āśritya* (taking shelter of); *duṣpuram̱* (adj◦-obj1◦ insatiable); *dambhamānamadānvitaḥ:* (subj◦ m◦ those people endowed with pride, vanity and arrogance); *mohāṯ* (out of delusion); *gṛhītvā* (having held); *asadgrāhāṉ* (obj2◦ wrong notions, misconceptions); *pravartante* (they undertake); *aśućivratāḥ:* (obj3◦ indecent austerities); (16.10)

(§4) āśritya duṣpuram̱ kāmam̱ dambhamānamadānvitaḥ: gṛhītvā asadgrāhāṉ mohāṯ pravartante aśućivratāḥ:;

(§5) Those people endowed with pride, vanity and arrogance, taking shelter of insatiable passion, and having held wrong notions out of delusion, they undertake indecent austerities; (16.10)

16.11 चिन्तामपरिमेयां च प्रलयान्तामुपाश्रिताः ।
कामोपभोगपरमा एतावदिति निश्चिताः ।।
ćintāmaparimeyāṁ ća pralayāntāmupāśritāḥ:,
kāmopabhogaparamā etāvaditi niśćitāḥ:. (16.11)

(§1) *ćintām̱* (r◦ 8/16) *aparimeyām̱* (r◦ 14/1) *ća pralayāntām̱* (r◦ 8/20) *upāśritāḥ:* (r◦ 22/8) *kāmopabhogaparamāḥ:* (r◦ 20/5) *etāvaṯ* (r◦ 8/4) *iti niśćitāḥ:* (r◦ 22/8)

📖 Remember, (i) भू = become, be, take birth, occur (ii) क्षयाय (Dative Case) = for the destruction.

(§2) 📖*ćintāṃ* (2acc∘ sing∘ ←f∘ *ćintā* ←√चिन्त्); 📖*aparimeyāṃ* (f∘ 2acc∘ sing∘ n.tatpu∘ ←adj∘ *parimeya* ←परि√मा); *ća* (1.1); 📖*pralayāntāṃ* (f∘ 2acc∘ sing∘ ←bahuvrī∘ adj∘ *pralayānta*, प्रलय: अन्त: यस्य ←m∘ *pralaya* 7.6 + m∘ *anta* 2.16); *upāśritāḥ:* (4.10); *kāmopabhogaparamāḥ:* (m∘ 1nom∘ plu∘ ←bahuvrī∘ *kāmopabhoga-parama*, कामानाम् उपभोग: परम: यस्य ←m∘ *kāma* 1.22 + m∘ *upabhoga* ←उप√भुज् + adj∘ *parama* 1.17); *etāvaṭ* (mode indicating ind∘ ←pron∘ *etad* 1.3); *iti* (1.25); *niśćitāḥ:* (m∘ 1nom∘ plu∘ ←ppp∘ adj∘ *niśćita* 2.7) (16.11)

(§3) *ćintāṃ* (obj∘ worry); *aparimeyāṃ* (adj1∘-obj∘ an infinite); *ća* (and); *pralayāntāṃ* (adj2∘-obj∘ that ends only with the death); *upāśritāḥ:* (adj1∘-subj∘ sheltered in); *kāmopabhogaparamāḥ:* (subj∘ those for whome passion and enjoyment is the ultimate goal); *etāvaṭ* ("this is it," that's all); *iti* (that); *niśćitāḥ:* (adj2∘-subj∘ convinced) (16.11)

(§4) ća upāśritāḥ: aparimeyāṃ ćintāṃ pralayāntāṃ kāmopabhogaparamāḥ: niśćitāḥ: iti etāvaṭ

(§5) and, sheltered in an infinite worry[779] that ends only with death, those for whom[780] passion and enjoyment is the ultimate goal (are) convinced[781] that "this is it." (16.11)

16.12 आशापाशशतैर्बद्धा: कामक्रोधपरायणा: ।
ईहन्ते कामभोगार्थमन्यायेनार्थसञ्चयान् ।।
āśāpāśaśatairbaddhāḥ: kāmakrodhaparāyaṇāḥ:,
īhante kāmabhogārthamanyāyenārthasañćayāṇ. (16.12)

(§1) *āśāpāśaśataiḥ:* (r∘ 16/11) *baddhāḥ:* (r∘ 22/1) *kāmakrodhaparāyaṇāḥ:* (r∘ 24/5, 22/8) *īhante kāmabhogārthaṃ* (r∘ 8/16) *anyāyena* (r∘ 1/1) *arthasañćayāṇ*

(§2) *āśāpāśaśataiḥ:* (m∘ 3inst∘ plu∘ ←tatpu∘ *āśāpāśa-śata*, आशाया: पाशानाम् शत: ←f∘ *āśā* 9.12 + m∘ 📖*pāśa* ←√पश् + num∘ adj∘ *śata* 11.5); *baddhāḥ:* (m∘ 1nom∘ plu∘ ←ppp∘ adj∘ *baddha* ←√बन्ध्); *kāmakrodhaparāyaṇāḥ:* (m∘ 1nom∘ plu∘ ←bahuvrī∘ *kāma-krodha-parāyaṇa*, काम: च क्रोध: च परम् अयनम्

---

[779] elsewhere∘ चिन्ताम् → fears, worries, cares, anxities, ...etc.

📖 चिन्ताम् is not plural noun.

[780] elsewhere∘ कामोभोगपरमा: → looking upon..., holding that..., they believe that..., they regard the..., giving themselves to..., ...etc.

📖 कामोभोगपरमा: is not a gerund or a verb. It is a *bahuvrihi* adjective of the subject.

[781] elsewhere∘ निश्चिता: → feeling sure, they believe hat, ...etc.

📖 निश्चिता: is not a verb or gerund. It is plural m. ppp. adjective of of the plural subject : कामोपभोग परमा: ।

यस्य ←m◦ *kāma* 1.22 + m◦ *krodha* 2.56 + ind◦ *param̦* 2.12 + n◦ *ayana* 1.11); *īhante* (3rd-per◦ plu◦ pres◦ वर्तमान्-लट् ātmane◦ ←class1◦ √ईह् 7.22); *kāmabhogārtham̦* (m◦ 2acc◦ sing◦ ←tatpu◦ *kāma-bhogārtha*, कामस्य भोगस्य अर्थः ←m◦ *kāma* 1.22 + m◦ *bhoga* 1.32 + m◦ *artha* 1.7); *anyāyena* (m◦ 3inst◦ sing◦ ←n.tatpu◦ *anyāya* ←m◦ nyāya ←नि√इ); *arthasañćayān̦* (m◦ 2acc◦ plu◦ ←tatpu◦ *artha-sañćaya*, अर्थस्य सञ्चयः ←m◦ *artha* 1.7 + m◦ 🕮*sañćaya* ←सम्√चि) (16.12)

(§3) *āśāpāśaśataiḥ: baddhāḥ:* (adj◦-subj◦ entangled in or bound by shackles of hundreds of desires); *kāmakrodhaparāyaṇāḥ:* (subj◦ those for whom passion and attachment are ultimate goals); *īhante* (they desire); *kāmabhogārtham̦* (for pleasure and enjoyment); *anyāyena* (with foul means); *arthasañćayān̦* (obj◦ hoards of wealth) (16.12)

(§4) āśāpāśaśataiḥ: baddhāḥ: kāmakrodhaparāyaṇāḥ: īhante arthasañćayān̦ kāmabhogārtham̦

(§5) Bound by shackles of hundreds of desires, those for whom[782] passion and attachment are ultimate goals, they desire hoards of wealth[783] with foul means for pleasure and enjoyment. (16.12)

16.13 इदमद्य मया लब्धमिमं प्राप्स्ये मनोरथम् ।
इदमस्तीदमपि मे भविष्यति पुनर्धनम् ।।
idamadya mayā labdhamimaṁ prāpsye manoratham̦,
idamastīdamapi me bhaviṣyati punardhanam̦. (16.13)

(§1) *idam̦* (r◦ 8/16) *adya mayā labdham̦* (r◦ 8/18) *imam̦* (r◦ 14/1) *prāpsye manoratham̦* (r◦ 14/2) *idam̦* (r◦ 8/16) *asti* (r◦ 1/5) *idam̦* (r◦ 8/16) *api me bhaviṣyati* (r◦ 25/6) *punardhanam̦* (r◦ 14/2)

(§2) *idam̦* (1nom◦ 1.10); *adya* (4.3); *mayā* (1.22); *labdham̦* (n◦ 1nom◦ sing◦ ←ppp◦ adj◦ *labdha* ←√लभ्); *imam̦* (2acc◦ 1.28); *prāpsye* (1st-per◦ sing◦ fut2◦ लृट् भविष्य◦ ātmane◦ ←class5◦ प्र√आप्); *manoratham̦* (n◦ 2acc◦ sing◦ ←bahuvrī◦ 🕮*manoratha*, मनसः रथः इव यत् तत् ←m◦ *manaș* 1.30 + m◦ *ratham̦* 1.4); *idam̦* (1nom◦ 1.10); *asti* (2.40); *idam̦* (1nom◦ 1.10); *api* (1.26); *me* (6pos◦ 1.21); *bhaviṣyati* (3rd-per◦ sing◦ fut2◦ लृट् भविष्य◦ parasmai◦ ←class1◦ √भू 11.32); *punar̦* (4.9); *dhanam̦* (1nom◦ sing◦ ←n◦ *dhana* 1.15)

---

[782] elsewhere◦ कामक्रोधपरायणाः → giving themselves wholly to..., giving themselves up to, are suceptible to..., ...etc.

🕮 कामक्रोधपरायणाः is not a gerund or क्त्वा participle. It is just a noun subject.

[783] elsewhere◦ ईहन्ते अर्थसञ्चयान् → to amass wealth, to obtain, to collect, to secure, ...etc.

🕮 ईहन्ते is not an infinitive. It is a simple लट् Present Tense.

(16.13)

(§3) *idam̦* (adj1◦-obj1◦ this); *adya* (today); *mayā* (by me); *labdham̦* (adj2◦-obj1◦ obtained, fulfilled); *imam̦* (adj3◦-obj1◦ this); *prāpsye* (I will obtain, fulfill); *manoratham̦* (obj1-2◦ desire); *idam̦* (adj◦-obj3◦ this); *asti* (is); *idam̦* (adj◦-obj4◦ this); *api* (also); *me* (mine); *bhaviṣyati* (will be); *punar̦* (again, and); *dhanam̦* (obj3/4◦ wealth) (16.13)

(§4) idam̦ manoratham̦ labdham̦ mayā adya imam̦ prāpsye idam̦ dhanam̦ asti me punar̦ idam̦ api bhaviṣyati

(§5) This desire (is) fulfilled by me today (and) this I will fulfill (tomorrow). This wealth is mine and this also will be (mine). (16.13)

16.14 असौ मया हत: शत्रुर्हनिष्ये चापरानपि ।
ईश्वरोऽहमहं भोगी सिद्धोऽहं बलवान्सुखी ।।

asau mayā hataḥ: śatrurhaniṣye ćāparānapi,
īśvaro'hamahaṁ bhogī siddho'haṁ balavānsukhī; (16.14)

(§1) *asau mayā hataḥ:* (r◦ 22/5) *śatruḥ:* (r◦ 16/8) *haniṣye* (r◦ 25/10) *ća* (r◦ 1/1) *aparān̦* (r◦ 8/11) *api* (r◦ 23/1) *īśvaraḥ:* (r◦ 15/1) *aham̦* (r◦ 8/16) *aham̦* (r◦ 14/1) *bhogī siddhaḥ:* (r◦ 15/1) *aham̦* (r◦ 14/1) *balavān̦* (r◦ 13/20) *sukhī;*

(§2) *asau* (1nom◦ 11.26); *mayā* (1.22); *hataḥ:* (2.37); *śatruḥ:* (m◦ 1nom◦ sing◦ ←m◦ *śatru* 3.43); *haniṣye* (1st-per◦ sing◦ fut2◦ लृट् भविष्य◦ ātmane◦ ←class2◦ √हन्); *ća* (1.1); *aparān̦* (m◦ 2acc◦ plu◦ ←adj◦ *apara* 2.22); *api* (1.26); *īśvaraḥ:* (4.6); *aham̦* (1.22); *aham̦* (↑); *bhogī* (m◦ 1nom◦ sing◦ ←m◦ or adj◦ *bhogin̦* ←√भुज्); 🕮*siddhaḥ:* (m◦ 1nom◦ sing◦ ←m◦ *siddha* 7.3); *aham̦* (↑); *balavān̦* (m◦ 1nom◦ sing◦ ←adj◦ *balavaț* 6.34); *sukhī* (5.23); (16.14)

(§3) *asau* (adj1◦-obj1◦ this); *mayā* (by me); *hataḥ:* (adj2◦-obj1◦killed); *śatruḥ:* (obj1◦ enemy); *haniṣye* (I will kill); *ća* (and); *aparān̦* (obj2◦ others); *api* (also); **(i)** *īśvaraḥ:* (adj1◦-subj1◦ the lord, god); *aham̦* (subj1◦ I am); *aham̦* (subj1◦ I am); **(ii)** *bhogī* (adj2◦-subj1◦ enjoyer); **(iii)** *siddhaḥ:* (adj3◦-subj1◦ the achiever, the accomplished one); *aham̦* (subj1◦ I am); **(iv)** *balavān̦* (adj4◦-subj1◦ the powerful); **(v)** *sukhī* (adj5◦-subj1◦ happy); (16.14)

(§4) asau śatruḥ: hataḥ: mayā ća haniṣye aparān̦ api aham̦ īśvaraḥ: aham̦ bhogī siddhaḥ: balavān̦ aham̦ sukhī;

(§5) (The demonic people deluded bu ignorance say that :) This[784] enemy (is) killed by me and I will kill others also. I am (i) the lord, I am (ii) the enjoyer, (iii) the accomplished one, (iv) the

[784] elsewhere◦ असौ → That

powerful (and) (v) I am happy; (16.14)

16.15 आढ्योऽभिजनवानस्मि कोऽन्योऽस्ति सदृशो मया ।
यक्ष्ये दास्यामि मोदिष्य इत्यज्ञानविमोहिता: ।।
āḍhyo‘bhijanavānasmi ko‘nyo‘sti sadṛśo mayā,
yakṣye dāsyāmi modiṣya ityajñānavimohitāḥ:; (16.15)

(§1) *āḍhyaḥ:* (r◦ 15/1) *abhijanavān* (r◦ 8/11) *asmi kaḥ:* (r◦ 15/1) *anyaḥ:* (r◦ 15/1) *asti sadṛśaḥ:* (r◦ 15/9) *mayā yakṣye dāsyāmi modiṣye* (r◦ 5/2, 25/10) *iti* (r◦ 4/1) *ajñānavimohitāḥ:* (r◦ 22/8)

(§2) 🕮*āḍhyaḥ:* (m◦ 1nom◦ sing◦ ←adj◦ *āḍhya* ←आ√ध्यै); *abhijanavān* (m◦ 1nom◦ sing◦ ←taddhita◦ adj◦ *abhijanavat* ←m◦ *abhijana* ←अभि√जन् + affix *vatup* 2.45); *asmi* (7.8); *kaḥ:* (8.2); *anyaḥ:* (2.29); *asti* (2.40); *sadṛśaḥ:* (m◦ 1nom◦ sing◦ ←adj◦ *sadṛśa* 3.33); *mayā* (1.22); *yakṣye* (1st-per◦ sing◦ fut2◦ लृट् भविष्य◦ ātmane◦ ←class1◦ √यज्); *dāsyāmi* (1st-per◦ sing◦ fut2◦ लृट् भविष्य◦ parasmai◦ ←class3◦ √दा); *modiṣye* (1st-per◦ sing◦ fut2◦ लृट् भविष्य◦ ātmane◦ ←class1◦ √मुद्); *iti* (1.25); *ajñānavimohitāḥ:* (m◦ 1nom◦ plu◦ ←tatpu◦ *ajñāna-vimohita*, अज्ञानेन विमोहित: ←n◦ *ajñāna* 4.42 + ppp◦ adj◦ 🕮*vimohita* ←वि√मुह्) (16.15)

(§3) **(vi)** *āḍhyaḥ:* (adj6◦-subj1◦ opulent, wealthy); **(vii)** *abhijanavān* (adj7◦-subj1◦ aristocratic); *asmi* (subj1◦ I am); *kaḥ:* (adj1◦-subj2◦ who); *anyaḥ:* (adj2◦-subj2◦ else); *asti* (is there); *sadṛśaḥ:* (adj3◦-subj2◦ equal); *mayā* (by me, to me); *yakṣye* (I will perform *yajña*); *dāsyāmi* (I will perform charity); *modiṣye* (I will rejoice); *iti* (thus, that); *ajñānavimohitāḥ:* (subj1◦ those demonic people who are deluded by ignorance) (16.15)

(§4) ajñānavimohitāḥ: iti asmi āḍhyaḥ: abhijanavān kaḥ: anyaḥ: asti sadṛśaḥ: mayā yakṣye dāsyāmi modiṣye

(§5) Those demonic people who are deluded by ignorance (boast about themselves by saying), "I am am (vi) opulent (and) (vii) aristocratic. Who else is there equal to me? I will perform *yajña,* I will perform charity, I will rejoice;" (16.15)

16.16 अनेकचित्तविभ्रान्ता मोहजालसमावृता: ।
प्रसक्ता: कामभोगेषु पतन्ति नरकेऽशुचौ ।।
anaekacittavibhrāntā mohajālasamāvṛtāḥ:,
prasaktāḥ: kāmabhogeṣu patanti narake‘śucau; (16.16)

(§1) *anaekacittavibhrāntāḥ:* (r◦ 20/13) *mohajālasamāvṛtāḥ:* (r◦ 22/8) *prasaktāḥ:* (r◦ 22/1) *kāmabhogeṣu patanti narake* (r◦ 6/1) *aśucau;*

(§2) *anaekaćittavibhrāntāḥ:* (m∘ 1nom∘ plu∘ ←tatpu∘ *anaeka-ćitta-vibhrānta,* अनेकेन चित्तेन विभ्रान्तः ←adj∘ *aneka* 6.45 + n∘ *ćitta* 4.21 + ppp∘ adj∘ 🕮*vibhrānta* ←वि√भ्रम्); *mohajālasamāvṛtāḥ:* (m∘ 1nom∘ plu∘ ←tatpu∘ *moha-jāla-samāvṛta,* मोहस्य जालेन समावृतः ←m∘ *moha* 2.52 + n∘ *jāla* ←√जल् + ppp∘ adj∘ *samāvṛta* 7.25); *prasaktāḥ:* (m∘ 1nom∘ plu∘ ←ppp∘ adj∘ *prasakta* 2.44); *kāmabhogeṣu* (m∘ 7loc∘ plu∘ ←tatpu∘ *kāma-bhoga,* कामस्य भोगः ←m∘ *kāma* 1.22 + m∘ *bhoga* 1.32); *patanti* (1.42); *narake* (1.44); *a-śućau* (m∘ 7loc∘ sing∘ ←adj∘ *śući* 6.11); (16.16)

(§3) **(viii)** *anaekaćittavibhrāntāḥ:* (adj8∘-subj1∘ those whose mind confused in many ways); **(ix)** *mohajālasamāvṛtāḥ:* (adj9∘-subj1∘ those who are caught up in the snare of delusion); **(x)** *prasaktāḥ: kāmabhogeṣu* (adj10∘-subj1∘ those who are attached to passions and enjoyment); *patanti* (they fall); *narake* (in the hell); *a-śućau* (in the foul); (16.16)

(§4) anaekaćittavibhrāntāḥ: mohajālasamāvṛtāḥ: prasaktāḥ: kāmabhogeṣu patanti a-śućau narake;

(§5) Those (viii) whose minds are confused in many ways, (ix) those who are caught up in the snare of delusion, and (x) those who are attached to passions and enjoyments, they fall in foul hell; (16.16)

16.17 आत्मसम्भाविताः स्तब्धा धनमानमदान्विताः ।
यजन्ते नामयज्ञैस्ते दम्भेनाविधिपूर्वकम् ।।

ātmasambhāvitāḥ: stabdhā dhanamānamadānvitāḥ:,
yajante nāmayajñaiste dambhenāvidhipūrvakam; (16.17)

(§1) *ātmasambhāvitāḥ:* (r∘ 22/7) *stabdhāḥ:* (r∘ 20/9) *dhanamānamadānvitāḥ:* (r∘ 22/8) *yajante nāmayajñaiḥ:* (r∘ 18/1) *te dambhena* (r∘ 1/1) *avidhipūrvakam* (r∘ 14/2);

(§2) *ātmasambhāvitāḥ:* (m∘ 1nom∘ plu∘ ←tatpu∘ *ātma-sambhāvita,* आत्मना सम्भावितः ←m∘ *ātman* 2.41 + ppp∘ adj∘ *sambhāvita* 2.34); *stabdhāḥ:* (m∘ 1nom∘ plu∘ ←ppp∘ adj∘ 🕮*stabdha* ←√स्तम्भ्); *dhanamānamadānvitāḥ:* (m∘ 1nom∘ plu∘ ←tatpu∘ *dhana-māna-madānvita,* धनेन च मानेन च मदेन च अन्वितः ←n∘ *dhana* 1.15 + m∘ *māna* 6.7 + m∘ *mada* 16.10 + ppp∘ adj∘ *anvita* 9.23); *yajante* (4.12); *nāmayajñaiḥ:* (m∘ 3inst∘ plu∘ ←tatpu∘ *nāma-yajña,* नाम्नः यज्ञः ←n∘ or adj∘ *nāman* ←√म्ना + m∘ *yajña* 3.9); *te* (1.33); *dambhena* (3inst∘ sing∘ ←m∘ *dambha* 13.8); *avidhipūrvakam* (9.23); (16.17)

(§3) **(xi)** *ātmasambhāvitāḥ:* (adj11∘-subj1∘ those who are conceited); **(xii)** *stabdhāḥ:* (adj12∘-subj1∘ obstinate); **(xiii)** *dhanamānamadānvitāḥ:* (adj13∘-subj1∘ intoxicated with the pride of wealth and fame); *yajante* (they perform); *nāmayajñaiḥ:* (with ostentatious *yajña; yajñna* for name sake); *te* (they); *dambhena* (with hypocrisy); *avidhipūrvakam* (not as prescribed rites; against what is preacribed by the scriptures);

(§4) ātmasambhāvitāḥ: stabdhāḥ: dhanamānamadānvitāḥ: te yajante nāmayajñaiḥ: dambhena avidhipūrvakam;

(§5) (xi) those who are conceited, (xii) obstinate, (and) (xiii) intoxicated with the pride of wealth and fame, - they perform *yajña* for name sake with hypocrisy, against tenets of the scriptures; (16.17)

16.18 अहङ्कारं बलं दर्पं कामं क्रोधं च संश्रिताः ।
मामात्मपरदेहेषु प्रद्विषन्तोऽभ्यसूयकाः ।।
ahaṅkāram balam darpam kāmam krodham ća saṁśritāḥ:,
māmātmapardeheṣu pradviṣanto'bhyasūyakāḥ:; (16.18)

(§1) *ahaṅkāram* (r◦ 14/1) *balam* (r◦ 14/1) *darpam* (r◦ 14/1) *kāmam* (r◦ 14/1) *krodham* (r◦ 14/1) *ća saṁśritāḥ:* (r◦ 22/8) *mām* (r◦ 8/17) *ātmapardeheṣu* (r◦ 25/5) *pradviṣantaḥ:* (r◦ 15/1) *abhyasūyakāḥ:* (r◦ 22/8);

(§2) *ahaṅkāram* (2acc◦ sing◦ ←m◦ *ahaṅkāra* 2.71); *balam* (1.10); *darpam* (2acc◦ sing◦ ←m◦ *darpa* 11.28); *kāmam* (16.10); *krodham* (2acc◦ sing◦ ←m◦ *krodha* 2.56); *ća* (1.1); 🕮*saṁśritāḥ:* (m◦ 1nom◦ plu◦ ←ppp◦ adj◦ *saṁśrita* ←सम्√श्रि); *mām* (1.46); *ātmapardeheṣu* (7loc◦ plu◦ ←tatpu◦ *ātma-pardehau* = आत्मनः च परस्य च देहौ ←m◦ *ātman* 2.41 + adj◦ *para* 2.3 + m◦ *deha* 2.13); *pradviṣantaḥ:* (1Nom◦ plu◦ ←śatṛ◦ adj◦ *pradviṣat* ←प्र√द्विष्); *abhyasūyakāḥ:* (m◦ 1nom◦ plu◦ ←adj◦ 🕮*abhyasūyaka* ←अभि√असू);
(16.18)

(§3) **(xiv)** *ahaṅkāram* (obj1◦ self-pride); *balam* (obj2◦ power); *darpam* (obj3◦ arrogance); *kāmam* (obj4◦ passion); *krodham* (obj5◦ anger); *ća* (and); *saṁśritāḥ:* (adj◦-obj1-5◦ Those who are possessed of 1-5); *mām* (obj6◦ me, to me); *ātmapardeheṣu* (in their own and in other's bodies); **(xv)** *pradviṣantaḥ:* (adj15◦-subj1◦ Those who are loathful); **(xvi)** *abhyasūyakāḥ:* (adj16◦-subj1◦ Those who are envious); (16.18)

(§4) saṁśritāḥ: ahaṅkāram balam darpam kāmam ća krodham pradviṣantaḥ: abhyasūyakāḥ: mām ātmapardeheṣu

(§5) Those who are (xiv) possessed[785] of self-pride, power, arrogance, passion and anger; (xv)

---

[785] elsewhere◦ संश्रिताः → Clinging to..., Resorting to..., on account of..., Given to..., Given over to..., Dominated by..., ...etc.

🕮 संश्रिताः is not a gerund. It is just a ppp. adj. of the noun subject.

those who are loathful[786] (and) (xvi) those who are envious[787] of Me (who is) in their own and in others' bodies; (16.18)

16.19 तानहं द्विषतः क्रूरान्संसारेषु नराधमान् ।
क्षिपाम्यजस्रमशुभानासुरीष्वेव योनिषु ॥
tānaham dviṣataḥ: krūrānsaṁsāreṣu narādhamān,
kṣipāmyajasramaśubhānāsurīṣveva yoniṣu. (16.19)

(§1) *tān* (r◦ 8/11) *aham* (r◦ 14/1) *dviṣataḥ:* (r◦ 22/1) *krūrān* (r◦ 13/20) *saṁsāreṣu* (r◦ 25/5) *narādhamān* (r◦ 23/1) *kṣipāmi* (r◦ 4/1) *ajasram* (r◦ 8/16) *aśubhān* (r◦ 8/12) *āsurīṣu* (r◦ 25/5, 4/9) *eva* *yoniṣu* (r◦ 25/5)

(§2) *tān* (1.7); *aham* (1.22); *dviṣataḥ:* (m◦ 2acc◦ plu◦ ←śatṛ◦ adj◦ *dviṣat* ←√द्विष्); *krūrān* (m◦ 2acc◦ plu◦ ←adj◦ *krūra* ←√कृत्); *saṁsāreṣu* (7loc◦ plu◦ ←m◦ *saṁsāra* 9.3); *narādhamān* (m◦ 2acc◦ plu◦ ←adj◦ *narādhama* 7.15); *kṣipāmi* (1st-per◦ sing◦ pres◦ वर्तमान्-लट् parasmai◦ ←class6◦ √क्षिप्); *ajasram* (adv◦ ind◦ ←adj◦ *ajasra* ←√जस्); *aśubhān* (m◦ 2acc◦ plu◦ ←adj◦ *aśubha* 2.57); *āsurīṣu* (f◦ 7loc◦ plu◦ ←adj◦ *āsurī* 9.12); *eva* (1.1); *yoniṣu* (7loc◦ plu◦ ←f◦ *yoni* 5.22) (16.19)

(§3) *tān* (obj◦ to those people - mentioned as subj1-16◦ above); *aham* (subj◦ I); *dviṣataḥ:* (adj1◦-obj◦ to those loathful people); *krūrān* (adj2◦-obj◦ to those cruel people); *saṁsāreṣu* (in the worldly cycles of rebirth); *narādhamān* (adj3◦-obj◦ wretches, to those base people); *kṣipāmi* (I throw); *ajasram* (adv◦ perpetually); *aśubhān* (adj4◦-obj◦ to those vicious people); *āsurīṣu* (in the demonic); *eva* (only); *yoniṣu* (in the wombs) (16.19)

(§4) tān dviṣataḥ: krūrān narādhamān aśubhān aham ajasram kṣipāmi eva āsurīṣu yoniṣu saṁsāreṣu

(§5) (Lord Krishna says :) To those loathful people, to those cruel people, to those base people, to those vicious people, I perpetually cast only in the demonic wombs (of) the worldly cycles of rebirth. (16.19)

16.20 आसुरीं योनिमापन्ना मूढा जन्मनि जन्मनि ।

---

[786] elsewhere◦ मां...प्रद्विषन्तः → they hate me, despise Me, hating me, while hating me, they feel extreme hatred..., blasphame againsi the real religion ...etc.

📖 प्रद्विषन्तः is not a verb or gerund. It is a ppp. adj. of the noun subject.

[787] elsewhere◦ अभ्यसूयकाः → they become envious, ...etc.

📖 अभ्यसूयकाः is not a verb. It is a ppp. adj. of the subject.

मामप्राप्यैव कौन्तेय ततो यान्त्यधमां गतिम् ।।

āsurīṁ yonimāpannā mūḍhā janmani janmani,

māmaprāpyaiva kaunteya tato yāntyadhamāṁ gatim. (16.20)

(§1) *āsurīm* (r◦ 14/1) *yonim* (r◦ 8/17) *āpannāḥ:* (r◦ 20/13) *mūḍhāḥ:* (r◦ 20/7) *janmani janmani mām* (r◦ 8/16) *aprāpya* (r◦ 3/1) *eva kaunteya tataḥ:* (r◦ 15/10) *yānti* (r◦ 4/1) *adhamām* (r◦ 14/1) *gatim* (r◦ 14/2)

(§2) *āsurīm* (9.12); *yonim* (2acc◦ sing◦ ←f◦ *yoni* 5.22); *āpannāḥ:* (m◦ 1nom◦ plu◦ ←ppp◦ adj◦ *āpanna* 7.24); *mūḍhāḥ:* (7.15); *janmani* (7loc◦ sing◦ ←n◦ *janman* 2.27); *janmani* (↑); *mām* (1.46); *aprāpya* (6.37); *eva* (1.1); *kaunteya* (2.14); *tataḥ:* (1.13); *yānti* (3.33); *adhamām* (f◦ 2acc◦ sing◦ ←adj◦ *adhama* 7.15); *gatim* (6.37) (16.20)

(§3) () *āsurīm yonim āpannāḥ:* (adj18◦-subj1◦ those who have attained demonic births); *mūḍhāḥ:* **(xxviii)** (adj19◦-subj1◦ those deluded people); *janmani janmani* (life after life); *mām* (obj1◦ me); *aprāpya* (having not attained); *eva* (only); *kaunteya* (O Arjuna!); *tataḥ:* (thus); *yānti* (they attain); *adhamām* (adj◦-obj2◦ the lowest); *gatim* (obj2◦ state, condition) (16.20)

(§4) kaunteya mūḍhāḥ: āsurīm yonim āpannāḥ: janmani janmani aprāpya mām tataḥ: yānti eva adhamām gatim

(§5) O Arjuna! those (xvii) deluded people (xviii) who have attained[788] demonic births life after life, having not attained me thus, they attain only the lowest state.[789] (16.20)

16.21 त्रिविधं नरकस्येदं द्वारं नाशनमात्मन: ।

कामः क्रोधस्तथा लोभस्तस्मादेतत्त्रयं त्यजेत् ।।

trividhaṁ naraksyedaṁ dvāraṁ nāśanamātmanaḥ:,

kāmaḥ: krodhastathā lobhastasmādetattrayaṁ tyajet. (16.21)

(§1) *trividham* (r◦ 14/1) *naraksya* (r◦ 2/1) *idam* (r◦ 14/1) *dvāram* (r◦ 14/1) *nāśanam* (r◦ 8/17) *ātmanaḥ:* (r◦ 22/8) *kāmaḥ:* (r◦ 22/1) *krodhaḥ:* (r◦ 18/1) *tathā lobhaḥ:* (r◦ 18/1) *tasmāt* (r◦ 8/9) *etat* (r◦ 1/10) *trayam* (r◦ 14/1) *tyajet*

(§2) *trividham* (n◦ 1nom◦ sing◦ ←adj◦ dvigu◦ *tri-vidha*, त्रयाणाम् विधीनाम् समाहार: ←adj◦ *tri* 2.45 + m◦

---

[788] elsewhere◦ आपन्ना: → Entering into, Being born, Having entered, having come to possess, Obtaining, Attaining, ...etc.

📖 आपन्ना: is not a gerund. It is just a ppp. adj. of the noun subject.

[789] elsewhere◦ गतिम् → Goal.

vidhi 9.23); *naraksya* (6pos sing◦ ←m◦ *naraka* 1.42); *idam̜* (1.10); *dvāram̜* (1nom◦ sing◦ ←n◦ *dvāra* 2.32); *nāśanam̜* (n◦ 1nom◦ sing◦ ←adj◦ *nāśana* 3.41); *ātmanaḥ:* (4.42); *kāmaḥ:* (2.62); *krodhaḥ:* (2.62); *tathā* (1.8); *lobhaḥ:* (14.12); *tasmāt̜* (1.37); *etat̜* (2acc◦ 2.6); *trayam̜* (n◦ 2acc◦ sing◦ ←n◦ *traya* 11.20); *tyajet̜* (3rd-per◦ sing◦ potential◦ विधि◦ parasmai◦ ←class1◦ √त्यज्) (16.21)

(§3) *trividham̜* (adj1◦-subj◦ of three inlets, with three inlets, with a triple inlet); *naraksya* (of, to the hell); *idam̜* (adj2◦-subj1◦ this); *dvāram̜* (subj◦ door); *nāśanam̜* (adj3◦-subj◦ destroyer); *ātmanaḥ:* (one's); *kāmaḥ:* (subj2◦ passion); *krodhaḥ:* (subj3◦ anger); *tathā* (and, as well as); *lobhaḥ:* (subj4◦ greed); *tasmāt̜* (therefore); *etat̜* (obj◦ this); *trayam̜* (triplet, triad); *tyajet̜* (one must forsake) (16.21)

(§4) idam̜ dvāram̜ naraksya trividham̜ kāmaḥ: krodhaḥ: tathā lobhaḥ: ātmanaḥ: nāśanam̜ tasmāt̜ tyajet̜ etat̜ trayam̜

(§5) This door to hell, with three inlets, (namely) (i) passion, (ii) anger and (iii) greed (is) one's[790] destroyer. Therefore,[791] one must forsake this triplet.[792] (16.21)

16.22 एतैर्विमुक्तः कौन्तेय तमोद्वारैस्त्रिभिर्नरः ।
आचरत्यात्मनः श्रेयस्ततो याति परां गतिम् ।।
etairvimuktaḥ: kaunteya tamodvāraistribhirnaraḥ:,
āćaratyātmanaḥ: śreyastato yāti parām̐ gatim̜. (16.22)

(§1) *etaiḥ:* (r◦ 16/11) *vimuktaḥ:* (r◦ 22/1) *kaunteya tamodvāraiḥ:* (r◦ 18/1) *tribhiḥ:* (r◦ 16/6) *naraḥ:* (r◦ 22/8) *āćarati* (r◦ 4/2) *ātmanaḥ:* (r◦ 22/5) *śreyaḥ:* (r◦ 18/1) *tataḥ:* (r◦ 15/10) *yāti parām̜* (r◦ 14/1) *gatim̜* (r◦ 14/2)

(§2) *etaiḥ:* (1.43); *vimuktaḥ:* (9.28); *kaunteya* (2.14); *tamodvāraiḥ:* (n◦ 3inst◦ plu◦ ←tatpu◦ *tamo-dvāraiḥ:*, तमसः द्वारम् ←n◦ *tamas̜* 7.12 + n◦ *dvāra* 2.32); *tribhiḥ:* (7.13); *naraḥ:* (2.22); *āćarati* (3.21); *ātmanaḥ:* (4.42); *śreyaḥ:* (1.31); *tataḥ:* (1.13); *yāti* (6.45); *parām̜* (4.39); *gatim̜* (6.37) (16.22)

(§3) *etaiḥ:* (from these); *vimuktaḥ:* (adj1◦-subj◦ he who is free); *kaunteya* (O Aujuna!); *tamodvāraiḥ:* (from the gates of darkness); *tribhiḥ:* (from the three); *naraḥ:* (subj◦ the person); *āćarati* (he does);

---

[790] elsewhere◦ आत्मनः → of the atma, of the soul, the self, ...etc.

📖 Remember, the *ātmā* is अक्षरः अविनशी, अछेद्यः, अव्ययः, अजरः, अमरः, शाश्वतः ।

[791] elsewhere◦ तस्मात् → Please see footnote for *hi* हि in 2.15.

📖 एतत् is not plural.

[792] elsewhere◦ एतत् → these three, these, ...etc.

📖 एतत् is not plural.

ātmanaḥ: (adj◦-obj1◦ his own); *śreyaḥ:* (obj1◦ good); *tataḥ:* (thus, thereafter); *yāti* (he attains); *parām̩* (adj◦-obj2◦ the highest) *gatim̩* (obj2◦ state) (16.22)

(§4) kaunteya naraḥ: vimuktaḥ: etaiḥ: tribhiḥ: tamodvāraiḥ: āćarati ātmanaḥ: śreyaḥ: tataḥ: yāti parām̩ gatim̩

(§5) O Arjuna! the person who is free from these three gates of darkness, he does[793] his own[794] good, and thus he attains the highest state. (16.22)

16.23 यः शास्त्रविधिमुत्सृज्य वर्तते कामकारतः ।
न स सिद्धिमवाप्नोति न सुखं न परां गतिम् ।।
yaḥ: śāstravidhimutsṛjya vartate kāmakārataḥ:,
na sa siddhimavāpnoti na sukhaṁ na parāṁ gatim̩. (16.23)

(§1) *yaḥ:* (r◦ 22/5) *śāstravidhim̩* (r◦ 8/20) *utsṛjya vartate kāmakārataḥ:* (r◦ 22/8) *na saḥ:* (r◦ 21/2) *siddhim̩* (r◦ 8/16) *avāpnoti na sukham̩* (r◦ 14/1) *na parām̩* (r◦ 14/1) *gatim̩* (r◦ 14/2)

(§2) *yaḥ:* (2.19); *śāstravidhim̩* (m◦ 2acc◦ sing◦ ←tatpu◦ *śāstra-vidhi*, शास्त्राणाम् विधिः ←n◦ *śāstra* 15.20 + m◦ *vidhi* 9.23); *utsṛjya* (lyp◦ past-participle ind◦ ←उद्√सृज्); *vartate* (5.26); *kāmakārataḥ:* (m◦ 5abl◦ sing◦ ←adv◦ *kāma-kārat̩* ←काम√कृ); *na* (1.30); *saḥ:* (1.13); *siddhim̩* (3.4); *avāpnoti* (15.8); *na* (1.30); *sukham̩* (2acc◦ 5.13); *na* (1.30); *parām̩* (4.39); *gatim̩* (6.37) (16.23)

(§3) *yaḥ:* (adj1◦-subj◦ he who); *śāstravidhim̩* (obj1◦ the precepts of the scripture); *utsṛjya* (ignoring); *vartate* (acts); *kāmakārataḥ:* (adj2◦-subj◦ he who acts with the impulse of his desire); *na* (neither); *saḥ:* (subj◦ he); *siddhim̩* (obj2◦ success); *avāpnoti* (attains); *na* (nor); *sukham̩* (obj3◦ happiness); *na* (nor); *parām̩* (adj◦-obj4◦ the higher); *gatim̩* (obj4◦ state) (16.23)

(§4) utsṛjya śāstravidhim̩ yaḥ: vartate kāmakārataḥ: saḥ: na avāpnoti siddhim̩ na sukham̩ na parām̩ gatim̩

(§5) Ignoring the precepts of the scripture, he who acts with the impulse of his desire, neither attains success[795] nor happiness nor the higher[796] state. (16.23)

---

[793] elsewhere◦ आचरति → strives for, ...etc.

[794] elsewhere◦ आत्मनः → of the soul, for the soul, for the self, ...etc.

📖 Remember, the *ātmā* is अक्षरः, अजरः, अव्ययः ।

[795] elsewhere◦ सिद्धिम् → perfection.

📖 If one acts against the scriptures, there is no question of his being perfect or imperfect. One does not attain perfection even otherwise. See footnote in 4.12

[796] elsewhere◦ पराम् → of the soul, for the soul, for the self, ...etc.

📖 If one acts against the scriptures, there is no question of his attaining highest state.

16.24 तस्माच्छास्त्रं प्रमाणं ते कार्याकार्यव्यवस्थितौ ।
ज्ञात्वा शास्त्रविधानोक्तं कर्म कर्तुमिहार्हसि ।।

tasmaććhāstraṁ pramāṇaṁ te kāryākāryavyavasthitau,
jñātvā śāstravidhānoktaṁ karma kartumihārhasi. (16.24)

(§1) *tasmāt* (r◦ 11/4) *śāstram* (r◦ 14/1) *pramāṇam* (r◦ 14/1, 24/3) *te kāryākāryavyavasthitau jñātvā śāstravidhānoktam* (r◦ 14/1) *karma kartum* (r◦ 8/18) *iha* (r◦ 1/1) *arhasi*

(§2) *tasmāt* (1.37); *śāstram* (2acc◦ 15.20); *pramāṇam* (2acc◦ 3.21); *te* (4dat◦ 2.7); *kāryākāryavyavasthitau* (f◦ 7loc◦ dual◦ ←dvandva rooted tatpu◦ कार्यस्य अकार्यस्य च व्यवस्थिती ←pot◦ adj◦ *kārya* 3.17 + pot◦ adj◦ *akārya* ←अ√कृ + f◦ *vyavasthiti* ←वि–अव√स्था 1.20); *jñātvā* (4.15); *śāstravidhānoktam* (n◦ 2acc◦ sing◦ ←tatpu◦ *śāstra-vidhānokta*, शास्त्रस्य विधानेन उक्तम् ←n◦ *śāstra* 15.20 + n◦ *akārya* ←वि√धा + ppp◦ adj◦ *ukta* 1.24); *karma* (2acc◦ 3.8); *kartum* (1.45); *iha* (2.5); *arhasi* (2.25) (16.24)

(§3) *tasmāt* (therefore); *śāstram* (obj1◦ the scripture); *pramāṇam* (adj1◦-obj1◦ authority); *te* (adj2◦-obj1◦ your); *kāryākāryavyavasthitau* (in the determination of what ought to be done and what ought not to be done); *jñātvā* (having known, having understood); *śāstravidhānoktam* (the sayings of the precepts of the scriptures); *karma* (obj2◦ *karma*, deed, work, duty); *kartum* (to perfom); *iha* (in this world); *arhasi* (you ought to) (16.24)

(§4) tasmāt kāryākāryavyavasthitau śāstram te pramāṇam jñātvā śāstravidhānoktam arhasi kartum karma iha

(§5) Therefore,[797] in the determination of what ought to be done and what ought not to be done, the scripture (is) your authority. Having understood the sayings of the scriptures you ought to perfom *karma* in this world. (16.24)

इति श्रीमद्भगवद्गीतासूपनिषत्सु ब्रह्मविद्यायां योगशास्त्रे
श्रीकृष्णार्जुनसंवादे दैवासुरसम्पद्विभागयोगो नाम षोडशोऽध्यायः ।

iti śrīmadbhagavadgītāsūpaniṣatsu brahmavidyāyāṁ yogaśāstre
śrīkṛṣṇārjunasaṁvāde daivāsurasampadvibhāgayogo nāma ṣoḍaśo'dhyāyaḥ:

(§1) *iti śrīmadbhagavadgītāsu* (r◦ 1/8) *upaniṣatsu brahmavidyāyām* (r◦ 14/1) *yogaśāstre śrīkṛṣṇārjuna-saṁvāde daivāsurasampadvibhāgayogaḥ:* (r◦ 15/6) *nāma ṣoḍaśaḥ:* (r◦ 15/1) *adhyāyaḥ:* (r◦ 22/8)

(§2) *iti* (1.25); *śrīmadbhagavadgītāsu* (1.1); *upaniṣatsu* (1.1); *brahmavidyāyām* (1.1); *yogaśāstre* (1.1);

---

[797] elsewhere◦ तस्मात् → Please see footnote for *hi* हि in 2.15.

śrīkṛṣṇārjunasaṁvāde (1.1); *daivāsurasampadvibhāgayogaḥ:* (m◦ 1nom◦ sing◦ ←tatpu◦ *daivāsura-sampadvibhāga-yoga*, दैवी च आसुरी च सम्पदो: विभागस्य योग: ←adj◦ *daivī* 7.14 + adj◦ āsurī 9.12 + f◦ *sampaḍ* 16.3 + m◦ *vibhāga* 3.28 + m◦ *yoga* 2.39). *nāma* (1.1); *ṣoḍaśaḥ:* (m◦ 1nom◦ sing◦ ←sequence indicating num◦ adj◦ *ṣoḍaśa* ←num◦ *ṣaṣṭha* 15.7 + num◦ *daśa* 13.6); *adhyāyaḥ:* (1.1)

(§3) *iti* (thus); *śrīmadbhagavadgītāsu upaniṣatsu* (among the upaniṣads of Śrīmad-Bhagavadgītā); *brahmavidyāyāṃ* (of the eternal wisdoms); *yogaśāstre* (in the science of Yoga); *śrī-kṛṣṇārjuna-saṁvāde* (in the dialogue between Śrī Kṛṣṇa and Arjuna); *daivāsurasampadvibhāgayogaḥ:* (subj◦ the yoga pertaining to the divine and demonic attitudes). *nāma* (called) *ṣoḍaśaḥ:* (adj◦-subj◦ the sixteenth); *adhyāyaḥ:* (subj◦ discourse)

(§4) śrīmadbhagavadgītāsu upaniṣatsu yogaśāstre daivāsurasampadvibhāgayogaḥ: iti ṣoḍaśaḥ: adhyāyaḥ: nāma guṇatrayavibhāgayogaḥ: śrīkṛṣṇārjunasaṁvāde

(§5) Among the upaniṣads of the Śrīmad-Bhagavadgītā, in the science of Yoga of self realization, thus (is) the sixteenth discourse pertaining to the divine and demonic attitudes, in the dialogue between Śrī Kṛṣṇa and Arjuna.

CHAPTER 17

saptaḍaśo'dhyāyaḥ:

सप्तदशोऽध्याय: ।

THE YOGA PERTAINING TO "THE THREE FORMS OF FAITH"

śraddhātrayavibhāgayogaḥ:

श्रद्धात्रयविभागयोग: ।

Arjuna said (arjuna uvāća अर्जुन उवाच ।)

17.1 ये शास्त्रविधिमुत्सृज्य यजन्ते श्रद्धयान्विता: ।
तेषां निष्ठा तु का कृष्ण सत्त्वमाहो रजस्तम: ।।

ye śāstravidhimutsrujya yajante śraddhayānvitāḥ:,
teṣāṁ niṣṭhā tu kā kṛṣṇa sattvamāho rajastamaḥ:. (17.1)

(§1) *saptadaśaḥ:* (r◦ 15/1) *adhyāyaḥ:* (r◦ 22/8). *śraddhātrayavibhāgayogaḥ:* (r◦ 22/8). *arjunaḥ:* (r◦

19/4) *uvāća. ye śāstravidhiṃ* (r◦ 8/20) *utsṛjya yajante śraddhayā* (r◦ 1/3) *anvitāḥ:* (r◦ 22/8) *teṣāṃ* (r◦ 25/3, 14/1) *niṣṭhā tu kā kṛṣṇa sattvaṃ* (r◦ 8/17) *āho rajaḥ:* (r◦ 18/1) *tamaḥ:* (r◦ 22/8)

(§2) *saptadaśaḥ:* (m◦ 1nom◦ sing◦ ←sequence indicating num◦ adj◦ *sapta-daśa* ←adj◦ *sapta* 10.6 + adj◦ *daśa* 13.6); *adhyāyaḥ:* (1nom◦ sing◦ ←m◦ *adhyāya* ←अधि√इ). *śraddhātrayavibhāgayogaḥ:* (m◦ 1nom◦ sing◦ ←tatpu◦ *śraddhā-traya-vibhāga-yoga,* श्रद्धानाम् त्रयस्य विभागस्य योगः ←f◦ *śraddhā* 3.31 + n◦ *traya* 11.20 + m◦ *vibhāga* 3.28 + m◦ *yoga* 2.39). *arjunaḥ:* (1.28); *uvāća* (1.25). *ye* (1.7); *śāstravidhiṃ* (16.23); *utsṛjya* (16.23); *yajante* (4.12); *śraddhayā* (6.37); *anvitāḥ:* (9.23); *teṣāṃ* (5.16); *niṣṭhā* (3.3); *tu* (1.2); *kā* (1.36); *kṛṣṇa* (1.28); *sattvaṃ* (10.36); *āho* (interrogative ind◦ ←आ√हन्); *rajaḥ:* (14.5); *tamaḥ:* (1nom◦ 14.5) (17.1)

(§3) *saptadaśaḥ:* (adj◦-subj◦ seventeenth); *adhyāyaḥ:* (subj◦ chapter, discourse). *śraddhātrayavibhāgayogaḥ:* (subj◦ the yoga pertaining to the three forms of faith). *arjunaḥ:* (subj◦ Arjuna); *uvāća* (said).

ye (subj1◦ those who); *śāstravidhiṃ* (obj◦ the teaching of the sctiptures); *utsṛjya* (having kept aside, ignoring); *yajante* (worship); *śraddhayā* (with devotion); *anvitāḥ:* (adj◦-subj1◦ endowed); *teṣāṃ* (their); *niṣṭhā* (subj2◦ faith); *tu* (but, or); *kā* (what, what is); *kṛṣṇa* (O Kṛṣṇa!); *sattvaṃ* (adj1◦-subj2◦ sāttvic); *āho* (please tell me); *rajaḥ:* (adj2◦-subj2◦ rājasī); *tamaḥ:* (adj3◦-subj2◦ tāmasī) (17.1)

(§4) saptadaśaḥ: adhyāyaḥ:. śraddhātrayavibhāgayogaḥ:. Arjuna uvāća. kṛṣṇa utsṛjya śāstravidhiṃ ye yajante anvitāḥ: śraddhayā kā teṣāṃ niṣṭhā āho sattvaṃ rajaḥ: tu tamaḥ:

(§5) Seventeenth discourse. The *yoga* pertaining to the three forms of faith.

Arjuna said : O Kṛṣṇa! having kept aside the teaching of the sctiptures, those who endowed with devotion,[798] worship (you), what is their faith? Please tell me is it *sāttvic, rājasī* or *tāmasī.* (17.1)

The Lord said (śrībhagavānuvāća श्रीभगवानुवाच ।)

17.2 त्रिविधा भवति श्रद्धा देहिनां सा स्वभावजा ।
सात्त्विकी राजसी चैव तामसी चेति तां शृणु ।।

trividhā bhavati śraddhā dehināṃ sā svabhāvajā,
sāttvikī rājasī ćaiva tāmasī ćeti tāṃ śruṇu. (17.2)

(§1) *śrībhagavān* (r◦ 8/14) *uvāća. trividhā bhavati śraddhā dehināṃ* (r◦ 14/1) *sā svabhāvajā sāttvikī rājasī ća* (r◦ 3/1) *eva tāmasī ća* (r◦ 2/1) *iti tāṃ* (r◦ 14/1) *śṛṇu*

[798] elsewhere◦ श्रद्धयान्विता: → according to their own imagination, according to his own desire, ...etc,

(§2) *śrībhagavān̩* (2.2); *uvāća* (1.25). *trividhā* (f◦ 1nom◦ sing◦ ←adj◦ *tri-vidha* ←adj◦ *tri* 2.45 + m◦ *vidha* 3.3); *bhavati* (1.44); *śraddhā* (1nom◦ sing◦ ←f◦ *śraddhā* 3.31); *dehinām̩* (6pos plu◦ ←m◦ *dehin* 2.13); *sā* (2.69); *svabhāvajā* (f◦ 1nom◦ sing◦ bahuvrī◦ स्वभावे जायते या ←m◦ *svabhāva* 2.7 + m◦ *ja* 1.7); *sāttvikī* (f◦ 1nom◦ sing◦ ←adj◦ *sāttvika* 7.12); *rājasī* (f◦ 1nom◦ sing◦ ←adj◦ *rajasa* 7.12); *ća* (1.1); *eva* (1.1); *tāmasī* (f◦ 1nom◦ sing◦ ←adj◦ *tāmasa* 7.12); *ća* (1.1); *iti* (1.25); *tām̩* (7.21); *śṛṇu* (2.39) (17.2)

(§3) *śrībhagavān̩* (subj◦ Lord Kṛṣṇa); *uvāća* (said). *trividhā* (adj1◦-subj◦ of three kinds); *bhavati* (is); *śraddhā* (subj◦ devotion, the faith); *dehinām̩* (adj2◦-subj◦ of the embodied beings); *sā* (adj3◦-subj◦ that); *svabhāvajā* (adj4◦-subj◦ iinborn of their own *guṇas*); *sāttvikī* (adj5◦-subj◦ sāttvikī); *rājasī* (adj6◦-subj◦ rajasī); *ća* (and); *eva* (also); *tāmasī* (adj7◦-subj◦ tāmasī); *ća* (and); *iti* (namely); *tām̩* (obj◦ it, about it); *śṛṇu* (hear) (17.2)

(§4) śrībhagavān̩ uvāća śraddhā dehinām̩ sā svabhāvajā bhavati trividhā iti sāttvikī ća rājasī ća eva tāmasī śṛṇu tām̩

(§5) Lord Kṛṣṇa said : The faith of the embodied beings,[799] that (is) born of their own *guṇas,* (is) of three kinds namely *sāttvikī* and *rajasī* and also tāmasī. Hear about it :
(17.2)

17.3 सत्त्वानुरूपा सर्वस्य श्रद्धा भवति भारत ।
श्रद्धामयोऽयं पुरुषो यो यच्छ्रद्धः स एव सः ।।
sattvānurūpā sarvasya śraddhā bhavati bhārata,
śraddhāmayo'yaṁ puruṣo yo yaććhraddhaḥ: sa eva saḥ:. (17.3)

(§1) *sattvānurūpā sarvasya śraddhā bhavati bhārata śraddhāmayaḥ:* (r◦ 15/1) *ayam̩* (r◦ 14/1) *puruṣaḥ:* (r◦ 15/10) *yaḥ:* (r◦ 15/10) *yaṭ* (11.4) *śhraddhaḥ:* (r◦ 22/7) *saḥ:* (r◦ 21/2) *eva saḥ:* (r◦ 22/8)

(§2) *sattvānurūpā* (f◦ 1nom◦ sing◦ tatpu◦ सत्त्वस्य अनुरूपा ←n◦ *sattva* 2.45 + adj◦ *anurūpa* ←अनु√रूप्); *sarvasya* (2.30); *śraddhā* (17.2); *bhavati* (1.44); *bhārata* (1.24); *śraddhāmayaḥ:* (m◦ 1nom◦ sing◦ ←taddhita◦ adj◦ *śraddhāmaya* ←f◦ *śraddhā* 3.31 + adj◦ *maya* 4.10); *ayam̩* (2.19); *puruṣaḥ:* (2.21); *yaḥ:* (2.19); *yaṭ* (1.45); *śraddhaḥ:* (m◦ 1nom◦ sing◦ ←adj◦ *śraddha* ←श्रत्√धा); *saḥ:* (1.13); *eva* (1.1); *saḥ:* (1.13) (17.3)

(§3) *sattvānurūpā* (adj◦-subj1◦ according to his inborn nature); *sarvasya* (adj2◦-subj1◦ of everyone); *śraddhā* (subj1◦ the faith); *bhavati* (is); *bhārata* (O Arjuna!); *śraddhāmayaḥ:* (adj1◦-subj2◦ full of faith);

---

[799] NOTE : In 14.20, 14.5, 14.7 and 17.4 देही does not mean *ātma* (soul or self as some may read elsewhere). Here it means the embodied being, body beared, a person or भूतम् ।

ayaṃ puruṣaḥ: (subj2◦ a person); *yaḥ:* (adj1◦-subj3◦ he who, one); *yaṭ-śraddhaḥ:* (adj2◦-subj3◦ of whatever faith one is); *saḥ:* (adj3◦-subj3◦ that is what); *eva* (only); *saḥ:* (subj3◦ he) (17.3)

(§4) bhārata śraddhā sarvasya bhavati sattvānurūpā ayaṃ puruṣaḥ: śraddhāmayaḥ: yaḥ: yaṭ-śraddhaḥ: eva saḥ:

(§5) O Arjuna! the faith of everyone is according to hes inborn nature. a person (is) full of faith. Of whatever faith one is, only that is what he (is). (17.3)

17.4 यजन्ते सात्त्विका देवान्यक्षरक्षांसि राजसाः ।
प्रेतान्भूतगणांश्चान्ये यजन्ते तामसा जनाः ।।
yajante sāttvikā devānyakṣarkṣāṁsi rājasaḥ:,
pretānbhūtagaṇāṁśćānye yajante tāmasā janāḥ:. (17.4)

(§1) *yajante sāttvikāḥ:* (r◦ 20/8) *devāṇ* (r◦ 13/17) *yakṣarakṣāṁsi rajasāḥ:* (r◦ 22/8) *pretāṇ* (r◦ 13/15) *bhūtagaṇāṇ* (r◦ 13/6) *ća* (r◦ 1/1) *anye yajante tāmasāḥ:* (r◦ 20/7) *janāḥ:* (r◦ 22/8)

(§2) *yajante* (4.12); *sāttvikāḥ:* (7.12); *devāṇ* (3.11); *yakṣarakṣāṁsi* (n◦ 1nom◦ 2acc◦ plu◦ ←dvandva◦ यक्षाः च रक्षांसि च ←*yakṣa-rakṣaṣ* 10.23); *rajasāḥ:* (7.12); *pretāṇ* (2acc◦ plu◦ ←m◦ or ppp◦ adj◦ 🕮*preta* ←प्र√इ); *bhūtagaṇāṇ* (m◦ 2acc◦ plu◦ ←tatpu◦ *bhūta-gaṇa*, भूतानाम् गणः ←n◦ *bhūta* 2.28 + m◦ *gaṇa* 7.7); *ća* (1.1); *anye* (1.9); *yajante* (4.12); *tāmasāḥ:* (7.12); *janāḥ:* (7.16) (17.4)

(§3) *yajante* (they worship); *sāttvikāḥ:* (subj1◦ the *sāttvic* people); *devāṇ* (obj1◦ gods); *yakṣarakṣāṁsi* (obj2◦ the demi-gods and demons); *rajasāḥ:* (subj2◦ the *rajasī* people); *pretāṇ* (obj3◦ the departed beings); *bhūtagaṇāṇ* (obj4◦ the ghosts); *ća* (and); *anye* (adj◦-subj3◦ the other); *yajante* (they worship); *tāmasāḥ: janāḥ:* (subj3◦ *tāmasic* people); (17.4)

(§4) sāttvikāḥ: yajante devāṇ rajasāḥ: yakṣarakṣāṁsi anye tāmasāḥ: janāḥ: yajante pretāṇ ća bhūtagaṇāṇ

(§5) The *sāttvic* people worship gods. The *rajasī* people (worship) the demi-gods and demons. And, the other *tāmasic* people worship the departed beings and ghosts.
(17.4)

17.5 अशास्त्रविहितं घोरं तप्यन्ते ये तपो जनाः ।
दम्भाहङ्कारसंयुक्ताः कामरागबलान्विताः ।।
aśāstravihitaṁ ghoraṁ tapyante ye tapo janāḥ:,
dambhāhaṅkārasaṁyuktāḥ: kāmarāgabalānvitāḥ:. (17.5)

(§1) *aśāstravihitaṃ* (r◦ 14/1) *ghoraṃ* (r◦ 14/1) *tapyante ye tapaḥ:* (r◦ 15/3) *janāḥ:* (r◦ 22/8) *dambhāhaṅkārasaṁyuktāḥ:* (r◦ 22/1) *kāmarāgabalānvitāḥ:* (r◦ 22/8)

(§2) *aśāstravihitaṃ* (n∘ 2acc∘ sing∘ ←tatpu∘ *a-śāstra-vihita*, न शास्त्रेण विहितम् ←ind∘ *na* 1.30 + n∘ *śāstra* 15.20 + adj∘ *vihita* 7.22); *ghoraṃ* (2acc∘ 11.49); *tapyante* (3rd-per∘ plu∘ pres∘ वर्तमान्-लट् ātmane∘ ←class4∘ √तप्); *ye* (1.7); *tapaḥ:* (2acc∘ 7.9); *janāḥ:* (7.16); *dambhāhaṅkārasaṁyuktāḥ:* (m∘ 1nom∘ plu∘ ←tatpu∘ adj∘ *dambhāhaṅkāra- saṁyukta*, दम्भेन च अहङ्कारेण च संयुक्तः ←m∘ *dambha* 13.8 + m∘ *ahaṅkāra* 2.71 + ppp∘ adj∘ *saṁyukta* ←सम्√युज्); *kāmarāgabalānvitāḥ:* (m∘ 1nom∘ plu∘ ←tatpu∘ *kāma-rāga-balānvita*, कामस्य च रागस्य च बलेन अन्वितः ←m∘ *kāma* 1.22 + m∘ *rāga* 2.56 + n∘ *bala* 1.10 + adj∘ *anvita* 9.23) (17.5)

(§3) *aśāstravihitaṃ* (adj1∘-obj∘ not prescribed by the scriptures); *ghoraṃ* (adj2∘-obj∘ severe); *tapyante* (they undertake); *ye* (adj1∘-subj∘ those, those who); *tapaḥ:* (obj∘ austerity); *janāḥ:* (subj∘ people); *dambhāhaṅkārasaṁyuktāḥ:* (adj2∘-subj∘ those who are endowed with pertension and ego); *kāmarāgabalānvitāḥ:* (adj3∘-subj∘ those who are endowed with the passion of desire and attachment) (17.5)

(§4) ye janāḥ: dambhāhaṅkārasaṁyuktāḥ: kāmarāgabalānvitāḥ: tapyante ghoraṃ tapaḥ: aśāstravihitaṃ

(§5) Those people who are endowed with pertension and ego, those who are endowed with the passion of desire and attachment, they undertake severe austerity thet is not prescribed by the scriptures. (17.5)

17.6 कर्षयन्तः शरीरस्थं भूतग्राममचेतसः ।
मां चैवान्तःशरीरस्थं तान्विद्ध्यासुरनिश्चयान् ।।
karṣayantaḥ: śarīrasthaṁ bhūtagrāmamaćetasaḥ:,
maṁ ćaivāntaḥ:śarīrasthaṁ tānviddhyāsuraniśćayāṇ. (17.6)

(§1) *karṣayantaḥ:* (r∘ 22/5) *śarīrasthaṃ* (r∘ 14/1) *bhūtagrāmaṃ* (r∘ 8/16) *aćetasaḥ:* (r∘ 22/8) *māṃ* (r∘ 14/1) *ća* (r∘ 3/1) *eva* (r∘ 1/1) *antaḥ:śarīrasthaṃ* (r∘ 14/1) *tāṇ* (r∘ 13/19) *viddhi* (r∘ 4/2) *āsuraniśćayāṇ*

(§2) *karṣayantaḥ:* (1nom∘ plu∘ ←śatṛ∘ caus∘-adj∘ *karṣayat* ←√कृष्); *śarīrasthaṃ* (2acc∘ sing∘ ←bahuvrī∘ adj∘ *śarīrastha* 13.32); *bhūtagrāmaṃ* (9.8); *aćetasaḥ:* (3.32); *māṃ* (1.46); *ća* (1.1); *eva* (1.1); *antaḥ:śarīrasthaṃ* (m∘ 2acc∘ sing∘ ←bahuvrī∘ *antaḥ:-śarīra-stha*, अन्तः शरीरस्थः यः ←ind∘ *ante* 5.24 + adj∘ *śarīrastha* 13.32); *tāṇ* (1.7); *viddhi* (2.17); *āsuraniśćayāṇ* (m∘ 2acc∘ plu∘ ←bahuvrī∘ *āsura-niśćaya*, आसुरवत् निश्चयः यस्य ←adj∘ *āsura* 7.15 + m∘ *niśćaya* 2.37) (17.6)

(§3) *karṣayantaḥ:* (adj1∘-subj∘ torturing, while torturing); *śarīrasthaṃ* (adj∘-obj1∘ the one that is present in the body); *bhūtagrāmaṃ* (obj1∘ the aggregate of organs); *aćetasaḥ:* (adj2∘-subj∘ the mindless people); *māṃ* (obj2∘ me); *ća* (and); *eva* (also); *antaḥ:śarīrasthaṃ* (adj∘-obj2∘ he who is present in the body); *tān̦* (adj3◦-subj◦ them); *viddhi* (know); *āsuraniśćayān̦* (adj4◦-subj◦ those of demonic tendency) (17.6)

(§4) aćetasaḥ: karṣayantaḥ: bhūtagrāmam̦ śarīrastham̦ ća eva mām̦ antaḥ:śarīrastham̦ viddhi tān̦ āsuraniśćayān̦

(§5) The mindless people[800] (who are) torturing[801] the aggregate[802] of organs present in the body, and also torturing me, who is present in the body, know[803] them (to be) of demonic tendency. (17.6)

17.7 आहारस्त्वपि सर्वस्य त्रिविधो भवति प्रियः ।
यज्ञस्तपस्तथा दानं तेषां भेदमिमं शृणु ।।
āhārastvapi sarvasya trividho bhavati priyaḥ:,
yajñastapastathā dānaṁ teṣāṁ bhedamimaṁ śruṇu. (17.7)

(§1) *āhāraḥ:* (r◦ 18/1) *tu* (r◦ 4/6) *api sarvasya trividhaḥ:* (r◦ 15/8) *bhavati priyaḥ:* (r◦ 22/8) *yajñaḥ:* (r◦ 18/1) *tapaḥ:* (r◦ 18/1) *tathā dānam̦* (r◦ 14/1) *teṣām̦* (r◦ 25/3, 14/1) *bhedam̦* (r◦ 8/18) *imam̦* (r◦ 14/1) *śṛṇu*

(§2) *āhāraḥ:* (1nom◦ sing◦ ←m◦ *āhāra* 2.59); *tu* (1.2); *api* (1.26); *sarvasya* (2.30); *trividhaḥ:* (m◦ 1nom◦ sing◦ ←adj◦ *tri-vidha* 17.2); *bhavati* (1.44); *priyaḥ:* (7.17); *yajñaḥ:* (3.14); *tapaḥ:* (1nom◦ 7.9); *tathā* (1.8); 🕮*dānam̦* (1nom◦ 10.5); *teṣām̦* (5.16); *bhedam̦* (2acc◦ sing◦ ←m◦ *bheda* 3.26); *imam̦* (1.28); *śṛṇu* (2.39) (17.7)

(§3) *āhāraḥ:* (adj1◦-subj1◦ the food, diet); *tu* (and); *api* (also); *sarvasya* (adj2◦-subj1◦ of everyone); *trividhaḥ:* (adj3◦-subj1◦ of three types); *bhavati* (is); *priyaḥ:* (adj4◦-subj1◦ favourite, pleasing); *yajñaḥ:* (subj2◦ the austerity); *tapaḥ:* (subj3◦ penance); *tathā* (so also, as well as); *dānam̦* (subj4◦ charity); *teṣām̦*

---

[800] elsewhere◦ अचेतसः → being non-discriminating, senselessly, ...etc.

🕮 अचेतसः is not a gerund or an adverb.

[801] elsewhere◦ कर्षयन्तः → who torture, who emaciate, ...etc.

🕮 कर्षयन्तः is not a verb.

[802] elsewhere◦ भूतग्रामम् → all the organs, bodily organs, all the elements in the body, the elements in the body, material elements, elements contitituting theri body, the vitals in the body, ...etc.

🕮 भूतग्रामम् is not a plural noun.

[803] elsewhere◦ विद्धि → are to be known as, are called as, ...etc.

🕮 विद्धि is not a passive (कर्मणि) verb. It is an active (कर्तरि) verb

(adj∘-subj2-4∘ their); *bhedam̨* (obj∘ classification); *imam̨* (adj∘-obj∘ this); *śṛṇu* (please listen) **(17.7)**

(§4) āhārah̤: priyah̤: sarvasya bhavati api trividhah̤: tathā yajñah̤: tapah̤: tu dānam̨ śṛṇu imam̨ teṣām̨ bhedam̨.

(§5) The favourite foods of everyone is also of three types; so also (are) the austerity, penance and charity.[804] Please listen to this for their classification. **(17.7)**

17.8 आयु:सत्त्वबलारोग्यसुखप्रीतिविवर्धना: ।
रस्या: स्निग्धा: स्थिरा हृद्या आहारा: सात्त्विकप्रिया: ।।

āyuh̤:sattvabalārogyasukhaprītivivardhanāh̤:,
rasyāh̤: snigdhāh̤: sthirā hṛdyā āhārah̤: sāttvikapriyāh̤:. **(17.8)**

(§1) *āyuh̤:sattvabalārogyasukhaprītivivardhanāh̤:* (r∘ 22/8) *rasyāh̤:* (r∘ 22/7) *snigdhāh̤:* (r∘ 22/7) *sthirāh̤:* (r∘ 20/18) *hṛdyāh̤:* (r∘ 20/2) *āhārāh̤:* (r∘ 22/7) *sāttvikapriyāh̤:* (r∘ 22/8)

(§2) *āyuh̤:sattvabalārogyasukhaprītivivardhanāh̤:* (m∘ 1nom∘ plu∘ ←bahuvrī∘ *āyuh̤:-sattva-balārogya-sukha- prīti-vivardhana*, आयो: च सत्त्वस्य च बलस्य च आरोग्यस्य च सुखस्य च प्रीते: च विवर्धनं करोति य: स: ←n∘ *āyu* or 🕮*āyuṣ* 3.16 + n∘ *sattva* 2.45 + n∘ *bala* 1.10 + n∘ 🕮*ārogya* ←m∘ *roga* ←√रुज् + n∘ *sukha* 1.32 + f∘ *prīti* 1.36 + n∘ *vivardhana* ←वि√वृध्); *rasyāh̤:* (m∘ 1nom∘ plu∘ ←adj∘ 🕮*rasya* ←m∘ *rasa* 2.59); *snigdhāh̤:* (m∘ 1nom∘ plu∘ ←ppp∘ adj∘ 🕮*snigdha* ←√स्निह); *sthirāh̤:* (m∘ 1nom∘ plu∘ ←adj∘ *sthira* 1.16); *hṛdyāh̤:* (m∘ 1nom∘ plu∘ ←deriv∘ adj∘ 🕮*hṛdya* ←√हृद्); *āhārāh̤:* (m∘ 1nom∘ plu∘ ←m∘ 🕮*āhāra* 2.59); *sāttvikapriyāh̤:* (m∘ 1nom∘ plu∘ ←tatpu∘ adj∘ *sāttvika-priya*, सात्त्विकानाम् प्रिय: ←adj∘ m∘ *sāttvika* 7.12 + adj∘ *priya* 1.23) **(17.8)**

(§3) *āyuh̤:sattvabalārogyasukhaprītivivardhanāh̤:* (adj1-6∘-subj∘ the ones that augment life, righteousness, strength, fitness of health, happiness and delight); *rasyāh̤:* (adj7∘-subj∘ that are juicy, savory); *snigdhāh̤:* (adj8∘-subj∘ that are smooth); *sthirāh̤:* (adj9∘-subj∘ that give stability); *hṛdyāh̤:* (adj10∘-subj∘ that are dainty, pleasant); *āhārāh̤:* (subj∘ the foods); *sāttvikapriyāh̤:* (adj11∘-subj∘ are dear to the people with preponderant sattvic attribute) **(17.8)**

(§4) āhārāh̤: āyuh̤:sattvabalārogyasukhaprītivivardhanāh̤: rasyāh̤: snigdhāh̤: sthirāh̤: hṛdyāh̤: sāttvikapriyāh̤:

(§5) The foods that augment life, righteousness, strength, fitness of health, happiness and delight; that are savory; that are smooth; that give stability (and) that are pleasant, are dear to the

---

[804] elsewhere∘ यज्ञस्तपस्तथा दानं → sacrifices, austerities and gifts; Yajnas, austerities and gifts, ...etc.

🕮 यज्ञ: तप: and दानम् are not plural nouns.

people with preponderant[805] *sāttvic* attribute. (17.8)

17.9 कट्वम्ललवणात्युष्णतीक्ष्णरूक्षविदाहिनः ।
आहारा राजसस्येष्टा दुःखशोकामयप्रदाः ।।
kaṭvāmlalavaṇātyuṣṇatīkṣṇarūkṣavidāhinaḥ:,
āhārā rājasasyeṣṭā duḥ:khaśokāmayapradāḥ:. (17.9)

(§1) *kaṭvāmlalavaṇātyuṣṇatīkṣṇarūkṣavidāhinaḥ:* (r◦ 22/8) *āhārāḥ:* (r◦ 20/15) *rājasasya* (r◦ 2/1) *iṣṭāḥ:* (r◦ 20/8) *duḥ:khaśokāmayapradāḥ:* (r◦ 22/8)

(§2) *kaṭvāmlalavaṇātyuṣṇatīkṣṇarūkṣavidāhinaḥ:* (m◦ 1nom◦ plu◦ ←dvandva◦ कट्वः च अम्लाः च लवणाः च अत्युष्णाः च तीक्ष्णाः च रूक्षाः च विदाहिनः च ←adj◦ 🕮*kaṭu* ←√कट् + adj◦ 🕮*amla* ←√अम् + adj◦ 🕮*lavaṇa* ←√लू + adj◦ *ati* 6.11 + adj◦ 🕮*uṣṇa* 2.14 + adj◦ 🕮*tīkṣṇa* ←√तिज् + adj◦ 🕮*rūkṣa* ←√रूक्ष् + adj◦ 🕮*vidāhin* ←वि√दह); *āhārāḥ:* (17.8); *rājasasya* (m◦ 6pos◦ sing◦ ←adj◦ *rajasa* 7.12); *iṣṭāḥ:* (m◦ 1nom◦ plu◦ ←adj◦ *iṣṭa* 3.10); *duḥ:khaśokāmayapradāḥ:* (m◦ 1nom◦ plu◦ ←tatpu◦ *duḥ:kha-śokāmaya-prada*, दुःखम् च शोकम् च आमयम् च प्रददाति इति ←n◦ *duḥ:kha* 2.14 + m◦ *śoka* 1.47 + m◦ 🕮*āmaya* 2.51 + adjective forming affix प्रद *prada* ←प्र√दा) (17.9)

(§3) *kaṭvāmlalavaṇātyuṣṇatīkṣṇarūkṣavidāhinaḥ:* (adj1-7◦-subj◦ that are bitter, sour, salty, very hot, pungent, dry and burning); *āhārāḥ:* (subj◦ the foods); *rājasasya iṣṭāḥ:* (adj8◦-subj◦ dear to the people with preponderant *rājasic* attribute); *duḥ:khaśokāmayapradāḥ:* (adj9-11◦-subj◦ that produce pain, grief and sickness) (17.9)

(§4) āhārāḥ: kaṭvāmlalavaṇātyuṣṇatīkṣṇarūkṣavidāhinaḥ: duḥ:khaśokāmayapradāḥ: rājasasya iṣṭāḥ:

(§5) The foods that are bitter, sour, salty, very hot, pungent, dry and burning (and) that produce

---

[805] elsewhere◦ सात्त्विकप्रियाः → dear to one endowed with sattva, dear to the pure, such foods are juicy..., ...etc.

🕮 (i) सात्त्विकः is not the one with or endowed with *sat-guṇa*, but 'the one who has subdued his *rajoguṇa* and *tamoguṇa* and thus made his *sat-guṇa* more active or dominant over the other two guṇas.' **Everyone is endowed with all three *guṇas* in equal proportion**, The difference, however, is their ratio of preponderance. Please read the 'Introductory Essay' in Volume I, Chapter 2. The same footnote is good for the राजसस्येष्टाः and तामसप्रियम् mentioned in the following two verses.

(ii) such foods are juicy, fatty, ...etc : This verse does not say "the foods that sattvic people like are juicy, fatty, ...etc.," it also does not say that "the juicy, ...etc. foods are sattvic," rather what it says is that, "the juicy, ...etc. foods are dear to the *sāttavic* people." Whatever are the problems in thses three sentences, the same is good for the राजसस्येष्टाः and तामसप्रियम् in the next two verses.

pain, grief and sickness (are) dear to the people with preponderant *rājasic* attribute.[806] (17.9)

17.10 यातयामं गतरसं पूति पर्युषितं च यत् ।
उच्छिष्टमपि चामेध्यं भोजनं तामसप्रियम् ।।
yātayāmaṁ gatarasaṁ pūti paryuṣitaṁ ća yat,
uććhiṣṭamapi ćāmedhyaṁ bhojanaṁ tāmasapriyaṃ. (17.10)

(§1) *yātayāmaṃ* (r∘ 14/1) *gatarasaṃ* (r∘ 14/1) *pūti paryuṣitaṃ* (r∘ 14/1) *ća yaṭ* (r∘ 23/1) *uććhiṣṭaṃ* (r∘ 8/16) *api ća* (r∘ 1/1) *amedhyaṃ* (r∘ 14/1) *bhojanaṃ* (r∘ 14/1) *tāmasapriyaṃ* (r∘ 14/2)

(§2) 🕮*yātayāmaṃ* (n∘ 1nom∘ sing∘ ←bahuvrī∘ *yāta-yāma*, यात: याम: यस्य तत् ←ppp∘ adj∘ *yāta* ←√या + m∘ *yāma* ←√या); 🕮*gatarasaṃ* (n∘ 1nom∘ sing∘ ←bahuvrī∘ *gata-rasa*, गत: रस: यस्य तत् ←adj∘ *gata* 2.11 + m∘ *rasa* 2.59); 🕮*pūti* (n∘ 1nom∘ sing∘ ←adj∘ *pūti* ←√पूय्); 🕮*paryuṣitaṃ* (n∘ 1nom∘ sing∘ ←ppp∘ adj∘ *paryuṣita* ←परि√वस्); *ća* (1.1); *yaṭ* (2.67); 🕮*uććhiṣṭaṃ* (n∘ 1nom∘ sing∘ ←ppp∘ adj∘ *uććhiṣṭa* ←उद्√शिष्); *api* (1.26); *ća* (1.1); 🕮*amedhyaṃ* (n∘ 1nom∘ sing∘ ←ppp∘ adj∘ *amedhya* ←अ√मेध्); *bhojanaṃ* (n∘ 1nom∘ sing∘ ←n∘ *bhojana* 11.42); *tāmasapriyaṃ* (n∘ 1nom∘ sing∘ ←tatpu∘ adj∘ *tāmasa-priya*, तामसानाम् प्रियम् ←adj∘ *tāmasa* 7.12 + adj∘ *priya* 1.23) (17.10)

(§3) *yātayāmaṃ* (adj1∘-subj∘ stale, more than three hours old); *gatarasaṃ* (adj2∘-subj∘ flavorless); *pūti* (adj3∘-subj∘ putrid); *paryuṣitaṃ* (adj4∘-subj∘ decomposed); *ća* (and); *yaṭ* (adj5∘-subj∘ which is, that is); *uććhiṣṭaṃ* (adj6∘-subj∘ leftover); *api ća* (as well as); *amedhyaṃ* (adj7∘-subj∘ foul); *bhojanaṃ* (subj∘ the food); *tāmasapriyaṃ* (adj8∘-subj∘ dear to the people with preponderant *tāmasic* attribute) (17.10)

(§4) bhojanaṃ yaṭ yātayāmaṃ gatarasaṃ pūti paryuṣitaṃ ća uććhiṣṭaṃ api ća amedhyaṃ tāmasapriyaṃ

(§5) The food that is stale, flvorless, putrid, decomposed and/or leftover as well as foul (is) dear to the people with preponderant *tāmasic* attribute.[807] (17.10)

17.11 अफलाकाङ्क्षिभिर्यज्ञो विधिदृष्टो य इज्यते ।
यष्टव्यमेवेति मन: समाधाय स सात्त्विक: ।।
aphalākāṅkṣibhiryajño vidhidṛṣṭo ya ijjyate,
yaṣṭavyameveti manaḥ: samādhāya sa sāttvikaḥ:. (17.11)

(§1) *aphalākāṅkṣibhiḥ:* (r∘ 16/6) *yajñaḥ:* (r∘ 15/13) *vidhidṛṣṭaḥ:* (r∘ 15/10) *yaḥ:* (r∘ 19/2) *ijjyate*

[806] Please see the footnote in 7.8

[807] Please see the footnote in 7.8

yaṣṭavyam̩ (r◦ 8/22) *eva* (r◦ 2/1) *iti manaḥ:* (r◦ 22/7) *samādhāya saḥ:* (r◦ 21/2) *sāttvikaḥ:* (r◦ 22/8)

(§2) *a-phalākāṅkṣibhiḥ:* (3inst◦ plu◦ n.tatpu◦ ←m◦ *phalākāṅkṣin̩,* फलस्य आकांक्षी ←n◦ *phala* 2.43 + adj◦ *ākāṅkṣin̩* ←आ√कांक्ष्); *yajñaḥ:* (3.14); *vidhidṛṣṭaḥ:* (1nom◦ sing◦ ←tatpu◦ *vidhi-dṛṣṭa,* विध्या दृष्टः ←m◦ *vidhi* 9.23 + ppp◦ adj◦ *dṛṣṭa* 2.16); *yaḥ:* (2.19); *ijjyate* (3rd-per◦ sing◦ pres◦ वर्तमान्–लट् ātmane◦ ←class1◦ √यज्); *yaṣṭavyam̩* (2acc◦ sing◦ ←pot◦ adj◦ *yaṣṭavya* ←√यज्); *eva* (1.1); *iti* (1.25); *manaḥ:* (2acc◦ 6.12); *samādhāya* (lyp◦ past-participle ind◦ ←सम्–आ√धा 5.10); *saḥ:* (1.13); *sāttvikaḥ:* (m◦ 1nom◦ sing◦ ←adj◦ *sāttvika* 7.12) (17.11)

(§3) *a-phalākāṅkṣibhiḥ:* (adj◦-subj1◦ by persons who do not perform duty with the derire for its fruit); *yajñaḥ:* (obj1◦ the *yajña,* austirity); *vidhidṛṣṭaḥ:* (adj1◦-obj1◦ the one that which is as observed in the scriptures); *yaḥ:* (adj2◦-obj1◦ that which); *ijjyate* (is performed); *yaṣṭavyam̩* (adj◦-obj2◦ the obligatory); *eva* (indeed); *iti* (thus); *manaḥ:* (obj2◦ mind); *samādhāya* (having fixed); *saḥ:* (adj1◦-subj2◦ that, that *yajña*); *sāttvikaḥ:* (adj2◦-subj2◦ *sāttvika*) (17.11)

(§4) yajñaḥ: yaḥ: ijjyate vidhidṛṣṭaḥ: a-phalākāṅkṣibhiḥ: eva iti samādhāya yaṣṭavyam̩ manaḥ: saḥ: sāttvikaḥ:

(§5) The *yajña,* the one that is[808] as observed in the scriptures, that is performed by persons who do not do their duty with the derire for its fruit, having fixed the obligatory mind[809] thus, that *yajña* (is) *sāttvika.* (17.11)

17.12 अभिसन्धाय तु फलं दम्भार्थमपि चैव यत् ।
इज्यते भरतश्रेष्ठ तं यज्ञं विद्धि राजसम् ।।

abhisandhāya tu phalaṁ dambhārthamapi ćaiva yat̩,
ijyate bharataśreṣṭha taṁ yajñaṁ viddhi rājasam̩. (17.12)

(§1) *abhisandhāya tu phalam̩* (r◦ 14/1) *dambhārtham̩* (r◦ 8/16) *api ća* (r◦ 3/1) *eva yat̩* (r◦ 23/1) *ijjyate bharataśreṣṭha tam̩* (r◦ 14/1) *yajñam̩* (r◦ 14/1) *viddhi rājasam̩* (r◦ 14/2)

(§2) *abhisandhāya* (lyp◦ past-participle ind◦ ←अभि–सम्√धा); *tu* (1.2); *phalam̩* (2acc◦ 2.51); *dambhārtham̩* (adv◦ ←tatpu◦ *dambhārtha,* दम्भस्य अर्थः ←m◦ *dambha* 13.8 + m◦ *artha* 1.7); *api* (1.26); *ća* (1.1); *eva* (1.1);

---

[808] elsewhere◦ विधिदृष्टः → observing the scriptures.

📖 विधिदृष्टः is not a gerund or lyp. participle. It is ppp. adj. of the *yajña.*

[809] elsewhere◦ यष्टव्यम् → under the belief that sacrifice is a duty, it is surely obligatory, the sacrifece...as a matter of duty, ...etc.

📖 Remember, यष्टव्यम् in a neuter gender adjective of the neuter gender object मनः । It is not the adjective of the masculine subject *yajña.*

yat̹ (1nom◦ 3.21); *ijjyate* (17.11); *bharataśreṣṭha* (m◦ 8voc◦ sing◦ ←bahuvrī◦ *bharata-śreṣṭha*, भरतेषु श्रेष्ठ: य: ←m◦ *bharata* 3.41 + adj◦ *śreṣṭha* 3.21); *tam̹* (2.1); *yajñam̹* (4.25); *viddhi* (2.17); *rājasam̹* (m◦ 2acc◦ sing◦ ←adj◦ *rajasa* 7.12) (17.12)

(§3) *abhisandhāya* (having a desire for); *tu* (but); *phalam̹* (obj1◦ 2acc◦ fruit); *dambhārtham̹* (adv◦ hypocritically); *api ća eva* (only); *yat̹* (adj1◦-obj2◦ whatever); *ijjyate* (is observed, austerity performed, is sacrificed); *bharataśreṣṭha* (O Arjuna!); *tam̹* (adj1◦-obj3◦ that); *yajñam̹* (obj3◦ *yajña*); *viddhi* (know, know it to be); *rājasam̹* (adj2◦-obj3◦ *rajasic*) (17.12)

(§4) tu bharataśreṣṭha yat̹ api ća eva api ća dambhārtham̹ ijjyate abhisandhāya phalam̹ eva tam̹ yajñam̹ viddhi rājasam̹

(§5) But, O Arjuna! whatever[810] is sacrificed hypocritically, having a desire for its fruit only, that *yajña*, know it to be *rajasic*. (17.12)

17.13 विधिहीनमसृष्टान्नं मन्त्रहीनमदक्षिणम् ।
श्रद्धाविरहितं यज्ञं तामसं परिचक्षते ।।
vidhihīnamasṛṣṭānnaṁ mantrahīnamadakṣiṇam̹,
śraddhāvirahitaṁ yajñaṁ tāmasaṁ parićakṣate. (17.13)

(§1) *vidhihīnam̹* (r◦ 8/16) *asṛṣṭānnam̹* (r◦ 14/1) *mantrahīnam̹* (r◦ 8/16) *adakṣiṇam̹* (r◦ 14/2, 24/3) *śraddhāvirahitam̹* (r◦ 14/1) *yajñam̹* (r◦ 14/1) *tāmasam̹* (r◦ 14/1) *parićakṣate*

(§2) *vidhihīnam̹* (m◦ 2acc◦ sing◦ ←adj◦ tatpu◦ *vidhi-hīna*, विधिना हीनम् ←m◦ *vidhi* 9.23 + adj◦ *hīna* ←√हा); *asṛṣṭānnam̹* (m◦ 2acc◦ sing◦ ←bahuvrī◦ *a-sṛṣṭānna*, अन्नम् न सृष्टम् यस्मिन् ←ind◦ *na* 1.30 + adj◦ *sṛṣṭa* 4.13 + n◦ *anna* 3.14); *mantrahīnam̹* (m◦ 2acc◦ sing◦ ←adj◦ *mantra-hīna*, मन्त्रेण हीनम् ←m◦ *mantra* 9.16 + adj◦ *hīna* ↑); *adakṣiṇam̹* (m◦ 2acc◦ sing◦ ←n.tatpu◦ *a-dakṣiṇa*, दक्षिणया विरहितम् ←f◦ *dakṣiṇā* ←√दक्ष्); *śraddhāvirahitam̹* (n◦ 2acc◦ sing◦ ←tatpu◦ *śraddhā-virahita*, श्रद्धया विरहितम् ←f◦ *śraddhā* 3.31 + ppp◦ adj◦ *virahita* ←वि√रह्); *yajñam̹* (4.25); *tāmasam̹* (m◦ 2acc◦ sing◦ ←adj◦ *tāmasa* 7.12); *parićakṣate* (3rd-per◦ sing◦ pres◦ वर्तमान्–लट् ātmane◦ ←class2◦ परि√चक्ष्) (17.13)

(§3) *vidhihīnam̹* (adj1◦-obj◦ that is performed without observing observing the instructions of the scriptures); *asṛṣṭānnam̹* (adj2◦-obj◦ without the offering of food); *mantrahīnam̹* (adj3◦-obj◦ without

---

[810] elsewhere◦ यत् इज्यते → the sacrifice which is performed.

📖 Remember, neuter gender यत् is not adjective of masculine object sacrifice. It is n. adjective of n. 'whatever' work (कर्म) performed as a *yajña*.

chanting hymns from scritpures); *adakṣiṇam̩* (adj4◦-obj◦ without offering a donation); *śraddhāvirahitam̩* (adj5◦-obj◦ without offering oblation); *yajñam̩* (obj◦ a *yajña*); *tāmasam̩* (adj6◦-obj◦ *tamasic*); *parićakṣate* (they regard it, they see it) (17.13)

(§4) yajñam̩ vidhihīnam̩ asr̥ṣṭānnam̩ mantrahīnam̩ adakṣiṇam̩ śraddhāvirahitam̩ parićakṣate tāmasam̩

(§5) A *yajña* that is performed without observing observing the instructions of the scriptures, without the offering of food, without chanting hymns from scritpures, without offering a donation (and) without offering oblation, they regard[811] it as a *tamasic yajnā.*

(17.13)

17.14 देवद्विजगुरुप्राज्ञपूजनं शौचमार्जवम् ।
ब्रह्मचर्यमहिंसा च शारीरं तप उच्यते ।।
devadvijagurupr̄ajñapūjanaṁ śaućamārjavam̩,
brahmaćaryamahiṁsā ća śārīraṁ tapa ućyate. (17.14)

(§1) *devadvijagurupr̄ajñapūjanam̩* (r◦ 14/1) *śaućam̩* (r◦ 8/17) *ārjavam̩* (r◦ 14/2) *brahmaćaryam̩* (r◦ 8/16) *ahimsā ća śārīram̩* (r◦ 14/1) *tapaḥ:* (r◦ 19/4) *ućyate*

(§2) *devadvijagurupr̄ajñapūjanam̩* (n◦ 1nom◦ sing◦ ←tatpu◦ *deva-dvija-guru-prājña-pūjana*, देवानाम् च द्विजानाम् च गुरूणाम् च प्राज्ञानाम् च पूजनम् ←m◦ *deva* 3.11 + m◦ *dvija* 1.7 + m◦ *guru* 2.5 + f◦ *prājñā* ←प्र√ज्ञा + n◦ *pūjana* ←√पूज्); *śaućamārjavam̩* (n◦ 1nom◦ sing◦ ←dvandva◦ शौचम् च आर्जवम् च ←n◦ *śauća* 13.8 + m◦ *ārjava* 13.8); *brahmaćaryam̩* (1nom◦ sing◦ ←n◦ *brahmaćarya* 8.11); *ahimsā* (10.5); *ća* (1.1); *śārīram̩* (1nom◦ 4.21); *tapaḥ:* (1nom◦ 7.9); *ućyate* (2.25) (17.14)

(§3) *devadvijagurupr̄ajñapūjanam̩* (adj1◦-subj◦ the worship of gods, twice-borns, teachers and the wise); *śaućamārjavam̩* (adj2-3◦-subj◦ purity and straightforwardness); *brahmaćaryam̩* (adj4-subj◦ celibacy); *ahimsā* (adj5◦-subj◦ non-violence); *ća* (and); *śārīram̩* (adj6◦-subj◦ bodily); *tapaḥ:* (subj◦ austerity); *ućyate* (known as) (17.14)

(§4) devadvijagurupr̄ajñapūjanam̩ śaućamārjavam̩ brahmaćaryam̩ ća ahimsā ućyate śārīram̩ tapaḥ:

(§5) (i) The worship of gods, twice-borns, teachers and the wise; (ii) purity and straight-forwardness; (iii) celibacy and (iv) non-violence are known as bodily austerity. (17.14)

---

[811] elsewhere◦ परिचक्षते → is said to be, is considered to be, ...etc.

📖 परिचक्षते is not a Passive voice. It is *ātmanepadī* verb, but in Active voice (कर्तरि प्रयोग:). An ātmanepadī verb does not have to be in Passive voice (कर्मणि प्रयोग:).

17.15 अनुद्वेगकरं वाक्यं सत्यं प्रियहितं च यत् ।
स्वाध्यायाभ्यसनं चैव वाङ्मयं तप उच्यते ।।

anudvegakaraṁ vākyaṁ satyaṁ priyahitaṁ ća yaṭ,
svādhyāyābhyasanaṁ ćaiva vāṅgmayaṁ tapa ućyate. (17.15)

(§1) *anudvegakaraṃ* (r◦ 14/1) *vākyaṃ* (r◦ 14/1) *satyaṃ* (r◦ 14/1) *priyahitaṃ* (r◦ 14/1) *ća yaṭ* (r◦ 23/1) *svādhyāyābhyasanaṃ* (r◦ 14/1) *ća* (r◦ 3/1) *eva vāṅgmayaṃ* (r◦ 14/1) *tapaḥ:* (r◦ 19/4) *ućyate*

(§2) 🕮*anudvegakaraṃ* (n◦ 1nom◦ sing◦ ←n.tatpu◦ *anudvega-kara* ←adj◦ *udvega-kara*, उद्वेगम् करोति इति ←m◦ *udvega* 2.56 + adj◦ <u>*kara*</u> 2.2); 🕮*vākyaṃ* (1nom◦ 1.21); *satyaṃ* (1nom◦ 10.4); *priyahitaṃ* (n◦ 1nom◦ sing◦ ←dvandva◦ प्रियम् च हितम् च ←adj◦ *priya* 1.23 + deriv◦ adj◦ *hita* 5.25); *ća* (1.1); *yaṭ* (1.45); *svādhyāyābhyasanaṃ* (n◦ 1nom◦ sing◦ ←tatpu◦ *svādhyāyābhyasana*, स्वाध्यायस्य अभ्यसनम् ←m◦ *svādhyāya* 4.28 + n◦ *abhyasana* ←अभि√अस्); *ća* (1.1); *eva* (1.1); *vāṅgmayaṃ* (1nom◦ sing◦ ←n◦ *vāṅgmaya* ←f◦ *vāć* 2.42 + adj◦ *maya* 4.10); *tapaḥ:* (1nom◦ 7.9); *ućyate* (2.25) (17.15)

(§3) *anudvegakaraṃ* (adj1◦-subj◦ that does not cause agitation); *vākyaṃ* (subj◦ the speech, the language); *satyaṃ* (adj2◦-subj◦ that is true); *priyahitaṃ* (adj3-4◦-subj◦ pleasant and beneficial); *ća* (and); *yaṭ* (adj5◦-subj◦ that which); *svādhyāyābhyasanaṃ* (adj6◦-subj◦ the practice of study of the scriptures); *ća eva* (as well as); *vāṅgmayaṃ* (adj7◦-subj◦ of speech); *tapaḥ:* (subj◦ austerity); *ućyate* (is known as) (17.15)

(§4) vākyaṃ anudvegakaraṃ satyaṃ priyahitaṃ ća yaṭ ća eva svādhyāyābhyasanaṃ ućyate tapaḥ: vāṅgmayaṃ

(§5) The language (i) that does not cause agitation, (ii) that is true, pleasant and beneficial as well as (iii) that which (comes with) the practice of study of the scriptures, is known as austerity of speech. (17.15)

17.16 मन:प्रसाद: सौम्यत्वं मौनमात्मविनिग्रह: ।
भावसंशुद्धिरित्येतत्तपो मानसमुच्यते ।।
manaḥ:prasādaḥ: saumyatvaṁ maunamātmavinigrahaḥ:,
bhāvasam̃śuddhirityetattapo mānasamućyate. (17.16)

(§1) *manaḥ:prasādaḥ:* (r◦ 22/7) *saumyatvaṃ* (r◦ 14/1) *maunaṃ* (r◦ 8/17) *ātmavinigrahaḥ:* (r◦ 22/8) *bhāvasam̃śuddhiḥ:* (r◦ 16/1) *iti* (r◦ 4/4) *etaṭ* (r◦ 1/10) *tapaḥ:* (r◦ 15/9) *mānasaṃ* (r◦ 8/20) *ućyate*

(§2) *manaḥ:prasādaḥ:* (m◦ 1nom◦ sing◦ ←tatpu◦ *manaḥ:-prasāda*, मनस: प्रसाद: ←n◦ *manaṣ* 1.30 + m◦ *prasāda* 2.14); *saumyatvaṃ* (1nom◦ sing◦ ←n◦ *saumyatva* ←adj◦ *saumya* 11.50); *maunaṃ* (10.38); *ātmavinigrahaḥ:* (13.8); *bhāvasam̃śuddhiḥ:* (f◦ 1nom◦ sing◦ ←tatpu◦ *bhāva-sam̃śuddhi*, भावस्य संशुद्धि:

←m∘ *bhāva* 2.7 + f∘ *saṁśuddhiḥ:* 16.1); *iti* (1.25); *etaṭ* (1nom∘ 2.3); *tapaḥ:* (1nom∘ 7.9); *mānasaṃ* (1nom∘ sing∘ ←n∘ *mānasa* 1.47); *ućyate* (2.25) (17.16)

(§3) *manaḥ:prasādaḥ:* (adj1∘-subj∘ soothing, contentment, pleasure of mind); *saumyatvaṃ* (adj2∘-subj∘ mildness, gentleness); *maunaṃ* (adj3∘-subj∘ calmness); *ātmavinigrahaḥ:* (adj4∘-subj∘ self-control); *bhāvasaṁśuddhiḥ:* (adj5∘-subj∘ purity in thought); *iti* (thus); *etaṭ* (adj6∘-subj∘ this); *tapaḥ:* (subj∘ austerity); *mānasaṃ* (adj7∘-subj∘ mental); *ućyate* (is known as) (17.16)

(§4) manaḥ:prasādaḥ: saumyatvaṃ maunaṃ ātmavinigrahaḥ: bhāvasaṁśuddhiḥ: iti etaṭ ućyate mānasaṃ tapaḥ:

(§5) Contentment of mind, mildness, calmness, self-control (and) purity in thought, thus this is[812] known as mental austerity. (17.16)

17.17 श्रद्धया परया तप्तं तपस्तत्त्रिविधं नरैः ।
अफलाकाङ्क्षिभिर्युक्तैः सात्त्विकं परिचक्षते ।।
śraddhayā parayā taptaṁ tapastattrividhaṁ naraiḥ:,
aphalākāṅkṣibhiryuktaiḥ: sāttvikaṁ parićakṣate. (17.17)

(§1) *śraddhayā parayā taptaṃ* (r∘ 14/1) *tapaḥ:* (r∘ 18/1) *taṭ* (r∘ 1/10) *trividhaṃ* (r∘ 14/1) *naraiḥ:* (r∘ 22/8) *aphalākāṅkṣibhiḥ:* (r∘ 16/6) *yuktaiḥ:* (r∘ 22/7) *sāttvikaṃ* (r∘ 14/1) *parićakṣate*

(§2) *śraddhayā* (6.37); *parayā* (1.27); *taptaṃ* (n∘ 1nom∘ sing∘ ←ppp∘ adj∘ *tapta* ←√तप्); *tapaḥ:* (7.9); *taṭ* (1.10); *trividhaṃ* (16.21); *naraiḥ:* (3inst∘ plu∘ ←m∘ *nara* 1.5); *aphalākāṅkṣibhiḥ:* (17.11); *yuktaiḥ:* (m∘ 3inst∘ plu∘ ←adj∘ *yukta* 1.14); ***sāttvikaṃ*** (1nom∘ sing∘ ←adj∘ *sāttvika* 14.16); *parićakṣate* (17.13) (17.17)

(§3) *śraddhayā parayā* (with full faith); *taptaṃ* (adj1∘-obj∘ the penance that is observed); *tapaḥ:* (obj∘ the austerity); *taṭ* (adj2∘-obj∘ that); *trividhaṃ* (adj3∘-obj∘ threefold); *naraiḥ:* (subj∘ by people); *aphalākāṅkṣibhiḥ:* (by them who do not expect fruit from his duty); *yuktaiḥ:* (by those who are equipped with *buddhi yoga*); *sāttvikaṃ* (adj4∘-subj∘ *sāttvika*); *parićakṣate* (they regard it as) (17.17)

(§4) trividhaṃ taṭ taptaṃ śraddhayā parayā naraiḥ: aphalākāṅkṣibhiḥ: yuktaiḥ: parićakṣate sāttvikaṃ tapaḥ:

(§5) The threefold penance that is observed with full faith by people who do not expect fruit

[812] elsewhere∘ उच्यते → are called, these are, ...etc.

📖 उच्यते is not plural.

from his duty (and) by those who are equipped with *buddhi yoga,* they regard[813] it as *sāttvika* austerity. (17.17)

17.18 सत्कारमानपूजार्थं तपो दम्भेन चैव यत् ।
क्रियते तदिह प्रोक्तं राजसं चलमध्रुवम् ।।
satkāramānapūjārthaṁ tapo dambhena ćaiva yat̩,
kriyate tadiha proktaṁ rājasaṁ ćalamadhruvam̩. (17.18)

(§1) *satkāramānapūjārtham̩* (r∘ 14/1) *tapaḥ:* (r∘ 15/4) *dambhena ća* (r∘ 3/1) *eva yat̩* (r∘ 23/1) *kriyate tat̩* (r∘ 8/4) *iha proktam̩* (r∘ 14/1) *rājasam̩* (r∘ 14/1) *ćalam̩* (r∘ 8/16) *adhruvam̩* (r∘ 14/2)

(§2) *satkāramānapūjārtham̩* (adv∘ ←bahuvrī∘ *satkāra-māna-pūjārtha,* सत्कारस्य च मानस्य च पूजाया: अर्थ: यस्मिन् ←m∘ 🕮*satkāra* ←√अस् + m∘ *māna* 6.7 + f∘ 🕮*pūjā* 2.4 + m∘ *artha* 1.7); *tapaḥ:* (7.9); *dambhena* (16.17); *ća* (1.1); *eva* (1.1); *yat̩* (1nom∘ 2.67); <u>*kriyate*</u> (3rd-per∘ sing∘ pres∘ वर्तमान्-लट् ātmane∘ ←class8∘ √कृ); *tat̩* (1nom∘ 1.10); *iha* (2.5); *proktam̩* (1mon∘ 8.1); *rājasam̩* (1nom∘ 17.12); *ćalam̩* (1nom∘ 6.35); *adhruvam̩* (n∘ 1nom∘ sing∘ ←n.bahuvrī∘ *a-dhruva* ←adj∘ *dhruva* 2.27) (17.18)

(§3) *satkāramānapūjārtham̩* (adv∘ for earning name, fame and respect); *tapaḥ:* (subj∘ the austerity); *dambhena* (ostentatiously); *ća eva* (and); *yat̩* (adj1∘-subj∘ which); *kriyate* (is performed); *tat̩* (adj2∘-subj∘ that); *iha* (here, in this world); *proktam̩* (is called as); *rājasam̩* (adj3∘-subj∘ rājasic); *ćalam̩* (adj4∘-subj∘ unstable); *adhruvam̩* (adj4∘-subj∘ impermanent) (17.18)

(§4) ća eva tapaḥ: yat̩ kriyate dambhena satkāramānapūjārtham̩ tat̩ ćalam̩ adhruvam̩ proktam̩ rājasam̩ iha

(§5) And, the austerity which is performed ostentatiously for earning name, fame and respect, that unstable impermanent (austerity) is called as *rājasic* in[814] this world. (17.18)

17.19 मूढग्राहेणात्मनो यत्पीडया क्रियते तप: ।
परस्योत्सादनार्थं वा तत्तामसमुदाहृतम् ।।
mūḍhagrāheṇātmano yatpīḍayā kriyate tapaḥ:,
parasyotsādanārthaṁ vā tattāmasamudahṛtam̩. (17.19)

---

[813] elsewhere∘ परिचक्षते → is said to be, is considered to be, ...etc.

🕮 Please see footnote in verse 17.13

[814] elsewhere∘ इह → belonging to this world.

🕮 इह is not an adjective.

(§1) *mūḍhagrāheṇa* (r◦ 24/1, 1/2) *ātmanaḥ:* (r◦ 15/10) *yaṭ* (r◦ 10/6) *pīḍayā kriyate tapaḥ:* (r◦ 22/8) *parasya* (r◦ 2/2) *utsādanārthaṃ* (r◦ 14/1) *vā taṭ* (r◦ 1/10) *tāmasaṃ* (r◦ 8/20) *udāhṛtaṃ* (r◦ 14/2)

(§2) *mūḍhagrāheṇa* (m◦ 3inst◦ sing◦ ←tatpu◦ *mūḍha-grāha,* मूढः ग्राहः ←adj◦ *mūḍha* 7.15 + m◦ *grāha* 16.10); *ātmanaḥ:* (4.42); *yaṭ* (1nom◦ 1.45); *pīḍayā* (3inst◦ sing◦ ←f◦ *pīḍā* ←√पीड्); *kriyate* (17.18); *tapaḥ:* (1nom◦ 7.9); *parasya* (6pos sing◦ ←adj◦ *para* 2.3); *utsādanārthaṃ* (n◦ 1nom◦ sing◦ ←tatpu◦ *utsādanārtha,* उत्सादनस्य अर्थः यस्मिन् ←n◦ 🕮*utsādana* ←उद्√सद् + m◦ *artha* 1.7); *vā* (1.32); *taṭ* (1nom◦ 1.10); *tāmasaṃ* (17.13); *udāhṛtaṃ* (13.7) (17.19)

(§3) *mūḍhagrāheṇa* (adv◦ with a delusion); *ātmanaḥ:* (of oneself, to oneself, oneself); *yaṭ* (adj1◦-subj◦ which); *pīḍayā* (for torturing); *kriyate* (is performed); *tapaḥ:* (subj◦ the austerity); *parasya utsādanārthaṃ* (for the destruction of others); *vā* (or); *taṭ* (adj2◦-subj◦ that); *tāmasaṃ* (adj3◦-subj◦ tāmasic); *udāhṛtaṃ* (is known as) (17.19)

(§4) tapaḥ: yaṭ kriyate mūḍhagrāheṇa pīḍayā ātmanaḥ: vā parasya utsādanārthaṃ taṭ udāhṛtaṃ tāmasaṃ

(§5) The austerity which is performed with a delusion for torturing oneself[815] or for the destruction of others, that (austerity) is known as *tāmasic.* (17.19)

17.20 दातव्यमिति यद्दानं दीयतेऽनुपकारिणे ।
देशे काले च पात्रे च तद्दानं सात्त्विकं स्मृतम् ।।
dātavyamiti yaddānaṃ dīyate'nupakāriṇe,
deśe kāle ća pātre ća taddānaṃ sāttvikaṃ smṛtaṃ. (17.20)

(§1) *dātavyaṃ* (r◦ 8/18) *iti yaṭ* (r◦ 9/5) *dānaṃ* (r◦ 14/1) *dīyate* (r◦ 6/1) *anupakāriṇe* (r◦ 24/9) *deśe kāle ća pātre ća taṭ* (r◦ 9/5) *dānaṃ* (r◦ 14/1) *sāttvikaṃ* (r◦ 14/1) *smṛtaṃ* (r◦ 14/2)

(§2) *dātavyaṃ* (n◦ 1nom◦ sing◦ ←pot◦ adj◦ *dātavya* ←√दा); *iti* (1.25); *yaṭ* (1.45); *dānaṃ* (10.5); *dīyate* (3rd-per◦ sing◦ pres◦ वर्तमान्–लट् ātmane◦ ←class1◦ √दा); *anupakāriṇe* (m◦ 4dat◦ sing◦ n.tatpu◦ ←adj◦ *upakāriṇ* ←उप√कृ); 🕮*deśe* (6.11); 🕮*kāle* (8.23); *ća* (1.1); *pātre* (4dat◦ sing◦ ←n◦ 🕮*pātra* ←√पा); *ća* (1.1); *taṭ* (1.10); *dānaṃ* (1nom◦ 10.5); *sāttvikaṃ* (1nom◦ 17.17); *smṛtaṃ* (n◦ 1nom◦ sing◦ ←adj◦ *smṛta* 6.19) (

---

[815] elsewhere◦ आत्मनः पीडया → with torture of the self, torturing the self, ...etc.

🕮 As said in the footnote of verse 14.21, remember, the *ātmā* is अविनशी, अछेद्यः, अक्षरः, अव्ययः, अजरः, अमरः, शाश्वतः । One can not torture or hurt of destroy *ātmā* or the self. One can do torturing of oneself. Also, for the same reason, one can cause others (परस्य) destruction, but not destruction of others self or others selves.

17.20

(§3) *dātavyam̩* (adj1◦-subj◦ which is ought to be given); *iti* (such); *yat̩* (adj1◦-subj◦ which); *dānam̩* (subj◦ the charity); *dīyate* (is given); *anupakāriṇe* (to one who has not done you any favour, to one whom you do not owe any favour); *deśe* (at a place); *kāle* (at a time); *ća* (and); *pātre* (at right person); *ća* (and); *tat̩* (adj2◦-subj◦ that); *dānam̩* (subj◦ charity); *sāttvikam̩* (adj3◦-subj◦ sāttvic); *smṛtam̩* (is known as) **(17.20)**

(§4) dānam̩ yat̩ dātavyam̩ iti ća dīyate pātre kāle ća deśe anupakāriṇe tat̩ dānam̩ smṛtam̩ sāttvikam̩

(§5) The charity which is ought to be given and is given at right time, place and person,[816] to one whom you do not owe any favour, that charity is known as a *sāttvic* (charity). **(17.20)**

17.21 यत्तु प्रत्युपकारार्थं फलमुद्दिश्य वा पुनः ।
दीयते च परिक्लिष्टं तद्दानं राजसं स्मृतम् ।।

yattu pratyupakārārthaṁ phalamuddiśya vā punaḥ:,
dīyate ća parikliṣṭaṁ taddānaṁ rājasaṁ smṛtam̩. **(17.21)**

(§1) *yat̩* (r◦ 1/10) *tu pratyupakārārtham̩* (r◦ 14/1) *phalam̩* (r◦ 8/20) *uddiśya vā punaḥ:* (r◦ 22/8) *dīyate ća parikliṣṭam̩* (r◦ 14/1) *tat̩* (r◦ 9/5) *dānam̩* (r◦ 14/1) *rājasam̩* (r◦ 14/1) *smṛtam̩* (r◦ 14/2)

(§2) *yat̩* (1nom◦ 1.45); *tu* (1.2); *pratyupakārārtham̩* (n◦ 1nom◦ sing◦ ←bahuvrī◦ *pratyupakārārtha*, प्रत्युपकारस्य अर्थः यस्मिन् ←m◦ *pratyupakāra* ←प्रति–उप√कृ + m◦ *artha* 1.7); *phalam̩* (2.51); *uddiśya* (lyp◦ past-participle ind◦ ←उद्√दिश्); *vā* (1.32); *punaḥ:* (4.35); *dīyate* (17.20); *ća* (1.1); *parikliṣṭam̩* (n◦ 1nom◦ sing◦ ←ppp◦ adj◦ *parikliṣṭa* ←परि√क्लिश्); *tat̩* (1.10); *dānam̩* (1nom◦ 10.5); *rājasam̩* (1nom◦ 17.12); *smṛtam̩* (17.20) **(17.21)**

(§3) *yat̩* (adj1◦-subj◦ which); *tu* (however); *pratyupakārārtham̩* (adv◦ for returning a favour); *phalam̩ uddiśya* (expecting a fruit thereof); *vā* (or); *punaḥ:* (and, again); *dīyate* (is given); *ća* (and); 🕮*parikliṣṭam̩* (adv◦ unwillingly, reluctantly); *tat̩* (adj2◦-subj◦ that); *dānam̩* (subj◦ the charity); *rājasam̩* (adj3◦-subj◦ rājasic); *smṛtam̩* (is known as) **(17.21)**

(§4) tu dānam̩ yat̩ dīyate pratyupakārārtham̩ punaḥ: vā phalam̩ uddiśya ća parikliṣṭam̩ tat̩ smṛtam̩ rājasam̩

(§5) However, The charity which is given for returning a favour and or expecting a fruit thereof and reluctantly, that (charity) is known as *rājasic*. **(17.21)**

---

[816] elsewhere◦ दीयतेऽनुपकारिणे देशे काले च → without expecting anything in return at right time and place, to one who will do no service in return, in a fit place and time,, ...etc.

17.22 अदेशकाले यद्दानमपात्रेभ्यश्च दीयते ।
असत्कृतमवज्ञातं तत्तामसमुदाहृतम् ।।

adeśakāle yaddānamapātrebhyaśća dīyate,
asatkṛtamavajñātaṁ tattāmasamudāhṛtam̩. (17.22)

(§1) *adeśakāle yat̩* (r◦ 9/5) *dānam̩* (r◦ 8/16) *apātrebhyaḥ:* (r◦ 17/1) *ća dīyate* (r◦ 23/1) *asatkṛtam̩* (r◦ 8/16) *avajñātam̩* (r◦ 14/1) *tat̩* (r◦ 1/10) *tāmasam̩* (r◦ 8/20) *udāhṛtam̩* (r◦ 14/2)

(§2) *adeśakāle* (m◦ 7loc◦ sing◦ ←dvandva◦ अदेशे च अकाले च ←m◦ *deśa* 6.11 + m◦ *kāla* 2.72); *yat̩* (1.45); *dānam̩* (1nom◦ 10.5); *apātrebhyaḥ:* (4dat◦ plu◦ ←n.tatpu◦ *apātra* ←n◦ *pātra* 17.20); *ća* (1.1); *dīyate* (17.20); *asatkṛtam̩* (adv◦ ←adj◦ *satkṛt̩* 11.42); *avajñātam̩* (adv◦ ←ppp◦ adj◦ *avajñāta* ←f◦ *avajñā* ←अव√ज्ञा); *tat̩* (1nom◦ 1.10); *tāmasam̩* (1nom◦ 17.13); *udāhṛtam̩* (13.7) (17.22)

(§3) *adeśakāle* (at wrong time and at wrong place); *yat̩* (adj1◦-subj◦ which); *dānam̩* (subj◦ the charity); *apātrebhyaḥ:* (to an unfit person, to an unworthy person); *ća* (and); *dīyate* (is given); *asatkṛtam̩* (adv◦ disrespectfully); *avajñātam̩* (adv◦ with contempt); *tat̩* (adj2◦-subj◦ that); *tāmasam̩* (adj1◦-subj◦ tāmasic); *udāhṛtam̩* (is known as) (17.22)

(§4) dānam̩ yat̩ dīyate apātrebhyaḥ: adeśakāle asatkṛtam̩ ća avajñātam̩ tat̩ udāhṛtam̩ tāmasam̩

(§5) The charity which is given to an unworthy person at wrong time and at wrong place, disrespectfully and with contempt, that (charity) is known as *tāmasic.* (17.22)

17.23 ॐ तत्सदिति निर्देशो ब्रह्मणस्त्रिविधः स्मृतः ।
ब्राह्मणास्तेन वेदाश्च यज्ञाश्च विहिताः पुरा ।।

oṁ tatsaditi nirdeśo brahmaṇastrividhaḥ: smṛtaḥ:,
brāhmaṇāstena vedāśća yajñāśća vihitāḥ: purā. (17.23)

(§1) *om̩ tat̩* (r◦ 10/7) *sat̩* (r◦ 8/4) *iti nirdeśaḥ:* (r◦ 15/7) *brahmaṇaḥ:* (r◦ 18/1) *trividhaḥ:* (r◦ 22/7) *smṛtaḥ:* (r◦ 22/8) *brāhmaṇāḥ:* (r◦ 24/5, 18/1) *tena vedāḥ:* (r◦ 17/1) *ća yajñāḥ:* (r◦ 17/1) *ća vihitāḥ:* (r◦ 22/3) *purā*

(§2) *om̩* (8.13); *tat* (1.10); *sat̩* (2.16); *iti* (1.25); 📖*nirdeśaḥ:* (1nom◦ sing◦ ←m◦ *nirdeśa* ←निर्√दिश्); *brahmaṇaḥ:* (4.32); *trividhaḥ:* (17.7); *smṛtaḥ:* (m◦ 1nom◦ sing◦ ←adj◦ *smṛta* 6.19); *brāhmaṇāḥ:* (9.33); *tena* (3.38); *vedāḥ:* (2.45); *ća* (1.1); *yajñāḥ:* (4.32); *ća* (1.1); *vihitāḥ:* (1nom◦ plu◦ ←adj◦ *vihita* 7.22); *purā* (3.3) (17.23)

(§3) *om̩* (om); *tat* (tat); *sat̩* (sat); *iti* (thus); *nirdeśaḥ:* (subj1◦ designation); *brahmaṇaḥ:* (of *brahma*); *trividhaḥ:* (adj1◦-subj1◦ the threefold); *smṛtaḥ:* (adj2◦-subj1◦ the one that is known as); *brāhmaṇāḥ:*

(subj2∘ the brāhmaṇas); *tena* (with that); *vedāḥ:* (subj3∘ the vedas); *ća* (and); *yajñāḥ:* (subj4∘ the yajñas); *ća* (and); *vihitāḥ:* (adj1∘-subj2-4∘ ordained); *purā* (adv∘ anciently, in olden times) (17.23)

(§4)   oṃ tat saṭ iti smṛtaḥ: trividhaḥ: nirdeśaḥ: brahmaṇaḥ: brāhmaṇāḥ: ća vedāḥ: ća yajñāḥ: purā vihitāḥ: tena

(§5)   "om-taṭ-saṭ" is known as the threefold designation of *brahma*. The *brāhmaṇas*, and the *vedas* and the *yajñas* (are) anciently ordained with that designation. (17.23)

17.24   तस्मादोमित्युदाहृत्य यज्ञदानतप:क्रिया: ।
प्रवर्तन्ते विधानोक्ता: सततं ब्रह्मवादिनाम् ॥

tasmādomityudāhṛtya yajñadānatapaḥ:kriyāḥ:,
pravartante vidhānoktāḥ: satataṃ brahmavādinām. (17.24)

(§1) *tasmāṭ* (r∘ 8/10) *oṃ* (r∘ 8/18) *iti* (r∘ 4/3) *udāhṛtya yajñadānatapaḥ:kriyāḥ:* (r∘ 22/8) *pravartante vidhānoktāḥ:* (r∘ 22/7) *satataṃ* (r∘ 14/1) *brahmavādinām* (r∘ 14/2)

(§2) *tasmāṭ* (1.37); *oṃ* (8.13); *iti* (1.25); *udāhṛtya* (lyp∘ past-participle ind∘ ←उद्-आ√ह); *yajñadānatapaḥ:kriyāḥ:* (f∘ 1nom∘ plu∘ ←tatpu∘ *yajña-dāna-tapaḥ:-kriyā*, यज्ञस्य च दानस्य च तपस: च क्रिया ←m∘ *yajña* 3.9 + n∘ *dāna* 8.28 + n∘ *tapas* 4.10 + f∘ *kriyā* 1.42); *pravartante* (16.10); *vidhānoktāḥ:* (1nom∘ plu∘ ←tatpu∘ *vidhānokta*, विधानेन उक्त: ←n∘ *vidhāna* 16.24 + ppp∘ adj∘ *ukta* 1.24); ▣*satataṃ* (3.19); *brahmavādinām* (m∘ 6pos∘ plu∘ ←tatpu∘ *brahmavādin*, ब्रह्मण: वादी ←n∘ *brahman* 2.72 + m∘ *vādin* 2.42) (17.24)

(§3) *tasmāṭ* (therefore); *oṃ* (om); *iti* (thus); *udāhṛtya* (uttering); *yajñadānatapaḥ:kriyāḥ:* (subj1-3∘ the acts of *yajña*, charity and austerity); *pravartante* (commence); *vidhānoktāḥ:* (adj1∘-subj1-3∘ prescribed by the scriptures); *satataṃ* (adv∘ always); *brahmavādinām* (of the knowers of the *brahma*) (17.24)

(§4)   brahmavādinām tasmāṭ yajñadānatapaḥ:kriyāḥ: vidhānoktāḥ: satataṃ pravartante udāhṛtya oṃ iti

(§5)   Of the knowers of the *brahma*, therefore, the acts of *yajña*, charity and austerity, prescribed[817] by the scriptures, always commence uttering *om*. (17.24)

17.25   तदित्यनभिसन्धाय फलं यज्ञतप:क्रिया: ।
दानक्रियाश्च विविधा: क्रियन्ते मोक्षकाङ्क्षिभि: ॥

tadityanabhisandhāya phalam yajñatapaḥ:kriyāḥ:,

---

[817] elsewhere∘ विधानोक्ता: → as prescribed.

📖 Remember, विधानोक्ता: is the adjective of यज्ञदानतप:क्रिया: । It not the adverb of प्रवर्तन्ते ।

dānakriyāśća vividhāḥ: kriyante mokṣakāṅkṣibhiḥ:. (17.25)

(§1) *taṭ* (r◦ 8/4) *iti* (r◦ 4/1) *anabhisandhāya phalaṃ* (r◦ 14/1) *yajñatapaḥ:kriyāḥ:* (r◦ 22/8) *dānakriyāḥ:* (r◦ 17/1) *ća vividhāḥ:* (r◦ 22/1) *kriyante mokṣakāṅkṣibhiḥ:* (r◦ 22/8)

(§2) *taṭ* (1.10); *iti* (1.25); *anabhisandhāya* (n.tatpu◦ ←lyp◦ past-participle ind◦ ←ind◦ *aṇ* 3.36 + अभि-सम्√धा); *phalaṃ* (2.51); *yajñatapaḥ:kriyāḥ:* (f◦ 1nom◦ plu◦ ←tatpu◦ *yajña-tapaḥ:-kriyā*, यज्ञस्य च तपसः च क्रिया ←m◦ *yajña* 3.9 + n◦ *tapaṣ* 4.10 + f◦ *kriyā* 1.42); *dānakriyāḥ:* (f◦ 1nom◦ plu◦ ←tatpu◦ *dāna-kriyā*, दानस्य क्रिया ←n◦ *dāna* 8.28 + f◦ *kriyā* 1.42); *ća* (1.1); *vividhāḥ:* (f◦ 1nom◦ plu◦ ←adj◦ *vividha* 13.5); *kriyante* (3rd-per◦ plu◦ pres◦ वर्तमान्-लट् ātmane◦ ←class8◦ √कृ 17.18); *mokṣakāṅkṣibhiḥ:* (m◦ 3inst◦ plu◦ ←tatpu◦ *mokṣa-kāṅkṣiṇ*, मोक्षस्य कांक्षी ←m◦ *mokṣa* 5.28 + m◦ *kāṅkṣiṇ* ←√कांक्ष्) (17.25)

(§3) *taṭ* (taṭ); *iti* (thus); *anabhisandhāya* (without expecting); *phalaṃ* (obj◦ the fruit); *yajñatapaḥ:kriyāḥ:* (subj1-2◦ the acts of *yajña* and austerity); *dānakriyāḥ:* (subj3◦ charity); *ća* (and); *vividhāḥ:* (adj◦-subj1-3◦ the various); *kriyante* (are performed); *mokṣakāṅkṣibhiḥ:* (by those who desire freedom from the cycle of rebirth) (17.25)

(§4) vividhāḥ: yajñatapaḥ:kriyāḥ: ća dānakriyāḥ: anabhisandhāya phalaṃ mokṣakāṅkṣibhiḥ: iti taṭ.

(§5) The various acts of *yajña* and austerity and charity are performed, without expecting the fruit, by those who desire freedom from the cycle of rebirth, (by uttering the word) *taṭ*. (17.25)

17.26 सद्भावे साधुभावे च सदित्येतत्प्रयुज्यते ।
प्रशस्ते कर्मणि तथा सच्छब्दः पार्थ युज्यते ।।
sadbhāve sādhubhāve ća sadityetatprayujyate,
praśaste karmaṇi tathā saććhabdaḥ: pārtha yujyate. (17.26)

(§1) *sadbhāve sādhubhāve ća saṭ* (r◦ 8/4) *iti* (r◦ 4/4) *etaṭ* (r◦ 10/6) *prayujyate praśaste karmaṇi* (r◦ 24/7) *tathā saṭ* (r◦ 11/4) *śabdaḥ:* (r◦ 22/3) *pārtha yujyate*

(§2) *sadbhāve* (m◦ 7loc◦ sing◦ ←tatpu◦ *sadbhāva*, सतः भावः ←adj◦ *saṭ* 2.16 + m◦ *bhāva* 2.7); *sādhubhāve* (m◦ 7loc◦ sing◦ ←tatpu◦ *sādhu-bhāva*, साधोः भावः ←m◦ *sādhu* 4.8 + m◦ *bhāva* 2.7); *ća* (1.1); *saṭ* (1nom◦ 2.16); *iti* (1.25); *etaṭ* (1nom◦ 2.3); *prayujyate* (3rd-per◦ sing◦ pres◦ वर्तमान्-लट् ātmane◦ ←class7◦ प्र√युज् 10.7); *praśaste* (7loc◦ sing◦ ←ppp◦ adj◦ 🕮*praśasta* ←प्र√शंस्); *karmaṇi* (2.47); *tathā* (1.8); *saṭ* (1nom◦ 2.16); *śabdaḥ:* (1.13); *pārtha* (1.25); *yujyate* (10.7) (17.26)

(§3) *sadbhāve* (in the meaning of righteousness); *sādhubhāve* (in the meaning of goodness); *ća* (and); *saṭ iti* (*saṭ*); *etaṭ* (adj◦-subj◦ this); *prayujyate* (is used); *praśaste* (in the laudable); *karmaṇi* (in acts); *tathā* (also); *saṭ śabdaḥ:* (subj◦ the word *saṭ*); *pārtha* (O Arjuna!); *yujyate* (is used) (17.26)

(§4) pārtha sadbhāve ća sādhubhāve iti saṭ prayujyate tathā praśaste karmaṇi saṭ etaṭ śabdaḥ: saṭ yujyate

(§5) O Arjuna! in the meaning of righteousness and in the meaning of goodness *saṭ* is used; also in the laudable acts this word *saṭ* is used. (17.26)

17.27 यज्ञे तपसि दाने च स्थितिः सदिति चोच्यते ।
कर्म चैव तदर्थीयं सदित्येवाभिधीयते ।।

yajñe tapasi dāne ća sthitiḥ: saditi oćyate,
karma ćaiva tadarthiyaṁ sadityevābhidhīyate. (17.27)

(§1) *yajñe tapasi dāne ća sthitiḥ:* (r∘ 22/7) *saṭ* (r∘ 8/4) *iti ća* (r∘ 2/2) *ućyate karma ća* (r∘ 3/1) *eva tadarthiyaṃ* (r∘ 14/1) *saṭ* (r∘ 8/4) *iti* (r∘ 4/4) *eva* (r∘ 1/1) *abhidhīyate*

(§2) *yajñe* (3.15); *tapasi* (7loc∘ sing∘ ←n∘ *tapaṣ* (4.10); *dāne* (7loc∘ sing∘ ←n∘ *dāna* 8.28); *ća* (1.1); *sthitiḥ:* (2.72); *saṭ* (2.16); *iti* (1.25); *ća* (1.1); *ućyate* (2.25); *karma* (2.49); *ća* (1.1); *eva* (1.1); *tadarthiyaṃ* (n∘ 1nom∘ sing∘ ←bahuvrī∘ *tadarthiya,* सः यस्य अर्थः यस्मिन् ←pron∘ *taṭ* 1.10 + m∘ *artha* 1.7); *saṭ* (2.16); *iti* (1.25); *eva* (1.1); *abhidhīyate* (13.2) (17.27)

(§3) *yajñe* (in *yajña*); *tapasi* (in austerity); *dāne* (in charity); *ća* (and); *sthitiḥ:* (subj1∘ the steady state); *saṭ iti* (sat); *ća* (and); *ućyate* (is called); *karma* (subj2∘ the act, deed); *ća eva* (also); *tadarthiyaṃ* (adj∘-subj2∘ related to it); *saṭ iti* (*sat*); *eva* (also); *abhidhīyate* (is known as)

(§4) sthitiḥ: yajñe ća tapasi ća dāne ućyate saṭ iti ća eva karma tadarthiyaṃ abhidhīyate eva saṭ iti

(§5) The steady state in *yajña,* and in austerity and in charity is called *saṭ;* also the deed related to it is also known as *saṭ.* (17.27)

17.28 अश्रद्धया हुतं दत्तं तपस्तप्तं कृतं च यत् ।
असदित्युच्यते पार्थ न च तत्प्रेत्य नो इह ।।

aśraddhayā hutaṁ dattaṁ tapastaptaṁ kṛtaṁ ća yaṭ,
asadityućyate pārtha na ća tatpretya no iha. (17.28)

(§1) *aśraddhayā hutaṃ* (r∘ 14/1) *dattaṃ* (r∘ 14/1) *tapaḥ:* (r∘ 18/1) *taptaṃ* (r∘ 14/1) *kṛtaṃ* (r∘ 14/1) *ća yaṭ* (r∘ 23/1) *asaṭ* (r∘ 8/4) *iti* (r∘ 4/3) *ućyate pārtha na ća taṭ* (r∘ 10/6) *pretya no iha*

(§2) *a-śraddhayā* (n.tatpu∘ ←adj∘ *śraddhayā* 6.37); *hutaṃ* (1nom∘ 4.24); *dattaṃ* (1nom∘ sing∘ ←adj∘ *datta* 3.12); *tapaḥ:* (1nom∘ 7.9); *taptaṃ* (1nom∘ 17.17); *kṛtaṃ* (1nom∘ 4.15); *ća* (1.1); *yaṭ* (1nom∘ 2.67); *asaṭ* (1nom∘ 9.19); *iti* (1.25); *ućyate* (2.25); *pārtha* (1.25); *na* (1.30); *ća* (1.1); *taṭ* (1nom∘ 1.10); *pretya* (lyp∘ past-participle ind∘ ←प्र√इ); *naḥ* (Dat∘ *asmaḍ*); *iha* (2.5) (17.28)

(§3) *a-śraddhayā* (without faith); *hutam̩* (subj1◦ oblation offered); *dattam̩* (subj2◦ charity given); *tapaḥ: taptam̩* (subj3◦ austerity performed); *kr̥tam̩* (subj4◦ act done); *ća* (and); *yat̩* (adj1◦-subj1◦ which, whatever); *asat̩* (subj5◦ *asat̩*); *iti* (thus); *ućyate* (is called as); *pārtha* (O Arjuna!); *na ća* (is not); *tat̩* (adj1◦-subj1-4◦ that); *pretya* (adj2◦-subj1-4◦ hereafter, after death); *naḥ* (for us); *iha* (in this world) (17.28)

(§4) a-śraddhayā yat̩ hutam̩ dattam̩ tapaḥ: taptam̩ ća kr̥tam̩ ućyate asat̩. pārtha tat̩ na naḥ iha ća pretya.

(§5) Without faith, whatever oblation (is) offered, charity given, austerity performed and act done, it is called as *asat̩*. O Arjuna! that is not (good) for us in this world and hereafter. (17.28)

इति श्रीमद्भगवद्गीतासूपनिषत्सु ब्रह्मविद्यायां योगशास्त्रे
श्रीकृष्णार्जुनसंवादे श्रद्धात्रयविभागयोगो नाम सप्तदशोऽध्याय: ।

iti śrīmadbhagavadgītāsūpaniṣatsu brahmavidyāyām̐ yogaśāstre
śrīkr̥ṣṇārjunasam̐vāde śraddhātrayavibhāgayogo nāma saptadaśo'dhyāyaḥ:

(§1) *iti śrīmadbhagavadgītāsu* (r◦ 1/8) *upaniṣatsu brahmavidyāyām̩* (r◦ 14/1) *yogaśāstre śrīkr̥ṣṇārjunasam̐vāde śraddhātrayavibhāgayogaḥ:* (r◦ 15/6) *nāma saptadaśaḥ:* (r◦ 15/1) *adhyāyaḥ:* (r◦ 22/8)

(§2) *iti* (1.25); *śrīmadbhagavadgītāsu* (1.1); *upaniṣatsu* (1.1); *brahmavidyāyām̩* (1.1); *yogaśāstre* (1.1); *śrīkr̥ṣṇārjunasam̐vāde* (1.1); *śraddhātrayavibhāgayogaḥ:* (m◦ 1nom◦ sing◦ ←tatpu◦ *śraddhā-traya-vibhāga-yoga,* श्रद्धानाम् त्रयस्य विभागस्य योग: ←f◦ *śraddhā* 3.31 + n◦ *traya* 11.20 + m◦ *vibhāga* 3.28 + m◦ *yoga* 2.39). *nāma* (1.1); *saptadaśaḥ:* (m◦ 1nom◦ sing◦ ←sequence indicating num◦ adj◦ *sapta-daśa* ←adj◦ *sapta* 10.6 + adj◦ *daśa* 13.6); *adhyāyaḥ:* (1.1)

(§3) *iti* (thus); *śrīmadbhagavadgītāsu upaniṣatsu* (among the upaniṣads of Śrīmad-Bhagavadgītā); *brahmavidyāyām̩* (of the eternal wisdoms); *yogaśāstre* (in the science of Yoga); *śrī-kr̥ṣṇārjuna-sam̐vāde* (in the dialogue between Śrī Kr̥ṣṇa and Arjuna); *śraddhātrayavibhāgayogaḥ:* (subj◦ the yoga pertaining to the three forms of faith). *nāma* (called) *saptaḍaśaḥ:* (adj◦-subj◦ the seventeenth); *adhyāyaḥ:* (subj◦ discourse)

(§4) śrīmadbhagavadgītāsu upaniṣatsu yogaśāstre śraddhātrayavibhāgayogaḥ: iti saptaḍaśaḥ: adhyāyaḥ: nāma guṇatrayavibhāgayogaḥ: śrīkr̥ṣṇārjunasam̐vāde

(§5) Among the upaniṣads of the Śrīmad-Bhagavadgītā, in the science of Yoga of self realization, thus (is) the seventeenth discourse pertaining to the three forms of faith, in the dialogue between Śrī Kr̥ṣṇa and Arjuna.

CHAPTER 18

aṣṭādaśo'dhyāyaḥ:
अष्टादशोऽध्यायः ।

THE YOGA PERTAINING TO "THE RENUNCIATION AND LIBERATION"

mokṣasannyāsayogaḥ:
मोक्षसंन्यासयोगः ।

Arjuna said (arjuna uvāća अर्जुन उवाच ।)

18.1 संन्यासस्य महाबाहो तत्त्वमिच्छामि वेदितुम् ।
त्यागस्य च हृषीकेश पृथक्केशिनिषूदन ।।

sannyāsasya mahābāho tattvamiććhāmi veditum,
tyāgasya ća hṛṣīkeśa pṛthakkeśiniṣūdana. (18.1)

(§1) *aṣṭādaśaḥ:* (r◦ 15/1) *adhyāyaḥ:* (r◦ 22/8). *mokṣasannyāsayogaḥ:* (r◦ 22/8). *arjunaḥ:* (r◦ 19/4) *uvāća. sannyāsasya mahābāho tattvam* (r◦ 8/18) *iććhāmi veditum* (r◦ 14/2) *tyāgasya ća hṛṣīkeśa pṛthak* (r◦ 1/9) *keśiniṣūdana*

(§2) *aṣṭādaśaḥ:* (m◦ 1nom◦ sing◦ ←sequence indicating num◦ adj◦ *aṣṭādaśa* ←num◦ adj◦ *aṣṭan* 7.4 + num◦ adj◦ *daśa* 13.6); *adhyāyaḥ:* (1nom◦ sing◦ ←m◦ *adhyāya* ←अधि√इ). *mokṣasannyāsayogaḥ:* (m◦ 1nom◦ sing◦ ←tatpu◦ *mokṣa-sannyāsa-yoga,* मोक्षस्य च संन्यासस्य च योगः ←m◦ *mokṣa* 5.28 + m◦ *sannyāsa* 5.1 + m◦ *yoga* 2.39). *arjunaḥ:* (1.28); *uvāća* (1.25). *sannyāsasya* (6pos sing◦ ←m◦ *sannyāsa* 5.1); *mahābāho* (2.26); *tattvam* (2acc◦ sing◦ ←n◦ *tattva* 2.16); *iććhāmi* (1.35); <u>*veditum*</u> (inf◦ ind◦ ←√विद्); *tyāgasya* (6pos sing◦ ←m◦ *tyāga* 12.11); *ća* (1.1); *hṛṣīkeśa* (11.36); 🕮*pṛthak* (1.18); *keśiniṣūdana* (m◦ 8voc◦ sing◦ ←bahuvrī◦ *keśi-niṣūdana,* केशिनः निषूदनः ←m◦ prop◦ *keśin* + n◦ *niṣūdana* ←नि√सूद्) (18.1)

(§3) *aṣṭādaśaḥ:* (adj1◦-subj◦ eighteenth); *adhyāyaḥ:* (subj◦ chapter). *mokṣasannyāsayogaḥ:* (subj1◦ the *yoga* of renunciation and liberation). *arjunaḥ:* (subj◦ Arjuna); *uvāća* (said). *sannyāsasya* (of the rununciation of authorship of karma); *mahābāho* (O Śrī Kṛṣṇa!); *tattvam* (obj1◦ the principle); *iććhāmi* (I wish); *veditum* (to know); *tyāgasya* (of the renunciation); *ća* (and); *hṛṣīkeśa* (O Śrī Kṛṣṇa!); *pṛthak* (separately); *keśiniṣūdana* (O Śrī Kṛṣṇa!) (18.1)

(§4) aṣṭādaśaḥ: adhyāyaḥ: mokṣasannyāsayogaḥ: arjunaḥ: uvāća mahābāho iććhāmi veditum pṛthak tattvam sannyāsasya ća hṛṣīkeśa tyāgasya keśiniṣūdana

(§5) Eighteenth chapter. The *yoga* of renunciation and liberation. Arjuna said :

O Śrī Kṛṣṇa! I wish to know separately the principle of the rununciation of authorship of *karma* and, O Śrī Kṛṣṇa! of the renunciation of *karma*, O Śrī Kṛṣṇa!
(18.1)

The Lord said (śrībhagavānuvāća श्रीभगवानुवाच ।)

18.2 काम्यानां कर्मणां न्यासं संन्यासं कवयो विदुः ।
सर्वकर्मफलत्यागं प्राहुस्त्यागं विचक्षणाः ।।
kāmyānāṁ karmaṇāṁ nyāsaṁ sannyāsaṁ kavayo viduḥ:,
sarvakarmaphalatyāgaṁ prāhustyāgaṁ vićakṣaṇāḥ:. **(18.2)**

(§1) *śrībhagavān̩* (r◦ 8/14) *uvāća. kāmyānām̩* (r◦ 14/1) *karmaṇām̩* (r◦ 14/1) *nyāsam̩* (r◦ 14/1) *sannyāsam̩* (r◦ 14/1) *kavayaḥ:* (r◦ 15/13) *viduḥ:* (r◦ 22/8) *sarvakarmaphalatyāgam̩* (r◦ 14/1) *prāhuḥ:* (r◦ 18/1) *tyāgam̩* (r◦ 14/1) *vićakṣaṇāḥ:* (r◦ 24/5, 22/8)

(§2) *śrībhagavān̩* (2.2); *uvāća* (1.25). *kāmyānām̩* (n◦ 6pos◦ plu◦ ←pot◦ adj◦ *kāmya* 10.1); *karmaṇām̩* (3.4); *nyāsam̩* (2acc◦ sing◦ ←m◦ *nyāsa* ←नि√अस्); *sannyāsam̩* (5.1); *kavayaḥ:* (4.16); *viduḥ:* (4.2); *sarvakarmaphalatyāgam̩* (12.11); *prāhuḥ:* (6.2); *tyāgam̩* (2acc◦ sing◦ ←m◦ *tyāga* 12.11); *vićakṣaṇāḥ:* (m◦ 1nom◦ plu◦ ←adj◦ 📖*vićakṣaṇa* ←वि√चक्ष्) **(18.2)**

(§3) *śrībhagavān̩* (Lord Kṛṣṇa); *uvāća* (said). *kāmyānām̩ karmaṇām̩* (of the *karmas* prompted by desires); *nyāsam̩* (obj1◦ the renunciation); *sannyāsam̩* (obj2◦ renunciation); *kavayaḥ:* (subj1◦ wise men); *viduḥ:* (say); *sarvakarmaphalatyāgam̩* (adj◦-obj3◦ the renunciation of the desire for the fruit of all *karmas*); *prāhuḥ:* (say); *tyāgam̩* (obj3◦ renunciation); *vićakṣaṇāḥ:* (subj2◦ the clear-sighted opeple, far-seeing, circumspect) **(18.2)**

(§4) śrībhagavān̩ uvāća kavayaḥ: viduḥ: nyāsam̩ kāmyānām̩ karmaṇām̩ sannyāsam̩ vićakṣaṇāḥ: prāhuḥ: sarvakarmaphalatyāgam̩ tyāgam̩

(§5) Lord Kṛṣṇa said : (Some) wise men say, the renunciation of the *karmas* prompted by desires (is) renunciation. (While other) clear-sighted people say, the renunciation of the desire[818] for the fruit of all *karmas is* renunciation. (18.2)

18.3 त्याज्यं दोषवदित्येके कर्म प्राहुर्मनीषिणः ।

---

[818] elsewhere◦ फलत्यागम् → renunciation of all actions.

📖 Please see the NOTE in the footnote of Verse 12.12 in Volume I of this book.

यज्ञदानतपःकर्म न त्याज्यमिति चापरे ।।

tyājyaṁ doṣavadityeke karma prāhurmanīṣiṇaḥ:,

yajñadānatapaḥ:karma na tyājyamiti ćāpare. (18.3)

(§1) *tyājyaṃ* (r◦ 14/1) *doṣavaṭ* (r◦ 8/4) *iti* (r◦ 4/4) *eke karma prāhuḥ:* (r◦ 16/8) *manīṣiṇaḥ:* (r◦ 22/8) *yajñadānatapaḥ:karma na tyājyaṃ* (r◦ 8/18) *iti ća* (r◦ 1/1) *apare*

(§2) *tyājyaṃ* (n◦ 1Nom◦ sing◦ ←pot◦ adj◦ *tyājya* ←√त्यज्); *doṣavaṭ* (n◦ 1Nom◦ sing◦ ←śatṛ◦ adj◦ *doṣavaṭ* ←√दुष्); *iti* (1.25); *eke* (m◦ 1nom◦ plu◦ ←adj◦ *eka* 2.41); *karma* (2acc◦ 2.49); *prāhuḥ:* (6.2); *manīṣiṇaḥ:* (2.51); *yajñadānatapaḥ:karma* (n◦ 1Nom◦ sing◦ ←tatpu◦ *yajña-dāna-tapaḥ:-karma,* यज्ञस्य च दानस्य च तपसः च कर्म ←m◦ *yajña* 3.9 + n◦ *dāna* 8.28 + n◦ *tapaṣ* (4.10); + n◦ *karmaṇ* 1.15); *na* (1.30); *tyājyaṃ* (↑); *iti* (1.25); *ća* (1.1); *apare* (1nom◦ plu◦ ←pron◦ *apara* 4.25) (18.3)

(§3) *tyājyaṃ* (adj1◦-subj1◦ ought to be renounced); *doṣavaṭ* (adj2◦-subj1◦ faulty, defective); *iti* (that); *eke* (adj1◦-subj2◦ some); *karma* (subj1◦ *karma*); *prāhuḥ:* (they say); *manīṣiṇaḥ:* (adj2◦-subj2◦ thinkers); *yajñadānatapaḥ:karma* (subj3◦ act of *yajña,* charity and austerity); *na* (is not); *tyājyaṃ* (ought to be renounced); *iti* (that); *ća* (and); *apare* (subj4◦ other, other thinkers)

(§4) eke manīṣiṇaḥ: prāhuḥ: iti karma doṣavaṭ ća tyājyaṃ apare iti yajñadānatapaḥ:karma na tyājyaṃ

(§5) Some thinkers say that *karma* (is) defective[819] and ought to be renounced; (while) other thinkers (say) that act of *yajña,* charity and austerity is ought not to be renounced. (18.3)

18.4 निश्चयं शृणु मे तत्र त्यागे भरतसत्तम ।

त्यागो हि पुरुषव्याघ्र त्रिविधः सम्प्रकीर्तितः ।।

niśćayaṁ śruṇu me tatra tyāge bharatasattama,

tyago hi puruṣavyāghra trividhaḥ: samprakīrtitaḥ:. (18.4)

(§1) *niśćayaṃ* (r◦ 14/1) *śṛṇu me tatra tyāge bharatasattama tyāgaḥ:* (r◦ 15/14) *hi puruṣavyāghra trividhaḥ:* (r◦ 22/7) *samprakīrtitaḥ:* (r◦ 22/8)

(§2) 🕮*niśćayaṃ* (2acc◦ sing◦ ←m◦ *niśćaya* 2.37); *śṛṇu* (2.39); *me* (1.21); *tatra* (1.26); *tyāge* (7loc◦ sing◦ ←m◦ *tyāga* 12..11); *bharatasattama* (m◦ 8voc◦ sing◦ ←bahuvrī◦ *bharata-sattama,* भरतेषु सत्तमः यः ←m◦ *bharata* 3.41 + adj◦ *sattama* 4.31); *tyāgaḥ:* (16.2); *hi* (1.11); *puruṣavyāghra* (m◦ 8voc◦ sing◦ ←bahuvrī◦ *puruṣa-vyāghra,* पुरुषेषु व्याघ्रः यः ←m◦ *puruṣa* 2.15 + m◦ *vyāghra* ←वि–आ√घ्रा); *trividhaḥ:* (17.7);

---

[819] elsewhere◦ दोषवत् → full of evil, as evil, as an evil, measure of evil, ...etc.

samprakīrtitaḥ: (m◦ 1nom◦ sing◦ ←ppp◦ adj◦ *samprakīrtita* ←सम्-प्र√कृ) (18.4)

(§3) *niśćayam̧* (obj◦ decision); *śṛṇu* (please hear); *me* (my); *tatra* (in the matter of); *tyāge* (renunciation); *bharatasattama* (O Arjuna!); *tyāgaḥ:* (subj◦ renunciation); *hi* (because, for); *puruṣavyāghra* (O Arjuna!); *trividhaḥ:* (adj1◦-subj◦ of three kinds); *samprakīrtitaḥ:* (adj2◦-subj◦ designated) (18.4)

(§4) bharatasattama śṛṇu me niśćayam̧ tatra tyāge hi puruṣavyāghra tyāgaḥ: samprakīrtitaḥ: trividhaḥ:

(§5) O Arjuna! please hear my decision in the matter of renunciation. Because,[820] O Arjuna! renunciation (is) designated of three kinds. (18.4)

18.5 यज्ञदानतप:कर्म न त्याज्यं कार्यमेव तत् ।
यज्ञो दानं तपश्चैव पावनानि मनीषिणाम् ।।
yajñadānatapaḥ:karma na tyājyaṁ kāryameva taţ,
yajño dānaṁ tapaśćaiva pāvanāni manīṣiṇām̧. (18.5)

(§1) *yajñadānatapaḥ:karma na tyājyam̧* (r◦ 14/1) *kāryam̧* (r◦ 8/22) *eva taţ* (r◦ 23/1) *yajñaḥ:* (r◦ 15/4) *dānam̧* (r◦ 14/1) *tapaḥ:* (r◦ 17/1) *ća* (r◦ 3/1) *eva pāvanāni manīṣiṇām̧* (r◦ 24/6, 14/2)

(§2) *yajñadānatapaḥ:karma* (1nom◦ 18.3); *na* (1.30); *tyājyam̧* (18.3); *kāryam̧* (1nom◦ 3.17); *eva* (1.1); *taţ* (1nom◦ 1.10); *yajñaḥ:* (3.14); *dānam̧* (1nom◦ 10.5); *tapaḥ:* (1nom◦ 7.9); *ća* (1.1); *eva* (1.1); *pāvanāni* (n◦ 1nom◦ plu◦ ←adj◦ 🕮*pāvana* ←√पू); *manīṣiṇām̧* (m◦ 6pos◦ plu◦ ←adj◦ *manīṣiņ* 2.51) (18.5)

(§3) *yajñadānatapaḥ:karma* (subj1◦ the act of *yajña,* charity and austerity); *na tyājyam̧* (adj1◦-subj1◦ ought not to be renounced); *kāryam̧* (adj2◦-subj◦ ought to be performed); *eva* (certainly); *taţ* (adj3◦-subj1◦ it, that); *yajñaḥ:* (subj2◦ *yajñaḥ:*); *dānam̧* (subj3◦ charity); *tapaḥ:* (subj4◦ austerity); *ća eva* (and); *pāvanāni* (adj1◦-subj2-4◦ the purifiers); *manīṣiṇām̧* (of the thinkers) (18.5)

(§4) yajñadānatapaḥ:karma na tyājyam̧ taţ eva kāryam̧ yajñaḥ: dānam̧ ća eva tapaḥ: pāvanāni manīṣiṇām̧ .

(§5) The act of *yajña,* charity and austerity ought not to be renounced. That certainly ought to be performed. Yajñaḥ:, charity and austerity (are) the purifiers for the thinkers. (18.5)

18.6 एतान्यपि तु कर्माणि सङ्गं त्यक्त्वा फलानि च ।
कर्तव्यानीति मे पार्थ निश्चितं मतमुत्तमम् ।।

---

[820] elsewhere◦ हि → See the footnote in 2.16

etānyapi tu karmāṇi saṅgaṁ tyaktvā phalāni ća,
kartavyānīti me pārtha niśćitaṁ matamuttamam̥. (18.6)

(§1) *etāni* (r∘ 4/1) *api tu karmāṇi* (r∘ 24/7) *saṅgam̥* (r∘ 14/1) *tyaktvā phalāni ća kartavyāni* (r∘ 1/5) *iti me pārtha niśćitam̥* (r∘ 14/1) *matam̥* (r∘ 8/20) *uttamam̥* (r∘ 14/2)

(§2) *etāni* (1nom∘ 14.12); *api* (1.26); *tu* (1.2); *karmāṇi* (1nom∘ 2.48); *saṅgam̥* (2.48); *tyaktvā* (1.33); *phalāni* (1nom∘ plu∘ ←n∘ *phala* 2.43); *ća* (1.1); *kartavyāni* (n∘ 1nom∘ plu∘ ←adj∘ *kartavya* 3.22); *iti* (1.25); *me* (1.21); *pārtha* (1.25); *niśćitam̥* (1nom∘ 2.7); *matam̥* (1nom∘ 3.31); *uttamam̥* (1nom∘ 4.3) (18.6)

(§3) *etāni* (adj1∘-subj1∘ these); *api* (even); *tu* (but); *karmāṇi* (subj1∘ acts, acts of *yajña,* charity and austerity); *saṅgam̥* (obj∘ attachment); *tyaktvā* (having renounced); *phalāni* (obj∘ to the desire for the fruit); *ća* (and); *kartavyāni* (adj2∘-subj∘ are to be performed); *iti* (thus, thus is); *me* (adj1∘-subj2∘ my); *pārtha* (O Arjuna!); *niśćitam̥* (adj2∘-subj2∘ firm); *matam̥* (subj2∘ opinion); *uttamam̥* (adj1∘-subj2∘ adj3∘-subj2∘ best) (18.6)

(§4) tu api etāni karmāṇi kartavyāni tyaktvā saṅgam̥ phalāni pārtha iti me niśćitam̥ ća uttamam̥ matam̥

(§5) But, even these acts of *yajña,* charity and austerity are to be performed, having renounced attachment to the desire[821] for the fruit. O Arjuna! thus is my firm and best opinion. (18.6)

18.7 नियतस्य तु संन्यास: कर्मणो नोपपद्यते ।
मोहात्तस्य परित्यागस्तामस: परिकीर्तित: ।।

niyatasya tu sannyāsaḥ: karmaṇo nopapadyate,
mohattasya parityāgastāmasaḥ: parikīrtitaḥ:. (18.7)

(§1) *niyatasya tu sannyāsaḥ:* (r∘ 22/1) *karmaṇaḥ:* (r∘ 15/6, 24/2) *na* (r∘ 2/2) *upapadyate mohāt̥* (r∘ 1/10) *tasya parityāgaḥ:* (r∘ 18/1) *tāmasaḥ:* (r∘ 22/3) *parikīrtitaḥ:* (r∘ 22/8)

(§2) *niyatasya* (6pos sing∘ ←adj∘ *niyata* 1.44); *tu* (1.2); *sannyāsaḥ:* (5.2); *karmaṇaḥ:* (4.17); *na* (1.30); *upapadyate* (2.3); *mohāt̥* (16.10); *tasya* (1.12); *parityāgaḥ:* (m∘ 1nom∘ sing∘ ←m∘ *parityāga* ←परि√त्यज्); *tāmasaḥ:* (1nom∘ sing∘ ←adj∘ *tāmasa* 7.12); *parikīrtitaḥ:* (m∘ 1nom∘ sing∘ ←ppp∘ adj∘ *parikīrtita* ←परि√कीर्त्) (18.7)

(§3) *niyatasya* (of the prescribed); *tu* (however); *sannyāsaḥ:* (subj1∘ renouncement); *karmaṇaḥ:* (of the

---

[821] elsewhere∘ फलम् → fruit.

📖 Please see the NOTE in the footnote of Verse 12.12 in Volume I of this book.

karma); *na upapadyate* (is not proper); *mohāt* (out of delusion); *tasya* (its); *parityāgaḥ:* (subj2∘ renouncement); *tāmasaḥ:* (adj∘-subj2∘ tāmasic); *parikīrtitaḥ:* (adj2∘-subj2∘ called) (18.7)

(§4) tu sannyāsaḥ: niyatasya karmaṇaḥ: na upapadyate tasya parityāgaḥ: mohāt parikīrtitaḥ: tāmasaḥ:

(§5) However, renouncement of the prescribed *karma* is not proper. Its renouncement out of delusion (is) called *tāmasic* (*tyāga*). (18.7)

18.8 दु:खमित्येव यत्कर्म कायक्लेशभयात्त्यजेत् ।

स कृत्वा राजसं त्यागं नैव त्यागफलं लभेत् ।।

duḥ:khamityeva yatkarma kāyakleśabhayāttyajet,

sa kṛtvā rājasaṁ tyāgaṁ naiva tyāgaphalaṁ labhet. (18.8)

(§1) *duḥ:kham* (r∘ 8/18) *iti* (r∘ 4/4) *eva yat* (r∘ 10/5) *karma kāyakleśabhayāt* (r∘ 1/10) *tyajet* (r∘ 23/1) *saḥ:* (r∘ 21/2) *kṛtvā rājasam* (r∘ 14/1) *tyāgam* (r∘ 14/1) *na* (r∘ 3/1) *eva tyāgaphalam* (r∘ 14/1) *labhet*

(§2) *duḥ:kham* (2acc∘ 5.6); *iti* (1.25); *eva* (1.1); *yat* (2acc∘ 1.45); *karma* (2acc∘ 2.49); *kāyakleśabhayāt* (n∘ 5abl∘ sing∘ ←tatpu∘ *kāya-kleśa-bhaya,* कायस्य क्लेशस्य भयम् ←n∘ *kāya* 5.11 + m∘ *kleśa* 12.5 + n∘ *bhaya* 2.35); *tyajet* (16.21); *saḥ:* (1.13); *kṛtvā* (2.38); *rājasam* (2acc∘ 17.12); *tyāgam* (18.2); *na* (1.30); *eva* (1.1); *tyāgaphalam* (n∘ 2acc∘ sing∘ ←tatpu∘ *tyāga-phala,* त्यागस्य फलम् ←m∘ *tyāga* 12.11 + n∘ *phala* 2.43); *labhet* (3rd-per∘ sing∘ potential∘ विधि∘ parasmai∘ ←class1∘ √लभ्) (18.8)

(§3) *duḥ:kham* (adj1∘-obj1∘ painful); *iti eva* (merely); *yat* (adj2∘-obj1∘ which); *karma* (obj1∘ a duty); *kāyakleśabhayāt* (from the fear of physical stress); *tyajet* (one may renounce); *saḥ:* (subj∘ he); *kṛtvā* (having performed); *rājasam* (adj∘-obj2∘ rājasic); *tyāgam* (obj2∘ renunciation); *na eva* (not); *tyāgaphalam* (obj3∘ the fruit of the renunciation); *labhet* (may attain) (18.8)

(§4) tyajet karma yat duḥ:kham iti eva kāyakleśabhayāt saḥ: kṛtvā rājasam tyāgam labhet na eva tyāgaphalam

(§5) One may renounce a duty which (is) painful, merely from the fear of physical stress. Having performed such *rājasic* renunciation, he may not attain the fruit of the renunciation. (18.8)

18.9 कार्यमित्येव यत्कर्म नियतं क्रियतेऽर्जुन ।

सङ्गं त्यक्त्वा फलं चैव स त्याग: सात्त्विको मत: ।।

kāryamityeva yatkarma niyataṁ kriyate'rjuna,

saṅgaṁ tyaktvā phalaṁ ćaiva sa tyāgaḥ: sāttviko mataḥ:. (18.9)

(§1) *kāryam* (r∘ 8/18) *iti* (r∘ 4/4) *eva yat* (r∘ 10/5) *karma niyatam* (r∘ 14/1) *kriyate* (r∘ 6/1) *arjuna saṅgam̧* (r◦ 14/1) *tyaktvā phalam̧* (r◦ 14/1) *ćа* (r◦ 3/1) *eva saḥ:* (r◦ 21/2) *tyāgaḥ:* (r◦ 22/7) *sāttvikaḥ:* (r◦ 15/9) *mataḥ:* (r◦ 22/8)

(§2) *kāryam̧* (1nom◦ 3.17); *iti* (1.25); *eva* (1.1); *yaț* (1nom◦ 1.45); *karma* (1nom◦ 2.49); *niyatam̧* (1nom◦ sing◦ ←adjo *niyata* 3.8); *kriyate* (17.18); *arjuna* (2.2); *saṅgam̧* (2.48); *tyaktvā* (1.33); *phalam̧* (2acc◦ 2.51); *ćа* (1.1); *eva* (1.1); *saḥ:* (1.13); *tyāgaḥ:* (16.2); *sāttvikaḥ:* (17.11); *mataḥ:* (6.32) (18.9)

(§3) *kāryam̧* (adj1◦-subj1◦ ought to be done); *iti eva* (merely); *yaț* (adj2◦-subj1◦ which); *karma* (subj1◦ a duty); *niyatam̧* (adj3◦-subj1◦ prescribed); *kriyate* (is performed); *arjuna* (O Arjuna!); *saṅgam̧* (obj1◦ attachment); *tyaktvā* (having renounced); *phalam̧* (obj2◦ the desire for the fruit); *ćа eva* (as well as); *saḥ:* (adj1◦-subj2◦ that); *tyāgaḥ:* (subj2◦ renunciation); *sāttvikaḥ:* (adj2◦-subj2◦ *sāttvic*); *mataḥ:* (adj1◦-subj1◦ considered) (18.9)

(§4) arjuna niyatam̧ karma yaț kāryam̧ iti eva kriyate tyaktvā saṅgam̧ ćа eva phalam̧ saḥ: tyāgaḥ: mataḥ: sāttvikaḥ:

(§5) O Arjuna! a prescribed duty which ought to be done, is performed having renounced attachment as well as the desire[822] for the fruit, that renunciation (is) considered *sāttvic.* (18.9)

18.10 न द्वेष्ट्यकुशलं कर्म कुशले नानुषज्जते ।
त्यागी सत्त्वसमाविष्टो मेधावी छिन्नसंशयः ।।
na dveṣṭyakuśalaṁ karma kuśale nānuṣajjate,
tyāgī sattvasamāviṣṭo medhāvī ćhinnasaṁśayaḥ:; (18.10)

(§1) *na dveṣṭi* (r◦ 4/1) *akuśalam̧* (r◦ 14/1) *karma kuśale na* (r◦ 1/1) *anuṣajjate tyāgī sattvasamāviṣṭaḥ:* (r◦ 15/9) *medhāvī ćhinnasaṁśayaḥ:* (r◦ 22/8);

(§2) *na* (1.30); *dveṣṭi* (2.57); 📖*a-kuśalam̧* (nbahuvrī◦ n◦ 2acc◦ sing◦ ←adj◦ *kuśala* ←√कुश्); *karma* (2acc◦ 2.49); *kuśale* (n◦ 7loc◦ sing◦ ←adj◦ 📖*kuśala* ↑); *na* (1.30); *anuṣajjate* (6.4); *tyāgī* (m◦ 1nom◦ sing◦ ←m◦ *tyāgiņ* ←√त्यज्); *sattvasamāviṣṭaḥ:* (m◦ 1nom◦ sing◦ ←bahuvrī◦ adj◦ *sattva-samāviṣṭa*, सत्त्वेन समाविष्टः यः ←n◦ *sattva* 2.45 + ppp◦ adj◦ *samāviṣṭa* ←सम्–आ√विश्); 📖*medhāvī* (m◦ 1nom◦ sing◦ ←adj◦ *medhāviņ* ←√मेध्); *ćhinnasaṁśayaḥ:* (m◦ 1nom◦ sing◦ ←bahuvrī◦ *ćhinna-saṁśaya*, छिन्नः संशयः यस्य ←ppp◦ adj◦ *ćhinna* 5.25 + m◦ *saṁśaya* 4.40); (18.10)

(§3) *na* (does not); *dveṣṭi* (detest, hate); *akuśalam̧* (adj1◦-obj◦ difficult, undesirable); *karma* (obj◦ duty);

---

[822] elsewhere◦ फलम् → fruit, result, ...etc.

📖 Please see the NOTE in the footnote of Verse 12.12 in Volume I of this book.

kuśale (adj2◦-obj◦ in the desirable task); *na* (he who does not); *anuṣajjate* (he gets indulged); *tyāgī* (subj◦ a person who renounces, the renouncing person); *sattvasamāviṣṭaḥ:* (adj1◦-subj◦ the one whose *sat-guṇa* is preponderant); *medhāvī* (adj2◦-subj◦ the wise person, intelligent); *ćhinnasaṁśayaḥ:* (adj3◦-subj◦ one whose doubts are dispelled); (18.10)

(§4) tyāgī sattvasamāviṣṭaḥ: na dveṣṭi akuśalaṃ karma na anuṣajjate kuśale medhāvī ćhinnasaṁśayaḥ:

(§5) The renouncing person, whose *sat-guṇa* is preponderant, he who does not detest difficult duty (and) does not get indulged in the desirable task, the wise person whose doubts are dispelled; (18.10)

18.11 न हि देहभृता शक्यं त्यक्तुं कर्माण्यशेषत: ।
यस्तु कर्मफलत्यागी स त्यागीत्यभिधीयते ।।
na hi dehabhṛtā śakyaṁ tyaktuṁ karmāṇyaśeṣataḥ:,
yastu karmaphalatyāgī sa tyāgītyabhidhīyate. (18.11)

(§1) *na hi dehabhṛtā śakyaṃ* (r◦ 14/1) *tyaktuṃ* (r◦ 14/1) *karmāṇi* (r◦ 24/7, 4/1) *aśeṣataḥ:* (r◦ 22/8) *yaḥ:* (r◦ 18/1) *tu karmaphalatyāgī saḥ:* (r◦ 21/2) *tyāgī* (r◦ 1/7) *iti* (r◦ 4/1) *abhidhīyate*

(§2) *na* (1.30); *hi* (1.11); *dehabhṛtā* (m◦ 3inst◦ sing◦ ←bahuvrī◦ adj◦ *dehabhṛṭ* 14.14); *śakyaṃ* (11.4); *tyaktuṃ* (inf◦ ind◦ ←√त्यज्); *karmāṇi* (2acc◦ 2.48); *aśeṣataḥ:* (6.24); *yaḥ:* (2.19); *tu* (1.2); *karmaphalatyāgī* (m◦ 1nom◦ sing◦ ←tatpu◦ *karma-phala-tyāgin*, कर्मण: फलस्य त्यागी ←n◦ *karmaṇ* 1.15 + n◦ *phala* 2.43 + m◦ or adj◦ *tyāgiṇ* 18.10); *saḥ:* (1.13); *tyāgī* (18.10); *iti* (1.25); *abhidhīyate* (13.2) (18.11)

(§3) *na* (it is not); *hi* (because); *dehabhṛtā* (by a body-bearer); *śakyaṃ* (possible); *tyaktuṃ* (to renounce); *karmāṇi* (duties); *aśeṣataḥ:* (adv◦ totally); *yaḥ:* (adj1◦-subj◦ he who); *tu* (however); *karmaphalatyāgī* (adj2◦-subj◦ a person who has renounces the desire for the fruit of his dutiful acts); *saḥ:* (subj◦ he); *tyāgī* (adj3◦-subj◦ *tyāgī*, renouncer); *iti* (as); *abhidhīyate* (is called) (18.11)

(§4) hi na aśeṣataḥ: śakyaṃ tyaktuṃ karmāṇi dehabhṛtā yaḥ: tu karmaphalatyāgī saḥ: abhidhīyate iti tyāgī

(§5) Because,[823] it is not totally possible to renounce duties by a body-bearer, however, a person who renounces the desire for the fruit of his dutiful acts, he is called as *tyāgī*. (18.11)

18.12 अनिष्टमिष्टं मिश्रं च त्रिविधं कर्मण: फलम् ।
भवत्यत्यागिनां प्रेत्य न तु संन्यासिनां क्वचित् ।।

[823] Please see the footnote in verse 2.15in volume I of this book.

aniṣṭamiṣṭaṁ miśraṁ ća trividhaṁ karmaṇaḥ: phalaṃ,

bhavatyatyāgināṁ pretya na tu sannyāsināṁ kvaćiṭ. (18.12)

(§1) *aniṣṭaṃ* (r◦ 8/18) *iṣṭaṃ* (r◦ 14/1) *miśraṃ* (r◦ 14/1) *ća trividhaṃ* (r◦ 14/1) *karmaṇaḥ:* (r◦ 22/4, 24/2) *phalaṃ* (r◦ 14/2) *bhavati* (r◦ 4/1) *atyāgināṃ* (r◦ 14/1) *pretya na tu sannyāsināṃ* (r◦ 14/1) *kvaćiṭ*

(§2) *aniṣṭaṃ* (n◦ 1nom◦ sing◦ ←adj◦ *aniṣṭa* 13.10); *iṣṭaṃ* (n◦ 1nom◦ sing◦ ←adj◦ 🕮*iṣṭa* 3.10); 🕮*miśraṃ* (n◦ 1nom◦ sing◦ ←ppp◦ adj◦ *miśra* ←√मिश्र्); *ća* (1.1); *trividhaṃ* (1nom◦ 16.21); *karmaṇaḥ:* (4.17); *phalaṃ* (1nom◦ 7.23); *bhavati* (1.44); *atyāgināṃ* (m◦ 6pos◦ plu◦ n.tatpu◦ ←m◦ *tyāgiṇ* 18.10); *pretya* (17.28); *na* (1.30); *tu* (1.2); *sannyāsināṃ* (6pos plu◦ ←m◦ *saṃnyāsiṇ* 5.3); *kvaćiṭ* (frequency indicating ind◦ ←ind◦ *kva* ←pron◦ *kiṃ* 1.1 + indeclinable affix *ćiṭ* 2.17) (18.12)

(§3) *aniṣṭaṃ* (adj1◦-subj◦ undesirable); *iṣṭaṃ* (adj2◦-subj◦ desirable); *miśraṃ* (adj3◦-subj◦ mixed); *ća* (and); *trividhaṃ* (adj4◦-subj◦ threefold); *karmaṇaḥ:* (for the actions); *phalaṃ* (subj◦ the fruit); *bhavati* (is, becomes); *atyāgināṃ* (of the people who do not renounce the desire for the fruit for their actions); *pretya* (after death, having died); *na* (not); *tu* (but); *sannyāsināṃ* (for the people who renounce the authorship of their actions); *kvaćiṭ* (any, such) (18.12)

(§4) trividhaṃ aniṣṭaṃ iṣṭaṃ ća miśraṃ bhavati phalaṃ pretya karmaṇaḥ: atyāgināṃ tu na kvaćiṭ sannyāsināṃ

(§5) For the actions of the people who do not renounce the desire for the fruit for their actions, threefold - desirable, undesirable and mixed - is the fruit after death, but not such for the people who renounce the authorship of their actions. (18.12)

18.13 पञ्चैतानि महाबाहो कारणानि निबोध मे ।

साङ्ख्ये कृतान्ते प्रोक्तानि सिद्धये सर्वकर्मणाम् ।।

pañćaitāni mahābāho kāraṇāni nibodha me,

sāṅkhye kṛtānte proktāni siddhaye sarvakarmaṇāṃ. (18.13)

(§1) *pañća* (r◦ 3/1) *etāni mahābāho kāraṇāni nibodha me sāṅkhye kṛtānte proktāni siddhaye sarvakarmaṇāṃ* (r◦ 24/6, 14/2)

(§2) *pañća* (13.6); *etāni* (2acc◦ 14.12); *mahābāho* (2.26); *kāraṇāni* (2acc◦ plu◦ ←n◦ 🕮*kāraṇa* 3.13); *nibodha* (1.7); *me* (1.21); *sāṅkhye* (2.39); *kṛtānte* (7loc◦ sing◦ ←tatpu◦ 🕮*kṛtānta*, कृतस्य अन्तः ←ppp◦ adj◦ *kṛta* 1.35 + m◦ *anta* 2.16); *proktāni* (n◦ 2acc◦ plu◦ ←ppp◦ adj◦ *prokta* 3.3); *siddhaye* (7.3); *sarva* (1.6); *karmaṇāṃ* (3.4) (18.13)

(§3) *pañća* (adj1◦-subj◦ five); *etāni* (adj2◦-subj◦ five); *mahābāho* (O Arjuna!); *kāraṇāni* (subj◦ reasons);

nibodha (please understand); *me* (from me); *sāṅkhye kṛtānte* (m◦ in the *Sāṅkhya* discipline); *proktāni* (adj3◦-subj◦ told); *siddhaye* (for the success, accomplishment); *sarva-karmaṇām̦* (of all duties) (18.13)

(§4) mahābāho nibodha me etāni pañća kāraṇāni proktāni sāṅkhye kṛtānte siddhaye sarva-karmaṇām̦

(§5) O Arjuna! please understand from me the five reasons, (as) told in the *Sāṅkhya* discipline, for the success[824] of all duties : (18.13)

18.14 अधिष्ठानं तथा कर्ता करणं च पृथग्विधम् ।
विविधाश्च पृथक्चेष्टा दैवं चैवात्र पञ्चमम् ।।
adhiṣṭhanaṁ tathā kartā karaṇaṁ ća pṛthagvidham̦,
vividhāśća pṛthakćeṣṭā daivaṁ ćaivātra pañćamam̦. (18.14)

(§1) *adhiṣṭhānam̦* (r◦ 14/1) *tathā kartā karaṇam̦* (r◦ 14/1, 24/3) *ća pṛthagvidham̦* (r◦ 14/2) *vividhāḥ:* (r◦ 17/1) *ća pṛthak̦* (r◦ 10/1) *ćeṣṭāḥ:* (r◦ 20/8) *daivam̦* (r◦ 14/1) *ća* (r◦ 3/1) *eva* (r◦ 1/1) *atra pañćamam̦* (r◦ 14/2)

(§2) *adhiṣṭhānam̦* (3.40); *tathā* (1.8); *kartā* (3.24); *karaṇam̦* (n◦ 1nom◦ sing◦ ←n◦ *karaṇa* 13.21); *ća* (1.1); *pṛthagvidham̦* (used adverbially, n◦ 1nom◦ 2acc◦ sing◦ ←adj◦ *pṛthagvidha* 10.5); *vividhāḥ:* (17.5); *ća* (1.1); *pṛthak̦* (1.18); *ćeṣṭāḥ:* (1nom◦ plu◦ ←f◦ *ćeṣṭā* 6.17); *daivam̦* (1nom◦ sing◦ ←n◦ daiva 4.25); *ća* (1.1); *eva* (1.1); *atra* (1.4); *pañćamam̦* (n◦ 1nom◦ sing◦ ←sequense indicating adj◦ *pañćama* ←num◦ *pañćan̦* 13.6) (18.14)

(§3) *adhiṣṭhānam̦* (subj1◦ the substratum, seat); *tathā* (as well as); *kartā* (subj2◦ the doer); *karaṇam̦* (subj3◦ the cause, the reason, the ground); *ća* (and); *pṛthagvidham̦* (adv◦ separately); *vividhāḥ:* (adj1◦-subj4◦ various kinds of); *ća* (and); *pṛthak̦* (adj2◦-subj4◦ distinct); *ćeṣṭāḥ:* (subj4◦ efforts); *daivam̦* (subj5◦ the destiny, providence, fate, luck); *ća eva* (and); *atra* (here); *pañćamam̦* (adj1◦-subj5◦ the fifth) (18.14)

(§4) pṛthagvidham̦ atra adhiṣṭhānam̦ tathā kartā ća karaṇam̦ ća vividhāḥ: pṛthak̦ ćeṣṭāḥ: ća eva daivam̦ pañćamam̦

(§5) Separately[825] (i) the substratum[826] as well as (ii) the doer[827] and (iii) the ground[828] and

---

[824] elsewhere◦ सिद्धये → terminate, perfection, ...etc.

📖 Please see the NOTE (सिद्धिम्) in the footnote of Verse 4.12 in Volume II of this book.

[825] elsewhere◦ पृथग्विधम् → different kinds of organs... (adjective).

[826] elsewhere◦ अधिष्ठानम् → locus.

(iv) various kinds of distinct efforts[829] and the (v) destiny[830] (is) the fifth. (18.14)

18.15 शरीरवाङ्मनोभिर्यत्कर्म प्रारभते नरः ।
न्याय्यं वा विपरीतं वा पञ्चैते तस्य हेतवः ।।
śarīravāṅgmanobhiryatkarma prārabhate naraḥ:,
nyāyyaṁ vā viparītaṁ vā pañćaite tasya hetavaḥ:. (18.15)

(§1) *śarīravāṅgmanobhiḥ:* (r∘ 16/6) *yaț* (r∘ 10/5) *karma prārabhate naraḥ:* (r∘ 22/8) *nyāyyam̦* (r∘ 14/1) *vā viparītam̦* (r∘ 14/1) *vā pañća* (r∘ 3/1) *ete tasya hetavaḥ:* (r∘ 22/8)

(§2) *śarīra-vāṅgmanobhiḥ:* (n∘ 3inst∘ plu∘ ←dvandva∘ शरीरेण च वाचे च मनसा च ←n∘ *śarīra* 1.29 + f∘ *vāć* 2.42 + n∘ *manaș* 1.30); *yaț* (2acc∘ 3.21); *karma* (2acc∘ 2.49); *prārabhate* (3rd-per∘ sing∘ pres∘ वर्तमान्–लट् ātmane∘ ←class1∘ प्र–आ√रभ् 3.7); *naraḥ:* (2.22); *nyāyyam̦* (n∘ 2acc∘ sing∘ ←pot∘ adj∘ *nyāyya* ←m∘ *nyāya* 16.12); *vā* (1.32); *viparītam̦* (n∘ 2acc∘ sing∘ ←adj∘ *viparita* 1.31); *vā* (1.32); *pañća* (13.6); *ete* (m∘ plu∘ *etad̦* 1.23); *tasya* (1.12); *hetavaḥ:* (1nom∘ plu∘ ←m∘ *hetu* 1.35) (18.15)

(§3) *śarīravāṅgmanobhiḥ:* (with the body, with speech and mind; with action, with words and thought); *yaț* (adj1∘-obj∘ which); *karma* (obj∘ an action); *prārabhate* (he commences, begins); *naraḥ:* (subj1∘ a person); *nyāyyam̦* (adj2∘-obj∘ just, righteous); *vā* (or); *viparītam̦* (adj3∘-obj∘ otherwise); *vā* (else); *pañća* (adj1∘-subj2∘ the five); *ete* (adj2∘-subj2∘ these); *tasya* (for it, its); *hetavaḥ:* (subj2∘ reasons) (18.15)

(§4) karma nyāyyam̦ vā vā viparītam̦ yaț naraḥ: prārabhate śarīravāṅgmanobhiḥ: ete pañća hetavaḥ:

(§5) An action, just or otherwise, which a person commences[831] with his body, speech and mind, these (are) the five reasons for it. (18.15)

18.16 तत्रैवं सति कर्तारमात्मानं केवलं तु यः ।
पश्यत्यकृतबुद्धित्वान्न स पश्यति दुर्मतिः ।।
tatraivaṁ sati kartāramātmānaṁ kevalaṁ tu yaḥ:,
paśyatyakṛtabuddhitvānna sa paśyati durmatiḥ:. (18.16)

---

[827] elsewhere∘ कर्ता → agent.

[828] elsewhere∘ करणम् → organs, instruments, senses, ...etc.

[829] elsewhere∘ चेष्टाः → activities.

[830] elsewhere∘ दैवम् → divine.

[831] elsewhere∘ प्रारभते → performs,

(§1) *tatra* (r◦ 3/1) *evam̦* (r◦ 14/1) *sati kartāram̦* (r◦ 8/17) *ātmānam̦* (r◦ 14/1) *kevalam̦* (r◦ 14/1) *tu yaḥ:* (r◦ 22/8) *paśyati* (r◦ 4/1) *akṛtabuddhitvāț* (r◦ 12/1) *na saḥ:* (r◦ 21/2) *paśyati durmatiḥ:* (r◦ 22/8)

(§2) *tatra* (1.26); *evam̦* (1nom◦ 1.24); *sati* (n◦ 7loc◦ sing◦ ←adj◦ *saț* 2.16); *kartāram̦* (2acc◦ 4.13); *ātmānam̦* (3.43); *kevalam̦* (4.21); *tu* (1.2); *yaḥ:* (2.19); *paśyati* (2.29); *akṛtabuddhitvāț* (n◦ 5abl◦ sing◦ ←bahuvrī◦ adj◦ or n◦ *akṛta-buddhitva*, न कृता बुद्धिः येन तत् प्रमाणम् ←adj◦ *akṛta* 3.18 + f◦ *buddhi* 1.23); *na* (1.30); *saḥ:* (1.13); *paśyati* (2.29); 🕮*durmatiḥ:* (m◦ 1nom◦ sing◦ ←bahuvrī◦ adj◦ *durmati* मूढा मतिः यस्य सः ←ind◦ *dur̦* 1.2 + f◦ *mati* 6.36) (18.16)

(§3) *tatra* (there, in that matter); *evam̦* (adj◦-subj1◦ such); *sati* (subj1◦ having been the case, even such being the reality); *kartāram̦* (adj◦-obj◦ doer, doer of the actions); *ātmānam̦* (obj◦ to himself); *kevalam̦* (only, the sole); *tu* (but); *yaḥ:* (adj1◦-subj2◦ he who, who); *paśyati* (sees, perceives); *akṛtabuddhitvāț* (for not having proper thinking); *na* (does not); *saḥ:* (subj2◦ he, that person); *paśyati* (sees, perceives); *durmatiḥ:* (adj2◦-subj2◦ of improper understanding) (18.16)

(§4) tu evam̦ sati tatra yaḥ: paśyati ātmānam̦ kevalam̦ kartāram̦ saḥ: durmatiḥ: na paśyati akṛtabuddhitvāț

(§5) But, even such being the reality in that matter, he who perceives himself[832] the sole doer[833] of the actions, that person of improper understanding[834] does not perceive (the reality), for not having proper understanding.[835] (18.16)

18.17 यस्य नाहङ्कृतो भावो बुद्धिर्यस्य न लिप्यते ।
हत्वापि स इमाँल्लोकान्न हन्ति न निबध्यते ।।
yasya nāhaṁkṛto bhāvo buddhiryasya na lipyate,
hatvāpi sa imām̐llokānna hanti na nibadhyate. (18.17)

(§1) *yasya na* (r◦ 1/1) *ahaṁkṛtaḥ:* (r◦ 15/8) *bhāvaḥ:* (r◦ 15/7) *buddhiḥ:* (r◦ 16/6) *yasya na lipyate hatvā* (r◦ 1/3) *api saḥ:* (r◦ 21/2) *imān̦* (r◦ 13/8) *lokān̦* (r◦ 1/11) *na hanti na nibadhyate*

(§2) *yasya* (2.61); *na* (1.30); *ahaṁkṛtaḥ:* (m◦ 1nom◦ sing◦ ←tatpu◦ adj◦ *ahaṁkṛta*, अहङ्कारेण सह कृतः ←pron◦ *aham̦* or *ahan̦* + ppp◦ adj◦ *kṛta* 1.35); *bhāvaḥ:* (2.16); *buddhiḥ:* (2.39); *yasya* (2.61); *na* (1.30);

---

[832] elsewhere◦ आत्मानम् → the absolute Self.

[833] elsewhere◦ कर्तारम् → agent.

[834] elsewhere◦ दुर्मतिः → person of deluded intellect, the man of impure intellect, has a perverted intellect, ...etc.

[835] elsewhere◦ अकृतबुद्धित्वात् → owing to the imperfection of the intellect, on account of imperfect understanding, person of deluded intellect, owing to the dullness of his wit, untrained in understanding, on account of untrained understanding, ...etc.

lipyate (5.7); *hatvā* (1.31); *api* (1.26); *saḥ:* (1.13); *imān̩* (10.16); *lokān̩* (6.41); *na* (1.30); *hanti* (2.19); *na* (1.30); *nibadhyate* (4.22) (18.17)

(§3) *yasya na* (he who does not have); *ahaṁkṛtaḥ:* (adj∘-subj1∘ I am the doer, that I am the author of the action); *bhāvaḥ:* (subj1∘ a feeling); *buddhiḥ:* (subj2∘ thinking); *yasya* (adj∘-subj3∘ he whose); *na* (does not); *lipyate* (it gets bound); *hatvā* (killing); *api* (even, also); *saḥ:* (subj3∘ he); *imān̩* (adj∘-obj∘ these); *lokān̩* (adj∘-obj∘ people); *na* (neither); *hanti* (kills); *na* (nor); *nibadhyate* (gets bound) (18.17)

(§4) yasya na bhāvaḥ: ahaṁkṛtaḥ: yasya buddhiḥ: na lipyate saḥ: api hatvā imān̩ lokān̩ na hanti na nibadhyate

(§5) He who does not have a feeling that I am the doer[836] of the action, he whose thinking[837] does not get bound[838] (this way), he, even killing these people[839] neither kills nor gets bound (by the fruit). (18.17)

18.18 ज्ञानं ज्ञेयं परिज्ञाता त्रिविधा कर्मचोदना ।
करणं कर्म कर्तेति त्रिविधः कर्मसङ्ग्रहः ।।
jñānaṁ jñeyaṁ parijñātā trividhā karmaćodanā,
karaṇaṁ karma karteti trividhaḥ: karmasaṁgrahaḥ:. (18.18)

(§1) *jñānam̩* (r∘ 14/1) *jñeyam̩* (r∘ 14/1) *parijñātā trividhā karmaćodanā karaṇam̩* (r∘ 14/1, 24/3) *karma kartā* (r∘ 2/3) *iti trividhaḥ:* (r∘ 22/1) *karmasaṁgrahaḥ:* (r∘ 22/8)

(§2) *jñānam̩* (1nom∘ 3.39); *jñeyam̩* (1nom∘ 1.39); *parijñātā* (m∘ 1nom∘ sing∘ ←m∘ *parijñātṛ* ←परि√ज्ञा); *trividhā* (17.2); *karmaćodanā* (f∘ 1nom∘ sing∘ ←tatpu∘ *karma-ćodanā*, कर्मणाम् चोदना ←n∘ *karman̩* 1.15 + f∘ *ćodanā* ←√चुद्); *karaṇam̩* (18.14); *karma* (2.49); *kartā* (3.24); *iti* (1.25); *trividhaḥ:* (17.7); *karmasaṁgrahaḥ:* (m∘ 1nom∘ sing∘ ←tatpu∘ *karma-saṁgraha*, कर्मणः सङ्ग्रहः ←n∘ *karman̩* 1.15 + m∘ *saṅgraha* 3.20) (18.18)

---

[836] elsewhere∘ अहङ्कृतः → egotism, ego sense, consciousness of ego, notion of egoism, egoistic notion of I-ness, feeling of egoism, egoistic notion, self-sense, ... etc.

[837] elsewhere∘ बुद्धिः → intellect, intelligence, ...etc.

📖 Please see footnote (बुद्धिः) in verse 2.52, in volume I.

[838] elsewhere∘ लिप्यते → is tainted,

📖 इमान् is not an adj of worlds, creatures, beings etc. It is the adj∘ of people इमान् लोकान्।

[839] elsewhere∘ इमाँल्लोकान् → men in the world, people in this world, these worlds, these creatures, these beings, ...etc.

📖 Please see footnote (बुद्धिः) in verse 2.52, in volume I.

(§3) *jñānam* (subj1◦ the knowledge); *jñeyam* (subj2◦ that which ought to be known); *parijñātā* (subj3◦ the knower); *trividhā* (adj◦-subj4◦ the threefold); *karmaćodanā* (subj4◦ stimulation, inspirations for *karma*); *karaṇam* (subj5◦ the means); *karma* (subj6◦ the deed); *kartā* (subj7◦ the doer); *iti trividhaḥ:* (adj◦-subj8◦ are the threefold); *karmasaṁgrahaḥ:* (subj8◦ aggregate of *karma*) (18.18)

(§4) jñānam jñeyam parijñātā trividhakarmaćodanā karaṇam karma kartā iti trividhaḥ: karmasaṁgrahaḥ:

(§5) (i) The Knowledge, (ii) that which ought to be known, (and) (iii) the knower (are) the threefold stimulations for *karma*. The (i) means, ii) the deed (and) (iii) the doer are the threefold aggregate[840] of *karma*. (18.18)

18.19 ज्ञानं कर्म च कर्ता च त्रिधैव गुणभेदतः ।
प्रोच्यते गुणसङ्ख्याने यथावच्छृणु तान्यपि ।।
jñānaṁ karma ća kartā ća tridhaiva guṇabhedataḥ:,
proćyate guṇasaṅkhyāne yathāvaććhruṇu tānyapi. (18.19)

(§1) *jñānam* (r◦ 14/1) *karma ća kartā ća tridhā* (r◦ 3/3) *eva guṇabhedataḥ:* (r◦ 22/8) *proćyate guṇasaṅkhyāne yathāvat* (r◦ 11/4) *śṛṇu tāni* (r◦ 4/1) *api*

(§2) *jñānam* (1nom◦ 3.39); *karma* (1nom◦ 2.49); *ća* (1.1); *kartā* (3.24); *ća* (1.1); *tridhā* (mode indicating ind◦ ←adj◦ *tri* 2.45); *eva* (1.1); *guṇabhedataḥ:* (adv◦ ←tatpu◦ *guṇa-bheda*, गुणानाम् भेदः ←m◦ *guṇa* 2.45 + m◦ *bheda* 3.26); *proćyate* (3rd-per◦ sing◦ pres◦ वर्तमान्–लट् ātmane◦ ←class2◦ प्र√वच्); *guṇasaṅkhyāne* (n◦ 7loc◦ sing◦ ←tatpu◦ *guṇa-saṅkhyāna*, गुणस्य संख्यानम् ←m◦ *guṇa* 2.45 + n◦ *saṅkhyāna* ←सम्√ख्या); *yathāvat* (mode indicating adv◦ ind◦ ←pron◦ *yad* 1.7); *śṛṇu* (2.39); *tāni* (2.61); *api* (1.26) (18.19)

(§3) *jñānam* (subj1◦ the knowledge); *karma* (subj2◦ *karma*); *ća* (and); *kartā* (subj3◦ the doer); *ća* (and); *tridhā* (adj◦-subj1-3◦ three types); *eva* (only); *guṇabhedataḥ:* (according to the differences in the *guṇas*); *proćyate* (are declared); *guṇasaṅkhyāne* (in the doctrine of *guṇa*); *yathāvat* (duly, rightly); *śṛṇu* (please listen); *tāni* (obj◦ them, those differences); *api* (also) (18.19)

(§4) guṇabhedataḥ: jñānam ća karma ća kartā proćyate tridhā eva api śṛṇu tāni yathāvat guṇasaṅkhyāne

(§5) According to the differences in the *guṇas* - the knowledge, *karma* and the doer are also declared of three types. Also, please listen those three differences rightly in the doctrine of *guṇa* : (18.19)

[840] elsewhere◦ कर्मसङ्ग्रहः → comprehension, basis, constituents, ...etc.

18.20 सर्वभूतेषु येनैकं भावमव्ययमीक्षते ।
अविभक्तं विभक्तेषु तज्ज्ञानं विद्धि सात्त्विकम् ।।

sarvabhūteṣu yenaikaṁ bhāvamavyayamīkṣate,
avibhaktaṁ vibhakteṣu tajjñānaṁ viddhi sāttvikam. (18.20)

(§1) *sarvabhūteṣu* (r◦ 25/5) *yena* (r◦ 3/1) *ekam* (r◦ 14/1) *bhāvam* (r◦ 8/16) *avyayam* (r◦ 8/19) *īkṣate* (r◦ 23/1) *avibhaktam* (r◦ 14/1) *vibhakteṣu* (r◦ 25/5) *tat* (r◦ 11/2) *jñānam* (r◦ 14/1) *viddhi sāttvikam* (r◦ 14/2)

(§2) *sarvabhūteṣu* (3.18); *yena* (2.17); *ekam* (m◦ 2acc◦ 3.2); *bhāvam* (7.15); *avyayam* (2acc◦ 2.21); *īkṣate* (6.29); *avibhaktam* (13.17); *vibhakteṣu* (m◦ 7loc◦ sing◦ ←adj◦ *vibhakta* 13.17); *tat* (2acc◦ 2.7); *jñānam* (2acc◦ 3.40); *viddhi* (2.17); *sāttvikam* (2acc◦ 14.16) (18.20)

(§3) *sarvabhūteṣu* (in all beings); *yena* (by which); *ekam* (adj1◦-obj1◦ one, a single); *bhāvam* (obj1◦ being, existence); *avyayam* (adj2◦-obj1◦ eternal); *īkṣate* (one sees); *avibhaktam* (adj3◦-obj1◦ uniform); *vibhakteṣu* (among the ununiform); *tat* (adj1◦-obj2◦ that); *jñānam* (obj2◦ the knowledge, thinking, understanding); *viddhi* (please know. know to be); *sāttvikam* (adj2◦-obj2◦ *sāttvic*) (18.20)

(§4) viddhi tat jñānam sāttvikam yena īkṣate ekam avyayam bhāvam sarvabhūteṣu avibhaktam vibhakteṣu

(§5) That 'understanding' is known as *sāttvic* by which one sees a single eternal existence[841] (of ātmā) in all beings, uniform among the ununiform. (18.20)

18.21 पृथक्त्वेन तु यज्ज्ञानं नानाभावान्पृथग्विधान् ।
वेत्ति सर्वेषु भूतेषु तज्ज्ञानं विद्धि राजसम् ।।

pṛthaktvena tu yatjjñānaṁ nānābhāvānpṛthagvidhān,
vetti sarveṣu bhūteṣu tajjñānam viddhi rājasam. (18.21)

(§1) *pṛthaktvena tu yat* (r◦ 11/2) *jñānam* (r◦ 14/1) *nānābhāvān* (r◦ 13/13) *pṛthagvidhān* (r◦ 23/1) *vetti sarveṣu* (r◦ 25/5) *bhūteṣu* (r◦ 25/5) *tat* (r◦ 11/2) *jñānam* (r◦ 14/1) *viddhi rājasam* (r◦ 14/2)

(§2) *pṛthaktvena* (9.15); *tu* (1.2); *yat* (1nom◦ 1.45); *jñānam* (1nom◦ 3.39); *nānā* (1.9); *bhāvān* (2acc◦ plu◦ ←m◦ *bhāva* 2.7); *pṛthagvidhān* (m◦ 2acc◦ plu◦ ←adj◦ *pṛthagvidha* 10.5); *vetti* (2.19); *sarveṣu* (1.11); *bhūteṣu* (7.11); *tat* (2acc◦ 2.7); *jñānam* (2acc◦ 3.40); *viddhi* (2.17); *rājasam* (17.12) (18.21)

(§3) *pṛthaktvena* (separately); *tu* (but); *yat* (adj◦-obj1◦ which); *jñānam* (obj1◦ the knowledge, thinking,

---

[841] elsewhere◦ भावम् → situation, substance, Reality, ...etc.

📖 भावम् = single eternal existence = ātmā.

understanding); *nānā* (adj∘-obj2∘ different); *bhāvān̦* (obj2∘ existences); *pṛthagvidhān̦* (adj2∘-obj2∘ various); *vetti* (one thinks); *sarveṣu* (in all); *bhūteṣu* (beings); *taț* (adj1∘-obj1∘ that); *jñānam̦* (obj1∘ knowledge, thinking, understanding); *viddhi* (know, know it to be); *rājasam̦* (adj2∘-obj1∘ *rājasic*). (18.21)

(§4) tu jñānam̦ yaț vetti nānā bhāvān̦ pṛthaktvena sarveṣu pṛthagvidhān̦ bhūteṣu viddhi taț jñānam̦ rājasam̦

(§5) But, the understanding (by) which one thinks different existences separately[842] (separate ātmās) in all various beings, know that understanding to be *rājasic.* (18.21)

18.22 यत्तु कृत्स्नवदेकस्मिन्कार्ये सक्तमहैतुकम् ।
अतत्त्वार्थवदल्पं च तत्तामसमुदाहृतम् ।।
yattu kṛtsnavadekasminkārye saktamahaitukam̦,
atattvārthavadalpaṁ ća tattāmasamudāhṛtam̦. (18.22)

(§1) *yaț* (r∘ 1/10) *tu kṛtsnavaț* (r∘ 8/9) *ekasmin̦* (r∘ 13/9) *kārye saktam̦* (r∘ 8/16) *ahaitukam̦* (r∘ 14/2) *atattvārthavaț* (r∘ 8/2) *alpam̦* (r∘ 14/1) *ća taț* (r∘ 1/10) *tāmasam̦* (r∘ 8/20) *udāhṛtam̦* (r∘ 14/2)

(§2) *yaț* (1nom∘ 1.45); *tu* (1.2); *kṛtsnavaț* (n∘ 1nom∘ sing∘ ←adj∘ *kṛtsnavaț* ←adj∘ *kṛtsna* 1.40 + ind∘ affix *vaț* 2.29); *ekasmin̦* (7loc∘ sing∘ ←adj∘ *eka* 2.41); *kārye* (7loc∘ sing∘ ←n∘ *kārya* 13.21); *saktam̦* (n∘ 1nom∘ sing∘ ←adj∘ *sakta* 3.25); *a-haitukam̦* (n∘ 1nom∘ sing∘ n.tatpu∘ ←adj∘ taddhita∘ *haituka* 16.8); *a-tattvārthavaț* (n∘ 1nom∘ sing∘ n.tatpu∘ ←adj∘ *tattvārtha-vaț*, तत्त्वस्य अर्थवत् ←n∘ *tattva* 2.16 + m∘ *artha* 1.7 + taddhi∘ affix *vaț* 1.5); *alpam̦* (n∘ 1nom∘ sing∘ ←adj∘ *alpa* 7.23); *ća* (1.1); *taț* (1nom∘ 1.10); *tāmasam̦* (1nom∘ 17.13); *udāhṛtam̦* (13.7) (18.22)

(§3) *yaț* (adj∘-subj∘ which, that which); *tu* (however); *kṛtsnavaț* (adj1∘-subj∘ as though it were all); *ekasmin̦* (in one); *kārye* (in form); *saktam̦* (adj2∘-subj∘ attached, confined); *ahaitukam̦* (adj3∘-subj∘ baseless); *atattvārthavaț* (adj4∘-subj∘ irrational); *alpam̦* (adj5∘-subj∘ insignificant); *ća* (and); *taț* (adj6∘-subj∘ that); *tāmasam̦* (adj7∘-subj∘ *tāmasic*); *udāhṛtam̦* (declared, declared to be) (18.22)

(§4) tu yaț saktam̦ ekasmin̦ kārye kṛtsnavaț taț ahaitukam̦ atattvārthavaț ća alpam̦ udāhṛtam̦ tāmasam̦

(§5) However, (the understanding) which (is) confined in one form od deity as though it were all, that baseless, irrational, and insignificant understanding is declared, declared to be *tāmasic.* (18.22)

---

[842] elsewhere∘ पृथक्त्वेन → distince, separate, different, ...etc.

📖 पृथक्त्वेन is adverb of the verb वेत्ति । It is not an adjective.

18.23 नियतं सङ्गरहितमरागद्वेषतः कृतम् ।
अफलप्रेप्सुना कर्म यत्तत्सात्त्विकमुच्यते ।।

niyataṁ saṅgarahitamarāgadveṣataḥ: kṛtaṃ,
aphalaprepsunā karma yattatsāttvikamućyate. (18.23)

(§1) *niyataṃ* (r◦ 14/1) *saṅgarahitaṃ* (r◦ 8/16) *arāgadveṣataḥ:* (r◦ 22/1) *kṛtaṃ* (r◦ 14/2) *aphalaprepsunā karma yaṭ* (r◦ 1/10) *taṭ* (r◦ 10/7) *sāttvikaṃ* (r◦ 8/20) *ućyate*

(§2) *niyataṃ* (1nom◦ 18.9); *saṅgarahitaṃ* (adv◦ ←tatpu◦ adj◦ *saṅga-rahita,* सङ्गेन रहितम् ←m◦ *saṅga* 2.47 + ppp◦ adj◦ *rahita* ←√रह्); *arāgadveṣataḥ:* (adv◦ ←n.tatpu◦ śānać◦ adj◦ *a-rāga-dveṣaṭ* ←m◦ *rāga* 2.56 + m◦ *dveṣa* 2.64); *kṛtaṃ* (4.15); *aphalaprepsunā* (adv◦ ←desi◦ adj◦ *phala-prepsu* ←n◦ *phala* 2.43 + adj◦ *prepsu* ←प्र√आप्); *karma* (2.49); *yaṭ* (1nom◦ 1.45); *taṭ* (1nom◦ 1.10); *sāttvikaṃ* (1nom◦ 17.17); *ućyate* (2.25) (18.23)

(§3) *niyataṃ* (adj1◦-subj◦ the prescribed); *saṅgarahitaṃ* (adv◦ without attachment); *arāgadveṣataḥ:* (adv◦ without without liking or disliking); *kṛtaṃ* (ppp◦ adj◦ done); *aphalaprepsunā* (adv◦ without a desire for its fruiṭ); *karma* (subj◦ *karma*); *yaṭ* (adj2◦-subj◦ which); *taṭ* (adj3◦-subj◦ that); *sāttvikaṃ* (adj4◦-subj◦ *sāttvic*); *ućyate* (is called) (18.23)

(§4) niyataṃ karma yaṭ kṛtaṃ saṅgarahitaṃ aphalaprepsunā arāgadveṣataḥ: taṭ ućyate sāttvikaṃ

(§5) The prescribed *karma* which (is) done without attachment, without a desire for its fruiṭ, (and) without liking or disliking,[843] that (*karma*) is called *sāttvic.* (18.23)

18.24 यत्तु कामेप्सुना कर्म साहङ्कारेण वा पुनः ।
क्रियते बहुलायासं तद्राजसमुदाहृतम् ।।

yattu kāmaprepsunā karma sāhaṅkāreṇa vā punaḥ:,
kriyate bahulāyāsaṁ tadrājasamudāhṛtaṃ. (18.24)

(§1) *yaṭ* (r◦ 1/10) *tu kāmaprepsunā karma sāhaṅkāreṇa* (r◦ 24/1) *vā punaḥ:* (r◦ 22/8) *kriyate bahulāyāsaṃ* (r◦ 14/1) *taṭ* (r◦ 9/10) *rājasaṃ* (r◦ 8/20) *udāhṛtaṃ* (r◦ 14/2)

(§2) *yaṭ* (1nom◦ 1.45); *tu* (1.2); *kāmaprepsunā* (m◦ 3inst◦ sing◦ ←tatpu◦ -desi◦ adj◦ *kāma-prepsu,* कामस्य इप्सुः ←n◦ *kāma* 1.22 + adj◦ *prepsu* ←√आप्); *karma* (1nom◦ 2.49); *sāhaṅkāreṇa* (m◦ 3inst◦ sing◦ ←bahuvrī◦

---

[843] elsewhere◦ सङ्गरहितमरागद्वेषतः कृतम् अफलप्रेप्सुना → The action which is ...etc.

📖 Remember, सङ्गरहितम्, अरागद्वेषतः and अफलप्रेप्सुना are not adjectives of the subject कर्म । These are adverbs of the ppp. adjective कृतम used as a verb. Adjective of an adjective is also an adverb.

sāhankāra, अस्ति साहङ्कारः यस्य सः ←m◦ adj◦ *saha* 1.22 + m◦ *ahankāra* 2.71); *vā* (1.32); *punaḥ:* (4.35); *kriyate* (17.18); 🕮*bahulāyāsam̦* (n◦ 1nom◦ sing◦ ←bahuvrī◦ *bahulāyāsa*, बहुलाः आयासः यस्मिन् ←adj◦ *bahula* 2.43 + m◦ *āyāsa* ←आ√यस्); *taț* (1nom◦ 1.10); *rājasam̦* (1nom◦ 17.12); *udāhṛtam̦* (13.7) (18.24)

(§3) *yaț* (adj1◦-subj◦ which, that which); *tu* (but); *kāmaprepsunā* (adv◦ with the desire of fruit); *karma* (subj◦ the *karma*); *sāhankāreṇa* (adv◦ with ego of authorship); *vā punaḥ:* (and); *kriyate* (is done); *bahulāyāsam̦* (adv◦ with great strain); *taț* (adj2◦-subj◦ that); *rājasam̦* (adj3◦-subj◦ *rājasic*); *udāhṛtam̦* (called) (18.24)

(§4) tu karma yaț kriyate kāmaprepsunā sāhankāreṇa vā punaḥ: bahulāyāsam̦ taț udāhṛtam̦ rājasam̦

(§5) But, the *karma* which is done with the desire of fruit, with ego of authorship and with great strain,[844] that (*karma* is) called *rājasic.* (18.24)

18.25 अनुबन्धं क्षयं हिंसामनवेक्ष्य च पौरुषम् ।
मोहादारभ्यते कर्म यत्तत्तामसमुच्यते ।।
anubandham kṣayam hiṁsāmanavekṣya ća paurusam̦,
mohādārabhyate karma yattattāmasamućyate. (18.25)

(§1) *anubandham̦* (r◦ 14/1) *kṣayam̦* (r◦ 14/1) *hiṁsām̦* (r◦ 8/16) *anavekṣya ća pauruṣam̦* (r◦ 14/2) *mohāț* (r◦ 8/3) *ārabhyate karma yaț* (r◦ 1/10) *taț* (r◦ 1/10) *tāmasam̦* (r◦ 8/20) *ućyate*

(§2) *anubandham̦* (2acc◦ sing◦ ←m◦ *anubandha* 15.2); *kṣayam̦* (2acc◦ sing◦ ←m◦ *kṣaya* 1.38); *hiṁsām̦* (2acc◦ sing◦ ←f◦ *hiṁsā* 10.5); *anavekṣya* (lyp◦ past-participle ind◦ ←अन्–अव√ईक्ष्); *ća* (1.1); *pauruṣam̦* (2acc◦ 7.8); *mohāț* (16.10); *ārabhyate* (3rd-per◦ sing◦ pres◦ वर्तमान्–लट् ātmane◦ ←class1◦ आ√रभ 3.7); *karma* (2acc◦ 2.49); *yaț* (2acc◦ 1.45); *taț* (1nom◦ 1.10); *tāmasam̦* (1nom◦ 17.13); *ućyate* (2.25) (18.25)

(§3) *anubandham̦* (obj1◦ the consequence); *kṣayam̦* (obj2◦ loss); *hiṁsām̦* (obj3◦ damage, harm); *anavekṣya* (disregarding); *ća* (and); *pauruṣam̦* (obj4◦ ability, one's own ability); *mohāț* (out of delusion); *ārabhyate* (is commensed); *karma* (subj◦ the *karma*); *yaț* (adj1◦-subj◦ which); *taț* (adj2◦-subj◦ that, that *karma*); *tāmasam̦* (adj3◦-subj◦ *tāmasic*); *ućyate* (is called) (18.25)

(§4) karma yaț ārabhyate mohāț anavekṣya anubandham̦ kṣayam̦ hiṁsām̦ ća pauruṣam̦ taț ućyate tāmasam̦

(§5) The *karma* which is commensed out of delusion, disregarding the consequence, loss, harm

---

[844] elsewhere◦ क्रियते बहुलायासम् → action which is highly strenous.

🕮 Remember again, as said in the previous footnote, बहुलायासम् is not adjective of the subject कर्म । It is an adverb of the verb क्रियते ।

and one’s own ability, that ***karma*** is called ***tāmasic.*** (18.25)

18.26 मुक्तसङ्गोऽनहंवादी धृत्युत्साहसमन्वित: ।
सिद्ध्यसिद्ध्योर्निर्विकार: कर्ता सात्त्विक उच्यते ।।
muktasaṅgo‘nahaṁvādī dhṛtyutsāhasamanvitaḥ:,
siddhyasiddhyornirvikāraḥ: kartā sāttvika ućyate. (18.26)

(§1) *muktasaṅgaḥ:* (r◦ 15/1) *anahaṁvādī dhṛtyutsāhasamanvitaḥ:* (r◦ 22/8) *siddhyasiddhyaoḥ:* (r◦ 16/12) *nirvikāraḥ:* (r◦ 22/1) *kartā sāttvikaḥ:* (r◦ 19/4) *ućyate*

(§2) *muktasaṅgaḥ:* (m◦ 1nom◦ sing◦ ←bahuvrī◦ *mukta-saṅga* 3.9); *anahaṁvādī* (m◦ 1nom◦ sing◦ n.tatpu◦ ←adj◦ *ahaṁvādiṇ*, अहम् वदति इति ←pron◦ *ahaṃ* 1.22 + m◦ *vādiṇ* 2.42); *dhṛtyutsāhasamanvitaḥ:* (m◦ 1nom◦ sing◦ ←tatpu◦ *dhṛtyutsāha-samanvita*, धृत्या च उत्साहेन च समन्वित: ←f◦ *dhṛti* 6.25 + m◦ *utsāha* ←उद्√सह् + adj◦ *samanvita* 10.8); *siddhyasiddhyaoḥ:* (2.48); *nirvikāraḥ:* (m◦ 1nom◦ sing◦ ←bahuvrī◦ *nir-vikāra*, नास्ति विकार: यस्य ←ind◦ *nir* 2.45 + m◦ *vikāra* 13.4); *kartā* (3.24); *sāttvikaḥ:* (17.11); *ućyate* (2.25) (18.26)

(§3) *muktasaṅgaḥ:* (adj1◦-subj◦ he who is free from attachment); *anahaṁvādī* (adj2◦-subj◦ he who is free from the feeling of the ego of authorship of *karma*); *dhṛtyutsāhasamanvitaḥ:* (adj3◦-subj◦ he who is equipped with courage and promptness); *siddhyasiddhyaoḥ: nirvikāraḥ:* (adj4◦-subj◦ he who is indifferent to achieving success and not achieving success); *kartā* (subj◦ the doer); *sāttvikaḥ:* (adj5◦-subj◦ *sāttvic*); *ućyate* (is called) (18.26)

(§4) kartā muktasaṅgaḥ: anahaṁvādī dhṛtyutsāhasamanvitaḥ: siddhyasiddhyaoḥ: nirvikāraḥ: ućyate sāttvikaḥ:

(§5) The doer who is (i) free from attachment, (ii) who is free from the feeling of the ego of authorship[845] of *karma,* (iii) who is equipped with courage and promptness (and) (iv) who is indifferent to achieving success[846] and not achieving success, is called *sāttvic.* (18.26)

18.27 रागी कर्मफलप्रेप्सुर्लुब्धो हिंसात्मकोऽशुचि: ।
हर्षशोकान्वित: कर्ता राजस: परिकीर्तित: ।।

---

[845] elsewhere◦ अनहंवादी → not egotistic, not egoistic, non-egoistic, reverse to speech of egoism, feeling of I, devoid of egoism, ...etc,

📖 Remember the definition of बुद्धियोग: given in the footnote of verse 2.39, in volume I

[846] elsewhere◦ सिद्धि → perfection.

📖 See the footnote of verse 2.10, in volume I

rāgī karmaphalaprepsurlubdho hiṁsātmako‘śućiḥ:,
harṣaśokānvitaḥ: kartā rājasaḥ: parikīrtitaḥ:. (18.27)

(§1) *rāgī karmaphalaprepsuḥ:* (r◦ 16/8) *lubdhaḥ:* (r◦ 15/14) *hiṁsātmakaḥ:* (r◦ 15/1) *aśućiḥ:* (r◦ 22/8) *harṣaśokānvitaḥ:* (r◦ 22/1) *kartā rājasaḥ:* (r◦ 22/3) *parikīrtitaḥ:* (r◦ 22/8)

(§2) 🕮*rāgī* (m◦ 1nom◦ sing◦ ←adj◦ *rāgiṇ* ←√रञ्ज्); *karmaphalaprepsuḥ:* (m◦ 1nom◦ sing◦ ←adj◦ *karma-phala-prepsu,* कर्मण: फलस्य प्रेप्सु: ←n◦ *karmaṇ* 1.15 + n◦ *phala* 2.43 + adj◦ *prepsu* 18.23); 🕮*lubdhaḥ:* (m◦ 1nom◦ sing◦ ←ppp◦ adj◦ *lubdha* ←√लुभ्); 🕮*hiṁsātmakaḥ:* (m◦ 1nom◦ sing◦ ←taddhita◦ adj◦ *hiṁsātmaka* ←f◦ *hiṁsā* 10.5 + adj◦ *ātmaka* 14.7); *aśućiḥ:* (m◦ 1nom◦ sing◦ ←adj◦ *aśući* 16.10); *harṣaśokānvitaḥ:* (m◦ 1nom◦ sing◦ ←tatpu◦ adj◦ *harṣa-śokānvita,* हर्षेण च शोकेण च अन्वित: ←m◦ *harṣa* 1.12 + m◦ *śoka* 1.47 + adj◦ *anvita* 9.23); *kartā* (3.24); *rājasaḥ:* (m◦ 1nom◦ sing◦ ←taddhita◦ adj◦ *rajasa* 7.12); *parikīrtitaḥ:* (18.7) (18.27)

(§3) *rāgī* (= *anurāgī* adj1◦-subj◦ attached, one who is attached to desires); *karmaphalaprepsuḥ:* (adj2◦-subj◦ one who performs karma with the desire of its fruit); *lubdhaḥ:* (adj3◦-subj◦ one who is greedy); *hiṁsātmakaḥ:* (adj4◦-subj◦ one whose nature is violent); *aśućiḥ:* (adj5◦-subj◦ one who is not pure at heart); *harṣaśokānvitaḥ:* (adj6◦-subj◦ one who affected by the feelings of joy and sorrow); *kartā* (subj◦ the doer); *rājasaḥ:* (adj7◦-subj◦ *rājasic*); *parikīrtitaḥ:* (adj8◦-subj◦ is known as) (18.27)

(§4) kartā rāgī karmaphalaprepsuḥ: lubdhaḥ: hiṁsātmakaḥ: aśućiḥ: harṣaśokānvitaḥ: parikīrtitaḥ: rājasaḥ:

(§5) The doer (i) who is attached to desires, (ii) who performs *karma* with the desire of its fruit, (iii) who is greedy, whose nature is violent, (iv) who is not pure at heart, (iv) who is affected by the feelings of joy and sorrow, such *kartā* is known as *rājasic.* (18.27)

18.28 अयुक्त: प्राकृत: स्तब्ध: शठो नैष्कृतिकोऽलस: ।
विषादी दीर्घसूत्री च कर्ता तामस उच्यते ।।
ayuktaḥ: prākṛtaḥ: stabdhaḥ: śaṭho naiṣkṛtiko‘lasaḥ:,
viṣādī dīrghasūtrī ća kartā tāmasa ućyate. (18.28)

(§1) *ayuktaḥ:* (r◦ 22/3) *prākṛtaḥ:* (r◦ 22/7) *stabdhaḥ:* (r◦ 22/5) *śaṭhaḥ:* (r◦ 15/6) *naiṣkṛtika* (r◦ 15/1) *alasaḥ:* (r◦ 22/8) *viṣādī dīrghasūtrī ća kartā tāmasaḥ:* (r◦ 19/4) *ućyate*

(§2) *ayuktaḥ:* (5.12); 🕮*prākṛtaḥ:* (m◦ 1nom◦ sing◦ ←ppp◦ adj◦ *prākṛta* ←प्र√कृ); *stabdhaḥ:* (m◦ 1nom◦ sing◦ ←adj◦ *stabdha* 16.17); 🕮*śaṭhaḥ:* (m◦ 1nom◦ sing◦ ←adj◦ *śaṭha* ←√शठ्); *naiṣkṛtikaḥ:* (m◦ 1nom◦ sing◦ ←taddhita◦ adj◦ *naiṣkṛtika* ←f◦ *niṣkṛti* ←निर्√कृ); *alasaḥ:* (m◦ 1nom◦ sing◦ ←adj◦ n.tatpu◦ *alasa* ←अ√लस्); *viṣādī* (m◦ 1nom◦ sing◦ ←adj◦ *viṣādiṇ* ←वि√सद् 1.27); 🕮*dīrghasūtrī* (m◦ 1nom◦ sing◦ ←adj◦

dīrghasūtriṇ ←adj◦ *dīrgha* ←√द्रु + adj◦ *sūtriṇ* ←√सूत्र्); *ća* (1.1); *kartā* (3.24); *tāmasaḥ:* (18.7); *ućyate* (2.25) (18.28)

(§3) *ayuktaḥ:* (adj1◦-subj◦ one who is not disciplined with *yoga*); *prākṛtaḥ:* (adj2◦-subj◦ uncultured, uncivilized); *stabdhaḥ:* (adj3◦-subj◦ obstinate); *śaṭhaḥ:* (adj4◦-subj◦ deceitful); *naiṣkṛtikaḥ:* (adj5◦-subj◦ malicious, malevolent, spiteful); *alasaḥ:* (adj6◦-subj◦ lazy); *viṣādī* (adj7◦-subj◦ despondent); *dīrghasūtrī* (adj8◦-subj◦ procrastinating); *ća* (and); *kartā* (subj◦ the doer); *tāmasaḥ:* (adj9◦-subj◦ *tāmasic*); *ućyate* (is called) (18.28)

(§4) kartā ayuktaḥ: prākṛtaḥ: stabdhaḥ: śaṭhaḥ: naiṣkṛtikaḥ: alasaḥ: viṣādī ća dīrghasūtrī ućyate tāmasaḥ:

(§5) The doer (i) who is not disciplined with *yoga,* who is (ii) uncivilized, (iii) obstinate, (iv) deceitful, (v) malevolent, (vi) lazy, (vii) despondent and (viii) procrastinating, (such *kartā*) is called *tāmasic.*

(18.28)

18.29 बुद्धेर्भेदं धृतेश्चैव गुणतस्त्रिविधं शृणु ।
प्रोच्यमानमशेषेण पृथक्त्वेन धनञ्जय ।।

buddherbhedaṁ dhṛteśćaiva guṇatastrividhaṁ śṛṇu,
proćyamānamaśeṣeṇa pṛthaktvena dhanañjaya. (18.29)

(§1) *buddheḥ:* (r◦ 16/10) *bhedaṃ* (r◦ 14/1) *dhṛteḥ:* (r◦ 17/1) *ća* (r◦ 3/1) *eva guṇataḥ:* (r◦ 18/1) *trividhaṃ* (r◦ 14/1) *śṛṇu proćyamānaṃ* (r◦ 8/16) *aśeṣeṇa* (r◦ 24/1) *pṛthaktvena dhanañjaya*

(§2) *buddheḥ:* (3.42); *bhedaṃ* (17.7); *dhṛteḥ:* (6pos sing◦ ←f◦ *dhṛti* 6.5); *ća* (1.1); *eva* (1.1); *guṇataḥ:* (ind◦ *guṇataṣ* ←m◦ *guṇa* 2.45); *trividhaṃ* (2acc◦ 16.21); *śṛṇu* (2.39); *proćyamānaṃ* (2acc◦ sing◦ ←śānać◦ adj◦ *proćyamāna* ←प्र√वच्); *aśeṣeṇa* (4.35); *pṛthaktvena* (9.15); *dhanañjaya* (2.48) (18.29)

(§3) *buddheḥ:* (of the thinking, understanding); *bhedaṃ* (obj◦ distinction); *dhṛteḥ:* (of the courage); *ća eva* (and); *guṇataḥ:* (adv◦ according to their *guṇas*); *trividhaṃ* (adj◦-obj◦ the threefold); *śṛṇu* (please listen to); *proćyamānaṃ* (being told); *aśeṣeṇa* (adv◦ fully); *pṛthaktvena* (adv◦ separately); *dhanañjaya* (O Arjuna!) (18.29)

(§4) dhanañjaya śṛṇu trividhaṃ bhedaṃ buddheḥ: ća eva dhṛteḥ: proćyamānaṃ aśeṣeṇa pṛthaktvena guṇataḥ:

(§5) O Arjuna! please listen to the threefold distinction of the thinking, and of courage, being told fully (and) separately, according to their *guṇas*. (18.29)

18.30 प्रवृत्तिं च निवृत्तिं च कार्याकार्ये भयाभये ।
बन्धं मोक्षं च या वेत्ति बुद्धिः सा पार्थ सात्त्विकी ।।

pravṛttiṁ ća nivṛttiṁ ća kāryākārye bhayābhaye,
bandhaṁ mokṣaṁ ća yā vetti buddhiḥ: sā pārtha sāttvikī. (18.30)

(§1) *pravṛttiṃ* (r◦ 14/1) *ća nivṛttiṃ* (r◦ 14/1) *ća kāryākārye bhayābhaye bandhaṃ* (r◦ 14/1) *mokṣaṃ* (r◦ 14/1) *ća yā vetti buddhiḥ:* (r◦ 22/7) *sā pārtha sāttvikī*

(§2) *pravṛttiṃ* (11.31); *ća* (1.1); *nivṛttiṃ* (16.7); *ća* (1.1); *kāryākārye* (n◦ 2acc◦ dual◦ ←dvandva◦ कार्यम् च अकार्यम् च 16.24); *bhayābhaye* (n◦ 2acc◦ dual◦ ←dvandva◦ भयम् च अभयम् च ←n◦ *bhaya* 2.35 + n◦ n.tatpu◦ *abhaya* 10.4); *bandhaṃ* (2acc◦ sing◦ ←m◦ *bandha* 1.27); *mokṣaṃ* (2acc◦ sing◦ ←m◦ *mokṣa* 5.28); *ća* (1.1); *yā* (2.69); *vetti* (2.19); *buddhiḥ:* (2.39); *sā* (2.69); *pārtha* (1.25); *sāttvikī* (17.2) (18.30)

(§3) *pravṛttiṃ* (obj1◦ indulgence); *ća* (and); *nivṛttiṃ* (obj2◦ abstention, refraining); *ća* (and); *kāryākārye* (obj3-4◦ what ought to be done and what ought not to be done); *bhayābhaye* (obj4-5◦ fear and fearlessness; concern and carelessness); *bandhaṃ* (obj6◦ bondage); *mokṣaṃ* (obj7◦ freedom); *ća* (and); *yā* (adj1◦-subj◦ which); *vetti* (nderstands); *buddhiḥ:* (subj◦ the thinking); *sā* (adj2◦-subj◦ that); *pārtha* (O Arjuna!); *sāttvikī* (adj3◦-subj◦ *sāttvic*) (18.30)

(§4) pārtha buddhiḥ: yā vetti pravṛttiṃ ća nivṛttiṃ ća kāryākārye bhayābhaye bandhaṃ ća mokṣaṃ sā sāttvikī

(§5) O Arjuna! the thinking which understands (i) indulgence and abstention; and (ii) what ought to be done and what ought not to be done; (iii) concern and carelessness; (iv) bondage and freedom, that (thinking is) *sāttvic.* (18.30)

18.31 यया धर्ममधर्मं च कार्यं चाकार्यमेव च ।
अयथावत्प्रजानाति बुद्धिः सा पार्थ राजसी ।।

yayā dharmamadharmaṁ ća karyaṁ ćākāryameva ća,
ayathāvatprajānāti buddhiḥ: sā pārtha rājasī. (18.31)

(§1) *yayā dharmaṃ* (r◦ 8/16) *adharmaṃ* (r◦ 14/1) *ća kāryaṃ* (r◦ 14/1) *ća* (r◦ 1/1) *akāryaṃ* (r◦ 8/22) *eva ća* (r◦ 23/1) *ayathāvaṭ* (r◦ 10/6) *prajānāti buddhiḥ:* (r◦ 22/7) *sā pārtha rājasī*

(§2) *yayā* (2.39); *dharmaṃ* (2acc◦ sing◦ ←m◦ *dharma* 1.1); *adharmaṃ* (2acc◦ sing◦ ←m◦ *adharma* 1.40); *ća* (1.1); *kāryaṃ* (3.19); *ća* (1.1); *akāryaṃ* (n◦ 2acc◦ sing◦ ←adj◦ *akārya* 16.24); *eva* (1.1); *ća* (1.1); *ayathāvaṭ* (ind◦ *a* अ 1.10 + mode indicating ind◦ *yathāvaṭ* 18.19); *prajānāti* (3rd-per◦ sing◦ pres◦ वर्तमान्-लट् parasmai◦ ←class9◦ प्र√ज्ञा 11.31); *buddhiḥ:* (2.39); *sā* (2.69); *pārtha* (1.25); *rājasī* (17.2) (18.31)

(§3) *yayā* (by which); *dharmaṃ* (obj1◦ righteousness, virtue); *adharmaṃ* (obj2◦ unrighteousness, vice); *ća* (and); *kāryaṃ* (obj3◦ what ought to be done); *ća* (and); *akāryaṃ* (obj4◦ what ought not to be done);

eva ća (and); *ayathāvat̥* (adv◦ wrongly); *prajānāti* (one understands,); *buddhiḥ:* (subj◦ the thinking); *sā* (obj1◦-subj◦ that); *pārtha* (O Arjuna!); *rājasī* (obj2◦-subj◦ *rājasīc*) (18.31)

(§4) pārtha buddhiḥ: yayā ayathāvat̥ prajānāti dharmam̥ ća adharmam̥ eva ća kāryam̥ ća akāryam̥ sā rājasī

(§5) O Arjuna! the thinking by which one wrongly understands virtue[847] and vice;[848] and what ought to be done and what ought not to be done; that (thinking is) *rājasīc.*
(18.31)

18.32 अधर्मं धर्ममिति या मन्यते तमसावृता ।
सर्वार्थान्विपरीतांश्च बुद्धिः सा पार्थ तामसी ।।
adharmaṁ dharmamiti yā manyate tamasāvṛtā,
sarvārthānviparitāṁśća buddhiḥ: sā pārtha tāmasī. (18.32)

(§1) *adharmam̥* (r◦ 14/1) *dharmam̥* (r◦ 8/18) *iti yā manyate tamasā* (r◦ 1/4) *āvṛtā sarvārthān̥* (r◦ 13/19) *viparitān̥* (r◦ 13/6) *ća buddhiḥ:* (r◦ 22/7) *sā pārtha tāmasī*

(§2) *adharmam̥* (18.31); *dharmam̥* (18.31); *iti* (1.25); *yā* (2.69); *manyate* (2.19); *tamasā* (3inst◦ sing◦ ←n◦ *tamas̥* 7.12); *āvṛtā* (f◦ 1nom◦ sing◦ ←adj◦ *āvṛta* 3.38); *sarvārthān̥* (m◦ 2acc◦ plu◦ ←tatpu◦ *sarvārtha* ←pron◦ *sarva* 1.6 + m◦ *artha* 1.7); *viparitān̥* (m◦ 2acc◦ plu◦ ←adj◦ *viparita* 1.31); *ća* (1.1); *buddhiḥ:* (2.39); *sā* (2.69); *pārtha* (1.25); *tāmasī* (17.2) (18.32)

(§3) *adharmam̥* (obj1◦ unrighteousness, vice); *dharmam̥* (obj2◦ righteousness, virtue); *iti* (as); *yā* (subj1◦ which); *manyate* (understands); *tamasā* (with darkness); *āvṛtā* (adj◦-subj1◦ covered, enveloped); *sarvārthān̥* (obj3◦ all things); *viparitān̥* (adj◦-obj3◦ reverse, contrary); *ća* (and); *buddhiḥ:* (subj1◦ the thinking); *sā* (adj1◦-subj◦ that); *pārtha* (O Arjuna!); *tāmasī* (adj2◦-subj◦ *tāmasīc*) (18.32)

(§4) pārtha buddhiḥ: yā āvṛtā tamasā manyate adharmam̥ iti dharmam̥ ća sarvārthān̥ viparitān̥ sā tāmasī

(§5) O Arjuna! the thinking which, covered[849] with darkness, understands vice as virtue and all things contrary, that (thinking is) *tāmasīc.* (18.32)

---

[847] elsewhere◦ धर्मम् → religion.

📖 Please see the footnote धर्म in verse 2.31 in Volume I of this book.

[848] elsewhere◦ अधर्मम् → irreligion.

[849] elsewhere◦ आवृता → being covered by.

📖 आवृता is a simple ppp. adjective.

18.33 धृत्या यया धारयते मन:प्राणेन्द्रियक्रिया: ।
योगेनाव्यभिचारिण्या धृति: सा पार्थ सात्त्विकी ।।

dhṛtyā yayā dhārayate manaḥ:prāṇendriyakriyāḥ:,
yogenāvyabhićāriṇyā dhṛtiḥ: sā pārtha sāttvikī. (18.33)

(§1) *dhṛtyā yayā dhārayate manaḥ:prāṇendriyakriyāḥ:* (r◦ 22/8) *yogena* (r◦ 1/1) *avyabhićāriṇyā dhṛtiḥ:* (r◦ 22/7) *sā pārtha sāttvikī*

(§2) *dhṛtyā* (3inst◦ sing◦ ←f◦ *dhṛti* 6.25); *yayā* (2.39); *dhārayate* (3rd-per◦ sing◦ pres◦ वर्तमान्-लट् ātmane◦ caus◦ ←class1◦ √धृ 15.13); *manaḥ:prāṇendriyakriyāḥ:* (f◦ 2acc◦ plu◦ ←tatpu◦ *manaḥ:-prāṇendriya-kriyā*, मनस: च प्राणस्य च इन्द्रियाणां च क्रियाणां समाहार: ←n◦ *manas* 1.3 + m◦ *prāṇa* 1.33 + n◦ *indriya* 2.8 + f◦ *kriyā* 1.42); *yogena* (10.7); *avyabhićāriṇyā* (3inst◦ sing◦ ←f◦ *a-vyabhićāriṇī* 13.11); *dhṛtiḥ:* (10.34); *sā* (2.69); *pārtha* (1.25); *sāttvikī* (17.2) (18.33)

(§3) *dhṛtyā yayā* (by the courage with which); *dhārayate* (one retains, one bears); *manaḥ:prāṇendriyakriyāḥ:* (obj◦ the functions of the body, organs and mind); *yogena* (with *buddhiyoga*, with *sama-buddhiyoga*); *avyabhićāriṇyā* (by unwavering); *dhṛtiḥ:* (subj◦ courage); *sā* (adj◦-subj◦ that); *pārtha* (O Arjuna!); *sāttvikī* (*sāttvic*). (18.33)

(§4) pārtha avyabhićāriṇyā dhṛtyā yayā dhārayate manaḥ:prāṇendriyakriyāḥ: yogena sā dhṛtiḥ: sāttvikī

(§5) O Arjuna! by unwavering courage with which one retains[850] the functions of the body, organs and mind with *sama-buddhiyoga*,[851] that courage (is) *sāttvic*. (18.33)

18.34 यया तु धर्मकामार्थान्धृत्या धारयतेऽर्जुन ।
प्रसङ्गेन फलाकाङ्क्षी धृति: सा पार्थ राजसी ।।

yayā tu dharmakāmārthāndhṛtyā dhārayate'rjuna,
prasaṅgena phalākāṅkṣī dhṛtiḥ: sā pārtha rājasī. (18.34)

(§1) *yayā tu dharmakāmārthān* (r◦ 13/12) *dhṛtyā dhārayate* (r◦ 6/1) *arjuna prasaṅgena phalākāṅkṣī dhṛtiḥ:* (r◦ 22/7) *sā pārtha rājasī*

---

[850] elsewhere◦ धारयते → restrains.

📖 Please check, in the next verse (18.34) the verb धारयते is then translated as "one holds on." Remember the root verb √धृ = to bear, to retain. Quite opposite of restrain.

[851] elsewhere◦ योगेन → with yoga, through Yoga, with yoga practice, by yoga practice, through the yoga of meditation, by meditation, through concentration, ...etc,

(§2) *yayā* (2.39); *tu* (1.2); *dharma-kāmārthān* (m◦ 2acc◦ plu◦ ←dvandva◦ धर्मम् च कामम् च अर्थम् च ←m◦ *dharma* 1.1 + m◦ *kāma* 1.22 + m◦ *artha* 1.7); *dhṛtyā* (18.33); *dhārayate* (18.33); *arjuna* (2.2); *prasaṅgena* (3inst◦ sing◦ ←m◦ *prasaṅga* ←प्र√सञ्ज्); *phalākāṅkṣī* (m◦ 1nom◦ sing◦ ←desi◦ adj◦ *phalākāṅkṣin* 17.11); *dhṛtiḥ:* (10.34); *sā* (2.69); *pārtha* (1.25); *rājasī* (17.2) (18.34)

(§3) *yayā* (with which); *tu* (but); *dharma-kāmārthān* (obj◦ virtues, passions and possessions); *dhṛtyā* (with courage); *dhārayate* (bears); *arjuna* (O Arjuna!); *prasaṅgena* (= *saṅgena,* with attachment); *phalākāṅkṣī* (subj1◦ one who performs *karma* with the desire of its fruit); *dhṛtiḥ:* (subj2◦ courage); *sā* (adj◦-subj2◦ that); *pārtha* (O Arjuna!); *rājasī* (*rājasic*). (18.34)

(§4) tu arjuna dhṛtyā yayā phalākāṅkṣī dhārayate dharmakāmārthān prasaṅgena pārtha sā dhṛtiḥ: rājasī

(§5) But, O Arjuna! the courage with which 'a fruit wisher'[852] bears virtues, passions and possessions with attachment to them, O Arjuna! that courage (is) *rājasic*. (18.34)

18.35 यया स्वप्नं भयं शोकं विषादं मदमेव च ।
न विमुञ्चति दुर्मेधा धृतिः सा पार्थ तामसी ।।
yayā svapnaṁ bhayaṁ śokaṁ viṣādaṁ madameva ća,
na vimuñćati durmedhā dhṛti sā pārtha tāmasī. (18.35)

(§1) *yayā svapnam* (r◦ 14/1) *bhayam* (r◦ 14/1) *śokam* (r◦ 14/1) *viṣādam* (r◦ 14/1) *madam* (r◦ 8/22) *eva ća na vimuñćati durmedhā* (r◦ 20.9) *dhṛtiḥ:* (r◦ 22/7) *sā pārtha tāmasī*

(§2) *yayā* (2.39); *svapnam* (2acc◦ sing◦ ←m◦ *svapna* 6.16); *bhayam* (10.4); *śokam* (2.8); *viṣādam* (2acc◦ sing◦ ←m◦ *viṣāda* 1.27); *madam* (2acc◦ sing◦ ←m◦ *mada* 16.10); *eva* (1.1); *ća* (1.1); *na* (1.30); *vimuñćati* (3rd-per◦ sing◦ pres◦ वर्तमान्-लट् parasmai◦ ←class6◦ वि√मुच्); 📖*durmedhāḥ:* (m◦ 1nom◦ sing◦ ←bahuvrī◦ *durmedhas*, दुर्-मेधा यस्य सः ←ind◦ *dur* 1.2 + f◦ *medhā* 7.23); *dhṛtiḥ:* (10.34); *sā* (2.69); *pārtha* (1.25); *tāmasī* (17.2) (18.35)

(§3) *yayā* (with which); *svapnam* (obj1◦ sleep); *bhayam* (obj2◦ fear); *śokam* (obj3◦ grief); *viṣādam* (obj4◦ despair); *madam* (obj5◦ vanity); *eva ća* (and); *na vimuñćati* (he does not let go of, give up); *durmedhāḥ:* (adj◦-subj◦ a person of deluded thinking); *dhṛtiḥ:* (subj◦ the courage); *sā* (adj1◦-subj◦ that); *pārtha* (O Arjuna!); *tāmasī* (adj2◦-subj◦ *tāmasic*). (18.35)

---

[852] elsewhere◦ फलाकाङ्क्षी → being desirous of fruit..., with desire for the fruit..., and expects fruit, desiring their fruit because of attachment, fruitive results, desires of fruitive results, induces him to desire the fruit, ...etc.

📖 फलाकाङ्क्षी is a simple Nominative adjective. It is not a gerund or verb.

(§4) pārtha dhṛtiḥ: yayā durmedhāḥ: a person of deluded thinking does not let go svapnam̦ fear, śokam̦ viṣādam̦ eva ća madam̦ sā that tāmasī

(§5) O Arjuna! the courage with which <u>a person</u>[853] of deluded thinking <u>does not let go</u>[854] of sleep, fear, grief, despair and vanity, that (courage is) *tāmasic.* (18.35)

18.36 सुखं त्विदानीं त्रिविधं शृणु मे भरतर्षभ ।
अभ्यासाद्रमते यत्र दुःखान्तं च निगच्छति ।।

sukhaṁ tvidānīṁ trividhaṁ sṛṇu me bharatarṣabha,
abhyāsādramate yatra duḥ:khāntaṁ ća nigaććhati. (18.36)

(§1) *sukham̦* (r◦ 14/1) *tu* (r◦ 4/8) *idānīm̦* (r◦ 14/1) *trividham̦* (r◦ 14/1) *śṛṇu me bharatarṣabha* (r◦ 23/1) *abhyāsāț* (r◦ 9/10) *ramate yatra duḥ:khāntam̦* (r◦ 14/1) *ća nigaććhati*

(§2) *sukham̦* (2acc◦ 2.66); *tu* (1.2); *idānīm̦* (2acc◦ 11.51); *trividham̦* (adv◦); *śṛṇu* (2.39); *me* (1.21); *bharatarṣabha* (3.41); *abhyāsāț* (12.12); *ramate* (5.22); *yatra* (6.20); *duḥ:khāntam̦* (m◦ 2acc◦ sing◦ ←tatpu◦ *duḥ:khānta,* दुःखस्य अन्तः ←n◦ *duḥ:kha* 2.14 + m◦ *anta* 2.16); *ća* (1.1); *nigaććhati* (9.31) (18.36)

(§3) *sukham̦* (obj1◦ happiness); *tu* (but); *idānīm̦* (now); *trividham̦* (adj◦-obj1◦ the threefold); *śṛṇu* (please listen); *me* (from me); *bharatarṣabha* (O Arjuna!); *abhyāsāț* (from the practice); *ramate* (one feels delighted); *yatra* (of which); *duḥ:khāntam̦* (obj2◦ the end of woes); *ća* (and); *nigaććhati* (one attains, one reaches) (18.36)

(§4) tu idānīm̦ bharatarṣabha śṛṇu me trividham̦ sukham̦ abhyāsāț yatra ramate ća nigaććhati duḥ:khāntam̦

(§5) But now, O Arjuna! please listen from me the threefold happiness, from the practice of which one feels delighted and one attains the end of woes. (18.36)

18.37 यत्तदग्रे विषमिव परिणामेऽमृतोपमम् ।
तत्सुखं सात्त्विकं प्रोक्तमात्मबुद्धिप्रसादजम् ।।

---

[853] elsewhere◦ दुर्मेधा: → from <u>stupidity</u>, unintelligent <u>determination</u>, ...etc.

🕮 Please note that : it is not f◦ दुर्मेधा it is m◦ दुर्मेधा: an adjective of a masculine noun, a person दुर्मेधस् (दुर्मेधा: दुर्मेधसौ दुर्मेधस:) of दुर्मेधा (deluded thinking). The visarga of दुर्मेधा: is deleted by its sandhi with the following word धृति: ।

[854] elsewhere◦ विमुञ्चति → cannot go beyond.

🕮 Please note, धृति: is not the subject of विमुञ्चति । m◦ दुर्मेधा: is the subject of the verb विमुञ्चति ।

yattadagre viṣamiva pariṇāme'mṛtopamam,
tatsukhaṁ sāttvikaṁ proktamātmabuddhiprasādajam. (18.37)

(§1) *yat* (r◦ 1/10) *tat* (r◦ 8/2) *agre viṣam* (r◦ 8/18) *iva pariṇāme* (r◦ 6/1) *amṛtopamam* (r◦ 14/2) *tat* (r◦ 10/7) *sukham* (r◦ 14/1) *sāttvikam* (r◦ 14/1) *proktam* (r◦ 8/17) *ātmabuddhiprasādajam* (r◦ 14/2)

(§2) *yat* (1nom◦ 1.45); *tat* (1nom◦ 1.10); 🕮*agre* (7loc◦ sing◦ ←n◦ *agra* 6.12); *viṣam* (1nom◦ sing◦ ←n◦ *viṣa* ←√विष्); *iva* (1.30); 🕮*pariṇāme* (7loc◦ sing◦ ←m◦ *pariṇāma* ←परि√नम्); *amṛtopamam* (1nom◦ sing◦ ←bahuvrī◦ *amṛtopama*, अमृतम् उपमा यस्य ←n◦ *amṛta* 2.15 + f◦ *upamā* 6.19); *tat* (1nom◦ 1.10); *sukham* (1nom◦ 2.66); *sāttvikam* (1nom◦ 17.17); *proktam* (1nom◦ 8.1); *ātmabuddhiprasādajam* (1nom◦ sing◦ ←bahuvrī◦ *ātma-buddhi-prasāda-ja*, आत्मनः बुद्धेः or बुद्ध्याः प्रसादात् जातम् यत् ←n◦ *ātman* 2.41 + f◦ *buddhi* 1.23 + m◦ *prasāda* 2.64 + adj◦ *ja* 1.7) (18.37)

(§3) *yat* (adj1◦-subj◦ which); *tat* (adj2◦-subj◦ that); *agre* (in the beginning, at the outset); *viṣam iva* (like a poison, bitter); *pariṇāme* (in the end); *amṛtopamam* (like the nectar of immortality); *tat* (adj2◦-subj◦ that, that happiness); *sukham* (subj◦ happiness); *sāttvikam* (adj3◦-subj◦ *sāttvic*); *proktam* (adj4◦-subj◦ called); *ātmabuddhiprasādajam* (adj5◦-subj◦ born from the tranquility of one's own mind) (18.37)

(§4) tat sukham yat viṣam iva agre pariṇāme amṛtopamam tat ātmabuddhiprasādajam proktam sāttvikam

(§5) That happiness which is bitter like a poison at the outset (but) in the end (sweet) like the nectar of immortality, that happiness born from the tranquility of one's own mind[855] (is) called *sāttvic*. (18.37)

18.38 विषयेन्द्रियसंयोगाद्यत्तदग्रेऽमृतोपमम् ।
परिणामे विषमिव तत्सुखं राजसं स्मृतम् ॥
viṣayendriyasaṁyogādyattadagre'mṛtopamam,
pariṇāme viṣamiva tatsukhaṁ rājasaṁ smṛtam. (18.38)

(§1) *viṣayendriyasaṁyogāt* (r◦ 9/9) *yat* (r◦ 1/10) *tat* (r◦ 8/2) *agre* (r◦ 6/1) *amṛtopamam* (r◦ 14/2) *pariṇāme viṣam* (r◦ 8/18) *iva tat* (r◦ 10/7) *sukham* (r◦ 14/1) *rājasam* (r◦ 14/1) *smṛtam* (r◦ 14/2)

(§2) *viṣayendriyasaṁyogāt* (m◦ 5abl◦ sing◦ ←tatpu◦ *viṣayendriya-saṁyoga*, विषयाणां च इन्द्रियाणाम् च संयोगः ←m◦ *viṣaya* 2.45 + n◦ *indriya* 2.8 + m◦ *saṁyoga* 5.14); *yat* (1nom◦ 2.67); *tat* (nom◦ 1.10); *agre* (18.37); *amṛtopamam* (1nom◦ 18.37); *pariṇāme* (18.37); *viṣam* (1nom◦ 18.37); *iva* (1.30); *tat* (1nom◦

---

[855] elsewhere◦ आत्मबुद्धिप्रसादजम् → which awakens one to delf-realization, which arises from the purity of one's intellect, transluscence of intellect due to self-Realization, born of a clear understanding of the Self,

1.10); *sukham̩* (1nom∘ 2.66); *rājasam̩* (1nom∘ 17.12); *smṛtam̩* (17.20) (18.38)

(§3) *viṣayendriyasam̐yogāt̩* (from the intercourse of organs with their sense objects); *yat̩* (adj1∘-subj∘ which); *tat̩* (adj2∘-subj∘ that); *agre* (at the outset); *amṛtopamam̩* (adj3∘-subj∘ like the nectar); *pariṇāme* (in the end); *viṣam̩ iva* (like a poison); *tat̩* (adj2∘-subj∘ that happiness); *sukham̩* (subj∘ the happiness); *rājasam̩* (adj4∘-subj∘ *rājasic*); *smṛtam̩* (adj5∘-subj∘ known as) (18.38)

(§4) sukham̩ yat̩ viṣayendriyasam̐yogāt̩ tat̩ amṛtopamam̩ agre viṣam̩ iva pariṇāme tat̩ smṛtam̩ rājasam̩

(§5) The happiness which (is born) from the intercourse of organs with their sense objects (and) that (is) like the nectar at the outset (and) like a poison in the end, that happiness (is) known as *rājasic.* (18.38)

18.39 यदग्रे चानुबन्धे च सुखं मोहनमात्मनः ।
निद्रालस्यप्रमादोत्थं तत्तामसमुदाहृतम् ।।
yadagre ćānubandhe ća sukhaṁ mohanamātmanaḥ:,
nidrālasyapramādotthaṁ tattāmasamudahṛtam̩. (18.39)

(§1) *yat̩* (r∘ 8/2) *agre ća* (r∘ 1/1) *anubandhe ća sukham̩* (r∘ 14/1) *mohanam̩* (r∘ 8/17) *ātmanaḥ:* (r∘ 22/8) *nidrālasyapramādottham̩* (r∘ 14/1) *tat̩* (r∘ 1/10) *tāmasam̩* (r∘ 8/20) *udāhṛtam̩* (r∘ 14/2)

(§2) *yat̩* (1nom∘ 1.45); *agre* (18.37); *ća* (1.1); 🕮*anubandhe* (7loc∘ sing∘ ←m∘ *anubandha* 15.2); *ća* (1.1); *sukham̩* (1nom∘ 2.66); *mohanam̩* (1nom∘ 14.8); *ātmanaḥ:* (4.42); *nidrālasyapramādottham̩* (n∘ 1nom∘ sing∘ ←bahuvrī∘ *nidrālasya-pramādottha*, निद्रया च आलस्येन च प्रमादेन च उत्थितं यत ←f∘ *nidrā* 14.8 + n∘ *ālasya* 14.8 + m∘ *pramāda* 11.41 + adj∘ *utthita* 11.12 or ppp∘ adj∘ *uttha* ←उद्√स्था); *tat̩* (1nom∘ 1.10); *tāmasam̩* (1nom∘ 17.13); *udāhṛtam̩* (1nom∘ 13.7) (18.39)

(§3) *yat̩* (adj1∘-subj∘ which); *agre* (at the outset); *ća* (and); *anubandhe* (at the end); *ća* (and); *sukham̩* (subj∘ the happiness); *mohanam̩* (adj2∘-subj∘ hypnotizing, delusive); *ātmanaḥ:* (to oneself); *nidrālasyapramādottham̩* (adj3∘-subj∘ which is born of sleep, laziness and inadvertence); *tat̩* (adj4∘-subj∘ that happiness); *tāmasam̩* (adj5∘-subj∘ *tāmasic*); *udāhṛtam̩* (adj6∘-subj∘ called) (18.39)

(§4) sukham̩ yat̩ nidrālasyapramādottham̩ ća mohanam̩ ātmanaḥ: agre ća anubandhe tat̩ udāhṛtam̩ tāmasam̩

(§5) The happiness which is born of sleep, laziness and inadvertence and (which is) delusive to oneself at the outset (and) at the end, that happiness (is) called *tāmasic.* (18.39)

18.40 न तदस्ति पृथिव्यां वा दिवि देवेषु वा पुनः ।
सत्त्वं प्रकृतिजैर्मुक्तं यदेभिः स्यात्त्रिभिर्गुणैः ।।
na tadasti pṛthivyāṁ vā divi deveṣu vā punaḥ:,

sattvaṁ prakṛtijairmuktaṁ yadebhiḥ: syāttribhirguṇaiḥ:. (18.40)

(§1) *na taṭ* (r◦ 8/2) *asti pṛthivyāṃ* (r◦ 14/1) *vā divi deveṣu* (r◦ 25/5) *vā punaḥ:* (r◦ 22/8) *sattvaṃ* (r◦ 14/1) *prakṛtijaiḥ:* (r◦ 16/11) *muktaṃ* (r◦ 14/1) *yaṭ* (r◦ 8/9) *ebhiḥ:* (r◦ 22/7) *syāṭ* (r◦ 1/10) *tribhiḥ:* (r◦ 16/6) *guṇaiḥ:* (r◦ 22/8)

(§2) *na* (1.30); *taṭ* (1nom◦ 1.10); *asti* (2.40); *pṛthivyāṃ* (7.9); *vā* (1.32); *divi* (9.20); *deveṣu* (7loc◦ plu◦ ←m◦ *deva* 3.11); *vā* (1.32); *punaḥ:* (4.35); *sattvaṃ* (1nom◦ 10.36); *prakṛtijaiḥ:* (3.5); *muktaṃ* (n◦ 1nom◦ sing◦ ←ppp◦ adj◦ *mukta* 3.9); *yaṭ* (1.45); **ebhiḥ:* (7.13); *syāṭ* (1.36); *tribhiḥ:* (7.13); *guṇaiḥ:* (3.5) (18.40)

(§3) *na* (no such); *taṭ* (adj1◦-subj◦ that); *asti* (is, there is); *pṛthivyāṃ* (in the world, on the earth); *vā* (either); *divi* (in the heaven); *deveṣu* (in the gods); *vā* (or); *punaḥ:* (also); *sattvaṃ* (subj◦ entity, thing); *prakṛtijaiḥ:* (adj1◦-subj◦ by the - born of *prakṛtiḥ,* produced by nature); *muktaṃ* (adj2◦-subj◦ free of); *yaṭ* (adj1◦-subj◦ which); *ebhiḥ:* (by these); *syāṭ* (may be); *tribhiḥ:* (by three); *guṇaiḥ:* (by *guṇas*) (18.40)

(§4) asti na sattvaṃ vā pṛthivyāṃ vā divi deveṣu punaḥ: taṭ yaṭ syāṭ muktaṃ ebhiḥ: tribhiḥ: guṇaiḥ: prakṛtijaiḥ:

(§5) There is no such thing either in the world or in the heaven in the gods also that may be free of these three *guṇas* born of *prakṛtiḥ*. (18.40)

18.41 ब्राह्मणक्षत्रियविशां शूद्राणां च परन्तप ।
कर्माणि प्रविभक्तानि स्वभावप्रभवैर्गुणैः ।।
brāhmaṇakṣtriyaviśāṁ śūdrāṇāṁ ća parantapa,
karmāṇi pravibhaktāni svabhāvaprabhavairguṇaiḥ:. (18.41)

(§1) *brāhmaṇakṣtriyaviśāṃ* (r◦ 14/1) *śūdrāṇāṃ* (r◦ 24/6, 14/1) *ća parantapa karmāṇi* (r◦ 24/7) *pravibhaktāni svabhāvaprabhavaiḥ:* (r◦ 16/11) *guṇaiḥ:* (r◦ 22/8)

(§2) *brāhmaṇakṣtriyaviśāṃ* (m◦ 6pos◦ plu◦ ←dvandva◦ ब्राह्मणानाम् क्षत्रियाणाम् विशाम् च ←adj◦ *brāhmaṇa* 2.46 + adj◦ *kṣatriya* 2.31 + adj◦ *viś* ←√विश्); *śūdrāṇāṃ* (m◦ 6pos plu◦ ←adj◦ *śūdra* 9.32); *ća* (1.1); *parantapa* (2.3); *karmāṇi* (1nom◦ 3.27); *pravibhaktāni* (n◦ 1nom◦ plu◦ ←ppp◦ adj◦ *pravibhakta* 11.13); *svabhāvaprabhavaiḥ:* (m◦ 3inst◦ plu◦ ←tatpu◦ *svabhāva-prabhava,* स्वभावतः प्रभवः यस्य ←m◦ *svabhāva* 2.7 + m◦ *prabhava* 6.24); *guṇaiḥ:* (3.5) (18.41)

(§3) *brāhmaṇakṣtriyaviśāṃ* (of the brahmaṇas, kṣatriyas, vaishyas; of the intellectuals; warriors, tradesmen); *śūdrāṇāṃ* (of the sūdras; of the people of serving class); *ća* (and); *parantapa* (O Arjuna!); *karmāṇi* (subj◦ the duties); *pravibhaktāni* (adj◦-subj◦ apportioned); *svabhāvaprabhavaiḥ:* (according to the inborn, innate); *guṇaiḥ:* (*guṇas,* attributes, nature) (18.41)

(§4) parantapa karmāṇi brāhmaṇakṣtriyaviśāṃ ća śūdrāṇāṃ pravibhaktāni svabhāvaprabhavaiḥ: guṇaiḥ:

(§5) O Arjuna! the duties of the intellectuals;[856] warriors,[857] tradesmen[858] and of the people of serving class[859] (are) apportioned according to their inborn nature. (18.41)

18.42 शमो दमस्तपः शौचं क्षान्तिरार्जवमेव च ।
ज्ञानं विज्ञानमास्तिक्यं ब्रह्मकर्म स्वभावजम् ।।
śamo damastapaḥ: śaućaṁ kṣāntirārjavameva ća,
jñānaṁ vijñānamāstikyaṁ brahmakarma svabhāvajaṃ. (18.42)

(§1) *śamaḥ:* (r◦ 15/4) *damaḥ:* (r◦ 18/1) *tapaḥ:* (r◦ 22/5) *śaućaṃ* (r◦ 14/1) *kṣāntiḥ:* (r◦ 16/1) *ārjavaṃ* (r◦ 8/22) *eva ća jñānaṃ* (r◦ 14/1) *vijñānaṃ* (r◦ 8/17) *āstikyaṃ* (r◦ 14/1) *brahmakarma svabhājaṃ* (r◦ 14/2)

(§2) *śamaḥ:* (6.3); *damaḥ:* (10.4); *tapaḥ:* (7.9); *śaućaṃ* (13.8); *kṣāntiḥ:* (13.8); *ārjavaṃ* (13.8); *eva* (1.1); *ća* (1.1); *jñānaṃ* (1nom◦ 3.39); *vijñānaṃ* (1nom◦ sing◦ ←n◦ *vijñāna* 3.41); *āstikyaṃ* (1nom◦ sing◦ ←n◦ *āstikya* ←adj◦ *āstika* ←√अस्); *brahmakarma* (n◦ 1nom◦ sing◦ ←tatpu◦ *brahma-karman*, ब्रह्मणः कर्म 4.24); *svabhājaṃ* (n◦ 1nom◦ sing◦ ←bahuvrī◦ *svabhāva-ja* 17.2) (18.42)

(§3) *śamaḥ:* (subj1◦ calmness); *damaḥ:* (subj2◦ self-control, restraint); *tapaḥ:* (subj3◦ austerity); *śaućaṃ* (subj4◦ purity, internal and external purity); *kṣāntiḥ:* (subj5◦ patience); *ārjavaṃ* (subj6◦ uprightness, sincerity, honesty); *eva ća* (and); *jñānaṃ* (subj6◦ knowledge, wisdom); *vijñānaṃ* (subj7◦ practical experience, science); *āstikyaṃ* (subj8◦ theism, piety); *brahmakarma* (subj9◦ duty or qualities for the members of the intellectual class); *svabhājaṃ* (adj◦-subj9◦ the inborn, innate) (18.42)

(§4) śamaḥ: damaḥ: tapaḥ: śaućaṃ kṣāntiḥ: ārjavaṃ jñānaṃ vijñānaṃ eva ća āstikyaṃ svabhājaṃ brahmakarma

(§5) Calmness, self-control, austerity, internal and external purity, patience, honesty, wisdom, practical experience and piety (are) the inborn qualities for the members of the intellectual class. (18.42)

---

[856] elsewhere◦ ब्राह्मण → member of the of the brāhmana caste, Please see footnote in verse 1.42

[857] elsewhere◦ क्षत्रिय → member of the warrior caste. Please see footnote in verse 2.31

[858] elsewhere◦ विशाम् → of the members of the farmer caste. Please see footnote in verse 1.42

[859] elsewhere◦ शूद्राणाम् → of the members of the fourth or servant caste. Please see footnote in verse 1.42

18.43 शौर्यं तेजो धृतिर्दाक्ष्यं युद्धे चाप्यपलायनम् ।
दानमीश्वरभावश्च क्षात्रं कर्म स्वभावजम् ।।

śauryaṁ tejo dhṛtirdākṣyaṁ yuddhe ćāpyapalāyanaṃ,
dānamīśvarabhāvaśća kṣātraṁ karma svabhāvajaṃ. (18.43)

(§1) *śauryaṃ* (r◦ 14/1) *tejaḥ:* (r◦ 15/5) *dhṛtiḥ:* (r◦ 16/6) *dākṣyaṃ* (r◦ 14/1) *yuddhe ća* (r◦ 1/1) *api* (r◦ 4/1) *apalāyanaṃ* (r◦ 14/2) *dānaṃ* (r◦ 8/19) *īśvarabhāvaḥ:* (r◦ 17/1) *ća kṣātraṃ* (r◦ 14/1) *karma svabhājaṃ* (r◦ 14/2)

(§2) 🕮*śauryaṃ* (1nom◦ sing◦ ←n◦ *śaurya* ←√शुर्); *tejaḥ:* (7.9); *dhṛtiḥ:* (10.34); 🕮*dākṣyaṃ* (1nom◦ sing◦ ←n◦ *dākṣya* ←√दक्ष्); *yuddhe* (1.23); *ća* (1.1); *api* (1.26); *ća* (1.1) *a-palāyanaṃ* (1nom◦ sing◦ n.tatpu◦ ←n◦ *palāyana* ←परा√अय्); *dānaṃ* (10.5); *īśvarabhāvaḥ:* (m◦ 1nom◦ sing◦ ←tatpu◦ *īśvara-bhāva,* ईश्वरः इव भावः ←m◦ *īśvara* 4.6 + m◦ *bhāva* 2.7); *ća* (1.1); *kṣātraṃ* (n◦ 1nom◦ sing◦ ←adj◦ *kṣātra* ←√क्षण्); *karma* (2.49); *svabhājaṃ* (18.42) (18.43)

(§3) *śauryaṃ* (subj1◦ valour); *tejaḥ:* (subj2◦ power, prowess); *dhṛtiḥ:* (subj3◦ courage); *dākṣyaṃ* (subj4◦ skill); *yuddhe* (in war); *ća* (and); *api ća* (and) *apalāyanaṃ* (subj5◦ not running away, staying firm); *dānaṃ* (subj6◦ charity); *īśvarabhāvaḥ:* (subj7◦ lordliness); *ća* (and); *kṣātraṃ karma* (subj8◦ nature for a member of the warroir class); *svabhājaṃ* (adj◦-subj8◦ the inborn) (18.43)

(§4) śauryaṃ tejaḥ: dhṛtiḥ: ća dākṣyaṃ ća apalāyanaṃ yuddhe api ća dānaṃ īśvarabhāvaḥ: svabhājaṃ kṣātraṃ karma

(§5) Valour, prowess, courage and skill and staying firm in the war, and charity, lordliness (are) the inborn for a member of the warroir class. (18.43)

18.44 कृषिगौरक्ष्यवाणिज्यं वैश्यकर्म स्वभावजम् ।
परिचर्यात्मकं कर्म शूद्रस्यापि स्वभावजम् ।।

kṛṣigaurakṣyavāṇijyaṁ vaiśyakarma svabhāvajaṃ,
parićaryātmakaṁ karma śūdrasyāpi svabhāvajaṃ. (18.44)

(§1) *kṛṣigaurakṣyavāṇijyaṃ* (r◦ 14/1) *vaiśyakarma svabhājaṃ* (r◦ 14/2) *parićaryātmakaṃ* (r◦ 14/1) *karma śūdrasya* (r◦ 1/1) *api svabhājaṃ* (r◦ 14/2)

(§2) *kṛṣi-gau-rakṣya-vāṇijyaṃ* (n◦ 1nom◦ sing◦ ←dvandva◦ कृषिः च गौरक्ष्यम् च वाणिज्यम् च ←f◦ *kṛṣi* ←√कृष् + f◦ *go* 5.18 + n◦ *rakṣa* ←√रक्ष् + n◦ *vāṇijya* ←√पण्); *vaiśyakarma* (n◦ 1nom◦ sing◦ ←tatpu◦ *vaiśya-karmaṇ,* वैश्यानाम् कर्म ←m◦ *vaiśya* 9.32 + n◦ *karmaṇ* 1.15); *svabhājaṃ* (18.42); *parićaryātmakaṃ* (n◦ 1nom◦ sing◦ ←adj◦ *parićaryātmaka* ←f◦ *parićaryā* ←परि√चर् + adj◦ *ātmaka* 14.7); *karma* (2.49); *śūdrasya*

(6pos sing◦ ←m◦ *śūdra* 9.32); *api* (1.26); *svabhājam̧* (18.42) (18.44)

(§3) *kr̥ṣigaurakṣyavāṇijyam̧* (subj1-3◦ farming, cattle raising and trade); *vaiśyakarma* (subj2◦ duty for a member of the tradesmen's class); *svabhājam̧* (adj◦-subj2◦ the inborn); *paricaryātmakam̧* (adj1◦-subj4◦ consisting of service); *karma* (subj4◦ the duty); *śūdrasya* (for a member of the service class); *api* (also); *svabhājam̧* (adj2◦-subj4◦ inborn) (18.44)

(§4) kr̥ṣigaurakṣyavāṇijyam̧ svabhājam̧ vaiśyakarma api karma paricaryātmakam̧ svabhājam̧ śūdrasya

(§5) Farming, cattle raising and trade (is) the inborn duty for a member of the tradesmen's class. Also, the duty consisting of service (is) inborn for a member of the service class. (18.44)

18.45 स्वे स्वे कर्मण्यभिरत: संसिद्धिं लभते नर: ।
स्वकर्मनिरत: सिद्धिं यथा विन्दति तच्छृणु ।।
sve sve karmaṇyabhiratah̤: saṁsiddhiṁ labhate narah̤:,
svakarmaniratah̤: siddhiṁ yathā vindati taććhruṇu. (18.45)

(§1) *sve sve karmaṇi* (r◦ 24/7, 4/1) *abhiratah̤:* (r◦ 22/7) *saṁsiddhim̧* (r◦ 14/1) *labhate narah̤:* (r◦ 22/8) *svakarmaniratah̤:* (r◦ 22/7) *siddhim̧* (r◦ 14/1) *yathā vindati taţ* (r◦ 11/4) *śr̥ṇu*

(§2) *svae* (m◦ 7loc◦ sing◦ ←pron◦ adj◦ *sva* 1.28); *svae* (↑); *karmaṇi* (2.47); *abhiratah̤:* (m◦ 1nom◦ sing◦ ←ppp◦ adj◦ *abhirata* ←अभि√रम्); *saṁsiddhim̧* (3.20); *labhate* (4.39); *narah̤:* (2.22); *svakarmaniratah̤:* (m◦ 1nom◦ sing◦ ←tatpu◦ *svakarma-nirata*, स्वस्य कर्मणि निरत: ←adj◦ *sva* 1.28 + n◦ *karmaņ* 1.15 + ppp◦ adj◦ *nirata* ←नि√रम्); *siddhim̧* (3.4); *yathā* (1.11); *vindati* (4.38); *taţ* (2acc◦ 2.7); *śr̥ṇu* (2.39) (18.45)

(§3) *svae svae* (in one's own); *karmaṇi* (in duty); *abhiratah̤:* (adj1◦-subj◦ engaged); *saṁsiddhim̧* (obj◦ success); *labhate* (one attains); *narah̤:* (subj◦ a person); *svakarmaniratah̤:* (adj2◦-subj◦ engaged in one's own duty); *siddhim̧* (obj◦ success); *yathā* (how); *vindati* (one attains); *taţ* (adj◦-obj◦ that); *śr̥ṇu* (please listen) (18.45)

(§4) abhiratah̤: svae svae karmaṇi narah̤: labhate saṁsiddhim̧ śr̥ṇu yathā vindati taţ siddhim̧ svakarmaniratah̤:

(§5) Engaged[860] in one's own[861] duty a person attains success.[862] Please listen how one attains

[860] elsewhere◦ निरत: → being devoted.

📖 निरत: is not a gerund. It is a simple ppp. adjective.

[861] elsewhere◦ स्वे स्वे कर्मणि → repeated kind of action.

[862] elsewhere◦ संसिद्धिम्, सिद्धिम् → perfection.

📖 Please footnote सिद्धिम् in verse 2.10, in volume I of this book..

that success engaged in one's own duty. (18.45)

18.46 यत: प्रवृत्तिर्भूतानां येन सर्वमिदं ततम् ।
स्वकर्मणा तमभ्यर्च्य सिद्धिं विन्दति मानव: ।।

yataḥ: pravṛttirbhūtānām yena sarvamidam tatam,

svakarmaṇā tamabhyarćya siddhim vindati mānavaḥ:. (18.46)

(§1) *yataḥ:* (r◦ 22/3) *pravṛttiḥ:* (r◦ 16/6) *bhūtānām* (r◦ 14/1) *yena sarvam* (r◦ 8/18) *idam* (r◦ 14/1) *tatam* (r◦ 14/2) *svakarmaṇā* (r◦ 24/4) *tam* (r◦ 8/16) *abhyarćya siddhim* (r◦ 14/1) *vindati mānavaḥ:* (r◦ 22/8)

(§2) *yataḥ:* (6.26); *pravṛttiḥ:* (14.12); *bhūtānām* (2.69); *yena* (2.17); *sarvam* (2.17); *idam* (1.10); *tatam* (2.17); *svakarmaṇā* (n◦ 3inst◦ sing◦ ←tatpu◦ *sva-karman* ←adj◦ *sva* 1.28 + n◦ *karman* 1.15); *tam* (2.1); *abhyarćya* (lyp◦ past-participle ind◦ ←अभि√अर्च्); *siddhim* (3.4); *vindati* (4.38); *mānavaḥ:* (3.17)
(18.46)

(§3) *yataḥ:* (from whom); *pravṛttiḥ:* (subj1◦ origin); *bhūtānām* (of the beings); *yena* (by whom); *sarvam* (adj1◦-subj2◦ all); *idam* (subj2◦ this, this universe); *tatam* (adj2◦-subj2◦ evolved); *svakarmaṇā* (through his own duty); *tam* (obj1◦ him); *abhyarćya* (worshipping); *siddhim* (obj2◦ success); *vindati* (one attains); *mānavaḥ:* (subj3◦ a person)
(18.46)

(§4) mānavaḥ: vindati siddhim svakarmaṇā abhyarćya tam yataḥ: pravṛttiḥ bhūtānām yena sarvam idam tatam

(§5) A person[863] attains success,[864] through his own duty,[865] worshipping Him, from whom origin of the beings (takes place), (and) by whom all this (is) evolved.[866]
(18.46)

18.47 श्रेयान्स्वधर्मो विगुण: परधर्मात्स्वनुष्ठितात् ।

---

[863] elsewhere◦ मानव: → Man

[864] elsewhere◦ सिद्धिम् → perfection.

   📖 Please footnote सिद्धिम् in verse 2.10, in volume I of this book..

[865] elsewhere◦ स्वकर्मणा → with his own action.

[866] elsewhere◦ ततम् → pervaded.

   📖 Please footnote ततम् in verse 2.17, in volume I of this book..

स्वभावनियतं कर्म कुर्वन्नाप्नोति किल्बिषम् ।।

śreyān svadharmo viguṇaḥ: paradharmātsvanuṣṭhitāta,

svabhāvaniyataṁ karma kurvannāpnoti kilbiṣam. (18.47)

(§1) *śreyān* (r◦ 13/20) *svadharmaḥ:* (r◦ 15/13) *viguṇaḥ:* (r◦ 22/3) *paradharmāt* (r◦ 10/7) *svanuṣṭhitāt* (r◦ 23/1) *svabhāvaniyatam* (r◦ 14/1) *karma kurvan* (r◦ 1/11) *na* (r◦ 1/2) *āpnoti kilbiṣam* (r◦ 14/2)

(§2) *śreyān* (3.35); *svadharmaḥ:* (3.35); *viguṇaḥ:* (3.35); *paradharmāt* (3.35); *svanuṣṭhitāt* (3.35); *svabhāvaniyatam* (n◦ 2acc◦ sing◦ ←adj◦ *svabhāva-niyata,* स्वभावेन नियतम् ←m◦ *svabhāva* 2.7 + ppp◦ adv◦ *niyata* 1.44); *karma* (2acc◦ 3.8); *kurvan* (1nom◦ 4.21); *na* (1.30); *āpnoti* (2.70); *kilbiṣam* (2acc◦ 4.21) (18.47)

(§3) *śreyān* (adj1◦-subj◦ superior, better); *svadharmaḥ:* (subj◦ one's own duty); *viguṇaḥ:* (adj2◦-subj◦ defective); *paradharmāt* (than other person's duty); *svanuṣṭhitāt* (than well performed); *svabhāvaniyatam* (adj◦-obj1◦ prescribed by one's own inborn nature); *karma* (obj1◦ a duty); *kurvan* (while doing); *na āpnoti* (one does not incur); *kilbiṣam* (obj2◦ sin) (18.47)

(§4) svadharmaḥ: viguṇaḥ: śreyān paradharmāt svanuṣṭhitāt na āpnoti kilbiṣam karma svabhāvaniyatam

(§5) One's own duty[867] (even) defective (is) better than other person's duty well performed. One does not incur sin while doing a duty[868] prescribed by one's own inborn nature. (18.47)

18.48 सहजं कर्म कौन्तेय सदोषमपि न त्यजेत् ।

सर्वारम्भा हि दोषेण धूमेनाग्निरिवावृताः ।।

sahajaṁ karma kaunteya sadoṣamapi na tyajet,

sarvārambhā hi doṣeṇa dhūmenāgnirivāvṛtāḥ:. (18.48)

(§1) *sahajam* (r◦ 14/1) *karma kaunteya sadoṣam* (r◦ 8/16) *api na tyajet* (r◦ 23/1) *sarvārambhāḥ:* (r◦ 20/18) *hi doṣeṇa dhūmena* (r◦ 1/1) *agniḥ:* (r◦ 16/1) *iva* (r◦ 1/2) *āvṛtāḥ:* (r◦ 22/8)

(§2) *sahajam* (n◦ 2acc◦ sing◦ ←bahuvrī◦ adj◦ *sahaja,* सहेन जायते यत् ←ind◦ *saha* 1.22 + m◦ *ja* 1.7); *karma* (2acc◦ 3.8); *kaunteya* (2.14); *sadoṣam* (n◦ 2acc◦ sing◦ ←bahuvrī◦ adj◦ *sa-doṣa,* दोषेण सहितम् यत् ←m◦ *doṣa* 1.38 + adj◦ *sahita* 9.1); *api* (1.26); *na* (1.30); *tyajet* (16.21); *sarvārambhāḥ:* (m◦ 1nom◦ plu◦ ←tatpu◦ *sarvārambha* 12.16); *hi* (1.11); *doṣeṇa* (3inst◦ sing◦ ←m◦ *doṣa* 1.38); *dhūmena* (3.38); *agniḥ:* (4.37); *iva* (1.30); *āvṛtāḥ:* (m◦ 1nom◦ plu◦ ←adj◦ *āvṛta* 3.38) (18.48)

---

[867] elsewhere◦ स्वधर्मः → own occupation, own religion.

[868] elsewhere◦ कर्म → action.

(§3) *sahajam̦* (adj1◦-obj◦ that with which one is born); *karma* (obj◦ a duty); *kaunteya* (O Arjuna!); *sadoṣam̦* (adj2◦-obj◦ a defective); *api* (even); *na tyajeț* (one ought not renounce, leave); *sarvārambhāḥ:* (adj◦-subj1◦ all undertakings); *hi* (because, for); *doṣeṇa* (with defect); *dhūmena* (with smoke); *agniḥ:* (subj2◦ the fire); *iva* (as); *āvṛtāḥ:* (adj◦-subj2◦ covered) (18.48)

(§4) kaunteya na tyajeț api sadoṣam̦ karma sahajam̦ hi sarvārambhāḥ: doṣeṇa iva agniḥ: āvṛtāḥ: dhūmena

(§5) O Arjuna! one ought not renounce even a defective duty with which one is born, because[869] all undertakings (are) with defect, as the fire covered with smoke. (18.48)

18.49 असक्तबुद्धिः सर्वत्र जितात्मा विगतस्पृहः ।
नैष्कर्म्यसिद्धिं परमां संन्यासेनाधिगच्छति ।।

asaktabuddhiḥ: sarvatra jitātmā vigataspṛhaḥ:,
naiṣkarmyasiddhiṁ paramaṁ sannyāsenādhigac̍c̍hati. (18.49)

(§1) *asaktabuddhiḥ:* (r◦ 22/7) *sarvatra jitātmā vigataspṛhaḥ:* (r◦ 22/8) *naiṣkarmyasiddhim̦* (r◦ 14/1) *paramām̦* (r◦ 14/1) *sannyāsena* (r◦ 1/1) *adhigac̍c̍hati*

(§2) *asaktabuddhiḥ:* (m◦ 1nom◦ sing◦ ←bahuvrī◦ *asakta-buddhi,* असक्ता बुद्धिः यस्य ←adj◦ *asakta* 3.7 + f◦ *buddhi* 1.23); *sarvatra* (2.57); *jitātmā* (m◦ 1nom◦ sing◦ ←bahuvrī◦ *jitātman̦* 6.7); *vigataspṛhaḥ:* (2.56); *naiṣkarmyasiddhim̦* (f◦ 2acc◦ sing◦ ←tatpu◦ *naiṣkarmya-siddhi,* नैष्कर्म्यस्य सिद्धिः ←n◦ *naiṣkarmya* 3.4 + f◦ *siddhi* 2.48); *paramām̦* (8.13); *sannyāsena* (3inst◦ sing◦ ←m◦ *sannyāsa* 5.1); *adhigac̍c̍hati* (2.64) (18.49)

(§3) *asaktabuddhiḥ:* (adj1◦-subj◦ he whose mind is unattached, he whose mind is free from attachment); *sarvatra* (adv◦ in every which way); *jitātmā* (adj2◦-subj◦ he who has conquered his senses); *vigataspṛhaḥ:* (adj3◦-subj◦ he whose desires have subsided); *naiṣkarmyasiddhim̦* (obj◦ success in selfless duty); *paramām̦* (adj◦-obj◦ supreme); *sannyāsena* (by *jñānayoga,* by renouncing the authorship of *karma*); *adhigac̍c̍hati* (he attains) (18.49)

(§4) asaktabuddhiḥ: sarvatra jitātmā vigataspṛhaḥ: adhigac̍c̍hati paramām̦ naiṣkarmyasiddhim̦ sannyāsena

(§5) He whose mind[870] free from attachment in every which way, he who has conquered his senses[871] (and) he whose desires have subsided, he attains supreme success[872] in selfless duty[873]

---

[869] हि → Please see footnote of verse 3.5 in volume II of this book.

[870] elsewhere◦ बुद्धिः → intellect.

[871] elsewhere◦ जितात्मा → conquered internal organs.

by renouncing the authorship of ***karma.***[874] (18.49)

18.50 सिद्धिं प्राप्तो यथा ब्रह्म तथाप्नोति निबोध मे ।
समासेनैव कौन्तेय निष्ठा ज्ञानस्य या परा ।।

siddhiṁ prāpto yathā brahma tathāpnoti nibodha me,
samāsenaiva kaunteya niṣṭhā jñānasya yā parā. (18.50)

(§1) *siddhiṃ* (r◦ 14/1) *prāptaḥ:* (r◦ 15/10) *yathā brahma tathā* (r◦ 1/4) *āpnoti nibodha me samāsena* (r◦ 3/1) *eva kaunteya niṣṭhā jñānasya yā parā*

(§2) *siddhiṃ* (3.4); *prāptaḥ:* (m◦ 1nom◦ sing◦ ←adj◦ *prāpta* 4.2); *yathā* (1.11); *brahma* (3.15); *tathā* (1.8); *āpnoti* (2.70); *nibodha* (1.7); *me* (1.21); *samāsena* (13.4); *eva* (1.1); *kaunteya* (2.14); *niṣṭhā* (3.3); *jñānasya* (6pos sing◦ ←n◦ *jñāna* 3.3); *yā* (2.69); *parā* (3.42) (18.50)

(§3) *siddhiṃ* (obj◦ success); *prāptaḥ:* (adj◦-subj1◦ one who has achieved); *yathā* (how); *brahma* (*brahma*); *tathā* (thus); *āpnoti* (he attains); *nibodha* (please know, please understnd); *me* (from me); *samāsena* (in essence); *eva* (only); *kaunteya* (O Arjuna!); *niṣṭhā* (subj2◦ faith; goal); *jñānasya* (of knowledge); *yā* (adj1◦-subj2◦ which); *parā* (adj2◦-subj2◦ the supreme) (18.50)

(§4) kaunteya nibodha me samāsena eva yathā prāptaḥ: siddhiṃ tathā āpnoti brahma yā parā niṣṭhā jñānasya

(§5) O Arjuna! please understnd from me, in essence only, (as to) how one who has achieved success[875] thus, attains *brahma*[876] which (is) the supreme goal[877] of knowledge. (18.50)

---

[872] elsewhere◦ सिद्धिं परमाम् → supreme perfection, highest perfection.

🕮 (i) Please see footnote isaiī in verse 4.12, in Volume II of this book. (ii) Not only that only *brahma* is perfect, when perfection itself is the ultimate thing, there is no such thing as 'supreme perfection' as much as there is no such thing as 'slight perfection.' A thing is either imperfect or perfect.

[873] elsewhere◦ नैष्कर्म्यसिद्धिम् → perfection consisting in the state of one free from duties, perfection of actionlessness, highest perfection of actionlessness, freedom from reaction, perfection of nonreaction, ...etc.

🕮 (i) Please see footnote on नैष्कर्म्य of verse 3.4 in volume II of this book.

(ii) Please also note that there is no such thing as 'actionlessness.' For details please see footnotes अकर्म in verses 6.1 and 3.8 in volume II of this book.

[874] elsewhere◦ संन्यासेन → by the renounced order of life, through renunciation, ...etc.

[875] elsewhere◦ सिद्धि → success (not perfection).

[876] elsewhere◦ ब्रह्म → brahman.

🕮 Nominatine of brahman is *brahma.* Please see the chart given at the very outset of the volume I of this

18.51 बुद्ध्या विशुद्धया युक्तो धृत्यात्मानं नियम्य च ।
शब्दादीन्विषयांस्त्यक्त्वा रागद्वेषौ व्युदस्य च ॥

buddhyā viśuddhayā yukto dhṛtyātmānaṁ niyamya ća,
śabdādīnviṣayāṁstyaktvā rāgadveṣau vyudasya ća; (18.51)

(§1) *buddhyā viśuddhayā yuktaḥ:* (r◦ 15/5) *dhṛtyā* (r◦ 1/4) *ātmānam̦* (r◦ 14/1) *niyamya ća śabdādīn̦* (r◦ 13/19) *viṣayān̦* (r◦ 13/7) *tyaktvā rāgadveṣau vyudasya ća;*

(§2) *buddhyā* (2.39); *viśuddhayā* (f◦ 3inst◦ sing◦ ←adj◦ *viśuddhā* ←f◦ *viśuddhi* 6.12); *yuktaḥ:* (2.39); *dhṛtyā* (18.33); *ātmānam̦* (3.43); *niyamya* (3.7); *ća* (1.1); *śabdādīn̦* (4.26); *viṣayān̦* (2.62); *tyaktvā* (1.33); *rāgadveṣau* (2acc◦ 3.34); *vyudasya* (lyp◦ past-participle ind◦ ←वि-उद्√अस्); *ća* (1.1); (18.51)

(§3) *buddhyā* (with thinking, with mind); *viśuddhayā* (with unadultrated, with undeluded); *yuktaḥ:* (adj◦-subj◦ equipped with *buddhiyoga*); *dhṛtyā* (with courage); *ātmānam̦* (obj1◦ himself); *niyamya* (controlling, having controlled); *ća* (and); *śabdādīn̦* (similar to *śrotrādīni* 4.26, adj◦-obj2◦ such as hearing etc.); *viṣayān̦* (obj2◦ the sense objects); *tyaktvā* (leaving aside, ignoring, not indulging in); *rāgadveṣau* (obj3◦ attachment and detestation); *vyudasya* (keeping aside, having kept aside); *ća* (and); (18.51)

(§4) viśuddhayā buddhyā yuktaḥ: ća niyamya ātmānam̦ dhṛtyā tyaktvā viṣayān̦ śabdādīn̦ ća vyudasya rāgadveṣau

(§5) With undeluded mind,[878] equipped with *buddhiyoga,*[879] and controlling himself[880] with courage, not indulging in the sense objects such as hearing[881] etc. and keeping aside attachment

---

book.

[877] elsewhere◦ निष्ठा ज्ञानस्य परा → state of highest and supreme knowledge, the stage of highest knowledge, culmination of knowledge, ...etc.

📖 (i) Please note that परा (supreme) is a feminine adjective, it can not qualify the neuter noun ज्ञानस्य (knowledge). It can only qualify the feminine noun निष्ठा (goal).

[878] elsewhere◦ बुद्ध्या विशुद्धया → with pure intellect, with pure intelligence, being purified by his intelligence, with the purity of intellect, ...etc.

[879] elsewhere◦ युक्तः → being endowed.

📖 युक्तः is not a gerund. It is a simple ppp. adjective.

[880] elsewhere◦ आत्मानम् → the self, the Self.

[881] elsewhere◦ शब्दादीन् त्यक्त्वा → abandoning sound,

and detestation; (18.51)

18.52 विविक्तसेवी लघ्वाशी यतवाक्कायमानसः ।
ध्यानयोगपरो नित्यं वैराग्यं समुपाश्रितः ।।
viviktasevī laghvāśī yatavākkāyamānasaḥ:,
dhyānayogaparo nityaṁ vairāgyaṁ samupāśritaḥ:; (18.52)

(§1) *viviktasevī laghvāśī yatavākkāyamānasaḥ:* (r◦ 22/8) *dhyānayogaparaḥ:* (r◦ 15/6) *nityam̧* (r◦ 14/1) *vairāgyam̧* (r◦ 14/1) *samupāśritaḥ:* (r◦ 22/8);

(§2) 🕮*viviktasevī* (m◦ 1nom◦ sing◦ ←tatpu◦ *viviktaseviņ*, विविक्तम् सेवते इति ←adj◦ *vivikta* 13.11 + adj◦ *seviņ* ←√सेव्); 🕮*laghvāśī* (m◦ 1nom◦ sing◦ ←tatpu◦ *laghvāśiņ* ←adj◦ *laghu* ←√लङ्घ् + m◦ *āśiņ* 3.13); *yatavākkāyamānasaḥ:* (m◦ 1nom◦ sing◦ ←bahuvrī◦ *yata-vāk-kāya-mānasa,* यता वाक् च कायम् च मानसम् च यस्य ←adj◦ *yaţ* 1.45 + f◦ *vāć* 2.42 + n◦ *kāya* 5.11 + n◦ *mānasa* 1.47); *dhyānayogaparaḥ:* (m◦ 1nom◦ sing◦ ←bahuvrī◦ *dhyāna-yoga-para,* ध्यानम् च योगः च परः यस्य ←n◦ *dhyāna* 12.12 + m◦ *yoga* 2.39 + adj◦ *para* 2.3); *nityam̧* (2.21); *vairāgyam̧* (13.9); *samupāśritaḥ:* (m◦ 1nom◦ sing◦ ←ppp◦ adj◦ *samupāśrita* ←सम्–उप–आ√श्रि); (18.52)

(§3) *viviktasevī* (adj1◦-subj◦ one who stays in solitude); *laghvāśī* (adj2◦-subj◦ one who is a moderate eater); *yatavākkāyamānasaḥ:* (adj3◦-subj◦ one who has control over his body, speech and mind); *dhyānayogaparaḥ:* (adj4◦-subj◦ one who is equipped with the yoga of contemplation); *nityam̧* (adj◦-obj◦ incessant); *vairāgyam̧* (obj◦ indifference to the world); *samupāśritaḥ:* (adj5◦-subj◦ one who has taken shelter of); (18.52)

(§4) viviktasevī laghvāśī yatavākkāyamānasaḥ: dhyānayogaparaḥ: samupāśritaḥ: nityam̧ vairāgyam̧

(§5) One (i) who stays in solitude, (ii) one who is a moderate eater, (iii) one who has control over his body, speech and mind; (iv) one whom the *yoga* of contemplation[882] is the highest goal, (v) one who has taken[883] shelter of incessant indifference to the world; (18.52)

18.53 अहङ्कारं बलं दर्पं कामं क्रोधं परिग्रहम् ।
विमुच्य निर्ममः शान्तो ब्रह्मभूयाय कल्पते ।।
ahaṅkāraṁ balaṁ darpaṁ kāmaṁ krodhaṁ parigraham̧,

---

[882] elsewhere◦ ध्यानयोगपरः → who is always in trance.

[883] elsewhere◦ समुपाश्रितः → taking refuge, having taken shelter of, ...etc.

🕮 समुपाश्रितः is not a gerund. It is a simple ppp. adjective.

vimućya nirmamaḥ: śānto brahmabhūyāya kalpate. (18.53)

(§1) *ahaṅkāraṃ* (r◦ 14/1) *balaṃ* (r◦ 14/1) *darpaṃ* (r◦ 14/1) *kāmaṃ* (r◦ 14/1) *krodhaṃ* (r◦ 14/1) *parigrahaṃ* (r◦ 14/2) *vimućya nirmamaḥ:* (r◦ 22/5) *śāntaḥ:* (r◦ 15/7) *brahmabhūyāya kalpate*

(§2) *ahaṅkāraṃ* (16.8); *balaṃ* (1.10); *darpaṃ* (16.18); *kāmaṃ* (16.10); *krodhaṃ* (16.18); *parigrahaṃ* (2acc◦ sing◦ ←m◦ *parigraha* 4.21); *vimućya* (lyp◦ past-participle ind◦ ←वि√मुच्); *nirmamaḥ:* (2.71); *śāntaḥ:* (m◦ 1nom◦ sing◦ ←adj◦ *śānta* 6.27); *brahmabhūyāya* (14.26); *kalpate* (2.15) (18.53)

(§3) *ahaṅkāraṃ* (obj1◦ 'I'-ness, ego); *balaṃ* (obj2◦ force, imposition); *darpaṃ* (obj3◦ arrogance); *kāmaṃ* (obj4◦ desire, longing); *krodhaṃ* (obj5◦ anger); *parigrahaṃ* (obj1◦ possession); *vimućya* (having renounced); *nirmamaḥ:* (adj6◦-subj◦ one who does not have 'my'-ness); *śāntaḥ:* (adj7◦-subj◦ one who is peaceful, tranquil); *brahmabhūyāya* (for becoming one with *brahma*); *kalpate* (he is fit) (18.53)

(§4) vimućya ahaṅkāraṃ balaṃ darpaṃ kāmaṃ krodhaṃ parigrahaṃ nirmamaḥ: śāntaḥ: kalpate brahmabhūyāya

(§5) Having renounced 'I'-ness, force, arrogance, longing, anger (and) possession, (vi) one who does not have 'my'-ness, (and) (vii) one who is peaceful, he is fit for becoming one with *brahma*.[884] (18.53)

18.54 ब्रह्मभूत: प्रसन्नात्मा न शोचति न काङ्क्षति ।
सम: सर्वेषु भूतेषु मद्भक्तिं लभते पराम् ।।
brahmabhūtaḥ: prasannātmā na śoćati na kāṅkṣati,
samaḥ: sarveṣu bhūteṣu madbhaktiṃ labhate parāṃ. (18.54)

(§1) *brahmabhūtaḥ:* (r◦ 22/3) *prasannātmā na śoćati na kāṅkṣati samaḥ:* (r◦ 22/7) *sarveṣu* (r◦ 25/5) *bhūteṣu* (r◦ 25/5) *madbhaktiṃ* (r◦ 14/1) *labhate parāṃ* (r◦ 14/2)

(§2) *brahmabhūtaḥ:* (5.24); *prasannātmā* (m◦ 1nom◦ sing◦ ←bahuvrī◦ *prasannātman*, प्रसन्न: आत्मा यस्य ←adj◦ *prasanna* 2.65 + m◦ *ātman* 2.41); *na* (1.30); *śoćati* (12.17); *na* (1.30); *kāṅkṣati* (5.3); *samaḥ:* (2.48); *sarveṣu* (1.11); *bhūteṣu* (7.11); *madbhaktiṃ* (f◦ 2acc◦ sing◦ ←tatpu◦ *madbhakti*, मयि भक्ति: ←pron◦ *mat* 1.9 + f◦ *bhakti* 7.17); *labhate* (4.39); *parāṃ* (4.39) (18.54)

(§3) *brahmabhūtaḥ:* (adj1◦-subj◦ one who has become one with *brahma*); *prasannātmā* (adj2◦-subj◦ the person who is happy at heart); *na śoćati* (neither he laments); *na kāṅkṣati* (nor he desires); *samaḥ:*

---

[884] elsewhere◦ ब्रह्मभूयाय → for becoming brahman, for self-realization, ...etc.

(adj3◦-subj◦ equanimous, indifferent); *sarveṣu bhūteṣu* (towards all beings); *madbhaktiṃ* (obj◦ my grace); *labhate* (he attains); *parāṃ* (adj◦-obj◦ divine) (18.54)

(§4) brahmabhūtaḥ: prasannātmā na śoćati na kāṅkṣati samaḥ: sarveṣu bhūteṣu labhate parāṃ madbhaktiṃ.

(§5) The person (i) who has become one with *brahma,* the person[885] (ii) who is happy at heart, he neither laments nor he desires. (iii) He who is equanimous[886] towards all beings, he attains my divine grace. (18.54)

18.55 भक्त्या मामभिजानाति यावान्यश्चास्मि तत्त्वत: ।
तती मां तत्त्वती ज्ञात्वा विशते तदनन्तरम् ।।
bhaktyā māmabhijānāti yāvānyaśćāsmi tattvataḥ:,
tato māṁ tattvato jñatvā viśate tadanantaraṃ. (18.55)

(§1) *bhaktyā māṃ* (r◦ 8/16) *abhijānāti yāvāṇ* (r◦ 13/17) *yaḥ:* (r◦ 17/1) *ća* (r◦ 1/1) *asmi tattvataḥ:* (r◦ 22/8) *tataḥ:* (r◦ 15/9) *māṃ* (r◦ 14/1) *tattvataḥ:* (r◦ 15/3) *jñātvā viśate tadanantaraṃ* (r◦ 14/2)

(§2) *bhaktyā* (8.10); *māṃ* (1.46); *abhijānāti* (4.14); *yāvāṇ* (2.46); *yaḥ:* (2.19); *ća* (1.1); *asmi* (7.8); *tattvataḥ:* (4.9); *tataḥ:* (1.13); *māṃ* (1.46); *tattvataḥ:* (4.9); *jñātvā* (4.15); *viśate* (3rd-per◦ sing◦ pres◦ वर्तमान्-लट् ātmane◦ ←class6◦ √विश् 2.70); *tadanantaraṃ* (adv◦ ind◦ ←pron◦ *tad* 1.2 + adj◦ *anantara* 12.12) (18.55)

(§3) *bhaktyā* (with devotion); *māṃ* (obj◦ me); *abhijānāti* (he properly understands); *yāvāṇ* (adj◦-subj1◦ how); *yaḥ:* (adj◦-subj2◦ who); *ća* (and); *asmi* (subj1◦ I am); *tattvataḥ:* (adv◦ in principle, truly); *tataḥ:* (then, from that); *māṃ* (obj◦ me); *tattvataḥ:* (in principle, truly); *jñātvā* (having understood); *viśate* (he enters, he attains); *tadanantaraṃ* (adv◦ after that, after that forever) (18.55)

(§4) bhaktyā abhijānāti māṃ tattvataḥ: yāvāṇ ća yaḥ: asmi jñātvā tattvataḥ: tataḥ: viśate māṃ tadanantaraṃ

(§5) With devotion he properly understands[887] me truly how and who I am. Having understood (me) in principle, then he attains[888] me after that forever.[889] (18.55)

---

[885] elsewhere◦ प्रसन्नात्मा → he whose self is serene, serene in the SELF, whose Self is serene, ...etc.

📖 Please see the footnote आत्मा (self) in verse 16.12

[886] elsewhere◦ सम: → “*regarding his own ātman (self) as identical with the ātmans of all beings.*”

[887] elsewhere◦ अभिजानाति → one can undrstand me, he comes to know me, ...etc,

[888] elsewhere◦ विशते → he can enter.

[889] elsewhere◦ तदनन्तरम् → immediately.

18.56 सर्वकर्माण्यपि सदा कुर्वाणो मद्व्यपाश्रय: ।
मत्प्रसादादवाप्नोति शाश्वतं पदमव्ययम् ।।

sarvakarmāṇyapi sadā kurvāṇo madvyapāśrayaḥ:,
matprasādādavāpnoti śāśvataṁ padamavyayam. (18.56)

(§1) *sarvakarmāṇi* (r∘ 24/7, 4/1) *api sadā kurvāṇaḥ:* (r∘ 15/9, 24/2) *madvyapāśrayaḥ:* (r∘ 22/8) *matprasādāt* (r∘ 8/2) *avāpnoti śāśvatam* (r∘ 14/1) *padam* (r∘ 8/16) *avyayam* (r∘ 14/2)

(§2) *sarvakarmāṇi* (3.26); *api* (1.26); *sadā* (1.40); *kurvāṇaḥ:* (m∘ 1nom∘ sing∘ ←śānać∘ adj∘ *kurvāṇa* or *kurvat* ←√कृ); *madvyapāśrayaḥ:* (m∘ 1nom∘ sing∘ ←bahuvrī∘ *madvyapāśrayaḥ:*, अहम् व्यपाश्रय: यस्य ←pron∘ *mat* 1.9 + m∘ *vyapāśraya* 3.18); *matprasādāt* (m∘ 5abl∘ sing∘ ←tatpu∘ *mat-prasāda*, मम प्रसाद: ←pron∘ *mat* 1.9 + m∘ *prasāda* 2.64); *avāpnoti* (15.8); *śāśvatam* (10.12); *padam* (2.51); *avyayam* (2.21) (18.56)

(§3) *sarvakarmāṇi* (obj1∘ all undertakings); *api* (even); *sadā* (always); *kurvāṇaḥ:* (adj1∘-subj1∘ doing, while performing); *madvyapāśrayaḥ:* (adj2∘-subj1∘ he whose reliance is on me); *matprasādāt* (from my grace, with my grace, blessing); *avāpnoti* (he attains); *śāśvatam* (adj∘-obj2∘ everlasting); *padam* (obj2∘ state); *avyayam* (adj2∘-oubj2∘ immutable) (18.56)

(§4) api kurvāṇaḥ: sarvakarmāṇi sadā madvyapāśrayaḥ: avāpnoti śāśvatam avyayam padam matprasādāt

(§5) Even while performing all undertakings he whose reliance is always on me, he attains everlasting immutable state with my blessing. (18.56)

18.57 चेतसा सर्वकर्माणि मयि संन्यस्य मत्पर: ।
बुद्धियोगमुपाश्रित्य मच्चित्त: सततं भव ।।

ćetasā sarvakarmāṇi mayi sannyasta matparaḥ:,
buddhiyogamupāśritya maććittaḥ: satataṁ bhava. (18.57)

(§1) *ćetasā sarvakarmāṇi* (r∘ 24/7) *mayi sannyasya matparaḥ:* (r∘ 22/8) *buddhiyogam* (r∘ 8/20) *upāśritya maććittaḥ:* (r∘ 22/7) *satatam* (r∘ 14/1) *bhava*

(§2) *ćetasā* (8.8); *sarvakarmāṇi* (3.26); *mayi* (3.30); *sannyasya* (3.30); *matparaḥ:* (2.61); *buddhiyogam* (10.10); *upāśritya* (14.2); *maććittaḥ:* (6.14); *satatam* (3.19); *bhava* (2.45) (18.57)

(§3) *ćetasā* (by mind, with mind); *sarvakarmāṇi* (obj1∘ all undertakings); *mayi* (in me); *sannyasya*

📖 Please see the footnote अनन्तरम् in verse 12.12 in volume 1 of this book. Also see the next verse शाश्वतम् पदम् (18.56।

(having relinquished); *matparaḥ:* (adj1◦-subj◦ he for whom I am the ultimate goal); *buddhiyogam̩* (obj2◦ buddhiyoga, yoga of equanimous thinking); *upāśritya* (depending on); *maććittaḥ:* (adj2◦-subj◦ he whose heart is fixed on me); *satatam̩* (always); *bhava* (be, you please be!) (18.57)

(§4) ćetasā sannyasya sarvakarmāṇi mayi satatam̩ upāśritya buddhiyogam̩ bhava matparaḥ: maććittaḥ:

(§5) With his mind, having relinquished all undertakings in me (and) always depending on the *yoga* of equanimous thinking,[890] (O Arjuna!) you please be the one whom I am the ultimate goal, and the one whose heart is fixed on me. (18.57)

18.58 मच्चित्त: सर्वदुर्गाणि मत्प्रसादात्तरिष्यसि ।
अथ चेत्त्वमहङ्कारान्न श्रोष्यसि विनङ्क्ष्यसि ।।
maććitaḥ: sarvadurgāṇi matprasādāttariṣyasi,
atha ćettvamahaṅkārānna śroṣyasi vinaṅkṣyasi. (18.58)

(§1) *maććittaḥ:* (r◦ 22/7) *sarvadurgāṇi* (r◦ 24/7) *matprasādāt̩* (r◦ 1/10) *tariṣyasi* (r◦ 23/1) *atha ćet̩* (r◦ 1/10) *tvam̩* (r◦ 8/16) *ahaṅkārāt̩* (r◦ 12/1) *na śroṣyasi vinaṅkṣyasi*

(§2) *maććittaḥ:* (6.14); *sarvadurgāṇi* (सर्वाणि दुर्गाणि n◦ 2acc◦ plu◦ tatpu◦ ←pron◦ *sarva* 1.6 + n◦ 🕮*durga* ←ind◦ *dur̩* 1.2 + adj◦ *ga* ←√गै); *matprasādāt̩* (18.56); *tariṣyasi* (2nd-per◦ sing◦ fut2◦ लृट् भविष्य◦ parasmai◦ ←class1◦ √तृ 7.14); *atha* (1.20); *ćet̩* (2.33); *tvam̩* (2.11); *ahaṅkārāt̩* (5abl◦ sing◦ ←m◦ *ahaṅkāra* 2.71); *na* (1.30); *śroṣyasi* (2nd-per◦ sing◦ fut2◦ लृट् भविष्य◦ parasmai◦ ←class1◦ √श्रु); *vinaṅkṣyasi* (2nd-per◦ sing◦ fut2◦ लृट् भविष्य◦ parasmai◦ ←class4◦ वि√नश्) (18.58)

(§3) *maććittaḥ:* (adj1◦-subj◦ he whose heart is fixed on me); *sarvadurgāṇi* (Obj◦ all obstacles); *matprasādāt̩* (with my blessing); *tariṣyasi* (you will cross over); *atha ćet̩* (if, on the other hand); *tvam̩* (subj◦ you); *ahaṅkārāt̩* (out of self pride); *na śroṣyasi* (you will not listen); *vinaṅkṣyasi* (you will perish). (18.58)

(§4) maććittaḥ: tariṣyasi sarvadurgāṇi matprasādāt̩ atha ćet̩ tvam̩ na śroṣyasi ahaṅkārāt̩ vinaṅkṣyasi .

(§5) With the heart fixed on me,[891] you will cross over all obstacles with my blessing. If, on the

---

[890] elsewhere◦ बुद्धियोगम् → Yoga of intelligence, intuitive determination, trained intuition, devotional activities, devotional service, ...etc.

🕮 Please see the footnotes बुद्धियोग in verse 2.50 and 2.39 in volume 1 of this book.

[891] elsewhere◦ मच्चित्त: → Having your mind fixed on me.

🕮 मच्चित्त: is not a gerund. It is a simple m◦ *bahuvrihi* adjective.

other hand, you will not listen (to me) out of self pride, you will perish.
(18.58)

18.59 यदहङ्कारमाश्रित्य न योत्स्य इति मन्यसे ।
मिथ्यैष व्यवसायस्ते प्रकृतिस्त्वां नियोक्ष्यति ।।

yadahaṅkāramāśritya na yotsya iti manyase,
mithyaiṣa vyavasāyaste prakṛtistvāṁ niyokṣyati. (18.59)

(§1) *yaṭ* (r◦ 8/2) *ahaṅkāraṃ* (r◦ 8/17) *āśritya na yotse* (r◦ 5/2) *iti manyase mithyā* (r◦ 3/3) *eṣaḥ:* (r◦ 25/1, 21/1) *vyavasāyaḥ:* (r◦ 18/1) *te prakṛtiḥ:* (r◦ 18/1) *tvāṃ* (r◦ 14/1) *niyokṣyati*

(§2) *yaṭ* (1.45) *ahaṅkāraṃ* (16.18) *āśritya* (7.29) *na* (1.30) *yotse* (2.9) *iti* (1.25) *manyase* (2.26) *mithyā* (3.6) *eṣaḥ:* (3.10) *vyavasāyaḥ:* (10.36) *te* (2.7) *prakṛtiḥ:* (7.4) *tvāṃ* (2.7) *niyokṣyati* (3rd-per◦ sing◦ fut2◦ लृट् भविष्य◦ parasmai◦ ←class7◦नि√युज्)

(§3) *yaṭ* (adj◦-obj1◦ which); *ahaṅkāraṃ* (obj1◦ self-pride, ego); *āśritya* (having relied on, taking shelter of); *na yotse* ('I shall not fight'); *iti* (that); *manyase* (you think); *mithyā* (adj1◦-subj1◦ false, vain); *eṣaḥ:* (adj2◦-subj1◦ this); *vyavasāyaḥ:* (subj1◦ resolve); *te* (your); *prakṛtiḥ:* (subj2◦ your inborn nature); *tvāṃ* (obj2◦ to you); *niyokṣyati* (will impel, will appoint) (18.59)

(§4) āśritya ahaṅkāraṃ yaṭ manyase iti na yotse mithyā eṣaḥ: te vyavasāyaḥ: prakṛtiḥ: niyokṣyati tvāṃ

(§5) Taking shelter of self-pride, with which you think that 'I shall not fight,' vain (is) this your resolve. Your inborn nature will impel you. (18.59)

18.60 स्वभावजेन कौन्तेय निबद्धः स्वेन कर्मणा ।
कर्तुं नेच्छसि यन्मोहात्करिष्यस्यवशोऽपि तत् ।।

svabhāvajena kaunteya nibaddhaḥ: svena karmaṇā,
kartuṁ neććhasi yanmohātkariṣyasyavaśo'pi taṭ. (18.60)

(§1) *svabhāvajena kaunteya nibaddhaḥ:* (r◦ 22/7) *svena karmaṇā* (r◦ 24/4) *kartuṃ* (r◦ 14/1) *na* (r◦ 2/1) *iććhasi yaṭ* (r◦ 12/2) *mohāṭ* (r◦ 10/5) *kariṣyasi* (r◦ 4/1) *avaśaḥ:* (r◦ 15/1) *api taṭ*

(§2) *svabhāvajena* (n◦ 3inst◦ sing◦ ←bahuvrī◦ *svabhāvaja* 17.2); *kaunteya* (2.14); *nibaddhaḥ:* (m◦ 1nom◦ sing◦ ←ppp◦ adj◦ *nibaddha* ←नि√बन्ध्); *svena* (3inst◦ sing◦ ←adj◦ *sva* 1.28); *karmaṇā* (3.20); *kartuṃ* (1.45); *na* (1.30); *iććhasi* (11.7); *yaṭ* (2acc◦ 2.31); *mohāṭ* (16.10); *kariṣyasi* (2.33); *avaśaḥ:* (3.5); *api* (1.26); *taṭ* (2acc◦ 2.7) (18.60)

(§3) *svabhāvajena* (with your inborn nature); *kaunteya* (O Arjuna!); *nibaddhaḥ:* (adj◦-subj1◦ bound);

svena (with your); *karmaṇā* (by duty); *kartuṃ* (to perform); *na iććhasi* (you do not wish); *yat̤* (adj1∘-obj∘ that resolve with which); *mohāt̤* (out of delusion); *kariṣyasi* (you will do); *avaśaḥ:* (against will, against your will); *api* (also, even); *tat̤* (adj2∘-obj∘ that) (18.60)

(§4) kaunteya yat̤ na iććhasi kartuṃ mohāt̤ kariṣyasi tat̤ nibaddhaḥ: svabhāvajena svena karmaṇā api avaśaḥ:

(§5) O Arjuna! that resolve with which you do not wish to perform out of delusion, you will do that bound by your inborn nature (and) as your duty, even against your will. (18.60)

18.61 ईश्वरः सर्वभूतानां हृद्देशेऽर्जुन तिष्ठति ।
भ्रामयन्सर्वभूतानि यन्त्रारूढानि मायया ।।
īśvaraḥ: sarvabhūtānāṁ hṛddeśe'rjuna tiṣṭhati,
bhrāmayansarvabhūtāni yantrārūḍhāni māyayā. (18.61)

(§1) *īśvaraḥ:* (r∘ 22/7) *sarvabhūtānāṃ* (r∘ 14/1) *hṛddeśe* (r∘ 6/1) *arjuna tiṣṭhati bhrāmayan̤* (r∘ 13/20) *sarvabhūtāni yantrārūḍhāni māyayā*

(§2) *īśvaraḥ:* (4.6); *sarva* (1.6); *bhūtānāṃ* (2.69); *hṛddeśe* (m∘ 7loc∘ sing∘ ←tatpu∘ *hṛddeśa*, हृदः देशः ←n∘ *hṛd* 4.40 + m∘ *deśa* 6.11); *arjuna* (2.2); *tiṣṭhati* (3.5); *bhrāmayan̤* (m∘ 1nom∘ sing∘ ←śatṛ∘ adj∘ caus∘*bhrāmayat̤* ←√भ्रम्); *sarvabhūtāni* (2acc∘ 6.29); *yantrārūḍhāni* (n∘ 2acc∘ plu∘ ←bahuvrī∘ adj∘ *yantrārūḍha*, यन्त्रे आरूढम् यत् ←n∘ *yantra* ←√यन्त्र् + ppp∘ adj∘ *ārūḍha* 6.3); *māyayā* (7.15) (18.61)

(§3) *īśvaraḥ:* (subj∘ the Lord, God); *sarva bhūtānāṃ* (of all beings); *hṛddeśe* (in the realm of the heart); *arjuna* (O Arjuna!); *tiṣṭhati* (stays, exists); *bhrāmayan̤* (adj1∘-obj∘ revolving); *sarvabhūtāni* (obj∘ all beings); *yantrārūḍhāni* (adj2∘-obj∘ mounted on the wheel); *māyayā* (with his invisible power, according to his will) (18.61)

(§4) arjuna īśvaraḥ: tiṣṭhati hṛddeśe sarva bhūtānāṃ bhrāmayan̤ sarvabhūtāni yantrārūḍhāni māyayā

(§5) O Arjuna! the Lord exists[892] in the realm[893] of the heart of all beings, revolving all beings (as though) mounted on the wheel (of birth and death) with his invisible power, according to His will.[894] (18.61)

---

[892] elsewhere∘ तिष्ठति → sits, dwells, resides, is situated, abides, ...etc.

[893] elsewhere∘ हृद्देशे → in the heart.

[894] elsewhere∘ मायया → material energy, magic, power of illusion, ...etc.

📖 Same meaning applies here (also in 18.61), as we used in the verse 4.6, (please see it in voulme II of

18.62 तमेव शरणं गच्छ सर्वभावेन भारत ।
तत्प्रसादात्परां शान्तिं स्थानं प्राप्स्यसि शाश्वतम् ।।
tameva śaraṇaṁ gaćcha sarvabhāvena bhārata,
tatprasādātparāṁ śāntiṁ sthānaṁ prāpsyasi śāśvatam. (18.62)

(§1) *tam* (r◦ 8/22) *eva śaraṇam* (r◦ 14/1, 24/3) *gaćcha sarvabhāvena bhārata taṭ* (r◦10.6) *prasādāṭ* (r◦ 10/6) *parām* (r◦ 14/1) *śāntim* (r◦ 14/1) *sthānam* (r◦ 14/1) *prāpsyasi śāśvatam* (r◦ 14/2)

(§2) *tam* (2.1); *eva* (1.1); *śaraṇam* (2.49); *gaćcha* (2nd-per◦ sing◦ imperative◦ उपदेशार्थ-लोट् parasmai◦ ←class1◦ √गम्); *sarvabhāvena* (15.19); *bhārata* (1.24); *tatprasādāṭ* (m◦ 5abl◦ sing◦ ←tatpu◦ *tat-prasāda*, तस्य प्रसाद: ←pron◦ *taṭ* 1.10 + m◦ *prasāda* 2.64); *parām* (4.39); *śāntim* (2.70); *sthānam* (2acc◦ 8.28); *prāpsyasi* (2.37); *śāśvatam* (10.12) (18.62)

(§3) *tam* (adj◦-obj1◦ to him, unto him); *eva* (only); *śaraṇam* (obj2◦ refuge); *gaćcha* (go, you please go); *sarvabhāvena* (with all your devotion); *bhārata* (O Arjuna!); *tatprasādāṭ* (with that grace); *parām* (adj◦-obj3◦ supreme); *śāntim* (obj3◦ peace); *sthānam* (obj4◦ place, abode); *prāpsyasi* (you will attain); *śāśvatam* (adj◦-obj4◦ the eternal) (18.62)

(§4) bhārata gaćcha tam eva śaraṇam sarvabhāvena tatprasādāṭ prāpsyasi parām śāntim śāśvatam sthānam

(§5) O Arjuna! you please go only unto Him (for) refuge with all your devotion. With that grace you will attain supreme peace (and) the eternal abode. (18.62)

18.63 इति ते ज्ञानमाख्यातं गुह्याद्गुह्यतरं मया ।
विमृश्यैतदशेषेण यथेच्छसि तथा कुरु ।।
iti te jñānamākhyātaṁ guhyādguhyataraṁ mayā,
vimṛśyaitadaśeṣeṇa yatheććhasi tathā kuru. (18.63)

(§1) *iti te jñānam* (r◦ 8/17) *ākhyātam* (r◦ 14/1) *guhyāṭ* (r◦ 9/4) *guhyataram* (r◦ 14/1) *mayā vimṛśya* (r◦ 3/1) *etaṭ* (r◦ 8/2) *aśeṣeṇa* (r◦ 24/1) *yathā* (r◦ 2/3) *ićchasi tathā kuru*

(§2) *iti* (1.25); *te* (1.7); *jñānam* (1nom◦ 3.39); *ākhyātam* (n◦ 1nom◦ sing◦ ←ppp◦ adj◦ *ākhyāta* ←आ√ख्या); *guhyāṭ* (5abl◦ sing◦ ←n◦ *guhya* 9.1); *guhyataram* (1nom◦ sing◦ ←n◦ *guhya* 9.1 + comparative affix *tara* 1.46); *mayā* (1.22); *vimṛśya* (lyp◦ past-participle ind◦ ←वि√मृश्); *etaṭ* (2.3); *aśeṣeṇa* (4.35); *yathā* (1.11); *ićchasi* (11.7); *tathā* (1.8); *kuru* (2.48) (18.63)

---

this book)

(§3) *iti* (thus); *te* (for you, to you); *jñānam̩* (obj1◦ the knowledge); *ākhyātam̩* (adj1◦-obj1◦ explained, told); *guhyāt̩ guhyataram̩* (most secret among the secrets); *mayā* (by me); *vimṛśya* (pondering over); *etat̩* (adj2◦-obj1◦ it); *aśeṣeṇa* (adv◦ fully); *yathā* (as); *ićchasi* (you wish); *tathā* (so); *kuru* (you please do) (18.63)

(§4) iti jñānam̩ guhyāt̩ guhyataram̩ ākhyātam̩ te mayā vimṛśya etat̩ aśeṣeṇa kuru tathā yathā ićchasi

(§5) Thus knowledge, most secret among the secrets, (is) told to you by me. Pondering over it fully, you please do so as you wish. (18.63)

18.64 सर्वगुह्यतमं भूयः शृणु मे परमं वचः ।
इष्टोऽसि मे दृढमिति ततो वक्ष्यामि ते हितम् ।।

sarvaguhyatamaṁ bhūya: śṛṇu me paramaṁ vaćaḥ:,
iṣṭo'si me dṛḍhamiti tato vakṣyāmi te hitam̩. (18.64)

(§1) *sarvaguhyatamam̩* (r◦ 14/1) *bhūyaḥ:* (r◦ 22/5) *śṛṇu me paramam̩* (r◦ 14/1) *vaćaḥ:* (r◦ 22/8) *iṣṭaḥ:* (r◦ 15/1) *asi me dṛḍham̩* (r◦ 8/18) *iti tataḥ:* (r◦ 15/13) *vakṣyāmi te hitam̩* (r◦ 14/2)

(§2) *sarvaguhyatamam̩* (n◦ 2acc◦ sing◦ ←pron◦ *sarva* 1.6 + n◦ *guhya* 9.1 + superlative affix *tama* 1.7); *bhūyaḥ:* (2.20); *śṛṇu* (2.39); *me* (1.21); *paramam̩* (2acc◦ 8.8); *vaćaḥ:* (2acc◦ 2.10); *iṣṭaḥ:* (m◦ 1nom◦ sing◦ ←adj◦ *iṣta* 3.10); *asi* (4.3); *me* (1.21); *dṛḍham̩* (6.34); *iti* (1.25); *tataḥ:* (1.13); *vakṣyāmi* (7.2); *te* (2.7); 🕮*hitam̩* (n◦ 2acc◦ sing◦ ←adj◦ *hita* 5.25) (18.64)

(§3) *sarvaguhyatamam̩* (adj1◦-obj1◦ most secret); *bhūyaḥ:* (adv◦ again); *śṛṇu* (please listen to); *me* (my); *paramam̩* (adj2◦-obj1◦ supreme); *vaćaḥ:* (obj1◦ word); *iṣṭaḥ:* (adj◦-subj◦ dear, beloved); *asi* (subj◦ you are); *me* (my); *dṛḍham̩* (adv◦ fittingly), *iti* (thus); *tataḥ:* (therefore); *vakṣyāmi* (I shall tell); *te* (for your); *hitam̩* (obj2◦ good, benefit) (18.64)

(§4) śṛṇu bhūyaḥ: me sarvaguhyatamam̩ paramam̩ vaćaḥ: asi me iṣṭaḥ: tataḥ: vakṣyāmi dṛḍham̩ iti te hitam̩

(§5) Please listen again my most secret supreme word. You are my beloved, therefore, I shall tell fittingly[895] thus for your good. (18.64)

18.65 मन्मना भव मद्भक्तो मद्याजी मां नमस्कुरु ।
मामेवैष्यसि सत्यं ते प्रतिजाने प्रियोऽसि मे ।।

manmanā bhava madbhakto madyājī māṁ namaskuru,

---

[895] elsewhere◦ दृढम् → well beloved, very dear, ever dear, ...etc.

🕮 Remember : In दृढम् वक्ष्यामि n◦ दृढम् is not a adjective of m◦ Arjuna. It is adv◦ of the verb वक्ष्यामि ।

māmevaiṣyasi satyaṁ te pratijāne priyo'si me. (18.65)

(§1) *manmanāḥ:* (r◦ 20/12) *bhava madbhaktaḥ:* (r◦ 15/9) *madyājī māṃ* (r◦ 14/1) *namaskuru māṃ* (r◦ 8/22) *eva* (r◦ 3/1) *eṣyasi satyaṃ* (r◦ 14/1) *te pratijāne priyaḥ:* (r◦ 15/1) *asi me*

(§2) *manmanāḥ:* (9.34); *bhava* (2.45); *madbhaktaḥ:* (9.34); *madyājī* (9.34); *māṃ* (1.46); *namaskuru* (9.34); *māṃ* (1.46); *eva* (1.1); *eṣyasi* (8.7); *satyaṃ* (10.4); *te* (1.7); *pratijāne* (1st-per◦ sing◦ pres◦ वर्तमान्-लट् ātmane◦ ←class9◦ प्रति√ज्ञा); *priyaḥ:* (7.17); *asi* (4.3); *me* (1.21) (18.65)

(§3) *manmanāḥ:* (adj1◦-subj◦ he whose mind is fixed on me); *bhava* (you please be!); *madbhaktaḥ:* (adj2◦-subj◦ he who is my devotee); *madyājī* (adj3◦-subj1◦ he who worships me); *māṃ* (adj◦-obj◦ to me); *namaskuru* (make reverence); *māṃ* (adj◦-obj◦ to me); *eva* (alone); *eṣyasi* (you will come); *satyaṃ* (adv◦ truly); *te* (you, to you); *pratijāne* (I promise); *priyaḥ:* (adj4◦-subj◦ dear); *asi* (subj◦ you are); *me* (my) (18.65)

(§4) bhava manmanāḥ: madbhaktaḥ: madyājī namaskuru māṃ pratijāne satyaṃ te eṣyasi māṃ eva asi me priyaḥ:

(§5) You please be he whose mind is fixed on me, he who is my devotee, he who worships me. Make reverence to me. I truly[896] promise you, you will come to me alone. You are my dear. (18.65)

18.66 सर्वधर्मान्परित्यज्य मामेकं शरणं व्रज ।
अहं त्वां सर्वपापेभ्यो मोक्षयिष्यामि मा शुचः ।।
sarvadharmānparityajya māmekaṁ śaraṇaṁ vraja,
ahaṁ tvāṁ sarvapāpebhyo mokṣayiṣyāmi mā śucaḥ:. (18.66)

(§1) *sarvadharmān* (r◦ 13/13) *parityajya māṃ* (r◦ 3/1) *ekaṃ* (r◦ 14/1) *śaraṇaṃ* (r◦ 14/1, 24/3) *vraja* (r◦ 23/1) *ahaṃ* (r◦ 14/1) *tvāṃ* (14.1) *sarvapāpebhyaḥ:* (r◦ 15/9) *mokṣayiṣyāmi* (r◦ 25/9) *mā śucaḥ:* (r◦ 22/8)

(§2) *sarvadharmān* (सर्वान् धर्मान् m◦ 2acc◦ plu◦ ←pron◦ *sarva* 1.6 + m◦ *dharma* 1.1); *parityajya* (lyp◦ past-participle ind◦ ←परि√त्यज्); *māṃ* (1.46); *ekaṃ* (2acc◦ 3.2); *śaraṇaṃ* (2acc◦ 2.49); *vraja* (2nd-per◦ sing◦ imperative◦ उपदेशार्थ-लोट् parasmai◦ ←class1◦ √व्रज्); *ahaṃ* (1.22); *tvāṃ* (2.7); *sarvapāpebhyaḥ:* (सर्वेभ्यः पापेभ्यः m◦ 5abl◦ plu◦ ←pron◦ *sarva* 1.6 + n◦ *pāpa* 1.36); *mokṣayiṣyāmi* (1st-per◦ sing◦ fut2◦ लृट् भविष्य◦ parasmai◦ caus◦ ←class2◦ √मुच्); *mā* (2.3); *śucaḥ:* (16.5) (18.66)

---

[896] elsewhere◦ सत्यम् → Truth.

(§3) *sarvadharmān̦* (obj1◦ all duties); *mām̦ parityajya* (having performed in my name, having relinquished to my name); *ekam̦* (adv◦ alone); *śaraṇam̦* (obj2◦ refuge); *vraja* (please take!); *aham̦* (subj◦ I); *tvām̦* (obj3◦ you); *sarvapāpebhyaḥ:* (from all sins); *mokṣayiṣyāmi* (I shall release); *mā* (please don't); *śućaḥ:* (lament) (18.66)

(§4) parityajya sarvadharmān̦ vraja mām̦ ekam̦ śaraṇam̦ aham̦ mokṣayiṣyāmi tvām̦ sarvapāpebhyaḥ: mā śućaḥ:

(§5) Having performed[897] all duties[898] in my name, please take me alone (for) refuge. I shall release you from all sins. Please don't lament. (18.66)

18.67 इदं ते नातपस्काय नाभक्ताय कदाचन ।
न चाशुश्रूषवे वाच्यं न च मां योऽभ्यसूयति ।।
idaṁ te nātapaskāya nābhaktāya kadāćana,
na ćāśuśrūṣave vāćyaṁ na ća māṁ yo'bhyasūyati. (18.67)

(§1) *idam̦* (r◦ 14/1) *te na* (r◦ 1/1) *atapaskāya na* (r◦ 1/1) *abhaktāya kadāćana na ća* (r◦ 1/1) *aśuśrūṣave vāćyam̦* (r◦ 14/1) *na ća mām̦* (r◦ 14/1) *yaḥ:* (r◦ 15/1) *abhyasūyati*

(§2) *idam̦* (1nom◦ 1.10); *te* (2.7) *na* (3.38); *a-tapaskāya* (4dat◦ sing◦ n.bahuvrī◦ ←m◦ *tapaska*, तपसः कायम् यस्य ←n◦ *tapaṣ* 4.10 + n◦ *kāya* 5.11); *na* (1.30); *a-bhaktāya* (4dat◦ sing◦ n.tatpu◦ ←m◦ *bhakta* 4.3); *kadāćana* (2.47); *na* (1.30); *ća* (1.1); *a-śuśrūṣave* (m◦ 4dat◦ sing◦ n.tatpu◦ ←desi◦ adj◦ *śuśrūṣu* ←√श्रु); *vāćyam̦* (n◦ 1nom◦ sing◦ ←pot◦ adj◦ *vāćya* ←√वच्); *na* (1.30); *ća* (1.1); *mām̦* (1.46); *yaḥ:* (2.19); *abhyasūyati* (3rd-per◦ sing◦ pres◦ वर्तमान्–लट् parasmai◦ ←class3◦ √असू) (18.67)

(§3) *idam̦* (subj1◦ this); *te* (of you, from you, by you) *na* (not); *atapaskāya* (to one who does not have austerity); *na* (nor); *abhaktāya* (to one who is not my devotee); *kadāćana na* (never); *ća* (and); *aśuśrūṣave* (to one who does not wish to listen); *vāćyam̦* (obj1◦ dialogue); *na* (nor); *ća* (and); *mām̦* (obj2◦ me); *yaḥ:* (subj2◦ he who); *abhyasūyati* (criticizes) (18.67)

(§4) na kadāćana idam̦ vāćyam̦ te atapaskāya ća na abhaktāya na aśuśrūṣave ća na yaḥ: abhyasūyati mām̦

(§5) Never this dialogue (to be told) by you (i) to one who does not have austerity, and (ii) nor to

---

[897] elsewhere◦ परित्यज्य → abandon.

📖 परित्यज्य is not imperative लोट्

[898] elsewhere◦ सर्वधर्मान् → all varieties of religion.

📖 Please see footnote धर्म in verse 2.31, in the volume I of this book.

one who is not my devotee, (iii) nor to one who does not wish to listen, and (iv) not he who criticizes me. (18.67)

18.68 य इदं परमं गुह्यं मद्भक्तेष्वभिधास्यति ।
भक्तिं मयि परां कृत्वा मामेवैष्यत्यसंशयः ।।

ya idaṁ paramaṁ guhyaṁ madbhakteṣvabhidhāsyati,
bhaktiṁ mayi parāṁ kṛtvā māmevaiṣyatyasam̐śayaḥ:; (18.68)

(§1) *yaḥ:* (r◦ 19/2) *idaṃ* (r◦ 14/1) *paramaṃ* (r◦ 14/1) *guhyaṃ* (r◦ 14/1) *madbhakteṣu* (r◦ 25/5, 4/6) *abhidhāsyati bhaktiṃ* (r◦ 14/1) *mayi parāṃ* (r◦ 14/1) *kṛtvā māṃ* (r◦ 8/22) *eva* (r◦ 3/1) *eṣyati* (r◦ 25/6, 4/1) *asam̐śayaḥ:* (r◦ 22/8)

(§2) *yaḥ:* (2.19); *idaṃ* (2acc◦ 1.10); *paramaṃ* (2acc◦ 8.3); *guhyaṃ* (2acc◦ sing◦ ←n◦ *guhya* 11.1); *madbhakteṣu* (m◦ 7loc◦ plu◦ ←tatpu◦ *madbhakta* 7.23); *abhidhāsyati* (3rd-per◦ sing◦ fut2◦ लृट् भविष्य◦ parasmai◦ ←class3◦ अभि√धा); *bhaktiṃ* (2acc◦ sing◦ ←f◦ *bhakti* 7.17); *mayi* (3.30); *parāṃ* (4.39); *kṛtvā* (2.38); *māṃ* (1.46); *eva* (1.1); *eṣyati* (3rd-per◦ sing◦ fut2◦ लृट् भविष्य◦ parasmai◦ ←class2◦ √इ 8.7); *asam̐śayaḥ:* (1nom◦ sing◦ ←adv◦ *asam̐śaya* 6.35) (18.68)

(§3) *yaḥ:* (adj1◦-subj◦ he who); *idaṃ* (adj1◦-obj1◦ this); *paramaṃ* (adj2◦-obj1◦ supreme); *guhyaṃ* (obj1◦ secret); *madbhakteṣu* (in, to my devotees); *abhidhāsyati* (shall speak, set forth); *bhaktiṃ* (obj2◦ devotion); *mayi* (in me); *parāṃ* (adj◦-obj2◦ great); *kṛtvā* (having done); *māṃ* (obj3◦ me); *eva* (only); *eṣyati* (he will come, will attain); *asam̐śayaḥ:* (adj2◦-subj◦ one who has no doubt, the doubtless person) (18.68)

(§4) yaḥ: abhidhāsyati idaṃ paramaṃ guhyaṃ madbhakteṣu kṛtvā parāṃ bhaktiṃ mayi asam̐śayaḥ: eṣyati māṃ eva

(§5) He who shall speak this supreme secret to my devotees, having done great devotion in me, the doubtless person[899] will attain me only; (18.68)

18.69 न च तस्मान्मनुष्येषु कश्चिन्मे प्रियकृत्तमः ।
भविता न च मे तस्मादन्यः प्रियतरः भुवि ।।

na ća tasmānmanuṣyeṣu kaśćinme priyakṛttamaḥ:,
bhavitā na ća me tasmādanyaḥ: priyataraḥ: bhuvi. (18.69)

---

[899] elsewhere◦ असंशयः → without doubt reaches Me.

📖 Please note that : असंशयः is not an adverb. It is m◦ adjective of 'he.'

(§1) *na ća tasmāṭ* (r◦ 12/2) *manuṣyeṣu* (r◦ 25/5) *kaśćiṭ* (r◦ 12/2) *me priyakṛttamaḥ:* (r◦ 22/8) *bhavitā na ća me tasmāṭ* (r◦ 8/2) *anyaḥ:* (r◦ 22/3) *priyataraḥ:* (r◦ 15/8) *bhuvi*

(§2) *na* (1.30); *ća* (1.1); *tasmāṭ* (5abl◦ 1.37); *manuṣyeṣu* (4.18); *kaśćiṭ* (2.17); *me* (1.21); *priyakṛttamaḥ:* (m◦ 1nom◦ sing◦ ←adj◦ *priyakṛṭ* ←प्रिय√कृत् + superlative suffix *tama* 1.7); *bhavitā* (2.20); *na* (1.30); *ća* (1.1); *me* (1.21); *tasmāṭ* (1.37); *anyaḥ:* (2.29); *priyataraḥ:* (m◦ 1nom◦ sing◦ *priya-tara*, ←adj◦ *priya* 1.23 + comparative affix *tara* 1.46); *bhuvi* (7loc◦ sing◦ ←f◦ *bhū* ←√भू) (18.69)

(§3) *na* (not); *ća* (and); *tasmāṭ* (than him); *manuṣyeṣu* (among people); *kaśćiṭ* (anyone); *me* (for me, to me); *priyakṛttamaḥ:* (adj◦-subj1◦ best, most superior dear doer); *bhavitā* (he shall be); *na* (nor); *ća* (moreover, and); *me* (for me, to me); *tasmāṭ* (than him); *anyaḥ:* (subj2◦ anyone else); *priyataraḥ:* (adj◦-subj2◦ more dear); *bhuvi* (on the earth) (18.69)

(§4) ća manuṣyeṣu na kaśćiṭ priyakṛttamaḥ: me tasmāṭ ća na anyaḥ: bhavitā priyataraḥ: me tasmāṭ bhuvi

(§5) and among people, he is the most[900] superior 'dear-doer'[901] for me. Moreover, nor anyone else shall be more dear to me than him, on the earth.

(18.69)

18.70 अध्येष्यते च य इमं धर्म्यं संवादमावयोः ।
ज्ञानयज्ञेन तेनाहमिष्टः स्यामिति मे मतिः ।।
adhyeṣyate ća ya imam dharmyam saṁvādamāvayoḥ:,
jñānayajñena tenāhamiṣṭaḥ: syāmiti me matiḥ:. (18.70)

(§1) *adhyeṣyate* (r◦ 25/8) *ća yaḥ:* (r◦ 19/2) *imaṃ* (r◦ 14/1) *dharmyaṃ* (r◦ 14/1) *saṁvādaṃ* (r◦ 8/17) *āvayoḥ:* (r◦ 22/8) *jñānayajñena tena* (r◦ 1/1) *ahaṃ* (r◦ 8/18) *iṣṭaḥ:* (r◦ 22/7) *syāṃ* (r◦ 8/18) *iti me matiḥ:* (r◦ 22/8)

(§2) *adhyeṣyate* (3rd-per◦ sing◦ fut2◦ लृट् भविष्य◦ ātmane◦ ←class2◦ अधि√इ); *ća* (1.1); *yaḥ:* (2.19); *imaṃ* (1.28); *dharmyaṃ* (2.33); *saṁvādaṃ* (2acc◦ sing◦ ←m◦ *saṁvāda* ←सम्√वद्); *āvayoḥ:* (6pos◦ dual◦ ←pron◦ *asmad* 1.7); *jñānayajñena* (9.15); *tena* (3.38); *ahaṃ* (1.22); *iṣṭaḥ:* (18.64); *syāṃ* (3.24); *iti* (1.25); *me* (1.21); *matiḥ:* (6.36) (18.70)

---

[900] elsewhere◦ प्रियकृत्तमः → better dear, more dear, dearer, etc.

📖 कृत्तमः is superlative adjective, not a comparative adjective.

[901] elsewhere◦ न च कश्चिन्मे प्रियकृत्तमः → there is none dearer to me,

📖 Please note that मे प्रियकृत् is 'dear doer' to me, NOT 'dear' to me.

(§3) *adhyeṣyate* (he shall study); *ća* (and); *yaḥ:* (subj1◦ he who); *imaṃ* (adj1◦-obj◦ this); *dharmyaṃ* (adj2◦-obj◦ virtuous); *sam̃vādaṃ* (obj◦ dialogue); *āvayoḥ:* (our, between both of us); *jñānayajñena* (with austerity of knowledge); *tena* (by him); *ahaṃ* (subj2◦ I); *iṣṭaḥ:* (adj◦-subj2◦ adored); *syāṃ* (I shall be, may be); *iti* (thus is); *me* (my); *matiḥ:* (subj3◦ opinion) (18.70)

(§4) ća yaḥ: adhyeṣyate imaṃ dharmyaṃ sam̃vādaṃ āvayoḥ: ahaṃ syāṃ iṣṭaḥ: tena jñānayajñena iti me matiḥ:

(§5) And, he who shall study this virtuous[902] dialogue between both of us, I shall be adored by him with austerity[903] of knowledge, thus is my opinion. (18.70)

18.71 श्रद्धावाननसूयश्च शृणुयादपि यो नरः ।
सोऽपि मुक्तः शुभाँल्लोकान्प्राप्नुयात्पुण्यकर्मणाम् ।।
śraddhāvānanasūyaśća śṛṇuyādapi yo nara:,
so'pi muktaḥ: śubhām̃llokānprāpnuyātpuṇyakarmaṇāṃ. (18.71)

(§1) *śraddhāvāṇ* (r◦ 8/11) *anasūyaḥ:* (r◦ 17/1) *ća śṛṇuyāṭ* (r◦ 8/2) *api yaḥ:* (r◦ 15/6) *naraḥ:* (r◦ 22/8) *saḥ:* (r◦ 15/1) *api muktaḥ:* (r◦ 22/5) *śubhāṇ* (r◦ 13/8) *lokāṇ* (r◦ 13/13) *prāpnuyāṭ* (r◦ 10/6) *puṇyakarmaṇāṃ* (r◦ 24/6, 14/2)

(§2) *śraddhāvāṇ* (4.39); *anasūyaḥ:* (m◦ 1nom◦ sing◦ ←bahuvrī◦ *anasūya* 9.1); *ća* (1.1); *śṛṇuyāṭ* (3rd-per◦ sing◦ potential◦ विधि◦ parasmai◦ ←class1◦ √श्रु); *api* (1.26); *yaḥ:* (2.19); *naraḥ:* (2.22); *saḥ:* (1.13); *api* (1.26); *muktaḥ:* (5.28); *śubhāṇ* (m◦ 2acc◦ plu◦ ←adj◦ *śubha* 2.57); *lokāṇ* (6.41); *prāpnuyāṭ* (3rd-per◦ sing◦ potential◦ विधि◦ parasmai◦ ←class5◦ प्र√आप्); *puṇyakarmaṇāṃ* (7.28) (18.71)

(§3) *śraddhāvāṇ* (adj1◦-subj◦ faithful); *anasūyaḥ:* (adj2◦-subj◦ non-envious, trusting); *ća* (and); *śṛṇuyāṭ* (he should listen); *api* (also); *yaḥ:* (adj3◦-subj◦ he who); *naraḥ:* (subj◦ a person); *saḥ:* (adj4◦-subj◦ he); *api* (also); *muktaḥ:* (adj5◦-subj◦ freed); *śubhāṇ* (adj◦-obj◦ the auspicious); *lokāṇ* (obj◦ worlds); *prāpnuyāṭ* (he should attain, shall attain); *puṇyakarmaṇāṃ* (of virtuous people) (18.71)

(§4) naraḥ: yaḥ: śraddhāvāṇ ća anasūyaḥ: śṛṇuyāṭ api muktaḥ: saḥ: api prāpnuyāṭ śubhāṇ lokāṇ puṇyakarmaṇāṃ

(§5) A person who (is) faithful[904] ◌ோல் trusting should listen (this). Freed,[905] he also shall

---

[902] elsewhere◦ धमर्यम् → religious, sacred, ...etc.

[903] elsewhere◦ ज्ञानयज्ञेन → through the Sacrifice in the form of knowledge, with the knowledge sacrifice, sacrifice through knowledge, by his intelligence, ...etc.

[904] elsewhere◦ श्रद्धावान्→ being reverential, listens with faith, ...etc.

attain the auspicious worlds of virtuous people. (18.71)

18.72 कच्चिदेतच्छ्रुतं पार्थ त्वयैकाग्रेण चेतसा ।
कच्चिदज्ञानसम्मोहः प्रनष्टस्ते धनञ्जय ।।

kaććidetaććhrutaṁ pārtha tvayaikāgreṇa ćetasā,
kaććidajñānasammohaḥ: pranaṣṭaste dhanañjaya. (18.72)

(§1) *kaććit* (r◦ 8/9) *etat* (r◦ 11/4) *śrutam* (r◦ 14/1) *pārtha tvayā* (r◦ 3/3) *ekāgreṇa* (r◦ 24/1) *ćetasā kaććit* (r◦ 8/2) *ajñānasammohaḥ:* (r◦ 22/3) *pranaṣṭaḥ:* (r◦ 18/1) *te dhanañjaya*

(§2) *kaććit* (6.38); *etat* (1nom◦ 2.6); *śrutam* (n◦ 1nom◦ sing◦ ←adj◦ *śruta* 2.52); *pārtha* (1.25); *tvayā* (6.3); *ekāgreṇa* (n◦ 3inst◦ sing◦ ←adj◦ *ekāgar* 6.12); *ćetasā* (8.8); *kaććit* (6.38); *ajñānasammohaḥ:* (m◦ 1nom◦ sing◦ ←tatpu◦ *ajñāna-sammoha*, अज्ञानस्य सम्मोहः ←n◦ *ajñāna* 4.42 + m◦ *sammoha* 2.63); *pranaṣṭaḥ:* (m◦ 1nom◦ sing◦ ←ppp◦ adj◦ *pranaṣṭa* ←प्र√नश्); *te* (2.7); *dhanañjaya* (2.48) (18.72)

(§3) *kaććit* (whether); *etat* (obj1◦ this, this secret); *śrutam* (adj◦-obj◦ heard, listened); *pārtha* (O Arjuna!); *tvayā* (subj◦ by you); *ekāgreṇa* (with one pointed); *ćetasā* (with mind); *kaććit* (whether); *ajñānasammohaḥ:* (subj2◦ delusion born out of ignorance); *pranaṣṭaḥ:* (adj1◦-subj2◦ subsided, quietened); *te* (adj2◦-subj2◦ your); *dhanañjaya* (O Arjuna!) (18.72)

(§4) pārtha kaććit etat śrutam tvayā ekāgreṇa ćetasā dhanañjaya kaććit te ajñānasammohaḥ: pranaṣṭaḥ:

(§5) O Arjuna! is this secret listened by you with one pointed mind? O Arjuna! has your delusion born out of ignorance subsided?[906] (18.72)

Arjuna said (arjuna uvāća अर्जुन उवाच ।)

18.73 नष्टो मोहः स्मृतिर्लब्धा त्वत्प्रसादान्मयाच्युत ।
स्थितोऽस्मि गतसन्देहः करिष्ये वचनं तव ।।

naṣṭo mohaḥ: smṛtirlabdhā tvatprasādānmayāćyuta,
sthito'smigatasandehaḥ: kariṣye vaćanaṁ tava. (18.73)

(§1) *arjunaḥ:* (r◦ 19/4) *uvāća. naṣṭaḥ:* (r◦ 15/9) *mohaḥ:* (r◦ 22/7) *smṛtiḥ:* (r◦ 16/6) *labdhā tvatprasādāt* (r◦ 12/2) *mayā* (r◦ 1/3) *aćyuta sthitaḥ:* (r◦ 15/1) *asmi gatasandehaḥ:* (r◦ 22/1) *kariṣye* (r◦ 25/10)

📖 श्रद्धावान् is not a gerund. It is a present perticiple adjective.

[905] elsewhere◦ मुक्तः → becoming free, becomes free, etc.

📖 मुक्तः is not a gerund or present tense verb. It is a m◦ ppp. adjective of m◦ subj◦ सः ।.

[906] elsewhere◦ प्रशान्तः → destroyed.

vaćanaṃ (r◦ 14/1) *tava*

(§2) *arjunaḥ:* (1.47); *uvāća* (1.25), *naṣṭaḥ:* (4.2); *mohaḥ:* (11.1); 📖*smṛtiḥ:* (10.34); *labdhā* (f◦ 1nom◦ sing◦ ←adj◦ *labdha* 16.13); *tvatprasādāṭ* (m◦ 5abl◦ sing◦ ←tatpu◦ *tvat-prasāda,* तव प्रसाद: ←pron◦ *tvaṭ* 6.39 + m◦ *prasāda* 2.64); *mayā* (1.22); *aćyuta* (1.21); *sthitaḥ:* (5.20); *asmi* (7.8); *gatasandehaḥ:* (m◦ 1nom◦ sing◦ ←bahuvrī◦ *gata-sandeha,* गत: सन्देह: यस्य ←adj◦ *gata* 2.11 + m◦ *sandeh* ←सम्√दिह); *kariṣye* (1st-per◦ sing◦ fut2◦ लृट् भविष्य◦ ātmane◦ ←class8◦ √कृ); *vaćanaṃ* (1.2); *tava* (1.3) (18.73)

(§3) *arjunaḥ:* (Arjuna); *uvāća* (said), *naṣṭaḥ:* (adj◦-subj1◦ overcome); *mohaḥ:* (subj1◦ the delusion); *smṛtiḥ:* (subj2◦ the right thinking, wisdom, good sense); *labdhā* (adj◦-subj2◦ gained, regained); *tvatprasādāṭ* (through your grace); *mayā* (by me); *aćyuta* (O Kṛṣṇa!); *sthitaḥ:* (adj1◦-subj3◦ calmed down, settled down); *asmi* (subj3◦ I am); *gatasandehaḥ:* (adj◦-subj3◦ he whose doubts have gone away, doubtless); *kariṣye* (shall do. I shall obey); *vaćanaṃ* (obj◦ word); *tava* (adj◦-obj◦ your) (18.73)

(§4) arjunaḥ: uvāća aćyuta tvatprasādāṭ mohaḥ: naṣṭaḥ: smṛtiḥ: labdhā mayā asmi sthitaḥ: gatasandehaḥ: kariṣye tava vaćanaṃ

(§5) Arjuna said : O Kṛṣṇa! through your grace, the delusion (is) overcome[907] (and) the good sense[908] (is) regained[909] by me. I am (now) settled down[910] (and) doubtless. I shall obey your word. (18.73)

Sanjaya said (sañjaya uvāća सजय उवाच ।)

18.74 इत्यहं वासुदेवस्य पार्थस्य च महात्मन: ।
संवादमिममश्रौषमद्भुतं रोमहर्षणम् ।।

ityahaṁ vāsudevasya pārthasya ća mahātmanaḥ:,
saṁvādamimamaśrauṣamadbhutaṁ romaharsaṇaṃ. (18.74)

(§1) *sañjayaḥ:* (r◦ 19/4) *uvāća. iti* (r◦ 4/1) *ahaṃ* (r◦ 14/1) *vāsudevasya pārthasya ća mahātmana:* (r◦ 22/8) *saṁvādaṃ* (r◦ 8/18) *imaṃ* (r◦ 8/16) *aśrauṣaṃ* (r◦ 8/16) *adhbutaṃ* (r◦ 14/1) *romaharsaṇaṃ* (r◦ 14/2, 24/3)

(§2) *sañjayaḥ:* (1.2); *uvāća* (1.25). *iti* (1.25); *ahaṃ* (1.22); *vāsudevasya* (m◦ 6pos◦ sing◦ ←prop◦

---

[907] elsewhere◦ नष्ट: → destroyed.

[908] elsewhere◦ स्मृति: → memory.

[909] elsewhere◦ लब्धा → back to his senses.

[910] elsewhere◦ स्थित: अस्मि → I am now firm, I stand, ...etc.

📖 स्थित: is not a present tense. It is m◦ ppp. adjective of m◦ subject I.

vāsudeva 7.19); *pārthasya* (m∘ 6pos∘ sing∘ ←m∘ *pārtha* 1.26); *ća* (1.1); *mahātmana:* (8.15); *saṁvādaṃ* (18.70); *imaṃ* (1.28); *aśrauṣaṃ* (1st-per∘ sing∘ -pastind∘ लुङ् भूत parasmai∘ ←class1∘ √श्रु); *adhbutaṃ* (11.20); *romaharsaṇaṃ* (2acc∘ sing∘ ←n∘ *roma-harsaṇa* ←n∘ *romaṇ* 1.29 + adj∘ *harṣaṇa* ←m∘ *harṣa* 1.29) (18.74)

(§3) *sañjayaḥ:* (Sañjaya); *uvāća* (said). *iti* (thus); *ahaṃ* (subj1∘ I); *vāsudevasya* (of Lord Śrī Kṛṣṇa); *pārthasya* (of Arjuna); *ća* (and); *mahātmana:* (adj∘-subj1∘ noble soul); *saṁvādaṃ* (obj∘ conversation, dialogue); *imaṃ* (adj1∘-obj1∘ this); *aśrauṣaṃ* (I have heard); *adhbutaṃ* (adj2∘-obj∘ unique, never heard before); *romaharsaṇaṃ* (adj3∘-obj∘ inspiring, exciting, invigorating, hair raising) (18.74)

(§4) sañjayaḥ: uvāća iti ahaṃ aśrauṣaṃ imaṃ adhbutaṃ romaharsaṇaṃ saṁvādaṃ vāsudevasya ća mahātmana: pārthasya

(§5) Sañjaya said : Thus I have heard this unique[911] (and) hair raising dialogue of Lord Śrī Kṛṣṇa and noble soul Arjuna. (18.74)

18.75 व्यासप्रसादाच्छ्रुतवानेतद्गुह्यमहं परम् ।
योगं योगेश्वरात्कृष्णात्साक्षात्कथयतः स्वयम् ।।
vyāsaprasādāććhrutavānetadguhyamahaṁ paraṃ,
yogaṁ yogeśvarātkṛṣṇātsākṣātkathayataḥ: svayaṃ. (18.75)

(§1) *vyāsaprasādāṭ* (r∘ 11/4) *śrutavāṇ* (r∘ 8/15) *etaṭ* (r∘ 9/4) *guhyaṃ* (r∘ 8/16) *ahaṃ* (r∘ 14/1) *paraṃ* (r∘ 14/2) *yogaṃ* (r∘ 14/1) *yogeśvarāṭ* (r∘ 10/5) *kṛṣṇāṭ* (r∘ 10/7) *sākṣāṭ* (r∘ 10/5) *kathayataḥ:* (r∘ 22/7) *svayaṃ* (r∘ 14/2)

(§2) *vyāsaprasādāṭ* (m∘ 5abl∘ sing∘ ←tatpu∘ *vyāsa-prasāda*, व्यासस्य प्रसाद: ←prop∘ *vyāsa* 10.13 + m∘ *prasāda* 2.64); *śrutavāṇ* (m∘ 1nom∘ sing∘ ←śatṛ∘ adj∘ *śrutavaṭ* ←√श्रु); *etaṭ* (2acc∘ 2.6); *guhyaṃ* (2acc∘ 18.68); *ahaṃ* (1.22); *paraṃ* (2acc∘ 2.59); *yogaṃ* (2.53); *yogeśvarāṭ* (m∘ 5abl∘ sing∘ ←bahuvrī∘ *yogeśvara* 11.4); *kṛṣṇāṭ* (m∘ 5abl∘ sing∘ ←prop∘ *kṛṣṇa* 1.28); 🕮*sākṣāṭ* (adv∘ ind∘ ←सह√अक्ष्); *kathayataḥ:* (m∘ 5abl∘ sing∘ ←adj∘ *kathayaṭ* 10.9); *svayaṃ* (4.38) (18.75)

(§3) *vyāsaprasādāṭ* (through the grace of Vyāsa); *śrutavāṇ* (adj∘-subj1∘ he who has heard); *etaṭ* (adj1∘-obj∘ this); *guhyaṃ* (adj2∘-obj∘ secret); *ahaṃ* (subj1∘ I); *paraṃ* (adj3∘-obj∘ supreme); *yogaṃ* (obj∘ *yoga*); *yogeśvarāṭ* (from the Lord of *yoga*); *kṛṣṇāṭ* (from Śrī Kṛṣṇa); *sākṣāṭ* (personally); *kathayataḥ:* (adj∘-subj2∘ telling); *svayaṃ* (subj2∘ Himself) (18.75)

[911] elsewhere∘ अद्भुतम् → wonderous, wonderful, ...etc.

(§4) vyāsaprasādāt aham śrutavān etat param guhyam yogam kṛṣṇāt yogeśvarāt kathayataḥ: sākṣāt svayam

(§5) Through the grace of Vyāsa, I (am the one who has) heard[912] this supreme secret *yoga* from Śrī Kṛṣṇa, the Lord of *yoga*, telling Himself personally to (Arjuna). (18.75)

18.76 राजन्संस्मृत्य संस्मृत्य संवादमिममद्भुतम् ।
केशवार्जुनयोः पुण्यं हृष्यामि च मुहुर्मुहुः ।।
rājansam̐smṛtya sam̐smṛtya sam̐vādamimamadbhutam,
keśavārjunayoḥ: puṇyam̐ hṛṣyāmi ća muhurmuhuḥ:. (18.76)

(§1) *rājan* (r∘ 13/20) *sam̐smṛtya sam̐smṛtya* (r∘ 8/18) *imam* (r∘ 8/16) *adhbutam* (r∘ 14/2) *keśavārjunayoḥ:* (r∘ 22/3) *puṇyam* (r∘ 14/1) *hṛṣyāmi* (r∘ 25/9) *ća muhu: (16.8) muhuḥ:* (r∘ 22/8)

(§2) *rājan* (2.7); *sam̐smṛtya* (lyp∘ past-participle ind∘ ←सम्√स्मृ); *sam̐smṛtya* (↑); *sam̐vādam* (18.70); *imam* (1.28); *adhbutam* (11.20); *keśavārjunayoḥ:* (m∘ 6pos∘ dual∘ ←dvandva∘ केशवस्य च अर्जुनस्य च ←m∘ *keśava* 1.31 + m∘ prop∘ *arjuna* 1.4); *puṇyam* (9.20); *hṛṣyāmi* (1st-per∘ sing∘ pres∘ वर्तमान्-लट् parasmai∘ ←class1∘ √हृष् 12.17); *ća* (1.1); 🕮*muhurmuhuḥ:* (= mauhu: mauhu: ←frequency indicating ind∘ *muhus* ←√मुह) (18.76)

(§3) *rājan* (O King Dhṛtarāṣṭra!); *sam̐smṛtya sam̐smṛtya* (having remembered over and over); *sam̐vādam* (obj∘ dialogue); *imam* (adj1∘-obj∘ this); *adhbutam* (adj2∘-obj∘ unique); *keśavārjunayoḥ:* (adj3∘-obj∘ of Lord Kṛṣṇa and Arjuna); *puṇyam* (adj1∘-obj∘ sacred); *hṛṣyāmi* (I rejoice); *ća* (and); *muhurmuhuḥ:* (again and again) (18.76)

(§4) rājan sam̐smṛtya sam̐smṛtya imam adhbutam ća puṇyam sam̐vādam keśavārjunayoḥ: hṛṣyāmi muhurmuhuḥ:

(§5) O King Dhṛtarāṣṭra! having remembered[913] over and over this unique[914] and sacred dialogue of Lord Kṛṣṇa and Arjuna, I rejoice[915] again and again. (18.76)

---

[912] elsewhere∘ श्रुतवान् → I have heard.

🕮 Please remember, श्रुतवान् is not a verb. It is a participle adjective of subject I.

[913] elsewhere∘ संस्मृत्य संस्मृत्य → I repeatedly recall, I recall to mind again and again, ...etc.

🕮 Please remember, संस्मृत्य is not a verb. It is a lyp. participle.

[914] अद्भुतम् → Please see the footnote in the previous verse 18.74

[915] elsewhere∘ हृष्यामि → being thrilled, thrilled, ...etc.

🕮 हृष्यामि is not a gerund or adjective. It is a simple present tense.

18.77 तच्च संस्मृत्य संस्मृत्य रूपमत्यद्भुतं हरेः ।
विस्मयो मे महान्राजन्हृष्यामि च पुनः पुनः ।।

taćća saṁsmṛtya saṁsmṛtya rūpamatyadbhutaṁ hareḥ:,
vismayo me mahān̖ rājanhṛṣyāmi ća punaḥ: punaḥ:. (18.77)

(§1) *tat̖* (r◦ 11/1) *ća saṁsmṛtya saṁsmṛtya rūpam̖* (r◦ 8/16) *ati* (r◦ 4/1) *adhbutam̖* (r◦ 14/1) *hareḥ:* (r◦ 22/8) *vismayaḥ:* (r◦ 15/9) *me mahān̖* (r◦ 13/18) *rājan̖* (r◦ 13/21) *hṛṣyāmi* (r◦ 25/9) *ća punaḥ:* (r◦ 22/3) *punaḥ:* (r◦ 22/8)

(§2) *tat̖* (1.10); *ća* (1.1); *saṁsmṛtya* (18.76); *saṁsmṛtya* (18.76); *rūpam̖* (11.3); *ati* (6.11); *adhbutam̖* (11.20); *hareḥ:* (m◦ 6pos◦ sing◦ ←bahuvrī◦ *hari* 11.9); *vismayaḥ:* (m◦ 1nom◦ sing◦ ←m◦ *vismaya* 11.14); *me* (1.21); *mahān̖* (9.6); *rājan̖* (11.9); *hṛṣyāmi* (18.76); *ća* (1.1); *punaḥ:* (4.35); *punaḥ:* (4.35) (18.77)

(§3) *tat̖* (adj1◦-obj◦ that); *ća* (and); *saṁsmṛtya saṁsmṛtya* (having remembered over and over); *rūpam̖* (obj◦ form, figure); *ati* (very much); *adhbutam̖* (adj1◦-obj◦ unique); *hareḥ:* (adj2◦-obj◦ of Lord Kṛṣṇa); *vismayaḥ:* (subj◦ amazement); *me* (my); *mahān̖* (adj◦-subj◦ great); *rājan̖* (O King Dhritarāṣtra!); *hṛṣyāmi* (I rejoice); *ća* (and); *punaḥ: punaḥ:* (again and again) (18.77)

(§4) ća rājan̖ saṁsmṛtya saṁsmṛtya tat̖ adhbutam̖ rūpam̖ hareḥ: hṛṣyāmi ati punaḥ: punaḥ: ća me vismayaḥ: mahān̖

(§5) And, O King Dhritarāṣtra! having remembered over and over, that unique[916] figure of Lord Kṛṣṇa, I rejoice[917] very much again and again; and my amazement (is) great. (18.77)

18.78 यत्र योगेश्वरः कृष्णो यत्र पार्थो धनुर्धरः ।
तत्र श्रीर्विजयो भूतिर्ध्रुवा नीतिर्मतिर्मम ।।

yatra yogeśvaraḥ: kṛṣṇo yatra pārtho dhanurdharaḥ:,
tatra śrīrvijayo bhūtirdhruvā nītirmatirmama. (18.78)

(§1) *yatra yogeśvaraḥ:* (r◦ 22/1) *kṛṣṇaḥ:* (r◦ 15/10) *yatra pārthaḥ:* (r◦ 15/5) *dhanurdharaḥ:* (r◦ 22/8) *tatra śrīḥ:* (r◦ 16/7) *vijayaḥ:* (r◦ 15/8) *bhūtiḥ:* (r◦ 16/6) *dhruvā nītiḥ:* (r◦ 16/6) *matiḥ:* (r◦ 16/6) *mama*

(§2) *yatra* (6.20); 🕮*yogeśvaraḥ:* (m◦ 1nom◦ sing◦ ←bahuvrī◦ *yogeśvara* 11.4); *kṛṣṇaḥ:* (8.25); *yatra*

---

[916] अद्भुतम् → Please see the footnote in verse 18.74

[917] elsewhere◦ हृष्यामि → Please see in footnote of the previous verse.

(6.20); *pārthaḥ:* (1.26); 📖*dhanurdharaḥ:* (m◦ 1nom◦ sing◦ ←bahuvrī◦ *dhanurdhara,* धनु: धारयति य: ←m◦ *dhanu* 1.20 + adj◦ *dhara* 11.11); *tatra* (1.26); 📖*śrīḥ:* (10.34); *vijayaḥ:* (1nom◦ sing◦ ←m◦ *vijaya* 1.32); 📖*bhūtiḥ:* (1nom◦ sing◦ ←f◦ *bhūti* ←√भू); *dhruvā* (f◦ 1nom◦ sing◦ ←adj◦ *dhruva* 2.27); *nītiḥ:* (10.38); *matiḥ:* (6.36); *mama* (1.7) (18.78)

(§3) *yatra* (wherever); *yogeśvaraḥ:* (adj◦-subj1◦ the Lord of *yoga*); *kṛṣṇaḥ:* (subj1◦ Śrī Kṛṣṇa); *yatra* (wherever); *pārthaḥ:* (subj2◦ Arjuna); *dhanurdharaḥ:* (adj◦-subj2◦ the great archer); *tatra* (there); *śrīḥ:* (subj3◦ opulence); *vijayaḥ:* (subj4◦ victory); *bhūtiḥ:* (subj5◦ prosperity); *dhruvā* (adj◦-subj6◦ firm, unfailing); *nītiḥ:* (subj6◦ morality); *matiḥ:* (subj7◦ opinion); *mama* (adj◦-subj7◦ my) (18.78)

(§4) yatra kṛṣṇaḥ: yogeśvaraḥ: yatra pārthaḥ: dhanurdharaḥ: tatra śrīḥ: vijayaḥ: bhūtiḥ: dhruvā nītiḥ: mama matiḥ:

(§5) Wherever (is) Śrī Kṛṣṇa, the Lord of *yoga,* (and) wherever (is) Arjuna, the Great archer, there (is) opulence, victory, prosperity, (and) unfailing morality.[918] (This is) my opinion. (18.78)

इति श्रीमद्भगवद्गीतासूपनिषत्सु ब्रह्मविद्यायां योगशास्त्रे
श्रीकृष्णार्जुनसंवादे मोक्षसंन्यासयोगो नाम अष्टादशोऽध्याय: ।

iti śrīmadbhagavadgītāsūpaniṣatsu brahmavidyāyāṁ yogaśāstre
śrīkṛṣṇārjunasaṁvāde mokṣasannyāsayogo nāma aṣṭādaśo'dhyāyaḥ:.

(§1) *iti śrīmadbhagavadgītāsu* (r◦ 1/8) *upaniṣatsu brahmavidyāyām* (r◦ 14/1) *yogaśāstre śrīkṛṣṇārjunasaṁvāde mokṣasannyāsayogaḥ:* (r◦ 15/6) *nāma* (r◦ 1/1) *aṣṭādaśaḥ:* (r◦ 15/1) *adhyāyaḥ:* (r◦ 22/8); *iti śrīmadbhagavadgītā samāpyate.*

iti (1.25); *śrīmadbhagavadgītāsu* (f◦ 7loc◦ plu◦ ←tatpu◦ *śrīmadbhagavadgītā* ←adj◦ *śrīmat* 6.41 + adj◦ *bhagavat* 10.14 + f◦ *gītā* ←√गै); *upaniṣatsu* (7loc◦ plu◦ ←f◦ *upaniṣat* ←उप-नि√सद्); *brahmavidyāyām* (f◦ 7loc◦ sing◦ tatpu◦ *brahma-vidyā,* ब्रह्मण: विद्या ←n◦ *brahman* 2.72 + *vidyā* 5.18); *yogaśāstre* (n◦ 7loc◦ sing◦ ←tatpu◦ *yoga-śāstra,* योगस्य शास्त्रम् ←m◦ *yoga* 2.39 + n◦ *śāstra* 15.20); *śrīkṛṣṇārjunasaṁvāde* (m◦ 7loc◦ sing◦ ←tatpu◦ *śrīkṛṣṇārjuna-saṁvāda,* श्रीकृष्णस्य च अर्जुनस्य च संवाद: ←adj◦ *śrī* 10.34 + m◦ prop◦ *kṛṣṇa* 1.28 + m◦ prop◦ *arjuna* 1.4 + m◦ *saṁvāda* 18.70); *aṣṭādaśaḥ:* (m◦ 1nom◦ sing◦ num◦ adj◦ *aṣṭādaśa*

---

[918] elsewhere◦ ध्रुवा नीति: → there are sure fortune...; there will indeed abide Fortune..., such is my firm conviction, there are certain fortune..., there will surely be fortune..., there will also certainly be opulence..., there will surely be Splendor..., etc.

📖 Please ध्रुवा is a singular feminine adjective. It muse be attached to a feminine singular noun, which normally follows it. ध्रुवा is not plural. It is not an adverb. ध्रुवा does not qualify मतिर्मम ।

←num◦ *aṣṭan* 7.4 + num◦ *daśa* 13.6); *adhyāyaḥ:* (1nom◦ sing◦ ←m◦ *adhyāya* ←अधि√इ); *iti* (1.25); *śrīmadbhagavadgītā* (↑); *samāpyate* (3rd-per◦ sing◦ pres◦ वर्तमान्–लट् ātmane◦ ←class5◦ सम्√आप्)

(§2) *iti* (1.25); *śrīmadbhagavadgītāsu* (f◦ 7loc◦ plu◦ tatpu◦ *śrīmad-bhagavad-gītā* ←adj◦ *śrīmaṭ* 6.41↓ + adj◦ *bhagavaṭ* 10.14↓ + f◦ *gītā* ←5◦√गै); *upaniṣatsu* (7loc◦ plu◦ ←f◦ *upaniṣaḍ* ←6◦उप–नि√सद्); *brahmavidyāyāṃ* (f◦ 7loc◦ sing◦ ←tatpu◦ *brahma-vidyā*, ब्रह्मण: विद्या ←n◦ *brahmaṇ* 2.72↓ + *vidyā* 5.18↓); *yogaśāstre* (n◦ 7loc◦ sing◦ ←tatpu◦ *yoga-śāstra*, योगानाम् शास्त्रम् । योगस्य शास्त्रम् । ←m◦ *yoga* 2.39↓ + n◦ *śāstra* 15.20↓); *śrīkṛṣṇārjunasaṁvāde* (m◦ 7loc◦ sing◦ ←tatpu◦ *śrī-kṛṣṇārjuna-saṁvāda*, श्रीकृष्णस्य च अर्जुनस्य च संवाद: ←adj◦ *śrī* 10.34↓ + m◦ prop◦ *kṛṣṇa* 1.28 + m◦ prop◦ *arjuna* 1.4 + m◦ *saṁvāda* 18.70↓); *mokṣasannyāsayogaḥ:* (m◦ 1nom◦ sing◦ ←tatpu◦ *mokṣa-sannyāsa-yogaḥ:*, मोक्षस्य च संन्यासस्य योग: ←n◦ *mokṣa* 5.28 + m◦ *sannyāsa* 5.1 + m◦ *yoga* 2.39); *nāma* (1nom◦ sing◦ ←n◦ *nāmaṇ* ←1◦√म्ना); *aṣṭādaśaḥ:* (m◦ 1nom◦ sing◦ ←num◦ adj◦ *aṣṭā* 7.4 *daśa* 13.6); *adhyāyaḥ:* (1nom◦ sing◦ ←m◦ *adhyāya* ←1◦अधि√इ)

(§3) *iti* (thus); *śrīmadbhagavadgītāsu upaniṣatsu* (among the upaniṣads of Śrīmad-Bhagavadgītā); *brahmavidyāyāṃ* (of the eternal wisdoms); *yogaśāstre* (in the science of Yoga); *śrīkṛṣṇārjunasaṁvāde* (in the dialogue between Śrī Kṛṣṇa and Arjuna); *mokṣasannyāsayogaḥ:* (adj1◦-subj◦ mokṣa-sannyāsa-yoga); *nāma* (called) *aṣṭādaśaḥ:* (adj2◦-subj◦ eighteenth); *adhyāyaḥ:* (subj◦ discourse)

(§4) śrīmadbhagavadgītāsu upaniṣatsu yogaśāstre brahmavidyāyāṃ iti aṣṭādaśaḥ: adhyāyaḥ: nāma mokṣasannyāsayogaḥ: śrīkṛṣṇārjunasaṁvāde

(§5) Among the upaniṣads of the Śrīmad-Bhagavadgītā, in the science of Yoga of self realization, thus (is) the thirteenth discourse called *mokṣasannyāsayogaḥ:* in the dialogue between Śrī Kṛṣṇa and Arjuna.

REFERENCES

आधारसूचिः

Apte, Vaman Shivram; *The Practical Sanskrit English Dictionary*; MLBD Pubulishers. Pvt. Ltd, Dehli, 1998.

Kale, M.R.; *A Higher Sanskrit Grammar*; Motilal Banarasidas, Delhi, 1995

Monir-Williams, Sir Monir; *A Sanskrit-English Dictionary*; Motilal Banarasidass Pvt. Ltd, Dehli, 1993.

Monir-Williams, Sir Monir; *A Practical Grammar of Sanskrit Language*; Oriental Books Reprint Co., New Dehli, 1978

Narale, Ratnakar; *Sanskrit Grammar and Reference Book,* Books-India, Toronto, 2013.

Whitney, William Dwight; *The Roots Verb-forms And Primary Derivatives of the Sanskrit Language*; MLBD, Delhi 1997

Wilson, Prof. H.H.; *An Introduction to the Grammar of Sanskrit Language*; Choukhamba Sanskrit Series XI., Varanasi, 1979

The Book Images on the Front Cover are the additional references

आप्टे, वामन शिवराम; संस्कृत हिन्दी कोश, मोतीलाल बनारसीदास पब्लिशर्स, प्रा॰ लि॰, दिल्ली, 1997.

झा, पं. रामचंद्र व्याकरणाचार्य; रूपचन्द्रिका; हरिदास संस्कृत ग्रंथमाला 156; चौखंबा संस्कृत सीरीज, वाराणसी, सं 2051.

द्विवेदी, पद्मश्री डॉ. आचार्य कपिलदेव; संस्कृत-व्याकरण एवं लघुसिद्धान्तकौमुदी; विश्वविद्यालय प्रकाशन, वाराणसी, 1996.

नराले, रत्नाकर; गीता दर्शन, प्रभात प्रकाशन, नई दिल्ली, 2005.

पाण्डेय, पण्डितरामनरायणदत्त शास्त्री; महाभारत (हिंदी) : 1-4 खण्ड; गीताप्रेस, गोरखपुर, सं. 2051.

मिश्र, पं. गोमतीप्रसादशास्त्री; श्री वरदाचार्यकृत लघुसिद्धान्तकौमुदी, चौखम्बा सुरभारती प्रकाशन, वाराणसी, 1999

शर्मा, चतुर्वेदी द्वारकाप्रसाद; झा, पण्डित तारिणीश; संस्कृत-शब्दार्थ-कौस्तुभ; रामनारायणलाल बेनीप्रसाद; इलाहाबाद 1928

सोमयाजी, पं. धन्वाडगोपलकृष्णाचार्य; तिङन्तार्णवतरणि; कृष्णदास संस्कृत सी. 31; कृष्णदास अकादमी, वाराणसी, 1980

www.ingramcontent.com/pod-product-compliance
Lightning Source LLC
Chambersburg PA
CBHW080942120626
46546CB00010B/2813
* 9 7 8 1 9 8 9 4 1 6 7 9 2 *